PostgreSQL 11.2 Docum

CW00735183

The PostgreSQL Global Development Group

This book contains the following sections of the original manual.
The original page numbers were kept intact.

Preface
Chapters 37-50 & Reference
Bibliography
Index

This is book two of a three-book series.
Book 1 - ISBN 9781680922738
Book 2 - ISBN 9781680922745
Book 3 - ISBN 9781680922752

You may download the original document as a PDF
for free from https://www.postgresql.org/docs/manuals/

PostgreSQL 11.2 Documentation

The PostgreSQL Global Development Group
Copyright © 1996-2019 The PostgreSQL Global Development Group

Legal Notice

Table of Contents

List of Figures

List of Tables

List of Examples

Preface

This book is the official documentation of PostgreSQL. It has been written by the PostgreSQL developers and other volunteers in parallel to the development of the PostgreSQL software. It describes all the functionality that the current version of PostgreSQL officially supports.

To make the large amount of information about PostgreSQL manageable, this book has been organized in several parts. Each part is targeted at a different class of users, or at users in different stages of their PostgreSQL experience:

- Part I is an informal introduction for new users.

- Part II documents the SQL query language environment, including data types and functions, as well as user-level performance tuning. Every PostgreSQL user should read this.

- Part III describes the installation and administration of the server. Everyone who runs a PostgreSQL server, be it for private use or for others, should read this part.

- Part IV describes the programming interfaces for PostgreSQL client programs.

- Part V contains information for advanced users about the extensibility capabilities of the server. Topics include user-defined data types and functions.

- Part VI contains reference information about SQL commands, client and server programs. This part supports the other parts with structured information sorted by command or program.

- Part VII contains assorted information that might be of use to PostgreSQL developers.

1. What is PostgreSQL?

PostgreSQL is an object-relational database management system (ORDBMS) based on POSTGRES, Version 4.2[1], developed at the University of California at Berkeley Computer Science Department. POSTGRES pioneered many concepts that only became available in some commercial database systems much later.

PostgreSQL is an open-source descendant of this original Berkeley code. It supports a large part of the SQL standard and offers many modern features:

- complex queries
- foreign keys
- triggers
- updatable views
- transactional integrity
- multiversion concurrency control

Also, PostgreSQL can be extended by the user in many ways, for example by adding new

- data types
- functions
- operators
- aggregate functions

---

[1] http://db.cs.berkeley.edu/postgres.html

- index methods
- procedural languages

And because of the liberal license, PostgreSQL can be used, modified, and distributed by anyone free of charge for any purpose, be it private, commercial, or academic.

2. A Brief History of PostgreSQL

The object-relational database management system now known as PostgreSQL is derived from the POST-GRES package written at the University of California at Berkeley. With over two decades of development behind it, PostgreSQL is now the most advanced open-source database available anywhere.

2.1. The Berkeley POSTGRES Project

The POSTGRES project, led by Professor Michael Stonebraker, was sponsored by the Defense Advanced Research Projects Agency (DARPA), the Army Research Office (ARO), the National Science Foundation (NSF), and ESL, Inc. The implementation of POSTGRES began in 1986. The initial concepts for the system were presented in [ston86], and the definition of the initial data model appeared in [rowe87]. The design of the rule system at that time was described in [ston87a]. The rationale and architecture of the storage manager were detailed in [ston87b].

POSTGRES has undergone several major releases since then. The first "demoware" system became operational in 1987 and was shown at the 1988 ACM-SIGMOD Conference. Version 1, described in [ston90a], was released to a few external users in June 1989. In response to a critique of the first rule system ([ston89]), the rule system was redesigned ([ston90b]), and Version 2 was released in June 1990 with the new rule system. Version 3 appeared in 1991 and added support for multiple storage managers, an improved query executor, and a rewritten rule system. For the most part, subsequent releases until Postgres95 (see below) focused on portability and reliability.

POSTGRES has been used to implement many different research and production applications. These include: a financial data analysis system, a jet engine performance monitoring package, an asteroid tracking database, a medical information database, and several geographic information systems. POSTGRES has also been used as an educational tool at several universities. Finally, Illustra Information Technologies (later merged into Informix[2], which is now owned by IBM[3]) picked up the code and commercialized it. In late 1992, POSTGRES became the primary data manager for the Sequoia 2000 scientific computing project[4].

The size of the external user community nearly doubled during 1993. It became increasingly obvious that maintenance of the prototype code and support was taking up large amounts of time that should have been devoted to database research. In an effort to reduce this support burden, the Berkeley POSTGRES project officially ended with Version 4.2.

2.2. Postgres95

In 1994, Andrew Yu and Jolly Chen added an SQL language interpreter to POSTGRES. Under a new name, Postgres95 was subsequently released to the web to find its own way in the world as an open-source descendant of the original POSTGRES Berkeley code.

Postgres95 code was completely ANSI C and trimmed in size by 25%. Many internal changes improved performance and maintainability. Postgres95 release 1.0.x ran about 30-50% faster on the Wisconsin

---

[2] https://www.ibm.com/analytics/informix
[3] https://www.ibm.com/
[4] http://meteora.ucsd.edu/s2k/s2k_home.html

Benchmark compared to POSTGRES, Version 4.2. Apart from bug fixes, the following were the major enhancements:

- The query language PostQUEL was replaced with SQL (implemented in the server). (Interface library libpq was named after PostQUEL.) Subqueries were not supported until PostgreSQL (see below), but they could be imitated in Postgres95 with user-defined SQL functions. Aggregate functions were re-implemented. Support for the GROUP BY query clause was also added.

- A new program (psql) was provided for interactive SQL queries, which used GNU Readline. This largely superseded the old monitor program.

- A new front-end library, libpgtcl, supported Tcl-based clients. A sample shell, pgtclsh, provided new Tcl commands to interface Tcl programs with the Postgres95 server.

- The large-object interface was overhauled. The inversion large objects were the only mechanism for storing large objects. (The inversion file system was removed.)

- The instance-level rule system was removed. Rules were still available as rewrite rules.

- A short tutorial introducing regular SQL features as well as those of Postgres95 was distributed with the source code

- GNU make (instead of BSD make) was used for the build. Also, Postgres95 could be compiled with an unpatched GCC (data alignment of doubles was fixed).

2.3. PostgreSQL

By 1996, it became clear that the name "Postgres95" would not stand the test of time. We chose a new name, PostgreSQL, to reflect the relationship between the original POSTGRES and the more recent versions with SQL capability. At the same time, we set the version numbering to start at 6.0, putting the numbers back into the sequence originally begun by the Berkeley POSTGRES project.

Many people continue to refer to PostgreSQL as "Postgres" (now rarely in all capital letters) because of tradition or because it is easier to pronounce. This usage is widely accepted as a nickname or alias.

The emphasis during development of Postgres95 was on identifying and understanding existing problems in the server code. With PostgreSQL, the emphasis has shifted to augmenting features and capabilities, although work continues in all areas.

Details about what has happened in PostgreSQL since then can be found in Appendix E.

3. Conventions

The following conventions are used in the synopsis of a command: brackets ([and]) indicate optional parts. (In the synopsis of a Tcl command, question marks (?) are used instead, as is usual in Tcl.) Braces ({ and }) and vertical lines (|) indicate that you must choose one alternative. Dots (...) mean that the preceding element can be repeated.

Where it enhances the clarity, SQL commands are preceded by the prompt =>, and shell commands are preceded by the prompt $. Normally, prompts are not shown, though.

An *administrator* is generally a person who is in charge of installing and running the server. A *user* could be anyone who is using, or wants to use, any part of the PostgreSQL system. These terms should not be interpreted too narrowly; this book does not have fixed presumptions about system administration procedures.

4. Further Information

Besides the documentation, that is, this book, there are other resources about PostgreSQL:

Wiki

The PostgreSQL wiki[5] contains the project's FAQ[6] (Frequently Asked Questions) list, TODO[7] list, and detailed information about many more topics.

Web Site

The PostgreSQL web site[8] carries details on the latest release and other information to make your work or play with PostgreSQL more productive.

Mailing Lists

The mailing lists are a good place to have your questions answered, to share experiences with other users, and to contact the developers. Consult the PostgreSQL web site for details.

Yourself!

PostgreSQL is an open-source project. As such, it depends on the user community for ongoing support. As you begin to use PostgreSQL, you will rely on others for help, either through the documentation or through the mailing lists. Consider contributing your knowledge back. Read the mailing lists and answer questions. If you learn something which is not in the documentation, write it up and contribute it. If you add features to the code, contribute them.

5. Bug Reporting Guidelines

When you find a bug in PostgreSQL we want to hear about it. Your bug reports play an important part in making PostgreSQL more reliable because even the utmost care cannot guarantee that every part of PostgreSQL will work on every platform under every circumstance.

The following suggestions are intended to assist you in forming bug reports that can be handled in an effective fashion. No one is required to follow them but doing so tends to be to everyone's advantage.

We cannot promise to fix every bug right away. If the bug is obvious, critical, or affects a lot of users, chances are good that someone will look into it. It could also happen that we tell you to update to a newer version to see if the bug happens there. Or we might decide that the bug cannot be fixed before some major rewrite we might be planning is done. Or perhaps it is simply too hard and there are more important things on the agenda. If you need help immediately, consider obtaining a commercial support contract.

5.1. Identifying Bugs

Before you report a bug, please read and re-read the documentation to verify that you can really do whatever it is you are trying. If it is not clear from the documentation whether you can do something or not, please report that too; it is a bug in the documentation. If it turns out that a program does something different from what the documentation says, that is a bug. That might include, but is not limited to, the following circumstances:

---

[5] https://wiki.postgresql.org
[6] https://wiki.postgresql.org/wiki/Frequently_Asked_Questions
[7] https://wiki.postgresql.org/wiki/Todo
[8] https://www.postgresql.org

- A program terminates with a fatal signal or an operating system error message that would point to a problem in the program. (A counterexample might be a "disk full" message, since you have to fix that yourself.)

- A program produces the wrong output for any given input.

- A program refuses to accept valid input (as defined in the documentation).

- A program accepts invalid input without a notice or error message. But keep in mind that your idea of invalid input might be our idea of an extension or compatibility with traditional practice.

- PostgreSQL fails to compile, build, or install according to the instructions on supported platforms.

Here "program" refers to any executable, not only the backend process.

Being slow or resource-hogging is not necessarily a bug. Read the documentation or ask on one of the mailing lists for help in tuning your applications. Failing to comply to the SQL standard is not necessarily a bug either, unless compliance for the specific feature is explicitly claimed.

Before you continue, check on the TODO list and in the FAQ to see if your bug is already known. If you cannot decode the information on the TODO list, report your problem. The least we can do is make the TODO list clearer.

5.2. What to Report

The most important thing to remember about bug reporting is to state all the facts and only facts. Do not speculate what you think went wrong, what "it seemed to do", or which part of the program has a fault. If you are not familiar with the implementation you would probably guess wrong and not help us a bit. And even if you are, educated explanations are a great supplement to but no substitute for facts. If we are going to fix the bug we still have to see it happen for ourselves first. Reporting the bare facts is relatively straightforward (you can probably copy and paste them from the screen) but all too often important details are left out because someone thought it does not matter or the report would be understood anyway.

The following items should be contained in every bug report:

- The exact sequence of steps *from program start-up* necessary to reproduce the problem. This should be self-contained; it is not enough to send in a bare SELECT statement without the preceding CREATE TABLE and INSERT statements, if the output should depend on the data in the tables. We do not have the time to reverse-engineer your database schema, and if we are supposed to make up our own data we would probably miss the problem.

  The best format for a test case for SQL-related problems is a file that can be run through the psql frontend that shows the problem. (Be sure to not have anything in your ~/.psqlrc start-up file.) An easy way to create this file is to use pg_dump to dump out the table declarations and data needed to set the scene, then add the problem query. You are encouraged to minimize the size of your example, but this is not absolutely necessary. If the bug is reproducible, we will find it either way.

  If your application uses some other client interface, such as PHP, then please try to isolate the offending queries. We will probably not set up a web server to reproduce your problem. In any case remember to provide the exact input files; do not guess that the problem happens for "large files" or "midsize databases", etc. since this information is too inexact to be of use.

- The output you got. Please do not say that it "didn't work" or "crashed". If there is an error message, show it, even if you do not understand it. If the program terminates with an operating system error, say which. If nothing at all happens, say so. Even if the result of your test case is a program crash or otherwise obvious it might not happen on our platform. The easiest thing is to copy the output from the terminal, if possible.

Note

If you are reporting an error message, please obtain the most verbose form of the message. In psql, say `\set VERBOSITY verbose` beforehand. If you are extracting the message from the server log, set the run-time parameter log_error_verbosity to `verbose` so that all details are logged.

Note

In case of fatal errors, the error message reported by the client might not contain all the information available. Please also look at the log output of the database server. If you do not keep your server's log output, this would be a good time to start doing so.

- The output you expected is very important to state. If you just write "This command gives me that output." or "This is not what I expected.", we might run it ourselves, scan the output, and think it looks OK and is exactly what we expected. We should not have to spend the time to decode the exact semantics behind your commands. Especially refrain from merely saying that "This is not what SQL says/Oracle does." Digging out the correct behavior from SQL is not a fun undertaking, nor do we all know how all the other relational databases out there behave. (If your problem is a program crash, you can obviously omit this item.)

- Any command line options and other start-up options, including any relevant environment variables or configuration files that you changed from the default. Again, please provide exact information. If you are using a prepackaged distribution that starts the database server at boot time, you should try to find out how that is done.

- Anything you did at all differently from the installation instructions.

- The PostgreSQL version. You can run the command `SELECT version();` to find out the version of the server you are connected to. Most executable programs also support a `--version` option; at least `postgres --version` and `psql --version` should work. If the function or the options do not exist then your version is more than old enough to warrant an upgrade. If you run a prepackaged version, such as RPMs, say so, including any subversion the package might have. If you are talking about a Git snapshot, mention that, including the commit hash.

  If your version is older than 11.2 we will almost certainly tell you to upgrade. There are many bug fixes and improvements in each new release, so it is quite possible that a bug you have encountered in an older release of PostgreSQL has already been fixed. We can only provide limited support for sites using older releases of PostgreSQL; if you require more than we can provide, consider acquiring a commercial support contract.

- Platform information. This includes the kernel name and version, C library, processor, memory information, and so on. In most cases it is sufficient to report the vendor and version, but do not assume everyone knows what exactly "Debian" contains or that everyone runs on i386s. If you have installation problems then information about the toolchain on your machine (compiler, make, and so on) is also necessary.

Do not be afraid if your bug report becomes rather lengthy. That is a fact of life. It is better to report everything the first time than us having to squeeze the facts out of you. On the other hand, if your input files are huge, it is fair to ask first whether somebody is interested in looking into it. Here is an article[9] that outlines some more tips on reporting bugs.

Do not spend all your time to figure out which changes in the input make the problem go away. This will probably not help solving it. If it turns out that the bug cannot be fixed right away, you will still have time to find and share your work-around. Also, once again, do not waste your time guessing why the bug exists. We will find that out soon enough.

When writing a bug report, please avoid confusing terminology. The software package in total is called "PostgreSQL", sometimes "Postgres" for short. If you are specifically talking about the backend process, mention that, do not just say "PostgreSQL crashes". A crash of a single backend process is quite different from crash of the parent "postgres" process; please don't say "the server crashed" when you mean a single backend process went down, nor vice versa. Also, client programs such as the interactive frontend "psql" are completely separate from the backend. Please try to be specific about whether the problem is on the client or server side.

5.3. Where to Report Bugs

In general, send bug reports to the bug report mailing list at `<pgsql-bugs@lists.post-gresql.org>`. You are requested to use a descriptive subject for your email message, perhaps parts of the error message.

Another method is to fill in the bug report web-form available at the project's web site[10]. Entering a bug report this way causes it to be mailed to the `<pgsql-bugs@lists.postgresql.org>` mailing list.

If your bug report has security implications and you'd prefer that it not become immediately visible in public archives, don't send it to `pgsql-bugs`. Security issues can be reported privately to `<security@postgresql.org>`.

Do not send bug reports to any of the user mailing lists, such as `<pgsql-sql@lists.post-gresql.org>` or `<pgsql-general@lists.postgresql.org>`. These mailing lists are for answering user questions, and their subscribers normally do not wish to receive bug reports. More importantly, they are unlikely to fix them.

Also, please do *not* send reports to the developers' mailing list `<pgsql-hackers@lists.post-gresql.org>`. This list is for discussing the development of PostgreSQL, and it would be nice if we could keep the bug reports separate. We might choose to take up a discussion about your bug report on `pgsql-hackers`, if the problem needs more review.

If you have a problem with the documentation, the best place to report it is the documentation mailing list `<pgsql-docs@lists.postgresql.org>`. Please be specific about what part of the documentation you are unhappy with.

If your bug is a portability problem on a non-supported platform, send mail to `<pgsql-hacker-s@lists.postgresql.org>`, so we (and you) can work on porting PostgreSQL to your platform.

Note

Due to the unfortunate amount of spam going around, all of the above lists will be moderated unless you are subscribed. That means there will be some delay before the email

---

[9] https://www.chiark.greenend.org.uk/~sgtatham/bugs.html
[10] https://www.postgresql.org/

is delivered. If you wish to subscribe to the lists, please visit https://lists.postgresql.org/ for instructions.

PostgreSQL 11.2 Documentation

The PostgreSQL Global Development Group

PostgreSQL 11.2 Documentation

The PostgreSQL Global Development Group

Copyright © 1996-2019 The PostgreSQL Global Development Group

Legal Notice

Table of Contents

List of Figures

List of Tables

List of Examples

Preface

This book is the official documentation of PostgreSQL. It has been written by the PostgreSQL developers and other volunteers in parallel to the development of the PostgreSQL software. It describes all the functionality that the current version of PostgreSQL officially supports.

To make the large amount of information about PostgreSQL manageable, this book has been organized in several parts. Each part is targeted at a different class of users, or at users in different stages of their PostgreSQL experience:

- Part I is an informal introduction for new users.

- Part II documents the SQL query language environment, including data types and functions, as well as user-level performance tuning. Every PostgreSQL user should read this.

- Part III describes the installation and administration of the server. Everyone who runs a PostgreSQL server, be it for private use or for others, should read this part.

- Part IV describes the programming interfaces for PostgreSQL client programs.

- Part V contains information for advanced users about the extensibility capabilities of the server. Topics include user-defined data types and functions.

- Part VI contains reference information about SQL commands, client and server programs. This part supports the other parts with structured information sorted by command or program.

- Part VII contains assorted information that might be of use to PostgreSQL developers.

1. What is PostgreSQL?

PostgreSQL is an object-relational database management system (ORDBMS) based on POSTGRES, Version 4.2[1], developed at the University of California at Berkeley Computer Science Department. POST-GRES pioneered many concepts that only became available in some commercial database systems much later.

PostgreSQL is an open-source descendant of this original Berkeley code. It supports a large part of the SQL standard and offers many modern features:

- complex queries
- foreign keys
- triggers
- updatable views
- transactional integrity
- multiversion concurrency control

Also, PostgreSQL can be extended by the user in many ways, for example by adding new

- data types
- functions
- operators
- aggregate functions

---

[1] http://db.cs.berkeley.edu/postgres.html

- index methods
- procedural languages

And because of the liberal license, PostgreSQL can be used, modified, and distributed by anyone free of charge for any purpose, be it private, commercial, or academic.

2. A Brief History of PostgreSQL

The object-relational database management system now known as PostgreSQL is derived from the POST-GRES package written at the University of California at Berkeley. With over two decades of development behind it, PostgreSQL is now the most advanced open-source database available anywhere.

2.1. The Berkeley POSTGRES Project

The POSTGRES project, led by Professor Michael Stonebraker, was sponsored by the Defense Advanced Research Projects Agency (DARPA), the Army Research Office (ARO), the National Science Foundation (NSF), and ESL, Inc. The implementation of POSTGRES began in 1986. The initial concepts for the system were presented in [ston86], and the definition of the initial data model appeared in [rowe87]. The design of the rule system at that time was described in [ston87a]. The rationale and architecture of the storage manager were detailed in [ston87b].

POSTGRES has undergone several major releases since then. The first "demoware" system became operational in 1987 and was shown at the 1988 ACM-SIGMOD Conference. Version 1, described in [ston90a], was released to a few external users in June 1989. In response to a critique of the first rule system ([ston89]), the rule system was redesigned ([ston90b]), and Version 2 was released in June 1990 with the new rule system. Version 3 appeared in 1991 and added support for multiple storage managers, an improved query executor, and a rewritten rule system. For the most part, subsequent releases until Postgres95 (see below) focused on portability and reliability.

POSTGRES has been used to implement many different research and production applications. These include: a financial data analysis system, a jet engine performance monitoring package, an asteroid tracking database, a medical information database, and several geographic information systems. POSTGRES has also been used as an educational tool at several universities. Finally, Illustra Information Technologies (later merged into Informix[2], which is now owned by IBM[3]) picked up the code and commercialized it. In late 1992, POSTGRES became the primary data manager for the Sequoia 2000 scientific computing project[4].

The size of the external user community nearly doubled during 1993. It became increasingly obvious that maintenance of the prototype code and support was taking up large amounts of time that should have been devoted to database research. In an effort to reduce this support burden, the Berkeley POSTGRES project officially ended with Version 4.2.

2.2. Postgres95

In 1994, Andrew Yu and Jolly Chen added an SQL language interpreter to POSTGRES. Under a new name, Postgres95 was subsequently released to the web to find its own way in the world as an open-source descendant of the original POSTGRES Berkeley code.

Postgres95 code was completely ANSI C and trimmed in size by 25%. Many internal changes improved performance and maintainability. Postgres95 release 1.0.x ran about 30-50% faster on the Wisconsin

---

[2] https://www.ibm.com/analytics/informix
[3] https://www.ibm.com/
[4] http://meteora.ucsd.edu/s2k/s2k_home.html

Benchmark compared to POSTGRES, Version 4.2. Apart from bug fixes, the following were the major enhancements:

- The query language PostQUEL was replaced with SQL (implemented in the server). (Interface library libpq was named after PostQUEL.) Subqueries were not supported until PostgreSQL (see below), but they could be imitated in Postgres95 with user-defined SQL functions. Aggregate functions were re-implemented. Support for the GROUP BY query clause was also added.

- A new program (psql) was provided for interactive SQL queries, which used GNU Readline. This largely superseded the old monitor program.

- A new front-end library, libpgtcl, supported Tcl-based clients. A sample shell, pgtclsh, provided new Tcl commands to interface Tcl programs with the Postgres95 server.

- The large-object interface was overhauled. The inversion large objects were the only mechanism for storing large objects. (The inversion file system was removed.)

- The instance-level rule system was removed. Rules were still available as rewrite rules.

- A short tutorial introducing regular SQL features as well as those of Postgres95 was distributed with the source code

- GNU make (instead of BSD make) was used for the build. Also, Postgres95 could be compiled with an unpatched GCC (data alignment of doubles was fixed).

2.3. PostgreSQL

By 1996, it became clear that the name "Postgres95" would not stand the test of time. We chose a new name, PostgreSQL, to reflect the relationship between the original POSTGRES and the more recent versions with SQL capability. At the same time, we set the version numbering to start at 6.0, putting the numbers back into the sequence originally begun by the Berkeley POSTGRES project.

Many people continue to refer to PostgreSQL as "Postgres" (now rarely in all capital letters) because of tradition or because it is easier to pronounce. This usage is widely accepted as a nickname or alias.

The emphasis during development of Postgres95 was on identifying and understanding existing problems in the server code. With PostgreSQL, the emphasis has shifted to augmenting features and capabilities, although work continues in all areas.

Details about what has happened in PostgreSQL since then can be found in Appendix E.

3. Conventions

The following conventions are used in the synopsis of a command: brackets ([and]) indicate optional parts. (In the synopsis of a Tcl command, question marks (?) are used instead, as is usual in Tcl.) Braces ({ and }) and vertical lines (|) indicate that you must choose one alternative. Dots (...) mean that the preceding element can be repeated.

Where it enhances the clarity, SQL commands are preceded by the prompt =>, and shell commands are preceded by the prompt $. Normally, prompts are not shown, though.

An *administrator* is generally a person who is in charge of installing and running the server. A *user* could be anyone who is using, or wants to use, any part of the PostgreSQL system. These terms should not be interpreted too narrowly; this book does not have fixed presumptions about system administration procedures.

4. Further Information

Besides the documentation, that is, this book, there are other resources about PostgreSQL:

Wiki

> The PostgreSQL wiki[5] contains the project's FAQ[6] (Frequently Asked Questions) list, TODO[7] list, and detailed information about many more topics.

Web Site

> The PostgreSQL web site[8] carries details on the latest release and other information to make your work or play with PostgreSQL more productive.

Mailing Lists

> The mailing lists are a good place to have your questions answered, to share experiences with other users, and to contact the developers. Consult the PostgreSQL web site for details.

Yourself!

> PostgreSQL is an open-source project. As such, it depends on the user community for ongoing support. As you begin to use PostgreSQL, you will rely on others for help, either through the documentation or through the mailing lists. Consider contributing your knowledge back. Read the mailing lists and answer questions. If you learn something which is not in the documentation, write it up and contribute it. If you add features to the code, contribute them.

5. Bug Reporting Guidelines

When you find a bug in PostgreSQL we want to hear about it. Your bug reports play an important part in making PostgreSQL more reliable because even the utmost care cannot guarantee that every part of PostgreSQL will work on every platform under every circumstance.

The following suggestions are intended to assist you in forming bug reports that can be handled in an effective fashion. No one is required to follow them but doing so tends to be to everyone's advantage.

We cannot promise to fix every bug right away. If the bug is obvious, critical, or affects a lot of users, chances are good that someone will look into it. It could also happen that we tell you to update to a newer version to see if the bug happens there. Or we might decide that the bug cannot be fixed before some major rewrite we might be planning is done. Or perhaps it is simply too hard and there are more important things on the agenda. If you need help immediately, consider obtaining a commercial support contract.

5.1. Identifying Bugs

Before you report a bug, please read and re-read the documentation to verify that you can really do whatever it is you are trying. If it is not clear from the documentation whether you can do something or not, please report that too; it is a bug in the documentation. If it turns out that a program does something different from what the documentation says, that is a bug. That might include, but is not limited to, the following circumstances:

---

[5] https://wiki.postgresql.org
[6] https://wiki.postgresql.org/wiki/Frequently_Asked_Questions
[7] https://wiki.postgresql.org/wiki/Todo
[8] https://www.postgresql.org

- A program terminates with a fatal signal or an operating system error message that would point to a problem in the program. (A counterexample might be a "disk full" message, since you have to fix that yourself.)

- A program produces the wrong output for any given input.

- A program refuses to accept valid input (as defined in the documentation).

- A program accepts invalid input without a notice or error message. But keep in mind that your idea of invalid input might be our idea of an extension or compatibility with traditional practice.

- PostgreSQL fails to compile, build, or install according to the instructions on supported platforms.

Here "program" refers to any executable, not only the backend process.

Being slow or resource-hogging is not necessarily a bug. Read the documentation or ask on one of the mailing lists for help in tuning your applications. Failing to comply to the SQL standard is not necessarily a bug either, unless compliance for the specific feature is explicitly claimed.

Before you continue, check on the TODO list and in the FAQ to see if your bug is already known. If you cannot decode the information on the TODO list, report your problem. The least we can do is make the TODO list clearer.

5.2. What to Report

The most important thing to remember about bug reporting is to state all the facts and only facts. Do not speculate what you think went wrong, what "it seemed to do", or which part of the program has a fault. If you are not familiar with the implementation you would probably guess wrong and not help us a bit. And even if you are, educated explanations are a great supplement to but no substitute for facts. If we are going to fix the bug we still have to see it happen for ourselves first. Reporting the bare facts is relatively straightforward (you can probably copy and paste them from the screen) but all too often important details are left out because someone thought it does not matter or the report would be understood anyway.

The following items should be contained in every bug report:

- The exact sequence of steps *from program start-up* necessary to reproduce the problem. This should be self-contained; it is not enough to send in a bare SELECT statement without the preceding CREATE TABLE and INSERT statements, if the output should depend on the data in the tables. We do not have the time to reverse-engineer your database schema, and if we are supposed to make up our own data we would probably miss the problem.

  The best format for a test case for SQL-related problems is a file that can be run through the psql frontend that shows the problem. (Be sure to not have anything in your ~/.psqlrc start-up file.) An easy way to create this file is to use pg_dump to dump out the table declarations and data needed to set the scene, then add the problem query. You are encouraged to minimize the size of your example, but this is not absolutely necessary. If the bug is reproducible, we will find it either way.

  If your application uses some other client interface, such as PHP, then please try to isolate the offending queries. We will probably not set up a web server to reproduce your problem. In any case remember to provide the exact input files; do not guess that the problem happens for "large files" or "midsize databases", etc. since this information is too inexact to be of use.

- The output you got. Please do not say that it "didn't work" or "crashed". If there is an error message, show it, even if you do not understand it. If the program terminates with an operating system error, say which. If nothing at all happens, say so. Even if the result of your test case is a program crash or otherwise obvious it might not happen on our platform. The easiest thing is to copy the output from the terminal, if possible.

Note

If you are reporting an error message, please obtain the most verbose form of the message. In psql, say \set VERBOSITY verbose beforehand. If you are extracting the message from the server log, set the run-time parameter log_error_verbosity to verbose so that all details are logged.

Note

In case of fatal errors, the error message reported by the client might not contain all the information available. Please also look at the log output of the database server. If you do not keep your server's log output, this would be a good time to start doing so.

- The output you expected is very important to state. If you just write "This command gives me that output." or "This is not what I expected.", we might run it ourselves, scan the output, and think it looks OK and is exactly what we expected. We should not have to spend the time to decode the exact semantics behind your commands. Especially refrain from merely saying that "This is not what SQL says/Oracle does." Digging out the correct behavior from SQL is not a fun undertaking, nor do we all know how all the other relational databases out there behave. (If your problem is a program crash, you can obviously omit this item.)

- Any command line options and other start-up options, including any relevant environment variables or configuration files that you changed from the default. Again, please provide exact information. If you are using a prepackaged distribution that starts the database server at boot time, you should try to find out how that is done.

- Anything you did at all differently from the installation instructions.

- The PostgreSQL version. You can run the command SELECT version(); to find out the version of the server you are connected to. Most executable programs also support a --version option; at least postgres --version and psql --version should work. If the function or the options do not exist then your version is more than old enough to warrant an upgrade. If you run a prepackaged version, such as RPMs, say so, including any subversion the package might have. If you are talking about a Git snapshot, mention that, including the commit hash.

  If your version is older than 11.2 we will almost certainly tell you to upgrade. There are many bug fixes and improvements in each new release, so it is quite possible that a bug you have encountered in an older release of PostgreSQL has already been fixed. We can only provide limited support for sites using older releases of PostgreSQL; if you require more than we can provide, consider acquiring a commercial support contract.

- Platform information. This includes the kernel name and version, C library, processor, memory information, and so on. In most cases it is sufficient to report the vendor and version, but do not assume everyone knows what exactly "Debian" contains or that everyone runs on i386s. If you have installation problems then information about the toolchain on your machine (compiler, make, and so on) is also necessary.

Do not be afraid if your bug report becomes rather lengthy. That is a fact of life. It is better to report everything the first time than us having to squeeze the facts out of you. On the other hand, if your input files are huge, it is fair to ask first whether somebody is interested in looking into it. Here is an article[9] that outlines some more tips on reporting bugs.

Do not spend all your time to figure out which changes in the input make the problem go away. This will probably not help solving it. If it turns out that the bug cannot be fixed right away, you will still have time to find and share your work-around. Also, once again, do not waste your time guessing why the bug exists. We will find that out soon enough.

When writing a bug report, please avoid confusing terminology. The software package in total is called "PostgreSQL", sometimes "Postgres" for short. If you are specifically talking about the backend process, mention that, do not just say "PostgreSQL crashes". A crash of a single backend process is quite different from crash of the parent "postgres" process; please don't say "the server crashed" when you mean a single backend process went down, nor vice versa. Also, client programs such as the interactive frontend "psql" are completely separate from the backend. Please try to be specific about whether the problem is on the client or server side.

5.3. Where to Report Bugs

In general, send bug reports to the bug report mailing list at `<pgsql-bugs@lists.post-gresql.org>`. You are requested to use a descriptive subject for your email message, perhaps parts of the error message.

Another method is to fill in the bug report web-form available at the project's web site[10]. Entering a bug report this way causes it to be mailed to the `<pgsql-bugs@lists.postgresql.org>` mailing list.

If your bug report has security implications and you'd prefer that it not become immediately visible in public archives, don't send it to `pgsql-bugs`. Security issues can be reported privately to `<security@postgresql.org>`.

Do not send bug reports to any of the user mailing lists, such as `<pgsql-sql@lists.post-gresql.org>` or `<pgsql-general@lists.postgresql.org>`. These mailing lists are for answering user questions, and their subscribers normally do not wish to receive bug reports. More importantly, they are unlikely to fix them.

Also, please do *not* send reports to the developers' mailing list `<pgsql-hackers@lists.post-gresql.org>`. This list is for discussing the development of PostgreSQL, and it would be nice if we could keep the bug reports separate. We might choose to take up a discussion about your bug report on `pgsql-hackers`, if the problem needs more review.

If you have a problem with the documentation, the best place to report it is the documentation mailing list `<pgsql-docs@lists.postgresql.org>`. Please be specific about what part of the documentation you are unhappy with.

If your bug is a portability problem on a non-supported platform, send mail to `<pgsql-hacker-s@lists.postgresql.org>`, so we (and you) can work on porting PostgreSQL to your platform.

> ## Note
>
> Due to the unfortunate amount of spam going around, all of the above lists will be moderated unless you are subscribed. That means there will be some delay before the email

---

[9] https://www.chiark.greenend.org.uk/~sgtatham/bugs.html
[10] https://www.postgresql.org/

is delivered. If you wish to subscribe to the lists, please visit https://lists.postgresql.org/ for instructions.

Chapter 37. The Information Schema

The information schema consists of a set of views that contain information about the objects defined in the current database. The information schema is defined in the SQL standard and can therefore be expected to be portable and remain stable — unlike the system catalogs, which are specific to PostgreSQL and are modeled after implementation concerns. The information schema views do not, however, contain information about PostgreSQL-specific features; to inquire about those you need to query the system catalogs or other PostgreSQL-specific views.

Note

When querying the database for constraint information, it is possible for a standard-compliant query that expects to return one row to return several. This is because the SQL standard requires constraint names to be unique within a schema, but PostgreSQL does not enforce this restriction. PostgreSQL automatically-generated constraint names avoid duplicates in the same schema, but users can specify such duplicate names.

This problem can appear when querying information schema views such as `check_constraint_routine_usage`, `check_constraints`, `domain_constraints`, and `referential_constraints`. Some other views have similar issues but contain the table name to help distinguish duplicate rows, e.g., `constraint_column_usage`, `constraint_table_usage`, `table_constraints`.

37.1. The Schema

The information schema itself is a schema named `information_schema`. This schema automatically exists in all databases. The owner of this schema is the initial database user in the cluster, and that user naturally has all the privileges on this schema, including the ability to drop it (but the space savings achieved by that are minuscule).

By default, the information schema is not in the schema search path, so you need to access all objects in it through qualified names. Since the names of some of the objects in the information schema are generic names that might occur in user applications, you should be careful if you want to put the information schema in the path.

37.2. Data Types

The columns of the information schema views use special data types that are defined in the information schema. These are defined as simple domains over ordinary built-in types. You should not use these types for work outside the information schema, but your applications must be prepared for them if they select from the information schema.

These types are:

`cardinal_number`

   A nonnegative integer.

`character_data`

   A character string (without specific maximum length).

`sql_identifier`

> A character string. This type is used for SQL identifiers, the type `character_data` is used for any other kind of text data.

`time_stamp`

> A domain over the type `timestamp with time zone`

`yes_or_no`

> A character string domain that contains either `YES` or `NO`. This is used to represent Boolean (true/false) data in the information schema. (The information schema was invented before the type `boolean` was added to the SQL standard, so this convention is necessary to keep the information schema backward compatible.)

Every column in the information schema has one of these five types.

37.3. `information_schema_catalog_name`

`information_schema_catalog_name` is a table that always contains one row and one column containing the name of the current database (current catalog, in SQL terminology).

Table 37.1. `information_schema_catalog_name` Columns

Name	Data Type	Description
catalog_name	sql_identifier	Name of the database that contains this information schema

37.4. `administrable_role_authorizations`

The view `administrable_role_authorizations` identifies all roles that the current user has the admin option for.

Table 37.2. `administrable_role_authorizations` Columns

Name	Data Type	Description
grantee	sql_identifier	Name of the role to which this role membership was granted (can be the current user, or a different role in case of nested role memberships)
role_name	sql_identifier	Name of a role
is_grantable	yes_or_no	Always YES

37.5. `applicable_roles`

The view `applicable_roles` identifies all roles whose privileges the current user can use. This means there is some chain of role grants from the current user to the role in question. The current user itself is also an applicable role. The set of applicable roles is generally used for permission checking.

Table 37.3. `applicable_roles` Columns

Name	Data Type	Description
grantee	sql_identifier	Name of the role to which this role membership was granted (can be the current user, or a different role in case of nested role memberships)
role_name	sql_identifier	Name of a role
is_grantable	yes_or_no	YES if the grantee has the admin option on the role, NO if not

37.6. attributes

The view `attributes` contains information about the attributes of composite data types defined in the database. (Note that the view does not give information about table columns, which are sometimes called attributes in PostgreSQL contexts.) Only those attributes are shown that the current user has access to (by way of being the owner of or having some privilege on the type).

Table 37.4. `attributes` Columns

Name	Data Type	Description
udt_catalog	sql_identifier	Name of the database containing the data type (always the current database)
udt_schema	sql_identifier	Name of the schema containing the data type
udt_name	sql_identifier	Name of the data type
attribute_name	sql_identifier	Name of the attribute
ordinal_position	cardinal_number	Ordinal position of the attribute within the data type (count starts at 1)
attribute_default	character_data	Default expression of the attribute
is_nullable	yes_or_no	YES if the attribute is possibly nullable, NO if it is known not nullable.
data_type	character_data	Data type of the attribute, if it is a built-in type, or ARRAY if it is some array (in that case, see the view element_types), else USER-DEFINED (in that case, the type is identified in attribute_udt_name and associated columns).
character_maximum_length	cardinal_number	If data_type identifies a character or bit string type, the declared maximum length; null for all other data types or if no maximum length was declared.

Name	Data Type	Description
`character_octet_length`	`cardinal_number`	If `data_type` identifies a character type, the maximum possible length in octets (bytes) of a datum; null for all other data types. The maximum octet length depends on the declared character maximum length (see above) and the server encoding.
`character_set_catalog`	`sql_identifier`	Applies to a feature not available in PostgreSQL
`character_set_schema`	`sql_identifier`	Applies to a feature not available in PostgreSQL
`character_set_name`	`sql_identifier`	Applies to a feature not available in PostgreSQL
`collation_catalog`	`sql_identifier`	Name of the database containing the collation of the attribute (always the current database), null if default or the data type of the attribute is not collatable
`collation_schema`	`sql_identifier`	Name of the schema containing the collation of the attribute, null if default or the data type of the attribute is not collatable
`collation_name`	`sql_identifier`	Name of the collation of the attribute, null if default or the data type of the attribute is not collatable
`numeric_precision`	`cardinal_number`	If `data_type` identifies a numeric type, this column contains the (declared or implicit) precision of the type for this attribute. The precision indicates the number of significant digits. It can be expressed in decimal (base 10) or binary (base 2) terms, as specified in the column `numeric_precision_radix`. For all other data types, this column is null.
`numeric_precision_radix`	`cardinal_number`	If `data_type` identifies a numeric type, this column indicates in which base the values in the columns `numeric_precision` and `numeric_scale` are expressed. The value is either 2 or 10. For all other data types, this column is null.
`numeric_scale`	`cardinal_number`	If `data_type` identifies an exact numeric type, this column contains the (declared or implicit)

Name	Data Type	Description
		scale of the type for this attribute. The scale indicates the number of significant digits to the right of the decimal point. It can be expressed in decimal (base 10) or binary (base 2) terms, as specified in the column `numeric_precision_radix`. For all other data types, this column is null.
datetime_precision	cardinal_number	If `data_type` identifies a date, time, timestamp, or interval type, this column contains the (declared or implicit) fractional seconds precision of the type for this attribute, that is, the number of decimal digits maintained following the decimal point in the seconds value. For all other data types, this column is null.
interval_type	character_data	If `data_type` identifies an interval type, this column contains the specification which fields the intervals include for this attribute, e.g., `YEAR TO MONTH`, `DAY TO SECOND`, etc. If no field restrictions were specified (that is, the interval accepts all fields), and for all other data types, this field is null.
interval_precision	cardinal_number	Applies to a feature not available in PostgreSQL (see `datetime_precision` for the fractional seconds precision of interval type attributes)
attribute_udt_catalog	sql_identifier	Name of the database that the attribute data type is defined in (always the current database)
attribute_udt_schema	sql_identifier	Name of the schema that the attribute data type is defined in
attribute_udt_name	sql_identifier	Name of the attribute data type
scope_catalog	sql_identifier	Applies to a feature not available in PostgreSQL
scope_schema	sql_identifier	Applies to a feature not available in PostgreSQL
scope_name	sql_identifier	Applies to a feature not available in PostgreSQL

Name	Data Type	Description
maximum_cardinality	cardinal_number	Always null, because arrays always have unlimited maximum cardinality in PostgreSQL
dtd_identifier	sql_identifier	An identifier of the data type descriptor of the column, unique among the data type descriptors pertaining to the table. This is mainly useful for joining with other instances of such identifiers. (The specific format of the identifier is not defined and not guaranteed to remain the same in future versions.)
is_derived_reference_attribute	yes_or_no	Applies to a feature not available in PostgreSQL

See also under Section 37.16, a similarly structured view, for further information on some of the columns.

37.7. character_sets

The view character_sets identifies the character sets available in the current database. Since PostgreSQL does not support multiple character sets within one database, this view only shows one, which is the database encoding.

Take note of how the following terms are used in the SQL standard:

character repertoire

An abstract collection of characters, for example UNICODE, UCS, or LATIN1. Not exposed as an SQL object, but visible in this view.

character encoding form

An encoding of some character repertoire. Most older character repertoires only use one encoding form, and so there are no separate names for them (e.g., LATIN1 is an encoding form applicable to the LATIN1 repertoire). But for example Unicode has the encoding forms UTF8, UTF16, etc. (not all supported by PostgreSQL). Encoding forms are not exposed as an SQL object, but are visible in this view.

character set

A named SQL object that identifies a character repertoire, a character encoding, and a default collation. A predefined character set would typically have the same name as an encoding form, but users could define other names. For example, the character set UTF8 would typically identify the character repertoire UCS, encoding form UTF8, and some default collation.

You can think of an "encoding" in PostgreSQL either as a character set or a character encoding form. They will have the same name, and there can only be one in one database.

Table 37.5. `character_sets` Columns

Name	Data Type	Description
character_set_catalog	sql_identifier	Character sets are currently not implemented as schema objects, so this column is null.
character_set_schema	sql_identifier	Character sets are currently not implemented as schema objects, so this column is null.
character_set_name	sql_identifier	Name of the character set, currently implemented as showing the name of the database encoding
character_repertoire	sql_identifier	Character repertoire, showing UCS if the encoding is UTF8, else just the encoding name
form_of_use	sql_identifier	Character encoding form, same as the database encoding
default_collate_catalog	sql_identifier	Name of the database containing the default collation (always the current database, if any collation is identified)
default_collate_schema	sql_identifier	Name of the schema containing the default collation
default_collate_name	sql_identifier	Name of the default collation. The default collation is identified as the collation that matches the COLLATE and CTYPE settings of the current database. If there is no such collation, then this column and the associated schema and catalog columns are null.

37.8. `check_constraint_routine_usage`

The view `check_constraint_routine_usage` identifies routines (functions and procedures) that are used by a check constraint. Only those routines are shown that are owned by a currently enabled role.

Table 37.6. `check_constraint_routine_usage` Columns

Name	Data Type	Description
constraint_catalog	sql_identifier	Name of the database containing the constraint (always the current database)
constraint_schema	sql_identifier	Name of the schema containing the constraint
constraint_name	sql_identifier	Name of the constraint
specific_catalog	sql_identifier	Name of the database containing the function (always the current database)

Name	Data Type	Description
specific_schema	sql_identifier	Name of the schema containing the function
specific_name	sql_identifier	The "specific name" of the function. See Section 37.40 for more information.

37.9. check_constraints

The view check_constraints contains all check constraints, either defined on a table or on a domain, that are owned by a currently enabled role. (The owner of the table or domain is the owner of the constraint.)

Table 37.7. check_constraints Columns

Name	Data Type	Description
constraint_catalog	sql_identifier	Name of the database containing the constraint (always the current database)
constraint_schema	sql_identifier	Name of the schema containing the constraint
constraint_name	sql_identifier	Name of the constraint
check_clause	character_data	The check expression of the check constraint

37.10. collations

The view collations contains the collations available in the current database.

Table 37.8. collations Columns

Name	Data Type	Description
collation_catalog	sql_identifier	Name of the database containing the collation (always the current database)
collation_schema	sql_identifier	Name of the schema containing the collation
collation_name	sql_identifier	Name of the default collation
pad_attribute	character_data	Always NO PAD (The alternative PAD SPACE is not supported by PostgreSQL.)

37.11. collation_character_set_applicability

The view collation_character_set_applicability identifies which character set the available collations are applicable to. In PostgreSQL, there is only one character set per database (see explanation in Section 37.7), so this view does not provide much useful information.

Table 37.9. `collation_character_set_applicability` Columns

Name	Data Type	Description
collation_catalog	sql_identifier	Name of the database containing the collation (always the current database)
collation_schema	sql_identifier	Name of the schema containing the collation
collation_name	sql_identifier	Name of the default collation
character_set_catalog	sql_identifier	Character sets are currently not implemented as schema objects, so this column is null
character_set_schema	sql_identifier	Character sets are currently not implemented as schema objects, so this column is null
character_set_name	sql_identifier	Name of the character set

37.12. `column_domain_usage`

The view `column_domain_usage` identifies all columns (of a table or a view) that make use of some domain defined in the current database and owned by a currently enabled role.

Table 37.10. `column_domain_usage` Columns

Name	Data Type	Description
domain_catalog	sql_identifier	Name of the database containing the domain (always the current database)
domain_schema	sql_identifier	Name of the schema containing the domain
domain_name	sql_identifier	Name of the domain
table_catalog	sql_identifier	Name of the database containing the table (always the current database)
table_schema	sql_identifier	Name of the schema containing the table
table_name	sql_identifier	Name of the table
column_name	sql_identifier	Name of the column

37.13. `column_options`

The view `column_options` contains all the options defined for foreign table columns in the current database. Only those foreign table columns are shown that the current user has access to (by way of being the owner or having some privilege).

Table 37.11. `column_options` Columns

Name	Data Type	Description
table_catalog	sql_identifier	Name of the database that contains the foreign table (always the current database)
table_schema	sql_identifier	Name of the schema that contains the foreign table
table_name	sql_identifier	Name of the foreign table
column_name	sql_identifier	Name of the column
option_name	sql_identifier	Name of an option
option_value	character_data	Value of the option

37.14. `column_privileges`

The view `column_privileges` identifies all privileges granted on columns to a currently enabled role or by a currently enabled role. There is one row for each combination of column, grantor, and grantee.

If a privilege has been granted on an entire table, it will show up in this view as a grant for each column, but only for the privilege types where column granularity is possible: SELECT, INSERT, UPDATE, REFERENCES.

Table 37.12. `column_privileges` Columns

Name	Data Type	Description
grantor	sql_identifier	Name of the role that granted the privilege
grantee	sql_identifier	Name of the role that the privilege was granted to
table_catalog	sql_identifier	Name of the database that contains the table that contains the column (always the current database)
table_schema	sql_identifier	Name of the schema that contains the table that contains the column
table_name	sql_identifier	Name of the table that contains the column
column_name	sql_identifier	Name of the column
privilege_type	character_data	Type of the privilege: SELECT, INSERT, UPDATE, or REFERENCES
is_grantable	yes_or_no	YES if the privilege is grantable, NO if not

37.15. `column_udt_usage`

The view `column_udt_usage` identifies all columns that use data types owned by a currently enabled role. Note that in PostgreSQL, built-in data types behave like user-defined types, so they are included here as well. See also Section 37.16 for details.

Table 37.13. `column_udt_usage` Columns

Name	Data Type	Description
udt_catalog	sql_identifier	Name of the database that the column data type (the underlying type of the domain, if applicable) is defined in (always the current database)
udt_schema	sql_identifier	Name of the schema that the column data type (the underlying type of the domain, if applicable) is defined in
udt_name	sql_identifier	Name of the column data type (the underlying type of the domain, if applicable)
table_catalog	sql_identifier	Name of the database containing the table (always the current database)
table_schema	sql_identifier	Name of the schema containing the table
table_name	sql_identifier	Name of the table
column_name	sql_identifier	Name of the column

37.16. `columns`

The view `columns` contains information about all table columns (or view columns) in the database. System columns (`oid`, etc.) are not included. Only those columns are shown that the current user has access to (by way of being the owner or having some privilege).

Table 37.14. `columns` Columns

Name	Data Type	Description
table_catalog	sql_identifier	Name of the database containing the table (always the current database)
table_schema	sql_identifier	Name of the schema containing the table
table_name	sql_identifier	Name of the table
column_name	sql_identifier	Name of the column
ordinal_position	cardinal_number	Ordinal position of the column within the table (count starts at 1)
column_default	character_data	Default expression of the column

Name	Data Type	Description
is_nullable	yes_or_no	YES if the column is possibly nullable, NO if it is known not nullable. A not-null constraint is one way a column can be known not nullable, but there can be others.
data_type	character_data	Data type of the column, if it is a built-in type, or ARRAY if it is some array (in that case, see the view element_types), else USER-DEFINED (in that case, the type is identified in udt_name and associated columns). If the column is based on a domain, this column refers to the type underlying the domain (and the domain is identified in domain_name and associated columns).
character_maximum_length	cardinal_number	If data_type identifies a character or bit string type, the declared maximum length; null for all other data types or if no maximum length was declared.
character_octet_length	cardinal_number	If data_type identifies a character type, the maximum possible length in octets (bytes) of a datum; null for all other data types. The maximum octet length depends on the declared character maximum length (see above) and the server encoding.
numeric_precision	cardinal_number	If data_type identifies a numeric type, this column contains the (declared or implicit) precision of the type for this column. The precision indicates the number of significant digits. It can be expressed in decimal (base 10) or binary (base 2) terms, as specified in the column numeric_precision_radix. For all other data types, this column is null.
numeric_precision_radix	cardinal_number	If data_type identifies a numeric type, this column indicates in which base the values in the columns numeric_precision and numeric_scale are expressed. The value is either 2 or 10. For all other data types, this column is null.

Name	Data Type	Description
numeric_scale	cardinal_number	If data_type identifies an exact numeric type, this column contains the (declared or implicit) scale of the type for this column. The scale indicates the number of significant digits to the right of the decimal point. It can be expressed in decimal (base 10) or binary (base 2) terms, as specified in the column numeric_precision_radix. For all other data types, this column is null.
datetime_precision	cardinal_number	If data_type identifies a date, time, timestamp, or interval type, this column contains the (declared or implicit) fractional seconds precision of the type for this column, that is, the number of decimal digits maintained following the decimal point in the seconds value. For all other data types, this column is null.
interval_type	character_data	If data_type identifies an interval type, this column contains the specification which fields the intervals include for this column, e.g., YEAR TO MONTH, DAY TO SECOND, etc. If no field restrictions were specified (that is, the interval accepts all fields), and for all other data types, this field is null.
interval_precision	cardinal_number	Applies to a feature not available in PostgreSQL (see datetime_precision for the fractional seconds precision of interval type columns)
character_set_catalog	sql_identifier	Applies to a feature not available in PostgreSQL
character_set_schema	sql_identifier	Applies to a feature not available in PostgreSQL
character_set_name	sql_identifier	Applies to a feature not available in PostgreSQL
collation_catalog	sql_identifier	Name of the database containing the collation of the column (always the current database), null if default or the data type of the column is not collatable

Name	Data Type	Description
collation_schema	sql_identifier	Name of the schema containing the collation of the column, null if default or the data type of the column is not collatable
collation_name	sql_identifier	Name of the collation of the column, null if default or the data type of the column is not collatable
domain_catalog	sql_identifier	If the column has a domain type, the name of the database that the domain is defined in (always the current database), else null.
domain_schema	sql_identifier	If the column has a domain type, the name of the schema that the domain is defined in, else null.
domain_name	sql_identifier	If the column has a domain type, the name of the domain, else null.
udt_catalog	sql_identifier	Name of the database that the column data type (the underlying type of the domain, if applicable) is defined in (always the current database)
udt_schema	sql_identifier	Name of the schema that the column data type (the underlying type of the domain, if applicable) is defined in
udt_name	sql_identifier	Name of the column data type (the underlying type of the domain, if applicable)
scope_catalog	sql_identifier	Applies to a feature not available in PostgreSQL
scope_schema	sql_identifier	Applies to a feature not available in PostgreSQL
scope_name	sql_identifier	Applies to a feature not available in PostgreSQL
maximum_cardinality	cardinal_number	Always null, because arrays always have unlimited maximum cardinality in PostgreSQL
dtd_identifier	sql_identifier	An identifier of the data type descriptor of the column, unique among the data type descriptors pertaining to the table. This is mainly useful for joining with other instances of such identifiers. (The specific format of the identifier is not defined and not guaran-

Name	Data Type	Description
		teed to remain the same in future versions.)
is_self_referencing	yes_or_no	Applies to a feature not available in PostgreSQL
is_identity	yes_or_no	If the column is an identity column, then YES, else NO.
identity_generation	character_data	If the column is an identity column, then ALWAYS or BY DE-FAULT, reflecting the definition of the column.
identity_start	character_data	If the column is an identity column, then the start value of the internal sequence, else null.
identity_increment	character_data	If the column is an identity column, then the increment of the internal sequence, else null.
identity_maximum	character_data	If the column is an identity column, then the maximum value of the internal sequence, else null.
identity_minimum	character_data	If the column is an identity column, then the minimum value of the internal sequence, else null.
identity_cycle	yes_or_no	If the column is an identity column, then YES if the internal sequence cycles or NO if it does not; otherwise null.
is_generated	character_data	Applies to a feature not available in PostgreSQL
generation_expression	character_data	Applies to a feature not available in PostgreSQL
is_updatable	yes_or_no	YES if the column is updatable, NO if not (Columns in base tables are always updatable, columns in views not necessarily)

Since data types can be defined in a variety of ways in SQL, and PostgreSQL contains additional ways to define data types, their representation in the information schema can be somewhat difficult. The column data_type is supposed to identify the underlying built-in type of the column. In PostgreSQL, this means that the type is defined in the system catalog schema pg_catalog. This column might be useful if the application can handle the well-known built-in types specially (for example, format the numeric types differently or use the data in the precision columns). The columns udt_name, udt_schema, and udt_catalog always identify the underlying data type of the column, even if the column is based on a domain. (Since PostgreSQL treats built-in types like user-defined types, built-in types appear here as well. This is an extension of the SQL standard.) These columns should be used if an application wants to process data differently according to the type, because in that case it wouldn't matter if the column is really based on a domain. If the column is based on a domain, the identity of the domain is stored in the columns domain_name, domain_schema, and domain_catalog. If you want to pair up columns with their associated data types and treat domains as separate types, you could write `coalesce(domain_name, udt_name)`, etc.

37.17. `constraint_column_usage`

The view `constraint_column_usage` identifies all columns in the current database that are used by some constraint. Only those columns are shown that are contained in a table owned by a currently enabled role. For a check constraint, this view identifies the columns that are used in the check expression. For a foreign key constraint, this view identifies the columns that the foreign key references. For a unique or primary key constraint, this view identifies the constrained columns.

Table 37.15. `constraint_column_usage` Columns

Name	Data Type	Description
table_catalog	sql_identifier	Name of the database that contains the table that contains the column that is used by some constraint (always the current database)
table_schema	sql_identifier	Name of the schema that contains the table that contains the column that is used by some constraint
table_name	sql_identifier	Name of the table that contains the column that is used by some constraint
column_name	sql_identifier	Name of the column that is used by some constraint
constraint_catalog	sql_identifier	Name of the database that contains the constraint (always the current database)
constraint_schema	sql_identifier	Name of the schema that contains the constraint
constraint_name	sql_identifier	Name of the constraint

37.18. `constraint_table_usage`

The view `constraint_table_usage` identifies all tables in the current database that are used by some constraint and are owned by a currently enabled role. (This is different from the view `table_constraints`, which identifies all table constraints along with the table they are defined on.) For a foreign key constraint, this view identifies the table that the foreign key references. For a unique or primary key constraint, this view simply identifies the table the constraint belongs to. Check constraints and not-null constraints are not included in this view.

Table 37.16. `constraint_table_usage` Columns

Name	Data Type	Description
table_catalog	sql_identifier	Name of the database that contains the table that is used by

Name	Data Type	Description
		some constraint (always the current database)
table_schema	sql_identifier	Name of the schema that contains the table that is used by some constraint
table_name	sql_identifier	Name of the table that is used by some constraint
constraint_catalog	sql_identifier	Name of the database that contains the constraint (always the current database)
constraint_schema	sql_identifier	Name of the schema that contains the constraint
constraint_name	sql_identifier	Name of the constraint

37.19. data_type_privileges

The view data_type_privileges identifies all data type descriptors that the current user has access to, by way of being the owner of the described object or having some privilege for it. A data type descriptor is generated whenever a data type is used in the definition of a table column, a domain, or a function (as parameter or return type) and stores some information about how the data type is used in that instance (for example, the declared maximum length, if applicable). Each data type descriptor is assigned an arbitrary identifier that is unique among the data type descriptor identifiers assigned for one object (table, domain, function). This view is probably not useful for applications, but it is used to define some other views in the information schema.

Table 37.17. data_type_privileges Columns

Name	Data Type	Description
object_catalog	sql_identifier	Name of the database that contains the described object (always the current database)
object_schema	sql_identifier	Name of the schema that contains the described object
object_name	sql_identifier	Name of the described object
object_type	character_data	The type of the described object: one of TABLE (the data type descriptor pertains to a column of that table), DOMAIN (the data type descriptors pertains to that domain), ROUTINE (the data type descriptor pertains to a parameter or the return data type of that function).
dtd_identifier	sql_identifier	The identifier of the data type descriptor, which is unique among the data type descriptors for that same object.

37.20. `domain_constraints`

The view `domain_constraints` contains all constraints belonging to domains defined in the current database. Only those domains are shown that the current user has access to (by way of being the owner or having some privilege).

Table 37.18. `domain_constraints` Columns

Name	Data Type	Description
`constraint_catalog`	`sql_identifier`	Name of the database that contains the constraint (always the current database)
`constraint_schema`	`sql_identifier`	Name of the schema that contains the constraint
`constraint_name`	`sql_identifier`	Name of the constraint
`domain_catalog`	`sql_identifier`	Name of the database that contains the domain (always the current database)
`domain_schema`	`sql_identifier`	Name of the schema that contains the domain
`domain_name`	`sql_identifier`	Name of the domain
`is_deferrable`	`yes_or_no`	YES if the constraint is deferrable, NO if not
`initially_deferred`	`yes_or_no`	YES if the constraint is deferrable and initially deferred, NO if not

37.21. `domain_udt_usage`

The view `domain_udt_usage` identifies all domains that are based on data types owned by a currently enabled role. Note that in PostgreSQL, built-in data types behave like user-defined types, so they are included here as well.

Table 37.19. `domain_udt_usage` Columns

Name	Data Type	Description
`udt_catalog`	`sql_identifier`	Name of the database that the domain data type is defined in (always the current database)
`udt_schema`	`sql_identifier`	Name of the schema that the domain data type is defined in
`udt_name`	`sql_identifier`	Name of the domain data type
`domain_catalog`	`sql_identifier`	Name of the database that contains the domain (always the current database)
`domain_schema`	`sql_identifier`	Name of the schema that contains the domain
`domain_name`	`sql_identifier`	Name of the domain

37.22. domains

The view domains contains all domains defined in the current database. Only those domains are shown that the current user has access to (by way of being the owner or having some privilege).

Table 37.20. domains Columns

Name	Data Type	Description
domain_catalog	sql_identifier	Name of the database that contains the domain (always the current database)
domain_schema	sql_identifier	Name of the schema that contains the domain
domain_name	sql_identifier	Name of the domain
data_type	character_data	Data type of the domain, if it is a built-in type, or ARRAY if it is some array (in that case, see the view element_types), else USER-DEFINED (in that case, the type is identified in udt_name and associated columns).
character_maximum_length	cardinal_number	If the domain has a character or bit string type, the declared maximum length; null for all other data types or if no maximum length was declared.
character_octet_length	cardinal_number	If the domain has a character type, the maximum possible length in octets (bytes) of a datum; null for all other data types. The maximum octet length depends on the declared character maximum length (see above) and the server encoding.
character_set_catalog	sql_identifier	Applies to a feature not available in PostgreSQL
character_set_schema	sql_identifier	Applies to a feature not available in PostgreSQL
character_set_name	sql_identifier	Applies to a feature not available in PostgreSQL
collation_catalog	sql_identifier	Name of the database containing the collation of the domain (always the current database), null if default or the data type of the domain is not collatable
collation_schema	sql_identifier	Name of the schema containing the collation of the domain, null if

Name	Data Type	Description
		default or the data type of the domain is not collatable
collation_name	sql_identifier	Name of the collation of the domain, null if default or the data type of the domain is not collatable
numeric_precision	cardinal_number	If the domain has a numeric type, this column contains the (declared or implicit) precision of the type for this domain. The precision indicates the number of significant digits. It can be expressed in decimal (base 10) or binary (base 2) terms, as specified in the column numeric_precision_radix. For all other data types, this column is null.
numeric_precision_radix	cardinal_number	If the domain has a numeric type, this column indicates in which base the values in the columns numeric_precision and numeric_scale are expressed. The value is either 2 or 10. For all other data types, this column is null.
numeric_scale	cardinal_number	If the domain has an exact numeric type, this column contains the (declared or implicit) scale of the type for this domain. The scale indicates the number of significant digits to the right of the decimal point. It can be expressed in decimal (base 10) or binary (base 2) terms, as specified in the column numeric_precision_radix. For all other data types, this column is null.
datetime_precision	cardinal_number	If data_type identifies a date, time, timestamp, or interval type, this column contains the (declared or implicit) fractional seconds precision of the type for this domain, that is, the number of decimal digits maintained following the decimal point in the seconds value. For all other data types, this column is null.
interval_type	character_data	If data_type identifies an interval type, this column contains the specification which fields the

Name	Data Type	Description
		intervals include for this domain, e.g., YEAR TO MONTH, DAY TO SECOND, etc. If no field restrictions were specified (that is, the interval accepts all fields), and for all other data types, this field is null.
interval_precision	cardinal_number	Applies to a feature not available in PostgreSQL (see datetime_precision for the fractional seconds precision of interval type domains)
domain_default	character_data	Default expression of the domain
udt_catalog	sql_identifier	Name of the database that the domain data type is defined in (always the current database)
udt_schema	sql_identifier	Name of the schema that the domain data type is defined in
udt_name	sql_identifier	Name of the domain data type
scope_catalog	sql_identifier	Applies to a feature not available in PostgreSQL
scope_schema	sql_identifier	Applies to a feature not available in PostgreSQL
scope_name	sql_identifier	Applies to a feature not available in PostgreSQL
maximum_cardinality	cardinal_number	Always null, because arrays always have unlimited maximum cardinality in PostgreSQL
dtd_identifier	sql_identifier	An identifier of the data type descriptor of the domain, unique among the data type descriptors pertaining to the domain (which is trivial, because a domain only contains one data type descriptor). This is mainly useful for joining with other instances of such identifiers. (The specific format of the identifier is not defined and not guaranteed to remain the same in future versions.)

37.23. element_types

The view element_types contains the data type descriptors of the elements of arrays. When a table column, composite-type attribute, domain, function parameter, or function return value is defined to be of an array type, the respective information schema view only contains ARRAY in the column data_type. To obtain information on the element type of the array, you can join the respective view with this view.

For example, to show the columns of a table with data types and array element types, if applicable, you could do:

```
SELECT c.column_name, c.data_type, e.data_type AS element_type
FROM information_schema.columns c LEFT JOIN
 information_schema.element_types e
     ON ((c.table_catalog, c.table_schema, c.table_name, 'TABLE',
c.dtd_identifier)
        = (e.object_catalog, e.object_schema, e.object_name,
e.object_type, e.collection_type_identifier))
WHERE c.table_schema = '...' AND c.table_name = '...'
ORDER BY c.ordinal_position;
```

This view only includes objects that the current user has access to, by way of being the owner or having some privilege.

Table 37.21. `element_types` Columns

Name	Data Type	Description
object_catalog	sql_identifier	Name of the database that contains the object that uses the array being described (always the current database)
object_schema	sql_identifier	Name of the schema that contains the object that uses the array being described
object_name	sql_identifier	Name of the object that uses the array being described
object_type	character_data	The type of the object that uses the array being described: one of TABLE (the array is used by a column of that table), USER-DEFINED TYPE (the array is used by an attribute of that composite type), DOMAIN (the array is used by that domain), ROUTINE (the array is used by a parameter or the return data type of that function).
collection_type_identifier	sql_identifier	The identifier of the data type descriptor of the array being described. Use this to join with the dtd_identifier columns of other information schema views.
data_type	character_data	Data type of the array elements, if it is a built-in type, else USER-DEFINED (in that case, the type is identified in udt_name and associated columns).
character_maximum_length	cardinal_number	Always null, since this information is not applied to array element data types in PostgreSQL

Name	Data Type	Description
`character_octet_length`	`cardinal_number`	Always null, since this information is not applied to array element data types in PostgreSQL
`character_set_catalog`	`sql_identifier`	Applies to a feature not available in PostgreSQL
`character_set_schema`	`sql_identifier`	Applies to a feature not available in PostgreSQL
`character_set_name`	`sql_identifier`	Applies to a feature not available in PostgreSQL
`collation_catalog`	`sql_identifier`	Name of the database containing the collation of the element type (always the current database), null if default or the data type of the element is not collatable
`collation_schema`	`sql_identifier`	Name of the schema containing the collation of the element type, null if default or the data type of the element is not collatable
`collation_name`	`sql_identifier`	Name of the collation of the element type, null if default or the data type of the element is not collatable
`numeric_precision`	`cardinal_number`	Always null, since this information is not applied to array element data types in PostgreSQL
`numeric_precision_radix`	`cardinal_number`	Always null, since this information is not applied to array element data types in PostgreSQL
`numeric_scale`	`cardinal_number`	Always null, since this information is not applied to array element data types in PostgreSQL
`datetime_precision`	`cardinal_number`	Always null, since this information is not applied to array element data types in PostgreSQL
`interval_type`	`character_data`	Always null, since this information is not applied to array element data types in PostgreSQL
`interval_precision`	`cardinal_number`	Always null, since this information is not applied to array element data types in PostgreSQL
`domain_default`	`character_data`	Not yet implemented
`udt_catalog`	`sql_identifier`	Name of the database that the data type of the elements is defined in (always the current database)
`udt_schema`	`sql_identifier`	Name of the schema that the data type of the elements is defined in

Name	Data Type	Description
udt_name	sql_identifier	Name of the data type of the elements
scope_catalog	sql_identifier	Applies to a feature not available in PostgreSQL
scope_schema	sql_identifier	Applies to a feature not available in PostgreSQL
scope_name	sql_identifier	Applies to a feature not available in PostgreSQL
maximum_cardinality	cardinal_number	Always null, because arrays always have unlimited maximum cardinality in PostgreSQL
dtd_identifier	sql_identifier	An identifier of the data type descriptor of the element. This is currently not useful.

37.24. enabled_roles

The view enabled_roles identifies the currently "enabled roles". The enabled roles are recursively defined as the current user together with all roles that have been granted to the enabled roles with automatic inheritance. In other words, these are all roles that the current user has direct or indirect, automatically inheriting membership in.

For permission checking, the set of "applicable roles" is applied, which can be broader than the set of enabled roles. So generally, it is better to use the view applicable_roles instead of this one; See Section 37.5 for details on applicable_roles view.

Table 37.22. enabled_roles Columns

Name	Data Type	Description
role_name	sql_identifier	Name of a role

37.25. foreign_data_wrapper_options

The view foreign_data_wrapper_options contains all the options defined for foreign-data wrappers in the current database. Only those foreign-data wrappers are shown that the current user has access to (by way of being the owner or having some privilege).

Table 37.23. foreign_data_wrapper_options Columns

Name	Data Type	Description
foreign_data_wrapper_catalog	sql_identifier	Name of the database that the foreign-data wrapper is defined in (always the current database)
foreign_data_wrapper_name	sql_identifier	Name of the foreign-data wrapper
option_name	sql_identifier	Name of an option

Name	Data Type	Description
option_value	character_data	Value of the option

37.26. foreign_data_wrappers

The view foreign_data_wrappers contains all foreign-data wrappers defined in the current database. Only those foreign-data wrappers are shown that the current user has access to (by way of being the owner or having some privilege).

Table 37.24. foreign_data_wrappers Columns

Name	Data Type	Description
foreign_data_wrapper_catalog	sql_identifier	Name of the database that contains the foreign-data wrapper (always the current database)
foreign_data_wrapper_name	sql_identifier	Name of the foreign-data wrapper
authorization_identifier	sql_identifier	Name of the owner of the foreign server
library_name	character_data	File name of the library that implementing this foreign-data wrapper
foreign_data_wrapper_language	character_data	Language used to implement this foreign-data wrapper

37.27. foreign_server_options

The view foreign_server_options contains all the options defined for foreign servers in the current database. Only those foreign servers are shown that the current user has access to (by way of being the owner or having some privilege).

Table 37.25. foreign_server_options Columns

Name	Data Type	Description
foreign_server_catalog	sql_identifier	Name of the database that the foreign server is defined in (always the current database)
foreign_server_name	sql_identifier	Name of the foreign server
option_name	sql_identifier	Name of an option
option_value	character_data	Value of the option

37.28. foreign_servers

The view foreign_servers contains all foreign servers defined in the current database. Only those foreign servers are shown that the current user has access to (by way of being the owner or having some privilege).

Table 37.26. `foreign_servers` Columns

Name	Data Type	Description
foreign_server_catalog	sql_identifier	Name of the database that the foreign server is defined in (always the current database)
foreign_server_name	sql_identifier	Name of the foreign server
foreign_data_wrapper_catalog	sql_identifier	Name of the database that contains the foreign-data wrapper used by the foreign server (always the current database)
foreign_data_wrapper_name	sql_identifier	Name of the foreign-data wrapper used by the foreign server
foreign_server_type	character_data	Foreign server type information, if specified upon creation
foreign_server_version	character_data	Foreign server version information, if specified upon creation
authorization_identifier	sql_identifier	Name of the owner of the foreign server

37.29. `foreign_table_options`

The view `foreign_table_options` contains all the options defined for foreign tables in the current database. Only those foreign tables are shown that the current user has access to (by way of being the owner or having some privilege).

Table 37.27. `foreign_table_options` Columns

Name	Data Type	Description
foreign_table_catalog	sql_identifier	Name of the database that contains the foreign table (always the current database)
foreign_table_schema	sql_identifier	Name of the schema that contains the foreign table
foreign_table_name	sql_identifier	Name of the foreign table
option_name	sql_identifier	Name of an option
option_value	character_data	Value of the option

37.30. `foreign_tables`

The view `foreign_tables` contains all foreign tables defined in the current database. Only those foreign tables are shown that the current user has access to (by way of being the owner or having some privilege).

Table 37.28. `foreign_tables` Columns

Name	Data Type	Description
foreign_table_catalog	sql_identifier	Name of the database that the foreign table is defined in (always the current database)
foreign_table_schema	sql_identifier	Name of the schema that contains the foreign table
foreign_table_name	sql_identifier	Name of the foreign table
foreign_server_catalog	sql_identifier	Name of the database that the foreign server is defined in (always the current database)
foreign_server_name	sql_identifier	Name of the foreign server

37.31. `key_column_usage`

The view `key_column_usage` identifies all columns in the current database that are restricted by some unique, primary key, or foreign key constraint. Check constraints are not included in this view. Only those columns are shown that the current user has access to, by way of being the owner or having some privilege.

Table 37.29. `key_column_usage` Columns

Name	Data Type	Description
constraint_catalog	sql_identifier	Name of the database that contains the constraint (always the current database)
constraint_schema	sql_identifier	Name of the schema that contains the constraint
constraint_name	sql_identifier	Name of the constraint
table_catalog	sql_identifier	Name of the database that contains the table that contains the column that is restricted by this constraint (always the current database)
table_schema	sql_identifier	Name of the schema that contains the table that contains the column that is restricted by this constraint
table_name	sql_identifier	Name of the table that contains the column that is restricted by this constraint
column_name	sql_identifier	Name of the column that is restricted by this constraint
ordinal_position	cardinal_number	Ordinal position of the column within the constraint key (count starts at 1)
position_in_u-nique_constraint	cardinal_number	For a foreign-key constraint, ordinal position of the referenced col-

Name	Data Type	Description
		umn within its unique constraint (count starts at 1); otherwise null

37.32. parameters

The view `parameters` contains information about the parameters (arguments) of all functions in the current database. Only those functions are shown that the current user has access to (by way of being the owner or having some privilege).

Table 37.30. parameters Columns

Name	Data Type	Description
specific_catalog	sql_identifier	Name of the database containing the function (always the current database)
specific_schema	sql_identifier	Name of the schema containing the function
specific_name	sql_identifier	The "specific name" of the function. See Section 37.40 for more information.
ordinal_position	cardinal_number	Ordinal position of the parameter in the argument list of the function (count starts at 1)
parameter_mode	character_data	IN for input parameter, OUT for output parameter, and INOUT for input/output parameter.
is_result	yes_or_no	Applies to a feature not available in PostgreSQL
as_locator	yes_or_no	Applies to a feature not available in PostgreSQL
parameter_name	sql_identifier	Name of the parameter, or null if the parameter has no name
data_type	character_data	Data type of the parameter, if it is a built-in type, or AR-RAY if it is some array (in that case, see the view element_types), else USER-DE-FINED (in that case, the type is identified in udt_name and associated columns).
character_maximum_length	cardinal_number	Always null, since this information is not applied to parameter data types in PostgreSQL
character_octet_length	cardinal_number	Always null, since this information is not applied to parameter data types in PostgreSQL

Name	Data Type	Description
character_set_catalog	sql_identifier	Applies to a feature not available in PostgreSQL
character_set_schema	sql_identifier	Applies to a feature not available in PostgreSQL
character_set_name	sql_identifier	Applies to a feature not available in PostgreSQL
collation_catalog	sql_identifier	Always null, since this information is not applied to parameter data types in PostgreSQL
collation_schema	sql_identifier	Always null, since this information is not applied to parameter data types in PostgreSQL
collation_name	sql_identifier	Always null, since this information is not applied to parameter data types in PostgreSQL
numeric_precision	cardinal_number	Always null, since this information is not applied to parameter data types in PostgreSQL
numeric_precision_radix	cardinal_number	Always null, since this information is not applied to parameter data types in PostgreSQL
numeric_scale	cardinal_number	Always null, since this information is not applied to parameter data types in PostgreSQL
datetime_precision	cardinal_number	Always null, since this information is not applied to parameter data types in PostgreSQL
interval_type	character_data	Always null, since this information is not applied to parameter data types in PostgreSQL
interval_precision	cardinal_number	Always null, since this information is not applied to parameter data types in PostgreSQL
udt_catalog	sql_identifier	Name of the database that the data type of the parameter is defined in (always the current database)
udt_schema	sql_identifier	Name of the schema that the data type of the parameter is defined in
udt_name	sql_identifier	Name of the data type of the parameter
scope_catalog	sql_identifier	Applies to a feature not available in PostgreSQL
scope_schema	sql_identifier	Applies to a feature not available in PostgreSQL

Name	Data Type	Description
scope_name	sql_identifier	Applies to a feature not available in PostgreSQL
maximum_cardinality	cardinal_number	Always null, because arrays always have unlimited maximum cardinality in PostgreSQL
dtd_identifier	sql_identifier	An identifier of the data type descriptor of the parameter, unique among the data type descriptors pertaining to the function. This is mainly useful for joining with other instances of such identifiers. (The specific format of the identifier is not defined and not guaranteed to remain the same in future versions.)
parameter_default	character_data	The default expression of the parameter, or null if none or if the function is not owned by a currently enabled role.

37.33. referential_constraints

The view referential_constraints contains all referential (foreign key) constraints in the current database. Only those constraints are shown for which the current user has write access to the referencing table (by way of being the owner or having some privilege other than SELECT).

Table 37.31. referential_constraints Columns

Name	Data Type	Description
constraint_catalog	sql_identifier	Name of the database containing the constraint (always the current database)
constraint_schema	sql_identifier	Name of the schema containing the constraint
constraint_name	sql_identifier	Name of the constraint
unique_constraint_catalog	sql_identifier	Name of the database that contains the unique or primary key constraint that the foreign key constraint references (always the current database)
unique_constraint_schema	sql_identifier	Name of the schema that contains the unique or primary key constraint that the foreign key constraint references
unique_constraint_name	sql_identifier	Name of the unique or primary key constraint that the foreign key constraint references

Name	Data Type	Description
match_option	character_data	Match option of the foreign key constraint: FULL, PARTIAL, or NONE.
update_rule	character_data	Update rule of the foreign key constraint: CASCADE, SET NULL, SET DEFAULT, RESTRICT, or NO ACTION.
delete_rule	character_data	Delete rule of the foreign key constraint: CASCADE, SET NULL, SET DEFAULT, RESTRICT, or NO ACTION.

37.34. role_column_grants

The view role_column_grants identifies all privileges granted on columns where the grantor or grantee is a currently enabled role. Further information can be found under column_privileges. The only effective difference between this view and column_privileges is that this view omits columns that have been made accessible to the current user by way of a grant to PUBLIC.

Table 37.32. role_column_grants Columns

Name	Data Type	Description
grantor	sql_identifier	Name of the role that granted the privilege
grantee	sql_identifier	Name of the role that the privilege was granted to
table_catalog	sql_identifier	Name of the database that contains the table that contains the column (always the current database)
table_schema	sql_identifier	Name of the schema that contains the table that contains the column
table_name	sql_identifier	Name of the table that contains the column
column_name	sql_identifier	Name of the column
privilege_type	character_data	Type of the privilege: SELECT, INSERT, UPDATE, or REFERENCES
is_grantable	yes_or_no	YES if the privilege is grantable, NO if not

37.35. role_routine_grants

The view role_routine_grants identifies all privileges granted on functions where the grantor or grantee is a currently enabled role. Further information can be found under routine_privileges. The only effective difference between this view and routine_privileges is that this view omits functions that have been made accessible to the current user by way of a grant to PUBLIC.

Table 37.33. `role_routine_grants` Columns

Name	Data Type	Description
grantor	sql_identifier	Name of the role that granted the privilege
grantee	sql_identifier	Name of the role that the privilege was granted to
specific_catalog	sql_identifier	Name of the database containing the function (always the current database)
specific_schema	sql_identifier	Name of the schema containing the function
specific_name	sql_identifier	The "specific name" of the function. See Section 37.40 for more information.
routine_catalog	sql_identifier	Name of the database containing the function (always the current database)
routine_schema	sql_identifier	Name of the schema containing the function
routine_name	sql_identifier	Name of the function (might be duplicated in case of overloading)
privilege_type	character_data	Always EXECUTE (the only privilege type for functions)
is_grantable	yes_or_no	YES if the privilege is grantable, NO if not

37.36. `role_table_grants`

The view `role_table_grants` identifies all privileges granted on tables or views where the grantor or grantee is a currently enabled role. Further information can be found under `table_privileges`. The only effective difference between this view and `table_privileges` is that this view omits tables that have been made accessible to the current user by way of a grant to PUBLIC.

Table 37.34. `role_table_grants` Columns

Name	Data Type	Description
grantor	sql_identifier	Name of the role that granted the privilege
grantee	sql_identifier	Name of the role that the privilege was granted to
table_catalog	sql_identifier	Name of the database that contains the table (always the current database)
table_schema	sql_identifier	Name of the schema that contains the table
table_name	sql_identifier	Name of the table

Name	Data Type	Description
privilege_type	character_data	Type of the privilege: SELECT, INSERT, UPDATE, DELETE, TRUNCATE, REFERENCES, or TRIGGER
is_grantable	yes_or_no	YES if the privilege is grantable, NO if not
with_hierarchy	yes_or_no	In the SQL standard, WITH HIERARCHY OPTION is a separate (sub-)privilege allowing certain operations on table inheritance hierarchies. In PostgreSQL, this is included in the SELECT privilege, so this column shows YES if the privilege is SELECT, else NO.

37.37. role_udt_grants

The view role_udt_grants is intended to identify USAGE privileges granted on user-defined types where the grantor or grantee is a currently enabled role. Further information can be found under udt_privileges. The only effective difference between this view and udt_privileges is that this view omits objects that have been made accessible to the current user by way of a grant to PUBLIC. Since data types do not have real privileges in PostgreSQL, but only an implicit grant to PUBLIC, this view is empty.

Table 37.35. role_udt_grants Columns

Name	Data Type	Description
grantor	sql_identifier	The name of the role that granted the privilege
grantee	sql_identifier	The name of the role that the privilege was granted to
udt_catalog	sql_identifier	Name of the database containing the type (always the current database)
udt_schema	sql_identifier	Name of the schema containing the type
udt_name	sql_identifier	Name of the type
privilege_type	character_data	Always TYPE USAGE
is_grantable	yes_or_no	YES if the privilege is grantable, NO if not

37.38. role_usage_grants

The view role_usage_grants identifies USAGE privileges granted on various kinds of objects where the grantor or grantee is a currently enabled role. Further information can be found under usage_privileges. The only effective difference between this view and usage_privileges is that this view omits objects that have been made accessible to the current user by way of a grant to PUBLIC.

Table 37.36. `role_usage_grants` Columns

Name	Data Type	Description
grantor	sql_identifier	The name of the role that granted the privilege
grantee	sql_identifier	The name of the role that the privilege was granted to
object_catalog	sql_identifier	Name of the database containing the object (always the current database)
object_schema	sql_identifier	Name of the schema containing the object, if applicable, else an empty string
object_name	sql_identifier	Name of the object
object_type	character_data	COLLATION or DOMAIN or FOREIGN DATA WRAPPER or FOREIGN SERVER or SEQUENCE
privilege_type	character_data	Always USAGE
is_grantable	yes_or_no	YES if the privilege is grantable, NO if not

37.39. `routine_privileges`

The view `routine_privileges` identifies all privileges granted on functions to a currently enabled role or by a currently enabled role. There is one row for each combination of function, grantor, and grantee.

Table 37.37. `routine_privileges` Columns

Name	Data Type	Description
grantor	sql_identifier	Name of the role that granted the privilege
grantee	sql_identifier	Name of the role that the privilege was granted to
specific_catalog	sql_identifier	Name of the database containing the function (always the current database)
specific_schema	sql_identifier	Name of the schema containing the function
specific_name	sql_identifier	The "specific name" of the function. See Section 37.40 for more information.
routine_catalog	sql_identifier	Name of the database containing the function (always the current database)
routine_schema	sql_identifier	Name of the schema containing the function

Name	Data Type	Description
routine_name	sql_identifier	Name of the function (might be duplicated in case of overloading)
privilege_type	character_data	Always EXECUTE (the only privilege type for functions)
is_grantable	yes_or_no	YES if the privilege is grantable, NO if not

37.40. routines

The view routines contains all functions and procedures in the current database. Only those functions and procedures are shown that the current user has access to (by way of being the owner or having some privilege).

Table 37.38. routines Columns

Name	Data Type	Description
specific_catalog	sql_identifier	Name of the database containing the function (always the current database)
specific_schema	sql_identifier	Name of the schema containing the function
specific_name	sql_identifier	The "specific name" of the function. This is a name that uniquely identifies the function in the schema, even if the real name of the function is overloaded. The format of the specific name is not defined, it should only be used to compare it to other instances of specific routine names.
routine_catalog	sql_identifier	Name of the database containing the function (always the current database)
routine_schema	sql_identifier	Name of the schema containing the function
routine_name	sql_identifier	Name of the function (might be duplicated in case of overloading)
routine_type	character_data	FUNCTION for a function, PROCEDURE for a procedure
module_catalog	sql_identifier	Applies to a feature not available in PostgreSQL
module_schema	sql_identifier	Applies to a feature not available in PostgreSQL
module_name	sql_identifier	Applies to a feature not available in PostgreSQL
udt_catalog	sql_identifier	Applies to a feature not available in PostgreSQL

Name	Data Type	Description
udt_schema	sql_identifier	Applies to a feature not available in PostgreSQL
udt_name	sql_identifier	Applies to a feature not available in PostgreSQL
data_type	character_data	Return data type of the function, if it is a built-in type, or **ARRAY** if it is some array (in that case, see the view element_types), else **USER-DEFINED** (in that case, the type is identified in type_udt_name and associated columns). Null for a procedure.
character_maximum_length	cardinal_number	Always null, since this information is not applied to return data types in PostgreSQL
character_octet_length	cardinal_number	Always null, since this information is not applied to return data types in PostgreSQL
character_set_catalog	sql_identifier	Applies to a feature not available in PostgreSQL
character_set_schema	sql_identifier	Applies to a feature not available in PostgreSQL
character_set_name	sql_identifier	Applies to a feature not available in PostgreSQL
collation_catalog	sql_identifier	Always null, since this information is not applied to return data types in PostgreSQL
collation_schema	sql_identifier	Always null, since this information is not applied to return data types in PostgreSQL
collation_name	sql_identifier	Always null, since this information is not applied to return data types in PostgreSQL
numeric_precision	cardinal_number	Always null, since this information is not applied to return data types in PostgreSQL
numeric_precision_radix	cardinal_number	Always null, since this information is not applied to return data types in PostgreSQL
numeric_scale	cardinal_number	Always null, since this information is not applied to return data types in PostgreSQL
datetime_precision	cardinal_number	Always null, since this information is not applied to return data types in PostgreSQL

Name	Data Type	Description
interval_type	character_data	Always null, since this information is not applied to return data types in PostgreSQL
interval_precision	cardinal_number	Always null, since this information is not applied to return data types in PostgreSQL
type_udt_catalog	sql_identifier	Name of the database that the return data type of the function is defined in (always the current database). Null for a procedure.
type_udt_schema	sql_identifier	Name of the schema that the return data type of the function is defined in. Null for a procedure.
type_udt_name	sql_identifier	Name of the return data type of the function. Null for a procedure.
scope_catalog	sql_identifier	Applies to a feature not available in PostgreSQL
scope_schema	sql_identifier	Applies to a feature not available in PostgreSQL
scope_name	sql_identifier	Applies to a feature not available in PostgreSQL
maximum_cardinality	cardinal_number	Always null, because arrays always have unlimited maximum cardinality in PostgreSQL
dtd_identifier	sql_identifier	An identifier of the data type descriptor of the return data type of this function, unique among the data type descriptors pertaining to the function. This is mainly useful for joining with other instances of such identifiers. (The specific format of the identifier is not defined and not guaranteed to remain the same in future versions.)
routine_body	character_data	If the function is an SQL function, then SQL, else EXTERNAL.
routine_definition	character_data	The source text of the function (null if the function is not owned by a currently enabled role). (According to the SQL standard, this column is only applicable if routine_body is SQL, but in PostgreSQL it will contain whatever source text was specified when the function was created.)
external_name	character_data	If this function is a C function, then the external name (link sym-

Name	Data Type	Description
		bol) of the function; else null. (This works out to be the same value that is shown in `routine_definition`.)
external_language	character_data	The language the function is written in
parameter_style	character_data	Always GENERAL (The SQL standard defines other parameter styles, which are not available in PostgreSQL.)
is_deterministic	yes_or_no	If the function is declared immutable (called deterministic in the SQL standard), then YES, else NO. (You cannot query the other volatility levels available in PostgreSQL through the information schema.)
sql_data_access	character_data	Always MODIFIES, meaning that the function possibly modifies SQL data. This information is not useful for PostgreSQL.
is_null_call	yes_or_no	If the function automatically returns null if any of its arguments are null, then YES, else NO. Null for a procedure.
sql_path	character_data	Applies to a feature not available in PostgreSQL
schema_level_routine	yes_or_no	Always YES (The opposite would be a method of a user-defined type, which is a feature not available in PostgreSQL.)
max_dynamic_result_sets	cardinal_number	Applies to a feature not available in PostgreSQL
is_user_defined_cast	yes_or_no	Applies to a feature not available in PostgreSQL
is_implicitly_invocable	yes_or_no	Applies to a feature not available in PostgreSQL
security_type	character_data	If the function runs with the privileges of the current user, then INVOKER, if the function runs with the privileges of the user who defined it, then DEFINER.
to_sql_specific_catalog	sql_identifier	Applies to a feature not available in PostgreSQL
to_sql_specific_schema	sql_identifier	Applies to a feature not available in PostgreSQL

Name	Data Type	Description
to_sql_specific_name	sql_identifier	Applies to a feature not available in PostgreSQL
as_locator	yes_or_no	Applies to a feature not available in PostgreSQL
created	time_stamp	Applies to a feature not available in PostgreSQL
last_altered	time_stamp	Applies to a feature not available in PostgreSQL
new_savepoint_level	yes_or_no	Applies to a feature not available in PostgreSQL
is_udt_dependent	yes_or_no	Currently always NO. The alternative YES applies to a feature not available in PostgreSQL.
result_cast_from_data_type	character_data	Applies to a feature not available in PostgreSQL
result_cast_as_locator	yes_or_no	Applies to a feature not available in PostgreSQL
result_cast_char_max_length	cardinal_number	Applies to a feature not available in PostgreSQL
result_cast_char_octet_length	character_data	Applies to a feature not available in PostgreSQL
result_cast_char_set_catalog	sql_identifier	Applies to a feature not available in PostgreSQL
result_cast_char_set_schema	sql_identifier	Applies to a feature not available in PostgreSQL
result_cast_char_set_name	sql_identifier	Applies to a feature not available in PostgreSQL
result_cast_collation_catalog	sql_identifier	Applies to a feature not available in PostgreSQL
result_cast_collation_schema	sql_identifier	Applies to a feature not available in PostgreSQL
result_cast_collation_name	sql_identifier	Applies to a feature not available in PostgreSQL
result_cast_numeric_precision	cardinal_number	Applies to a feature not available in PostgreSQL
result_cast_numeric_precision_radix	cardinal_number	Applies to a feature not available in PostgreSQL
result_cast_numeric_scale	cardinal_number	Applies to a feature not available in PostgreSQL
result_cast_datetime_precision	character_data	Applies to a feature not available in PostgreSQL
result_cast_interval_type	character_data	Applies to a feature not available in PostgreSQL

Name	Data Type	Description
result_cast_interval_precision	cardinal_number	Applies to a feature not available in PostgreSQL
result_cast_type_udt_catalog	sql_identifier	Applies to a feature not available in PostgreSQL
result_cast_type_udt_schema	sql_identifier	Applies to a feature not available in PostgreSQL
result_cast_type_udt_name	sql_identifier	Applies to a feature not available in PostgreSQL
result_cast_scope_catalog	sql_identifier	Applies to a feature not available in PostgreSQL
result_cast_scope_schema	sql_identifier	Applies to a feature not available in PostgreSQL
result_cast_scope_name	sql_identifier	Applies to a feature not available in PostgreSQL
result_cast_maximum_cardinality	cardinal_number	Applies to a feature not available in PostgreSQL
result_cast_dtd_identifier	sql_identifier	Applies to a feature not available in PostgreSQL

37.41. schemata

The view schemata contains all schemas in the current database that the current user has access to (by way of being the owner or having some privilege).

Table 37.39. schemata Columns

Name	Data Type	Description
catalog_name	sql_identifier	Name of the database that the schema is contained in (always the current database)
schema_name	sql_identifier	Name of the schema
schema_owner	sql_identifier	Name of the owner of the schema
default_character_set_catalog	sql_identifier	Applies to a feature not available in PostgreSQL
default_character_set_schema	sql_identifier	Applies to a feature not available in PostgreSQL
default_character_set_name	sql_identifier	Applies to a feature not available in PostgreSQL
sql_path	character_data	Applies to a feature not available in PostgreSQL

37.42. sequences

The view sequences contains all sequences defined in the current database. Only those sequences are shown that the current user has access to (by way of being the owner or having some privilege).

Table 37.40. sequences Columns

Name	Data Type	Description
sequence_catalog	sql_identifier	Name of the database that contains the sequence (always the current database)
sequence_schema	sql_identifier	Name of the schema that contains the sequence
sequence_name	sql_identifier	Name of the sequence
data_type	character_data	The data type of the sequence.
numeric_precision	cardinal_number	This column contains the (declared or implicit) precision of the sequence data type (see above). The precision indicates the number of significant digits. It can be expressed in decimal (base 10) or binary (base 2) terms, as specified in the column numeric_precision_radix.
numeric_precision_radix	cardinal_number	This column indicates in which base the values in the columns numeric_precision and numeric_scale are expressed. The value is either 2 or 10.
numeric_scale	cardinal_number	This column contains the (declared or implicit) scale of the sequence data type (see above). The scale indicates the number of significant digits to the right of the decimal point. It can be expressed in decimal (base 10) or binary (base 2) terms, as specified in the column numeric_precision_radix.
start_value	character_data	The start value of the sequence
minimum_value	character_data	The minimum value of the sequence
maximum_value	character_data	The maximum value of the sequence
increment	character_data	The increment of the sequence
cycle_option	yes_or_no	YES if the sequence cycles, else NO

Note that in accordance with the SQL standard, the start, minimum, maximum, and increment values are returned as character strings.

37.43. `sql_features`

The table `sql_features` contains information about which formal features defined in the SQL standard are supported by PostgreSQL. This is the same information that is presented in Appendix D. There you can also find some additional background information.

Table 37.41. `sql_features` Columns

Name	Data Type	Description
feature_id	character_data	Identifier string of the feature
feature_name	character_data	Descriptive name of the feature
sub_feature_id	character_data	Identifier string of the subfeature, or a zero-length string if not a subfeature
sub_feature_name	character_data	Descriptive name of the subfeature, or a zero-length string if not a subfeature
is_supported	yes_or_no	YES if the feature is fully supported by the current version of PostgreSQL, NO if not
is_verified_by	character_data	Always null, since the PostgreSQL development group does not perform formal testing of feature conformance
comments	character_data	Possibly a comment about the supported status of the feature

37.44. `sql_implementation_info`

The table `sql_implementation_info` contains information about various aspects that are left implementation-defined by the SQL standard. This information is primarily intended for use in the context of the ODBC interface; users of other interfaces will probably find this information to be of little use. For this reason, the individual implementation information items are not described here; you will find them in the description of the ODBC interface.

Table 37.42. `sql_implementation_info` Columns

Name	Data Type	Description
implementation_info_id	character_data	Identifier string of the implementation information item
implementation_info_name	character_data	Descriptive name of the implementation information item
integer_value	cardinal_number	Value of the implementation information item, or null if the value is contained in the column character_value
character_value	character_data	Value of the implementation information item, or null if the value

Name	Data Type	Description
		is contained in the column `integer_value`
`comments`	`character_data`	Possibly a comment pertaining to the implementation information item

37.45. `sql_languages`

The table `sql_languages` contains one row for each SQL language binding that is supported by PostgreSQL. PostgreSQL supports direct SQL and embedded SQL in C; that is all you will learn from this table.

This table was removed from the SQL standard in SQL:2008, so there are no entries referring to standards later than SQL:2003.

Table 37.43. `sql_languages` Columns

Name	Data Type	Description
`sql_language_source`	`character_data`	The name of the source of the language definition; always `ISO 9075`, that is, the SQL standard
`sql_language_year`	`character_data`	The year the standard referenced in `sql_language_source` was approved.
`sql_language_conformance`	`character_data`	The standard conformance level for the language binding. For ISO 9075:2003 this is always `CORE`.
`sql_language_integrity`	`character_data`	Always null (This value is relevant to an earlier version of the SQL standard.)
`sql_language_implementation`	`character_data`	Always null
`sql_language_binding_style`	`character_data`	The language binding style, either `DIRECT` or `EMBEDDED`
`sql_language_programming_language`	`character_data`	The programming language, if the binding style is `EMBEDDED`, else null. PostgreSQL only supports the language C.

37.46. `sql_packages`

The table `sql_packages` contains information about which feature packages defined in the SQL standard are supported by PostgreSQL. Refer to Appendix D for background information on feature packages.

Table 37.44. `sql_packages` Columns

Name	Data Type	Description
`feature_id`	`character_data`	Identifier string of the package

Name	Data Type	Description
feature_name	character_data	Descriptive name of the package
is_supported	yes_or_no	YES if the package is fully supported by the current version of PostgreSQL, NO if not
is_verified_by	character_data	Always null, since the PostgreSQL development group does not perform formal testing of feature conformance
comments	character_data	Possibly a comment about the supported status of the package

37.47. sql_parts

The table sql_parts contains information about which of the several parts of the SQL standard are supported by PostgreSQL.

Table 37.45. sql_parts Columns

Name	Data Type	Description
feature_id	character_data	An identifier string containing the number of the part
feature_name	character_data	Descriptive name of the part
is_supported	yes_or_no	YES if the part is fully supported by the current version of PostgreSQL, NO if not
is_verified_by	character_data	Always null, since the PostgreSQL development group does not perform formal testing of feature conformance
comments	character_data	Possibly a comment about the supported status of the part

37.48. sql_sizing

The table sql_sizing contains information about various size limits and maximum values in PostgreSQL. This information is primarily intended for use in the context of the ODBC interface; users of other interfaces will probably find this information to be of little use. For this reason, the individual sizing items are not described here; you will find them in the description of the ODBC interface.

Table 37.46. sql_sizing Columns

Name	Data Type	Description
sizing_id	cardinal_number	Identifier of the sizing item
sizing_name	character_data	Descriptive name of the sizing item
supported_value	cardinal_number	Value of the sizing item, or 0 if the size is unlimited or cannot be de-

Name	Data Type	Description
		termined, or null if the features for which the sizing item is applicable are not supported
comments	character_data	Possibly a comment pertaining to the sizing item

37.49. sql_sizing_profiles

The table sql_sizing_profiles contains information about the sql_sizing values that are required by various profiles of the SQL standard. PostgreSQL does not track any SQL profiles, so this table is empty.

Table 37.47. sql_sizing_profiles Columns

Name	Data Type	Description
sizing_id	cardinal_number	Identifier of the sizing item
sizing_name	character_data	Descriptive name of the sizing item
profile_id	character_data	Identifier string of a profile
required_value	cardinal_number	The value required by the SQL profile for the sizing item, or 0 if the profile places no limit on the sizing item, or null if the profile does not require any of the features for which the sizing item is applicable
comments	character_data	Possibly a comment pertaining to the sizing item within the profile

37.50. table_constraints

The view table_constraints contains all constraints belonging to tables that the current user owns or has some privilege other than SELECT on.

Table 37.48. table_constraints Columns

Name	Data Type	Description
constraint_catalog	sql_identifier	Name of the database that contains the constraint (always the current database)
constraint_schema	sql_identifier	Name of the schema that contains the constraint
constraint_name	sql_identifier	Name of the constraint
table_catalog	sql_identifier	Name of the database that contains the table (always the current database)

Name	Data Type	Description
table_schema	sql_identifier	Name of the schema that contains the table
table_name	sql_identifier	Name of the table
constraint_type	character_data	Type of the constraint: CHECK, FOREIGN KEY, PRIMARY KEY, or UNIQUE
is_deferrable	yes_or_no	YES if the constraint is deferrable, NO if not
initially_deferred	yes_or_no	YES if the constraint is deferrable and initially deferred, NO if not
enforced	yes_or_no	Applies to a feature not available in PostgreSQL (currently always YES)

37.51. `table_privileges`

The view `table_privileges` identifies all privileges granted on tables or views to a currently enabled role or by a currently enabled role. There is one row for each combination of table, grantor, and grantee.

Table 37.49. `table_privileges` Columns

Name	Data Type	Description
grantor	sql_identifier	Name of the role that granted the privilege
grantee	sql_identifier	Name of the role that the privilege was granted to
table_catalog	sql_identifier	Name of the database that contains the table (always the current database)
table_schema	sql_identifier	Name of the schema that contains the table
table_name	sql_identifier	Name of the table
privilege_type	character_data	Type of the privilege: SELECT, INSERT, UPDATE, DELETE, TRUNCATE, REFERENCES, or TRIGGER
is_grantable	yes_or_no	YES if the privilege is grantable, NO if not
with_hierarchy	yes_or_no	In the SQL standard, WITH HIERARCHY OPTION is a separate (sub-)privilege allowing certain operations on table inheritance hierarchies. In PostgreSQL, this is included in the SELECT privilege, so this column shows YES if the privilege is SELECT, else NO.

37.52. `tables`

The view `tables` contains all tables and views defined in the current database. Only those tables and views are shown that the current user has access to (by way of being the owner or having some privilege).

Table 37.50. `tables` Columns

Name	Data Type	Description
`table_catalog`	`sql_identifier`	Name of the database that contains the table (always the current database)
`table_schema`	`sql_identifier`	Name of the schema that contains the table
`table_name`	`sql_identifier`	Name of the table
`table_type`	`character_data`	Type of the table: `BASE TABLE` for a persistent base table (the normal table type), `VIEW` for a view, `FOREIGN` for a foreign table, or `LOCAL TEMPORARY` for a temporary table
`self_referencing_column_name`	`sql_identifier`	Applies to a feature not available in PostgreSQL
`reference_generation`	`character_data`	Applies to a feature not available in PostgreSQL
`user_defined_type_catalog`	`sql_identifier`	If the table is a typed table, the name of the database that contains the underlying data type (always the current database), else null.
`user_defined_type_schema`	`sql_identifier`	If the table is a typed table, the name of the schema that contains the underlying data type, else null.
`user_defined_type_name`	`sql_identifier`	If the table is a typed table, the name of the underlying data type, else null.
`is_insertable_into`	`yes_or_no`	`YES` if the table is insertable into, `NO` if not (Base tables are always insertable into, views not necessarily.)
`is_typed`	`yes_or_no`	`YES` if the table is a typed table, `NO` if not
`commit_action`	`character_data`	Not yet implemented

37.53. `transforms`

The view `transforms` contains information about the transforms defined in the current database. More precisely, it contains a row for each function contained in a transform (the "from SQL" or "to SQL" function).

Table 37.51. transforms Columns

Name	Data Type	Description
udt_catalog	sql_identifier	Name of the database that contains the type the transform is for (always the current database)
udt_schema	sql_identifier	Name of the schema that contains the type the transform is for
udt_name	sql_identifier	Name of the type the transform is for
specific_catalog	sql_identifier	Name of the database containing the function (always the current database)
specific_schema	sql_identifier	Name of the schema containing the function
specific_name	sql_identifier	The "specific name" of the function. See Section 37.40 for more information.
group_name	sql_identifier	The SQL standard allows defining transforms in "groups", and selecting a group at run time. PostgreSQL does not support this. Instead, transforms are specific to a language. As a compromise, this field contains the language the transform is for.
transform_type	character_data	FROM SQL or TO SQL

37.54. triggered_update_columns

For triggers in the current database that specify a column list (like UPDATE OF column1, column2), the view triggered_update_columns identifies these columns. Triggers that do not specify a column list are not included in this view. Only those columns are shown that the current user owns or has some privilege other than SELECT on.

Table 37.52. triggered_update_columns Columns

Name	Data Type	Description
trigger_catalog	sql_identifier	Name of the database that contains the trigger (always the current database)
trigger_schema	sql_identifier	Name of the schema that contains the trigger
trigger_name	sql_identifier	Name of the trigger
event_object_catalog	sql_identifier	Name of the database that contains the table that the trigger is defined on (always the current database)

Name	Data Type	Description
`event_object_schema`	`sql_identifier`	Name of the schema that contains the table that the trigger is defined on
`event_object_table`	`sql_identifier`	Name of the table that the trigger is defined on
`event_object_column`	`sql_identifier`	Name of the column that the trigger is defined on

37.55. `triggers`

The view `triggers` contains all triggers defined in the current database on tables and views that the current user owns or has some privilege other than `SELECT` on.

Table 37.53. `triggers` Columns

Name	Data Type	Description
`trigger_catalog`	`sql_identifier`	Name of the database that contains the trigger (always the current database)
`trigger_schema`	`sql_identifier`	Name of the schema that contains the trigger
`trigger_name`	`sql_identifier`	Name of the trigger
`event_manipulation`	`character_data`	Event that fires the trigger (`INSERT`, `UPDATE`, or `DELETE`)
`event_object_catalog`	`sql_identifier`	Name of the database that contains the table that the trigger is defined on (always the current database)
`event_object_schema`	`sql_identifier`	Name of the schema that contains the table that the trigger is defined on
`event_object_table`	`sql_identifier`	Name of the table that the trigger is defined on
`action_order`	`cardinal_number`	Firing order among triggers on the same table having the same `event_manipulation`, `action_timing`, and `action_orientation`. In PostgreSQL, triggers are fired in name order, so this column reflects that.
`action_condition`	`character_data`	`WHEN` condition of the trigger, null if none (also null if the table is not owned by a currently enabled role)
`action_statement`	`character_data`	Statement that is executed by the trigger (currently always `EXE-`

Name	Data Type	Description
		CUTE FUNCTION func-tion(...))
action_orientation	character_data	Identifies whether the trigger fires once for each processed row or once for each statement (ROW or STATEMENT)
action_timing	character_data	Time at which the trigger fires (BEFORE, AFTER, or INSTEAD OF)
action_refer-ence_old_table	sql_identifier	Name of the "old" transition table, or null if none
action_refer-ence_new_table	sql_identifier	Name of the "new" transition table, or null if none
action_refer-ence_old_row	sql_identifier	Applies to a feature not available in PostgreSQL
action_refer-ence_new_row	sql_identifier	Applies to a feature not available in PostgreSQL
created	time_stamp	Applies to a feature not available in PostgreSQL

Triggers in PostgreSQL have two incompatibilities with the SQL standard that affect the representation in the information schema. First, trigger names are local to each table in PostgreSQL, rather than being independent schema objects. Therefore there can be duplicate trigger names defined in one schema, so long as they belong to different tables. (trigger_catalog and trigger_schema are really the values pertaining to the table that the trigger is defined on.) Second, triggers can be defined to fire on multiple events in PostgreSQL (e.g., ON INSERT OR UPDATE), whereas the SQL standard only allows one. If a trigger is defined to fire on multiple events, it is represented as multiple rows in the information schema, one for each type of event. As a consequence of these two issues, the primary key of the view trig-gers is really (trigger_catalog, trigger_schema, event_object_table, trig-ger_name, event_manipulation) instead of (trigger_catalog, trigger_schema, trigger_name), which is what the SQL standard specifies. Nonetheless, if you define your triggers in a manner that conforms with the SQL standard (trigger names unique in the schema and only one event type per trigger), this will not affect you.

> **Note**
>
> Prior to PostgreSQL 9.1, this view's columns action_timing, action_ref-erence_old_table, action_reference_new_table, action_refer-ence_old_row, and action_reference_new_row were named condi-tion_timing, condition_reference_old_table, condition_refer-ence_new_table, condition_reference_old_row, and condition_ref-erence_new_row respectively. That was how they were named in the SQL:1999 stan-dard. The new naming conforms to SQL:2003 and later.

37.56. udt_privileges

The view udt_privileges identifies USAGE privileges granted on user-defined types to a currently enabled role or by a currently enabled role. There is one row for each combination of type, grantor, and grantee. This view shows only composite types (see under Section 37.58 for why); see Section 37.57 for domain privileges.

Table 37.54. `udt_privileges` Columns

Name	Data Type	Description
grantor	sql_identifier	Name of the role that granted the privilege
grantee	sql_identifier	Name of the role that the privilege was granted to
udt_catalog	sql_identifier	Name of the database containing the type (always the current database)
udt_schema	sql_identifier	Name of the schema containing the type
udt_name	sql_identifier	Name of the type
privilege_type	character_data	Always `TYPE USAGE`
is_grantable	yes_or_no	`YES` if the privilege is grantable, `NO` if not

37.57. usage_privileges

The view `usage_privileges` identifies `USAGE` privileges granted on various kinds of objects to a currently enabled role or by a currently enabled role. In PostgreSQL, this currently applies to collations, domains, foreign-data wrappers, foreign servers, and sequences. There is one row for each combination of object, grantor, and grantee.

Since collations do not have real privileges in PostgreSQL, this view shows implicit non-grantable `USAGE` privileges granted by the owner to `PUBLIC` for all collations. The other object types, however, show real privileges.

In PostgreSQL, sequences also support `SELECT` and `UPDATE` privileges in addition to the `USAGE` privilege. These are nonstandard and therefore not visible in the information schema.

Table 37.55. `usage_privileges` Columns

Name	Data Type	Description
grantor	sql_identifier	Name of the role that granted the privilege
grantee	sql_identifier	Name of the role that the privilege was granted to
object_catalog	sql_identifier	Name of the database containing the object (always the current database)
object_schema	sql_identifier	Name of the schema containing the object, if applicable, else an empty string
object_name	sql_identifier	Name of the object
object_type	character_data	`COLLATION` or `DOMAIN` or `FOREIGN DATA WRAPPER`

Name	Data Type	Description
		or FOREIGN SERVER or SEQUENCE
privilege_type	character_data	Always USAGE
is_grantable	yes_or_no	YES if the privilege is grantable, NO if not

37.58. user_defined_types

The view user_defined_types currently contains all composite types defined in the current database. Only those types are shown that the current user has access to (by way of being the owner or having some privilege).

SQL knows about two kinds of user-defined types: structured types (also known as composite types in PostgreSQL) and distinct types (not implemented in PostgreSQL). To be future-proof, use the column user_defined_type_category to differentiate between these. Other user-defined types such as base types and enums, which are PostgreSQL extensions, are not shown here. For domains, see Section 37.22 instead.

Table 37.56. user_defined_types Columns

Name	Data Type	Description
user_defined_type_catalog	sql_identifier	Name of the database that contains the type (always the current database)
user_defined_type_schema	sql_identifier	Name of the schema that contains the type
user_defined_type_name	sql_identifier	Name of the type
user_defined_type_category	character_data	Currently always STRUCTURED
is_instantiable	yes_or_no	Applies to a feature not available in PostgreSQL
is_final	yes_or_no	Applies to a feature not available in PostgreSQL
ordering_form	character_data	Applies to a feature not available in PostgreSQL
ordering_category	character_data	Applies to a feature not available in PostgreSQL
ordering_routine_catalog	sql_identifier	Applies to a feature not available in PostgreSQL
ordering_routine_schema	sql_identifier	Applies to a feature not available in PostgreSQL
ordering_routine_name	sql_identifier	Applies to a feature not available in PostgreSQL
reference_type	character_data	Applies to a feature not available in PostgreSQL

Name	Data Type	Description
data_type	character_data	Applies to a feature not available in PostgreSQL
character_maxi-mum_length	cardinal_number	Applies to a feature not available in PostgreSQL
character_octet_length	cardinal_number	Applies to a feature not available in PostgreSQL
character_set_catalog	sql_identifier	Applies to a feature not available in PostgreSQL
character_set_schema	sql_identifier	Applies to a feature not available in PostgreSQL
character_set_name	sql_identifier	Applies to a feature not available in PostgreSQL
collation_catalog	sql_identifier	Applies to a feature not available in PostgreSQL
collation_schema	sql_identifier	Applies to a feature not available in PostgreSQL
collation_name	sql_identifier	Applies to a feature not available in PostgreSQL
numeric_precision	cardinal_number	Applies to a feature not available in PostgreSQL
numeric_preci-sion_radix	cardinal_number	Applies to a feature not available in PostgreSQL
numeric_scale	cardinal_number	Applies to a feature not available in PostgreSQL
datetime_precision	cardinal_number	Applies to a feature not available in PostgreSQL
interval_type	character_data	Applies to a feature not available in PostgreSQL
interval_precision	cardinal_number	Applies to a feature not available in PostgreSQL
source_dtd_identifier	sql_identifier	Applies to a feature not available in PostgreSQL
ref_dtd_identifier	sql_identifier	Applies to a feature not available in PostgreSQL

37.59. `user_mapping_options`

The view `user_mapping_options` contains all the options defined for user mappings in the current database. Only those user mappings are shown where the current user has access to the corresponding foreign server (by way of being the owner or having some privilege).

Table 37.57. `user_mapping_options` Columns

Name	Data Type	Description
authorization_identi-fier	sql_identifier	Name of the user being mapped, or PUBLIC if the mapping is public
foreign_server_catalog	sql_identifier	Name of the database that the foreign server used by this mapping is defined in (always the current database)
foreign_server_name	sql_identifier	Name of the foreign server used by this mapping
option_name	sql_identifier	Name of an option
option_value	character_data	Value of the option. This column will show as null unless the current user is the user being mapped, or the mapping is for PUBLIC and the current user is the server owner, or the current user is a superuser. The intent is to protect password information stored as user mapping option.

37.60. `user_mappings`

The view `user_mappings` contains all user mappings defined in the current database. Only those user mappings are shown where the current user has access to the corresponding foreign server (by way of being the owner or having some privilege).

Table 37.58. `user_mappings` Columns

Name	Data Type	Description
authorization_identi-fier	sql_identifier	Name of the user being mapped, or PUBLIC if the mapping is public
foreign_server_catalog	sql_identifier	Name of the database that the foreign server used by this mapping is defined in (always the current database)
foreign_server_name	sql_identifier	Name of the foreign server used by this mapping

37.61. `view_column_usage`

The view `view_column_usage` identifies all columns that are used in the query expression of a view (the SELECT statement that defines the view). A column is only included if the table that contains the column is owned by a currently enabled role.

> **Note**
>
> Columns of system tables are not included. This should be fixed sometime.

Table 37.59. `view_column_usage` Columns

Name	Data Type	Description
view_catalog	sql_identifier	Name of the database that contains the view (always the current database)
view_schema	sql_identifier	Name of the schema that contains the view
view_name	sql_identifier	Name of the view
table_catalog	sql_identifier	Name of the database that contains the table that contains the column that is used by the view (always the current database)
table_schema	sql_identifier	Name of the schema that contains the table that contains the column that is used by the view
table_name	sql_identifier	Name of the table that contains the column that is used by the view
column_name	sql_identifier	Name of the column that is used by the view

37.62. `view_routine_usage`

The view `view_routine_usage` identifies all routines (functions and procedures) that are used in the query expression of a view (the `SELECT` statement that defines the view). A routine is only included if that routine is owned by a currently enabled role.

Table 37.60. `view_routine_usage` Columns

Name	Data Type	Description
table_catalog	sql_identifier	Name of the database containing the view (always the current database)
table_schema	sql_identifier	Name of the schema containing the view
table_name	sql_identifier	Name of the view
specific_catalog	sql_identifier	Name of the database containing the function (always the current database)
specific_schema	sql_identifier	Name of the schema containing the function

Name	Data Type	Description
specific_name	sql_identifier	The "specific name" of the function. See Section 37.40 for more information.

37.63. `view_table_usage`

The view `view_table_usage` identifies all tables that are used in the query expression of a view (the `SELECT` statement that defines the view). A table is only included if that table is owned by a currently enabled role.

Note

System tables are not included. This should be fixed sometime.

Table 37.61. `view_table_usage` Columns

Name	Data Type	Description
view_catalog	sql_identifier	Name of the database that contains the view (always the current database)
view_schema	sql_identifier	Name of the schema that contains the view
view_name	sql_identifier	Name of the view
table_catalog	sql_identifier	Name of the database that contains the table that is used by the view (always the current database)
table_schema	sql_identifier	Name of the schema that contains the table that is used by the view
table_name	sql_identifier	Name of the table that is used by the view

37.64. `views`

The view `views` contains all views defined in the current database. Only those views are shown that the current user has access to (by way of being the owner or having some privilege).

Table 37.62. `views` Columns

Name	Data Type	Description
table_catalog	sql_identifier	Name of the database that contains the view (always the current database)
table_schema	sql_identifier	Name of the schema that contains the view

Name	Data Type	Description
table_name	sql_identifier	Name of the view
view_definition	character_data	Query expression defining the view (null if the view is not owned by a currently enabled role)
check_option	character_data	Applies to a feature not available in PostgreSQL
is_updatable	yes_or_no	YES if the view is updatable (allows UPDATE and DELETE), NO if not
is_insertable_into	yes_or_no	YES if the view is insertable into (allows INSERT), NO if not
is_trigger_updatable	yes_or_no	YES if the view has an INSTEAD OF UPDATE trigger defined on it, NO if not
is_trigger_deletable	yes_or_no	YES if the view has an INSTEAD OF DELETE trigger defined on it, NO if not
is_trigger_in-sertable_into	yes_or_no	YES if the view has an INSTEAD OF INSERT trigger defined on it, NO if not

Part V. Server Programming

This part is about extending the server functionality with user-defined functions, data types, triggers, etc. These are advanced topics which should probably be approached only after all the other user documentation about PostgreSQL has been understood. Later chapters in this part describe the server-side programming languages available in the PostgreSQL distribution as well as general issues concerning server-side programming languages. It is essential to read at least the earlier sections of Chapter 38 (covering functions) before diving into the material about server-side programming languages.

Table of Contents

Chapter 38. Extending SQL

In the sections that follow, we will discuss how you can extend the PostgreSQL SQL query language by adding:

- functions (starting in Section 38.3)
- aggregates (starting in Section 38.11)
- data types (starting in Section 38.12)
- operators (starting in Section 38.13)
- operator classes for indexes (starting in Section 38.15)
- packages of related objects (starting in Section 38.16)

38.1. How Extensibility Works

PostgreSQL is extensible because its operation is catalog-driven. If you are familiar with standard relational database systems, you know that they store information about databases, tables, columns, etc., in what are commonly known as system catalogs. (Some systems call this the data dictionary.) The catalogs appear to the user as tables like any other, but the DBMS stores its internal bookkeeping in them. One key difference between PostgreSQL and standard relational database systems is that PostgreSQL stores much more information in its catalogs: not only information about tables and columns, but also information about data types, functions, access methods, and so on. These tables can be modified by the user, and since PostgreSQL bases its operation on these tables, this means that PostgreSQL can be extended by users. By comparison, conventional database systems can only be extended by changing hardcoded procedures in the source code or by loading modules specially written by the DBMS vendor.

The PostgreSQL server can moreover incorporate user-written code into itself through dynamic loading. That is, the user can specify an object code file (e.g., a shared library) that implements a new type or function, and PostgreSQL will load it as required. Code written in SQL is even more trivial to add to the server. This ability to modify its operation "on the fly" makes PostgreSQL uniquely suited for rapid prototyping of new applications and storage structures.

38.2. The PostgreSQL Type System

PostgreSQL data types can be divided into base types, container types, domains, and pseudo-types.

38.2.1. Base Types

Base types are those, like `integer`, that are implemented below the level of the SQL language (typically in a low-level language such as C). They generally correspond to what are often known as abstract data types. PostgreSQL can only operate on such types through functions provided by the user and only understands the behavior of such types to the extent that the user describes them. The built-in base types are described in Chapter 8.

Enumerated (enum) types can be considered as a subcategory of base types. The main difference is that they can be created using just SQL commands, without any low-level programming. Refer to Section 8.7 for more information.

38.2.2. Container Types

PostgreSQL has three kinds of "container" types, which are types that contain multiple values of other types. These are arrays, composites, and ranges.

Arrays can hold multiple values that are all of the same type. An array type is automatically created for each base type, composite type, range type, and domain type. But there are no arrays of arrays. So far as the type system is concerned, multi-dimensional arrays are the same as one-dimensional arrays. Refer to Section 8.15 for more information.

Composite types, or row types, are created whenever the user creates a table. It is also possible to use CREATE TYPE to define a "stand-alone" composite type with no associated table. A composite type is simply a list of types with associated field names. A value of a composite type is a row or record of field values. Refer to Section 8.16 for more information.

A range type can hold two values of the same type, which are the lower and upper bounds of the range. Range types are user-created, although a few built-in ones exist. Refer to Section 8.17 for more information.

38.2.3. Domains

A domain is based on a particular underlying type and for many purposes is interchangeable with its underlying type. However, a domain can have constraints that restrict its valid values to a subset of what the underlying type would allow. Domains are created using the SQL command CREATE DOMAIN. Refer to Section 8.18 for more information.

38.2.4. Pseudo-Types

There are a few "pseudo-types" for special purposes. Pseudo-types cannot appear as columns of tables or components of container types, but they can be used to declare the argument and result types of functions. This provides a mechanism within the type system to identify special classes of functions. Table 8.25 lists the existing pseudo-types.

38.2.5. Polymorphic Types

Five pseudo-types of special interest are `anyelement`, `anyarray`, `anynonarray`, `anyenum`, and `anyrange`, which are collectively called *polymorphic types*. Any function declared using these types is said to be a *polymorphic function*. A polymorphic function can operate on many different data types, with the specific data type(s) being determined by the data types actually passed to it in a particular call.

Polymorphic arguments and results are tied to each other and are resolved to a specific data type when a query calling a polymorphic function is parsed. Each position (either argument or return value) declared as `anyelement` is allowed to have any specific actual data type, but in any given call they must all be the *same* actual type. Each position declared as `anyarray` can have any array data type, but similarly they must all be the same type. And similarly, positions declared as `anyrange` must all be the same range type. Furthermore, if there are positions declared `anyarray` and others declared `anyelement`, the actual array type in the `anyarray` positions must be an array whose elements are the same type appearing in the `anyelement` positions. Similarly, if there are positions declared `anyrange` and others declared `anyelement`, the actual range type in the `anyrange` positions must be a range whose subtype is the same type appearing in the `anyelement` positions. `anynonarray` is treated exactly the same as `anyelement`, but adds the additional constraint that the actual type must not be an array type. `anyenum` is treated exactly the same as `anyelement`, but adds the additional constraint that the actual type must be an enum type.

Thus, when more than one argument position is declared with a polymorphic type, the net effect is that only certain combinations of actual argument types are allowed. For example, a function declared as `equal(anyelement, anyelement)` will take any two input values, so long as they are of the same data type.

When the return value of a function is declared as a polymorphic type, there must be at least one argument position that is also polymorphic, and the actual data type supplied as the argument determines the actual result type for that call. For example, if there were not already an array subscripting mechanism, one could define a function that implements subscripting as `subscript(anyarray, integer) returns anyelement`. This declaration constrains the actual first argument to be an array type, and allows the parser to infer the correct result type from the actual first argument's type. Another example is that a function declared as `f(anyarray) returns anyenum` will only accept arrays of enum types.

Note that `anynonarray` and `anyenum` do not represent separate type variables; they are the same type as `anyelement`, just with an additional constraint. For example, declaring a function as `f(anyelement, anyenum)` is equivalent to declaring it as `f(anyenum, anyenum)`: both actual arguments have to be the same enum type.

A variadic function (one taking a variable number of arguments, as in Section 38.5.5) can be polymorphic: this is accomplished by declaring its last parameter as `VARIADIC anyarray`. For purposes of argument matching and determining the actual result type, such a function behaves the same as if you had written the appropriate number of `anynonarray` parameters.

38.3. User-defined Functions

PostgreSQL provides four kinds of functions:

- query language functions (functions written in SQL) (Section 38.5)

- procedural language functions (functions written in, for example, PL/pgSQL or PL/Tcl) (Section 38.8)

- internal functions (Section 38.9)

- C-language functions (Section 38.10)

Every kind of function can take base types, composite types, or combinations of these as arguments (parameters). In addition, every kind of function can return a base type or a composite type. Functions can also be defined to return sets of base or composite values.

Many kinds of functions can take or return certain pseudo-types (such as polymorphic types), but the available facilities vary. Consult the description of each kind of function for more details.

It's easiest to define SQL functions, so we'll start by discussing those. Most of the concepts presented for SQL functions will carry over to the other types of functions.

Throughout this chapter, it can be useful to look at the reference page of the CREATE FUNCTION command to understand the examples better. Some examples from this chapter can be found in `funcs.sql` and `funcs.c` in the `src/tutorial` directory in the PostgreSQL source distribution.

38.4. User-defined Procedures

A procedure is a database object similar to a function. The difference is that a procedure does not return a value, so there is no return type declaration. While a function is called as part of a query or DML command, a procedure is called explicitly using the CALL statement.

The explanations on how to define user-defined functions in the rest of this chapter apply to procedures as well, except that the CREATE PROCEDURE command is used instead, there is no return type, and some other features such as strictness don't apply.

Collectively, functions and procedures are also known as *routines*. There are commands such as ALTER ROUTINE and DROP ROUTINE that can operate on functions and procedures without having to know which kind it is. Note, however, that there is no `CREATE ROUTINE` command.

38.5. Query Language (SQL) Functions

SQL functions execute an arbitrary list of SQL statements, returning the result of the last query in the list. In the simple (non-set) case, the first row of the last query's result will be returned. (Bear in mind that "the first row" of a multirow result is not well-defined unless you use ORDER BY.) If the last query happens to return no rows at all, the null value will be returned.

Alternatively, an SQL function can be declared to return a set (that is, multiple rows) by specifying the function's return type as SETOF *sometype*, or equivalently by declaring it as RETURNS TABLE(*columns*). In this case all rows of the last query's result are returned. Further details appear below.

The body of an SQL function must be a list of SQL statements separated by semicolons. A semicolon after the last statement is optional. Unless the function is declared to return void, the last statement must be a SELECT, or an INSERT, UPDATE, or DELETE that has a RETURNING clause.

Any collection of commands in the SQL language can be packaged together and defined as a function. Besides SELECT queries, the commands can include data modification queries (INSERT, UPDATE, and DELETE), as well as other SQL commands. (You cannot use transaction control commands, e.g. COMMIT, SAVEPOINT, and some utility commands, e.g. VACUUM, in SQL functions.) However, the final command must be a SELECT or have a RETURNING clause that returns whatever is specified as the function's return type. Alternatively, if you want to define a SQL function that performs actions but has no useful value to return, you can define it as returning void. For example, this function removes rows with negative salaries from the emp table:

```
CREATE FUNCTION clean_emp() RETURNS void AS '
    DELETE FROM emp
        WHERE salary < 0;
' LANGUAGE SQL;

SELECT clean_emp();

 clean_emp
-----------

(1 row)
```

> ## Note
>
> The entire body of a SQL function is parsed before any of it is executed. While a SQL function can contain commands that alter the system catalogs (e.g., CREATE TABLE), the effects of such commands will not be visible during parse analysis of later commands in the function. Thus, for example, CREATE TABLE foo (...); INSERT INTO foo VALUES(...); will not work as desired if packaged up into a single SQL function, since foo won't exist yet when the INSERT command is parsed. It's recommended to use PL/pgSQL instead of a SQL function in this type of situation.

The syntax of the CREATE FUNCTION command requires the function body to be written as a string constant. It is usually most convenient to use dollar quoting (see Section 4.1.2.4) for the string constant. If you choose to use regular single-quoted string constant syntax, you must double single quote marks (') and backslashes (\) (assuming escape string syntax) in the body of the function (see Section 4.1.2.1).

38.5.1. Arguments for SQL Functions

Arguments of a SQL function can be referenced in the function body using either names or numbers. Examples of both methods appear below.

To use a name, declare the function argument as having a name, and then just write that name in the function body. If the argument name is the same as any column name in the current SQL command within the function, the column name will take precedence. To override this, qualify the argument name with the name of the function itself, that is *function_name.argument_name*. (If this would conflict with a qualified column name, again the column name wins. You can avoid the ambiguity by choosing a different alias for the table within the SQL command.)

In the older numeric approach, arguments are referenced using the syntax $n: $1 refers to the first input argument, $2 to the second, and so on. This will work whether or not the particular argument was declared with a name.

If an argument is of a composite type, then the dot notation, e.g., *argname.fieldname* or $1.*fieldname*, can be used to access attributes of the argument. Again, you might need to qualify the argument's name with the function name to make the form with an argument name unambiguous.

SQL function arguments can only be used as data values, not as identifiers. Thus for example this is reasonable:

```
INSERT INTO mytable VALUES ($1);
```

but this will not work:

```
INSERT INTO $1 VALUES (42);
```

> **Note**
>
> The ability to use names to reference SQL function arguments was added in PostgreSQL 9.2. Functions to be used in older servers must use the $n notation.

38.5.2. SQL Functions on Base Types

The simplest possible SQL function has no arguments and simply returns a base type, such as `integer`:

```
CREATE FUNCTION one() RETURNS integer AS $$
    SELECT 1 AS result;
$$ LANGUAGE SQL;

-- Alternative syntax for string literal:
CREATE FUNCTION one() RETURNS integer AS '
    SELECT 1 AS result;
' LANGUAGE SQL;

SELECT one();

 one
```

```
-----
    1
```

Notice that we defined a column alias within the function body for the result of the function (with the name `result`), but this column alias is not visible outside the function. Hence, the result is labeled `one` instead of `result`.

It is almost as easy to define SQL functions that take base types as arguments:

```
CREATE FUNCTION add_em(x integer, y integer) RETURNS integer AS $$
    SELECT x + y;
$$ LANGUAGE SQL;

SELECT add_em(1, 2) AS answer;

 answer
--------
      3
```

Alternatively, we could dispense with names for the arguments and use numbers:

```
CREATE FUNCTION add_em(integer, integer) RETURNS integer AS $$
    SELECT $1 + $2;
$$ LANGUAGE SQL;

SELECT add_em(1, 2) AS answer;

 answer
--------
      3
```

Here is a more useful function, which might be used to debit a bank account:

```
CREATE FUNCTION tf1 (accountno integer, debit numeric) RETURNS numeric
  AS $$
    UPDATE bank
        SET balance = balance - debit
        WHERE accountno = tf1.accountno;
    SELECT 1;
$$ LANGUAGE SQL;
```

A user could execute this function to debit account 17 by $100.00 as follows:

```
SELECT tf1(17, 100.0);
```

In this example, we chose the name `accountno` for the first argument, but this is the same as the name of a column in the `bank` table. Within the `UPDATE` command, `accountno` refers to the column `bank.accountno`, so `tf1.accountno` must be used to refer to the argument. We could of course avoid this by using a different name for the argument.

In practice one would probably like a more useful result from the function than a constant 1, so a more likely definition is:

```
CREATE FUNCTION tf1 (accountno integer, debit numeric) RETURNS numeric
 AS $$
    UPDATE bank
        SET balance = balance - debit
        WHERE accountno = tf1.accountno;
    SELECT balance FROM bank WHERE accountno = tf1.accountno;
$$ LANGUAGE SQL;
```

which adjusts the balance and returns the new balance. The same thing could be done in one command using RETURNING:

```
CREATE FUNCTION tf1 (accountno integer, debit numeric) RETURNS numeric
 AS $$
    UPDATE bank
        SET balance = balance - debit
        WHERE accountno = tf1.accountno
    RETURNING balance;
$$ LANGUAGE SQL;
```

A SQL function must return exactly its declared result type. This may require inserting an explicit cast. For example, suppose we wanted the previous add_em function to return type float8 instead. This won't work:

```
CREATE FUNCTION add_em(integer, integer) RETURNS float8 AS $$
    SELECT $1 + $2;
$$ LANGUAGE SQL;
```

even though in other contexts PostgreSQL would be willing to insert an implicit cast to convert integer to float8. We need to write it as

```
CREATE FUNCTION add_em(integer, integer) RETURNS float8 AS $$
    SELECT ($1 + $2)::float8;
$$ LANGUAGE SQL;
```

38.5.3. SQL Functions on Composite Types

When writing functions with arguments of composite types, we must not only specify which argument we want but also the desired attribute (field) of that argument. For example, suppose that emp is a table containing employee data, and therefore also the name of the composite type of each row of the table. Here is a function double_salary that computes what someone's salary would be if it were doubled:

```
CREATE TABLE emp (
    name        text,
    salary      numeric,
    age         integer,
    cubicle     point
);

INSERT INTO emp VALUES ('Bill', 4200, 45, '(2,1)');
```

```
CREATE FUNCTION double_salary(emp) RETURNS numeric AS $$
    SELECT $1.salary * 2 AS salary;
$$ LANGUAGE SQL;

SELECT name, double_salary(emp.*) AS dream
    FROM emp
    WHERE emp.cubicle ~= point '(2,1)';

 name | dream
------+-------
 Bill |  8400
```

Notice the use of the syntax $1.salary to select one field of the argument row value. Also notice how the calling SELECT command uses *table_name*.* to select the entire current row of a table as a composite value. The table row can alternatively be referenced using just the table name, like this:

```
SELECT name, double_salary(emp) AS dream
    FROM emp
    WHERE emp.cubicle ~= point '(2,1)';
```

but this usage is deprecated since it's easy to get confused. (See Section 8.16.5 for details about these two notations for the composite value of a table row.)

Sometimes it is handy to construct a composite argument value on-the-fly. This can be done with the ROW construct. For example, we could adjust the data being passed to the function:

```
SELECT name, double_salary(ROW(name, salary*1.1, age, cubicle)) AS
 dream
    FROM emp;
```

It is also possible to build a function that returns a composite type. This is an example of a function that returns a single emp row:

```
CREATE FUNCTION new_emp() RETURNS emp AS $$
    SELECT text 'None' AS name,
        1000.0 AS salary,
        25 AS age,
        point '(2,2)' AS cubicle;
$$ LANGUAGE SQL;
```

In this example we have specified each of the attributes with a constant value, but any computation could have been substituted for these constants.

Note two important things about defining the function:

- The select list order in the query must be exactly the same as that in which the columns appear in the table associated with the composite type. (Naming the columns, as we did above, is irrelevant to the system.)

- We must ensure each expression's type matches the corresponding column of the composite type, inserting a cast if necessary. Otherwise we'll get errors like this:

```
ERROR:  function declared to return emp returns varchar instead of
  text at column 1
```

As with the base-type case, the function will not insert any casts automatically.

A different way to define the same function is:

```
CREATE FUNCTION new_emp() RETURNS emp AS $$
    SELECT ROW('None', 1000.0, 25, '(2,2)')::emp;
$$ LANGUAGE SQL;
```

Here we wrote a SELECT that returns just a single column of the correct composite type. This isn't really better in this situation, but it is a handy alternative in some cases — for example, if we need to compute the result by calling another function that returns the desired composite value. Another example is that if we are trying to write a function that returns a domain over composite, rather than a plain composite type, it is always necessary to write it as returning a single column, since there is no other way to produce a value that is exactly of the domain type.

We could call this function directly either by using it in a value expression:

```
SELECT new_emp();

         new_emp
-------------------------
 (None,1000.0,25,"(2,2)")
```

or by calling it as a table function:

```
SELECT * FROM new_emp();

 name | salary | age | cubicle
------+--------+-----+---------
 None | 1000.0 |  25 | (2,2)
```

The second way is described more fully in Section 38.5.7.

When you use a function that returns a composite type, you might want only one field (attribute) from its result. You can do that with syntax like this:

```
SELECT (new_emp()).name;

 name
------
 None
```

The extra parentheses are needed to keep the parser from getting confused. If you try to do it without them, you get something like this:

```
SELECT new_emp().name;
ERROR:  syntax error at or near "."
LINE 1: SELECT new_emp().name;
```

Another option is to use functional notation for extracting an attribute:

```
SELECT name(new_emp());

 name
------
 None
```

As explained in Section 8.16.5, the field notation and functional notation are equivalent.

Another way to use a function returning a composite type is to pass the result to another function that accepts the correct row type as input:

```
CREATE FUNCTION getname(emp) RETURNS text AS $$
    SELECT $1.name;
$$ LANGUAGE SQL;

SELECT getname(new_emp());
 getname
---------
 None
(1 row)
```

38.5.4. SQL Functions with Output Parameters

An alternative way of describing a function's results is to define it with *output parameters*, as in this example:

```
CREATE FUNCTION add_em (IN x int, IN y int, OUT sum int)
AS 'SELECT x + y'
LANGUAGE SQL;

SELECT add_em(3,7);
 add_em
--------
     10
(1 row)
```

This is not essentially different from the version of **add_em** shown in Section 38.5.2. The real value of output parameters is that they provide a convenient way of defining functions that return several columns. For example,

```
CREATE FUNCTION sum_n_product (x int, y int, OUT sum int, OUT product
 int)
AS 'SELECT x + y, x * y'
LANGUAGE SQL;

 SELECT * FROM sum_n_product(11,42);
 sum | product
```

```
-----+---------
 53  |      462
(1 row)
```

What has essentially happened here is that we have created an anonymous composite type for the result of the function. The above example has the same end result as

```
CREATE TYPE sum_prod AS (sum int, product int);

CREATE FUNCTION sum_n_product (int, int) RETURNS sum_prod
AS 'SELECT $1 + $2, $1 * $2'
LANGUAGE SQL;
```

but not having to bother with the separate composite type definition is often handy. Notice that the names attached to the output parameters are not just decoration, but determine the column names of the anonymous composite type. (If you omit a name for an output parameter, the system will choose a name on its own.)

Notice that output parameters are not included in the calling argument list when invoking such a function from SQL. This is because PostgreSQL considers only the input parameters to define the function's calling signature. That means also that only the input parameters matter when referencing the function for purposes such as dropping it. We could drop the above function with either of

```
DROP FUNCTION sum_n_product (x int, y int, OUT sum int, OUT product
 int);
DROP FUNCTION sum_n_product (int, int);
```

Parameters can be marked as IN (the default), OUT, INOUT, or VARIADIC. An INOUT parameter serves as both an input parameter (part of the calling argument list) and an output parameter (part of the result record type). VARIADIC parameters are input parameters, but are treated specially as described next.

38.5.5. SQL Functions with Variable Numbers of Arguments

SQL functions can be declared to accept variable numbers of arguments, so long as all the "optional" arguments are of the same data type. The optional arguments will be passed to the function as an array. The function is declared by marking the last parameter as VARIADIC; this parameter must be declared as being of an array type. For example:

```
CREATE FUNCTION mleast(VARIADIC arr numeric[]) RETURNS numeric AS $$
    SELECT min($1[i]) FROM generate_subscripts($1, 1) g(i);
$$ LANGUAGE SQL;

SELECT mleast(10, -1, 5, 4.4);
 mleast
--------
     -1
(1 row)
```

Effectively, all the actual arguments at or beyond the VARIADIC position are gathered up into a one-dimensional array, as if you had written

```
SELECT mleast(ARRAY[10, -1, 5, 4.4]);    -- doesn't work
```

You can't actually write that, though — or at least, it will not match this function definition. A parameter marked `VARIADIC` matches one or more occurrences of its element type, not of its own type.

Sometimes it is useful to be able to pass an already-constructed array to a variadic function; this is particularly handy when one variadic function wants to pass on its array parameter to another one. Also, this is the only secure way to call a variadic function found in a schema that permits untrusted users to create objects; see Section 10.3. You can do this by specifying `VARIADIC` in the call:

```
SELECT mleast(VARIADIC ARRAY[10, -1, 5, 4.4]);
```

This prevents expansion of the function's variadic parameter into its element type, thereby allowing the array argument value to match normally. `VARIADIC` can only be attached to the last actual argument of a function call.

Specifying `VARIADIC` in the call is also the only way to pass an empty array to a variadic function, for example:

```
SELECT mleast(VARIADIC ARRAY[]::numeric[]);
```

Simply writing `SELECT mleast()` does not work because a variadic parameter must match at least one actual argument. (You could define a second function also named `mleast`, with no parameters, if you wanted to allow such calls.)

The array element parameters generated from a variadic parameter are treated as not having any names of their own. This means it is not possible to call a variadic function using named arguments (Section 4.3), except when you specify `VARIADIC`. For example, this will work:

```
SELECT mleast(VARIADIC arr => ARRAY[10, -1, 5, 4.4]);
```

but not these:

```
SELECT mleast(arr => 10);
SELECT mleast(arr => ARRAY[10, -1, 5, 4.4]);
```

38.5.6. SQL Functions with Default Values for Arguments

Functions can be declared with default values for some or all input arguments. The default values are inserted whenever the function is called with insufficiently many actual arguments. Since arguments can only be omitted from the end of the actual argument list, all parameters after a parameter with a default value have to have default values as well. (Although the use of named argument notation could allow this restriction to be relaxed, it's still enforced so that positional argument notation works sensibly.) Whether or not you use it, this capability creates a need for precautions when calling functions in databases where some users mistrust other users; see Section 10.3.

For example:

```
CREATE FUNCTION foo(a int, b int DEFAULT 2, c int DEFAULT 3)
RETURNS int
```

```
LANGUAGE SQL
AS $$
    SELECT $1 + $2 + $3;
$$;

SELECT foo(10, 20, 30);
 foo
-----
  60
(1 row)

SELECT foo(10, 20);
 foo
-----
  33
(1 row)

SELECT foo(10);
 foo
-----
  15
(1 row)

SELECT foo();  -- fails since there is no default for the first
 argument
ERROR:  function foo() does not exist
```

The = sign can also be used in place of the key word DEFAULT.

38.5.7. SQL Functions as Table Sources

All SQL functions can be used in the FROM clause of a query, but it is particularly useful for functions returning composite types. If the function is defined to return a base type, the table function produces a one-column table. If the function is defined to return a composite type, the table function produces a column for each attribute of the composite type.

Here is an example:

```
CREATE TABLE foo (fooid int, foosubid int, fooname text);
INSERT INTO foo VALUES (1, 1, 'Joe');
INSERT INTO foo VALUES (1, 2, 'Ed');
INSERT INTO foo VALUES (2, 1, 'Mary');

CREATE FUNCTION getfoo(int) RETURNS foo AS $$
    SELECT * FROM foo WHERE fooid = $1;
$$ LANGUAGE SQL;

SELECT *, upper(fooname) FROM getfoo(1) AS t1;

 fooid | foosubid | fooname | upper
-------+----------+---------+-------
     1 |        1 | Joe     | JOE
(1 row)
```

As the example shows, we can work with the columns of the function's result just the same as if they were columns of a regular table.

Note that we only got one row out of the function. This is because we did not use SETOF. That is described in the next section.

38.5.8. SQL Functions Returning Sets

When an SQL function is declared as returning SETOF *sometype*, the function's final query is executed to completion, and each row it outputs is returned as an element of the result set.

This feature is normally used when calling the function in the FROM clause. In this case each row returned by the function becomes a row of the table seen by the query. For example, assume that table foo has the same contents as above, and we say:

```
CREATE FUNCTION getfoo(int) RETURNS SETOF foo AS $$
    SELECT * FROM foo WHERE fooid = $1;
$$ LANGUAGE SQL;

SELECT * FROM getfoo(1) AS t1;
```

Then we would get:

```
 fooid | foosubid | fooname
-------+----------+---------
     1 |        1 | Joe
     1 |        2 | Ed
(2 rows)
```

It is also possible to return multiple rows with the columns defined by output parameters, like this:

```
CREATE TABLE tab (y int, z int);
INSERT INTO tab VALUES (1, 2), (3, 4), (5, 6), (7, 8);

CREATE FUNCTION sum_n_product_with_tab (x int, OUT sum int, OUT
 product int)
RETURNS SETOF record
AS $$
    SELECT $1 + tab.y, $1 * tab.y FROM tab;
$$ LANGUAGE SQL;

SELECT * FROM sum_n_product_with_tab(10);
 sum | product
-----+---------
  11 |      10
  13 |      30
  15 |      50
  17 |      70
(4 rows)
```

The key point here is that you must write RETURNS SETOF record to indicate that the function returns multiple rows instead of just one. If there is only one output parameter, write that parameter's type instead of record.

It is frequently useful to construct a query's result by invoking a set-returning function multiple times, with the parameters for each invocation coming from successive rows of a table or subquery. The preferred way to do this is to use the LATERAL key word, which is described in Section 7.2.1.5. Here is an example using a set-returning function to enumerate elements of a tree structure:

```
SELECT * FROM nodes;
   name     | parent
-----------+--------
 Top       |
 Child1    | Top
 Child2    | Top
 Child3    | Top
 SubChild1 | Child1
 SubChild2 | Child1
(6 rows)

CREATE FUNCTION listchildren(text) RETURNS SETOF text AS $$
    SELECT name FROM nodes WHERE parent = $1
$$ LANGUAGE SQL STABLE;

SELECT * FROM listchildren('Top');
 listchildren
--------------
 Child1
 Child2
 Child3
(3 rows)

SELECT name, child FROM nodes, LATERAL listchildren(name) AS child;
  name   |   child
---------+-----------
 Top     | Child1
 Top     | Child2
 Top     | Child3
 Child1  | SubChild1
 Child1  | SubChild2
(5 rows)
```

This example does not do anything that we couldn't have done with a simple join, but in more complex calculations the option to put some of the work into a function can be quite convenient.

Functions returning sets can also be called in the select list of a query. For each row that the query generates by itself, the set-returning function is invoked, and an output row is generated for each element of the function's result set. The previous example could also be done with queries like these:

```
SELECT listchildren('Top');
 listchildren
--------------
 Child1
 Child2
 Child3
(3 rows)
```

```
SELECT name, listchildren(name) FROM nodes;
  name  | listchildren
--------+--------------
 Top    | Child1
 Top    | Child2
 Top    | Child3
 Child1 | SubChild1
 Child1 | SubChild2
(5 rows)
```

In the last SELECT, notice that no output row appears for Child2, Child3, etc. This happens because listchildren returns an empty set for those arguments, so no result rows are generated. This is the same behavior as we got from an inner join to the function result when using the LATERAL syntax.

PostgreSQL's behavior for a set-returning function in a query's select list is almost exactly the same as if the set-returning function had been written in a LATERAL FROM-clause item instead. For example,

```
SELECT x, generate_series(1,5) AS g FROM tab;
```

is almost equivalent to

```
SELECT x, g FROM tab, LATERAL generate_series(1,5) AS g;
```

It would be exactly the same, except that in this specific example, the planner could choose to put g on the outside of the nestloop join, since g has no actual lateral dependency on tab. That would result in a different output row order. Set-returning functions in the select list are always evaluated as though they are on the inside of a nestloop join with the rest of the FROM clause, so that the function(s) are run to completion before the next row from the FROM clause is considered.

If there is more than one set-returning function in the query's select list, the behavior is similar to what you get from putting the functions into a single LATERAL ROWS FROM(...) FROM-clause item. For each row from the underlying query, there is an output row using the first result from each function, then an output row using the second result, and so on. If some of the set-returning functions produce fewer outputs than others, null values are substituted for the missing data, so that the total number of rows emitted for one underlying row is the same as for the set-returning function that produced the most outputs. Thus the set-returning functions run "in lockstep" until they are all exhausted, and then execution continues with the next underlying row.

Set-returning functions can be nested in a select list, although that is not allowed in FROM-clause items. In such cases, each level of nesting is treated separately, as though it were a separate LATERAL ROWS FROM(...) item. For example, in

```
SELECT srf1(srf2(x), srf3(y)), srf4(srf5(z)) FROM tab;
```

the set-returning functions srf2, srf3, and srf5 would be run in lockstep for each row of tab, and then srf1 and srf4 would be applied in lockstep to each row produced by the lower functions.

Set-returning functions cannot be used within conditional-evaluation constructs, such as CASE or COALESCE. For example, consider

```
SELECT x, CASE WHEN x > 0 THEN generate_series(1, 5) ELSE 0 END FROM
  tab;
```

It might seem that this should produce five repetitions of input rows that have x > 0, and a single repetition of those that do not; but actually, because generate_series(1, 5) would be run in an implicit LATERAL FROM item before the CASE expression is ever evaluated, it would produce five repetitions of every input row. To reduce confusion, such cases produce a parse-time error instead.

Note

If a function's last command is INSERT, UPDATE, or DELETE with RETURNING, that command will always be executed to completion, even if the function is not declared with SETOF or the calling query does not fetch all the result rows. Any extra rows produced by the RETURNING clause are silently dropped, but the commanded table modifications still happen (and are all completed before returning from the function).

Note

Before PostgreSQL 10, putting more than one set-returning function in the same select list did not behave very sensibly unless they always produced equal numbers of rows. Otherwise, what you got was a number of output rows equal to the least common multiple of the numbers of rows produced by the set-returning functions. Also, nested set-returning functions did not work as described above; instead, a set-returning function could have at most one set-returning argument, and each nest of set-returning functions was run independently. Also, conditional execution (set-returning functions inside CASE etc) was previously allowed, complicating things even more. Use of the LATERAL syntax is recommended when writing queries that need to work in older PostgreSQL versions, because that will give consistent results across different versions. If you have a query that is relying on conditional execution of a set-returning function, you may be able to fix it by moving the conditional test into a custom set-returning function. For example,

```
SELECT x, CASE WHEN y > 0 THEN generate_series(1, z) ELSE 5
 END FROM tab;
```

could become

```
CREATE FUNCTION case_generate_series(cond bool, start int,
 fin int, els int)
  RETURNS SETOF int AS $$
BEGIN
  IF cond THEN
    RETURN QUERY SELECT generate_series(start, fin);
  ELSE
    RETURN QUERY SELECT els;
  END IF;
END$$ LANGUAGE plpgsql;

SELECT x, case_generate_series(y > 0, 1, z, 5) FROM tab;
```

This formulation will work the same in all versions of PostgreSQL.

38.5.9. SQL Functions Returning TABLE

There is another way to declare a function as returning a set, which is to use the syntax RETURNS TA-BLE(*columns*). This is equivalent to using one or more OUT parameters plus marking the function as returning SETOF record (or SETOF a single output parameter's type, as appropriate). This notation is specified in recent versions of the SQL standard, and thus may be more portable than using SETOF.

For example, the preceding sum-and-product example could also be done this way:

```
CREATE FUNCTION sum_n_product_with_tab (x int)
RETURNS TABLE(sum int, product int) AS $$
    SELECT $1 + tab.y, $1 * tab.y FROM tab;
$$ LANGUAGE SQL;
```

It is not allowed to use explicit OUT or INOUT parameters with the RETURNS TABLE notation — you must put all the output columns in the TABLE list.

38.5.10. Polymorphic SQL Functions

SQL functions can be declared to accept and return the polymorphic types anyelement, anyarray, anynonarray, anyenum, and anyrange. See Section 38.2.5 for a more detailed explanation of polymorphic functions. Here is a polymorphic function make_array that builds up an array from two arbitrary data type elements:

```
CREATE FUNCTION make_array(anyelement, anyelement) RETURNS anyarray AS
 $$
    SELECT ARRAY[$1, $2];
$$ LANGUAGE SQL;

SELECT make_array(1, 2) AS intarray, make_array('a'::text, 'b') AS
 textarray;
 intarray | textarray
----------+-----------
 {1,2}    | {a,b}
(1 row)
```

Notice the use of the typecast 'a'::text to specify that the argument is of type text. This is required if the argument is just a string literal, since otherwise it would be treated as type unknown, and array of unknown is not a valid type. Without the typecast, you will get errors like this:

```
ERROR:  could not determine polymorphic type because input has type
 "unknown"
```

It is permitted to have polymorphic arguments with a fixed return type, but the converse is not. For example:

```
CREATE FUNCTION is_greater(anyelement, anyelement) RETURNS boolean AS
 $$
    SELECT $1 > $2;
$$ LANGUAGE SQL;
```

```
SELECT is_greater(1, 2);
 is_greater
------------
 f
(1 row)

CREATE FUNCTION invalid_func() RETURNS anyelement AS $$
    SELECT 1;
$$ LANGUAGE SQL;
ERROR:  cannot determine result data type
DETAIL:  A function returning a polymorphic type must have at least
 one polymorphic argument.
```

Polymorphism can be used with functions that have output arguments. For example:

```
CREATE FUNCTION dup (f1 anyelement, OUT f2 anyelement, OUT f3
 anyarray)
AS 'select $1, array[$1,$1]' LANGUAGE SQL;

SELECT * FROM dup(22);
 f2 |    f3
----+----------
 22 | {22,22}
(1 row)
```

Polymorphism can also be used with variadic functions. For example:

```
CREATE FUNCTION anyleast (VARIADIC anyarray) RETURNS anyelement AS $$
    SELECT min($1[i]) FROM generate_subscripts($1, 1) g(i);
$$ LANGUAGE SQL;

SELECT anyleast(10, -1, 5, 4);
 anyleast
----------
       -1
(1 row)

SELECT anyleast('abc'::text, 'def');
 anyleast
----------
 abc
(1 row)

CREATE FUNCTION concat_values(text, VARIADIC anyarray) RETURNS text AS
 $$
    SELECT array_to_string($2, $1);
$$ LANGUAGE SQL;

SELECT concat_values('|', 1, 4, 2);
 concat_values
---------------
 1|4|2
(1 row)
```

38.5.11. SQL Functions with Collations

When a SQL function has one or more parameters of collatable data types, a collation is identified for each function call depending on the collations assigned to the actual arguments, as described in Section 23.2. If a collation is successfully identified (i.e., there are no conflicts of implicit collations among the arguments) then all the collatable parameters are treated as having that collation implicitly. This will affect the behavior of collation-sensitive operations within the function. For example, using the `anyleast` function described above, the result of

```
SELECT anyleast('abc'::text, 'ABC');
```

will depend on the database's default collation. In C locale the result will be ABC, but in many other locales it will be abc. The collation to use can be forced by adding a COLLATE clause to any of the arguments, for example

```
SELECT anyleast('abc'::text, 'ABC' COLLATE "C");
```

Alternatively, if you wish a function to operate with a particular collation regardless of what it is called with, insert COLLATE clauses as needed in the function definition. This version of `anyleast` would always use en_US locale to compare strings:

```
CREATE FUNCTION anyleast (VARIADIC anyarray) RETURNS anyelement AS $$
    SELECT min($1[i] COLLATE "en_US") FROM generate_subscripts($1, 1)
 g(i);
$$ LANGUAGE SQL;
```

But note that this will throw an error if applied to a non-collatable data type.

If no common collation can be identified among the actual arguments, then a SQL function treats its parameters as having their data types' default collation (which is usually the database's default collation, but could be different for parameters of domain types).

The behavior of collatable parameters can be thought of as a limited form of polymorphism, applicable only to textual data types.

38.6. Function Overloading

More than one function can be defined with the same SQL name, so long as the arguments they take are different. In other words, function names can be *overloaded*. Whether or not you use it, this capability entails security precautions when calling functions in databases where some users mistrust other users; see Section 10.3. When a query is executed, the server will determine which function to call from the data types and the number of the provided arguments. Overloading can also be used to simulate functions with a variable number of arguments, up to a finite maximum number.

When creating a family of overloaded functions, one should be careful not to create ambiguities. For instance, given the functions:

```
CREATE FUNCTION test(int, real) RETURNS ...
CREATE FUNCTION test(smallint, double precision) RETURNS ...
```

it is not immediately clear which function would be called with some trivial input like test(1, 1.5). The currently implemented resolution rules are described in Chapter 10, but it is unwise to design a system that subtly relies on this behavior.

A function that takes a single argument of a composite type should generally not have the same name as any attribute (field) of that type. Recall that *attribute(table)* is considered equivalent to *table.attribute*. In the case that there is an ambiguity between a function on a composite type and an attribute of the composite type, the attribute will always be used. It is possible to override that choice by schema-qualifying the function name (that is, *schema.func(table)*) but it's better to avoid the problem by not choosing conflicting names.

Another possible conflict is between variadic and non-variadic functions. For instance, it is possible to create both foo(numeric) and foo(VARIADIC numeric[]). In this case it is unclear which one should be matched to a call providing a single numeric argument, such as foo(10.1). The rule is that the function appearing earlier in the search path is used, or if the two functions are in the same schema, the non-variadic one is preferred.

When overloading C-language functions, there is an additional constraint: The C name of each function in the family of overloaded functions must be different from the C names of all other functions, either internal or dynamically loaded. If this rule is violated, the behavior is not portable. You might get a run-time linker error, or one of the functions will get called (usually the internal one). The alternative form of the AS clause for the SQL CREATE FUNCTION command decouples the SQL function name from the function name in the C source code. For instance:

```
CREATE FUNCTION test(int) RETURNS int
    AS 'filename', 'test_1arg'
    LANGUAGE C;
CREATE FUNCTION test(int, int) RETURNS int
    AS 'filename', 'test_2arg'
    LANGUAGE C;
```

The names of the C functions here reflect one of many possible conventions.

38.7. Function Volatility Categories

Every function has a *volatility* classification, with the possibilities being VOLATILE, STABLE, or IMMUTABLE. VOLATILE is the default if the CREATE FUNCTION command does not specify a category. The volatility category is a promise to the optimizer about the behavior of the function:

- A VOLATILE function can do anything, including modifying the database. It can return different results on successive calls with the same arguments. The optimizer makes no assumptions about the behavior of such functions. A query using a volatile function will re-evaluate the function at every row where its value is needed.

- A STABLE function cannot modify the database and is guaranteed to return the same results given the same arguments for all rows within a single statement. This category allows the optimizer to optimize multiple calls of the function to a single call. In particular, it is safe to use an expression containing such a function in an index scan condition. (Since an index scan will evaluate the comparison value only once, not once at each row, it is not valid to use a VOLATILE function in an index scan condition.)

- An IMMUTABLE function cannot modify the database and is guaranteed to return the same results given the same arguments forever. This category allows the optimizer to pre-evaluate the function when a query calls it with constant arguments. For example, a query like SELECT ... WHERE x = 2 + 2 can be simplified on sight to SELECT ... WHERE x = 4, because the function underlying the integer addition operator is marked IMMUTABLE.

For best optimization results, you should label your functions with the strictest volatility category that is valid for them.

Any function with side-effects *must* be labeled VOLATILE, so that calls to it cannot be optimized away. Even a function with no side-effects needs to be labeled VOLATILE if its value can change within a single query; some examples are random(), currval(), timeofday().

Another important example is that the current_timestamp family of functions qualify as STABLE, since their values do not change within a transaction.

There is relatively little difference between STABLE and IMMUTABLE categories when considering simple interactive queries that are planned and immediately executed: it doesn't matter a lot whether a function is executed once during planning or once during query execution startup. But there is a big difference if the plan is saved and reused later. Labeling a function IMMUTABLE when it really isn't might allow it to be prematurely folded to a constant during planning, resulting in a stale value being re-used during subsequent uses of the plan. This is a hazard when using prepared statements or when using function languages that cache plans (such as PL/pgSQL).

For functions written in SQL or in any of the standard procedural languages, there is a second important property determined by the volatility category, namely the visibility of any data changes that have been made by the SQL command that is calling the function. A VOLATILE function will see such changes, a STABLE or IMMUTABLE function will not. This behavior is implemented using the snapshotting behavior of MVCC (see Chapter 13): STABLE and IMMUTABLE functions use a snapshot established as of the start of the calling query, whereas VOLATILE functions obtain a fresh snapshot at the start of each query they execute.

Note

Functions written in C can manage snapshots however they want, but it's usually a good idea to make C functions work this way too.

Because of this snapshotting behavior, a function containing only SELECT commands can safely be marked STABLE, even if it selects from tables that might be undergoing modifications by concurrent queries. PostgreSQL will execute all commands of a STABLE function using the snapshot established for the calling query, and so it will see a fixed view of the database throughout that query.

The same snapshotting behavior is used for SELECT commands within IMMUTABLE functions. It is generally unwise to select from database tables within an IMMUTABLE function at all, since the immutability will be broken if the table contents ever change. However, PostgreSQL does not enforce that you do not do that.

A common error is to label a function IMMUTABLE when its results depend on a configuration parameter. For example, a function that manipulates timestamps might well have results that depend on the TimeZone setting. For safety, such functions should be labeled STABLE instead.

Note

PostgreSQL requires that STABLE and IMMUTABLE functions contain no SQL commands other than SELECT to prevent data modification. (This is not a completely bulletproof test, since such functions could still call VOLATILE functions that modify the database. If you do that, you will find that the STABLE or IMMUTABLE function does not notice the database changes applied by the called function, since they are hidden from its snapshot.)

38.8. Procedural Language Functions

PostgreSQL allows user-defined functions to be written in other languages besides SQL and C. These other languages are generically called *procedural languages* (PLs). Procedural languages aren't built into the PostgreSQL server; they are offered by loadable modules. See Chapter 42 and following chapters for more information.

38.9. Internal Functions

Internal functions are functions written in C that have been statically linked into the PostgreSQL server. The "body" of the function definition specifies the C-language name of the function, which need not be the same as the name being declared for SQL use. (For reasons of backward compatibility, an empty body is accepted as meaning that the C-language function name is the same as the SQL name.)

Normally, all internal functions present in the server are declared during the initialization of the database cluster (see Section 18.2), but a user could use CREATE FUNCTION to create additional alias names for an internal function. Internal functions are declared in CREATE FUNCTION with language name internal. For instance, to create an alias for the sqrt function:

```
CREATE FUNCTION square_root(double precision) RETURNS double precision
    AS 'dsqrt'
    LANGUAGE internal
    STRICT;
```

(Most internal functions expect to be declared "strict".)

Note

Not all "predefined" functions are "internal" in the above sense. Some predefined functions are written in SQL.

38.10. C-Language Functions

User-defined functions can be written in C (or a language that can be made compatible with C, such as C ++). Such functions are compiled into dynamically loadable objects (also called shared libraries) and are loaded by the server on demand. The dynamic loading feature is what distinguishes "C language" functions from "internal" functions — the actual coding conventions are essentially the same for both. (Hence, the standard internal function library is a rich source of coding examples for user-defined C functions.)

Currently only one calling convention is used for C functions ("version 1"). Support for that calling convention is indicated by writing a PG_FUNCTION_INFO_V1() macro call for the function, as illustrated below.

38.10.1. Dynamic Loading

The first time a user-defined function in a particular loadable object file is called in a session, the dynamic loader loads that object file into memory so that the function can be called. The CREATE FUNCTION for a user-defined C function must therefore specify two pieces of information for the function: the name of the loadable object file, and the C name (link symbol) of the specific function to call within that object file. If the C name is not explicitly specified then it is assumed to be the same as the SQL function name.

The following algorithm is used to locate the shared object file based on the name given in the CREATE FUNCTION command:

1. If the name is an absolute path, the given file is loaded.

2. If the name starts with the string $libdir, that part is replaced by the PostgreSQL package library directory name, which is determined at build time.

3. If the name does not contain a directory part, the file is searched for in the path specified by the configuration variable dynamic_library_path.

4. Otherwise (the file was not found in the path, or it contains a non-absolute directory part), the dynamic loader will try to take the name as given, which will most likely fail. (It is unreliable to depend on the current working directory.)

If this sequence does not work, the platform-specific shared library file name extension (often .so) is appended to the given name and this sequence is tried again. If that fails as well, the load will fail.

It is recommended to locate shared libraries either relative to $libdir or through the dynamic library path. This simplifies version upgrades if the new installation is at a different location. The actual directory that $libdir stands for can be found out with the command pg_config --pkglibdir.

The user ID the PostgreSQL server runs as must be able to traverse the path to the file you intend to load. Making the file or a higher-level directory not readable and/or not executable by the postgres user is a common mistake.

In any case, the file name that is given in the CREATE FUNCTION command is recorded literally in the system catalogs, so if the file needs to be loaded again the same procedure is applied.

Note

PostgreSQL will not compile a C function automatically. The object file must be compiled before it is referenced in a CREATE FUNCTION command. See Section 38.10.5 for additional information.

To ensure that a dynamically loaded object file is not loaded into an incompatible server, PostgreSQL checks that the file contains a "magic block" with the appropriate contents. This allows the server to detect obvious incompatibilities, such as code compiled for a different major version of PostgreSQL. To include a magic block, write this in one (and only one) of the module source files, after having included the header fmgr.h:

```
PG_MODULE_MAGIC;
```

After it is used for the first time, a dynamically loaded object file is retained in memory. Future calls in the same session to the function(s) in that file will only incur the small overhead of a symbol table lookup. If you need to force a reload of an object file, for example after recompiling it, begin a fresh session.

Optionally, a dynamically loaded file can contain initialization and finalization functions. If the file includes a function named _PG_init, that function will be called immediately after loading the file. The function receives no parameters and should return void. If the file includes a function named _PG_fini, that function will be called immediately before unloading the file. Likewise, the function receives no parameters and should return void. Note that _PG_fini will only be called during an unload of the file, not during process termination. (Presently, unloads are disabled and will never occur, but this may change in the future.)

38.10.2. Base Types in C-Language Functions

To know how to write C-language functions, you need to know how PostgreSQL internally represents base data types and how they can be passed to and from functions. Internally, PostgreSQL regards a base type as a "blob of memory". The user-defined functions that you define over a type in turn define the way that PostgreSQL can operate on it. That is, PostgreSQL will only store and retrieve the data from disk and use your user-defined functions to input, process, and output the data.

Base types can have one of three internal formats:

- pass by value, fixed-length

- pass by reference, fixed-length

- pass by reference, variable-length

By-value types can only be 1, 2, or 4 bytes in length (also 8 bytes, if `sizeof(Datum)` is 8 on your machine). You should be careful to define your types such that they will be the same size (in bytes) on all architectures. For example, the `long` type is dangerous because it is 4 bytes on some machines and 8 bytes on others, whereas `int` type is 4 bytes on most Unix machines. A reasonable implementation of the `int4` type on Unix machines might be:

```
/* 4-byte integer, passed by value */
typedef int int4;
```

(The actual PostgreSQL C code calls this type `int32`, because it is a convention in C that `intXX` means *XX bits*. Note therefore also that the C type `int8` is 1 byte in size. The SQL type `int8` is called `int64` in C. See also Table 38.1.)

On the other hand, fixed-length types of any size can be passed by-reference. For example, here is a sample implementation of a PostgreSQL type:

```
/* 16-byte structure, passed by reference */
typedef struct
{
    double  x, y;
} Point;
```

Only pointers to such types can be used when passing them in and out of PostgreSQL functions. To return a value of such a type, allocate the right amount of memory with `palloc`, fill in the allocated memory, and return a pointer to it. (Also, if you just want to return the same value as one of your input arguments that's of the same data type, you can skip the extra `palloc` and just return the pointer to the input value.)

Finally, all variable-length types must also be passed by reference. All variable-length types must begin with an opaque length field of exactly 4 bytes, which will be set by `SET_VARSIZE`; never set this field directly! All data to be stored within that type must be located in the memory immediately following that length field. The length field contains the total length of the structure, that is, it includes the size of the length field itself.

Another important point is to avoid leaving any uninitialized bits within data type values; for example, take care to zero out any alignment padding bytes that might be present in structs. Without this, logically-equivalent constants of your data type might be seen as unequal by the planner, leading to inefficient (though not incorrect) plans.

Warning

Never modify the contents of a pass-by-reference input value. If you do so you are likely to corrupt on-disk data, since the pointer you are given might point directly into a disk buffer. The sole exception to this rule is explained in Section 38.11.

As an example, we can define the type `text` as follows:

```
typedef struct {
    int32 length;
    char data[FLEXIBLE_ARRAY_MEMBER];
} text;
```

The `[FLEXIBLE_ARRAY_MEMBER]` notation means that the actual length of the data part is not specified by this declaration.

When manipulating variable-length types, we must be careful to allocate the correct amount of memory and set the length field correctly. For example, if we wanted to store 40 bytes in a `text` structure, we might use a code fragment like this:

```
#include "postgres.h"
...
char buffer[40]; /* our source data */
...
text *destination = (text *) palloc(VARHDRSZ + 40);
SET_VARSIZE(destination, VARHDRSZ + 40);
memcpy(destination->data, buffer, 40);
...
```

VARHDRSZ is the same as `sizeof(int32)`, but it's considered good style to use the macro VARHDRSZ to refer to the size of the overhead for a variable-length type. Also, the length field *must* be set using the SET_VARSIZE macro, not by simple assignment.

Table 38.1 specifies which C type corresponds to which SQL type when writing a C-language function that uses a built-in type of PostgreSQL. The "Defined In" column gives the header file that needs to be included to get the type definition. (The actual definition might be in a different file that is included by the listed file. It is recommended that users stick to the defined interface.) Note that you should always include `postgres.h` first in any source file, because it declares a number of things that you will need anyway.

Table 38.1. Equivalent C Types for Built-in SQL Types

SQL Type	C Type	Defined In
abstime	AbsoluteTime	utils/nabstime.h
bigint (int8)	int64	postgres.h
boolean	bool	postgres.h (maybe compiler built-in)

SQL Type	C Type	Defined In
box	BOX*	utils/geo_decls.h
bytea	bytea*	postgres.h
"char"	char	(compiler built-in)
character	BpChar*	postgres.h
cid	CommandId	postgres.h
date	DateADT	utils/date.h
smallint (int2)	int16	postgres.h
int2vector	int2vector*	postgres.h
integer (int4)	int32	postgres.h
real (float4)	float4*	postgres.h
double precision (float8)	float8*	postgres.h
interval	Interval*	datatype/timestamp.h
lseg	LSEG*	utils/geo_decls.h
name	Name	postgres.h
oid	Oid	postgres.h
oidvector	oidvector*	postgres.h
path	PATH*	utils/geo_decls.h
point	POINT*	utils/geo_decls.h
regproc	regproc	postgres.h
reltime	RelativeTime	utils/nabstime.h
text	text*	postgres.h
tid	ItemPointer	storage/itemptr.h
time	TimeADT	utils/date.h
time with time zone	TimeTzADT	utils/date.h
timestamp	Timestamp*	datatype/timestamp.h
tinterval	TimeInterval	utils/nabstime.h
varchar	VarChar*	postgres.h
xid	TransactionId	postgres.h

Now that we've gone over all of the possible structures for base types, we can show some examples of real functions.

38.10.3. Version 1 Calling Conventions

The version-1 calling convention relies on macros to suppress most of the complexity of passing arguments and results. The C declaration of a version-1 function is always:

```
Datum funcname(PG_FUNCTION_ARGS)
```

In addition, the macro call:

```
PG_FUNCTION_INFO_V1(funcname);
```

must appear in the same source file. (Conventionally, it's written just before the function itself.) This macro call is not needed for `internal`-language functions, since PostgreSQL assumes that all internal functions use the version-1 convention. It is, however, required for dynamically-loaded functions.

In a version-1 function, each actual argument is fetched using a `PG_GETARG_xxx()` macro that corresponds to the argument's data type. In non-strict functions there needs to be a previous check about argument null-ness using `PG_ARGNULL_xxx()`. The result is returned using a `PG_RETURN_xxx()` macro for the return type. `PG_GETARG_xxx()` takes as its argument the number of the function argument to fetch, where the count starts at 0. `PG_RETURN_xxx()` takes as its argument the actual value to return.

Here are some examples using the version-1 calling convention:

```c
#include "postgres.h"
#include <string.h>
#include "fmgr.h"
#include "utils/geo_decls.h"

PG_MODULE_MAGIC;

/* by value */

PG_FUNCTION_INFO_V1(add_one);

Datum
add_one(PG_FUNCTION_ARGS)
{
    int32   arg = PG_GETARG_INT32(0);

    PG_RETURN_INT32(arg + 1);
}

/* by reference, fixed length */

PG_FUNCTION_INFO_V1(add_one_float8);

Datum
add_one_float8(PG_FUNCTION_ARGS)
{
    /* The macros for FLOAT8 hide its pass-by-reference nature. */
    float8   arg = PG_GETARG_FLOAT8(0);

    PG_RETURN_FLOAT8(arg + 1.0);
}

PG_FUNCTION_INFO_V1(makepoint);

Datum
makepoint(PG_FUNCTION_ARGS)
{
    /* Here, the pass-by-reference nature of Point is not hidden. */
    Point      *pointx = PG_GETARG_POINT_P(0);
```

```
    Point       *pointy = PG_GETARG_POINT_P(1);
    Point       *new_point = (Point *) palloc(sizeof(Point));

    new_point->x = pointx->x;
    new_point->y = pointy->y;

    PG_RETURN_POINT_P(new_point);
}

/* by reference, variable length */

PG_FUNCTION_INFO_V1(copytext);

Datum
copytext(PG_FUNCTION_ARGS)
{
    text       *t = PG_GETARG_TEXT_PP(0);

    /*
     * VARSIZE_ANY_EXHDR is the size of the struct in bytes, minus the
     * VARHDRSZ or VARHDRSZ_SHORT of its header.  Construct the copy
 with a
     * full-length header.
     */
    text       *new_t = (text *) palloc(VARSIZE_ANY_EXHDR(t) +
 VARHDRSZ);
    SET_VARSIZE(new_t, VARSIZE_ANY_EXHDR(t) + VARHDRSZ);

    /*
     * VARDATA is a pointer to the data region of the new struct.  The
 source
     * could be a short datum, so retrieve its data through
 VARDATA_ANY.
     */
    memcpy((void *) VARDATA(new_t), /* destination */
           (void *) VARDATA_ANY(t), /* source */
           VARSIZE_ANY_EXHDR(t));   /* how many bytes */
    PG_RETURN_TEXT_P(new_t);
}

PG_FUNCTION_INFO_V1(concat_text);

Datum
concat_text(PG_FUNCTION_ARGS)
{
    text  *arg1 = PG_GETARG_TEXT_PP(0);
    text  *arg2 = PG_GETARG_TEXT_PP(1);
    int32 arg1_size = VARSIZE_ANY_EXHDR(arg1);
    int32 arg2_size = VARSIZE_ANY_EXHDR(arg2);
    int32 new_text_size = arg1_size + arg2_size + VARHDRSZ;
    text *new_text = (text *) palloc(new_text_size);

    SET_VARSIZE(new_text, new_text_size);
    memcpy(VARDATA(new_text), VARDATA_ANY(arg1), arg1_size);
```

```
    memcpy(VARDATA(new_text) + arg1_size, VARDATA_ANY(arg2),
 arg2_size);
    PG_RETURN_TEXT_P(new_text);
}
```

Supposing that the above code has been prepared in file `funcs.c` and compiled into a shared object, we could define the functions to PostgreSQL with commands like this:

```
CREATE FUNCTION add_one(integer) RETURNS integer
    AS 'DIRECTORY/funcs', 'add_one'
    LANGUAGE C STRICT;

-- note overloading of SQL function name "add_one"
CREATE FUNCTION add_one(double precision) RETURNS double precision
    AS 'DIRECTORY/funcs', 'add_one_float8'
    LANGUAGE C STRICT;

CREATE FUNCTION makepoint(point, point) RETURNS point
    AS 'DIRECTORY/funcs', 'makepoint'
    LANGUAGE C STRICT;

CREATE FUNCTION copytext(text) RETURNS text
    AS 'DIRECTORY/funcs', 'copytext'
    LANGUAGE C STRICT;

CREATE FUNCTION concat_text(text, text) RETURNS text
    AS 'DIRECTORY/funcs', 'concat_text'
    LANGUAGE C STRICT;
```

Here, *DIRECTORY* stands for the directory of the shared library file (for instance the PostgreSQL tutorial directory, which contains the code for the examples used in this section). (Better style would be to use just `'funcs'` in the AS clause, after having added *DIRECTORY* to the search path. In any case, we can omit the system-specific extension for a shared library, commonly `.so`.)

Notice that we have specified the functions as "strict", meaning that the system should automatically assume a null result if any input value is null. By doing this, we avoid having to check for null inputs in the function code. Without this, we'd have to check for null values explicitly, using `PG_ARGISNULL()`.

At first glance, the version-1 coding conventions might appear to be just pointless obscurantism, over using plain C calling conventions. They do however allow to deal with NULLable arguments/return values, and "toasted" (compressed or out-of-line) values.

The macro `PG_ARGISNULL(n)` allows a function to test whether each input is null. (Of course, doing this is only necessary in functions not declared "strict".) As with the `PG_GETARG_xxx()` macros, the input arguments are counted beginning at zero. Note that one should refrain from executing `PG_GETARG_xxx()` until one has verified that the argument isn't null. To return a null result, execute `PG_RETURN_NULL()`; this works in both strict and nonstrict functions.

Other options provided by the version-1 interface are two variants of the `PG_GETARG_xxx()` macros. The first of these, `PG_GETARG_xxx_COPY()`, guarantees to return a copy of the specified argument that is safe for writing into. (The normal macros will sometimes return a pointer to a value that is physically stored in a table, which must not be written to. Using the `PG_GETARG_xxx_COPY()` macros guarantees a writable result.) The second variant consists of the `PG_GETARG_xxx_SLICE()` macros which take three arguments. The first is the number of the function argument (as above). The second and third are the offset and length of the segment to be returned. Offsets are counted from zero, and a negative length requests that the remainder of the value be returned. These macros provide more efficient access to parts of large values in the case where they have storage type "external". (The storage type of a column can be specified using ALTER TABLE *tablename* ALTER COLUMN *colname* SET STORAGE *storagetype*. *storagetype* is one of plain, external, extended, or main.)

Finally, the version-1 function call conventions make it possible to return set results (Section 38.10.8) and implement trigger functions (Chapter 39) and procedural-language call handlers (Chapter 56). For more details see src/backend/utils/fmgr/README in the source distribution.

38.10.4. Writing Code

Before we turn to the more advanced topics, we should discuss some coding rules for PostgreSQL C-language functions. While it might be possible to load functions written in languages other than C into PostgreSQL, this is usually difficult (when it is possible at all) because other languages, such as C++, FORTRAN, or Pascal often do not follow the same calling convention as C. That is, other languages do not pass argument and return values between functions in the same way. For this reason, we will assume that your C-language functions are actually written in C.

The basic rules for writing and building C functions are as follows:

- Use pg_config --includedir-server to find out where the PostgreSQL server header files are installed on your system (or the system that your users will be running on).

- Compiling and linking your code so that it can be dynamically loaded into PostgreSQL always requires special flags. See Section 38.10.5 for a detailed explanation of how to do it for your particular operating system.

- Remember to define a "magic block" for your shared library, as described in Section 38.10.1.

- When allocating memory, use the PostgreSQL functions palloc and pfree instead of the corresponding C library functions malloc and free. The memory allocated by palloc will be freed automatically at the end of each transaction, preventing memory leaks.

- Always zero the bytes of your structures using memset (or allocate them with palloc0 in the first place). Even if you assign to each field of your structure, there might be alignment padding (holes in the structure) that contain garbage values. Without this, it's difficult to support hash indexes or hash joins, as you must pick out only the significant bits of your data structure to compute a hash. The planner also sometimes relies on comparing constants via bitwise equality, so you can get undesirable planning results if logically-equivalent values aren't bitwise equal.

- Most of the internal PostgreSQL types are declared in postgres.h, while the function manager interfaces (PG_FUNCTION_ARGS, etc.) are in fmgr.h, so you will need to include at least these two files. For portability reasons it's best to include postgres.h *first*, before any other system or user header files. Including postgres.h will also include elog.h and palloc.h for you.

- Symbol names defined within object files must not conflict with each other or with symbols defined in the PostgreSQL server executable. You will have to rename your functions or variables if you get error messages to this effect.

38.10.5. Compiling and Linking Dynamically-loaded Functions

Before you are able to use your PostgreSQL extension functions written in C, they must be compiled and linked in a special way to produce a file that can be dynamically loaded by the server. To be precise, a *shared library* needs to be created.

For information beyond what is contained in this section you should read the documentation of your operating system, in particular the manual pages for the C compiler, cc, and the link editor, ld. In addition, the PostgreSQL source code contains several working examples in the contrib directory. If you rely on these examples you will make your modules dependent on the availability of the PostgreSQL source code, however.

Creating shared libraries is generally analogous to linking executables: first the source files are compiled into object files, then the object files are linked together. The object files need to be created as *position-independent code* (PIC), which conceptually means that they can be placed at an arbitrary location in memory when they are loaded by the executable. (Object files intended for executables are usually not compiled that way.) The command to link a shared library contains special flags to distinguish it from linking an executable (at least in theory — on some systems the practice is much uglier).

In the following examples we assume that your source code is in a file foo.c and we will create a shared library foo.so. The intermediate object file will be called foo.o unless otherwise noted. A shared library can contain more than one object file, but we only use one here.

FreeBSD

The compiler flag to create PIC is -fPIC. To create shared libraries the compiler flag is -shared.

```
gcc -fPIC -c foo.c
gcc -shared -o foo.so foo.o
```

This is applicable as of version 3.0 of FreeBSD.

HP-UX

The compiler flag of the system compiler to create PIC is +z. When using GCC it's -fPIC. The linker flag for shared libraries is -b. So:

```
cc +z -c foo.c
```

or:

```
gcc -fPIC -c foo.c
```

and then:

```
ld -b -o foo.sl foo.o
```

HP-UX uses the extension .sl for shared libraries, unlike most other systems.

Linux

The compiler flag to create PIC is -fPIC. The compiler flag to create a shared library is -shared. A complete example looks like this:

```
cc -fPIC -c foo.c
cc -shared -o foo.so foo.o
```

macOS

Here is an example. It assumes the developer tools are installed.

```
cc -c foo.c
cc -bundle -flat_namespace -undefined suppress -o foo.so foo.o
```

NetBSD

The compiler flag to create PIC is -fPIC. For ELF systems, the compiler with the flag -shared is used to link shared libraries. On the older non-ELF systems, ld -Bshareable is used.

```
gcc -fPIC -c foo.c
gcc -shared -o foo.so foo.o
```

OpenBSD

The compiler flag to create PIC is -fPIC. ld -Bshareable is used to link shared libraries.

```
gcc -fPIC -c foo.c
ld -Bshareable -o foo.so foo.o
```

Solaris

The compiler flag to create PIC is -KPIC with the Sun compiler and -fPIC with GCC. To link shared libraries, the compiler option is -G with either compiler or alternatively -shared with GCC.

```
cc -KPIC -c foo.c
cc -G -o foo.so foo.o
```

or

```
gcc -fPIC -c foo.c
gcc -G -o foo.so foo.o
```

> ### Tip
>
> If this is too complicated for you, you should consider using GNU Libtool[1], which hides the platform differences behind a uniform interface.

The resulting shared library file can then be loaded into PostgreSQL. When specifying the file name to the CREATE FUNCTION command, one must give it the name of the shared library file, not the intermediate object file. Note that the system's standard shared-library extension (usually .so or .sl) can be omitted from the CREATE FUNCTION command, and normally should be omitted for best portability.

Refer back to Section 38.10.1 about where the server expects to find the shared library files.

38.10.6. Composite-type Arguments

Composite types do not have a fixed layout like C structures. Instances of a composite type can contain null fields. In addition, composite types that are part of an inheritance hierarchy can have different fields than

---

[1] http://www.gnu.org/software/libtool/

other members of the same inheritance hierarchy. Therefore, PostgreSQL provides a function interface for accessing fields of composite types from C.

Suppose we want to write a function to answer the query:

```
SELECT name, c_overpaid(emp, 1500) AS overpaid
    FROM emp
    WHERE name = 'Bill' OR name = 'Sam';
```

Using the version-1 calling conventions, we can define c_overpaid as:

```
#include "postgres.h"
#include "executor/executor.h"  /* for GetAttributeByName() */

PG_MODULE_MAGIC;

PG_FUNCTION_INFO_V1(c_overpaid);

Datum
c_overpaid(PG_FUNCTION_ARGS)
{
    HeapTupleHeader  t = PG_GETARG_HEAPTUPLEHEADER(0);
    int32            limit = PG_GETARG_INT32(1);
    bool isnull;
    Datum salary;

    salary = GetAttributeByName(t, "salary", &isnull);
    if (isnull)
        PG_RETURN_BOOL(false);
    /* Alternatively, we might prefer to do PG_RETURN_NULL() for null
 salary. */

    PG_RETURN_BOOL(DatumGetInt32(salary) > limit);
}
```

GetAttributeByName is the PostgreSQL system function that returns attributes out of the specified row. It has three arguments: the argument of type HeapTupleHeader passed into the function, the name of the desired attribute, and a return parameter that tells whether the attribute is null. GetAttribute-ByName returns a Datum value that you can convert to the proper data type by using the appropriate DatumGet*XXX*( ) macro. Note that the return value is meaningless if the null flag is set; always check the null flag before trying to do anything with the result.

There is also GetAttributeByNum, which selects the target attribute by column number instead of name.

The following command declares the function c_overpaid in SQL:

```
CREATE FUNCTION c_overpaid(emp, integer) RETURNS boolean
    AS 'DIRECTORY/funcs', 'c_overpaid'
    LANGUAGE C STRICT;
```

Notice we have used STRICT so that we did not have to check whether the input arguments were NULL.

38.10.7. Returning Rows (Composite Types)

To return a row or composite-type value from a C-language function, you can use a special API that provides macros and functions to hide most of the complexity of building composite data types. To use this API, the source file must include:

```
#include "funcapi.h"
```

There are two ways you can build a composite data value (henceforth a "tuple"): you can build it from an array of Datum values, or from an array of C strings that can be passed to the input conversion functions of the tuple's column data types. In either case, you first need to obtain or construct a `TupleDesc` descriptor for the tuple structure. When working with Datums, you pass the `TupleDesc` to `BlessTupleDesc`, and then call `heap_form_tuple` for each row. When working with C strings, you pass the `TupleDesc` to `TupleDescGetAttInMetadata`, and then call `BuildTupleFromCStrings` for each row. In the case of a function returning a set of tuples, the setup steps can all be done once during the first call of the function.

Several helper functions are available for setting up the needed `TupleDesc`. The recommended way to do this in most functions returning composite values is to call:

```
TypeFuncClass get_call_result_type(FunctionCallInfo fcinfo,
                                   Oid *resultTypeId,
                                   TupleDesc *resultTupleDesc)
```

passing the same `fcinfo` struct passed to the calling function itself. (This of course requires that you use the version-1 calling conventions.) `resultTypeId` can be specified as NULL or as the address of a local variable to receive the function's result type OID. `resultTupleDesc` should be the address of a local `TupleDesc` variable. Check that the result is `TYPEFUNC_COMPOSITE`; if so, `resultTupleDesc` has been filled with the needed `TupleDesc`. (If it is not, you can report an error along the lines of "function returning record called in context that cannot accept type record".)

Tip

`get_call_result_type` can resolve the actual type of a polymorphic function result; so it is useful in functions that return scalar polymorphic results, not only functions that return composites. The `resultTypeId` output is primarily useful for functions returning polymorphic scalars.

Note

`get_call_result_type` has a sibling `get_expr_result_type`, which can be used to resolve the expected output type for a function call represented by an expression tree. This can be used when trying to determine the result type from outside the function itself. There is also `get_func_result_type`, which can be used when only the function's OID is available. However these functions are not able to deal with functions declared to return `record`, and `get_func_result_type` cannot resolve polymorphic types, so you should preferentially use `get_call_result_type`.

Older, now-deprecated functions for obtaining `TupleDesc`s are:

```
TupleDesc RelationNameGetTupleDesc(const char *relname)
```

to get a `TupleDesc` for the row type of a named relation, and:

```
TupleDesc TypeGetTupleDesc(Oid typeoid, List *colaliases)
```

to get a `TupleDesc` based on a type OID. This can be used to get a `TupleDesc` for a base or composite type. It will not work for a function that returns `record`, however, and it cannot resolve polymorphic types.

Once you have a `TupleDesc`, call:

```
TupleDesc BlessTupleDesc(TupleDesc tupdesc)
```

if you plan to work with Datums, or:

```
AttInMetadata *TupleDescGetAttInMetadata(TupleDesc tupdesc)
```

if you plan to work with C strings. If you are writing a function returning set, you can save the results of these functions in the `FuncCallContext` structure — use the `tuple_desc` or `attinmeta` field respectively.

When working with Datums, use:

```
HeapTuple heap_form_tuple(TupleDesc tupdesc, Datum *values, bool
 *isnull)
```

to build a `HeapTuple` given user data in Datum form.

When working with C strings, use:

```
HeapTuple BuildTupleFromCStrings(AttInMetadata *attinmeta, char
 **values)
```

to build a `HeapTuple` given user data in C string form. *values* is an array of C strings, one for each attribute of the return row. Each C string should be in the form expected by the input function of the attribute data type. In order to return a null value for one of the attributes, the corresponding pointer in the *values* array should be set to `NULL`. This function will need to be called again for each row you return.

Once you have built a tuple to return from your function, it must be converted into a `Datum`. Use:

```
HeapTupleGetDatum(HeapTuple tuple)
```

to convert a `HeapTuple` into a valid Datum. This `Datum` can be returned directly if you intend to return just a single row, or it can be used as the current return value in a set-returning function.

An example appears in the next section.

38.10.8. Returning Sets

There is also a special API that provides support for returning sets (multiple rows) from a C-language function. A set-returning function must follow the version-1 calling conventions. Also, source files must include funcapi.h, as above.

A set-returning function (SRF) is called once for each item it returns. The SRF must therefore save enough state to remember what it was doing and return the next item on each call. The structure FuncCallContext is provided to help control this process. Within a function, fcinfo->flinfo->fn_extra is used to hold a pointer to FuncCallContext across calls.

```
typedef struct FuncCallContext
{
    /*
     * Number of times we've been called before
     *
     * call_cntr is initialized to 0 for you by SRF_FIRSTCALL_INIT(),
 and
     * incremented for you every time SRF_RETURN_NEXT() is called.
     */
    uint64 call_cntr;

    /*
     * OPTIONAL maximum number of calls
     *
     * max_calls is here for convenience only and setting it is
 optional.
     * If not set, you must provide alternative means to know when the
     * function is done.
     */
    uint64 max_calls;

    /*
     * OPTIONAL pointer to result slot
     *
     * This is obsolete and only present for backward compatibility,
 viz,
     * user-defined SRFs that use the deprecated TupleDescGetSlot().
     */
    TupleTableSlot *slot;

    /*
     * OPTIONAL pointer to miscellaneous user-provided context
 information
     *
     * user_fctx is for use as a pointer to your own data to retain
     * arbitrary context information between calls of your function.
     */
    void *user_fctx;

    /*
     * OPTIONAL pointer to struct containing attribute type input
 metadata
```

```
     *
     * attinmeta is for use when returning tuples (i.e., composite
data types)
     * and is not used when returning base data types. It is only
needed
     * if you intend to use BuildTupleFromCStrings() to create the
return
     * tuple.
     */
    AttInMetadata *attinmeta;

    /*
     * memory context used for structures that must live for multiple
calls
     *
     * multi_call_memory_ctx is set by SRF_FIRSTCALL_INIT() for you,
and used
     * by SRF_RETURN_DONE() for cleanup. It is the most appropriate
memory
     * context for any memory that is to be reused across multiple
calls
     * of the SRF.
     */
    MemoryContext multi_call_memory_ctx;

    /*
     * OPTIONAL pointer to struct containing tuple description
     *
     * tuple_desc is for use when returning tuples (i.e., composite
data types)
     * and is only needed if you are going to build the tuples with
     * heap_form_tuple() rather than with BuildTupleFromCStrings().
Note that
     * the TupleDesc pointer stored here should usually have been run
through
     * BlessTupleDesc() first.
     */
    TupleDesc tuple_desc;

} FuncCallContext;
```

An SRF uses several functions and macros that automatically manipulate the FuncCallContext structure (and expect to find it via fn_extra). Use:

```
SRF_IS_FIRSTCALL()
```

to determine if your function is being called for the first or a subsequent time. On the first call (only) use:

```
SRF_FIRSTCALL_INIT()
```

to initialize the FuncCallContext. On every function call, including the first, use:

```
SRF_PERCALL_SETUP()
```

to properly set up for using the `FuncCallContext` and clearing any previously returned data left over from the previous pass.

If your function has data to return, use:

```
SRF_RETURN_NEXT(funcctx, result)
```

to return it to the caller. (`result` must be of type `Datum`, either a single value or a tuple prepared as described above.) Finally, when your function is finished returning data, use:

```
SRF_RETURN_DONE(funcctx)
```

to clean up and end the SRF.

The memory context that is current when the SRF is called is a transient context that will be cleared between calls. This means that you do not need to call `pfree` on everything you allocated using `palloc`; it will go away anyway. However, if you want to allocate any data structures to live across calls, you need to put them somewhere else. The memory context referenced by `multi_call_memory_ctx` is a suitable location for any data that needs to survive until the SRF is finished running. In most cases, this means that you should switch into `multi_call_memory_ctx` while doing the first-call setup.

> # Warning
>
> While the actual arguments to the function remain unchanged between calls, if you detoast the argument values (which is normally done transparently by the `PG_GETARG_xxx` macro) in the transient context then the detoasted copies will be freed on each cycle. Accordingly, if you keep references to such values in your `user_fctx`, you must either copy them into the `multi_call_memory_ctx` after detoasting, or ensure that you detoast the values only in that context.

A complete pseudo-code example looks like the following:

```
Datum
my_set_returning_function(PG_FUNCTION_ARGS)
{
    FuncCallContext   *funcctx;
    Datum              result;
    further declarations as needed

    if (SRF_IS_FIRSTCALL())
    {
        MemoryContext oldcontext;

        funcctx = SRF_FIRSTCALL_INIT();
        oldcontext = MemoryContextSwitchTo(funcctx-
>multi_call_memory_ctx);
        /* One-time setup code appears here: */
        user code
        if returning composite
```

```
                build TupleDesc, and perhaps AttInMetadata
            endif returning composite
            user code
            MemoryContextSwitchTo(oldcontext);
    }

    /* Each-time setup code appears here: */
    user code
    funcctx = SRF_PERCALL_SETUP();
    user code

    /* this is just one way we might test whether we are done: */
    if (funcctx->call_cntr < funcctx->max_calls)
    {
        /* Here we want to return another item: */
        user code
        obtain result Datum
        SRF_RETURN_NEXT(funcctx, result);
    }
    else
    {
        /* Here we are done returning items and just need to clean up:
 */
        user code
        SRF_RETURN_DONE(funcctx);
    }
}
```

A complete example of a simple SRF returning a composite type looks like:

```
PG_FUNCTION_INFO_V1(retcomposite);

Datum
retcomposite(PG_FUNCTION_ARGS)
{
    FuncCallContext     *funcctx;
    int                 call_cntr;
    int                 max_calls;
    TupleDesc           tupdesc;
    AttInMetadata       *attinmeta;

    /* stuff done only on the first call of the function */
    if (SRF_IS_FIRSTCALL())
    {
        MemoryContext    oldcontext;

        /* create a function context for cross-call persistence */
        funcctx = SRF_FIRSTCALL_INIT();

        /* switch to memory context appropriate for multiple function
 calls */
        oldcontext = MemoryContextSwitchTo(funcctx-
>multi_call_memory_ctx);
```

```
        /* total number of tuples to be returned */
        funcctx->max_calls = PG_GETARG_UINT32(0);

        /* Build a tuple descriptor for our result type */
        if (get_call_result_type(fcinfo, NULL, &tupdesc) !=
TYPEFUNC_COMPOSITE)
            ereport(ERROR,
                    (errcode(ERRCODE_FEATURE_NOT_SUPPORTED),
                     errmsg("function returning record called in
context "
                            "that cannot accept type record")));

        /*
         * generate attribute metadata needed later to produce tuples
from raw
         * C strings
         */
        attinmeta = TupleDescGetAttInMetadata(tupdesc);
        funcctx->attinmeta = attinmeta;

        MemoryContextSwitchTo(oldcontext);
    }

    /* stuff done on every call of the function */
    funcctx = SRF_PERCALL_SETUP();

    call_cntr = funcctx->call_cntr;
    max_calls = funcctx->max_calls;
    attinmeta = funcctx->attinmeta;

    if (call_cntr < max_calls)      /* do when there is more left to
send */
    {
        char        **values;
        HeapTuple   tuple;
        Datum       result;

        /*
         * Prepare a values array for building the returned tuple.
         * This should be an array of C strings which will
         * be processed later by the type input functions.
         */
        values = (char **) palloc(3 * sizeof(char *));
        values[0] = (char *) palloc(16 * sizeof(char));
        values[1] = (char *) palloc(16 * sizeof(char));
        values[2] = (char *) palloc(16 * sizeof(char));

        snprintf(values[0], 16, "%d", 1 * PG_GETARG_INT32(1));
        snprintf(values[1], 16, "%d", 2 * PG_GETARG_INT32(1));
        snprintf(values[2], 16, "%d", 3 * PG_GETARG_INT32(1));

        /* build a tuple */
        tuple = BuildTupleFromCStrings(attinmeta, values);
```

```
        /* make the tuple into a datum */
        result = HeapTupleGetDatum(tuple);

        /* clean up (this is not really necessary) */
        pfree(values[0]);
        pfree(values[1]);
        pfree(values[2]);
        pfree(values);

        SRF_RETURN_NEXT(funcctx, result);
    }
    else    /* do when there is no more left */
    {
        SRF_RETURN_DONE(funcctx);
    }
}
```

One way to declare this function in SQL is:

```
CREATE TYPE __retcomposite AS (f1 integer, f2 integer, f3 integer);

CREATE OR REPLACE FUNCTION retcomposite(integer, integer)
    RETURNS SETOF __retcomposite
    AS 'filename', 'retcomposite'
    LANGUAGE C IMMUTABLE STRICT;
```

A different way is to use OUT parameters:

```
CREATE OR REPLACE FUNCTION retcomposite(IN integer, IN integer,
    OUT f1 integer, OUT f2 integer, OUT f3 integer)
    RETURNS SETOF record
    AS 'filename', 'retcomposite'
    LANGUAGE C IMMUTABLE STRICT;
```

Notice that in this method the output type of the function is formally an anonymous `record` type.

The directory `contrib/tablefunc` module in the source distribution contains more examples of set-returning functions.

38.10.9. Polymorphic Arguments and Return Types

C-language functions can be declared to accept and return the polymorphic types `anyelement`, `anyarray`, `anynonarray`, `anyenum`, and `anyrange`. See Section 38.2.5 for a more detailed explanation of polymorphic functions. When function arguments or return types are defined as polymorphic types, the function author cannot know in advance what data type it will be called with, or need to return. There are two routines provided in `fmgr.h` to allow a version-1 C function to discover the actual data types of its arguments and the type it is expected to return. The routines are called `get_fn_expr_rettype(FmgrInfo *flinfo)` and `get_fn_expr_argtype(FmgrInfo *flinfo, int argnum)`. They return the result or argument type OID, or `InvalidOid` if the information is not available. The structure `flinfo` is normally accessed as `fcinfo->flinfo`. The parameter `argnum` is zero based. `get_call_result_type` can also be used as an alternative to `get_fn_expr_rettype`. There is also `get_fn_expr_variadic`, which can be used to find out whether variadic arguments have been merged into an array. This is primarily useful for `VARIADIC "any"` functions, since such merging will always have occurred for variadic functions taking ordinary array types.

For example, suppose we want to write a function to accept a single element of any type, and return a one-dimensional array of that type:

```
PG_FUNCTION_INFO_V1(make_array);
Datum
make_array(PG_FUNCTION_ARGS)
{
    ArrayType   *result;
    Oid          element_type = get_fn_expr_argtype(fcinfo->flinfo, 0);
    Datum        element;
    bool         isnull;
    int16        typlen;
    bool         typbyval;
    char         typalign;
    int          ndims;
    int          dims[MAXDIM];
    int          lbs[MAXDIM];

    if (!OidIsValid(element_type))
        elog(ERROR, "could not determine data type of input");

    /* get the provided element, being careful in case it's NULL */
    isnull = PG_ARGISNULL(0);
    if (isnull)
        element = (Datum) 0;
    else
        element = PG_GETARG_DATUM(0);

    /* we have one dimension */
    ndims = 1;
    /* and one element */
    dims[0] = 1;
    /* and lower bound is 1 */
    lbs[0] = 1;

    /* get required info about the element type */
    get_typlenbyvalalign(element_type, &typlen, &typbyval, &typalign);

    /* now build the array */
    result = construct_md_array(&element, &isnull, ndims, dims, lbs,
                                element_type, typlen, typbyval,
 typalign);

    PG_RETURN_ARRAYTYPE_P(result);
}
```

The following command declares the function `make_array` in SQL:

```
CREATE FUNCTION make_array(anyelement) RETURNS anyarray
```

```
AS 'DIRECTORY/funcs', 'make_array'
LANGUAGE C IMMUTABLE;
```

There is a variant of polymorphism that is only available to C-language functions: they can be declared to take parameters of type `"any"`. (Note that this type name must be double-quoted, since it's also a SQL reserved word.) This works like `anyelement` except that it does not constrain different `"any"` arguments to be the same type, nor do they help determine the function's result type. A C-language function can also declare its final parameter to be `VARIADIC "any"`. This will match one or more actual arguments of any type (not necessarily the same type). These arguments will *not* be gathered into an array as happens with normal variadic functions; they will just be passed to the function separately. The `PG_NARGS()` macro and the methods described above must be used to determine the number of actual arguments and their types when using this feature. Also, users of such a function might wish to use the `VARIADIC` keyword in their function call, with the expectation that the function would treat the array elements as separate arguments. The function itself must implement that behavior if wanted, after using `get_fn_expr_variadic` to detect that the actual argument was marked with `VARIADIC`.

38.10.10. Transform Functions

Some function calls can be simplified during planning based on properties specific to the function. For example, `int4mul(n, 1)` could be simplified to just n. To define such function-specific optimizations, write a *transform function* and place its OID in the `protransform` field of the primary function's `pg_proc` entry. The transform function must have the SQL signature `protransform(internal)` `RETURNS internal`. The argument, actually `FuncExpr *`, is a dummy node representing a call to the primary function. If the transform function's study of the expression tree proves that a simplified expression tree can substitute for all possible concrete calls represented thereby, build and return that simplified expression. Otherwise, return a `NULL` pointer (*not* a SQL null).

We make no guarantee that PostgreSQL will never call the primary function in cases that the transform function could simplify. Ensure rigorous equivalence between the simplified expression and an actual call to the primary function.

Currently, this facility is not exposed to users at the SQL level because of security concerns, so it is only practical to use for optimizing built-in functions.

38.10.11. Shared Memory and LWLocks

Add-ins can reserve LWLocks and an allocation of shared memory on server startup. The add-in's shared library must be preloaded by specifying it in shared_preload_libraries. Shared memory is reserved by calling:

```
void RequestAddinShmemSpace(int size)
```

from your `_PG_init` function.

LWLocks are reserved by calling:

```
void RequestNamedLWLockTranche(const char *tranche_name, int
 num_lwlocks)
```

from `_PG_init`. This will ensure that an array of `num_lwlocks` LWLocks is available under the name `tranche_name`. Use `GetNamedLWLockTranche` to get a pointer to this array.

To avoid possible race-conditions, each backend should use the LWLock `AddinShmemInitLock` when connecting to and initializing its allocation of shared memory, as shown here:

```
static mystruct *ptr = NULL;

if (!ptr)
{
        bool    found;

        LWLockAcquire(AddinShmemInitLock, LW_EXCLUSIVE);
        ptr = ShmemInitStruct("my struct name", size, &found);
        if (!found)
        {
                initialize contents of shmem area;
                acquire any requested LWLocks using:
                ptr->locks = GetNamedLWLockTranche("my tranche name");
        }
        LWLockRelease(AddinShmemInitLock);
}
```

38.10.12. Using C++ for Extensibility

Although the PostgreSQL backend is written in C, it is possible to write extensions in C++ if these guidelines are followed:

- All functions accessed by the backend must present a C interface to the backend; these C functions can then call C++ functions. For example, `extern C` linkage is required for backend-accessed functions. This is also necessary for any functions that are passed as pointers between the backend and C++ code.

- Free memory using the appropriate deallocation method. For example, most backend memory is allocated using `palloc()`, so use `pfree()` to free it. Using C++ `delete` in such cases will fail.

- Prevent exceptions from propagating into the C code (use a catch-all block at the top level of all `extern C` functions). This is necessary even if the C++ code does not explicitly throw any exceptions, because events like out-of-memory can still throw exceptions. Any exceptions must be caught and appropriate errors passed back to the C interface. If possible, compile C++ with `-fno-exceptions` to eliminate exceptions entirely; in such cases, you must check for failures in your C++ code, e.g. check for NULL returned by `new()`.

- If calling backend functions from C++ code, be sure that the C++ call stack contains only plain old data structures (POD). This is necessary because backend errors generate a distant `longjmp()` that does not properly unroll a C++ call stack with non-POD objects.

In summary, it is best to place C++ code behind a wall of `extern C` functions that interface to the backend, and avoid exception, memory, and call stack leakage.

38.11. User-defined Aggregates

Aggregate functions in PostgreSQL are defined in terms of *state values* and *state transition functions*. That is, an aggregate operates using a state value that is updated as each successive input row is processed. To define a new aggregate function, one selects a data type for the state value, an initial value for the state, and a state transition function. The state transition function takes the previous state value and the aggregate's input value(s) for the current row, and returns a new state value. A *final function* can also be specified, in case the desired result of the aggregate is different from the data that needs to be kept in the running state value. The final function takes the ending state value and returns whatever is wanted as the aggregate result. In principle, the transition and final functions are just ordinary functions that could also be used outside the context of the aggregate. (In practice, it's often helpful for performance reasons to create specialized transition functions that can only work when called as part of an aggregate.)

Thus, in addition to the argument and result data types seen by a user of the aggregate, there is an internal state-value data type that might be different from both the argument and result types.

If we define an aggregate that does not use a final function, we have an aggregate that computes a running function of the column values from each row. sum is an example of this kind of aggregate. sum starts at zero and always adds the current row's value to its running total. For example, if we want to make a sum aggregate to work on a data type for complex numbers, we only need the addition function for that data type. The aggregate definition would be:

```
CREATE AGGREGATE sum (complex)
(
    sfunc = complex_add,
    stype = complex,
    initcond = '(0,0)'
);
```

which we might use like this:

```
SELECT sum(a) FROM test_complex;

   sum
-----------
 (34,53.9)
```

(Notice that we are relying on function overloading: there is more than one aggregate named sum, but PostgreSQL can figure out which kind of sum applies to a column of type complex.)

The above definition of sum will return zero (the initial state value) if there are no nonnull input values. Perhaps we want to return null in that case instead — the SQL standard expects sum to behave that way. We can do this simply by omitting the initcond phrase, so that the initial state value is null. Ordinarily this would mean that the sfunc would need to check for a null state-value input. But for sum and some other simple aggregates like max and min, it is sufficient to insert the first nonnull input value into the state variable and then start applying the transition function at the second nonnull input value. PostgreSQL will do that automatically if the initial state value is null and the transition function is marked "strict" (i.e., not to be called for null inputs).

Another bit of default behavior for a "strict" transition function is that the previous state value is retained unchanged whenever a null input value is encountered. Thus, null values are ignored. If you need some other behavior for null inputs, do not declare your transition function as strict; instead code it to test for null inputs and do whatever is needed.

avg (average) is a more complex example of an aggregate. It requires two pieces of running state: the sum of the inputs and the count of the number of inputs. The final result is obtained by dividing these quantities. Average is typically implemented by using an array as the state value. For example, the built-in implementation of avg(float8) looks like:

```
CREATE AGGREGATE avg (float8)
(
    sfunc = float8_accum,
```

```
stype = float8[],
finalfunc = float8_avg,
initcond = '{0,0,0}'
);
```

> **Note**
>
> `float8_accum` requires a three-element array, not just two elements, because it accumulates the sum of squares as well as the sum and count of the inputs. This is so that it can be used for some other aggregates as well as `avg`.

Aggregate function calls in SQL allow `DISTINCT` and `ORDER BY` options that control which rows are fed to the aggregate's transition function and in what order. These options are implemented behind the scenes and are not the concern of the aggregate's support functions.

For further details see the CREATE AGGREGATE command.

38.11.1. Moving-Aggregate Mode

Aggregate functions can optionally support *moving-aggregate mode*, which allows substantially faster execution of aggregate functions within windows with moving frame starting points. (See Section 3.5 and Section 4.2.8 for information about use of aggregate functions as window functions.) The basic idea is that in addition to a normal "forward" transition function, the aggregate provides an *inverse transition function*, which allows rows to be removed from the aggregate's running state value when they exit the window frame. For example a `sum` aggregate, which uses addition as the forward transition function, would use subtraction as the inverse transition function. Without an inverse transition function, the window function mechanism must recalculate the aggregate from scratch each time the frame starting point moves, resulting in run time proportional to the number of input rows times the average frame length. With an inverse transition function, the run time is only proportional to the number of input rows.

The inverse transition function is passed the current state value and the aggregate input value(s) for the earliest row included in the current state. It must reconstruct what the state value would have been if the given input row had never been aggregated, but only the rows following it. This sometimes requires that the forward transition function keep more state than is needed for plain aggregation mode. Therefore, the moving-aggregate mode uses a completely separate implementation from the plain mode: it has its own state data type, its own forward transition function, and its own final function if needed. These can be the same as the plain mode's data type and functions, if there is no need for extra state.

As an example, we could extend the `sum` aggregate given above to support moving-aggregate mode like this:

```
CREATE AGGREGATE sum (complex)
(
    sfunc = complex_add,
    stype = complex,
    initcond = '(0,0)',
    msfunc = complex_add,
    minvfunc = complex_sub,
    mstype = complex,
    minitcond = '(0,0)'
);
```

The parameters whose names begin with m define the moving-aggregate implementation. Except for the inverse transition function minvfunc, they correspond to the plain-aggregate parameters without m.

The forward transition function for moving-aggregate mode is not allowed to return null as the new state value. If the inverse transition function returns null, this is taken as an indication that the inverse function cannot reverse the state calculation for this particular input, and so the aggregate calculation will be redone from scratch for the current frame starting position. This convention allows moving-aggregate mode to be used in situations where there are some infrequent cases that are impractical to reverse out of the running state value. The inverse transition function can "punt" on these cases, and yet still come out ahead so long as it can work for most cases. As an example, an aggregate working with floating-point numbers might choose to punt when a NaN (not a number) input has to be removed from the running state value.

When writing moving-aggregate support functions, it is important to be sure that the inverse transition function can reconstruct the correct state value exactly. Otherwise there might be user-visible differences in results depending on whether the moving-aggregate mode is used. An example of an aggregate for which adding an inverse transition function seems easy at first, yet where this requirement cannot be met is sum over float4 or float8 inputs. A naive declaration of sum(float8) could be

```
CREATE AGGREGATE unsafe_sum (float8)
(
    stype = float8,
    sfunc = float8pl,
    mstype = float8,
    msfunc = float8pl,
    minvfunc = float8mi
);
```

This aggregate, however, can give wildly different results than it would have without the inverse transition function. For example, consider

```
SELECT
  unsafe_sum(x) OVER (ORDER BY n ROWS BETWEEN CURRENT ROW AND 1
  FOLLOWING)
FROM (VALUES (1, 1.0e20::float8),
             (2, 1.0::float8)) AS v (n,x);
```

This query returns 0 as its second result, rather than the expected answer of 1. The cause is the limited precision of floating-point values: adding 1 to 1e20 results in 1e20 again, and so subtracting 1e20 from that yields 0, not 1. Note that this is a limitation of floating-point arithmetic in general, not a limitation of PostgreSQL.

38.11.2. Polymorphic and Variadic Aggregates

Aggregate functions can use polymorphic state transition functions or final functions, so that the same functions can be used to implement multiple aggregates. See Section 38.2.5 for an explanation of polymorphic functions. Going a step further, the aggregate function itself can be specified with polymorphic input type(s) and state type, allowing a single aggregate definition to serve for multiple input data types. Here is an example of a polymorphic aggregate:

```
CREATE AGGREGATE array_accum (anyelement)
(
    sfunc = array_append,
```

```
    stype = anyarray,
    initcond = '{}'
);
```

Here, the actual state type for any given aggregate call is the array type having the actual input type as elements. The behavior of the aggregate is to concatenate all the inputs into an array of that type. (Note: the built-in aggregate `array_agg` provides similar functionality, with better performance than this definition would have.)

Here's the output using two different actual data types as arguments:

```
SELECT attrelid::regclass, array_accum(attname)
    FROM pg_attribute
    WHERE attnum > 0 AND attrelid = 'pg_tablespace'::regclass
    GROUP BY attrelid;

    attrelid    |                array_accum
----------------+-------------------------------------------
 pg_tablespace  | {spcname,spcowner,spcacl,spcoptions}
(1 row)

SELECT attrelid::regclass, array_accum(atttypid::regtype)
    FROM pg_attribute
    WHERE attnum > 0 AND attrelid = 'pg_tablespace'::regclass
    GROUP BY attrelid;

    attrelid    |         array_accum
----------------+--------------------------
 pg_tablespace  | {name,oid,aclitem[],text[]}
(1 row)
```

Ordinarily, an aggregate function with a polymorphic result type has a polymorphic state type, as in the above example. This is necessary because otherwise the final function cannot be declared sensibly: it would need to have a polymorphic result type but no polymorphic argument type, which CREATE FUNCTION will reject on the grounds that the result type cannot be deduced from a call. But sometimes it is inconvenient to use a polymorphic state type. The most common case is where the aggregate support functions are to be written in C and the state type should be declared as `internal` because there is no SQL-level equivalent for it. To address this case, it is possible to declare the final function as taking extra "dummy" arguments that match the input arguments of the aggregate. Such dummy arguments are always passed as null values since no specific value is available when the final function is called. Their only use is to allow a polymorphic final function's result type to be connected to the aggregate's input type(s). For example, the definition of the built-in aggregate `array_agg` is equivalent to

```
CREATE FUNCTION array_agg_transfn(internal, anynonarray)
  RETURNS internal ...;
CREATE FUNCTION array_agg_finalfn(internal, anynonarray)
  RETURNS anyarray ...;

CREATE AGGREGATE array_agg (anynonarray)
(
    sfunc = array_agg_transfn,
    stype = internal,
    finalfunc = array_agg_finalfn,
```

```
    finalfunc_extra
);
```

Here, the `finalfunc_extra` option specifies that the final function receives, in addition to the state value, extra dummy argument(s) corresponding to the aggregate's input argument(s). The extra `anynonarray` argument allows the declaration of `array_agg_finalfn` to be valid.

An aggregate function can be made to accept a varying number of arguments by declaring its last argument as a `VARIADIC` array, in much the same fashion as for regular functions; see Section 38.5.5. The aggregate's transition function(s) must have the same array type as their last argument. The transition function(s) typically would also be marked `VARIADIC`, but this is not strictly required.

Note

Variadic aggregates are easily misused in connection with the `ORDER BY` option (see Section 4.2.7), since the parser cannot tell whether the wrong number of actual arguments have been given in such a combination. Keep in mind that everything to the right of `ORDER BY` is a sort key, not an argument to the aggregate. For example, in

```
SELECT myaggregate(a ORDER BY a, b, c) FROM ...
```

the parser will see this as a single aggregate function argument and three sort keys. However, the user might have intended

```
SELECT myaggregate(a, b, c ORDER BY a) FROM ...
```

If `myaggregate` is variadic, both these calls could be perfectly valid.

For the same reason, it's wise to think twice before creating aggregate functions with the same names and different numbers of regular arguments.

38.11.3. Ordered-Set Aggregates

The aggregates we have been describing so far are "normal" aggregates. PostgreSQL also supports *ordered-set aggregates*, which differ from normal aggregates in two key ways. First, in addition to ordinary aggregated arguments that are evaluated once per input row, an ordered-set aggregate can have "direct" arguments that are evaluated only once per aggregation operation. Second, the syntax for the ordinary aggregated arguments specifies a sort ordering for them explicitly. An ordered-set aggregate is usually used to implement a computation that depends on a specific row ordering, for instance rank or percentile, so that the sort ordering is a required aspect of any call. For example, the built-in definition of `percentile_disc` is equivalent to:

```
CREATE FUNCTION ordered_set_transition(internal, anyelement)
  RETURNS internal ...;
CREATE FUNCTION percentile_disc_final(internal, float8, anyelement)
  RETURNS anyelement ...;

CREATE AGGREGATE percentile_disc (float8 ORDER BY anyelement)
(
    sfunc = ordered_set_transition,
    stype = internal,
```

```
    finalfunc = percentile_disc_final,
    finalfunc_extra
);
```

This aggregate takes a `float8` direct argument (the percentile fraction) and an aggregated input that can be of any sortable data type. It could be used to obtain a median household income like this:

```
SELECT percentile_disc(0.5) WITHIN GROUP (ORDER BY income) FROM
 households;
 percentile_disc
-----------------
           50489
```

Here, `0.5` is a direct argument; it would make no sense for the percentile fraction to be a value varying across rows.

Unlike the case for normal aggregates, the sorting of input rows for an ordered-set aggregate is *not* done behind the scenes, but is the responsibility of the aggregate's support functions. The typical implementation approach is to keep a reference to a "tuplesort" object in the aggregate's state value, feed the incoming rows into that object, and then complete the sorting and read out the data in the final function. This design allows the final function to perform special operations such as injecting additional "hypothetical" rows into the data to be sorted. While normal aggregates can often be implemented with support functions written in PL/pgSQL or another PL language, ordered-set aggregates generally have to be written in C, since their state values aren't definable as any SQL data type. (In the above example, notice that the state value is declared as type `internal` — this is typical.) Also, because the final function performs the sort, it is not possible to continue adding input rows by executing the transition function again later. This means the final function is not `READ_ONLY`; it must be declared in CREATE AGGREGATE as `READ_WRITE`, or as `SHAREABLE` if it's possible for additional final-function calls to make use of the already-sorted state.

The state transition function for an ordered-set aggregate receives the current state value plus the aggregated input values for each row, and returns the updated state value. This is the same definition as for normal aggregates, but note that the direct arguments (if any) are not provided. The final function receives the last state value, the values of the direct arguments if any, and (if `finalfunc_extra` is specified) null values corresponding to the aggregated input(s). As with normal aggregates, `finalfunc_extra` is only really useful if the aggregate is polymorphic; then the extra dummy argument(s) are needed to connect the final function's result type to the aggregate's input type(s).

Currently, ordered-set aggregates cannot be used as window functions, and therefore there is no need for them to support moving-aggregate mode.

38.11.4. Partial Aggregation

Optionally, an aggregate function can support *partial aggregation*. The idea of partial aggregation is to run the aggregate's state transition function over different subsets of the input data independently, and then to combine the state values resulting from those subsets to produce the same state value that would have resulted from scanning all the input in a single operation. This mode can be used for parallel aggregation by having different worker processes scan different portions of a table. Each worker produces a partial state value, and at the end those state values are combined to produce a final state value. (In the future this mode might also be used for purposes such as combining aggregations over local and remote tables; but that is not implemented yet.)

To support partial aggregation, the aggregate definition must provide a *combine function*, which takes two values of the aggregate's state type (representing the results of aggregating over two subsets of the input rows) and produces a new value of the state type, representing what the state would have been after aggregating over the combination of those sets of rows. It is unspecified what the relative order of the input rows from the two sets would have been. This means that it's usually impossible to define a useful combine function for aggregates that are sensitive to input row order.

As simple examples, MAX and MIN aggregates can be made to support partial aggregation by specifying the combine function as the same greater-of-two or lesser-of-two comparison function that is used as their transition function. SUM aggregates just need an addition function as combine function. (Again, this is the same as their transition function, unless the state value is wider than the input data type.)

The combine function is treated much like a transition function that happens to take a value of the state type, not of the underlying input type, as its second argument. In particular, the rules for dealing with null values and strict functions are similar. Also, if the aggregate definition specifies a non-null initcond, keep in mind that that will be used not only as the initial state for each partial aggregation run, but also as the initial state for the combine function, which will be called to combine each partial result into that state.

If the aggregate's state type is declared as internal, it is the combine function's responsibility that its result is allocated in the correct memory context for aggregate state values. This means in particular that when the first input is NULL it's invalid to simply return the second input, as that value will be in the wrong context and will not have sufficient lifespan.

When the aggregate's state type is declared as internal, it is usually also appropriate for the aggregate definition to provide a *serialization function* and a *deserialization function*, which allow such a state value to be copied from one process to another. Without these functions, parallel aggregation cannot be performed, and future applications such as local/remote aggregation will probably not work either.

A serialization function must take a single argument of type internal and return a result of type bytea, which represents the state value packaged up into a flat blob of bytes. Conversely, a deserialization function reverses that conversion. It must take two arguments of types bytea and internal, and return a result of type internal. (The second argument is unused and is always zero, but it is required for type-safety reasons.) The result of the deserialization function should simply be allocated in the current memory context, as unlike the combine function's result, it is not long-lived.

Worth noting also is that for an aggregate to be executed in parallel, the aggregate itself must be marked PARALLEL SAFE. The parallel-safety markings on its support functions are not consulted.

38.11.5. Support Functions for Aggregates

A function written in C can detect that it is being called as an aggregate support function by calling Agg-CheckCallContext, for example:

```
if (AggCheckCallContext(fcinfo, NULL))
```

One reason for checking this is that when it is true, the first input must be a temporary state value and can therefore safely be modified in-place rather than allocating a new copy. See int8inc() for an example. (While aggregate transition functions are always allowed to modify the transition value in-place, aggregate final functions are generally discouraged from doing so; if they do so, the behavior must be declared when creating the aggregate. See CREATE AGGREGATE for more detail.)

The second argument of AggCheckCallContext can be used to retrieve the memory context in which aggregate state values are being kept. This is useful for transition functions that wish to use "expanded" objects (see Section 38.12.1) as their state values. On first call, the transition function should return an expanded object whose memory context is a child of the aggregate state context, and then keep returning the same expanded object on subsequent calls. See array_append() for an example. (array_append() is not the transition function of any built-in aggregate, but it is written to behave efficiently when used as transition function of a custom aggregate.)

Another support routine available to aggregate functions written in C is `AggGetAggref`, which returns the `Aggref` parse node that defines the aggregate call. This is mainly useful for ordered-set aggregates, which can inspect the substructure of the `Aggref` node to find out what sort ordering they are supposed to implement. Examples can be found in `orderedsetaggs.c` in the PostgreSQL source code.

38.12. User-defined Types

As described in Section 38.2, PostgreSQL can be extended to support new data types. This section describes how to define new base types, which are data types defined below the level of the SQL language. Creating a new base type requires implementing functions to operate on the type in a low-level language, usually C.

The examples in this section can be found in `complex.sql` and `complex.c` in the `src/tutorial` directory of the source distribution. See the `README` file in that directory for instructions about running the examples.

A user-defined type must always have input and output functions. These functions determine how the type appears in strings (for input by the user and output to the user) and how the type is organized in memory. The input function takes a null-terminated character string as its argument and returns the internal (in memory) representation of the type. The output function takes the internal representation of the type as argument and returns a null-terminated character string. If we want to do anything more with the type than merely store it, we must provide additional functions to implement whatever operations we'd like to have for the type.

Suppose we want to define a type `complex` that represents complex numbers. A natural way to represent a complex number in memory would be the following C structure:

```
typedef struct Complex {
    double      x;
    double      y;
} Complex;
```

We will need to make this a pass-by-reference type, since it's too large to fit into a single `Datum` value.

As the external string representation of the type, we choose a string of the form `(x,y)`.

The input and output functions are usually not hard to write, especially the output function. But when defining the external string representation of the type, remember that you must eventually write a complete and robust parser for that representation as your input function. For instance:

```
PG_FUNCTION_INFO_V1(complex_in);

Datum
complex_in(PG_FUNCTION_ARGS)
{
    char        *str = PG_GETARG_CSTRING(0);
    double      x,
                y;
    Complex     *result;

    if (sscanf(str, " ( %lf , %lf )", &x, &y) != 2)
        ereport(ERROR,
```

```
                    (errcode(ERRCODE_INVALID_TEXT_REPRESENTATION),
                     errmsg("invalid input syntax for complex: \"%s\"",
                            str)));

    result = (Complex *) palloc(sizeof(Complex));
    result->x = x;
    result->y = y;
    PG_RETURN_POINTER(result);
}
```

The output function can simply be:

```
PG_FUNCTION_INFO_V1(complex_out);

Datum
complex_out(PG_FUNCTION_ARGS)
{
    Complex    *complex = (Complex *) PG_GETARG_POINTER(0);
    char       *result;

    result = psprintf("(%g,%g)", complex->x, complex->y);
    PG_RETURN_CSTRING(result);
}
```

You should be careful to make the input and output functions inverses of each other. If you do not, you will have severe problems when you need to dump your data into a file and then read it back in. This is a particularly common problem when floating-point numbers are involved.

Optionally, a user-defined type can provide binary input and output routines. Binary I/O is normally faster but less portable than textual I/O. As with textual I/O, it is up to you to define exactly what the external binary representation is. Most of the built-in data types try to provide a machine-independent binary representation. For complex, we will piggy-back on the binary I/O converters for type float8:

```
PG_FUNCTION_INFO_V1(complex_recv);

Datum
complex_recv(PG_FUNCTION_ARGS)
{
    StringInfo  buf = (StringInfo) PG_GETARG_POINTER(0);
    Complex     *result;

    result = (Complex *) palloc(sizeof(Complex));
    result->x = pq_getmsgfloat8(buf);
    result->y = pq_getmsgfloat8(buf);
    PG_RETURN_POINTER(result);
}

PG_FUNCTION_INFO_V1(complex_send);

Datum
complex_send(PG_FUNCTION_ARGS)
```

```
{
    Complex      *complex = (Complex *) PG_GETARG_POINTER(0);
    StringInfoData buf;

    pq_begintypsend(&buf);
    pq_sendfloat8(&buf, complex->x);
    pq_sendfloat8(&buf, complex->y);
    PG_RETURN_BYTEA_P(pq_endtypsend(&buf));
}
```

Once we have written the I/O functions and compiled them into a shared library, we can define the **complex** type in SQL. First we declare it as a shell type:

```
CREATE TYPE complex;
```

This serves as a placeholder that allows us to reference the type while defining its I/O functions. Now we can define the I/O functions:

```
CREATE FUNCTION complex_in(cstring)
    RETURNS complex
    AS 'filename'
    LANGUAGE C IMMUTABLE STRICT;

CREATE FUNCTION complex_out(complex)
    RETURNS cstring
    AS 'filename'
    LANGUAGE C IMMUTABLE STRICT;

CREATE FUNCTION complex_recv(internal)
    RETURNS complex
    AS 'filename'
    LANGUAGE C IMMUTABLE STRICT;

CREATE FUNCTION complex_send(complex)
    RETURNS bytea
    AS 'filename'
    LANGUAGE C IMMUTABLE STRICT;
```

Finally, we can provide the full definition of the data type:

```
CREATE TYPE complex (
   internallength = 16,
   input = complex_in,
   output = complex_out,
   receive = complex_recv,
   send = complex_send,
   alignment = double
);
```

When you define a new base type, PostgreSQL automatically provides support for arrays of that type. The array type typically has the same name as the base type with the underscore character (_) prepended.

Once the data type exists, we can declare additional functions to provide useful operations on the data type. Operators can then be defined atop the functions, and if needed, operator classes can be created to support indexing of the data type. These additional layers are discussed in following sections.

If the internal representation of the data type is variable-length, the internal representation must follow the standard layout for variable-length data: the first four bytes must be a `char[4]` field which is never accessed directly (customarily named `vl_len_`). You must use the `SET_VARSIZE()` macro to store the total size of the datum (including the length field itself) in this field and `VARSIZE()` to retrieve it. (These macros exist because the length field may be encoded depending on platform.)

For further details see the description of the CREATE TYPE command.

38.12.1. TOAST Considerations

If the values of your data type vary in size (in internal form), it's usually desirable to make the data type TOAST-able (see Section 68.2). You should do this even if the values are always too small to be compressed or stored externally, because TOAST can save space on small data too, by reducing header overhead.

To support TOAST storage, the C functions operating on the data type must always be careful to unpack any toasted values they are handed by using `PG_DETOAST_DATUM`. (This detail is customarily hidden by defining type-specific `GETARG_DATATYPE_P` macros.) Then, when running the `CREATE TYPE` command, specify the internal length as `variable` and select some appropriate storage option other than `plain`.

If data alignment is unimportant (either just for a specific function or because the data type specifies byte alignment anyway) then it's possible to avoid some of the overhead of `PG_DETOAST_DATUM`. You can use `PG_DETOAST_DATUM_PACKED` instead (customarily hidden by defining a `GETARG_DATATYPE_PP` macro) and using the macros `VARSIZE_ANY_EXHDR` and `VARDATA_ANY` to access a potentially-packed datum. Again, the data returned by these macros is not aligned even if the data type definition specifies an alignment. If the alignment is important you must go through the regular `PG_DETOAST_DATUM` interface.

> ## Note
>
> Older code frequently declares `vl_len_` as an `int32` field instead of `char[4]`. This is OK as long as the struct definition has other fields that have at least `int32` alignment. But it is dangerous to use such a struct definition when working with a potentially unaligned datum; the compiler may take it as license to assume the datum actually is aligned, leading to core dumps on architectures that are strict about alignment.

Another feature that's enabled by TOAST support is the possibility of having an *expanded* in-memory data representation that is more convenient to work with than the format that is stored on disk. The regular or "flat" varlena storage format is ultimately just a blob of bytes; it cannot for example contain pointers, since it may get copied to other locations in memory. For complex data types, the flat format may be quite expensive to work with, so PostgreSQL provides a way to "expand" the flat format into a representation that is more suited to computation, and then pass that format in-memory between functions of the data type.

To use expanded storage, a data type must define an expanded format that follows the rules given in `src/include/utils/expandeddatum.h`, and provide functions to "expand" a flat varlena value into expanded format and "flatten" the expanded format back to the regular varlena representation. Then ensure that all C functions for the data type can accept either representation, possibly by converting one into the other immediately upon receipt. This does not require fixing all existing functions for the data type at once, because the standard `PG_DETOAST_DATUM` macro is defined to convert expanded inputs into regular flat format. Therefore, existing functions that work with the flat varlena format will continue to work, though slightly inefficiently, with expanded inputs; they need not be converted until and unless better performance is important.

C functions that know how to work with an expanded representation typically fall into two categories: those that can only handle expanded format, and those that can handle either expanded or flat varlena inputs. The former are easier to write but may be less efficient overall, because converting a flat input to expanded form for use by a single function may cost more than is saved by operating on the expanded format. When only expanded format need be handled, conversion of flat inputs to expanded form can be hidden inside an argument-fetching macro, so that the function appears no more complex than one working with traditional varlena input. To handle both types of input, write an argument-fetching function that will detoast external, short-header, and compressed varlena inputs, but not expanded inputs. Such a function can be defined as returning a pointer to a union of the flat varlena format and the expanded format. Callers can use the `VARATT_IS_EXPANDED_HEADER()` macro to determine which format they received.

The TOAST infrastructure not only allows regular varlena values to be distinguished from expanded values, but also distinguishes "read-write" and "read-only" pointers to expanded values. C functions that only need to examine an expanded value, or will only change it in safe and non-semantically-visible ways, need not care which type of pointer they receive. C functions that produce a modified version of an input value are allowed to modify an expanded input value in-place if they receive a read-write pointer, but must not modify the input if they receive a read-only pointer; in that case they have to copy the value first, producing a new value to modify. A C function that has constructed a new expanded value should always return a read-write pointer to it. Also, a C function that is modifying a read-write expanded value in-place should take care to leave the value in a sane state if it fails partway through.

For examples of working with expanded values, see the standard array infrastructure, particularly `src/backend/utils/adt/array_expanded.c`.

38.13. User-defined Operators

Every operator is "syntactic sugar" for a call to an underlying function that does the real work; so you must first create the underlying function before you can create the operator. However, an operator is *not merely* syntactic sugar, because it carries additional information that helps the query planner optimize queries that use the operator. The next section will be devoted to explaining that additional information.

PostgreSQL supports left unary, right unary, and binary operators. Operators can be overloaded; that is, the same operator name can be used for different operators that have different numbers and types of operands. When a query is executed, the system determines the operator to call from the number and types of the provided operands.

Here is an example of creating an operator for adding two complex numbers. We assume we've already created the definition of type `complex` (see Section 38.12). First we need a function that does the work, then we can define the operator:

```
CREATE FUNCTION complex_add(complex, complex)
    RETURNS complex
    AS 'filename', 'complex_add'
    LANGUAGE C IMMUTABLE STRICT;

CREATE OPERATOR + (
    leftarg = complex,
    rightarg = complex,
    function = complex_add,
```

```
        commutator = +
);
```

Now we could execute a query like this:

```
SELECT (a + b) AS c FROM test_complex;

        c
-----------------
 (5.2,6.05)
 (133.42,144.95)
```

We've shown how to create a binary operator here. To create unary operators, just omit one of `leftarg` (for left unary) or `rightarg` (for right unary). The `function` clause and the argument clauses are the only required items in CREATE OPERATOR. The `commutator` clause shown in the example is an optional hint to the query optimizer. Further details about `commutator` and other optimizer hints appear in the next section.

38.14. Operator Optimization Information

A PostgreSQL operator definition can include several optional clauses that tell the system useful things about how the operator behaves. These clauses should be provided whenever appropriate, because they can make for considerable speedups in execution of queries that use the operator. But if you provide them, you must be sure that they are right! Incorrect use of an optimization clause can result in slow queries, subtly wrong output, or other Bad Things. You can always leave out an optimization clause if you are not sure about it; the only consequence is that queries might run slower than they need to.

Additional optimization clauses might be added in future versions of PostgreSQL. The ones described here are all the ones that release 11.2 understands.

38.14.1. COMMUTATOR

The COMMUTATOR clause, if provided, names an operator that is the commutator of the operator being defined. We say that operator A is the commutator of operator B if (x A y) equals (y B x) for all possible input values x, y. Notice that B is also the commutator of A. For example, operators < and > for a particular data type are usually each others' commutators, and operator + is usually commutative with itself. But operator – is usually not commutative with anything.

The left operand type of a commutable operator is the same as the right operand type of its commutator, and vice versa. So the name of the commutator operator is all that PostgreSQL needs to be given to look up the commutator, and that's all that needs to be provided in the COMMUTATOR clause.

It's critical to provide commutator information for operators that will be used in indexes and join clauses, because this allows the query optimizer to "flip around" such a clause to the forms needed for different plan types. For example, consider a query with a WHERE clause like `tab1.x = tab2.y`, where `tab1.x` and `tab2.y` are of a user-defined type, and suppose that `tab2.y` is indexed. The optimizer cannot generate an index scan unless it can determine how to flip the clause around to `tab2.y = tab1.x`, because the index-scan machinery expects to see the indexed column on the left of the operator it is given. PostgreSQL will *not* simply assume that this is a valid transformation — the creator of the = operator must specify that it is valid, by marking the operator with commutator information.

When you are defining a self-commutative operator, you just do it. When you are defining a pair of commutative operators, things are a little trickier: how can the first one to be defined refer to the other one, which you haven't defined yet? There are two solutions to this problem:

- One way is to omit the COMMUTATOR clause in the first operator that you define, and then provide one in the second operator's definition. Since PostgreSQL knows that commutative operators come in pairs, when it sees the second definition it will automatically go back and fill in the missing COMMUTATOR clause in the first definition.

- The other, more straightforward way is just to include COMMUTATOR clauses in both definitions. When PostgreSQL processes the first definition and realizes that COMMUTATOR refers to a nonexistent operator, the system will make a dummy entry for that operator in the system catalog. This dummy entry will have valid data only for the operator name, left and right operand types, and result type, since that's all that PostgreSQL can deduce at this point. The first operator's catalog entry will link to this dummy entry. Later, when you define the second operator, the system updates the dummy entry with the additional information from the second definition. If you try to use the dummy operator before it's been filled in, you'll just get an error message.

38.14.2. NEGATOR

The NEGATOR clause, if provided, names an operator that is the negator of the operator being defined. We say that operator A is the negator of operator B if both return Boolean results and (x A y) equals NOT (x B y) for all possible inputs x, y. Notice that B is also the negator of A. For example, < and >= are a negator pair for most data types. An operator can never validly be its own negator.

Unlike commutators, a pair of unary operators could validly be marked as each other's negators; that would mean (A x) equals NOT (B x) for all x, or the equivalent for right unary operators.

An operator's negator must have the same left and/or right operand types as the operator to be defined, so just as with COMMUTATOR, only the operator name need be given in the NEGATOR clause.

Providing a negator is very helpful to the query optimizer since it allows expressions like NOT (x = y) to be simplified into x <> y. This comes up more often than you might think, because NOT operations can be inserted as a consequence of other rearrangements.

Pairs of negator operators can be defined using the same methods explained above for commutator pairs.

38.14.3. RESTRICT

The RESTRICT clause, if provided, names a restriction selectivity estimation function for the operator. (Note that this is a function name, not an operator name.) RESTRICT clauses only make sense for binary operators that return boolean. The idea behind a restriction selectivity estimator is to guess what fraction of the rows in a table will satisfy a WHERE-clause condition of the form:

```
column OP constant
```

for the current operator and a particular constant value. This assists the optimizer by giving it some idea of how many rows will be eliminated by WHERE clauses that have this form. (What happens if the constant is on the left, you might be wondering? Well, that's one of the things that COMMUTATOR is for...)

Writing new restriction selectivity estimation functions is far beyond the scope of this chapter, but fortunately you can usually just use one of the system's standard estimators for many of your own operators. These are the standard restriction estimators:

eqsel for =
neqsel for <>
scalarltsel for <
scalarlesel for <=

```
scalargtsel for >
scalargesel for >=
```

You can frequently get away with using either `eqsel` or `neqsel` for operators that have very high or very low selectivity, even if they aren't really equality or inequality. For example, the approximate-equality geometric operators use `eqsel` on the assumption that they'll usually only match a small fraction of the entries in a table.

You can use `scalarltsel`, `scalarlesel`, `scalargtsel` and `scalargesel` for comparisons on data types that have some sensible means of being converted into numeric scalars for range comparisons. If possible, add the data type to those understood by the function `convert_to_scalar()` in `src/backend/utils/adt/selfuncs.c`. (Eventually, this function should be replaced by per-data-type functions identified through a column of the `pg_type` system catalog; but that hasn't happened yet.) If you do not do this, things will still work, but the optimizer's estimates won't be as good as they could be.

There are additional selectivity estimation functions designed for geometric operators in `src/backend/utils/adt/geo_selfuncs.c`: `areasel`, `positionsel`, and `contsel`. At this writing these are just stubs, but you might want to use them (or even better, improve them) anyway.

38.14.4. JOIN

The `JOIN` clause, if provided, names a join selectivity estimation function for the operator. (Note that this is a function name, not an operator name.) `JOIN` clauses only make sense for binary operators that return `boolean`. The idea behind a join selectivity estimator is to guess what fraction of the rows in a pair of tables will satisfy a `WHERE`-clause condition of the form:

```
table1.column1 OP table2.column2
```

for the current operator. As with the `RESTRICT` clause, this helps the optimizer very substantially by letting it figure out which of several possible join sequences is likely to take the least work.

As before, this chapter will make no attempt to explain how to write a join selectivity estimator function, but will just suggest that you use one of the standard estimators if one is applicable:

```
eqjoinsel for =
neqjoinsel for <>
scalarltjoinsel for <
scalarlejoinsel for <=
scalargtjoinsel for >
scalargejoinsel for >=
areajoinsel for 2D area-based comparisons
positionjoinsel for 2D position-based comparisons
contjoinsel for 2D containment-based comparisons
```

38.14.5. HASHES

The `HASHES` clause, if present, tells the system that it is permissible to use the hash join method for a join based on this operator. `HASHES` only makes sense for a binary operator that returns `boolean`, and in practice the operator must represent equality for some data type or pair of data types.

The assumption underlying hash join is that the join operator can only return true for pairs of left and right values that hash to the same hash code. If two values get put in different hash buckets, the join will never compare them at all, implicitly assuming that the result of the join operator must be false. So it never makes sense to specify HASHES for operators that do not represent some form of equality. In most cases it is only practical to support hashing for operators that take the same data type on both sides. However, sometimes it is possible to design compatible hash functions for two or more data types; that is, functions that will generate the same hash codes for "equal" values, even though the values have different representations. For example, it's fairly simple to arrange this property when hashing integers of different widths.

To be marked HASHES, the join operator must appear in a hash index operator family. This is not enforced when you create the operator, since of course the referencing operator family couldn't exist yet. But attempts to use the operator in hash joins will fail at run time if no such operator family exists. The system needs the operator family to find the data-type-specific hash function(s) for the operator's input data type(s). Of course, you must also create suitable hash functions before you can create the operator family.

Care should be exercised when preparing a hash function, because there are machine-dependent ways in which it might fail to do the right thing. For example, if your data type is a structure in which there might be uninteresting pad bits, you cannot simply pass the whole structure to hash_any. (Unless you write your other operators and functions to ensure that the unused bits are always zero, which is the recommended strategy.) Another example is that on machines that meet the IEEE floating-point standard, negative zero and positive zero are different values (different bit patterns) but they are defined to compare equal. If a float value might contain negative zero then extra steps are needed to ensure it generates the same hash value as positive zero.

A hash-joinable operator must have a commutator (itself if the two operand data types are the same, or a related equality operator if they are different) that appears in the same operator family. If this is not the case, planner errors might occur when the operator is used. Also, it is a good idea (but not strictly required) for a hash operator family that supports multiple data types to provide equality operators for every combination of the data types; this allows better optimization.

Note

The function underlying a hash-joinable operator must be marked immutable or stable. If it is volatile, the system will never attempt to use the operator for a hash join.

Note

If a hash-joinable operator has an underlying function that is marked strict, the function must also be complete: that is, it should return true or false, never null, for any two non-null inputs. If this rule is not followed, hash-optimization of IN operations might generate wrong results. (Specifically, IN might return false where the correct answer according to the standard would be null; or it might yield an error complaining that it wasn't prepared for a null result.)

38.14.6. MERGES

The MERGES clause, if present, tells the system that it is permissible to use the merge-join method for a join based on this operator. MERGES only makes sense for a binary operator that returns boolean, and in practice the operator must represent equality for some data type or pair of data types.

Merge join is based on the idea of sorting the left- and right-hand tables into order and then scanning them in parallel. So, both data types must be capable of being fully ordered, and the join operator must be one that can only succeed for pairs of values that fall at the "same place" in the sort order. In practice this means that the join operator must behave like equality. But it is possible to merge-join two distinct data types so long as they are logically compatible. For example, the smallint-versus-integer equality operator is merge-joinable. We only need sorting operators that will bring both data types into a logically compatible sequence.

To be marked MERGES, the join operator must appear as an equality member of a btree index operator family. This is not enforced when you create the operator, since of course the referencing operator family couldn't exist yet. But the operator will not actually be used for merge joins unless a matching operator family can be found. The MERGES flag thus acts as a hint to the planner that it's worth looking for a matching operator family.

A merge-joinable operator must have a commutator (itself if the two operand data types are the same, or a related equality operator if they are different) that appears in the same operator family. If this is not the case, planner errors might occur when the operator is used. Also, it is a good idea (but not strictly required) for a btree operator family that supports multiple data types to provide equality operators for every combination of the data types; this allows better optimization.

Note

The function underlying a merge-joinable operator must be marked immutable or stable. If it is volatile, the system will never attempt to use the operator for a merge join.

38.15. Interfacing Extensions To Indexes

The procedures described thus far let you define new types, new functions, and new operators. However, we cannot yet define an index on a column of a new data type. To do this, we must define an *operator class* for the new data type. Later in this section, we will illustrate this concept in an example: a new operator class for the B-tree index method that stores and sorts complex numbers in ascending absolute value order.

Operator classes can be grouped into *operator families* to show the relationships between semantically compatible classes. When only a single data type is involved, an operator class is sufficient, so we'll focus on that case first and then return to operator families.

38.15.1. Index Methods and Operator Classes

The pg_am table contains one row for every index method (internally known as access method). Support for regular access to tables is built into PostgreSQL, but all index methods are described in pg_am. It is possible to add a new index access method by writing the necessary code and then creating an entry in pg_am — but that is beyond the scope of this chapter (see Chapter 61).

The routines for an index method do not directly know anything about the data types that the index method will operate on. Instead, an *operator class* identifies the set of operations that the index method needs to use to work with a particular data type. Operator classes are so called because one thing they specify is the set of WHERE-clause operators that can be used with an index (i.e., can be converted into an index-scan qualification). An operator class can also specify some *support function* that are needed by the internal operations of the index method, but do not directly correspond to any WHERE-clause operator that can be used with the index.

It is possible to define multiple operator classes for the same data type and index method. By doing this, multiple sets of indexing semantics can be defined for a single data type. For example, a B-tree index requires a sort ordering to be defined for each data type it works on. It might be useful for a complex-number data type to have one B-tree operator class that sorts the data by complex absolute value, another that sorts by real part, and so on. Typically, one of the operator classes will be deemed most commonly useful and will be marked as the default operator class for that data type and index method.

The same operator class name can be used for several different index methods (for example, both B-tree and hash index methods have operator classes named `int4_ops`), but each such class is an independent entity and must be defined separately.

38.15.2. Index Method Strategies

The operators associated with an operator class are identified by "strategy numbers", which serve to identify the semantics of each operator within the context of its operator class. For example, B-trees impose a strict ordering on keys, lesser to greater, and so operators like "less than" and "greater than or equal to" are interesting with respect to a B-tree. Because PostgreSQL allows the user to define operators, PostgreSQL cannot look at the name of an operator (e.g., < or >=) and tell what kind of comparison it is. Instead, the index method defines a set of "strategies", which can be thought of as generalized operators. Each operator class specifies which actual operator corresponds to each strategy for a particular data type and interpretation of the index semantics.

The B-tree index method defines five strategies, shown in Table 38.2.

Table 38.2. B-tree Strategies

Operation	Strategy Number
less than	1
less than or equal	2
equal	3
greater than or equal	4
greater than	5

Hash indexes support only equality comparisons, and so they use only one strategy, shown in Table 38.3.

Table 38.3. Hash Strategies

Operation	Strategy Number
equal	1

GiST indexes are more flexible: they do not have a fixed set of strategies at all. Instead, the "consistency" support routine of each particular GiST operator class interprets the strategy numbers however it likes. As an example, several of the built-in GiST index operator classes index two-dimensional geometric objects, providing the "R-tree" strategies shown in Table 38.4. Four of these are true two-dimensional tests (overlaps, same, contains, contained by); four of them consider only the X direction; and the other four provide the same tests in the Y direction.

Table 38.4. GiST Two-Dimensional "R-tree" Strategies

Operation	Strategy Number
strictly left of	1
does not extend to right of	2
overlaps	3
does not extend to left of	4

Operation	Strategy Number
strictly right of	5
same	6
contains	7
contained by	8
does not extend above	9
strictly below	10
strictly above	11
does not extend below	12

SP-GiST indexes are similar to GiST indexes in flexibility: they don't have a fixed set of strategies. Instead the support routines of each operator class interpret the strategy numbers according to the operator class's definition. As an example, the strategy numbers used by the built-in operator classes for points are shown in Table 38.5.

Table 38.5. SP-GiST Point Strategies

Operation	Strategy Number
strictly left of	1
strictly right of	5
same	6
contained by	8
strictly below	10
strictly above	11

GIN indexes are similar to GiST and SP-GiST indexes, in that they don't have a fixed set of strategies either. Instead the support routines of each operator class interpret the strategy numbers according to the operator class's definition. As an example, the strategy numbers used by the built-in operator class for arrays are shown in Table 38.6.

Table 38.6. GIN Array Strategies

Operation	Strategy Number
overlap	1
contains	2
is contained by	3
equal	4

BRIN indexes are similar to GiST, SP-GiST and GIN indexes in that they don't have a fixed set of strategies either. Instead the support routines of each operator class interpret the strategy numbers according to the operator class's definition. As an example, the strategy numbers used by the built-in Minmax operator classes are shown in Table 38.7.

Table 38.7. BRIN Minmax Strategies

Operation	Strategy Number
less than	1

Operation	Strategy Number
less than or equal	2
equal	3
greater than or equal	4
greater than	5

Notice that all the operators listed above return Boolean values. In practice, all operators defined as index method search operators must return type `boolean`, since they must appear at the top level of a `WHERE` clause to be used with an index. (Some index access methods also support *ordering operators*, which typically don't return Boolean values; that feature is discussed in Section 38.15.7.)

38.15.3. Index Method Support Routines

Strategies aren't usually enough information for the system to figure out how to use an index. In practice, the index methods require additional support routines in order to work. For example, the B-tree index method must be able to compare two keys and determine whether one is greater than, equal to, or less than the other. Similarly, the hash index method must be able to compute hash codes for key values. These operations do not correspond to operators used in qualifications in SQL commands; they are administrative routines used by the index methods, internally.

Just as with strategies, the operator class identifies which specific functions should play each of these roles for a given data type and semantic interpretation. The index method defines the set of functions it needs, and the operator class identifies the correct functions to use by assigning them to the "support function numbers" specified by the index method.

B-trees require a comparison support function, and allow two additional support functions to be supplied at the operator class author's option, as shown in Table 38.8. The requirements for these support functions are explained further in Section 63.3.

Table 38.8. B-tree Support Functions

Function	Support Number
Compare two keys and return an integer less than zero, zero, or greater than zero, indicating whether the first key is less than, equal to, or greater than the second	1
Return the addresses of C-callable sort support function(s) (optional)	2
Compare a test value to a base value plus/minus an offset, and return true or false according to the comparison result (optional)	3

Hash indexes require one support function, and allow a second one to be supplied at the operator class author's option, as shown in Table 38.9.

Table 38.9. Hash Support Functions

Function	Support Number
Compute the 32-bit hash value for a key	1
Compute the 64-bit hash value for a key given a 64-bit salt; if the salt is 0, the low 32 bits of the result	2

Function	Support Number
must match the value that would have been computed by function 1 (optional)	

GiST indexes have nine support functions, two of which are optional, as shown in Table 38.10. (For more information see Chapter 64.)

Table 38.10. GiST Support Functions

Function	Description	Support Number
consistent	determine whether key satisfies the query qualifier	1
union	compute union of a set of keys	2
compress	compute a compressed representation of a key or value to be indexed	3
decompress	compute a decompressed representation of a compressed key	4
penalty	compute penalty for inserting new key into subtree with given subtree's key	5
picksplit	determine which entries of a page are to be moved to the new page and compute the union keys for resulting pages	6
equal	compare two keys and return true if they are equal	7
distance	determine distance from key to query value (optional)	8
fetch	compute original representation of a compressed key for index-only scans (optional)	9

SP-GiST indexes require five support functions, as shown in Table 38.11. (For more information see Chapter 65.)

Table 38.11. SP-GiST Support Functions

Function	Description	Support Number
config	provide basic information about the operator class	1
choose	determine how to insert a new value into an inner tuple	2
picksplit	determine how to partition a set of values	3
inner_consistent	determine which sub-partitions need to be searched for a query	4
leaf_consistent	determine whether key satisfies the query qualifier	5

GIN indexes have six support functions, three of which are optional, as shown in Table 38.12. (For more information see Chapter 66.)

Table 38.12. GIN Support Functions

Function	Description	Support Number
compare	compare two keys and return an integer less than zero, zero, or greater than zero, indicating whether the first key is less than, equal to, or greater than the second	1
extractValue	extract keys from a value to be indexed	2
extractQuery	extract keys from a query condition	3
consistent	determine whether value matches query condition (Boolean variant) (optional if support function 6 is present)	4
comparePartial	compare partial key from query and key from index, and return an integer less than zero, zero, or greater than zero, indicating whether GIN should ignore this index entry, treat the entry as a match, or stop the index scan (optional)	5
triConsistent	determine whether value matches query condition (ternary variant) (optional if support function 4 is present)	6

BRIN indexes have four basic support functions, as shown in Table 38.13; those basic functions may require additional support functions to be provided. (For more information see Section 67.3.)

Table 38.13. BRIN Support Functions

Function	Description	Support Number
opcInfo	return internal information describing the indexed columns' summary data	1
add_value	add a new value to an existing summary index tuple	2
consistent	determine whether value matches query condition	3
union	compute union of two summary tuples	4

Unlike search operators, support functions return whichever data type the particular index method expects; for example in the case of the comparison function for B-trees, a signed integer. The number and types of the arguments to each support function are likewise dependent on the index method. For B-tree and hash the comparison and hashing support functions take the same input data types as do the operators included in the operator class, but this is not the case for most GiST, SP-GiST, GIN, and BRIN support functions.

38.15.4. An Example

Now that we have seen the ideas, here is the promised example of creating a new operator class. (You can find a working copy of this example in `src/tutorial/complex.c` and `src/tutorial/complex.sql` in the source distribution.) The operator class encapsulates operators that sort complex numbers in absolute value order, so we choose the name `complex_abs_ops`. First, we need a set of operators. The procedure for defining operators was discussed in Section 38.13. For an operator class on B-trees, the operators we require are:

- absolute-value less-than (strategy 1)
- absolute-value less-than-or-equal (strategy 2)
- absolute-value equal (strategy 3)
- absolute-value greater-than-or-equal (strategy 4)
- absolute-value greater-than (strategy 5)

The least error-prone way to define a related set of comparison operators is to write the B-tree comparison support function first, and then write the other functions as one-line wrappers around the support function. This reduces the odds of getting inconsistent results for corner cases. Following this approach, we first write:

```
#define Mag(c)  ((c)->x*(c)->x + (c)->y*(c)->y)

static int
complex_abs_cmp_internal(Complex *a, Complex *b)
{
    double      amag = Mag(a),
                bmag = Mag(b);

    if (amag < bmag)
        return -1;
    if (amag > bmag)
        return 1;
    return 0;
}
```

Now the less-than function looks like:

```
PG_FUNCTION_INFO_V1(complex_abs_lt);

Datum
complex_abs_lt(PG_FUNCTION_ARGS)
{
    Complex     *a = (Complex *) PG_GETARG_POINTER(0);
    Complex     *b = (Complex *) PG_GETARG_POINTER(1);

    PG_RETURN_BOOL(complex_abs_cmp_internal(a, b) < 0);
}
```

The other four functions differ only in how they compare the internal function's result to zero.

Next we declare the functions and the operators based on the functions to SQL:

```
CREATE FUNCTION complex_abs_lt(complex, complex) RETURNS bool
    AS 'filename', 'complex_abs_lt'
    LANGUAGE C IMMUTABLE STRICT;

CREATE OPERATOR < (
    leftarg = complex, rightarg = complex, procedure = complex_abs_lt,
    commutator = > , negator = >= ,
    restrict = scalarltsel, join = scalarltjoinsel
);
```

It is important to specify the correct commutator and negator operators, as well as suitable restriction and join selectivity functions, otherwise the optimizer will be unable to make effective use of the index.

Other things worth noting are happening here:

- There can only be one operator named, say, = and taking type `complex` for both operands. In this case we don't have any other operator = for `complex`, but if we were building a practical data type we'd probably want = to be the ordinary equality operation for complex numbers (and not the equality of the absolute values). In that case, we'd need to use some other operator name for `complex_abs_eq`.

- Although PostgreSQL can cope with functions having the same SQL name as long as they have different argument data types, C can only cope with one global function having a given name. So we shouldn't name the C function something simple like `abs_eq`. Usually it's a good practice to include the data type name in the C function name, so as not to conflict with functions for other data types.

- We could have made the SQL name of the function `abs_eq`, relying on PostgreSQL to distinguish it by argument data types from any other SQL function of the same name. To keep the example simple, we make the function have the same names at the C level and SQL level.

The next step is the registration of the support routine required by B-trees. The example C code that implements this is in the same file that contains the operator functions. This is how we declare the function:

```
CREATE FUNCTION complex_abs_cmp(complex, complex)
    RETURNS integer
    AS 'filename'
    LANGUAGE C IMMUTABLE STRICT;
```

Now that we have the required operators and support routine, we can finally create the operator class:

```
CREATE OPERATOR CLASS complex_abs_ops
    DEFAULT FOR TYPE complex USING btree AS
        OPERATOR        1        < ,
        OPERATOR        2        <= ,
        OPERATOR        3        = ,
        OPERATOR        4        >= ,
        OPERATOR        5        > ,
        FUNCTION        1        complex_abs_cmp(complex, complex);
```

And we're done! It should now be possible to create and use B-tree indexes on `complex` columns.

We could have written the operator entries more verbosely, as in:

```
OPERATOR        1         < (complex, complex) ,
```

but there is no need to do so when the operators take the same data type we are defining the operator class for.

The above example assumes that you want to make this new operator class the default B-tree operator class for the `complex` data type. If you don't, just leave out the word `DEFAULT`.

38.15.5. Operator Classes and Operator Families

So far we have implicitly assumed that an operator class deals with only one data type. While there certainly can be only one data type in a particular index column, it is often useful to index operations that compare an indexed column to a value of a different data type. Also, if there is use for a cross-data-type operator in connection with an operator class, it is often the case that the other data type has a related operator class of its own. It is helpful to make the connections between related classes explicit, because this can aid the planner in optimizing SQL queries (particularly for B-tree operator classes, since the planner contains a great deal of knowledge about how to work with them).

To handle these needs, PostgreSQL uses the concept of an *operator family*. An operator family contains one or more operator classes, and can also contain indexable operators and corresponding support functions that belong to the family as a whole but not to any single class within the family. We say that such operators and functions are "loose" within the family, as opposed to being bound into a specific class. Typically each operator class contains single-data-type operators while cross-data-type operators are loose in the family.

All the operators and functions in an operator family must have compatible semantics, where the compatibility requirements are set by the index method. You might therefore wonder why bother to single out particular subsets of the family as operator classes; and indeed for many purposes the class divisions are irrelevant and the family is the only interesting grouping. The reason for defining operator classes is that they specify how much of the family is needed to support any particular index. If there is an index using an operator class, then that operator class cannot be dropped without dropping the index — but other parts of the operator family, namely other operator classes and loose operators, could be dropped. Thus, an operator class should be specified to contain the minimum set of operators and functions that are reasonably needed to work with an index on a specific data type, and then related but non-essential operators can be added as loose members of the operator family.

As an example, PostgreSQL has a built-in B-tree operator family `integer_ops`, which includes operator classes `int8_ops`, `int4_ops`, and `int2_ops` for indexes on `bigint` (int8), `integer` (int4), and `smallint` (int2) columns respectively. The family also contains cross-data-type comparison operators allowing any two of these types to be compared, so that an index on one of these types can be searched using a comparison value of another type. The family could be duplicated by these definitions:

```
CREATE OPERATOR FAMILY integer_ops USING btree;

CREATE OPERATOR CLASS int8_ops
DEFAULT FOR TYPE int8 USING btree FAMILY integer_ops AS
  -- standard int8 comparisons
  OPERATOR 1 < ,
  OPERATOR 2 <= ,
  OPERATOR 3 = ,
  OPERATOR 4 >= ,
  OPERATOR 5 > ,
```

```
  FUNCTION 1 btint8cmp(int8, int8) ,
  FUNCTION 2 btint8sortsupport(internal) ,
  FUNCTION 3 in_range(int8, int8, int8, boolean, boolean) ;

CREATE OPERATOR CLASS int4_ops
DEFAULT FOR TYPE int4 USING btree FAMILY integer_ops AS
  -- standard int4 comparisons
  OPERATOR 1 < ,
  OPERATOR 2 <= ,
  OPERATOR 3 = ,
  OPERATOR 4 >= ,
  OPERATOR 5 > ,
  FUNCTION 1 btint4cmp(int4, int4) ,
  FUNCTION 2 btint4sortsupport(internal) ,
  FUNCTION 3 in_range(int4, int4, int4, boolean, boolean) ;

CREATE OPERATOR CLASS int2_ops
DEFAULT FOR TYPE int2 USING btree FAMILY integer_ops AS
  -- standard int2 comparisons
  OPERATOR 1 < ,
  OPERATOR 2 <= ,
  OPERATOR 3 = ,
  OPERATOR 4 >= ,
  OPERATOR 5 > ,
  FUNCTION 1 btint2cmp(int2, int2) ,
  FUNCTION 2 btint2sortsupport(internal) ,
  FUNCTION 3 in_range(int2, int2, int2, boolean, boolean) ;

ALTER OPERATOR FAMILY integer_ops USING btree ADD
  -- cross-type comparisons int8 vs int2
  OPERATOR 1 < (int8, int2) ,
  OPERATOR 2 <= (int8, int2) ,
  OPERATOR 3 = (int8, int2) ,
  OPERATOR 4 >= (int8, int2) ,
  OPERATOR 5 > (int8, int2) ,
  FUNCTION 1 btint82cmp(int8, int2) ,

  -- cross-type comparisons int8 vs int4
  OPERATOR 1 < (int8, int4) ,
  OPERATOR 2 <= (int8, int4) ,
  OPERATOR 3 = (int8, int4) ,
  OPERATOR 4 >= (int8, int4) ,
  OPERATOR 5 > (int8, int4) ,
  FUNCTION 1 btint84cmp(int8, int4) ,

  -- cross-type comparisons int4 vs int2
  OPERATOR 1 < (int4, int2) ,
  OPERATOR 2 <= (int4, int2) ,
  OPERATOR 3 = (int4, int2) ,
  OPERATOR 4 >= (int4, int2) ,
  OPERATOR 5 > (int4, int2) ,
  FUNCTION 1 btint42cmp(int4, int2) ,

  -- cross-type comparisons int4 vs int8
```

```
OPERATOR 1 < (int4, int8) ,
OPERATOR 2 <= (int4, int8) ,
OPERATOR 3 = (int4, int8) ,
OPERATOR 4 >= (int4, int8) ,
OPERATOR 5 > (int4, int8) ,
FUNCTION 1 btint48cmp(int4, int8) ,

-- cross-type comparisons int2 vs int8
OPERATOR 1 < (int2, int8) ,
OPERATOR 2 <= (int2, int8) ,
OPERATOR 3 = (int2, int8) ,
OPERATOR 4 >= (int2, int8) ,
OPERATOR 5 > (int2, int8) ,
FUNCTION 1 btint28cmp(int2, int8) ,

-- cross-type comparisons int2 vs int4
OPERATOR 1 < (int2, int4) ,
OPERATOR 2 <= (int2, int4) ,
OPERATOR 3 = (int2, int4) ,
OPERATOR 4 >= (int2, int4) ,
OPERATOR 5 > (int2, int4) ,
FUNCTION 1 btint24cmp(int2, int4) ,

-- cross-type in_range functions
FUNCTION 3 in_range(int4, int4, int8, boolean, boolean) ,
FUNCTION 3 in_range(int4, int4, int2, boolean, boolean) ,
FUNCTION 3 in_range(int2, int2, int8, boolean, boolean) ,
FUNCTION 3 in_range(int2, int2, int4, boolean, boolean) ;
```

Notice that this definition "overloads" the operator strategy and support function numbers: each number occurs multiple times within the family. This is allowed so long as each instance of a particular number has distinct input data types. The instances that have both input types equal to an operator class's input type are the primary operators and support functions for that operator class, and in most cases should be declared as part of the operator class rather than as loose members of the family.

In a B-tree operator family, all the operators in the family must sort compatibly, as is specified in detail in Section 63.2. For each operator in the family there must be a support function having the same two input data types as the operator. It is recommended that a family be complete, i.e., for each combination of data types, all operators are included. Each operator class should include just the non-cross-type operators and support function for its data type.

To build a multiple-data-type hash operator family, compatible hash support functions must be created for each data type supported by the family. Here compatibility means that the functions are guaranteed to return the same hash code for any two values that are considered equal by the family's equality operators, even when the values are of different types. This is usually difficult to accomplish when the types have different physical representations, but it can be done in some cases. Furthermore, casting a value from one data type represented in the operator family to another data type also represented in the operator family via an implicit or binary coercion cast must not change the computed hash value. Notice that there is only one support function per data type, not one per equality operator. It is recommended that a family be complete, i.e., provide an equality operator for each combination of data types. Each operator class should include just the non-cross-type equality operator and the support function for its data type.

GiST, SP-GiST, and GIN indexes do not have any explicit notion of cross-data-type operations. The set of operators supported is just whatever the primary support functions for a given operator class can handle.

In BRIN, the requirements depends on the framework that provides the operator classes. For operator classes based on `minmax`, the behavior required is the same as for B-tree operator families: all the operators in the family must sort compatibly, and casts must not change the associated sort ordering.

Note

Prior to PostgreSQL 8.3, there was no concept of operator families, and so any cross-data-type operators intended to be used with an index had to be bound directly into the index's operator class. While this approach still works, it is deprecated because it makes an index's dependencies too broad, and because the planner can handle cross-data-type comparisons more effectively when both data types have operators in the same operator family.

38.15.6. System Dependencies on Operator Classes

PostgreSQL uses operator classes to infer the properties of operators in more ways than just whether they can be used with indexes. Therefore, you might want to create operator classes even if you have no intention of indexing any columns of your data type.

In particular, there are SQL features such as `ORDER BY` and `DISTINCT` that require comparison and sorting of values. To implement these features on a user-defined data type, PostgreSQL looks for the default B-tree operator class for the data type. The "equals" member of this operator class defines the system's notion of equality of values for `GROUP BY` and `DISTINCT`, and the sort ordering imposed by the operator class defines the default `ORDER BY` ordering.

If there is no default B-tree operator class for a data type, the system will look for a default hash operator class. But since that kind of operator class only provides equality, it is only able to support grouping not sorting.

When there is no default operator class for a data type, you will get errors like "could not identify an ordering operator" if you try to use these SQL features with the data type.

Note

In PostgreSQL versions before 7.4, sorting and grouping operations would implicitly use operators named =, <, and >. The new behavior of relying on default operator classes avoids having to make any assumption about the behavior of operators with particular names.

Sorting by a non-default B-tree operator class is possible by specifying the class's less-than operator in a `USING` option, for example

```
SELECT * FROM mytable ORDER BY somecol USING ~<~;
```

Alternatively, specifying the class's greater-than operator in `USING` selects a descending-order sort.

Comparison of arrays of a user-defined type also relies on the semantics defined by the type's default B-tree operator class. If there is no default B-tree operator class, but there is a default hash operator class, then array equality is supported, but not ordering comparisons.

Another SQL feature that requires even more data-type-specific knowledge is the RANGE *offset* PRECEDING/FOLLOWING framing option for window functions (see Section 4.2.8). For a query such as

```
SELECT sum(x) OVER (ORDER BY x RANGE BETWEEN 5 PRECEDING AND 10
 FOLLOWING)
  FROM mytable;
```

it is not sufficient to know how to order by x; the database must also understand how to "subtract 5" or "add 10" to the current row's value of x to identify the bounds of the current window frame. Comparing the resulting bounds to other rows' values of x is possible using the comparison operators provided by the B-tree operator class that defines the ORDER BY ordering — but addition and subtraction operators are not part of the operator class, so which ones should be used? Hard-wiring that choice would be undesirable, because different sort orders (different B-tree operator classes) might need different behavior. Therefore, a B-tree operator class can specify an *in_range* support function that encapsulates the addition and subtraction behaviors that make sense for its sort order. It can even provide more than one in_range support function, in case there is more than one data type that makes sense to use as the offset in RANGE clauses. If the B-tree operator class associated with the window's ORDER BY clause does not have a matching in_range support function, the RANGE *offset* PRECEDING/FOLLOWING option is not supported.

Another important point is that an equality operator that appears in a hash operator family is a candidate for hash joins, hash aggregation, and related optimizations. The hash operator family is essential here since it identifies the hash function(s) to use.

38.15.7. Ordering Operators

Some index access methods (currently, only GiST) support the concept of *ordering operators*. What we have been discussing so far are *search operators*. A search operator is one for which the index can be searched to find all rows satisfying WHERE *indexed_column operator constant*. Note that nothing is promised about the order in which the matching rows will be returned. In contrast, an ordering operator does not restrict the set of rows that can be returned, but instead determines their order. An ordering operator is one for which the index can be scanned to return rows in the order represented by ORDER BY *indexed_column operator constant*. The reason for defining ordering operators that way is that it supports nearest-neighbor searches, if the operator is one that measures distance. For example, a query like

```
SELECT * FROM places ORDER BY location <-> point '(101,456)' LIMIT 10;
```

finds the ten places closest to a given target point. A GiST index on the location column can do this efficiently because <-> is an ordering operator.

While search operators have to return Boolean results, ordering operators usually return some other type, such as float or numeric for distances. This type is normally not the same as the data type being indexed. To avoid hard-wiring assumptions about the behavior of different data types, the definition of an ordering operator is required to name a B-tree operator family that specifies the sort ordering of the result data type. As was stated in the previous section, B-tree operator families define PostgreSQL's notion of ordering, so this is a natural representation. Since the point <-> operator returns float8, it could be specified in an operator class creation command like this:

```
OPERATOR 15     <-> (point, point) FOR ORDER BY float_ops
```

where `float_ops` is the built-in operator family that includes operations on `float8`. This declaration states that the index is able to return rows in order of increasing values of the `<->` operator.

38.15.8. Special Features of Operator Classes

There are two special features of operator classes that we have not discussed yet, mainly because they are not useful with the most commonly used index methods.

Normally, declaring an operator as a member of an operator class (or family) means that the index method can retrieve exactly the set of rows that satisfy a `WHERE` condition using the operator. For example:

```
SELECT * FROM table WHERE integer_column < 4;
```

can be satisfied exactly by a B-tree index on the integer column. But there are cases where an index is useful as an inexact guide to the matching rows. For example, if a GiST index stores only bounding boxes for geometric objects, then it cannot exactly satisfy a `WHERE` condition that tests overlap between nonrectangular objects such as polygons. Yet we could use the index to find objects whose bounding box overlaps the bounding box of the target object, and then do the exact overlap test only on the objects found by the index. If this scenario applies, the index is said to be "lossy" for the operator. Lossy index searches are implemented by having the index method return a *recheck* flag when a row might or might not really satisfy the query condition. The core system will then test the original query condition on the retrieved row to see whether it should be returned as a valid match. This approach works if the index is guaranteed to return all the required rows, plus perhaps some additional rows, which can be eliminated by performing the original operator invocation. The index methods that support lossy searches (currently, GiST, SP-GiST and GIN) allow the support functions of individual operator classes to set the recheck flag, and so this is essentially an operator-class feature.

Consider again the situation where we are storing in the index only the bounding box of a complex object such as a polygon. In this case there's not much value in storing the whole polygon in the index entry — we might as well store just a simpler object of type `box`. This situation is expressed by the `STORAGE` option in `CREATE OPERATOR CLASS`: we'd write something like:

```
CREATE OPERATOR CLASS polygon_ops
    DEFAULT FOR TYPE polygon USING gist AS
        ...
        STORAGE box;
```

At present, only the GiST, GIN and BRIN index methods support a `STORAGE` type that's different from the column data type. The GiST `compress` and `decompress` support routines must deal with data-type conversion when `STORAGE` is used. In GIN, the `STORAGE` type identifies the type of the "key" values, which normally is different from the type of the indexed column — for example, an operator class for integer-array columns might have keys that are just integers. The GIN `extractValue` and `extractQuery` support routines are responsible for extracting keys from indexed values. BRIN is similar to GIN: the `STORAGE` type identifies the type of the stored summary values, and operator classes' support procedures are responsible for interpreting the summary values correctly.

38.16. Packaging Related Objects into an Extension

A useful extension to PostgreSQL typically includes multiple SQL objects; for example, a new data type will require new functions, new operators, and probably new index operator classes. It is helpful to collect all these objects into a single package to simplify database management. PostgreSQL calls such a package an *extension*. To define an extension, you need at least a *script file* that contains the SQL commands to create the extension's objects, and a *control file* that specifies a few basic properties of the extension itself. If the extension includes C code, there will typically also be a shared library file into which the C code has been built. Once you have these files, a simple CREATE EXTENSION command loads the objects into your database.

The main advantage of using an extension, rather than just running the SQL script to load a bunch of "loose" objects into your database, is that PostgreSQL will then understand that the objects of the extension go together. You can drop all the objects with a single DROP EXTENSION command (no need to maintain a separate "uninstall" script). Even more useful, pg_dump knows that it should not dump the individual member objects of the extension — it will just include a CREATE EXTENSION command in dumps, instead. This vastly simplifies migration to a new version of the extension that might contain more or different objects than the old version. Note however that you must have the extension's control, script, and other files available when loading such a dump into a new database.

PostgreSQL will not let you drop an individual object contained in an extension, except by dropping the whole extension. Also, while you can change the definition of an extension member object (for example, via CREATE OR REPLACE FUNCTION for a function), bear in mind that the modified definition will not be dumped by pg_dump. Such a change is usually only sensible if you concurrently make the same change in the extension's script file. (But there are special provisions for tables containing configuration data; see Section 38.16.4.) In production situations, it's generally better to create an extension update script to perform changes to extension member objects.

The extension script may set privileges on objects that are part of the extension via GRANT and REVOKE statements. The final set of privileges for each object (if any are set) will be stored in the pg_init_privs system catalog. When pg_dump is used, the CREATE EXTENSION command will be included in the dump, followed by the set of GRANT and REVOKE statements necessary to set the privileges on the objects to what they were at the time the dump was taken.

PostgreSQL does not currently support extension scripts issuing CREATE POLICY or SECURITY LABEL statements. These are expected to be set after the extension has been created. All RLS policies and security labels on extension objects will be included in dumps created by pg_dump.

The extension mechanism also has provisions for packaging modification scripts that adjust the definitions of the SQL objects contained in an extension. For example, if version 1.1 of an extension adds one function and changes the body of another function compared to 1.0, the extension author can provide an *update script* that makes just those two changes. The ALTER EXTENSION UPDATE command can then be used to apply these changes and track which version of the extension is actually installed in a given database.

The kinds of SQL objects that can be members of an extension are shown in the description of ALTER EXTENSION. Notably, objects that are database-cluster-wide, such as databases, roles, and tablespaces, cannot be extension members since an extension is only known within one database. (Although an extension script is not prohibited from creating such objects, if it does so they will not be tracked as part of the extension.) Also notice that while a table can be a member of an extension, its subsidiary objects such as indexes are not directly considered members of the extension. Another important point is that schemas can belong to extensions, but not vice versa: an extension as such has an unqualified name and does not exist "within" any schema. The extension's member objects, however, will belong to schemas whenever appropriate for their object types. It may or may not be appropriate for an extension to own the schema(s) its member objects are within.

If an extension's script creates any temporary objects (such as temp tables), those objects are treated as extension members for the remainder of the current session, but are automatically dropped at session end, as any temporary object would be. This is an exception to the rule that extension member objects cannot be dropped without dropping the whole extension.

38.16.1. Defining Extension Objects

Widely-distributed extensions should assume little about the database they occupy. In particular, unless you issued `SET search_path = pg_temp`, assume each unqualified name could resolve to an object that a malicious user has defined. Beware of constructs that depend on `search_path` implicitly: `IN` and `CASE` *expression* `WHEN` always select an operator using the search path. In their place, use `OPERATOR(`*schema.=*`)` `ANY` and `CASE WHEN` *expression*.

38.16.2. Extension Files

The CREATE EXTENSION command relies on a control file for each extension, which must be named the same as the extension with a suffix of `.control`, and must be placed in the installation's `SHAREDIR/extension` directory. There must also be at least one SQL script file, which follows the naming pattern *extension--version*`.sql` (for example, `foo--1.0.sql` for version `1.0` of extension `foo`). By default, the script file(s) are also placed in the `SHAREDIR/extension` directory; but the control file can specify a different directory for the script file(s).

The file format for an extension control file is the same as for the `postgresql.conf` file, namely a list of *parameter_name* = *value* assignments, one per line. Blank lines and comments introduced by # are allowed. Be sure to quote any value that is not a single word or number.

A control file can set the following parameters:

`directory` (`string`)

> The directory containing the extension's SQL script file(s). Unless an absolute path is given, the name is relative to the installation's `SHAREDIR` directory. The default behavior is equivalent to specifying `directory = 'extension'`.

`default_version` (`string`)

> The default version of the extension (the one that will be installed if no version is specified in `CREATE EXTENSION`). Although this can be omitted, that will result in `CREATE EXTENSION` failing if no `VERSION` option appears, so you generally don't want to do that.

`comment` (`string`)

> A comment (any string) about the extension. The comment is applied when initially creating an extension, but not during extension updates (since that might override user-added comments). Alternatively, the extension's comment can be set by writing a COMMENT command in the script file.

`encoding` (`string`)

> The character set encoding used by the script file(s). This should be specified if the script files contain any non-ASCII characters. Otherwise the files will be assumed to be in the database encoding.

`module_pathname` (`string`)

> The value of this parameter will be substituted for each occurrence of `MODULE_PATHNAME` in the script file(s). If it is not set, no substitution is made. Typically, this is set to `$libdir/`*shared_library_name* and then `MODULE_PATHNAME` is used in `CREATE FUNCTION` commands for C-language functions, so that the script files do not need to hard-wire the name of the shared library.

`requires` (`string`)

> A list of names of extensions that this extension depends on, for example `requires = 'foo, bar'`. Those extensions must be installed before this one can be installed.

superuser (boolean)

> If this parameter is true (which is the default), only superusers can create the extension or update it to a new version. If it is set to false, just the privileges required to execute the commands in the installation or update script are required.

relocatable (boolean)

> An extension is *relocatable* if it is possible to move its contained objects into a different schema after initial creation of the extension. The default is false, i.e. the extension is not relocatable. See Section 38.16.3 for more information.

schema (string)

> This parameter can only be set for non-relocatable extensions. It forces the extension to be loaded into exactly the named schema and not any other. The schema parameter is consulted only when initially creating an extension, not during extension updates. See Section 38.16.3 for more information.

In addition to the primary control file *extension*.control, an extension can have secondary control files named in the style *extension--version*.control. If supplied, these must be located in the script file directory. Secondary control files follow the same format as the primary control file. Any parameters set in a secondary control file override the primary control file when installing or updating to that version of the extension. However, the parameters directory and default_version cannot be set in a secondary control file.

An extension's SQL script files can contain any SQL commands, except for transaction control commands (BEGIN, COMMIT, etc) and commands that cannot be executed inside a transaction block (such as VACUUM). This is because the script files are implicitly executed within a transaction block.

An extension's SQL script files can also contain lines beginning with \echo, which will be ignored (treated as comments) by the extension mechanism. This provision is commonly used to throw an error if the script file is fed to psql rather than being loaded via CREATE EXTENSION (see example script in Section 38.16.7). Without that, users might accidentally load the extension's contents as "loose" objects rather than as an extension, a state of affairs that's a bit tedious to recover from.

While the script files can contain any characters allowed by the specified encoding, control files should contain only plain ASCII, because there is no way for PostgreSQL to know what encoding a control file is in. In practice this is only an issue if you want to use non-ASCII characters in the extension's comment. Recommended practice in that case is to not use the control file comment parameter, but instead use COMMENT ON EXTENSION within a script file to set the comment.

38.16.3. Extension Relocatability

Users often wish to load the objects contained in an extension into a different schema than the extension's author had in mind. There are three supported levels of relocatability:

- A fully relocatable extension can be moved into another schema at any time, even after it's been loaded into a database. This is done with the ALTER EXTENSION SET SCHEMA command, which automatically renames all the member objects into the new schema. Normally, this is only possible if the extension contains no internal assumptions about what schema any of its objects are in. Also, the extension's objects must all be in one schema to begin with (ignoring objects that do not belong to any schema, such as procedural languages). Mark a fully relocatable extension by setting relocatable = true in its control file.

- An extension might be relocatable during installation but not afterwards. This is typically the case if the extension's script file needs to reference the target schema explicitly, for example in setting search_path properties for SQL functions. For such an extension, set `relocatable = false` in its control file, and use `@extschema@` to refer to the target schema in the script file. All occurrences of this string will be replaced by the actual target schema's name before the script is executed. The user can set the target schema using the `SCHEMA` option of `CREATE EXTENSION`.

- If the extension does not support relocation at all, set `relocatable = false` in its control file, and also set `schema` to the name of the intended target schema. This will prevent use of the `SCHEMA` option of `CREATE EXTENSION`, unless it specifies the same schema named in the control file. This choice is typically necessary if the extension contains internal assumptions about schema names that can't be replaced by uses of `@extschema@`. The `@extschema@` substitution mechanism is available in this case too, although it is of limited use since the schema name is determined by the control file.

In all cases, the script file will be executed with search_path initially set to point to the target schema; that is, `CREATE EXTENSION` does the equivalent of this:

```
SET LOCAL search_path TO @extschema@;
```

This allows the objects created by the script file to go into the target schema. The script file can change `search_path` if it wishes, but that is generally undesirable. `search_path` is restored to its previous setting upon completion of `CREATE EXTENSION`.

The target schema is determined by the `schema` parameter in the control file if that is given, otherwise by the `SCHEMA` option of `CREATE EXTENSION` if that is given, otherwise the current default object creation schema (the first one in the caller's `search_path`). When the control file `schema` parameter is used, the target schema will be created if it doesn't already exist, but in the other two cases it must already exist.

If any prerequisite extensions are listed in `requires` in the control file, their target schemas are appended to the initial setting of `search_path`. This allows their objects to be visible to the new extension's script file.

Although a non-relocatable extension can contain objects spread across multiple schemas, it is usually desirable to place all the objects meant for external use into a single schema, which is considered the extension's target schema. Such an arrangement works conveniently with the default setting of `search_path` during creation of dependent extensions.

38.16.4. Extension Configuration Tables

Some extensions include configuration tables, which contain data that might be added or changed by the user after installation of the extension. Ordinarily, if a table is part of an extension, neither the table's definition nor its content will be dumped by pg_dump. But that behavior is undesirable for a configuration table; any data changes made by the user need to be included in dumps, or the extension will behave differently after a dump and reload.

To solve this problem, an extension's script file can mark a table or a sequence it has created as a configuration relation, which will cause pg_dump to include the table's or the sequence's contents (not its definition) in dumps. To do that, call the function **pg_extension_config_dump(regclass, text)** after creating the table or the sequence, for example

```
CREATE TABLE my_config (key text, value text);
CREATE SEQUENCE my_config_seq;

SELECT pg_catalog.pg_extension_config_dump('my_config', '');
SELECT pg_catalog.pg_extension_config_dump('my_config_seq', '');
```

Any number of tables or sequences can be marked this way. Sequences associated with `serial` or `bigserial` columns can be marked as well.

When the second argument of `pg_extension_config_dump` is an empty string, the entire contents of the table are dumped by pg_dump. This is usually only correct if the table is initially empty as created by the extension script. If there is a mixture of initial data and user-provided data in the table, the second argument of `pg_extension_config_dump` provides a `WHERE` condition that selects the data to be dumped. For example, you might do

```
CREATE TABLE my_config (key text, value text, standard_entry boolean);

SELECT pg_catalog.pg_extension_config_dump('my_config', 'WHERE NOT
 standard_entry');
```

and then make sure that `standard_entry` is true only in the rows created by the extension's script.

For sequences, the second argument of `pg_extension_config_dump` has no effect.

More complicated situations, such as initially-provided rows that might be modified by users, can be handled by creating triggers on the configuration table to ensure that modified rows are marked correctly.

You can alter the filter condition associated with a configuration table by calling `pg_extension_config_dump` again. (This would typically be useful in an extension update script.) The only way to mark a table as no longer a configuration table is to dissociate it from the extension with `ALTER EXTENSION ... DROP TABLE`.

Note that foreign key relationships between these tables will dictate the order in which the tables are dumped out by pg_dump. Specifically, pg_dump will attempt to dump the referenced-by table before the referencing table. As the foreign key relationships are set up at CREATE EXTENSION time (prior to data being loaded into the tables) circular dependencies are not supported. When circular dependencies exist, the data will still be dumped out but the dump will not be able to be restored directly and user intervention will be required.

Sequences associated with `serial` or `bigserial` columns need to be directly marked to dump their state. Marking their parent relation is not enough for this purpose.

38.16.5. Extension Updates

One advantage of the extension mechanism is that it provides convenient ways to manage updates to the SQL commands that define an extension's objects. This is done by associating a version name or number with each released version of the extension's installation script. In addition, if you want users to be able to update their databases dynamically from one version to the next, you should provide *update scripts* that make the necessary changes to go from one version to the next. Update scripts have names following the pattern *extension--oldversion--newversion*.sql (for example, `foo--1.0--1.1.sql` contains the commands to modify version `1.0` of extension `foo` into version `1.1`).

Given that a suitable update script is available, the command `ALTER EXTENSION UPDATE` will update an installed extension to the specified new version. The update script is run in the same environment that `CREATE EXTENSION` provides for installation scripts: in particular, `search_path` is set up in the same way, and any new objects created by the script are automatically added to the extension. Also, if the script chooses to drop extension member objects, they are automatically dissociated from the extension.

If an extension has secondary control files, the control parameters that are used for an update script are those associated with the script's target (new) version.

The update mechanism can be used to solve an important special case: converting a "loose" collection of objects into an extension. Before the extension mechanism was added to PostgreSQL (in 9.1), many people wrote extension modules that simply created assorted unpackaged objects. Given an existing database containing such objects, how can we convert the objects into a properly packaged extension? Dropping them and then doing a plain `CREATE EXTENSION` is one way, but it's not desirable if the objects have dependencies (for example, if there are table columns of a data type created by the extension). The way to fix this situation is to create an empty extension, then use `ALTER EXTENSION ADD` to attach each pre-existing object to the extension, then finally create any new objects that are in the current extension version but were not in the unpackaged release. `CREATE EXTENSION` supports this case with its `FROM old_version` option, which causes it to not run the normal installation script for the target version, but instead the update script named *extension--old_version--target_version*.`sql`. The choice of the dummy version name to use as *old_version* is up to the extension author, though `unpackaged` is a common convention. If you have multiple prior versions you need to be able to update into extension style, use multiple dummy version names to identify them.

`ALTER EXTENSION` is able to execute sequences of update script files to achieve a requested update. For example, if only `foo--1.0--1.1.sql` and `foo--1.1--2.0.sql` are available, `ALTER EXTENSION` will apply them in sequence if an update to version `2.0` is requested when `1.0` is currently installed.

PostgreSQL doesn't assume anything about the properties of version names: for example, it does not know whether `1.1` follows `1.0`. It just matches up the available version names and follows the path that requires applying the fewest update scripts. (A version name can actually be any string that doesn't contain `--` or leading or trailing `-`.)

Sometimes it is useful to provide "downgrade" scripts, for example `foo--1.1--1.0.sql` to allow reverting the changes associated with version `1.1`. If you do that, be careful of the possibility that a downgrade script might unexpectedly get applied because it yields a shorter path. The risky case is where there is a "fast path" update script that jumps ahead several versions as well as a downgrade script to the fast path's start point. It might take fewer steps to apply the downgrade and then the fast path than to move ahead one version at a time. If the downgrade script drops any irreplaceable objects, this will yield undesirable results.

To check for unexpected update paths, use this command:

```
SELECT * FROM pg_extension_update_paths('extension_name');
```

This shows each pair of distinct known version names for the specified extension, together with the update path sequence that would be taken to get from the source version to the target version, or `NULL` if there is no available update path. The path is shown in textual form with `--` separators. You can use `regexp_split_to_array(path,'--')` if you prefer an array format.

38.16.6. Installing Extensions using Update Scripts

An extension that has been around for awhile will probably exist in several versions, for which the author will need to write update scripts. For example, if you have released a `foo` extension in versions `1.0`, `1.1`, and `1.2`, there should be update scripts `foo--1.0--1.1.sql` and `foo--1.1--1.2.sql`. Before PostgreSQL 10, it was necessary to also create new script files `foo--1.1.sql` and `foo--1.2.sql` that directly build the newer extension versions, or else the newer versions could not be installed directly, only by installing `1.0` and then updating. That was tedious and duplicative, but now it's unnecessary, because `CREATE EXTENSION` can follow update chains automatically. For example, if only the script files `foo--1.0.sql`, `foo--1.0--1.1.sql`, and `foo--1.1--1.2.sql` are available then a request to install version `1.2` is honored by running those three scripts in sequence. The processing is the same as if you'd first installed 1.0 and then updated to 1.2. (As with ALTER EXTENSION UPDATE, if multiple pathways are available then the shortest is preferred.) Arranging an extension's script files in this style can reduce the amount of maintenance effort needed to produce small updates.

If you use secondary (version-specific) control files with an extension maintained in this style, keep in mind that each version needs a control file even if it has no stand-alone installation script, as that control file will determine how the implicit update to that version is performed. For example, if foo--1.0.control specifies requires = 'bar' but foo's other control files do not, the extension's dependency on bar will be dropped when updating from 1.0 to another version.

38.16.7. Extension Example

Here is a complete example of an SQL-only extension, a two-element composite type that can store any type of value in its slots, which are named "k" and "v". Non-text values are automatically coerced to text for storage.

The script file pair--1.0.sql looks like this:

```
-- complain if script is sourced in psql, rather than via CREATE
 EXTENSION
\echo Use "CREATE EXTENSION pair" to load this file. \quit

CREATE TYPE pair AS ( k text, v text );

CREATE OR REPLACE FUNCTION pair(text, text)
RETURNS pair LANGUAGE SQL AS 'SELECT ROW($1, $2)::@extschema@.pair;';

CREATE OPERATOR ~> (LEFTARG = text, RIGHTARG = text, FUNCTION = pair);

-- "SET search_path" is easy to get right, but qualified names perform
 better.
CREATE OR REPLACE FUNCTION lower(pair)
RETURNS pair LANGUAGE SQL
AS 'SELECT ROW(lower($1.k), lower($1.v))::@extschema@.pair;'
SET search_path = pg_temp;

CREATE OR REPLACE FUNCTION pair_concat(pair, pair)
RETURNS pair LANGUAGE SQL
AS 'SELECT ROW($1.k OPERATOR(pg_catalog.||) $2.k,
               $1.v OPERATOR(pg_catalog.||) $2.v)::@extschema@.pair;';
```

The control file pair.control looks like this:

```
# pair extension
comment = 'A key/value pair data type'
default_version = '1.0'
relocatable = false
```

While you hardly need a makefile to install these two files into the correct directory, you could use a Makefile containing this:

```
EXTENSION = pair
DATA = pair--1.0.sql

PG_CONFIG = pg_config
PGXS := $(shell $(PG_CONFIG) --pgxs)
include $(PGXS)
```

This makefile relies on PGXS, which is described in Section 38.17. The command `make install` will install the control and script files into the correct directory as reported by pg_config.

Once the files are installed, use the CREATE EXTENSION command to load the objects into any particular database.

38.17. Extension Building Infrastructure

If you are thinking about distributing your PostgreSQL extension modules, setting up a portable build system for them can be fairly difficult. Therefore the PostgreSQL installation provides a build infrastructure for extensions, called PGXS, so that simple extension modules can be built simply against an already installed server. PGXS is mainly intended for extensions that include C code, although it can be used for pure-SQL extensions too. Note that PGXS is not intended to be a universal build system framework that can be used to build any software interfacing to PostgreSQL; it simply automates common build rules for simple server extension modules. For more complicated packages, you might need to write your own build system.

To use the PGXS infrastructure for your extension, you must write a simple makefile. In the makefile, you need to set some variables and include the global PGXS makefile. Here is an example that builds an extension module named `isbn_issn`, consisting of a shared library containing some C code, an extension control file, a SQL script, an include file (only needed if other modules might need to access the extension functions without going via SQL), and a documentation text file:

```
MODULES = isbn_issn
EXTENSION = isbn_issn
DATA = isbn_issn--1.0.sql
DOCS = README.isbn_issn
HEADERS_isbn_issn = isbn_issn.h

PG_CONFIG = pg_config
PGXS := $(shell $(PG_CONFIG) --pgxs)
include $(PGXS)
```

The last three lines should always be the same. Earlier in the file, you assign variables or add custom make rules.

Set one of these three variables to specify what is built:

MODULES

> list of shared-library objects to be built from source files with same stem (do not include library suffixes in this list)

MODULE_big

> a shared library to build from multiple source files (list object files in OBJS)

PROGRAM

> an executable program to build (list object files in `OBJS`)

The following variables can also be set:

EXTENSION

> extension name(s); for each name you must provide an *extension*.`control` file, which will be installed into *prefix*/`share/extension`

MODULEDIR

> subdirectory of *prefix*/`share` into which DATA and DOCS files should be installed (if not set, default is `extension` if `EXTENSION` is set, or `contrib` if not)

DATA

> random files to install into *prefix*/`share/$MODULEDIR`

DATA_built

> random files to install into *prefix*/`share/$MODULEDIR`, which need to be built first

DATA_TSEARCH

> random files to install under *prefix*/`share/tsearch_data`

DOCS

> random files to install under *prefix*/`doc/$MODULEDIR`

HEADERS
HEADERS_built

> Files to (optionally build and) install under *prefix*/`include/server/$MODULEDIR/$MODULE_big`.
>
> Unlike `DATA_built`, files in `HEADERS_built` are not removed by the `clean` target; if you want them removed, also add them to `EXTRA_CLEAN` or add your own rules to do it.

HEADERS_$MODULE
HEADERS_built_$MODULE

> Files to install (after building if specified) under *prefix*/`include/server/$MODULEDIR/$MODULE`, where `$MODULE` must be a module name used in `MODULES` or `MODULE_big`.
>
> Unlike `DATA_built`, files in `HEADERS_built_$MODULE` are not removed by the `clean` target; if you want them removed, also add them to `EXTRA_CLEAN` or add your own rules to do it.
>
> It is legal to use both variables for the same module, or any combination, unless you have two module names in the `MODULES` list that differ only by the presence of a prefix `built_`, which would cause ambiguity. In that (hopefully unlikely) case, you should use only the `HEADERS_built_$MODULE` variables.

SCRIPTS

> script files (not binaries) to install into *prefix*/`bin`

`SCRIPTS_built`

script files (not binaries) to install into *prefix*/bin, which need to be built first

`REGRESS`

list of regression test cases (without suffix), see below

`REGRESS_OPTS`

additional switches to pass to pg_regress

`NO_INSTALLCHECK`

don't define an `installcheck` target, useful e.g. if tests require special configuration, or don't use pg_regress

`EXTRA_CLEAN`

extra files to remove in `make clean`

`PG_CPPFLAGS`

will be prepended to `CPPFLAGS`

`PG_CFLAGS`

will be appended to `CFLAGS`

`PG_CXXFLAGS`

will be appended to `CXXFLAGS`

`PG_LDFLAGS`

will be prepended to `LDFLAGS`

`PG_LIBS`

will be added to `PROGRAM` link line

`SHLIB_LINK`

will be added to `MODULE_big` link line

`PG_CONFIG`

path to pg_config program for the PostgreSQL installation to build against (typically just `pg_config` to use the first one in your `PATH`)

Put this makefile as `Makefile` in the directory which holds your extension. Then you can do `make` to compile, and then `make install` to install your module. By default, the extension is compiled and installed for the PostgreSQL installation that corresponds to the first `pg_config` program found in your `PATH`. You can use a different installation by setting `PG_CONFIG` to point to its `pg_config` program, either within the makefile or on the `make` command line.

You can also run `make` in a directory outside the source tree of your extension, if you want to keep the build directory separate. This procedure is also called a *VPATH* build. Here's how:

```
mkdir build_dir
cd build_dir
make -f /path/to/extension/source/tree/Makefile
make -f /path/to/extension/source/tree/Makefile install
```

Alternatively, you can set up a directory for a VPATH build in a similar way to how it is done for the core code. One way to do this is using the core script `config/prep_buildtree`. Once this has been done you can build by setting the `make` variable `VPATH` like this:

```
make VPATH=/path/to/extension/source/tree
make VPATH=/path/to/extension/source/tree install
```

This procedure can work with a greater variety of directory layouts.

The scripts listed in the `REGRESS` variable are used for regression testing of your module, which can be invoked by `make installcheck` after doing `make install`. For this to work you must have a running PostgreSQL server. The script files listed in `REGRESS` must appear in a subdirectory named `sql/` in your extension's directory. These files must have extension `.sql`, which must not be included in the `REGRESS` list in the makefile. For each test there should also be a file containing the expected output in a subdirectory named `expected/`, with the same stem and extension `.out`. `make installcheck` executes each test script with psql, and compares the resulting output to the matching expected file. Any differences will be written to the file `regression.diffs` in `diff -c` format. Note that trying to run a test that is missing its expected file will be reported as "trouble", so make sure you have all expected files.

Tip

The easiest way to create the expected files is to create empty files, then do a test run (which will of course report differences). Inspect the actual result files found in the `results/` directory, then copy them to `expected/` if they match what you expect from the test.

Chapter 39. Triggers

This chapter provides general information about writing trigger functions. Trigger functions can be written in most of the available procedural languages, including PL/pgSQL (Chapter 43), PL/Tcl (Chapter 44), PL/Perl (Chapter 45), and PL/Python (Chapter 46). After reading this chapter, you should consult the chapter for your favorite procedural language to find out the language-specific details of writing a trigger in it.

It is also possible to write a trigger function in C, although most people find it easier to use one of the procedural languages. It is not currently possible to write a trigger function in the plain SQL function language.

39.1. Overview of Trigger Behavior

A trigger is a specification that the database should automatically execute a particular function whenever a certain type of operation is performed. Triggers can be attached to tables (partitioned or not), views, and foreign tables.

On tables and foreign tables, triggers can be defined to execute either before or after any `INSERT`, `UPDATE`, or `DELETE` operation, either once per modified row, or once per SQL statement. `UPDATE` triggers can moreover be set to fire only if certain columns are mentioned in the `SET` clause of the `UPDATE` statement. Triggers can also fire for `TRUNCATE` statements. If a trigger event occurs, the trigger's function is called at the appropriate time to handle the event.

On views, triggers can be defined to execute instead of `INSERT`, `UPDATE`, or `DELETE` operations. Such `INSTEAD OF` triggers are fired once for each row that needs to be modified in the view. It is the responsibility of the trigger's function to perform the necessary modifications to the view's underlying base table(s) and, where appropriate, return the modified row as it will appear in the view. Triggers on views can also be defined to execute once per SQL statement, before or after `INSERT`, `UPDATE`, or `DELETE` operations. However, such triggers are fired only if there is also an `INSTEAD OF` trigger on the view. Otherwise, any statement targeting the view must be rewritten into a statement affecting its underlying base table(s), and then the triggers that will be fired are the ones attached to the base table(s).

The trigger function must be defined before the trigger itself can be created. The trigger function must be declared as a function taking no arguments and returning type `trigger`. (The trigger function receives its input through a specially-passed `TriggerData` structure, not in the form of ordinary function arguments.)

Once a suitable trigger function has been created, the trigger is established with CREATE TRIGGER. The same trigger function can be used for multiple triggers.

PostgreSQL offers both *per-row* triggers and *per-statement* triggers. With a per-row trigger, the trigger function is invoked once for each row that is affected by the statement that fired the trigger. In contrast, a per-statement trigger is invoked only once when an appropriate statement is executed, regardless of the number of rows affected by that statement. In particular, a statement that affects zero rows will still result in the execution of any applicable per-statement triggers. These two types of triggers are sometimes called *row-level* triggers and *statement-level* triggers, respectively. Triggers on `TRUNCATE` may only be defined at statement level, not per-row.

Triggers are also classified according to whether they fire *before*, *after*, or *instead of* the operation. These are referred to as `BEFORE` triggers, `AFTER` triggers, and `INSTEAD OF` triggers respectively. Statement-level `BEFORE` triggers naturally fire before the statement starts to do anything, while statement-level `AFTER` triggers fire at the very end of the statement. These types of triggers may be defined on tables, views, or foreign tables. Row-level `BEFORE` triggers fire immediately before a particular row is operated on, while row-level AFTER triggers fire at the end of the statement (but before any statement-level AFTER triggers). These types of triggers may only be defined on non-partitioned tables and foreign tables, not views. INSTEAD OF triggers may only be defined on views, and only at row level; they fire immediately as each row in the view is identified as needing to be operated on.

A statement that targets a parent table in an inheritance or partitioning hierarchy does not cause the statement-level triggers of affected child tables to be fired; only the parent table's statement-level triggers are fired. However, row-level triggers of any affected child tables will be fired.

If an INSERT contains an ON CONFLICT DO UPDATE clause, it is possible that the effects of row-level BEFORE INSERT triggers and row-level BEFORE UPDATE triggers can both be applied in a way that is apparent from the final state of the updated row, if an EXCLUDED column is referenced. There need not be an EXCLUDED column reference for both sets of row-level BEFORE triggers to execute, though. The possibility of surprising outcomes should be considered when there are both BEFORE INSERT and BEFORE UPDATE row-level triggers that change a row being inserted/updated (this can be problematic even if the modifications are more or less equivalent, if they're not also idempotent). Note that statement-level UPDATE triggers are executed when ON CONFLICT DO UPDATE is specified, regardless of whether or not any rows were affected by the UPDATE (and regardless of whether the alternative UPDATE path was ever taken). An INSERT with an ON CONFLICT DO UPDATE clause will execute statement-level BEFORE INSERT triggers first, then statement-level BEFORE UPDATE triggers, followed by statement-level AFTER UPDATE triggers and finally statement-level AFTER INSERT triggers.

If an UPDATE on a partitioned table causes a row to move to another partition, it will be performed as a DELETE from the original partition followed by an INSERT into the new partition. In this case, all row-level BEFORE UPDATE triggers and all row-level BEFORE DELETE triggers are fired on the original partition. Then all row-level BEFORE INSERT triggers are fired on the destination partition. The possibility of surprising outcomes should be considered when all these triggers affect the row being moved. As far as AFTER ROW triggers are concerned, AFTER DELETE and AFTER INSERT triggers are applied; but AFTER UPDATE triggers are not applied because the UPDATE has been converted to a DELETE and an INSERT. As far as statement-level triggers are concerned, none of the DELETE or INSERT triggers are fired, even if row movement occurs; only the UPDATE triggers defined on the target table used in the UPDATE statement will be fired.

Trigger functions invoked by per-statement triggers should always return NULL. Trigger functions invoked by per-row triggers can return a table row (a value of type HeapTuple) to the calling executor, if they choose. A row-level trigger fired before an operation has the following choices:

- It can return NULL to skip the operation for the current row. This instructs the executor to not perform the row-level operation that invoked the trigger (the insertion, modification, or deletion of a particular table row).

- For row-level INSERT and UPDATE triggers only, the returned row becomes the row that will be inserted or will replace the row being updated. This allows the trigger function to modify the row being inserted or updated.

A row-level BEFORE trigger that does not intend to cause either of these behaviors must be careful to return as its result the same row that was passed in (that is, the NEW row for INSERT and UPDATE triggers, the OLD row for DELETE triggers).

A row-level INSTEAD OF trigger should either return NULL to indicate that it did not modify any data from the view's underlying base tables, or it should return the view row that was passed in (the NEW row for INSERT and UPDATE operations, or the OLD row for DELETE operations). A nonnull return value is used to signal that the trigger performed the necessary data modifications in the view. This will cause the count of the number of rows affected by the command to be incremented. For INSERT and UPDATE operations, the trigger may modify the NEW row before returning it. This will change the data returned by

INSERT RETURNING or UPDATE RETURNING, and is useful when the view will not show exactly the same data that was provided.

The return value is ignored for row-level triggers fired after an operation, and so they can return NULL.

If more than one trigger is defined for the same event on the same relation, the triggers will be fired in alphabetical order by trigger name. In the case of BEFORE and INSTEAD OF triggers, the possibly-modified row returned by each trigger becomes the input to the next trigger. If any BEFORE or INSTEAD OF trigger returns NULL, the operation is abandoned for that row and subsequent triggers are not fired (for that row).

A trigger definition can also specify a Boolean WHEN condition, which will be tested to see whether the trigger should be fired. In row-level triggers the WHEN condition can examine the old and/or new values of columns of the row. (Statement-level triggers can also have WHEN conditions, although the feature is not so useful for them.) In a BEFORE trigger, the WHEN condition is evaluated just before the function is or would be executed, so using WHEN is not materially different from testing the same condition at the beginning of the trigger function. However, in an AFTER trigger, the WHEN condition is evaluated just after the row update occurs, and it determines whether an event is queued to fire the trigger at the end of statement. So when an AFTER trigger's WHEN condition does not return true, it is not necessary to queue an event nor to re-fetch the row at end of statement. This can result in significant speedups in statements that modify many rows, if the trigger only needs to be fired for a few of the rows. INSTEAD OF triggers do not support WHEN conditions.

Typically, row-level BEFORE triggers are used for checking or modifying the data that will be inserted or updated. For example, a BEFORE trigger might be used to insert the current time into a timestamp column, or to check that two elements of the row are consistent. Row-level AFTER triggers are most sensibly used to propagate the updates to other tables, or make consistency checks against other tables. The reason for this division of labor is that an AFTER trigger can be certain it is seeing the final value of the row, while a BEFORE trigger cannot; there might be other BEFORE triggers firing after it. If you have no specific reason to make a trigger BEFORE or AFTER, the BEFORE case is more efficient, since the information about the operation doesn't have to be saved until end of statement.

If a trigger function executes SQL commands then these commands might fire triggers again. This is known as cascading triggers. There is no direct limitation on the number of cascade levels. It is possible for cascades to cause a recursive invocation of the same trigger; for example, an INSERT trigger might execute a command that inserts an additional row into the same table, causing the INSERT trigger to be fired again. It is the trigger programmer's responsibility to avoid infinite recursion in such scenarios.

When a trigger is being defined, arguments can be specified for it. The purpose of including arguments in the trigger definition is to allow different triggers with similar requirements to call the same function. As an example, there could be a generalized trigger function that takes as its arguments two column names and puts the current user in one and the current time stamp in the other. Properly written, this trigger function would be independent of the specific table it is triggering on. So the same function could be used for INSERT events on any table with suitable columns, to automatically track creation of records in a transaction table for example. It could also be used to track last-update events if defined as an UPDATE trigger.

Each programming language that supports triggers has its own method for making the trigger input data available to the trigger function. This input data includes the type of trigger event (e.g., INSERT or UPDATE) as well as any arguments that were listed in CREATE TRIGGER. For a row-level trigger, the input data also includes the NEW row for INSERT and UPDATE triggers, and/or the OLD row for UPDATE and DELETE triggers.

By default, statement-level triggers do not have any way to examine the individual row(s) modified by the statement. But an AFTER STATEMENT trigger can request that *transition tables* be created to make the sets of affected rows available to the trigger. AFTER ROW triggers can also request transition tables, so that they can see the total changes in the table as well as the change in the individual row they are currently being fired for. The method for examining the transition tables again depends on the programming language that is being used, but the typical approach is to make the transition tables act like read-only temporary tables that can be accessed by SQL commands issued within the trigger function.

39.2. Visibility of Data Changes

If you execute SQL commands in your trigger function, and these commands access the table that the trigger is for, then you need to be aware of the data visibility rules, because they determine whether these SQL commands will see the data change that the trigger is fired for. Briefly:

- Statement-level triggers follow simple visibility rules: none of the changes made by a statement are visible to statement-level BEFORE triggers, whereas all modifications are visible to statement-level AFTER triggers.

- The data change (insertion, update, or deletion) causing the trigger to fire is naturally *not* visible to SQL commands executed in a row-level BEFORE trigger, because it hasn't happened yet.

- However, SQL commands executed in a row-level BEFORE trigger *will* see the effects of data changes for rows previously processed in the same outer command. This requires caution, since the ordering of these change events is not in general predictable; a SQL command that affects multiple rows can visit the rows in any order.

- Similarly, a row-level INSTEAD OF trigger will see the effects of data changes made by previous firings of INSTEAD OF triggers in the same outer command.

- When a row-level AFTER trigger is fired, all data changes made by the outer command are already complete, and are visible to the invoked trigger function.

If your trigger function is written in any of the standard procedural languages, then the above statements apply only if the function is declared VOLATILE. Functions that are declared STABLE or IMMUTABLE will not see changes made by the calling command in any case.

Further information about data visibility rules can be found in Section 47.5. The example in Section 39.4 contains a demonstration of these rules.

39.3. Writing Trigger Functions in C

This section describes the low-level details of the interface to a trigger function. This information is only needed when writing trigger functions in C. If you are using a higher-level language then these details are handled for you. In most cases you should consider using a procedural language before writing your triggers in C. The documentation of each procedural language explains how to write a trigger in that language.

Trigger functions must use the "version 1" function manager interface.

When a function is called by the trigger manager, it is not passed any normal arguments, but it is passed a "context" pointer pointing to a TriggerData structure. C functions can check whether they were called from the trigger manager or not by executing the macro:

```
CALLED_AS_TRIGGER(fcinfo)
```

which expands to:

```
((fcinfo)->context != NULL && IsA((fcinfo)->context, TriggerData))
```

If this returns true, then it is safe to cast `fcinfo->context` to type `TriggerData *` and make use of the pointed-to `TriggerData` structure. The function must *not* alter the `TriggerData` structure or any of the data it points to.

`struct TriggerData` is defined in `commands/trigger.h`:

```
typedef struct TriggerData
{
    NodeTag         type;
    TriggerEvent    tg_event;
    Relation        tg_relation;
    HeapTuple       tg_trigtuple;
    HeapTuple       tg_newtuple;
    Trigger         *tg_trigger;
    Buffer          tg_trigtuplebuf;
    Buffer          tg_newtuplebuf;
    Tuplestorestate *tg_oldtable;
    Tuplestorestate *tg_newtable;
} TriggerData;
```

where the members are defined as follows:

`type`

Always `T_TriggerData`.

`tg_event`

Describes the event for which the function is called. You can use the following macros to examine `tg_event`:

`TRIGGER_FIRED_BEFORE(tg_event)`

Returns true if the trigger fired before the operation.

`TRIGGER_FIRED_AFTER(tg_event)`

Returns true if the trigger fired after the operation.

`TRIGGER_FIRED_INSTEAD(tg_event)`

Returns true if the trigger fired instead of the operation.

`TRIGGER_FIRED_FOR_ROW(tg_event)`

Returns true if the trigger fired for a row-level event.

`TRIGGER_FIRED_FOR_STATEMENT(tg_event)`

Returns true if the trigger fired for a statement-level event.

`TRIGGER_FIRED_BY_INSERT(tg_event)`

Returns true if the trigger was fired by an `INSERT` command.

`TRIGGER_FIRED_BY_UPDATE(tg_event)`

Returns true if the trigger was fired by an UPDATE command.

`TRIGGER_FIRED_BY_DELETE(tg_event)`

Returns true if the trigger was fired by a DELETE command.

`TRIGGER_FIRED_BY_TRUNCATE(tg_event)`

Returns true if the trigger was fired by a TRUNCATE command.

`tg_relation`

A pointer to a structure describing the relation that the trigger fired for. Look at `utils/rel.h` for details about this structure. The most interesting things are `tg_relation->rd_att` (descriptor of the relation tuples) and `tg_relation->rd_rel->relname` (relation name; the type is not `char*` but `NameData`; use `SPI_getrelname(tg_relation)` to get a `char*` if you need a copy of the name).

`tg_trigtuple`

A pointer to the row for which the trigger was fired. This is the row being inserted, updated, or deleted. If this trigger was fired for an INSERT or DELETE then this is what you should return from the function if you don't want to replace the row with a different one (in the case of INSERT) or skip the operation. For triggers on foreign tables, values of system columns herein are unspecified.

`tg_newtuple`

A pointer to the new version of the row, if the trigger was fired for an UPDATE, and NULL if it is for an INSERT or a DELETE. This is what you have to return from the function if the event is an UPDATE and you don't want to replace this row by a different one or skip the operation. For triggers on foreign tables, values of system columns herein are unspecified.

`tg_trigger`

A pointer to a structure of type `Trigger`, defined in `utils/reltrigger.h`:

```
typedef struct Trigger
{
    Oid         tgoid;
    char        *tgname;
    Oid         tgfoid;
    int16       tgtype;
    char        tgenabled;
    bool        tgisinternal;
    Oid         tgconstrrelid;
    Oid         tgconstrindid;
    Oid         tgconstraint;
    bool        tgdeferrable;
    bool        tginitdeferred;
    int16       tgnargs;
    int16       tgnattr;
    int16       *tgattr;
    char        **tgargs;
```

```
    char      *tgqual;
    char      *tgoldtable;
    char      *tgnewtable;
} Trigger;
```

where `tgname` is the trigger's name, `tgnargs` is the number of arguments in `tgargs`, and `tgargs` is an array of pointers to the arguments specified in the `CREATE TRIGGER` statement. The other members are for internal use only.

`tg_trigtuplebuf`

The buffer containing `tg_trigtuple`, or `InvalidBuffer` if there is no such tuple or it is not stored in a disk buffer.

`tg_newtuplebuf`

The buffer containing `tg_newtuple`, or `InvalidBuffer` if there is no such tuple or it is not stored in a disk buffer.

`tg_oldtable`

A pointer to a structure of type `Tuplestorestate` containing zero or more rows in the format specified by `tg_relation`, or a NULL pointer if there is no `OLD TABLE` transition relation.

`tg_newtable`

A pointer to a structure of type `Tuplestorestate` containing zero or more rows in the format specified by `tg_relation`, or a NULL pointer if there is no `NEW TABLE` transition relation.

To allow queries issued through SPI to reference transition tables, see SPI_register_trigger_data.

A trigger function must return either a `HeapTuple` pointer or a `NULL` pointer (*not* an SQL null value, that is, do not set *isNull* true). Be careful to return either `tg_trigtuple` or `tg_newtuple`, as appropriate, if you don't want to modify the row being operated on.

39.4. A Complete Trigger Example

Here is a very simple example of a trigger function written in C. (Examples of triggers written in procedural languages can be found in the documentation of the procedural languages.)

The function `trigf` reports the number of rows in the table `ttest` and skips the actual operation if the command attempts to insert a null value into the column `x`. (So the trigger acts as a not-null constraint but doesn't abort the transaction.)

First, the table definition:

```
CREATE TABLE ttest (
    x integer
);
```

This is the source code of the trigger function:

```
#include "postgres.h"
#include "fmgr.h"
```

```
#include "executor/spi.h"      /* this is what you need to work with
 SPI */
#include "commands/trigger.h"   /* ... triggers ... */
#include "utils/rel.h"          /* ... and relations */

PG_MODULE_MAGIC;

PG_FUNCTION_INFO_V1(trigf);

Datum
trigf(PG_FUNCTION_ARGS)
{
    TriggerData *trigdata = (TriggerData *) fcinfo->context;
    TupleDesc   tupdesc;
    HeapTuple   rettuple;
    char        *when;
    bool        checknull = false;
    bool        isnull;
    int         ret, i;

    /* make sure it's called as a trigger at all */
    if (!CALLED_AS_TRIGGER(fcinfo))
        elog(ERROR, "trigf: not called by trigger manager");

    /* tuple to return to executor */
    if (TRIGGER_FIRED_BY_UPDATE(trigdata->tg_event))
        rettuple = trigdata->tg_newtuple;
    else
        rettuple = trigdata->tg_trigtuple;

    /* check for null values */
    if (!TRIGGER_FIRED_BY_DELETE(trigdata->tg_event)
        && TRIGGER_FIRED_BEFORE(trigdata->tg_event))
        checknull = true;

    if (TRIGGER_FIRED_BEFORE(trigdata->tg_event))
        when = "before";
    else
        when = "after ";

    tupdesc = trigdata->tg_relation->rd_att;

    /* connect to SPI manager */
    if ((ret = SPI_connect()) < 0)
        elog(ERROR, "trigf (fired %s): SPI_connect returned %d", when,
 ret);

    /* get number of rows in table */
    ret = SPI_exec("SELECT count(*) FROM ttest", 0);

    if (ret < 0)
        elog(ERROR, "trigf (fired %s): SPI_exec returned %d", when,
 ret);
```

```
    /* count(*) returns int8, so be careful to convert */
    i = DatumGetInt64(SPI_getbinval(SPI_tuptable->vals[0],
                                    SPI_tuptable->tupdesc,
                                    1,
                                    &isnull));

    elog (INFO, "trigf (fired %s): there are %d rows in ttest", when,
i);

    SPI_finish();

    if (checknull)
    {
        SPI_getbinval(rettuple, tupdesc, 1, &isnull);
        if (isnull)
            rettuple = NULL;
    }

    return PointerGetDatum(rettuple);
}
```

After you have compiled the source code (see Section 38.10.5), declare the function and the triggers:

```
CREATE FUNCTION trigf() RETURNS trigger
    AS 'filename'
    LANGUAGE C;

CREATE TRIGGER tbefore BEFORE INSERT OR UPDATE OR DELETE ON ttest
    FOR EACH ROW EXECUTE FUNCTION trigf();

CREATE TRIGGER tafter AFTER INSERT OR UPDATE OR DELETE ON ttest
    FOR EACH ROW EXECUTE FUNCTION trigf();
```

Now you can test the operation of the trigger:

```
=> INSERT INTO ttest VALUES (NULL);
INFO:  trigf (fired before): there are 0 rows in ttest
INSERT 0 0

-- Insertion skipped and AFTER trigger is not fired

=> SELECT * FROM ttest;
 x
---
(0 rows)

=> INSERT INTO ttest VALUES (1);
INFO:  trigf (fired before): there are 0 rows in ttest
INFO:  trigf (fired after ): there are 1 rows in ttest
                                             ^^^^^^^^
                            remember what we said about visibility.
INSERT 167793 1
```

```
vac=> SELECT * FROM ttest;
 x
---
 1
(1 row)

=> INSERT INTO ttest SELECT x * 2 FROM ttest;
INFO:  trigf (fired before): there are 1 rows in ttest
INFO:  trigf (fired after ): there are 2 rows in ttest
                                              ^^^^^^

                         remember what we said about visibility.
INSERT 167794 1
=> SELECT * FROM ttest;
 x
---
 1
 2
(2 rows)

=> UPDATE ttest SET x = NULL WHERE x = 2;
INFO:  trigf (fired before): there are 2 rows in ttest
UPDATE 0
=> UPDATE ttest SET x = 4 WHERE x = 2;
INFO:  trigf (fired before): there are 2 rows in ttest
INFO:  trigf (fired after ): there are 2 rows in ttest
UPDATE 1
vac=> SELECT * FROM ttest;
 x
---
 1
 4
(2 rows)

=> DELETE FROM ttest;
INFO:  trigf (fired before): there are 2 rows in ttest
INFO:  trigf (fired before): there are 1 rows in ttest
INFO:  trigf (fired after ): there are 0 rows in ttest
INFO:  trigf (fired after ): there are 0 rows in ttest
                                              ^^^^^^

                         remember what we said about visibility.
DELETE 2
=> SELECT * FROM ttest;
 x
---
(0 rows)
```

There are more complex examples in `src/test/regress/regress.c` and in spi.

Chapter 40. Event Triggers

To supplement the trigger mechanism discussed in Chapter 39, PostgreSQL also provides event triggers. Unlike regular triggers, which are attached to a single table and capture only DML events, event triggers are global to a particular database and are capable of capturing DDL events.

Like regular triggers, event triggers can be written in any procedural language that includes event trigger support, or in C, but not in plain SQL.

40.1. Overview of Event Trigger Behavior

An event trigger fires whenever the event with which it is associated occurs in the database in which it is defined. Currently, the only supported events are `ddl_command_start`, `ddl_command_end`, `table_rewrite` and `sql_drop`. Support for additional events may be added in future releases.

The `ddl_command_start` event occurs just before the execution of a CREATE, ALTER, DROP, SECURITY LABEL, COMMENT, GRANT or REVOKE command. No check whether the affected object exists or doesn't exist is performed before the event trigger fires. As an exception, however, this event does not occur for DDL commands targeting shared objects — databases, roles, and tablespaces — or for commands targeting event triggers themselves. The event trigger mechanism does not support these object types. `ddl_command_start` also occurs just before the execution of a SELECT INTO command, since this is equivalent to CREATE TABLE AS.

The `ddl_command_end` event occurs just after the execution of this same set of commands. To obtain more details on the DDL operations that took place, use the set-returning function `pg_event_trigger_ddl_commands()` from the `ddl_command_end` event trigger code (see Section 9.28). Note that the trigger fires after the actions have taken place (but before the transaction commits), and thus the system catalogs can be read as already changed.

The `sql_drop` event occurs just before the `ddl_command_end` event trigger for any operation that drops database objects. To list the objects that have been dropped, use the set-returning function `pg_event_trigger_dropped_objects()` from the `sql_drop` event trigger code (see Section 9.28). Note that the trigger is executed after the objects have been deleted from the system catalogs, so it's not possible to look them up anymore.

The `table_rewrite` event occurs just before a table is rewritten by some actions of the commands ALTER TABLE and ALTER TYPE. While other control statements are available to rewrite a table, like CLUSTER and VACUUM, the `table_rewrite` event is not triggered by them.

Event triggers (like other functions) cannot be executed in an aborted transaction. Thus, if a DDL command fails with an error, any associated `ddl_command_end` triggers will not be executed. Conversely, if a `ddl_command_start` trigger fails with an error, no further event triggers will fire, and no attempt will be made to execute the command itself. Similarly, if a `ddl_command_end` trigger fails with an error, the effects of the DDL statement will be rolled back, just as they would be in any other case where the containing transaction aborts.

For a complete list of commands supported by the event trigger mechanism, see Section 40.2.

Event triggers are created using the command CREATE EVENT TRIGGER. In order to create an event trigger, you must first create a function with the special return type `event_trigger`. This function need not (and may not) return a value; the return type serves merely as a signal that the function is to be invoked as an event trigger.

If more than one event trigger is defined for a particular event, they will fire in alphabetical order by trigger name.

A trigger definition can also specify a WHEN condition so that, for example, a ddl_command_start trigger can be fired only for particular commands which the user wishes to intercept. A common use of such triggers is to restrict the range of DDL operations which users may perform.

40.2. Event Trigger Firing Matrix

Table 40.1 lists all commands for which event triggers are supported.

Table 40.1. Event Trigger Support by Command Tag

Command Tag	ddl_command_start	ddl_command_end	sql_drop	table_rewrite	Notes
ALTER AGGREGATE	X	X	-	-	
ALTER COLLATION	X	X	-	-	
ALTER CONVERSION	X	X	-	-	
ALTER DOMAIN	X	X	-	-	
ALTER EXTENSION	X	X	-	-	
ALTER FOREIGN DATA WRAPPER	X	X	-	-	
ALTER FOREIGN TABLE	X	X	X	-	
ALTER FUNCTION	X	X	-	-	
ALTER LANGUAGE	X	X	-	-	
ALTER OPERATOR	X	X	-	-	
ALTER OPERATOR CLASS	X	X	-	-	
ALTER OPERATOR FAMILY	X	X	-	-	
ALTER POLICY	X	X	-	-	
ALTER SCHEMA	X	X	-	-	
ALTER SEQUENCE	X	X	-	-	

Command Tag	ddl_command_start	ddl_command_end	sql_drop	table_rewrite	Notes
ALTER SERVER	X	X	-	-	
ALTER TABLE	X	X	X	X	
ALTER TEXT SEARCH CONFIGURATION	X	X	-	-	
ALTER TEXT SEARCH DICTIONARY	X	X	-	-	
ALTER TEXT SEARCH PARSER	X	X	-	-	
ALTER TEXT SEARCH TEMPLATE	X	X	-	-	
ALTER TRIGGER	X	X	-	-	
ALTER TYPE	X	X	-	X	
ALTER USER MAPPING	X	X	-	-	
ALTER VIEW	X	X	-	-	
CREATE AGGREGATE	X	X	-	-	
COMMENT	X	X	-	-	Only for local objects
CREATE CAST	X	X	-	-	
CREATE COLLATION	X	X	-	-	
CREATE CONVERSION	X	X	-	-	
CREATE DOMAIN	X	X	-	-	
CREATE EXTENSION	X	X	-	-	
CREATE FOREIGN DATA WRAPPER	X	X	-	-	
CREATE FOREIGN TABLE	X	X	-	-	

Command Tag	ddl_command_start	ddl_command_end	sql_drop	table_rewrite	Notes
CREATE FUNCTION	X	X	-	-	
CREATE INDEX	X	X	-	-	
CREATE LANGUAGE	X	X	-	-	
CREATE OPERATOR	X	X	-	-	
CREATE OPERATOR CLASS	X	X	-	-	
CREATE OPERATOR FAMILY	X	X	-	-	
CREATE POLICY	X	X	-	-	
CREATE RULE	X	X	-	-	
CREATE SCHEMA	X	X	-	-	
CREATE SEQUENCE	X	X	-	-	
CREATE SERVER	X	X	-	-	
CREATE STATISTICS	X	X	-	-	
CREATE TABLE	X	X	-	-	
CREATE TABLE AS	X	X	-	-	
CREATE TEXT SEARCH CONFIGURATION	X	X	-	-	
CREATE TEXT SEARCH DICTIONARY	X	X	-	-	
CREATE TEXT SEARCH PARSER	X	X	-	-	
CREATE TEXT	X	X	-	-	

Command Tag	ddl_command_start	ddl_command_end	sql_drop	table_rewrite	Notes
SEARCH TEMPLATE					
CREATE TRIGGER	X	X	-	-	
CREATE TYPE	X	X	-	-	
CREATE USER MAPPING	X	X	-	-	
CREATE VIEW	X	X	-	-	
DROP AGGREGATE	X	X	X	-	
DROP CAST	X	X	X	-	
DROP COLLATION	X	X	X	-	
DROP CONVERSION	X	X	X	-	
DROP DOMAIN	X	X	X	-	
DROP EXTENSION	X	X	X	-	
DROP FOREIGN DATA WRAPPER	X	X	X	-	
DROP FOREIGN TABLE	X	X	X	-	
DROP FUNCTION	X	X	X	-	
DROP INDEX	X	X	X	-	
DROP LANGUAGE	X	X	X	-	
DROP OPERATOR	X	X	X	-	
DROP OPERATOR CLASS	X	X	X	-	
DROP OPERATOR FAMILY	X	X	X	-	
DROP OWNED	X	X	X	-	

Command Tag	ddl_command_start	ddl_command_end	sql_drop	table_rewrite	Notes
DROP POLICY	X	X	X	–	
DROP RULE	X	X	X	–	
DROP SCHEMA	X	X	X	–	
DROP SEQUENCE	X	X	X	–	
DROP SERVER	X	X	X	–	
DROP STATISTICS	X	X	X	–	
DROP TABLE	X	X	X	–	
DROP TEXT SEARCH CONFIGURATION	X	X	X	–	
DROP TEXT SEARCH DICTIONARY	X	X	X	–	
DROP TEXT SEARCH PARSER	X	X	X	–	
DROP TEXT SEARCH TEMPLATE	X	X	X	–	
DROP TRIGGER	X	X	X	–	
DROP TYPE	X	X	X	–	
DROP USER MAPPING	X	X	X	–	
DROP VIEW	X	X	X	–	
GRANT	X	X	–	–	Only for local objects
IMPORT FOREIGN SCHEMA	X	X	–	–	
REVOKE	X	X	–	–	Only for local objects
SECURITY LABEL	X	X	–	–	Only for local objects
SELECT INTO	X	X	–	–	

40.3. Writing Event Trigger Functions in C

This section describes the low-level details of the interface to an event trigger function. This information is only needed when writing event trigger functions in C. If you are using a higher-level language then these details are handled for you. In most cases you should consider using a procedural language before writing your event triggers in C. The documentation of each procedural language explains how to write an event trigger in that language.

Event trigger functions must use the "version 1" function manager interface.

When a function is called by the event trigger manager, it is not passed any normal arguments, but it is passed a "context" pointer pointing to a `EventTriggerData` structure. C functions can check whether they were called from the event trigger manager or not by executing the macro:

```
CALLED_AS_EVENT_TRIGGER(fcinfo)
```

which expands to:

```
((fcinfo)->context != NULL && IsA((fcinfo)->context,
 EventTriggerData))
```

If this returns true, then it is safe to cast `fcinfo->context` to type `EventTriggerData *` and make use of the pointed-to `EventTriggerData` structure. The function must *not* alter the `EventTriggerData` structure or any of the data it points to.

`struct EventTriggerData` is defined in `commands/event_trigger.h`:

```
typedef struct EventTriggerData
{
    NodeTag     type;
    const char *event;      /* event name */
    Node       *parsetree;  /* parse tree */
    const char *tag;        /* command tag */
} EventTriggerData;
```

where the members are defined as follows:

`type`

  Always `T_EventTriggerData`.

`event`

  Describes the event for which the function is called, one of `"ddl_command_start"`, `"ddl_command_end"`, `"sql_drop"`, `"table_rewrite"`. See Section 40.1 for the meaning of these events.

`parsetree`

  A pointer to the parse tree of the command. Check the PostgreSQL source code for details. The parse tree structure is subject to change without notice.

tag

The command tag associated with the event for which the event trigger is run, for example "CREATE FUNCTION".

An event trigger function must return a NULL pointer (*not* an SQL null value, that is, do not set *isNull* true).

40.4. A Complete Event Trigger Example

Here is a very simple example of an event trigger function written in C. (Examples of triggers written in procedural languages can be found in the documentation of the procedural languages.)

The function noddl raises an exception each time it is called. The event trigger definition associated the function with the ddl_command_start event. The effect is that all DDL commands (with the exceptions mentioned in Section 40.1) are prevented from running.

This is the source code of the trigger function:

```
#include "postgres.h"
#include "commands/event_trigger.h"


PG_MODULE_MAGIC;

PG_FUNCTION_INFO_V1(noddl);

Datum
noddl(PG_FUNCTION_ARGS)
{
    EventTriggerData *trigdata;

    if (!CALLED_AS_EVENT_TRIGGER(fcinfo))  /* internal error */
        elog(ERROR, "not fired by event trigger manager");

    trigdata = (EventTriggerData *) fcinfo->context;

    ereport(ERROR,
        (errcode(ERRCODE_INSUFFICIENT_PRIVILEGE),
                errmsg("command \"%s\" denied", trigdata->tag)));

    PG_RETURN_NULL();
}
```

After you have compiled the source code (see Section 38.10.5), declare the function and the triggers:

```
CREATE FUNCTION noddl() RETURNS event_trigger
    AS 'noddl' LANGUAGE C;

CREATE EVENT TRIGGER noddl ON ddl_command_start
    EXECUTE FUNCTION noddl();
```

Now you can test the operation of the trigger:

```
=# \dy
                    List of event triggers
  Name  |        Event        | Owner | Enabled | Function | Tags
--------+---------------------+-------+---------+----------+------
 noddl  | ddl_command_start   | dim   | enabled | noddl    |
(1 row)

=# CREATE TABLE foo(id serial);
ERROR:  command "CREATE TABLE" denied
```

In this situation, in order to be able to run some DDL commands when you need to do so, you have to either drop the event trigger or disable it. It can be convenient to disable the trigger for only the duration of a transaction:

```
BEGIN;
ALTER EVENT TRIGGER noddl DISABLE;
CREATE TABLE foo (id serial);
ALTER EVENT TRIGGER noddl ENABLE;
COMMIT;
```

(Recall that DDL commands on event triggers themselves are not affected by event triggers.)

40.5. A Table Rewrite Event Trigger Example

Thanks to the `table_rewrite` event, it is possible to implement a table rewriting policy only allowing the rewrite in maintenance windows.

Here's an example implementing such a policy.

```
CREATE OR REPLACE FUNCTION no_rewrite()
 RETURNS event_trigger
 LANGUAGE plpgsql AS
$$
---
--- Implement local Table Rewriting policy:
---     public.foo is not allowed rewriting, ever
---     other tables are only allowed rewriting between 1am and 6am
---     unless they have more than 100 blocks
---
DECLARE
  table_oid oid := pg_event_trigger_table_rewrite_oid();
  current_hour integer := extract('hour' from current_time);
  pages integer;
  max_pages integer := 100;
BEGIN
  IF pg_event_trigger_table_rewrite_oid() = 'public.foo'::regclass
  THEN
        RAISE EXCEPTION 'you''re not allowed to rewrite the table %',
                        table_oid::regclass;
  END IF;
```

```
     SELECT INTO pages relpages FROM pg_class WHERE oid = table_oid;
     IF pages > max_pages
     THEN
            RAISE EXCEPTION 'rewrites only allowed for table with less
  than % pages',
                              max_pages;
     END IF;

     IF current_hour NOT BETWEEN 1 AND 6
     THEN
            RAISE EXCEPTION 'rewrites only allowed between 1am and 6am';
     END IF;
END;
$$;

CREATE EVENT TRIGGER no_rewrite_allowed
                 ON table_rewrite
   EXECUTE FUNCTION no_rewrite();
```

Chapter 41. The Rule System

This chapter discusses the rule system in PostgreSQL. Production rule systems are conceptually simple, but there are many subtle points involved in actually using them.

Some other database systems define active database rules, which are usually stored procedures and triggers. In PostgreSQL, these can be implemented using functions and triggers as well.

The rule system (more precisely speaking, the query rewrite rule system) is totally different from stored procedures and triggers. It modifies queries to take rules into consideration, and then passes the modified query to the query planner for planning and execution. It is very powerful, and can be used for many things such as query language procedures, views, and versions. The theoretical foundations and the power of this rule system are also discussed in [ston90b] and [ong90].

41.1. The Query Tree

To understand how the rule system works it is necessary to know when it is invoked and what its input and results are.

The rule system is located between the parser and the planner. It takes the output of the parser, one query tree, and the user-defined rewrite rules, which are also query trees with some extra information, and creates zero or more query trees as result. So its input and output are always things the parser itself could have produced and thus, anything it sees is basically representable as an SQL statement.

Now what is a query tree? It is an internal representation of an SQL statement where the single parts that it is built from are stored separately. These query trees can be shown in the server log if you set the configuration parameters `debug_print_parse`, `debug_print_rewritten`, or `debug_print_plan`. The rule actions are also stored as query trees, in the system catalog `pg_rewrite`. They are not formatted like the log output, but they contain exactly the same information.

Reading a raw query tree requires some experience. But since SQL representations of query trees are sufficient to understand the rule system, this chapter will not teach how to read them.

When reading the SQL representations of the query trees in this chapter it is necessary to be able to identify the parts the statement is broken into when it is in the query tree structure. The parts of a query tree are

the command type

> This is a simple value telling which command (SELECT, INSERT, UPDATE, DELETE) produced the query tree.

the range table

> The range table is a list of relations that are used in the query. In a SELECT statement these are the relations given after the FROM key word.

> Every range table entry identifies a table or view and tells by which name it is called in the other parts of the query. In the query tree, the range table entries are referenced by number rather than by name, so here it doesn't matter if there are duplicate names as it would in an SQL statement. This can happen after the range tables of rules have been merged in. The examples in this chapter will not have this situation.

the result relation

> This is an index into the range table that identifies the relation where the results of the query go.

SELECT queries don't have a result relation. (The special case of SELECT INTO is mostly identical to CREATE TABLE followed by INSERT ... SELECT, and is not discussed separately here.)

For INSERT, UPDATE, and DELETE commands, the result relation is the table (or view!) where the changes are to take effect.

the target list

The target list is a list of expressions that define the result of the query. In the case of a SELECT, these expressions are the ones that build the final output of the query. They correspond to the expressions between the key words SELECT and FROM. (* is just an abbreviation for all the column names of a relation. It is expanded by the parser into the individual columns, so the rule system never sees it.)

DELETE commands don't need a normal target list because they don't produce any result. Instead, the planner adds a special CTID entry to the empty target list, to allow the executor to find the row to be deleted. (CTID is added when the result relation is an ordinary table. If it is a view, a whole-row variable is added instead, by the rule system, as described in Section 41.2.4.)

For INSERT commands, the target list describes the new rows that should go into the result relation. It consists of the expressions in the VALUES clause or the ones from the SELECT clause in INSERT ... SELECT. The first step of the rewrite process adds target list entries for any columns that were not assigned to by the original command but have defaults. Any remaining columns (with neither a given value nor a default) will be filled in by the planner with a constant null expression.

For UPDATE commands, the target list describes the new rows that should replace the old ones. In the rule system, it contains just the expressions from the SET column = expression part of the command. The planner will handle missing columns by inserting expressions that copy the values from the old row into the new one. Just as for DELETE, a CTID or whole-row variable is added so that the executor can identify the old row to be updated.

Every entry in the target list contains an expression that can be a constant value, a variable pointing to a column of one of the relations in the range table, a parameter, or an expression tree made of function calls, constants, variables, operators, etc.

the qualification

The query's qualification is an expression much like one of those contained in the target list entries. The result value of this expression is a Boolean that tells whether the operation (INSERT, UPDATE, DELETE, or SELECT) for the final result row should be executed or not. It corresponds to the WHERE clause of an SQL statement.

the join tree

The query's join tree shows the structure of the FROM clause. For a simple query like SELECT ... FROM a, b, c, the join tree is just a list of the FROM items, because we are allowed to join them in any order. But when JOIN expressions, particularly outer joins, are used, we have to join in the order shown by the joins. In that case, the join tree shows the structure of the JOIN expressions. The restrictions associated with particular JOIN clauses (from ON or USING expressions) are stored as qualification expressions attached to those join-tree nodes. It turns out to be convenient to store the top-level WHERE expression as a qualification attached to the top-level join-tree item, too. So really the join tree represents both the FROM and WHERE clauses of a SELECT.

the others

The other parts of the query tree like the ORDER BY clause aren't of interest here. The rule system substitutes some entries there while applying rules, but that doesn't have much to do with the fundamentals of the rule system.

41.2. Views and the Rule System

Views in PostgreSQL are implemented using the rule system. In fact, there is essentially no difference between:

```
CREATE VIEW myview AS SELECT * FROM mytab;
```

compared against the two commands:

```
CREATE TABLE myview (same column list as mytab);
CREATE RULE "_RETURN" AS ON SELECT TO myview DO INSTEAD
    SELECT * FROM mytab;
```

because this is exactly what the `CREATE VIEW` command does internally. This has some side effects. One of them is that the information about a view in the PostgreSQL system catalogs is exactly the same as it is for a table. So for the parser, there is absolutely no difference between a table and a view. They are the same thing: relations.

41.2.1. How SELECT Rules Work

Rules `ON SELECT` are applied to all queries as the last step, even if the command given is an `INSERT`, `UPDATE` or `DELETE`. And they have different semantics from rules on the other command types in that they modify the query tree in place instead of creating a new one. So `SELECT` rules are described first.

Currently, there can be only one action in an `ON SELECT` rule, and it must be an unconditional `SELECT` action that is `INSTEAD`. This restriction was required to make rules safe enough to open them for ordinary users, and it restricts `ON SELECT` rules to act like views.

The examples for this chapter are two join views that do some calculations and some more views using them in turn. One of the two first views is customized later by adding rules for `INSERT`, `UPDATE`, and `DELETE` operations so that the final result will be a view that behaves like a real table with some magic functionality. This is not such a simple example to start from and this makes things harder to get into. But it's better to have one example that covers all the points discussed step by step rather than having many different ones that might mix up in mind.

For the example, we need a little `min` function that returns the lower of 2 integer values. We create that as:

```
CREATE FUNCTION min(integer, integer) RETURNS integer AS $$
    SELECT CASE WHEN $1 < $2 THEN $1 ELSE $2 END
$$ LANGUAGE SQL STRICT;
```

The real tables we need in the first two rule system descriptions are these:

```
CREATE TABLE shoe_data (
    shoename    text,           -- primary key
    sh_avail    integer,        -- available number of pairs
    slcolor     text,           -- preferred shoelace color
    slminlen    real,           -- minimum shoelace length
    slmaxlen    real,           -- maximum shoelace length
    slunit      text            -- length unit
```

```
);

CREATE TABLE shoelace_data (
    sl_name     text,        -- primary key
    sl_avail    integer,     -- available number of pairs
    sl_color    text,        -- shoelace color
    sl_len      real,        -- shoelace length
    sl_unit     text         -- length unit
);

CREATE TABLE unit (
    un_name     text,        -- primary key
    un_fact     real         -- factor to transform to cm
);
```

As you can see, they represent shoe-store data.

The views are created as:

```
CREATE VIEW shoe AS
    SELECT sh.shoename,
           sh.sh_avail,
           sh.slcolor,
           sh.slminlen,
           sh.slminlen * un.un_fact AS slminlen_cm,
           sh.slmaxlen,
           sh.slmaxlen * un.un_fact AS slmaxlen_cm,
           sh.slunit
      FROM shoe_data sh, unit un
     WHERE sh.slunit = un.un_name;

CREATE VIEW shoelace AS
    SELECT s.sl_name,
           s.sl_avail,
           s.sl_color,
           s.sl_len,
           s.sl_unit,
           s.sl_len * u.un_fact AS sl_len_cm
      FROM shoelace_data s, unit u
     WHERE s.sl_unit = u.un_name;

CREATE VIEW shoe_ready AS
    SELECT rsh.shoename,
           rsh.sh_avail,
           rsl.sl_name,
           rsl.sl_avail,
           min(rsh.sh_avail, rsl.sl_avail) AS total_avail
      FROM shoe rsh, shoelace rsl
     WHERE rsl.sl_color = rsh.slcolor
       AND rsl.sl_len_cm >= rsh.slminlen_cm
       AND rsl.sl_len_cm <= rsh.slmaxlen_cm;
```

The CREATE VIEW command for the shoelace view (which is the simplest one we have) will create a relation shoelace and an entry in pg_rewrite that tells that there is a rewrite rule that must be applied whenever the relation shoelace is referenced in a query's range table. The rule has no rule qualification (discussed later, with the non-SELECT rules, since SELECT rules currently cannot have them) and it is INSTEAD. Note that rule qualifications are not the same as query qualifications. The action of our rule has a query qualification. The action of the rule is one query tree that is a copy of the SELECT statement in the view creation command.

Note

The two extra range table entries for NEW and OLD that you can see in the pg_rewrite entry aren't of interest for SELECT rules.

Now we populate unit, shoe_data and shoelace_data and run a simple query on a view:

```
INSERT INTO unit VALUES ('cm', 1.0);
INSERT INTO unit VALUES ('m', 100.0);
INSERT INTO unit VALUES ('inch', 2.54);

INSERT INTO shoe_data VALUES ('sh1', 2, 'black', 70.0, 90.0, 'cm');
INSERT INTO shoe_data VALUES ('sh2', 0, 'black', 30.0, 40.0, 'inch');
INSERT INTO shoe_data VALUES ('sh3', 4, 'brown', 50.0, 65.0, 'cm');
INSERT INTO shoe_data VALUES ('sh4', 3, 'brown', 40.0, 50.0, 'inch');

INSERT INTO shoelace_data VALUES ('sl1', 5, 'black', 80.0, 'cm');
INSERT INTO shoelace_data VALUES ('sl2', 6, 'black', 100.0, 'cm');
INSERT INTO shoelace_data VALUES ('sl3', 0, 'black', 35.0 , 'inch');
INSERT INTO shoelace_data VALUES ('sl4', 8, 'black', 40.0 , 'inch');
INSERT INTO shoelace_data VALUES ('sl5', 4, 'brown', 1.0 , 'm');
INSERT INTO shoelace_data VALUES ('sl6', 0, 'brown', 0.9 , 'm');
INSERT INTO shoelace_data VALUES ('sl7', 7, 'brown', 60 , 'cm');
INSERT INTO shoelace_data VALUES ('sl8', 1, 'brown', 40 , 'inch');

SELECT * FROM shoelace;
```

sl_name	sl_avail	sl_color	sl_len	sl_unit	sl_len_cm
sl1	5	black	80	cm	80
sl2	6	black	100	cm	100
sl7	7	brown	60	cm	60
sl3	0	black	35	inch	88.9
sl4	8	black	40	inch	101.6
sl8	1	brown	40	inch	101.6
sl5	4	brown	1	m	100
sl6	0	brown	0.9	m	90

(8 rows)

This is the simplest SELECT you can do on our views, so we take this opportunity to explain the basics of view rules. The SELECT * FROM shoelace was interpreted by the parser and produced the query tree:

```
SELECT shoelace.sl_name, shoelace.sl_avail,
       shoelace.sl_color, shoelace.sl_len,
       shoelace.sl_unit, shoelace.sl_len_cm
```

```
FROM shoelace shoelace;
```

and this is given to the rule system. The rule system walks through the range table and checks if there are rules for any relation. When processing the range table entry for `shoelace` (the only one up to now) it finds the `_RETURN` rule with the query tree:

```
SELECT s.sl_name, s.sl_avail,
       s.sl_color, s.sl_len, s.sl_unit,
       s.sl_len * u.un_fact AS sl_len_cm
  FROM shoelace old, shoelace new,
       shoelace_data s, unit u
 WHERE s.sl_unit = u.un_name;
```

To expand the view, the rewriter simply creates a subquery range-table entry containing the rule's action query tree, and substitutes this range table entry for the original one that referenced the view. The resulting rewritten query tree is almost the same as if you had typed:

```
SELECT shoelace.sl_name, shoelace.sl_avail,
       shoelace.sl_color, shoelace.sl_len,
       shoelace.sl_unit, shoelace.sl_len_cm
  FROM (SELECT s.sl_name,
               s.sl_avail,
               s.sl_color,
               s.sl_len,
               s.sl_unit,
               s.sl_len * u.un_fact AS sl_len_cm
          FROM shoelace_data s, unit u
         WHERE s.sl_unit = u.un_name) shoelace;
```

There is one difference however: the subquery's range table has two extra entries `shoelace old` and `shoelace new`. These entries don't participate directly in the query, since they aren't referenced by the subquery's join tree or target list. The rewriter uses them to store the access privilege check information that was originally present in the range-table entry that referenced the view. In this way, the executor will still check that the user has proper privileges to access the view, even though there's no direct use of the view in the rewritten query.

That was the first rule applied. The rule system will continue checking the remaining range-table entries in the top query (in this example there are no more), and it will recursively check the range-table entries in the added subquery to see if any of them reference views. (But it won't expand `old` or `new` — otherwise we'd have infinite recursion!) In this example, there are no rewrite rules for `shoelace_data` or `unit`, so rewriting is complete and the above is the final result given to the planner.

Now we want to write a query that finds out for which shoes currently in the store we have the matching shoelaces (color and length) and where the total number of exactly matching pairs is greater or equal to two.

```
SELECT * FROM shoe_ready WHERE total_avail >= 2;
```

shoename	sh_avail	sl_name	sl_avail	total_avail
sh1	2	sl1	5	2
sh3	4	sl7	7	4

(2 rows)

The output of the parser this time is the query tree:

```
SELECT shoe_ready.shoename, shoe_ready.sh_avail,
       shoe_ready.sl_name, shoe_ready.sl_avail,
       shoe_ready.total_avail
  FROM shoe_ready shoe_ready
 WHERE shoe_ready.total_avail >= 2;
```

The first rule applied will be the one for the shoe_ready view and it results in the query tree:

```
SELECT shoe_ready.shoename, shoe_ready.sh_avail,
       shoe_ready.sl_name, shoe_ready.sl_avail,
       shoe_ready.total_avail
  FROM (SELECT rsh.shoename,
               rsh.sh_avail,
               rsl.sl_name,
               rsl.sl_avail,
               min(rsh.sh_avail, rsl.sl_avail) AS total_avail
          FROM shoe rsh, shoelace rsl
         WHERE rsl.sl_color = rsh.slcolor
           AND rsl.sl_len_cm >= rsh.slminlen_cm
           AND rsl.sl_len_cm <= rsh.slmaxlen_cm) shoe_ready
 WHERE shoe_ready.total_avail >= 2;
```

Similarly, the rules for shoe and shoelace are substituted into the range table of the subquery, leading to a three-level final query tree:

```
SELECT shoe_ready.shoename, shoe_ready.sh_avail,
       shoe_ready.sl_name, shoe_ready.sl_avail,
       shoe_ready.total_avail
  FROM (SELECT rsh.shoename,
               rsh.sh_avail,
               rsl.sl_name,
               rsl.sl_avail,
               min(rsh.sh_avail, rsl.sl_avail) AS total_avail
          FROM (SELECT sh.shoename,
                       sh.sh_avail,
                       sh.slcolor,
                       sh.slminlen,
                       sh.slminlen * un.un_fact AS slminlen_cm,
                       sh.slmaxlen,
                       sh.slmaxlen * un.un_fact AS slmaxlen_cm,
                       sh.slunit
                  FROM shoe_data sh, unit un
                 WHERE sh.slunit = un.un_name) rsh,
               (SELECT s.sl_name,
                       s.sl_avail,
                       s.sl_color,
                       s.sl_len,
                       s.sl_unit,
                       s.sl_len * u.un_fact AS sl_len_cm
                  FROM shoelace_data s, unit u
```

```
                    WHERE s.sl_unit = u.un_name) rsl
            WHERE rsl.sl_color = rsh.slcolor
                AND rsl.sl_len_cm >= rsh.slminlen_cm
                AND rsl.sl_len_cm <= rsh.slmaxlen_cm) shoe_ready
    WHERE shoe_ready.total_avail > 2;
```

It turns out that the planner will collapse this tree into a two-level query tree: the bottommost SELECT commands will be "pulled up" into the middle SELECT since there's no need to process them separately. But the middle SELECT will remain separate from the top, because it contains aggregate functions. If we pulled those up it would change the behavior of the topmost SELECT, which we don't want. However, collapsing the query tree is an optimization that the rewrite system doesn't have to concern itself with.

41.2.2. View Rules in Non-SELECT Statements

Two details of the query tree aren't touched in the description of view rules above. These are the command type and the result relation. In fact, the command type is not needed by view rules, but the result relation may affect the way in which the query rewriter works, because special care needs to be taken if the result relation is a view.

There are only a few differences between a query tree for a SELECT and one for any other command. Obviously, they have a different command type and for a command other than a SELECT, the result relation points to the range-table entry where the result should go. Everything else is absolutely the same. So having two tables t1 and t2 with columns a and b, the query trees for the two statements:

```
SELECT t2.b FROM t1, t2 WHERE t1.a = t2.a;
```

```
UPDATE t1 SET b = t2.b FROM t2 WHERE t1.a = t2.a;
```

are nearly identical. In particular:

- The range tables contain entries for the tables t1 and t2.

- The target lists contain one variable that points to column b of the range table entry for table t2.

- The qualification expressions compare the columns a of both range-table entries for equality.

- The join trees show a simple join between t1 and t2.

The consequence is, that both query trees result in similar execution plans: They are both joins over the two tables. For the UPDATE the missing columns from t1 are added to the target list by the planner and the final query tree will read as:

```
UPDATE t1 SET a = t1.a, b = t2.b FROM t2 WHERE t1.a = t2.a;
```

and thus the executor run over the join will produce exactly the same result set as:

```
SELECT t1.a, t2.b FROM t1, t2 WHERE t1.a = t2.a;
```

But there is a little problem in UPDATE: the part of the executor plan that does the join does not care what the results from the join are meant for. It just produces a result set of rows. The fact that one is a SELECT command and the other is an UPDATE is handled higher up in the executor, where it knows that this is an UPDATE, and it knows that this result should go into table t1. But which of the rows that are there has to be replaced by the new row?

To resolve this problem, another entry is added to the target list in UPDATE (and also in DELETE) statements: the current tuple ID (CTID). This is a system column containing the file block number and position in the block for the row. Knowing the table, the CTID can be used to retrieve the original row of t1 to be updated. After adding the CTID to the target list, the query actually looks like:

```
SELECT t1.a, t2.b, t1.ctid FROM t1, t2 WHERE t1.a = t2.a;
```

Now another detail of PostgreSQL enters the stage. Old table rows aren't overwritten, and this is why ROLLBACK is fast. In an UPDATE, the new result row is inserted into the table (after stripping the CTID) and in the row header of the old row, which the CTID pointed to, the cmax and xmax entries are set to the current command counter and current transaction ID. Thus the old row is hidden, and after the transaction commits the vacuum cleaner can eventually remove the dead row.

Knowing all that, we can simply apply view rules in absolutely the same way to any command. There is no difference.

41.2.3. The Power of Views in PostgreSQL

The above demonstrates how the rule system incorporates view definitions into the original query tree. In the second example, a simple SELECT from one view created a final query tree that is a join of 4 tables (unit was used twice with different names).

The benefit of implementing views with the rule system is, that the planner has all the information about which tables have to be scanned plus the relationships between these tables plus the restrictive qualifications from the views plus the qualifications from the original query in one single query tree. And this is still the situation when the original query is already a join over views. The planner has to decide which is the best path to execute the query, and the more information the planner has, the better this decision can be. And the rule system as implemented in PostgreSQL ensures, that this is all information available about the query up to that point.

41.2.4. Updating a View

What happens if a view is named as the target relation for an INSERT, UPDATE, or DELETE? Doing the substitutions described above would give a query tree in which the result relation points at a subquery range-table entry, which will not work. There are several ways in which PostgreSQL can support the appearance of updating a view, however.

If the subquery selects from a single base relation and is simple enough, the rewriter can automatically replace the subquery with the underlying base relation so that the INSERT, UPDATE, or DELETE is applied to the base relation in the appropriate way. Views that are "simple enough" for this are called *automatically updatable*. For detailed information on the kinds of view that can be automatically updated, see CREATE VIEW.

Alternatively, the operation may be handled by a user-provided INSTEAD OF trigger on the view. Rewriting works slightly differently in this case. For INSERT, the rewriter does nothing at all with the view, leaving it as the result relation for the query. For UPDATE and DELETE, it's still necessary to expand the view query to produce the "old" rows that the command will attempt to update or delete. So the view is expanded as normal, but another unexpanded range-table entry is added to the query to represent the view in its capacity as the result relation.

The problem that now arises is how to identify the rows to be updated in the view. Recall that when the result relation is a table, a special CTID entry is added to the target list to identify the physical locations of the rows to be updated. This does not work if the result relation is a view, because a view does not have any CTID, since its rows do not have actual physical locations. Instead, for an UPDATE or DELETE operation, a special `wholerow` entry is added to the target list, which expands to include all columns from the view. The executor uses this value to supply the "old" row to the `INSTEAD OF` trigger. It is up to the trigger to work out what to update based on the old and new row values.

Another possibility is for the user to define `INSTEAD` rules that specify substitute actions for `INSERT`, `UPDATE`, and `DELETE` commands on a view. These rules will rewrite the command, typically into a command that updates one or more tables, rather than views. That is the topic of Section 41.4.

Note that rules are evaluated first, rewriting the original query before it is planned and executed. Therefore, if a view has `INSTEAD OF` triggers as well as rules on `INSERT`, `UPDATE`, or `DELETE`, then the rules will be evaluated first, and depending on the result, the triggers may not be used at all.

Automatic rewriting of an `INSERT`, `UPDATE`, or `DELETE` query on a simple view is always tried last. Therefore, if a view has rules or triggers, they will override the default behavior of automatically updatable views.

If there are no `INSTEAD` rules or `INSTEAD OF` triggers for the view, and the rewriter cannot automatically rewrite the query as an update on the underlying base relation, an error will be thrown because the executor cannot update a view as such.

41.3. Materialized Views

Materialized views in PostgreSQL use the rule system like views do, but persist the results in a table-like form. The main differences between:

```
CREATE MATERIALIZED VIEW mymatview AS SELECT * FROM mytab;
```

and:

```
CREATE TABLE mymatview AS SELECT * FROM mytab;
```

are that the materialized view cannot subsequently be directly updated and that the query used to create the materialized view is stored in exactly the same way that a view's query is stored, so that fresh data can be generated for the materialized view with:

```
REFRESH MATERIALIZED VIEW mymatview;
```

The information about a materialized view in the PostgreSQL system catalogs is exactly the same as it is for a table or view. So for the parser, a materialized view is a relation, just like a table or a view. When a materialized view is referenced in a query, the data is returned directly from the materialized view, like from a table; the rule is only used for populating the materialized view.

While access to the data stored in a materialized view is often much faster than accessing the underlying tables directly or through a view, the data is not always current; yet sometimes current data is not needed. Consider a table which records sales:

```
CREATE TABLE invoice (
    invoice_no      integer         PRIMARY KEY,
    seller_no       integer,        -- ID of salesperson
    invoice_date    date,           -- date of sale
    invoice_amt     numeric(13,2)   -- amount of sale
);
```

If people want to be able to quickly graph historical sales data, they might want to summarize, and they may not care about the incomplete data for the current date:

```
CREATE MATERIALIZED VIEW sales_summary AS
  SELECT
      seller_no,
      invoice_date,
      sum(invoice_amt)::numeric(13,2) as sales_amt
    FROM invoice
    WHERE invoice_date < CURRENT_DATE
    GROUP BY
      seller_no,
      invoice_date
    ORDER BY
      seller_no,
      invoice_date;

CREATE UNIQUE INDEX sales_summary_seller
  ON sales_summary (seller_no, invoice_date);
```

This materialized view might be useful for displaying a graph in the dashboard created for salespeople. A job could be scheduled to update the statistics each night using this SQL statement:

```
REFRESH MATERIALIZED VIEW sales_summary;
```

Another use for a materialized view is to allow faster access to data brought across from a remote system through a foreign data wrapper. A simple example using `file_fdw` is below, with timings, but since this is using cache on the local system the performance difference compared to access to a remote system would usually be greater than shown here. Notice we are also exploiting the ability to put an index on the materialized view, whereas `file_fdw` does not support indexes; this advantage might not apply for other sorts of foreign data access.

Setup:

```
CREATE EXTENSION file_fdw;
CREATE SERVER local_file FOREIGN DATA WRAPPER file_fdw;
CREATE FOREIGN TABLE words (word text NOT NULL)
  SERVER local_file
  OPTIONS (filename '/usr/share/dict/words');
CREATE MATERIALIZED VIEW wrd AS SELECT * FROM words;
CREATE UNIQUE INDEX wrd_word ON wrd (word);
CREATE EXTENSION pg_trgm;
CREATE INDEX wrd_trgm ON wrd USING gist (word gist_trgm_ops);
VACUUM ANALYZE wrd;
```

Now let's spell-check a word. Using `file_fdw` directly:

```
SELECT count(*) FROM words WHERE word = 'caterpiler';

 count
-------
```

```
        0
(1 row)
```

With EXPLAIN ANALYZE, we see:

```
 Aggregate  (cost=21763.99..21764.00 rows=1 width=0) (actual
time=188.180..188.181 rows=1 loops=1)
   -> Foreign Scan on words  (cost=0.00..21761.41 rows=1032 width=0)
(actual time=188.177..188.177 rows=0 loops=1)
         Filter: (word = 'caterpiler'::text)
         Rows Removed by Filter: 479829
         Foreign File: /usr/share/dict/words
         Foreign File Size: 4953699
 Planning time: 0.118 ms
 Execution time: 188.273 ms
```

If the materialized view is used instead, the query is much faster:

```
 Aggregate  (cost=4.44..4.45 rows=1 width=0) (actual time=0.042..0.042
rows=1 loops=1)
   -> Index Only Scan using wrd_word on wrd  (cost=0.42..4.44 rows=1
width=0) (actual time=0.039..0.039 rows=0 loops=1)
         Index Cond: (word = 'caterpiler'::text)
         Heap Fetches: 0
 Planning time: 0.164 ms
 Execution time: 0.117 ms
```

Either way, the word is spelled wrong, so let's look for what we might have wanted. Again using file_fdw:

```
SELECT word FROM words ORDER BY word <-> 'caterpiler' LIMIT 10;

     word
---------------
 cater
 caterpillar
 Caterpillar
 caterpillars
 caterpillar's
 Caterpillar's
 caterer
 caterer's
 caters
 catered
(10 rows)
```

```
 Limit  (cost=11583.61..11583.64 rows=10 width=32) (actual
time=1431.591..1431.594 rows=10 loops=1)
   -> Sort  (cost=11583.61..11804.76 rows=88459 width=32) (actual
time=1431.589..1431.591 rows=10 loops=1)
         Sort Key: ((word <-> 'caterpiler'::text))
```

```
        Sort Method: top-N heapsort  Memory: 25kB
        -> Foreign Scan on words  (cost=0.00..9672.05 rows=88459
width=32) (actual time=0.057..1286.455 rows=479829 loops=1)
              Foreign File: /usr/share/dict/words
              Foreign File Size: 4953699
Planning time: 0.128 ms
Execution time: 1431.679 ms
```

Using the materialized view:

```
Limit  (cost=0.29..1.06 rows=10 width=10) (actual
time=187.222..188.257 rows=10 loops=1)
  -> Index Scan using wrd_trgm on wrd  (cost=0.29..37020.87
rows=479829 width=10) (actual time=187.219..188.252 rows=10 loops=1)
        Order By: (word <-> 'caterpiler'::text)
Planning time: 0.196 ms
Execution time: 198.640 ms
```

If you can tolerate periodic update of the remote data to the local database, the performance benefit can be substantial.

41.4. Rules on INSERT, UPDATE, and DELETE

Rules that are defined on INSERT, UPDATE, and DELETE are significantly different from the view rules described in the previous section. First, their CREATE RULE command allows more:

- They are allowed to have no action.

- They can have multiple actions.

- They can be INSTEAD or ALSO (the default).

- The pseudorelations NEW and OLD become useful.

- They can have rule qualifications.

Second, they don't modify the query tree in place. Instead they create zero or more new query trees and can throw away the original one.

Caution

In many cases, tasks that could be performed by rules on INSERT/UPDATE/DELETE are better done with triggers. Triggers are notationally a bit more complicated, but their semantics are much simpler to understand. Rules tend to have surprising results when the original query contains volatile functions: volatile functions may get executed more times than expected in the process of carrying out the rules.

Also, there are some cases that are not supported by these types of rules at all, notably including WITH clauses in the original query and multiple-assignment sub-SELECTs in the SET list of UPDATE queries. This is because copying these constructs into a rule query would result in multiple evaluations of the sub-query, contrary to the express intent of the query's author.

41.4.1. How Update Rules Work

Keep the syntax:

```
CREATE [ OR REPLACE ] RULE name AS ON event
    TO table [ WHERE condition ]
    DO [ ALSO | INSTEAD ] { NOTHING | command | ( command ; command
 ... ) }
```

in mind. In the following, *update rules* means rules that are defined on INSERT, UPDATE, or DELETE.

Update rules get applied by the rule system when the result relation and the command type of a query tree are equal to the object and event given in the CREATE RULE command. For update rules, the rule system creates a list of query trees. Initially the query-tree list is empty. There can be zero (NOTHING key word), one, or multiple actions. To simplify, we will look at a rule with one action. This rule can have a qualification or not and it can be INSTEAD or ALSO (the default).

What is a rule qualification? It is a restriction that tells when the actions of the rule should be done and when not. This qualification can only reference the pseudorelations NEW and/or OLD, which basically represent the relation that was given as object (but with a special meaning).

So we have three cases that produce the following query trees for a one-action rule.

No qualification, with either ALSO or INSTEAD

   the query tree from the rule action with the original query tree's qualification added

Qualification given and ALSO

   the query tree from the rule action with the rule qualification and the original query tree's qualification added

Qualification given and INSTEAD

   the query tree from the rule action with the rule qualification and the original query tree's qualification; and the original query tree with the negated rule qualification added

Finally, if the rule is ALSO, the unchanged original query tree is added to the list. Since only qualified INSTEAD rules already add the original query tree, we end up with either one or two output query trees for a rule with one action.

For ON INSERT rules, the original query (if not suppressed by INSTEAD) is done before any actions added by rules. This allows the actions to see the inserted row(s). But for ON UPDATE and ON DELETE rules, the original query is done after the actions added by rules. This ensures that the actions can see the to-be-updated or to-be-deleted rows; otherwise, the actions might do nothing because they find no rows matching their qualifications.

The query trees generated from rule actions are thrown into the rewrite system again, and maybe more rules get applied resulting in more or less query trees. So a rule's actions must have either a different command type or a different result relation than the rule itself is on, otherwise this recursive process will end up in an infinite loop. (Recursive expansion of a rule will be detected and reported as an error.)

The query trees found in the actions of the `pg_rewrite` system catalog are only templates. Since they can reference the range-table entries for NEW and OLD, some substitutions have to be made before they can be used. For any reference to NEW, the target list of the original query is searched for a corresponding entry. If found, that entry's expression replaces the reference. Otherwise, NEW means the same as OLD (for an UPDATE) or is replaced by a null value (for an INSERT). Any reference to OLD is replaced by a reference to the range-table entry that is the result relation.

After the system is done applying update rules, it applies view rules to the produced query tree(s). Views cannot insert new update actions so there is no need to apply update rules to the output of view rewriting.

41.4.1.1. A First Rule Step by Step

Say we want to trace changes to the sl_avail column in the shoelace_data relation. So we set up a log table and a rule that conditionally writes a log entry when an UPDATE is performed on shoelace_data.

```
CREATE TABLE shoelace_log (
    sl_name     text,            -- shoelace changed
    sl_avail    integer,         -- new available value
    log_who     text,            -- who did it
    log_when    timestamp        -- when
);

CREATE RULE log_shoelace AS ON UPDATE TO shoelace_data
    WHERE NEW.sl_avail <> OLD.sl_avail
    DO INSERT INTO shoelace_log VALUES (
                                NEW.sl_name,
                                NEW.sl_avail,
                                current_user,
                                current_timestamp
                    );
```

Now someone does:

```
UPDATE shoelace_data SET sl_avail = 6 WHERE sl_name = 'sl7';
```

and we look at the log table:

```
SELECT * FROM shoelace_log;

 sl_name | sl_avail | log_who | log_when
---------+----------+---------+-------------------------------
 sl7     |        6 | Al      | Tue Oct 20 16:14:45 1998 MET DST
(1 row)
```

That's what we expected. What happened in the background is the following. The parser created the query tree:

```
UPDATE shoelace_data SET sl_avail = 6
  FROM shoelace_data shoelace_data
 WHERE shoelace_data.sl_name = 'sl7';
```

There is a rule log_shoelace that is ON UPDATE with the rule qualification expression:

```
NEW.sl_avail <> OLD.sl_avail
```

and the action:

```
INSERT INTO shoelace_log VALUES (
        new.sl_name, new.sl_avail,
        current_user, current_timestamp )
  FROM shoelace_data new, shoelace_data old;
```

(This looks a little strange since you cannot normally write INSERT ... VALUES ... FROM. The FROM clause here is just to indicate that there are range-table entries in the query tree for new and old. These are needed so that they can be referenced by variables in the INSERT command's query tree.)

The rule is a qualified ALSO rule, so the rule system has to return two query trees: the modified rule action and the original query tree. In step 1, the range table of the original query is incorporated into the rule's action query tree. This results in:

```
INSERT INTO shoelace_log VALUES (
        new.sl_name, new.sl_avail,
        current_user, current_timestamp )
  FROM shoelace_data new, shoelace_data old,
       shoelace_data shoelace_data;
```

In step 2, the rule qualification is added to it, so the result set is restricted to rows where sl_avail changes:

```
INSERT INTO shoelace_log VALUES (
        new.sl_name, new.sl_avail,
        current_user, current_timestamp )
  FROM shoelace_data new, shoelace_data old,
       shoelace_data shoelace_data
 WHERE new.sl_avail <> old.sl_avail;
```

(This looks even stranger, since INSERT ... VALUES doesn't have a WHERE clause either, but the planner and executor will have no difficulty with it. They need to support this same functionality anyway for INSERT ... SELECT.)

In step 3, the original query tree's qualification is added, restricting the result set further to only the rows that would have been touched by the original query:

```
INSERT INTO shoelace_log VALUES (
        new.sl_name, new.sl_avail,
        current_user, current_timestamp )
  FROM shoelace_data new, shoelace_data old,
       shoelace_data shoelace_data
 WHERE new.sl_avail <> old.sl_avail
   AND shoelace_data.sl_name = 'sl7';
```

Step 4 replaces references to NEW by the target list entries from the original query tree or by the matching variable references from the result relation:

```
INSERT INTO shoelace_log VALUES (
       shoelace_data.sl_name, 6,
       current_user, current_timestamp )
  FROM shoelace_data new, shoelace_data old,
       shoelace_data shoelace_data
 WHERE 6 <> old.sl_avail
   AND shoelace_data.sl_name = 'sl7';
```

Step 5 changes OLD references into result relation references:

```
INSERT INTO shoelace_log VALUES (
       shoelace_data.sl_name, 6,
       current_user, current_timestamp )
  FROM shoelace_data new, shoelace_data old,
       shoelace_data shoelace_data
 WHERE 6 <> shoelace_data.sl_avail
   AND shoelace_data.sl_name = 'sl7';
```

That's it. Since the rule is ALSO, we also output the original query tree. In short, the output from the rule system is a list of two query trees that correspond to these statements:

```
INSERT INTO shoelace_log VALUES (
       shoelace_data.sl_name, 6,
       current_user, current_timestamp )
  FROM shoelace_data
 WHERE 6 <> shoelace_data.sl_avail
   AND shoelace_data.sl_name = 'sl7';

UPDATE shoelace_data SET sl_avail = 6
 WHERE sl_name = 'sl7';
```

These are executed in this order, and that is exactly what the rule was meant to do.

The substitutions and the added qualifications ensure that, if the original query would be, say:

```
UPDATE shoelace_data SET sl_color = 'green'
 WHERE sl_name = 'sl7';
```

no log entry would get written. In that case, the original query tree does not contain a target list entry for sl_avail, so NEW.sl_avail will get replaced by shoelace_data.sl_avail. Thus, the extra command generated by the rule is:

```
INSERT INTO shoelace_log VALUES (
       shoelace_data.sl_name, shoelace_data.sl_avail,
       current_user, current_timestamp )
  FROM shoelace_data
 WHERE shoelace_data.sl_avail <> shoelace_data.sl_avail
   AND shoelace_data.sl_name = 'sl7';
```

and that qualification will never be true.

It will also work if the original query modifies multiple rows. So if someone issued the command:

```
UPDATE shoelace_data SET sl_avail = 0
 WHERE sl_color = 'black';
```

four rows in fact get updated (sl1, sl2, sl3, and sl4). But sl3 already has sl_avail = 0. In this case, the original query trees qualification is different and that results in the extra query tree:

```
INSERT INTO shoelace_log
SELECT shoelace_data.sl_name, 0,
       current_user, current_timestamp
  FROM shoelace_data
 WHERE 0 <> shoelace_data.sl_avail
   AND shoelace_data.sl_color = 'black';
```

being generated by the rule. This query tree will surely insert three new log entries. And that's absolutely correct.

Here we can see why it is important that the original query tree is executed last. If the UPDATE had been executed first, all the rows would have already been set to zero, so the logging INSERT would not find any row where 0 <> shoelace_data.sl_avail.

41.4.2. Cooperation with Views

A simple way to protect view relations from the mentioned possibility that someone can try to run INSERT, UPDATE, or DELETE on them is to let those query trees get thrown away. So we could create the rules:

```
CREATE RULE shoe_ins_protect AS ON INSERT TO shoe
    DO INSTEAD NOTHING;
CREATE RULE shoe_upd_protect AS ON UPDATE TO shoe
    DO INSTEAD NOTHING;
CREATE RULE shoe_del_protect AS ON DELETE TO shoe
    DO INSTEAD NOTHING;
```

If someone now tries to do any of these operations on the view relation shoe, the rule system will apply these rules. Since the rules have no actions and are INSTEAD, the resulting list of query trees will be empty and the whole query will become nothing because there is nothing left to be optimized or executed after the rule system is done with it.

A more sophisticated way to use the rule system is to create rules that rewrite the query tree into one that does the right operation on the real tables. To do that on the shoelace view, we create the following rules:

```
CREATE RULE shoelace_ins AS ON INSERT TO shoelace
    DO INSTEAD
    INSERT INTO shoelace_data VALUES (
          NEW.sl_name,
          NEW.sl_avail,
          NEW.sl_color,
          NEW.sl_len,
          NEW.sl_unit
    );

CREATE RULE shoelace_upd AS ON UPDATE TO shoelace
```

```
    DO INSTEAD
    UPDATE shoelace_data
       SET sl_name = NEW.sl_name,
           sl_avail = NEW.sl_avail,
           sl_color = NEW.sl_color,
           sl_len = NEW.sl_len,
           sl_unit = NEW.sl_unit
     WHERE sl_name = OLD.sl_name;

CREATE RULE shoelace_del AS ON DELETE TO shoelace
    DO INSTEAD
    DELETE FROM shoelace_data
     WHERE sl_name = OLD.sl_name;
```

If you want to support RETURNING queries on the view, you need to make the rules include RETURNING clauses that compute the view rows. This is usually pretty trivial for views on a single table, but it's a bit tedious for join views such as shoelace. An example for the insert case is:

```
CREATE RULE shoelace_ins AS ON INSERT TO shoelace
    DO INSTEAD
    INSERT INTO shoelace_data VALUES (
            NEW.sl_name,
            NEW.sl_avail,
            NEW.sl_color,
            NEW.sl_len,
            NEW.sl_unit
    )
    RETURNING
            shoelace_data.*,
            (SELECT shoelace_data.sl_len * u.un_fact
             FROM unit u WHERE shoelace_data.sl_unit = u.un_name);
```

Note that this one rule supports both INSERT and INSERT RETURNING queries on the view — the RETURNING clause is simply ignored for INSERT.

Now assume that once in a while, a pack of shoelaces arrives at the shop and a big parts list along with it. But you don't want to manually update the shoelace view every time. Instead we set up two little tables: one where you can insert the items from the part list, and one with a special trick. The creation commands for these are:

```
CREATE TABLE shoelace_arrive (
    arr_name    text,
    arr_quant   integer
);

CREATE TABLE shoelace_ok (
    ok_name     text,
    ok_quant    integer
);

CREATE RULE shoelace_ok_ins AS ON INSERT TO shoelace_ok
    DO INSTEAD
    UPDATE shoelace
```

```
            SET sl_avail = sl_avail + NEW.ok_quant
        WHERE sl_name = NEW.ok_name;
```

Now you can fill the table `shoelace_arrive` with the data from the parts list:

```
SELECT * FROM shoelace_arrive;

 arr_name | arr_quant
----------+-----------
 sl3      |        10
 sl6      |        20
 sl8      |        20
(3 rows)
```

Take a quick look at the current data:

```
SELECT * FROM shoelace;

 sl_name  | sl_avail | sl_color | sl_len | sl_unit | sl_len_cm
----------+----------+----------+--------+---------+-----------
 sl1      |        5 | black    |     80 | cm      |        80
 sl2      |        6 | black    |    100 | cm      |       100
 sl7      |        6 | brown    |     60 | cm      |        60
 sl3      |        0 | black    |     35 | inch    |      88.9
 sl4      |        8 | black    |     40 | inch    |     101.6
 sl8      |        1 | brown    |     40 | inch    |     101.6
 sl5      |        4 | brown    |      1 | m       |       100
 sl6      |        0 | brown    |    0.9 | m       |        90
(8 rows)
```

Now move the arrived shoelaces in:

```
INSERT INTO shoelace_ok SELECT * FROM shoelace_arrive;
```

and check the results:

```
SELECT * FROM shoelace ORDER BY sl_name;

 sl_name  | sl_avail | sl_color | sl_len | sl_unit | sl_len_cm
----------+----------+----------+--------+---------+-----------
 sl1      |        5 | black    |     80 | cm      |        80
 sl2      |        6 | black    |    100 | cm      |       100
 sl7      |        6 | brown    |     60 | cm      |        60
 sl4      |        8 | black    |     40 | inch    |     101.6
 sl3      |       10 | black    |     35 | inch    |      88.9
 sl8      |       21 | brown    |     40 | inch    |     101.6
 sl5      |        4 | brown    |      1 | m       |       100
 sl6      |       20 | brown    |    0.9 | m       |        90
(8 rows)
```

```
SELECT * FROM shoelace_log;
```

```
 sl_name | sl_avail | log_who| log_when
---------+----------+--------+-------------------------------
 sl7     |        6 | Al     | Tue Oct 20 19:14:45 1998 MET DST
 sl3     |       10 | Al     | Tue Oct 20 19:25:16 1998 MET DST
 sl6     |       20 | Al     | Tue Oct 20 19:25:16 1998 MET DST
 sl8     |       21 | Al     | Tue Oct 20 19:25:16 1998 MET DST
(4 rows)
```

It's a long way from the one `INSERT ... SELECT` to these results. And the description of the query-tree transformation will be the last in this chapter. First, there is the parser's output:

```
INSERT INTO shoelace_ok
SELECT shoelace_arrive.arr_name, shoelace_arrive.arr_quant
  FROM shoelace_arrive shoelace_arrive, shoelace_ok shoelace_ok;
```

Now the first rule `shoelace_ok_ins` is applied and turns this into:

```
UPDATE shoelace
   SET sl_avail = shoelace.sl_avail + shoelace_arrive.arr_quant
  FROM shoelace_arrive shoelace_arrive, shoelace_ok shoelace_ok,
       shoelace_ok old, shoelace_ok new,
       shoelace shoelace
 WHERE shoelace.sl_name = shoelace_arrive.arr_name;
```

and throws away the original `INSERT` on `shoelace_ok`. This rewritten query is passed to the rule system again, and the second applied rule `shoelace_upd` produces:

```
UPDATE shoelace_data
   SET sl_name = shoelace.sl_name,
       sl_avail = shoelace.sl_avail + shoelace_arrive.arr_quant,
       sl_color = shoelace.sl_color,
       sl_len = shoelace.sl_len,
       sl_unit = shoelace.sl_unit
  FROM shoelace_arrive shoelace_arrive, shoelace_ok shoelace_ok,
       shoelace_ok old, shoelace_ok new,
       shoelace shoelace, shoelace old,
       shoelace new, shoelace_data shoelace_data
 WHERE shoelace.sl_name = shoelace_arrive.arr_name
   AND shoelace_data.sl_name = shoelace.sl_name;
```

Again it's an `INSTEAD` rule and the previous query tree is trashed. Note that this query still uses the view `shoelace`. But the rule system isn't finished with this step, so it continues and applies the `_RETURN` rule on it, and we get:

```
UPDATE shoelace_data
   SET sl_name = s.sl_name,
       sl_avail = s.sl_avail + shoelace_arrive.arr_quant,
       sl_color = s.sl_color,
       sl_len = s.sl_len,
       sl_unit = s.sl_unit
```

```
    FROM shoelace_arrive shoelace_arrive, shoelace_ok shoelace_ok,
         shoelace_ok old, shoelace_ok new,
         shoelace shoelace, shoelace old,
         shoelace new, shoelace_data shoelace_data,
         shoelace old, shoelace new,
         shoelace_data s, unit u
   WHERE s.sl_name = shoelace_arrive.arr_name
     AND shoelace_data.sl_name = s.sl_name;
```

Finally, the rule `log_shoelace` gets applied, producing the extra query tree:

```
INSERT INTO shoelace_log
SELECT s.sl_name,
       s.sl_avail + shoelace_arrive.arr_quant,
       current_user,
       current_timestamp
  FROM shoelace_arrive shoelace_arrive, shoelace_ok shoelace_ok,
       shoelace_ok old, shoelace_ok new,
       shoelace shoelace, shoelace old,
       shoelace new, shoelace_data shoelace_data,
       shoelace old, shoelace new,
       shoelace_data s, unit u,
       shoelace_data old, shoelace_data new
       shoelace_log shoelace_log
 WHERE s.sl_name = shoelace_arrive.arr_name
   AND shoelace_data.sl_name = s.sl_name
   AND (s.sl_avail + shoelace_arrive.arr_quant) <> s.sl_avail;
```

After that the rule system runs out of rules and returns the generated query trees.

So we end up with two final query trees that are equivalent to the SQL statements:

```
INSERT INTO shoelace_log
SELECT s.sl_name,
       s.sl_avail + shoelace_arrive.arr_quant,
       current_user,
       current_timestamp
  FROM shoelace_arrive shoelace_arrive, shoelace_data shoelace_data,
       shoelace_data s
 WHERE s.sl_name = shoelace_arrive.arr_name
   AND shoelace_data.sl_name = s.sl_name
   AND s.sl_avail + shoelace_arrive.arr_quant <> s.sl_avail;

UPDATE shoelace_data
   SET sl_avail = shoelace_data.sl_avail + shoelace_arrive.arr_quant
  FROM shoelace_arrive shoelace_arrive,
       shoelace_data shoelace_data,
       shoelace_data s
 WHERE s.sl_name = shoelace_arrive.sl_name
   AND shoelace_data.sl_name = s.sl_name;
```

The result is that data coming from one relation inserted into another, changed into updates on a third, changed into updating a fourth plus logging that final update in a fifth gets reduced into two queries.

There is a little detail that's a bit ugly. Looking at the two queries, it turns out that the `shoelace_data` relation appears twice in the range table where it could definitely be reduced to one. The planner does not handle it and so the execution plan for the rule systems output of the `INSERT` will be

```
Nested Loop
  -> Merge Join
        -> Seq Scan
              -> Sort
                    -> Seq Scan on s
        -> Seq Scan
              -> Sort
                    -> Seq Scan on shoelace_arrive
  -> Seq Scan on shoelace_data
```

while omitting the extra range table entry would result in a

```
Merge Join
  -> Seq Scan
        -> Sort
              -> Seq Scan on s
  -> Seq Scan
        -> Sort
              -> Seq Scan on shoelace_arrive
```

which produces exactly the same entries in the log table. Thus, the rule system caused one extra scan on the table `shoelace_data` that is absolutely not necessary. And the same redundant scan is done once more in the `UPDATE`. But it was a really hard job to make that all possible at all.

Now we make a final demonstration of the PostgreSQL rule system and its power. Say you add some shoelaces with extraordinary colors to your database:

```
INSERT INTO shoelace VALUES ('sl9', 0, 'pink', 35.0, 'inch', 0.0);
INSERT INTO shoelace VALUES ('sl10', 1000, 'magenta', 40.0, 'inch',
  0.0);
```

We would like to make a view to check which `shoelace` entries do not fit any shoe in color. The view for this is:

```
CREATE VIEW shoelace_mismatch AS
    SELECT * FROM shoelace WHERE NOT EXISTS
        (SELECT shoename FROM shoe WHERE slcolor = sl_color);
```

Its output is:

```
SELECT * FROM shoelace_mismatch;
```

sl_name	sl_avail	sl_color	sl_len	sl_unit	sl_len_cm
sl9	0	pink	35	inch	88.9
sl10	1000	magenta	40	inch	101.6

Now we want to set it up so that mismatching shoelaces that are not in stock are deleted from the database. To make it a little harder for PostgreSQL, we don't delete it directly. Instead we create one more view:

```
CREATE VIEW shoelace_can_delete AS
    SELECT * FROM shoelace_mismatch WHERE sl_avail = 0;
```

and do it this way:

```
DELETE FROM shoelace WHERE EXISTS
    (SELECT * FROM shoelace_can_delete
            WHERE sl_name = shoelace.sl_name);
```

Voilà:

```
SELECT * FROM shoelace;
```

sl_name	sl_avail	sl_color	sl_len	sl_unit	sl_len_cm
sl1	5	black	80	cm	80
sl2	6	black	100	cm	100
sl7	6	brown	60	cm	60
sl4	8	black	40	inch	101.6
sl3	10	black	35	inch	88.9
sl8	21	brown	40	inch	101.6
sl10	1000	magenta	40	inch	101.6
sl5	4	brown	1	m	100
sl6	20	brown	0.9	m	90

```
(9 rows)
```

A DELETE on a view, with a subquery qualification that in total uses 4 nesting/joined views, where one of them itself has a subquery qualification containing a view and where calculated view columns are used, gets rewritten into one single query tree that deletes the requested data from a real table.

There are probably only a few situations out in the real world where such a construct is necessary. But it makes you feel comfortable that it works.

41.5. Rules and Privileges

Due to rewriting of queries by the PostgreSQL rule system, other tables/views than those used in the original query get accessed. When update rules are used, this can include write access to tables.

Rewrite rules don't have a separate owner. The owner of a relation (table or view) is automatically the owner of the rewrite rules that are defined for it. The PostgreSQL rule system changes the behavior of the default access control system. Relations that are used due to rules get checked against the privileges of the rule owner, not the user invoking the rule. This means that users only need the required privileges for the tables/views that are explicitly named in their queries.

For example: A user has a list of phone numbers where some of them are private, the others are of interest for the assistant of the office. The user can construct the following:

```
CREATE TABLE phone_data (person text, phone text, private boolean);
```

```
CREATE VIEW phone_number AS
    SELECT person, CASE WHEN NOT private THEN phone END AS phone
    FROM phone_data;
GRANT SELECT ON phone_number TO assistant;
```

Nobody except that user (and the database superusers) can access the phone_data table. But because of the GRANT, the assistant can run a SELECT on the phone_number view. The rule system will rewrite the SELECT from phone_number into a SELECT from phone_data. Since the user is the owner of phone_number and therefore the owner of the rule, the read access to phone_data is now checked against the user's privileges and the query is permitted. The check for accessing phone_number is also performed, but this is done against the invoking user, so nobody but the user and the assistant can use it.

The privileges are checked rule by rule. So the assistant is for now the only one who can see the public phone numbers. But the assistant can set up another view and grant access to that to the public. Then, anyone can see the phone_number data through the assistant's view. What the assistant cannot do is to create a view that directly accesses phone_data. (Actually the assistant can, but it will not work since every access will be denied during the permission checks.) And as soon as the user notices that the assistant opened their phone_number view, the user can revoke the assistant's access. Immediately, any access to the assistant's view would fail.

One might think that this rule-by-rule checking is a security hole, but in fact it isn't. But if it did not work this way, the assistant could set up a table with the same columns as phone_number and copy the data to there once per day. Then it's the assistant's own data and the assistant can grant access to everyone they want. A GRANT command means, "I trust you". If someone you trust does the thing above, it's time to think it over and then use REVOKE.

Note that while views can be used to hide the contents of certain columns using the technique shown above, they cannot be used to reliably conceal the data in unseen rows unless the security_barrier flag has been set. For example, the following view is insecure:

```
CREATE VIEW phone_number AS
    SELECT person, phone FROM phone_data WHERE phone NOT LIKE '412%';
```

This view might seem secure, since the rule system will rewrite any SELECT from phone_number into a SELECT from phone_data and add the qualification that only entries where phone does not begin with 412 are wanted. But if the user can create their own functions, it is not difficult to convince the planner to execute the user-defined function prior to the NOT LIKE expression. For example:

```
CREATE FUNCTION tricky(text, text) RETURNS bool AS $$
BEGIN
    RAISE NOTICE '% => %', $1, $2;
    RETURN true;
END
$$ LANGUAGE plpgsql COST 0.0000000000000000000001;

SELECT * FROM phone_number WHERE tricky(person, phone);
```

Every person and phone number in the phone_data table will be printed as a NOTICE, because the planner will choose to execute the inexpensive tricky function before the more expensive NOT LIKE. Even if the user is prevented from defining new functions, built-in functions can be used in similar attacks. (For example, most casting functions include their input values in the error messages they produce.)

Similar considerations apply to update rules. In the examples of the previous section, the owner of the tables in the example database could grant the privileges SELECT, INSERT, UPDATE, and DELETE on the shoelace view to someone else, but only SELECT on shoelace_log. The rule action to write log entries will still be executed successfully, and that other user could see the log entries. But they could not create fake entries, nor could they manipulate or remove existing ones. In this case, there is no possibility of subverting the rules by convincing the planner to alter the order of operations, because the only rule which references shoelace_log is an unqualified INSERT. This might not be true in more complex scenarios.

When it is necessary for a view to provide row level security, the security_barrier attribute should be applied to the view. This prevents maliciously-chosen functions and operators from being passed values from rows until after the view has done its work. For example, if the view shown above had been created like this, it would be secure:

```
CREATE VIEW phone_number WITH (security_barrier) AS
    SELECT person, phone FROM phone_data WHERE phone NOT LIKE '412%';
```

Views created with the security_barrier may perform far worse than views created without this option. In general, there is no way to avoid this: the fastest possible plan must be rejected if it may compromise security. For this reason, this option is not enabled by default.

The query planner has more flexibility when dealing with functions that have no side effects. Such functions are referred to as LEAKPROOF, and include many simple, commonly used operators, such as many equality operators. The query planner can safely allow such functions to be evaluated at any point in the query execution process, since invoking them on rows invisible to the user will not leak any information about the unseen rows. Further, functions which do not take arguments or which are not passed any arguments from the security barrier view do not have to be marked as LEAKPROOF to be pushed down, as they never receive data from the view. In contrast, a function that might throw an error depending on the values received as arguments (such as one that throws an error in the event of overflow or division by zero) is not leak-proof, and could provide significant information about the unseen rows if applied before the security view's row filters.

It is important to understand that even a view created with the security_barrier option is intended to be secure only in the limited sense that the contents of the invisible tuples will not be passed to possibly-insecure functions. The user may well have other means of making inferences about the unseen data; for example, they can see the query plan using EXPLAIN, or measure the run time of queries against the view. A malicious attacker might be able to infer something about the amount of unseen data, or even gain some information about the data distribution or most common values (since these things may affect the run time of the plan; or even, since they are also reflected in the optimizer statistics, the choice of plan). If these types of "covert channel" attacks are of concern, it is probably unwise to grant any access to the data at all.

41.6. Rules and Command Status

The PostgreSQL server returns a command status string, such as INSERT 149592 1, for each command it receives. This is simple enough when there are no rules involved, but what happens when the query is rewritten by rules?

Rules affect the command status as follows:

- If there is no unconditional INSTEAD rule for the query, then the originally given query will be executed, and its command status will be returned as usual. (But note that if there were any conditional INSTEAD rules, the negation of their qualifications will have been added to the original query. This might reduce the number of rows it processes, and if so the reported status will be affected.)

- If there is any unconditional INSTEAD rule for the query, then the original query will not be executed at all. In this case, the server will return the command status for the last query that was inserted by an

INSTEAD rule (conditional or unconditional) and is of the same command type (INSERT, UPDATE, or DELETE) as the original query. If no query meeting those requirements is added by any rule, then the returned command status shows the original query type and zeroes for the row-count and OID fields.

The programmer can ensure that any desired INSTEAD rule is the one that sets the command status in the second case, by giving it the alphabetically last rule name among the active rules, so that it gets applied last.

41.7. Rules Versus Triggers

Many things that can be done using triggers can also be implemented using the PostgreSQL rule system. One of the things that cannot be implemented by rules are some kinds of constraints, especially foreign keys. It is possible to place a qualified rule that rewrites a command to NOTHING if the value of a column does not appear in another table. But then the data is silently thrown away and that's not a good idea. If checks for valid values are required, and in the case of an invalid value an error message should be generated, it must be done by a trigger.

In this chapter, we focused on using rules to update views. All of the update rule examples in this chapter can also be implemented using INSTEAD OF triggers on the views. Writing such triggers is often easier than writing rules, particularly if complex logic is required to perform the update.

For the things that can be implemented by both, which is best depends on the usage of the database. A trigger is fired once for each affected row. A rule modifies the query or generates an additional query. So if many rows are affected in one statement, a rule issuing one extra command is likely to be faster than a trigger that is called for every single row and must re-determine what to do many times. However, the trigger approach is conceptually far simpler than the rule approach, and is easier for novices to get right.

Here we show an example of how the choice of rules versus triggers plays out in one situation. There are two tables:

```
CREATE TABLE computer (
    hostname        text,       -- indexed
    manufacturer    text        -- indexed
);

CREATE TABLE software (
    software        text,       -- indexed
    hostname        text        -- indexed
);
```

Both tables have many thousands of rows and the indexes on hostname are unique. The rule or trigger should implement a constraint that deletes rows from software that reference a deleted computer. The trigger would use this command:

```
DELETE FROM software WHERE hostname = $1;
```

Since the trigger is called for each individual row deleted from computer, it can prepare and save the plan for this command and pass the hostname value in the parameter. The rule would be written as:

```
CREATE RULE computer_del AS ON DELETE TO computer
    DO DELETE FROM software WHERE hostname = OLD.hostname;
```

Now we look at different types of deletes. In the case of a:

```
DELETE FROM computer WHERE hostname = 'mypc.local.net';
```

the table `computer` is scanned by index (fast), and the command issued by the trigger would also use an index scan (also fast). The extra command from the rule would be:

```
DELETE FROM software WHERE computer.hostname = 'mypc.local.net'
                      AND software.hostname = computer.hostname;
```

Since there are appropriate indexes set up, the planner will create a plan of

```
Nestloop
  ->  Index Scan using comp_hostidx on computer
  ->  Index Scan using soft_hostidx on software
```

So there would be not that much difference in speed between the trigger and the rule implementation.

With the next delete we want to get rid of all the 2000 computers where the `hostname` starts with `old`. There are two possible commands to do that. One is:

```
DELETE FROM computer WHERE hostname >= 'old'
                      AND hostname <  'ole'
```

The command added by the rule will be:

```
DELETE FROM software WHERE computer.hostname >= 'old' AND
 computer.hostname < 'ole'
                      AND software.hostname = computer.hostname;
```

with the plan

```
Hash Join
  ->  Seq Scan on software
  ->  Hash
    ->  Index Scan using comp_hostidx on computer
```

The other possible command is:

```
DELETE FROM computer WHERE hostname ~ '^old';
```

which results in the following executing plan for the command added by the rule:

```
Nestloop
  ->  Index Scan using comp_hostidx on computer
  ->  Index Scan using soft_hostidx on software
```

This shows, that the planner does not realize that the qualification for `hostname` in `computer` could also be used for an index scan on `software` when there are multiple qualification expressions combined with AND, which is what it does in the regular-expression version of the command. The trigger will get invoked once for each of the 2000 old computers that have to be deleted, and that will result in one index scan over `computer` and 2000 index scans over `software`. The rule implementation will do it with two commands that use indexes. And it depends on the overall size of the table `software` whether the rule will still be faster in the sequential scan situation. 2000 command executions from the trigger over the SPI manager take some time, even if all the index blocks will soon be in the cache.

The last command we look at is:

```
DELETE FROM computer WHERE manufacturer = 'bim';
```

Again this could result in many rows to be deleted from `computer`. So the trigger will again run many commands through the executor. The command generated by the rule will be:

```
DELETE FROM software WHERE computer.manufacturer = 'bim'
                     AND software.hostname = computer.hostname;
```

The plan for that command will again be the nested loop over two index scans, only using a different index on `computer`:

```
Nestloop
   ->  Index Scan using comp_manufidx on computer
   ->  Index Scan using soft_hostidx on software
```

In any of these cases, the extra commands from the rule system will be more or less independent from the number of affected rows in a command.

The summary is, rules will only be significantly slower than triggers if their actions result in large and badly qualified joins, a situation where the planner fails.

Chapter 42. Procedural Languages

PostgreSQL allows user-defined functions to be written in other languages besides SQL and C. These other languages are generically called *procedural languages* (PLs). For a function written in a procedural language, the database server has no built-in knowledge about how to interpret the function's source text. Instead, the task is passed to a special handler that knows the details of the language. The handler could either do all the work of parsing, syntax analysis, execution, etc. itself, or it could serve as "glue" between PostgreSQL and an existing implementation of a programming language. The handler itself is a C language function compiled into a shared object and loaded on demand, just like any other C function.

There are currently four procedural languages available in the standard PostgreSQL distribution: PL/pgSQL (Chapter 43), PL/Tcl (Chapter 44), PL/Perl (Chapter 45), and PL/Python (Chapter 46). There are additional procedural languages available that are not included in the core distribution. Appendix H has information about finding them. In addition other languages can be defined by users; the basics of developing a new procedural language are covered in Chapter 56.

42.1. Installing Procedural Languages

A procedural language must be "installed" into each database where it is to be used. But procedural languages installed in the database `template1` are automatically available in all subsequently created databases, since their entries in `template1` will be copied by `CREATE DATABASE`. So the database administrator can decide which languages are available in which databases and can make some languages available by default if desired.

For the languages supplied with the standard distribution, it is only necessary to execute `CREATE EXTENSION language_name` to install the language into the current database. The manual procedure described below is only recommended for installing languages that have not been packaged as extensions.

Manual Procedural Language Installation

A procedural language is installed in a database in five steps, which must be carried out by a database superuser. In most cases the required SQL commands should be packaged as the installation script of an "extension", so that `CREATE EXTENSION` can be used to execute them.

1. The shared object for the language handler must be compiled and installed into an appropriate library directory. This works in the same way as building and installing modules with regular user-defined C functions does; see Section 38.10.5. Often, the language handler will depend on an external library that provides the actual programming language engine; if so, that must be installed as well.

2. The handler must be declared with the command

   ```
   CREATE FUNCTION handler_function_name()
       RETURNS language_handler
       AS 'path-to-shared-object'
       LANGUAGE C;
   ```

   The special return type of `language_handler` tells the database system that this function does not return one of the defined SQL data types and is not directly usable in SQL statements.

3. (Optional) Optionally, the language handler can provide an "inline" handler function that executes anonymous code blocks (DO commands) written in this language. If an inline handler function is provided by the language, declare it with a command like

---

```
CREATE FUNCTION inline_function_name(internal)
    RETURNS void
    AS 'path-to-shared-object'
    LANGUAGE C;
```

4. (Optional) Optionally, the language handler can provide a "validator" function that checks a function definition for correctness without actually executing it. The validator function is called by CREATE FUNCTION if it exists. If a validator function is provided by the language, declare it with a command like

```
CREATE FUNCTION validator_function_name(oid)
    RETURNS void
    AS 'path-to-shared-object'
    LANGUAGE C STRICT;
```

5. Finally, the PL must be declared with the command

```
CREATE [TRUSTED] [PROCEDURAL] LANGUAGE language-name
    HANDLER handler_function_name
    [INLINE inline_function_name]
    [VALIDATOR validator_function_name] ;
```

The optional key word TRUSTED specifies that the language does not grant access to data that the user would not otherwise have. Trusted languages are designed for ordinary database users (those without superuser privilege) and allows them to safely create functions and procedures. Since PL functions are executed inside the database server, the TRUSTED flag should only be given for languages that do not allow access to database server internals or the file system. The languages PL/pgSQL, PL/Tcl, and PL/Perl are considered trusted; the languages PL/TclU, PL/PerlU, and PL/PythonU are designed to provide unlimited functionality and should *not* be marked trusted.

Example 42.1 shows how the manual installation procedure would work with the language PL/Perl.

Example 42.1. Manual Installation of PL/Perl

The following command tells the database server where to find the shared object for the PL/Perl language's call handler function:

```
CREATE FUNCTION plperl_call_handler() RETURNS language_handler AS
    '$libdir/plperl' LANGUAGE C;
```

PL/Perl has an inline handler function and a validator function, so we declare those too:

```
CREATE FUNCTION plperl_inline_handler(internal) RETURNS void AS
    '$libdir/plperl' LANGUAGE C;
```

```
CREATE FUNCTION plperl_validator(oid) RETURNS void AS
    '$libdir/plperl' LANGUAGE C STRICT;
```

The command:

```
CREATE TRUSTED PROCEDURAL LANGUAGE plperl
    HANDLER plperl_call_handler
    INLINE plperl_inline_handler
    VALIDATOR plperl_validator;
```

then defines that the previously declared functions should be invoked for functions and procedures where the language attribute is plperl.

In a default PostgreSQL installation, the handler for the PL/pgSQL language is built and installed into the "library" directory; furthermore, the PL/pgSQL language itself is installed in all databases. If Tcl support is configured in, the handlers for PL/Tcl and PL/TclU are built and installed in the library directory, but the language itself is not installed in any database by default. Likewise, the PL/Perl and PL/PerlU handlers are built and installed if Perl support is configured, and the PL/PythonU handler is installed if Python support is configured, but these languages are not installed by default.

Chapter 43. PL/pgSQL - SQL Procedural Language

43.1. Overview

PL/pgSQL is a loadable procedural language for the PostgreSQL database system. The design goals of PL/pgSQL were to create a loadable procedural language that

- can be used to create functions and triggers,

- adds control structures to the SQL language,

- can perform complex computations,

- inherits all user-defined types, functions, and operators,

- can be defined to be trusted by the server,

- is easy to use.

Functions created with PL/pgSQL can be used anywhere that built-in functions could be used. For example, it is possible to create complex conditional computation functions and later use them to define operators or use them in index expressions.

In PostgreSQL 9.0 and later, PL/pgSQL is installed by default. However it is still a loadable module, so especially security-conscious administrators could choose to remove it.

43.1.1. Advantages of Using PL/pgSQL

SQL is the language PostgreSQL and most other relational databases use as query language. It's portable and easy to learn. But every SQL statement must be executed individually by the database server.

That means that your client application must send each query to the database server, wait for it to be processed, receive and process the results, do some computation, then send further queries to the server. All this incurs interprocess communication and will also incur network overhead if your client is on a different machine than the database server.

With PL/pgSQL you can group a block of computation and a series of queries *inside* the database server, thus having the power of a procedural language and the ease of use of SQL, but with considerable savings of client/server communication overhead.

- Extra round trips between client and server are eliminated

- Intermediate results that the client does not need do not have to be marshaled or transferred between server and client

- Multiple rounds of query parsing can be avoided

This can result in a considerable performance increase as compared to an application that does not use stored functions.

Also, with PL/pgSQL you can use all the data types, operators and functions of SQL.

43.1.2. Supported Argument and Result Data Types

Functions written in PL/pgSQL can accept as arguments any scalar or array data type supported by the server, and they can return a result of any of these types. They can also accept or return any composite type (row type) specified by name. It is also possible to declare a PL/pgSQL function as accepting `record`, which means that any composite type will do as input, or as returning `record`, which means that the result is a row type whose columns are determined by specification in the calling query, as discussed in Section 7.2.1.4.

PL/pgSQL functions can be declared to accept a variable number of arguments by using the `VARIADIC` marker. This works exactly the same way as for SQL functions, as discussed in Section 38.5.5.

PL/pgSQL functions can also be declared to accept and return the polymorphic types `anyelement`, `anyarray`, `anynonarray`, `anyenum`, and `anyrange`. The actual data types handled by a polymorphic function can vary from call to call, as discussed in Section 38.2.5. An example is shown in Section 43.3.1.

PL/pgSQL functions can also be declared to return a "set" (or table) of any data type that can be returned as a single instance. Such a function generates its output by executing `RETURN NEXT` for each desired element of the result set, or by using `RETURN QUERY` to output the result of evaluating a query.

Finally, a PL/pgSQL function can be declared to return `void` if it has no useful return value. (Alternatively, it could be written as a procedure in that case.)

PL/pgSQL functions can also be declared with output parameters in place of an explicit specification of the return type. This does not add any fundamental capability to the language, but it is often convenient, especially for returning multiple values. The `RETURNS TABLE` notation can also be used in place of `RETURNS SETOF`.

Specific examples appear in Section 43.3.1 and Section 43.6.1.

43.2. Structure of PL/pgSQL

Functions written in PL/pgSQL are defined to the server by executing CREATE FUNCTION commands. Such a command would normally look like, say,

```
CREATE FUNCTION somefunc(integer, text) RETURNS integer
AS 'function body text'
LANGUAGE plpgsql;
```

The function body is simply a string literal so far as `CREATE FUNCTION` is concerned. It is often helpful to use dollar quoting (see Section 4.1.2.4) to write the function body, rather than the normal single quote syntax. Without dollar quoting, any single quotes or backslashes in the function body must be escaped by doubling them. Almost all the examples in this chapter use dollar-quoted literals for their function bodies.

PL/pgSQL is a block-structured language. The complete text of a function body must be a *block*. A block is defined as:

```
[ <<label>> ]
[ DECLARE
    declarations ]
BEGIN
```

```
    statements
END [ label ];
```

Each declaration and each statement within a block is terminated by a semicolon. A block that appears within another block must have a semicolon after END, as shown above; however the final END that concludes a function body does not require a semicolon.

Tip

A common mistake is to write a semicolon immediately after BEGIN. This is incorrect and will result in a syntax error.

A *label* is only needed if you want to identify the block for use in an EXIT statement, or to qualify the names of the variables declared in the block. If a label is given after END, it must match the label at the block's beginning.

All key words are case-insensitive. Identifiers are implicitly converted to lower case unless double-quoted, just as they are in ordinary SQL commands.

Comments work the same way in PL/pgSQL code as in ordinary SQL. A double dash (--) starts a comment that extends to the end of the line. A /* starts a block comment that extends to the matching occurrence of */. Block comments nest.

Any statement in the statement section of a block can be a *subblock*. Subblocks can be used for logical grouping or to localize variables to a small group of statements. Variables declared in a subblock mask any similarly-named variables of outer blocks for the duration of the subblock; but you can access the outer variables anyway if you qualify their names with their block's label. For example:

```
CREATE FUNCTION somefunc() RETURNS integer AS $$
<< outerblock >>
DECLARE
    quantity integer := 30;
BEGIN
    RAISE NOTICE 'Quantity here is %', quantity;  -- Prints 30
    quantity := 50;
    --
    -- Create a subblock
    --
    DECLARE
        quantity integer := 80;
    BEGIN
        RAISE NOTICE 'Quantity here is %', quantity;  -- Prints 80
        RAISE NOTICE 'Outer quantity here is %', outerblock.quantity;
  -- Prints 50
    END;

    RAISE NOTICE 'Quantity here is %', quantity;  -- Prints 50

    RETURN quantity;
END;
$$ LANGUAGE plpgsql;
```

> **Note**
>
> There is actually a hidden "outer block" surrounding the body of any PL/pgSQL function. This block provides the declarations of the function's parameters (if any), as well as some special variables such as FOUND (see Section 43.5.5). The outer block is labeled with the function's name, meaning that parameters and special variables can be qualified with the function's name.

It is important not to confuse the use of BEGIN/END for grouping statements in PL/pgSQL with the similarly-named SQL commands for transaction control. PL/pgSQL's BEGIN/END are only for grouping; they do not start or end a transaction. See Section 43.8 for information on managing transactions in PL/pgSQL. Also, a block containing an EXCEPTION clause effectively forms a subtransaction that can be rolled back without affecting the outer transaction. For more about that see Section 43.6.8.

43.3. Declarations

All variables used in a block must be declared in the declarations section of the block. (The only exceptions are that the loop variable of a FOR loop iterating over a range of integer values is automatically declared as an integer variable, and likewise the loop variable of a FOR loop iterating over a cursor's result is automatically declared as a record variable.)

PL/pgSQL variables can have any SQL data type, such as integer, varchar, and char.

Here are some examples of variable declarations:

```
user_id integer;
quantity numeric(5);
url varchar;
myrow tablename%ROWTYPE;
myfield tablename.columnname%TYPE;
arow RECORD;
```

The general syntax of a variable declaration is:

```
name [ CONSTANT ] type [ COLLATE collation_name ] [ NOT NULL ]
    [ { DEFAULT | := | = } expression ];
```

The DEFAULT clause, if given, specifies the initial value assigned to the variable when the block is entered. If the DEFAULT clause is not given then the variable is initialized to the SQL null value. The CONSTANT option prevents the variable from being assigned to after initialization, so that its value will remain constant for the duration of the block. The COLLATE option specifies a collation to use for the variable (see Section 43.3.6). If NOT NULL is specified, an assignment of a null value results in a run-time error. All variables declared as NOT NULL must have a nonnull default value specified. Equal (=) can be used instead of PL/SQL-compliant :=.

A variable's default value is evaluated and assigned to the variable each time the block is entered (not just once per function call). So, for example, assigning now() to a variable of type timestamp causes the variable to have the time of the current function call, not the time when the function was precompiled.

Examples:

```
quantity integer DEFAULT 32;
url varchar := 'http://mysite.com';
user_id CONSTANT integer := 10;
```

43.3.1. Declaring Function Parameters

Parameters passed to functions are named with the identifiers $1, $2, etc. Optionally, aliases can be declared for $n parameter names for increased readability. Either the alias or the numeric identifier can then be used to refer to the parameter value.

There are two ways to create an alias. The preferred way is to give a name to the parameter in the CREATE FUNCTION command, for example:

```
CREATE FUNCTION sales_tax(subtotal real) RETURNS real AS $$
BEGIN
    RETURN subtotal * 0.06;
END;
$$ LANGUAGE plpgsql;
```

The other way is to explicitly declare an alias, using the declaration syntax

```
name ALIAS FOR $n;
```

The same example in this style looks like:

```
CREATE FUNCTION sales_tax(real) RETURNS real AS $$
DECLARE
    subtotal ALIAS FOR $1;
BEGIN
    RETURN subtotal * 0.06;
END;
$$ LANGUAGE plpgsql;
```

Note

These two examples are not perfectly equivalent. In the first case, subtotal could be referenced as sales_tax.subtotal, but in the second case it could not. (Had we attached a label to the inner block, subtotal could be qualified with that label, instead.)

Some more examples:

```
CREATE FUNCTION instr(varchar, integer) RETURNS integer AS $$
DECLARE
    v_string ALIAS FOR $1;
    index ALIAS FOR $2;
BEGIN
    -- some computations using v_string and index here
END;
$$ LANGUAGE plpgsql;
```

```
CREATE FUNCTION concat_selected_fields(in_t sometablename) RETURNS
 text AS $$
BEGIN
    RETURN in_t.f1 || in_t.f3 || in_t.f5 || in_t.f7;
END;
$$ LANGUAGE plpgsql;
```

When a PL/pgSQL function is declared with output parameters, the output parameters are given n names and optional aliases in just the same way as the normal input parameters. An output parameter is effectively a variable that starts out NULL; it should be assigned to during the execution of the function. The final value of the parameter is what is returned. For instance, the sales-tax example could also be done this way:

```
CREATE FUNCTION sales_tax(subtotal real, OUT tax real) AS $$
BEGIN
    tax := subtotal * 0.06;
END;
$$ LANGUAGE plpgsql;
```

Notice that we omitted RETURNS real — we could have included it, but it would be redundant.

Output parameters are most useful when returning multiple values. A trivial example is:

```
CREATE FUNCTION sum_n_product(x int, y int, OUT sum int, OUT prod int)
 AS $$
BEGIN
    sum := x + y;
    prod := x * y;
END;
$$ LANGUAGE plpgsql;
```

As discussed in Section 38.5.4, this effectively creates an anonymous record type for the function's results. If a RETURNS clause is given, it must say RETURNS record.

Another way to declare a PL/pgSQL function is with RETURNS TABLE, for example:

```
CREATE FUNCTION extended_sales(p_itemno int)
RETURNS TABLE(quantity int, total numeric) AS $$
BEGIN
    RETURN QUERY SELECT s.quantity, s.quantity * s.price FROM sales AS
 s
                WHERE s.itemno = p_itemno;
END;
$$ LANGUAGE plpgsql;
```

This is exactly equivalent to declaring one or more OUT parameters and specifying RETURNS SETOF *sometype*.

When the return type of a PL/pgSQL function is declared as a polymorphic type (anyelement, anyarray, anynonarray, anyenum, or anyrange), a special parameter $0 is created. Its data type is the actual return type of the function, as deduced from the actual input types (see Section 38.2.5). This allows the function to access its actual return type as shown in Section 43.3.3. $0 is initialized to null and can be modified by the function, so it can be used to hold the return value if desired, though that is not required. $0 can also be given an alias. For example, this function works on any data type that has a + operator:

```
CREATE FUNCTION add_three_values(v1 anyelement, v2 anyelement, v3
 anyelement)
RETURNS anyelement AS $$
DECLARE
    result ALIAS FOR $0;
BEGIN
    result := v1 + v2 + v3;
    RETURN result;
END;
$$ LANGUAGE plpgsql;
```

The same effect can be obtained by declaring one or more output parameters as polymorphic types. In this case the special $0 parameter is not used; the output parameters themselves serve the same purpose. For example:

```
CREATE FUNCTION add_three_values(v1 anyelement, v2 anyelement, v3
 anyelement,
                                  OUT sum anyelement)
AS $$
BEGIN
    sum := v1 + v2 + v3;
END;
$$ LANGUAGE plpgsql;
```

43.3.2. ALIAS

```
newname ALIAS FOR oldname;
```

The ALIAS syntax is more general than is suggested in the previous section: you can declare an alias for any variable, not just function parameters. The main practical use for this is to assign a different name for variables with predetermined names, such as NEW or OLD within a trigger function.

Examples:

```
DECLARE
  prior ALIAS FOR old;
  updated ALIAS FOR new;
```

Since ALIAS creates two different ways to name the same object, unrestricted use can be confusing. It's best to use it only for the purpose of overriding predetermined names.

43.3.3. Copying Types

```
variable%TYPE
```

%TYPE provides the data type of a variable or table column. You can use this to declare variables that will hold database values. For example, let's say you have a column named user_id in your users table. To declare a variable with the same data type as users.user_id you write:

```
user_id users.user_id%TYPE;
```

By using %TYPE you don't need to know the data type of the structure you are referencing, and most importantly, if the data type of the referenced item changes in the future (for instance: you change the type of user_id from integer to real), you might not need to change your function definition.

%TYPE is particularly valuable in polymorphic functions, since the data types needed for internal variables can change from one call to the next. Appropriate variables can be created by applying %TYPE to the function's arguments or result placeholders.

43.3.4. Row Types

```
name table_name%ROWTYPE;
name composite_type_name;
```

A variable of a composite type is called a *row* variable (or *row-type* variable). Such a variable can hold a whole row of a SELECT or FOR query result, so long as that query's column set matches the declared type of the variable. The individual fields of the row value are accessed using the usual dot notation, for example rowvar.field.

A row variable can be declared to have the same type as the rows of an existing table or view, by using the *table_name*%ROWTYPE notation; or it can be declared by giving a composite type's name. (Since every table has an associated composite type of the same name, it actually does not matter in PostgreSQL whether you write %ROWTYPE or not. But the form with %ROWTYPE is more portable.)

Parameters to a function can be composite types (complete table rows). In that case, the corresponding identifier $n will be a row variable, and fields can be selected from it, for example $1.user_id.

Here is an example of using composite types. table1 and table2 are existing tables having at least the mentioned fields:

```
CREATE FUNCTION merge_fields(t_row table1) RETURNS text AS $$
DECLARE
    t2_row table2%ROWTYPE;
BEGIN
    SELECT * INTO t2_row FROM table2 WHERE ... ;
    RETURN t_row.f1 || t2_row.f3 || t_row.f5 || t2_row.f7;
END;
$$ LANGUAGE plpgsql;

SELECT merge_fields(t.*) FROM table1 t WHERE ... ;
```

43.3.5. Record Types

```
name RECORD;
```

Record variables are similar to row-type variables, but they have no predefined structure. They take on the actual row structure of the row they are assigned during a SELECT or FOR command. The substructure of a record variable can change each time it is assigned to. A consequence of this is that until a record variable is first assigned to, it has no substructure, and any attempt to access a field in it will draw a run-time error.

Note that RECORD is not a true data type, only a placeholder. One should also realize that when a PL/pgSQL function is declared to return type record, this is not quite the same concept as a record variable, even though such a function might use a record variable to hold its result. In both cases the actual row structure is unknown when the function is written, but for a function returning record the actual structure is determined when the calling query is parsed, whereas a record variable can change its row structure on-the-fly.

43.3.6. Collation of PL/pgSQL Variables

When a PL/pgSQL function has one or more parameters of collatable data types, a collation is identified for each function call depending on the collations assigned to the actual arguments, as described in Section 23.2. If a collation is successfully identified (i.e., there are no conflicts of implicit collations among the arguments) then all the collatable parameters are treated as having that collation implicitly. This will affect the behavior of collation-sensitive operations within the function. For example, consider

```
CREATE FUNCTION less_than(a text, b text) RETURNS boolean AS $$
BEGIN
    RETURN a < b;
END;
$$ LANGUAGE plpgsql;

SELECT less_than(text_field_1, text_field_2) FROM table1;
SELECT less_than(text_field_1, text_field_2 COLLATE "C") FROM table1;
```

The first use of less_than will use the common collation of text_field_1 and text_field_2 for the comparison, while the second use will use C collation.

Furthermore, the identified collation is also assumed as the collation of any local variables that are of collatable types. Thus this function would not work any differently if it were written as

```
CREATE FUNCTION less_than(a text, b text) RETURNS boolean AS $$
DECLARE
    local_a text := a;
    local_b text := b;
BEGIN
    RETURN local_a < local_b;
END;
$$ LANGUAGE plpgsql;
```

If there are no parameters of collatable data types, or no common collation can be identified for them, then parameters and local variables use the default collation of their data type (which is usually the database's default collation, but could be different for variables of domain types).

A local variable of a collatable data type can have a different collation associated with it by including the COLLATE option in its declaration, for example

```
DECLARE
    local_a text COLLATE "en_US";
```

This option overrides the collation that would otherwise be given to the variable according to the rules above.

Also, of course explicit COLLATE clauses can be written inside a function if it is desired to force a particular collation to be used in a particular operation. For example,

```
CREATE FUNCTION less_than_c(a text, b text) RETURNS boolean AS $$
BEGIN
    RETURN a < b COLLATE "C";
END;
$$ LANGUAGE plpgsql;
```

This overrides the collations associated with the table columns, parameters, or local variables used in the expression, just as would happen in a plain SQL command.

43.4. Expressions

All expressions used in PL/pgSQL statements are processed using the server's main SQL executor. For example, when you write a PL/pgSQL statement like

```
IF expression THEN ...
```

PL/pgSQL will evaluate the expression by feeding a query like

```
SELECT expression
```

to the main SQL engine. While forming the SELECT command, any occurrences of PL/pgSQL variable names are replaced by parameters, as discussed in detail in Section 43.11.1. This allows the query plan for the SELECT to be prepared just once and then reused for subsequent evaluations with different values of the variables. Thus, what really happens on first use of an expression is essentially a PREPARE command. For example, if we have declared two integer variables x and y, and we write

```
IF x < y THEN ...
```

what happens behind the scenes is equivalent to

```
PREPARE statement_name(integer, integer) AS SELECT $1 < $2;
```

and then this prepared statement is EXECUTEd for each execution of the IF statement, with the current values of the PL/pgSQL variables supplied as parameter values. Normally these details are not important to a PL/pgSQL user, but they are useful to know when trying to diagnose a problem. More information appears in Section 43.11.2.

43.5. Basic Statements

In this section and the following ones, we describe all the statement types that are explicitly understood by PL/pgSQL. Anything not recognized as one of these statement types is presumed to be an SQL command and is sent to the main database engine to execute, as described in Section 43.5.2 and Section 43.5.3.

43.5.1. Assignment

An assignment of a value to a PL/pgSQL variable is written as:

```
variable { := | = } expression;
```

As explained previously, the expression in such a statement is evaluated by means of an SQL SELECT command sent to the main database engine. The expression must yield a single value (possibly a row value, if the variable is a row or record variable). The target variable can be a simple variable (optionally qualified with a block name), a field of a row or record variable, or an element of an array that is a simple variable or field. Equal (=) can be used instead of PL/SQL-compliant :=.

If the expression's result data type doesn't match the variable's data type, the value will be coerced as though by an assignment cast (see Section 10.4). If no assignment cast is known for the pair of data types involved, the PL/pgSQL interpreter will attempt to convert the result value textually, that is by applying the result type's output function followed by the variable type's input function. Note that this could result in run-time errors generated by the input function, if the string form of the result value is not acceptable to the input function.

Examples:

```
tax := subtotal * 0.06;
my_record.user_id := 20;
```

43.5.2. Executing a Command With No Result

For any SQL command that does not return rows, for example INSERT without a RETURNING clause, you can execute the command within a PL/pgSQL function just by writing the command.

Any PL/pgSQL variable name appearing in the command text is treated as a parameter, and then the current value of the variable is provided as the parameter value at run time. This is exactly like the processing described earlier for expressions; for details see Section 43.11.1.

When executing a SQL command in this way, PL/pgSQL may cache and re-use the execution plan for the command, as discussed in Section 43.11.2.

Sometimes it is useful to evaluate an expression or SELECT query but discard the result, for example when calling a function that has side-effects but no useful result value. To do this in PL/pgSQL, use the PERFORM statement:

```
PERFORM query;
```

This executes query and discards the result. Write the query the same way you would write an SQL SELECT command, but replace the initial keyword SELECT with PERFORM. For WITH queries, use PER-FORM and then place the query in parentheses. (In this case, the query can only return one row.) PL/pgSQL variables will be substituted into the query just as for commands that return no result, and the plan is cached in the same way. Also, the special variable FOUND is set to true if the query produced at least one row, or false if it produced no rows (see Section 43.5.5).

> ### Note
>
> One might expect that writing SELECT directly would accomplish this result, but at present the only accepted way to do it is PERFORM. A SQL command that can return rows, such as SELECT, will be rejected as an error unless it has an INTO clause as discussed in the next section.

An example:

```
PERFORM create_mv('cs_session_page_requests_mv', my_query);
```

43.5.3. Executing a Query with a Single-row Result

The result of a SQL command yielding a single row (possibly of multiple columns) can be assigned to a record variable, row-type variable, or list of scalar variables. This is done by writing the base SQL command and adding an INTO clause. For example,

```
SELECT select_expressions INTO [STRICT] target FROM ...;
INSERT ... RETURNING expressions INTO [STRICT] target;
UPDATE ... RETURNING expressions INTO [STRICT] target;
DELETE ... RETURNING expressions INTO [STRICT] target;
```

where *target* can be a record variable, a row variable, or a comma-separated list of simple variables and record/row fields. PL/pgSQL variables will be substituted into the rest of the query, and the plan is cached, just as described above for commands that do not return rows. This works for SELECT, INSERT/UP-DATE/DELETE with RETURNING, and utility commands that return row-set results (such as EXPLAIN). Except for the INTO clause, the SQL command is the same as it would be written outside PL/pgSQL.

Tip

Note that this interpretation of SELECT with INTO is quite different from PostgreSQL's regular SELECT INTO command, wherein the INTO target is a newly created table. If you want to create a table from a SELECT result inside a PL/pgSQL function, use the syntax CREATE TABLE ... AS SELECT.

If a row or a variable list is used as target, the query's result columns must exactly match the structure of the target as to number and data types, or else a run-time error occurs. When a record variable is the target, it automatically configures itself to the row type of the query result columns.

The INTO clause can appear almost anywhere in the SQL command. Customarily it is written either just before or just after the list of *select_expressions* in a SELECT command, or at the end of the command for other command types. It is recommended that you follow this convention in case the PL/pgSQL parser becomes stricter in future versions.

If STRICT is not specified in the INTO clause, then *target* will be set to the first row returned by the query, or to nulls if the query returned no rows. (Note that "the first row" is not well-defined unless you've used ORDER BY.) Any result rows after the first row are discarded. You can check the special FOUND variable (see Section 43.5.5) to determine whether a row was returned:

```
SELECT * INTO myrec FROM emp WHERE empname = myname;
IF NOT FOUND THEN
    RAISE EXCEPTION 'employee % not found', myname;
END IF;
```

If the STRICT option is specified, the query must return exactly one row or a run-time error will be reported, either NO_DATA_FOUND (no rows) or TOO_MANY_ROWS (more than one row). You can use an exception block if you wish to catch the error, for example:

```
BEGIN
    SELECT * INTO STRICT myrec FROM emp WHERE empname = myname;
    EXCEPTION
        WHEN NO_DATA_FOUND THEN
            RAISE EXCEPTION 'employee % not found', myname;
        WHEN TOO_MANY_ROWS THEN
            RAISE EXCEPTION 'employee % not unique', myname;
END;
```

Successful execution of a command with STRICT always sets FOUND to true.

For INSERT/UPDATE/DELETE with RETURNING, PL/pgSQL reports an error for more than one returned row, even when STRICT is not specified. This is because there is no option such as ORDER BY with which to determine which affected row should be returned.

If print_strict_params is enabled for the function, then when an error is thrown because the requirements of STRICT are not met, the DETAIL part of the error message will include information about the parameters passed to the query. You can change the print_strict_params setting for all functions by setting plpgsql.print_strict_params, though only subsequent function compilations will be affected. You can also enable it on a per-function basis by using a compiler option, for example:

```
CREATE FUNCTION get_userid(username text) RETURNS int
AS $$
#print_strict_params on
DECLARE
userid int;
BEGIN
    SELECT users.userid INTO STRICT userid
        FROM users WHERE users.username = get_userid.username;
    RETURN userid;
END
$$ LANGUAGE plpgsql;
```

On failure, this function might produce an error message such as

```
ERROR:  query returned no rows
DETAIL:  parameters: $1 = 'nosuchuser'
CONTEXT:  PL/pgSQL function get_userid(text) line 6 at SQL statement
```

Note

The STRICT option matches the behavior of Oracle PL/SQL's SELECT INTO and related statements.

To handle cases where you need to process multiple result rows from a SQL query, see Section 43.6.6.

43.5.4. Executing Dynamic Commands

Oftentimes you will want to generate dynamic commands inside your PL/pgSQL functions, that is, commands that will involve different tables or different data types each time they are executed. PL/pgSQL's normal attempts to cache plans for commands (as discussed in Section 43.11.2) will not work in such scenarios. To handle this sort of problem, the EXECUTE statement is provided:

```
EXECUTE command-string [ INTO [STRICT] target ] [ USING expression
 [, ... ] ];
```

where *command-string* is an expression yielding a string (of type text) containing the command to be executed. The optional *target* is a record variable, a row variable, or a comma-separated list of simple variables and record/row fields, into which the results of the command will be stored. The optional USING expressions supply values to be inserted into the command.

No substitution of PL/pgSQL variables is done on the computed command string. Any required variable values must be inserted in the command string as it is constructed; or you can use parameters as described below.

Also, there is no plan caching for commands executed via EXECUTE. Instead, the command is always planned each time the statement is run. Thus the command string can be dynamically created within the function to perform actions on different tables and columns.

The INTO clause specifies where the results of a SQL command returning rows should be assigned. If a row or variable list is provided, it must exactly match the structure of the query's results (when a record variable is used, it will configure itself to match the result structure automatically). If multiple rows are returned, only the first will be assigned to the INTO variable. If no rows are returned, NULL is assigned to the INTO variable(s). If no INTO clause is specified, the query results are discarded.

If the STRICT option is given, an error is reported unless the query produces exactly one row.

The command string can use parameter values, which are referenced in the command as $1, $2, etc. These symbols refer to values supplied in the USING clause. This method is often preferable to inserting data values into the command string as text: it avoids run-time overhead of converting the values to text and back, and it is much less prone to SQL-injection attacks since there is no need for quoting or escaping. An example is:

```
EXECUTE 'SELECT count(*) FROM mytable WHERE inserted_by = $1 AND
 inserted <= $2'
   INTO c
   USING checked_user, checked_date;
```

Note that parameter symbols can only be used for data values — if you want to use dynamically determined table or column names, you must insert them into the command string textually. For example, if the preceding query needed to be done against a dynamically selected table, you could do this:

```
EXECUTE 'SELECT count(*) FROM '
    || quote_ident(tabname)
    || ' WHERE inserted_by = $1 AND inserted <= $2'
   INTO c
   USING checked_user, checked_date;
```

A cleaner approach is to use format()'s %I specification for table or column names (strings separated by a newline are concatenated):

```
EXECUTE format('SELECT count(*) FROM %I '
   'WHERE inserted_by = $1 AND inserted <= $2', tabname)
```

```
INTO c
USING checked_user, checked_date;
```

Another restriction on parameter symbols is that they only work in SELECT, INSERT, UPDATE, and DELETE commands. In other statement types (generically called utility statements), you must insert values textually even if they are just data values.

An EXECUTE with a simple constant command string and some USING parameters, as in the first example above, is functionally equivalent to just writing the command directly in PL/pgSQL and allowing replacement of PL/pgSQL variables to happen automatically. The important difference is that EXECUTE will replan the command on each execution, generating a plan that is specific to the current parameter values; whereas PL/pgSQL may otherwise create a generic plan and cache it for re-use. In situations where the best plan depends strongly on the parameter values, it can be helpful to use EXECUTE to positively ensure that a generic plan is not selected.

SELECT INTO is not currently supported within EXECUTE; instead, execute a plain SELECT command and specify INTO as part of the EXECUTE itself.

Note

The PL/pgSQL EXECUTE statement is not related to the EXECUTE SQL statement supported by the PostgreSQL server. The server's EXECUTE statement cannot be used directly within PL/pgSQL functions (and is not needed).

Example 43.1. Quoting Values In Dynamic Queries

When working with dynamic commands you will often have to handle escaping of single quotes. The recommended method for quoting fixed text in your function body is dollar quoting. (If you have legacy code that does not use dollar quoting, please refer to the overview in Section 43.12.1, which can save you some effort when translating said code to a more reasonable scheme.)

Dynamic values require careful handling since they might contain quote characters. An example using format() (this assumes that you are dollar quoting the function body so quote marks need not be doubled):

```
EXECUTE format('UPDATE tbl SET %I = $1 '
    'WHERE key = $2', colname) USING newvalue, keyvalue;
```

It is also possible to call the quoting functions directly:

```
EXECUTE 'UPDATE tbl SET '
        || quote_ident(colname)
        || ' = '
        || quote_literal(newvalue)
        || ' WHERE key = '
        || quote_literal(keyvalue);
```

This example demonstrates the use of the quote_ident and quote_literal functions (see Section 9.4). For safety, expressions containing column or table identifiers should be passed through quote_ident before insertion in a dynamic query. Expressions containing values that should be literal strings in the constructed command should be passed through quote_literal. These functions take the appropriate steps to return the input text enclosed in double or single quotes respectively, with any embedded special characters properly escaped.

Because `quote_literal` is labeled `STRICT`, it will always return null when called with a null argument. In the above example, if `newvalue` or `keyvalue` were null, the entire dynamic query string would become null, leading to an error from `EXECUTE`. You can avoid this problem by using the `quote_nullable` function, which works the same as `quote_literal` except that when called with a null argument it returns the string `NULL`. For example,

```
EXECUTE 'UPDATE tbl SET '
        || quote_ident(colname)
        || ' = '
        || quote_nullable(newvalue)
        || ' WHERE key = '
        || quote_nullable(keyvalue);
```

If you are dealing with values that might be null, you should usually use `quote_nullable` in place of `quote_literal`.

As always, care must be taken to ensure that null values in a query do not deliver unintended results. For example the `WHERE` clause

```
'WHERE key = ' || quote_nullable(keyvalue)
```

will never succeed if `keyvalue` is null, because the result of using the equality operator = with a null operand is always null. If you wish null to work like an ordinary key value, you would need to rewrite the above as

```
'WHERE key IS NOT DISTINCT FROM ' || quote_nullable(keyvalue)
```

(At present, `IS NOT DISTINCT FROM` is handled much less efficiently than =, so don't do this unless you must. See Section 9.2 for more information on nulls and `IS DISTINCT`.)

Note that dollar quoting is only useful for quoting fixed text. It would be a very bad idea to try to write this example as:

```
EXECUTE 'UPDATE tbl SET '
        || quote_ident(colname)
        || ' = $$'
        || newvalue
        || '$$ WHERE key = '
        || quote_literal(keyvalue);
```

because it would break if the contents of `newvalue` happened to contain $$. The same objection would apply to any other dollar-quoting delimiter you might pick. So, to safely quote text that is not known in advance, you *must* use `quote_literal`, `quote_nullable`, or `quote_ident`, as appropriate.

Dynamic SQL statements can also be safely constructed using the `format` function (see Section 9.4.1). For example:

```
EXECUTE format('UPDATE tbl SET %I = %L '
    'WHERE key = %L', colname, newvalue, keyvalue);
```

%I is equivalent to `quote_ident`, and %L is equivalent to `quote_nullable`. The `format` function can be used in conjunction with the `USING` clause:

```
EXECUTE format('UPDATE tbl SET %I = $1 WHERE key = $2', colname)
    USING newvalue, keyvalue;
```

This form is better because the variables are handled in their native data type format, rather than uncondi-tionally converting them to text and quoting them via %L. It is also more efficient.

A much larger example of a dynamic command and `EXECUTE` can be seen in Example 43.10, which builds and executes a `CREATE FUNCTION` command to define a new function.

43.5.5. Obtaining the Result Status

There are several ways to determine the effect of a command. The first method is to use the `GET DIAG-NOSTICS` command, which has the form:

```
GET [ CURRENT ] DIAGNOSTICS variable { = | := } item [ , ... ];
```

This command allows retrieval of system status indicators. `CURRENT` is a noise word (but see also `GET STACKED DIAGNOSTICS` in Section 43.6.8.1). Each *item* is a key word identifying a status value to be assigned to the specified *variable* (which should be of the right data type to receive it). The currently available status items are shown in Table 43.1. Colon-equal (:=) can be used instead of the SQL-standard = token. An example:

```
GET DIAGNOSTICS integer_var = ROW_COUNT;
```

Table 43.1. Available Diagnostics Items

Name	Type	Description
ROW_COUNT	bigint	the number of rows processed by the most recent SQL command
RESULT_OID	oid	the OID of the last row in-serted by the most recent SQL command (only useful after an INSERT command into a table having OIDs)
PG_CONTEXT	text	line(s) of text describing the cur-rent call stack (see Section 43.6.9)

The second method to determine the effects of a command is to check the special variable named `FOUND`, which is of type `boolean`. `FOUND` starts out false within each PL/pgSQL function call. It is set by each of the following types of statements:

- A `SELECT INTO` statement sets `FOUND` true if a row is assigned, false if no row is returned.

- A `PERFORM` statement sets `FOUND` true if it produces (and discards) one or more rows, false if no row is produced.

- `UPDATE`, `INSERT`, and `DELETE` statements set `FOUND` true if at least one row is affected, false if no row is affected.

- A FETCH statement sets FOUND true if it returns a row, false if no row is returned.

- A MOVE statement sets FOUND true if it successfully repositions the cursor, false otherwise.

- A FOR or FOREACH statement sets FOUND true if it iterates one or more times, else false. FOUND is set this way when the loop exits; inside the execution of the loop, FOUND is not modified by the loop statement, although it might be changed by the execution of other statements within the loop body.

- RETURN QUERY and RETURN QUERY EXECUTE statements set FOUND true if the query returns at least one row, false if no row is returned.

Other PL/pgSQL statements do not change the state of FOUND. Note in particular that EXECUTE changes the output of GET DIAGNOSTICS, but does not change FOUND.

FOUND is a local variable within each PL/pgSQL function; any changes to it affect only the current function.

43.5.6. Doing Nothing At All

Sometimes a placeholder statement that does nothing is useful. For example, it can indicate that one arm of an if/then/else chain is deliberately empty. For this purpose, use the NULL statement:

```
NULL;
```

For example, the following two fragments of code are equivalent:

```
BEGIN
    y := x / 0;
EXCEPTION
    WHEN division_by_zero THEN
        NULL;  -- ignore the error
END;
```

```
BEGIN
    y := x / 0;
EXCEPTION
    WHEN division_by_zero THEN  -- ignore the error
END;
```

Which is preferable is a matter of taste.

Note

In Oracle's PL/SQL, empty statement lists are not allowed, and so NULL statements are *required* for situations such as this. PL/pgSQL allows you to just write nothing, instead.

43.6. Control Structures

Control structures are probably the most useful (and important) part of PL/pgSQL. With PL/pgSQL's control structures, you can manipulate PostgreSQL data in a very flexible and powerful way.

43.6.1. Returning From a Function

There are two commands available that allow you to return data from a function: RETURN and RETURN NEXT.

43.6.1.1. RETURN

```
RETURN expression;
```

RETURN with an expression terminates the function and returns the value of *expression* to the caller. This form is used for PL/pgSQL functions that do not return a set.

In a function that returns a scalar type, the expression's result will automatically be cast into the function's return type as described for assignments. But to return a composite (row) value, you must write an expression delivering exactly the requested column set. This may require use of explicit casting.

If you declared the function with output parameters, write just RETURN with no expression. The current values of the output parameter variables will be returned.

If you declared the function to return void, a RETURN statement can be used to exit the function early; but do not write an expression following RETURN.

The return value of a function cannot be left undefined. If control reaches the end of the top-level block of the function without hitting a RETURN statement, a run-time error will occur. This restriction does not apply to functions with output parameters and functions returning void, however. In those cases a RETURN statement is automatically executed if the top-level block finishes.

Some examples:

```
-- functions returning a scalar type
RETURN 1 + 2;
RETURN scalar_var;

-- functions returning a composite type
RETURN composite_type_var;
RETURN (1, 2, 'three'::text);   -- must cast columns to correct types
```

43.6.1.2. RETURN NEXT and RETURN QUERY

```
RETURN NEXT expression;
RETURN QUERY query;
RETURN QUERY EXECUTE command-string [ USING expression [, ... ] ];
```

When a PL/pgSQL function is declared to return SETOF *sometype*, the procedure to follow is slightly different. In that case, the individual items to return are specified by a sequence of RETURN NEXT or RETURN QUERY commands, and then a final RETURN command with no argument is used to indicate that the function has finished executing. RETURN NEXT can be used with both scalar and composite data types; with a composite result type, an entire "table" of results will be returned. RETURN QUERY appends the results of executing a query to the function's result set. RETURN NEXT and RETURN QUERY can be freely intermixed in a single set-returning function, in which case their results will be concatenated.

RETURN NEXT and RETURN QUERY do not actually return from the function — they simply append zero or more rows to the function's result set. Execution then continues with the next statement in the PL/

pgSQL function. As successive RETURN NEXT or RETURN QUERY commands are executed, the result set is built up. A final RETURN, which should have no argument, causes control to exit the function (or you can just let control reach the end of the function).

RETURN QUERY has a variant RETURN QUERY EXECUTE, which specifies the query to be executed dynamically. Parameter expressions can be inserted into the computed query string via USING, in just the same way as in the EXECUTE command.

If you declared the function with output parameters, write just RETURN NEXT with no expression. On each execution, the current values of the output parameter variable(s) will be saved for eventual return as a row of the result. Note that you must declare the function as returning SETOF record when there are multiple output parameters, or SETOF *sometype* when there is just one output parameter of type *sometype*, in order to create a set-returning function with output parameters.

Here is an example of a function using RETURN NEXT:

```
CREATE TABLE foo (fooid INT, foosubid INT, fooname TEXT);
INSERT INTO foo VALUES (1, 2, 'three');
INSERT INTO foo VALUES (4, 5, 'six');

CREATE OR REPLACE FUNCTION get_all_foo() RETURNS SETOF foo AS
$BODY$
DECLARE
    r foo%rowtype;
BEGIN
    FOR r IN
        SELECT * FROM foo WHERE fooid > 0
    LOOP
        -- can do some processing here
        RETURN NEXT r; -- return current row of SELECT
    END LOOP;
    RETURN;
END
$BODY$
LANGUAGE plpgsql;

SELECT * FROM get_all_foo();
```

Here is an example of a function using RETURN QUERY:

```
CREATE FUNCTION get_available_flightid(date) RETURNS SETOF integer AS
$BODY$
BEGIN
    RETURN QUERY SELECT flightid
                   FROM flight
                  WHERE flightdate >= $1
                    AND flightdate < ($1 + 1);

    -- Since execution is not finished, we can check whether rows were
returned
    -- and raise exception if not.
    IF NOT FOUND THEN
        RAISE EXCEPTION 'No flight at %.', $1;
```

```
    END IF;

    RETURN;
 END
$BODY$
LANGUAGE plpgsql;

-- Returns available flights or raises exception if there are no
-- available flights.
SELECT * FROM get_available_flightid(CURRENT_DATE);
```

> ### Note
>
> The current implementation of RETURN NEXT and RETURN QUERY stores the entire result set before returning from the function, as discussed above. That means that if a PL/pgSQL function produces a very large result set, performance might be poor: data will be written to disk to avoid memory exhaustion, but the function itself will not return until the entire result set has been generated. A future version of PL/pgSQL might allow users to define set-returning functions that do not have this limitation. Currently, the point at which data begins being written to disk is controlled by the work_mem configuration variable. Administrators who have sufficient memory to store larger result sets in memory should consider increasing this parameter.

43.6.2. Returning From a Procedure

A procedure does not have a return value. A procedure can therefore end without a RETURN statement. If you wish to use a RETURN statement to exit the code early, write just RETURN with no expression.

If the procedure has output parameters, the final values of the output parameter variables will be returned to the caller.

43.6.3. Calling a Procedure

A PL/pgSQL function, procedure, or DO block can call a procedure using CALL. Output parameters are handled differently from the way that CALL works in plain SQL. Each INOUT parameter of the procedure must correspond to a variable in the CALL statement, and whatever the procedure returns is assigned back to that variable after it returns. For example:

```
CREATE PROCEDURE triple(INOUT x int)
LANGUAGE plpgsql
AS $$
BEGIN
    x := x * 3;
END;
$$;

DO $$
DECLARE myvar int := 5;
BEGIN
  CALL triple(myvar);
  RAISE NOTICE 'myvar = %', myvar;  -- prints 15
```

```
END
$$;
```

43.6.4. Conditionals

IF and CASE statements let you execute alternative commands based on certain conditions. PL/pgSQL has three forms of IF:

- IF ... THEN ... END IF

- IF ... THEN ... ELSE ... END IF

- IF ... THEN ... ELSIF ... THEN ... ELSE ... END IF

and two forms of CASE:

- CASE ... WHEN ... THEN ... ELSE ... END CASE

- CASE WHEN ... THEN ... ELSE ... END CASE

43.6.4.1. IF-THEN

```
IF boolean-expression THEN
    statements
END IF;
```

IF-THEN statements are the simplest form of IF. The statements between THEN and END IF will be executed if the condition is true. Otherwise, they are skipped.

Example:

```
IF v_user_id <> 0 THEN
    UPDATE users SET email = v_email WHERE user_id = v_user_id;
END IF;
```

43.6.4.2. IF-THEN-ELSE

```
IF boolean-expression THEN
    statements
ELSE
    statements
END IF;
```

IF-THEN-ELSE statements add to IF-THEN by letting you specify an alternative set of statements that should be executed if the condition is not true. (Note this includes the case where the condition evaluates to NULL.)

Examples:

```
IF parentid IS NULL OR parentid = ''
THEN
    RETURN fullname;
```

```
ELSE
    RETURN hp_true_filename(parentid) || '/' || fullname;
END IF;
```

```
IF v_count > 0 THEN
    INSERT INTO users_count (count) VALUES (v_count);
    RETURN 't';
ELSE
    RETURN 'f';
END IF;
```

43.6.4.3. IF-THEN-ELSIF

```
IF boolean-expression THEN
    statements
[ ELSIF boolean-expression THEN
    statements
[ ELSIF boolean-expression THEN
    statements
    ...
]
]
[ ELSE
    statements ]
END IF;
```

Sometimes there are more than just two alternatives. IF-THEN-ELSIF provides a convenient method of checking several alternatives in turn. The IF conditions are tested successively until the first one that is true is found. Then the associated statement(s) are executed, after which control passes to the next statement after END IF. (Any subsequent IF conditions are *not* tested.) If none of the IF conditions is true, then the ELSE block (if any) is executed.

Here is an example:

```
IF number = 0 THEN
    result := 'zero';
ELSIF number > 0 THEN
    result := 'positive';
ELSIF number < 0 THEN
    result := 'negative';
ELSE
    -- hmm, the only other possibility is that number is null
    result := 'NULL';
END IF;
```

The key word ELSIF can also be spelled ELSEIF.

An alternative way of accomplishing the same task is to nest IF-THEN-ELSE statements, as in the following example:

```
IF demo_row.sex = 'm' THEN
```

```
        pretty_sex := 'man';
ELSE
    IF demo_row.sex = 'f' THEN
        pretty_sex := 'woman';
    END IF;
END IF;
```

However, this method requires writing a matching END IF for each IF, so it is much more cumbersome than using ELSIF when there are many alternatives.

43.6.4.4. Simple CASE

```
CASE search-expression
    WHEN expression [, expression [ ... ]] THEN
        statements
  [ WHEN expression [, expression [ ... ]] THEN
        statements
    ... ]
  [ ELSE
        statements ]
END CASE;
```

The simple form of CASE provides conditional execution based on equality of operands. The *search-expression* is evaluated (once) and successively compared to each *expression* in the WHEN clauses. If a match is found, then the corresponding *statements* are executed, and then control passes to the next statement after END CASE. (Subsequent WHEN expressions are not evaluated.) If no match is found, the ELSE *statements* are executed; but if ELSE is not present, then a CASE_NOT_FOUND exception is raised.

Here is a simple example:

```
CASE x
    WHEN 1, 2 THEN
        msg := 'one or two';
    ELSE
        msg := 'other value than one or two';
END CASE;
```

43.6.4.5. Searched CASE

```
CASE
    WHEN boolean-expression THEN
        statements
  [ WHEN boolean-expression THEN
        statements
    ... ]
  [ ELSE
        statements ]
END CASE;
```

The searched form of CASE provides conditional execution based on truth of Boolean expressions. Each WHEN clause's *boolean-expression* is evaluated in turn, until one is found that yields true. Then the corresponding *statements* are executed, and then control passes to the next statement after END CASE. (Subsequent WHEN expressions are not evaluated.) If no true result is found, the ELSE *statements* are executed; but if ELSE is not present, then a CASE_NOT_FOUND exception is raised.

Here is an example:

```
CASE
    WHEN x BETWEEN 0 AND 10 THEN
        msg := 'value is between zero and ten';
    WHEN x BETWEEN 11 AND 20 THEN
        msg := 'value is between eleven and twenty';
END CASE;
```

This form of CASE is entirely equivalent to IF-THEN-ELSIF, except for the rule that reaching an omitted ELSE clause results in an error rather than doing nothing.

43.6.5. Simple Loops

With the LOOP, EXIT, CONTINUE, WHILE, FOR, and FOREACH statements, you can arrange for your PL/pgSQL function to repeat a series of commands.

43.6.5.1. LOOP

```
[ <<label>> ]
LOOP
    statements
END LOOP [ label ];
```

LOOP defines an unconditional loop that is repeated indefinitely until terminated by an EXIT or RETURN statement. The optional *label* can be used by EXIT and CONTINUE statements within nested loops to specify which loop those statements refer to.

43.6.5.2. EXIT

```
EXIT [ label ] [ WHEN boolean-expression ];
```

If no *label* is given, the innermost loop is terminated and the statement following END LOOP is executed next. If *label* is given, it must be the label of the current or some outer level of nested loop or block. Then the named loop or block is terminated and control continues with the statement after the loop's/block's corresponding END.

If WHEN is specified, the loop exit occurs only if *boolean-expression* is true. Otherwise, control passes to the statement after EXIT.

EXIT can be used with all types of loops; it is not limited to use with unconditional loops.

When used with a BEGIN block, EXIT passes control to the next statement after the end of the block. Note that a label must be used for this purpose; an unlabeled EXIT is never considered to match a BEGIN block. (This is a change from pre-8.4 releases of PostgreSQL, which would allow an unlabeled EXIT to match a BEGIN block.)

Examples:

```
LOOP
    -- some computations
    IF count > 0 THEN
        EXIT;  -- exit loop
    END IF;
END LOOP;

LOOP
    -- some computations
    EXIT WHEN count > 0;  -- same result as previous example
END LOOP;

<<ablock>>
BEGIN
    -- some computations
    IF stocks > 100000 THEN
        EXIT ablock;  -- causes exit from the BEGIN block
    END IF;
    -- computations here will be skipped when stocks > 100000
END;
```

43.6.5.3. CONTINUE

```
CONTINUE [ label ] [ WHEN boolean-expression ];
```

If no *label* is given, the next iteration of the innermost loop is begun. That is, all statements remaining in the loop body are skipped, and control returns to the loop control expression (if any) to determine whether another loop iteration is needed. If *label* is present, it specifies the label of the loop whose execution will be continued.

If WHEN is specified, the next iteration of the loop is begun only if *boolean-expression* is true. Otherwise, control passes to the statement after CONTINUE.

CONTINUE can be used with all types of loops; it is not limited to use with unconditional loops.

Examples:

```
LOOP
    -- some computations
    EXIT WHEN count > 100;
    CONTINUE WHEN count < 50;
    -- some computations for count IN [50 .. 100]
END LOOP;
```

43.6.5.4. WHILE

```
[ <<label>> ]
WHILE boolean-expression LOOP
    statements
END LOOP [ label ];
```

The WHILE statement repeats a sequence of statements so long as the *boolean-expression* evaluates to true. The expression is checked just before each entry to the loop body.

For example:

```
WHILE amount_owed > 0 AND gift_certificate_balance > 0 LOOP
    -- some computations here
END LOOP;

WHILE NOT done LOOP
    -- some computations here
END LOOP;
```

43.6.5.5. FOR (Integer Variant)

```
[ <<label>> ]
FOR name IN [ REVERSE ] expression .. expression [ BY expression ]
 LOOP
    statements
END LOOP [ label ];
```

This form of FOR creates a loop that iterates over a range of integer values. The variable *name* is automatically defined as type integer and exists only inside the loop (any existing definition of the variable name is ignored within the loop). The two expressions giving the lower and upper bound of the range are evaluated once when entering the loop. If the BY clause isn't specified the iteration step is 1, otherwise it's the value specified in the BY clause, which again is evaluated once on loop entry. If REVERSE is specified then the step value is subtracted, rather than added, after each iteration.

Some examples of integer FOR loops:

```
FOR i IN 1..10 LOOP
    -- i will take on the values 1,2,3,4,5,6,7,8,9,10 within the loop
END LOOP;

FOR i IN REVERSE 10..1 LOOP
    -- i will take on the values 10,9,8,7,6,5,4,3,2,1 within the loop
END LOOP;

FOR i IN REVERSE 10..1 BY 2 LOOP
    -- i will take on the values 10,8,6,4,2 within the loop
END LOOP;
```

If the lower bound is greater than the upper bound (or less than, in the REVERSE case), the loop body is not executed at all. No error is raised.

If a *label* is attached to the FOR loop then the integer loop variable can be referenced with a qualified name, using that *label*.

43.6.6. Looping Through Query Results

Using a different type of FOR loop, you can iterate through the results of a query and manipulate that data accordingly. The syntax is:

```
[ <<label>> ]
FOR target IN query LOOP
    statements
END LOOP [ label ];
```

The *target* is a record variable, row variable, or comma-separated list of scalar variables. The *target* is successively assigned each row resulting from the *query* and the loop body is executed for each row. Here is an example:

```
CREATE FUNCTION cs_refresh_mviews() RETURNS integer AS $$
DECLARE
    mviews RECORD;
BEGIN
    RAISE NOTICE 'Refreshing materialized views...';

    FOR mviews IN SELECT * FROM cs_materialized_views ORDER BY
sort_key LOOP

        -- Now "mviews" has one record from cs_materialized_views

        RAISE NOTICE 'Refreshing materialized view %s ...',
quote_ident(mviews.mv_name);
        EXECUTE format('TRUNCATE TABLE %I', mviews.mv_name);
        EXECUTE format('INSERT INTO %I %s', mviews.mv_name,
mviews.mv_query);
    END LOOP;

    RAISE NOTICE 'Done refreshing materialized views.';
    RETURN 1;
END;
$$ LANGUAGE plpgsql;
```

If the loop is terminated by an EXIT statement, the last assigned row value is still accessible after the loop.

The *query* used in this type of FOR statement can be any SQL command that returns rows to the caller: SELECT is the most common case, but you can also use INSERT, UPDATE, or DELETE with a RE-TURNING clause. Some utility commands such as EXPLAIN will work too.

PL/pgSQL variables are substituted into the query text, and the query plan is cached for possible re-use, as discussed in detail in Section 43.11.1 and Section 43.11.2.

The FOR-IN-EXECUTE statement is another way to iterate over rows:

```
[ <<label>> ]
FOR target IN EXECUTE text_expression [ USING expression [, ... ] ]
 LOOP
    statements
END LOOP [ label ];
```

This is like the previous form, except that the source query is specified as a string expression, which is evaluated and replanned on each entry to the FOR loop. This allows the programmer to choose the speed of a preplanned query or the flexibility of a dynamic query, just as with a plain EXECUTE statement. As with EXECUTE, parameter values can be inserted into the dynamic command via USING.

Another way to specify the query whose results should be iterated through is to declare it as a cursor. This is described in Section 43.7.4.

43.6.7. Looping Through Arrays

The FOREACH loop is much like a FOR loop, but instead of iterating through the rows returned by a SQL query, it iterates through the elements of an array value. (In general, FOREACH is meant for looping through components of a composite-valued expression; variants for looping through composites besides arrays may be added in future.) The FOREACH statement to loop over an array is:

```
[ <<label>> ]
FOREACH target [ SLICE number ] IN ARRAY expression LOOP
    statements
END LOOP [ label ];
```

Without SLICE, or if SLICE 0 is specified, the loop iterates through individual elements of the array produced by evaluating the *expression*. The *target* variable is assigned each element value in sequence, and the loop body is executed for each element. Here is an example of looping through the elements of an integer array:

```
CREATE FUNCTION sum(int[]) RETURNS int8 AS $$
DECLARE
  s int8 := 0;
  x int;
BEGIN
  FOREACH x IN ARRAY $1
  LOOP
    s := s + x;
  END LOOP;
  RETURN s;
END;
$$ LANGUAGE plpgsql;
```

The elements are visited in storage order, regardless of the number of array dimensions. Although the *target* is usually just a single variable, it can be a list of variables when looping through an array of composite values (records). In that case, for each array element, the variables are assigned from successive columns of the composite value.

With a positive SLICE value, FOREACH iterates through slices of the array rather than single elements. The SLICE value must be an integer constant not larger than the number of dimensions of the array. The *target* variable must be an array, and it receives successive slices of the array value, where each slice is of the number of dimensions specified by SLICE. Here is an example of iterating through one-dimensional slices:

```
CREATE FUNCTION scan_rows(int[]) RETURNS void AS $$
DECLARE
  x int[];
BEGIN
  FOREACH x SLICE 1 IN ARRAY $1
  LOOP
    RAISE NOTICE 'row = %', x;
```

```
    END LOOP;
END;
$$ LANGUAGE plpgsql;

SELECT scan_rows(ARRAY[[1,2,3],[4,5,6],[7,8,9],[10,11,12]]);

NOTICE:  row = {1,2,3}
NOTICE:  row = {4,5,6}
NOTICE:  row = {7,8,9}
NOTICE:  row = {10,11,12}
```

43.6.8. Trapping Errors

By default, any error occurring in a PL/pgSQL function aborts execution of the function, and indeed of the surrounding transaction as well. You can trap errors and recover from them by using a BEGIN block with an EXCEPTION clause. The syntax is an extension of the normal syntax for a BEGIN block:

```
[ <<label>> ]
[ DECLARE
    declarations ]
BEGIN
    statements
EXCEPTION
    WHEN condition [ OR condition ... ] THEN
        handler_statements
    [ WHEN condition [ OR condition ... ] THEN
        handler_statements
      ... ]
END;
```

If no error occurs, this form of block simply executes all the *statements*, and then control passes to the next statement after END. But if an error occurs within the *statements*, further processing of the *statements* is abandoned, and control passes to the EXCEPTION list. The list is searched for the first *condition* matching the error that occurred. If a match is found, the corresponding *handler_statements* are executed, and then control passes to the next statement after END. If no match is found, the error propagates out as though the EXCEPTION clause were not there at all: the error can be caught by an enclosing block with EXCEPTION, or if there is none it aborts processing of the function.

The *condition* names can be any of those shown in Appendix A. A category name matches any error within its category. The special condition name OTHERS matches every error type except QUERY_CAN-CELED and ASSERT_FAILURE. (It is possible, but often unwise, to trap those two error types by name.) Condition names are not case-sensitive. Also, an error condition can be specified by SQLSTATE code; for example these are equivalent:

```
WHEN division_by_zero THEN ...
WHEN SQLSTATE '22012' THEN ...
```

If a new error occurs within the selected *handler_statements*, it cannot be caught by this EXCEP-TION clause, but is propagated out. A surrounding EXCEPTION clause could catch it.

When an error is caught by an EXCEPTION clause, the local variables of the PL/pgSQL function remain as they were when the error occurred, but all changes to persistent database state within the block are rolled back. As an example, consider this fragment:

```
INSERT INTO mytab(firstname, lastname) VALUES('Tom', 'Jones');
BEGIN
    UPDATE mytab SET firstname = 'Joe' WHERE lastname = 'Jones';
    x := x + 1;
    y := x / 0;
EXCEPTION
    WHEN division_by_zero THEN
        RAISE NOTICE 'caught division_by_zero';
        RETURN x;
END;
```

When control reaches the assignment to y, it will fail with a division_by_zero error. This will be caught by the EXCEPTION clause. The value returned in the RETURN statement will be the incremented value of x, but the effects of the UPDATE command will have been rolled back. The INSERT command preceding the block is not rolled back, however, so the end result is that the database contains Tom Jones not Joe Jones.

Tip

A block containing an EXCEPTION clause is significantly more expensive to enter and exit than a block without one. Therefore, don't use EXCEPTION without need.

Example 43.2. Exceptions with UPDATE/INSERT

This example uses exception handling to perform either UPDATE or INSERT, as appropriate. It is recommended that applications use INSERT with ON CONFLICT DO UPDATE rather than actually using this pattern. This example serves primarily to illustrate use of PL/pgSQL control flow structures:

```
CREATE TABLE db (a INT PRIMARY KEY, b TEXT);

CREATE FUNCTION merge_db(key INT, data TEXT) RETURNS VOID AS
$$
BEGIN
    LOOP
        -- first try to update the key
        UPDATE db SET b = data WHERE a = key;
        IF found THEN
            RETURN;
        END IF;
        -- not there, so try to insert the key
        -- if someone else inserts the same key concurrently,
        -- we could get a unique-key failure
        BEGIN
            INSERT INTO db(a,b) VALUES (key, data);
            RETURN;
        EXCEPTION WHEN unique_violation THEN
            -- Do nothing, and loop to try the UPDATE again.
        END;
    END LOOP;
END;
```

```
$$
LANGUAGE plpgsql;

SELECT merge_db(1, 'david');
SELECT merge_db(1, 'dennis');
```

This coding assumes the `unique_violation` error is caused by the `INSERT`, and not by, say, an `INSERT` in a trigger function on the table. It might also misbehave if there is more than one unique index on the table, since it will retry the operation regardless of which index caused the error. More safety could be had by using the features discussed next to check that the trapped error was the one expected.

43.6.8.1. Obtaining Information About an Error

Exception handlers frequently need to identify the specific error that occurred. There are two ways to get information about the current exception in PL/pgSQL: special variables and the `GET STACKED DIAGNOSTICS` command.

Within an exception handler, the special variable `SQLSTATE` contains the error code that corresponds to the exception that was raised (refer to Table A.1 for a list of possible error codes). The special variable `SQLERRM` contains the error message associated with the exception. These variables are undefined outside exception handlers.

Within an exception handler, one may also retrieve information about the current exception by using the `GET STACKED DIAGNOSTICS` command, which has the form:

```
GET STACKED DIAGNOSTICS variable { = | := } item [ , ... ];
```

Each `item` is a key word identifying a status value to be assigned to the specified `variable` (which should be of the right data type to receive it). The currently available status items are shown in Table 43.2.

Table 43.2. Error Diagnostics Items

Name	Type	Description
RETURNED_SQLSTATE	text	the SQLSTATE error code of the exception
COLUMN_NAME	text	the name of the column related to exception
CONSTRAINT_NAME	text	the name of the constraint related to exception
PG_DATATYPE_NAME	text	the name of the data type related to exception
MESSAGE_TEXT	text	the text of the exception's primary message
TABLE_NAME	text	the name of the table related to exception
SCHEMA_NAME	text	the name of the schema related to exception
PG_EXCEPTION_DETAIL	text	the text of the exception's detail message, if any
PG_EXCEPTION_HINT	text	the text of the exception's hint message, if any

Name	Type	Description
PG_EXCEPTION_CONTEXT	text	line(s) of text describing the call stack at the time of the exception (see Section 43.6.9)

If the exception did not set a value for an item, an empty string will be returned.

Here is an example:

```
DECLARE
  text_var1 text;
  text_var2 text;
  text_var3 text;
BEGIN
  -- some processing which might cause an exception
  ...
EXCEPTION WHEN OTHERS THEN
  GET STACKED DIAGNOSTICS text_var1 = MESSAGE_TEXT,
                          text_var2 = PG_EXCEPTION_DETAIL,
                          text_var3 = PG_EXCEPTION_HINT;
END;
```

43.6.9. Obtaining Execution Location Information

The GET DIAGNOSTICS command, previously described in Section 43.5.5, retrieves information about current execution state (whereas the GET STACKED DIAGNOSTICS command discussed above reports information about the execution state as of a previous error). Its PG_CONTEXT status item is useful for identifying the current execution location. PG_CONTEXT returns a text string with line(s) of text describing the call stack. The first line refers to the current function and currently executing GET DIAGNOSTICS command. The second and any subsequent lines refer to calling functions further up the call stack. For example:

```
CREATE OR REPLACE FUNCTION outer_func() RETURNS integer AS $$
BEGIN
  RETURN inner_func();
END;
$$ LANGUAGE plpgsql;

CREATE OR REPLACE FUNCTION inner_func() RETURNS integer AS $$
DECLARE
  stack text;
BEGIN
  GET DIAGNOSTICS stack = PG_CONTEXT;
  RAISE NOTICE E'--- Call Stack ---\n%', stack;
  RETURN 1;
END;
$$ LANGUAGE plpgsql;

SELECT outer_func();

NOTICE:  --- Call Stack ---
PL/pgSQL function inner_func() line 5 at GET DIAGNOSTICS
```

```
PL/pgSQL function outer_func() line 3 at RETURN
CONTEXT:  PL/pgSQL function outer_func() line 3 at RETURN
 outer_func
 ------------
          1
(1 row)
```

GET STACKED DIAGNOSTICS ... PG_EXCEPTION_CONTEXT returns the same sort of stack trace, but describing the location at which an error was detected, rather than the current location.

43.7. Cursors

Rather than executing a whole query at once, it is possible to set up a *cursor* that encapsulates the query, and then read the query result a few rows at a time. One reason for doing this is to avoid memory overrun when the result contains a large number of rows. (However, PL/pgSQL users do not normally need to worry about that, since FOR loops automatically use a cursor internally to avoid memory problems.) A more interesting usage is to return a reference to a cursor that a function has created, allowing the caller to read the rows. This provides an efficient way to return large row sets from functions.

43.7.1. Declaring Cursor Variables

All access to cursors in PL/pgSQL goes through cursor variables, which are always of the special data type refcursor. One way to create a cursor variable is just to declare it as a variable of type refcursor. Another way is to use the cursor declaration syntax, which in general is:

```
name [ [ NO ] SCROLL ] CURSOR [ ( arguments ) ] FOR query;
```

(FOR can be replaced by IS for Oracle compatibility.) If SCROLL is specified, the cursor will be capable of scrolling backward; if NO SCROLL is specified, backward fetches will be rejected; if neither specification appears, it is query-dependent whether backward fetches will be allowed. *arguments*, if specified, is a comma-separated list of pairs *name datatype* that define names to be replaced by parameter values in the given query. The actual values to substitute for these names will be specified later, when the cursor is opened.

Some examples:

```
DECLARE
    curs1 refcursor;
    curs2 CURSOR FOR SELECT * FROM tenk1;
    curs3 CURSOR (key integer) FOR SELECT * FROM tenk1 WHERE unique1 =
key;
```

All three of these variables have the data type refcursor, but the first can be used with any query, while the second has a fully specified query already *bound* to it, and the last has a parameterized query bound to it. (key will be replaced by an integer parameter value when the cursor is opened.) The variable curs1 is said to be *unbound* since it is not bound to any particular query.

43.7.2. Opening Cursors

Before a cursor can be used to retrieve rows, it must be *opened*. (This is the equivalent action to the SQL command DECLARE CURSOR.) PL/pgSQL has three forms of the OPEN statement, two of which use unbound cursor variables while the third uses a bound cursor variable.

> ### Note
>
> Bound cursor variables can also be used without explicitly opening the cursor, via the FOR
> statement described in Section 43.7.4.

43.7.2.1. OPEN FOR *query*

```
OPEN unbound_cursorvar [ [ NO ] SCROLL ] FOR query;
```

The cursor variable is opened and given the specified query to execute. The cursor cannot be open already,
and it must have been declared as an unbound cursor variable (that is, as a simple refcursor variable).
The query must be a SELECT, or something else that returns rows (such as EXPLAIN). The query is treated
in the same way as other SQL commands in PL/pgSQL: PL/pgSQL variable names are substituted, and the
query plan is cached for possible reuse. When a PL/pgSQL variable is substituted into the cursor query,
the value that is substituted is the one it has at the time of the OPEN; subsequent changes to the variable
will not affect the cursor's behavior. The SCROLL and NO SCROLL options have the same meanings as
for a bound cursor.

An example:

```
OPEN curs1 FOR SELECT * FROM foo WHERE key = mykey;
```

43.7.2.2. OPEN FOR EXECUTE

```
OPEN unbound_cursorvar [ [ NO ] SCROLL ] FOR EXECUTE query_string
                                 [ USING expression [, ... ] ];
```

The cursor variable is opened and given the specified query to execute. The cursor cannot be open already,
and it must have been declared as an unbound cursor variable (that is, as a simple refcursor variable).
The query is specified as a string expression, in the same way as in the EXECUTE command. As usual,
this gives flexibility so the query plan can vary from one run to the next (see Section 43.11.2), and it also
means that variable substitution is not done on the command string. As with EXECUTE, parameter values
can be inserted into the dynamic command via format() and USING. The SCROLL and NO SCROLL
options have the same meanings as for a bound cursor.

An example:

```
OPEN curs1 FOR EXECUTE format('SELECT * FROM %I WHERE col1 =
$1',tabname) USING keyvalue;
```

In this example, the table name is inserted into the query via format(). The comparison value for col1
is inserted via a USING parameter, so it needs no quoting.

43.7.2.3. Opening a Bound Cursor

```
OPEN bound_cursorvar [ ( [ argument_name := ] argument_value
[, ...] ) ];
```

This form of OPEN is used to open a cursor variable whose query was bound to it when it was declared. The cursor cannot be open already. A list of actual argument value expressions must appear if and only if the cursor was declared to take arguments. These values will be substituted in the query.

The query plan for a bound cursor is always considered cacheable; there is no equivalent of EXECUTE in this case. Notice that SCROLL and NO SCROLL cannot be specified in OPEN, as the cursor's scrolling behavior was already determined.

Argument values can be passed using either *positional* or *named* notation. In positional notation, all arguments are specified in order. In named notation, each argument's name is specified using := to separate it from the argument expression. Similar to calling functions, described in Section 4.3, it is also allowed to mix positional and named notation.

Examples (these use the cursor declaration examples above):

```
OPEN curs2;
OPEN curs3(42);
OPEN curs3(key := 42);
```

Because variable substitution is done on a bound cursor's query, there are really two ways to pass values into the cursor: either with an explicit argument to OPEN, or implicitly by referencing a PL/pgSQL variable in the query. However, only variables declared before the bound cursor was declared will be substituted into it. In either case the value to be passed is determined at the time of the OPEN. For example, another way to get the same effect as the curs3 example above is

```
DECLARE
    key integer;
    curs4 CURSOR FOR SELECT * FROM tenk1 WHERE unique1 = key;
BEGIN
    key := 42;
    OPEN curs4;
```

43.7.3. Using Cursors

Once a cursor has been opened, it can be manipulated with the statements described here.

These manipulations need not occur in the same function that opened the cursor to begin with. You can return a refcursor value out of a function and let the caller operate on the cursor. (Internally, a refcursor value is simply the string name of a so-called portal containing the active query for the cursor. This name can be passed around, assigned to other refcursor variables, and so on, without disturbing the portal.)

All portals are implicitly closed at transaction end. Therefore a refcursor value is usable to reference an open cursor only until the end of the transaction.

43.7.3.1. FETCH

```
FETCH [ direction { FROM | IN } ] cursor INTO target;
```

FETCH retrieves the next row from the cursor into a target, which might be a row variable, a record variable, or a comma-separated list of simple variables, just like SELECT INTO. If there is no next row, the target is set to NULL(s). As with SELECT INTO, the special variable FOUND can be checked to see whether a row was obtained or not.

The *direction* clause can be any of the variants allowed in the SQL FETCH command except the ones that can fetch more than one row; namely, it can be NEXT, PRIOR, FIRST, LAST, ABSOLUTE *count*, RELATIVE *count*, FORWARD, or BACKWARD. Omitting *direction* is the same as specifying NEXT. In the forms using a *count*, the *count* can be any integer-valued expression (unlike the SQL FETCH command, which only allows an integer constant). *direction* values that require moving backward are likely to fail unless the cursor was declared or opened with the SCROLL option.

cursor must be the name of a refcursor variable that references an open cursor portal.

Examples:

```
FETCH curs1 INTO rowvar;
FETCH curs2 INTO foo, bar, baz;
FETCH LAST FROM curs3 INTO x, y;
FETCH RELATIVE -2 FROM curs4 INTO x;
```

43.7.3.2. MOVE

```
MOVE [ direction { FROM | IN } ] cursor;
```

MOVE repositions a cursor without retrieving any data. MOVE works exactly like the FETCH command, except it only repositions the cursor and does not return the row moved to. As with SELECT INTO, the special variable FOUND can be checked to see whether there was a next row to move to.

Examples:

```
MOVE curs1;
MOVE LAST FROM curs3;
MOVE RELATIVE -2 FROM curs4;
MOVE FORWARD 2 FROM curs4;
```

43.7.3.3. UPDATE/DELETE WHERE CURRENT OF

```
UPDATE table SET ... WHERE CURRENT OF cursor;
DELETE FROM table WHERE CURRENT OF cursor;
```

When a cursor is positioned on a table row, that row can be updated or deleted using the cursor to identify the row. There are restrictions on what the cursor's query can be (in particular, no grouping) and it's best to use FOR UPDATE in the cursor. For more information see the DECLARE reference page.

An example:

```
UPDATE foo SET dataval = myval WHERE CURRENT OF curs1;
```

43.7.3.4. CLOSE

```
CLOSE cursor;
```

CLOSE closes the portal underlying an open cursor. This can be used to release resources earlier than end of transaction, or to free up the cursor variable to be opened again.

An example:

```
CLOSE curs1;
```

43.7.3.5. Returning Cursors

PL/pgSQL functions can return cursors to the caller. This is useful to return multiple rows or columns, especially with very large result sets. To do this, the function opens the cursor and returns the cursor name to the caller (or simply opens the cursor using a portal name specified by or otherwise known to the caller). The caller can then fetch rows from the cursor. The cursor can be closed by the caller, or it will be closed automatically when the transaction closes.

The portal name used for a cursor can be specified by the programmer or automatically generated. To specify a portal name, simply assign a string to the refcursor variable before opening it. The string value of the refcursor variable will be used by OPEN as the name of the underlying portal. However, if the refcursor variable is null, OPEN automatically generates a name that does not conflict with any existing portal, and assigns it to the refcursor variable.

Note

A bound cursor variable is initialized to the string value representing its name, so that the portal name is the same as the cursor variable name, unless the programmer overrides it by assignment before opening the cursor. But an unbound cursor variable defaults to the null value initially, so it will receive an automatically-generated unique name, unless overridden.

The following example shows one way a cursor name can be supplied by the caller:

```
CREATE TABLE test (col text);
INSERT INTO test VALUES ('123');

CREATE FUNCTION reffunc(refcursor) RETURNS refcursor AS '
BEGIN
    OPEN $1 FOR SELECT col FROM test;
    RETURN $1;
END;
' LANGUAGE plpgsql;

BEGIN;
SELECT reffunc('funccursor');
FETCH ALL IN funccursor;
COMMIT;
```

The following example uses automatic cursor name generation:

```
CREATE FUNCTION reffunc2() RETURNS refcursor AS '
DECLARE
    ref refcursor;
BEGIN
    OPEN ref FOR SELECT col FROM test;
    RETURN ref;
END;
' LANGUAGE plpgsql;

-- need to be in a transaction to use cursors.
BEGIN;
SELECT reffunc2();

      reffunc2
--------------------
 <unnamed cursor 1>
(1 row)

FETCH ALL IN "<unnamed cursor 1>";
COMMIT;
```

The following example shows one way to return multiple cursors from a single function:

```
CREATE FUNCTION myfunc(refcursor, refcursor) RETURNS SETOF refcursor
 AS $$
BEGIN
    OPEN $1 FOR SELECT * FROM table_1;
    RETURN NEXT $1;
    OPEN $2 FOR SELECT * FROM table_2;
    RETURN NEXT $2;
END;
$$ LANGUAGE plpgsql;

-- need to be in a transaction to use cursors.
BEGIN;

SELECT * FROM myfunc('a', 'b');

FETCH ALL FROM a;
FETCH ALL FROM b;
COMMIT;
```

43.7.4. Looping Through a Cursor's Result

There is a variant of the FOR statement that allows iterating through the rows returned by a cursor. The syntax is:

```
[ <<label>> ]
FOR recordvar IN bound_cursorvar [ ( [ argument_name
 := ] argument_value [, ...] ) ] LOOP
    statements
END LOOP [ label ];
```

The cursor variable must have been bound to some query when it was declared, and it *cannot* be open already. The FOR statement automatically opens the cursor, and it closes the cursor again when the loop exits. A list of actual argument value expressions must appear if and only if the cursor was declared to take arguments. These values will be substituted in the query, in just the same way as during an OPEN (see Section 43.7.2.3).

The variable *recordvar* is automatically defined as type record and exists only inside the loop (any existing definition of the variable name is ignored within the loop). Each row returned by the cursor is successively assigned to this record variable and the loop body is executed.

43.8. Transaction Management

In procedures invoked by the CALL command as well as in anonymous code blocks (DO command), it is possible to end transactions using the commands COMMIT and ROLLBACK. A new transaction is started automatically after a transaction is ended using these commands, so there is no separate START TRANSACTION command. (Note that BEGIN and END have different meanings in PL/pgSQL.)

Here is a simple example:

```
CREATE PROCEDURE transaction_test1()
LANGUAGE plpgsql
AS $$
BEGIN
    FOR i IN 0..9 LOOP
        INSERT INTO test1 (a) VALUES (i);
        IF i % 2 = 0 THEN
            COMMIT;
        ELSE
            ROLLBACK;
        END IF;
    END LOOP;
END
$$;

CALL transaction_test1();
```

Transaction control is only possible in CALL or DO invocations from the top level or nested CALL or DO invocations without any other intervening command. For example, if the call stack is CALL proc1() → CALL proc2() → CALL proc3(), then the second and third procedures can perform transaction control actions. But if the call stack is CALL proc1() → SELECT func2() → CALL proc3(), then the last procedure cannot do transaction control, because of the SELECT in between.

Special considerations apply to cursor loops. Consider this example:

```
CREATE PROCEDURE transaction_test2()
LANGUAGE plpgsql
AS $$
DECLARE
    r RECORD;
BEGIN
    FOR r IN SELECT * FROM test2 ORDER BY x LOOP
        INSERT INTO test1 (a) VALUES (r.x);
```

```
        COMMIT;
    END LOOP;
END;
$$;

CALL transaction_test2();
```

Normally, cursors are automatically closed at transaction commit. However, a cursor created as part of a loop like this is automatically converted to a holdable cursor by the first COMMIT or ROLLBACK. That means that the cursor is fully evaluated at the first COMMIT or ROLLBACK rather than row by row. The cursor is still removed automatically after the loop, so this is mostly invisible to the user.

Transaction commands are not allowed in cursor loops driven by commands that are not read-only (for example UPDATE ... RETURNING).

A transaction cannot be ended inside a block with exception handlers.

43.9. Errors and Messages

43.9.1. Reporting Errors and Messages

Use the RAISE statement to report messages and raise errors.

```
RAISE [ level ] 'format' [, expression [, ... ]] [ USING option
 = expression [, ... ] ];
RAISE [ level ] condition_name [ USING option = expression [, ... ] ];
RAISE [ level ] SQLSTATE 'sqlstate' [ USING option = expression
 [, ... ] ];
RAISE [ level ] USING option = expression [, ... ];
RAISE ;
```

The *level* option specifies the error severity. Allowed levels are DEBUG, LOG, INFO, NOTICE, WARNING, and EXCEPTION, with EXCEPTION being the default. EXCEPTION raises an error (which normally aborts the current transaction); the other levels only generate messages of different priority levels. Whether messages of a particular priority are reported to the client, written to the server log, or both is controlled by the log_min_messages and client_min_messages configuration variables. See Chapter 19 for more information.

After *level* if any, you can write a *format* (which must be a simple string literal, not an expression). The format string specifies the error message text to be reported. The format string can be followed by optional argument expressions to be inserted into the message. Inside the format string, % is replaced by the string representation of the next optional argument's value. Write %% to emit a literal %. The number of arguments must match the number of % placeholders in the format string, or an error is raised during the compilation of the function.

In this example, the value of v_job_id will replace the % in the string:

```
RAISE NOTICE 'Calling cs_create_job(%)', v_job_id;
```

You can attach additional information to the error report by writing USING followed by *option* = *expression* items. Each *expression* can be any string-valued expression. The allowed *option* key words are:

MESSAGE

Sets the error message text. This option can't be used in the form of RAISE that includes a format string before USING.

DETAIL

Supplies an error detail message.

HINT

Supplies a hint message.

ERRCODE

Specifies the error code (SQLSTATE) to report, either by condition name, as shown in Appendix A, or directly as a five-character SQLSTATE code.

COLUMN
CONSTRAINT
DATATYPE
TABLE
SCHEMA

Supplies the name of a related object.

This example will abort the transaction with the given error message and hint:

```
RAISE EXCEPTION 'Nonexistent ID --> %', user_id
    USING HINT = 'Please check your user ID';
```

These two examples show equivalent ways of setting the SQLSTATE:

```
RAISE 'Duplicate user ID: %', user_id USING ERRCODE =
 'unique_violation';
RAISE 'Duplicate user ID: %', user_id USING ERRCODE = '23505';
```

There is a second RAISE syntax in which the main argument is the condition name or SQLSTATE to be reported, for example:

```
RAISE division_by_zero;
RAISE SQLSTATE '22012';
```

In this syntax, USING can be used to supply a custom error message, detail, or hint. Another way to do the earlier example is

```
RAISE unique_violation USING MESSAGE = 'Duplicate user ID: ' ||
 user_id;
```

Still another variant is to write RAISE USING or RAISE *level* USING and put everything else into the USING list.

The last variant of RAISE has no parameters at all. This form can only be used inside a BEGIN block's EXCEPTION clause; it causes the error currently being handled to be re-thrown.

Note

Before PostgreSQL 9.1, `RAISE` without parameters was interpreted as re-throwing the error from the block containing the active exception handler. Thus an `EXCEPTION` clause nested within that handler could not catch it, even if the `RAISE` was within the nested `EXCEPTION` clause's block. This was deemed surprising as well as being incompatible with Oracle's PL/SQL.

If no condition name nor SQLSTATE is specified in a `RAISE EXCEPTION` command, the default is to use `RAISE_EXCEPTION (P0001)`. If no message text is specified, the default is to use the condition name or SQLSTATE as message text.

Note

When specifying an error code by SQLSTATE code, you are not limited to the predefined error codes, but can select any error code consisting of five digits and/or upper-case ASCII letters, other than `00000`. It is recommended that you avoid throwing error codes that end in three zeroes, because these are category codes and can only be trapped by trapping the whole category.

43.9.2. Checking Assertions

The `ASSERT` statement is a convenient shorthand for inserting debugging checks into PL/pgSQL functions.

```
ASSERT condition [ , message ];
```

The `condition` is a Boolean expression that is expected to always evaluate to true; if it does, the `ASSERT` statement does nothing further. If the result is false or null, then an `ASSERT_FAILURE` exception is raised. (If an error occurs while evaluating the `condition`, it is reported as a normal error.)

If the optional `message` is provided, it is an expression whose result (if not null) replaces the default error message text "assertion failed", should the `condition` fail. The `message` expression is not evaluated in the normal case where the assertion succeeds.

Testing of assertions can be enabled or disabled via the configuration parameter `plpgsql.check_as-serts`, which takes a Boolean value; the default is `on`. If this parameter is `off` then `ASSERT` statements do nothing.

Note that `ASSERT` is meant for detecting program bugs, not for reporting ordinary error conditions. Use the `RAISE` statement, described above, for that.

43.10. Trigger Functions

PL/pgSQL can be used to define trigger functions on data changes or database events. A trigger function is created with the `CREATE FUNCTION` command, declaring it as a function with no arguments and a return type of `trigger` (for data change triggers) or `event_trigger` (for database event triggers). Special local variables named `TG_something` are automatically defined to describe the condition that triggered the call.

43.10.1. Triggers on Data Changes

A data change trigger is declared as a function with no arguments and a return type of `trigger`. Note that the function must be declared with no arguments even if it expects to receive some arguments specified in `CREATE TRIGGER` — such arguments are passed via `TG_ARGV`, as described below.

When a PL/pgSQL function is called as a trigger, several special variables are created automatically in the top-level block. They are:

NEW

> Data type `RECORD`; variable holding the new database row for `INSERT`/`UPDATE` operations in row-level triggers. This variable is null in statement-level triggers and for `DELETE` operations.

OLD

> Data type `RECORD`; variable holding the old database row for `UPDATE`/`DELETE` operations in row-level triggers. This variable is null in statement-level triggers and for `INSERT` operations.

TG_NAME

> Data type `name`; variable that contains the name of the trigger actually fired.

TG_WHEN

> Data type `text`; a string of `BEFORE`, `AFTER`, or `INSTEAD OF`, depending on the trigger's definition.

TG_LEVEL

> Data type `text`; a string of either `ROW` or `STATEMENT` depending on the trigger's definition.

TG_OP

> Data type `text`; a string of `INSERT`, `UPDATE`, `DELETE`, or `TRUNCATE` telling for which operation the trigger was fired.

TG_RELID

> Data type `oid`; the object ID of the table that caused the trigger invocation.

TG_RELNAME

> Data type `name`; the name of the table that caused the trigger invocation. This is now deprecated, and could disappear in a future release. Use `TG_TABLE_NAME` instead.

TG_TABLE_NAME

> Data type `name`; the name of the table that caused the trigger invocation.

TG_TABLE_SCHEMA

> Data type `name`; the name of the schema of the table that caused the trigger invocation.

TG_NARGS

> Data type `integer`; the number of arguments given to the trigger function in the `CREATE TRIGGER` statement.

`TG_ARGV[]`

> Data type array of `text`; the arguments from the `CREATE TRIGGER` statement. The index counts from 0. Invalid indexes (less than 0 or greater than or equal to `tg_nargs`) result in a null value.

A trigger function must return either `NULL` or a record/row value having exactly the structure of the table the trigger was fired for.

Row-level triggers fired `BEFORE` can return null to signal the trigger manager to skip the rest of the operation for this row (i.e., subsequent triggers are not fired, and the `INSERT/UPDATE/DELETE` does not occur for this row). If a nonnull value is returned then the operation proceeds with that row value. Returning a row value different from the original value of `NEW` alters the row that will be inserted or updated. Thus, if the trigger function wants the triggering action to succeed normally without altering the row value, `NEW` (or a value equal thereto) has to be returned. To alter the row to be stored, it is possible to replace single values directly in `NEW` and return the modified `NEW`, or to build a complete new record/row to return. In the case of a before-trigger on `DELETE`, the returned value has no direct effect, but it has to be nonnull to allow the trigger action to proceed. Note that `NEW` is null in `DELETE` triggers, so returning that is usually not sensible. The usual idiom in `DELETE` triggers is to return `OLD`.

`INSTEAD OF` triggers (which are always row-level triggers, and may only be used on views) can return null to signal that they did not perform any updates, and that the rest of the operation for this row should be skipped (i.e., subsequent triggers are not fired, and the row is not counted in the rows-affected status for the surrounding `INSERT/UPDATE/DELETE`). Otherwise a nonnull value should be returned, to signal that the trigger performed the requested operation. For `INSERT` and `UPDATE` operations, the return value should be `NEW`, which the trigger function may modify to support `INSERT RETURNING` and `UPDATE RETURNING` (this will also affect the row value passed to any subsequent triggers, or passed to a special `EXCLUDED` alias reference within an `INSERT` statement with an `ON CONFLICT DO UPDATE` clause). For `DELETE` operations, the return value should be `OLD`.

The return value of a row-level trigger fired `AFTER` or a statement-level trigger fired `BEFORE` or `AFTER` is always ignored; it might as well be null. However, any of these types of triggers might still abort the entire operation by raising an error.

Example 43.3 shows an example of a trigger function in PL/pgSQL.

Example 43.3. A PL/pgSQL Trigger Function

This example trigger ensures that any time a row is inserted or updated in the table, the current user name and time are stamped into the row. And it checks that an employee's name is given and that the salary is a positive value.

```
CREATE TABLE emp (
    empname text,
    salary integer,
    last_date timestamp,
    last_user text
);

CREATE FUNCTION emp_stamp() RETURNS trigger AS $emp_stamp$
    BEGIN
        -- Check that empname and salary are given
        IF NEW.empname IS NULL THEN
            RAISE EXCEPTION 'empname cannot be null';
        END IF;
        IF NEW.salary IS NULL THEN
```

```
            RAISE EXCEPTION '% cannot have null salary', NEW.empname;
        END IF;

        -- Who works for us when they must pay for it?
        IF NEW.salary < 0 THEN
            RAISE EXCEPTION '% cannot have a negative salary',
  NEW.empname;
        END IF;

        -- Remember who changed the payroll when
        NEW.last_date := current_timestamp;
        NEW.last_user := current_user;
        RETURN NEW;
    END;
$emp_stamp$ LANGUAGE plpgsql;

CREATE TRIGGER emp_stamp BEFORE INSERT OR UPDATE ON emp
    FOR EACH ROW EXECUTE FUNCTION emp_stamp();
```

Another way to log changes to a table involves creating a new table that holds a row for each insert, update, or delete that occurs. This approach can be thought of as auditing changes to a table. Example 43.4 shows an example of an audit trigger function in PL/pgSQL.

Example 43.4. A PL/pgSQL Trigger Function For Auditing

This example trigger ensures that any insert, update or delete of a row in the emp table is recorded (i.e., audited) in the emp_audit table. The current time and user name are stamped into the row, together with the type of operation performed on it.

```
CREATE TABLE emp (
    empname             text NOT NULL,
    salary              integer
);

CREATE TABLE emp_audit(
    operation           char(1)   NOT NULL,
    stamp               timestamp NOT NULL,
    userid              text      NOT NULL,
    empname             text      NOT NULL,
    salary integer
);

CREATE OR REPLACE FUNCTION process_emp_audit() RETURNS TRIGGER AS
 $emp_audit$
    BEGIN
        --
        -- Create a row in emp_audit to reflect the operation
  performed on emp,
        -- making use of the special variable TG_OP to work out the
  operation.
        --
        IF (TG_OP = 'DELETE') THEN
            INSERT INTO emp_audit SELECT 'D', now(), user, OLD.*;
```

```
        ELSIF (TG_OP = 'UPDATE') THEN
            INSERT INTO emp_audit SELECT 'U', now(), user, NEW.*;
        ELSIF (TG_OP = 'INSERT') THEN
            INSERT INTO emp_audit SELECT 'I', now(), user, NEW.*;
        END IF;
        RETURN NULL; -- result is ignored since this is an AFTER
 trigger
    END;
$emp_audit$ LANGUAGE plpgsql;

CREATE TRIGGER emp_audit
AFTER INSERT OR UPDATE OR DELETE ON emp
    FOR EACH ROW EXECUTE FUNCTION process_emp_audit();
```

A variation of the previous example uses a view joining the main table to the audit table, to show when each entry was last modified. This approach still records the full audit trail of changes to the table, but also presents a simplified view of the audit trail, showing just the last modified timestamp derived from the audit trail for each entry. Example 43.5 shows an example of an audit trigger on a view in PL/pgSQL.

Example 43.5. A PL/pgSQL View Trigger Function For Auditing

This example uses a trigger on the view to make it updatable, and ensure that any insert, update or delete of a row in the view is recorded (i.e., audited) in the emp_audit table. The current time and user name are recorded, together with the type of operation performed, and the view displays the last modified time of each row.

```
CREATE TABLE emp (
    empname             text PRIMARY KEY,
    salary              integer
);

CREATE TABLE emp_audit(
    operation           char(1)   NOT NULL,
    userid              text      NOT NULL,
    empname             text      NOT NULL,
    salary              integer,
    stamp               timestamp NOT NULL
);

CREATE VIEW emp_view AS
    SELECT e.empname,
           e.salary,
           max(ea.stamp) AS last_updated
      FROM emp e
      LEFT JOIN emp_audit ea ON ea.empname = e.empname
     GROUP BY 1, 2;

CREATE OR REPLACE FUNCTION update_emp_view() RETURNS TRIGGER AS $$
    BEGIN
        --
        -- Perform the required operation on emp, and create a row in
 emp_audit
        -- to reflect the change made to emp.
```

```
    --
    IF (TG_OP = 'DELETE') THEN
        DELETE FROM emp WHERE empname = OLD.empname;
        IF NOT FOUND THEN RETURN NULL; END IF;

        OLD.last_updated = now();
        INSERT INTO emp_audit VALUES('D', user, OLD.*);
        RETURN OLD;
    ELSIF (TG_OP = 'UPDATE') THEN
        UPDATE emp SET salary = NEW.salary WHERE empname =
OLD.empname;
        IF NOT FOUND THEN RETURN NULL; END IF;

        NEW.last_updated = now();
        INSERT INTO emp_audit VALUES('U', user, NEW.*);
        RETURN NEW;
    ELSIF (TG_OP = 'INSERT') THEN
        INSERT INTO emp VALUES(NEW.empname, NEW.salary);

        NEW.last_updated = now();
        INSERT INTO emp_audit VALUES('I', user, NEW.*);
        RETURN NEW;
    END IF;
END;
$$ LANGUAGE plpgsql;

CREATE TRIGGER emp_audit
INSTEAD OF INSERT OR UPDATE OR DELETE ON emp_view
    FOR EACH ROW EXECUTE FUNCTION update_emp_view();
```

One use of triggers is to maintain a summary table of another table. The resulting summary can be used in place of the original table for certain queries — often with vastly reduced run times. This technique is commonly used in Data Warehousing, where the tables of measured or observed data (called fact tables) might be extremely large. Example 43.6 shows an example of a trigger function in PL/pgSQL that maintains a summary table for a fact table in a data warehouse.

Example 43.6. A PL/pgSQL Trigger Function For Maintaining A Summary Table

The schema detailed here is partly based on the *Grocery Store* example from *The Data Warehouse Toolkit* by Ralph Kimball.

```
--
-- Main tables - time dimension and sales fact.
--
CREATE TABLE time_dimension (
    time_key                integer NOT NULL,
    day_of_week             integer NOT NULL,
    day_of_month            integer NOT NULL,
    month                   integer NOT NULL,
    quarter                 integer NOT NULL,
    year                    integer NOT NULL
);
CREATE UNIQUE INDEX time_dimension_key ON time_dimension(time_key);
```

```
CREATE TABLE sales_fact (
    time_key                        integer NOT NULL,
    product_key                     integer NOT NULL,
    store_key                       integer NOT NULL,
    amount_sold                     numeric(12,2) NOT NULL,
    units_sold                      integer NOT NULL,
    amount_cost                     numeric(12,2) NOT NULL
);
CREATE INDEX sales_fact_time ON sales_fact(time_key);


--
-- Summary table - sales by time.
--
CREATE TABLE sales_summary_bytime (
    time_key                        integer NOT NULL,
    amount_sold                     numeric(15,2) NOT NULL,
    units_sold                      numeric(12) NOT NULL,
    amount_cost                     numeric(15,2) NOT NULL
);
CREATE UNIQUE INDEX sales_summary_bytime_key ON
 sales_summary_bytime(time_key);


--
-- Function and trigger to amend summarized column(s) on UPDATE,
 INSERT, DELETE.
--
CREATE OR REPLACE FUNCTION maint_sales_summary_bytime() RETURNS
 TRIGGER
AS $maint_sales_summary_bytime$
    DECLARE
        delta_time_key              integer;
        delta_amount_sold           numeric(15,2);
        delta_units_sold            numeric(12);
        delta_amount_cost           numeric(15,2);
    BEGIN

        -- Work out the increment/decrement amount(s).
        IF (TG_OP = 'DELETE') THEN

            delta_time_key = OLD.time_key;
            delta_amount_sold = -1 * OLD.amount_sold;
            delta_units_sold = -1 * OLD.units_sold;
            delta_amount_cost = -1 * OLD.amount_cost;

        ELSIF (TG_OP = 'UPDATE') THEN

            -- forbid updates that change the time_key -
            -- (probably not too onerous, as DELETE + INSERT is how
 most
            -- changes will be made).
            IF ( OLD.time_key != NEW.time_key) THEN
                RAISE EXCEPTION 'Update of time_key : % -> % not
 allowed',
```

```
                                                        OLD.time_key,
        NEW.time_key;
                END IF;

                delta_time_key = OLD.time_key;
                delta_amount_sold = NEW.amount_sold - OLD.amount_sold;
                delta_units_sold = NEW.units_sold - OLD.units_sold;
                delta_amount_cost = NEW.amount_cost - OLD.amount_cost;

            ELSIF (TG_OP = 'INSERT') THEN

                delta_time_key = NEW.time_key;
                delta_amount_sold = NEW.amount_sold;
                delta_units_sold = NEW.units_sold;
                delta_amount_cost = NEW.amount_cost;

            END IF;


            -- Insert or update the summary row with the new values.
            <<insert_update>>
            LOOP
                UPDATE sales_summary_bytime
                    SET amount_sold = amount_sold + delta_amount_sold,
                        units_sold = units_sold + delta_units_sold,
                        amount_cost = amount_cost + delta_amount_cost
                    WHERE time_key = delta_time_key;

                EXIT insert_update WHEN found;

                BEGIN
                    INSERT INTO sales_summary_bytime (
                                time_key,
                                amount_sold,
                                units_sold,
                                amount_cost)
                        VALUES (
                                delta_time_key,
                                delta_amount_sold,
                                delta_units_sold,
                                delta_amount_cost
                                );

                    EXIT insert_update;

                EXCEPTION
                    WHEN UNIQUE_VIOLATION THEN
                        -- do nothing
                END;
            END LOOP insert_update;

            RETURN NULL;

        END;
```

```
$maint_sales_summary_bytime$ LANGUAGE plpgsql;

CREATE TRIGGER maint_sales_summary_bytime
AFTER INSERT OR UPDATE OR DELETE ON sales_fact
    FOR EACH ROW EXECUTE FUNCTION maint_sales_summary_bytime();

INSERT INTO sales_fact VALUES(1,1,1,10,3,15);
INSERT INTO sales_fact VALUES(1,2,1,20,5,35);
INSERT INTO sales_fact VALUES(2,2,1,40,15,135);
INSERT INTO sales_fact VALUES(2,3,1,10,1,13);
SELECT * FROM sales_summary_bytime;
DELETE FROM sales_fact WHERE product_key = 1;
SELECT * FROM sales_summary_bytime;
UPDATE sales_fact SET units_sold = units_sold * 2;
SELECT * FROM sales_summary_bytime;
```

AFTER triggers can also make use of *transition tables* to inspect the entire set of rows changed by the triggering statement. The CREATE TRIGGER command assigns names to one or both transition tables, and then the function can refer to those names as though they were read-only temporary tables. Example 43.7 shows an example.

Example 43.7. Auditing with Transition Tables

This example produces the same results as Example 43.4, but instead of using a trigger that fires for every row, it uses a trigger that fires once per statement, after collecting the relevant information in a transition table. This can be significantly faster than the row-trigger approach when the invoking statement has modified many rows. Notice that we must make a separate trigger declaration for each kind of event, since the REFERENCING clauses must be different for each case. But this does not stop us from using a single trigger function if we choose. (In practice, it might be better to use three separate functions and avoid the run-time tests on TG_OP.)

```
CREATE TABLE emp (
    empname             text NOT NULL,
    salary              integer
);

CREATE TABLE emp_audit(
    operation           char(1)   NOT NULL,
    stamp               timestamp NOT NULL,
    userid              text      NOT NULL,
    empname             text      NOT NULL,
    salary integer
);

CREATE OR REPLACE FUNCTION process_emp_audit() RETURNS TRIGGER AS
 $emp_audit$
    BEGIN
        --
        -- Create rows in emp_audit to reflect the operations
 performed on emp,
        -- making use of the special variable TG_OP to work out the
 operation.
        --
```

```
        IF (TG_OP = 'DELETE') THEN
            INSERT INTO emp_audit
                SELECT 'D', now(), user, o.* FROM old_table o;
        ELSIF (TG_OP = 'UPDATE') THEN
            INSERT INTO emp_audit
                SELECT 'U', now(), user, n.* FROM new_table n;
        ELSIF (TG_OP = 'INSERT') THEN
            INSERT INTO emp_audit
                SELECT 'I', now(), user, n.* FROM new_table n;
        END IF;
        RETURN NULL; -- result is ignored since this is an AFTER
 trigger
    END;
$emp_audit$ LANGUAGE plpgsql;

CREATE TRIGGER emp_audit_ins
    AFTER INSERT ON emp
    REFERENCING NEW TABLE AS new_table
    FOR EACH STATEMENT EXECUTE FUNCTION process_emp_audit();
CREATE TRIGGER emp_audit_upd
    AFTER UPDATE ON emp
    REFERENCING OLD TABLE AS old_table NEW TABLE AS new_table
    FOR EACH STATEMENT EXECUTE FUNCTION process_emp_audit();
CREATE TRIGGER emp_audit_del
    AFTER DELETE ON emp
    REFERENCING OLD TABLE AS old_table
    FOR EACH STATEMENT EXECUTE FUNCTION process_emp_audit();
```

43.10.2. Triggers on Events

PL/pgSQL can be used to define event triggers. PostgreSQL requires that a function that is to be called as an event trigger must be declared as a function with no arguments and a return type of event_trigger.

When a PL/pgSQL function is called as an event trigger, several special variables are created automatically in the top-level block. They are:

TG_EVENT

Data type text; a string representing the event the trigger is fired for.

TG_TAG

Data type text; variable that contains the command tag for which the trigger is fired.

Example 43.8 shows an example of an event trigger function in PL/pgSQL.

Example 43.8. A PL/pgSQL Event Trigger Function

This example trigger simply raises a NOTICE message each time a supported command is executed.

```
CREATE OR REPLACE FUNCTION snitch() RETURNS event_trigger AS $$
BEGIN
    RAISE NOTICE 'snitch: % %', tg_event, tg_tag;
END;
```

```
$$ LANGUAGE plpgsql;

CREATE EVENT TRIGGER snitch ON ddl_command_start EXECUTE FUNCTION
 snitch();
```

43.11. PL/pgSQL Under the Hood

This section discusses some implementation details that are frequently important for PL/pgSQL users to
know.

43.11.1. Variable Substitution

SQL statements and expressions within a PL/pgSQL function can refer to variables and parameters of
the function. Behind the scenes, PL/pgSQL substitutes query parameters for such references. Parameters
will only be substituted in places where a parameter or column reference is syntactically allowed. As an
extreme case, consider this example of poor programming style:

```
INSERT INTO foo (foo) VALUES (foo);
```

The first occurrence of `foo` must syntactically be a table name, so it will not be substituted, even if the
function has a variable named `foo`. The second occurrence must be the name of a column of the table, so
it will not be substituted either. Only the third occurrence is a candidate to be a reference to the function's
variable.

> ### Note
>
> PostgreSQL versions before 9.0 would try to substitute the variable in all three cases, lead-
> ing to syntax errors.

Since the names of variables are syntactically no different from the names of table columns, there can be
ambiguity in statements that also refer to tables: is a given name meant to refer to a table column, or a
variable? Let's change the previous example to

```
INSERT INTO dest (col) SELECT foo + bar FROM src;
```

Here, `dest` and `src` must be table names, and `col` must be a column of `dest`, but `foo` and `bar` might
reasonably be either variables of the function or columns of `src`.

By default, PL/pgSQL will report an error if a name in a SQL statement could refer to either a variable
or a table column. You can fix such a problem by renaming the variable or column, or by qualifying the
ambiguous reference, or by telling PL/pgSQL which interpretation to prefer.

The simplest solution is to rename the variable or column. A common coding rule is to use a different
naming convention for PL/pgSQL variables than you use for column names. For example, if you consistently name function variables *v_something* while none of your column names start with *v_*, no conflicts will occur.

Alternatively you can qualify ambiguous references to make them clear. In the above example, `src.foo`
would be an unambiguous reference to the table column. To create an unambiguous reference to a variable,
declare it in a labeled block and use the block's label (see Section 43.2). For example,

```
<<block>>
DECLARE
    foo int;
BEGIN
    foo := ...;
    INSERT INTO dest (col) SELECT block.foo + bar FROM src;
```

Here block.foo means the variable even if there is a column foo in src. Function parameters, as well as special variables such as FOUND, can be qualified by the function's name, because they are implicitly declared in an outer block labeled with the function's name.

Sometimes it is impractical to fix all the ambiguous references in a large body of PL/pgSQL code. In such cases you can specify that PL/pgSQL should resolve ambiguous references as the variable (which is compatible with PL/pgSQL's behavior before PostgreSQL 9.0), or as the table column (which is compatible with some other systems such as Oracle).

To change this behavior on a system-wide basis, set the configuration parameter plpgsql.variable_conflict to one of error, use_variable, or use_column (where error is the factory default). This parameter affects subsequent compilations of statements in PL/pgSQL functions, but not statements already compiled in the current session. Because changing this setting can cause unexpected changes in the behavior of PL/pgSQL functions, it can only be changed by a superuser.

You can also set the behavior on a function-by-function basis, by inserting one of these special commands at the start of the function text:

```
#variable_conflict error
#variable_conflict use_variable
#variable_conflict use_column
```

These commands affect only the function they are written in, and override the setting of plpgsql.variable_conflict. An example is

```
CREATE FUNCTION stamp_user(id int, comment text) RETURNS void AS $$
    #variable_conflict use_variable
    DECLARE
        curtime timestamp := now();
    BEGIN
        UPDATE users SET last_modified = curtime, comment = comment
          WHERE users.id = id;
    END;
$$ LANGUAGE plpgsql;
```

In the UPDATE command, curtime, comment, and id will refer to the function's variable and parameters whether or not users has columns of those names. Notice that we had to qualify the reference to users.id in the WHERE clause to make it refer to the table column. But we did not have to qualify the reference to comment as a target in the UPDATE list, because syntactically that must be a column of users. We could write the same function without depending on the variable_conflict setting in this way:

```
CREATE FUNCTION stamp_user(id int, comment text) RETURNS void AS $$
    <<fn>>
```

```
DECLARE
    curtime timestamp := now();
BEGIN
    UPDATE users SET last_modified = fn.curtime, comment =
stamp_user.comment
        WHERE users.id = stamp_user.id;
END;
$$ LANGUAGE plpgsql;
```

Variable substitution does not happen in the command string given to EXECUTE or one of its variants. If you need to insert a varying value into such a command, do so as part of constructing the string value, or use USING, as illustrated in Section 43.5.4.

Variable substitution currently works only in SELECT, INSERT, UPDATE, and DELETE commands, because the main SQL engine allows query parameters only in these commands. To use a non-constant name or value in other statement types (generically called utility statements), you must construct the utility statement as a string and EXECUTE it.

43.11.2. Plan Caching

The PL/pgSQL interpreter parses the function's source text and produces an internal binary instruction tree the first time the function is called (within each session). The instruction tree fully translates the PL/pgSQL statement structure, but individual SQL expressions and SQL commands used in the function are not translated immediately.

As each expression and SQL command is first executed in the function, the PL/pgSQL interpreter parses and analyzes the command to create a prepared statement, using the SPI manager's SPI_prepare function. Subsequent visits to that expression or command reuse the prepared statement. Thus, a function with conditional code paths that are seldom visited will never incur the overhead of analyzing those commands that are never executed within the current session. A disadvantage is that errors in a specific expression or command cannot be detected until that part of the function is reached in execution. (Trivial syntax errors will be detected during the initial parsing pass, but anything deeper will not be detected until execution.)

PL/pgSQL (or more precisely, the SPI manager) can furthermore attempt to cache the execution plan associated with any particular prepared statement. If a cached plan is not used, then a fresh execution plan is generated on each visit to the statement, and the current parameter values (that is, PL/pgSQL variable values) can be used to optimize the selected plan. If the statement has no parameters, or is executed many times, the SPI manager will consider creating a *generic* plan that is not dependent on specific parameter values, and caching that for re-use. Typically this will happen only if the execution plan is not very sensitive to the values of the PL/pgSQL variables referenced in it. If it is, generating a plan each time is a net win. See PREPARE for more information about the behavior of prepared statements.

Because PL/pgSQL saves prepared statements and sometimes execution plans in this way, SQL commands that appear directly in a PL/pgSQL function must refer to the same tables and columns on every execution; that is, you cannot use a parameter as the name of a table or column in an SQL command. To get around this restriction, you can construct dynamic commands using the PL/pgSQL EXECUTE statement — at the price of performing new parse analysis and constructing a new execution plan on every execution.

The mutable nature of record variables presents another problem in this connection. When fields of a record variable are used in expressions or statements, the data types of the fields must not change from one call of the function to the next, since each expression will be analyzed using the data type that is present when the expression is first reached. EXECUTE can be used to get around this problem when necessary.

If the same function is used as a trigger for more than one table, PL/pgSQL prepares and caches statements independently for each such table — that is, there is a cache for each trigger function and table combination, not just for each function. This alleviates some of the problems with varying data types; for instance, a trigger function will be able to work successfully with a column named key even if it happens to have different types in different tables.

Likewise, functions having polymorphic argument types have a separate statement cache for each combination of actual argument types they have been invoked for, so that data type differences do not cause unexpected failures.

Statement caching can sometimes have surprising effects on the interpretation of time-sensitive values. For example there is a difference between what these two functions do:

```
CREATE FUNCTION logfunc1(logtxt text) RETURNS void AS $$
    BEGIN
        INSERT INTO logtable VALUES (logtxt, 'now');
    END;
$$ LANGUAGE plpgsql;
```

and:

```
CREATE FUNCTION logfunc2(logtxt text) RETURNS void AS $$
    DECLARE
        curtime timestamp;
    BEGIN
        curtime := 'now';
        INSERT INTO logtable VALUES (logtxt, curtime);
    END;
$$ LANGUAGE plpgsql;
```

In the case of logfunc1, the PostgreSQL main parser knows when analyzing the INSERT that the string 'now' should be interpreted as timestamp, because the target column of logtable is of that type. Thus, 'now' will be converted to a timestamp constant when the INSERT is analyzed, and then used in all invocations of logfunc1 during the lifetime of the session. Needless to say, this isn't what the programmer wanted. A better idea is to use the now() or current_timestamp function.

In the case of logfunc2, the PostgreSQL main parser does not know what type 'now' should become and therefore it returns a data value of type text containing the string now. During the ensuing assignment to the local variable curtime, the PL/pgSQL interpreter casts this string to the timestamp type by calling the text_out and timestamp_in functions for the conversion. So, the computed time stamp is updated on each execution as the programmer expects. Even though this happens to work as expected, it's not terribly efficient, so use of the now() function would still be a better idea.

43.12. Tips for Developing in PL/pgSQL

One good way to develop in PL/pgSQL is to use the text editor of your choice to create your functions, and in another window, use psql to load and test those functions. If you are doing it this way, it is a good idea to write the function using CREATE OR REPLACE FUNCTION. That way you can just reload the file to update the function definition. For example:

```
CREATE OR REPLACE FUNCTION testfunc(integer) RETURNS integer AS $$
        ....
$$ LANGUAGE plpgsql;
```

While running psql, you can load or reload such a function definition file with:

```
\i filename.sql
```

and then immediately issue SQL commands to test the function.

Another good way to develop in PL/pgSQL is with a GUI database access tool that facilitates development in a procedural language. One example of such a tool is pgAdmin, although others exist. These tools often provide convenient features such as escaping single quotes and making it easier to recreate and debug functions.

43.12.1. Handling of Quotation Marks

The code of a PL/pgSQL function is specified in CREATE FUNCTION as a string literal. If you write the string literal in the ordinary way with surrounding single quotes, then any single quotes inside the function body must be doubled; likewise any backslashes must be doubled (assuming escape string syntax is used). Doubling quotes is at best tedious, and in more complicated cases the code can become downright incomprehensible, because you can easily find yourself needing half a dozen or more adjacent quote marks. It's recommended that you instead write the function body as a "dollar-quoted" string literal (see Section 4.1.2.4). In the dollar-quoting approach, you never double any quote marks, but instead take care to choose a different dollar-quoting delimiter for each level of nesting you need. For example, you might write the CREATE FUNCTION command as:

```
CREATE OR REPLACE FUNCTION testfunc(integer) RETURNS integer AS $PROC$
    ....
$PROC$ LANGUAGE plpgsql;
```

Within this, you might use quote marks for simple literal strings in SQL commands and $$ to delimit fragments of SQL commands that you are assembling as strings. If you need to quote text that includes $$, you could use Q, and so on.

The following chart shows what you have to do when writing quote marks without dollar quoting. It might be useful when translating pre-dollar quoting code into something more comprehensible.

1 quotation mark

> To begin and end the function body, for example:

> ```
> CREATE FUNCTION foo() RETURNS integer AS '
>     ....
> ' LANGUAGE plpgsql;
> ```

> Anywhere within a single-quoted function body, quote marks *must* appear in pairs.

2 quotation marks

> For string literals inside the function body, for example:

> ```
> a_output := ''Blah'';
> SELECT * FROM users WHERE f_name=''foobar'';
> ```

> In the dollar-quoting approach, you'd just write:

```
a_output := 'Blah';
SELECT * FROM users WHERE f_name='foobar';
```

which is exactly what the PL/pgSQL parser would see in either case.

4 quotation marks

When you need a single quotation mark in a string constant inside the function body, for example:

```
a_output := a_output || '' AND name LIKE ''''foobar'''' AND xyz''
```

The value actually appended to `a_output` would be: `AND name LIKE 'foobar' AND xyz`.

In the dollar-quoting approach, you'd write:

```
a_output := a_output || $$ AND name LIKE 'foobar' AND xyz$$
```

being careful that any dollar-quote delimiters around this are not just `$$`.

6 quotation marks

When a single quotation mark in a string inside the function body is adjacent to the end of that string constant, for example:

```
a_output := a_output || '' AND name LIKE ''''foobar'''''
```

The value appended to `a_output` would then be: `AND name LIKE 'foobar'`.

In the dollar-quoting approach, this becomes:

```
a_output := a_output || $$ AND name LIKE 'foobar'$$
```

10 quotation marks

When you want two single quotation marks in a string constant (which accounts for 8 quotation marks) and this is adjacent to the end of that string constant (2 more). You will probably only need that if you are writing a function that generates other functions, as in Example 43.10. For example:

```
a_output := a_output || '' if v_'' ||
    referrer_keys.kind || '' like '''''''''
    || referrer_keys.key_string || '''''''''
    then return '''''' || referrer_keys.referrer_type
    || ''''''; end if;'';
```

The value of `a_output` would then be:

```
if v_... like ''...'' then return ''...''; end if;
```

In the dollar-quoting approach, this becomes:

```
a_output := a_output || $$ if v_$$ || referrer_keys.kind || $$ like
 '$$
    || referrer_keys.key_string || $$'
    then return '$$  || referrer_keys.referrer_type
    || $$'; end if;$$;
```

where we assume we only need to put single quote marks into a_output, because it will be re-quoted before use.

43.12.2. Additional Compile-time Checks

To aid the user in finding instances of simple but common problems before they cause harm, PL/pgSQL provides additional *checks*. When enabled, depending on the configuration, they can be used to emit either a WARNING or an ERROR during the compilation of a function. A function which has received a WARNING can be executed without producing further messages, so you are advised to test in a separate development environment.

These additional checks are enabled through the configuration variables plpgsql.extra_warnings for warnings and plpgsql.extra_errors for errors. Both can be set either to a comma-separated list of checks, "none" or "all". The default is "none". Currently the list of available checks includes only one:

shadowed_variables

Checks if a declaration shadows a previously defined variable.

The following example shows the effect of plpgsql.extra_warnings set to shadowed_variables:

```
SET plpgsql.extra_warnings TO 'shadowed_variables';

CREATE FUNCTION foo(f1 int) RETURNS int AS $$
DECLARE
f1 int;
BEGIN
RETURN f1;
END
$$ LANGUAGE plpgsql;
WARNING:  variable "f1" shadows a previously defined variable
LINE 3: f1 int;
        ^
CREATE FUNCTION
```

43.13. Porting from Oracle PL/SQL

This section explains differences between PostgreSQL's PL/pgSQL language and Oracle's PL/SQL language, to help developers who port applications from Oracle® to PostgreSQL.

PL/pgSQL is similar to PL/SQL in many aspects. It is a block-structured, imperative language, and all variables have to be declared. Assignments, loops, and conditionals are similar. The main differences you should keep in mind when porting from PL/SQL to PL/pgSQL are:

- If a name used in a SQL command could be either a column name of a table or a reference to a variable of the function, PL/SQL treats it as a column name. This corresponds to PL/pgSQL's `plpgsql.variable_conflict` = `use_column` behavior, which is not the default, as explained in Section 43.11.1. It's often best to avoid such ambiguities in the first place, but if you have to port a large amount of code that depends on this behavior, setting `variable_conflict` may be the best solution.

- In PostgreSQL the function body must be written as a string literal. Therefore you need to use dollar quoting or escape single quotes in the function body. (See Section 43.12.1.)

- Data type names often need translation. For example, in Oracle string values are commonly declared as being of type `varchar2`, which is a non-SQL-standard type. In PostgreSQL, use type `varchar` or `text` instead. Similarly, replace type `number` with `numeric`, or use some other numeric data type if there's a more appropriate one.

- Instead of packages, use schemas to organize your functions into groups.

- Since there are no packages, there are no package-level variables either. This is somewhat annoying. You can keep per-session state in temporary tables instead.

- Integer `FOR` loops with `REVERSE` work differently: PL/SQL counts down from the second number to the first, while PL/pgSQL counts down from the first number to the second, requiring the loop bounds to be swapped when porting. This incompatibility is unfortunate but is unlikely to be changed. (See Section 43.6.5.5.)

- `FOR` loops over queries (other than cursors) also work differently: the target variable(s) must have been declared, whereas PL/SQL always declares them implicitly. An advantage of this is that the variable values are still accessible after the loop exits.

- There are various notational differences for the use of cursor variables.

43.13.1. Porting Examples

Example 43.9 shows how to port a simple function from PL/SQL to PL/pgSQL.

Example 43.9. Porting a Simple Function from PL/SQL to PL/pgSQL

Here is an Oracle PL/SQL function:

```
CREATE OR REPLACE FUNCTION cs_fmt_browser_version(v_name varchar2,
                                                  v_version varchar2)
RETURN varchar2 IS
BEGIN
    IF v_version IS NULL THEN
        RETURN v_name;
    END IF;
    RETURN v_name || '/' || v_version;
END;
/
show errors;
```

Let's go through this function and see the differences compared to PL/pgSQL:

- The type name `varchar2` has to be changed to `varchar` or `text`. In the examples in this section, we'll use `varchar`, but `text` is often a better choice if you do not need specific string length limits.

- The RETURN key word in the function prototype (not the function body) becomes RETURNS in Post-greSQL. Also, IS becomes AS, and you need to add a LANGUAGE clause because PL/pgSQL is not the only possible function language.

- In PostgreSQL, the function body is considered to be a string literal, so you need to use quote marks or dollar quotes around it. This substitutes for the terminating / in the Oracle approach.

- The show errors command does not exist in PostgreSQL, and is not needed since errors are reported automatically.

This is how this function would look when ported to PostgreSQL:

```
CREATE OR REPLACE FUNCTION cs_fmt_browser_version(v_name varchar,
                                                  v_version varchar)
RETURNS varchar AS $$
BEGIN
    IF v_version IS NULL THEN
        RETURN v_name;
    END IF;
    RETURN v_name || '/' || v_version;
END;
$$ LANGUAGE plpgsql;
```

Example 43.10 shows how to port a function that creates another function and how to handle the ensuing quoting problems.

Example 43.10. Porting a Function that Creates Another Function from PL/SQL to PL/pgSQL

The following procedure grabs rows from a SELECT statement and builds a large function with the results in IF statements, for the sake of efficiency.

This is the Oracle version:

```
CREATE OR REPLACE PROCEDURE cs_update_referrer_type_proc IS
    CURSOR referrer_keys IS
        SELECT * FROM cs_referrer_keys
        ORDER BY try_order;
    func_cmd VARCHAR(4000);
BEGIN
    func_cmd := 'CREATE OR REPLACE FUNCTION
 cs_find_referrer_type(v_host IN VARCHAR2,
                v_domain IN VARCHAR2, v_url IN VARCHAR2) RETURN
 VARCHAR2 IS BEGIN';

    FOR referrer_key IN referrer_keys LOOP
        func_cmd := func_cmd ||
            ' IF v_' || referrer_key.kind
            || ' LIKE ''' || referrer_key.key_string
            || ''' THEN RETURN ''' || referrer_key.referrer_type
            || '''; END IF;';
    END LOOP;

    func_cmd := func_cmd || ' RETURN NULL; END;';
```

```
        EXECUTE IMMEDIATE func_cmd;
END;
/
show errors;
```

Here is how this function would end up in PostgreSQL:

```
CREATE OR REPLACE PROCEDURE cs_update_referrer_type_proc() AS $func$
DECLARE
    referrer_keys CURSOR IS
        SELECT * FROM cs_referrer_keys
        ORDER BY try_order;
    func_body text;
    func_cmd text;
BEGIN
    func_body := 'BEGIN';

    FOR referrer_key IN referrer_keys LOOP
        func_body := func_body ||
          ' IF v_' || referrer_key.kind
          || ' LIKE ' || quote_literal(referrer_key.key_string)
          || ' THEN RETURN ' ||
  quote_literal(referrer_key.referrer_type)
          || '; END IF;' ;
    END LOOP;

    func_body := func_body || ' RETURN NULL; END;';

    func_cmd :=
      'CREATE OR REPLACE FUNCTION cs_find_referrer_type(v_host
varchar,
                                                        v_domain
varchar,
                                                        v_url varchar)
        RETURNS varchar AS '
      || quote_literal(func_body)
      || ' LANGUAGE plpgsql;' ;

    EXECUTE func_cmd;
END;
$func$ LANGUAGE plpgsql;
```

Notice how the body of the function is built separately and passed through quote_literal to double any quote marks in it. This technique is needed because we cannot safely use dollar quoting for defining the new function: we do not know for sure what strings will be interpolated from the refer-rer_key.key_string field. (We are assuming here that referrer_key.kind can be trusted to always be host, domain, or url, but referrer_key.key_string might be anything, in particular it might contain dollar signs.) This function is actually an improvement on the Oracle original, because it will not generate broken code when referrer_key.key_string or referrer_key.refer-rer_type contain quote marks.

Example 43.11 shows how to port a function with OUT parameters and string manipulation. PostgreSQL does not have a built-in instr function, but you can create one using a combination of other functions.

In Section 43.13.3 there is a PL/pgSQL implementation of `instr` that you can use to make your porting easier.

Example 43.11. Porting a Procedure With String Manipulation and OUT Parameters from PL/SQL to PL/pgSQL

The following Oracle PL/SQL procedure is used to parse a URL and return several elements (host, path, and query).

This is the Oracle version:

```
CREATE OR REPLACE PROCEDURE cs_parse_url(
    v_url IN VARCHAR2,
    v_host OUT VARCHAR2,  -- This will be passed back
    v_path OUT VARCHAR2,  -- This one too
    v_query OUT VARCHAR2) -- And this one
IS
    a_pos1 INTEGER;
    a_pos2 INTEGER;
BEGIN
    v_host := NULL;
    v_path := NULL;
    v_query := NULL;
    a_pos1 := instr(v_url, '//');

    IF a_pos1 = 0 THEN
        RETURN;
    END IF;
    a_pos2 := instr(v_url, '/', a_pos1 + 2);
    IF a_pos2 = 0 THEN
        v_host := substr(v_url, a_pos1 + 2);
        v_path := '/';
        RETURN;
    END IF;

    v_host := substr(v_url, a_pos1 + 2, a_pos2 - a_pos1 - 2);
    a_pos1 := instr(v_url, '?', a_pos2 + 1);

    IF a_pos1 = 0 THEN
        v_path := substr(v_url, a_pos2);
        RETURN;
    END IF;

    v_path := substr(v_url, a_pos2, a_pos1 - a_pos2);
    v_query := substr(v_url, a_pos1 + 1);
END;
/
show errors;
```

Here is a possible translation into PL/pgSQL:

```
CREATE OR REPLACE FUNCTION cs_parse_url(
    v_url IN VARCHAR,
```

```
    v_host OUT VARCHAR,  -- This will be passed back
    v_path OUT VARCHAR,  -- This one too
    v_query OUT VARCHAR) -- And this one
AS $$
DECLARE
    a_pos1 INTEGER;
    a_pos2 INTEGER;
BEGIN
    v_host := NULL;
    v_path := NULL;
    v_query := NULL;
    a_pos1 := instr(v_url, '//');

    IF a_pos1 = 0 THEN
        RETURN;
    END IF;
    a_pos2 := instr(v_url, '/', a_pos1 + 2);
    IF a_pos2 = 0 THEN
        v_host := substr(v_url, a_pos1 + 2);
        v_path := '/';
        RETURN;
    END IF;

    v_host := substr(v_url, a_pos1 + 2, a_pos2 - a_pos1 - 2);
    a_pos1 := instr(v_url, '?', a_pos2 + 1);

    IF a_pos1 = 0 THEN
        v_path := substr(v_url, a_pos2);
        RETURN;
    END IF;

    v_path := substr(v_url, a_pos2, a_pos1 - a_pos2);
    v_query := substr(v_url, a_pos1 + 1);
END;
$$ LANGUAGE plpgsql;
```

This function could be used like this:

```
SELECT * FROM cs_parse_url('http://foobar.com/query.cgi?baz');
```

Example 43.12 shows how to port a procedure that uses numerous features that are specific to Oracle.

Example 43.12. Porting a Procedure from PL/SQL to PL/pgSQL

The Oracle version:

```
CREATE OR REPLACE PROCEDURE cs_create_job(v_job_id IN INTEGER) IS
    a_running_job_count INTEGER;
BEGIN
    LOCK TABLE cs_jobs IN EXCLUSIVE MODE;

    SELECT count(*) INTO a_running_job_count FROM cs_jobs WHERE
 end_stamp IS NULL;
```

```
    IF a_running_job_count > 0 THEN
        COMMIT; -- free lock
        raise_application_error(-20000,
                    'Unable to create a new job: a job is currently
running.');
    END IF;

    DELETE FROM cs_active_job;
    INSERT INTO cs_active_job(job_id) VALUES (v_job_id);

    BEGIN
        INSERT INTO cs_jobs (job_id, start_stamp) VALUES (v_job_id,
sysdate);
    EXCEPTION
        WHEN dup_val_on_index THEN NULL; -- don't worry if it already
 exists
    END;
    COMMIT;
END;
/
show errors
```

This is how we could port this procedure to PL/pgSQL:

```
CREATE OR REPLACE PROCEDURE cs_create_job(v_job_id integer) AS $$
DECLARE
    a_running_job_count integer;
BEGIN
    LOCK TABLE cs_jobs IN EXCLUSIVE MODE;

    SELECT count(*) INTO a_running_job_count FROM cs_jobs WHERE
 end_stamp IS NULL;

    IF a_running_job_count > 0 THEN
        COMMIT; -- free lock
        RAISE EXCEPTION 'Unable to create a new job: a job is
currently running'; -- ❶
    END IF;

    DELETE FROM cs_active_job;
    INSERT INTO cs_active_job(job_id) VALUES (v_job_id);

    BEGIN
        INSERT INTO cs_jobs (job_id, start_stamp) VALUES (v_job_id,
now());
    EXCEPTION
        WHEN unique_violation THEN -- ❷
            -- don't worry if it already exists
    END;
    COMMIT;
END;
$$ LANGUAGE plpgsql;
```

■ The syntax of RAISE is considerably different from Oracle's statement, although the basic case RAISE *exception_name* works similarly.

■ The exception names supported by PL/pgSQL are different from Oracle's. The set of built-in exception names is much larger (see Appendix A). There is not currently a way to declare user-defined exception names, although you can throw user-chosen SQLSTATE values instead.

43.13.2. Other Things to Watch For

This section explains a few other things to watch for when porting Oracle PL/SQL functions to PostgreSQL.

43.13.2.1. Implicit Rollback after Exceptions

In PL/pgSQL, when an exception is caught by an EXCEPTION clause, all database changes since the block's BEGIN are automatically rolled back. That is, the behavior is equivalent to what you'd get in Oracle with:

```
BEGIN
    SAVEPOINT s1;
    ... code here ...
EXCEPTION
    WHEN ... THEN
        ROLLBACK TO s1;
        ... code here ...
    WHEN ... THEN
        ROLLBACK TO s1;
        ... code here ...
END;
```

If you are translating an Oracle procedure that uses SAVEPOINT and ROLLBACK TO in this style, your task is easy: just omit the SAVEPOINT and ROLLBACK TO. If you have a procedure that uses SAVEPOINT and ROLLBACK TO in a different way then some actual thought will be required.

43.13.2.2. EXECUTE

The PL/pgSQL version of EXECUTE works similarly to the PL/SQL version, but you have to remember to use quote_literal and quote_ident as described in Section 43.5.4. Constructs of the type EXECUTE 'SELECT * FROM $1'; will not work reliably unless you use these functions.

43.13.2.3. Optimizing PL/pgSQL Functions

PostgreSQL gives you two function creation modifiers to optimize execution: "volatility" (whether the function always returns the same result when given the same arguments) and "strictness" (whether the function returns null if any argument is null). Consult the CREATE FUNCTION reference page for details.

When making use of these optimization attributes, your CREATE FUNCTION statement might look something like this:

```
CREATE FUNCTION foo(...) RETURNS integer AS $$
...
$$ LANGUAGE plpgsql STRICT IMMUTABLE;
```

43.13.3. Appendix

This section contains the code for a set of Oracle-compatible `instr` functions that you can use to simplify your porting efforts.

```
--
-- instr functions that mimic Oracle's counterpart
-- Syntax: instr(string1, string2 [, n [, m]])
-- where [] denotes optional parameters.
--
-- Search string1, beginning at the nth character, for the mth
 occurrence
-- of string2.  If n is negative, search backwards, starting at the
 abs(n)'th
-- character from the end of string1.
-- If n is not passed, assume 1 (search starts at first character).
-- If m is not passed, assume 1 (find first occurrence).
-- Returns starting index of string2 in string1, or 0 if string2 is
 not found.
--

CREATE FUNCTION instr(varchar, varchar) RETURNS integer AS $$
BEGIN
    RETURN instr($1, $2, 1);
END;
$$ LANGUAGE plpgsql STRICT IMMUTABLE;


CREATE FUNCTION instr(string varchar, string_to_search_for varchar,
                      beg_index integer)
RETURNS integer AS $$
DECLARE
    pos integer NOT NULL DEFAULT 0;
    temp_str varchar;
    beg integer;
    length integer;
    ss_length integer;
BEGIN
    IF beg_index > 0 THEN
        temp_str := substring(string FROM beg_index);
        pos := position(string_to_search_for IN temp_str);

        IF pos = 0 THEN
            RETURN 0;
        ELSE
            RETURN pos + beg_index - 1;
        END IF;
    ELSIF beg_index < 0 THEN
        ss_length := char_length(string_to_search_for);
        length := char_length(string);
        beg := length + 1 + beg_index;
```

```
            WHILE beg > 0 LOOP
                temp_str := substring(string FROM beg FOR ss_length);
                IF string_to_search_for = temp_str THEN
                    RETURN beg;
                END IF;

                beg := beg - 1;
            END LOOP;

            RETURN 0;
        ELSE
            RETURN 0;
        END IF;
    END;
    $$ LANGUAGE plpgsql STRICT IMMUTABLE;


    CREATE FUNCTION instr(string varchar, string_to_search_for varchar,
                          beg_index integer, occur_index integer)
    RETURNS integer AS $$
    DECLARE
        pos integer NOT NULL DEFAULT 0;
        occur_number integer NOT NULL DEFAULT 0;
        temp_str varchar;
        beg integer;
        i integer;
        length integer;
        ss_length integer;
    BEGIN
        IF occur_index <= 0 THEN
            RAISE 'argument ''%'' is out of range', occur_index
              USING ERRCODE = '22003';
        END IF;

        IF beg_index > 0 THEN
            beg := beg_index - 1;
            FOR i IN 1..occur_index LOOP
                temp_str := substring(string FROM beg + 1);
                pos := position(string_to_search_for IN temp_str);
                IF pos = 0 THEN
                    RETURN 0;
                END IF;
                beg := beg + pos;
            END LOOP;

            RETURN beg;
        ELSIF beg_index < 0 THEN
            ss_length := char_length(string_to_search_for);
            length := char_length(string);
            beg := length + 1 + beg_index;

            WHILE beg > 0 LOOP
                temp_str := substring(string FROM beg FOR ss_length);
                IF string_to_search_for = temp_str THEN
```

```
            occur_number := occur_number + 1;
            IF occur_number = occur_index THEN
                RETURN beg;
            END IF;
        END IF;

        beg := beg - 1;
    END LOOP;

    RETURN 0;
ELSE
    RETURN 0;
END IF;
END;
$$ LANGUAGE plpgsql STRICT IMMUTABLE;
```

Chapter 44. PL/Tcl - Tcl Procedural Language

PL/Tcl is a loadable procedural language for the PostgreSQL database system that enables the Tcl language[1] to be used to write PostgreSQL functions.

44.1. Overview

PL/Tcl offers most of the capabilities a function writer has in the C language, with a few restrictions, and with the addition of the powerful string processing libraries that are available for Tcl.

One compelling *good* restriction is that everything is executed from within the safety of the context of a Tcl interpreter. In addition to the limited command set of safe Tcl, only a few commands are available to access the database via SPI and to raise messages via `elog()`. PL/Tcl provides no way to access internals of the database server or to gain OS-level access under the permissions of the PostgreSQL server process, as a C function can do. Thus, unprivileged database users can be trusted to use this language; it does not give them unlimited authority.

The other notable implementation restriction is that Tcl functions cannot be used to create input/output functions for new data types.

Sometimes it is desirable to write Tcl functions that are not restricted to safe Tcl. For example, one might want a Tcl function that sends email. To handle these cases, there is a variant of PL/Tcl called `PL/TclU` (for untrusted Tcl). This is exactly the same language except that a full Tcl interpreter is used. *If PL/TclU is used, it must be installed as an untrusted procedural language* so that only database superusers can create functions in it. The writer of a PL/TclU function must take care that the function cannot be used to do anything unwanted, since it will be able to do anything that could be done by a user logged in as the database administrator.

The shared object code for the PL/Tcl and PL/TclU call handlers is automatically built and installed in the PostgreSQL library directory if Tcl support is specified in the configuration step of the installation procedure. To install PL/Tcl and/or PL/TclU in a particular database, use the `CREATE EXTENSION` command, for example `CREATE EXTENSION pltcl` or `CREATE EXTENSION pltclu`.

44.2. PL/Tcl Functions and Arguments

To create a function in the PL/Tcl language, use the standard CREATE FUNCTION syntax:

```
CREATE FUNCTION funcname (argument-types) RETURNS return-type AS $$
    # PL/Tcl function body
$$ LANGUAGE pltcl;
```

PL/TclU is the same, except that the language has to be specified as `pltclu`.

The body of the function is simply a piece of Tcl script. When the function is called, the argument values are passed to the Tcl script as variables named 1 ... *n*. The result is returned from the Tcl code in the usual way, with a `return` statement. In a procedure, the return value from the Tcl code is ignored.

---

[1] http://www.tcl.tk/

For example, a function returning the greater of two integer values could be defined as:

```
CREATE FUNCTION tcl_max(integer, integer) RETURNS integer AS $$
    if {$1 > $2} {return $1}
    return $2
$$ LANGUAGE pltcl STRICT;
```

Note the clause STRICT, which saves us from having to think about null input values: if a null value is passed, the function will not be called at all, but will just return a null result automatically.

In a nonstrict function, if the actual value of an argument is null, the corresponding $n variable will be set to an empty string. To detect whether a particular argument is null, use the function argisnull. For example, suppose that we wanted tcl_max with one null and one nonnull argument to return the nonnull argument, rather than null:

```
CREATE FUNCTION tcl_max(integer, integer) RETURNS integer AS $$
    if {[argisnull 1]} {
        if {[argisnull 2]} { return_null }
        return $2
    }
    if {[argisnull 2]} { return $1 }
    if {$1 > $2} {return $1}
    return $2
$$ LANGUAGE pltcl;
```

As shown above, to return a null value from a PL/Tcl function, execute return_null. This can be done whether the function is strict or not.

Composite-type arguments are passed to the function as Tcl arrays. The element names of the array are the attribute names of the composite type. If an attribute in the passed row has the null value, it will not appear in the array. Here is an example:

```
CREATE TABLE employee (
    name text,
    salary integer,
    age integer
);

CREATE FUNCTION overpaid(employee) RETURNS boolean AS $$
    if {200000.0 < $1(salary)} {
        return "t"
    }
    if {$1(age) < 30 && 100000.0 < $1(salary)} {
        return "t"
    }
    return "f"
$$ LANGUAGE pltcl;
```

PL/Tcl functions can return composite-type results, too. To do this, the Tcl code must return a list of column name/value pairs matching the expected result type. Any column names omitted from the list are returned as nulls, and an error is raised if there are unexpected column names. Here is an example:

```
CREATE FUNCTION square_cube(in int, out squared int, out cubed int) AS
  $$
    return [list squared [expr {$1 * $1}] cubed [expr {$1 * $1 * $1}]]
$$ LANGUAGE pltcl;
```

Output arguments of procedures are returned in the same way, for example:

```
CREATE PROCEDURE tcl_triple(INOUT a integer, INOUT b integer) AS $$
    return [list a [expr {$1 * 3}] b [expr {$2 * 3}]]
$$ LANGUAGE pltcl;

CALL tcl_triple(5, 10);
```

Tip

The result list can be made from an array representation of the desired tuple with the `array get` Tcl command. For example:

```
CREATE FUNCTION raise_pay(employee, delta int) RETURNS
 employee AS $$
    set 1(salary) [expr {$1(salary) + $2}]
    return [array get 1]
$$ LANGUAGE pltcl;
```

PL/Tcl functions can return sets. To do this, the Tcl code should call `return_next` once per row to be returned, passing either the appropriate value when returning a scalar type, or a list of column name/value pairs when returning a composite type. Here is an example returning a scalar type:

```
CREATE FUNCTION sequence(int, int) RETURNS SETOF int AS $$
    for {set i $1} {$i < $2} {incr i} {
        return_next $i
    }
$$ LANGUAGE pltcl;
```

and here is one returning a composite type:

```
CREATE FUNCTION table_of_squares(int, int) RETURNS TABLE (x int, x2
 int) AS $$
    for {set i $1} {$i < $2} {incr i} {
        return_next [list x $i x2 [expr {$i * $i}]]
    }
$$ LANGUAGE pltcl;
```

44.3. Data Values in PL/Tcl

The argument values supplied to a PL/Tcl function's code are simply the input arguments converted to text form (just as if they had been displayed by a SELECT statement). Conversely, the `return` and `return_next` commands will accept any string that is acceptable input format for the function's declared result type, or for the specified column of a composite result type.

44.4. Global Data in PL/Tcl

Sometimes it is useful to have some global data that is held between two calls to a function or is shared between different functions. This is easily done in PL/Tcl, but there are some restrictions that must be understood.

For security reasons, PL/Tcl executes functions called by any one SQL role in a separate Tcl interpreter for that role. This prevents accidental or malicious interference by one user with the behavior of another user's PL/Tcl functions. Each such interpreter will have its own values for any "global" Tcl variables. Thus, two PL/Tcl functions will share the same global variables if and only if they are executed by the same SQL role. In an application wherein a single session executes code under multiple SQL roles (via SECURITY DEFINER functions, use of SET ROLE, etc) you may need to take explicit steps to ensure that PL/Tcl functions can share data. To do that, make sure that functions that should communicate are owned by the same user, and mark them SECURITY DEFINER. You must of course take care that such functions can't be used to do anything unintended.

All PL/TclU functions used in a session execute in the same Tcl interpreter, which of course is distinct from the interpreter(s) used for PL/Tcl functions. So global data is automatically shared between PL/TclU functions. This is not considered a security risk because all PL/TclU functions execute at the same trust level, namely that of a database superuser.

To help protect PL/Tcl functions from unintentionally interfering with each other, a global array is made available to each function via the upvar command. The global name of this variable is the function's internal name, and the local name is GD. It is recommended that GD be used for persistent private data of a function. Use regular Tcl global variables only for values that you specifically intend to be shared among multiple functions. (Note that the GD arrays are only global within a particular interpreter, so they do not bypass the security restrictions mentioned above.)

An example of using GD appears in the spi_execp example below.

44.5. Database Access from PL/Tcl

The following commands are available to access the database from the body of a PL/Tcl function:

spi_exec ?-count n? ?-array name? command ?loop-body?

> Executes an SQL command given as a string. An error in the command causes an error to be raised. Otherwise, the return value of spi_exec is the number of rows processed (selected, inserted, updated, or deleted) by the command, or zero if the command is a utility statement. In addition, if the command is a SELECT statement, the values of the selected columns are placed in Tcl variables as described below.

> The optional -count value tells spi_exec the maximum number of rows to process in the command. The effect of this is comparable to setting up a query as a cursor and then saying FETCH n.

> If the command is a SELECT statement, the values of the result columns are placed into Tcl variables named after the columns. If the -array option is given, the column values are instead stored into elements of the named associative array, with the column names used as array indexes. In addition, the current row number within the result (counting from zero) is stored into the array element named ".tupno", unless that name is in use as a column name in the result.

> If the command is a SELECT statement and no loop-body script is given, then only the first row of results are stored into Tcl variables or array elements; remaining rows, if any, are ignored. No storing

occurs if the query returns no rows. (This case can be detected by checking the result of `spi_exec`.) For example:

```
spi_exec "SELECT count(*) AS cnt FROM pg_proc"
```

will set the Tcl variable `$cnt` to the number of rows in the `pg_proc` system catalog.

If the optional *loop-body* argument is given, it is a piece of Tcl script that is executed once for each row in the query result. (*loop-body* is ignored if the given command is not a SELECT.) The values of the current row's columns are stored into Tcl variables or array elements before each iteration. For example:

```
spi_exec -array C "SELECT * FROM pg_class" {
    elog DEBUG "have table $C(relname)"
}
```

will print a log message for every row of `pg_class`. This feature works similarly to other Tcl looping constructs; in particular `continue` and `break` work in the usual way inside the loop body.

If a column of a query result is null, the target variable for it is "unset" rather than being set.

spi_prepare *query typelist*

Prepares and saves a query plan for later execution. The saved plan will be retained for the life of the current session.

The query can use parameters, that is, placeholders for values to be supplied whenever the plan is actually executed. In the query string, refer to parameters by the symbols $1 ... $*n*. If the query uses parameters, the names of the parameter types must be given as a Tcl list. (Write an empty list for *typelist* if no parameters are used.)

The return value from `spi_prepare` is a query ID to be used in subsequent calls to `spi_execp`. See `spi_execp` for an example.

spi_execp ?-count *n*? ?-array *name*? ?-nulls *string*? *queryid* ?*value-list*? ?*loop-body*?

Executes a query previously prepared with `spi_prepare`. *queryid* is the ID returned by `spi_prepare`. If the query references parameters, a *value-list* must be supplied. This is a Tcl list of actual values for the parameters. The list must be the same length as the parameter type list previously given to `spi_prepare`. Omit *value-list* if the query has no parameters.

The optional value for `-nulls` is a string of spaces and `'n'` characters telling `spi_execp` which of the parameters are null values. If given, it must have exactly the same length as the *value-list*. If it is not given, all the parameter values are nonnull.

Except for the way in which the query and its parameters are specified, `spi_execp` works just like `spi_exec`. The `-count`, `-array`, and *loop-body* options are the same, and so is the result value.

Here's an example of a PL/Tcl function using a prepared plan:

```
CREATE FUNCTION t1_count(integer, integer) RETURNS integer AS $$
    if {![ info exists GD(plan) ]} {
```

```
        # prepare the saved plan on the first call
        set GD(plan) [ spi_prepare \
                "SELECT count(*) AS cnt FROM t1 WHERE num >= \$1
AND num <= \$2" \
                [ list int4 int4 ] ]
    }
    spi_execp -count 1 $GD(plan) [ list $1 $2 ]
    return $cnt
$$ LANGUAGE pltcl;
```

We need backslashes inside the query string given to `spi_prepare` to ensure that the $n markers will be passed through to `spi_prepare` as-is, and not replaced by Tcl variable substitution.

`spi_lastoid`

Returns the OID of the row inserted by the last `spi_exec` or `spi_execp`, if the command was a single-row `INSERT` and the modified table contained OIDs. (If not, you get zero.)

`subtransaction` *command*

The Tcl script contained in *command* is executed within a SQL subtransaction. If the script returns an error, that entire subtransaction is rolled back before returning the error out to the surrounding Tcl code. See Section 44.9 for more details and an example.

`quote` *string*

Doubles all occurrences of single quote and backslash characters in the given string. This can be used to safely quote strings that are to be inserted into SQL commands given to `spi_exec` or `spi_prepare`. For example, think about an SQL command string like:

```
"SELECT '$val' AS ret"
```

where the Tcl variable `val` actually contains `doesn't`. This would result in the final command string:

```
SELECT 'doesn't' AS ret
```

which would cause a parse error during `spi_exec` or `spi_prepare`. To work properly, the submitted command should contain:

```
SELECT 'doesn''t' AS ret
```

which can be formed in PL/Tcl using:

```
"SELECT '[ quote $val ]' AS ret"
```

One advantage of `spi_execp` is that you don't have to quote parameter values like this, since the parameters are never parsed as part of an SQL command string.

`elog` *level msg*

Emits a log or error message. Possible levels are `DEBUG`, `LOG`, `INFO`, `NOTICE`, `WARNING`, `ERROR`, and `FATAL`. `ERROR` raises an error condition; if this is not trapped by the surrounding Tcl code, the error propagates out to the calling query, causing the current transaction or subtransaction to be aborted. This is effectively the same as the Tcl `error` command. `FATAL` aborts the transaction and causes the current session to shut down. (There is probably no good reason to use this error level in PL/Tcl functions, but it's provided for completeness.) The other levels only generate messages of different priority levels. Whether messages of a particular priority are reported to the client, written to the server log, or both is controlled by the log_min_messages and client_min_messages configuration variables. See Chapter 19 and Section 44.8 for more information.

44.6. Trigger Functions in PL/Tcl

Trigger functions can be written in PL/Tcl. PostgreSQL requires that a function that is to be called as a trigger must be declared as a function with no arguments and a return type of `trigger`.

The information from the trigger manager is passed to the function body in the following variables:

$TG_name

The name of the trigger from the `CREATE TRIGGER` statement.

$TG_relid

The object ID of the table that caused the trigger function to be invoked.

$TG_table_name

The name of the table that caused the trigger function to be invoked.

$TG_table_schema

The schema of the table that caused the trigger function to be invoked.

$TG_relatts

A Tcl list of the table column names, prefixed with an empty list element. So looking up a column name in the list with Tcl's `lsearch` command returns the element's number starting with 1 for the first column, the same way the columns are customarily numbered in PostgreSQL. (Empty list elements also appear in the positions of columns that have been dropped, so that the attribute numbering is correct for columns to their right.)

$TG_when

The string `BEFORE`, `AFTER`, or `INSTEAD OF`, depending on the type of trigger event.

$TG_level

The string `ROW` or `STATEMENT` depending on the type of trigger event.

$TG_op

The string `INSERT`, `UPDATE`, `DELETE`, or `TRUNCATE` depending on the type of trigger event.

$NEW

An associative array containing the values of the new table row for `INSERT` or `UPDATE` actions, or empty for `DELETE`. The array is indexed by column name. Columns that are null will not appear in the array. This is not set for statement-level triggers.

$OLD

An associative array containing the values of the old table row for UPDATE or DELETE actions, or empty for INSERT. The array is indexed by column name. Columns that are null will not appear in the array. This is not set for statement-level triggers.

$args

A Tcl list of the arguments to the function as given in the CREATE TRIGGER statement. These arguments are also accessible as $1 ... $n in the function body.

The return value from a trigger function can be one of the strings OK or SKIP, or a list of column name/value pairs. If the return value is OK, the operation (INSERT/UPDATE/DELETE) that fired the trigger will proceed normally. SKIP tells the trigger manager to silently suppress the operation for this row. If a list is returned, it tells PL/Tcl to return a modified row to the trigger manager; the contents of the modified row are specified by the column names and values in the list. Any columns not mentioned in the list are set to null. Returning a modified row is only meaningful for row-level BEFORE INSERT or UPDATE triggers, for which the modified row will be inserted instead of the one given in $NEW; or for row-level INSTEAD OF INSERT or UPDATE triggers where the returned row is used as the source data for INSERT RETURNING or UPDATE RETURNING clauses. In row-level BEFORE DELETE or INSTEAD OF DELETE triggers, returning a modified row has the same effect as returning OK, that is the operation proceeds. The trigger return value is ignored for all other types of triggers.

Tip

The result list can be made from an array representation of the modified tuple with the `array get` Tcl command.

Here's a little example trigger function that forces an integer value in a table to keep track of the number of updates that are performed on the row. For new rows inserted, the value is initialized to 0 and then incremented on every update operation.

```
CREATE FUNCTION trigfunc_modcount() RETURNS trigger AS $$
    switch $TG_op {
        INSERT {
            set NEW($1) 0
        }
        UPDATE {
            set NEW($1) $OLD($1)
            incr NEW($1)
        }
        default {
            return OK
        }
    }
    return [array get NEW]
$$ LANGUAGE pltcl;

CREATE TABLE mytab (num integer, description text, modcnt integer);

CREATE TRIGGER trig_mytab_modcount BEFORE INSERT OR UPDATE ON mytab
```

```
FOR EACH ROW EXECUTE FUNCTION trigfunc_modcount('modcnt');
```

Notice that the trigger function itself does not know the column name; that's supplied from the trigger arguments. This lets the trigger function be reused with different tables.

44.7. Event Trigger Functions in PL/Tcl

Event trigger functions can be written in PL/Tcl. PostgreSQL requires that a function that is to be called as an event trigger must be declared as a function with no arguments and a return type of `event_trigger`.

The information from the trigger manager is passed to the function body in the following variables:

`$TG_event`

> The name of the event the trigger is fired for.

`$TG_tag`

> The command tag for which the trigger is fired.

The return value of the trigger function is ignored.

Here's a little example event trigger function that simply raises a `NOTICE` message each time a supported command is executed:

```
CREATE OR REPLACE FUNCTION tclsnitch() RETURNS event_trigger AS $$
  elog NOTICE "tclsnitch: $TG_event $TG_tag"
$$ LANGUAGE pltcl;

CREATE EVENT TRIGGER tcl_a_snitch ON ddl_command_start EXECUTE
 FUNCTION tclsnitch();
```

44.8. Error Handling in PL/Tcl

Tcl code within or called from a PL/Tcl function can raise an error, either by executing some invalid operation or by generating an error using the Tcl `error` command or PL/Tcl's `elog` command. Such errors can be caught within Tcl using the Tcl `catch` command. If an error is not caught but is allowed to propagate out to the top level of execution of the PL/Tcl function, it is reported as a SQL error in the function's calling query.

Conversely, SQL errors that occur within PL/Tcl's `spi_exec`, `spi_prepare`, and `spi_execp` commands are reported as Tcl errors, so they are catchable by Tcl's `catch` command. (Each of these PL/Tcl commands runs its SQL operation in a subtransaction, which is rolled back on error, so that any partially-completed operation is automatically cleaned up.) Again, if an error propagates out to the top level without being caught, it turns back into a SQL error.

Tcl provides an `errorCode` variable that can represent additional information about an error in a form that is easy for Tcl programs to interpret. The contents are in Tcl list format, and the first word identifies the subsystem or library reporting the error; beyond that the contents are left to the individual subsystem or library. For database errors reported by PL/Tcl commands, the first word is `POSTGRES`, the second word is the PostgreSQL version number, and additional words are field name/value pairs providing detailed information about the error. Fields `SQLSTATE`, `condition`, and `message` are always supplied (the first two represent the error code and condition name as shown in Appendix A). Fields that may be present include detail, hint, context, schema, table, column, datatype, constraint, statement, cursor_position, filename, lineno, and funcname.

A convenient way to work with PL/Tcl's errorCode information is to load it into an array, so that the field names become array subscripts. Code for doing that might look like

```
if {[catch { spi_exec $sql_command }]} {
    if {[lindex $::errorCode 0] == "POSTGRES"} {
        array set errorArray $::errorCode
        if {$errorArray(condition) == "undefined_table"} {
            # deal with missing table
        } else {
            # deal with some other type of SQL error
        }
    }
}
```

(The double colons explicitly specify that errorCode is a global variable.)

44.9. Explicit Subtransactions in PL/Tcl

Recovering from errors caused by database access as described in Section 44.8 can lead to an undesirable situation where some operations succeed before one of them fails, and after recovering from that error the data is left in an inconsistent state. PL/Tcl offers a solution to this problem in the form of explicit subtransactions.

Consider a function that implements a transfer between two accounts:

```
CREATE FUNCTION transfer_funds() RETURNS void AS $$
    if [catch {
        spi_exec "UPDATE accounts SET balance = balance - 100 WHERE
account_name = 'joe'"
        spi_exec "UPDATE accounts SET balance = balance + 100 WHERE
account_name = 'mary'"
    } errormsg] {
        set result [format "error transferring funds: %s" $errormsg]
    } else {
        set result "funds transferred successfully"
    }
    spi_exec "INSERT INTO operations (result) VALUES ('[quote
$result]')"
$$ LANGUAGE pltcl;
```

If the second UPDATE statement results in an exception being raised, this function will log the failure, but the result of the first UPDATE will nevertheless be committed. In other words, the funds will be withdrawn from Joe's account, but will not be transferred to Mary's account. This happens because each spi_exec is a separate subtransaction, and only one of those subtransactions got rolled back.

To handle such cases, you can wrap multiple database operations in an explicit subtransaction, which will succeed or roll back as a whole. PL/Tcl provides a subtransaction command to manage this. We can rewrite our function as:

```
CREATE FUNCTION transfer_funds2() RETURNS void AS $$
    if [catch {
        subtransaction {
            spi_exec "UPDATE accounts SET balance = balance - 100
WHERE account_name = 'joe'"
            spi_exec "UPDATE accounts SET balance = balance + 100
WHERE account_name = 'mary'"
        }
    } errormsg] {
        set result [format "error transferring funds: %s" $errormsg]
    } else {
        set result "funds transferred successfully"
    }
    spi_exec "INSERT INTO operations (result) VALUES ('[quote
$result]')"
$$ LANGUAGE pltcl;
```

Note that use of catch is still required for this purpose. Otherwise the error would propagate to the top level of the function, preventing the desired insertion into the operations table. The subtransaction command does not trap errors, it only assures that all database operations executed inside its scope will be rolled back together when an error is reported.

A rollback of an explicit subtransaction occurs on any error reported by the contained Tcl code, not only errors originating from database access. Thus a regular Tcl exception raised inside a subtransaction command will also cause the subtransaction to be rolled back. However, non-error exits out of the contained Tcl code (for instance, due to return) do not cause a rollback.

44.10. Transaction Management

In a procedure called from the top level or an anonymous code block (DO command) called from the top level it is possible to control transactions. To commit the current transaction, call the commit command. To roll back the current transaction, call the rollback command. (Note that it is not possible to run the SQL commands COMMIT or ROLLBACK via spi_exec or similar. It has to be done using these functions.) After a transaction is ended, a new transaction is automatically started, so there is no separate command for that.

Here is an example:

```
CREATE PROCEDURE transaction_test1()
LANGUAGE pltcl
AS $$
for {set i 0} {$i < 10} {incr i} {
    spi_exec "INSERT INTO test1 (a) VALUES ($i)"
    if {$i % 2 == 0} {
        commit
    } else {
        rollback
    }
}
$$;

CALL transaction_test1();
```

Transactions cannot be ended when an explicit subtransaction is active.

44.11. PL/Tcl Configuration

This section lists configuration parameters that affect PL/Tcl.

`pltcl.start_proc (string)`

> This parameter, if set to a nonempty string, specifies the name (possibly schema-qualified) of a parameterless PL/Tcl function that is to be executed whenever a new Tcl interpreter is created for PL/Tcl. Such a function can perform per-session initialization, such as loading additional Tcl code. A new Tcl interpreter is created when a PL/Tcl function is first executed in a database session, or when an additional interpreter has to be created because a PL/Tcl function is called by a new SQL role.

> The referenced function must be written in the `pltcl` language, and must not be marked SECURITY DEFINER. (These restrictions ensure that it runs in the interpreter it's supposed to initialize.) The current user must have permission to call it, too.

> If the function fails with an error it will abort the function call that caused the new interpreter to be created and propagate out to the calling query, causing the current transaction or subtransaction to be aborted. Any actions already done within Tcl won't be undone; however, that interpreter won't be used again. If the language is used again the initialization will be attempted again within a fresh Tcl interpreter.

> Only superusers can change this setting. Although this setting can be changed within a session, such changes will not affect Tcl interpreters that have already been created.

`pltclu.start_proc (string)`

> This parameter is exactly like `pltcl.start_proc`, except that it applies to PL/TclU. The referenced function must be written in the `pltclu` language.

44.12. Tcl Procedure Names

In PostgreSQL, the same function name can be used for different function definitions as long as the number of arguments or their types differ. Tcl, however, requires all procedure names to be distinct. PL/Tcl deals with this by making the internal Tcl procedure names contain the object ID of the function from the system table `pg_proc` as part of their name. Thus, PostgreSQL functions with the same name and different argument types will be different Tcl procedures, too. This is not normally a concern for a PL/Tcl programmer, but it might be visible when debugging.

Chapter 45. PL/Perl - Perl Procedural Language

PL/Perl is a loadable procedural language that enables you to write PostgreSQL functions in the Perl programming language[1].

The main advantage to using PL/Perl is that this allows use, within stored functions, of the manyfold "string munging" operators and functions available for Perl. Parsing complex strings might be easier using Perl than it is with the string functions and control structures provided in PL/pgSQL.

To install PL/Perl in a particular database, use CREATE EXTENSION plperl.

Tip

If a language is installed into `template1`, all subsequently created databases will have the language installed automatically.

Note

Users of source packages must specially enable the build of PL/Perl during the installation process. (Refer to Chapter 16 for more information.) Users of binary packages might find PL/Perl in a separate subpackage.

45.1. PL/Perl Functions and Arguments

To create a function in the PL/Perl language, use the standard CREATE FUNCTION syntax:

```
CREATE FUNCTION funcname (argument-types) RETURNS return-type AS $$
    # PL/Perl function body
$$ LANGUAGE plperl;
```

The body of the function is ordinary Perl code. In fact, the PL/Perl glue code wraps it inside a Perl subroutine. A PL/Perl function is called in a scalar context, so it can't return a list. You can return non-scalar values (arrays, records, and sets) by returning a reference, as discussed below.

In a PL/Perl procedure, any return value from the Perl code is ignored.

PL/Perl also supports anonymous code blocks called with the DO statement:

```
DO $$
    # PL/Perl code
$$ LANGUAGE plperl;
```

---

[1] http://www.perl.org

An anonymous code block receives no arguments, and whatever value it might return is discarded. Otherwise it behaves just like a function.

Note

The use of named nested subroutines is dangerous in Perl, especially if they refer to lexical variables in the enclosing scope. Because a PL/Perl function is wrapped in a subroutine, any named subroutine you place inside one will be nested. In general, it is far safer to create anonymous subroutines which you call via a coderef. For more information, see the entries for `Variable "%s" will not stay shared` and `Variable "%s" is not available` in the perldiag man page, or search the Internet for "perl nested named subroutine".

The syntax of the `CREATE FUNCTION` command requires the function body to be written as a string constant. It is usually most convenient to use dollar quoting (see Section 4.1.2.4) for the string constant. If you choose to use escape string syntax `E''`, you must double any single quote marks (`'`) and backslashes (`\`) used in the body of the function (see Section 4.1.2.1).

Arguments and results are handled as in any other Perl subroutine: arguments are passed in `@_`, and a result value is returned with `return` or as the last expression evaluated in the function.

For example, a function returning the greater of two integer values could be defined as:

```
CREATE FUNCTION perl_max (integer, integer) RETURNS integer AS $$
    if ($_[0] > $_[1]) { return $_[0]; }
    return $_[1];
$$ LANGUAGE plperl;
```

Note

Arguments will be converted from the database's encoding to UTF-8 for use inside PL/Perl, and then converted from UTF-8 back to the database encoding upon return.

If an SQL null value is passed to a function, the argument value will appear as "undefined" in Perl. The above function definition will not behave very nicely with null inputs (in fact, it will act as though they are zeroes). We could add `STRICT` to the function definition to make PostgreSQL do something more reasonable: if a null value is passed, the function will not be called at all, but will just return a null result automatically. Alternatively, we could check for undefined inputs in the function body. For example, suppose that we wanted `perl_max` with one null and one nonnull argument to return the nonnull argument, rather than a null value:

```
CREATE FUNCTION perl_max (integer, integer) RETURNS integer AS $$
    my ($x, $y) = @_;
    if (not defined $x) {
        return undef if not defined $y;
        return $y;
    }
    return $x if not defined $y;
    return $x if $x > $y;
```

```
    return $y;
$$ LANGUAGE plperl;
```

As shown above, to return an SQL null value from a PL/Perl function, return an undefined value. This can be done whether the function is strict or not.

Anything in a function argument that is not a reference is a string, which is in the standard PostgreSQL external text representation for the relevant data type. In the case of ordinary numeric or text types, Perl will just do the right thing and the programmer will normally not have to worry about it. However, in other cases the argument will need to be converted into a form that is more usable in Perl. For example, the decode_bytea function can be used to convert an argument of type bytea into unescaped binary.

Similarly, values passed back to PostgreSQL must be in the external text representation format. For example, the encode_bytea function can be used to escape binary data for a return value of type bytea.

Perl can return PostgreSQL arrays as references to Perl arrays. Here is an example:

```
CREATE OR REPLACE function returns_array()
RETURNS text[][] AS $$
    return [['a"b','c,d'],['e\\f','g']];
$$ LANGUAGE plperl;

select returns_array();
```

Perl passes PostgreSQL arrays as a blessed PostgreSQL::InServer::ARRAY object. This object may be treated as an array reference or a string, allowing for backward compatibility with Perl code written for PostgreSQL versions below 9.1 to run. For example:

```
CREATE OR REPLACE FUNCTION concat_array_elements(text[]) RETURNS TEXT
  AS $$
    my $arg = shift;
    my $result = "";
    return undef if (!defined $arg);

    # as an array reference
    for (@$arg) {
        $result .= $_;
    }

    # also works as a string
    $result .= $arg;

    return $result;
$$ LANGUAGE plperl;

SELECT concat_array_elements(ARRAY['PL','/','Perl']);
```

Note

Multidimensional arrays are represented as references to lower-dimensional arrays of references in a way common to every Perl programmer.

Composite-type arguments are passed to the function as references to hashes. The keys of the hash are the attribute names of the composite type. Here is an example:

```
CREATE TABLE employee (
    name text,
    basesalary integer,
    bonus integer
);

CREATE FUNCTION empcomp(employee) RETURNS integer AS $$
    my ($emp) = @_;
    return $emp->{basesalary} + $emp->{bonus};
$$ LANGUAGE plperl;

SELECT name, empcomp(employee.*) FROM employee;
```

A PL/Perl function can return a composite-type result using the same approach: return a reference to a hash that has the required attributes. For example:

```
CREATE TYPE testrowperl AS (f1 integer, f2 text, f3 text);

CREATE OR REPLACE FUNCTION perl_row() RETURNS testrowperl AS $$
    return {f2 => 'hello', f1 => 1, f3 => 'world'};
$$ LANGUAGE plperl;

SELECT * FROM perl_row();
```

Any columns in the declared result data type that are not present in the hash will be returned as null values.

Similarly, output arguments of procedures can be returned as a hash reference:

```
CREATE PROCEDURE perl_triple(INOUT a integer, INOUT b integer) AS $$
    my ($a, $b) = @_;
    return {a => $a * 3, b => $b * 3};
$$ LANGUAGE plperl;

CALL perl_triple(5, 10);
```

PL/Perl functions can also return sets of either scalar or composite types. Usually you'll want to return rows one at a time, both to speed up startup time and to keep from queuing up the entire result set in memory. You can do this with return_next as illustrated below. Note that after the last return_next, you must put either return or (better) return undef.

```
CREATE OR REPLACE FUNCTION perl_set_int(int)
RETURNS SETOF INTEGER AS $$
    foreach (0..$_[0]) {
        return_next($_);
    }
    return undef;
$$ LANGUAGE plperl;
```

```
SELECT * FROM perl_set_int(5);

CREATE OR REPLACE FUNCTION perl_set()
RETURNS SETOF testrowperl AS $$
    return_next({ f1 => 1, f2 => 'Hello', f3 => 'World' });
    return_next({ f1 => 2, f2 => 'Hello', f3 => 'PostgreSQL' });
    return_next({ f1 => 3, f2 => 'Hello', f3 => 'PL/Perl' });
    return undef;
$$ LANGUAGE plperl;
```

For small result sets, you can return a reference to an array that contains either scalars, references to arrays, or references to hashes for simple types, array types, and composite types, respectively. Here are some simple examples of returning the entire result set as an array reference:

```
CREATE OR REPLACE FUNCTION perl_set_int(int) RETURNS SETOF INTEGER AS
 $$
    return [0..$_[0]];
$$ LANGUAGE plperl;

SELECT * FROM perl_set_int(5);

CREATE OR REPLACE FUNCTION perl_set() RETURNS SETOF testrowperl AS $$
    return [
        { f1 => 1, f2 => 'Hello', f3 => 'World' },
        { f1 => 2, f2 => 'Hello', f3 => 'PostgreSQL' },
        { f1 => 3, f2 => 'Hello', f3 => 'PL/Perl' }
    ];
$$ LANGUAGE plperl;

SELECT * FROM perl_set();
```

If you wish to use the `strict` pragma with your code you have a few options. For temporary global use you can `SET plperl.use_strict` to true. This will affect subsequent compilations of PL/Perl functions, but not functions already compiled in the current session. For permanent global use you can set `plperl.use_strict` to true in the `postgresql.conf` file.

For permanent use in specific functions you can simply put:

```
use strict;
```

at the top of the function body.

The `feature` pragma is also available to `use` if your Perl is version 5.10.0 or higher.

45.2. Data Values in PL/Perl

The argument values supplied to a PL/Perl function's code are simply the input arguments converted to text form (just as if they had been displayed by a `SELECT` statement). Conversely, the `return` and `return_next` commands will accept any string that is acceptable input format for the function's declared return type.

45.3. Built-in Functions

45.3.1. Database Access from PL/Perl

Access to the database itself from your Perl function can be done via the following functions:

spi_exec_query(*query* [, *max-rows*])

> spi_exec_query executes an SQL command and returns the entire row set as a reference to an array of hash references. *You should only use this command when you know that the result set will be relatively small.* Here is an example of a query (SELECT command) with the optional maximum number of rows:

> ```
> $rv = spi_exec_query('SELECT * FROM my_table', 5);
> ```

> This returns up to 5 rows from the table my_table. If my_table has a column my_column, you can get that value from row $i of the result like this:

> ```
> $foo = $rv->{rows}[$i]->{my_column};
> ```

> The total number of rows returned from a SELECT query can be accessed like this:

> ```
> $nrows = $rv->{processed}
> ```

> Here is an example using a different command type:

> ```
> $query = "INSERT INTO my_table VALUES (1, 'test')";
> $rv = spi_exec_query($query);
> ```

> You can then access the command status (e.g., SPI_OK_INSERT) like this:

> ```
> $res = $rv->{status};
> ```

> To get the number of rows affected, do:

> ```
> $nrows = $rv->{processed};
> ```

> Here is a complete example:

```
CREATE TABLE test (
    i int,
    v varchar
);

INSERT INTO test (i, v) VALUES (1, 'first line');
INSERT INTO test (i, v) VALUES (2, 'second line');
INSERT INTO test (i, v) VALUES (3, 'third line');
INSERT INTO test (i, v) VALUES (4, 'immortal');
```

```
CREATE OR REPLACE FUNCTION test_munge() RETURNS SETOF test AS $$
    my $rv = spi_exec_query('select i, v from test;');
    my $status = $rv->{status};
    my $nrows = $rv->{processed};
    foreach my $rn (0 .. $nrows - 1) {
        my $row = $rv->{rows}[$rn];
        $row->{i} += 200 if defined($row->{i});
        $row->{v} =~ tr/A-Za-z/a-zA-Z/ if (defined($row->{v}));
        return_next($row);
    }
    return undef;
$$ LANGUAGE plperl;

SELECT * FROM test_munge();
```

spi_query(*command*)
spi_fetchrow(*cursor*)
spi_cursor_close(*cursor*)

spi_query and spi_fetchrow work together as a pair for row sets which might be large, or for cases where you wish to return rows as they arrive. spi_fetchrow works *only* with spi_query. The following example illustrates how you use them together:

```
CREATE TYPE foo_type AS (the_num INTEGER, the_text TEXT);

CREATE OR REPLACE FUNCTION lotsa_md5 (INTEGER) RETURNS SETOF
 foo_type AS $$
    use Digest::MD5 qw(md5_hex);
    my $file = '/usr/share/dict/words';
    my $t = localtime;
    elog(NOTICE, "opening file $file at $t" );
    open my $fh, '<', $file # ooh, it's a file access!
        or elog(ERROR, "cannot open $file for reading: $!");
    my @words = <$fh>;
    close $fh;
    $t = localtime;
    elog(NOTICE, "closed file $file at $t");
    chomp(@words);
    my $row;
    my $sth = spi_query("SELECT * FROM generate_series(1,$_[0]) AS
 b(a)");
    while (defined ($row = spi_fetchrow($sth))) {
        return_next({
            the_num => $row->{a},
            the_text => md5_hex($words[rand @words])
        });
    }
    return;
$$ LANGUAGE plperlu;

SELECT * from lotsa_md5(500);
```

Normally, spi_fetchrow should be repeated until it returns undef, indicating that there are no more rows to read. The cursor returned by spi_query is automatically freed when spi_fetchrow returns undef. If you do not wish to read all the rows, instead call spi_cursor_close to free the cursor. Failure to do so will result in memory leaks.

```
spi_prepare(command, argument types)
spi_query_prepared(plan, arguments)
spi_exec_prepared(plan [, attributes], arguments)
spi_freeplan(plan)
```

spi_prepare, spi_query_prepared, spi_exec_prepared, and spi_freeplan implement the same functionality but for prepared queries. spi_prepare accepts a query string with numbered argument placeholders ($1, $2, etc) and a string list of argument types:

```
$plan = spi_prepare('SELECT * FROM test WHERE id > $1 AND name =
 $2',
                                                    'INTEGER',
 'TEXT');
```

Once a query plan is prepared by a call to spi_prepare, the plan can be used instead of the string query, either in spi_exec_prepared, where the result is the same as returned by spi_exec_query, or in spi_query_prepared which returns a cursor exactly as spi_query does, which can be later passed to spi_fetchrow. The optional second parameter to spi_exec_prepared is a hash reference of attributes; the only attribute currently supported is limit, which sets the maximum number of rows returned by a query.

The advantage of prepared queries is that is it possible to use one prepared plan for more than one query execution. After the plan is not needed anymore, it can be freed with spi_freeplan:

```
CREATE OR REPLACE FUNCTION init() RETURNS VOID AS $$
        $_SHARED{my_plan} = spi_prepare('SELECT (now() + $1)::date
 AS now',
                                        'INTERVAL');
$$ LANGUAGE plperl;

CREATE OR REPLACE FUNCTION add_time( INTERVAL ) RETURNS TEXT AS $$
        return spi_exec_prepared(
                $_SHARED{my_plan},
                $_[0]
        )->{rows}->[0]->{now};
$$ LANGUAGE plperl;

CREATE OR REPLACE FUNCTION done() RETURNS VOID AS $$
        spi_freeplan( $_SHARED{my_plan});
        undef $_SHARED{my_plan};
$$ LANGUAGE plperl;

SELECT init();
SELECT add_time('1 day'), add_time('2 days'), add_time('3 days');
SELECT done();

  add_time  |  add_time  |  add_time
------------+------------+------------
 2005-12-10 | 2005-12-11 | 2005-12-12
```

Note that the parameter subscript in `spi_prepare` is defined via $1, $2, $3, etc, so avoid declaring query strings in double quotes that might easily lead to hard-to-catch bugs.

Another example illustrates usage of an optional parameter in `spi_exec_prepared`:

```
CREATE TABLE hosts AS SELECT id, ('192.168.1.'||id)::inet AS
  address
                        FROM generate_series(1,3) AS id;

CREATE OR REPLACE FUNCTION init_hosts_query() RETURNS VOID AS $$
        $_SHARED{plan} = spi_prepare('SELECT * FROM hosts
                                      WHERE address << $1',
  'inet');
$$ LANGUAGE plperl;

CREATE OR REPLACE FUNCTION query_hosts(inet) RETURNS SETOF hosts AS
  $$
        return spi_exec_prepared(
                $_SHARED{plan},
                {limit => 2},
                $_[0]
        )->{rows};
$$ LANGUAGE plperl;

CREATE OR REPLACE FUNCTION release_hosts_query() RETURNS VOID AS $$
        spi_freeplan($_SHARED{plan});
        undef $_SHARED{plan};
$$ LANGUAGE plperl;

SELECT init_hosts_query();
SELECT query_hosts('192.168.1.0/30');
SELECT release_hosts_query();

    query_hosts
-----------------
  (1,192.168.1.1)
  (2,192.168.1.2)
(2 rows)
```

```
spi_commit()
spi_rollback()
```

Commit or roll back the current transaction. This can only be called in a procedure or anonymous code block (DO command) called from the top level. (Note that it is not possible to run the SQL commands COMMIT or ROLLBACK via `spi_exec_query` or similar. It has to be done using these functions.) After a transaction is ended, a new transaction is automatically started, so there is no separate function for that.

Here is an example:

```
CREATE PROCEDURE transaction_test1()
LANGUAGE plperl
AS $$
```

```
foreach my $i (0..9) {
    spi_exec_query("INSERT INTO test1 (a) VALUES ($i)");
    if ($i % 2 == 0) {
        spi_commit();
    } else {
        spi_rollback();
    }
}
$$;

CALL transaction_test1();
```

45.3.2. Utility Functions in PL/Perl

elog(*level*, *msg*)

Emit a log or error message. Possible levels are DEBUG, LOG, INFO, NOTICE, WARNING, and ER-ROR. ERROR raises an error condition; if this is not trapped by the surrounding Perl code, the error propagates out to the calling query, causing the current transaction or subtransaction to be aborted. This is effectively the same as the Perl die command. The other levels only generate messages of different priority levels. Whether messages of a particular priority are reported to the client, written to the server log, or both is controlled by the log_min_messages and client_min_messages configuration variables. See Chapter 19 for more information.

quote_literal(*string*)

Return the given string suitably quoted to be used as a string literal in an SQL statement string. Embedded single-quotes and backslashes are properly doubled. Note that quote_literal returns undef on undef input; if the argument might be undef, quote_nullable is often more suitable.

quote_nullable(*string*)

Return the given string suitably quoted to be used as a string literal in an SQL statement string; or, if the argument is undef, return the unquoted string "NULL". Embedded single-quotes and backslashes are properly doubled.

quote_ident(*string*)

Return the given string suitably quoted to be used as an identifier in an SQL statement string. Quotes are added only if necessary (i.e., if the string contains non-identifier characters or would be case-folded). Embedded quotes are properly doubled.

decode_bytea(*string*)

Return the unescaped binary data represented by the contents of the given string, which should be bytea encoded.

encode_bytea(*string*)

Return the bytea encoded form of the binary data contents of the given string.

encode_array_literal(*array*)
encode_array_literal(*array*, *delimiter*)

Returns the contents of the referenced array as a string in array literal format (see Section 8.15.2). Returns the argument value unaltered if it's not a reference to an array. The delimiter used between elements of the array literal defaults to ", " if a delimiter is not specified or is undef.

encode_typed_literal(*value*, *typename*)

Converts a Perl variable to the value of the data type passed as a second argument and returns a string representation of this value. Correctly handles nested arrays and values of composite types.

encode_array_constructor(*array*)

Returns the contents of the referenced array as a string in array constructor format (see Section 4.2.12). Individual values are quoted using quote_nullable. Returns the argument value, quoted using quote_nullable, if it's not a reference to an array.

looks_like_number(*string*)

Returns a true value if the content of the given string looks like a number, according to Perl, returns false otherwise. Returns undef if the argument is undef. Leading and trailing space is ignored. Inf and Infinity are regarded as numbers.

is_array_ref(*argument*)

Returns a true value if the given argument may be treated as an array reference, that is, if ref of the argument is ARRAY or PostgreSQL::InServer::ARRAY. Returns false otherwise.

45.4. Global Values in PL/Perl

You can use the global hash %_SHARED to store data, including code references, between function calls for the lifetime of the current session.

Here is a simple example for shared data:

```
CREATE OR REPLACE FUNCTION set_var(name text, val text) RETURNS text
  AS $$
    if ($_SHARED{$_[0]} = $_[1]) {
        return 'ok';
    } else {
        return "cannot set shared variable $_[0] to $_[1]";
    }
$$ LANGUAGE plperl;

CREATE OR REPLACE FUNCTION get_var(name text) RETURNS text AS $$
    return $_SHARED{$_[0]};
$$ LANGUAGE plperl;

SELECT set_var('sample', 'Hello, PL/Perl!  How''s tricks?');
SELECT get_var('sample');
```

Here is a slightly more complicated example using a code reference:

```
CREATE OR REPLACE FUNCTION myfuncs() RETURNS void AS $$
    $_SHARED{myquote} = sub {
        my $arg = shift;
        $arg =~ s/(['\\])/\\$1/g;
        return "'$arg'";
    };
```

```
$$ LANGUAGE plperl;

SELECT myfuncs(); /* initializes the function */

/* Set up a function that uses the quote function */

CREATE OR REPLACE FUNCTION use_quote(TEXT) RETURNS text AS $$
    my $text_to_quote = shift;
    my $qfunc = $_SHARED{myquote};
    return &$qfunc($text_to_quote);
$$ LANGUAGE plperl;
```

(You could have replaced the above with the one-liner `return $_SHARED{myquote}->($_[0]);` at the expense of readability.)

For security reasons, PL/Perl executes functions called by any one SQL role in a separate Perl interpreter for that role. This prevents accidental or malicious interference by one user with the behavior of another user's PL/Perl functions. Each such interpreter has its own value of the `%_SHARED` variable and other global state. Thus, two PL/Perl functions will share the same value of `%_SHARED` if and only if they are executed by the same SQL role. In an application wherein a single session executes code under multiple SQL roles (via `SECURITY DEFINER` functions, use of `SET ROLE`, etc) you may need to take explicit steps to ensure that PL/Perl functions can share data via `%_SHARED`. To do that, make sure that functions that should communicate are owned by the same user, and mark them `SECURITY DEFINER`. You must of course take care that such functions can't be used to do anything unintended.

45.5. Trusted and Untrusted PL/Perl

Normally, PL/Perl is installed as a "trusted" programming language named `plperl`. In this setup, certain Perl operations are disabled to preserve security. In general, the operations that are restricted are those that interact with the environment. This includes file handle operations, `require`, and `use` (for external modules). There is no way to access internals of the database server process or to gain OS-level access with the permissions of the server process, as a C function can do. Thus, any unprivileged database user can be permitted to use this language.

Here is an example of a function that will not work because file system operations are not allowed for security reasons:

```
CREATE FUNCTION badfunc() RETURNS integer AS $$
    my $tmpfile = "/tmp/badfile";
    open my $fh, '>', $tmpfile
        or elog(ERROR, qq{could not open the file "$tmpfile": $!});
    print $fh "Testing writing to a file\n";
    close $fh or elog(ERROR, qq{could not close the file "$tmpfile":
 $!});
    return 1;
$$ LANGUAGE plperl;
```

The creation of this function will fail as its use of a forbidden operation will be caught by the validator.

Sometimes it is desirable to write Perl functions that are not restricted. For example, one might want a Perl function that sends mail. To handle these cases, PL/Perl can also be installed as an "untrusted" language (usually called PL/PerlU). In this case the full Perl language is available. When installing the language, the language name `plperlu` will select the untrusted PL/Perl variant.

The writer of a PL/PerlU function must take care that the function cannot be used to do anything unwanted, since it will be able to do anything that could be done by a user logged in as the database administrator. Note that the database system allows only database superusers to create functions in untrusted languages.

If the above function was created by a superuser using the language `plperlu`, execution would succeed.

In the same way, anonymous code blocks written in Perl can use restricted operations if the language is specified as `plperlu` rather than `plperl`, but the caller must be a superuser.

Note

While PL/Perl functions run in a separate Perl interpreter for each SQL role, all PL/PerlU functions executed in a given session run in a single Perl interpreter (which is not any of the ones used for PL/Perl functions). This allows PL/PerlU functions to share data freely, but no communication can occur between PL/Perl and PL/PerlU functions.

Note

Perl cannot support multiple interpreters within one process unless it was built with the appropriate flags, namely either `usemultiplicity` or `useithreads`. (`usemultiplicity` is preferred unless you actually need to use threads. For more details, see the perlembed man page.) If PL/Perl is used with a copy of Perl that was not built this way, then it is only possible to have one Perl interpreter per session, and so any one session can only execute either PL/PerlU functions, or PL/Perl functions that are all called by the same SQL role.

45.6. PL/Perl Triggers

PL/Perl can be used to write trigger functions. In a trigger function, the hash reference `$_TD` contains information about the current trigger event. `$_TD` is a global variable, which gets a separate local value for each invocation of the trigger. The fields of the `$_TD` hash reference are:

`$_TD->{new}{foo}`

>   NEW value of column `foo`

`$_TD->{old}{foo}`

>   OLD value of column `foo`

`$_TD->{name}`

>   Name of the trigger being called

`$_TD->{event}`

>   Trigger event: INSERT, UPDATE, DELETE, TRUNCATE, or UNKNOWN

`$_TD->{when}`

>   When the trigger was called: BEFORE, AFTER, INSTEAD OF, or UNKNOWN

`$_TD->{level}`

> The trigger level: ROW, STATEMENT, or UNKNOWN

`$_TD->{relid}`

> OID of the table on which the trigger fired

`$_TD->{table_name}`

> Name of the table on which the trigger fired

`$_TD->{relname}`

> Name of the table on which the trigger fired. This has been deprecated, and could be removed in a future release. Please use $_TD->{table_name} instead.

`$_TD->{table_schema}`

> Name of the schema in which the table on which the trigger fired, is

`$_TD->{argc}`

> Number of arguments of the trigger function

`@{$_TD->{args}}`

> Arguments of the trigger function. Does not exist if `$_TD->{argc}` is 0.

Row-level triggers can return one of the following:

`return;`

> Execute the operation

`"SKIP"`

> Don't execute the operation

`"MODIFY"`

> Indicates that the NEW row was modified by the trigger function

Here is an example of a trigger function, illustrating some of the above:

```
CREATE TABLE test (
    i int,
    v varchar
);

CREATE OR REPLACE FUNCTION valid_id() RETURNS trigger AS $$
    if (($_TD->{new}{i} >= 100) || ($_TD->{new}{i} <= 0)) {
        return "SKIP";    # skip INSERT/UPDATE command
    } elsif ($_TD->{new}{v} ne "immortal") {
        $_TD->{new}{v} .= "(modified by trigger)";
        return "MODIFY";  # modify row and execute INSERT/UPDATE
  command
```

```
    } else {
        return;              # execute INSERT/UPDATE command
    }
$$ LANGUAGE plperl;

CREATE TRIGGER test_valid_id_trig
    BEFORE INSERT OR UPDATE ON test
    FOR EACH ROW EXECUTE FUNCTION valid_id();
```

45.7. PL/Perl Event Triggers

PL/Perl can be used to write event trigger functions. In an event trigger function, the hash reference $_TD contains information about the current trigger event. $_TD is a global variable, which gets a separate local value for each invocation of the trigger. The fields of the $_TD hash reference are:

$_TD->{event}

> The name of the event the trigger is fired for.

$_TD->{tag}

> The command tag for which the trigger is fired.

The return value of the trigger function is ignored.

Here is an example of an event trigger function, illustrating some of the above:

```
CREATE OR REPLACE FUNCTION perlsnitch() RETURNS event_trigger AS $$
  elog(NOTICE, "perlsnitch: " . $_TD->{event} . " " . $_TD->{tag} . "
  ");
$$ LANGUAGE plperl;

CREATE EVENT TRIGGER perl_a_snitch
    ON ddl_command_start
    EXECUTE FUNCTION perlsnitch();
```

45.8. PL/Perl Under the Hood

45.8.1. Configuration

This section lists configuration parameters that affect PL/Perl.

plperl.on_init (string)

> Specifies Perl code to be executed when a Perl interpreter is first initialized, before it is specialized for use by plperl or plperlu. The SPI functions are not available when this code is executed. If the code fails with an error it will abort the initialization of the interpreter and propagate out to the calling query, causing the current transaction or subtransaction to be aborted.

> The Perl code is limited to a single string. Longer code can be placed into a module and loaded by the on_init string. Examples:

```
plperl.on_init = 'require "plperlinit.pl"'
plperl.on_init = 'use lib "/my/app"; use MyApp::PgInit;'
```

Any modules loaded by `plperl.on_init`, either directly or indirectly, will be available for use by `plperl`. This may create a security risk. To see what modules have been loaded you can use:

```
DO 'elog(WARNING, join ", ", sort keys %INC)' LANGUAGE plperl;
```

Initialization will happen in the postmaster if the `plperl` library is included in shared_preload_libraries, in which case extra consideration should be given to the risk of destabilizing the postmaster. The principal reason for making use of this feature is that Perl modules loaded by `plperl.on_init` need be loaded only at postmaster start, and will be instantly available without loading overhead in individual database sessions. However, keep in mind that the overhead is avoided only for the first Perl interpreter used by a database session — either PL/PerlU, or PL/Perl for the first SQL role that calls a PL/Perl function. Any additional Perl interpreters created in a database session will have to execute `plperl.on_init` afresh. Also, on Windows there will be no savings whatsoever from preloading, since the Perl interpreter created in the postmaster process does not propagate to child processes.

This parameter can only be set in the `postgresql.conf` file or on the server command line.

`plperl.on_plperl_init(string)`
`plperl.on_plperlu_init(string)`

These parameters specify Perl code to be executed when a Perl interpreter is specialized for `plperl` or `plperlu` respectively. This will happen when a PL/Perl or PL/PerlU function is first executed in a database session, or when an additional interpreter has to be created because the other language is called or a PL/Perl function is called by a new SQL role. This follows any initialization done by `plperl.on_init`. The SPI functions are not available when this code is executed. The Perl code in `plperl.on_plperl_init` is executed after "locking down" the interpreter, and thus it can only perform trusted operations.

If the code fails with an error it will abort the initialization and propagate out to the calling query, causing the current transaction or subtransaction to be aborted. Any actions already done within Perl won't be undone; however, that interpreter won't be used again. If the language is used again the initialization will be attempted again within a fresh Perl interpreter.

Only superusers can change these settings. Although these settings can be changed within a session, such changes will not affect Perl interpreters that have already been used to execute functions.

`plperl.use_strict(boolean)`

When set true subsequent compilations of PL/Perl functions will have the `strict` pragma enabled. This parameter does not affect functions already compiled in the current session.

45.8.2. Limitations and Missing Features

The following features are currently missing from PL/Perl, but they would make welcome contributions.

- PL/Perl functions cannot call each other directly.

- SPI is not yet fully implemented.

- If you are fetching very large data sets using `spi_exec_query`, you should be aware that these will all go into memory. You can avoid this by using `spi_query`/`spi_fetchrow` as illustrated earlier.

A similar problem occurs if a set-returning function passes a large set of rows back to PostgreSQL via `return`. You can avoid this problem too by instead using `return_next` for each row returned, as shown previously.

- When a session ends normally, not due to a fatal error, any `END` blocks that have been defined are executed. Currently no other actions are performed. Specifically, file handles are not automatically flushed and objects are not automatically destroyed.

Chapter 46. PL/Python - Python Procedural Language

The PL/Python procedural language allows PostgreSQL functions to be written in the Python language[1].

To install PL/Python in a particular database, use `CREATE EXTENSION plpythonu` (but see also Section 46.1).

Tip

If a language is installed into `template1`, all subsequently created databases will have the language installed automatically.

PL/Python is only available as an "untrusted" language, meaning it does not offer any way of restricting what users can do in it and is therefore named `plpythonu`. A trusted variant `plpython` might become available in the future if a secure execution mechanism is developed in Python. The writer of a function in untrusted PL/Python must take care that the function cannot be used to do anything unwanted, since it will be able to do anything that could be done by a user logged in as the database administrator. Only superusers can create functions in untrusted languages such as `plpythonu`.

Note

Users of source packages must specially enable the build of PL/Python during the installation process. (Refer to the installation instructions for more information.) Users of binary packages might find PL/Python in a separate subpackage.

46.1. Python 2 vs. Python 3

PL/Python supports both the Python 2 and Python 3 language variants. (The PostgreSQL installation instructions might contain more precise information about the exact supported minor versions of Python.) Because the Python 2 and Python 3 language variants are incompatible in some important aspects, the following naming and transitioning scheme is used by PL/Python to avoid mixing them:

- The PostgreSQL language named `plpython2u` implements PL/Python based on the Python 2 language variant.

- The PostgreSQL language named `plpython3u` implements PL/Python based on the Python 3 language variant.

- The language named `plpythonu` implements PL/Python based on the default Python language variant, which is currently Python 2. (This default is independent of what any local Python installations might consider to be their "default", for example, what `/usr/bin/python` might be.) The default will probably be changed to Python 3 in a distant future release of PostgreSQL, depending on the progress of the migration to Python 3 in the Python community.

---

[1] https://www.python.org

This scheme is analogous to the recommendations in PEP 394[2] regarding the naming and transitioning of the `python` command.

It depends on the build configuration or the installed packages whether PL/Python for Python 2 or Python 3 or both are available.

Tip

The built variant depends on which Python version was found during the installation or which version was explicitly set using the `PYTHON` environment variable; see Section 16.4. To make both variants of PL/Python available in one installation, the source tree has to be configured and built twice.

This results in the following usage and migration strategy:

- Existing users and users who are currently not interested in Python 3 use the language name `plpythonu` and don't have to change anything for the foreseeable future. It is recommended to gradually "future-proof" the code via migration to Python 2.6/2.7 to simplify the eventual migration to Python 3.

  In practice, many PL/Python functions will migrate to Python 3 with few or no changes.

- Users who know that they have heavily Python 2 dependent code and don't plan to ever change it can make use of the `plpython2u` language name. This will continue to work into the very distant future, until Python 2 support might be completely dropped by PostgreSQL.

- Users who want to dive into Python 3 can use the `plpython3u` language name, which will keep working forever by today's standards. In the distant future, when Python 3 might become the default, they might like to remove the "3" for aesthetic reasons.

- Daredevils, who want to build a Python-3-only operating system environment, can change the contents of `pg_pltemplate` to make `plpythonu` be equivalent to `plpython3u`, keeping in mind that this would make their installation incompatible with most of the rest of the world.

See also the document What's New In Python 3.0[3] for more information about porting to Python 3.

It is not allowed to use PL/Python based on Python 2 and PL/Python based on Python 3 in the same session, because the symbols in the dynamic modules would clash, which could result in crashes of the PostgreSQL server process. There is a check that prevents mixing Python major versions in a session, which will abort the session if a mismatch is detected. It is possible, however, to use both PL/Python variants in the same database, from separate sessions.

46.2. PL/Python Functions

Functions in PL/Python are declared via the standard CREATE FUNCTION syntax:

```
CREATE FUNCTION funcname (argument-list)
  RETURNS return-type
AS $$
```

---

[2] https://www.python.org/dev/peps/pep-0394/
[3] https://docs.python.org/3/whatsnew/3.0.html

```
  # PL/Python function body
$$ LANGUAGE plpythonu;
```

The body of a function is simply a Python script. When the function is called, its arguments are passed as elements of the list `args`; named arguments are also passed as ordinary variables to the Python script. Use of named arguments is usually more readable. The result is returned from the Python code in the usual way, with `return` or `yield` (in case of a result-set statement). If you do not provide a return value, Python returns the default `None`. PL/Python translates Python's `None` into the SQL null value. In a procedure, the result from the Python code must be `None` (typically achieved by ending the procedure without a `return` statement or by using a `return` statement without argument); otherwise, an error will be raised.

For example, a function to return the greater of two integers can be defined as:

```
CREATE FUNCTION pymax (a integer, b integer)
  RETURNS integer
AS $$
  if a > b:
    return a
  return b
$$ LANGUAGE plpythonu;
```

The Python code that is given as the body of the function definition is transformed into a Python function. For example, the above results in:

```
def __plpython_procedure_pymax_23456():
  if a > b:
    return a
  return b
```

assuming that 23456 is the OID assigned to the function by PostgreSQL.

The arguments are set as global variables. Because of the scoping rules of Python, this has the subtle consequence that an argument variable cannot be reassigned inside the function to the value of an expression that involves the variable name itself, unless the variable is redeclared as global in the block. For example, the following won't work:

```
CREATE FUNCTION pystrip(x text)
  RETURNS text
AS $$
  x = x.strip()  # error
  return x
$$ LANGUAGE plpythonu;
```

because assigning to `x` makes `x` a local variable for the entire block, and so the `x` on the right-hand side of the assignment refers to a not-yet-assigned local variable `x`, not the PL/Python function parameter. Using the `global` statement, this can be made to work:

```
CREATE FUNCTION pystrip(x text)
  RETURNS text
AS $$
  global x
  x = x.strip()  # ok now
```

```
    return x
$$ LANGUAGE plpythonu;
```

But it is advisable not to rely on this implementation detail of PL/Python. It is better to treat the function parameters as read-only.

46.3. Data Values

Generally speaking, the aim of PL/Python is to provide a "natural" mapping between the PostgreSQL and the Python worlds. This informs the data mapping rules described below.

46.3.1. Data Type Mapping

When a PL/Python function is called, its arguments are converted from their PostgreSQL data type to a corresponding Python type:

- PostgreSQL `boolean` is converted to Python `bool`.

- PostgreSQL `smallint` and `int` are converted to Python `int`. PostgreSQL `bigint` and `oid` are converted to `long` in Python 2 and to `int` in Python 3.

- PostgreSQL `real` and `double` are converted to Python `float`.

- PostgreSQL `numeric` is converted to Python `Decimal`. This type is imported from the `cdecimal` package if that is available. Otherwise, `decimal.Decimal` from the standard library will be used. `cdecimal` is significantly faster than `decimal`. In Python 3.3 and up, however, `cdecimal` has been integrated into the standard library under the name `decimal`, so there is no longer any difference.

- PostgreSQL `bytea` is converted to Python `str` in Python 2 and to `bytes` in Python 3. In Python 2, the string should be treated as a byte sequence without any character encoding.

- All other data types, including the PostgreSQL character string types, are converted to a Python `str`. In Python 2, this string will be in the PostgreSQL server encoding; in Python 3, it will be a Unicode string like all strings.

- For nonscalar data types, see below.

When a PL/Python function returns, its return value is converted to the function's declared PostgreSQL return data type as follows:

- When the PostgreSQL return type is `boolean`, the return value will be evaluated for truth according to the *Python* rules. That is, 0 and empty string are false, but notably `'f'` is true.

- When the PostgreSQL return type is `bytea`, the return value will be converted to a string (Python 2) or bytes (Python 3) using the respective Python built-ins, with the result being converted to `bytea`.

- For all other PostgreSQL return types, the return value is converted to a string using the Python built-in `str`, and the result is passed to the input function of the PostgreSQL data type. (If the Python value is a `float`, it is converted using the `repr` built-in instead of `str`, to avoid loss of precision.)

  Strings in Python 2 are required to be in the PostgreSQL server encoding when they are passed to PostgreSQL. Strings that are not valid in the current server encoding will raise an error, but not all encoding mismatches can be detected, so garbage data can still result when this is not done correctly. Unicode strings are converted to the correct encoding automatically, so it can be safer and more convenient to use those. In Python 3, all strings are Unicode strings.

- For nonscalar data types, see below.

Note that logical mismatches between the declared PostgreSQL return type and the Python data type of the actual return object are not flagged; the value will be converted in any case.

46.3.2. Null, None

If an SQL null value is passed to a function, the argument value will appear as None in Python. For example, the function definition of pymax shown in Section 46.2 will return the wrong answer for null inputs. We could add STRICT to the function definition to make PostgreSQL do something more reasonable: if a null value is passed, the function will not be called at all, but will just return a null result automatically. Alternatively, we could check for null inputs in the function body:

```
CREATE FUNCTION pymax (a integer, b integer)
  RETURNS integer
AS $$
  if (a is None) or (b is None):
    return None
  if a > b:
    return a
  return b
$$ LANGUAGE plpythonu;
```

As shown above, to return an SQL null value from a PL/Python function, return the value None. This can be done whether the function is strict or not.

46.3.3. Arrays, Lists

SQL array values are passed into PL/Python as a Python list. To return an SQL array value out of a PL/Python function, return a Python list:

```
CREATE FUNCTION return_arr()
  RETURNS int[]
AS $$
return [1, 2, 3, 4, 5]
$$ LANGUAGE plpythonu;

SELECT return_arr();
 return_arr
-------------
 {1,2,3,4,5}
(1 row)
```

Multidimensional arrays are passed into PL/Python as nested Python lists. A 2-dimensional array is a list of lists, for example. When returning a multi-dimensional SQL array out of a PL/Python function, the inner lists at each level must all be of the same size. For example:

```
CREATE FUNCTION test_type_conversion_array_int4(x int4[]) RETURNS
  int4[] AS $$
plpy.info(x, type(x))
return x
```

```
$$ LANGUAGE plpythonu;

SELECT * FROM test_type_conversion_array_int4(ARRAY[[1,2,3],[4,5,6]]);
INFO:  ([[1, 2, 3], [4, 5, 6]], <type 'list'>)
 test_type_conversion_array_int4
---------------------------------
 {{1,2,3},{4,5,6}}
(1 row)
```

Other Python sequences, like tuples, are also accepted for backwards-compatibility with PostgreSQL versions 9.6 and below, when multi-dimensional arrays were not supported. However, they are always treated as one-dimensional arrays, because they are ambiguous with composite types. For the same reason, when a composite type is used in a multi-dimensional array, it must be represented by a tuple, rather than a list.

Note that in Python, strings are sequences, which can have undesirable effects that might be familiar to Python programmers:

```
CREATE FUNCTION return_str_arr()
  RETURNS varchar[]
AS $$
return "hello"
$$ LANGUAGE plpythonu;

SELECT return_str_arr();
 return_str_arr
----------------
 {h,e,l,l,o}
(1 row)
```

46.3.4. Composite Types

Composite-type arguments are passed to the function as Python mappings. The element names of the mapping are the attribute names of the composite type. If an attribute in the passed row has the null value, it has the value None in the mapping. Here is an example:

```
CREATE TABLE employee (
  name text,
  salary integer,
  age integer
);

CREATE FUNCTION overpaid (e employee)
  RETURNS boolean
AS $$
  if e["salary"] > 200000:
    return True
  if (e["age"] < 30) and (e["salary"] > 100000):
    return True
  return False
$$ LANGUAGE plpythonu;
```

There are multiple ways to return row or composite types from a Python function. The following examples assume we have:

```
CREATE TYPE named_value AS (
  name    text,
  value   integer
);
```

A composite result can be returned as a:

Sequence type (a tuple or list, but not a set because it is not indexable)

Returned sequence objects must have the same number of items as the composite result type has fields. The item with index 0 is assigned to the first field of the composite type, 1 to the second and so on. For example:

```
CREATE FUNCTION make_pair (name text, value integer)
  RETURNS named_value
AS $$
  return ( name, value )
  # or alternatively, as tuple: return [ name, value ]
$$ LANGUAGE plpythonu;
```

To return a SQL null for any column, insert None at the corresponding position.

When an array of composite types is returned, it cannot be returned as a list, because it is ambiguous whether the Python list represents a composite type, or another array dimension.

Mapping (dictionary)

The value for each result type column is retrieved from the mapping with the column name as key. Example:

```
CREATE FUNCTION make_pair (name text, value integer)
  RETURNS named_value
AS $$
  return { "name": name, "value": value }
$$ LANGUAGE plpythonu;
```

Any extra dictionary key/value pairs are ignored. Missing keys are treated as errors. To return a SQL null value for any column, insert None with the corresponding column name as the key.

Object (any object providing method __getattr__)

This works the same as a mapping. Example:

```
CREATE FUNCTION make_pair (name text, value integer)
  RETURNS named_value
AS $$
  class named_value:
    def __init__ (self, n, v):
      self.name = n
      self.value = v
  return named_value(name, value)
```

```
    # or simply
    class nv: pass
    nv.name = name
    nv.value = value
    return nv
$$ LANGUAGE plpythonu;
```

Functions with OUT parameters are also supported. For example:

```
CREATE FUNCTION multiout_simple(OUT i integer, OUT j integer) AS $$
return (1, 2)
$$ LANGUAGE plpythonu;

SELECT * FROM multiout_simple();
```

Output parameters of procedures are passed back the same way. For example:

```
CREATE PROCEDURE python_triple(INOUT a integer, INOUT b integer) AS $$
return (a * 3, b * 3)
$$ LANGUAGE plpythonu;

CALL python_triple(5, 10);
```

46.3.5. Set-returning Functions

A PL/Python function can also return sets of scalar or composite types. There are several ways to achieve this because the returned object is internally turned into an iterator. The following examples assume we have composite type:

```
CREATE TYPE greeting AS (
  how text,
  who text
);
```

A set result can be returned from a:

Sequence type (tuple, list, set)

```
    CREATE FUNCTION greet (how text)
      RETURNS SETOF greeting
    AS $$
      # return tuple containing lists as composite types
      # all other combinations work also
      return ( [ how, "World" ], [ how, "PostgreSQL" ], [ how, "PL/
Python" ] )
    $$ LANGUAGE plpythonu;
```

Iterator (any object providing __iter__ and next methods)

```
    CREATE FUNCTION greet (how text)
```

```
    RETURNS SETOF greeting
AS $$
  class producer:
    def __init__ (self, how, who):
      self.how = how
      self.who = who
      self.ndx = -1

    def __iter__ (self):
      return self

    def next (self):
      self.ndx += 1
      if self.ndx == len(self.who):
        raise StopIteration
      return ( self.how, self.who[self.ndx] )

  return producer(how, [ "World", "PostgreSQL", "PL/Python" ])
$$ LANGUAGE plpythonu;
```

Generator (`yield`)

```
  CREATE FUNCTION greet (how text)
    RETURNS SETOF greeting
  AS $$
    for who in [ "World", "PostgreSQL", "PL/Python" ]:
      yield ( how, who )
  $$ LANGUAGE plpythonu;
```

Set-returning functions with OUT parameters (using RETURNS SETOF record) are also supported. For example:

```
CREATE FUNCTION multiout_simple_setof(n integer, OUT integer, OUT
 integer) RETURNS SETOF record AS $$
return [(1, 2)] * n
$$ LANGUAGE plpythonu;

SELECT * FROM multiout_simple_setof(3);
```

46.4. Sharing Data

The global dictionary SD is available to store private data between repeated calls to the same function. The global dictionary GD is public data, that is available to all Python functions within a session; use with care.

Each function gets its own execution environment in the Python interpreter, so that global data and function arguments from myfunc are not available to myfunc2. The exception is the data in the GD dictionary, as mentioned above.

46.5. Anonymous Code Blocks

PL/Python also supports anonymous code blocks called with the DO statement:

```
DO $$
    # PL/Python code
$$ LANGUAGE plpythonu;
```

An anonymous code block receives no arguments, and whatever value it might return is discarded. Otherwise it behaves just like a function.

46.6. Trigger Functions

When a function is used as a trigger, the dictionary TD contains trigger-related values:

TD["event"]

> contains the event as a string: INSERT, UPDATE, DELETE, or TRUNCATE.

TD["when"]

> contains one of BEFORE, AFTER, or INSTEAD OF.

TD["level"]

> contains ROW or STATEMENT.

TD["new"]
TD["old"]

> For a row-level trigger, one or both of these fields contain the respective trigger rows, depending on the trigger event.

TD["name"]

> contains the trigger name.

TD["table_name"]

> contains the name of the table on which the trigger occurred.

TD["table_schema"]

> contains the schema of the table on which the trigger occurred.

TD["relid"]

> contains the OID of the table on which the trigger occurred.

TD["args"]

> If the CREATE TRIGGER command included arguments, they are available in TD["args"][0] to TD["args"][n-1].

If TD["when"] is BEFORE or INSTEAD OF and TD["level"] is ROW, you can return None or "OK" from the Python function to indicate the row is unmodified, "SKIP" to abort the event, or if TD["event"] is INSERT or UPDATE you can return "MODIFY" to indicate you've modified the new row. Otherwise the return value is ignored.

46.7. Database Access

The PL/Python language module automatically imports a Python module called `plpy`. The functions and constants in this module are available to you in the Python code as `plpy.foo`.

46.7.1. Database Access Functions

The `plpy` module provides several functions to execute database commands:

`plpy.execute(query [, max-rows])`

Calling `plpy.execute` with a query string and an optional row limit argument causes that query to be run and the result to be returned in a result object.

The result object emulates a list or dictionary object. The result object can be accessed by row number and column name. For example:

```
rv = plpy.execute("SELECT * FROM my_table", 5)
```

returns up to 5 rows from `my_table`. If `my_table` has a column `my_column`, it would be accessed as:

```
foo = rv[i]["my_column"]
```

The number of rows returned can be obtained using the built-in `len` function.

The result object has these additional methods:

`nrows()`

Returns the number of rows processed by the command. Note that this is not necessarily the same as the number of rows returned. For example, an `UPDATE` command will set this value but won't return any rows (unless `RETURNING` is used).

`status()`

The `SPI_execute()` return value.

`colnames()`
`coltypes()`
`coltypmods()`

Return a list of column names, list of column type OIDs, and list of type-specific type modifiers for the columns, respectively.

These methods raise an exception when called on a result object from a command that did not produce a result set, e.g., `UPDATE` without `RETURNING`, or `DROP TABLE`. But it is OK to use these methods on a result set containing zero rows.

`__str__()`

The standard `__str__` method is defined so that it is possible for example to debug query execution results using `plpy.debug(rv)`.

The result object can be modified.

Note that calling `plpy.execute` will cause the entire result set to be read into memory. Only use that function when you are sure that the result set will be relatively small. If you don't want to risk excessive memory usage when fetching large results, use `plpy.cursor` rather than `plpy.execute`.

```
plpy.prepare(query [, argtypes])
plpy.execute(plan [, arguments [, max-rows]])
```

`plpy.prepare` prepares the execution plan for a query. It is called with a query string and a list of parameter types, if you have parameter references in the query. For example:

```
plan = plpy.prepare("SELECT last_name FROM my_users WHERE
 first_name = $1", ["text"])
```

`text` is the type of the variable you will be passing for `$1`. The second argument is optional if you don't want to pass any parameters to the query.

After preparing a statement, you use a variant of the function `plpy.execute` to run it:

```
rv = plpy.execute(plan, ["name"], 5)
```

Pass the plan as the first argument (instead of the query string), and a list of values to substitute into the query as the second argument. The second argument is optional if the query does not expect any parameters. The third argument is the optional row limit as before.

Alternatively, you can call the `execute` method on the plan object:

```
rv = plan.execute(["name"], 5)
```

Query parameters and result row fields are converted between PostgreSQL and Python data types as described in Section 46.3.

When you prepare a plan using the PL/Python module it is automatically saved. Read the SPI documentation (Chapter 47) for a description of what this means. In order to make effective use of this across function calls one needs to use one of the persistent storage dictionaries SD or GD (see Section 46.4). For example:

```
CREATE FUNCTION usesavedplan() RETURNS trigger AS $$
    if "plan" in SD:
        plan = SD["plan"]
    else:
        plan = plpy.prepare("SELECT 1")
        SD["plan"] = plan
    # rest of function
$$ LANGUAGE plpythonu;
```

```
plpy.cursor(query)
plpy.cursor(plan [, arguments])
```

The `plpy.cursor` function accepts the same arguments as `plpy.execute` (except for the row limit) and returns a cursor object, which allows you to process large result sets in smaller chunks. As with `plpy.execute`, either a query string or a plan object along with a list of arguments can be used, or the `cursor` function can be called as a method of the plan object.

The cursor object provides a `fetch` method that accepts an integer parameter and returns a result object. Each time you call `fetch`, the returned object will contain the next batch of rows, never larger than the parameter value. Once all rows are exhausted, `fetch` starts returning an empty result object. Cursor objects also provide an iterator interface[4], yielding one row at a time until all rows are exhausted. Data fetched that way is not returned as result objects, but rather as dictionaries, each dictionary corresponding to a single result row.

An example of two ways of processing data from a large table is:

```
CREATE FUNCTION count_odd_iterator() RETURNS integer AS $$
odd = 0
for row in plpy.cursor("select num from largetable"):
    if row['num'] % 2:
        odd += 1
return odd
$$ LANGUAGE plpythonu;

CREATE FUNCTION count_odd_fetch(batch_size integer) RETURNS integer
 AS $$
odd = 0
cursor = plpy.cursor("select num from largetable")
while True:
    rows = cursor.fetch(batch_size)
    if not rows:
        break
    for row in rows:
        if row['num'] % 2:
            odd += 1
return odd
$$ LANGUAGE plpythonu;

CREATE FUNCTION count_odd_prepared() RETURNS integer AS $$
odd = 0
plan = plpy.prepare("select num from largetable where num % $1 <>
 0", ["integer"])
rows = list(plpy.cursor(plan, [2]))  # or: = list(plan.cursor([2]))

return len(rows)
$$ LANGUAGE plpythonu;
```

Cursors are automatically disposed of. But if you want to explicitly release all resources held by a cursor, use the `close` method. Once closed, a cursor cannot be fetched from anymore.

Tip

Do not confuse objects created by `plpy.cursor` with DB-API cursors as defined by the Python Database API specification[5]. They don't have anything in common except for the name.

---

[4] https://docs.python.org/library/stdtypes.html#iterator-types
[5] https://www.python.org/dev/peps/pep-0249/

46.7.2. Trapping Errors

Functions accessing the database might encounter errors, which will cause them to abort and raise an exception. Both `plpy.execute` and `plpy.prepare` can raise an instance of a subclass of `plpy.SPIError`, which by default will terminate the function. This error can be handled just like any other Python exception, by using the `try/except` construct. For example:

```
CREATE FUNCTION try_adding_joe() RETURNS text AS $$
    try:
        plpy.execute("INSERT INTO users(username) VALUES ('joe')")
    except plpy.SPIError:
        return "something went wrong"
    else:
        return "Joe added"
$$ LANGUAGE plpythonu;
```

The actual class of the exception being raised corresponds to the specific condition that caused the error. Refer to Table A.1 for a list of possible conditions. The module `plpy.spiexceptions` defines an exception class for each PostgreSQL condition, deriving their names from the condition name. For instance, `division_by_zero` becomes `DivisionByZero`, `unique_violation` becomes `UniqueViolation`, `fdw_error` becomes `FdwError`, and so on. Each of these exception classes inherits from `SPIError`. This separation makes it easier to handle specific errors, for instance:

```
CREATE FUNCTION insert_fraction(numerator int, denominator int)
 RETURNS text AS $$
from plpy import spiexceptions
try:
    plan = plpy.prepare("INSERT INTO fractions (frac) VALUES ($1 /
$2)", ["int", "int"])
    plpy.execute(plan, [numerator, denominator])
except spiexceptions.DivisionByZero:
    return "denominator cannot equal zero"
except spiexceptions.UniqueViolation:
    return "already have that fraction"
except plpy.SPIError, e:
    return "other error, SQLSTATE %s" % e.sqlstate
else:
    return "fraction inserted"
$$ LANGUAGE plpythonu;
```

Note that because all exceptions from the `plpy.spiexceptions` module inherit from `SPIError`, an `except` clause handling it will catch any database access error.

As an alternative way of handling different error conditions, you can catch the `SPIError` exception and determine the specific error condition inside the `except` block by looking at the `sqlstate` attribute of the exception object. This attribute is a string value containing the "SQLSTATE" error code. This approach provides approximately the same functionality

46.8. Explicit Subtransactions

Recovering from errors caused by database access as described in Section 46.7.2 can lead to an undesirable situation where some operations succeed before one of them fails, and after recovering from that error the data is left in an inconsistent state. PL/Python offers a solution to this problem in the form of explicit subtransactions.

46.8.1. Subtransaction Context Managers

Consider a function that implements a transfer between two accounts:

```
CREATE FUNCTION transfer_funds() RETURNS void AS $$
try:
    plpy.execute("UPDATE accounts SET balance = balance - 100 WHERE
 account_name = 'joe'")
    plpy.execute("UPDATE accounts SET balance = balance + 100 WHERE
 account_name = 'mary'")
except plpy.SPIError, e:
    result = "error transferring funds: %s" % e.args
else:
    result = "funds transferred correctly"
plan = plpy.prepare("INSERT INTO operations (result) VALUES ($1)",
 ["text"])
plpy.execute(plan, [result])
$$ LANGUAGE plpythonu;
```

If the second UPDATE statement results in an exception being raised, this function will report the error, but the result of the first UPDATE will nevertheless be committed. In other words, the funds will be withdrawn from Joe's account, but will not be transferred to Mary's account.

To avoid such issues, you can wrap your plpy.execute calls in an explicit subtransaction. The plpy module provides a helper object to manage explicit subtransactions that gets created with the plpy.subtransaction() function. Objects created by this function implement the context manager interface[6]. Using explicit subtransactions we can rewrite our function as:

```
CREATE FUNCTION transfer_funds2() RETURNS void AS $$
try:
    with plpy.subtransaction():
        plpy.execute("UPDATE accounts SET balance = balance - 100
 WHERE account_name = 'joe'")
        plpy.execute("UPDATE accounts SET balance = balance + 100
 WHERE account_name = 'mary'")
except plpy.SPIError, e:
    result = "error transferring funds: %s" % e.args
else:
    result = "funds transferred correctly"
plan = plpy.prepare("INSERT INTO operations (result) VALUES ($1)",
 ["text"])
plpy.execute(plan, [result])
$$ LANGUAGE plpythonu;
```

Note that the use of try/catch is still required. Otherwise the exception would propagate to the top of the Python stack and would cause the whole function to abort with a PostgreSQL error, so that the operations table would not have any row inserted into it. The subtransaction context manager does not trap errors, it only assures that all database operations executed inside its scope will be atomically

---

[6] https://docs.python.org/library/stdtypes.html#context-manager-types

committed or rolled back. A rollback of the subtransaction block occurs on any kind of exception exit, not only ones caused by errors originating from database access. A regular Python exception raised inside an explicit subtransaction block would also cause the subtransaction to be rolled back.

46.8.2. Older Python Versions

Context managers syntax using the `with` keyword is available by default in Python 2.6. If using PL/Python with an older Python version, it is still possible to use explicit subtransactions, although not as transparently. You can call the subtransaction manager's `__enter__` and `__exit__` functions using the `enter` and `exit` convenience aliases. The example function that transfers funds could be written as:

```
CREATE FUNCTION transfer_funds_old() RETURNS void AS $$
try:
    subxact = plpy.subtransaction()
    subxact.enter()
    try:
        plpy.execute("UPDATE accounts SET balance = balance - 100
 WHERE account_name = 'joe'")
        plpy.execute("UPDATE accounts SET balance = balance + 100
 WHERE account_name = 'mary'")
    except:
        import sys
        subxact.exit(*sys.exc_info())
        raise
    else:
        subxact.exit(None, None, None)
except plpy.SPIError, e:
    result = "error transferring funds: %s" % e.args
else:
    result = "funds transferred correctly"

plan = plpy.prepare("INSERT INTO operations (result) VALUES ($1)",
 ["text"])
plpy.execute(plan, [result])
$$ LANGUAGE plpythonu;
```

> ### Note
>
> Although context managers were implemented in Python 2.5, to use the `with` syntax in that version you need to use a future statement[7]. Because of implementation details, however, you cannot use future statements in PL/Python functions.

46.9. Transaction Management

In a procedure called from the top level or an anonymous code block (`DO` command) called from the top level it is possible to control transactions. To commit the current transaction, call `plpy.commit()`. To roll back the current transaction, call `plpy.rollback()`. (Note that it is not possible to run the SQL commands `COMMIT` or `ROLLBACK` via `plpy.execute` or similar. It has to be done using these

---

[7] https://docs.python.org/release/2.5/ref/future.html

functions.) After a transaction is ended, a new transaction is automatically started, so there is no separate function for that.

Here is an example:

```
CREATE PROCEDURE transaction_test1()
LANGUAGE plpythonu
AS $$
for i in range(0, 10):
    plpy.execute("INSERT INTO test1 (a) VALUES (%d)" % i)
    if i % 2 == 0:
        plpy.commit()
    else:
        plpy.rollback()
$$;

CALL transaction_test1();
```

Transactions cannot be ended when an explicit subtransaction is active.

46.10. Utility Functions

The `plpy` module also provides the functions

```
plpy.debug(msg, **kwargs)
plpy.log(msg, **kwargs)
plpy.info(msg, **kwargs)
plpy.notice(msg, **kwargs)
plpy.warning(msg, **kwargs)
plpy.error(msg, **kwargs)
plpy.fatal(msg, **kwargs)
```

`plpy.error` and `plpy.fatal` actually raise a Python exception which, if uncaught, propagates out to the calling query, causing the current transaction or subtransaction to be aborted. `raise plpy.Error(msg)` and `raise plpy.Fatal(msg)` are equivalent to calling `plpy.error(msg)` and `plpy.fatal(msg)`, respectively but the `raise` form does not allow passing keyword arguments. The other functions only generate messages of different priority levels. Whether messages of a particular priority are reported to the client, written to the server log, or both is controlled by the log_min_messages and client_min_messages configuration variables. See Chapter 19 for more information.

The *msg* argument is given as a positional argument. For backward compatibility, more than one positional argument can be given. In that case, the string representation of the tuple of positional arguments becomes the message reported to the client.

The following keyword-only arguments are accepted:

```
detail
hint
sqlstate
schema_name
table_name
column_name
datatype_name
constraint_name
```

The string representation of the objects passed as keyword-only arguments is used to enrich the messages reported to the client. For example:

```
CREATE FUNCTION raise_custom_exception() RETURNS void AS $$
plpy.error("custom exception message",
           detail="some info about exception",
           hint="hint for users")
$$ LANGUAGE plpythonu;

=# SELECT raise_custom_exception();
ERROR:  plpy.Error: custom exception message
DETAIL:  some info about exception
HINT:  hint for users
CONTEXT:  Traceback (most recent call last):
  PL/Python function "raise_custom_exception", line 4, in <module>
    hint="hint for users")
PL/Python function "raise_custom_exception"
```

Another set of utility functions are `plpy.quote_literal(string)`, `plpy.quote_nullable(string)`, and `plpy.quote_ident(string)`. They are equivalent to the built-in quoting functions described in Section 9.4. They are useful when constructing ad-hoc queries. A PL/Python equivalent of dynamic SQL from Example 43.1 would be:

```
plpy.execute("UPDATE tbl SET %s = %s WHERE key = %s" % (
    plpy.quote_ident(colname),
    plpy.quote_nullable(newvalue),
    plpy.quote_literal(keyvalue)))
```

46.11. Environment Variables

Some of the environment variables that are accepted by the Python interpreter can also be used to affect PL/Python behavior. They would need to be set in the environment of the main PostgreSQL server process, for example in a start script. The available environment variables depend on the version of Python; see the Python documentation for details. At the time of this writing, the following environment variables have an affect on PL/Python, assuming an adequate Python version:

- PYTHONHOME

- PYTHONPATH

- PYTHONY2K

- PYTHONOPTIMIZE

- PYTHONDEBUG

- PYTHONVERBOSE

- PYTHONCASEOK

- PYTHONDONTWRITEBYTECODE

- PYTHONIOENCODING

- `PYTHONUSERBASE`

- `PYTHONHASHSEED`

(It appears to be a Python implementation detail beyond the control of PL/Python that some of the environment variables listed on the `python` man page are only effective in a command-line interpreter and not an embedded Python interpreter.)

Chapter 47. Server Programming Interface

The *Server Programming Interface* (SPI) gives writers of user-defined C functions the ability to run SQL commands inside their functions. SPI is a set of interface functions to simplify access to the parser, planner, and executor. SPI also does some memory management.

Note

The available procedural languages provide various means to execute SQL commands from functions. Most of these facilities are based on SPI, so this documentation might be of use for users of those languages as well.

Note that if a command invoked via SPI fails, then control will not be returned to your C function. Rather, the transaction or subtransaction in which your C function executes will be rolled back. (This might seem surprising given that the SPI functions mostly have documented error-return conventions. Those conventions only apply for errors detected within the SPI functions themselves, however.) It is possible to recover control after an error by establishing your own subtransaction surrounding SPI calls that might fail.

SPI functions return a nonnegative result on success (either via a returned integer value or in the global variable `SPI_result`, as described below). On error, a negative result or `NULL` will be returned.

Source code files that use SPI must include the header file `executor/spi.h`.

47.1. Interface Functions

SPI_connect

SPI_connect, SPI_connect_ext — connect a C function to the SPI manager

Synopsis

```
int SPI_connect(void)
```

```
int SPI_connect_ext(int options)
```

Description

SPI_connect opens a connection from a C function invocation to the SPI manager. You must call this function if you want to execute commands through SPI. Some utility SPI functions can be called from unconnected C functions.

SPI_connect_ext does the same but has an argument that allows passing option flags. Currently, the following option values are available:

SPI_OPT_NONATOMIC

Sets the SPI connection to be *nonatomic*, which means that transaction control calls SPI_commit, SPI_rollback, and SPI_start_transaction are allowed. Otherwise, calling these functions will result in an immediate error.

SPI_connect() is equivalent to SPI_connect_ext(0).

Return Value

SPI_OK_CONNECT

on success

SPI_ERROR_CONNECT

on error

SPI_finish

SPI_finish — disconnect a C function from the SPI manager

Synopsis

```
int SPI_finish(void)
```

Description

SPI_finish closes an existing connection to the SPI manager. You must call this function after completing the SPI operations needed during your C function's current invocation. You do not need to worry about making this happen, however, if you abort the transaction via elog(ERROR). In that case SPI will clean itself up automatically.

Return Value

SPI_OK_FINISH

if properly disconnected

SPI_ERROR_UNCONNECTED

if called from an unconnected C function

SPI_execute

SPI_execute — execute a command

Synopsis

```
int SPI_execute(const char * command, bool read_only, long count)
```

Description

SPI_execute executes the specified SQL command for *count* rows. If *read_only* is true, the command must be read-only, and execution overhead is somewhat reduced.

This function can only be called from a connected C function.

If *count* is zero then the command is executed for all rows that it applies to. If *count* is greater than zero, then no more than *count* rows will be retrieved; execution stops when the count is reached, much like adding a LIMIT clause to the query. For example,

```
SPI_execute("SELECT * FROM foo", true, 5);
```

will retrieve at most 5 rows from the table. Note that such a limit is only effective when the command actually returns rows. For example,

```
SPI_execute("INSERT INTO foo SELECT * FROM bar", false, 5);
```

inserts all rows from bar, ignoring the *count* parameter. However, with

```
SPI_execute("INSERT INTO foo SELECT * FROM bar RETURNING *", false,
 5);
```

at most 5 rows would be inserted, since execution would stop after the fifth RETURNING result row is retrieved.

You can pass multiple commands in one string; SPI_execute returns the result for the command executed last. The *count* limit applies to each command separately (even though only the last result will actually be returned). The limit is not applied to any hidden commands generated by rules.

When *read_only* is false, SPI_execute increments the command counter and computes a new *snapshot* before executing each command in the string. The snapshot does not actually change if the current transaction isolation level is SERIALIZABLE or REPEATABLE READ, but in READ COMMITTED mode the snapshot update allows each command to see the results of newly committed transactions from other sessions. This is essential for consistent behavior when the commands are modifying the database.

When *read_only* is true, SPI_execute does not update either the snapshot or the command counter, and it allows only plain SELECT commands to appear in the command string. The commands are executed using the snapshot previously established for the surrounding query. This execution mode is somewhat faster than the read/write mode due to eliminating per-command overhead. It also allows genuinely *stable* functions to be built: since successive executions will all use the same snapshot, there will be no change in the results.

It is generally unwise to mix read-only and read-write commands within a single function using SPI; that could result in very confusing behavior, since the read-only queries would not see the results of any database updates done by the read-write queries.

The actual number of rows for which the (last) command was executed is returned in the global variable `SPI_processed`. If the return value of the function is `SPI_OK_SELECT`, `SPI_OK_INSERT_RE-TURNING`, `SPI_OK_DELETE_RETURNING`, or `SPI_OK_UPDATE_RETURNING`, then you can use the global pointer `SPITupleTable *SPI_tuptable` to access the result rows. Some utility commands (such as `EXPLAIN`) also return row sets, and `SPI_tuptable` will contain the result in these cases too. Some utility commands (`COPY`, `CREATE TABLE AS`) don't return a row set, so `SPI_tuptable` is NULL, but they still return the number of rows processed in `SPI_processed`.

The structure `SPITupleTable` is defined thus:

```
typedef struct
{
    MemoryContext tuptabcxt;    /* memory context of result table */
    uint64      alloced;        /* number of alloced vals */
    uint64      free;           /* number of free vals */
    TupleDesc   tupdesc;        /* row descriptor */
    HeapTuple   *vals;          /* rows */
} SPITupleTable;
```

`vals` is an array of pointers to rows. (The number of valid entries is given by `SPI_processed`.) `tupdesc` is a row descriptor which you can pass to SPI functions dealing with rows. `tuptabcxt`, `alloced`, and `free` are internal fields not intended for use by SPI callers.

`SPI_finish` frees all `SPITupleTable`s allocated during the current C function. You can free a particular result table earlier, if you are done with it, by calling `SPI_freetuptable`.

Arguments

const char * *command*

string containing command to execute

bool *read_only*

`true` for read-only execution

long *count*

maximum number of rows to return, or 0 for no limit

Return Value

If the execution of the command was successful then one of the following (nonnegative) values will be returned:

SPI_OK_SELECT

if a `SELECT` (but not `SELECT INTO`) was executed

`SPI_OK_SELINTO`

> if a `SELECT INTO` was executed

`SPI_OK_INSERT`

> if an `INSERT` was executed

`SPI_OK_DELETE`

> if a `DELETE` was executed

`SPI_OK_UPDATE`

> if an `UPDATE` was executed

`SPI_OK_INSERT_RETURNING`

> if an `INSERT RETURNING` was executed

`SPI_OK_DELETE_RETURNING`

> if a `DELETE RETURNING` was executed

`SPI_OK_UPDATE_RETURNING`

> if an `UPDATE RETURNING` was executed

`SPI_OK_UTILITY`

> if a utility command (e.g., `CREATE TABLE`) was executed

`SPI_OK_REWRITTEN`

> if the command was rewritten into another kind of command (e.g., `UPDATE` became an `INSERT`) by a rule.

On error, one of the following negative values is returned:

`SPI_ERROR_ARGUMENT`

> if *command* is `NULL` or *count* is less than 0

`SPI_ERROR_COPY`

> if `COPY TO stdout` or `COPY FROM stdin` was attempted

`SPI_ERROR_TRANSACTION`

> if a transaction manipulation command was attempted (`BEGIN`, `COMMIT`, `ROLLBACK`, `SAVEPOINT`, `PREPARE TRANSACTION`, `COMMIT PREPARED`, `ROLLBACK PREPARED`, or any variant thereof)

`SPI_ERROR_OPUNKNOWN`

> if the command type is unknown (shouldn't happen)

`SPI_ERROR_UNCONNECTED`

> if called from an unconnected C function

Notes

All SPI query-execution functions set both `SPI_processed` and `SPI_tuptable` (just the pointer, not the contents of the structure). Save these two global variables into local C function variables if you need to access the result table of `SPI_execute` or another query-execution function across later calls.

SPI_exec

SPI_exec — execute a read/write command

Synopsis

```
int SPI_exec(const char * command, long count)
```

Description

SPI_exec is the same as SPI_execute, with the latter's *read_only* parameter always taken as false.

Arguments

const char * *command*

string containing command to execute

long *count*

maximum number of rows to return, or 0 for no limit

Return Value

See SPI_execute.

SPI_execute_with_args

SPI_execute_with_args — execute a command with out-of-line parameters

Synopsis

```
int SPI_execute_with_args(const char *command,
                          int nargs, Oid *argtypes,
                          Datum *values, const char *nulls,
                          bool read_only, long count)
```

Description

SPI_execute_with_args executes a command that might include references to externally supplied parameters. The command text refers to a parameter as $n, and the call specifies data types and values for each such symbol. read_only and count have the same interpretation as in SPI_execute.

The main advantage of this routine compared to SPI_execute is that data values can be inserted into the command without tedious quoting/escaping, and thus with much less risk of SQL-injection attacks.

Similar results can be achieved with SPI_prepare followed by SPI_execute_plan; however, when using this function the query plan is always customized to the specific parameter values provided. For one-time query execution, this function should be preferred. If the same command is to be executed with many different parameters, either method might be faster, depending on the cost of re-planning versus the benefit of custom plans.

Arguments

const char * command

    command string

int nargs

    number of input parameters ($1, $2, etc.)

Oid * argtypes

    an array of length nargs, containing the OIDs of the data types of the parameters

Datum * values

    an array of length nargs, containing the actual parameter values

const char * nulls

    an array of length nargs, describing which parameters are null

    If nulls is NULL then SPI_execute_with_args assumes that no parameters are null. Otherwise, each entry of the nulls array should be ' ' if the corresponding parameter value is non-null, or 'n' if the corresponding parameter value is null. (In the latter case, the actual value in the corresponding values entry doesn't matter.) Note that nulls is not a text string, just an array: it does not need a '\0' terminator.

```
bool read_only
```

> true for read-only execution

```
long count
```

> maximum number of rows to return, or 0 for no limit

Return Value

The return value is the same as for `SPI_execute`.

`SPI_processed` and `SPI_tuptable` are set as in `SPI_execute` if successful.

SPI_prepare

SPI_prepare — prepare a statement, without executing it yet

Synopsis

```
SPIPlanPtr SPI_prepare(const char * command, int nargs, Oid
 * argtypes)
```

Description

SPI_prepare creates and returns a prepared statement for the specified command, but doesn't execute the command. The prepared statement can later be executed repeatedly using SPI_execute_plan.

When the same or a similar command is to be executed repeatedly, it is generally advantageous to perform parse analysis only once, and might furthermore be advantageous to re-use an execution plan for the command. SPI_prepare converts a command string into a prepared statement that encapsulates the results of parse analysis. The prepared statement also provides a place for caching an execution plan if it is found that generating a custom plan for each execution is not helpful.

A prepared command can be generalized by writing parameters ($1, $2, etc.) in place of what would be constants in a normal command. The actual values of the parameters are then specified when SPI_execute_plan is called. This allows the prepared command to be used over a wider range of situations than would be possible without parameters.

The statement returned by SPI_prepare can be used only in the current invocation of the C function, since SPI_finish frees memory allocated for such a statement. But the statement can be saved for longer using the functions SPI_keepplan or SPI_saveplan.

Arguments

const char * command

   command string

int nargs

   number of input parameters ($1, $2, etc.)

Oid * argtypes

   pointer to an array containing the OIDs of the data types of the parameters

Return Value

SPI_prepare returns a non-null pointer to an SPIPlan, which is an opaque struct representing a prepared statement. On error, NULL will be returned, and SPI_result will be set to one of the same error codes used by SPI_execute, except that it is set to SPI_ERROR_ARGUMENT if command is NULL, or if nargs is less than 0, or if nargs is greater than 0 and argtypes is NULL.

Notes

If no parameters are defined, a generic plan will be created at the first use of SPI_execute_plan, and used for all subsequent executions as well. If there are parameters, the first few uses of SPI_execute_plan will generate custom plans that are specific to the supplied parameter values. After enough uses of the same prepared statement, SPI_execute_plan will build a generic plan, and if that is not too much more expensive than the custom plans, it will start using the generic plan instead of re-planning each time. If this default behavior is unsuitable, you can alter it by passing the CURSOR_OP-T_GENERIC_PLAN or CURSOR_OPT_CUSTOM_PLAN flag to SPI_prepare_cursor, to force use of generic or custom plans respectively.

Although the main point of a prepared statement is to avoid repeated parse analysis and planning of the statement, PostgreSQL will force re-analysis and re-planning of the statement before using it whenever database objects used in the statement have undergone definitional (DDL) changes since the previous use of the prepared statement. Also, if the value of search_path changes from one use to the next, the statement will be re-parsed using the new search_path. (This latter behavior is new as of PostgreSQL 9.3.) See PREPARE for more information about the behavior of prepared statements.

This function should only be called from a connected C function.

SPIPlanPtr is declared as a pointer to an opaque struct type in spi.h. It is unwise to try to access its contents directly, as that makes your code much more likely to break in future revisions of PostgreSQL.

The name SPIPlanPtr is somewhat historical, since the data structure no longer necessarily contains an execution plan.

SPI_prepare_cursor

SPI_prepare_cursor — prepare a statement, without executing it yet

Synopsis

```
SPIPlanPtr SPI_prepare_cursor(const char * command, int nargs,
                              Oid * argtypes, int cursorOptions)
```

Description

SPI_prepare_cursor is identical to SPI_prepare, except that it also allows specification of the planner's "cursor options" parameter. This is a bit mask having the values shown in nodes/parsenodes.h for the options field of DeclareCursorStmt. SPI_prepare always takes the cursor options as zero.

Arguments

const char * command

   command string

int nargs

   number of input parameters ($1, $2, etc.)

Oid * argtypes

   pointer to an array containing the OIDs of the data types of the parameters

int cursorOptions

   integer bit mask of cursor options; zero produces default behavior

Return Value

SPI_prepare_cursor has the same return conventions as SPI_prepare.

Notes

Useful bits to set in cursorOptions include CURSOR_OPT_SCROLL, CURSOR_OPT_NO_SCROLL, CURSOR_OPT_FAST_PLAN, CURSOR_OPT_GENERIC_PLAN, and CURSOR_OPT_CUSTOM_PLAN. Note in particular that CURSOR_OPT_HOLD is ignored.

SPI_prepare_params

SPI_prepare_params — prepare a statement, without executing it yet

Synopsis

```
SPIPlanPtr SPI_prepare_params(const char * command,
                              ParserSetupHook parserSetup,
                              void * parserSetupArg,
                              int cursorOptions)
```

Description

SPI_prepare_params creates and returns a prepared statement for the specified command, but doesn't execute the command. This function is equivalent to SPI_prepare_cursor, with the addition that the caller can specify parser hook functions to control the parsing of external parameter references.

Arguments

const char * command

command string

ParserSetupHook parserSetup

Parser hook setup function

void * parserSetupArg

pass-through argument for parserSetup

int cursorOptions

integer bit mask of cursor options; zero produces default behavior

Return Value

SPI_prepare_params has the same return conventions as SPI_prepare.

SPI_getargcount

SPI_getargcount — return the number of arguments needed by a statement prepared by SPI_prepare

Synopsis

```
int SPI_getargcount(SPIPlanPtr plan)
```

Description

SPI_getargcount returns the number of arguments needed to execute a statement prepared by SPI_prepare.

Arguments

SPIPlanPtr *plan*

   prepared statement (returned by SPI_prepare)

Return Value

The count of expected arguments for the *plan*. If the *plan* is NULL or invalid, SPI_result is set to SPI_ERROR_ARGUMENT and -1 is returned.

SPI_getargtypeid

SPI_getargtypeid — return the data type OID for an argument of a statement prepared by SPI_prepare

Synopsis

```
Oid SPI_getargtypeid(SPIPlanPtr plan, int argIndex)
```

Description

SPI_getargtypeid returns the OID representing the type for the *argIndex*'th argument of a statement prepared by SPI_prepare. First argument is at index zero.

Arguments

SPIPlanPtr *plan*

> prepared statement (returned by SPI_prepare)

int *argIndex*

> zero based index of the argument

Return Value

The type OID of the argument at the given index. If the *plan* is NULL or invalid, or *argIndex* is less than 0 or not less than the number of arguments declared for the *plan*, SPI_result is set to SPI_ERROR_ARGUMENT and InvalidOid is returned.

SPI_is_cursor_plan

SPI_is_cursor_plan — return `true` if a statement prepared by `SPI_prepare` can be used with `SPI_cursor_open`

Synopsis

```
bool SPI_is_cursor_plan(SPIPlanPtr plan)
```

Description

`SPI_is_cursor_plan` returns `true` if a statement prepared by `SPI_prepare` can be passed as an argument to `SPI_cursor_open`, or `false` if that is not the case. The criteria are that the *plan* represents one single command and that this command returns tuples to the caller; for example, `SELECT` is allowed unless it contains an `INTO` clause, and `UPDATE` is allowed only if it contains a `RETURNING` clause.

Arguments

SPIPlanPtr *plan*

prepared statement (returned by `SPI_prepare`)

Return Value

`true` or `false` to indicate if the *plan* can produce a cursor or not, with `SPI_result` set to zero. If it is not possible to determine the answer (for example, if the *plan* is NULL or invalid, or if called when not connected to SPI), then `SPI_result` is set to a suitable error code and `false` is returned.

SPI_execute_plan

SPI_execute_plan — execute a statement prepared by SPI_prepare

Synopsis

```
int SPI_execute_plan(SPIPlanPtr plan, Datum * values, const char
* nulls,
                    bool read_only, long count)
```

Description

SPI_execute_plan executes a statement prepared by SPI_prepare or one of its siblings. read_only and count have the same interpretation as in SPI_execute.

Arguments

SPIPlanPtr plan

>   prepared statement (returned by SPI_prepare)

Datum * values

>   An array of actual parameter values. Must have same length as the statement's number of arguments.

const char * nulls

>   An array describing which parameters are null. Must have same length as the statement's number of arguments.

>   If nulls is NULL then SPI_execute_plan assumes that no parameters are null. Otherwise, each entry of the nulls array should be ' ' if the corresponding parameter value is non-null, or 'n' if the corresponding parameter value is null. (In the latter case, the actual value in the corresponding values entry doesn't matter.) Note that nulls is not a text string, just an array: it does not need a '\0' terminator.

bool read_only

>   true for read-only execution

long count

>   maximum number of rows to return, or 0 for no limit

Return Value

The return value is the same as for SPI_execute, with the following additional possible error (negative) results:

SPI_ERROR_ARGUMENT

>   if plan is NULL or invalid, or count is less than 0

SPI_ERROR_PARAM

if *values* is NULL and *plan* was prepared with some parameters

SPI_processed and SPI_tuptable are set as in SPI_execute if successful.

SPI_execute_plan_with_paramlist

SPI_execute_plan_with_paramlist — execute a statement prepared by SPI_prepare

Synopsis

```
int SPI_execute_plan_with_paramlist(SPIPlanPtr plan,
                                    ParamListInfo params,
                                    bool read_only,
                                    long count)
```

Description

SPI_execute_plan_with_paramlist executes a statement prepared by SPI_prepare. This function is equivalent to SPI_execute_plan except that information about the parameter values to be passed to the query is presented differently. The ParamListInfo representation can be convenient for passing down values that are already available in that format. It also supports use of dynamic parameter sets via hook functions specified in ParamListInfo.

Arguments

SPIPlanPtr plan

   prepared statement (returned by SPI_prepare)

ParamListInfo params

   data structure containing parameter types and values; NULL if none

bool read_only

   true for read-only execution

long count

   maximum number of rows to return, or 0 for no limit

Return Value

The return value is the same as for SPI_execute_plan.

SPI_processed and SPI_tuptable are set as in SPI_execute_plan if successful.

SPI_execp

SPI_execp — execute a statement in read/write mode

Synopsis

```
int SPI_execp(SPIPlanPtr plan, Datum * values, const char * nulls,
 long count)
```

Description

SPI_execp is the same as SPI_execute_plan, with the latter's *read_only* parameter always taken as false.

Arguments

SPIPlanPtr *plan*

> prepared statement (returned by SPI_prepare)

Datum * *values*

> An array of actual parameter values. Must have same length as the statement's number of arguments.

const char * *nulls*

> An array describing which parameters are null. Must have same length as the statement's number of arguments.

> If *nulls* is NULL then SPI_execp assumes that no parameters are null. Otherwise, each entry of the *nulls* array should be ' ' if the corresponding parameter value is non-null, or 'n' if the corresponding parameter value is null. (In the latter case, the actual value in the corresponding *values* entry doesn't matter.) Note that *nulls* is not a text string, just an array: it does not need a '\0' terminator.

long *count*

> maximum number of rows to return, or 0 for no limit

Return Value

See SPI_execute_plan.

SPI_processed and SPI_tuptable are set as in SPI_execute if successful.

SPI_cursor_open

SPI_cursor_open — set up a cursor using a statement created with SPI_prepare

Synopsis

```
Portal SPI_cursor_open(const char * name, SPIPlanPtr plan,
                       Datum * values, const char * nulls,
                       bool read_only)
```

Description

SPI_cursor_open sets up a cursor (internally, a portal) that will execute a statement prepared by SPI_prepare. The parameters have the same meanings as the corresponding parameters to SPI_execute_plan.

Using a cursor instead of executing the statement directly has two benefits. First, the result rows can be retrieved a few at a time, avoiding memory overrun for queries that return many rows. Second, a portal can outlive the current C function (it can, in fact, live to the end of the current transaction). Returning the portal name to the C function's caller provides a way of returning a row set as result.

The passed-in parameter data will be copied into the cursor's portal, so it can be freed while the cursor still exists.

Arguments

const char * name

name for portal, or NULL to let the system select a name

SPIPlanPtr plan

prepared statement (returned by SPI_prepare)

Datum * values

An array of actual parameter values. Must have same length as the statement's number of arguments.

const char * nulls

An array describing which parameters are null. Must have same length as the statement's number of arguments.

If nulls is NULL then SPI_cursor_open assumes that no parameters are null. Otherwise, each entry of the nulls array should be ' ' if the corresponding parameter value is non-null, or 'n' if the corresponding parameter value is null. (In the latter case, the actual value in the corresponding values entry doesn't matter.) Note that nulls is not a text string, just an array: it does not need a '\0' terminator.

bool read_only

true for read-only execution

Return Value

Pointer to portal containing the cursor. Note there is no error return convention; any error will be reported via `elog`.

SPI_cursor_open_with_args

SPI_cursor_open_with_args — set up a cursor using a query and parameters

Synopsis

```
Portal SPI_cursor_open_with_args(const char *name,
                                 const char *command,
                                 int nargs, Oid *argtypes,
                                 Datum *values, const char *nulls,
                                 bool read_only, int cursorOptions)
```

Description

SPI_cursor_open_with_args sets up a cursor (internally, a portal) that will execute the specified query. Most of the parameters have the same meanings as the corresponding parameters to SPI_prepare_cursor and SPI_cursor_open.

For one-time query execution, this function should be preferred over SPI_prepare_cursor followed by SPI_cursor_open. If the same command is to be executed with many different parameters, either method might be faster, depending on the cost of re-planning versus the benefit of custom plans.

The passed-in parameter data will be copied into the cursor's portal, so it can be freed while the cursor still exists.

Arguments

const char * name

  name for portal, or NULL to let the system select a name

const char * command

  command string

int nargs

  number of input parameters ($1, $2, etc.)

Oid * argtypes

  an array of length nargs, containing the OIDs of the data types of the parameters

Datum * values

  an array of length nargs, containing the actual parameter values

const char * nulls

  an array of length nargs, describing which parameters are null

  If nulls is NULL then SPI_cursor_open_with_args assumes that no parameters are null. Otherwise, each entry of the nulls array should be ' ' if the corresponding parameter value is non-null, or `'n'` if the corresponding parameter value is null. (In the latter case, the actual value in the corresponding `values` entry doesn't matter.) Note that `nulls` is not a text string, just an array: it does not need a `'\0'` terminator.

bool *read_only*

true for read-only execution

int *cursorOptions*

integer bit mask of cursor options; zero produces default behavior

Return Value

Pointer to portal containing the cursor. Note there is no error return convention; any error will be reported via elog.

SPI_cursor_open_with_paramlist

SPI_cursor_open_with_paramlist — set up a cursor using parameters

Synopsis

```
Portal SPI_cursor_open_with_paramlist(const char *name,
                                      SPIPlanPtr plan,
                                      ParamListInfo params,
                                      bool read_only)
```

Description

`SPI_cursor_open_with_paramlist` sets up a cursor (internally, a portal) that will execute a statement prepared by `SPI_prepare`. This function is equivalent to `SPI_cursor_open` except that information about the parameter values to be passed to the query is presented differently. The `ParamListInfo` representation can be convenient for passing down values that are already available in that format. It also supports use of dynamic parameter sets via hook functions specified in `ParamListInfo`.

The passed-in parameter data will be copied into the cursor's portal, so it can be freed while the cursor still exists.

Arguments

`const char * name`

name for portal, or `NULL` to let the system select a name

`SPIPlanPtr plan`

prepared statement (returned by `SPI_prepare`)

`ParamListInfo params`

data structure containing parameter types and values; NULL if none

`bool read_only`

`true` for read-only execution

Return Value

Pointer to portal containing the cursor. Note there is no error return convention; any error will be reported via `elog`.

SPI_cursor_find

SPI_cursor_find — find an existing cursor by name

Synopsis

```
Portal SPI_cursor_find(const char * name)
```

Description

SPI_cursor_find finds an existing portal by name. This is primarily useful to resolve a cursor name returned as text by some other function.

Arguments

const char * name

   name of the portal

Return Value

pointer to the portal with the specified name, or NULL if none was found

SPI_cursor_fetch

SPI_cursor_fetch — fetch some rows from a cursor

Synopsis

```
void SPI_cursor_fetch(Portal portal, bool forward, long count)
```

Description

`SPI_cursor_fetch` fetches some rows from a cursor. This is equivalent to a subset of the SQL command FETCH (see `SPI_scroll_cursor_fetch` for more functionality).

Arguments

Portal *portal*

portal containing the cursor

bool *forward*

true for fetch forward, false for fetch backward

long *count*

maximum number of rows to fetch

Return Value

`SPI_processed` and `SPI_tuptable` are set as in `SPI_execute` if successful.

Notes

Fetching backward may fail if the cursor's plan was not created with the `CURSOR_OPT_SCROLL` option.

SPI_cursor_move

SPI_cursor_move — move a cursor

Synopsis

```
void SPI_cursor_move(Portal portal, bool forward, long count)
```

Description

SPI_cursor_move skips over some number of rows in a cursor. This is equivalent to a subset of the SQL command MOVE (see SPI_scroll_cursor_move for more functionality).

Arguments

Portal *portal*

portal containing the cursor

bool *forward*

true for move forward, false for move backward

long *count*

maximum number of rows to move

Notes

Moving backward may fail if the cursor's plan was not created with the CURSOR_OPT_SCROLL option.

SPI_scroll_cursor_fetch

SPI_scroll_cursor_fetch — fetch some rows from a cursor

Synopsis

```
void SPI_scroll_cursor_fetch(Portal portal, FetchDirection direction,
                             long count)
```

Description

SPI_scroll_cursor_fetch fetches some rows from a cursor. This is equivalent to the SQL command FETCH.

Arguments

Portal *portal*

portal containing the cursor

FetchDirection *direction*

one of FETCH_FORWARD, FETCH_BACKWARD, FETCH_ABSOLUTE or FETCH_RELATIVE

long *count*

number of rows to fetch for FETCH_FORWARD or FETCH_BACKWARD; absolute row number to fetch for FETCH_ABSOLUTE; or relative row number to fetch for FETCH_RELATIVE

Return Value

SPI_processed and SPI_tuptable are set as in SPI_execute if successful.

Notes

See the SQL FETCH command for details of the interpretation of the *direction* and *count* parameters.

Direction values other than FETCH_FORWARD may fail if the cursor's plan was not created with the CURSOR_OPT_SCROLL option.

SPI_scroll_cursor_move

SPI_scroll_cursor_move — move a cursor

Synopsis

```
void SPI_scroll_cursor_move(Portal portal, FetchDirection direction,
                            long count)
```

Description

`SPI_scroll_cursor_move` skips over some number of rows in a cursor. This is equivalent to the SQL command `MOVE`.

Arguments

`Portal portal`

   portal containing the cursor

`FetchDirection direction`

   one of `FETCH_FORWARD`, `FETCH_BACKWARD`, `FETCH_ABSOLUTE` or `FETCH_RELATIVE`

`long count`

   number of rows to move for `FETCH_FORWARD` or `FETCH_BACKWARD`; absolute row number to move to for `FETCH_ABSOLUTE`; or relative row number to move to for `FETCH_RELATIVE`

Return Value

`SPI_processed` is set as in `SPI_execute` if successful. `SPI_tuptable` is set to `NULL`, since no rows are returned by this function.

Notes

See the SQL FETCH command for details of the interpretation of the *direction* and *count* parameters.

Direction values other than `FETCH_FORWARD` may fail if the cursor's plan was not created with the `CURSOR_OPT_SCROLL` option.

SPI_cursor_close

SPI_cursor_close — close a cursor

Synopsis

```
void SPI_cursor_close(Portal portal)
```

Description

SPI_cursor_close closes a previously created cursor and releases its portal storage.

All open cursors are closed automatically at the end of a transaction. SPI_cursor_close need only be invoked if it is desirable to release resources sooner.

Arguments

Portal portal

portal containing the cursor

SPI_keepplan

SPI_keepplan — save a prepared statement

Synopsis

```
int SPI_keepplan(SPIPlanPtr plan)
```

Description

SPI_keepplan saves a passed statement (prepared by SPI_prepare) so that it will not be freed by SPI_finish nor by the transaction manager. This gives you the ability to reuse prepared statements in the subsequent invocations of your C function in the current session.

Arguments

SPIPlanPtr plan

the prepared statement to be saved

Return Value

0 on success; SPI_ERROR_ARGUMENT if plan is NULL or invalid

Notes

The passed-in statement is relocated to permanent storage by means of pointer adjustment (no data copying is required). If you later wish to delete it, use SPI_freeplan on it.

SPI_saveplan

SPI_saveplan — save a prepared statement

Synopsis

```
SPIPlanPtr SPI_saveplan(SPIPlanPtr plan)
```

Description

SPI_saveplan copies a passed statement (prepared by SPI_prepare) into memory that will not be freed by SPI_finish nor by the transaction manager, and returns a pointer to the copied statement. This gives you the ability to reuse prepared statements in the subsequent invocations of your C function in the current session.

Arguments

SPIPlanPtr *plan*

> the prepared statement to be saved

Return Value

Pointer to the copied statement; or NULL if unsuccessful. On error, SPI_result is set thus:

SPI_ERROR_ARGUMENT

> if *plan* is NULL or invalid

SPI_ERROR_UNCONNECTED

> if called from an unconnected C function

Notes

The originally passed-in statement is not freed, so you might wish to do SPI_freeplan on it to avoid leaking memory until SPI_finish.

In most cases, SPI_keepplan is preferred to this function, since it accomplishes largely the same result without needing to physically copy the prepared statement's data structures.

SPI_register_relation

SPI_register_relation — make an ephemeral named relation available by name in SPI queries

Synopsis

```
int SPI_register_relation(EphemeralNamedRelation enr)
```

Description

`SPI_register_relation` makes an ephemeral named relation, with associated information, available to queries planned and executed through the current SPI connection.

Arguments

`EphemeralNamedRelation enr`

the ephemeral named relation registry entry

Return Value

If the execution of the command was successful then the following (nonnegative) value will be returned:

`SPI_OK_REL_REGISTER`

if the relation has been successfully registered by name

On error, one of the following negative values is returned:

`SPI_ERROR_ARGUMENT`

if *enr* is NULL or its `name` field is NULL

`SPI_ERROR_UNCONNECTED`

if called from an unconnected C function

`SPI_ERROR_REL_DUPLICATE`

if the name specified in the `name` field of *enr* is already registered for this connection

SPI_unregister_relation

SPI_unregister_relation — remove an ephemeral named relation from the registry

Synopsis

```
int SPI_unregister_relation(const char * name)
```

Description

SPI_unregister_relation removes an ephemeral named relation from the registry for the current connection.

Arguments

const char * name

> the relation registry entry name

Return Value

If the execution of the command was successful then the following (nonnegative) value will be returned:

SPI_OK_REL_UNREGISTER

> if the tuplestore has been successfully removed from the registry

On error, one of the following negative values is returned:

SPI_ERROR_ARGUMENT

> if name is NULL

SPI_ERROR_UNCONNECTED

> if called from an unconnected C function

SPI_ERROR_REL_NOT_FOUND

> if name is not found in the registry for the current connection

SPI_register_trigger_data

SPI_register_trigger_data — make ephemeral trigger data available in SPI queries

Synopsis

```
int SPI_register_trigger_data(TriggerData *tdata)
```

Description

SPI_register_trigger_data makes any ephemeral relations captured by a trigger available to queries planned and executed through the current SPI connection. Currently, this means the transition tables captured by an AFTER trigger defined with a REFERENCING OLD/NEW TABLE AS ... clause. This function should be called by a PL trigger handler function after connecting.

Arguments

TriggerData *tdata

> the TriggerData object passed to a trigger handler function as fcinfo->context

Return Value

If the execution of the command was successful then the following (nonnegative) value will be returned:

SPI_OK_TD_REGISTER

> if the captured trigger data (if any) has been successfully registered

On error, one of the following negative values is returned:

SPI_ERROR_ARGUMENT

> if tdata is NULL

SPI_ERROR_UNCONNECTED

> if called from an unconnected C function

SPI_ERROR_REL_DUPLICATE

> if the name of any trigger data transient relation is already registered for this connection

47.2. Interface Support Functions

The functions described here provide an interface for extracting information from result sets returned by SPI_execute and other SPI functions.

All functions described in this section can be used by both connected and unconnected C functions.

SPI_fname

SPI_fname — determine the column name for the specified column number

Synopsis

```
char * SPI_fname(TupleDesc rowdesc, int colnumber)
```

Description

SPI_fname returns a copy of the column name of the specified column. (You can use pfree to release the copy of the name when you don't need it anymore.)

Arguments

TupleDesc rowdesc

input row description

int colnumber

column number (count starts at 1)

Return Value

The column name; NULL if colnumber is out of range. SPI_result set to SPI_ERROR_NOAT-TRIBUTE on error.

SPI_fnumber

SPI_fnumber — determine the column number for the specified column name

Synopsis

```
int SPI_fnumber(TupleDesc rowdesc, const char * colname)
```

Description

SPI_fnumber returns the column number for the column with the specified name.

If colname refers to a system column (e.g., oid) then the appropriate negative column number will be returned. The caller should be careful to test the return value for exact equality to SPI_ERROR_NOAT-TRIBUTE to detect an error; testing the result for less than or equal to 0 is not correct unless system columns should be rejected.

Arguments

TupleDesc rowdesc

input row description

const char * colname

column name

Return Value

Column number (count starts at 1 for user-defined columns), or SPI_ERROR_NOATTRIBUTE if the named column was not found.

SPI_getvalue

SPI_getvalue — return the string value of the specified column

Synopsis

```
char * SPI_getvalue(HeapTuple row, TupleDesc rowdesc, int colnumber)
```

Description

`SPI_getvalue` returns the string representation of the value of the specified column.

The result is returned in memory allocated using `palloc`. (You can use `pfree` to release the memory when you don't need it anymore.)

Arguments

HeapTuple *row*

> input row to be examined

TupleDesc *rowdesc*

> input row description

int *colnumber*

> column number (count starts at 1)

Return Value

Column value, or `NULL` if the column is null, *colnumber* is out of range (`SPI_result` is set to `SPI_ERROR_NOATTRIBUTE`), or no output function is available (`SPI_result` is set to `SPI_ERROR_NOOUTFUNC`).

SPI_getbinval

SPI_getbinval — return the binary value of the specified column

Synopsis

```
Datum SPI_getbinval(HeapTuple row, TupleDesc rowdesc, int colnumber,
                    bool * isnull)
```

Description

SPI_getbinval returns the value of the specified column in the internal form (as type Datum).

This function does not allocate new space for the datum. In the case of a pass-by-reference data type, the return value will be a pointer into the passed row.

Arguments

HeapTuple row

　　input row to be examined

TupleDesc rowdesc

　　input row description

int colnumber

　　column number (count starts at 1)

bool * isnull

　　flag for a null value in the column

Return Value

The binary value of the column is returned. The variable pointed to by isnull is set to true if the column is null, else to false.

SPI_result is set to SPI_ERROR_NOATTRIBUTE on error.

SPI_gettype

SPI_gettype — return the data type name of the specified column

Synopsis

```
char * SPI_gettype(TupleDesc rowdesc, int colnumber)
```

Description

SPI_gettype returns a copy of the data type name of the specified column. (You can use pfree to release the copy of the name when you don't need it anymore.)

Arguments

TupleDesc *rowdesc*

> input row description

int *colnumber*

> column number (count starts at 1)

Return Value

The data type name of the specified column, or NULL on error. SPI_result is set to SPI_ERROR_NOATTRIBUTE on error.

SPI_gettypeid

SPI_gettypeid — return the data type OID of the specified column

Synopsis

```
Oid SPI_gettypeid(TupleDesc rowdesc, int colnumber)
```

Description

SPI_gettypeid returns the OID of the data type of the specified column.

Arguments

TupleDesc *rowdesc*

input row description

int *colnumber*

column number (count starts at 1)

Return Value

The OID of the data type of the specified column or InvalidOid on error. On error, SPI_result is set to SPI_ERROR_NOATTRIBUTE.

SPI_getrelname

SPI_getrelname — return the name of the specified relation

Synopsis

```
char * SPI_getrelname(Relation rel)
```

Description

SPI_getrelname returns a copy of the name of the specified relation. (You can use pfree to release the copy of the name when you don't need it anymore.)

Arguments

Relation rel

    input relation

Return Value

The name of the specified relation.

SPI_getnspname

SPI_getnspname — return the namespace of the specified relation

Synopsis

```
char * SPI_getnspname(Relation rel)
```

Description

SPI_getnspname returns a copy of the name of the namespace that the specified Relation belongs to. This is equivalent to the relation's schema. You should pfree the return value of this function when you are finished with it.

Arguments

Relation *rel*

input relation

Return Value

The name of the specified relation's namespace.

SPI_result_code_string

SPI_result_code_string — return error code as string

Synopsis

```
const char * SPI_result_code_string(int code);
```

Description

SPI_result_code_string returns a string representation of the result code returned by various SPI functions or stored in SPI_result.

Arguments

int *code*

result code

Return Value

A string representation of the result code.

47.3. Memory Management

PostgreSQL allocates memory within *memory contexts*, which provide a convenient method of managing allocations made in many different places that need to live for differing amounts of time. Destroying a context releases all the memory that was allocated in it. Thus, it is not necessary to keep track of individual objects to avoid memory leaks; instead only a relatively small number of contexts have to be managed. palloc and related functions allocate memory from the "current" context.

SPI_connect creates a new memory context and makes it current. SPI_finish restores the previous current memory context and destroys the context created by SPI_connect. These actions ensure that transient memory allocations made inside your C function are reclaimed at C function exit, avoiding memory leakage.

However, if your C function needs to return an object in allocated memory (such as a value of a pass-by-reference data type), you cannot allocate that memory using palloc, at least not while you are connected to SPI. If you try, the object will be deallocated by SPI_finish, and your C function will not work reliably. To solve this problem, use SPI_palloc to allocate memory for your return object. SPI_palloc allocates memory in the "upper executor context", that is, the memory context that was current when SPI_connect was called, which is precisely the right context for a value returned from your C function. Several of the other utility functions described in this section also return objects created in the upper executor context.

When SPI_connect is called, the private context of the C function, which is created by SPI_connect, is made the current context. All allocations made by palloc, repalloc, or SPI utility functions (except as described in this section) are made in this context. When a C function disconnects from the SPI manager (via SPI_finish) the current context is restored to the upper executor context, and all allocations made in the C function memory context are freed and cannot be used any more.

SPI_palloc

SPI_palloc — allocate memory in the upper executor context

Synopsis

```
void * SPI_palloc(Size size)
```

Description

SPI_palloc allocates memory in the upper executor context.

This function can only be used while connected to SPI. Otherwise, it throws an error.

Arguments

Size *size*

size in bytes of storage to allocate

Return Value

pointer to new storage space of the specified size

SPI_repalloc

SPI_repalloc — reallocate memory in the upper executor context

Synopsis

```
void * SPI_repalloc(void * pointer, Size size)
```

Description

SPI_repalloc changes the size of a memory segment previously allocated using SPI_palloc.

This function is no longer different from plain repalloc. It's kept just for backward compatibility of existing code.

Arguments

void * *pointer*

   pointer to existing storage to change

Size *size*

   size in bytes of storage to allocate

Return Value

pointer to new storage space of specified size with the contents copied from the existing area

SPI_pfree

SPI_pfree — free memory in the upper executor context

Synopsis

```
void SPI_pfree(void * pointer)
```

Description

`SPI_pfree` frees memory previously allocated using `SPI_palloc` or `SPI_repalloc`.

This function is no longer different from plain `pfree`. It's kept just for backward compatibility of existing code.

Arguments

`void * pointer`

pointer to existing storage to free

SPI_copytuple

SPI_copytuple — make a copy of a row in the upper executor context

Synopsis

```
HeapTuple SPI_copytuple(HeapTuple row)
```

Description

SPI_copytuple makes a copy of a row in the upper executor context. This is normally used to return a modified row from a trigger. In a function declared to return a composite type, use SPI_returntuple instead.

This function can only be used while connected to SPI. Otherwise, it returns NULL and sets SPI_result to SPI_ERROR_UNCONNECTED.

Arguments

HeapTuple row

row to be copied

Return Value

the copied row, or NULL on error (see SPI_result for an error indication)

SPI_returntuple

SPI_returntuple — prepare to return a tuple as a Datum

Synopsis

```
HeapTupleHeader SPI_returntuple(HeapTuple row, TupleDesc rowdesc)
```

Description

`SPI_returntuple` makes a copy of a row in the upper executor context, returning it in the form of a row type `Datum`. The returned pointer need only be converted to `Datum` via `PointerGetDatum` before returning.

This function can only be used while connected to SPI. Otherwise, it returns NULL and sets `SPI_result` to `SPI_ERROR_UNCONNECTED`.

Note that this should be used for functions that are declared to return composite types. It is not used for triggers; use `SPI_copytuple` for returning a modified row in a trigger.

Arguments

`HeapTuple row`

    row to be copied

`TupleDesc rowdesc`

    descriptor for row (pass the same descriptor each time for most effective caching)

Return Value

`HeapTupleHeader` pointing to copied row, or `NULL` on error (see `SPI_result` for an error indication)

SPI_modifytuple

SPI_modifytuple — create a row by replacing selected fields of a given row

Synopsis

```
HeapTuple SPI_modifytuple(Relation rel, HeapTuple row, int ncols,
                          int * colnum, Datum * values, const char
  * nulls)
```

Description

SPI_modifytuple creates a new row by substituting new values for selected columns, copying the original row's columns at other positions. The input row is not modified. The new row is returned in the upper executor context.

This function can only be used while connected to SPI. Otherwise, it returns NULL and sets SPI_result to SPI_ERROR_UNCONNECTED.

Arguments

Relation rel

Used only as the source of the row descriptor for the row. (Passing a relation rather than a row descriptor is a misfeature.)

HeapTuple row

row to be modified

int ncols

number of columns to be changed

int * colnum

an array of length ncols, containing the numbers of the columns that are to be changed (column numbers start at 1)

Datum * values

an array of length ncols, containing the new values for the specified columns

const char * nulls

an array of length ncols, describing which new values are null

If nulls is NULL then SPI_modifytuple assumes that no new values are null. Otherwise, each entry of the nulls array should be ' ' if the corresponding new value is non-null, or 'n' if the corresponding new value is null. (In the latter case, the actual value in the corresponding values entry doesn't matter.) Note that nulls is not a text string, just an array: it does not need a '\0' terminator.

Return Value

new row with modifications, allocated in the upper executor context, or NULL on error (see SPI_result for an error indication)

On error, SPI_result is set as follows:

SPI_ERROR_ARGUMENT

if *rel* is NULL, or if *row* is NULL, or if *ncols* is less than or equal to 0, or if *colnum* is NULL, or if *values* is NULL.

SPI_ERROR_NOATTRIBUTE

if *colnum* contains an invalid column number (less than or equal to 0 or greater than the number of columns in *row*)

SPI_ERROR_UNCONNECTED

if SPI is not active

SPI_freetuple

SPI_freetuple — free a row allocated in the upper executor context

Synopsis

```
void SPI_freetuple(HeapTuple row)
```

Description

SPI_freetuple frees a row previously allocated in the upper executor context.

This function is no longer different from plain heap_freetuple. It's kept just for backward compatibility of existing code.

Arguments

HeapTuple *row*

row to free

SPI_freetuptable

SPI_freetuptable — free a row set created by `SPI_execute` or a similar function

Synopsis

```
void SPI_freetuptable(SPITupleTable * tuptable)
```

Description

`SPI_freetuptable` frees a row set created by a prior SPI command execution function, such as `SPI_execute`. Therefore, this function is often called with the global variable `SPI_tuptable` as argument.

This function is useful if an SPI-using C function needs to execute multiple commands and does not want to keep the results of earlier commands around until it ends. Note that any unfreed row sets will be freed anyway at `SPI_finish`. Also, if a subtransaction is started and then aborted within execution of an SPI-using C function, SPI automatically frees any row sets created while the subtransaction was running.

Beginning in PostgreSQL 9.3, `SPI_freetuptable` contains guard logic to protect against duplicate deletion requests for the same row set. In previous releases, duplicate deletions would lead to crashes.

Arguments

`SPITupleTable * tuptable`

pointer to row set to free, or NULL to do nothing

SPI_freeplan

SPI_freeplan — free a previously saved prepared statement

Synopsis

```
int SPI_freeplan(SPIPlanPtr plan)
```

Description

SPI_freeplan releases a prepared statement previously returned by SPI_prepare or saved by SPI_keepplan or SPI_saveplan.

Arguments

SPIPlanPtr *plan*

   pointer to statement to free

Return Value

0 on success; SPI_ERROR_ARGUMENT if *plan* is NULL or invalid

47.4. Transaction Management

It is not possible to run transaction control commands such as COMMIT and ROLLBACK through SPI functions such as SPI_execute. There are, however, separate interface functions that allow transaction control through SPI.

It is not generally safe and sensible to start and end transactions in arbitrary user-defined SQL-callable functions without taking into account the context in which they are called. For example, a transaction boundary in the middle of a function that is part of a complex SQL expression that is part of some SQL command will probably result in obscure internal errors or crashes. The interface functions presented here are primarily intended to be used by procedural language implementations to support transaction management in SQL-level procedures that are invoked by the CALL command, taking the context of the CALL invocation into account. SPI-using procedures implemented in C can implement the same logic, but the details of that are beyond the scope of this documentation.

SPI_commit

SPI_commit — commit the current transaction

Synopsis

```
void SPI_commit(void)
```

Description

SPI_commit commits the current transaction. It is approximately equivalent to running the SQL command COMMIT. After a transaction is committed, a new transaction has to be started using SPI_start_transaction before further database actions can be executed.

This function can only be executed if the SPI connection has been set as nonatomic in the call to SPI_connect_ext.

SPI_rollback

SPI_rollback — abort the current transaction

Synopsis

```
void SPI_rollback(void)
```

Description

SPI_rollback rolls back the current transaction. It is approximately equivalent to running the SQL command ROLLBACK. After a transaction is rolled back, a new transaction has to be started using SPI_start_transaction before further database actions can be executed.

This function can only be executed if the SPI connection has been set as nonatomic in the call to SPI_connect_ext.

SPI_start_transaction

SPI_start_transaction — start a new transaction

Synopsis

```
void SPI_start_transaction(void)
```

Description

SPI_start_transaction starts a new transaction. It can only be called after SPI_commit or SPI_rollback, as there is no transaction active at that point. Normally, when an SPI-using procedure is called, there is already a transaction active, so attempting to start another one before closing out the current one will result in an error.

This function can only be executed if the SPI connection has been set as nonatomic in the call to SPI_connect_ext.

47.5. Visibility of Data Changes

The following rules govern the visibility of data changes in functions that use SPI (or any other C function):

- During the execution of an SQL command, any data changes made by the command are invisible to the command itself. For example, in:

```
INSERT INTO a SELECT * FROM a;
```

the inserted rows are invisible to the SELECT part.

- Changes made by a command C are visible to all commands that are started after C, no matter whether they are started inside C (during the execution of C) or after C is done.

- Commands executed via SPI inside a function called by an SQL command (either an ordinary function or a trigger) follow one or the other of the above rules depending on the read/write flag passed to SPI. Commands executed in read-only mode follow the first rule: they cannot see changes of the calling command. Commands executed in read-write mode follow the second rule: they can see all changes made so far.

- All standard procedural languages set the SPI read-write mode depending on the volatility attribute of the function. Commands of STABLE and IMMUTABLE functions are done in read-only mode, while commands of VOLATILE functions are done in read-write mode. While authors of C functions are able to violate this convention, it's unlikely to be a good idea to do so.

The next section contains an example that illustrates the application of these rules.

47.6. Examples

This section contains a very simple example of SPI usage. The C function execq takes an SQL command as its first argument and a row count as its second, executes the command using SPI_exec and returns the number of rows that were processed by the command. You can find more complex examples for SPI in the source tree in src/test/regress/regress.c and in the spi module.

```c
#include "postgres.h"

#include "executor/spi.h"
#include "utils/builtins.h"

PG_MODULE_MAGIC;

PG_FUNCTION_INFO_V1(execq);

Datum
execq(PG_FUNCTION_ARGS)
{
    char *command;
    int cnt;
    int ret;
    uint64 proc;

    /* Convert given text object to a C string */
    command = text_to_cstring(PG_GETARG_TEXT_PP(0));
    cnt = PG_GETARG_INT32(1);

    SPI_connect();

    ret = SPI_exec(command, cnt);

    proc = SPI_processed;

    /*
     * If some rows were fetched, print them via elog(INFO).
     */
    if (ret > 0 && SPI_tuptable != NULL)
    {
        TupleDesc tupdesc = SPI_tuptable->tupdesc;
        SPITupleTable *tuptable = SPI_tuptable;
        char buf[8192];
        uint64 j;

        for (j = 0; j < proc; j++)
        {
            HeapTuple tuple = tuptable->vals[j];
            int i;

            for (i = 1, buf[0] = 0; i <= tupdesc->natts; i++)
                snprintf(buf + strlen(buf), sizeof(buf) - strlen(buf),
 " %s%s",
                        SPI_getvalue(tuple, tupdesc, i),
                        (i == tupdesc->natts) ? " " : " |");
            elog(INFO, "EXECQ: %s", buf);
        }
    }

    SPI_finish();
    pfree(command);
```

```
        PG_RETURN_INT64(proc);
}
```

This is how you declare the function after having compiled it into a shared library (details are in Section 38.10.5.):

```
CREATE FUNCTION execq(text, integer) RETURNS int8
    AS 'filename'
    LANGUAGE C STRICT;
```

Here is a sample session:

```
=> SELECT execq('CREATE TABLE a (x integer)', 0);
 execq
-------
     0
(1 row)

=> INSERT INTO a VALUES (execq('INSERT INTO a VALUES (0)', 0));
INSERT 0 1
=> SELECT execq('SELECT * FROM a', 0);
INFO:  EXECQ:  0     -- inserted by execq
INFO:  EXECQ:  1     -- returned by execq and inserted by upper INSERT

 execq
-------
     2
(1 row)

=> SELECT execq('INSERT INTO a SELECT x + 2 FROM a', 1);
 execq
-------
     1
(1 row)

=> SELECT execq('SELECT * FROM a', 10);
INFO:  EXECQ:  0
INFO:  EXECQ:  1
INFO:  EXECQ:  2     -- 0 + 2, only one row inserted - as specified

 execq
-------
     3               -- 10 is the max value only, 3 is the real number
 of rows
(1 row)

=> DELETE FROM a;
DELETE 3
=> INSERT INTO a VALUES (execq('SELECT * FROM a', 0) + 1);
INSERT 0 1
=> SELECT * FROM a;
 x
```

```
 ---
  1                        -- no rows in a (0) + 1
(1 row)

=> INSERT INTO a VALUES (execq('SELECT * FROM a', 0) + 1);
INFO:  EXECQ:  1
INSERT 0 1
=> SELECT * FROM a;
 x
 ---
  1
  2                        -- there was one row in a + 1
(2 rows)

-- This demonstrates the data changes visibility rule:

=> INSERT INTO a SELECT execq('SELECT * FROM a', 0) * x FROM a;
INFO:  EXECQ:  1
INFO:  EXECQ:  2
INFO:  EXECQ:  1
INFO:  EXECQ:  2
INFO:  EXECQ:  2
INSERT 0 2
=> SELECT * FROM a;
 x
 ---
  1
  2
  2                        -- 2 rows * 1 (x in first row)
  6                        -- 3 rows (2 + 1 just inserted) * 2 (x in second
 row)
(4 rows)                        ^^^^^^
                                rows visible to execq() in different
 invocations
```

Chapter 48. Background Worker Processes

PostgreSQL can be extended to run user-supplied code in separate processes. Such processes are started, stopped and monitored by `postgres`, which permits them to have a lifetime closely linked to the server's status. These processes have the option to attach to PostgreSQL's shared memory area and to connect to databases internally; they can also run multiple transactions serially, just like a regular client-connected server process. Also, by linking to libpq they can connect to the server and behave like a regular client application.

Warning

There are considerable robustness and security risks in using background worker processes because, being written in the C language, they have unrestricted access to data. Administrators wishing to enable modules that include background worker process should exercise extreme caution. Only carefully audited modules should be permitted to run background worker processes.

Background workers can be initialized at the time that PostgreSQL is started by including the module name in `shared_preload_libraries`. A module wishing to run a background worker can register it by calling `RegisterBackgroundWorker(BackgroundWorker *worker)` from its `_PG_init()`. Background workers can also be started after the system is up and running by calling the function `RegisterDynamicBackgroundWorker(BackgroundWorker *worker, BackgroundWorkerHandle **handle)`. Unlike `RegisterBackgroundWorker`, which can only be called from within the postmaster, `RegisterDynamicBackgroundWorker` must be called from a regular backend or another background worker.

The structure `BackgroundWorker` is defined thus:

```
typedef void (*bgworker_main_type)(Datum main_arg);
typedef struct BackgroundWorker
{
    char        bgw_name[BGW_MAXLEN];
    char        bgw_type[BGW_MAXLEN];
    int         bgw_flags;
    BgWorkerStartTime bgw_start_time;
    int         bgw_restart_time;        /* in seconds, or
 BGW_NEVER_RESTART */
    char        bgw_library_name[BGW_MAXLEN];
    char        bgw_function_name[BGW_MAXLEN];
    Datum       bgw_main_arg;
    char        bgw_extra[BGW_EXTRALEN];
    int         bgw_notify_pid;
} BackgroundWorker;
```

`bgw_name` and `bgw_type` are strings to be used in log messages, process listings and similar contexts. `bgw_type` should be the same for all background workers of the same type, so that it is possible to group such workers in a process listing, for example. `bgw_name` on the other hand can contain additional information about the specific process. (Typically, the string for `bgw_name` will contain the type somehow, but that is not strictly required.)

`bgw_flags` is a bitwise-or'd bit mask indicating the capabilities that the module wants. Possible values are:

BGWORKER_SHMEM_ACCESS

Requests shared memory access. Workers without shared memory access cannot access any of PostgreSQL's shared data structures, such as heavyweight or lightweight locks, shared buffers, or any custom data structures which the worker itself may wish to create and use.

BGWORKER_BACKEND_DATABASE_CONNECTION

Requests the ability to establish a database connection through which it can later run transactions and queries. A background worker using BGWORKER_BACKEND_DATABASE_CONNECTION to connect to a database must also attach shared memory using BGWORKER_SHMEM_ACCESS, or worker start-up will fail.

`bgw_start_time` is the server state during which `postgres` should start the process; it can be one of BgWorkerStart_PostmasterStart (start as soon as `postgres` itself has finished its own initialization; processes requesting this are not eligible for database connections), BgWorkerStart_ConsistentState (start as soon as a consistent state has been reached in a hot standby, allowing processes to connect to databases and run read-only queries), and BgWorkerStart_RecoveryFinished (start as soon as the system has entered normal read-write state). Note the last two values are equivalent in a server that's not a hot standby. Note that this setting only indicates when the processes are to be started; they do not stop when a different state is reached.

`bgw_restart_time` is the interval, in seconds, that `postgres` should wait before restarting the process, in case it crashes. It can be any positive value, or BGW_NEVER_RESTART, indicating not to restart the process in case of a crash.

`bgw_library_name` is the name of a library in which the initial entry point for the background worker should be sought. The named library will be dynamically loaded by the worker process and `bgw_function_name` will be used to identify the function to be called. If loading a function from the core code, this must be set to "postgres".

`bgw_function_name` is the name of a function in a dynamically loaded library which should be used as the initial entry point for a new background worker.

`bgw_main_arg` is the `Datum` argument to the background worker main function. This main function should take a single argument of type `Datum` and return `void`. `bgw_main_arg` will be passed as the argument. In addition, the global variable `MyBgworkerEntry` points to a copy of the `BackgroundWorker` structure passed at registration time; the worker may find it helpful to examine this structure.

On Windows (and anywhere else where `EXEC_BACKEND` is defined) or in dynamic background workers it is not safe to pass a `Datum` by reference, only by value. If an argument is required, it is safest to pass an int32 or other small value and use that as an index into an array allocated in shared memory. If a value like a `cstring` or `text` is passed then the pointer won't be valid from the new background worker process.

`bgw_extra` can contain extra data to be passed to the background worker. Unlike `bgw_main_arg`, this data is not passed as an argument to the worker's main function, but it can be accessed via `MyBgworkerEntry`, as discussed above.

`bgw_notify_pid` is the PID of a PostgreSQL backend process to which the postmaster should send SIGUSR1 when the process is started or exits. It should be 0 for workers registered at postmaster startup time, or when the backend registering the worker does not wish to wait for the worker to start up. Otherwise, it should be initialized to `MyProcPid`.

Once running, the process can connect to a database by calling `BackgroundWorkerInitialize-Connection(char *dbname, char *username, uint32 flags)` or `BackgroundWorkerInitializeConnectionByOid(Oid dboid, Oid useroid, uint32 flags)`. This allows the process to run transactions and queries using the `SPI` interface. If `dbname` is NULL or `dboid` is `InvalidOid`, the session is not connected to any particular database, but shared catalogs can be accessed. If `username` is NULL or `useroid` is `InvalidOid`, the process will run as the superuser created during `initdb`. If `BGWORKER_BYPASS_ALLOWCONN` is specified as `flags` it is possible to bypass the restriction to connect to databases not allowing user connections. A background worker can only call one of these two functions, and only once. It is not possible to switch databases.

Signals are initially blocked when control reaches the background worker's main function, and must be unblocked by it; this is to allow the process to customize its signal handlers, if necessary. Signals can be unblocked in the new process by calling `BackgroundWorkerUnblockSignals` and blocked by calling `BackgroundWorkerBlockSignals`.

If `bgw_restart_time` for a background worker is configured as `BGW_NEVER_RESTART`, or if it exits with an exit code of 0 or is terminated by `TerminateBackgroundWorker`, it will be automatically unregistered by the postmaster on exit. Otherwise, it will be restarted after the time period configured via `bgw_restart_time`, or immediately if the postmaster reinitializes the cluster due to a backend failure. Backends which need to suspend execution only temporarily should use an interruptible sleep rather than exiting; this can be achieved by calling `WaitLatch()`. Make sure the `WL_POSTMASTER_DEATH` flag is set when calling that function, and verify the return code for a prompt exit in the emergency case that `postgres` itself has terminated.

When a background worker is registered using the `RegisterDynamicBackgroundWorker` function, it is possible for the backend performing the registration to obtain information regarding the status of the worker. Backends wishing to do this should pass the address of a `BackgroundWorkerHandle *` as the second argument to `RegisterDynamicBackgroundWorker`. If the worker is successfully registered, this pointer will be initialized with an opaque handle that can subsequently be passed to `GetBackgroundWorkerPid(BackgroundWorkerHandle *, pid_t *)` or `TerminateBackgroundWorker(BackgroundWorkerHandle *)`. `GetBackgroundWorkerPid` can be used to poll the status of the worker: a return value of `BGWH_NOT_YET_STARTED` indicates that the worker has not yet been started by the postmaster; `BGWH_STOPPED` indicates that it has been started but is no longer running; and `BGWH_STARTED` indicates that it is currently running. In this last case, the PID will also be returned via the second argument. `TerminateBackgroundWorker` causes the postmaster to send `SIGTERM` to the worker if it is running, and to unregister it as soon as it is not.

In some cases, a process which registers a background worker may wish to wait for the worker to start up. This can be accomplished by initializing `bgw_notify_pid` to `MyProcPid` and then passing the `BackgroundWorkerHandle *` obtained at registration time to `WaitForBackgroundWorkerStartup(BackgroundWorkerHandle *handle, pid_t *)` function. This function will block until the postmaster has attempted to start the background worker, or until the postmaster dies. If the background worker is running, the return value will be `BGWH_STARTED`, and the PID will be written to the provided address. Otherwise, the return value will be `BGWH_STOPPED` or `BGWH_POSTMASTER_DIED`.

A process can also wait for a background worker to shut down, by using the `WaitForBackgroundWorkerShutdown(BackgroundWorkerHandle *handle)` function and passing the `BackgroundWorkerHandle *` obtained at registration. This function will block until the background worker exits, or postmaster dies. When the background worker exits, the return value is `BGWH_STOPPED`, if postmaster dies it will return `BGWH_POSTMASTER_DIED`.

If a background worker sends asynchronous notifications with the `NOTIFY` command via the Server Programming Interface (SPI), it should call `ProcessCompletedNotifies` explicitly after committing the enclosing transaction so that any notifications can be delivered. If a background worker registers to receive asynchronous notifications with the `LISTEN` through SPI, the worker will log those notifications, but there is no programmatic way for the worker to intercept and respond to those notifications.

The `src/test/modules/worker_spi` module contains a working example, which demonstrates some useful techniques.

The maximum number of registered background workers is limited by max_worker_processes.

Chapter 49. Logical Decoding

PostgreSQL provides infrastructure to stream the modifications performed via SQL to external consumers. This functionality can be used for a variety of purposes, including replication solutions and auditing.

Changes are sent out in streams identified by logical replication slots.

The format in which those changes are streamed is determined by the output plugin used. An example plugin is provided in the PostgreSQL distribution. Additional plugins can be written to extend the choice of available formats without modifying any core code. Every output plugin has access to each individual new row produced by INSERT and the new row version created by UPDATE. Availability of old row versions for UPDATE and DELETE depends on the configured replica identity (see REPLICA IDENTITY).

Changes can be consumed either using the streaming replication protocol (see Section 53.4 and Section 49.3), or by calling functions via SQL (see Section 49.4). It is also possible to write additional methods of consuming the output of a replication slot without modifying core code (see Section 49.7).

49.1. Logical Decoding Examples

The following example demonstrates controlling logical decoding using the SQL interface.

Before you can use logical decoding, you must set wal_level to logical and max_replication_slots to at least 1. Then, you should connect to the target database (in the example below, postgres) as a superuser.

```
postgres=# -- Create a slot named 'regression_slot' using the output
 plugin 'test_decoding'
postgres=# SELECT * FROM
 pg_create_logical_replication_slot('regression_slot',
 'test_decoding');
    slot_name     |    lsn
-----------------+-----------
 regression_slot | 0/16B1970
(1 row)

postgres=# SELECT slot_name, plugin, slot_type, database, active,
 restart_lsn, confirmed_flush_lsn FROM pg_replication_slots;
    slot_name    |    plugin     | slot_type | database | active |
 restart_lsn | confirmed_flush_lsn
-----------------+---------------+-----------+----------+--------
+-------------+-----------------
 regression_slot | test_decoding | logical   | postgres | f      |
 0/16A4408   | 0/16A4440
(1 row)

postgres=# -- There are no changes to see yet
postgres=# SELECT * FROM
 pg_logical_slot_get_changes('regression_slot', NULL, NULL);
 lsn | xid | data
-----+-----+------
(0 rows)

postgres=# CREATE TABLE data(id serial primary key, data text);
```

```
CREATE TABLE

postgres=# -- DDL isn't replicated, so all you'll see is the
 transaction
postgres=# SELECT * FROM
 pg_logical_slot_get_changes('regression_slot', NULL, NULL);
    lsn    |  xid  |     data
-----------+-------+--------------
 0/BA2DA58 | 10297 | BEGIN 10297
 0/BA5A5A0 | 10297 | COMMIT 10297
(2 rows)

postgres=# -- Once changes are read, they're consumed and not emitted
postgres=# -- in a subsequent call:
postgres=# SELECT * FROM
 pg_logical_slot_get_changes('regression_slot', NULL, NULL);
 lsn | xid | data
-----+-----+------
(0 rows)

postgres=# BEGIN;
postgres=# INSERT INTO data(data) VALUES('1');
postgres=# INSERT INTO data(data) VALUES('2');
postgres=# COMMIT;

postgres=# SELECT * FROM
 pg_logical_slot_get_changes('regression_slot', NULL, NULL);
    lsn    |  xid  |                         data

-----------+-------
+----------------------------------------------------------
 0/BA5A688 | 10298 | BEGIN 10298
 0/BA5A6F0 | 10298 | table public.data: INSERT: id[integer]:1
data[text]:'1'
 0/BA5A7F8 | 10298 | table public.data: INSERT: id[integer]:2
data[text]:'2'
 0/BA5A8A8 | 10298 | COMMIT 10298
(4 rows)

postgres=# INSERT INTO data(data) VALUES('3');

postgres=# -- You can also peek ahead in the change stream without
 consuming changes
postgres=# SELECT * FROM
 pg_logical_slot_peek_changes('regression_slot', NULL, NULL);
    lsn    |  xid  |                         data

-----------+-------
+----------------------------------------------------------
 0/BA5A8E0 | 10299 | BEGIN 10299
 0/BA5A8E0 | 10299 | table public.data: INSERT: id[integer]:3
data[text]:'3'
 0/BA5A990 | 10299 | COMMIT 10299
(3 rows)
```

```
postgres=# -- The next call to pg_logical_slot_peek_changes() returns
  the same changes again
postgres=# SELECT * FROM
  pg_logical_slot_peek_changes('regression_slot', NULL, NULL);
    lsn     |  xid  |                         data

-----------+-------
+-----------------------------------------------------------
 0/BA5A8E0 | 10299 | BEGIN 10299
 0/BA5A8E0 | 10299 | table public.data: INSERT: id[integer]:3
 data[text]:'3'
 0/BA5A990 | 10299 | COMMIT 10299
(3 rows)

postgres=# -- options can be passed to output plugin, to influence the
  formatting
postgres=# SELECT * FROM
  pg_logical_slot_peek_changes('regression_slot', NULL, NULL, 'include-
timestamp', 'on');
    lsn     |  xid  |                         data

-----------+-------
+-----------------------------------------------------------
 0/BA5A8E0 | 10299 | BEGIN 10299
 0/BA5A8E0 | 10299 | table public.data: INSERT: id[integer]:3
 data[text]:'3'
 0/BA5A990 | 10299 | COMMIT 10299 (at 2017-05-10 12:07:21.272494-04)
(3 rows)

postgres=# -- Remember to destroy a slot you no longer need to stop it
  consuming
postgres=# -- server resources:
postgres=# SELECT pg_drop_replication_slot('regression_slot');
 pg_drop_replication_slot
-----------------------

(1 row)
```

The following example shows how logical decoding is controlled over the streaming replication protocol, using the program pg_recvlogical included in the PostgreSQL distribution. This requires that client authentication is set up to allow replication connections (see Section 26.2.5.1) and that max_wal_senders is set sufficiently high to allow an additional connection.

```
$ pg_recvlogical -d postgres --slot=test --create-slot
$ pg_recvlogical -d postgres --slot=test --start -f -
Control+Z
$ psql -d postgres -c "INSERT INTO data(data) VALUES('4');"
$ fg
BEGIN 693
table public.data: INSERT: id[integer]:4 data[text]:'4'
COMMIT 693
Control+C
```

```
$ pg_recvlogical -d postgres --slot=test --drop-slot
```

49.2. Logical Decoding Concepts

49.2.1. Logical Decoding

Logical decoding is the process of extracting all persistent changes to a database's tables into a coherent, easy to understand format which can be interpreted without detailed knowledge of the database's internal state.

In PostgreSQL, logical decoding is implemented by decoding the contents of the write-ahead log, which describe changes on a storage level, into an application-specific form such as a stream of tuples or SQL statements.

49.2.2. Replication Slots

In the context of logical replication, a slot represents a stream of changes that can be replayed to a client in the order they were made on the origin server. Each slot streams a sequence of changes from a single database.

> ### Note
>
> PostgreSQL also has streaming replication slots (see Section 26.2.5), but they are used somewhat differently there.

A replication slot has an identifier that is unique across all databases in a PostgreSQL cluster. Slots persist independently of the connection using them and are crash-safe.

A logical slot will emit each change just once in normal operation. The current position of each slot is persisted only at checkpoint, so in the case of a crash the slot may return to an earlier LSN, which will then cause recent changes to be resent when the server restarts. Logical decoding clients are responsible for avoiding ill effects from handling the same message more than once. Clients may wish to record the last LSN they saw when decoding and skip over any repeated data or (when using the replication protocol) request that decoding start from that LSN rather than letting the server determine the start point. The Replication Progress Tracking feature is designed for this purpose, refer to replication origins.

Multiple independent slots may exist for a single database. Each slot has its own state, allowing different consumers to receive changes from different points in the database change stream. For most applications, a separate slot will be required for each consumer.

A logical replication slot knows nothing about the state of the receiver(s). It's even possible to have multiple different receivers using the same slot at different times; they'll just get the changes following on from when the last receiver stopped consuming them. Only one receiver may consume changes from a slot at any given time.

> ### Caution
>
> Replication slots persist across crashes and know nothing about the state of their consumer(s). They will prevent removal of required resources even when there is no connection using them. This consumes storage because neither required WAL nor required rows from the system catalogs can be removed by VACUUM as long as they are required by a replication slot. In extreme cases this could cause the database to shut down to prevent

transaction ID wraparound (see Section 24.1.5). So if a slot is no longer required it should be dropped.

49.2.3. Output Plugins

Output plugins transform the data from the write-ahead log's internal representation into the format the consumer of a replication slot desires.

49.2.4. Exported Snapshots

When a new replication slot is created using the streaming replication interface (see CREATE_REPLI-CATION_SLOT), a snapshot is exported (see Section 9.26.5), which will show exactly the state of the database after which all changes will be included in the change stream. This can be used to create a new replica by using SET TRANSACTION SNAPSHOT to read the state of the database at the moment the slot was created. This transaction can then be used to dump the database's state at that point in time, which afterwards can be updated using the slot's contents without losing any changes.

Creation of a snapshot is not always possible. In particular, it will fail when connected to a hot standby. Applications that do not require snapshot export may suppress it with the NOEXPORT_SNAPSHOT option.

49.3. Streaming Replication Protocol Interface

The commands

- CREATE_REPLICATION_SLOT *slot_name* LOGICAL *output_plugin*

- DROP_REPLICATION_SLOT *slot_name* [WAIT]

- START_REPLICATION SLOT *slot_name* LOGICAL ...

are used to create, drop, and stream changes from a replication slot, respectively. These commands are only available over a replication connection; they cannot be used via SQL. See Section 53.4 for details on these commands.

The command pg_recvlogical can be used to control logical decoding over a streaming replication connection. (It uses these commands internally.)

49.4. Logical Decoding SQL Interface

See Section 9.26.6 for detailed documentation on the SQL-level API for interacting with logical decoding.

Synchronous replication (see Section 26.2.8) is only supported on replication slots used over the streaming replication interface. The function interface and additional, non-core interfaces do not support synchronous replication.

49.5. System Catalogs Related to Logical Decoding

The pg_replication_slots view and the pg_stat_replication view provide information about the current state of replication slots and streaming replication connections respectively. These views apply to both physical and logical replication.

49.6. Logical Decoding Output Plugins

An example output plugin can be found in the `contrib/test_decoding` subdirectory of the PostgreSQL source tree.

49.6.1. Initialization Function

An output plugin is loaded by dynamically loading a shared library with the output plugin's name as the library base name. The normal library search path is used to locate the library. To provide the required output plugin callbacks and to indicate that the library is actually an output plugin it needs to provide a function named `_PG_output_plugin_init`. This function is passed a struct that needs to be filled with the callback function pointers for individual actions.

```
typedef struct OutputPluginCallbacks
{
    LogicalDecodeStartupCB startup_cb;
    LogicalDecodeBeginCB begin_cb;
    LogicalDecodeChangeCB change_cb;
    LogicalDecodeTruncateCB truncate_cb;
    LogicalDecodeCommitCB commit_cb;
    LogicalDecodeMessageCB message_cb;
    LogicalDecodeFilterByOriginCB filter_by_origin_cb;
    LogicalDecodeShutdownCB shutdown_cb;
} OutputPluginCallbacks;

typedef void (*LogicalOutputPluginInit) (struct OutputPluginCallbacks
 *cb);
```

The `begin_cb`, `change_cb` and `commit_cb` callbacks are required, while `startup_cb`, `filter_by_origin_cb`, `truncate_cb`, and `shutdown_cb` are optional. If `truncate_cb` is not set but a TRUNCATE is to be decoded, the action will be ignored.

49.6.2. Capabilities

To decode, format and output changes, output plugins can use most of the backend's normal infrastructure, including calling output functions. Read only access to relations is permitted as long as only relations are accessed that either have been created by `initdb` in the `pg_catalog` schema, or have been marked as user provided catalog tables using

```
ALTER TABLE user_catalog_table SET (user_catalog_table = true);
CREATE TABLE another_catalog_table(data text) WITH (user_catalog_table
 = true);
```

Any actions leading to transaction ID assignment are prohibited. That, among others, includes writing to tables, performing DDL changes, and calling `txid_current()`.

49.6.3. Output Modes

Output plugin callbacks can pass data to the consumer in nearly arbitrary formats. For some use cases, like viewing the changes via SQL, returning data in a data type that can contain arbitrary data (e.g., `bytea`) is cumbersome. If the output plugin only outputs textual data in the server's encoding, it can declare that by setting OutputPluginOptions.output_type to OUTPUT_PLUGIN_TEXTUAL_OUTPUT instead of OUTPUT_PLUGIN_BINARY_OUTPUT in the startup callback. In that case, all the data has to be in the server's encoding so that a text datum can contain it. This is checked in assertion-enabled builds.

49.6.4. Output Plugin Callbacks

An output plugin gets notified about changes that are happening via various callbacks it needs to provide.

Concurrent transactions are decoded in commit order, and only changes belonging to a specific transaction are decoded between the begin and commit callbacks. Transactions that were rolled back explicitly or implicitly never get decoded. Successful savepoints are folded into the transaction containing them in the order they were executed within that transaction.

Note

Only transactions that have already safely been flushed to disk will be decoded. That can lead to a COMMIT not immediately being decoded in a directly following pg_logical_slot_get_changes() when synchronous_commit is set to off.

49.6.4.1. Startup Callback

The optional startup_cb callback is called whenever a replication slot is created or asked to stream changes, independent of the number of changes that are ready to be put out.

```
typedef void (*LogicalDecodeStartupCB) (struct LogicalDecodingContext
 *ctx,
                                        OutputPluginOptions *options,
                                        bool is_init);
```

The is_init parameter will be true when the replication slot is being created and false otherwise. *options* points to a struct of options that output plugins can set:

```
typedef struct OutputPluginOptions
{
    OutputPluginOutputType output_type;
    bool        receive_rewrites;
} OutputPluginOptions;
```

output_type has to either be set to OUTPUT_PLUGIN_TEXTUAL_OUTPUT or OUTPUT_PLUGIN_BINARY_OUTPUT. See also Section 49.6.3. If receive_rewrites is true, the output plugin will also be called for changes made by heap rewrites during certain DDL operations. These are of interest to plugins that handle DDL replication, but they require special handling.

The startup callback should validate the options present in ctx->output_plugin_options. If the output plugin needs to have a state, it can use ctx->output_plugin_private to store it.

49.6.4.2. Shutdown Callback

The optional shutdown_cb callback is called whenever a formerly active replication slot is not used anymore and can be used to deallocate resources private to the output plugin. The slot isn't necessarily being dropped, streaming is just being stopped.

```
typedef void (*LogicalDecodeShutdownCB) (struct LogicalDecodingContext
 *ctx);
```

49.6.4.3. Transaction Begin Callback

The required `begin_cb` callback is called whenever a start of a committed transaction has been decoded. Aborted transactions and their contents never get decoded.

```
typedef void (*LogicalDecodeBeginCB) (struct LogicalDecodingContext
 *ctx,
                                      ReorderBufferTXN *txn);
```

The *txn* parameter contains meta information about the transaction, like the time stamp at which it has been committed and its XID.

49.6.4.4. Transaction End Callback

The required `commit_cb` callback is called whenever a transaction commit has been decoded. The `change_cb` callbacks for all modified rows will have been called before this, if there have been any modified rows.

```
typedef void (*LogicalDecodeCommitCB) (struct LogicalDecodingContext
 *ctx,
                                       ReorderBufferTXN *txn,
                                       XLogRecPtr commit_lsn);
```

49.6.4.5. Change Callback

The required `change_cb` callback is called for every individual row modification inside a transaction, may it be an `INSERT`, `UPDATE`, or `DELETE`. Even if the original command modified several rows at once the callback will be called individually for each row.

```
typedef void (*LogicalDecodeChangeCB) (struct LogicalDecodingContext
 *ctx,
                                       ReorderBufferTXN *txn,
                                       Relation relation,
                                       ReorderBufferChange *change);
```

The *ctx* and *txn* parameters have the same contents as for the `begin_cb` and `commit_cb` callbacks, but additionally the relation descriptor *relation* points to the relation the row belongs to and a struct *change* describing the row modification are passed in.

Note

Only changes in user defined tables that are not unlogged (see `UNLOGGED`) and not temporary (see `TEMPORARY` or `TEMP`) can be extracted using logical decoding.

49.6.4.6. Truncate Callback

The `truncate_cb` callback is called for a `TRUNCATE` command.

```
typedef void (*LogicalDecodeTruncateCB) (struct LogicalDecodingContext
    *ctx,
                                         ReorderBufferTXN *txn,
                                         int nrelations,
                                         Relation relations[],
                                         ReorderBufferChange *change);
```

The parameters are analogous to the change_cb callback. However, because TRUNCATE actions on tables connected by foreign keys need to be executed together, this callback receives an array of relations instead of just a single one. See the description of the TRUNCATE statement for details.

49.6.4.7. Origin Filter Callback

The optional filter_by_origin_cb callback is called to determine whether data that has been re-played from *origin_id* is of interest to the output plugin.

```
typedef bool (*LogicalDecodeFilterByOriginCB) (struct
    LogicalDecodingContext *ctx,
                                         RepOriginId origin_id);
```

The *ctx* parameter has the same contents as for the other callbacks. No information but the origin is available. To signal that changes originating on the passed in node are irrelevant, return true, causing them to be filtered away; false otherwise. The other callbacks will not be called for transactions and changes that have been filtered away.

This is useful when implementing cascading or multidirectional replication solutions. Filtering by the origin allows to prevent replicating the same changes back and forth in such setups. While transactions and changes also carry information about the origin, filtering via this callback is noticeably more efficient.

49.6.4.8. Generic Message Callback

The optional message_cb callback is called whenever a logical decoding message has been decoded.

```
typedef void (*LogicalDecodeMessageCB) (struct LogicalDecodingContext
    *ctx,
                                         ReorderBufferTXN *txn,
                                         XLogRecPtr message_lsn,
                                         bool transactional,
                                         const char *prefix,
                                         Size message_size,
                                         const char *message);
```

The *txn* parameter contains meta information about the transaction, like the time stamp at which it has been committed and its XID. Note however that it can be NULL when the message is non-transactional and the XID was not assigned yet in the transaction which logged the message. The *lsn* has WAL location of the message. The *transactional* says if the message was sent as transactional or not. The *prefix* is arbitrary null-terminated prefix which can be used for identifying interesting messages for the current plugin. And finally the *message* parameter holds the actual message of *message_size* size.

Extra care should be taken to ensure that the prefix the output plugin considers interesting is unique. Using name of the extension or the output plugin itself is often a good choice.

49.6.5. Functions for Producing Output

To actually produce output, output plugins can write data to the `StringInfo` output buffer in `ctx->out` when inside the `begin_cb`, `commit_cb`, or `change_cb` callbacks. Before writing to the output buffer, `OutputPluginPrepareWrite(ctx, last_write)` has to be called, and after finishing writing to the buffer, `OutputPluginWrite(ctx, last_write)` has to be called to perform the write. The *last_write* indicates whether a particular write was the callback's last write.

The following example shows how to output data to the consumer of an output plugin:

```
OutputPluginPrepareWrite(ctx, true);
appendStringInfo(ctx->out, "BEGIN %u", txn->xid);
OutputPluginWrite(ctx, true);
```

49.7. Logical Decoding Output Writers

It is possible to add more output methods for logical decoding. For details, see `src/backend/replication/logical/logicalfuncs.c`. Essentially, three functions need to be provided: one to read WAL, one to prepare writing output, and one to write the output (see Section 49.6.5).

49.8. Synchronous Replication Support for Logical Decoding

Logical decoding can be used to build synchronous replication solutions with the same user interface as synchronous replication for streaming replication. To do this, the streaming replication interface (see Section 49.3) must be used to stream out data. Clients have to send `Standby status update (F)` (see Section 53.4) messages, just like streaming replication clients do.

Note

A synchronous replica receiving changes via logical decoding will work in the scope of a single database. Since, in contrast to that, *synchronous_standby_names* currently is server wide, this means this technique will not work properly if more than one database is actively used.

Chapter 50. Replication Progress Tracking

Replication origins are intended to make it easier to implement logical replication solutions on top of logical decoding. They provide a solution to two common problems:

- How to safely keep track of replication progress

- How to change replication behavior based on the origin of a row; for example, to prevent loops in bidirectional replication setups

Replication origins have just two properties, a name and an OID. The name, which is what should be used to refer to the origin across systems, is free-form `text`. It should be used in a way that makes conflicts between replication origins created by different replication solutions unlikely; e.g. by prefixing the replication solution's name to it. The OID is used only to avoid having to store the long version in situations where space efficiency is important. It should never be shared across systems.

Replication origins can be created using the function `pg_replication_origin_create()`; dropped using `pg_replication_origin_drop()`; and seen in the `pg_replication_origin` system catalog.

One nontrivial part of building a replication solution is to keep track of replay progress in a safe manner. When the applying process, or the whole cluster, dies, it needs to be possible to find out up to where data has successfully been replicated. Naive solutions to this, such as updating a row in a table for every replayed transaction, have problems like run-time overhead and database bloat.

Using the replication origin infrastructure a session can be marked as replaying from a remote node (using the `pg_replication_origin_session_setup()` function). Additionally the LSN and commit time stamp of every source transaction can be configured on a per transaction basis using `pg_replication_origin_xact_setup()`. If that's done replication progress will persist in a crash safe manner. Replay progress for all replication origins can be seen in the `pg_replication_origin_status` view. An individual origin's progress, e.g. when resuming replication, can be acquired using `pg_replication_origin_progress()` for any origin or `pg_replication_origin_session_progress()` for the origin configured in the current session.

In replication topologies more complex than replication from exactly one system to one other system, another problem can be that it is hard to avoid replicating replayed rows again. That can lead both to cycles in the replication and inefficiencies. Replication origins provide an optional mechanism to recognize and prevent that. When configured using the functions referenced in the previous paragraph, every change and transaction passed to output plugin callbacks (see Section 49.6) generated by the session is tagged with the replication origin of the generating session. This allows treating them differently in the output plugin, e.g. ignoring all but locally-originating rows. Additionally the `filter_by_origin_cb` callback can be used to filter the logical decoding change stream based on the source. While less flexible, filtering via that callback is considerably more efficient than doing it in the output plugin.

Part VI. Reference

The entries in this Reference are meant to provide in reasonable length an authoritative, complete, and formal summary about their respective subjects. More information about the use of PostgreSQL, in narrative, tutorial, or example form, can be found in other parts of this book. See the cross-references listed on each reference page.

The reference entries are also available as traditional "man" pages.

Table of Contents

SQL Commands

This part contains reference information for the SQL commands supported by PostgreSQL. By "SQL" the language in general is meant; information about the standards conformance and compatibility of each command can be found on the respective reference page.

Table of Contents

ABORT

ABORT — abort the current transaction

Synopsis

```
ABORT [ WORK | TRANSACTION ]
```

Description

ABORT rolls back the current transaction and causes all the updates made by the transaction to be discarded. This command is identical in behavior to the standard SQL command ROLLBACK, and is present only for historical reasons.

Parameters

WORK
TRANSACTION

Optional key words. They have no effect.

Notes

Use COMMIT to successfully terminate a transaction.

Issuing ABORT outside of a transaction block emits a warning and otherwise has no effect.

Examples

To abort all changes:

```
ABORT;
```

Compatibility

This command is a PostgreSQL extension present for historical reasons. ROLLBACK is the equivalent standard SQL command.

See Also

BEGIN, COMMIT, ROLLBACK

ALTER AGGREGATE

ALTER AGGREGATE — change the definition of an aggregate function

Synopsis

```
ALTER AGGREGATE name ( aggregate_signature ) RENAME TO new_name
ALTER AGGREGATE name ( aggregate_signature )
                OWNER TO { new_owner | CURRENT_USER | SESSION_USER }
ALTER AGGREGATE name ( aggregate_signature ) SET SCHEMA new_schema

where aggregate_signature is:

* |
[ argmode ] [ argname ] argtype [ , ... ] |
[ [ argmode ] [ argname ] argtype [ , ... ] ] ORDER BY [ argmode ]
 [ argname ] argtype [ , ... ]
```

Description

ALTER AGGREGATE changes the definition of an aggregate function.

You must own the aggregate function to use ALTER AGGREGATE. To change the schema of an aggregate function, you must also have CREATE privilege on the new schema. To alter the owner, you must also be a direct or indirect member of the new owning role, and that role must have CREATE privilege on the aggregate function's schema. (These restrictions enforce that altering the owner doesn't do anything you couldn't do by dropping and recreating the aggregate function. However, a superuser can alter ownership of any aggregate function anyway.)

Parameters

name

The name (optionally schema-qualified) of an existing aggregate function.

argmode

The mode of an argument: IN or VARIADIC. If omitted, the default is IN.

argname

The name of an argument. Note that ALTER AGGREGATE does not actually pay any attention to argument names, since only the argument data types are needed to determine the aggregate function's identity.

argtype

An input data type on which the aggregate function operates. To reference a zero-argument aggregate function, write * in place of the list of argument specifications. To reference an ordered-set aggregate function, write ORDER BY between the direct and aggregated argument specifications.

new_name

> The new name of the aggregate function.

new_owner

> The new owner of the aggregate function.

new_schema

> The new schema for the aggregate function.

Notes

The recommended syntax for referencing an ordered-set aggregate is to write ORDER BY between the direct and aggregated argument specifications, in the same style as in CREATE AGGREGATE. However, it will also work to omit ORDER BY and just run the direct and aggregated argument specifications into a single list. In this abbreviated form, if VARIADIC "any" was used in both the direct and aggregated argument lists, write VARIADIC "any" only once.

Examples

To rename the aggregate function myavg for type integer to my_average:

```
ALTER AGGREGATE myavg(integer) RENAME TO my_average;
```

To change the owner of the aggregate function myavg for type integer to joe:

```
ALTER AGGREGATE myavg(integer) OWNER TO joe;
```

To move the ordered-set aggregate mypercentile with direct argument of type float8 and aggregated argument of type integer into schema myschema:

```
ALTER AGGREGATE mypercentile(float8 ORDER BY integer) SET SCHEMA
 myschema;
```

This will work too:

```
ALTER AGGREGATE mypercentile(float8, integer) SET SCHEMA myschema;
```

Compatibility

There is no ALTER AGGREGATE statement in the SQL standard.

See Also
CREATE AGGREGATE, DROP AGGREGATE

ALTER COLLATION

ALTER COLLATION — change the definition of a collation

Synopsis

```
ALTER COLLATION name REFRESH VERSION

ALTER COLLATION name RENAME TO new_name
ALTER COLLATION name OWNER TO { new_owner | CURRENT_USER |
  SESSION_USER }
ALTER COLLATION name SET SCHEMA new_schema
```

Description

ALTER COLLATION changes the definition of a collation.

You must own the collation to use ALTER COLLATION. To alter the owner, you must also be a direct or indirect member of the new owning role, and that role must have CREATE privilege on the collation's schema. (These restrictions enforce that altering the owner doesn't do anything you couldn't do by dropping and recreating the collation. However, a superuser can alter ownership of any collation anyway.)

Parameters

name

> The name (optionally schema-qualified) of an existing collation.

new_name

> The new name of the collation.

new_owner

> The new owner of the collation.

new_schema

> The new schema for the collation.

REFRESH VERSION

> Update the collation's version. See Notes below.

Notes

When using collations provided by the ICU library, the ICU-specific version of the collator is recorded in the system catalog when the collation object is created. When the collation is used, the current version is checked against the recorded version, and a warning is issued when there is a mismatch, for example:

```
WARNING:  collation "xx-x-icu" has version mismatch
DETAIL:  The collation in the database was created using version
 1.2.3.4, but the operating system provides version 2.3.4.5.
HINT:  Rebuild all objects affected by this collation and run ALTER
 COLLATION pg_catalog."xx-x-icu" REFRESH VERSION, or build PostgreSQL
 with the right library version.
```

A change in collation definitions can lead to corrupt indexes and other problems because the database system relies on stored objects having a certain sort order. Generally, this should be avoided, but it can happen in legitimate circumstances, such as when using pg_upgrade to upgrade to server binaries linked with a newer version of ICU. When this happens, all objects depending on the collation should be rebuilt, for example, using REINDEX. When that is done, the collation version can be refreshed using the command ALTER COLLATION ... REFRESH VERSION. This will update the system catalog to record the current collator version and will make the warning go away. Note that this does not actually check whether all affected objects have been rebuilt correctly.

The following query can be used to identify all collations in the current database that need to be refreshed and the objects that depend on them:

```
SELECT pg_describe_object(refclassid, refobjid, refobjsubid) AS
  "Collation",
       pg_describe_object(classid, objid, objsubid) AS "Object"
  FROM pg_depend d JOIN pg_collation c
      ON refclassid = 'pg_collation'::regclass AND refobjid = c.oid
  WHERE c.collversion <> pg_collation_actual_version(c.oid)
  ORDER BY 1, 2;
```

Examples

To rename the collation de_DE to german:

```
ALTER COLLATION "de_DE" RENAME TO german;
```

To change the owner of the collation en_US to joe:

```
ALTER COLLATION "en_US" OWNER TO joe;
```

Compatibility

There is no ALTER COLLATION statement in the SQL standard.

See Also

CREATE COLLATION, DROP COLLATION

ALTER CONVERSION

ALTER CONVERSION — change the definition of a conversion

Synopsis

```
ALTER CONVERSION name RENAME TO new_name
ALTER CONVERSION name OWNER TO { new_owner | CURRENT_USER |
 SESSION_USER }
ALTER CONVERSION name SET SCHEMA new_schema
```

Description

`ALTER CONVERSION` changes the definition of a conversion.

You must own the conversion to use `ALTER CONVERSION`. To alter the owner, you must also be a direct or indirect member of the new owning role, and that role must have `CREATE` privilege on the conversion's schema. (These restrictions enforce that altering the owner doesn't do anything you couldn't do by dropping and recreating the conversion. However, a superuser can alter ownership of any conversion anyway.)

Parameters

name

>   The name (optionally schema-qualified) of an existing conversion.

new_name

>   The new name of the conversion.

new_owner

>   The new owner of the conversion.

new_schema

>   The new schema for the conversion.

Examples

To rename the conversion `iso_8859_1_to_utf8` to `latin1_to_unicode`:

```
ALTER CONVERSION iso_8859_1_to_utf8 RENAME TO latin1_to_unicode;
```

To change the owner of the conversion `iso_8859_1_to_utf8` to `joe`:

```
ALTER CONVERSION iso_8859_1_to_utf8 OWNER TO joe;
```

Compatibility

There is no ALTER CONVERSION statement in the SQL standard.

See Also

CREATE CONVERSION, DROP CONVERSION

ALTER DATABASE

ALTER DATABASE — change a database

Synopsis

```
ALTER DATABASE name [ [ WITH ] option [ ... ] ]

where option can be:

    ALLOW_CONNECTIONS allowconn
    CONNECTION LIMIT connlimit
    IS_TEMPLATE istemplate

ALTER DATABASE name RENAME TO new_name

ALTER DATABASE name OWNER TO { new_owner | CURRENT_USER |
 SESSION_USER }

ALTER DATABASE name SET TABLESPACE new_tablespace

ALTER DATABASE name SET configuration_parameter { TO | = } { value |
 DEFAULT }
ALTER DATABASE name SET configuration_parameter FROM CURRENT
ALTER DATABASE name RESET configuration_parameter
ALTER DATABASE name RESET ALL
```

Description

ALTER DATABASE changes the attributes of a database.

The first form changes certain per-database settings. (See below for details.) Only the database owner or a superuser can change these settings.

The second form changes the name of the database. Only the database owner or a superuser can rename a database; non-superuser owners must also have the CREATEDB privilege. The current database cannot be renamed. (Connect to a different database if you need to do that.)

The third form changes the owner of the database. To alter the owner, you must own the database and also be a direct or indirect member of the new owning role, and you must have the CREATEDB privilege. (Note that superusers have all these privileges automatically.)

The fourth form changes the default tablespace of the database. Only the database owner or a superuser can do this; you must also have create privilege for the new tablespace. This command physically moves any tables or indexes in the database's old default tablespace to the new tablespace. The new default tablespace must be empty for this database, and no one can be connected to the database. Tables and indexes in non-default tablespaces are unaffected.

The remaining forms change the session default for a run-time configuration variable for a PostgreSQL database. Whenever a new session is subsequently started in that database, the specified value becomes the session default value. The database-specific default overrides whatever setting is present in postgresql.conf or has been received from the `postgres` command line. Only the database owner or a superuser can change the session defaults for a database. Certain variables cannot be set this way, or can only be set by a superuser.

Parameters

name

The name of the database whose attributes are to be altered.

allowconn

If false then no one can connect to this database.

connlimit

How many concurrent connections can be made to this database. -1 means no limit.

istemplate

If true, then this database can be cloned by any user with `CREATEDB` privileges; if false, then only superusers or the owner of the database can clone it.

new_name

The new name of the database.

new_owner

The new owner of the database.

new_tablespace

The new default tablespace of the database.

This form of the command cannot be executed inside a transaction block.

configuration_parameter
value

Set this database's session default for the specified configuration parameter to the given value. If *value* is DEFAULT or, equivalently, RESET is used, the database-specific setting is removed, so the system-wide default setting will be inherited in new sessions. Use `RESET ALL` to clear all database-specific settings. `SET FROM CURRENT` saves the session's current value of the parameter as the database-specific value.

See SET and Chapter 19 for more information about allowed parameter names and values.

Notes

It is also possible to tie a session default to a specific role rather than to a database; see ALTER ROLE. Role-specific settings override database-specific ones if there is a conflict.

Examples

To disable index scans by default in the database `test`:

```
ALTER DATABASE test SET enable_indexscan TO off;
```

Compatibility

The ALTER DATABASE statement is a PostgreSQL extension.

See Also

CREATE DATABASE, DROP DATABASE, SET, CREATE TABLESPACE

ALTER DEFAULT PRIVILEGES

ALTER DEFAULT PRIVILEGES — define default access privileges

Synopsis

```
ALTER DEFAULT PRIVILEGES
    [ FOR { ROLE | USER } target_role [, ...] ]
    [ IN SCHEMA schema_name [, ...] ]
    abbreviated_grant_or_revoke

where abbreviated_grant_or_revoke is one of:

GRANT { { SELECT | INSERT | UPDATE | DELETE | TRUNCATE | REFERENCES |
 TRIGGER }
    [, ...] | ALL [ PRIVILEGES ] }
    ON TABLES
    TO { [ GROUP ] role_name | PUBLIC } [, ...] [ WITH GRANT OPTION ]

GRANT { { USAGE | SELECT | UPDATE }
    [, ...] | ALL [ PRIVILEGES ] }
    ON SEQUENCES
    TO { [ GROUP ] role_name | PUBLIC } [, ...] [ WITH GRANT OPTION ]

GRANT { EXECUTE | ALL [ PRIVILEGES ] }
    ON { FUNCTIONS | ROUTINES }
    TO { [ GROUP ] role_name | PUBLIC } [, ...] [ WITH GRANT OPTION ]

GRANT { USAGE | ALL [ PRIVILEGES ] }
    ON TYPES
    TO { [ GROUP ] role_name | PUBLIC } [, ...] [ WITH GRANT OPTION ]

GRANT { USAGE | CREATE | ALL [ PRIVILEGES ] }
    ON SCHEMAS
    TO { [ GROUP ] role_name | PUBLIC } [, ...] [ WITH GRANT OPTION ]

REVOKE [ GRANT OPTION FOR ]
    { { SELECT | INSERT | UPDATE | DELETE | TRUNCATE | REFERENCES |
 TRIGGER }
    [, ...] | ALL [ PRIVILEGES ] }
    ON TABLES
    FROM { [ GROUP ] role_name | PUBLIC } [, ...]
    [ CASCADE | RESTRICT ]

REVOKE [ GRANT OPTION FOR ]
    { { USAGE | SELECT | UPDATE }
    [, ...] | ALL [ PRIVILEGES ] }
    ON SEQUENCES
    FROM { [ GROUP ] role_name | PUBLIC } [, ...]
    [ CASCADE | RESTRICT ]
```

```
REVOKE [ GRANT OPTION FOR ]
    { EXECUTE | ALL [ PRIVILEGES ] }
    ON { FUNCTIONS | ROUTINES }
    FROM { [ GROUP ] role_name | PUBLIC } [, ...]
    [ CASCADE | RESTRICT ]

REVOKE [ GRANT OPTION FOR ]
    { USAGE | ALL [ PRIVILEGES ] }
    ON TYPES
    FROM { [ GROUP ] role_name | PUBLIC } [, ...]
    [ CASCADE | RESTRICT ]

REVOKE [ GRANT OPTION FOR ]
    { USAGE | CREATE | ALL [ PRIVILEGES ] }
    ON SCHEMAS
    FROM { [ GROUP ] role_name | PUBLIC } [, ...]
    [ CASCADE | RESTRICT ]
```

Description

ALTER DEFAULT PRIVILEGES allows you to set the privileges that will be applied to objects created in the future. (It does not affect privileges assigned to already-existing objects.) Currently, only the privileges for schemas, tables (including views and foreign tables), sequences, functions, and types (including domains) can be altered. For this command, functions include aggregates and procedures. The words FUNCTIONS and ROUTINES are equivalent in this command. (ROUTINES is preferred going forward as the standard term for functions and procedures taken together. In earlier PostgreSQL releases, only the word FUNCTIONS was allowed. It is not possible to set default privileges for functions and procedures separately.)

You can change default privileges only for objects that will be created by yourself or by roles that you are a member of. The privileges can be set globally (i.e., for all objects created in the current database), or just for objects created in specified schemas. Default privileges that are specified per-schema are added to whatever the global default privileges are for the particular object type.

As explained under GRANT, the default privileges for any object type normally grant all grantable permissions to the object owner, and may grant some privileges to PUBLIC as well. However, this behavior can be changed by altering the global default privileges with ALTER DEFAULT PRIVILEGES.

Parameters

target_role

> The name of an existing role of which the current role is a member. If FOR ROLE is omitted, the current role is assumed.

schema_name

> The name of an existing schema. If specified, the default privileges are altered for objects later created in that schema. If IN SCHEMA is omitted, the global default privileges are altered. IN SCHEMA is not allowed when using ON SCHEMAS as schemas can't be nested.

role_name

> The name of an existing role to grant or revoke privileges for. This parameter, and all the other parameters in *abbreviated_grant_or_revoke*, act as described under GRANT or REVOKE, except that one is setting permissions for a whole class of objects rather than specific named objects.

Notes

Use psql's \ddp command to obtain information about existing assignments of default privileges. The meaning of the privilege values is the same as explained for \dp under GRANT.

If you wish to drop a role for which the default privileges have been altered, it is necessary to reverse the changes in its default privileges or use DROP OWNED BY to get rid of the default privileges entry for the role.

Examples

Grant SELECT privilege to everyone for all tables (and views) you subsequently create in schema myschema, and allow role webuser to INSERT into them too:

```
ALTER DEFAULT PRIVILEGES IN SCHEMA myschema GRANT SELECT ON TABLES TO
 PUBLIC;
ALTER DEFAULT PRIVILEGES IN SCHEMA myschema GRANT INSERT ON TABLES TO
 webuser;
```

Undo the above, so that subsequently-created tables won't have any more permissions than normal:

```
ALTER DEFAULT PRIVILEGES IN SCHEMA myschema REVOKE SELECT ON TABLES
 FROM PUBLIC;
ALTER DEFAULT PRIVILEGES IN SCHEMA myschema REVOKE INSERT ON TABLES
 FROM webuser;
```

Remove the public EXECUTE permission that is normally granted on functions, for all functions subsequently created by role admin:

```
ALTER DEFAULT PRIVILEGES FOR ROLE admin REVOKE EXECUTE ON FUNCTIONS
 FROM PUBLIC;
```

Compatibility

There is no ALTER DEFAULT PRIVILEGES statement in the SQL standard.

See Also

GRANT, REVOKE

ALTER DOMAIN

ALTER DOMAIN — change the definition of a domain

Synopsis

```
ALTER DOMAIN name
    { SET DEFAULT expression | DROP DEFAULT }
ALTER DOMAIN name
    { SET | DROP } NOT NULL
ALTER DOMAIN name
    ADD domain_constraint [ NOT VALID ]
ALTER DOMAIN name
    DROP CONSTRAINT [ IF EXISTS ] constraint_name [ RESTRICT |
 CASCADE ]
ALTER DOMAIN name
     RENAME CONSTRAINT constraint_name TO new_constraint_name
ALTER DOMAIN name
    VALIDATE CONSTRAINT constraint_name
ALTER DOMAIN name
    OWNER TO { new_owner | CURRENT_USER | SESSION_USER }
ALTER DOMAIN name
    RENAME TO new_name
ALTER DOMAIN name
    SET SCHEMA new_schema
```

Description

ALTER DOMAIN changes the definition of an existing domain. There are several sub-forms:

SET/DROP DEFAULT

These forms set or remove the default value for a domain. Note that defaults only apply to subsequent INSERT commands; they do not affect rows already in a table using the domain.

SET/DROP NOT NULL

These forms change whether a domain is marked to allow NULL values or to reject NULL values. You can only SET NOT NULL when the columns using the domain contain no null values.

ADD domain_constraint [NOT VALID]

This form adds a new constraint to a domain using the same syntax as CREATE DOMAIN. When a new constraint is added to a domain, all columns using that domain will be checked against the newly added constraint. These checks can be suppressed by adding the new constraint using the NOT VALID option; the constraint can later be made valid using ALTER DOMAIN ... VALIDATE CONSTRAINT. Newly inserted or updated rows are always checked against all constraints, even those marked NOT VALID. NOT VALID is only accepted for CHECK constraints.

DROP CONSTRAINT [IF EXISTS]

This form drops constraints on a domain. If IF EXISTS is specified and the constraint does not exist, no error is thrown. In this case a notice is issued instead.

RENAME CONSTRAINT

This form changes the name of a constraint on a domain.

VALIDATE CONSTRAINT

This form validates a constraint previously added as NOT VALID, that is, verify that all data in columns using the domain satisfy the specified constraint.

OWNER

This form changes the owner of the domain to the specified user.

RENAME

This form changes the name of the domain.

SET SCHEMA

This form changes the schema of the domain. Any constraints associated with the domain are moved into the new schema as well.

You must own the domain to use ALTER DOMAIN. To change the schema of a domain, you must also have CREATE privilege on the new schema. To alter the owner, you must also be a direct or indirect member of the new owning role, and that role must have CREATE privilege on the domain's schema. (These restrictions enforce that altering the owner doesn't do anything you couldn't do by dropping and recreating the domain. However, a superuser can alter ownership of any domain anyway.)

Parameters

name

The name (possibly schema-qualified) of an existing domain to alter.

domain_constraint

New domain constraint for the domain.

constraint_name

Name of an existing constraint to drop or rename.

NOT VALID

Do not verify existing column data for constraint validity.

CASCADE

Automatically drop objects that depend on the constraint, and in turn all objects that depend on those objects (see Section 5.13).

RESTRICT

Refuse to drop the constraint if there are any dependent objects. This is the default behavior.

new_name

The new name for the domain.

new_constraint_name

> The new name for the constraint.

new_owner

> The user name of the new owner of the domain.

new_schema

> The new schema for the domain.

Notes

Currently, `ALTER DOMAIN ADD CONSTRAINT`, `ALTER DOMAIN VALIDATE CONSTRAINT`, and `ALTER DOMAIN SET NOT NULL` will fail if the named domain or any derived domain is used within a container-type column (a composite, array, or range column) in any table in the database. They should eventually be improved to be able to verify the new constraint for such nested values.

Examples

To add a `NOT NULL` constraint to a domain:

```
ALTER DOMAIN zipcode SET NOT NULL;
```

To remove a `NOT NULL` constraint from a domain:

```
ALTER DOMAIN zipcode DROP NOT NULL;
```

To add a check constraint to a domain:

```
ALTER DOMAIN zipcode ADD CONSTRAINT zipchk CHECK (char_length(VALUE) =
 5);
```

To remove a check constraint from a domain:

```
ALTER DOMAIN zipcode DROP CONSTRAINT zipchk;
```

To rename a check constraint on a domain:

```
ALTER DOMAIN zipcode RENAME CONSTRAINT zipchk TO zip_check;
```

To move the domain into a different schema:

```
ALTER DOMAIN zipcode SET SCHEMA customers;
```

Compatibility

`ALTER DOMAIN` conforms to the SQL standard, except for the `OWNER`, `RENAME`, `SET SCHEMA`, and `VALIDATE CONSTRAINT` variants, which are PostgreSQL extensions. The `NOT VALID` clause of the `ADD CONSTRAINT` variant is also a PostgreSQL extension.

See Also

CREATE DOMAIN, DROP DOMAIN

ALTER EVENT TRIGGER

ALTER EVENT TRIGGER — change the definition of an event trigger

Synopsis

```
ALTER EVENT TRIGGER name DISABLE
ALTER EVENT TRIGGER name ENABLE [ REPLICA | ALWAYS ]
ALTER EVENT TRIGGER name OWNER TO { new_owner | CURRENT_USER |
 SESSION_USER }
ALTER EVENT TRIGGER name RENAME TO new_name
```

Description

ALTER EVENT TRIGGER changes properties of an existing event trigger.

You must be superuser to alter an event trigger.

Parameters

name

The name of an existing trigger to alter.

new_owner

The user name of the new owner of the event trigger.

new_name

The new name of the event trigger.

DISABLE/ENABLE [REPLICA | ALWAYS] TRIGGER

These forms configure the firing of event triggers. A disabled trigger is still known to the system, but is not executed when its triggering event occurs. See also session_replication_role.

Compatibility

There is no ALTER EVENT TRIGGER statement in the SQL standard.

See Also

CREATE EVENT TRIGGER, DROP EVENT TRIGGER

ALTER EXTENSION

ALTER EXTENSION — change the definition of an extension

Synopsis

```
ALTER EXTENSION name UPDATE [ TO new_version ]
ALTER EXTENSION name SET SCHEMA new_schema
ALTER EXTENSION name ADD member_object
ALTER EXTENSION name DROP member_object

where member_object is:

  ACCESS METHOD object_name |
  AGGREGATE aggregate_name ( aggregate_signature ) |
  CAST (source_type AS target_type) |
  COLLATION object_name |
  CONVERSION object_name |
  DOMAIN object_name |
  EVENT TRIGGER object_name |
  FOREIGN DATA WRAPPER object_name |
  FOREIGN TABLE object_name |
  FUNCTION function_name [ ( [ [ argmode ] [ argname ] argtype
[, ...] ] ) ] |
  MATERIALIZED VIEW object_name |
  OPERATOR operator_name (left_type, right_type) |
  OPERATOR CLASS object_name USING index_method |
  OPERATOR FAMILY object_name USING index_method |
  [ PROCEDURAL ] LANGUAGE object_name |
  PROCEDURE procedure_name [ ( [ [ argmode ] [ argname ] argtype
[, ...] ] ) ] |
  ROUTINE routine_name [ ( [ [ argmode ] [ argname ] argtype
[, ...] ] ) ] |
  SCHEMA object_name |
  SEQUENCE object_name |
  SERVER object_name |
  TABLE object_name |
  TEXT SEARCH CONFIGURATION object_name |
  TEXT SEARCH DICTIONARY object_name |
  TEXT SEARCH PARSER object_name |
  TEXT SEARCH TEMPLATE object_name |
  TRANSFORM FOR type_name LANGUAGE lang_name |
  TYPE object_name |
  VIEW object_name

and aggregate_signature is:

* |
[ argmode ] [ argname ] argtype [ , ... ] |
```

```
[ [ argmode ] [ argname ] argtype [ , ... ] ] ORDER BY [ argmode ]
[ argname ] argtype [ , ... ]
```

Description

ALTER EXTENSION changes the definition of an installed extension. There are several subforms:

UPDATE

> This form updates the extension to a newer version. The extension must supply a suitable update script (or series of scripts) that can modify the currently-installed version into the requested version.

SET SCHEMA

> This form moves the extension's objects into another schema. The extension has to be *relocatable* for this command to succeed.

ADD *member_object*

> This form adds an existing object to the extension. This is mainly useful in extension update scripts. The object will subsequently be treated as a member of the extension; notably, it can only be dropped by dropping the extension.

DROP *member_object*

> This form removes a member object from the extension. This is mainly useful in extension update scripts. The object is not dropped, only disassociated from the extension.

See Section 38.16 for more information about these operations.

You must own the extension to use ALTER EXTENSION. The ADD/DROP forms require ownership of the added/dropped object as well.

Parameters

name

> The name of an installed extension.

new_version

> The desired new version of the extension. This can be written as either an identifier or a string literal. If not specified, ALTER EXTENSION UPDATE attempts to update to whatever is shown as the default version in the extension's control file.

new_schema

> The new schema for the extension.

object_name
aggregate_name
function_name
operator_name
procedure_name
routine_name

> The name of an object to be added to or removed from the extension. Names of tables, aggregates, domains, foreign tables, functions, operators, operator classes, operator families, procedures, routines, sequences, text search objects, types, and views can be schema-qualified.

source_type

> The name of the source data type of the cast.

target_type

> The name of the target data type of the cast.

argmode

> The mode of a function, procedure, or aggregate argument: IN, OUT, INOUT, or VARIADIC. If omitted, the default is IN. Note that ALTER EXTENSION does not actually pay any attention to OUT arguments, since only the input arguments are needed to determine the function's identity. So it is sufficient to list the IN, INOUT, and VARIADIC arguments.

argname

> The name of a function, procedure, or aggregate argument. Note that ALTER EXTENSION does not actually pay any attention to argument names, since only the argument data types are needed to determine the function's identity.

argtype

> The data type of a function, procedure, or aggregate argument.

left_type
right_type

> The data type(s) of the operator's arguments (optionally schema-qualified). Write NONE for the missing argument of a prefix or postfix operator.

PROCEDURAL

> This is a noise word.

type_name

> The name of the data type of the transform.

lang_name

> The name of the language of the transform.

Examples

To update the `hstore` extension to version 2.0:

```
ALTER EXTENSION hstore UPDATE TO '2.0';
```

To change the schema of the `hstore` extension to `utils`:

```
ALTER EXTENSION hstore SET SCHEMA utils;
```

To add an existing function to the `hstore` extension:

```
ALTER EXTENSION hstore ADD FUNCTION populate_record(anyelement,
 hstore);
```

Compatibility

`ALTER EXTENSION` is a PostgreSQL extension.

See Also

CREATE EXTENSION, DROP EXTENSION

ALTER FOREIGN DATA WRAPPER

ALTER FOREIGN DATA WRAPPER — change the definition of a foreign-data wrapper

Synopsis

```
ALTER FOREIGN DATA WRAPPER name
    [ HANDLER handler_function | NO HANDLER ]
    [ VALIDATOR validator_function | NO VALIDATOR ]
    [ OPTIONS ( [ ADD | SET | DROP ] option ['value'] [, ... ]) ]
ALTER FOREIGN DATA WRAPPER name OWNER TO { new_owner | CURRENT_USER |
 SESSION_USER }
ALTER FOREIGN DATA WRAPPER name RENAME TO new_name
```

Description

ALTER FOREIGN DATA WRAPPER changes the definition of a foreign-data wrapper. The first form of the command changes the support functions or the generic options of the foreign-data wrapper (at least one clause is required). The second form changes the owner of the foreign-data wrapper.

Only superusers can alter foreign-data wrappers. Additionally, only superusers can own foreign-data wrappers.

Parameters

name

The name of an existing foreign-data wrapper.

HANDLER *handler_function*

Specifies a new handler function for the foreign-data wrapper.

NO HANDLER

This is used to specify that the foreign-data wrapper should no longer have a handler function.

Note that foreign tables that use a foreign-data wrapper with no handler cannot be accessed.

VALIDATOR *validator_function*

Specifies a new validator function for the foreign-data wrapper.

Note that it is possible that pre-existing options of the foreign-data wrapper, or of dependent servers, user mappings, or foreign tables, are invalid according to the new validator. PostgreSQL does not check for this. It is up to the user to make sure that these options are correct before using the modified foreign-data wrapper. However, any options specified in this ALTER FOREIGN DATA WRAPPER command will be checked using the new validator.

NO VALIDATOR

This is used to specify that the foreign-data wrapper should no longer have a validator function.

OPTIONS ([ADD | SET | DROP] *option* ['*value*'] [, ...])

Change options for the foreign-data wrapper. ADD, SET, and DROP specify the action to be performed. ADD is assumed if no operation is explicitly specified. Option names must be unique; names and values are also validated using the foreign data wrapper's validator function, if any.

new_owner

The user name of the new owner of the foreign-data wrapper.

new_name

The new name for the foreign-data wrapper.

Examples

Change a foreign-data wrapper dbi, add option foo, drop bar:

```
ALTER FOREIGN DATA WRAPPER dbi OPTIONS (ADD foo '1', DROP 'bar');
```

Change the foreign-data wrapper dbi validator to bob.myvalidator:

```
ALTER FOREIGN DATA WRAPPER dbi VALIDATOR bob.myvalidator;
```

Compatibility

ALTER FOREIGN DATA WRAPPER conforms to ISO/IEC 9075-9 (SQL/MED), except that the HANDLER, VALIDATOR, OWNER TO, and RENAME clauses are extensions.

See Also

CREATE FOREIGN DATA WRAPPER, DROP FOREIGN DATA WRAPPER

ALTER FOREIGN TABLE

ALTER FOREIGN TABLE — change the definition of a foreign table

Synopsis

```
ALTER FOREIGN TABLE [ IF EXISTS ] [ ONLY ] name [ * ]
    action [, ... ]
ALTER FOREIGN TABLE [ IF EXISTS ] [ ONLY ] name [ * ]
    RENAME [ COLUMN ] column_name TO new_column_name
ALTER FOREIGN TABLE [ IF EXISTS ] name
    RENAME TO new_name
ALTER FOREIGN TABLE [ IF EXISTS ] name
    SET SCHEMA new_schema

where action is one of:

    ADD [ COLUMN ] column_name data_type [ COLLATE collation ]
 [ column_constraint [ ... ] ]
    DROP [ COLUMN ] [ IF EXISTS ] column_name [ RESTRICT | CASCADE ]
    ALTER [ COLUMN ] column_name [ SET DATA ] TYPE data_type
 [ COLLATE collation ]
    ALTER [ COLUMN ] column_name SET DEFAULT expression
    ALTER [ COLUMN ] column_name DROP DEFAULT
    ALTER [ COLUMN ] column_name { SET | DROP } NOT NULL
    ALTER [ COLUMN ] column_name SET STATISTICS integer
    ALTER [ COLUMN ] column_name SET ( attribute_option = value
 [, ... ] )
    ALTER [ COLUMN ] column_name RESET ( attribute_option [, ... ] )
    ALTER [ COLUMN ] column_name SET STORAGE { PLAIN | EXTERNAL |
EXTENDED | MAIN }
    ALTER [ COLUMN ] column_name OPTIONS ( [ ADD | SET | DROP ] option
['value'] [, ... ])
    ADD table_constraint [ NOT VALID ]
    VALIDATE CONSTRAINT constraint_name
    DROP CONSTRAINT [ IF EXISTS ]  constraint_name [ RESTRICT |
CASCADE ]
    DISABLE TRIGGER [ trigger_name | ALL | USER ]
    ENABLE TRIGGER [ trigger_name | ALL | USER ]
    ENABLE REPLICA TRIGGER trigger_name
    ENABLE ALWAYS TRIGGER trigger_name
    SET WITH OIDS
    SET WITHOUT OIDS
    INHERIT parent_table
    NO INHERIT parent_table
    OWNER TO { new_owner | CURRENT_USER | SESSION_USER }
    OPTIONS ( [ ADD | SET | DROP ] option ['value'] [, ... ])
```

Description

ALTER FOREIGN TABLE changes the definition of an existing foreign table. There are several subforms:

ADD COLUMN

This form adds a new column to the foreign table, using the same syntax as CREATE FOREIGN TABLE. Unlike the case when adding a column to a regular table, nothing happens to the underlying storage: this action simply declares that some new column is now accessible through the foreign table.

DROP COLUMN [IF EXISTS]

This form drops a column from a foreign table. You will need to say CASCADE if anything outside the table depends on the column; for example, views. If IF EXISTS is specified and the column does not exist, no error is thrown. In this case a notice is issued instead.

SET DATA TYPE

This form changes the type of a column of a foreign table. Again, this has no effect on any underlying storage: this action simply changes the type that PostgreSQL believes the column to have.

SET/DROP DEFAULT

These forms set or remove the default value for a column. Default values only apply in subsequent INSERT or UPDATE commands; they do not cause rows already in the table to change.

SET/DROP NOT NULL

Mark a column as allowing, or not allowing, null values.

SET STATISTICS

This form sets the per-column statistics-gathering target for subsequent ANALYZE operations. See the similar form of ALTER TABLE for more details.

SET (attribute_option = value [, ...])
RESET (attribute_option [, ...])

This form sets or resets per-attribute options. See the similar form of ALTER TABLE for more details.

SET STORAGE

This form sets the storage mode for a column. See the similar form of ALTER TABLE for more details. Note that the storage mode has no effect unless the table's foreign-data wrapper chooses to pay attention to it.

ADD table_constraint [NOT VALID]

This form adds a new constraint to a foreign table, using the same syntax as CREATE FOREIGN TABLE. Currently only CHECK constraints are supported.

Unlike the case when adding a constraint to a regular table, nothing is done to verify the constraint is correct; rather, this action simply declares that some new condition should be assumed to hold for all rows in the foreign table. (See the discussion in CREATE FOREIGN TABLE.) If the constraint is marked NOT VALID, then it isn't assumed to hold, but is only recorded for possible future use.

VALIDATE CONSTRAINT

This form marks as valid a constraint that was previously marked as NOT VALID. No action is taken to verify the constraint, but future queries will assume that it holds.

DROP CONSTRAINT [IF EXISTS]

This form drops the specified constraint on a foreign table. If IF EXISTS is specified and the constraint does not exist, no error is thrown. In this case a notice is issued instead.

DISABLE/ENABLE [REPLICA | ALWAYS] TRIGGER

These forms configure the firing of trigger(s) belonging to the foreign table. See the similar form of ALTER TABLE for more details.

SET WITH OIDS

This form adds an oid system column to the table (see Section 5.4). It does nothing if the table already has OIDs. Unless the table's foreign-data wrapper supports OIDs, this column will simply read as zeroes.

Note that this is not equivalent to ADD COLUMN oid oid; that would add a normal column that happened to be named oid, not a system column.

SET WITHOUT OIDS

This form removes the oid system column from the table. This is exactly equivalent to DROP COLUMN oid RESTRICT, except that it will not complain if there is already no oid column.

INHERIT *parent_table*

This form adds the target foreign table as a new child of the specified parent table. See the similar form of ALTER TABLE for more details.

NO INHERIT *parent_table*

This form removes the target foreign table from the list of children of the specified parent table.

OWNER

This form changes the owner of the foreign table to the specified user.

OPTIONS ([ADD | SET | DROP] *option* ['*value*'] [, ...])

Change options for the foreign table or one of its columns. ADD, SET, and DROP specify the action to be performed. ADD is assumed if no operation is explicitly specified. Duplicate option names are not allowed (although it's OK for a table option and a column option to have the same name). Option names and values are also validated using the foreign data wrapper library.

RENAME

The RENAME forms change the name of a foreign table or the name of an individual column in a foreign table.

SET SCHEMA

This form moves the foreign table into another schema.

All the actions except RENAME and SET SCHEMA can be combined into a list of multiple alterations to apply in parallel. For example, it is possible to add several columns and/or alter the type of several columns in a single command.

If the command is written as ALTER FOREIGN TABLE IF EXISTS ... and the foreign table does not exist, no error is thrown. A notice is issued in this case.

You must own the table to use ALTER FOREIGN TABLE. To change the schema of a foreign table, you must also have CREATE privilege on the new schema. To alter the owner, you must also be a direct or indirect member of the new owning role, and that role must have CREATE privilege on the table's schema. (These restrictions enforce that altering the owner doesn't do anything you couldn't do by dropping and recreating the table. However, a superuser can alter ownership of any table anyway.) To add a column or alter a column type, you must also have USAGE privilege on the data type.

Parameters

name

> The name (possibly schema-qualified) of an existing foreign table to alter. If ONLY is specified before the table name, only that table is altered. If ONLY is not specified, the table and all its descendant tables (if any) are altered. Optionally, * can be specified after the table name to explicitly indicate that descendant tables are included.

column_name

> Name of a new or existing column.

new_column_name

> New name for an existing column.

new_name

> New name for the table.

data_type

> Data type of the new column, or new data type for an existing column.

table_constraint

> New table constraint for the foreign table.

constraint_name

> Name of an existing constraint to drop.

CASCADE

> Automatically drop objects that depend on the dropped column or constraint (for example, views referencing the column), and in turn all objects that depend on those objects (see Section 5.13).

RESTRICT

> Refuse to drop the column or constraint if there are any dependent objects. This is the default behavior.

trigger_name

> Name of a single trigger to disable or enable.

ALL

> Disable or enable all triggers belonging to the foreign table. (This requires superuser privilege if any of the triggers are internally generated triggers. The core system does not add such triggers to foreign tables, but add-on code could do so.)

USER

> Disable or enable all triggers belonging to the foreign table except for internally generated triggers.

parent_table

> A parent table to associate or de-associate with this foreign table.

new_owner

> The user name of the new owner of the table.

new_schema

> The name of the schema to which the table will be moved.

Notes

The key word COLUMN is noise and can be omitted.

Consistency with the foreign server is not checked when a column is added or removed with ADD COLUMN or DROP COLUMN, a NOT NULL or CHECK constraint is added, or a column type is changed with SET DATA TYPE. It is the user's responsibility to ensure that the table definition matches the remote side.

Refer to CREATE FOREIGN TABLE for a further description of valid parameters.

Examples

To mark a column as not-null:

```
ALTER FOREIGN TABLE distributors ALTER COLUMN street SET NOT NULL;
```

To change options of a foreign table:

```
ALTER FOREIGN TABLE myschema.distributors OPTIONS (ADD opt1 'value',
  SET opt2 'value2', DROP opt3 'value3');
```

Compatibility

The forms ADD, DROP, and SET DATA TYPE conform with the SQL standard. The other forms are PostgreSQL extensions of the SQL standard. Also, the ability to specify more than one manipulation in a single ALTER FOREIGN TABLE command is an extension.

ALTER FOREIGN TABLE DROP COLUMN can be used to drop the only column of a foreign table, leaving a zero-column table. This is an extension of SQL, which disallows zero-column foreign tables.

See Also

CREATE FOREIGN TABLE, DROP FOREIGN TABLE

ALTER FUNCTION

ALTER FUNCTION — change the definition of a function

Synopsis

```
ALTER FUNCTION name [ ( [ [ argmode ] [ argname ] argtype
[, ...] ] ) ]
    action [ ... ] [ RESTRICT ]
ALTER FUNCTION name [ ( [ [ argmode ] [ argname ] argtype
[, ...] ] ) ]
    RENAME TO new_name
ALTER FUNCTION name [ ( [ [ argmode ] [ argname ] argtype
[, ...] ] ) ]
    OWNER TO { new_owner | CURRENT_USER | SESSION_USER }
ALTER FUNCTION name [ ( [ [ argmode ] [ argname ] argtype
[, ...] ] ) ]
    SET SCHEMA new_schema
ALTER FUNCTION name [ ( [ [ argmode ] [ argname ] argtype
[, ...] ] ) ]
    DEPENDS ON EXTENSION extension_name

where action is one of:

    CALLED ON NULL INPUT | RETURNS NULL ON NULL INPUT | STRICT
    IMMUTABLE | STABLE | VOLATILE | [ NOT ] LEAKPROOF
    [ EXTERNAL ] SECURITY INVOKER | [ EXTERNAL ] SECURITY DEFINER
    PARALLEL { UNSAFE | RESTRICTED | SAFE }
    COST execution_cost
    ROWS result_rows
    SET configuration_parameter { TO | = } { value | DEFAULT }
    SET configuration_parameter FROM CURRENT
    RESET configuration_parameter
    RESET ALL
```

Description

ALTER FUNCTION changes the definition of a function.

You must own the function to use ALTER FUNCTION. To change a function's schema, you must also have CREATE privilege on the new schema. To alter the owner, you must also be a direct or indirect member of the new owning role, and that role must have CREATE privilege on the function's schema. (These restrictions enforce that altering the owner doesn't do anything you couldn't do by dropping and recreating the function. However, a superuser can alter ownership of any function anyway.)

Parameters

name

> The name (optionally schema-qualified) of an existing function. If no argument list is specified, the name must be unique in its schema.

argmode

> The mode of an argument: IN, OUT, INOUT, or VARIADIC. If omitted, the default is IN. Note that ALTER FUNCTION does not actually pay any attention to OUT arguments, since only the input arguments are needed to determine the function's identity. So it is sufficient to list the IN, INOUT, and VARIADIC arguments.

argname

> The name of an argument. Note that ALTER FUNCTION does not actually pay any attention to argument names, since only the argument data types are needed to determine the function's identity.

argtype

> The data type(s) of the function's arguments (optionally schema-qualified), if any.

new_name

> The new name of the function.

new_owner

> The new owner of the function. Note that if the function is marked SECURITY DEFINER, it will subsequently execute as the new owner.

new_schema

> The new schema for the function.

extension_name

> The name of the extension that the function is to depend on.

CALLED ON NULL INPUT
RETURNS NULL ON NULL INPUT
STRICT

> CALLED ON NULL INPUT changes the function so that it will be invoked when some or all of its arguments are null. RETURNS NULL ON NULL INPUT or STRICT changes the function so that it is not invoked if any of its arguments are null; instead, a null result is assumed automatically. See CREATE FUNCTION for more information.

IMMUTABLE
STABLE
VOLATILE

> Change the volatility of the function to the specified setting. See CREATE FUNCTION for details.

[EXTERNAL] SECURITY INVOKER
[EXTERNAL] SECURITY DEFINER

> Change whether the function is a security definer or not. The key word EXTERNAL is ignored for SQL conformance. See CREATE FUNCTION for more information about this capability.

PARALLEL

> Change whether the function is deemed safe for parallelism. See CREATE FUNCTION for details.

LEAKPROOF

Change whether the function is considered leakproof or not. See CREATE FUNCTION for more information about this capability.

COST *execution_cost*

Change the estimated execution cost of the function. See CREATE FUNCTION for more information.

ROWS *result_rows*

Change the estimated number of rows returned by a set-returning function. See CREATE FUNCTION for more information.

configuration_parameter
value

Add or change the assignment to be made to a configuration parameter when the function is called. If *value* is DEFAULT or, equivalently, RESET is used, the function-local setting is removed, so that the function executes with the value present in its environment. Use RESET ALL to clear all function-local settings. SET FROM CURRENT saves the value of the parameter that is current when ALTER FUNCTION is executed as the value to be applied when the function is entered.

See SET and Chapter 19 for more information about allowed parameter names and values.

RESTRICT

Ignored for conformance with the SQL standard.

Examples

To rename the function sqrt for type integer to square_root:

ALTER FUNCTION sqrt(integer) RENAME TO square_root;

To change the owner of the function sqrt for type integer to joe:

ALTER FUNCTION sqrt(integer) OWNER TO joe;

To change the schema of the function sqrt for type integer to maths:

ALTER FUNCTION sqrt(integer) SET SCHEMA maths;

To mark the function sqrt for type integer as being dependent on the extension mathlib:

ALTER FUNCTION sqrt(integer) DEPENDS ON EXTENSION mathlib;

To adjust the search path that is automatically set for a function:

ALTER FUNCTION check_password(text) SET search_path = admin, pg_temp;

To disable automatic setting of search_path for a function:

```
ALTER FUNCTION check_password(text) RESET search_path;
```

The function will now execute with whatever search path is used by its caller.

Compatibility

This statement is partially compatible with the `ALTER FUNCTION` statement in the SQL standard. The standard allows more properties of a function to be modified, but does not provide the ability to rename a function, make a function a security definer, attach configuration parameter values to a function, or change the owner, schema, or volatility of a function. The standard also requires the `RESTRICT` key word, which is optional in PostgreSQL.

See Also

CREATE FUNCTION, DROP FUNCTION, ALTER PROCEDURE, ALTER ROUTINE

ALTER GROUP

ALTER GROUP — change role name or membership

Synopsis

```
ALTER GROUP role_specification ADD USER user_name [, ... ]
ALTER GROUP role_specification DROP USER user_name [, ... ]

where role_specification can be:

    role_name
  | CURRENT_USER
  | SESSION_USER

ALTER GROUP group_name RENAME TO new_name
```

Description

ALTER GROUP changes the attributes of a user group. This is an obsolete command, though still accepted for backwards compatibility, because groups (and users too) have been superseded by the more general concept of roles.

The first two variants add users to a group or remove them from a group. (Any role can play the part of either a "user" or a "group" for this purpose.) These variants are effectively equivalent to granting or revoking membership in the role named as the "group"; so the preferred way to do this is to use GRANT or REVOKE.

The third variant changes the name of the group. This is exactly equivalent to renaming the role with ALTER ROLE.

Parameters

group_name

    The name of the group (role) to modify.

user_name

    Users (roles) that are to be added to or removed from the group. The users must already exist; ALTER GROUP does not create or drop users.

new_name

    The new name of the group.

Examples

Add users to a group:

```
ALTER GROUP staff ADD USER karl, john;
```

Remove a user from a group:

```
ALTER GROUP workers DROP USER beth;
```

Compatibility

There is no **ALTER GROUP** statement in the SQL standard.

See Also

GRANT, REVOKE, ALTER ROLE

ALTER INDEX

ALTER INDEX — change the definition of an index

Synopsis

```
ALTER INDEX [ IF EXISTS ] name RENAME TO new_name
ALTER INDEX [ IF EXISTS ] name SET TABLESPACE tablespace_name
ALTER INDEX name ATTACH PARTITION index_name
ALTER INDEX name DEPENDS ON EXTENSION extension_name
ALTER INDEX [ IF EXISTS ] name SET ( storage_parameter = value
[, ... ] )
ALTER INDEX [ IF EXISTS ] name RESET ( storage_parameter [, ... ] )
ALTER INDEX [ IF EXISTS ] name ALTER [ COLUMN ] column_number
    SET STATISTICS integer
ALTER INDEX ALL IN TABLESPACE name [ OWNED BY role_name [, ... ] ]
    SET TABLESPACE new_tablespace [ NOWAIT ]
```

Description

ALTER INDEX changes the definition of an existing index. There are several subforms:

RENAME

The RENAME form changes the name of the index. If the index is associated with a table constraint (either UNIQUE, PRIMARY KEY, or EXCLUDE), the constraint is renamed as well. There is no effect on the stored data.

SET TABLESPACE

This form changes the index's tablespace to the specified tablespace and moves the data file(s) associated with the index to the new tablespace. To change the tablespace of an index, you must own the index and have CREATE privilege on the new tablespace. All indexes in the current database in a tablespace can be moved by using the ALL IN TABLESPACE form, which will lock all indexes to be moved and then move each one. This form also supports OWNED BY, which will only move indexes owned by the roles specified. If the NOWAIT option is specified then the command will fail if it is unable to acquire all of the locks required immediately. Note that system catalogs will not be moved by this command, use ALTER DATABASE or explicit ALTER INDEX invocations instead if desired. See also CREATE TABLESPACE.

ATTACH PARTITION

Causes the named index to become attached to the altered index. The named index must be on a partition of the table containing the index being altered, and have an equivalent definition. An attached index cannot be dropped by itself, and will automatically be dropped if its parent index is dropped.

DEPENDS ON EXTENSION

This form marks the index as dependent on the extension, such that if the extension is dropped, the index will automatically be dropped as well.

```
SET ( storage_parameter = value [, ... ] )
```

This form changes one or more index-method-specific storage parameters for the index. See CREATE INDEX for details on the available parameters. Note that the index contents will not be modified immediately by this command; depending on the parameter you might need to rebuild the index with REINDEX to get the desired effects.

```
RESET ( storage_parameter [, ... ] )
```

This form resets one or more index-method-specific storage parameters to their defaults. As with SET, a REINDEX might be needed to update the index entirely.

```
ALTER [ COLUMN ] column_number SET STATISTICS integer
```

This form sets the per-column statistics-gathering target for subsequent ANALYZE operations, though can be used only on index columns that are defined as an expression. Since expressions lack a unique name, we refer to them using the ordinal number of the index column. The target can be set in the range 0 to 10000; alternatively, set it to -1 to revert to using the system default statistics target (default_statistics_target). For more information on the use of statistics by the PostgreSQL query planner, refer to Section 14.2.

Parameters

IF EXISTS

Do not throw an error if the index does not exist. A notice is issued in this case.

column_number

The ordinal number refers to the ordinal (left-to-right) position of the index column.

name

The name (possibly schema-qualified) of an existing index to alter.

new_name

The new name for the index.

tablespace_name

The tablespace to which the index will be moved.

extension_name

The name of the extension that the index is to depend on.

storage_parameter

The name of an index-method-specific storage parameter.

value

The new value for an index-method-specific storage parameter. This might be a number or a word depending on the parameter.

Notes

These operations are also possible using ALTER TABLE. `ALTER INDEX` is in fact just an alias for the forms of `ALTER TABLE` that apply to indexes.

There was formerly an `ALTER INDEX OWNER` variant, but this is now ignored (with a warning). An index cannot have an owner different from its table's owner. Changing the table's owner automatically changes the index as well.

Changing any part of a system catalog index is not permitted.

Examples

To rename an existing index:

```
ALTER INDEX distributors RENAME TO suppliers;
```

To move an index to a different tablespace:

```
ALTER INDEX distributors SET TABLESPACE fasttablespace;
```

To change an index's fill factor (assuming that the index method supports it):

```
ALTER INDEX distributors SET (fillfactor = 75);
REINDEX INDEX distributors;
```

Set the statistics-gathering target for an expression index:

```
CREATE INDEX coord_idx ON measured (x, y, (z + t));
ALTER INDEX coord_idx ALTER COLUMN 3 SET STATISTICS 1000;
```

Compatibility

`ALTER INDEX` is a PostgreSQL extension.

See Also

CREATE INDEX, REINDEX

ALTER LANGUAGE

ALTER LANGUAGE — change the definition of a procedural language

Synopsis

```
ALTER [ PROCEDURAL ] LANGUAGE name RENAME TO new_name
ALTER [ PROCEDURAL ] LANGUAGE name OWNER TO { new_owner | CURRENT_USER
  | SESSION_USER }
```

Description

ALTER LANGUAGE changes the definition of a procedural language. The only functionality is to rename the language or assign a new owner. You must be superuser or owner of the language to use ALTER LANGUAGE.

Parameters

name

Name of a language

new_name

The new name of the language

new_owner

The new owner of the language

Compatibility

There is no ALTER LANGUAGE statement in the SQL standard.

See Also

CREATE LANGUAGE, DROP LANGUAGE

ALTER LARGE OBJECT

ALTER LARGE OBJECT — change the definition of a large object

Synopsis

```
ALTER LARGE OBJECT large_object_oid OWNER TO { new_owner |
CURRENT_USER | SESSION_USER }
```

Description

ALTER LARGE OBJECT changes the definition of a large object.

You must own the large object to use ALTER LARGE OBJECT. To alter the owner, you must also be a direct or indirect member of the new owning role. (However, a superuser can alter any large object anyway.) Currently, the only functionality is to assign a new owner, so both restrictions always apply.

Parameters

large_object_oid

   OID of the large object to be altered

new_owner

   The new owner of the large object

Compatibility

There is no ALTER LARGE OBJECT statement in the SQL standard.

See Also

Chapter 35

ALTER MATERIALIZED VIEW

ALTER MATERIALIZED VIEW — change the definition of a materialized view

Synopsis

```
ALTER MATERIALIZED VIEW [ IF EXISTS ] name
    action [, ... ]
ALTER MATERIALIZED VIEW name
    DEPENDS ON EXTENSION extension_name
ALTER MATERIALIZED VIEW [ IF EXISTS ] name
    RENAME [ COLUMN ] column_name TO new_column_name
ALTER MATERIALIZED VIEW [ IF EXISTS ] name
    RENAME TO new_name
ALTER MATERIALIZED VIEW [ IF EXISTS ] name
    SET SCHEMA new_schema
ALTER MATERIALIZED VIEW ALL IN TABLESPACE name [ OWNED BY role_name
 [, ... ] ]
    SET TABLESPACE new_tablespace [ NOWAIT ]

where action is one of:

    ALTER [ COLUMN ] column_name SET STATISTICS integer
    ALTER [ COLUMN ] column_name SET ( attribute_option = value
 [, ... ] )
    ALTER [ COLUMN ] column_name RESET ( attribute_option [, ... ] )
    ALTER [ COLUMN ] column_name SET STORAGE { PLAIN | EXTERNAL |
 EXTENDED | MAIN }
    CLUSTER ON index_name
    SET WITHOUT CLUSTER
    SET ( storage_parameter = value [, ... ] )
    RESET ( storage_parameter [, ... ] )
    OWNER TO { new_owner | CURRENT_USER | SESSION_USER }
```

Description

ALTER MATERIALIZED VIEW changes various auxiliary properties of an existing materialized view.

You must own the materialized view to use ALTER MATERIALIZED VIEW. To change a materialized view's schema, you must also have CREATE privilege on the new schema. To alter the owner, you must also be a direct or indirect member of the new owning role, and that role must have CREATE privilege on the materialized view's schema. (These restrictions enforce that altering the owner doesn't do anything you couldn't do by dropping and recreating the materialized view. However, a superuser can alter ownership of any view anyway.)

The DEPENDS ON EXTENSION form marks the materialized view as dependent on an extension, such that the materialized view will automatically be dropped if the extension is dropped.

The statement subforms and actions available for ALTER MATERIALIZED VIEW are a subset of those available for ALTER TABLE, and have the same meaning when used for materialized views. See the descriptions for ALTER TABLE for details.

Parameters

name

The name (optionally schema-qualified) of an existing materialized view.

column_name

Name of a new or existing column.

extension_name

The name of the extension that the materialized view is to depend on.

new_column_name

New name for an existing column.

new_owner

The user name of the new owner of the materialized view.

new_name

The new name for the materialized view.

new_schema

The new schema for the materialized view.

Examples

To rename the materialized view `foo` to `bar`:

```
ALTER MATERIALIZED VIEW foo RENAME TO bar;
```

Compatibility

`ALTER MATERIALIZED VIEW` is a PostgreSQL extension.

See Also

CREATE MATERIALIZED VIEW, DROP MATERIALIZED VIEW, REFRESH MATERIALIZED VIEW

ALTER OPERATOR

ALTER OPERATOR — change the definition of an operator

Synopsis

```
ALTER OPERATOR name ( { left_type | NONE } , { right_type | NONE } )
    OWNER TO { new_owner | CURRENT_USER | SESSION_USER }

ALTER OPERATOR name ( { left_type | NONE } , { right_type | NONE } )
    SET SCHEMA new_schema

ALTER OPERATOR name ( { left_type | NONE } , { right_type | NONE } )
    SET ( { RESTRICT = { res_proc | NONE }
          | JOIN = { join_proc | NONE }
        } [, ... ] )
```

Description

`ALTER OPERATOR` changes the definition of an operator.

You must own the operator to use `ALTER OPERATOR`. To alter the owner, you must also be a direct or indirect member of the new owning role, and that role must have `CREATE` privilege on the operator's schema. (These restrictions enforce that altering the owner doesn't do anything you couldn't do by dropping and recreating the operator. However, a superuser can alter ownership of any operator anyway.)

Parameters

name

> The name (optionally schema-qualified) of an existing operator.

left_type

> The data type of the operator's left operand; write `NONE` if the operator has no left operand.

right_type

> The data type of the operator's right operand; write `NONE` if the operator has no right operand.

new_owner

> The new owner of the operator.

new_schema

> The new schema for the operator.

res_proc

> The restriction selectivity estimator function for this operator; write `NONE` to remove existing selectivity estimator.

join_proc

The join selectivity estimator function for this operator; write NONE to remove existing selectivity estimator.

Examples

Change the owner of a custom operator a @@ b for type text:

```
ALTER OPERATOR @@ (text, text) OWNER TO joe;
```

Change the restriction and join selectivity estimator functions of a custom operator a && b for type int[]:

```
ALTER OPERATOR && (_int4, _int4) SET (RESTRICT = _int_contsel, JOIN =
_int_contjoinsel);
```

Compatibility

There is no ALTER OPERATOR statement in the SQL standard.

See Also

CREATE OPERATOR, DROP OPERATOR

ALTER OPERATOR CLASS

ALTER OPERATOR CLASS — change the definition of an operator class

Synopsis

```
ALTER OPERATOR CLASS name USING index_method
    RENAME TO new_name

ALTER OPERATOR CLASS name USING index_method
    OWNER TO { new_owner | CURRENT_USER | SESSION_USER }

ALTER OPERATOR CLASS name USING index_method
    SET SCHEMA new_schema
```

Description

ALTER OPERATOR CLASS changes the definition of an operator class.

You must own the operator class to use ALTER OPERATOR CLASS. To alter the owner, you must also be a direct or indirect member of the new owning role, and that role must have CREATE privilege on the operator class's schema. (These restrictions enforce that altering the owner doesn't do anything you couldn't do by dropping and recreating the operator class. However, a superuser can alter ownership of any operator class anyway.)

Parameters

name

   The name (optionally schema-qualified) of an existing operator class.

index_method

   The name of the index method this operator class is for.

new_name

   The new name of the operator class.

new_owner

   The new owner of the operator class.

new_schema

   The new schema for the operator class.

Compatibility

There is no ALTER OPERATOR CLASS statement in the SQL standard.

See Also

CREATE OPERATOR CLASS, DROP OPERATOR CLASS, ALTER OPERATOR FAMILY

ALTER OPERATOR FAMILY

ALTER OPERATOR FAMILY — change the definition of an operator family

Synopsis

```
ALTER OPERATOR FAMILY name USING index_method ADD
  {  OPERATOR strategy_number operator_name ( op_type, op_type )
             [ FOR SEARCH | FOR ORDER BY sort_family_name ]
   | FUNCTION support_number [ ( op_type [ , op_type ] ) ]
             function_name [ ( argument_type [, ...] ) ]
  } [, ... ]

ALTER OPERATOR FAMILY name USING index_method DROP
  {  OPERATOR strategy_number ( op_type [ , op_type ] )
   | FUNCTION support_number ( op_type [ , op_type ] )
  } [, ... ]

ALTER OPERATOR FAMILY name USING index_method
    RENAME TO new_name

ALTER OPERATOR FAMILY name USING index_method
    OWNER TO { new_owner | CURRENT_USER | SESSION_USER }

ALTER OPERATOR FAMILY name USING index_method
    SET SCHEMA new_schema
```

Description

ALTER OPERATOR FAMILY changes the definition of an operator family. You can add operators and support functions to the family, remove them from the family, or change the family's name or owner.

When operators and support functions are added to a family with ALTER OPERATOR FAMILY, they are not part of any specific operator class within the family, but are just "loose" within the family. This indicates that these operators and functions are compatible with the family's semantics, but are not required for correct functioning of any specific index. (Operators and functions that are so required should be declared as part of an operator class, instead; see CREATE OPERATOR CLASS.) PostgreSQL will allow loose members of a family to be dropped from the family at any time, but members of an operator class cannot be dropped without dropping the whole class and any indexes that depend on it. Typically, single-data-type operators and functions are part of operator classes because they are needed to support an index on that specific data type, while cross-data-type operators and functions are made loose members of the family.

You must be a superuser to use ALTER OPERATOR FAMILY. (This restriction is made because an erroneous operator family definition could confuse or even crash the server.)

ALTER OPERATOR FAMILY does not presently check whether the operator family definition includes all the operators and functions required by the index method, nor whether the operators and functions form a self-consistent set. It is the user's responsibility to define a valid operator family.

Refer to Section 38.15 for further information.

Parameters

name

> The name (optionally schema-qualified) of an existing operator family.

index_method

> The name of the index method this operator family is for.

strategy_number

> The index method's strategy number for an operator associated with the operator family.

operator_name

> The name (optionally schema-qualified) of an operator associated with the operator family.

op_type

> In an OPERATOR clause, the operand data type(s) of the operator, or NONE to signify a left-unary or right-unary operator. Unlike the comparable syntax in CREATE OPERATOR CLASS, the operand data types must always be specified.

> In an ADD FUNCTION clause, the operand data type(s) the function is intended to support, if different from the input data type(s) of the function. For B-tree comparison functions and hash functions it is not necessary to specify *op_type* since the function's input data type(s) are always the correct ones to use. For B-tree sort support functions and all functions in GiST, SP-GiST and GIN operator classes, it is necessary to specify the operand data type(s) the function is to be used with.

> In a DROP FUNCTION clause, the operand data type(s) the function is intended to support must be specified.

sort_family_name

> The name (optionally schema-qualified) of an existing btree operator family that describes the sort ordering associated with an ordering operator.

> If neither FOR SEARCH nor FOR ORDER BY is specified, FOR SEARCH is the default.

support_number

> The index method's support function number for a function associated with the operator family.

function_name

> The name (optionally schema-qualified) of a function that is an index method support function for the operator family. If no argument list is specified, the name must be unique in its schema.

argument_type

> The parameter data type(s) of the function.

new_name

> The new name of the operator family.

new_owner

The new owner of the operator family.

new_schema

The new schema for the operator family.

The OPERATOR and FUNCTION clauses can appear in any order.

Notes

Notice that the DROP syntax only specifies the "slot" in the operator family, by strategy or support number and input data type(s). The name of the operator or function occupying the slot is not mentioned. Also, for DROP FUNCTION the type(s) to specify are the input data type(s) the function is intended to support; for GiST, SP-GiST and GIN indexes this might have nothing to do with the actual input argument types of the function.

Because the index machinery does not check access permissions on functions before using them, including a function or operator in an operator family is tantamount to granting public execute permission on it. This is usually not an issue for the sorts of functions that are useful in an operator family.

The operators should not be defined by SQL functions. A SQL function is likely to be inlined into the calling query, which will prevent the optimizer from recognizing that the query matches an index.

Before PostgreSQL 8.4, the OPERATOR clause could include a RECHECK option. This is no longer supported because whether an index operator is "lossy" is now determined on-the-fly at run time. This allows efficient handling of cases where an operator might or might not be lossy.

Examples

The following example command adds cross-data-type operators and support functions to an operator family that already contains B-tree operator classes for data types int4 and int2.

```
ALTER OPERATOR FAMILY integer_ops USING btree ADD

  -- int4 vs int2
  OPERATOR 1 < (int4, int2) ,
  OPERATOR 2 <= (int4, int2) ,
  OPERATOR 3 = (int4, int2) ,
  OPERATOR 4 >= (int4, int2) ,
  OPERATOR 5 > (int4, int2) ,
  FUNCTION 1 btint42cmp(int4, int2) ,

  -- int2 vs int4
  OPERATOR 1 < (int2, int4) ,
  OPERATOR 2 <= (int2, int4) ,
  OPERATOR 3 = (int2, int4) ,
  OPERATOR 4 >= (int2, int4) ,
  OPERATOR 5 > (int2, int4) ,
  FUNCTION 1 btint24cmp(int2, int4) ;
```

To remove these entries again:

```
ALTER OPERATOR FAMILY integer_ops USING btree DROP

    -- int4 vs int2
    OPERATOR 1 (int4, int2) ,
    OPERATOR 2 (int4, int2) ,
    OPERATOR 3 (int4, int2) ,
    OPERATOR 4 (int4, int2) ,
    OPERATOR 5 (int4, int2) ,
    FUNCTION 1 (int4, int2) ,

    -- int2 vs int4
    OPERATOR 1 (int2, int4) ,
    OPERATOR 2 (int2, int4) ,
    OPERATOR 3 (int2, int4) ,
    OPERATOR 4 (int2, int4) ,
    OPERATOR 5 (int2, int4) ,
    FUNCTION 1 (int2, int4) ;
```

Compatibility

There is no ALTER OPERATOR FAMILY statement in the SQL standard.

See Also

CREATE OPERATOR FAMILY, DROP OPERATOR FAMILY, CREATE OPERATOR CLASS, ALTER OPERATOR CLASS, DROP OPERATOR CLASS

ALTER POLICY

ALTER POLICY — change the definition of a row level security policy

Synopsis

```
ALTER POLICY name ON table_name RENAME TO new_name

ALTER POLICY name ON table_name
    [ TO { role_name | PUBLIC | CURRENT_USER | SESSION_USER }
 [, ...] ]
    [ USING ( using_expression ) ]
    [ WITH CHECK ( check_expression ) ]
```

Description

ALTER POLICY changes the definition of an existing row-level security policy. Note that ALTER POLICY only allows the set of roles to which the policy applies and the USING and WITH CHECK expressions to be modified. To change other properties of a policy, such as the command to which it applies or whether it is permissive or restrictive, the policy must be dropped and recreated.

To use ALTER POLICY, you must own the table that the policy applies to.

In the second form of ALTER POLICY, the role list, using_expression, and check_expression are replaced independently if specified. When one of those clauses is omitted, the corresponding part of the policy is unchanged.

Parameters

name

The name of an existing policy to alter.

table_name

The name (optionally schema-qualified) of the table that the policy is on.

new_name

The new name for the policy.

role_name

The role(s) to which the policy applies. Multiple roles can be specified at one time. To apply the policy to all roles, use PUBLIC.

using_expression

The USING expression for the policy. See CREATE POLICY for details.

check_expression

The WITH CHECK expression for the policy. See CREATE POLICY for details.

Compatibility

`ALTER POLICY` is a PostgreSQL extension.

See Also

CREATE POLICY, DROP POLICY

ALTER PROCEDURE

ALTER PROCEDURE — change the definition of a procedure

Synopsis

```
ALTER PROCEDURE name [ ( [ [ argmode ] [ argname ] argtype
[, ...] ] ) ]
    action [ ... ] [ RESTRICT ]
ALTER PROCEDURE name [ ( [ [ argmode ] [ argname ] argtype
[, ...] ] ) ]
    RENAME TO new_name
ALTER PROCEDURE name [ ( [ [ argmode ] [ argname ] argtype
[, ...] ] ) ]
    OWNER TO { new_owner | CURRENT_USER | SESSION_USER }
ALTER PROCEDURE name [ ( [ [ argmode ] [ argname ] argtype
[, ...] ] ) ]
    SET SCHEMA new_schema
ALTER PROCEDURE name [ ( [ [ argmode ] [ argname ] argtype
[, ...] ] ) ]
    DEPENDS ON EXTENSION extension_name

where action is one of:

    [ EXTERNAL ] SECURITY INVOKER | [ EXTERNAL ] SECURITY DEFINER
    SET configuration_parameter { TO | = } { value | DEFAULT }
    SET configuration_parameter FROM CURRENT
    RESET configuration_parameter
    RESET ALL
```

Description

ALTER PROCEDURE changes the definition of a procedure.

You must own the procedure to use ALTER PROCEDURE. To change a procedure's schema, you must also have CREATE privilege on the new schema. To alter the owner, you must also be a direct or indirect member of the new owning role, and that role must have CREATE privilege on the procedure's schema. (These restrictions enforce that altering the owner doesn't do anything you couldn't do by dropping and recreating the procedure. However, a superuser can alter ownership of any procedure anyway.)

Parameters

name

> The name (optionally schema-qualified) of an existing procedure. If no argument list is specified, the name must be unique in its schema.

argmode

> The mode of an argument: IN or VARIADIC. If omitted, the default is IN.

argname

> The name of an argument. Note that `ALTER PROCEDURE` does not actually pay any attention to argument names, since only the argument data types are needed to determine the procedure's identity.

argtype

> The data type(s) of the procedure's arguments (optionally schema-qualified), if any.

new_name

> The new name of the procedure.

new_owner

> The new owner of the procedure. Note that if the procedure is marked `SECURITY DEFINER`, it will subsequently execute as the new owner.

new_schema

> The new schema for the procedure.

extension_name

> The name of the extension that the procedure is to depend on.

```
[ EXTERNAL ] SECURITY INVOKER
[ EXTERNAL ] SECURITY DEFINER
```

> Change whether the procedure is a security definer or not. The key word `EXTERNAL` is ignored for SQL conformance. See CREATE PROCEDURE for more information about this capability.

configuration_parameter
value

> Add or change the assignment to be made to a configuration parameter when the procedure is called. If *value* is `DEFAULT` or, equivalently, `RESET` is used, the procedure-local setting is removed, so that the procedure executes with the value present in its environment. Use `RESET ALL` to clear all procedure-local settings. `SET FROM CURRENT` saves the value of the parameter that is current when `ALTER PROCEDURE` is executed as the value to be applied when the procedure is entered.

> See SET and Chapter 19 for more information about allowed parameter names and values.

`RESTRICT`

> Ignored for conformance with the SQL standard.

Examples

To rename the procedure `insert_data` with two arguments of type `integer` to `insert_record`:

```
ALTER PROCEDURE insert_data(integer, integer) RENAME TO insert_record;
```

To change the owner of the procedure `insert_data` with two arguments of type `integer` to `joe`:

```
ALTER PROCEDURE insert_data(integer, integer) OWNER TO joe;
```

To change the schema of the procedure `insert_data` with two arguments of type `integer` to accounting:

```
ALTER PROCEDURE insert_data(integer, integer) SET SCHEMA accounting;
```

To mark the procedure `insert_data(integer, integer)` as being dependent on the extension `myext`:

```
ALTER PROCEDURE insert_data(integer, integer) DEPENDS ON EXTENSION
 myext;
```

To adjust the search path that is automatically set for a procedure:

```
ALTER PROCEDURE check_password(text) SET search_path = admin, pg_temp;
```

To disable automatic setting of `search_path` for a procedure:

```
ALTER PROCEDURE check_password(text) RESET search_path;
```

The procedure will now execute with whatever search path is used by its caller.

Compatibility

This statement is partially compatible with the **ALTER PROCEDURE** statement in the SQL standard. The standard allows more properties of a procedure to be modified, but does not provide the ability to rename a procedure, make a procedure a security definer, attach configuration parameter values to a procedure, or change the owner, schema, or volatility of a procedure. The standard also requires the **RESTRICT** key word, which is optional in PostgreSQL.

See Also

CREATE PROCEDURE, DROP PROCEDURE, ALTER FUNCTION, ALTER ROUTINE

ALTER PUBLICATION

ALTER PUBLICATION — change the definition of a publication

Synopsis

```
ALTER PUBLICATION name ADD TABLE [ ONLY ] table_name [ * ] [, ...]
ALTER PUBLICATION name SET TABLE [ ONLY ] table_name [ * ] [, ...]
ALTER PUBLICATION name DROP TABLE [ ONLY ] table_name [ * ] [, ...]
ALTER PUBLICATION name SET ( publication_parameter [= value]
[, ... ] )
ALTER PUBLICATION name OWNER TO { new_owner | CURRENT_USER |
SESSION_USER }
ALTER PUBLICATION name RENAME TO new_name
```

Description

The command ALTER PUBLICATION can change the attributes of a publication.

The first three variants change which tables are part of the publication. The SET TABLE clause will replace the list of tables in the publication with the specified one. The ADD TABLE and DROP TABLE clauses will add and remove one or more tables from the publication. Note that adding tables to a publication that is already subscribed to will require a ALTER SUBSCRIPTION ... REFRESH PUBLICATION action on the subscribing side in order to become effective.

The fourth variant of this command listed in the synopsis can change all of the publication properties specified in CREATE PUBLICATION. Properties not mentioned in the command retain their previous settings.

The remaining variants change the owner and the name of the publication.

You must own the publication to use ALTER PUBLICATION. To alter the owner, you must also be a direct or indirect member of the new owning role. The new owner must have CREATE privilege on the database. Also, the new owner of a FOR ALL TABLES publication must be a superuser. However, a superuser can change the ownership of a publication while circumventing these restrictions.

Parameters

name

The name of an existing publication whose definition is to be altered.

table_name

Name of an existing table. If ONLY is specified before the table name, only that table is affected. If ONLY is not specified, the table and all its descendant tables (if any) are affected. Optionally, * can be specified after the table name to explicitly indicate that descendant tables are included.

SET (*publication_parameter* [= *value*] [, ...])

This clause alters publication parameters originally set by CREATE PUBLICATION. See there for more information.

---

new_owner

The user name of the new owner of the publication.

new_name

The new name for the publication.

Examples

Change the publication to publish only deletes and updates:

```
ALTER PUBLICATION noinsert SET (publish = 'update, delete');
```

Add some tables to the publication:

```
ALTER PUBLICATION mypublication ADD TABLE users, departments;
```

Compatibility

`ALTER PUBLICATION` is a PostgreSQL extension.

See Also

CREATE PUBLICATION, DROP PUBLICATION, CREATE SUBSCRIPTION, ALTER SUBSCRIPTION

ALTER ROLE

ALTER ROLE — change a database role

Synopsis

```
ALTER ROLE role_specification [ WITH ] option [ ... ]

where option can be:

      SUPERUSER | NOSUPERUSER
    | CREATEDB | NOCREATEDB
    | CREATEROLE | NOCREATEROLE
    | INHERIT | NOINHERIT
    | LOGIN | NOLOGIN
    | REPLICATION | NOREPLICATION
    | BYPASSRLS | NOBYPASSRLS
    | CONNECTION LIMIT connlimit
    | [ ENCRYPTED ] PASSWORD 'password' | PASSWORD NULL
    | VALID UNTIL 'timestamp'

ALTER ROLE name RENAME TO new_name

ALTER ROLE { role_specification | ALL } [ IN DATABASE database_name ]
  SET configuration_parameter { TO | = } { value | DEFAULT }
ALTER ROLE { role_specification | ALL } [ IN DATABASE database_name ]
  SET configuration_parameter FROM CURRENT
ALTER ROLE { role_specification | ALL } [ IN DATABASE database_name ]
  RESET configuration_parameter
ALTER ROLE { role_specification | ALL } [ IN DATABASE database_name ]
  RESET ALL

where role_specification can be:

    role_name
  | CURRENT_USER
  | SESSION_USER
```

Description

ALTER ROLE changes the attributes of a PostgreSQL role.

The first variant of this command listed in the synopsis can change many of the role attributes that can be specified in CREATE ROLE. (All the possible attributes are covered, except that there are no options for adding or removing memberships; use GRANT and REVOKE for that.) Attributes not mentioned in the command retain their previous settings. Database superusers can change any of these settings for any role. Roles having CREATEROLE privilege can change any of these settings, but only for non-superuser and non-replication roles. Ordinary roles can only change their own password.

The second variant changes the name of the role. Database superusers can rename any role. Roles having CREATEROLE privilege can rename non-superuser roles. The current session user cannot be renamed.

(Connect as a different user if you need to do that.) Because MD5-encrypted passwords use the role name as cryptographic salt, renaming a role clears its password if the password is MD5-encrypted.

The remaining variants change a role's session default for a configuration variable, either for all databases or, when the `IN  DATABASE` clause is specified, only for sessions in the named database. If `ALL` is specified instead of a role name, this changes the setting for all roles. Using `ALL` with `IN  DATABASE` is effectively the same as using the command `ALTER DATABASE ... SET ...`.

Whenever the role subsequently starts a new session, the specified value becomes the session default, overriding whatever setting is present in `postgresql.conf` or has been received from the `postgres` command line. This only happens at login time; executing SET ROLE or SET SESSION AUTHORIZATION does not cause new configuration values to be set. Settings set for all databases are overridden by database-specific settings attached to a role. Settings for specific databases or specific roles override settings for all roles.

Superusers can change anyone's session defaults. Roles having `CREATEROLE` privilege can change defaults for non-superuser roles. Ordinary roles can only set defaults for themselves. Certain configuration variables cannot be set this way, or can only be set if a superuser issues the command. Only superusers can change a setting for all roles in all databases.

Parameters

`name`

> The name of the role whose attributes are to be altered.

`CURRENT_USER`

> Alter the current user instead of an explicitly identified role.

`SESSION_USER`

> Alter the current session user instead of an explicitly identified role.

```
SUPERUSER
NOSUPERUSER
CREATEDB
NOCREATEDB
CREATEROLE
NOCREATEROLE
INHERIT
NOINHERIT
LOGIN
NOLOGIN
REPLICATION
NOREPLICATION
BYPASSRLS
NOBYPASSRLS
CONNECTION LIMIT connlimit
[ ENCRYPTED ] PASSWORD 'password'
PASSWORD NULL
VALID UNTIL 'timestamp'
```

> These clauses alter attributes originally set by CREATE ROLE. For more information, see the `CREATE ROLE` reference page.

new_name

    The new name of the role.

database_name

    The name of the database the configuration variable should be set in.

configuration_parameter
value

    Set this role's session default for the specified configuration parameter to the given value. If `value` is `DEFAULT` or, equivalently, `RESET` is used, the role-specific variable setting is removed, so the role will inherit the system-wide default setting in new sessions. Use `RESET ALL` to clear all role-specific settings. `SET FROM CURRENT` saves the session's current value of the parameter as the role-specific value. If `IN DATABASE` is specified, the configuration parameter is set or removed for the given role and database only.

    Role-specific variable settings take effect only at login; SET ROLE and SET SESSION AUTHORIZATION do not process role-specific variable settings.

    See SET and Chapter 19 for more information about allowed parameter names and values.

Notes

Use CREATE ROLE to add new roles, and DROP ROLE to remove a role.

`ALTER ROLE` cannot change a role's memberships. Use GRANT and REVOKE to do that.

Caution must be exercised when specifying an unencrypted password with this command. The password will be transmitted to the server in cleartext, and it might also be logged in the client's command history or the server log. psql contains a command `\password` that can be used to change a role's password without exposing the cleartext password.

It is also possible to tie a session default to a specific database rather than to a role; see ALTER DATABASE. If there is a conflict, database-role-specific settings override role-specific ones, which in turn override database-specific ones.

Examples

Change a role's password:

```
ALTER ROLE davide WITH PASSWORD 'hu8jmn3';
```

Remove a role's password:

```
ALTER ROLE davide WITH PASSWORD NULL;
```

Change a password expiration date, specifying that the password should expire at midday on 4th May 2015 using the time zone which is one hour ahead of UTC:

```
ALTER ROLE chris VALID UNTIL 'May 4 12:00:00 2015 +1';
```

Make a password valid forever:

```
ALTER ROLE fred VALID UNTIL 'infinity';
```

Give a role the ability to create other roles and new databases:

```
ALTER ROLE miriam CREATEROLE CREATEDB;
```

Give a role a non-default setting of the maintenance_work_mem parameter:

```
ALTER ROLE worker_bee SET maintenance_work_mem = 100000;
```

Give a role a non-default, database-specific setting of the client_min_messages parameter:

```
ALTER ROLE fred IN DATABASE devel SET client_min_messages = DEBUG;
```

Compatibility

The ALTER ROLE statement is a PostgreSQL extension.

See Also

CREATE ROLE, DROP ROLE, ALTER DATABASE, SET

ALTER ROUTINE

ALTER ROUTINE — change the definition of a routine

Synopsis

```
ALTER ROUTINE name [ ( [ [ argmode ] [ argname ] argtype [, ...] ] ) ]
    action [ ... ] [ RESTRICT ]
ALTER ROUTINE name [ ( [ [ argmode ] [ argname ] argtype [, ...] ] ) ]
    RENAME TO new_name
ALTER ROUTINE name [ ( [ [ argmode ] [ argname ] argtype [, ...] ] ) ]
    OWNER TO { new_owner | CURRENT_USER | SESSION_USER }
ALTER ROUTINE name [ ( [ [ argmode ] [ argname ] argtype [, ...] ] ) ]
    SET SCHEMA new_schema
ALTER ROUTINE name [ ( [ [ argmode ] [ argname ] argtype [, ...] ] ) ]
    DEPENDS ON EXTENSION extension_name

where action is one of:

    IMMUTABLE | STABLE | VOLATILE | [ NOT ] LEAKPROOF
    [ EXTERNAL ] SECURITY INVOKER | [ EXTERNAL ] SECURITY DEFINER
    PARALLEL { UNSAFE | RESTRICTED | SAFE }
    COST execution_cost
    ROWS result_rows
    SET configuration_parameter { TO | = } { value | DEFAULT }
    SET configuration_parameter FROM CURRENT
    RESET configuration_parameter
    RESET ALL
```

Description

ALTER ROUTINE changes the definition of a routine, which can be an aggregate function, a normal function, or a procedure. See under ALTER AGGREGATE, ALTER FUNCTION, and ALTER PROCEDURE for the description of the parameters, more examples, and further details.

Examples

To rename the routine `foo` for type `integer` to `foobar`:

```
ALTER ROUTINE foo(integer) RENAME TO foobar;
```

This command will work independent of whether `foo` is an aggregate, function, or procedure.

Compatibility

This statement is partially compatible with the ALTER ROUTINE statement in the SQL standard. See under ALTER FUNCTION and ALTER PROCEDURE for more details. Allowing routine names to refer to aggregate functions is a PostgreSQL extension.

See Also

ALTER AGGREGATE, ALTER FUNCTION, ALTER PROCEDURE, DROP ROUTINE

Note that there is no CREATE ROUTINE command.

ALTER RULE

ALTER RULE — change the definition of a rule

Synopsis

```
ALTER RULE name ON table_name RENAME TO new_name
```

Description

`ALTER RULE` changes properties of an existing rule. Currently, the only available action is to change the rule's name.

To use `ALTER RULE`, you must own the table or view that the rule applies to.

Parameters

name

The name of an existing rule to alter.

table_name

The name (optionally schema-qualified) of the table or view that the rule applies to.

new_name

The new name for the rule.

Examples

To rename an existing rule:

```
ALTER RULE notify_all ON emp RENAME TO notify_me;
```

Compatibility

`ALTER RULE` is a PostgreSQL language extension, as is the entire query rewrite system.

See Also

CREATE RULE, DROP RULE

ALTER SCHEMA

ALTER SCHEMA — change the definition of a schema

Synopsis

```
ALTER SCHEMA name RENAME TO new_name
ALTER SCHEMA name OWNER TO { new_owner | CURRENT_USER | SESSION_USER }
```

Description

ALTER SCHEMA changes the definition of a schema.

You must own the schema to use ALTER SCHEMA. To rename a schema you must also have the CREATE privilege for the database. To alter the owner, you must also be a direct or indirect member of the new owning role, and you must have the CREATE privilege for the database. (Note that superusers have all these privileges automatically.)

Parameters

name

> The name of an existing schema.

new_name

> The new name of the schema. The new name cannot begin with pg_, as such names are reserved for system schemas.

new_owner

> The new owner of the schema.

Compatibility

There is no ALTER SCHEMA statement in the SQL standard.

See Also

CREATE SCHEMA, DROP SCHEMA

ALTER SEQUENCE

ALTER SEQUENCE — change the definition of a sequence generator

Synopsis

```
ALTER SEQUENCE [ IF EXISTS ] name
    [ AS data_type ]
    [ INCREMENT [ BY ] increment ]
    [ MINVALUE minvalue | NO MINVALUE ] [ MAXVALUE maxvalue | NO
MAXVALUE ]
    [ START [ WITH ] start ]
    [ RESTART [ [ WITH ] restart ] ]
    [ CACHE cache ] [ [ NO ] CYCLE ]
    [ OWNED BY { table_name.column_name | NONE } ]
ALTER SEQUENCE [ IF EXISTS ] name OWNER TO { new_owner | CURRENT_USER
| SESSION_USER }
ALTER SEQUENCE [ IF EXISTS ] name RENAME TO new_name
ALTER SEQUENCE [ IF EXISTS ] name SET SCHEMA new_schema
```

Description

ALTER SEQUENCE changes the parameters of an existing sequence generator. Any parameters not specifically set in the ALTER SEQUENCE command retain their prior settings.

You must own the sequence to use ALTER SEQUENCE. To change a sequence's schema, you must also have CREATE privilege on the new schema. To alter the owner, you must also be a direct or indirect member of the new owning role, and that role must have CREATE privilege on the sequence's schema. (These restrictions enforce that altering the owner doesn't do anything you couldn't do by dropping and recreating the sequence. However, a superuser can alter ownership of any sequence anyway.)

Parameters

name

The name (optionally schema-qualified) of a sequence to be altered.

IF EXISTS

Do not throw an error if the sequence does not exist. A notice is issued in this case.

data_type

The optional clause AS data_type changes the data type of the sequence. Valid types are smallint, integer, and bigint.

Changing the data type automatically changes the minimum and maximum values of the sequence if and only if the previous minimum and maximum values were the minimum or maximum value of the old data type (in other words, if the sequence had been created using NO MINVALUE or NO MAXVALUE, implicitly or explicitly). Otherwise, the minimum and maximum values are preserved, unless new values are given as part of the same command. If the minimum and maximum values do not fit into the new data type, an error will be generated.

increment

The clause INCREMENT BY *increment* is optional. A positive value will make an ascending sequence, a negative one a descending sequence. If unspecified, the old increment value will be maintained.

minvalue
NO MINVALUE

The optional clause MINVALUE *minvalue* determines the minimum value a sequence can generate. If NO MINVALUE is specified, the defaults of 1 and the minimum value of the data type for ascending and descending sequences, respectively, will be used. If neither option is specified, the current minimum value will be maintained.

maxvalue
NO MAXVALUE

The optional clause MAXVALUE *maxvalue* determines the maximum value for the sequence. If NO MAXVALUE is specified, the defaults of the maximum value of the data type and -1 for ascending and descending sequences, respectively, will be used. If neither option is specified, the current maximum value will be maintained.

start

The optional clause START WITH *start* changes the recorded start value of the sequence. This has no effect on the *current* sequence value; it simply sets the value that future ALTER SEQUENCE RESTART commands will use.

restart

The optional clause RESTART [WITH *restart*] changes the current value of the sequence. This is similar to calling the setval function with is_called = false: the specified value will be returned by the *next* call of nextval. Writing RESTART with no *restart* value is equivalent to supplying the start value that was recorded by CREATE SEQUENCE or last set by ALTER SEQUENCE START WITH.

In contrast to a setval call, a RESTART operation on a sequence is transactional and blocks concurrent transactions from obtaining numbers from the same sequence. If that's not the desired mode of operation, setval should be used.

cache

The clause CACHE *cache* enables sequence numbers to be preallocated and stored in memory for faster access. The minimum value is 1 (only one value can be generated at a time, i.e., no cache). If unspecified, the old cache value will be maintained.

CYCLE

The optional CYCLE key word can be used to enable the sequence to wrap around when the *maxvalue* or *minvalue* has been reached by an ascending or descending sequence respectively. If the limit is reached, the next number generated will be the *minvalue* or *maxvalue*, respectively.

NO CYCLE

If the optional NO CYCLE key word is specified, any calls to nextval after the sequence has reached its maximum value will return an error. If neither CYCLE or NO CYCLE are specified, the old cycle behavior will be maintained.

OWNED BY *table_name.column_name*
OWNED BY NONE

> The OWNED BY option causes the sequence to be associated with a specific table column, such that if that column (or its whole table) is dropped, the sequence will be automatically dropped as well. If specified, this association replaces any previously specified association for the sequence. The specified table must have the same owner and be in the same schema as the sequence. Specifying OWNED BY NONE removes any existing association, making the sequence "free-standing".

new_owner

> The user name of the new owner of the sequence.

new_name

> The new name for the sequence.

new_schema

> The new schema for the sequence.

Notes

ALTER SEQUENCE will not immediately affect nextval results in backends, other than the current one, that have preallocated (cached) sequence values. They will use up all cached values prior to noticing the changed sequence generation parameters. The current backend will be affected immediately.

ALTER SEQUENCE does not affect the currval status for the sequence. (Before PostgreSQL 8.3, it sometimes did.)

ALTER SEQUENCE blocks concurrent nextval, currval, lastval, and setval calls.

For historical reasons, ALTER TABLE can be used with sequences too; but the only variants of ALTER TABLE that are allowed with sequences are equivalent to the forms shown above.

Examples

Restart a sequence called serial, at 105:

ALTER SEQUENCE serial RESTART WITH 105;

Compatibility

ALTER SEQUENCE conforms to the SQL standard, except for the AS, START WITH, OWNED BY, OWNER TO, RENAME TO, and SET SCHEMA clauses, which are PostgreSQL extensions.

See Also
CREATE SEQUENCE, DROP SEQUENCE

ALTER SERVER

ALTER SERVER — change the definition of a foreign server

Synopsis

```
ALTER SERVER name [ VERSION 'new_version' ]
    [ OPTIONS ( [ ADD | SET | DROP ] option ['value'] [, ... ] ) ]
ALTER SERVER name OWNER TO { new_owner | CURRENT_USER | SESSION_USER }
ALTER SERVER name RENAME TO new_name
```

Description

ALTER SERVER changes the definition of a foreign server. The first form changes the server version string or the generic options of the server (at least one clause is required). The second form changes the owner of the server.

To alter the server you must be the owner of the server. Additionally to alter the owner, you must own the server and also be a direct or indirect member of the new owning role, and you must have USAGE privilege on the server's foreign-data wrapper. (Note that superusers satisfy all these criteria automatically.)

Parameters

name

The name of an existing server.

new_version

New server version.

OPTIONS ([ADD | SET | DROP] option ['value'] [, ...])

Change options for the server. ADD, SET, and DROP specify the action to be performed. ADD is assumed if no operation is explicitly specified. Option names must be unique; names and values are also validated using the server's foreign-data wrapper library.

new_owner

The user name of the new owner of the foreign server.

new_name

The new name for the foreign server.

Examples

Alter server foo, add connection options:

```
ALTER SERVER foo OPTIONS (host 'foo', dbname 'foodb');
```

Alter server `foo`, change version, change `host` option:

```
ALTER SERVER foo VERSION '8.4' OPTIONS (SET host 'baz');
```

Compatibility

`ALTER  SERVER` conforms to ISO/IEC 9075-9 (SQL/MED). The `OWNER  TO` and `RENAME` forms are PostgreSQL extensions.

See Also

CREATE SERVER, DROP SERVER

ALTER STATISTICS

ALTER STATISTICS — change the definition of an extended statistics object

Synopsis

```
ALTER STATISTICS name OWNER TO { new_owner | CURRENT_USER |
 SESSION_USER }
ALTER STATISTICS name RENAME TO new_name
ALTER STATISTICS name SET SCHEMA new_schema
```

Description

ALTER STATISTICS changes the parameters of an existing extended statistics object. Any parameters not specifically set in the ALTER STATISTICS command retain their prior settings.

You must own the statistics object to use ALTER STATISTICS. To change a statistics object's schema, you must also have CREATE privilege on the new schema. To alter the owner, you must also be a direct or indirect member of the new owning role, and that role must have CREATE privilege on the statistics object's schema. (These restrictions enforce that altering the owner doesn't do anything you couldn't do by dropping and recreating the statistics object. However, a superuser can alter ownership of any statistics object anyway.)

Parameters

name

The name (optionally schema-qualified) of the statistics object to be altered.

new_owner

The user name of the new owner of the statistics object.

new_name

The new name for the statistics object.

new_schema

The new schema for the statistics object.

Compatibility

There is no ALTER STATISTICS command in the SQL standard.

See Also

CREATE STATISTICS, DROP STATISTICS

ALTER SUBSCRIPTION

ALTER SUBSCRIPTION — change the definition of a subscription

Synopsis

```
ALTER SUBSCRIPTION name CONNECTION 'conninfo'
ALTER SUBSCRIPTION name SET PUBLICATION publication_name [, ...]
[ WITH ( set_publication_option [= value] [, ... ] ) ]
ALTER SUBSCRIPTION name REFRESH PUBLICATION [ WITH ( refresh_option
[= value] [, ... ] ) ]
ALTER SUBSCRIPTION name ENABLE
ALTER SUBSCRIPTION name DISABLE
ALTER SUBSCRIPTION name SET ( subscription_parameter [= value]
[, ... ] )
ALTER SUBSCRIPTION name OWNER TO { new_owner | CURRENT_USER |
SESSION_USER }
ALTER SUBSCRIPTION name RENAME TO new_name
```

Description

ALTER SUBSCRIPTION can change most of the subscription properties that can be specified in CREATE SUBSCRIPTION.

You must own the subscription to use ALTER SUBSCRIPTION. To alter the owner, you must also be a direct or indirect member of the new owning role. The new owner has to be a superuser. (Currently, all subscription owners must be superusers, so the owner checks will be bypassed in practice. But this might change in the future.)

Parameters

name

The name of a subscription whose properties are to be altered.

CONNECTION 'conninfo'

This clause alters the connection property originally set by CREATE SUBSCRIPTION. See there for more information.

SET PUBLICATION *publication_name*

Changes list of subscribed publications. See CREATE SUBSCRIPTION for more information. By default this command will also act like REFRESH PUBLICATION.

set_publication_option specifies additional options for this operation. The supported options are:

refresh (boolean)

When false, the command will not try to refresh table information. REFRESH PUBLICATION should then be executed separately. The default is true.

Additionally, refresh options as described under REFRESH PUBLICATION may be specified.

REFRESH PUBLICATION

Fetch missing table information from publisher. This will start replication of tables that were added to the subscribed-to publications since the last invocation of REFRESH PUBLICATION or since CREATE SUBSCRIPTION.

refresh_option specifies additional options for the refresh operation. The supported options are:

copy_data (boolean)

Specifies whether the existing data in the publications that are being subscribed to should be copied once the replication starts. The default is true.

ENABLE

Enables the previously disabled subscription, starting the logical replication worker at the end of transaction.

DISABLE

Disables the running subscription, stopping the logical replication worker at the end of transaction.

SET (*subscription_parameter* [= *value*] [, ...])

This clause alters parameters originally set by CREATE SUBSCRIPTION. See there for more information. The allowed options are slot_name and synchronous_commit

new_owner

The user name of the new owner of the subscription.

new_name

The new name for the subscription.

Examples

Change the publication subscribed by a subscription to insert_only:

```
ALTER SUBSCRIPTION mysub SET PUBLICATION insert_only;
```

Disable (stop) the subscription:

```
ALTER SUBSCRIPTION mysub DISABLE;
```

Compatibility

ALTER SUBSCRIPTION is a PostgreSQL extension.

See Also

CREATE SUBSCRIPTION, DROP SUBSCRIPTION, CREATE PUBLICATION, ALTER PUBLICATION

ALTER SYSTEM

ALTER SYSTEM — change a server configuration parameter

Synopsis

```
ALTER SYSTEM SET configuration_parameter { TO | = } { value | 'value'
 | DEFAULT }

ALTER SYSTEM RESET configuration_parameter
ALTER SYSTEM RESET ALL
```

Description

`ALTER SYSTEM` is used for changing server configuration parameters across the entire database cluster. It can be more convenient than the traditional method of manually editing the `postgresql.conf` file. `ALTER SYSTEM` writes the given parameter setting to the `postgresql.auto.conf` file, which is read in addition to `postgresql.conf`. Setting a parameter to `DEFAULT`, or using the `RESET` variant, removes that configuration entry from the `postgresql.auto.conf` file. Use `RESET ALL` to remove all such configuration entries.

Values set with `ALTER SYSTEM` will be effective after the next server configuration reload, or after the next server restart in the case of parameters that can only be changed at server start. A server configuration reload can be commanded by calling the SQL function `pg_reload_conf()`, running `pg_ctl reload`, or sending a SIGHUP signal to the main server process.

Only superusers can use `ALTER SYSTEM`. Also, since this command acts directly on the file system and cannot be rolled back, it is not allowed inside a transaction block or function.

Parameters

configuration_parameter

Name of a settable configuration parameter. Available parameters are documented in Chapter 19.

value

New value of the parameter. Values can be specified as string constants, identifiers, numbers, or comma-separated lists of these, as appropriate for the particular parameter. `DEFAULT` can be written to specify removing the parameter and its value from `postgresql.auto.conf`.

Notes

This command can't be used to set data_directory, nor parameters that are not allowed in `postgresql.conf` (e.g., preset options).

See Section 19.1 for other ways to set the parameters.

Examples

Set the `wal_level`:

```
ALTER SYSTEM SET wal_level = replica;
```

Undo that, restoring whatever setting was effective in `postgresql.conf`:

```
ALTER SYSTEM RESET wal_level;
```

Compatibility

The `ALTER SYSTEM` statement is a PostgreSQL extension.

See Also

SET, SHOW

ALTER TABLE

ALTER TABLE — change the definition of a table

Synopsis

```
ALTER TABLE [ IF EXISTS ] [ ONLY ] name [ * ]
    action [, ... ]
ALTER TABLE [ IF EXISTS ] [ ONLY ] name [ * ]
    RENAME [ COLUMN ] column_name TO new_column_name
ALTER TABLE [ IF EXISTS ] [ ONLY ] name [ * ]
    RENAME CONSTRAINT constraint_name TO new_constraint_name
ALTER TABLE [ IF EXISTS ] name
    RENAME TO new_name
ALTER TABLE [ IF EXISTS ] name
    SET SCHEMA new_schema
ALTER TABLE ALL IN TABLESPACE name [ OWNED BY role_name [, ... ] ]
    SET TABLESPACE new_tablespace [ NOWAIT ]
ALTER TABLE [ IF EXISTS ] name
    ATTACH PARTITION partition_name { FOR VALUES partition_bound_spec
 | DEFAULT }
ALTER TABLE [ IF EXISTS ] name
    DETACH PARTITION partition_name

where action is one of:

    ADD [ COLUMN ] [ IF NOT EXISTS ] column_name data_type
 [ COLLATE collation ] [ column_constraint [ ... ] ]
    DROP [ COLUMN ] [ IF EXISTS ] column_name [ RESTRICT | CASCADE ]
    ALTER [ COLUMN ] column_name [ SET DATA ] TYPE data_type
 [ COLLATE collation ] [ USING expression ]
    ALTER [ COLUMN ] column_name SET DEFAULT expression
    ALTER [ COLUMN ] column_name DROP DEFAULT
    ALTER [ COLUMN ] column_name { SET | DROP } NOT NULL
    ALTER [ COLUMN ] column_name ADD GENERATED { ALWAYS | BY DEFAULT }
 AS IDENTITY [ ( sequence_options ) ]
    ALTER [ COLUMN ] column_name { SET GENERATED { ALWAYS | BY
 DEFAULT } | SET sequence_option | RESTART [ [ WITH ] restart ] }
 [...]
    ALTER [ COLUMN ] column_name DROP IDENTITY [ IF EXISTS ]
    ALTER [ COLUMN ] column_name SET STATISTICS integer
    ALTER [ COLUMN ] column_name SET ( attribute_option = value
 [, ... ] )
    ALTER [ COLUMN ] column_name RESET ( attribute_option [, ... ] )
    ALTER [ COLUMN ] column_name SET STORAGE { PLAIN | EXTERNAL |
 EXTENDED | MAIN }
    ADD table_constraint [ NOT VALID ]
    ADD table_constraint_using_index
    ALTER CONSTRAINT constraint_name [ DEFERRABLE | NOT DEFERRABLE ]
 [ INITIALLY DEFERRED | INITIALLY IMMEDIATE ]
```

```
    VALIDATE CONSTRAINT constraint_name
    DROP CONSTRAINT [ IF EXISTS ] constraint_name [ RESTRICT |
CASCADE ]
    DISABLE TRIGGER [ trigger_name | ALL | USER ]
    ENABLE TRIGGER [ trigger_name | ALL | USER ]
    ENABLE REPLICA TRIGGER trigger_name
    ENABLE ALWAYS TRIGGER trigger_name
    DISABLE RULE rewrite_rule_name
    ENABLE RULE rewrite_rule_name
    ENABLE REPLICA RULE rewrite_rule_name
    ENABLE ALWAYS RULE rewrite_rule_name
    DISABLE ROW LEVEL SECURITY
    ENABLE ROW LEVEL SECURITY
    FORCE ROW LEVEL SECURITY
    NO FORCE ROW LEVEL SECURITY
    CLUSTER ON index_name
    SET WITHOUT CLUSTER
    SET WITH OIDS
    SET WITHOUT OIDS
    SET TABLESPACE new_tablespace
    SET { LOGGED | UNLOGGED }
    SET ( storage_parameter = value [, ... ] )
    RESET ( storage_parameter [, ... ] )
    INHERIT parent_table
    NO INHERIT parent_table
    OF type_name
    NOT OF
    OWNER TO { new_owner | CURRENT_USER | SESSION_USER }
    REPLICA IDENTITY { DEFAULT | USING INDEX index_name | FULL |
 NOTHING }
```

and *partition_bound_spec* is:

```
IN ( { numeric_literal | string_literal | TRUE | FALSE | NULL }
 [, ...] ) |
FROM ( { numeric_literal | string_literal | TRUE | FALSE | MINVALUE |
 MAXVALUE } [, ...] )
  TO ( { numeric_literal | string_literal | TRUE | FALSE | MINVALUE |
 MAXVALUE } [, ...] ) |
WITH ( MODULUS numeric_literal, REMAINDER numeric_literal )
```

and *column_constraint* is:

```
[ CONSTRAINT constraint_name ]
{ NOT NULL |
  NULL |
  CHECK ( expression ) [ NO INHERIT ] |
  DEFAULT default_expr |
  GENERATED { ALWAYS | BY DEFAULT } AS IDENTITY [ ( sequence_options
  ) ] |
  UNIQUE index_parameters |
  PRIMARY KEY index_parameters |
  REFERENCES reftable [ ( refcolumn ) ] [ MATCH FULL | MATCH PARTIAL |
 MATCH SIMPLE ]
```

```
          [ ON DELETE action ] [ ON UPDATE action ] }
      [ DEFERRABLE | NOT DEFERRABLE ] [ INITIALLY DEFERRED | INITIALLY
      IMMEDIATE ]
```

and *table_constraint* is:

```
  [ CONSTRAINT constraint_name ]
  { CHECK ( expression ) [ NO INHERIT ] |
    UNIQUE ( column_name [, ... ] ) index_parameters |
    PRIMARY KEY ( column_name [, ... ] ) index_parameters |
    EXCLUDE [ USING index_method ] ( exclude_element WITH operator
  [, ... ] ) index_parameters [ WHERE ( predicate ) ] |
    FOREIGN KEY ( column_name [, ... ] ) REFERENCES reftable
  [ ( refcolumn [, ... ] ) ]
      [ MATCH FULL | MATCH PARTIAL | MATCH SIMPLE ] [ ON DELETE action ]
  [ ON UPDATE action ] }
  [ DEFERRABLE | NOT DEFERRABLE ] [ INITIALLY DEFERRED | INITIALLY
  IMMEDIATE ]
```

and *table_constraint_using_index* is:

```
      [ CONSTRAINT constraint_name ]
      { UNIQUE | PRIMARY KEY } USING INDEX index_name
      [ DEFERRABLE | NOT DEFERRABLE ] [ INITIALLY DEFERRED | INITIALLY
  IMMEDIATE ]
```

index_parameters in UNIQUE, PRIMARY KEY, and EXCLUDE constraints are:

```
  [ INCLUDE ( column_name [, ... ] ) ]
  [ WITH ( storage_parameter [= value] [, ... ] ) ]
  [ USING INDEX TABLESPACE tablespace_name ]
```

exclude_element in an EXCLUDE constraint is:

```
  { column_name | ( expression ) } [ opclass ] [ ASC | DESC ] [ NULLS
  { FIRST | LAST } ]
```

Description

ALTER TABLE changes the definition of an existing table. There are several subforms described below. Note that the lock level required may differ for each subform. An ACCESS EXCLUSIVE lock is held unless explicitly noted. When multiple subcommands are listed, the lock held will be the strictest one required from any subcommand.

ADD COLUMN [IF NOT EXISTS]

This form adds a new column to the table, using the same syntax as CREATE TABLE. If IF NOT EXISTS is specified and a column already exists with this name, no error is thrown.

DROP COLUMN [IF EXISTS]

This form drops a column from a table. Indexes and table constraints involving the column will be automatically dropped as well. Multivariate statistics referencing the dropped column will also be removed if the removal of the column would cause the statistics to contain data for only a single column. You will need to say CASCADE if anything outside the table depends on the column, for example, foreign key references or views. If `IF EXISTS` is specified and the column does not exist, no error is thrown. In this case a notice is issued instead.

`SET DATA TYPE`

This form changes the type of a column of a table. Indexes and simple table constraints involving the column will be automatically converted to use the new column type by reparsing the originally supplied expression. The optional `COLLATE` clause specifies a collation for the new column; if omitted, the collation is the default for the new column type. The optional `USING` clause specifies how to compute the new column value from the old; if omitted, the default conversion is the same as an assignment cast from old data type to new. A `USING` clause must be provided if there is no implicit or assignment cast from old to new type.

`SET/DROP DEFAULT`

These forms set or remove the default value for a column. Default values only apply in subsequent `INSERT` or `UPDATE` commands; they do not cause rows already in the table to change.

`SET/DROP NOT NULL`

These forms change whether a column is marked to allow null values or to reject null values. You can only use `SET NOT NULL` when the column contains no null values.

If this table is a partition, one cannot perform `DROP NOT NULL` on a column if it is marked `NOT NULL` in the parent table. To drop the `NOT NULL` constraint from all the partitions, perform `DROP NOT NULL` on the parent table. Even if there is no `NOT NULL` constraint on the parent, such a constraint can still be added to individual partitions, if desired; that is, the children can disallow nulls even if the parent allows them, but not the other way around.

```
ADD GENERATED { ALWAYS | BY DEFAULT } AS IDENTITY
SET GENERATED { ALWAYS | BY DEFAULT }
DROP IDENTITY [ IF EXISTS ]
```

These forms change whether a column is an identity column or change the generation attribute of an existing identity column. See CREATE TABLE for details.

If `DROP IDENTITY IF EXISTS` is specified and the column is not an identity column, no error is thrown. In this case a notice is issued instead.

`SET` *sequence_option*
`RESTART`

These forms alter the sequence that underlies an existing identity column. *sequence_option* is an option supported by ALTER SEQUENCE such as `INCREMENT BY`.

`SET STATISTICS`

This form sets the per-column statistics-gathering target for subsequent ANALYZE operations. The target can be set in the range 0 to 10000; alternatively, set it to -1 to revert to using the system default statistics target (default_statistics_target). For more information on the use of statistics by the PostgreSQL query planner, refer to Section 14.2.

`SET STATISTICS` acquires a `SHARE UPDATE EXCLUSIVE` lock.

```
SET ( attribute_option = value [, ... ] )
RESET ( attribute_option [, ... ] )
```

This form sets or resets per-attribute options. Currently, the only defined per-attribute options are `n_distinct` and `n_distinct_inherited`, which override the number-of-distinct-values estimates made by subsequent ANALYZE operations. `n_distinct` affects the statistics for the table itself, while `n_distinct_inherited` affects the statistics gathered for the table plus its inheritance children. When set to a positive value, `ANALYZE` will assume that the column contains exactly the specified number of distinct nonnull values. When set to a negative value, which must be greater than or equal to -1, `ANALYZE` will assume that the number of distinct nonnull values in the column is linear in the size of the table; the exact count is to be computed by multiplying the estimated table size by the absolute value of the given number. For example, a value of -1 implies that all values in the column are distinct, while a value of -0.5 implies that each value appears twice on the average. This can be useful when the size of the table changes over time, since the multiplication by the number of rows in the table is not performed until query planning time. Specify a value of 0 to revert to estimating the number of distinct values normally. For more information on the use of statistics by the PostgreSQL query planner, refer to Section 14.2.

Changing per-attribute options acquires a `SHARE UPDATE EXCLUSIVE` lock.

SET STORAGE

This form sets the storage mode for a column. This controls whether this column is held inline or in a secondary TOAST table, and whether the data should be compressed or not. `PLAIN` must be used for fixed-length values such as `integer` and is inline, uncompressed. `MAIN` is for inline, compressible data. `EXTERNAL` is for external, uncompressed data, and `EXTENDED` is for external, compressed data. `EXTENDED` is the default for most data types that support non-`PLAIN` storage. Use of `EXTERNAL` will make substring operations on very large `text` and `bytea` values run faster, at the penalty of increased storage space. Note that `SET STORAGE` doesn't itself change anything in the table, it just sets the strategy to be pursued during future table updates. See Section 68.2 for more information.

ADD *table_constraint* [NOT VALID]

This form adds a new constraint to a table using the same syntax as CREATE TABLE, plus the option `NOT VALID`, which is currently only allowed for foreign key and CHECK constraints. If the constraint is marked `NOT VALID`, the potentially-lengthy initial check to verify that all rows in the table satisfy the constraint is skipped. The constraint will still be enforced against subsequent inserts or updates (that is, they'll fail unless there is a matching row in the referenced table, in the case of foreign keys; and they'll fail unless the new row matches the specified check constraints). But the database will not assume that the constraint holds for all rows in the table, until it is validated by using the `VALIDATE CONSTRAINT` option. Foreign key constraints on partitioned tables may not be declared `NOT VALID` at present.

The addition of a foreign key constraint requires a `SHARE ROW EXCLUSIVE` lock on the referenced table.

Additional restrictions apply when unique or primary key constraints are added to partitioned tables; see CREATE TABLE.

ADD *table_constraint_using_index*

This form adds a new `PRIMARY KEY` or `UNIQUE` constraint to a table based on an existing unique index. All the columns of the index will be included in the constraint.

The index cannot have expression columns nor be a partial index. Also, it must be a b-tree index with default sort ordering. These restrictions ensure that the index is equivalent to one that would be built by a regular `ADD PRIMARY KEY` or `ADD UNIQUE` command.

If `PRIMARY KEY` is specified, and the index's columns are not already marked `NOT NULL`, then this command will attempt to do `ALTER COLUMN SET NOT NULL` against each such column. That requires a full table scan to verify the column(s) contain no nulls. In all other cases, this is a fast operation.

If a constraint name is provided then the index will be renamed to match the constraint name. Otherwise the constraint will be named the same as the index.

After this command is executed, the index is "owned" by the constraint, in the same way as if the index had been built by a regular ADD PRIMARY KEY or ADD UNIQUE command. In particular, dropping the constraint will make the index disappear too.

This form is not currently supported on partitioned tables.

> # Note
>
> Adding a constraint using an existing index can be helpful in situations where a new constraint needs to be added without blocking table updates for a long time. To do that, create the index using CREATE INDEX CONCURRENTLY, and then install it as an official constraint using this syntax. See the example below.

ALTER CONSTRAINT

This form alters the attributes of a constraint that was previously created. Currently only foreign key constraints may be altered.

VALIDATE CONSTRAINT

This form validates a foreign key or check constraint that was previously created as NOT VALID, by scanning the table to ensure there are no rows for which the constraint is not satisfied. Nothing happens if the constraint is already marked valid.

Validation can be a long process on larger tables. The value of separating validation from initial creation is that you can defer validation to less busy times, or can be used to give additional time to correct pre-existing errors while preventing new errors. Note also that validation on its own does not prevent normal write commands against the table while it runs.

Validation acquires only a SHARE UPDATE EXCLUSIVE lock on the table being altered. If the constraint is a foreign key then a ROW SHARE lock is also required on the table referenced by the constraint.

DROP CONSTRAINT [IF EXISTS]

This form drops the specified constraint on a table, along with any index underlying the constraint. If IF EXISTS is specified and the constraint does not exist, no error is thrown. In this case a notice is issued instead.

DISABLE/ENABLE [REPLICA | ALWAYS] TRIGGER

These forms configure the firing of trigger(s) belonging to the table. A disabled trigger is still known to the system, but is not executed when its triggering event occurs. For a deferred trigger, the enable status is checked when the event occurs, not when the trigger function is actually executed. One can disable or enable a single trigger specified by name, or all triggers on the table, or only user triggers (this option excludes internally generated constraint triggers such as those that are used to implement foreign key constraints or deferrable uniqueness and exclusion constraints). Disabling or enabling internally generated constraint triggers requires superuser privileges; it should be done with caution since of course the integrity of the constraint cannot be guaranteed if the triggers are not executed.

The trigger firing mechanism is also affected by the configuration variable session_replication_role. Simply enabled triggers (the default) will fire when the replication role is "origin" (the default) or "local". Triggers configured as `ENABLE REPLICA` will only fire if the session is in "replica" mode, and triggers configured as `ENABLE ALWAYS` will fire regardless of the current replication role.

The effect of this mechanism is that in the default configuration, triggers do not fire on replicas. This is useful because if a trigger is used on the origin to propagate data between tables, then the replication system will also replicate the propagated data, and the trigger should not fire a second time on the replica, because that would lead to duplication. However, if a trigger is used for another purpose such as creating external alerts, then it might be appropriate to set it to `ENABLE ALWAYS` so that it is also fired on replicas.

This command acquires a `SHARE ROW EXCLUSIVE` lock.

DISABLE/ENABLE [REPLICA | ALWAYS] RULE

These forms configure the firing of rewrite rules belonging to the table. A disabled rule is still known to the system, but is not applied during query rewriting. The semantics are as for disabled/enabled triggers. This configuration is ignored for `ON SELECT` rules, which are always applied in order to keep views working even if the current session is in a non-default replication role.

The rule firing mechanism is also affected by the configuration variable session_replication_role, analogous to triggers as described above.

DISABLE/ENABLE ROW LEVEL SECURITY

These forms control the application of row security policies belonging to the table. If enabled and no policies exist for the table, then a default-deny policy is applied. Note that policies can exist for a table even if row level security is disabled - in this case, the policies will NOT be applied and the policies will be ignored. See also CREATE POLICY.

NO FORCE/FORCE ROW LEVEL SECURITY

These forms control the application of row security policies belonging to the table when the user is the table owner. If enabled, row level security policies will be applied when the user is the table owner. If disabled (the default) then row level security will not be applied when the user is the table owner. See also CREATE POLICY.

CLUSTER ON

This form selects the default index for future CLUSTER operations. It does not actually re-cluster the table.

Changing cluster options acquires a `SHARE UPDATE EXCLUSIVE` lock.

SET WITHOUT CLUSTER

This form removes the most recently used CLUSTER index specification from the table. This affects future cluster operations that don't specify an index.

Changing cluster options acquires a `SHARE UPDATE EXCLUSIVE` lock.

SET WITH OIDS

This form adds an `oid` system column to the table (see Section 5.4). It does nothing if the table already has OIDs.

Note that this is not equivalent to `ADD COLUMN oid oid`; that would add a normal column that happened to be named `oid`, not a system column.

SET WITHOUT OIDS

This form removes the oid system column from the table. This is exactly equivalent to DROP COL-UMN oid RESTRICT, except that it will not complain if there is already no oid column.

SET TABLESPACE

This form changes the table's tablespace to the specified tablespace and moves the data file(s) associated with the table to the new tablespace. Indexes on the table, if any, are not moved; but they can be moved separately with additional SET TABLESPACE commands. All tables in the current database in a tablespace can be moved by using the ALL IN TABLESPACE form, which will lock all tables to be moved first and then move each one. This form also supports OWNED BY, which will only move tables owned by the roles specified. If the NOWAIT option is specified then the command will fail if it is unable to acquire all of the locks required immediately. Note that system catalogs are not moved by this command, use ALTER DATABASE or explicit ALTER TABLE invocations instead if desired. The information_schema relations are not considered part of the system catalogs and will be moved. See also CREATE TABLESPACE.

SET { LOGGED | UNLOGGED }

This form changes the table from unlogged to logged or vice-versa (see UNLOGGED). It cannot be applied to a temporary table.

SET (storage_parameter = value [, ...])

This form changes one or more storage parameters for the table. See Storage Parameters for details on the available parameters. Note that the table contents will not be modified immediately by this command; depending on the parameter you might need to rewrite the table to get the desired effects. That can be done with VACUUM FULL, CLUSTER or one of the forms of ALTER TABLE that forces a table rewrite. For planner related parameters, changes will take effect from the next time the table is locked so currently executing queries will not be affected.

SHARE UPDATE EXCLUSIVE lock will be taken for fillfactor, toast and autovacuum storage parameters, as well as the following planner related parameters: effective_io_concurrency, parallel_workers, seq_page_cost, random_page_cost, n_distinct and n_distinct_inherited.

Note

While CREATE TABLE allows OIDS to be specified in the WITH (storage_parameter) syntax, ALTER TABLE does not treat OIDS as a storage parameter. Instead use the SET WITH OIDS and SET WITHOUT OIDS forms to change OID status.

RESET (storage_parameter [, ...])

This form resets one or more storage parameters to their defaults. As with SET, a table rewrite might be needed to update the table entirely.

INHERIT parent_table

This form adds the target table as a new child of the specified parent table. Subsequently, queries against the parent will include records of the target table. To be added as a child, the target table must already contain all the same columns as the parent (it could have additional columns, too). The columns must have matching data types, and if they have NOT NULL constraints in the parent then they must also have NOT NULL constraints in the child.

There must also be matching child-table constraints for all CHECK constraints of the parent, except those marked non-inheritable (that is, created with ALTER TABLE ... ADD CONSTRAINT ... NO INHERIT) in the parent, which are ignored; all child-table constraints matched must not be marked non-inheritable. Currently UNIQUE, PRIMARY KEY, and FOREIGN KEY constraints are not considered, but this might change in the future.

NO INHERIT *parent_table*

This form removes the target table from the list of children of the specified parent table. Queries against the parent table will no longer include records drawn from the target table.

OF *type_name*

This form links the table to a composite type as though CREATE TABLE OF had formed it. The table's list of column names and types must precisely match that of the composite type; the presence of an oid system column is permitted to differ. The table must not inherit from any other table. These restrictions ensure that CREATE TABLE OF would permit an equivalent table definition.

NOT OF

This form dissociates a typed table from its type.

OWNER TO

This form changes the owner of the table, sequence, view, materialized view, or foreign table to the specified user.

REPLICA IDENTITY

This form changes the information which is written to the write-ahead log to identify rows which are updated or deleted. This option has no effect except when logical replication is in use. DEFAULT (the default for non-system tables) records the old values of the columns of the primary key, if any. USING INDEX records the old values of the columns covered by the named index, which must be unique, not partial, not deferrable, and include only columns marked NOT NULL. FULL records the old values of all columns in the row. NOTHING records no information about the old row. (This is the default for system tables.) In all cases, no old values are logged unless at least one of the columns that would be logged differs between the old and new versions of the row.

RENAME

The RENAME forms change the name of a table (or an index, sequence, view, materialized view, or foreign table), the name of an individual column in a table, or the name of a constraint of the table. When renaming a constraint that has an underlying index, the index is renamed as well. There is no effect on the stored data.

SET SCHEMA

This form moves the table into another schema. Associated indexes, constraints, and sequences owned by table columns are moved as well.

ATTACH PARTITION *partition_name* { FOR VALUES *partition_bound_spec* | DEFAULT }

This form attaches an existing table (which might itself be partitioned) as a partition of the target table. The table can be attached as a partition for specific values using FOR VALUES or as a default partition by using DEFAULT. For each index in the target table, a corresponding one will be created in the attached table; or, if an equivalent index already exists, will be attached to the target table's index, as if ALTER INDEX ATTACH PARTITION had been executed.

A partition using `FOR VALUES` uses same syntax for *partition_bound_spec* as CREATE TABLE. The partition bound specification must correspond to the partitioning strategy and partition key of the target table. The table to be attached must have all the same columns as the target table and no more; moreover, the column types must also match. Also, it must have all the `NOT NULL` and `CHECK` constraints of the target table. Currently `FOREIGN KEY` constraints are not considered. `UNIQUE` and `PRIMARY KEY` constraints from the parent table will be created in the partition, if they don't already exist. If any of the `CHECK` constraints of the table being attached is marked `NO INHERIT`, the command will fail; such a constraint must be recreated without the `NO INHERIT` clause.

If the new partition is a regular table, a full table scan is performed to check that no existing row in the table violates the partition constraint. It is possible to avoid this scan by adding a valid `CHECK` constraint to the table that would allow only the rows satisfying the desired partition constraint before running this command. It will be determined using such a constraint that the table need not be scanned to validate the partition constraint. This does not work, however, if any of the partition keys is an expression and the partition does not accept `NULL` values. If attaching a list partition that will not accept `NULL` values, also add `NOT NULL` constraint to the partition key column, unless it's an expression.

If the new partition is a foreign table, nothing is done to verify that all the rows in the foreign table obey the partition constraint. (See the discussion in CREATE FOREIGN TABLE about constraints on the foreign table.)

When a table has a default partition, defining a new partition changes the partition constraint for the default partition. The default partition can't contain any rows that would need to be moved to the new partition, and will be scanned to verify that none are present. This scan, like the scan of the new partition, can be avoided if an appropriate `CHECK` constraint is present. Also like the scan of the new partition, it is always skipped when the default partition is a foreign table.

`DETACH PARTITION` *partition_name*

> This form detaches specified partition of the target table. The detached partition continues to exist as a standalone table, but no longer has any ties to the table from which it was detached. Any indexes that were attached to the target table's indexes are detached.

All the forms of ALTER TABLE that act on a single table, except `RENAME`, `SET SCHEMA`, `ATTACH PARTITION`, and `DETACH PARTITION` can be combined into a list of multiple alterations to be applied together. For example, it is possible to add several columns and/or alter the type of several columns in a single command. This is particularly useful with large tables, since only one pass over the table need be made.

You must own the table to use `ALTER TABLE`. To change the schema or tablespace of a table, you must also have `CREATE` privilege on the new schema or tablespace. To add the table as a new child of a parent table, you must own the parent table as well. Also, to attach a table as a new partition of the table, you must own the table being attached. To alter the owner, you must also be a direct or indirect member of the new owning role, and that role must have `CREATE` privilege on the table's schema. (These restrictions enforce that altering the owner doesn't do anything you couldn't do by dropping and recreating the table. However, a superuser can alter ownership of any table anyway.) To add a column or alter a column type or use the `OF` clause, you must also have `USAGE` privilege on the data type.

Parameters

`IF EXISTS`

> Do not throw an error if the table does not exist. A notice is issued in this case.

name

The name (optionally schema-qualified) of an existing table to alter. If ONLY is specified before the table name, only that table is altered. If ONLY is not specified, the table and all its descendant tables (if any) are altered. Optionally, * can be specified after the table name to explicitly indicate that descendant tables are included.

column_name

Name of a new or existing column.

new_column_name

New name for an existing column.

new_name

New name for the table.

data_type

Data type of the new column, or new data type for an existing column.

table_constraint

New table constraint for the table.

constraint_name

Name of a new or existing constraint.

CASCADE

Automatically drop objects that depend on the dropped column or constraint (for example, views referencing the column), and in turn all objects that depend on those objects (see Section 5.13).

RESTRICT

Refuse to drop the column or constraint if there are any dependent objects. This is the default behavior.

trigger_name

Name of a single trigger to disable or enable.

ALL

Disable or enable all triggers belonging to the table. (This requires superuser privilege if any of the triggers are internally generated constraint triggers such as those that are used to implement foreign key constraints or deferrable uniqueness and exclusion constraints.)

USER

Disable or enable all triggers belonging to the table except for internally generated constraint triggers such as those that are used to implement foreign key constraints or deferrable uniqueness and exclusion constraints.

index_name

The name of an existing index.

storage_parameter

The name of a table storage parameter.

value

The new value for a table storage parameter. This might be a number or a word depending on the parameter.

parent_table

A parent table to associate or de-associate with this table.

new_owner

The user name of the new owner of the table.

new_tablespace

The name of the tablespace to which the table will be moved.

new_schema

The name of the schema to which the table will be moved.

partition_name

The name of the table to attach as a new partition or to detach from this table.

partition_bound_spec

The partition bound specification for a new partition. Refer to CREATE TABLE for more details on the syntax of the same.

Notes

The key word COLUMN is noise and can be omitted.

When a column is added with ADD COLUMN and a non-volatile DEFAULT is specified, the default is evaluated at the time of the statement and the result stored in the table's metadata. That value will be used for the column for all existing rows. If no DEFAULT is specified, NULL is used. In neither case is a rewrite of the table required.

Adding a column with a volatile DEFAULT or changing the type of an existing column will require the entire table and its indexes to be rewritten. As an exception, when changing the type of an existing column, if the USING clause does not change the column contents and the old type is either binary coercible to the new type or an unconstrained domain over the new type, a table rewrite is not needed; but any indexes on the affected columns must still be rebuilt. Adding or removing a system oid column also requires rewriting the entire table. Table and/or index rebuilds may take a significant amount of time for a large table; and will temporarily require as much as double the disk space.

Adding a CHECK or NOT NULL constraint requires scanning the table to verify that existing rows meet the constraint, but does not require a table rewrite.

Similarly, when attaching a new partition it may be scanned to verify that existing rows meet the partition constraint.

The main reason for providing the option to specify multiple changes in a single `ALTER TABLE` is that multiple table scans or rewrites can thereby be combined into a single pass over the table.

The `DROP COLUMN` form does not physically remove the column, but simply makes it invisible to SQL operations. Subsequent insert and update operations in the table will store a null value for the column. Thus, dropping a column is quick but it will not immediately reduce the on-disk size of your table, as the space occupied by the dropped column is not reclaimed. The space will be reclaimed over time as existing rows are updated. (These statements do not apply when dropping the system `oid` column; that is done with an immediate rewrite.)

To force immediate reclamation of space occupied by a dropped column, you can execute one of the forms of `ALTER TABLE` that performs a rewrite of the whole table. This results in reconstructing each row with the dropped column replaced by a null value.

The rewriting forms of `ALTER TABLE` are not MVCC-safe. After a table rewrite, the table will appear empty to concurrent transactions, if they are using a snapshot taken before the rewrite occurred. See Section 13.5 for more details.

The `USING` option of `SET DATA TYPE` can actually specify any expression involving the old values of the row; that is, it can refer to other columns as well as the one being converted. This allows very general conversions to be done with the `SET DATA TYPE` syntax. Because of this flexibility, the `USING` expression is not applied to the column's default value (if any); the result might not be a constant expression as required for a default. This means that when there is no implicit or assignment cast from old to new type, `SET DATA TYPE` might fail to convert the default even though a `USING` clause is supplied. In such cases, drop the default with `DROP DEFAULT`, perform the `ALTER TYPE`, and then use `SET DEFAULT` to add a suitable new default. Similar considerations apply to indexes and constraints involving the column.

If a table has any descendant tables, it is not permitted to add, rename, or change the type of a column in the parent table without doing the same to the descendants. This ensures that the descendants always have columns matching the parent. Similarly, a `CHECK` constraint cannot be renamed in the parent without also renaming it in all descendants, so that `CHECK` constraints also match between the parent and its descendants. (That restriction does not apply to index-based constraints, however.) Also, because selecting from the parent also selects from its descendants, a constraint on the parent cannot be marked valid unless it is also marked valid for those descendants. In all of these cases, `ALTER TABLE ONLY` will be rejected.

A recursive `DROP COLUMN` operation will remove a descendant table's column only if the descendant does not inherit that column from any other parents and never had an independent definition of the column. A nonrecursive `DROP COLUMN` (i.e., `ALTER TABLE ONLY ... DROP COLUMN`) never removes any descendant columns, but instead marks them as independently defined rather than inherited. A nonrecursive `DROP COLUMN` command will fail for a partitioned table, because all partitions of a table must have the same columns as the partitioning root.

The actions for identity columns (`ADD GENERATED`, `SET` etc., `DROP IDENTITY`), as well as the actions `TRIGGER`, `CLUSTER`, `OWNER`, and `TABLESPACE` never recurse to descendant tables; that is, they always act as though `ONLY` were specified. Adding a constraint recurses only for `CHECK` constraints that are not marked `NO INHERIT`.

Changing any part of a system catalog table is not permitted.

Refer to CREATE TABLE for a further description of valid parameters. Chapter 5 has further information on inheritance.

Examples

To add a column of type `varchar` to a table:

```
ALTER TABLE distributors ADD COLUMN address varchar(30);
```

To drop a column from a table:

```
ALTER TABLE distributors DROP COLUMN address RESTRICT;
```

To change the types of two existing columns in one operation:

```
ALTER TABLE distributors
    ALTER COLUMN address TYPE varchar(80),
    ALTER COLUMN name TYPE varchar(100);
```

To change an integer column containing Unix timestamps to `timestamp with time zone` via a `USING` clause:

```
ALTER TABLE foo
    ALTER COLUMN foo_timestamp SET DATA TYPE timestamp with time zone
    USING
        timestamp with time zone 'epoch' + foo_timestamp * interval '1
 second';
```

The same, when the column has a default expression that won't automatically cast to the new data type:

```
ALTER TABLE foo
    ALTER COLUMN foo_timestamp DROP DEFAULT,
    ALTER COLUMN foo_timestamp TYPE timestamp with time zone
    USING
        timestamp with time zone 'epoch' + foo_timestamp * interval '1
 second',
    ALTER COLUMN foo_timestamp SET DEFAULT now();
```

To rename an existing column:

```
ALTER TABLE distributors RENAME COLUMN address TO city;
```

To rename an existing table:

```
ALTER TABLE distributors RENAME TO suppliers;
```

To rename an existing constraint:

```
ALTER TABLE distributors RENAME CONSTRAINT zipchk TO zip_check;
```

To add a not-null constraint to a column:

```
ALTER TABLE distributors ALTER COLUMN street SET NOT NULL;
```

To remove a not-null constraint from a column:

```
ALTER TABLE distributors ALTER COLUMN street DROP NOT NULL;
```

To add a check constraint to a table and all its children:

```
ALTER TABLE distributors ADD CONSTRAINT zipchk CHECK
 (char_length(zipcode) = 5);
```

To add a check constraint only to a table and not to its children:

```
ALTER TABLE distributors ADD CONSTRAINT zipchk CHECK
 (char_length(zipcode) = 5) NO INHERIT;
```

(The check constraint will not be inherited by future children, either.)

To remove a check constraint from a table and all its children:

```
ALTER TABLE distributors DROP CONSTRAINT zipchk;
```

To remove a check constraint from one table only:

```
ALTER TABLE ONLY distributors DROP CONSTRAINT zipchk;
```

(The check constraint remains in place for any child tables.)

To add a foreign key constraint to a table:

```
ALTER TABLE distributors ADD CONSTRAINT distfk FOREIGN KEY (address)
 REFERENCES addresses (address);
```

To add a foreign key constraint to a table with the least impact on other work:

```
ALTER TABLE distributors ADD CONSTRAINT distfk FOREIGN KEY (address)
 REFERENCES addresses (address) NOT VALID;
ALTER TABLE distributors VALIDATE CONSTRAINT distfk;
```

To add a (multicolumn) unique constraint to a table:

```
ALTER TABLE distributors ADD CONSTRAINT dist_id_zipcode_key UNIQUE
 (dist_id, zipcode);
```

To add an automatically named primary key constraint to a table, noting that a table can only ever have one primary key:

```
ALTER TABLE distributors ADD PRIMARY KEY (dist_id);
```

To move a table to a different tablespace:

```
ALTER TABLE distributors SET TABLESPACE fasttablespace;
```

To move a table to a different schema:

```
ALTER TABLE myschema.distributors SET SCHEMA yourschema;
```

To recreate a primary key constraint, without blocking updates while the index is rebuilt:

```
CREATE UNIQUE INDEX CONCURRENTLY dist_id_temp_idx ON distributors
 (dist_id);
ALTER TABLE distributors DROP CONSTRAINT distributors_pkey,
    ADD CONSTRAINT distributors_pkey PRIMARY KEY USING INDEX
 dist_id_temp_idx;
```

To attach a partition to a range-partitioned table:

```
ALTER TABLE measurement
    ATTACH PARTITION measurement_y2016m07 FOR VALUES FROM
 ('2016-07-01') TO ('2016-08-01');
```

To attach a partition to a list-partitioned table:

```
ALTER TABLE cities
    ATTACH PARTITION cities_ab FOR VALUES IN ('a', 'b');
```

To attach a partition to a hash-partitioned table:

```
ALTER TABLE orders
    ATTACH PARTITION orders_p4 FOR VALUES WITH (MODULUS 4, REMAINDER
 3);
```

To attach a default partition to a partitioned table:

```
ALTER TABLE cities
    ATTACH PARTITION cities_partdef DEFAULT;
```

To detach a partition from a partitioned table:

```
ALTER TABLE measurement
    DETACH PARTITION measurement_y2015m12;
```

Compatibility

The forms ADD (without USING INDEX), DROP [COLUMN], DROP IDENTITY, RESTART, SET DEFAULT, SET DATA TYPE (without USING), SET GENERATED, and SET *sequence_option* conform with the SQL standard. The other forms are PostgreSQL extensions of the SQL standard. Also, the ability to specify more than one manipulation in a single ALTER TABLE command is an extension.

ALTER TABLE DROP COLUMN can be used to drop the only column of a table, leaving a zero-column table. This is an extension of SQL, which disallows zero-column tables.

See Also

CREATE TABLE

ALTER TABLESPACE

ALTER TABLESPACE — change the definition of a tablespace

Synopsis

```
ALTER TABLESPACE name RENAME TO new_name
ALTER TABLESPACE name OWNER TO { new_owner | CURRENT_USER |
 SESSION_USER }
ALTER TABLESPACE name SET ( tablespace_option = value [, ... ] )
ALTER TABLESPACE name RESET ( tablespace_option [, ... ] )
```

Description

ALTER TABLESPACE can be used to change the definition of a tablespace.

You must own the tablespace to change the definition of a tablespace. To alter the owner, you must also be a direct or indirect member of the new owning role. (Note that superusers have these privileges automatically.)

Parameters

name

The name of an existing tablespace.

new_name

The new name of the tablespace. The new name cannot begin with pg_, as such names are reserved for system tablespaces.

new_owner

The new owner of the tablespace.

tablespace_option

A tablespace parameter to be set or reset. Currently, the only available parameters are seq_page_cost, random_page_cost and effective_io_concurrency. Setting either value for a particular tablespace will override the planner's usual estimate of the cost of reading pages from tables in that tablespace, as established by the configuration parameters of the same name (see seq_page_cost, random_page_cost, effective_io_concurrency). This may be useful if one tablespace is located on a disk which is faster or slower than the remainder of the I/O subsystem.

Examples

Rename tablespace index_space to fast_raid:

```
ALTER TABLESPACE index_space RENAME TO fast_raid;
```

Change the owner of tablespace `index_space`:

```
ALTER TABLESPACE index_space OWNER TO mary;
```

Compatibility

There is no `ALTER TABLESPACE` statement in the SQL standard.

See Also

CREATE TABLESPACE, DROP TABLESPACE

ALTER TEXT SEARCH CONFIGURATION

ALTER TEXT SEARCH CONFIGURATION — change the definition of a text search configuration

Synopsis

```
ALTER TEXT SEARCH CONFIGURATION name
    ADD MAPPING FOR token_type [, ... ] WITH dictionary_name [, ... ]
ALTER TEXT SEARCH CONFIGURATION name
    ALTER MAPPING FOR token_type [, ... ] WITH dictionary_name
 [, ... ]
ALTER TEXT SEARCH CONFIGURATION name
    ALTER MAPPING REPLACE old_dictionary WITH new_dictionary
ALTER TEXT SEARCH CONFIGURATION name
    ALTER MAPPING FOR token_type [, ... ] REPLACE old_dictionary
 WITH new_dictionary
ALTER TEXT SEARCH CONFIGURATION name
    DROP MAPPING [ IF EXISTS ] FOR token_type [, ... ]
ALTER TEXT SEARCH CONFIGURATION name RENAME TO new_name
ALTER TEXT SEARCH CONFIGURATION name OWNER TO { new_owner |
 CURRENT_USER | SESSION_USER }
ALTER TEXT SEARCH CONFIGURATION name SET SCHEMA new_schema
```

Description

ALTER TEXT SEARCH CONFIGURATION changes the definition of a text search configuration. You can modify its mappings from token types to dictionaries, or change the configuration's name or owner.

You must be the owner of the configuration to use ALTER TEXT SEARCH CONFIGURATION.

Parameters

name

> The name (optionally schema-qualified) of an existing text search configuration.

token_type

> The name of a token type that is emitted by the configuration's parser.

dictionary_name

> The name of a text search dictionary to be consulted for the specified token type(s). If multiple dictionaries are listed, they are consulted in the specified order.

old_dictionary

> The name of a text search dictionary to be replaced in the mapping.

new_dictionary

> The name of a text search dictionary to be substituted for old_dictionary.

new_name

> The new name of the text search configuration.

new_owner

> The new owner of the text search configuration.

new_schema

> The new schema for the text search configuration.

The ADD MAPPING FOR form installs a list of dictionaries to be consulted for the specified token type(s); it is an error if there is already a mapping for any of the token types. The ALTER MAPPING FOR form does the same, but first removing any existing mapping for those token types. The ALTER MAPPING REPLACE forms substitute *new_dictionary* for *old_dictionary* anywhere the latter appears. This is done for only the specified token types when FOR appears, or for all mappings of the configuration when it doesn't. The DROP MAPPING form removes all dictionaries for the specified token type(s), causing tokens of those types to be ignored by the text search configuration. It is an error if there is no mapping for the token types, unless IF EXISTS appears.

Examples

The following example replaces the english dictionary with the swedish dictionary anywhere that english is used within my_config.

```
ALTER TEXT SEARCH CONFIGURATION my_config
  ALTER MAPPING REPLACE english WITH swedish;
```

Compatibility

There is no ALTER TEXT SEARCH CONFIGURATION statement in the SQL standard.

See Also
CREATE TEXT SEARCH CONFIGURATION, DROP TEXT SEARCH CONFIGURATION

ALTER TEXT SEARCH DICTIONARY

ALTER TEXT SEARCH DICTIONARY — change the definition of a text search dictionary

Synopsis

```
ALTER TEXT SEARCH DICTIONARY name (
    option [ = value ] [, ... ]
)
ALTER TEXT SEARCH DICTIONARY name RENAME TO new_name
ALTER TEXT SEARCH DICTIONARY name OWNER TO { new_owner | CURRENT_USER
 | SESSION_USER }
ALTER TEXT SEARCH DICTIONARY name SET SCHEMA new_schema
```

Description

ALTER TEXT SEARCH DICTIONARY changes the definition of a text search dictionary. You can change the dictionary's template-specific options, or change the dictionary's name or owner.

You must be the owner of the dictionary to use ALTER TEXT SEARCH DICTIONARY.

Parameters

name

The name (optionally schema-qualified) of an existing text search dictionary.

option

The name of a template-specific option to be set for this dictionary.

value

The new value to use for a template-specific option. If the equal sign and value are omitted, then any previous setting for the option is removed from the dictionary, allowing the default to be used.

new_name

The new name of the text search dictionary.

new_owner

The new owner of the text search dictionary.

new_schema

The new schema for the text search dictionary.

Template-specific options can appear in any order.

Examples

The following example command changes the stopword list for a Snowball-based dictionary. Other parameters remain unchanged.

```
ALTER TEXT SEARCH DICTIONARY my_dict ( StopWords = newrussian );
```

The following example command changes the language option to dutch, and removes the stopword option entirely.

```
ALTER TEXT SEARCH DICTIONARY my_dict ( language = dutch, StopWords );
```

The following example command "updates" the dictionary's definition without actually changing anything.

```
ALTER TEXT SEARCH DICTIONARY my_dict ( dummy );
```

(The reason this works is that the option removal code doesn't complain if there is no such option.) This trick is useful when changing configuration files for the dictionary: the ALTER will force existing database sessions to re-read the configuration files, which otherwise they would never do if they had read them earlier.

Compatibility

There is no ALTER TEXT SEARCH DICTIONARY statement in the SQL standard.

See Also

CREATE TEXT SEARCH DICTIONARY, DROP TEXT SEARCH DICTIONARY

ALTER TEXT SEARCH PARSER

ALTER TEXT SEARCH PARSER — change the definition of a text search parser

Synopsis

```
ALTER TEXT SEARCH PARSER name RENAME TO new_name
ALTER TEXT SEARCH PARSER name SET SCHEMA new_schema
```

Description

`ALTER TEXT SEARCH PARSER` changes the definition of a text search parser. Currently, the only supported functionality is to change the parser's name.

You must be a superuser to use `ALTER TEXT SEARCH PARSER`.

Parameters

name

> The name (optionally schema-qualified) of an existing text search parser.

new_name

> The new name of the text search parser.

new_schema

> The new schema for the text search parser.

Compatibility

There is no `ALTER TEXT SEARCH PARSER` statement in the SQL standard.

See Also

CREATE TEXT SEARCH PARSER, DROP TEXT SEARCH PARSER

ALTER TEXT SEARCH TEMPLATE

ALTER TEXT SEARCH TEMPLATE — change the definition of a text search template

Synopsis

```
ALTER TEXT SEARCH TEMPLATE name RENAME TO new_name
ALTER TEXT SEARCH TEMPLATE name SET SCHEMA new_schema
```

Description

ALTER TEXT SEARCH TEMPLATE changes the definition of a text search template. Currently, the only supported functionality is to change the template's name.

You must be a superuser to use ALTER TEXT SEARCH TEMPLATE.

Parameters

name

The name (optionally schema-qualified) of an existing text search template.

new_name

The new name of the text search template.

new_schema

The new schema for the text search template.

Compatibility

There is no ALTER TEXT SEARCH TEMPLATE statement in the SQL standard.

See Also

CREATE TEXT SEARCH TEMPLATE, DROP TEXT SEARCH TEMPLATE

ALTER TRIGGER

ALTER TRIGGER — change the definition of a trigger

Synopsis

```
ALTER TRIGGER name ON table_name RENAME TO new_name
ALTER TRIGGER name ON table_name DEPENDS ON EXTENSION extension_name
```

Description

`ALTER TRIGGER` changes properties of an existing trigger. The `RENAME` clause changes the name of the given trigger without otherwise changing the trigger definition. The `DEPENDS ON EXTENSION` clause marks the trigger as dependent on an extension, such that if the extension is dropped, the trigger will automatically be dropped as well.

You must own the table on which the trigger acts to be allowed to change its properties.

Parameters

name

The name of an existing trigger to alter.

table_name

The name of the table on which this trigger acts.

new_name

The new name for the trigger.

extension_name

The name of the extension that the trigger is to depend on.

Notes

The ability to temporarily enable or disable a trigger is provided by ALTER TABLE, not by `ALTER TRIGGER`, because `ALTER TRIGGER` has no convenient way to express the option of enabling or disabling all of a table's triggers at once.

Examples

To rename an existing trigger:

```
ALTER TRIGGER emp_stamp ON emp RENAME TO emp_track_chgs;
```

To mark a trigger as being dependent on an extension:

```
ALTER TRIGGER emp_stamp ON emp DEPENDS ON EXTENSION emplib;
```

Compatibility

ALTER TRIGGER is a PostgreSQL extension of the SQL standard.

See Also

ALTER TABLE

ALTER TYPE

ALTER TYPE — change the definition of a type

Synopsis

```
ALTER TYPE name action [, ... ]
ALTER TYPE name OWNER TO { new_owner | CURRENT_USER | SESSION_USER }
ALTER TYPE name RENAME ATTRIBUTE attribute_name TO new_attribute_name
 [ CASCADE | RESTRICT ]
ALTER TYPE name RENAME TO new_name
ALTER TYPE name SET SCHEMA new_schema
ALTER TYPE name ADD VALUE [ IF NOT EXISTS ] new_enum_value [ { BEFORE
 | AFTER } neighbor_enum_value ]
ALTER TYPE name RENAME VALUE existing_enum_value TO new_enum_value

where action is one of:

    ADD ATTRIBUTE attribute_name data_type [ COLLATE collation ]
 [ CASCADE | RESTRICT ]
    DROP ATTRIBUTE [ IF EXISTS ] attribute_name [ CASCADE | RESTRICT ]
    ALTER ATTRIBUTE attribute_name [ SET DATA ] TYPE data_type
 [ COLLATE collation ] [ CASCADE | RESTRICT ]
```

Description

`ALTER TYPE` changes the definition of an existing type. There are several subforms:

`ADD ATTRIBUTE`

This form adds a new attribute to a composite type, using the same syntax as CREATE TYPE.

`DROP ATTRIBUTE [ IF EXISTS ]`

This form drops an attribute from a composite type. If `IF EXISTS` is specified and the attribute does not exist, no error is thrown. In this case a notice is issued instead.

`SET DATA TYPE`

This form changes the type of an attribute of a composite type.

`OWNER`

This form changes the owner of the type.

`RENAME`

This form changes the name of the type or the name of an individual attribute of a composite type.

`SET SCHEMA`

This form moves the type into another schema.

```
ADD VALUE [ IF NOT EXISTS ] [ BEFORE | AFTER ]
```

This form adds a new value to an enum type. The new value's place in the enum's ordering can be specified as being BEFORE or AFTER one of the existing values. Otherwise, the new item is added at the end of the list of values.

If IF NOT EXISTS is specified, it is not an error if the type already contains the new value: a notice is issued but no other action is taken. Otherwise, an error will occur if the new value is already present.

```
RENAME VALUE
```

This form renames a value of an enum type. The value's place in the enum's ordering is not affected. An error will occur if the specified value is not present or the new name is already present.

The ADD ATTRIBUTE, DROP ATTRIBUTE, and ALTER ATTRIBUTE actions can be combined into a list of multiple alterations to apply in parallel. For example, it is possible to add several attributes and/ or alter the type of several attributes in a single command.

You must own the type to use ALTER TYPE. To change the schema of a type, you must also have CREATE privilege on the new schema. To alter the owner, you must also be a direct or indirect member of the new owning role, and that role must have CREATE privilege on the type's schema. (These restrictions enforce that altering the owner doesn't do anything you couldn't do by dropping and recreating the type. However, a superuser can alter ownership of any type anyway.) To add an attribute or alter an attribute type, you must also have USAGE privilege on the data type.

Parameters

name

The name (possibly schema-qualified) of an existing type to alter.

new_name

The new name for the type.

new_owner

The user name of the new owner of the type.

new_schema

The new schema for the type.

attribute_name

The name of the attribute to add, alter, or drop.

new_attribute_name

The new name of the attribute to be renamed.

data_type

The data type of the attribute to add, or the new type of the attribute to alter.

new_enum_value

The new value to be added to an enum type's list of values, or the new name to be given to an existing value. Like all enum literals, it needs to be quoted.

neighbor_enum_value

The existing enum value that the new value should be added immediately before or after in the enum type's sort ordering. Like all enum literals, it needs to be quoted.

existing_enum_value

The existing enum value that should be renamed. Like all enum literals, it needs to be quoted.

CASCADE

Automatically propagate the operation to typed tables of the type being altered, and their descendants.

RESTRICT

Refuse the operation if the type being altered is the type of a typed table. This is the default.

Notes

ALTER TYPE ... ADD VALUE (the form that adds a new value to an enum type) cannot be executed inside a transaction block.

Comparisons involving an added enum value will sometimes be slower than comparisons involving only original members of the enum type. This will usually only occur if BEFORE or AFTER is used to set the new value's sort position somewhere other than at the end of the list. However, sometimes it will happen even though the new value is added at the end (this occurs if the OID counter "wrapped around" since the original creation of the enum type). The slowdown is usually insignificant; but if it matters, optimal performance can be regained by dropping and recreating the enum type, or by dumping and reloading the database.

Examples

To rename a data type:

```
ALTER TYPE electronic_mail RENAME TO email;
```

To change the owner of the type email to joe:

```
ALTER TYPE email OWNER TO joe;
```

To change the schema of the type email to customers:

```
ALTER TYPE email SET SCHEMA customers;
```

To add a new attribute to a type:

```
ALTER TYPE compfoo ADD ATTRIBUTE f3 int;
```

To add a new value to an enum type in a particular sort position:

```
ALTER TYPE colors ADD VALUE 'orange' AFTER 'red';
```

To rename an enum value:

```
ALTER TYPE colors RENAME VALUE 'purple' TO 'mauve';
```

Compatibility

The variants to add and drop attributes are part of the SQL standard; the other variants are PostgreSQL extensions.

See Also

CREATE TYPE, DROP TYPE

ALTER USER

ALTER USER — change a database role

Synopsis

```
ALTER USER role_specification [ WITH ] option [ ... ]

where option can be:

    SUPERUSER | NOSUPERUSER
  | CREATEDB | NOCREATEDB
  | CREATEROLE | NOCREATEROLE
  | INHERIT | NOINHERIT
  | LOGIN | NOLOGIN
  | REPLICATION | NOREPLICATION
  | BYPASSRLS | NOBYPASSRLS
  | CONNECTION LIMIT connlimit
  | [ ENCRYPTED ] PASSWORD 'password' | PASSWORD NULL
  | VALID UNTIL 'timestamp'

ALTER USER name RENAME TO new_name

ALTER USER { role_specification | ALL } [ IN DATABASE database_name ]
 SET configuration_parameter { TO | = } { value | DEFAULT }
ALTER USER { role_specification | ALL } [ IN DATABASE database_name ]
 SET configuration_parameter FROM CURRENT
ALTER USER { role_specification | ALL } [ IN DATABASE database_name ]
 RESET configuration_parameter
ALTER USER { role_specification | ALL } [ IN DATABASE database_name ]
 RESET ALL

where role_specification can be:

    role_name
  | CURRENT_USER
  | SESSION_USER
```

Description

ALTER USER is now an alias for ALTER ROLE.

Compatibility

The ALTER USER statement is a PostgreSQL extension. The SQL standard leaves the definition of users to the implementation.

See Also

ALTER ROLE

ALTER USER MAPPING

ALTER USER MAPPING — change the definition of a user mapping

Synopsis

```
ALTER USER MAPPING FOR { user_name | USER | CURRENT_USER |
SESSION_USER | PUBLIC }
    SERVER server_name
    OPTIONS ( [ ADD | SET | DROP ] option ['value'] [, ... ] )
```

Description

ALTER USER MAPPING changes the definition of a user mapping.

The owner of a foreign server can alter user mappings for that server for any user. Also, a user can alter a user mapping for their own user name if USAGE privilege on the server has been granted to the user.

Parameters

user_name

> User name of the mapping. CURRENT_USER and USER match the name of the current user. PUBLIC is used to match all present and future user names in the system.

server_name

> Server name of the user mapping.

OPTIONS ([ADD | SET | DROP] option ['value'] [, ...])

> Change options for the user mapping. The new options override any previously specified options. ADD, SET, and DROP specify the action to be performed. ADD is assumed if no operation is explicitly specified. Option names must be unique; options are also validated by the server's foreign-data wrapper.

Examples

Change the password for user mapping bob, server foo:

```
ALTER USER MAPPING FOR bob SERVER foo OPTIONS (SET password 'public');
```

Compatibility

ALTER USER MAPPING conforms to ISO/IEC 9075-9 (SQL/MED). There is a subtle syntax issue: The standard omits the FOR key word. Since both CREATE USER MAPPING and DROP USER MAPPING use FOR in analogous positions, and IBM DB2 (being the other major SQL/MED implementation) also requires it for ALTER USER MAPPING, PostgreSQL diverges from the standard here in the interest of consistency and interoperability.

See Also

CREATE USER MAPPING, DROP USER MAPPING

ALTER VIEW

ALTER VIEW — change the definition of a view

Synopsis

```
ALTER VIEW [ IF EXISTS ] name ALTER [ COLUMN ] column_name SET
 DEFAULT expression
ALTER VIEW [ IF EXISTS ] name ALTER [ COLUMN ] column_name DROP
 DEFAULT
ALTER VIEW [ IF EXISTS ] name OWNER TO { new_owner | CURRENT_USER |
 SESSION_USER }
ALTER VIEW [ IF EXISTS ] name RENAME TO new_name
ALTER VIEW [ IF EXISTS ] name SET SCHEMA new_schema
ALTER VIEW [ IF EXISTS ] name SET ( view_option_name
 [= view_option_value] [, ... ] )
ALTER VIEW [ IF EXISTS ] name RESET ( view_option_name [, ... ] )
```

Description

ALTER VIEW changes various auxiliary properties of a view. (If you want to modify the view's defining query, use CREATE OR REPLACE VIEW.)

You must own the view to use ALTER VIEW. To change a view's schema, you must also have CREATE privilege on the new schema. To alter the owner, you must also be a direct or indirect member of the new owning role, and that role must have CREATE privilege on the view's schema. (These restrictions enforce that altering the owner doesn't do anything you couldn't do by dropping and recreating the view. However, a superuser can alter ownership of any view anyway.)

Parameters

name

> The name (optionally schema-qualified) of an existing view.

IF EXISTS

> Do not throw an error if the view does not exist. A notice is issued in this case.

SET/DROP DEFAULT

> These forms set or remove the default value for a column. A view column's default value is substituted into any INSERT or UPDATE command whose target is the view, before applying any rules or triggers for the view. The view's default will therefore take precedence over any default values from underlying relations.

new_owner

> The user name of the new owner of the view.

new_name

> The new name for the view.

new_schema

> The new schema for the view.

SET (*view_option_name* [= *view_option_value*] [, ...])
RESET (*view_option_name* [, ...])

> Sets or resets a view option. Currently supported options are:

check_option (string)

> Changes the check option of the view. The value must be local or cascaded.

security_barrier (boolean)

> Changes the security-barrier property of the view. The value must be Boolean value, such as true or false.

Notes

For historical reasons, ALTER TABLE can be used with views too; but the only variants of ALTER TABLE that are allowed with views are equivalent to the ones shown above.

Examples

To rename the view foo to bar:

```
ALTER VIEW foo RENAME TO bar;
```

To attach a default column value to an updatable view:

```
CREATE TABLE base_table (id int, ts timestamptz);
CREATE VIEW a_view AS SELECT * FROM base_table;
ALTER VIEW a_view ALTER COLUMN ts SET DEFAULT now();
INSERT INTO base_table(id) VALUES(1);  -- ts will receive a NULL
INSERT INTO a_view(id) VALUES(2);  -- ts will receive the current time
```

Compatibility

ALTER VIEW is a PostgreSQL extension of the SQL standard.

See Also

CREATE VIEW, DROP VIEW

ANALYZE

ANALYZE — collect statistics about a database

Synopsis

```
ANALYZE [ ( option [, ...] ) ] [ table_and_columns [, ...] ]
ANALYZE [ VERBOSE ] [ table_and_columns [, ...] ]

where option can be one of:

    VERBOSE

and table_and_columns is:

    table_name [ ( column_name [, ...] ) ]
```

Description

ANALYZE collects statistics about the contents of tables in the database, and stores the results in the **pg_s-tatistic** system catalog. Subsequently, the query planner uses these statistics to help determine the most efficient execution plans for queries.

Without a *table_and_columns* list, **ANALYZE** processes every table and materialized view in the current database that the current user has permission to analyze. With a list, **ANALYZE** processes only those table(s). It is further possible to give a list of column names for a table, in which case only the statistics for those columns are collected.

When the option list is surrounded by parentheses, the options can be written in any order. The parenthesized syntax was added in PostgreSQL 11; the unparenthesized syntax is deprecated.

Parameters

VERBOSE

Enables display of progress messages.

table_name

The name (possibly schema-qualified) of a specific table to analyze. If omitted, all regular tables, partitioned tables, and materialized views in the current database are analyzed (but not foreign tables). If the specified table is a partitioned table, both the inheritance statistics of the partitioned table as a whole and statistics of the individual partitions are updated.

column_name

The name of a specific column to analyze. Defaults to all columns.

Outputs

When VERBOSE is specified, ANALYZE emits progress messages to indicate which table is currently being processed. Various statistics about the tables are printed as well.

Notes

Foreign tables are analyzed only when explicitly selected. Not all foreign data wrappers support `ANALYZE`. If the table's wrapper does not support `ANALYZE`, the command prints a warning and does nothing.

In the default PostgreSQL configuration, the autovacuum daemon (see Section 24.1.6) takes care of automatic analyzing of tables when they are first loaded with data, and as they change throughout regular operation. When autovacuum is disabled, it is a good idea to run `ANALYZE` periodically, or just after making major changes in the contents of a table. Accurate statistics will help the planner to choose the most appropriate query plan, and thereby improve the speed of query processing. A common strategy for read-mostly databases is to run VACUUM and `ANALYZE` once a day during a low-usage time of day. (This will not be sufficient if there is heavy update activity.)

`ANALYZE` requires only a read lock on the target table, so it can run in parallel with other activity on the table.

The statistics collected by `ANALYZE` usually include a list of some of the most common values in each column and a histogram showing the approximate data distribution in each column. One or both of these can be omitted if `ANALYZE` deems them uninteresting (for example, in a unique-key column, there are no common values) or if the column data type does not support the appropriate operators. There is more information about the statistics in Chapter 24.

For large tables, `ANALYZE` takes a random sample of the table contents, rather than examining every row. This allows even very large tables to be analyzed in a small amount of time. Note, however, that the statistics are only approximate, and will change slightly each time `ANALYZE` is run, even if the actual table contents did not change. This might result in small changes in the planner's estimated costs shown by EXPLAIN. In rare situations, this non-determinism will cause the planner's choices of query plans to change after `ANALYZE` is run. To avoid this, raise the amount of statistics collected by `ANALYZE`, as described below.

The extent of analysis can be controlled by adjusting the default_statistics_target configuration variable, or on a column-by-column basis by setting the per-column statistics target with `ALTER TABLE ... ALTER COLUMN ... SET STATISTICS` (see ALTER TABLE). The target value sets the maximum number of entries in the most-common-value list and the maximum number of bins in the histogram. The default target value is 100, but this can be adjusted up or down to trade off accuracy of planner estimates against the time taken for `ANALYZE` and the amount of space occupied in `pg_statistic`. In particular, setting the statistics target to zero disables collection of statistics for that column. It might be useful to do that for columns that are never used as part of the `WHERE`, `GROUP BY`, or `ORDER BY` clauses of queries, since the planner will have no use for statistics on such columns.

The largest statistics target among the columns being analyzed determines the number of table rows sampled to prepare the statistics. Increasing the target causes a proportional increase in the time and space needed to do `ANALYZE`.

One of the values estimated by `ANALYZE` is the number of distinct values that appear in each column. Because only a subset of the rows are examined, this estimate can sometimes be quite inaccurate, even with the largest possible statistics target. If this inaccuracy leads to bad query plans, a more accurate value can be determined manually and then installed with `ALTER TABLE ... ALTER COLUMN ... SET (n_distinct = ...)` (see ALTER TABLE).

If the table being analyzed has one or more children, `ANALYZE` will gather statistics twice: once on the rows of the parent table only, and a second time on the rows of the parent table with all of its children. This second set of statistics is needed when planning queries that traverse the entire inheritance tree. The autovacuum daemon, however, will only consider inserts or updates on the parent table itself when deciding whether to trigger an automatic analyze for that table. If that table is rarely inserted into or updated, the inheritance statistics will not be up to date unless you run ANALYZE manually.

If any of the child tables are foreign tables whose foreign data wrappers do not support ANALYZE, those child tables are ignored while gathering inheritance statistics.

If the table being analyzed is completely empty, ANALYZE will not record new statistics for that table. Any existing statistics will be retained.

Compatibility

There is no ANALYZE statement in the SQL standard.

See Also

VACUUM, vacuumdb, Section 19.4.4, Section 24.1.6

BEGIN

BEGIN — start a transaction block

Synopsis

```
BEGIN [ WORK | TRANSACTION ] [ transaction_mode [, ...] ]

where transaction_mode is one of:

    ISOLATION LEVEL { SERIALIZABLE | REPEATABLE READ | READ COMMITTED
 | READ UNCOMMITTED }
    READ WRITE | READ ONLY
    [ NOT ] DEFERRABLE
```

Description

BEGIN initiates a transaction block, that is, all statements after a BEGIN command will be executed in a single transaction until an explicit COMMIT or ROLLBACK is given. By default (without BEGIN), PostgreSQL executes transactions in "autocommit" mode, that is, each statement is executed in its own transaction and a commit is implicitly performed at the end of the statement (if execution was successful, otherwise a rollback is done).

Statements are executed more quickly in a transaction block, because transaction start/commit requires significant CPU and disk activity. Execution of multiple statements inside a transaction is also useful to ensure consistency when making several related changes: other sessions will be unable to see the intermediate states wherein not all the related updates have been done.

If the isolation level, read/write mode, or deferrable mode is specified, the new transaction has those characteristics, as if SET TRANSACTION was executed.

Parameters

WORK
TRANSACTION

    Optional key words. They have no effect.

Refer to SET TRANSACTION for information on the meaning of the other parameters to this statement.

Notes

START TRANSACTION has the same functionality as BEGIN.

Use COMMIT or ROLLBACK to terminate a transaction block.

Issuing BEGIN when already inside a transaction block will provoke a warning message. The state of the transaction is not affected. To nest transactions within a transaction block, use savepoints (see SAVE-POINT).

For reasons of backwards compatibility, the commas between successive *transaction_modes* can be omitted.

Examples

To begin a transaction block:

```
BEGIN;
```

Compatibility

BEGIN is a PostgreSQL language extension. It is equivalent to the SQL-standard command START TRANSACTION, whose reference page contains additional compatibility information.

The DEFERRABLE *transaction_mode* is a PostgreSQL language extension.

Incidentally, the BEGIN key word is used for a different purpose in embedded SQL. You are advised to be careful about the transaction semantics when porting database applications.

See Also

COMMIT, ROLLBACK, START TRANSACTION, SAVEPOINT

CALL

CALL — invoke a procedure

Synopsis

```
CALL name ( [ argument ] [, ...] )
```

Description

CALL executes a procedure.

If the procedure has any output parameters, then a result row will be returned, containing the values of those parameters.

Parameters

name

The name (optionally schema-qualified) of the procedure.

argument

An input argument for the procedure call. See Section 4.3 for the full details on function and procedure call syntax, including use of named parameters.

Notes

The user must have EXECUTE privilege on the procedure in order to be allowed to invoke it.

To call a function (not a procedure), use SELECT instead.

If CALL is executed in a transaction block, then the called procedure cannot execute transaction control statements. Transaction control statements are only allowed if CALL is executed in its own transaction.

PL/pgSQL handles output parameters in CALL commands differently; see Section 43.6.3.

Examples

```
CALL do_db_maintenance();
```

Compatibility

CALL conforms to the SQL standard.

See Also

CREATE PROCEDURE

CHECKPOINT

CHECKPOINT — force a write-ahead log checkpoint

Synopsis

```
CHECKPOINT
```

Description

A checkpoint is a point in the write-ahead log sequence at which all data files have been updated to reflect the information in the log. All data files will be flushed to disk. Refer to Section 30.4 for more details about what happens during a checkpoint.

The CHECKPOINT command forces an immediate checkpoint when the command is issued, without waiting for a regular checkpoint scheduled by the system (controlled by the settings in Section 19.5.2). CHECKPOINT is not intended for use during normal operation.

If executed during recovery, the CHECKPOINT command will force a restartpoint (see Section 30.4) rather than writing a new checkpoint.

Only superusers can call CHECKPOINT.

Compatibility

The CHECKPOINT command is a PostgreSQL language extension.

CLOSE

CLOSE — close a cursor

Synopsis

```
CLOSE { name | ALL }
```

Description

CLOSE frees the resources associated with an open cursor. After the cursor is closed, no subsequent operations are allowed on it. A cursor should be closed when it is no longer needed.

Every non-holdable open cursor is implicitly closed when a transaction is terminated by COMMIT or ROLLBACK. A holdable cursor is implicitly closed if the transaction that created it aborts via ROLLBACK. If the creating transaction successfully commits, the holdable cursor remains open until an explicit CLOSE is executed, or the client disconnects.

Parameters

name

The name of an open cursor to close.

ALL

Close all open cursors.

Notes

PostgreSQL does not have an explicit OPEN cursor statement; a cursor is considered open when it is declared. Use the DECLARE statement to declare a cursor.

You can see all available cursors by querying the pg_cursors system view.

If a cursor is closed after a savepoint which is later rolled back, the CLOSE is not rolled back; that is, the cursor remains closed.

Examples

Close the cursor liahona:

```
CLOSE liahona;
```

Compatibility

CLOSE is fully conforming with the SQL standard. CLOSE ALL is a PostgreSQL extension.

See Also

DECLARE, FETCH, MOVE

CLUSTER

CLUSTER — cluster a table according to an index

Synopsis

```
CLUSTER [VERBOSE] table_name [ USING index_name ]
CLUSTER [VERBOSE]
```

Description

CLUSTER instructs PostgreSQL to cluster the table specified by *table_name* based on the index specified by *index_name*. The index must already have been defined on *table_name*.

When a table is clustered, it is physically reordered based on the index information. Clustering is a one-time operation: when the table is subsequently updated, the changes are not clustered. That is, no attempt is made to store new or updated rows according to their index order. (If one wishes, one can periodically recluster by issuing the command again. Also, setting the table's fillfactor storage parameter to less than 100% can aid in preserving cluster ordering during updates, since updated rows are kept on the same page if enough space is available there.)

When a table is clustered, PostgreSQL remembers which index it was clustered by. The form CLUSTER *table_name* reclusters the table using the same index as before. You can also use the CLUSTER or SET WITHOUT CLUSTER forms of ALTER TABLE to set the index to be used for future cluster operations, or to clear any previous setting.

CLUSTER without any parameter reclusters all the previously-clustered tables in the current database that the calling user owns, or all such tables if called by a superuser. This form of CLUSTER cannot be executed inside a transaction block.

When a table is being clustered, an ACCESS EXCLUSIVE lock is acquired on it. This prevents any other database operations (both reads and writes) from operating on the table until the CLUSTER is finished.

Parameters

table_name

The name (possibly schema-qualified) of a table.

index_name

The name of an index.

VERBOSE

Prints a progress report as each table is clustered.

Notes

In cases where you are accessing single rows randomly within a table, the actual order of the data in the table is unimportant. However, if you tend to access some data more than others, and there is an index

---

1545

that groups them together, you will benefit from using CLUSTER. If you are requesting a range of indexed values from a table, or a single indexed value that has multiple rows that match, CLUSTER will help because once the index identifies the table page for the first row that matches, all other rows that match are probably already on the same table page, and so you save disk accesses and speed up the query.

CLUSTER can re-sort the table using either an index scan on the specified index, or (if the index is a b-tree) a sequential scan followed by sorting. It will attempt to choose the method that will be faster, based on planner cost parameters and available statistical information.

When an index scan is used, a temporary copy of the table is created that contains the table data in the index order. Temporary copies of each index on the table are created as well. Therefore, you need free space on disk at least equal to the sum of the table size and the index sizes.

When a sequential scan and sort is used, a temporary sort file is also created, so that the peak temporary space requirement is as much as double the table size, plus the index sizes. This method is often faster than the index scan method, but if the disk space requirement is intolerable, you can disable this choice by temporarily setting enable_sort to off.

It is advisable to set maintenance_work_mem to a reasonably large value (but not more than the amount of RAM you can dedicate to the CLUSTER operation) before clustering.

Because the planner records statistics about the ordering of tables, it is advisable to run ANALYZE on the newly clustered table. Otherwise, the planner might make poor choices of query plans.

Because CLUSTER remembers which indexes are clustered, one can cluster the tables one wants clustered manually the first time, then set up a periodic maintenance script that executes CLUSTER without any parameters, so that the desired tables are periodically reclustered.

Examples

Cluster the table employees on the basis of its index employees_ind:

```
CLUSTER employees USING employees_ind;
```

Cluster the employees table using the same index that was used before:

```
CLUSTER employees;
```

Cluster all tables in the database that have previously been clustered:

```
CLUSTER;
```

Compatibility

There is no CLUSTER statement in the SQL standard.

The syntax

```
CLUSTER index_name ON table_name
```

is also supported for compatibility with pre-8.3 PostgreSQL versions.

See Also

clusterdb

COMMENT

COMMENT — define or change the comment of an object

Synopsis

```
COMMENT ON
{
    ACCESS METHOD object_name |
    AGGREGATE aggregate_name ( aggregate_signature ) |
    CAST (source_type AS target_type) |
    COLLATION object_name |
    COLUMN relation_name.column_name |
    CONSTRAINT constraint_name ON table_name |
    CONSTRAINT constraint_name ON DOMAIN domain_name |
    CONVERSION object_name |
    DATABASE object_name |
    DOMAIN object_name |
    EXTENSION object_name |
    EVENT TRIGGER object_name |
    FOREIGN DATA WRAPPER object_name |
    FOREIGN TABLE object_name |
    FUNCTION function_name [ ( [ [ argmode ] [ argname ] argtype
[, ...] ] ) ] |
    INDEX object_name |
    LARGE OBJECT large_object_oid |
    MATERIALIZED VIEW object_name |
    OPERATOR operator_name (left_type, right_type) |
    OPERATOR CLASS object_name USING index_method |
    OPERATOR FAMILY object_name USING index_method |
    POLICY policy_name ON table_name |
    [ PROCEDURAL ] LANGUAGE object_name |
    PROCEDURE procedure_name [ ( [ [ argmode ] [ argname ] argtype
[, ...] ] ) ] |
    PUBLICATION object_name |
    ROLE object_name |
    ROUTINE routine_name [ ( [ [ argmode ] [ argname ] argtype
[, ...] ] ) ] |
    RULE rule_name ON table_name |
    SCHEMA object_name |
    SEQUENCE object_name |
    SERVER object_name |
    STATISTICS object_name |
    SUBSCRIPTION object_name |
    TABLE object_name |
    TABLESPACE object_name |
    TEXT SEARCH CONFIGURATION object_name |
    TEXT SEARCH DICTIONARY object_name |
    TEXT SEARCH PARSER object_name |
    TEXT SEARCH TEMPLATE object_name |
```

```
    TRANSFORM FOR type_name LANGUAGE lang_name |
    TRIGGER trigger_name ON table_name |
    TYPE object_name |
    VIEW object_name
} IS 'text'
```

where *aggregate_signature* is:

```
* |
[ argmode ] [ argname ] argtype [ , ... ] |
[ [ argmode ] [ argname ] argtype [ , ... ] ] ORDER BY [ argmode ]
 [ argname ] argtype [ , ... ]
```

Description

COMMENT stores a comment about a database object.

Only one comment string is stored for each object, so to modify a comment, issue a new COMMENT command for the same object. To remove a comment, write NULL in place of the text string. Comments are automatically dropped when their object is dropped.

For most kinds of object, only the object's owner can set the comment. Roles don't have owners, so the rule for COMMENT ON ROLE is that you must be superuser to comment on a superuser role, or have the CREATEROLE privilege to comment on non-superuser roles. Likewise, access methods don't have owners either; you must be superuser to comment on an access method. Of course, a superuser can comment on anything.

Comments can be viewed using psql's \d family of commands. Other user interfaces to retrieve comments can be built atop the same built-in functions that psql uses, namely obj_description, col_description, and shobj_description (see Table 9.68).

Parameters

object_name
relation_name.column_name
aggregate_name
constraint_name
function_name
operator_name
policy_name
procedure_name
routine_name
rule_name
trigger_name

> The name of the object to be commented. Names of tables, aggregates, collations, conversions, domains, foreign tables, functions, indexes, operators, operator classes, operator families, procedures, routines, sequences, statistics, text search objects, types, and views can be schema-qualified. When commenting on a column, *relation_name* must refer to a table, view, composite type, or foreign table.

table_name
domain_name

When creating a comment on a constraint, a trigger, a rule or a policy these parameters specify the name of the table or domain on which that object is defined.

source_type

The name of the source data type of the cast.

target_type

The name of the target data type of the cast.

argmode

The mode of a function, procedure, or aggregate argument: IN, OUT, INOUT, or VARIADIC. If omitted, the default is IN. Note that COMMENT does not actually pay any attention to OUT arguments, since only the input arguments are needed to determine the function's identity. So it is sufficient to list the IN, INOUT, and VARIADIC arguments.

argname

The name of a function, procedure, or aggregate argument. Note that COMMENT does not actually pay any attention to argument names, since only the argument data types are needed to determine the function's identity.

argtype

The data type of a function, procedure, or aggregate argument.

large_object_oid

The OID of the large object.

left_type
right_type

The data type(s) of the operator's arguments (optionally schema-qualified). Write NONE for the missing argument of a prefix or postfix operator.

PROCEDURAL

This is a noise word.

type_name

The name of the data type of the transform.

lang_name

The name of the language of the transform.

text

The new comment, written as a string literal; or NULL to drop the comment.

Notes

There is presently no security mechanism for viewing comments: any user connected to a database can see all the comments for objects in that database. For shared objects such as databases, roles, and tablespaces, comments are stored globally so any user connected to any database in the cluster can see all the comments for shared objects. Therefore, don't put security-critical information in comments.

Examples

Attach a comment to the table `mytable`:

```
COMMENT ON TABLE mytable IS 'This is my table.';
```

Remove it again:

```
COMMENT ON TABLE mytable IS NULL;
```

Some more examples:

```
COMMENT ON ACCESS METHOD rtree IS 'R-Tree access method';
COMMENT ON AGGREGATE my_aggregate (double precision) IS 'Computes
 sample variance';
COMMENT ON CAST (text AS int4) IS 'Allow casts from text to int4';
COMMENT ON COLLATION "fr_CA" IS 'Canadian French';
COMMENT ON COLUMN my_table.my_column IS 'Employee ID number';
COMMENT ON CONVERSION my_conv IS 'Conversion to UTF8';
COMMENT ON CONSTRAINT bar_col_cons ON bar IS 'Constrains column col';
COMMENT ON CONSTRAINT dom_col_constr ON DOMAIN dom IS 'Constrains col
 of domain';
COMMENT ON DATABASE my_database IS 'Development Database';
COMMENT ON DOMAIN my_domain IS 'Email Address Domain';
COMMENT ON EXTENSION hstore IS 'implements the hstore data type';
COMMENT ON FOREIGN DATA WRAPPER mywrapper IS 'my foreign data
 wrapper';
COMMENT ON FOREIGN TABLE my_foreign_table IS 'Employee Information in
 other database';
COMMENT ON FUNCTION my_function (timestamp) IS 'Returns Roman
 Numeral';
COMMENT ON INDEX my_index IS 'Enforces uniqueness on employee ID';
COMMENT ON LANGUAGE plpython IS 'Python support for stored
 procedures';
COMMENT ON LARGE OBJECT 346344 IS 'Planning document';
COMMENT ON MATERIALIZED VIEW my_matview IS 'Summary of order history';
COMMENT ON OPERATOR ^ (text, text) IS 'Performs intersection of two
 texts';
COMMENT ON OPERATOR - (NONE, integer) IS 'Unary minus';
COMMENT ON OPERATOR CLASS int4ops USING btree IS '4 byte integer
 operators for btrees';
COMMENT ON OPERATOR FAMILY integer_ops USING btree IS 'all integer
 operators for btrees';
COMMENT ON POLICY my_policy ON mytable IS 'Filter rows by users';
```

```
COMMENT ON PROCEDURE my_proc (integer, integer) IS 'Runs a report';
COMMENT ON ROLE my_role IS 'Administration group for finance tables';
COMMENT ON RULE my_rule ON my_table IS 'Logs updates of employee
  records';
COMMENT ON SCHEMA my_schema IS 'Departmental data';
COMMENT ON SEQUENCE my_sequence IS 'Used to generate primary keys';
COMMENT ON SERVER myserver IS 'my foreign server';
COMMENT ON STATISTICS my_statistics IS 'Improves planner row
  estimations';
COMMENT ON TABLE my_schema.my_table IS 'Employee Information';
COMMENT ON TABLESPACE my_tablespace IS 'Tablespace for indexes';
COMMENT ON TEXT SEARCH CONFIGURATION my_config IS 'Special word
  filtering';
COMMENT ON TEXT SEARCH DICTIONARY swedish IS 'Snowball stemmer for
  Swedish language';
COMMENT ON TEXT SEARCH PARSER my_parser IS 'Splits text into words';
COMMENT ON TEXT SEARCH TEMPLATE snowball IS 'Snowball stemmer';
COMMENT ON TRANSFORM FOR hstore LANGUAGE plpythonu IS 'Transform
  between hstore and Python dict';
COMMENT ON TRIGGER my_trigger ON my_table IS 'Used for RI';
COMMENT ON TYPE complex IS 'Complex number data type';
COMMENT ON VIEW my_view IS 'View of departmental costs';
```

Compatibility

There is no COMMENT command in the SQL standard.

COMMIT

COMMIT — commit the current transaction

Synopsis

```
COMMIT [ WORK | TRANSACTION ]
```

Description

COMMIT commits the current transaction. All changes made by the transaction become visible to others and are guaranteed to be durable if a crash occurs.

Parameters

WORK
TRANSACTION

Optional key words. They have no effect.

Notes

Use ROLLBACK to abort a transaction.

Issuing COMMIT when not inside a transaction does no harm, but it will provoke a warning message.

Examples

To commit the current transaction and make all changes permanent:

```
COMMIT;
```

Compatibility

The SQL standard only specifies the two forms COMMIT and COMMIT WORK. Otherwise, this command is fully conforming.

See Also

BEGIN, ROLLBACK

COMMIT PREPARED

COMMIT PREPARED — commit a transaction that was earlier prepared for two-phase commit

Synopsis

```
COMMIT PREPARED transaction_id
```

Description

COMMIT PREPARED commits a transaction that is in prepared state.

Parameters

transaction_id

The transaction identifier of the transaction that is to be committed.

Notes

To commit a prepared transaction, you must be either the same user that executed the transaction originally, or a superuser. But you do not have to be in the same session that executed the transaction.

This command cannot be executed inside a transaction block. The prepared transaction is committed immediately.

All currently available prepared transactions are listed in the pg_prepared_xacts system view.

Examples

Commit the transaction identified by the transaction identifier foobar:

```
COMMIT PREPARED 'foobar';
```

Compatibility

COMMIT PREPARED is a PostgreSQL extension. It is intended for use by external transaction management systems, some of which are covered by standards (such as X/Open XA), but the SQL side of those systems is not standardized.

See Also

PREPARE TRANSACTION, ROLLBACK PREPARED

COPY

COPY — copy data between a file and a table

Synopsis

```
COPY table_name [ ( column_name [, ...] ) ]
    FROM { 'filename' | PROGRAM 'command' | STDIN }
    [ [ WITH ] ( option [, ...] ) ]

COPY { table_name [ ( column_name [, ...] ) ] | ( query ) }
    TO { 'filename' | PROGRAM 'command' | STDOUT }
    [ [ WITH ] ( option [, ...] ) ]

where option can be one of:

    FORMAT format_name
    OIDS [ boolean ]
    FREEZE [ boolean ]
    DELIMITER 'delimiter_character'
    NULL 'null_string'
    HEADER [ boolean ]
    QUOTE 'quote_character'
    ESCAPE 'escape_character'
    FORCE_QUOTE { ( column_name [, ...] ) | * }
    FORCE_NOT_NULL ( column_name [, ...] )
    FORCE_NULL ( column_name [, ...] )
    ENCODING 'encoding_name'
```

Description

COPY moves data between PostgreSQL tables and standard file-system files. COPY TO copies the contents of a table *to* a file, while COPY FROM copies data *from* a file to a table (appending the data to whatever is in the table already). COPY TO can also copy the results of a SELECT query.

If a list of columns is specified, COPY will only copy the data in the specified columns to or from the file. If there are any columns in the table that are not in the column list, COPY FROM will insert the default values for those columns.

COPY with a file name instructs the PostgreSQL server to directly read from or write to a file. The file must be accessible by the PostgreSQL user (the user ID the server runs as) and the name must be specified from the viewpoint of the server. When PROGRAM is specified, the server executes the given command and reads from the standard output of the program, or writes to the standard input of the program. The command must be specified from the viewpoint of the server, and be executable by the PostgreSQL user. When STDIN or STDOUT is specified, data is transmitted via the connection between the client and the server.

Parameters

table_name

The name (optionally schema-qualified) of an existing table.

column_name

An optional list of columns to be copied. If no column list is specified, all columns of the table will be copied.

query

A SELECT, VALUES, INSERT, UPDATE or DELETE command whose results are to be copied. Note that parentheses are required around the query.

For **INSERT**, **UPDATE** and **DELETE** queries a RETURNING clause must be provided, and the target relation must not have a conditional rule, nor an **ALSO** rule, nor an **INSTEAD** rule that expands to multiple statements.

filename

The path name of the input or output file. An input file name can be an absolute or relative path, but an output file name must be an absolute path. Windows users might need to use an **E** ' ' string and double any backslashes used in the path name.

PROGRAM

A command to execute. In **COPY FROM**, the input is read from standard output of the command, and in **COPY TO**, the output is written to the standard input of the command.

Note that the command is invoked by the shell, so if you need to pass any arguments to shell command that come from an untrusted source, you must be careful to strip or escape any special characters that might have a special meaning for the shell. For security reasons, it is best to use a fixed command string, or at least avoid passing any user input in it.

STDIN

Specifies that input comes from the client application.

STDOUT

Specifies that output goes to the client application.

boolean

Specifies whether the selected option should be turned on or off. You can write **TRUE**, **ON**, or **1** to enable the option, and **FALSE**, **OFF**, or **0** to disable it. The *boolean* value can also be omitted, in which case **TRUE** is assumed.

FORMAT

Selects the data format to be read or written: **text**, **csv** (Comma Separated Values), or **binary**. The default is **text**.

OIDS

Specifies copying the OID for each row. (An error is raised if **OIDS** is specified for a table that does not have OIDs, or in the case of copying a *query*.)

FREEZE

Requests copying the data with rows already frozen, just as they would be after running the **VACUUM FREEZE** command. This is intended as a performance option for initial data loading. Rows will be frozen only if the table being loaded has been created or truncated in the current subtransaction, there are no cursors open and there are no older snapshots held by this transaction. It is currently not possible to perform a `COPY FREEZE` on a partitioned table.

Note that all other sessions will immediately be able to see the data once it has been successfully loaded. This violates the normal rules of MVCC visibility and users specifying should be aware of the potential problems this might cause.

`DELIMITER`

Specifies the character that separates columns within each row (line) of the file. The default is a tab character in text format, a comma in `CSV` format. This must be a single one-byte character. This option is not allowed when using `binary` format.

`NULL`

Specifies the string that represents a null value. The default is `\N` (backslash-N) in text format, and an unquoted empty string in `CSV` format. You might prefer an empty string even in text format for cases where you don't want to distinguish nulls from empty strings. This option is not allowed when using `binary` format.

Note

When using `COPY FROM`, any data item that matches this string will be stored as a null value, so you should make sure that you use the same string as you used with `COPY TO`.

`HEADER`

Specifies that the file contains a header line with the names of each column in the file. On output, the first line contains the column names from the table, and on input, the first line is ignored. This option is allowed only when using `CSV` format.

`QUOTE`

Specifies the quoting character to be used when a data value is quoted. The default is double-quote. This must be a single one-byte character. This option is allowed only when using `CSV` format.

`ESCAPE`

Specifies the character that should appear before a data character that matches the `QUOTE` value. The default is the same as the `QUOTE` value (so that the quoting character is doubled if it appears in the data). This must be a single one-byte character. This option is allowed only when using `CSV` format.

`FORCE_QUOTE`

Forces quoting to be used for all non-`NULL` values in each specified column. `NULL` output is never quoted. If * is specified, non-`NULL` values will be quoted in all columns. This option is allowed only in `COPY TO`, and only when using `CSV` format.

`FORCE_NOT_NULL`

Do not match the specified columns' values against the null string. In the default case where the null string is empty, this means that empty values will be read as zero-length strings rather than nulls, even when they are not quoted. This option is allowed only in `COPY FROM`, and only when using `CSV` format.

FORCE_NULL

Match the specified columns' values against the null string, even if it has been quoted, and if a match is found set the value to NULL. In the default case where the null string is empty, this converts a quoted empty string into NULL. This option is allowed only in COPY FROM, and only when using CSV format.

ENCODING

Specifies that the file is encoded in the *encoding_name*. If this option is omitted, the current client encoding is used. See the Notes below for more details.

Outputs

On successful completion, a COPY command returns a command tag of the form

COPY *count*

The *count* is the number of rows copied.

> ## Note
>
> psql will print this command tag only if the command was not COPY ... TO STDOUT, or the equivalent psql meta-command \copy ... to stdout. This is to prevent confusing the command tag with the data that was just printed.

Notes

COPY TO can only be used with plain tables, not with views. However, you can write COPY (SELECT * FROM *viewname*) TO ... to copy the current contents of a view.

COPY FROM can be used with plain, foreign, or partitioned tables or with views that have INSTEAD OF INSERT triggers.

COPY only deals with the specific table named; it does not copy data to or from child tables. Thus for example COPY *table* TO shows the same data as SELECT * FROM ONLY *table*. But COPY (SELECT * FROM *table*) TO ... can be used to dump all of the data in an inheritance hierarchy.

You must have select privilege on the table whose values are read by COPY TO, and insert privilege on the table into which values are inserted by COPY FROM. It is sufficient to have column privileges on the column(s) listed in the command.

If row-level security is enabled for the table, the relevant SELECT policies will apply to COPY *table* TO statements. Currently, COPY FROM is not supported for tables with row-level security. Use equivalent INSERT statements instead.

Files named in a COPY command are read or written directly by the server, not by the client application. Therefore, they must reside on or be accessible to the database server machine, not the client. They must be accessible to and readable or writable by the PostgreSQL user (the user ID the server runs as), not the client. Similarly, the command specified with PROGRAM is executed directly by the server, not by the client application, must be executable by the PostgreSQL user. COPY naming a file or command is only allowed to database superusers or users who are granted one of the default roles `pg_read_server_files`, `pg_write_server_files`, or `pg_execute_server_program`, since it allows reading or writing any file or running a program that the server has privileges to access.

Do not confuse `COPY` with the psql instruction `\copy`. `\copy` invokes `COPY FROM STDIN` or `COPY TO STDOUT`, and then fetches/stores the data in a file accessible to the psql client. Thus, file accessibility and access rights depend on the client rather than the server when `\copy` is used.

It is recommended that the file name used in `COPY` always be specified as an absolute path. This is enforced by the server in the case of `COPY TO`, but for `COPY FROM` you do have the option of reading from a file specified by a relative path. The path will be interpreted relative to the working directory of the server process (normally the cluster's data directory), not the client's working directory.

Executing a command with `PROGRAM` might be restricted by the operating system's access control mechanisms, such as SELinux.

`COPY FROM` will invoke any triggers and check constraints on the destination table. However, it will not invoke rules.

For identity columns, the `COPY FROM` command will always write the column values provided in the input data, like the `INSERT` option `OVERRIDING SYSTEM VALUE`.

`COPY` input and output is affected by `DateStyle`. To ensure portability to other PostgreSQL installations that might use non-default `DateStyle` settings, `DateStyle` should be set to `ISO` before using `COPY TO`. It is also a good idea to avoid dumping data with `IntervalStyle` set to `sql_standard`, because negative interval values might be misinterpreted by a server that has a different setting for `IntervalStyle`.

Input data is interpreted according to `ENCODING` option or the current client encoding, and output data is encoded in `ENCODING` or the current client encoding, even if the data does not pass through the client but is read from or written to a file directly by the server.

`COPY` stops operation at the first error. This should not lead to problems in the event of a `COPY TO`, but the target table will already have received earlier rows in a `COPY FROM`. These rows will not be visible or accessible, but they still occupy disk space. This might amount to a considerable amount of wasted disk space if the failure happened well into a large copy operation. You might wish to invoke `VACUUM` to recover the wasted space.

`FORCE_NULL` and `FORCE_NOT_NULL` can be used simultaneously on the same column. This results in converting quoted null strings to null values and unquoted null strings to empty strings.

File Formats

Text Format

When the `text` format is used, the data read or written is a text file with one line per table row. Columns in a row are separated by the delimiter character. The column values themselves are strings generated by the output function, or acceptable to the input function, of each attribute's data type. The specified null string is used in place of columns that are null. `COPY FROM` will raise an error if any line of the input file contains more or fewer columns than are expected. If `OIDS` is specified, the OID is read or written as the first column, preceding the user data columns.

End of data can be represented by a single line containing just backslash-period (`\.`). An end-of-data marker is not necessary when reading from a file, since the end of file serves perfectly well; it is needed only when copying data to or from client applications using pre-3.0 client protocol.

Backslash characters (\) can be used in the COPY data to quote data characters that might otherwise be taken as row or column delimiters. In particular, the following characters *must* be preceded by a backslash if they appear as part of a column value: backslash itself, newline, carriage return, and the current delimiter character.

The specified null string is sent by COPY TO without adding any backslashes; conversely, COPY FROM matches the input against the null string before removing backslashes. Therefore, a null string such as \N cannot be confused with the actual data value \N (which would be represented as \\N).

The following special backslash sequences are recognized by COPY FROM:

Sequence	Represents
\b	Backspace (ASCII 8)
\f	Form feed (ASCII 12)
\n	Newline (ASCII 10)
\r	Carriage return (ASCII 13)
\t	Tab (ASCII 9)
\v	Vertical tab (ASCII 11)
digits	Backslash followed by one to three octal digits specifies the character with that numeric code
\x*digits*	Backslash x followed by one or two hex digits specifies the character with that numeric code

Presently, COPY TO will never emit an octal or hex-digits backslash sequence, but it does use the other sequences listed above for those control characters.

Any other backslashed character that is not mentioned in the above table will be taken to represent itself. However, beware of adding backslashes unnecessarily, since that might accidentally produce a string matching the end-of-data marker (\.) or the null string (\N by default). These strings will be recognized before any other backslash processing is done.

It is strongly recommended that applications generating COPY data convert data newlines and carriage returns to the \n and \r sequences respectively. At present it is possible to represent a data carriage return by a backslash and carriage return, and to represent a data newline by a backslash and newline. However, these representations might not be accepted in future releases. They are also highly vulnerable to corruption if the COPY file is transferred across different machines (for example, from Unix to Windows or vice versa).

COPY TO will terminate each row with a Unix-style newline ("\n"). Servers running on Microsoft Windows instead output carriage return/newline ("\r\n"), but only for COPY to a server file; for consistency across platforms, COPY TO STDOUT always sends "\n" regardless of server platform. COPY FROM can handle lines ending with newlines, carriage returns, or carriage return/newlines. To reduce the risk of error due to un-backslashed newlines or carriage returns that were meant as data, COPY FROM will complain if the line endings in the input are not all alike.

CSV Format

This format option is used for importing and exporting the Comma Separated Value (CSV) file format used by many other programs, such as spreadsheets. Instead of the escaping rules used by PostgreSQL's standard text format, it produces and recognizes the common CSV escaping mechanism.

The values in each record are separated by the DELIMITER character. If the value contains the delimiter character, the QUOTE character, the NULL string, a carriage return, or line feed character, then the whole value is prefixed and suffixed by the QUOTE character, and any occurrence within the value of a QUOTE character or the ESCAPE character is preceded by the escape character. You can also use FORCE_QUOTE to force quotes when outputting non-NULL values in specific columns.

The CSV format has no standard way to distinguish a NULL value from an empty string. PostgreSQL's COPY handles this by quoting. A NULL is output as the NULL parameter string and is not quoted, while a non-NULL value matching the NULL parameter string is quoted. For example, with the default settings, a NULL is written as an unquoted empty string, while an empty string data value is written with double quotes (""). Reading values follows similar rules. You can use FORCE_NOT_NULL to prevent NULL input comparisons for specific columns. You can also use FORCE_NULL to convert quoted null string data values to NULL.

Because backslash is not a special character in the CSV format, \., the end-of-data marker, could also appear as a data value. To avoid any misinterpretation, a \. data value appearing as a lone entry on a line is automatically quoted on output, and on input, if quoted, is not interpreted as the end-of-data marker. If you are loading a file created by another application that has a single unquoted column and might have a value of \., you might need to quote that value in the input file.

Note

In CSV format, all characters are significant. A quoted value surrounded by white space, or any characters other than DELIMITER, will include those characters. This can cause errors if you import data from a system that pads CSV lines with white space out to some fixed width. If such a situation arises you might need to preprocess the CSV file to remove the trailing white space, before importing the data into PostgreSQL.

Note

CSV format will both recognize and produce CSV files with quoted values containing embedded carriage returns and line feeds. Thus the files are not strictly one line per table row like text-format files.

Note

Many programs produce strange and occasionally perverse CSV files, so the file format is more a convention than a standard. Thus you might encounter some files that cannot be imported using this mechanism, and COPY might produce files that other programs cannot process.

Binary Format

The binary format option causes all data to be stored/read as binary format rather than as text. It is somewhat faster than the text and CSV formats, but a binary-format file is less portable across machine architectures and PostgreSQL versions. Also, the binary format is very data type specific; for example it will not work to output binary data from a smallint column and read it into an integer column, even though that would work fine in text format.

The binary file format consists of a file header, zero or more tuples containing the row data, and a file trailer. Headers and data are in network byte order.

Note

PostgreSQL releases before 7.4 used a different binary file format.

File Header

The file header consists of 15 bytes of fixed fields, followed by a variable-length header extension area. The fixed fields are:

Signature

11-byte sequence `PGCOPY\n\377\r\n\0` — note that the zero byte is a required part of the signature. (The signature is designed to allow easy identification of files that have been munged by a non-8-bit-clean transfer. This signature will be changed by end-of-line-translation filters, dropped zero bytes, dropped high bits, or parity changes.)

Flags field

32-bit integer bit mask to denote important aspects of the file format. Bits are numbered from 0 (LSB) to 31 (MSB). Note that this field is stored in network byte order (most significant byte first), as are all the integer fields used in the file format. Bits 16-31 are reserved to denote critical file format issues; a reader should abort if it finds an unexpected bit set in this range. Bits 0-15 are reserved to signal backwards-compatible format issues; a reader should simply ignore any unexpected bits set in this range. Currently only one flag bit is defined, and the rest must be zero:

Bit 16

if 1, OIDs are included in the data; if 0, not

Header extension area length

32-bit integer, length in bytes of remainder of header, not including self. Currently, this is zero, and the first tuple follows immediately. Future changes to the format might allow additional data to be present in the header. A reader should silently skip over any header extension data it does not know what to do with.

The header extension area is envisioned to contain a sequence of self-identifying chunks. The flags field is not intended to tell readers what is in the extension area. Specific design of header extension contents is left for a later release.

This design allows for both backwards-compatible header additions (add header extension chunks, or set low-order flag bits) and non-backwards-compatible changes (set high-order flag bits to signal such changes, and add supporting data to the extension area if needed).

Tuples

Each tuple begins with a 16-bit integer count of the number of fields in the tuple. (Presently, all tuples in a table will have the same count, but that might not always be true.) Then, repeated for each field in the tuple, there is a 32-bit length word followed by that many bytes of field data. (The length word does not include itself, and can be zero.) As a special case, -1 indicates a NULL field value. No value bytes follow in the NULL case.

There is no alignment padding or any other extra data between fields.

Presently, all data values in a binary-format file are assumed to be in binary format (format code one). It is anticipated that a future extension might add a header field that allows per-column format codes to be specified.

To determine the appropriate binary format for the actual tuple data you should consult the PostgreSQL source, in particular the `*send` and `*recv` functions for each column's data type (typically these functions are found in the `src/backend/utils/adt/` directory of the source distribution).

If OIDs are included in the file, the OID field immediately follows the field-count word. It is a normal field except that it's not included in the field-count. In particular it has a length word — this will allow handling of 4-byte vs. 8-byte OIDs without too much pain, and will allow OIDs to be shown as null if that ever proves desirable.

File Trailer

The file trailer consists of a 16-bit integer word containing -1. This is easily distinguished from a tuple's field-count word.

A reader should report an error if a field-count word is neither -1 nor the expected number of columns. This provides an extra check against somehow getting out of sync with the data.

Examples

The following example copies a table to the client using the vertical bar (`|`) as the field delimiter:

```
COPY country TO STDOUT (DELIMITER '|');
```

To copy data from a file into the `country` table:

```
COPY country FROM '/usr1/proj/bray/sql/country_data';
```

To copy into a file just the countries whose names start with 'A':

```
COPY (SELECT * FROM country WHERE country_name LIKE 'A%') TO '/usr1/proj/bray/sql/a_list_countries.copy';
```

To copy into a compressed file, you can pipe the output through an external compression program:

```
COPY country TO PROGRAM 'gzip > /usr1/proj/bray/sql/country_data.gz';
```

Here is a sample of data suitable for copying into a table from `STDIN`:

```
AF      AFGHANISTAN
AL      ALBANIA
DZ      ALGERIA
ZM      ZAMBIA
ZW      ZIMBABWE
```

Note that the white space on each line is actually a tab character.

The following is the same data, output in binary format. The data is shown after filtering through the Unix utility `od -c`. The table has three columns; the first has type `char(2)`, the second has type `text`, and the third has type `integer`. All the rows have a null value in the third column.

```
0000000    P    G    C    O    P    Y  \n 377 \r  \n  \0  \0  \0  \0  \0
\0
0000020   \0   \0   \0   \0 003   \0  \0  \0 002   A   F  \0  \0  \0 013
A
0000040    F    G    H    A    N    I   S   T   A   N 377 377 377 377  \0
003
0000060   \0   \0   \0 002    A    L   \0  \0  \0 007   A   L   B   A   N
I
0000100    A  377  377  377  377   \0 003  \0  \0  \0 002   D   Z  \0  \0
\0
0000120  007    A    L    G    E    R   I   A 377 377 377 377  \0 003  \0
\0
0000140   \0  002    Z    M   \0   \0  \0 006   Z   A   M   B   I   A 377
377
0000160  377  377   \0  003   \0   \0  \0 002   Z   W  \0  \0  \0  \b   z
I
0000200    M    B    A    B    W    E 377 377 377 377 377 377
```

Compatibility

There is no COPY statement in the SQL standard.

The following syntax was used before PostgreSQL version 9.0 and is still supported:

```
COPY table_name [ ( column_name [, ...] ) ]
    FROM { 'filename' | STDIN }
    [ [ WITH ]
          [ BINARY ]
          [ OIDS ]
          [ DELIMITER [ AS ] 'delimiter' ]
          [ NULL [ AS ] 'null string' ]
          [ CSV [ HEADER ]
                [ QUOTE [ AS ] 'quote' ]
                [ ESCAPE [ AS ] 'escape' ]
                [ FORCE NOT NULL column_name [, ...] ] ] ]

COPY { table_name [ ( column_name [, ...] ) ] | ( query ) }
    TO { 'filename' | STDOUT }
    [ [ WITH ]
          [ BINARY ]
          [ OIDS ]
          [ DELIMITER [ AS ] 'delimiter' ]
          [ NULL [ AS ] 'null string' ]
          [ CSV [ HEADER ]
                [ QUOTE [ AS ] 'quote' ]
                [ ESCAPE [ AS ] 'escape' ]
                [ FORCE QUOTE { column_name [, ...] | * } ] ] ]
```

Note that in this syntax, BINARY and CSV are treated as independent keywords, not as arguments of a FORMAT option.

The following syntax was used before PostgreSQL version 7.3 and is still supported:

```
COPY [ BINARY ] table_name [ WITH OIDS ]
    FROM { 'filename' | STDIN }
    [ [USING] DELIMITERS 'delimiter' ]
    [ WITH NULL AS 'null string' ]

COPY [ BINARY ] table_name [ WITH OIDS ]
    TO { 'filename' | STDOUT }
    [ [USING] DELIMITERS 'delimiter' ]
    [ WITH NULL AS 'null string' ]
```

CREATE ACCESS METHOD

CREATE ACCESS METHOD — define a new access method

Synopsis

```
CREATE ACCESS METHOD name
    TYPE access_method_type
    HANDLER handler_function
```

Description

CREATE ACCESS METHOD creates a new access method.

The access method name must be unique within the database.

Only superusers can define new access methods.

Parameters

name

> The name of the access method to be created.

access_method_type

> This clause specifies the type of access method to define. Only INDEX is supported at present.

handler_function

> *handler_function* is the name (possibly schema-qualified) of a previously registered function that represents the access method. The handler function must be declared to take a single argument of type internal, and its return type depends on the type of access method; for INDEX access methods, it must be index_am_handler. The C-level API that the handler function must implement varies depending on the type of access method. The index access method API is described in Chapter 61.

Examples

Create an index access method heptree with handler function heptree_handler:

```
CREATE ACCESS METHOD heptree TYPE INDEX HANDLER heptree_handler;
```

Compatibility

CREATE ACCESS METHOD is a PostgreSQL extension.

See Also

DROP ACCESS METHOD, CREATE OPERATOR CLASS, CREATE OPERATOR FAMILY

CREATE AGGREGATE

CREATE AGGREGATE — define a new aggregate function

Synopsis

```
CREATE AGGREGATE name ( [ argmode ] [ argname ] arg_data_type
[ , ... ] ) (
    SFUNC = sfunc,
    STYPE = state_data_type
    [ , SSPACE = state_data_size ]
    [ , FINALFUNC = ffunc ]
    [ , FINALFUNC_EXTRA ]
    [ , FINALFUNC_MODIFY = { READ_ONLY | SHAREABLE | READ_WRITE } ]
    [ , COMBINEFUNC = combinefunc ]
    [ , SERIALFUNC = serialfunc ]
    [ , DESERIALFUNC = deserialfunc ]
    [ , INITCOND = initial_condition ]
    [ , MSFUNC = msfunc ]
    [ , MINVFUNC = minvfunc ]
    [ , MSTYPE = mstate_data_type ]
    [ , MSSPACE = mstate_data_size ]
    [ , MFINALFUNC = mffunc ]
    [ , MFINALFUNC_EXTRA ]
    [ , MFINALFUNC_MODIFY = { READ_ONLY | SHAREABLE | READ_WRITE } ]
    [ , MINITCOND = minitial_condition ]
    [ , SORTOP = sort_operator ]
    [ , PARALLEL = { SAFE | RESTRICTED | UNSAFE } ]
)

CREATE AGGREGATE name ( [ [ argmode ] [ argname ] arg_data_type
[ , ... ] ]
                        ORDER BY [ argmode ] [ argname ] arg_data_type
[ , ... ] ) (
    SFUNC = sfunc,
    STYPE = state_data_type
    [ , SSPACE = state_data_size ]
    [ , FINALFUNC = ffunc ]
    [ , FINALFUNC_EXTRA ]
    [ , FINALFUNC_MODIFY = { READ_ONLY | SHAREABLE | READ_WRITE } ]
    [ , INITCOND = initial_condition ]
    [ , PARALLEL = { SAFE | RESTRICTED | UNSAFE } ]
    [ , HYPOTHETICAL ]
)

or the old syntax

CREATE AGGREGATE name (
    BASETYPE = base_type,
    SFUNC = sfunc,
```

```
        STYPE = state_data_type
      [ , SSPACE = state_data_size ]
      [ , FINALFUNC = ffunc ]
      [ , FINALFUNC_EXTRA ]
      [ , FINALFUNC_MODIFY = { READ_ONLY | SHAREABLE | READ_WRITE } ]
      [ , COMBINEFUNC = combinefunc ]
      [ , SERIALFUNC = serialfunc ]
      [ , DESERIALFUNC = deserialfunc ]
      [ , INITCOND = initial_condition ]
      [ , MSFUNC = msfunc ]
      [ , MINVFUNC = minvfunc ]
      [ , MSTYPE = mstate_data_type ]
      [ , MSSPACE = mstate_data_size ]
      [ , MFINALFUNC = mffunc ]
      [ , MFINALFUNC_EXTRA ]
      [ , MFINALFUNC_MODIFY = { READ_ONLY | SHAREABLE | READ_WRITE } ]
      [ , MINITCOND = minitial_condition ]
      [ , SORTOP = sort_operator ]
    )
```

Description

CREATE AGGREGATE defines a new aggregate function. Some basic and commonly-used aggregate functions are included with the distribution; they are documented in Section 9.20. If one defines new types or needs an aggregate function not already provided, then CREATE AGGREGATE can be used to provide the desired features.

If a schema name is given (for example, CREATE AGGREGATE myschema.myagg ...) then the aggregate function is created in the specified schema. Otherwise it is created in the current schema.

An aggregate function is identified by its name and input data type(s). Two aggregates in the same schema can have the same name if they operate on different input types. The name and input data type(s) of an aggregate must also be distinct from the name and input data type(s) of every ordinary function in the same schema. This behavior is identical to overloading of ordinary function names (see CREATE FUNCTION).

A simple aggregate function is made from one or two ordinary functions: a state transition function *sfunc*, and an optional final calculation function *ffunc*. These are used as follows:

```
sfunc( internal-state, next-data-values ) ---> next-internal-state
ffunc( internal-state ) ---> aggregate-value
```

PostgreSQL creates a temporary variable of data type *stype* to hold the current internal state of the aggregate. At each input row, the aggregate argument value(s) are calculated and the state transition function is invoked with the current state value and the new argument value(s) to calculate a new internal state value. After all the rows have been processed, the final function is invoked once to calculate the aggregate's return value. If there is no final function then the ending state value is returned as-is.

An aggregate function can provide an initial condition, that is, an initial value for the internal state value. This is specified and stored in the database as a value of type text, but it must be a valid external representation of a constant of the state value data type. If it is not supplied then the state value starts out null.

If the state transition function is declared "strict", then it cannot be called with null inputs. With such a transition function, aggregate execution behaves as follows. Rows with any null input values are ignored (the function is not called and the previous state value is retained). If the initial state value is null, then at the first row with all-nonnull input values, the first argument value replaces the state value, and the transition function is invoked at each subsequent row with all-nonnull input values. This is handy for implementing aggregates like max. Note that this behavior is only available when *state_data_type* is the same as the first *arg_data_type*. When these types are different, you must supply a nonnull initial condition or use a nonstrict transition function.

If the state transition function is not strict, then it will be called unconditionally at each input row, and must deal with null inputs and null state values for itself. This allows the aggregate author to have full control over the aggregate's handling of null values.

If the final function is declared "strict", then it will not be called when the ending state value is null; instead a null result will be returned automatically. (Of course this is just the normal behavior of strict functions.) In any case the final function has the option of returning a null value. For example, the final function for avg returns null when it sees there were zero input rows.

Sometimes it is useful to declare the final function as taking not just the state value, but extra parameters corresponding to the aggregate's input values. The main reason for doing this is if the final function is polymorphic and the state value's data type would be inadequate to pin down the result type. These extra parameters are always passed as NULL (and so the final function must not be strict when the FINAL-FUNC_EXTRA option is used), but nonetheless they are valid parameters. The final function could for example make use of get_fn_expr_argtype to identify the actual argument type in the current call.

An aggregate can optionally support *moving-aggregate mode*, as described in Section 38.11.1. This requires specifying the MSFUNC, MINVFUNC, and MSTYPE parameters, and optionally the MSPACE, MFI-NALFUNC, MFINALFUNC_EXTRA, MFINALFUNC_MODIFY, and MINITCOND parameters. Except for MINVFUNC, these parameters work like the corresponding simple-aggregate parameters without M; they define a separate implementation of the aggregate that includes an inverse transition function.

The syntax with ORDER BY in the parameter list creates a special type of aggregate called an *ordered-set aggregate*; or if HYPOTHETICAL is specified, then a *hypothetical-set aggregate* is created. These aggregates operate over groups of sorted values in order-dependent ways, so that specification of an input sort order is an essential part of a call. Also, they can have *direct* arguments, which are arguments that are evaluated only once per aggregation rather than once per input row. Hypothetical-set aggregates are a subclass of ordered-set aggregates in which some of the direct arguments are required to match, in number and data types, the aggregated argument columns. This allows the values of those direct arguments to be added to the collection of aggregate-input rows as an additional "hypothetical" row.

An aggregate can optionally support *partial aggregation*, as described in Section 38.11.4. This requires specifying the COMBINEFUNC parameter. If the *state_data_type* is internal, it's usually also appropriate to provide the SERIALFUNC and DESERIALFUNC parameters so that parallel aggregation is possible. Note that the aggregate must also be marked PARALLEL SAFE to enable parallel aggregation.

Aggregates that behave like MIN or MAX can sometimes be optimized by looking into an index instead of scanning every input row. If this aggregate can be so optimized, indicate it by specifying a *sort operator*. The basic requirement is that the aggregate must yield the first element in the sort ordering induced by the operator; in other words:

```
SELECT agg(col) FROM tab;
```

must be equivalent to:

```
SELECT col FROM tab ORDER BY col USING sortop LIMIT 1;
```

Further assumptions are that the aggregate ignores null inputs, and that it delivers a null result if and only if there were no non-null inputs. Ordinarily, a data type's < operator is the proper sort operator for MIN, and > is the proper sort operator for MAX. Note that the optimization will never actually take effect unless the specified operator is the "less than" or "greater than" strategy member of a B-tree index operator class.

To be able to create an aggregate function, you must have USAGE privilege on the argument types, the state type(s), and the return type, as well as EXECUTE privilege on the supporting functions.

Parameters

name

> The name (optionally schema-qualified) of the aggregate function to create.

argmode

> The mode of an argument: IN or VARIADIC. (Aggregate functions do not support OUT arguments.) If omitted, the default is IN. Only the last argument can be marked VARIADIC.

argname

> The name of an argument. This is currently only useful for documentation purposes. If omitted, the argument has no name.

arg_data_type

> An input data type on which this aggregate function operates. To create a zero-argument aggregate function, write * in place of the list of argument specifications. (An example of such an aggregate is count(*).)

base_type

> In the old syntax for CREATE AGGREGATE, the input data type is specified by a basetype parameter rather than being written next to the aggregate name. Note that this syntax allows only one input parameter. To define a zero-argument aggregate function with this syntax, specify the basetype as "ANY" (not *). Ordered-set aggregates cannot be defined with the old syntax.

sfunc

> The name of the state transition function to be called for each input row. For a normal *N*-argument aggregate function, the *sfunc* must take *N*+1 arguments, the first being of type *state_data_type* and the rest matching the declared input data type(s) of the aggregate. The function must return a value of type *state_data_type*. This function takes the current state value and the current input data value(s), and returns the next state value.

> For ordered-set (including hypothetical-set) aggregates, the state transition function receives only the current state value and the aggregated arguments, not the direct arguments. Otherwise it is the same.

state_data_type

> The data type for the aggregate's state value.

state_data_size

> The approximate average size (in bytes) of the aggregate's state value. If this parameter is omitted or is zero, a default estimate is used based on the *state_data_type*. The planner uses this value to estimate the memory required for a grouped aggregate query. The planner will consider using hash

aggregation for such a query only if the hash table is estimated to fit in work_mem; therefore, large values of this parameter discourage use of hash aggregation.

ffunc

The name of the final function called to compute the aggregate's result after all input rows have been traversed. For a normal aggregate, this function must take a single argument of type *state_data_type*. The return data type of the aggregate is defined as the return type of this function. If *ffunc* is not specified, then the ending state value is used as the aggregate's result, and the return type is *state_data_type*.

For ordered-set (including hypothetical-set) aggregates, the final function receives not only the final state value, but also the values of all the direct arguments.

If `FINALFUNC_EXTRA` is specified, then in addition to the final state value and any direct arguments, the final function receives extra NULL values corresponding to the aggregate's regular (aggregated) arguments. This is mainly useful to allow correct resolution of the aggregate result type when a polymorphic aggregate is being defined.

`FINALFUNC_MODIFY = { READ_ONLY | SHAREABLE | READ_WRITE }`

This option specifies whether the final function is a pure function that does not modify its arguments. `READ_ONLY` indicates it does not; the other two values indicate that it may change the transition state value. See Notes below for more detail. The default is `READ_ONLY`, except for ordered-set aggregates, for which the default is `READ_WRITE`.

combinefunc

The *combinefunc* function may optionally be specified to allow the aggregate function to support partial aggregation. If provided, the *combinefunc* must combine two *state_data_type* values, each containing the result of aggregation over some subset of the input values, to produce a new *state_data_type* that represents the result of aggregating over both sets of inputs. This function can be thought of as an *sfunc*, where instead of acting upon an individual input row and adding it to the running aggregate state, it adds another aggregate state to the running state.

The *combinefunc* must be declared as taking two arguments of the *state_data_type* and returning a value of the *state_data_type*. Optionally this function may be "strict". In this case the function will not be called when either of the input states are null; the other state will be taken as the correct result.

For aggregate functions whose *state_data_type* is internal, the *combinefunc* must not be strict. In this case the *combinefunc* must ensure that null states are handled correctly and that the state being returned is properly stored in the aggregate memory context.

serialfunc

An aggregate function whose *state_data_type* is internal can participate in parallel aggregation only if it has a *serialfunc* function, which must serialize the aggregate state into a bytea value for transmission to another process. This function must take a single argument of type internal and return type bytea. A corresponding *deserialfunc* is also required.

deserialfunc

Deserialize a previously serialized aggregate state back into *state_data_type*. This function must take two arguments of types bytea and internal, and produce a result of type internal. (Note: the second, internal argument is unused, but is required for type safety reasons.)

initial_condition

The initial setting for the state value. This must be a string constant in the form accepted for the data type *state_data_type*. If not specified, the state value starts out null.

msfunc

The name of the forward state transition function to be called for each input row in moving-aggregate mode. This is exactly like the regular transition function, except that its first argument and result are of type *mstate_data_type*, which might be different from *state_data_type*.

minvfunc

The name of the inverse state transition function to be used in moving-aggregate mode. This function has the same argument and result types as *msfunc*, but it is used to remove a value from the current aggregate state, rather than add a value to it. The inverse transition function must have the same strictness attribute as the forward state transition function.

mstate_data_type

The data type for the aggregate's state value, when using moving-aggregate mode.

mstate_data_size

The approximate average size (in bytes) of the aggregate's state value, when using moving-aggregate mode. This works the same as *state_data_size*.

mffunc

The name of the final function called to compute the aggregate's result after all input rows have been traversed, when using moving-aggregate mode. This works the same as *ffunc*, except that its first argument's type is *mstate_data_type* and extra dummy arguments are specified by writing MFI-NALFUNC_EXTRA. The aggregate result type determined by *mffunc* or *mstate_data_type* must match that determined by the aggregate's regular implementation.

MFINALFUNC_MODIFY = { READ_ONLY | SHAREABLE | READ_WRITE }

This option is like FINALFUNC_MODIFY, but it describes the behavior of the moving-aggregate final function.

minitial_condition

The initial setting for the state value, when using moving-aggregate mode. This works the same as *initial_condition*.

sort_operator

The associated sort operator for a MIN- or MAX-like aggregate. This is just an operator name (possibly schema-qualified). The operator is assumed to have the same input data types as the aggregate (which must be a single-argument normal aggregate).

PARALLEL = { SAFE | RESTRICTED | UNSAFE }

The meanings of PARALLEL SAFE, PARALLEL RESTRICTED, and PARALLEL UNSAFE are the same as in CREATE FUNCTION. An aggregate will not be considered for parallelization if it is marked PARALLEL UNSAFE (which is the default!) or PARALLEL RESTRICTED. Note that the parallel-safety markings of the aggregate's support functions are not consulted by the planner, only the marking of the aggregate itself.

HYPOTHETICAL

> For ordered-set aggregates only, this flag specifies that the aggregate arguments are to be processed according to the requirements for hypothetical-set aggregates: that is, the last few direct arguments must match the data types of the aggregated (WITHIN GROUP) arguments. The HYPOTHETICAL flag has no effect on run-time behavior, only on parse-time resolution of the data types and collations of the aggregate's arguments.

The parameters of CREATE AGGREGATE can be written in any order, not just the order illustrated above.

Notes

In parameters that specify support function names, you can write a schema name if needed, for example SFUNC = public.sum. Do not write argument types there, however — the argument types of the support functions are determined from other parameters.

Ordinarily, PostgreSQL functions are expected to be true functions that do not modify their input values. However, an aggregate transition function, *when used in the context of an aggregate*, is allowed to cheat and modify its transition-state argument in place. This can provide substantial performance benefits compared to making a fresh copy of the transition state each time.

Likewise, while an aggregate final function is normally expected not to modify its input values, sometimes it is impractical to avoid modifying the transition-state argument. Such behavior must be declared using the FINALFUNC_MODIFY parameter. The READ_WRITE value indicates that the final function modifies the transition state in unspecified ways. This value prevents use of the aggregate as a window function, and it also prevents merging of transition states for aggregate calls that share the same input values and transition functions. The SHAREABLE value indicates that the transition function cannot be applied after the final function, but multiple final-function calls can be performed on the ending transition state value. This value prevents use of the aggregate as a window function, but it allows merging of transition states. (That is, the optimization of interest here is not applying the same final function repeatedly, but applying different final functions to the same ending transition state value. This is allowed as long as none of the final functions are marked READ_WRITE.)

If an aggregate supports moving-aggregate mode, it will improve calculation efficiency when the aggregate is used as a window function for a window with moving frame start (that is, a frame start mode other than UNBOUNDED PRECEDING). Conceptually, the forward transition function adds input values to the aggregate's state when they enter the window frame from the bottom, and the inverse transition function removes them again when they leave the frame at the top. So, when values are removed, they are always removed in the same order they were added. Whenever the inverse transition function is invoked, it will thus receive the earliest added but not yet removed argument value(s). The inverse transition function can assume that at least one row will remain in the current state after it removes the oldest row. (When this would not be the case, the window function mechanism simply starts a fresh aggregation, rather than using the inverse transition function.)

The forward transition function for moving-aggregate mode is not allowed to return NULL as the new state value. If the inverse transition function returns NULL, this is taken as an indication that the inverse function cannot reverse the state calculation for this particular input, and so the aggregate calculation will be redone from scratch for the current frame starting position. This convention allows moving-aggregate mode to be used in situations where there are some infrequent cases that are impractical to reverse out of the running state value.

If no moving-aggregate implementation is supplied, the aggregate can still be used with moving frames, but PostgreSQL will recompute the whole aggregation whenever the start of the frame moves. Note that whether or not the aggregate supports moving-aggregate mode, PostgreSQL can handle a moving frame end without recalculation; this is done by continuing to add new values to the aggregate's state. This is why use of an aggregate as a window function requires that the final function be read-only: it must not damage the aggregate's state value, so that the aggregation can be continued even after an aggregate result value has been obtained for one set of frame boundaries.

The syntax for ordered-set aggregates allows `VARIADIC` to be specified for both the last direct parameter and the last aggregated (`WITHIN GROUP`) parameter. However, the current implementation restricts use of `VARIADIC` in two ways. First, ordered-set aggregates can only use `VARIADIC "any"`, not other variadic array types. Second, if the last direct parameter is `VARIADIC "any"`, then there can be only one aggregated parameter and it must also be `VARIADIC "any"`. (In the representation used in the system catalogs, these two parameters are merged into a single `VARIADIC "any"` item, since `pg_proc` cannot represent functions with more than one `VARIADIC` parameter.) If the aggregate is a hypothetical-set aggregate, the direct arguments that match the `VARIADIC "any"` parameter are the hypothetical ones; any preceding parameters represent additional direct arguments that are not constrained to match the aggregated arguments.

Currently, ordered-set aggregates do not need to support moving-aggregate mode, since they cannot be used as window functions.

Partial (including parallel) aggregation is currently not supported for ordered-set aggregates. Also, it will never be used for aggregate calls that include `DISTINCT` or `ORDER BY` clauses, since those semantics cannot be supported during partial aggregation.

Examples

See Section 38.11.

Compatibility

`CREATE AGGREGATE` is a PostgreSQL language extension. The SQL standard does not provide for user-defined aggregate functions.

See Also

ALTER AGGREGATE, DROP AGGREGATE

CREATE CAST

CREATE CAST — define a new cast

Synopsis

```
CREATE CAST (source_type AS target_type)
    WITH FUNCTION function_name [ (argument_type [, ...]) ]
    [ AS ASSIGNMENT | AS IMPLICIT ]

CREATE CAST (source_type AS target_type)
    WITHOUT FUNCTION
    [ AS ASSIGNMENT | AS IMPLICIT ]

CREATE CAST (source_type AS target_type)
    WITH INOUT
    [ AS ASSIGNMENT | AS IMPLICIT ]
```

Description

CREATE CAST defines a new cast. A cast specifies how to perform a conversion between two data types. For example,

```
SELECT CAST(42 AS float8);
```

converts the integer constant 42 to type `float8` by invoking a previously specified function, in this case `float8(int4)`. (If no suitable cast has been defined, the conversion fails.)

Two types can be *binary coercible*, which means that the conversion can be performed "for free" without invoking any function. This requires that corresponding values use the same internal representation. For instance, the types `text` and `varchar` are binary coercible both ways. Binary coercibility is not necessarily a symmetric relationship. For example, the cast from `xml` to `text` can be performed for free in the present implementation, but the reverse direction requires a function that performs at least a syntax check. (Two types that are binary coercible both ways are also referred to as binary compatible.)

You can define a cast as an *I/O conversion cast* by using the WITH INOUT syntax. An I/O conversion cast is performed by invoking the output function of the source data type, and passing the resulting string to the input function of the target data type. In many common cases, this feature avoids the need to write a separate cast function for conversion. An I/O conversion cast acts the same as a regular function-based cast; only the implementation is different.

By default, a cast can be invoked only by an explicit cast request, that is an explicit CAST(*x* AS *typename*) or *x*::*typename* construct.

If the cast is marked AS ASSIGNMENT then it can be invoked implicitly when assigning a value to a column of the target data type. For example, supposing that `foo.f1` is a column of type `text`, then:

```
INSERT INTO foo (f1) VALUES (42);
```

will be allowed if the cast from type `integer` to type `text` is marked `AS ASSIGNMENT`, otherwise not. (We generally use the term *assignment cast* to describe this kind of cast.)

If the cast is marked `AS IMPLICIT` then it can be invoked implicitly in any context, whether assignment or internally in an expression. (We generally use the term *implicit cast* to describe this kind of cast.) For example, consider this query:

```
SELECT 2 + 4.0;
```

The parser initially marks the constants as being of type `integer` and `numeric` respectively. There is no `integer + numeric` operator in the system catalogs, but there is a `numeric + numeric` operator. The query will therefore succeed if a cast from `integer` to `numeric` is available and is marked `AS IMPLICIT` — which in fact it is. The parser will apply the implicit cast and resolve the query as if it had been written

```
SELECT CAST ( 2 AS numeric ) + 4.0;
```

Now, the catalogs also provide a cast from `numeric` to `integer`. If that cast were marked `AS IMPLICIT` — which it is not — then the parser would be faced with choosing between the above interpretation and the alternative of casting the `numeric` constant to `integer` and applying the `integer + integer` operator. Lacking any knowledge of which choice to prefer, it would give up and declare the query ambiguous. The fact that only one of the two casts is implicit is the way in which we teach the parser to prefer resolution of a mixed `numeric`-and-`integer` expression as `numeric`; there is no built-in knowledge about that.

It is wise to be conservative about marking casts as implicit. An overabundance of implicit casting paths can cause PostgreSQL to choose surprising interpretations of commands, or to be unable to resolve commands at all because there are multiple possible interpretations. A good rule of thumb is to make a cast implicitly invokable only for information-preserving transformations between types in the same general type category. For example, the cast from `int2` to `int4` can reasonably be implicit, but the cast from `float8` to `int4` should probably be assignment-only. Cross-type-category casts, such as `text` to `int4`, are best made explicit-only.

Note

Sometimes it is necessary for usability or standards-compliance reasons to provide multiple implicit casts among a set of types, resulting in ambiguity that cannot be avoided as above. The parser has a fallback heuristic based on *type categories* and *preferred types* that can help to provide desired behavior in such cases. See CREATE TYPE for more information.

To be able to create a cast, you must own the source or the target data type and have `USAGE` privilege on the other type. To create a binary-coercible cast, you must be superuser. (This restriction is made because an erroneous binary-coercible cast conversion can easily crash the server.)

Parameters

source_type

The name of the source data type of the cast.

target_type

The name of the target data type of the cast.

function_name[(*argument_type* [, ...])]

> The function used to perform the cast. The function name can be schema-qualified. If it is not, the function will be looked up in the schema search path. The function's result data type must match the target type of the cast. Its arguments are discussed below. If no argument list is specified, the function name must be unique in its schema.

WITHOUT FUNCTION

> Indicates that the source type is binary-coercible to the target type, so no function is required to perform the cast.

WITH INOUT

> Indicates that the cast is an I/O conversion cast, performed by invoking the output function of the source data type, and passing the resulting string to the input function of the target data type.

AS ASSIGNMENT

> Indicates that the cast can be invoked implicitly in assignment contexts.

AS IMPLICIT

> Indicates that the cast can be invoked implicitly in any context.

Cast implementation functions can have one to three arguments. The first argument type must be identical to or binary-coercible from the cast's source type. The second argument, if present, must be type `integer`; it receives the type modifier associated with the destination type, or `-1` if there is none. The third argument, if present, must be type `boolean`; it receives `true` if the cast is an explicit cast, `false` otherwise. (Bizarrely, the SQL standard demands different behaviors for explicit and implicit casts in some cases. This argument is supplied for functions that must implement such casts. It is not recommended that you design your own data types so that this matters.)

The return type of a cast function must be identical to or binary-coercible to the cast's target type.

Ordinarily a cast must have different source and target data types. However, it is allowed to declare a cast with identical source and target types if it has a cast implementation function with more than one argument. This is used to represent type-specific length coercion functions in the system catalogs. The named function is used to coerce a value of the type to the type modifier value given by its second argument.

When a cast has different source and target types and a function that takes more than one argument, it supports converting from one type to another and applying a length coercion in a single step. When no such entry is available, coercion to a type that uses a type modifier involves two cast steps, one to convert between data types and a second to apply the modifier.

A cast to or from a domain type currently has no effect. Casting to or from a domain uses the casts associated with its underlying type.

Notes

Use DROP CAST to remove user-defined casts.

Remember that if you want to be able to convert types both ways you need to declare casts both ways explicitly.

It is normally not necessary to create casts between user-defined types and the standard string types (`text`, `varchar`, and `char(n)`, as well as user-defined types that are defined to be in the string category).

PostgreSQL provides automatic I/O conversion casts for that. The automatic casts to string types are treated as assignment casts, while the automatic casts from string types are explicit-only. You can override this behavior by declaring your own cast to replace an automatic cast, but usually the only reason to do so is if you want the conversion to be more easily invokable than the standard assignment-only or explicit-only setting. Another possible reason is that you want the conversion to behave differently from the type's I/O function; but that is sufficiently surprising that you should think twice about whether it's a good idea. (A small number of the built-in types do indeed have different behaviors for conversions, mostly because of requirements of the SQL standard.)

While not required, it is recommended that you continue to follow this old convention of naming cast implementation functions after the target data type. Many users are used to being able to cast data types using a function-style notation, that is *typename*(*x*). This notation is in fact nothing more nor less than a call of the cast implementation function; it is not specially treated as a cast. If your conversion functions are not named to support this convention then you will have surprised users. Since PostgreSQL allows overloading of the same function name with different argument types, there is no difficulty in having multiple conversion functions from different types that all use the target type's name.

Note

Actually the preceding paragraph is an oversimplification: there are two cases in which a function-call construct will be treated as a cast request without having matched it to an actual function. If a function call *name*(*x*) does not exactly match any existing function, but *name* is the name of a data type and pg_cast provides a binary-coercible cast to this type from the type of *x*, then the call will be construed as a binary-coercible cast. This exception is made so that binary-coercible casts can be invoked using functional syntax, even though they lack any function. Likewise, if there is no pg_cast entry but the cast would be to or from a string type, the call will be construed as an I/O conversion cast. This exception allows I/O conversion casts to be invoked using functional syntax.

Note

There is also an exception to the exception: I/O conversion casts from composite types to string types cannot be invoked using functional syntax, but must be written in explicit cast syntax (either CAST or :: notation). This exception was added because after the introduction of automatically-provided I/O conversion casts, it was found too easy to accidentally invoke such a cast when a function or column reference was intended.

Examples

To create an assignment cast from type bigint to type int4 using the function int4(bigint):

```
CREATE CAST (bigint AS int4) WITH FUNCTION int4(bigint) AS ASSIGNMENT;
```

(This cast is already predefined in the system.)

Compatibility

The CREATE CAST command conforms to the SQL standard, except that SQL does not make provisions for binary-coercible types or extra arguments to implementation functions. AS IMPLICIT is a PostgreSQL extension, too.

See Also

CREATE FUNCTION, CREATE TYPE, DROP CAST

CREATE COLLATION

CREATE COLLATION — define a new collation

Synopsis

```
CREATE COLLATION [ IF NOT EXISTS ] name (
    [ LOCALE = locale, ]
    [ LC_COLLATE = lc_collate, ]
    [ LC_CTYPE = lc_ctype, ]
    [ PROVIDER = provider, ]
    [ VERSION = version ]
)
CREATE COLLATION [ IF NOT EXISTS ] name FROM existing_collation
```

Description

CREATE COLLATION defines a new collation using the specified operating system locale settings, or by copying an existing collation.

To be able to create a collation, you must have CREATE privilege on the destination schema.

Parameters

IF NOT EXISTS

Do not throw an error if a collation with the same name already exists. A notice is issued in this case. Note that there is no guarantee that the existing collation is anything like the one that would have been created.

name

The name of the collation. The collation name can be schema-qualified. If it is not, the collation is defined in the current schema. The collation name must be unique within that schema. (The system catalogs can contain collations with the same name for other encodings, but these are ignored if the database encoding does not match.)

locale

This is a shortcut for setting LC_COLLATE and LC_CTYPE at once. If you specify this, you cannot specify either of those parameters.

lc_collate

Use the specified operating system locale for the LC_COLLATE locale category.

lc_ctype

Use the specified operating system locale for the LC_CTYPE locale category.

provider

> Specifies the provider to use for locale services associated with this collation. Possible values are: `icu`, `libc`. `libc` is the default. The available choices depend on the operating system and build options.

version

> Specifies the version string to store with the collation. Normally, this should be omitted, which will cause the version to be computed from the actual version of the collation as provided by the operating system. This option is intended to be used by `pg_upgrade` for copying the version from an existing installation.

> See also ALTER COLLATION for how to handle collation version mismatches.

existing_collation

> The name of an existing collation to copy. The new collation will have the same properties as the existing one, but it will be an independent object.

Notes

Use `DROP COLLATION` to remove user-defined collations.

See Section 23.2.2.3 for more information on how to create collations.

When using the `libc` collation provider, the locale must be applicable to the current database encoding. See CREATE DATABASE for the precise rules.

Examples

To create a collation from the operating system locale `fr_FR.utf8` (assuming the current database encoding is `UTF8`):

```
CREATE COLLATION french (locale = 'fr_FR.utf8');
```

To create a collation using the ICU provider using German phone book sort order:

```
CREATE COLLATION german_phonebook (provider = icu, locale = 'de-u-co-phonebk');
```

To create a collation from an existing collation:

```
CREATE COLLATION german FROM "de_DE";
```

This can be convenient to be able to use operating-system-independent collation names in applications.

Compatibility

There is a `CREATE COLLATION` statement in the SQL standard, but it is limited to copying an existing collation. The syntax to create a new collation is a PostgreSQL extension.

See Also

ALTER COLLATION, DROP COLLATION

CREATE CONVERSION

CREATE CONVERSION — define a new encoding conversion

Synopsis

```
CREATE [ DEFAULT ] CONVERSION name
    FOR source_encoding TO dest_encoding FROM function_name
```

Description

CREATE CONVERSION defines a new conversion between character set encodings. Also, conversions that are marked DEFAULT can be used for automatic encoding conversion between client and server. For this purpose, two conversions, from encoding A to B *and* from encoding B to A, must be defined.

To be able to create a conversion, you must have EXECUTE privilege on the function and CREATE privilege on the destination schema.

Parameters

DEFAULT

> The DEFAULT clause indicates that this conversion is the default for this particular source to destination encoding. There should be only one default encoding in a schema for the encoding pair.

name

> The name of the conversion. The conversion name can be schema-qualified. If it is not, the conversion is defined in the current schema. The conversion name must be unique within a schema.

source_encoding

> The source encoding name.

dest_encoding

> The destination encoding name.

function_name

> The function used to perform the conversion. The function name can be schema-qualified. If it is not, the function will be looked up in the path.

> The function must have the following signature:

```
conv_proc(
    integer,   -- source encoding ID
    integer,   -- destination encoding ID
    cstring,   -- source string (null terminated C string)
    internal,  -- destination (fill with a null terminated C string)
```

```
    integer   -- source string length
) RETURNS void;
```

Notes

Use DROP CONVERSION to remove user-defined conversions.

The privileges required to create a conversion might be changed in a future release.

Examples

To create a conversion from encoding UTF8 to LATIN1 using myfunc:

```
CREATE CONVERSION myconv FOR 'UTF8' TO 'LATIN1' FROM myfunc;
```

Compatibility

CREATE CONVERSION is a PostgreSQL extension. There is no CREATE CONVERSION statement in the SQL standard, but a CREATE TRANSLATION statement that is very similar in purpose and syntax.

See Also

ALTER CONVERSION, CREATE FUNCTION, DROP CONVERSION

CREATE DATABASE

CREATE DATABASE — create a new database

Synopsis

```
CREATE DATABASE name
    [ [ WITH ] [ OWNER [=] user_name ]
           [ TEMPLATE [=] template ]
           [ ENCODING [=] encoding ]
           [ LC_COLLATE [=] lc_collate ]
           [ LC_CTYPE [=] lc_ctype ]
           [ TABLESPACE [=] tablespace_name ]
           [ ALLOW_CONNECTIONS [=] allowconn ]
           [ CONNECTION LIMIT [=] connlimit ]
           [ IS_TEMPLATE [=] istemplate ] ]
```

Description

CREATE DATABASE creates a new PostgreSQL database.

To create a database, you must be a superuser or have the special CREATEDB privilege. See CREATE ROLE.

By default, the new database will be created by cloning the standard system database template1. A different template can be specified by writing TEMPLATE name. In particular, by writing TEMPLATE template0, you can create a virgin database containing only the standard objects predefined by your version of PostgreSQL. This is useful if you wish to avoid copying any installation-local objects that might have been added to template1.

Parameters

name

   The name of a database to create.

user_name

   The role name of the user who will own the new database, or DEFAULT to use the default (namely, the user executing the command). To create a database owned by another role, you must be a direct or indirect member of that role, or be a superuser.

template

   The name of the template from which to create the new database, or DEFAULT to use the default template (template1).

encoding

   Character set encoding to use in the new database. Specify a string constant (e.g., 'SQL_ASCII'), or an integer encoding number, or DEFAULT to use the default encoding (namely, the encoding of the template database). The character sets supported by the PostgreSQL server are described in Section 23.3.1. See below for additional restrictions.

lc_collate

Collation order (`LC_COLLATE`) to use in the new database. This affects the sort order applied to strings, e.g. in queries with ORDER BY, as well as the order used in indexes on text columns. The default is to use the collation order of the template database. See below for additional restrictions.

lc_ctype

Character classification (`LC_CTYPE`) to use in the new database. This affects the categorization of characters, e.g. lower, upper and digit. The default is to use the character classification of the template database. See below for additional restrictions.

tablespace_name

The name of the tablespace that will be associated with the new database, or `DEFAULT` to use the template database's tablespace. This tablespace will be the default tablespace used for objects created in this database. See CREATE TABLESPACE for more information.

allowconn

If false then no one can connect to this database. The default is true, allowing connections (except as restricted by other mechanisms, such as `GRANT/REVOKE CONNECT`).

connlimit

How many concurrent connections can be made to this database. -1 (the default) means no limit.

istemplate

If true, then this database can be cloned by any user with `CREATEDB` privileges; if false (the default), then only superusers or the owner of the database can clone it.

Optional parameters can be written in any order, not only the order illustrated above.

Notes

`CREATE DATABASE` cannot be executed inside a transaction block.

Errors along the line of "could not initialize database directory" are most likely related to insufficient permissions on the data directory, a full disk, or other file system problems.

Use DROP DATABASE to remove a database.

The program createdb is a wrapper program around this command, provided for convenience.

Database-level configuration parameters (set via ALTER DATABASE) are not copied from the template database.

Although it is possible to copy a database other than `template1` by specifying its name as the template, this is not (yet) intended as a general-purpose "COPY DATABASE" facility. The principal limitation is that no other sessions can be connected to the template database while it is being copied. `CREATE DATABASE` will fail if any other connection exists when it starts; otherwise, new connections to the template database are locked out until `CREATE DATABASE` completes. See Section 22.3 for more information.

The character set encoding specified for the new database must be compatible with the chosen locale settings (`LC_COLLATE` and `LC_CTYPE`). If the locale is C (or equivalently `POSIX`), then all encodings are allowed, but for other locale settings there is only one encoding that will work properly. (On Windows, however, UTF-8 encoding can be used with any locale.) CREATE DATABASE will allow superusers to specify SQL_ASCII encoding regardless of the locale settings, but this choice is deprecated and may result in misbehavior of character-string functions if data that is not encoding-compatible with the locale is stored in the database.

The encoding and locale settings must match those of the template database, except when template0 is used as template. This is because other databases might contain data that does not match the specified encoding, or might contain indexes whose sort ordering is affected by LC_COLLATE and LC_CTYPE. Copying such data would result in a database that is corrupt according to the new settings. template0, however, is known to not contain any data or indexes that would be affected.

The CONNECTION LIMIT option is only enforced approximately; if two new sessions start at about the same time when just one connection "slot" remains for the database, it is possible that both will fail. Also, the limit is not enforced against superusers or background worker processes.

Examples

To create a new database:

```
CREATE DATABASE lusiadas;
```

To create a database sales owned by user salesapp with a default tablespace of salesspace:

```
CREATE DATABASE sales OWNER salesapp TABLESPACE salesspace;
```

To create a database music with a different locale:

```
CREATE DATABASE music
    LC_COLLATE 'sv_SE.utf8' LC_CTYPE 'sv_SE.utf8'
    TEMPLATE template0;
```

In this example, the TEMPLATE template0 clause is required if the specified locale is different from the one in template1. (If it is not, then specifying the locale explicitly is redundant.)

To create a database music2 with a different locale and a different character set encoding:

```
CREATE DATABASE music2
    LC_COLLATE 'sv_SE.iso885915' LC_CTYPE 'sv_SE.iso885915'
    ENCODING LATIN9
    TEMPLATE template0;
```

The specified locale and encoding settings must match, or an error will be reported.

Note that locale names are specific to the operating system, so that the above commands might not work in the same way everywhere.

Compatibility

There is no CREATE DATABASE statement in the SQL standard. Databases are equivalent to catalogs, whose creation is implementation-defined.

See Also

ALTER DATABASE, DROP DATABASE

CREATE DOMAIN

CREATE DOMAIN — define a new domain

Synopsis

```
CREATE DOMAIN name [ AS ] data_type
    [ COLLATE collation ]
    [ DEFAULT expression ]
    [ constraint [ ... ] ]

where constraint is:

[ CONSTRAINT constraint_name ]
{ NOT NULL | NULL | CHECK (expression) }
```

Description

CREATE DOMAIN creates a new domain. A domain is essentially a data type with optional constraints (restrictions on the allowed set of values). The user who defines a domain becomes its owner.

If a schema name is given (for example, CREATE DOMAIN myschema.mydomain ...) then the domain is created in the specified schema. Otherwise it is created in the current schema. The domain name must be unique among the types and domains existing in its schema.

Domains are useful for abstracting common constraints on fields into a single location for maintenance. For example, several tables might contain email address columns, all requiring the same CHECK constraint to verify the address syntax. Define a domain rather than setting up each table's constraint individually.

To be able to create a domain, you must have USAGE privilege on the underlying type.

Parameters

name

The name (optionally schema-qualified) of a domain to be created.

data_type

The underlying data type of the domain. This can include array specifiers.

collation

An optional collation for the domain. If no collation is specified, the underlying data type's default collation is used. The underlying type must be collatable if COLLATE is specified.

DEFAULT expression

The DEFAULT clause specifies a default value for columns of the domain data type. The value is any variable-free expression (but subqueries are not allowed). The data type of the default expression must match the data type of the domain. If no default value is specified, then the default value is the null value.

The default expression will be used in any insert operation that does not specify a value for the column. If a default value is defined for a particular column, it overrides any default associated with the domain. In turn, the domain default overrides any default value associated with the underlying data type.

CONSTRAINT *constraint_name*

An optional name for a constraint. If not specified, the system generates a name.

NOT NULL

Values of this domain are prevented from being null (but see notes below).

NULL

Values of this domain are allowed to be null. This is the default.

This clause is only intended for compatibility with nonstandard SQL databases. Its use is discouraged in new applications.

CHECK (*expression*)

CHECK clauses specify integrity constraints or tests which values of the domain must satisfy. Each constraint must be an expression producing a Boolean result. It should use the key word VALUE to refer to the value being tested. Expressions evaluating to TRUE or UNKNOWN succeed. If the expression produces a FALSE result, an error is reported and the value is not allowed to be converted to the domain type.

Currently, CHECK expressions cannot contain subqueries nor refer to variables other than VALUE.

When a domain has multiple CHECK constraints, they will be tested in alphabetical order by name. (PostgreSQL versions before 9.5 did not honor any particular firing order for CHECK constraints.)

Notes

Domain constraints, particularly NOT NULL, are checked when converting a value to the domain type. It is possible for a column that is nominally of the domain type to read as null despite there being such a constraint. For example, this can happen in an outer-join query, if the domain column is on the nullable side of the outer join. A more subtle example is

```
INSERT INTO tab (domcol) VALUES ((SELECT domcol FROM tab WHERE
 false));
```

The empty scalar sub-SELECT will produce a null value that is considered to be of the domain type, so no further constraint checking is applied to it, and the insertion will succeed.

It is very difficult to avoid such problems, because of SQL's general assumption that a null value is a valid value of every data type. Best practice therefore is to design a domain's constraints so that a null value is allowed, and then to apply column NOT NULL constraints to columns of the domain type as needed, rather than directly to the domain type.

Examples

This example creates the us_postal_code data type and then uses the type in a table definition. A regular expression test is used to verify that the value looks like a valid US postal code:

```
CREATE DOMAIN us_postal_code AS TEXT
CHECK(
    VALUE ~ '^\d{5}$'
OR VALUE ~ '^\d{5}-\d{4}$'
);

CREATE TABLE us_snail_addy (
  address_id SERIAL PRIMARY KEY,
  street1 TEXT NOT NULL,
  street2 TEXT,
  street3 TEXT,
  city TEXT NOT NULL,
  postal us_postal_code NOT NULL
);
```

Compatibility

The command **CREATE DOMAIN** conforms to the SQL standard.

See Also

ALTER DOMAIN, DROP DOMAIN

CREATE EVENT TRIGGER

CREATE EVENT TRIGGER — define a new event trigger

Synopsis

```
CREATE EVENT TRIGGER name
    ON event
    [ WHEN filter_variable IN (filter_value [, ... ]) [ AND ... ] ]
    EXECUTE { FUNCTION | PROCEDURE } function_name()
```

Description

CREATE EVENT TRIGGER creates a new event trigger. Whenever the designated event occurs and the WHEN condition associated with the trigger, if any, is satisfied, the trigger function will be executed. For a general introduction to event triggers, see Chapter 40. The user who creates an event trigger becomes its owner.

Parameters

name

The name to give the new trigger. This name must be unique within the database.

event

The name of the event that triggers a call to the given function. See Section 40.1 for more information on event names.

filter_variable

The name of a variable used to filter events. This makes it possible to restrict the firing of the trigger to a subset of the cases in which it is supported. Currently the only supported *filter_variable* is TAG.

filter_value

A list of values for the associated *filter_variable* for which the trigger should fire. For TAG, this means a list of command tags (e.g. 'DROP FUNCTION').

function_name

A user-supplied function that is declared as taking no argument and returning type event_trigger.

In the syntax of CREATE EVENT TRIGGER, the keywords FUNCTION and PROCEDURE are equivalent, but the referenced function must in any case be a function, not a procedure. The use of the keyword PROCEDURE here is historical and deprecated.

Notes

Only superusers can create event triggers.

Event triggers are disabled in single-user mode (see postgres). If an erroneous event trigger disables the database so much that you can't even drop the trigger, restart in single-user mode and you'll be able to do that.

Examples

Forbid the execution of any DDL command:

```
CREATE OR REPLACE FUNCTION abort_any_command()
  RETURNS event_trigger
 LANGUAGE plpgsql
  AS $$
BEGIN
  RAISE EXCEPTION 'command % is disabled', tg_tag;
END;
$$;

CREATE EVENT TRIGGER abort_ddl ON ddl_command_start
   EXECUTE FUNCTION abort_any_command();
```

Compatibility

There is no CREATE EVENT TRIGGER statement in the SQL standard.

See Also
ALTER EVENT TRIGGER, DROP EVENT TRIGGER, CREATE FUNCTION

CREATE EXTENSION

CREATE EXTENSION — install an extension

Synopsis

```
CREATE EXTENSION [ IF NOT EXISTS ] extension_name
    [ WITH ] [ SCHEMA schema_name ]
             [ VERSION version ]
             [ FROM old_version ]
             [ CASCADE ]
```

Description

CREATE EXTENSION loads a new extension into the current database. There must not be an extension of the same name already loaded.

Loading an extension essentially amounts to running the extension's script file. The script will typically create new SQL objects such as functions, data types, operators and index support methods. CREATE EXTENSION additionally records the identities of all the created objects, so that they can be dropped again if DROP EXTENSION is issued.

Loading an extension requires the same privileges that would be required to create its component objects. For most extensions this means superuser or database owner privileges are needed. The user who runs CREATE EXTENSION becomes the owner of the extension for purposes of later privilege checks, as well as the owner of any objects created by the extension's script.

Parameters

IF NOT EXISTS

Do not throw an error if an extension with the same name already exists. A notice is issued in this case. Note that there is no guarantee that the existing extension is anything like the one that would have been created from the currently-available script file.

extension_name

The name of the extension to be installed. PostgreSQL will create the extension using details from the file SHAREDIR/extension/extension_name.control.

schema_name

The name of the schema in which to install the extension's objects, given that the extension allows its contents to be relocated. The named schema must already exist. If not specified, and the extension's control file does not specify a schema either, the current default object creation schema is used.

If the extension specifies a schema parameter in its control file, then that schema cannot be overridden with a SCHEMA clause. Normally, an error will be raised if a SCHEMA clause is given and it conflicts with the extension's schema parameter. However, if the CASCADE clause is also given, then schema_name is ignored when it conflicts. The given schema_name will be used for installation of any needed extensions that do not specify schema in their control files.

Remember that the extension itself is not considered to be within any schema: extensions have unqualified names that must be unique database-wide. But objects belonging to the extension can be within schemas.

version

The version of the extension to install. This can be written as either an identifier or a string literal. The default version is whatever is specified in the extension's control file.

old_version

FROM *old_version* must be specified when, and only when, you are attempting to install an extension that replaces an "old style" module that is just a collection of objects not packaged into an extension. This option causes CREATE EXTENSION to run an alternative installation script that absorbs the existing objects into the extension, instead of creating new objects. Be careful that SCHEMA specifies the schema containing these pre-existing objects.

The value to use for *old_version* is determined by the extension's author, and might vary if there is more than one version of the old-style module that can be upgraded into an extension. For the standard additional modules supplied with pre-9.1 PostgreSQL, use unpackaged for *old_version* when updating a module to extension style.

CASCADE

Automatically install any extensions that this extension depends on that are not already installed. Their dependencies are likewise automatically installed, recursively. The SCHEMA clause, if given, applies to all extensions that get installed this way. Other options of the statement are not applied to automatically-installed extensions; in particular, their default versions are always selected.

Notes

Before you can use CREATE EXTENSION to load an extension into a database, the extension's supporting files must be installed. Information about installing the extensions supplied with PostgreSQL can be found in Additional Supplied Modules.

The extensions currently available for loading can be identified from the pg_available_extensions or pg_available_extension_versions system views.

For information about writing new extensions, see Section 38.16.

Examples

Install the hstore extension into the current database:

```
CREATE EXTENSION hstore;
```

Update a pre-9.1 installation of hstore into extension style:

```
CREATE EXTENSION hstore SCHEMA public FROM unpackaged;
```

Be careful to specify the schema in which you installed the existing hstore objects.

Compatibility

CREATE EXTENSION is a PostgreSQL extension.

See Also

ALTER EXTENSION, DROP EXTENSION

CREATE FOREIGN DATA WRAPPER

CREATE FOREIGN DATA WRAPPER — define a new foreign-data wrapper

Synopsis

```
CREATE FOREIGN DATA WRAPPER name
    [ HANDLER handler_function | NO HANDLER ]
    [ VALIDATOR validator_function | NO VALIDATOR ]
    [ OPTIONS ( option 'value' [, ... ] ) ]
```

Description

`CREATE FOREIGN DATA WRAPPER` creates a new foreign-data wrapper. The user who defines a foreign-data wrapper becomes its owner.

The foreign-data wrapper name must be unique within the database.

Only superusers can create foreign-data wrappers.

Parameters

name

The name of the foreign-data wrapper to be created.

HANDLER *handler_function*

handler_function is the name of a previously registered function that will be called to retrieve the execution functions for foreign tables. The handler function must take no arguments, and its return type must be `fdw_handler`.

It is possible to create a foreign-data wrapper with no handler function, but foreign tables using such a wrapper can only be declared, not accessed.

VALIDATOR *validator_function*

validator_function is the name of a previously registered function that will be called to check the generic options given to the foreign-data wrapper, as well as options for foreign servers, user mappings and foreign tables using the foreign-data wrapper. If no validator function or `NO VALIDATOR` is specified, then options will not be checked at creation time. (Foreign-data wrappers will possibly ignore or reject invalid option specifications at run time, depending on the implementation.) The validator function must take two arguments: one of type `text[]`, which will contain the array of options as stored in the system catalogs, and one of type `oid`, which will be the OID of the system catalog containing the options. The return type is ignored; the function should report invalid options using the `ereport(ERROR)` function.

OPTIONS (*option* 'value' [, ...])

This clause specifies options for the new foreign-data wrapper. The allowed option names and values are specific to each foreign data wrapper and are validated using the foreign-data wrapper's validator function. Option names must be unique.

Notes

PostgreSQL's foreign-data functionality is still under active development. Optimization of queries is primitive (and mostly left to the wrapper, too). Thus, there is considerable room for future performance improvements.

Examples

Create a useless foreign-data wrapper dummy:

```
CREATE FOREIGN DATA WRAPPER dummy;
```

Create a foreign-data wrapper file with handler function file_fdw_handler:

```
CREATE FOREIGN DATA WRAPPER file HANDLER file_fdw_handler;
```

Create a foreign-data wrapper mywrapper with some options:

```
CREATE FOREIGN DATA WRAPPER mywrapper
    OPTIONS (debug 'true');
```

Compatibility

CREATE FOREIGN DATA WRAPPER conforms to ISO/IEC 9075-9 (SQL/MED), with the exception that the HANDLER and VALIDATOR clauses are extensions and the standard clauses LIBRARY and LANGUAGE are not implemented in PostgreSQL.

Note, however, that the SQL/MED functionality as a whole is not yet conforming.

See Also

ALTER FOREIGN DATA WRAPPER, DROP FOREIGN DATA WRAPPER, CREATE SERVER, CREATE USER MAPPING, CREATE FOREIGN TABLE

CREATE FOREIGN TABLE

CREATE FOREIGN TABLE — define a new foreign table

Synopsis

```
CREATE FOREIGN TABLE [ IF NOT EXISTS ] table_name ( [
  { column_name data_type [ OPTIONS ( option 'value' [, ... ] ) ]
  [ COLLATE collation ] [ column_constraint [ ... ] ]
    | table_constraint }
    [, ... ]
] )
[ INHERITS ( parent_table [, ... ] ) ]
  SERVER server_name
[ OPTIONS ( option 'value' [, ... ] ) ]

CREATE FOREIGN TABLE [ IF NOT EXISTS ] table_name
  PARTITION OF parent_table [ (
  { column_name [ WITH OPTIONS ] [ column_constraint [ ... ] ]
    | table_constraint }
    [, ... ]
) ] partition_bound_spec
  SERVER server_name
[ OPTIONS ( option 'value' [, ... ] ) ]

where column_constraint is:

[ CONSTRAINT constraint_name ]
{ NOT NULL |
  NULL |
  CHECK ( expression ) [ NO INHERIT ] |
  DEFAULT default_expr }

and table_constraint is:

[ CONSTRAINT constraint_name ]
CHECK ( expression ) [ NO INHERIT ]
```

Description

CREATE FOREIGN TABLE creates a new foreign table in the current database. The table will be owned by the user issuing the command.

If a schema name is given (for example, CREATE FOREIGN TABLE myschema.mytable ...) then the table is created in the specified schema. Otherwise it is created in the current schema. The name of the foreign table must be distinct from the name of any other foreign table, table, sequence, index, view, or materialized view in the same schema.

CREATE FOREIGN TABLE also automatically creates a data type that represents the composite type corresponding to one row of the foreign table. Therefore, foreign tables cannot have the same name as any existing data type in the same schema.

If `PARTITION OF` clause is specified then the table is created as a partition of `parent_table` with specified bounds.

To be able to create a foreign table, you must have `USAGE` privilege on the foreign server, as well as `USAGE` privilege on all column types used in the table.

Parameters

`IF NOT EXISTS`

Do not throw an error if a relation with the same name already exists. A notice is issued in this case. Note that there is no guarantee that the existing relation is anything like the one that would have been created.

`table_name`

The name (optionally schema-qualified) of the table to be created.

`column_name`

The name of a column to be created in the new table.

`data_type`

The data type of the column. This can include array specifiers. For more information on the data types supported by PostgreSQL, refer to Chapter 8.

`COLLATE collation`

The `COLLATE` clause assigns a collation to the column (which must be of a collatable data type). If not specified, the column data type's default collation is used.

`INHERITS ( parent_table [, ... ] )`

The optional `INHERITS` clause specifies a list of tables from which the new foreign table automatically inherits all columns. Parent tables can be plain tables or foreign tables. See the similar form of CREATE TABLE for more details.

`CONSTRAINT constraint_name`

An optional name for a column or table constraint. If the constraint is violated, the constraint name is present in error messages, so constraint names like `col must be positive` can be used to communicate helpful constraint information to client applications. (Double-quotes are needed to specify constraint names that contain spaces.) If a constraint name is not specified, the system generates a name.

`NOT NULL`

The column is not allowed to contain null values.

`NULL`

The column is allowed to contain null values. This is the default.

This clause is only provided for compatibility with non-standard SQL databases. Its use is discouraged in new applications.

CHECK (*expression*) [NO INHERIT]

The CHECK clause specifies an expression producing a Boolean result which each row in the foreign table is expected to satisfy; that is, the expression should produce TRUE or UNKNOWN, never FALSE, for all rows in the foreign table. A check constraint specified as a column constraint should reference that column's value only, while an expression appearing in a table constraint can reference multiple columns.

Currently, CHECK expressions cannot contain subqueries nor refer to variables other than columns of the current row. The system column `tableoid` may be referenced, but not any other system column.

A constraint marked with NO INHERIT will not propagate to child tables.

DEFAULT *default_expr*

The DEFAULT clause assigns a default data value for the column whose column definition it appears within. The value is any variable-free expression (subqueries and cross-references to other columns in the current table are not allowed). The data type of the default expression must match the data type of the column.

The default expression will be used in any insert operation that does not specify a value for the column. If there is no default for a column, then the default is null.

server_name

The name of an existing foreign server to use for the foreign table. For details on defining a server, see CREATE SERVER.

OPTIONS (*option* 'value' [, ...])

Options to be associated with the new foreign table or one of its columns. The allowed option names and values are specific to each foreign data wrapper and are validated using the foreign-data wrapper's validator function. Duplicate option names are not allowed (although it's OK for a table option and a column option to have the same name).

Notes

Constraints on foreign tables (such as CHECK or NOT NULL clauses) are not enforced by the core PostgreSQL system, and most foreign data wrappers do not attempt to enforce them either; that is, the constraint is simply assumed to hold true. There would be little point in such enforcement since it would only apply to rows inserted or updated via the foreign table, and not to rows modified by other means, such as directly on the remote server. Instead, a constraint attached to a foreign table should represent a constraint that is being enforced by the remote server.

Some special-purpose foreign data wrappers might be the only access mechanism for the data they access, and in that case it might be appropriate for the foreign data wrapper itself to perform constraint enforcement. But you should not assume that a wrapper does that unless its documentation says so.

Although PostgreSQL does not attempt to enforce constraints on foreign tables, it does assume that they are correct for purposes of query optimization. If there are rows visible in the foreign table that do not satisfy a declared constraint, queries on the table might produce incorrect answers. It is the user's responsibility to ensure that the constraint definition matches reality.

Examples

Create foreign table `films`, which will be accessed through the server `film_server`:

```
CREATE FOREIGN TABLE films (
    code        char(5) NOT NULL,
    title       varchar(40) NOT NULL,
    did         integer NOT NULL,
    date_prod   date,
    kind        varchar(10),
    len         interval hour to minute
)
SERVER film_server;
```

Create foreign table `measurement_y2016m07`, which will be accessed through the server `server_07`, as a partition of the range partitioned table `measurement`:

```
CREATE FOREIGN TABLE measurement_y2016m07
    PARTITION OF measurement FOR VALUES FROM ('2016-07-01') TO
    ('2016-08-01')
    SERVER server_07;
```

Compatibility

The `CREATE FOREIGN TABLE` command largely conforms to the SQL standard; however, much as with `CREATE TABLE`, `NULL` constraints and zero-column foreign tables are permitted. The ability to specify column default values is also a PostgreSQL extension. Table inheritance, in the form defined by PostgreSQL, is nonstandard.

See Also

ALTER FOREIGN TABLE, DROP FOREIGN TABLE, CREATE TABLE, CREATE SERVER, IMPORT FOREIGN SCHEMA

CREATE FUNCTION

CREATE FUNCTION — define a new function

Synopsis

```
CREATE [ OR REPLACE ] FUNCTION
    name ( [ [ argmode ] [ argname ] argtype [ { DEFAULT |
 = } default_expr ] [, ...] ] )
    [ RETURNS rettype
      | RETURNS TABLE ( column_name column_type [, ...] ) ]
  { LANGUAGE lang_name
    | TRANSFORM { FOR TYPE type_name } [, ... ]
    | WINDOW
    | IMMUTABLE | STABLE | VOLATILE | [ NOT ] LEAKPROOF
    | CALLED ON NULL INPUT | RETURNS NULL ON NULL INPUT | STRICT
    | [ EXTERNAL ] SECURITY INVOKER | [ EXTERNAL ] SECURITY DEFINER
    | PARALLEL { UNSAFE | RESTRICTED | SAFE }
    | COST execution_cost
    | ROWS result_rows
    | SET configuration_parameter { TO value | = value | FROM
 CURRENT }
    | AS 'definition'
    | AS 'obj_file', 'link_symbol'
  } ...
```

Description

CREATE FUNCTION defines a new function. CREATE OR REPLACE FUNCTION will either create a new function, or replace an existing definition. To be able to define a function, the user must have the USAGE privilege on the language.

If a schema name is included, then the function is created in the specified schema. Otherwise it is created in the current schema. The name of the new function must not match any existing function or procedure with the same input argument types in the same schema. However, functions and procedures of different argument types can share a name (this is called *overloading*).

To replace the current definition of an existing function, use CREATE OR REPLACE FUNCTION. It is not possible to change the name or argument types of a function this way (if you tried, you would actually be creating a new, distinct function). Also, CREATE OR REPLACE FUNCTION will not let you change the return type of an existing function. To do that, you must drop and recreate the function. (When using OUT parameters, that means you cannot change the types of any OUT parameters except by dropping the function.)

When CREATE OR REPLACE FUNCTION is used to replace an existing function, the ownership and permissions of the function do not change. All other function properties are assigned the values specified or implied in the command. You must own the function to replace it (this includes being a member of the owning role).

If you drop and then recreate a function, the new function is not the same entity as the old; you will have to drop existing rules, views, triggers, etc. that refer to the old function. Use CREATE OR REPLACE

FUNCTION to change a function definition without breaking objects that refer to the function. Also, ALTER FUNCTION can be used to change most of the auxiliary properties of an existing function.

The user that creates the function becomes the owner of the function.

To be able to create a function, you must have USAGE privilege on the argument types and the return type.

Parameters

name

> The name (optionally schema-qualified) of the function to create.

argmode

> The mode of an argument: IN, OUT, INOUT, or VARIADIC. If omitted, the default is IN. Only OUT arguments can follow a VARIADIC one. Also, OUT and INOUT arguments cannot be used together with the RETURNS TABLE notation.

argname

> The name of an argument. Some languages (including SQL and PL/pgSQL) let you use the name in the function body. For other languages the name of an input argument is just extra documentation, so far as the function itself is concerned; but you can use input argument names when calling a function to improve readability (see Section 4.3). In any case, the name of an output argument is significant, because it defines the column name in the result row type. (If you omit the name for an output argument, the system will choose a default column name.)

argtype

> The data type(s) of the function's arguments (optionally schema-qualified), if any. The argument types can be base, composite, or domain types, or can reference the type of a table column.

> Depending on the implementation language it might also be allowed to specify "pseudo-types" such as cstring. Pseudo-types indicate that the actual argument type is either incompletely specified, or outside the set of ordinary SQL data types.

> The type of a column is referenced by writing *table_name.column_name*%TYPE. Using this feature can sometimes help make a function independent of changes to the definition of a table.

default_expr

> An expression to be used as default value if the parameter is not specified. The expression has to be coercible to the argument type of the parameter. Only input (including INOUT) parameters can have a default value. All input parameters following a parameter with a default value must have default values as well.

rettype

> The return data type (optionally schema-qualified). The return type can be a base, composite, or domain type, or can reference the type of a table column. Depending on the implementation language it might also be allowed to specify "pseudo-types" such as cstring. If the function is not supposed to return a value, specify void as the return type.

> When there are OUT or INOUT parameters, the RETURNS clause can be omitted. If present, it must agree with the result type implied by the output parameters: RECORD if there are multiple output parameters, or the same type as the single output parameter.

The SETOF modifier indicates that the function will return a set of items, rather than a single item.

The type of a column is referenced by writing *table_name.column_name*%TYPE.

column_name

The name of an output column in the RETURNS TABLE syntax. This is effectively another way of declaring a named OUT parameter, except that RETURNS TABLE also implies RETURNS SETOF.

column_type

The data type of an output column in the RETURNS TABLE syntax.

lang_name

The name of the language that the function is implemented in. It can be sql, c, internal, or the name of a user-defined procedural language, e.g. plpgsql. Enclosing the name in single quotes is deprecated and requires matching case.

TRANSFORM { FOR TYPE *type_name* } [, ...] }

Lists which transforms a call to the function should apply. Transforms convert between SQL types and language-specific data types; see CREATE TRANSFORM. Procedural language implementations usually have hardcoded knowledge of the built-in types, so those don't need to be listed here. If a procedural language implementation does not know how to handle a type and no transform is supplied, it will fall back to a default behavior for converting data types, but this depends on the implementation.

WINDOW

WINDOW indicates that the function is a *window function* rather than a plain function. This is currently only useful for functions written in C. The WINDOW attribute cannot be changed when replacing an existing function definition.

IMMUTABLE
STABLE
VOLATILE

These attributes inform the query optimizer about the behavior of the function. At most one choice can be specified. If none of these appear, VOLATILE is the default assumption.

IMMUTABLE indicates that the function cannot modify the database and always returns the same result when given the same argument values; that is, it does not do database lookups or otherwise use information not directly present in its argument list. If this option is given, any call of the function with all-constant arguments can be immediately replaced with the function value.

STABLE indicates that the function cannot modify the database, and that within a single table scan it will consistently return the same result for the same argument values, but that its result could change across SQL statements. This is the appropriate selection for functions whose results depend on database lookups, parameter variables (such as the current time zone), etc. (It is inappropriate for AFTER triggers that wish to query rows modified by the current command.) Also note that the current_timestamp family of functions qualify as stable, since their values do not change within a transaction.

VOLATILE indicates that the function value can change even within a single table scan, so no optimizations can be made. Relatively few database functions are volatile in this sense; some examples are random(), currval(), timeofday(). But note that any function that has side-effects must be classified volatile, even if its result is quite predictable, to prevent calls from being optimized away; an example is setval().

For additional details see Section 38.7.

LEAKPROOF

LEAKPROOF indicates that the function has no side effects. It reveals no information about its arguments other than by its return value. For example, a function which throws an error message for some argument values but not others, or which includes the argument values in any error message, is not leakproof. This affects how the system executes queries against views created with the security_barrier option or tables with row level security enabled. The system will enforce conditions from security policies and security barrier views before any user-supplied conditions from the query itself that contain non-leakproof functions, in order to prevent the inadvertent exposure of data. Functions and operators marked as leakproof are assumed to be trustworthy, and may be executed before conditions from security policies and security barrier views. In addition, functions which do not take arguments or which are not passed any arguments from the security barrier view or table do not have to be marked as leakproof to be executed before security conditions. See CREATE VIEW and Section 41.5. This option can only be set by the superuser.

CALLED ON NULL INPUT
RETURNS NULL ON NULL INPUT
STRICT

CALLED ON NULL INPUT (the default) indicates that the function will be called normally when some of its arguments are null. It is then the function author's responsibility to check for null values if necessary and respond appropriately.

RETURNS NULL ON NULL INPUT or STRICT indicates that the function always returns null whenever any of its arguments are null. If this parameter is specified, the function is not executed when there are null arguments; instead a null result is assumed automatically.

[EXTERNAL] SECURITY INVOKER
[EXTERNAL] SECURITY DEFINER

SECURITY INVOKER indicates that the function is to be executed with the privileges of the user that calls it. That is the default. SECURITY DEFINER specifies that the function is to be executed with the privileges of the user that owns it.

The key word EXTERNAL is allowed for SQL conformance, but it is optional since, unlike in SQL, this feature applies to all functions not only external ones.

PARALLEL

PARALLEL UNSAFE indicates that the function can't be executed in parallel mode and the presence of such a function in an SQL statement forces a serial execution plan. This is the default. PARALLEL RESTRICTED indicates that the function can be executed in parallel mode, but the execution is restricted to parallel group leader. PARALLEL SAFE indicates that the function is safe to run in parallel mode without restriction.

Functions should be labeled parallel unsafe if they modify any database state, or if they make changes to the transaction such as using sub-transactions, or if they access sequences or attempt to make persistent changes to settings (e.g. setval). They should be labeled as parallel restricted if they access temporary tables, client connection state, cursors, prepared statements, or miscellaneous backend-local state which the system cannot synchronize in parallel mode (e.g. setseed cannot be executed other than by the group leader because a change made by another process would not be reflected in the leader). In general, if a function is labeled as being safe when it is restricted or unsafe, or if it is labeled as being restricted when it is in fact unsafe, it may throw errors or produce wrong answers when used in a parallel query. C-language functions could in theory exhibit totally undefined behavior if mislabeled, since there is no way for the system to protect itself against arbitrary C code, but in most likely cases the result will be no worse than for any other function. If in doubt, functions should be labeled as UNSAFE, which is the default.

COST *execution_cost*

A positive number giving the estimated execution cost for the function, in units of cpu_operator_cost. If the function returns a set, this is the cost per returned row. If the cost is not specified, 1 unit is assumed for C-language and internal functions, and 100 units for functions in all other languages. Larger values cause the planner to try to avoid evaluating the function more often than necessary.

ROWS *result_rows*

A positive number giving the estimated number of rows that the planner should expect the function to return. This is only allowed when the function is declared to return a set. The default assumption is 1000 rows.

configuration_parameter
value

The SET clause causes the specified configuration parameter to be set to the specified value when the function is entered, and then restored to its prior value when the function exits. SET FROM CURRENT saves the value of the parameter that is current when CREATE FUNCTION is executed as the value to be applied when the function is entered.

If a SET clause is attached to a function, then the effects of a SET LOCAL command executed inside the function for the same variable are restricted to the function: the configuration parameter's prior value is still restored at function exit. However, an ordinary SET command (without LOCAL) overrides the SET clause, much as it would do for a previous SET LOCAL command: the effects of such a command will persist after function exit, unless the current transaction is rolled back.

See SET and Chapter 19 for more information about allowed parameter names and values.

definition

A string constant defining the function; the meaning depends on the language. It can be an internal function name, the path to an object file, an SQL command, or text in a procedural language.

It is often helpful to use dollar quoting (see Section 4.1.2.4) to write the function definition string, rather than the normal single quote syntax. Without dollar quoting, any single quotes or backslashes in the function definition must be escaped by doubling them.

obj_file, *link_symbol*

This form of the AS clause is used for dynamically loadable C language functions when the function name in the C language source code is not the same as the name of the SQL function. The string *obj_file* is the name of the shared library file containing the compiled C function, and is interpreted as for the LOAD command. The string *link_symbol* is the function's link symbol, that is, the name of the function in the C language source code. If the link symbol is omitted, it is assumed to be the same as the name of the SQL function being defined. The C names of all functions must be different, so you must give overloaded C functions different C names (for example, use the argument types as part of the C names).

When repeated CREATE FUNCTION calls refer to the same object file, the file is only loaded once per session. To unload and reload the file (perhaps during development), start a new session.

Refer to Section 38.3 for further information on writing functions.

Overloading

PostgreSQL allows function *overloading*; that is, the same name can be used for several different functions so long as they have distinct input argument types. Whether or not you use it, this capability entails security precautions when calling functions in databases where some users mistrust other users; see Section 10.3.

Two functions are considered the same if they have the same names and *input* argument types, ignoring any OUT parameters. Thus for example these declarations conflict:

```
CREATE FUNCTION foo(int) ...
CREATE FUNCTION foo(int, out text) ...
```

Functions that have different argument type lists will not be considered to conflict at creation time, but if defaults are provided they might conflict in use. For example, consider

```
CREATE FUNCTION foo(int) ...
CREATE FUNCTION foo(int, int default 42) ...
```

A call foo(10) will fail due to the ambiguity about which function should be called.

Notes

The full SQL type syntax is allowed for declaring a function's arguments and return value. However, parenthesized type modifiers (e.g., the precision field for type numeric) are discarded by CREATE FUNCTION. Thus for example CREATE FUNCTION foo (varchar(10)) ... is exactly the same as CREATE FUNCTION foo (varchar) ....

When replacing an existing function with CREATE OR REPLACE FUNCTION, there are restrictions on changing parameter names. You cannot change the name already assigned to any input parameter (although you can add names to parameters that had none before). If there is more than one output parameter, you cannot change the names of the output parameters, because that would change the column names of the anonymous composite type that describes the function's result. These restrictions are made to ensure that existing calls of the function do not stop working when it is replaced.

If a function is declared STRICT with a VARIADIC argument, the strictness check tests that the variadic array *as a whole* is non-null. The function will still be called if the array has null elements.

Examples

Here are some trivial examples to help you get started. For more information and examples, see Section 38.3.

```
CREATE FUNCTION add(integer, integer) RETURNS integer
    AS 'select $1 + $2;'
    LANGUAGE SQL
    IMMUTABLE
    RETURNS NULL ON NULL INPUT;
```

Increment an integer, making use of an argument name, in PL/pgSQL:

```
CREATE OR REPLACE FUNCTION increment(i integer) RETURNS integer AS $$
        BEGIN
                RETURN i + 1;
        END;
$$ LANGUAGE plpgsql;
```

Return a record containing multiple output parameters:

```
CREATE FUNCTION dup(in int, out f1 int, out f2 text)
    AS $$ SELECT $1, CAST($1 AS text) || ' is text' $$
    LANGUAGE SQL;
```

```
SELECT * FROM dup(42);
```

You can do the same thing more verbosely with an explicitly named composite type:

```
CREATE TYPE dup_result AS (f1 int, f2 text);
```

```
CREATE FUNCTION dup(int) RETURNS dup_result
    AS $$ SELECT $1, CAST($1 AS text) || ' is text' $$
    LANGUAGE SQL;
```

```
SELECT * FROM dup(42);
```

Another way to return multiple columns is to use a TABLE function:

```
CREATE FUNCTION dup(int) RETURNS TABLE(f1 int, f2 text)
    AS $$ SELECT $1, CAST($1 AS text) || ' is text' $$
    LANGUAGE SQL;
```

```
SELECT * FROM dup(42);
```

However, a TABLE function is different from the preceding examples, because it actually returns a *set* of records, not just one record.

Writing SECURITY DEFINER Functions Safely

Because a SECURITY DEFINER function is executed with the privileges of the user that owns it, care is needed to ensure that the function cannot be misused. For security, search_path should be set to exclude any schemas writable by untrusted users. This prevents malicious users from creating objects (e.g., tables, functions, and operators) that mask objects intended to be used by the function. Particularly important in this regard is the temporary-table schema, which is searched first by default, and is normally writable by anyone. A secure arrangement can be obtained by forcing the temporary schema to be searched last. To do this, write pg_temp as the last entry in search_path. This function illustrates safe usage:

```
CREATE FUNCTION check_password(uname TEXT, pass TEXT)
RETURNS BOOLEAN AS $$
DECLARE passed BOOLEAN;
BEGIN
        SELECT  (pwd = $2) INTO passed
        FROM    pwds
```

```
        WHERE    username = $1;

        RETURN passed;
END;
$$  LANGUAGE plpgsql
    SECURITY DEFINER
    -- Set a secure search_path: trusted schema(s), then 'pg_temp'.
    SET search_path = admin, pg_temp;
```

This function's intention is to access a table `admin.pwds`. But without the `SET` clause, or with a `SET` clause mentioning only `admin`, the function could be subverted by creating a temporary table named `pwds`.

Before PostgreSQL version 8.3, the `SET` clause was not available, and so older functions may contain rather complicated logic to save, set, and restore `search_path`. The `SET` clause is far easier to use for this purpose.

Another point to keep in mind is that by default, execute privilege is granted to `PUBLIC` for newly created functions (see GRANT for more information). Frequently you will wish to restrict use of a security definer function to only some users. To do that, you must revoke the default `PUBLIC` privileges and then grant execute privilege selectively. To avoid having a window where the new function is accessible to all, create it and set the privileges within a single transaction. For example:

```
BEGIN;
CREATE FUNCTION check_password(uname TEXT, pass TEXT) ... SECURITY
 DEFINER;
REVOKE ALL ON FUNCTION check_password(uname TEXT, pass TEXT) FROM
 PUBLIC;
GRANT EXECUTE ON FUNCTION check_password(uname TEXT, pass TEXT) TO
 admins;
COMMIT;
```

Compatibility

A `CREATE FUNCTION` command is defined in the SQL standard. The PostgreSQL version is similar but not fully compatible. The attributes are not portable, neither are the different available languages.

For compatibility with some other database systems, *argmode* can be written either before or after *argname*. But only the first way is standard-compliant.

For parameter defaults, the SQL standard specifies only the syntax with the `DEFAULT` key word. The syntax with = is used in T-SQL and Firebird.

See Also
ALTER FUNCTION, DROP FUNCTION, GRANT, LOAD, REVOKE

CREATE GROUP

CREATE GROUP — define a new database role

Synopsis

```
CREATE GROUP name [ [ WITH ] option [ ... ] ]
```

where *option* can be:

```
    SUPERUSER | NOSUPERUSER
  | CREATEDB | NOCREATEDB
  | CREATEROLE | NOCREATEROLE
  | INHERIT | NOINHERIT
  | LOGIN | NOLOGIN
  | [ ENCRYPTED ] PASSWORD 'password'
  | VALID UNTIL 'timestamp'
  | IN ROLE role_name [, ...]
  | IN GROUP role_name [, ...]
  | ROLE role_name [, ...]
  | ADMIN role_name [, ...]
  | USER role_name [, ...]
  | SYSID uid
```

Description

CREATE GROUP is now an alias for CREATE ROLE.

Compatibility

There is no CREATE GROUP statement in the SQL standard.

See Also

CREATE ROLE

CREATE INDEX

CREATE INDEX — define a new index

Synopsis

```
CREATE [ UNIQUE ] INDEX [ CONCURRENTLY ] [ [ IF NOT EXISTS ] name ] ON
[ ONLY ] table_name [ USING method ]
    ( { column_name | ( expression ) } [ COLLATE collation ] [ opclass
] [ ASC | DESC ] [ NULLS { FIRST | LAST } ] [, ...] )
    [ INCLUDE ( column_name [, ...] ) ]
    [ WITH ( storage_parameter = value [, ... ] ) ]
    [ TABLESPACE tablespace_name ]
    [ WHERE predicate ]
```

Description

CREATE INDEX constructs an index on the specified column(s) of the specified relation, which can be a table or a materialized view. Indexes are primarily used to enhance database performance (though inappropriate use can result in slower performance).

The key field(s) for the index are specified as column names, or alternatively as expressions written in parentheses. Multiple fields can be specified if the index method supports multicolumn indexes.

An index field can be an expression computed from the values of one or more columns of the table row. This feature can be used to obtain fast access to data based on some transformation of the basic data. For example, an index computed on upper(col) would allow the clause WHERE upper(col) = 'JIM' to use an index.

PostgreSQL provides the index methods B-tree, hash, GiST, SP-GiST, GIN, and BRIN. Users can also define their own index methods, but that is fairly complicated.

When the WHERE clause is present, a *partial index* is created. A partial index is an index that contains entries for only a portion of a table, usually a portion that is more useful for indexing than the rest of the table. For example, if you have a table that contains both billed and unbilled orders where the unbilled orders take up a small fraction of the total table and yet that is an often used section, you can improve performance by creating an index on just that portion. Another possible application is to use WHERE with UNIQUE to enforce uniqueness over a subset of a table. See Section 11.8 for more discussion.

The expression used in the WHERE clause can refer only to columns of the underlying table, but it can use all columns, not just the ones being indexed. Presently, subqueries and aggregate expressions are also forbidden in WHERE. The same restrictions apply to index fields that are expressions.

All functions and operators used in an index definition must be "immutable", that is, their results must depend only on their arguments and never on any outside influence (such as the contents of another table or the current time). This restriction ensures that the behavior of the index is well-defined. To use a user-defined function in an index expression or WHERE clause, remember to mark the function immutable when you create it.

Parameters

UNIQUE

Causes the system to check for duplicate values in the table when the index is created (if data already exist) and each time data is added. Attempts to insert or update data which would result in duplicate entries will generate an error.

Additional restrictions apply when unique indexes are applied to partitioned tables; see CREATE TABLE.

CONCURRENTLY

When this option is used, PostgreSQL will build the index without taking any locks that prevent concurrent inserts, updates, or deletes on the table; whereas a standard index build locks out writes (but not reads) on the table until it's done. There are several caveats to be aware of when using this option — see Building Indexes Concurrently.

IF NOT EXISTS

Do not throw an error if a relation with the same name already exists. A notice is issued in this case. Note that there is no guarantee that the existing index is anything like the one that would have been created. Index name is required when IF NOT EXISTS is specified.

INCLUDE

The optional INCLUDE clause specifies a list of columns which will be included in the index as *non-key* columns. A non-key column cannot be used in an index scan search qualification, and it is disregarded for purposes of any uniqueness or exclusion constraint enforced by the index. However, an index-only scan can return the contents of non-key columns without having to visit the index's table, since they are available directly from the index entry. Thus, addition of non-key columns allows index-only scans to be used for queries that otherwise could not use them.

It's wise to be conservative about adding non-key columns to an index, especially wide columns. If an index tuple exceeds the maximum size allowed for the index type, data insertion will fail. In any case, non-key columns duplicate data from the index's table and bloat the size of the index, thus potentially slowing searches.

Columns listed in the INCLUDE clause don't need appropriate operator classes; the clause can include columns whose data types don't have operator classes defined for a given access method.

Expressions are not supported as included columns since they cannot be used in index-only scans.

Currently, only the B-tree index access method supports this feature. In B-tree indexes, the values of columns listed in the INCLUDE clause are included in leaf tuples which correspond to heap tuples, but are not included in upper-level index entries used for tree navigation.

name

The name of the index to be created. No schema name can be included here; the index is always created in the same schema as its parent table. If the name is omitted, PostgreSQL chooses a suitable name based on the parent table's name and the indexed column name(s).

ONLY

Indicates not to recurse creating indexes on partitions, if the table is partitioned. The default is to recurse.

table_name

The name (possibly schema-qualified) of the table to be indexed.

method

The name of the index method to be used. Choices are `btree`, `hash`, `gist`, `spgist`, `gin`, and `brin`. The default method is `btree`.

column_name

The name of a column of the table.

expression

An expression based on one or more columns of the table. The expression usually must be written with surrounding parentheses, as shown in the syntax. However, the parentheses can be omitted if the expression has the form of a function call.

collation

The name of the collation to use for the index. By default, the index uses the collation declared for the column to be indexed or the result collation of the expression to be indexed. Indexes with non-default collations can be useful for queries that involve expressions using non-default collations.

opclass

The name of an operator class. See below for details.

ASC

Specifies ascending sort order (which is the default).

DESC

Specifies descending sort order.

NULLS FIRST

Specifies that nulls sort before non-nulls. This is the default when `DESC` is specified.

NULLS LAST

Specifies that nulls sort after non-nulls. This is the default when `DESC` is not specified.

storage_parameter

The name of an index-method-specific storage parameter. See Index Storage Parameters for details.

tablespace_name

The tablespace in which to create the index. If not specified, default_tablespace is consulted, or temp_tablespaces for indexes on temporary tables.

predicate

The constraint expression for a partial index.

Index Storage Parameters

The optional `WITH` clause specifies *storage parameters* for the index. Each index method has its own set of allowed storage parameters. The B-tree, hash, GiST and SP-GiST index methods all accept this parameter:

fillfactor

The fillfactor for an index is a percentage that determines how full the index method will try to pack index pages. For B-trees, leaf pages are filled to this percentage during initial index build, and also when extending the index at the right (adding new largest key values). If pages subsequently become completely full, they will be split, leading to gradual degradation in the index's efficiency. B-trees use a default fillfactor of 90, but any integer value from 10 to 100 can be selected. If the table is static then fillfactor 100 is best to minimize the index's physical size, but for heavily updated tables a smaller fillfactor is better to minimize the need for page splits. The other index methods use fillfactor in different but roughly analogous ways; the default fillfactor varies between methods.

B-tree indexes additionally accept this parameter:

vacuum_cleanup_index_scale_factor

Per-index value for vacuum_cleanup_index_scale_factor.

GiST indexes additionally accept this parameter:

buffering

Determines whether the buffering build technique described in Section 64.4.1 is used to build the index. With OFF it is disabled, with ON it is enabled, and with AUTO it is initially disabled, but turned on on-the-fly once the index size reaches effective_cache_size. The default is AUTO.

GIN indexes accept different parameters:

fastupdate

This setting controls usage of the fast update technique described in Section 66.4.1. It is a Boolean parameter: ON enables fast update, OFF disables it. (Alternative spellings of ON and OFF are allowed as described in Section 19.1.) The default is ON.

Note

Turning `fastupdate` off via `ALTER INDEX` prevents future insertions from going into the list of pending index entries, but does not in itself flush previous entries. You might want to VACUUM the table or call `gin_clean_pending_list` function afterward to ensure the pending list is emptied.

---

gin_pending_list_limit

Custom gin_pending_list_limit parameter. This value is specified in kilobytes.

BRIN indexes accept different parameters:

pages_per_range

Defines the number of table blocks that make up one block range for each entry of a BRIN index (see Section 67.1 for more details). The default is 128.

autosummarize

Defines whether a summarization run is invoked for the previous page range whenever an insertion is detected on the next one.

Building Indexes Concurrently

Creating an index can interfere with regular operation of a database. Normally PostgreSQL locks the table to be indexed against writes and performs the entire index build with a single scan of the table. Other transactions can still read the table, but if they try to insert, update, or delete rows in the table they will block until the index build is finished. This could have a severe effect if the system is a live production database. Very large tables can take many hours to be indexed, and even for smaller tables, an index build can lock out writers for periods that are unacceptably long for a production system.

PostgreSQL supports building indexes without locking out writes. This method is invoked by specifying the CONCURRENTLY option of CREATE INDEX. When this option is used, PostgreSQL must perform two scans of the table, and in addition it must wait for all existing transactions that could potentially modify or use the index to terminate. Thus this method requires more total work than a standard index build and takes significantly longer to complete. However, since it allows normal operations to continue while the index is built, this method is useful for adding new indexes in a production environment. Of course, the extra CPU and I/O load imposed by the index creation might slow other operations.

In a concurrent index build, the index is actually entered into the system catalogs in one transaction, then two table scans occur in two more transactions. Before each table scan, the index build must wait for existing transactions that have modified the table to terminate. After the second scan, the index build must wait for any transactions that have a snapshot (see Chapter 13) predating the second scan to terminate. Then finally the index can be marked ready for use, and the CREATE INDEX command terminates. Even then, however, the index may not be immediately usable for queries: in the worst case, it cannot be used as long as transactions exist that predate the start of the index build.

If a problem arises while scanning the table, such as a deadlock or a uniqueness violation in a unique index, the CREATE INDEX command will fail but leave behind an "invalid" index. This index will be ignored for querying purposes because it might be incomplete; however it will still consume update overhead. The psql \d command will report such an index as INVALID:

```
postgres=# \d tab
        Table "public.tab"
 Column |  Type   | Collation | Nullable | Default
--------+---------+-----------+----------+---------
 col    | integer |           |          |
Indexes:
    "idx" btree (col) INVALID
```

The recommended recovery method in such cases is to drop the index and try again to perform CREATE INDEX CONCURRENTLY. (Another possibility is to rebuild the index with REINDEX. However, since REINDEX does not support concurrent builds, this option is unlikely to seem attractive.)

Another caveat when building a unique index concurrently is that the uniqueness constraint is already being enforced against other transactions when the second table scan begins. This means that constraint violations could be reported in other queries prior to the index becoming available for use, or even in cases where the index build eventually fails. Also, if a failure does occur in the second scan, the "invalid" index continues to enforce its uniqueness constraint afterwards.

Concurrent builds of expression indexes and partial indexes are supported. Errors occurring in the evaluation of these expressions could cause behavior similar to that described above for unique constraint violations.

Regular index builds permit other regular index builds on the same table to occur simultaneously, but only one concurrent index build can occur on a table at a time. In either case, schema modification of the table is not allowed while the index is being built. Another difference is that a regular CREATE INDEX command can be performed within a transaction block, but CREATE INDEX CONCURRENTLY cannot.

Notes

See Chapter 11 for information about when indexes can be used, when they are not used, and in which particular situations they can be useful.

Currently, only the B-tree, GiST, GIN, and BRIN index methods support multicolumn indexes. Up to 32 fields can be specified by default. (This limit can be altered when building PostgreSQL.) Only B-tree currently supports unique indexes.

An *operator class* can be specified for each column of an index. The operator class identifies the operators to be used by the index for that column. For example, a B-tree index on four-byte integers would use the int4_ops class; this operator class includes comparison functions for four-byte integers. In practice the default operator class for the column's data type is usually sufficient. The main point of having operator classes is that for some data types, there could be more than one meaningful ordering. For example, we might want to sort a complex-number data type either by absolute value or by real part. We could do this by defining two operator classes for the data type and then selecting the proper class when creating an index. More information about operator classes is in Section 11.10 and in Section 38.15.

When CREATE INDEX is invoked on a partitioned table, the default behavior is to recurse to all partitions to ensure they all have matching indexes. Each partition is first checked to determine whether an equivalent index already exists, and if so, that index will become attached as a partition index to the index being created, which will become its parent index. If no matching index exists, a new index will be created and automatically attached; the name of the new index in each partition will be determined as if no index name had been specified in the command. If the ONLY option is specified, no recursion is done, and the index is marked invalid. (ALTER INDEX ... ATTACH PARTITION marks the index valid, once all partitions acquire matching indexes.) Note, however, that any partition that is created in the future using CREATE TABLE ... PARTITION OF will automatically have a matching index, regardless of whether ONLY is specified.

For index methods that support ordered scans (currently, only B-tree), the optional clauses ASC, DESC, NULLS FIRST, and/or NULLS LAST can be specified to modify the sort ordering of the index. Since an ordered index can be scanned either forward or backward, it is not normally useful to create a single-column DESC index — that sort ordering is already available with a regular index. The value of these options is that multicolumn indexes can be created that match the sort ordering requested by a mixed-ordering query, such as SELECT ... ORDER BY x ASC, y DESC. The NULLS options are useful if you need to support "nulls sort low" behavior, rather than the default "nulls sort high", in queries that depend on indexes to avoid sorting steps.

For most index methods, the speed of creating an index is dependent on the setting of maintenance_work_mem. Larger values will reduce the time needed for index creation, so long as you don't make it larger than the amount of memory really available, which would drive the machine into swapping.

PostgreSQL can build indexes while leveraging multiple CPUs in order to process the table rows faster. This feature is known as *parallel index build*. For index methods that support building indexes in parallel (currently, only B-tree), maintenance_work_mem specifies the maximum amount of memory that can be used by each index build operation as a whole, regardless of how many worker processes were started. Generally, a cost model automatically determines how many worker processes should be requested, if any.

Parallel index builds may benefit from increasing maintenance_work_mem where an equivalent serial index build will see little or no benefit. Note that maintenance_work_mem may influence the number of worker processes requested, since parallel workers must have at least a 32MB share of the total maintenance_work_mem budget. There must also be a remaining 32MB share for the leader process.

Increasing max_parallel_maintenance_workers may allow more workers to be used, which will reduce the time needed for index creation, so long as the index build is not already I/O bound. Of course, there should also be sufficient CPU capacity that would otherwise lie idle.

Setting a value for `parallel_workers` via ALTER TABLE directly controls how many parallel worker processes will be requested by a `CREATE INDEX` against the table. This bypasses the cost model completely, and prevents `maintenance_work_mem` from affecting how many parallel workers are requested. Setting `parallel_workers` to 0 via `ALTER TABLE` will disable parallel index builds on the table in all cases.

Tip

You might want to reset `parallel_workers` after setting it as part of tuning an index build. This avoids inadvertent changes to query plans, since `parallel_workers` affects *all* parallel table scans.

While `CREATE INDEX` with the `CONCURRENTLY` option supports parallel builds without special restrictions, only the first table scan is actually performed in parallel.

Use DROP INDEX to remove an index.

Prior releases of PostgreSQL also had an R-tree index method. This method has been removed because it had no significant advantages over the GiST method. If USING `rtree` is specified, `CREATE INDEX` will interpret it as USING `gist`, to simplify conversion of old databases to GiST.

Examples

To create a unique B-tree index on the column `title` in the table `films`:

```
CREATE UNIQUE INDEX title_idx ON films (title);
```

To create a unique B-tree index on the column `title` with included columns `director` and `rating` in the table `films`:

```
CREATE UNIQUE INDEX title_idx ON films (title) INCLUDE (director,
 rating);
```

To create an index on the expression `lower(title)`, allowing efficient case-insensitive searches:

```
CREATE INDEX ON films ((lower(title)));
```

(In this example we have chosen to omit the index name, so the system will choose a name, typically `films_lower_idx`.)

To create an index with non-default collation:

```
CREATE INDEX title_idx_german ON films (title COLLATE "de_DE");
```

To create an index with non-default sort ordering of nulls:

```
CREATE INDEX title_idx_nulls_low ON films (title NULLS FIRST);
```

To create an index with non-default fill factor:

```
CREATE UNIQUE INDEX title_idx ON films (title) WITH (fillfactor = 70);
```

To create a GIN index with fast updates disabled:

```
CREATE INDEX gin_idx ON documents_table USING GIN (locations) WITH
  (fastupdate = off);
```

To create an index on the column code in the table films and have the index reside in the tablespace indexspace:

```
CREATE INDEX code_idx ON films (code) TABLESPACE indexspace;
```

To create a GiST index on a point attribute so that we can efficiently use box operators on the result of the conversion function:

```
CREATE INDEX pointloc
    ON points USING gist (box(location,location));
SELECT * FROM points
    WHERE box(location,location) && '(0,0),(1,1)'::box;
```

To create an index without locking out writes to the table:

```
CREATE INDEX CONCURRENTLY sales_quantity_index ON sales_table
  (quantity);
```

Compatibility

CREATE INDEX is a PostgreSQL language extension. There are no provisions for indexes in the SQL standard.

See Also

ALTER INDEX, DROP INDEX

CREATE LANGUAGE

CREATE LANGUAGE — define a new procedural language

Synopsis

```
CREATE [ OR REPLACE ] [ PROCEDURAL ] LANGUAGE name
CREATE [ OR REPLACE ] [ TRUSTED ] [ PROCEDURAL ] LANGUAGE name
    HANDLER call_handler [ INLINE inline_handler ]
  [ VALIDATOR valfunction ]
```

Description

CREATE LANGUAGE registers a new procedural language with a PostgreSQL database. Subsequently, functions and procedures can be defined in this new language.

Note

As of PostgreSQL 9.1, most procedural languages have been made into "extensions", and should therefore be installed with CREATE EXTENSION not CREATE LANGUAGE. Direct use of CREATE LANGUAGE should now be confined to extension installation scripts. If you have a "bare" language in your database, perhaps as a result of an upgrade, you can convert it to an extension using CREATE EXTENSION langname FROM unpackaged.

CREATE LANGUAGE effectively associates the language name with handler function(s) that are responsible for executing functions written in the language. Refer to Chapter 56 for more information about language handlers.

There are two forms of the CREATE LANGUAGE command. In the first form, the user supplies just the name of the desired language, and the PostgreSQL server consults the pg_pltemplate system catalog to determine the correct parameters. In the second form, the user supplies the language parameters along with the language name. The second form can be used to create a language that is not defined in pg_pltemplate, but this approach is considered obsolescent.

When the server finds an entry in the pg_pltemplate catalog for the given language name, it will use the catalog data even if the command includes language parameters. This behavior simplifies loading of old dump files, which are likely to contain out-of-date information about language support functions.

Ordinarily, the user must have the PostgreSQL superuser privilege to register a new language. However, the owner of a database can register a new language within that database if the language is listed in the pg_pltemplate catalog and is marked as allowed to be created by database owners (tmpldbacreate is true). The default is that trusted languages can be created by database owners, but this can be adjusted by superusers by modifying the contents of pg_pltemplate. The creator of a language becomes its owner and can later drop it, rename it, or assign it to a new owner.

CREATE OR REPLACE LANGUAGE will either create a new language, or replace an existing definition. If the language already exists, its parameters are updated according to the values specified or taken from pg_pltemplate, but the language's ownership and permissions settings do not change, and any existing functions written in the language are assumed to still be valid. In addition to the normal privilege requirements for creating a language, the user must be superuser or owner of the existing language. The REPLACE case is mainly meant to be used to ensure that the language exists. If the language has a pg_pltemplate entry then REPLACE will not actually change anything about an existing definition, except in the unusual case where the pg_pltemplate entry has been modified since the language was created.

Parameters

TRUSTED

> TRUSTED specifies that the language does not grant access to data that the user would not otherwise have. If this key word is omitted when registering the language, only users with the PostgreSQL superuser privilege can use this language to create new functions.

PROCEDURAL

> This is a noise word.

name

> The name of the new procedural language. The name must be unique among the languages in the database.

> For backward compatibility, the name can be enclosed by single quotes.

HANDLER *call_handler*

> *call_handler* is the name of a previously registered function that will be called to execute the procedural language's functions. The call handler for a procedural language must be written in a compiled language such as C with version 1 call convention and registered with PostgreSQL as a function taking no arguments and returning the language_handler type, a placeholder type that is simply used to identify the function as a call handler.

INLINE *inline_handler*

> *inline_handler* is the name of a previously registered function that will be called to execute an anonymous code block (DO command) in this language. If no *inline_handler* function is specified, the language does not support anonymous code blocks. The handler function must take one argument of type internal, which will be the DO command's internal representation, and it will typically return void. The return value of the handler is ignored.

VALIDATOR *valfunction*

> *valfunction* is the name of a previously registered function that will be called when a new function in the language is created, to validate the new function. If no validator function is specified, then a new function will not be checked when it is created. The validator function must take one argument of type oid, which will be the OID of the to-be-created function, and will typically return void.

> A validator function would typically inspect the function body for syntactical correctness, but it can also look at other properties of the function, for example if the language cannot handle certain argument types. To signal an error, the validator function should use the ereport() function. The return value of the function is ignored.

The TRUSTED option and the support function name(s) are ignored if the server has an entry for the specified language name in pg_pltemplate.

Notes

Use DROP LANGUAGE to drop procedural languages.

The system catalog `pg_language` (see Section 52.29) records information about the currently installed languages. Also, the psql command `\dL` lists the installed languages.

To create functions in a procedural language, a user must have the USAGE privilege for the language. By default, USAGE is granted to PUBLIC (i.e., everyone) for trusted languages. This can be revoked if desired.

Procedural languages are local to individual databases. However, a language can be installed into the `template1` database, which will cause it to be available automatically in all subsequently-created databases.

The call handler function, the inline handler function (if any), and the validator function (if any) must already exist if the server does not have an entry for the language in `pg_pltemplate`. But when there is an entry, the functions need not already exist; they will be automatically defined if not present in the database. (This might result in CREATE LANGUAGE failing, if the shared library that implements the language is not available in the installation.)

In PostgreSQL versions before 7.3, it was necessary to declare handler functions as returning the place-holder type `opaque`, rather than `language_handler`. To support loading of old dump files, CREATE LANGUAGE will accept a function declared as returning `opaque`, but it will issue a notice and change the function's declared return type to `language_handler`.

Examples

The preferred way of creating any of the standard procedural languages is just:

```
CREATE LANGUAGE plperl;
```

For a language not known in the `pg_pltemplate` catalog, a sequence such as this is needed:

```
CREATE FUNCTION plsample_call_handler() RETURNS language_handler
    AS '$libdir/plsample'
    LANGUAGE C;
CREATE LANGUAGE plsample
    HANDLER plsample_call_handler;
```

Compatibility

CREATE LANGUAGE is a PostgreSQL extension.

See Also

ALTER LANGUAGE, CREATE FUNCTION, DROP LANGUAGE, GRANT, REVOKE

CREATE MATERIALIZED VIEW

CREATE MATERIALIZED VIEW — define a new materialized view

Synopsis

```
CREATE MATERIALIZED VIEW [ IF NOT EXISTS ] table_name
    [ (column_name [, ...] ) ]
    [ WITH ( storage_parameter [= value] [, ... ] ) ]
    [ TABLESPACE tablespace_name ]
    AS query
    [ WITH [ NO ] DATA ]
```

Description

CREATE MATERIALIZED VIEW defines a materialized view of a query. The query is executed and used to populate the view at the time the command is issued (unless WITH NO DATA is used) and may be refreshed later using REFRESH MATERIALIZED VIEW.

CREATE MATERIALIZED VIEW is similar to CREATE TABLE AS, except that it also remembers the query used to initialize the view, so that it can be refreshed later upon demand. A materialized view has many of the same properties as a table, but there is no support for temporary materialized views or automatic generation of OIDs.

Parameters

IF NOT EXISTS

Do not throw an error if a materialized view with the same name already exists. A notice is issued in this case. Note that there is no guarantee that the existing materialized view is anything like the one that would have been created.

table_name

The name (optionally schema-qualified) of the materialized view to be created.

column_name

The name of a column in the new materialized view. If column names are not provided, they are taken from the output column names of the query.

WITH (storage_parameter [= value] [, ...])

This clause specifies optional storage parameters for the new materialized view; see Storage Parameters for more information. All parameters supported for CREATE TABLE are also supported for CREATE MATERIALIZED VIEW with the exception of OIDS. See CREATE TABLE for more information.

TABLESPACE tablespace_name

The tablespace_name is the name of the tablespace in which the new materialized view is to be created. If not specified, default_tablespace is consulted.

query

> A SELECT, TABLE, or VALUES command. This query will run within a security-restricted operation; in particular, calls to functions that themselves create temporary tables will fail.

WITH [NO] DATA

> This clause specifies whether or not the materialized view should be populated at creation time. If not, the materialized view will be flagged as unscannable and cannot be queried until REFRESH MATERIALIZED VIEW is used.

Compatibility

CREATE MATERIALIZED VIEW is a PostgreSQL extension.

See Also

ALTER MATERIALIZED VIEW, CREATE TABLE AS, CREATE VIEW, DROP MATERIALIZED VIEW, REFRESH MATERIALIZED VIEW

CREATE OPERATOR

CREATE OPERATOR — define a new operator

Synopsis

```
CREATE OPERATOR name (
    {FUNCTION|PROCEDURE} = function_name
    [, LEFTARG = left_type ] [, RIGHTARG = right_type ]
    [, COMMUTATOR = com_op ] [, NEGATOR = neg_op ]
    [, RESTRICT = res_proc ] [, JOIN = join_proc ]
    [, HASHES ] [, MERGES ]
)
```

Description

CREATE OPERATOR defines a new operator, *name*. The user who defines an operator becomes its owner. If a schema name is given then the operator is created in the specified schema. Otherwise it is created in the current schema.

The operator name is a sequence of up to NAMEDATALEN-1 (63 by default) characters from the following list:

+ - * / < > = ~ ! @ # % ^ & | ` ?

There are a few restrictions on your choice of name:

- `--` and `/*` cannot appear anywhere in an operator name, since they will be taken as the start of a comment.

- A multicharacter operator name cannot end in + or -, unless the name also contains at least one of these characters:

  ~ ! @ # % ^ & | ` ?

  For example, @- is an allowed operator name, but *- is not. This restriction allows PostgreSQL to parse SQL-compliant commands without requiring spaces between tokens.

- The use of => as an operator name is deprecated. It may be disallowed altogether in a future release.

The operator != is mapped to <> on input, so these two names are always equivalent.

At least one of LEFTARG and RIGHTARG must be defined. For binary operators, both must be defined. For right unary operators, only LEFTARG should be defined, while for left unary operators only RIGHTARG should be defined.

The *function_name* function must have been previously defined using CREATE FUNCTION and must be defined to accept the correct number of arguments (either one or two) of the indicated types.

In the syntax of **CREATE OPERATOR**, the keywords **FUNCTION** and **PROCEDURE** are equivalent, but the referenced function must in any case be a function, not a procedure. The use of the keyword **PROCEDURE** here is historical and deprecated.

The other clauses specify optional operator optimization clauses. Their meaning is detailed in Section 38.14.

To be able to create an operator, you must have **USAGE** privilege on the argument types and the return type, as well as **EXECUTE** privilege on the underlying function. If a commutator or negator operator is specified, you must own these operators.

Parameters

name

> The name of the operator to be defined. See above for allowable characters. The name can be schema-qualified, for example **CREATE OPERATOR myschema.+ (...)**. If not, then the operator is created in the current schema. Two operators in the same schema can have the same name if they operate on different data types. This is called *overloading*.

function_name

> The function used to implement this operator.

left_type

> The data type of the operator's left operand, if any. This option would be omitted for a left-unary operator.

right_type

> The data type of the operator's right operand, if any. This option would be omitted for a right-unary operator.

com_op

> The commutator of this operator.

neg_op

> The negator of this operator.

res_proc

> The restriction selectivity estimator function for this operator.

join_proc

> The join selectivity estimator function for this operator.

HASHES

> Indicates this operator can support a hash join.

MERGES

> Indicates this operator can support a merge join.

To give a schema-qualified operator name in *com_op* or the other optional arguments, use the OPERA-TOR( ) syntax, for example:

```
COMMUTATOR = OPERATOR(myschema.===) ,
```

Notes

Refer to Section 38.13 for further information.

It is not possible to specify an operator's lexical precedence in CREATE OPERATOR, because the parser's precedence behavior is hard-wired. See Section 4.1.6 for precedence details.

The obsolete options SORT1, SORT2, LTCMP, and GTCMP were formerly used to specify the names of sort operators associated with a merge-joinable operator. This is no longer necessary, since information about associated operators is found by looking at B-tree operator families instead. If one of these options is given, it is ignored except for implicitly setting MERGES true.

Use DROP OPERATOR to delete user-defined operators from a database. Use ALTER OPERATOR to modify operators in a database.

Examples

The following command defines a new operator, area-equality, for the data type box:

```
CREATE OPERATOR === (
    LEFTARG = box,
    RIGHTARG = box,
    FUNCTION = area_equal_function,
    COMMUTATOR = ===,
    NEGATOR = !==,
    RESTRICT = area_restriction_function,
    JOIN = area_join_function,
    HASHES, MERGES
);
```

Compatibility

CREATE OPERATOR is a PostgreSQL extension. There are no provisions for user-defined operators in the SQL standard.

See Also

ALTER OPERATOR, CREATE OPERATOR CLASS, DROP OPERATOR

CREATE OPERATOR CLASS

CREATE OPERATOR CLASS — define a new operator class

Synopsis

```
CREATE OPERATOR CLASS name [ DEFAULT ] FOR TYPE data_type
  USING index_method [ FAMILY family_name ] AS
  {  OPERATOR strategy_number operator_name [ ( op_type, op_type ) ]
  [ FOR SEARCH | FOR ORDER BY sort_family_name ]
    | FUNCTION support_number [ ( op_type [ , op_type
  ] ) ] function_name ( argument_type [, ...] )
    | STORAGE storage_type
  } [, ... ]
```

Description

CREATE OPERATOR CLASS creates a new operator class. An operator class defines how a particular data type can be used with an index. The operator class specifies that certain operators will fill particular roles or "strategies" for this data type and this index method. The operator class also specifies the support functions to be used by the index method when the operator class is selected for an index column. All the operators and functions used by an operator class must be defined before the operator class can be created.

If a schema name is given then the operator class is created in the specified schema. Otherwise it is created in the current schema. Two operator classes in the same schema can have the same name only if they are for different index methods.

The user who defines an operator class becomes its owner. Presently, the creating user must be a superuser. (This restriction is made because an erroneous operator class definition could confuse or even crash the server.)

CREATE OPERATOR CLASS does not presently check whether the operator class definition includes all the operators and functions required by the index method, nor whether the operators and functions form a self-consistent set. It is the user's responsibility to define a valid operator class.

Related operator classes can be grouped into *operator families*. To add a new operator class to an existing family, specify the FAMILY option in CREATE OPERATOR CLASS. Without this option, the new class is placed into a family named the same as the new class (creating that family if it doesn't already exist).

Refer to Section 38.15 for further information.

Parameters

name

> The name of the operator class to be created. The name can be schema-qualified.

DEFAULT

> If present, the operator class will become the default operator class for its data type. At most one operator class can be the default for a specific data type and index method.

data_type

The column data type that this operator class is for.

index_method

The name of the index method this operator class is for.

family_name

The name of the existing operator family to add this operator class to. If not specified, a family named the same as the operator class is used (creating it, if it doesn't already exist).

strategy_number

The index method's strategy number for an operator associated with the operator class.

operator_name

The name (optionally schema-qualified) of an operator associated with the operator class.

op_type

In an **OPERATOR** clause, the operand data type(s) of the operator, or **NONE** to signify a left-unary or right-unary operator. The operand data types can be omitted in the normal case where they are the same as the operator class's data type.

In a **FUNCTION** clause, the operand data type(s) the function is intended to support, if different from the input data type(s) of the function (for B-tree comparison functions and hash functions) or the class's data type (for B-tree sort support functions and all functions in GiST, SP-GiST, GIN and BRIN operator classes). These defaults are correct, and so *op_type* need not be specified in **FUNCTION** clauses, except for the case of a B-tree sort support function that is meant to support cross-data-type comparisons.

sort_family_name

The name (optionally schema-qualified) of an existing `btree` operator family that describes the sort ordering associated with an ordering operator.

If neither **FOR SEARCH** nor **FOR ORDER BY** is specified, **FOR SEARCH** is the default.

support_number

The index method's support function number for a function associated with the operator class.

function_name

The name (optionally schema-qualified) of a function that is an index method support function for the operator class.

argument_type

The parameter data type(s) of the function.

storage_type

The data type actually stored in the index. Normally this is the same as the column data type, but some index methods (currently GiST, GIN and BRIN) allow it to be different. The **STORAGE** clause must be omitted unless the index method allows a different type to be used. If the column *data_type* is specified as `anyarray`, the *storage_type* can be declared as `anyelement` to indicate that the index entries are members of the element type belonging to the actual array type that each particular index is created for.

The `OPERATOR`, `FUNCTION`, and `STORAGE` clauses can appear in any order.

Notes

Because the index machinery does not check access permissions on functions before using them, including a function or operator in an operator class is tantamount to granting public execute permission on it. This is usually not an issue for the sorts of functions that are useful in an operator class.

The operators should not be defined by SQL functions. A SQL function is likely to be inlined into the calling query, which will prevent the optimizer from recognizing that the query matches an index.

Before PostgreSQL 8.4, the `OPERATOR` clause could include a `RECHECK` option. This is no longer supported because whether an index operator is "lossy" is now determined on-the-fly at run time. This allows efficient handling of cases where an operator might or might not be lossy.

Examples

The following example command defines a GiST index operator class for the data type `_int4` (array of `int4`). See the intarray module for the complete example.

```
CREATE OPERATOR CLASS gist__int_ops
    DEFAULT FOR TYPE _int4 USING gist AS
        OPERATOR        3           &&,
        OPERATOR        6           = (anyarray, anyarray),
        OPERATOR        7           @>,
        OPERATOR        8           <@,
        OPERATOR        20          @@ (_int4, query_int),
        FUNCTION        1           g_int_consistent (internal, _int4,
smallint, oid, internal),
        FUNCTION        2           g_int_union (internal, internal),
        FUNCTION        3           g_int_compress (internal),
        FUNCTION        4           g_int_decompress (internal),
        FUNCTION        5           g_int_penalty (internal, internal,
internal),
        FUNCTION        6           g_int_picksplit (internal, internal),
        FUNCTION        7           g_int_same (_int4, _int4, internal);
```

Compatibility

`CREATE OPERATOR CLASS` is a PostgreSQL extension. There is no `CREATE OPERATOR CLASS` statement in the SQL standard.

See Also

ALTER OPERATOR CLASS, DROP OPERATOR CLASS, CREATE OPERATOR FAMILY, ALTER OPERATOR FAMILY

CREATE OPERATOR FAMILY

CREATE OPERATOR FAMILY — define a new operator family

Synopsis

```
CREATE OPERATOR FAMILY name USING index_method
```

Description

CREATE OPERATOR FAMILY creates a new operator family. An operator family defines a collection of related operator classes, and perhaps some additional operators and support functions that are compatible with these operator classes but not essential for the functioning of any individual index. (Operators and functions that are essential to indexes should be grouped within the relevant operator class, rather than being "loose" in the operator family. Typically, single-data-type operators are bound to operator classes, while cross-data-type operators can be loose in an operator family containing operator classes for both data types.)

The new operator family is initially empty. It should be populated by issuing subsequent CREATE OPERATOR CLASS commands to add contained operator classes, and optionally ALTER OPERATOR FAMILY commands to add "loose" operators and their corresponding support functions.

If a schema name is given then the operator family is created in the specified schema. Otherwise it is created in the current schema. Two operator families in the same schema can have the same name only if they are for different index methods.

The user who defines an operator family becomes its owner. Presently, the creating user must be a superuser. (This restriction is made because an erroneous operator family definition could confuse or even crash the server.)

Refer to Section 38.15 for further information.

Parameters

name

> The name of the operator family to be created. The name can be schema-qualified.

index_method

> The name of the index method this operator family is for.

Compatibility

CREATE OPERATOR FAMILY is a PostgreSQL extension. There is no CREATE OPERATOR FAMILY statement in the SQL standard.

See Also

ALTER OPERATOR FAMILY, DROP OPERATOR FAMILY, CREATE OPERATOR CLASS, ALTER OPERATOR CLASS, DROP OPERATOR CLASS

CREATE POLICY

CREATE POLICY — define a new row level security policy for a table

Synopsis

```
CREATE POLICY name ON table_name
    [ AS { PERMISSIVE | RESTRICTIVE } ]
    [ FOR { ALL | SELECT | INSERT | UPDATE | DELETE } ]
    [ TO { role_name | PUBLIC | CURRENT_USER | SESSION_USER }
[, ...] ]
    [ USING ( using_expression ) ]
    [ WITH CHECK ( check_expression ) ]
```

Description

The CREATE POLICY command defines a new row-level security policy for a table. Note that row-level security must be enabled on the table (using ALTER TABLE ... ENABLE ROW LEVEL SECURITY) in order for created policies to be applied.

A policy grants the permission to select, insert, update, or delete rows that match the relevant policy expression. Existing table rows are checked against the expression specified in USING, while new rows that would be created via INSERT or UPDATE are checked against the expression specified in WITH CHECK. When a USING expression returns true for a given row then that row is visible to the user, while if false or null is returned then the row is not visible. When a WITH CHECK expression returns true for a row then that row is inserted or updated, while if false or null is returned then an error occurs.

For INSERT and UPDATE statements, WITH CHECK expressions are enforced after BEFORE triggers are fired, and before any actual data modifications are made. Thus a BEFORE ROW trigger may modify the data to be inserted, affecting the result of the security policy check. WITH CHECK expressions are enforced before any other constraints.

Policy names are per-table. Therefore, one policy name can be used for many different tables and have a definition for each table which is appropriate to that table.

Policies can be applied for specific commands or for specific roles. The default for newly created policies is that they apply for all commands and roles, unless otherwise specified. Multiple policies may apply to a single command; see below for more details. Table 240 summarizes how the different types of policy apply to specific commands.

For policies that can have both USING and WITH CHECK expressions (ALL and UPDATE), if no WITH CHECK expression is defined, then the USING expression will be used both to determine which rows are visible (normal USING case) and which new rows will be allowed to be added (WITH CHECK case).

If row-level security is enabled for a table, but no applicable policies exist, a "default deny" policy is assumed, so that no rows will be visible or updatable.

Parameters

name

The name of the policy to be created. This must be distinct from the name of any other policy for the table.

table_name

> The name (optionally schema-qualified) of the table the policy applies to.

PERMISSIVE

> Specify that the policy is to be created as a permissive policy. All permissive policies which are applicable to a given query will be combined together using the Boolean "OR" operator. By creating permissive policies, administrators can add to the set of records which can be accessed. Policies are permissive by default.

RESTRICTIVE

> Specify that the policy is to be created as a restrictive policy. All restrictive policies which are applicable to a given query will be combined together using the Boolean "AND" operator. By creating restrictive policies, administrators can reduce the set of records which can be accessed as all restrictive policies must be passed for each record.

> Note that there needs to be at least one permissive policy to grant access to records before restrictive policies can be usefully used to reduce that access. If only restrictive policies exist, then no records will be accessible. When a mix of permissive and restrictive policies are present, a record is only accessible if at least one of the permissive policies passes, in addition to all the restrictive policies.

command

> The command to which the policy applies. Valid options are ALL, SELECT, INSERT, UPDATE, and DELETE. ALL is the default. See below for specifics regarding how these are applied.

role_name

> The role(s) to which the policy is to be applied. The default is PUBLIC, which will apply the policy to all roles.

using_expression

> Any SQL conditional expression (returning boolean). The conditional expression cannot contain any aggregate or window functions. This expression will be added to queries that refer to the table if row level security is enabled. Rows for which the expression returns true will be visible. Any rows for which the expression returns false or null will not be visible to the user (in a SELECT), and will not be available for modification (in an UPDATE or DELETE). Such rows are silently suppressed; no error is reported.

check_expression

> Any SQL conditional expression (returning boolean). The conditional expression cannot contain any aggregate or window functions. This expression will be used in INSERT and UPDATE queries against the table if row level security is enabled. Only rows for which the expression evaluates to true will be allowed. An error will be thrown if the expression evaluates to false or null for any of the records inserted or any of the records that result from the update. Note that the *check_expression* is evaluated against the proposed new contents of the row, not the original contents.

Per-Command Policies

ALL

> Using ALL for a policy means that it will apply to all commands, regardless of the type of command. If an ALL policy exists and more specific policies exist, then both the ALL policy and the more specific

policy (or policies) will be applied. Additionally, `ALL` policies will be applied to both the selection side of a query and the modification side, using the `USING` expression for both cases if only a `USING` expression has been defined.

As an example, if an `UPDATE` is issued, then the `ALL` policy will be applicable both to what the `UPDATE` will be able to select as rows to be updated (applying the `USING` expression), and to the resulting updated rows, to check if they are permitted to be added to the table (applying the `WITH CHECK` expression, if defined, and the `USING` expression otherwise). If an `INSERT` or `UPDATE` command attempts to add rows to the table that do not pass the `ALL` policy's `WITH CHECK` expression, the entire command will be aborted.

SELECT

Using `SELECT` for a policy means that it will apply to `SELECT` queries and whenever `SELECT` permissions are required on the relation the policy is defined for. The result is that only those records from the relation that pass the `SELECT` policy will be returned during a `SELECT` query, and that queries that require `SELECT` permissions, such as `UPDATE`, will also only see those records that are allowed by the `SELECT` policy. A `SELECT` policy cannot have a `WITH CHECK` expression, as it only applies in cases where records are being retrieved from the relation.

INSERT

Using `INSERT` for a policy means that it will apply to `INSERT` commands. Rows being inserted that do not pass this policy will result in a policy violation error, and the entire `INSERT` command will be aborted. An `INSERT` policy cannot have a `USING` expression, as it only applies in cases where records are being added to the relation.

Note that `INSERT` with `ON CONFLICT DO UPDATE` checks `INSERT` policies' `WITH CHECK` expressions only for rows appended to the relation by the `INSERT` path.

UPDATE

Using `UPDATE` for a policy means that it will apply to `UPDATE`, `SELECT FOR UPDATE` and `SELECT FOR SHARE` commands, as well as auxiliary `ON CONFLICT DO UPDATE` clauses of `INSERT` commands. Since `UPDATE` involves pulling an existing record and replacing it with a new modified record, `UPDATE` policies accept both a `USING` expression and a `WITH CHECK` expression. The `USING` expression determines which records the `UPDATE` command will see to operate against, while the `WITH CHECK` expression defines which modified rows are allowed to be stored back into the relation.

Any rows whose updated values do not pass the `WITH CHECK` expression will cause an error, and the entire command will be aborted. If only a `USING` clause is specified, then that clause will be used for both `USING` and `WITH CHECK` cases.

Typically an `UPDATE` command also needs to read data from columns in the relation being updated (e.g., in a `WHERE` clause or a `RETURNING` clause, or in an expression on the right hand side of the `SET` clause). In this case, `SELECT` rights are also required on the relation being updated, and the appropriate `SELECT` or `ALL` policies will be applied in addition to the `UPDATE` policies. Thus the user must have access to the row(s) being updated through a `SELECT` or `ALL` policy in addition to being granted permission to update the row(s) via an `UPDATE` or `ALL` policy.

When an `INSERT` command has an auxiliary `ON CONFLICT DO UPDATE` clause, if the `UPDATE` path is taken, the row to be updated is first checked against the `USING` expressions of any `UPDATE` policies, and then the new updated row is checked against the `WITH CHECK` expressions. Note, however, that unlike a standalone `UPDATE` command, if the existing row does not pass the `USING` expressions, an error will be thrown (the `UPDATE` path will *never* be silently avoided).

`DELETE`

Using `DELETE` for a policy means that it will apply to `DELETE` commands. Only rows that pass this policy will be seen by a `DELETE` command. There can be rows that are visible through a `SELECT` that are not available for deletion, if they do not pass the `USING` expression for the `DELETE` policy.

In most cases a `DELETE` command also needs to read data from columns in the relation that it is deleting from (e.g., in a `WHERE` clause or a `RETURNING` clause). In this case, `SELECT` rights are also required on the relation, and the appropriate `SELECT` or `ALL` policies will be applied in addition to the `DELETE` policies. Thus the user must have access to the row(s) being deleted through a `SELECT` or `ALL` policy in addition to being granted permission to delete the row(s) via a `DELETE` or `ALL` policy.

A `DELETE` policy cannot have a `WITH CHECK` expression, as it only applies in cases where records are being deleted from the relation, so that there is no new row to check.

Table 240. Policies Applied by Command Type

| Command | SELECT/ALL policy | INSERT/ALL policy | UPDATE/ALL policy | | DELETE/ALL policy |
	USING ex-pression	WITH CHECK expression	USING ex-pression	WITH CHECK expression	USING ex-pression
SELECT	Existing row	—	—	—	—
SELECT FOR UP-DATE/SHARE	Existing row	—	Existing row	—	—
INSERT	—	New row	—	—	—
INSERT ... RETURNING	New row [a]	New row	—	—	—
UPDATE	Existing & new rows [a]	—	Existing row	New row	—
DELETE	Existing row [a]	—	—	—	Existing row
ON CONFLICT DO UPDATE	Existing & new rows	—	Existing row	New row	—

[a] If read access is required to the existing or new row (for example, a `WHERE` or `RETURNING` clause that refers to columns from the relation).

Application of Multiple Policies

When multiple policies of different command types apply to the same command (for example, `SELECT` and `UPDATE` policies applied to an `UPDATE` command), then the user must have both types of permissions (for example, permission to select rows from the relation as well as permission to update them). Thus the expressions for one type of policy are combined with the expressions for the other type of policy using the `AND` operator.

When multiple policies of the same command type apply to the same command, then there must be at least one `PERMISSIVE` policy granting access to the relation, and all of the `RESTRICTIVE` policies must pass. Thus all the `PERMISSIVE` policy expressions are combined using `OR`, all the `RESTRICTIVE` policy expressions are combined using `AND`, and the results are combined using `AND`. If there are no `PERMISSIVE` policies, then access is denied.

Note that, for the purposes of combining multiple policies, `ALL` policies are treated as having the same type as whichever other type of policy is being applied.

For example, in an `UPDATE` command requiring both `SELECT` and `UPDATE` permissions, if there are multiple applicable policies of each type, they will be combined as follows:

```
expression from RESTRICTIVE SELECT/ALL policy 1
AND
expression from RESTRICTIVE SELECT/ALL policy 2
AND
...
AND
(
  expression from PERMISSIVE SELECT/ALL policy 1
  OR
  expression from PERMISSIVE SELECT/ALL policy 2
  OR
  ...
)
AND
expression from RESTRICTIVE UPDATE/ALL policy 1
AND
expression from RESTRICTIVE UPDATE/ALL policy 2
AND
...
AND
(
  expression from PERMISSIVE UPDATE/ALL policy 1
  OR
  expression from PERMISSIVE UPDATE/ALL policy 2
  OR
  ...
)
```

Notes

You must be the owner of a table to create or change policies for it.

While policies will be applied for explicit queries against tables in the database, they are not applied when the system is performing internal referential integrity checks or validating constraints. This means there are indirect ways to determine that a given value exists. An example of this is attempting to insert a duplicate value into a column that is a primary key or has a unique constraint. If the insert fails then the user can infer that the value already exists. (This example assumes that the user is permitted by policy to insert records which they are not allowed to see.) Another example is where a user is allowed to insert into a table which references another, otherwise hidden table. Existence can be determined by the user inserting values into the referencing table, where success would indicate that the value exists in the referenced table. These issues can be addressed by carefully crafting policies to prevent users from being able to insert, delete, or update records at all which might possibly indicate a value they are not otherwise able to see, or by using generated values (e.g., surrogate keys) instead of keys with external meanings.

Generally, the system will enforce filter conditions imposed using security policies prior to qualifications that appear in user queries, in order to prevent inadvertent exposure of the protected data to user-defined functions which might not be trustworthy. However, functions and operators marked by the system (or the system administrator) as LEAKPROOF may be evaluated before policy expressions, as they are assumed to be trustworthy.

Since policy expressions are added to the user's query directly, they will be run with the rights of the user running the overall query. Therefore, users who are using a given policy must be able to access any tables or functions referenced in the expression or they will simply receive a permission denied error when attempting to query the table that has row-level security enabled. This does not change how views work, however. As with normal queries and views, permission checks and policies for the tables which are referenced by a view will use the view owner's rights and any policies which apply to the view owner.

Additional discussion and practical examples can be found in Section 5.7.

Compatibility

CREATE POLICY is a PostgreSQL extension.

See Also

ALTER POLICY, DROP POLICY, ALTER TABLE

CREATE PROCEDURE

CREATE PROCEDURE — define a new procedure

Synopsis

```
CREATE [ OR REPLACE ] PROCEDURE
    name ( [ [ argmode ] [ argname ] argtype [ { DEFAULT |
 = } default_expr ] [, ...] ] )
  { LANGUAGE lang_name
    | TRANSFORM { FOR TYPE type_name } [, ... ]
    | [ EXTERNAL ] SECURITY INVOKER | [ EXTERNAL ] SECURITY DEFINER
    | SET configuration_parameter { TO value | = value | FROM
 CURRENT }
    | AS 'definition'
    | AS 'obj_file', 'link_symbol'
  } ...
```

Description

CREATE PROCEDURE defines a new procedure. CREATE OR REPLACE PROCEDURE will either create a new procedure, or replace an existing definition. To be able to define a procedure, the user must have the USAGE privilege on the language.

If a schema name is included, then the procedure is created in the specified schema. Otherwise it is created in the current schema. The name of the new procedure must not match any existing procedure or function with the same input argument types in the same schema. However, procedures and functions of different argument types can share a name (this is called *overloading*).

To replace the current definition of an existing procedure, use CREATE OR REPLACE PROCEDURE. It is not possible to change the name or argument types of a procedure this way (if you tried, you would actually be creating a new, distinct procedure).

When CREATE OR REPLACE PROCEDURE is used to replace an existing procedure, the ownership and permissions of the procedure do not change. All other procedure properties are assigned the values specified or implied in the command. You must own the procedure to replace it (this includes being a member of the owning role).

The user that creates the procedure becomes the owner of the procedure.

To be able to create a procedure, you must have USAGE privilege on the argument types.

Parameters

name

> The name (optionally schema-qualified) of the procedure to create.

argmode

> The mode of an argument: IN, INOUT, or VARIADIC. If omitted, the default is IN. (OUT arguments are currently not supported for procedures. Use INOUT instead.)

argname

> The name of an argument.

argtype

> The data type(s) of the procedure's arguments (optionally schema-qualified), if any. The argument types can be base, composite, or domain types, or can reference the type of a table column.

> Depending on the implementation language it might also be allowed to specify "pseudo-types" such as `cstring`. Pseudo-types indicate that the actual argument type is either incompletely specified, or outside the set of ordinary SQL data types.

> The type of a column is referenced by writing *table_name.column_name*`%TYPE`. Using this feature can sometimes help make a procedure independent of changes to the definition of a table.

default_expr

> An expression to be used as default value if the parameter is not specified. The expression has to be coercible to the argument type of the parameter. All input parameters following a parameter with a default value must have default values as well.

lang_name

> The name of the language that the procedure is implemented in. It can be `sql`, `c`, `internal`, or the name of a user-defined procedural language, e.g. `plpgsql`. Enclosing the name in single quotes is deprecated and requires matching case.

`TRANSFORM { FOR TYPE` *type_name* `} [, ... ] }`

> Lists which transforms a call to the procedure should apply. Transforms convert between SQL types and language-specific data types; see CREATE TRANSFORM. Procedural language implementations usually have hardcoded knowledge of the built-in types, so those don't need to be listed here. If a procedural language implementation does not know how to handle a type and no transform is supplied, it will fall back to a default behavior for converting data types, but this depends on the implementation.

`[EXTERNAL] SECURITY INVOKER`
`[EXTERNAL] SECURITY DEFINER`

> `SECURITY INVOKER` indicates that the procedure is to be executed with the privileges of the user that calls it. That is the default. `SECURITY DEFINER` specifies that the procedure is to be executed with the privileges of the user that owns it.

> The key word `EXTERNAL` is allowed for SQL conformance, but it is optional since, unlike in SQL, this feature applies to all procedures not only external ones.

> A `SECURITY DEFINER` procedure cannot execute transaction control statements (for example, `COMMIT` and `ROLLBACK`, depending on the language).

configuration_parameter
value

> The `SET` clause causes the specified configuration parameter to be set to the specified value when the procedure is entered, and then restored to its prior value when the procedure exits. `SET FROM CURRENT` saves the value of the parameter that is current when `CREATE PROCEDURE` is executed as the value to be applied when the procedure is entered.

If a `SET` clause is attached to a procedure, then the effects of a `SET LOCAL` command executed inside the procedure for the same variable are restricted to the procedure: the configuration parameter's prior value is still restored at procedure exit. However, an ordinary `SET` command (without `LOCAL`) overrides the `SET` clause, much as it would do for a previous `SET LOCAL` command: the effects of such a command will persist after procedure exit, unless the current transaction is rolled back.

If a `SET` clause is attached to a procedure, then that procedure cannot execute transaction control statements (for example, `COMMIT` and `ROLLBACK`, depending on the language).

See SET and Chapter 19 for more information about allowed parameter names and values.

definition

A string constant defining the procedure; the meaning depends on the language. It can be an internal procedure name, the path to an object file, an SQL command, or text in a procedural language.

It is often helpful to use dollar quoting (see Section 4.1.2.4) to write the procedure definition string, rather than the normal single quote syntax. Without dollar quoting, any single quotes or backslashes in the procedure definition must be escaped by doubling them.

obj_file, link_symbol

This form of the `AS` clause is used for dynamically loadable C language procedures when the procedure name in the C language source code is not the same as the name of the SQL procedure. The string *obj_file* is the name of the shared library file containing the compiled C procedure, and is interpreted as for the LOAD command. The string *link_symbol* is the procedure's link symbol, that is, the name of the procedure in the C language source code. If the link symbol is omitted, it is assumed to be the same as the name of the SQL procedure being defined.

When repeated `CREATE PROCEDURE` calls refer to the same object file, the file is only loaded once per session. To unload and reload the file (perhaps during development), start a new session.

Notes

See CREATE FUNCTION for more details on function creation that also apply to procedures.

Use CALL to execute a procedure.

Examples

```
CREATE PROCEDURE insert_data(a integer, b integer)
LANGUAGE SQL
AS $$
INSERT INTO tbl VALUES (a);
INSERT INTO tbl VALUES (b);
$$;

CALL insert_data(1, 2);
```

Compatibility

A `CREATE PROCEDURE` command is defined in the SQL standard. The PostgreSQL version is similar but not fully compatible. For details see also CREATE FUNCTION.

See Also

ALTER PROCEDURE, DROP PROCEDURE, CALL, CREATE FUNCTION

CREATE PUBLICATION

CREATE PUBLICATION — define a new publication

Synopsis

```
CREATE PUBLICATION name
    [ FOR TABLE [ ONLY ] table_name [ * ] [, ...]
      | FOR ALL TABLES ]
    [ WITH ( publication_parameter [= value] [, ... ] ) ]
```

Description

`CREATE PUBLICATION` adds a new publication into the current database. The publication name must be distinct from the name of any existing publication in the current database.

A publication is essentially a group of tables whose data changes are intended to be replicated through logical replication. See Section 31.1 for details about how publications fit into the logical replication setup.

Parameters

name

The name of the new publication.

FOR TABLE

Specifies a list of tables to add to the publication. If `ONLY` is specified before the table name, only that table is added to the publication. If `ONLY` is not specified, the table and all its descendant tables (if any) are added. Optionally, * can be specified after the table name to explicitly indicate that descendant tables are included.

Only persistent base tables can be part of a publication. Temporary tables, unlogged tables, foreign tables, materialized views, regular views, and partitioned tables cannot be part of a publication. To replicate a partitioned table, add the individual partitions to the publication.

FOR ALL TABLES

Marks the publication as one that replicates changes for all tables in the database, including tables created in the future.

WITH (*publication_parameter* [= *value*] [, ...])

This clause specifies optional parameters for a publication. The following parameters are supported:

publish (string)

This parameter determines which DML operations will be published by the new publication to the subscribers. The value is comma-separated list of operations. The allowed operations are `insert`, `update`, `delete`, and `truncate`. The default is to publish all actions, and so the default value for this option is `'insert, update, delete, truncate'`.

Notes

If neither FOR TABLE nor FOR ALL TABLES is specified, then the publication starts out with an empty set of tables. That is useful if tables are to be added later.

The creation of a publication does not start replication. It only defines a grouping and filtering logic for future subscribers.

To create a publication, the invoking user must have the CREATE privilege for the current database. (Of course, superusers bypass this check.)

To add a table to a publication, the invoking user must have ownership rights on the table. The FOR ALL TABLES clause requires the invoking user to be a superuser.

The tables added to a publication that publishes UPDATE and/or DELETE operations must have REPLICA IDENTITY defined. Otherwise those operations will be disallowed on those tables.

For an INSERT ... ON CONFLICT command, the publication will publish the operation that actually results from the command. So depending of the outcome, it may be published as either INSERT or UP-DATE, or it may not be published at all.

COPY ... FROM commands are published as INSERT operations.

DDL operations are not published.

Examples

Create a publication that publishes all changes in two tables:

```
CREATE PUBLICATION mypublication FOR TABLE users, departments;
```

Create a publication that publishes all changes in all tables:

```
CREATE PUBLICATION alltables FOR ALL TABLES;
```

Create a publication that only publishes INSERT operations in one table:

```
CREATE PUBLICATION insert_only FOR TABLE mydata
    WITH (publish = 'insert');
```

Compatibility

CREATE PUBLICATION is a PostgreSQL extension.

See Also

ALTER PUBLICATION, DROP PUBLICATION

CREATE ROLE

CREATE ROLE — define a new database role

Synopsis

```
CREATE ROLE name [ [ WITH ] option [ ... ] ]

where option can be:

      SUPERUSER | NOSUPERUSER
    | CREATEDB | NOCREATEDB
    | CREATEROLE | NOCREATEROLE
    | INHERIT | NOINHERIT
    | LOGIN | NOLOGIN
    | REPLICATION | NOREPLICATION
    | BYPASSRLS | NOBYPASSRLS
    | CONNECTION LIMIT connlimit
    | [ ENCRYPTED ] PASSWORD 'password' | PASSWORD NULL
    | VALID UNTIL 'timestamp'
    | IN ROLE role_name [, ...]
    | IN GROUP role_name [, ...]
    | ROLE role_name [, ...]
    | ADMIN role_name [, ...]
    | USER role_name [, ...]
    | SYSID uid
```

Description

CREATE ROLE adds a new role to a PostgreSQL database cluster. A role is an entity that can own database objects and have database privileges; a role can be considered a "user", a "group", or both depending on how it is used. Refer to Chapter 21 and Chapter 20 for information about managing users and authentication. You must have CREATEROLE privilege or be a database superuser to use this command.

Note that roles are defined at the database cluster level, and so are valid in all databases in the cluster.

Parameters

name

    The name of the new role.

SUPERUSER
NOSUPERUSER

    These clauses determine whether the new role is a "superuser", who can override all access restrictions within the database. Superuser status is dangerous and should be used only when really needed. You must yourself be a superuser to create a new superuser. If not specified, NOSUPERUSER is the default.

CREATEDB
NOCREATEDB

These clauses define a role's ability to create databases. If CREATEDB is specified, the role being defined will be allowed to create new databases. Specifying NOCREATEDB will deny a role the ability to create databases. If not specified, NOCREATEDB is the default.

CREATEROLE
NOCREATEROLE

These clauses determine whether a role will be permitted to create new roles (that is, execute CREATE ROLE). A role with CREATEROLE privilege can also alter and drop other roles. If not specified, NOCREATEROLE is the default.

INHERIT
NOINHERIT

These clauses determine whether a role "inherits" the privileges of roles it is a member of. A role with the INHERIT attribute can automatically use whatever database privileges have been granted to all roles it is directly or indirectly a member of. Without INHERIT, membership in another role only grants the ability to SET ROLE to that other role; the privileges of the other role are only available after having done so. If not specified, INHERIT is the default.

LOGIN
NOLOGIN

These clauses determine whether a role is allowed to log in; that is, whether the role can be given as the initial session authorization name during client connection. A role having the LOGIN attribute can be thought of as a user. Roles without this attribute are useful for managing database privileges, but are not users in the usual sense of the word. If not specified, NOLOGIN is the default, except when CREATE ROLE is invoked through its alternative spelling CREATE USER.

REPLICATION
NOREPLICATION

These clauses determine whether a role is a replication role. A role must have this attribute (or be a superuser) in order to be able to connect to the server in replication mode (physical or logical replication) and in order to be able to create or drop replication slots. A role having the REPLICATION attribute is a very highly privileged role, and should only be used on roles actually used for replication. If not specified, NOREPLICATION is the default.

BYPASSRLS
NOBYPASSRLS

These clauses determine whether a role bypasses every row-level security (RLS) policy. NOBY-PASSRLS is the default. Note that pg_dump will set row_security to OFF by default, to ensure all contents of a table are dumped out. If the user running pg_dump does not have appropriate permissions, an error will be returned. The superuser and owner of the table being dumped always bypass RLS.

CONNECTION LIMIT connlimit

If role can log in, this specifies how many concurrent connections the role can make. -1 (the default) means no limit. Note that only normal connections are counted towards this limit. Neither prepared transactions nor background worker connections are counted towards this limit.

[ENCRYPTED] PASSWORD '*password*'
PASSWORD NULL

> Sets the role's password. (A password is only of use for roles having the LOGIN attribute, but you can nonetheless define one for roles without it.) If you do not plan to use password authentication you can omit this option. If no password is specified, the password will be set to null and password authentication will always fail for that user. A null password can optionally be written explicitly as PASSWORD NULL.

> > ## Note
> >
> > Specifying an empty string will also set the password to null, but that was not the case before PostgreSQL version 10. In earlier versions, an empty string could be used, or not, depending on the authentication method and the exact version, and libpq would refuse to use it in any case. To avoid the ambiguity, specifying an empty string should be avoided.

> The password is always stored encrypted in the system catalogs. The ENCRYPTED keyword has no effect, but is accepted for backwards compatibility. The method of encryption is determined by the configuration parameter password_encryption. If the presented password string is already in MD5-encrypted or SCRAM-encrypted format, then it is stored as-is regardless of password_encryption (since the system cannot decrypt the specified encrypted password string, to encrypt it in a different format). This allows reloading of encrypted passwords during dump/restore.

VALID UNTIL '*timestamp*'

> The VALID UNTIL clause sets a date and time after which the role's password is no longer valid. If this clause is omitted the password will be valid for all time.

IN ROLE *role_name*

> The IN ROLE clause lists one or more existing roles to which the new role will be immediately added as a new member. (Note that there is no option to add the new role as an administrator; use a separate GRANT command to do that.)

IN GROUP *role_name*

> IN GROUP is an obsolete spelling of IN ROLE.

ROLE *role_name*

> The ROLE clause lists one or more existing roles which are automatically added as members of the new role. (This in effect makes the new role a "group".)

ADMIN *role_name*

> The ADMIN clause is like ROLE, but the named roles are added to the new role WITH ADMIN OPTION, giving them the right to grant membership in this role to others.

USER *role_name*

> The USER clause is an obsolete spelling of the ROLE clause.

SYSID *uid*

> The SYSID clause is ignored, but is accepted for backwards compatibility.

Notes

Use ALTER ROLE to change the attributes of a role, and DROP ROLE to remove a role. All the attributes specified by `CREATE ROLE` can be modified by later `ALTER ROLE` commands.

The preferred way to add and remove members of roles that are being used as groups is to use GRANT and REVOKE.

The `VALID UNTIL` clause defines an expiration time for a password only, not for the role *per se*. In particular, the expiration time is not enforced when logging in using a non-password-based authentication method.

The `INHERIT` attribute governs inheritance of grantable privileges (that is, access privileges for database objects and role memberships). It does not apply to the special role attributes set by `CREATE ROLE` and `ALTER ROLE`. For example, being a member of a role with `CREATEDB` privilege does not immediately grant the ability to create databases, even if `INHERIT` is set; it would be necessary to become that role via SET ROLE before creating a database.

The `INHERIT` attribute is the default for reasons of backwards compatibility: in prior releases of PostgreSQL, users always had access to all privileges of groups they were members of. However, `NOINHERIT` provides a closer match to the semantics specified in the SQL standard.

Be careful with the `CREATEROLE` privilege. There is no concept of inheritance for the privileges of a `CREATEROLE`-role. That means that even if a role does not have a certain privilege but is allowed to create other roles, it can easily create another role with different privileges than its own (except for creating roles with superuser privileges). For example, if the role "user" has the `CREATEROLE` privilege but not the `CREATEDB` privilege, nonetheless it can create a new role with the `CREATEDB` privilege. Therefore, regard roles that have the `CREATEROLE` privilege as almost-superuser-roles.

PostgreSQL includes a program createuser that has the same functionality as `CREATE ROLE` (in fact, it calls this command) but can be run from the command shell.

The `CONNECTION LIMIT` option is only enforced approximately; if two new sessions start at about the same time when just one connection "slot" remains for the role, it is possible that both will fail. Also, the limit is never enforced for superusers.

Caution must be exercised when specifying an unencrypted password with this command. The password will be transmitted to the server in cleartext, and it might also be logged in the client's command history or the server log. The command createuser, however, transmits the password encrypted. Also, psql contains a command `\password` that can be used to safely change the password later.

Examples

Create a role that can log in, but don't give it a password:

```
CREATE ROLE jonathan LOGIN;
```

Create a role with a password:

```
CREATE USER davide WITH PASSWORD 'jw8s0F4';
```

(`CREATE USER` is the same as `CREATE ROLE` except that it implies `LOGIN`.)

Create a role with a password that is valid until the end of 2004. After one second has ticked in 2005, the password is no longer valid.

```
CREATE ROLE miriam WITH LOGIN PASSWORD 'jw8s0F4' VALID UNTIL
  '2005-01-01';
```

Create a role that can create databases and manage roles:

```
CREATE ROLE admin WITH CREATEDB CREATEROLE;
```

Compatibility

The CREATE ROLE statement is in the SQL standard, but the standard only requires the syntax

```
CREATE ROLE name [ WITH ADMIN role_name ]
```

Multiple initial administrators, and all the other options of CREATE ROLE, are PostgreSQL extensions.

The SQL standard defines the concepts of users and roles, but it regards them as distinct concepts and leaves all commands defining users to be specified by each database implementation. In PostgreSQL we have chosen to unify users and roles into a single kind of entity. Roles therefore have many more optional attributes than they do in the standard.

The behavior specified by the SQL standard is most closely approximated by giving users the NOINHERIT attribute, while roles are given the INHERIT attribute.

See Also

SET ROLE, ALTER ROLE, DROP ROLE, GRANT, REVOKE, createuser

CREATE RULE

CREATE RULE — define a new rewrite rule

Synopsis

```
CREATE [ OR REPLACE ] RULE name AS ON event
    TO table_name [ WHERE condition ]
    DO [ ALSO | INSTEAD ] { NOTHING | command | ( command ; command
... ) }

where event can be one of:

    SELECT | INSERT | UPDATE | DELETE
```

Description

CREATE RULE defines a new rule applying to a specified table or view. CREATE OR REPLACE RULE will either create a new rule, or replace an existing rule of the same name for the same table.

The PostgreSQL rule system allows one to define an alternative action to be performed on insertions, updates, or deletions in database tables. Roughly speaking, a rule causes additional commands to be executed when a given command on a given table is executed. Alternatively, an INSTEAD rule can replace a given command by another, or cause a command not to be executed at all. Rules are used to implement SQL views as well. It is important to realize that a rule is really a command transformation mechanism, or command macro. The transformation happens before the execution of the command starts. If you actually want an operation that fires independently for each physical row, you probably want to use a trigger, not a rule. More information about the rules system is in Chapter 41.

Presently, ON SELECT rules must be unconditional INSTEAD rules and must have actions that consist of a single SELECT command. Thus, an ON SELECT rule effectively turns the table into a view, whose visible contents are the rows returned by the rule's SELECT command rather than whatever had been stored in the table (if anything). It is considered better style to write a CREATE VIEW command than to create a real table and define an ON SELECT rule for it.

You can create the illusion of an updatable view by defining ON INSERT, ON UPDATE, and ON DELETE rules (or any subset of those that's sufficient for your purposes) to replace update actions on the view with appropriate updates on other tables. If you want to support INSERT RETURNING and so on, then be sure to put a suitable RETURNING clause into each of these rules.

There is a catch if you try to use conditional rules for complex view updates: there *must* be an unconditional INSTEAD rule for each action you wish to allow on the view. If the rule is conditional, or is not INSTEAD, then the system will still reject attempts to perform the update action, because it thinks it might end up trying to perform the action on the dummy table of the view in some cases. If you want to handle all the useful cases in conditional rules, add an unconditional DO INSTEAD NOTHING rule to ensure that the system understands it will never be called on to update the dummy table. Then make the conditional rules non-INSTEAD; in the cases where they are applied, they add to the default INSTEAD NOTHING action. (This method does not currently work to support RETURNING queries, however.)

> ## Note
>
> A view that is simple enough to be automatically updatable (see CREATE VIEW) does not require a user-created rule in order to be updatable. While you can create an explicit rule anyway, the automatic update transformation will generally outperform an explicit rule.
>
> Another alternative worth considering is to use INSTEAD OF triggers (see CREATE TRIGGER) in place of rules.

Parameters

name

> The name of a rule to create. This must be distinct from the name of any other rule for the same table. Multiple rules on the same table and same event type are applied in alphabetical name order.

event

> The event is one of SELECT, INSERT, UPDATE, or DELETE. Note that an INSERT containing an ON CONFLICT clause cannot be used on tables that have either INSERT or UPDATE rules. Consider using an updatable view instead.

table_name

> The name (optionally schema-qualified) of the table or view the rule applies to.

condition

> Any SQL conditional expression (returning boolean). The condition expression cannot refer to any tables except NEW and OLD, and cannot contain aggregate functions.

INSTEAD

> INSTEAD indicates that the commands should be executed *instead of* the original command.

ALSO

> ALSO indicates that the commands should be executed *in addition to* the original command.
>
> If neither ALSO nor INSTEAD is specified, ALSO is the default.

command

> The command or commands that make up the rule action. Valid commands are SELECT, INSERT, UPDATE, DELETE, or NOTIFY.

Within *condition* and *command*, the special table names NEW and OLD can be used to refer to values in the referenced table. NEW is valid in ON INSERT and ON UPDATE rules to refer to the new row being inserted or updated. OLD is valid in ON UPDATE and ON DELETE rules to refer to the existing row being updated or deleted.

Notes

You must be the owner of a table to create or change rules for it.

In a rule for INSERT, UPDATE, or DELETE on a view, you can add a RETURNING clause that emits the view's columns. This clause will be used to compute the outputs if the rule is triggered by an INSERT RETURNING, UPDATE RETURNING, or DELETE RETURNING command respectively. When the rule is triggered by a command without RETURNING, the rule's RETURNING clause will be ignored. The current implementation allows only unconditional INSTEAD rules to contain RETURNING; furthermore there can be at most one RETURNING clause among all the rules for the same event. (This ensures that there is only one candidate RETURNING clause to be used to compute the results.) RETURNING queries on the view will be rejected if there is no RETURNING clause in any available rule.

It is very important to take care to avoid circular rules. For example, though each of the following two rule definitions are accepted by PostgreSQL, the SELECT command would cause PostgreSQL to report an error because of recursive expansion of a rule:

```
CREATE RULE "_RETURN" AS
    ON SELECT TO t1
    DO INSTEAD
        SELECT * FROM t2;

CREATE RULE "_RETURN" AS
    ON SELECT TO t2
    DO INSTEAD
        SELECT * FROM t1;

SELECT * FROM t1;
```

Presently, if a rule action contains a NOTIFY command, the NOTIFY command will be executed unconditionally, that is, the NOTIFY will be issued even if there are not any rows that the rule should apply to. For example, in:

```
CREATE RULE notify_me AS ON UPDATE TO mytable DO ALSO NOTIFY mytable;

UPDATE mytable SET name = 'foo' WHERE id = 42;
```

one NOTIFY event will be sent during the UPDATE, whether or not there are any rows that match the condition id = 42. This is an implementation restriction that might be fixed in future releases.

Compatibility

CREATE RULE is a PostgreSQL language extension, as is the entire query rewrite system.

See Also

ALTER RULE, DROP RULE

CREATE SCHEMA

CREATE SCHEMA — define a new schema

Synopsis

```
CREATE SCHEMA schema_name [ AUTHORIZATION role_specification ]
 [ schema_element [ ... ] ]
CREATE SCHEMA AUTHORIZATION role_specification [ schema_element
 [ ... ] ]
CREATE SCHEMA IF NOT EXISTS schema_name
 [ AUTHORIZATION role_specification ]
CREATE SCHEMA IF NOT EXISTS AUTHORIZATION role_specification

where role_specification can be:

    user_name
  | CURRENT_USER
  | SESSION_USER
```

Description

CREATE SCHEMA enters a new schema into the current database. The schema name must be distinct from the name of any existing schema in the current database.

A schema is essentially a namespace: it contains named objects (tables, data types, functions, and operators) whose names can duplicate those of other objects existing in other schemas. Named objects are accessed either by "qualifying" their names with the schema name as a prefix, or by setting a search path that includes the desired schema(s). A CREATE command specifying an unqualified object name creates the object in the current schema (the one at the front of the search path, which can be determined with the function current_schema).

Optionally, CREATE SCHEMA can include subcommands to create objects within the new schema. The subcommands are treated essentially the same as separate commands issued after creating the schema, except that if the AUTHORIZATION clause is used, all the created objects will be owned by that user.

Parameters

schema_name

   The name of a schema to be created. If this is omitted, the user_name is used as the schema name. The name cannot begin with pg_, as such names are reserved for system schemas.

user_name

   The role name of the user who will own the new schema. If omitted, defaults to the user executing the command. To create a schema owned by another role, you must be a direct or indirect member of that role, or be a superuser.

schema_element

   An SQL statement defining an object to be created within the schema. Currently, only CREATE TABLE, CREATE VIEW, CREATE INDEX, CREATE SEQUENCE, CREATE TRIGGER and GRANT are accepted as clauses within CREATE SCHEMA. Other kinds of objects may be created in separate commands after the schema is created.

IF NOT EXISTS

Do nothing (except issuing a notice) if a schema with the same name already exists. *schema_element* subcommands cannot be included when this option is used.

Notes

To create a schema, the invoking user must have the CREATE privilege for the current database. (Of course, superusers bypass this check.)

Examples

Create a schema:

CREATE SCHEMA myschema;

Create a schema for user joe; the schema will also be named joe:

CREATE SCHEMA AUTHORIZATION joe;

Create a schema named test that will be owned by user joe, unless there already is a schema named test. (It does not matter whether joe owns the pre-existing schema.)

CREATE SCHEMA IF NOT EXISTS test AUTHORIZATION joe;

Create a schema and create a table and view within it:

CREATE SCHEMA hollywood
    CREATE TABLE films (title text, release date, awards text[])
    CREATE VIEW winners AS
        SELECT title, release FROM films WHERE awards IS NOT NULL;

Notice that the individual subcommands do not end with semicolons.

The following is an equivalent way of accomplishing the same result:

CREATE SCHEMA hollywood;
CREATE TABLE hollywood.films (title text, release date, awards
 text[]);
CREATE VIEW hollywood.winners AS
    SELECT title, release FROM hollywood.films WHERE awards IS NOT
 NULL;

Compatibility

The SQL standard allows a DEFAULT CHARACTER SET clause in CREATE SCHEMA, as well as more subcommand types than are presently accepted by PostgreSQL.

The SQL standard specifies that the subcommands in CREATE SCHEMA can appear in any order. The present PostgreSQL implementation does not handle all cases of forward references in subcommands; it might sometimes be necessary to reorder the subcommands in order to avoid forward references.

According to the SQL standard, the owner of a schema always owns all objects within it. PostgreSQL allows schemas to contain objects owned by users other than the schema owner. This can happen only if the schema owner grants the CREATE privilege on their schema to someone else, or a superuser chooses to create objects in it.

The IF NOT EXISTS option is a PostgreSQL extension.

See Also

ALTER SCHEMA, DROP SCHEMA

CREATE SEQUENCE

CREATE SEQUENCE — define a new sequence generator

Synopsis

```
CREATE [ TEMPORARY | TEMP ] SEQUENCE [ IF NOT EXISTS ] name
    [ AS data_type ]
    [ INCREMENT [ BY ] increment ]
    [ MINVALUE minvalue | NO MINVALUE ] [ MAXVALUE maxvalue | NO
MAXVALUE ]
    [ START [ WITH ] start ] [ CACHE cache ] [ [ NO ] CYCLE ]
    [ OWNED BY { table_name.column_name | NONE } ]
```

Description

CREATE SEQUENCE creates a new sequence number generator. This involves creating and initializing a new special single-row table with the name name. The generator will be owned by the user issuing the command.

If a schema name is given then the sequence is created in the specified schema. Otherwise it is created in the current schema. Temporary sequences exist in a special schema, so a schema name cannot be given when creating a temporary sequence. The sequence name must be distinct from the name of any other sequence, table, index, view, or foreign table in the same schema.

After a sequence is created, you use the functions nextval, currval, and setval to operate on the sequence. These functions are documented in Section 9.16.

Although you cannot update a sequence directly, you can use a query like:

```
SELECT * FROM name;
```

to examine the parameters and current state of a sequence. In particular, the last_value field of the sequence shows the last value allocated by any session. (Of course, this value might be obsolete by the time it's printed, if other sessions are actively doing nextval calls.)

Parameters

TEMPORARY or TEMP

If specified, the sequence object is created only for this session, and is automatically dropped on session exit. Existing permanent sequences with the same name are not visible (in this session) while the temporary sequence exists, unless they are referenced with schema-qualified names.

IF NOT EXISTS

Do not throw an error if a relation with the same name already exists. A notice is issued in this case. Note that there is no guarantee that the existing relation is anything like the sequence that would have been created - it might not even be a sequence.

name

> The name (optionally schema-qualified) of the sequence to be created.

data_type

> The optional clause AS *data_type* specifies the data type of the sequence. Valid types are small-int, integer, and bigint. bigint is the default. The data type determines the default minimum and maximum values of the sequence.

increment

> The optional clause INCREMENT BY *increment* specifies which value is added to the current sequence value to create a new value. A positive value will make an ascending sequence, a negative one a descending sequence. The default value is 1.

minvalue
NO MINVALUE

> The optional clause MINVALUE *minvalue* determines the minimum value a sequence can generate. If this clause is not supplied or NO MINVALUE is specified, then defaults will be used. The default for an ascending sequence is 1. The default for a descending sequence is the minimum value of the data type.

maxvalue
NO MAXVALUE

> The optional clause MAXVALUE *maxvalue* determines the maximum value for the sequence. If this clause is not supplied or NO MAXVALUE is specified, then default values will be used. The default for an ascending sequence is the maximum value of the data type. The default for a descending sequence is -1.

start

> The optional clause START WITH *start* allows the sequence to begin anywhere. The default starting value is *minvalue* for ascending sequences and *maxvalue* for descending ones.

cache

> The optional clause CACHE *cache* specifies how many sequence numbers are to be preallocated and stored in memory for faster access. The minimum value is 1 (only one value can be generated at a time, i.e., no cache), and this is also the default.

CYCLE
NO CYCLE

> The CYCLE option allows the sequence to wrap around when the *maxvalue* or *minvalue* has been reached by an ascending or descending sequence respectively. If the limit is reached, the next number generated will be the *minvalue* or *maxvalue*, respectively.
>
> If NO CYCLE is specified, any calls to nextval after the sequence has reached its maximum value will return an error. If neither CYCLE or NO CYCLE are specified, NO CYCLE is the default.

OWNED BY *table_name.column_name*
OWNED BY NONE

> The OWNED BY option causes the sequence to be associated with a specific table column, such that if that column (or its whole table) is dropped, the sequence will be automatically dropped as well. The

specified table must have the same owner and be in the same schema as the sequence. OWNED BY NONE, the default, specifies that there is no such association.

Notes

Use DROP SEQUENCE to remove a sequence.

Sequences are based on bigint arithmetic, so the range cannot exceed the range of an eight-byte integer (-9223372036854775808 to 9223372036854775807).

Because nextval and setval calls are never rolled back, sequence objects cannot be used if "gapless" assignment of sequence numbers is needed. It is possible to build gapless assignment by using exclusive locking of a table containing a counter; but this solution is much more expensive than sequence objects, especially if many transactions need sequence numbers concurrently.

Unexpected results might be obtained if a *cache* setting greater than one is used for a sequence object that will be used concurrently by multiple sessions. Each session will allocate and cache successive sequence values during one access to the sequence object and increase the sequence object's last_value accordingly. Then, the next *cache*-1 uses of nextval within that session simply return the preallocated values without touching the sequence object. So, any numbers allocated but not used within a session will be lost when that session ends, resulting in "holes" in the sequence.

Furthermore, although multiple sessions are guaranteed to allocate distinct sequence values, the values might be generated out of sequence when all the sessions are considered. For example, with a *cache* setting of 10, session A might reserve values 1..10 and return nextval=1, then session B might reserve values 11..20 and return nextval=11 before session A has generated nextval=2. Thus, with a *cache* setting of one it is safe to assume that nextval values are generated sequentially; with a *cache* setting greater than one you should only assume that the nextval values are all distinct, not that they are generated purely sequentially. Also, last_value will reflect the latest value reserved by any session, whether or not it has yet been returned by nextval.

Another consideration is that a setval executed on such a sequence will not be noticed by other sessions until they have used up any preallocated values they have cached.

Examples

Create an ascending sequence called serial, starting at 101:

```
CREATE SEQUENCE serial START 101;
```

Select the next number from this sequence:

```
SELECT nextval('serial');

 nextval
---------
     101
```

Select the next number from this sequence:

```
SELECT nextval('serial');
```

```
nextval
---------
    102
```

Use this sequence in an `INSERT` command:

```
INSERT INTO distributors VALUES (nextval('serial'), 'nothing');
```

Update the sequence value after a `COPY FROM`:

```
BEGIN;
COPY distributors FROM 'input_file';
SELECT setval('serial', max(id)) FROM distributors;
END;
```

Compatibility

`CREATE SEQUENCE` conforms to the SQL standard, with the following exceptions:

- Obtaining the next value is done using the `nextval()` function instead of the standard's `NEXT VALUE FOR` expression.

- The `OWNED BY` clause is a PostgreSQL extension.

See Also

ALTER SEQUENCE, DROP SEQUENCE

CREATE SERVER

CREATE SERVER — define a new foreign server

Synopsis

```
CREATE SERVER [ IF NOT EXISTS ] server_name [ TYPE 'server_type' ]
 [ VERSION 'server_version' ]
    FOREIGN DATA WRAPPER fdw_name
    [ OPTIONS ( option 'value' [, ... ] ) ]
```

Description

CREATE SERVER defines a new foreign server. The user who defines the server becomes its owner.

A foreign server typically encapsulates connection information that a foreign-data wrapper uses to access an external data resource. Additional user-specific connection information may be specified by means of user mappings.

The server name must be unique within the database.

Creating a server requires USAGE privilege on the foreign-data wrapper being used.

Parameters

IF NOT EXISTS

Do not throw an error if a server with the same name already exists. A notice is issued in this case. Note that there is no guarantee that the existing server is anything like the one that would have been created.

server_name

The name of the foreign server to be created.

server_type

Optional server type, potentially useful to foreign-data wrappers.

server_version

Optional server version, potentially useful to foreign-data wrappers.

fdw_name

The name of the foreign-data wrapper that manages the server.

OPTIONS (option 'value' [, ...])

This clause specifies the options for the server. The options typically define the connection details of the server, but the actual names and values are dependent on the server's foreign-data wrapper.

Notes

When using the dblink module, a foreign server's name can be used as an argument of the dblink_connect function to indicate the connection parameters. It is necessary to have the USAGE privilege on the foreign server to be able to use it in this way.

Examples

Create a server `myserver` that uses the foreign-data wrapper `postgres_fdw`:

```
CREATE SERVER myserver FOREIGN DATA WRAPPER postgres_fdw OPTIONS (host
 'foo', dbname 'foodb', port '5432');
```

See postgres_fdw for more details.

Compatibility

CREATE SERVER conforms to ISO/IEC 9075-9 (SQL/MED).

See Also

ALTER SERVER, DROP SERVER, CREATE FOREIGN DATA WRAPPER, CREATE FOREIGN TA-BLE, CREATE USER MAPPING

CREATE STATISTICS

CREATE STATISTICS — define extended statistics

Synopsis

```
CREATE STATISTICS [ IF NOT EXISTS ] statistics_name
    [ ( statistics_kind [, ... ] ) ]
    ON column_name, column_name [, ...]
    FROM table_name
```

Description

CREATE STATISTICS will create a new extended statistics object tracking data about the specified table, foreign table or materialized view. The statistics object will be created in the current database and will be owned by the user issuing the command.

If a schema name is given (for example, CREATE STATISTICS myschema.mystat ...) then the statistics object is created in the specified schema. Otherwise it is created in the current schema. The name of the statistics object must be distinct from the name of any other statistics object in the same schema.

Parameters

IF NOT EXISTS

Do not throw an error if a statistics object with the same name already exists. A notice is issued in this case. Note that only the name of the statistics object is considered here, not the details of its definition.

statistics_name

The name (optionally schema-qualified) of the statistics object to be created.

statistics_kind

A statistics kind to be computed in this statistics object. Currently supported kinds are ndistinct, which enables n-distinct statistics, and dependencies, which enables functional dependency statistics. If this clause is omitted, all supported statistics kinds are included in the statistics object. For more information, see Section 14.2.2 and Section 70.2.

column_name

The name of a table column to be covered by the computed statistics. At least two column names must be given.

table_name

The name (optionally schema-qualified) of the table containing the column(s) the statistics are computed on.

Notes

You must be the owner of a table to create a statistics object reading it. Once created, however, the ownership of the statistics object is independent of the underlying table(s).

Examples

Create table t1 with two functionally dependent columns, i.e. knowledge of a value in the first column is sufficient for determining the value in the other column. Then functional dependency statistics are built on those columns:

```
CREATE TABLE t1 (
    a    int,
    b    int
);

INSERT INTO t1 SELECT i/100, i/500
                 FROM generate_series(1,1000000) s(i);

ANALYZE t1;

-- the number of matching rows will be drastically underestimated:
EXPLAIN ANALYZE SELECT * FROM t1 WHERE (a = 1) AND (b = 0);

CREATE STATISTICS s1 (dependencies) ON a, b FROM t1;

ANALYZE t1;

-- now the row count estimate is more accurate:
EXPLAIN ANALYZE SELECT * FROM t1 WHERE (a = 1) AND (b = 0);
```

Without functional-dependency statistics, the planner would assume that the two WHERE conditions are independent, and would multiply their selectivities together to arrive at a much-too-small row count estimate. With such statistics, the planner recognizes that the WHERE conditions are redundant and does not underestimate the row count.

Compatibility

There is no CREATE STATISTICS command in the SQL standard.

See Also

ALTER STATISTICS, DROP STATISTICS

CREATE SUBSCRIPTION

CREATE SUBSCRIPTION — define a new subscription

Synopsis

```
CREATE SUBSCRIPTION subscription_name
    CONNECTION 'conninfo'
    PUBLICATION publication_name [, ...]
    [ WITH ( subscription_parameter [= value] [, ... ] ) ]
```

Description

CREATE SUBSCRIPTION adds a new subscription for the current database. The subscription name must be distinct from the name of any existing subscription in the database.

The subscription represents a replication connection to the publisher. As such this command does not only add definitions in the local catalogs but also creates a replication slot on the publisher.

A logical replication worker will be started to replicate data for the new subscription at the commit of the transaction where this command is run.

Additional information about subscriptions and logical replication as a whole is available at Section 31.2 and Chapter 31.

Parameters

subscription_name

The name of the new subscription.

CONNECTION 'conninfo'

The connection string to the publisher. For details see Section 34.1.1.

PUBLICATION publication_name

Names of the publications on the publisher to subscribe to.

WITH (subscription_parameter [= value] [, ...])

This clause specifies optional parameters for a subscription. The following parameters are supported:

copy_data (boolean)

Specifies whether the existing data in the publications that are being subscribed to should be copied once the replication starts. The default is true.

create_slot (boolean)

Specifies whether the command should create the replication slot on the publisher. The default is true.

enabled (boolean)

Specifies whether the subscription should be actively replicating, or whether it should be just setup but not started yet. The default is true.

slot_name (string)

Name of the replication slot to use. The default behavior is to use the name of the subscription for the slot name.

When slot_name is set to NONE, there will be no replication slot associated with the subscription. This can be used if the replication slot will be created later manually. Such subscriptions must also have both enabled and create_slot set to false.

synchronous_commit (enum)

The value of this parameter overrides the synchronous_commit setting. The default value is off.

It is safe to use off for logical replication: If the subscriber loses transactions because of missing synchronization, the data will be resent from the publisher.

A different setting might be appropriate when doing synchronous logical replication. The logical replication workers report the positions of writes and flushes to the publisher, and when using synchronous replication, the publisher will wait for the actual flush. This means that setting synchronous_commit for the subscriber to off when the subscription is used for synchronous replication might increase the latency for COMMIT on the publisher. In this scenario, it can be advantageous to set synchronous_commit to local or higher.

connect (boolean)

Specifies whether the CREATE SUBSCRIPTION should connect to the publisher at all. Setting this to false will change default values of enabled, create_slot and copy_data to false.

It is not allowed to combine connect set to false and enabled, create_slot, or copy_data set to true.

Since no connection is made when this option is set to false, the tables are not subscribed, and so after you enable the subscription nothing will be replicated. It is required to run ALTER SUBSCRIPTION ... REFRESH PUBLICATION in order for tables to be subscribed.

Notes

See Section 31.7 for details on how to configure access control between the subscription and the publication instance.

When creating a replication slot (the default behavior), CREATE SUBSCRIPTION cannot be executed inside a transaction block.

Creating a subscription that connects to the same database cluster (for example, to replicate between databases in the same cluster or to replicate within the same database) will only succeed if the replication slot is not created as part of the same command. Otherwise, the CREATE SUBSCRIPTION call will hang. To make this work, create the replication slot separately (using the function pg_create_logical_replication_slot with the plugin name pgoutput) and create the subscription using the parameter create_slot = false. This is an implementation restriction that might be lifted in a future release.

Examples

Create a subscription to a remote server that replicates tables in the publications `mypublication` and `insert_only` and starts replicating immediately on commit:

```
CREATE SUBSCRIPTION mysub
        CONNECTION 'host=192.168.1.50 port=5432 user=foo
 dbname=foodb'
        PUBLICATION mypublication, insert_only;
```

Create a subscription to a remote server that replicates tables in the `insert_only` publication and does not start replicating until enabled at a later time.

```
CREATE SUBSCRIPTION mysub
        CONNECTION 'host=192.168.1.50 port=5432 user=foo
 dbname=foodb'
        PUBLICATION insert_only
               WITH (enabled = false);
```

Compatibility

`CREATE SUBSCRIPTION` is a PostgreSQL extension.

See Also

ALTER SUBSCRIPTION, DROP SUBSCRIPTION, CREATE PUBLICATION, ALTER PUBLICATION

CREATE TABLE

CREATE TABLE — define a new table

Synopsis

```
CREATE [ [ GLOBAL | LOCAL ] { TEMPORARY | TEMP } | UNLOGGED ] TABLE
[ IF NOT EXISTS ] table_name ( [
  { column_name data_type [ COLLATE collation ] [ column_constraint
[ ... ] ]
    | table_constraint
    | LIKE source_table [ like_option ... ] }
    [, ... ]
] )
[ INHERITS ( parent_table [, ... ] ) ]
[ PARTITION BY { RANGE | LIST | HASH } ( { column_name | ( expression
) } [ COLLATE collation ] [ opclass ] [, ... ] ) ]
[ WITH ( storage_parameter [= value] [, ... ] ) | WITH OIDS | WITHOUT
OIDS ]
[ ON COMMIT { PRESERVE ROWS | DELETE ROWS | DROP } ]
[ TABLESPACE tablespace_name ]

CREATE [ [ GLOBAL | LOCAL ] { TEMPORARY | TEMP } | UNLOGGED ] TABLE
[ IF NOT EXISTS ] table_name
    OF type_name [ (
  { column_name [ WITH OPTIONS ] [ column_constraint [ ... ] ]
    | table_constraint }
    [, ... ]
) ]
[ PARTITION BY { RANGE | LIST | HASH } ( { column_name | ( expression
) } [ COLLATE collation ] [ opclass ] [, ... ] ) ]
[ WITH ( storage_parameter [= value] [, ... ] ) | WITH OIDS | WITHOUT
OIDS ]
[ ON COMMIT { PRESERVE ROWS | DELETE ROWS | DROP } ]
[ TABLESPACE tablespace_name ]

CREATE [ [ GLOBAL | LOCAL ] { TEMPORARY | TEMP } | UNLOGGED ] TABLE
[ IF NOT EXISTS ] table_name
    PARTITION OF parent_table [ (
  { column_name [ WITH OPTIONS ] [ column_constraint [ ... ] ]
    | table_constraint }
    [, ... ]
) ] { FOR VALUES partition_bound_spec | DEFAULT }
[ PARTITION BY { RANGE | LIST | HASH } ( { column_name | ( expression
) } [ COLLATE collation ] [ opclass ] [, ... ] ) ]
[ WITH ( storage_parameter [= value] [, ... ] ) | WITH OIDS | WITHOUT
OIDS ]
[ ON COMMIT { PRESERVE ROWS | DELETE ROWS | DROP } ]
[ TABLESPACE tablespace_name ]
```

where *column_constraint* is:

```
[ CONSTRAINT constraint_name ]
{ NOT NULL |
  NULL |
  CHECK ( expression ) [ NO INHERIT ] |
  DEFAULT default_expr |
  GENERATED { ALWAYS | BY DEFAULT } AS IDENTITY [ ( sequence_options
) ] |
  UNIQUE index_parameters |
  PRIMARY KEY index_parameters |
  REFERENCES reftable [ ( refcolumn ) ] [ MATCH FULL | MATCH PARTIAL |
MATCH SIMPLE ]
    [ ON DELETE action ] [ ON UPDATE action ] }
[ DEFERRABLE | NOT DEFERRABLE ] [ INITIALLY DEFERRED | INITIALLY
 IMMEDIATE ]
```

and *table_constraint* is:

```
[ CONSTRAINT constraint_name ]
{ CHECK ( expression ) [ NO INHERIT ] |
  UNIQUE ( column_name [, ... ] ) index_parameters |
  PRIMARY KEY ( column_name [, ... ] ) index_parameters |
  EXCLUDE [ USING index_method ] ( exclude_element WITH operator
[, ... ] ) index_parameters [ WHERE ( predicate ) ] |
  FOREIGN KEY ( column_name [, ... ] ) REFERENCES reftable
[ ( refcolumn [, ... ] ) ]
    [ MATCH FULL | MATCH PARTIAL | MATCH SIMPLE ] [ ON DELETE action ]
[ ON UPDATE action ] }
[ DEFERRABLE | NOT DEFERRABLE ] [ INITIALLY DEFERRED | INITIALLY
 IMMEDIATE ]
```

and *like_option* is:

```
{ INCLUDING | EXCLUDING } { COMMENTS | CONSTRAINTS | DEFAULTS |
  IDENTITY | INDEXES | STATISTICS | STORAGE | ALL }
```

and *partition_bound_spec* is:

```
IN ( { numeric_literal | string_literal | TRUE | FALSE | NULL }
 [, ...] ) |
FROM ( { numeric_literal | string_literal | TRUE | FALSE | MINVALUE |
 MAXVALUE } [, ...] )
  TO ( { numeric_literal | string_literal | TRUE | FALSE | MINVALUE |
 MAXVALUE } [, ...] ) |
WITH ( MODULUS numeric_literal, REMAINDER numeric_literal )
```

index_parameters in UNIQUE, PRIMARY KEY, and EXCLUDE constraints are:

```
[ INCLUDE ( column_name [, ... ] ) ]
[ WITH ( storage_parameter [= value] [, ... ] ) ]
[ USING INDEX TABLESPACE tablespace_name ]
```

exclude_element in an EXCLUDE constraint is:

```
{ column_name | ( expression ) } [ opclass ] [ ASC | DESC ] [ NULLS
{ FIRST | LAST } ]
```

Description

CREATE TABLE will create a new, initially empty table in the current database. The table will be owned by the user issuing the command.

If a schema name is given (for example, CREATE TABLE myschema.mytable ...) then the table is created in the specified schema. Otherwise it is created in the current schema. Temporary tables exist in a special schema, so a schema name cannot be given when creating a temporary table. The name of the table must be distinct from the name of any other table, sequence, index, view, or foreign table in the same schema.

CREATE TABLE also automatically creates a data type that represents the composite type corresponding to one row of the table. Therefore, tables cannot have the same name as any existing data type in the same schema.

The optional constraint clauses specify constraints (tests) that new or updated rows must satisfy for an insert or update operation to succeed. A constraint is an SQL object that helps define the set of valid values in the table in various ways.

There are two ways to define constraints: table constraints and column constraints. A column constraint is defined as part of a column definition. A table constraint definition is not tied to a particular column, and it can encompass more than one column. Every column constraint can also be written as a table constraint; a column constraint is only a notational convenience for use when the constraint only affects one column.

To be able to create a table, you must have USAGE privilege on all column types or the type in the OF clause, respectively.

Parameters

TEMPORARY or TEMP

> If specified, the table is created as a temporary table. Temporary tables are automatically dropped at the end of a session, or optionally at the end of the current transaction (see ON COMMIT below). Existing permanent tables with the same name are not visible to the current session while the temporary table exists, unless they are referenced with schema-qualified names. Any indexes created on a temporary table are automatically temporary as well.

> The autovacuum daemon cannot access and therefore cannot vacuum or analyze temporary tables. For this reason, appropriate vacuum and analyze operations should be performed via session SQL commands. For example, if a temporary table is going to be used in complex queries, it is wise to run ANALYZE on the temporary table after it is populated.

> Optionally, GLOBAL or LOCAL can be written before TEMPORARY or TEMP. This presently makes no difference in PostgreSQL and is deprecated; see Compatibility.

UNLOGGED

> If specified, the table is created as an unlogged table. Data written to unlogged tables is not written to the write-ahead log (see Chapter 30), which makes them considerably faster than ordinary tables. However, they are not crash-safe: an unlogged table is automatically truncated after a crash or unclean

shutdown. The contents of an unlogged table are also not replicated to standby servers. Any indexes created on an unlogged table are automatically unlogged as well.

IF NOT EXISTS

Do not throw an error if a relation with the same name already exists. A notice is issued in this case. Note that there is no guarantee that the existing relation is anything like the one that would have been created.

table_name

The name (optionally schema-qualified) of the table to be created.

OF *type_name*

Creates a *typed table*, which takes its structure from the specified composite type (name optionally schema-qualified). A typed table is tied to its type; for example the table will be dropped if the type is dropped (with DROP TYPE ... CASCADE).

When a typed table is created, then the data types of the columns are determined by the underlying composite type and are not specified by the CREATE TABLE command. But the CREATE TABLE command can add defaults and constraints to the table and can specify storage parameters.

column_name

The name of a column to be created in the new table.

data_type

The data type of the column. This can include array specifiers. For more information on the data types supported by PostgreSQL, refer to Chapter 8.

COLLATE *collation*

The COLLATE clause assigns a collation to the column (which must be of a collatable data type). If not specified, the column data type's default collation is used.

INHERITS (*parent_table* [, ...])

The optional INHERITS clause specifies a list of tables from which the new table automatically inherits all columns. Parent tables can be plain tables or foreign tables.

Use of INHERITS creates a persistent relationship between the new child table and its parent table(s). Schema modifications to the parent(s) normally propagate to children as well, and by default the data of the child table is included in scans of the parent(s).

If the same column name exists in more than one parent table, an error is reported unless the data types of the columns match in each of the parent tables. If there is no conflict, then the duplicate columns are merged to form a single column in the new table. If the column name list of the new table contains a column name that is also inherited, the data type must likewise match the inherited column(s), and the column definitions are merged into one. If the new table explicitly specifies a default value for the column, this default overrides any defaults from inherited declarations of the column. Otherwise, any parents that specify default values for the column must all specify the same default, or an error will be reported.

CHECK constraints are merged in essentially the same way as columns: if multiple parent tables and/ or the new table definition contain identically-named CHECK constraints, these constraints must all have the same check expression, or an error will be reported. Constraints having the same name and expression will be merged into one copy. A constraint marked NO INHERIT in a parent will not be considered. Notice that an unnamed CHECK constraint in the new table will never be merged, since a unique name will always be chosen for it.

Column STORAGE settings are also copied from parent tables.

If a column in the parent table is an identity column, that property is not inherited. A column in the child table can be declared identity column if desired.

PARTITION BY { RANGE | LIST | HASH } ({ column_name | (expression) } [opclass] [, ...])

The optional PARTITION BY clause specifies a strategy of partitioning the table. The table thus created is called a *partitioned* table. The parenthesized list of columns or expressions forms the *partition key* for the table. When using range or hash partitioning, the partition key can include multiple columns or expressions (up to 32, but this limit can be altered when building PostgreSQL), but for list partitioning, the partition key must consist of a single column or expression.

Range and list partitioning require a btree operator class, while hash partitioning requires a hash operator class. If no operator class is specified explicitly, the default operator class of the appropriate type will be used; if no default operator class exists, an error will be raised. When hash partitioning is used, the operator class used must implement support function 2 (see Section 38.15.3 for details).

A partitioned table is divided into sub-tables (called partitions), which are created using separate CREATE TABLE commands. The partitioned table is itself empty. A data row inserted into the table is routed to a partition based on the value of columns or expressions in the partition key. If no existing partition matches the values in the new row, an error will be reported.

Partitioned tables do not support EXCLUDE constraints; however, you can define these constraints on individual partitions. Also, while it's possible to define PRIMARY KEY constraints on partitioned tables, creating foreign keys that reference a partitioned table is not yet supported.

See Section 5.10 for more discussion on table partitioning.

PARTITION OF parent_table { FOR VALUES partition_bound_spec | DEFAULT }

Creates the table as a *partition* of the specified parent table. The table can be created either as a partition for specific values using FOR VALUES or as a default partition using DEFAULT. This option is not available for hash-partitioned tables.

The *partition_bound_spec* must correspond to the partitioning method and partition key of the parent table, and must not overlap with any existing partition of that parent. The form with IN is used for list partitioning, the form with FROM and TO is used for range partitioning, and the form with WITH is used for hash partitioning.

Each of the values specified in the *partition_bound_spec* is a literal, NULL, MINVALUE, or MAXVALUE. Each literal value must be either a numeric constant that is coercible to the corresponding partition key column's type, or a string literal that is valid input for that type.

When creating a list partition, NULL can be specified to signify that the partition allows the partition key column to be null. However, there cannot be more than one such list partition for a given parent table. NULL cannot be specified for range partitions.

When creating a range partition, the lower bound specified with FROM is an inclusive bound, whereas the upper bound specified with TO is an exclusive bound. That is, the values specified in the FROM list are valid values of the corresponding partition key columns for this partition, whereas those in the TO list are not. Note that this statement must be understood according to the rules of row-wise comparison

(Section 9.23.5). For example, given `PARTITION BY RANGE (x,y)`, a partition bound `FROM (1, 2) TO (3, 4)` allows `x=1` with any `y>=2`, `x=2` with any non-null `y`, and `x=3` with any `y<4`.

The special values `MINVALUE` and `MAXVALUE` may be used when creating a range partition to indicate that there is no lower or upper bound on the column's value. For example, a partition defined using `FROM (MINVALUE) TO (10)` allows any values less than 10, and a partition defined using `FROM (10) TO (MAXVALUE)` allows any values greater than or equal to 10.

When creating a range partition involving more than one column, it can also make sense to use `MAXVALUE` as part of the lower bound, and `MINVALUE` as part of the upper bound. For example, a partition defined using `FROM (0, MAXVALUE) TO (10, MAXVALUE)` allows any rows where the first partition key column is greater than 0 and less than or equal to 10. Similarly, a partition defined using `FROM ('a', MINVALUE) TO ('b', MINVALUE)` allows any rows where the first partition key column starts with "a".

Note that if `MINVALUE` or `MAXVALUE` is used for one column of a partitioning bound, the same value must be used for all subsequent columns. For example, `(10, MINVALUE, 0)` is not a valid bound; you should write `(10, MINVALUE, MINVALUE)`.

Also note that some element types, such as `timestamp`, have a notion of "infinity", which is just another value that can be stored. This is different from `MINVALUE` and `MAXVALUE`, which are not real values that can be stored, but rather they are ways of saying that the value is unbounded. `MAXVALUE` can be thought of as being greater than any other value, including "infinity" and `MINVALUE` as being less than any other value, including "minus infinity". Thus the range `FROM ('infinity') TO (MAXVALUE)` is not an empty range; it allows precisely one value to be stored — "infinity".

If `DEFAULT` is specified, the table will be created as a default partition of the parent table. The parent can either be a list or range partitioned table. A partition key value not fitting into any other partition of the given parent will be routed to the default partition. There can be only one default partition for a given parent table.

When a table has an existing `DEFAULT` partition and a new partition is added to it, the existing default partition must be scanned to verify that it does not contain any rows which properly belong in the new partition. If the default partition contains a large number of rows, this may be slow. The scan will be skipped if the default partition is a foreign table or if it has a constraint which proves that it cannot contain rows which should be placed in the new partition.

When creating a hash partition, a modulus and remainder must be specified. The modulus must be a positive integer, and the remainder must be a non-negative integer less than the modulus. Typically, when initially setting up a hash-partitioned table, you should choose a modulus equal to the number of partitions and assign every table the same modulus and a different remainder (see examples, below). However, it is not required that every partition have the same modulus, only that every modulus which occurs among the partitions of a hash-partitioned table is a factor of the next larger modulus. This allows the number of partitions to be increased incrementally without needing to move all the data at once. For example, suppose you have a hash-partitioned table with 8 partitions, each of which has modulus 8, but find it necessary to increase the number of partitions to 16. You can detach one of the modulus-8 partitions, create two new modulus-16 partitions covering the same portion of the key space (one with a remainder equal to the remainder of the detached partition, and the other with a remainder equal to that value plus 8), and repopulate them with data. You can then repeat this -- perhaps at a later time -- for each modulus-8 partition until none remain. While this may still involve a large amount of data movement at each step, it is still better than having to create a whole new table and move all the data at once.

A partition must have the same column names and types as the partitioned table to which it belongs. If the parent is specified `WITH OIDS` then all partitions must have OIDs; the parent's OID column will be inherited by all partitions just like any other column. Modifications to the column names or types of a partitioned table, or the addition or removal of an OID column, will automatically propagate to all partitions. CHECK constraints will be inherited automatically by every partition, but an individual partition may specify additional CHECK constraints; additional constraints with the same name and condition as in the parent will be merged with the parent constraint. Defaults may be specified separately for each partition.

Rows inserted into a partitioned table will be automatically routed to the correct partition. If no suitable partition exists, an error will occur.

Operations such as TRUNCATE which normally affect a table and all of its inheritance children will cascade to all partitions, but may also be performed on an individual partition. Note that dropping a partition with DROP TABLE requires taking an ACCESS EXCLUSIVE lock on the parent table.

LIKE *source_table* [*like_option* ...]

The LIKE clause specifies a table from which the new table automatically copies all column names, their data types, and their not-null constraints.

Unlike INHERITS, the new table and original table are completely decoupled after creation is complete. Changes to the original table will not be applied to the new table, and it is not possible to include data of the new table in scans of the original table.

Default expressions for the copied column definitions will be copied only if INCLUDING DEFAULTS is specified. The default behavior is to exclude default expressions, resulting in the copied columns in the new table having null defaults. Note that copying defaults that call database-modification functions, such as nextval, may create a functional linkage between the original and new tables.

Any identity specifications of copied column definitions will only be copied if INCLUDING IDENTITY is specified. A new sequence is created for each identity column of the new table, separate from the sequences associated with the old table.

Not-null constraints are always copied to the new table. CHECK constraints will be copied only if INCLUDING CONSTRAINTS is specified. No distinction is made between column constraints and table constraints.

Extended statistics are copied to the new table if INCLUDING STATISTICS is specified.

Indexes, PRIMARY KEY, UNIQUE, and EXCLUDE constraints on the original table will be created on the new table only if INCLUDING INDEXES is specified. Names for the new indexes and constraints are chosen according to the default rules, regardless of how the originals were named. (This behavior avoids possible duplicate-name failures for the new indexes.)

STORAGE settings for the copied column definitions will be copied only if INCLUDING STORAGE is specified. The default behavior is to exclude STORAGE settings, resulting in the copied columns in the new table having type-specific default settings. For more on STORAGE settings, see Section 68.2.

Comments for the copied columns, constraints, and indexes will be copied only if INCLUDING COMMENTS is specified. The default behavior is to exclude comments, resulting in the copied columns and constraints in the new table having no comments.

INCLUDING ALL is an abbreviated form of INCLUDING COMMENTS INCLUDING CONSTRAINTS INCLUDING DEFAULTS INCLUDING IDENTITY INCLUDING INDEXES INCLUDING STATISTICS INCLUDING STORAGE.

Note that unlike INHERITS, columns and constraints copied by LIKE are not merged with similarly named columns and constraints. If the same name is specified explicitly or in another LIKE clause, an error is signaled.

The LIKE clause can also be used to copy column definitions from views, foreign tables, or composite types. Inapplicable options (e.g., INCLUDING INDEXES from a view) are ignored.

CONSTRAINT *constraint_name*

An optional name for a column or table constraint. If the constraint is violated, the constraint name is present in error messages, so constraint names like col must be positive can be used to communicate helpful constraint information to client applications. (Double-quotes are needed to specify constraint names that contain spaces.) If a constraint name is not specified, the system generates a name.

NOT NULL

The column is not allowed to contain null values.

NULL

The column is allowed to contain null values. This is the default.

This clause is only provided for compatibility with non-standard SQL databases. Its use is discouraged in new applications.

CHECK (*expression*) [NO INHERIT]

The CHECK clause specifies an expression producing a Boolean result which new or updated rows must satisfy for an insert or update operation to succeed. Expressions evaluating to TRUE or UNKNOWN succeed. Should any row of an insert or update operation produce a FALSE result, an error exception is raised and the insert or update does not alter the database. A check constraint specified as a column constraint should reference that column's value only, while an expression appearing in a table constraint can reference multiple columns.

Currently, CHECK expressions cannot contain subqueries nor refer to variables other than columns of the current row. The system column tableoid may be referenced, but not any other system column.

A constraint marked with NO INHERIT will not propagate to child tables.

When a table has multiple CHECK constraints, they will be tested for each row in alphabetical order by name, after checking NOT NULL constraints. (PostgreSQL versions before 9.5 did not honor any particular firing order for CHECK constraints.)

DEFAULT *default_expr*

The DEFAULT clause assigns a default data value for the column whose column definition it appears within. The value is any variable-free expression (subqueries and cross-references to other columns in the current table are not allowed). The data type of the default expression must match the data type of the column.

The default expression will be used in any insert operation that does not specify a value for the column. If there is no default for a column, then the default is null.

GENERATED { ALWAYS | BY DEFAULT } AS IDENTITY [(*sequence_options*)]

This clause creates the column as an *identity column*. It will have an implicit sequence attached to it and the column in new rows will automatically have values from the sequence assigned to it.

The clauses ALWAYS and BY DEFAULT determine how the sequence value is given precedence over a user-specified value in an INSERT statement. If ALWAYS is specified, a user-specified value is only accepted if the INSERT statement specifies OVERRIDING SYSTEM VALUE. If BY DEFAULT is specified, then the user-specified value takes precedence. See INSERT for details. (In the COPY command, user-specified values are always used regardless of this setting.)

The optional *sequence_options* clause can be used to override the options of the sequence. See CREATE SEQUENCE for details.

UNIQUE (column constraint)
UNIQUE (*column_name* [, ...]) [INCLUDE (*column_name* [, ...])] (table constraint)

The UNIQUE constraint specifies that a group of one or more columns of a table can contain only unique values. The behavior of the unique table constraint is the same as that for column constraints, with the additional capability to span multiple columns.

For the purpose of a unique constraint, null values are not considered equal.

Each unique table constraint must name a set of columns that is different from the set of columns named by any other unique or primary key constraint defined for the table. (Otherwise it would just be the same constraint listed twice.)

When establishing a unique constraint for a multi-level partition hierarchy, all the columns in the partition key of the target partitioned table, as well as those of all its descendant partitioned tables, must be included in the constraint definition.

Adding a unique constraint will automatically create a unique btree index on the column or group of columns used in the constraint. The optional clause INCLUDE adds to that index one or more columns on which the uniqueness is not enforced. Note that although the constraint is not enforced on the included columns, it still depends on them. Consequently, some operations on these columns (e.g. DROP COLUMN) can cause cascaded constraint and index deletion.

PRIMARY KEY (column constraint)
PRIMARY KEY (*column_name* [, ...]) [INCLUDE (*column_name* [, ...])] (table constraint)

The PRIMARY KEY constraint specifies that a column or columns of a table can contain only unique (non-duplicate), nonnull values. Only one primary key can be specified for a table, whether as a column constraint or a table constraint.

The primary key constraint should name a set of columns that is different from the set of columns named by any unique constraint defined for the same table. (Otherwise, the unique constraint is redundant and will be discarded.)

PRIMARY KEY enforces the same data constraints as a combination of UNIQUE and NOT NULL, but identifying a set of columns as the primary key also provides metadata about the design of the schema, since a primary key implies that other tables can rely on this set of columns as a unique identifier for rows.

PRIMARY KEY constraints share the restrictions that UNIQUE constraints have when placed on partitioned tables.

Adding a PRIMARY KEY constraint will automatically create a unique btree index on the column or group of columns used in the constraint. The optional INCLUDE clause allows a list of columns to be specified which will be included in the non-key portion of the index. Although uniqueness is not enforced on the included columns, the constraint still depends on them. Consequently, some operations on the included columns (e.g. DROP COLUMN) can cause cascaded constraint and index deletion.

```
EXCLUDE [ USING index_method ] ( exclude_element WITH operator [, ... ] )
index_parameters [ WHERE ( predicate ) ]
```

The EXCLUDE clause defines an exclusion constraint, which guarantees that if any two rows are compared on the specified column(s) or expression(s) using the specified operator(s), not all of these comparisons will return TRUE. If all of the specified operators test for equality, this is equivalent to a UNIQUE constraint, although an ordinary unique constraint will be faster. However, exclusion constraints can specify constraints that are more general than simple equality. For example, you can specify a constraint that no two rows in the table contain overlapping circles (see Section 8.8) by using the && operator.

Exclusion constraints are implemented using an index, so each specified operator must be associated with an appropriate operator class (see Section 11.10) for the index access method index_method. The operators are required to be commutative. Each exclude_element can optionally specify an operator class and/or ordering options; these are described fully under CREATE INDEX.

The access method must support amgettuple (see Chapter 61); at present this means GIN cannot be used. Although it's allowed, there is little point in using B-tree or hash indexes with an exclusion constraint, because this does nothing that an ordinary unique constraint doesn't do better. So in practice the access method will always be GiST or SP-GiST.

The predicate allows you to specify an exclusion constraint on a subset of the table; internally this creates a partial index. Note that parentheses are required around the predicate.

```
REFERENCES reftable [ ( refcolumn ) ] [ MATCH matchtype ] [ ON DELETE
action ] [ ON UPDATE action ] (column constraint)
FOREIGN KEY ( column_name [, ... ] ) REFERENCES reftable [ ( refcolumn
[, ... ] ) ] [ MATCH matchtype ] [ ON DELETE action ] [ ON UPDATE
action ] (table constraint)
```

These clauses specify a foreign key constraint, which requires that a group of one or more columns of the new table must only contain values that match values in the referenced column(s) of some row of the referenced table. If the refcolumn list is omitted, the primary key of the reftable is used. The referenced columns must be the columns of a non-deferrable unique or primary key constraint in the referenced table. The user must have REFERENCES permission on the referenced table (either the whole table, or the specific referenced columns). The addition of a foreign key constraint requires a SHARE ROW EXCLUSIVE lock on the referenced table. Note that foreign key constraints cannot be defined between temporary tables and permanent tables. Also note that while it is possible to define a foreign key on a partitioned table, it is not possible to declare a foreign key that references a partitioned table.

A value inserted into the referencing column(s) is matched against the values of the referenced table and referenced columns using the given match type. There are three match types: MATCH FULL, MATCH PARTIAL, and MATCH SIMPLE (which is the default). MATCH FULL will not allow one column of a multicolumn foreign key to be null unless all foreign key columns are null; if they are all null, the row is not required to have a match in the referenced table. MATCH SIMPLE allows any of the foreign key columns to be null; if any of them are null, the row is not required to have a match in the referenced table. MATCH PARTIAL is not yet implemented. (Of course, NOT NULL constraints can be applied to the referencing column(s) to prevent these cases from arising.)

In addition, when the data in the referenced columns is changed, certain actions are performed on the data in this table's columns. The ON DELETE clause specifies the action to perform when a referenced row in the referenced table is being deleted. Likewise, the ON UPDATE clause specifies the action to perform when a referenced column in the referenced table is being updated to a new value. If the row is updated, but the referenced column is not actually changed, no action is done. Referential actions other than the NO ACTION check cannot be deferred, even if the constraint is declared deferrable. There are the following possible actions for each clause:

NO ACTION

Produce an error indicating that the deletion or update would create a foreign key constraint violation. If the constraint is deferred, this error will be produced at constraint check time if there still exist any referencing rows. This is the default action.

RESTRICT

Produce an error indicating that the deletion or update would create a foreign key constraint violation. This is the same as NO ACTION except that the check is not deferrable.

CASCADE

Delete any rows referencing the deleted row, or update the values of the referencing column(s) to the new values of the referenced columns, respectively.

SET NULL

Set the referencing column(s) to null.

SET DEFAULT

Set the referencing column(s) to their default values. (There must be a row in the referenced table matching the default values, if they are not null, or the operation will fail.)

If the referenced column(s) are changed frequently, it might be wise to add an index to the referencing column(s) so that referential actions associated with the foreign key constraint can be performed more efficiently.

DEFERRABLE
NOT DEFERRABLE

This controls whether the constraint can be deferred. A constraint that is not deferrable will be checked immediately after every command. Checking of constraints that are deferrable can be postponed until the end of the transaction (using the SET CONSTRAINTS command). NOT DEFERRABLE is the default. Currently, only UNIQUE, PRIMARY KEY, EXCLUDE, and REFERENCES (foreign key) constraints accept this clause. NOT NULL and CHECK constraints are not deferrable. Note that deferrable constraints cannot be used as conflict arbitrators in an INSERT statement that includes an ON CONFLICT DO UPDATE clause.

INITIALLY IMMEDIATE
INITIALLY DEFERRED

If a constraint is deferrable, this clause specifies the default time to check the constraint. If the constraint is INITIALLY IMMEDIATE, it is checked after each statement. This is the default. If the constraint is INITIALLY DEFERRED, it is checked only at the end of the transaction. The constraint check time can be altered with the SET CONSTRAINTS command.

WITH (storage_parameter [= value] [, ...])

This clause specifies optional storage parameters for a table or index; see Storage Parameters for more information. The WITH clause for a table can also include OIDS=TRUE (or just OIDS) to specify that rows of the new table should have OIDs (object identifiers) assigned to them, or OIDS=FALSE to specify that the rows should not have OIDs. If OIDS is not specified, the default setting depends upon the default_with_oids configuration parameter. (If the new table inherits from any tables that have OIDs, then `OIDS=TRUE` is forced even if the command says `OIDS=FALSE`.)

If `OIDS=FALSE` is specified or implied, the new table does not store OIDs and no OID will be assigned for a row inserted into it. This is generally considered worthwhile, since it will reduce OID consumption and thereby postpone the wraparound of the 32-bit OID counter. Once the counter wraps around, OIDs can no longer be assumed to be unique, which makes them considerably less useful. In addition, excluding OIDs from a table reduces the space required to store the table on disk by 4 bytes per row (on most machines), slightly improving performance.

To remove OIDs from a table after it has been created, use ALTER TABLE.

`WITH OIDS`
`WITHOUT OIDS`

These are obsolescent syntaxes equivalent to `WITH (OIDS)` and `WITH (OIDS=FALSE)`, respectively. If you wish to give both an `OIDS` setting and storage parameters, you must use the `WITH ( ... )` syntax; see above.

`ON COMMIT`

The behavior of temporary tables at the end of a transaction block can be controlled using `ON COMMIT`. The three options are:

`PRESERVE ROWS`

No special action is taken at the ends of transactions. This is the default behavior.

`DELETE ROWS`

All rows in the temporary table will be deleted at the end of each transaction block. Essentially, an automatic TRUNCATE is done at each commit. When used on a partitioned table, this is not cascaded to its partitions.

`DROP`

The temporary table will be dropped at the end of the current transaction block. When used on a partitioned table, this action drops its partitions and when used on tables with inheritance children, it drops the dependent children.

`TABLESPACE tablespace_name`

The `tablespace_name` is the name of the tablespace in which the new table is to be created. If not specified, default_tablespace is consulted, or temp_tablespaces if the table is temporary.

`USING INDEX TABLESPACE tablespace_name`

This clause allows selection of the tablespace in which the index associated with a `UNIQUE`, `PRIMARY KEY`, or `EXCLUDE` constraint will be created. If not specified, default_tablespace is consulted, or temp_tablespaces if the table is temporary.

Storage Parameters

The `WITH` clause can specify *storage parameters* for tables, and for indexes associated with a `UNIQUE`, `PRIMARY KEY`, or `EXCLUDE` constraint. Storage parameters for indexes are documented in CREATE INDEX. The storage parameters currently available for tables are listed below. For many of these parameters, as shown, there is an additional parameter with the same name prefixed with `toast.`, which controls the behavior of the table's secondary TOAST table, if any (see Section 68.2 for more information about

TOAST). If a table parameter value is set and the equivalent `toast.` parameter is not, the TOAST table will use the table's parameter value. Specifying these parameters for partitioned tables is not supported, but you may specify them for individual leaf partitions.

`fillfactor` (`integer`)

The fillfactor for a table is a percentage between 10 and 100. 100 (complete packing) is the default. When a smaller fillfactor is specified, `INSERT` operations pack table pages only to the indicated percentage; the remaining space on each page is reserved for updating rows on that page. This gives `UPDATE` a chance to place the updated copy of a row on the same page as the original, which is more efficient than placing it on a different page. For a table whose entries are never updated, complete packing is the best choice, but in heavily updated tables smaller fillfactors are appropriate. This parameter cannot be set for TOAST tables.

`toast_tuple_target` (`integer`)

The toast_tuple_target specifies the minimum tuple length required before we try to move long column values into TOAST tables, and is also the target length we try to reduce the length below once toasting begins. This only affects columns marked as either External or Extended and applies only to new tuples - there is no effect on existing rows. By default this parameter is set to allow at least 4 tuples per block, which with the default blocksize will be 2040 bytes. Valid values are between 128 bytes and the (blocksize - header), by default 8160 bytes. Changing this value may not be useful for very short or very long rows. Note that the default setting is often close to optimal, and it is possible that setting this parameter could have negative effects in some cases. This parameter cannot be set for TOAST tables.

`parallel_workers` (`integer`)

This sets the number of workers that should be used to assist a parallel scan of this table. If not set, the system will determine a value based on the relation size. The actual number of workers chosen by the planner or by utility statements that use parallel scans may be less, for example due to the setting of max_worker_processes.

`autovacuum_enabled`, `toast.autovacuum_enabled` (`boolean`)

Enables or disables the autovacuum daemon for a particular table. If true, the autovacuum daemon will perform automatic `VACUUM` and/or `ANALYZE` operations on this table following the rules discussed in Section 24.1.6. If false, this table will not be autovacuumed, except to prevent transaction ID wraparound. See Section 24.1.5 for more about wraparound prevention. Note that the autovacuum daemon does not run at all (except to prevent transaction ID wraparound) if the autovacuum parameter is false; setting individual tables' storage parameters does not override that. Therefore there is seldom much point in explicitly setting this storage parameter to `true`, only to `false`.

`autovacuum_vacuum_threshold`, `toast.autovacuum_vacuum_threshold` (`integer`)

Per-table value for autovacuum_vacuum_threshold parameter.

`autovacuum_vacuum_scale_factor`, `toast.autovacuum_vacuum_scale_factor` (`float4`)

Per-table value for autovacuum_vacuum_scale_factor parameter.

`autovacuum_analyze_threshold` (`integer`)

Per-table value for autovacuum_analyze_threshold parameter.

`autovacuum_analyze_scale_factor` (`float4`)

Per-table value for autovacuum_analyze_scale_factor parameter.

`autovacuum_vacuum_cost_delay, toast.autovacuum_vacuum_cost_delay (integer)`

>   Per-table value for autovacuum_vacuum_cost_delay parameter.

`autovacuum_vacuum_cost_limit, toast.autovacuum_vacuum_cost_limit (integer)`

>   Per-table value for autovacuum_vacuum_cost_limit parameter.

`autovacuum_freeze_min_age, toast.autovacuum_freeze_min_age (integer)`

>   Per-table value for vacuum_freeze_min_age parameter. Note that autovacuum will ignore per-table `autovacuum_freeze_min_age` parameters that are larger than half the system-wide autovacuum_freeze_max_age setting.

`autovacuum_freeze_max_age, toast.autovacuum_freeze_max_age (integer)`

>   Per-table value for autovacuum_freeze_max_age parameter. Note that autovacuum will ignore per-table `autovacuum_freeze_max_age` parameters that are larger than the system-wide setting (it can only be set smaller).

`autovacuum_freeze_table_age, toast.autovacuum_freeze_table_age (integer)`

>   Per-table value for vacuum_freeze_table_age parameter.

`autovacuum_multixact_freeze_min_age,      toast.autovacuum_multixact_freeze_min_age (integer)`

>   Per-table value for vacuum_multixact_freeze_min_age parameter. Note that autovacuum will ignore per-table `autovacuum_multixact_freeze_min_age` parameters that are larger than half the system-wide autovacuum_multixact_freeze_max_age setting.

`autovacuum_multixact_freeze_max_age,      toast.autovacuum_multixact_freeze_max_age (integer)`

>   Per-table value for autovacuum_multixact_freeze_max_age parameter. Note that autovacuum will ignore per-table `autovacuum_multixact_freeze_max_age` parameters that are larger than the system-wide setting (it can only be set smaller).

`autovacuum_multixact_freeze_table_age,      toast.autovacuum_multixact_freeze_table_age (integer)`

>   Per-table value for vacuum_multixact_freeze_table_age parameter.

`log_autovacuum_min_duration, toast.log_autovacuum_min_duration (integer)`

>   Per-table value for log_autovacuum_min_duration parameter.

`user_catalog_table (boolean)`

>   Declare the table as an additional catalog table for purposes of logical replication. See Section 49.6.2 for details. This parameter cannot be set for TOAST tables.

Notes

Using OIDs in new applications is not recommended: where possible, using an identity column or other sequence generator as the table's primary key is preferred. However, if your application does make use of OIDs to identify specific rows of a table, it is recommended to create a unique constraint on the oid column of that table, to ensure that OIDs in the table will indeed uniquely identify rows even after counter wraparound. Avoid assuming that OIDs are unique across tables; if you need a database-wide unique identifier, use the combination of tableoid and row OID for the purpose.

Tip

The use of OIDS=FALSE is not recommended for tables with no primary key, since without either an OID or a unique data key, it is difficult to identify specific rows.

PostgreSQL automatically creates an index for each unique constraint and primary key constraint to enforce uniqueness. Thus, it is not necessary to create an index explicitly for primary key columns. (See CREATE INDEX for more information.)

Unique constraints and primary keys are not inherited in the current implementation. This makes the combination of inheritance and unique constraints rather dysfunctional.

A table cannot have more than 1600 columns. (In practice, the effective limit is usually lower because of tuple-length constraints.)

Examples

Create table films and table distributors:

```
CREATE TABLE films (
    code        char(5) CONSTRAINT firstkey PRIMARY KEY,
    title       varchar(40) NOT NULL,
    did         integer NOT NULL,
    date_prod   date,
    kind        varchar(10),
    len         interval hour to minute
);

CREATE TABLE distributors (
    did     integer PRIMARY KEY GENERATED BY DEFAULT AS IDENTITY,
    name    varchar(40) NOT NULL CHECK (name <> '')
);
```

Create a table with a 2-dimensional array:

```
CREATE TABLE array_int (
    vector  int[][]
);
```

Define a unique table constraint for the table films. Unique table constraints can be defined on one or more columns of the table:

```
CREATE TABLE films (
    code        char(5),
    title       varchar(40),
```

```
    did         integer,
    date_prod   date,
    kind        varchar(10),
    len         interval hour to minute,
    CONSTRAINT production UNIQUE(date_prod)
);
```

Define a check column constraint:

```
CREATE TABLE distributors (
    did         integer CHECK (did > 100),
    name        varchar(40)
);
```

Define a check table constraint:

```
CREATE TABLE distributors (
    did         integer,
    name        varchar(40),
    CONSTRAINT con1 CHECK (did > 100 AND name <> '')
);
```

Define a primary key table constraint for the table films:

```
CREATE TABLE films (
    code        char(5),
    title       varchar(40),
    did         integer,
    date_prod   date,
    kind        varchar(10),
    len         interval hour to minute,
    CONSTRAINT code_title PRIMARY KEY(code,title)
);
```

Define a primary key constraint for table distributors. The following two examples are equivalent, the first using the table constraint syntax, the second the column constraint syntax:

```
CREATE TABLE distributors (
    did         integer,
    name        varchar(40),
    PRIMARY KEY(did)
);
```

```
CREATE TABLE distributors (
    did         integer PRIMARY KEY,
    name        varchar(40)
);
```

Assign a literal constant default value for the column name, arrange for the default value of column did to be generated by selecting the next value of a sequence object, and make the default value of modtime be the time at which the row is inserted:

```
CREATE TABLE distributors (
    name       varchar(40) DEFAULT 'Luso Films',
    did        integer DEFAULT nextval('distributors_serial'),
    modtime    timestamp DEFAULT current_timestamp
);
```

Define two NOT NULL column constraints on the table distributors, one of which is explicitly given a name:

```
CREATE TABLE distributors (
    did      integer CONSTRAINT no_null NOT NULL,
    name     varchar(40) NOT NULL
);
```

Define a unique constraint for the name column:

```
CREATE TABLE distributors (
    did      integer,
    name     varchar(40) UNIQUE
);
```

The same, specified as a table constraint:

```
CREATE TABLE distributors (
    did      integer,
    name     varchar(40),
    UNIQUE(name)
);
```

Create the same table, specifying 70% fill factor for both the table and its unique index:

```
CREATE TABLE distributors (
    did      integer,
    name     varchar(40),
    UNIQUE(name) WITH (fillfactor=70)
)
WITH (fillfactor=70);
```

Create table circles with an exclusion constraint that prevents any two circles from overlapping:

```
CREATE TABLE circles (
    c circle,
    EXCLUDE USING gist (c WITH &&)
);
```

Create table cinemas in tablespace diskvol1:

```
CREATE TABLE cinemas (
        id serial,
        name text,
```

```
          location text
) TABLESPACE diskvol1;
```

Create a composite type and a typed table:

```
CREATE TYPE employee_type AS (name text, salary numeric);

CREATE TABLE employees OF employee_type (
    PRIMARY KEY (name),
    salary WITH OPTIONS DEFAULT 1000
);
```

Create a range partitioned table:

```
CREATE TABLE measurement (
    logdate         date not null,
    peaktemp        int,
    unitsales       int
) PARTITION BY RANGE (logdate);
```

Create a range partitioned table with multiple columns in the partition key:

```
CREATE TABLE measurement_year_month (
    logdate         date not null,
    peaktemp        int,
    unitsales       int
) PARTITION BY RANGE (EXTRACT(YEAR FROM logdate), EXTRACT(MONTH FROM
  logdate));
```

Create a list partitioned table:

```
CREATE TABLE cities (
    city_id      bigserial not null,
    name         text not null,
    population   bigint
) PARTITION BY LIST (left(lower(name), 1));
```

Create a hash partitioned table:

```
CREATE TABLE orders (
    order_id     bigint not null,
    cust_id      bigint not null,
    status       text
) PARTITION BY HASH (order_id);
```

Create partition of a range partitioned table:

```
CREATE TABLE measurement_y2016m07
    PARTITION OF measurement (
    unitsales DEFAULT 0
) FOR VALUES FROM ('2016-07-01') TO ('2016-08-01');
```

Create a few partitions of a range partitioned table with multiple columns in the partition key:

```
CREATE TABLE measurement_ym_older
    PARTITION OF measurement_year_month
    FOR VALUES FROM (MINVALUE, MINVALUE) TO (2016, 11);

CREATE TABLE measurement_ym_y2016m11
    PARTITION OF measurement_year_month
    FOR VALUES FROM (2016, 11) TO (2016, 12);

CREATE TABLE measurement_ym_y2016m12
    PARTITION OF measurement_year_month
    FOR VALUES FROM (2016, 12) TO (2017, 01);

CREATE TABLE measurement_ym_y2017m01
    PARTITION OF measurement_year_month
    FOR VALUES FROM (2017, 01) TO (2017, 02);
```

Create partition of a list partitioned table:

```
CREATE TABLE cities_ab
    PARTITION OF cities (
    CONSTRAINT city_id_nonzero CHECK (city_id != 0)
) FOR VALUES IN ('a', 'b');
```

Create partition of a list partitioned table that is itself further partitioned and then add a partition to it:

```
CREATE TABLE cities_ab
    PARTITION OF cities (
    CONSTRAINT city_id_nonzero CHECK (city_id != 0)
) FOR VALUES IN ('a', 'b') PARTITION BY RANGE (population);

CREATE TABLE cities_ab_10000_to_100000
    PARTITION OF cities_ab FOR VALUES FROM (10000) TO (100000);
```

Create partitions of a hash partitioned table:

```
CREATE TABLE orders_p1 PARTITION OF orders
    FOR VALUES WITH (MODULUS 4, REMAINDER 0);
CREATE TABLE orders_p2 PARTITION OF orders
    FOR VALUES WITH (MODULUS 4, REMAINDER 1);
CREATE TABLE orders_p3 PARTITION OF orders
    FOR VALUES WITH (MODULUS 4, REMAINDER 2);
CREATE TABLE orders_p4 PARTITION OF orders
    FOR VALUES WITH (MODULUS 4, REMAINDER 3);
```

Create a default partition:

```
CREATE TABLE cities_partdef
    PARTITION OF cities DEFAULT;
```

Compatibility

The CREATE TABLE command conforms to the SQL standard, with exceptions listed below.

Temporary Tables

Although the syntax of CREATE TEMPORARY TABLE resembles that of the SQL standard, the effect is not the same. In the standard, temporary tables are defined just once and automatically exist (starting with empty contents) in every session that needs them. PostgreSQL instead requires each session to issue its own CREATE TEMPORARY TABLE command for each temporary table to be used. This allows different sessions to use the same temporary table name for different purposes, whereas the standard's approach constrains all instances of a given temporary table name to have the same table structure.

The standard's definition of the behavior of temporary tables is widely ignored. PostgreSQL's behavior on this point is similar to that of several other SQL databases.

The SQL standard also distinguishes between global and local temporary tables, where a local temporary table has a separate set of contents for each SQL module within each session, though its definition is still shared across sessions. Since PostgreSQL does not support SQL modules, this distinction is not relevant in PostgreSQL.

For compatibility's sake, PostgreSQL will accept the GLOBAL and LOCAL keywords in a temporary table declaration, but they currently have no effect. Use of these keywords is discouraged, since future versions of PostgreSQL might adopt a more standard-compliant interpretation of their meaning.

The ON COMMIT clause for temporary tables also resembles the SQL standard, but has some differences. If the ON COMMIT clause is omitted, SQL specifies that the default behavior is ON COMMIT DELETE ROWS. However, the default behavior in PostgreSQL is ON COMMIT PRESERVE ROWS. The ON COMMIT DROP option does not exist in SQL.

Non-deferred Uniqueness Constraints

When a UNIQUE or PRIMARY KEY constraint is not deferrable, PostgreSQL checks for uniqueness immediately whenever a row is inserted or modified. The SQL standard says that uniqueness should be enforced only at the end of the statement; this makes a difference when, for example, a single command updates multiple key values. To obtain standard-compliant behavior, declare the constraint as DEFERRABLE but not deferred (i.e., INITIALLY IMMEDIATE). Be aware that this can be significantly slower than immediate uniqueness checking.

Column Check Constraints

The SQL standard says that CHECK column constraints can only refer to the column they apply to; only CHECK table constraints can refer to multiple columns. PostgreSQL does not enforce this restriction; it treats column and table check constraints alike.

EXCLUDE Constraint

The EXCLUDE constraint type is a PostgreSQL extension.

NULL "Constraint"

The NULL "constraint" (actually a non-constraint) is a PostgreSQL extension to the SQL standard that is included for compatibility with some other database systems (and for symmetry with the NOT NULL constraint). Since it is the default for any column, its presence is simply noise.

Constraint Naming

The SQL standard says that table and domain constraints must have names that are unique across the schema containing the table or domain. PostgreSQL is laxer: it only requires constraint names to be unique across the constraints attached to a particular table or domain. However, this extra freedom does not exist for index-based constraints (UNIQUE, PRIMARY KEY, and EXCLUDE constraints), because the associated index is named the same as the constraint, and index names must be unique across all relations within the same schema.

Currently, PostgreSQL does not record names for NOT NULL constraints at all, so they are not subject to the uniqueness restriction. This might change in a future release.

Inheritance

Multiple inheritance via the INHERITS clause is a PostgreSQL language extension. SQL:1999 and later define single inheritance using a different syntax and different semantics. SQL:1999-style inheritance is not yet supported by PostgreSQL.

Zero-column Tables

PostgreSQL allows a table of no columns to be created (for example, CREATE TABLE foo();). This is an extension from the SQL standard, which does not allow zero-column tables. Zero-column tables are not in themselves very useful, but disallowing them creates odd special cases for ALTER TABLE DROP COLUMN, so it seems cleaner to ignore this spec restriction.

Multiple Identity Columns

PostgreSQL allows a table to have more than one identity column. The standard specifies that a table can have at most one identity column. This is relaxed mainly to give more flexibility for doing schema changes or migrations. Note that the INSERT command supports only one override clause that applies to the entire statement, so having multiple identity columns with different behaviors is not well supported.

LIKE Clause

While a LIKE clause exists in the SQL standard, many of the options that PostgreSQL accepts for it are not in the standard, and some of the standard's options are not implemented by PostgreSQL.

WITH Clause

The WITH clause is a PostgreSQL extension; neither storage parameters nor OIDs are in the standard.

Tablespaces

The PostgreSQL concept of tablespaces is not part of the standard. Hence, the clauses TABLESPACE and USING INDEX TABLESPACE are extensions.

Typed Tables

Typed tables implement a subset of the SQL standard. According to the standard, a typed table has columns corresponding to the underlying composite type as well as one other column that is the "self-referencing column". PostgreSQL does not support these self-referencing columns explicitly, but the same effect can be had using the OID feature.

PARTITION BY Clause

The PARTITION BY clause is a PostgreSQL extension.

PARTITION OF Clause

The PARTITION OF clause is a PostgreSQL extension.

See Also

ALTER TABLE, DROP TABLE, CREATE TABLE AS, CREATE TABLESPACE, CREATE TYPE

CREATE TABLE AS

CREATE TABLE AS — define a new table from the results of a query

Synopsis

```
CREATE [ [ GLOBAL | LOCAL ] { TEMPORARY | TEMP } | UNLOGGED ] TABLE
 [ IF NOT EXISTS ] table_name
    [ (column_name [, ...] ) ]
    [ WITH ( storage_parameter [= value] [, ... ] ) | WITH OIDS |
WITHOUT OIDS ]
    [ ON COMMIT { PRESERVE ROWS | DELETE ROWS | DROP } ]
    [ TABLESPACE tablespace_name ]
    AS query
    [ WITH [ NO ] DATA ]
```

Description

CREATE TABLE AS creates a table and fills it with data computed by a SELECT command. The table columns have the names and data types associated with the output columns of the SELECT (except that you can override the column names by giving an explicit list of new column names).

CREATE TABLE AS bears some resemblance to creating a view, but it is really quite different: it creates a new table and evaluates the query just once to fill the new table initially. The new table will not track subsequent changes to the source tables of the query. In contrast, a view re-evaluates its defining SELECT statement whenever it is queried.

Parameters

GLOBAL or LOCAL

Ignored for compatibility. Use of these keywords is deprecated; refer to CREATE TABLE for details.

TEMPORARY or TEMP

If specified, the table is created as a temporary table. Refer to CREATE TABLE for details.

UNLOGGED

If specified, the table is created as an unlogged table. Refer to CREATE TABLE for details.

IF NOT EXISTS

Do not throw an error if a relation with the same name already exists. A notice is issued in this case. Refer to CREATE TABLE for details.

table_name

The name (optionally schema-qualified) of the table to be created.

`column_name`

> The name of a column in the new table. If column names are not provided, they are taken from the output column names of the query.

WITH (`storage_parameter` [= `value`] [, ...])

> This clause specifies optional storage parameters for the new table; see Storage Parameters for more information. The `WITH` clause can also include `OIDS=TRUE` (or just `OIDS`) to specify that rows of the new table should have OIDs (object identifiers) assigned to them, or `OIDS=FALSE` to specify that the rows should not have OIDs. See CREATE TABLE for more information.

WITH OIDS
WITHOUT OIDS

> These are obsolescent syntaxes equivalent to `WITH (OIDS)` and `WITH (OIDS=FALSE)`, respectively. If you wish to give both an `OIDS` setting and storage parameters, you must use the `WITH ( ... )` syntax; see above.

ON COMMIT

> The behavior of temporary tables at the end of a transaction block can be controlled using `ON COMMIT`. The three options are:

PRESERVE ROWS

> No special action is taken at the ends of transactions. This is the default behavior.

DELETE ROWS

> All rows in the temporary table will be deleted at the end of each transaction block. Essentially, an automatic TRUNCATE is done at each commit.

DROP

> The temporary table will be dropped at the end of the current transaction block.

TABLESPACE `tablespace_name`

> The `tablespace_name` is the name of the tablespace in which the new table is to be created. If not specified, default_tablespace is consulted, or temp_tablespaces if the table is temporary.

`query`

> A SELECT, TABLE, or VALUES command, or an EXECUTE command that runs a prepared SELECT, TABLE, or VALUES query.

WITH [NO] DATA

> This clause specifies whether or not the data produced by the query should be copied into the new table. If not, only the table structure is copied. The default is to copy the data.

Notes

This command is functionally similar to SELECT INTO, but it is preferred since it is less likely to be confused with other uses of the `SELECT INTO` syntax. Furthermore, `CREATE TABLE AS` offers a superset of the functionality offered by `SELECT INTO`.

The CREATE TABLE AS command allows the user to explicitly specify whether OIDs should be included. If the presence of OIDs is not explicitly specified, the default_with_oids configuration variable is used.

Examples

Create a new table films_recent consisting of only recent entries from the table films:

```
CREATE TABLE films_recent AS
  SELECT * FROM films WHERE date_prod >= '2002-01-01';
```

To copy a table completely, the short form using the TABLE command can also be used:

```
CREATE TABLE films2 AS
  TABLE films;
```

Create a new temporary table films_recent, consisting of only recent entries from the table films, using a prepared statement. The new table has OIDs and will be dropped at commit:

```
PREPARE recentfilms(date) AS
  SELECT * FROM films WHERE date_prod > $1;
CREATE TEMP TABLE films_recent WITH (OIDS) ON COMMIT DROP AS
  EXECUTE recentfilms('2002-01-01');
```

Compatibility

CREATE TABLE AS conforms to the SQL standard. The following are nonstandard extensions:

- The standard requires parentheses around the subquery clause; in PostgreSQL, these parentheses are optional.
- In the standard, the WITH [NO] DATA clause is required; in PostgreSQL it is optional.
- PostgreSQL handles temporary tables in a way rather different from the standard; see CREATE TABLE for details.
- The WITH clause is a PostgreSQL extension; neither storage parameters nor OIDs are in the standard.
- The PostgreSQL concept of tablespaces is not part of the standard. Hence, the clause TABLESPACE is an extension.

See Also

CREATE MATERIALIZED VIEW, CREATE TABLE, EXECUTE, SELECT, SELECT INTO, VALUES

CREATE TABLESPACE

CREATE TABLESPACE — define a new tablespace

Synopsis

```
CREATE TABLESPACE tablespace_name
    [ OWNER { new_owner | CURRENT_USER | SESSION_USER } ]
    LOCATION 'directory'
    [ WITH ( tablespace_option = value [, ... ] ) ]
```

Description

CREATE TABLESPACE registers a new cluster-wide tablespace. The tablespace name must be distinct from the name of any existing tablespace in the database cluster.

A tablespace allows superusers to define an alternative location on the file system where the data files containing database objects (such as tables and indexes) can reside.

A user with appropriate privileges can pass tablespace_name to CREATE DATABASE, CREATE TABLE, CREATE INDEX or ADD CONSTRAINT to have the data files for these objects stored within the specified tablespace.

Warning

A tablespace cannot be used independently of the cluster in which it is defined; see Section 22.6.

Parameters

tablespace_name

> The name of a tablespace to be created. The name cannot begin with pg_, as such names are reserved for system tablespaces.

user_name

> The name of the user who will own the tablespace. If omitted, defaults to the user executing the command. Only superusers can create tablespaces, but they can assign ownership of tablespaces to non-superusers.

directory

> The directory that will be used for the tablespace. The directory should be empty and must be owned by the PostgreSQL system user. The directory must be specified by an absolute path name.

tablespace_option

> A tablespace parameter to be set or reset. Currently, the only available parameters are seq_page_cost, random_page_cost and effective_io_concurrency. Setting either

value for a particular tablespace will override the planner's usual estimate of the cost of reading pages from tables in that tablespace, as established by the configuration parameters of the same name (see seq_page_cost, random_page_cost, effective_io_concurrency). This may be useful if one tablespace is located on a disk which is faster or slower than the remainder of the I/O subsystem.

Notes

Tablespaces are only supported on systems that support symbolic links.

CREATE TABLESPACE cannot be executed inside a transaction block.

Examples

Create a tablespace dbspace at /data/dbs:

CREATE TABLESPACE dbspace LOCATION '/data/dbs';

Create a tablespace indexspace at /data/indexes owned by user genevieve:

CREATE TABLESPACE indexspace OWNER genevieve LOCATION '/data/indexes';

Compatibility

CREATE TABLESPACE is a PostgreSQL extension.

See Also

CREATE DATABASE, CREATE TABLE, CREATE INDEX, DROP TABLESPACE, ALTER TABLESPACE

CREATE TEXT SEARCH CONFIGURATION

CREATE TEXT SEARCH CONFIGURATION — define a new text search configuration

Synopsis

```
CREATE TEXT SEARCH CONFIGURATION name (
    PARSER = parser_name |
    COPY = source_config
)
```

Description

CREATE TEXT SEARCH CONFIGURATION creates a new text search configuration. A text search configuration specifies a text search parser that can divide a string into tokens, plus dictionaries that can be used to determine which tokens are of interest for searching.

If only the parser is specified, then the new text search configuration initially has no mappings from token types to dictionaries, and therefore will ignore all words. Subsequent ALTER TEXT SEARCH CONFIGURATION commands must be used to create mappings to make the configuration useful. Alternatively, an existing text search configuration can be copied.

If a schema name is given then the text search configuration is created in the specified schema. Otherwise it is created in the current schema.

The user who defines a text search configuration becomes its owner.

Refer to Chapter 12 for further information.

Parameters

name

> The name of the text search configuration to be created. The name can be schema-qualified.

parser_name

> The name of the text search parser to use for this configuration.

source_config

> The name of an existing text search configuration to copy.

Notes

The PARSER and COPY options are mutually exclusive, because when an existing configuration is copied, its parser selection is copied too.

Compatibility

There is no CREATE TEXT SEARCH CONFIGURATION statement in the SQL standard.

See Also

ALTER TEXT SEARCH CONFIGURATION, DROP TEXT SEARCH CONFIGURATION

CREATE TEXT SEARCH DICTIONARY

CREATE TEXT SEARCH DICTIONARY — define a new text search dictionary

Synopsis

```
CREATE TEXT SEARCH DICTIONARY name (
    TEMPLATE = template
    [, option = value [, ... ]]
)
```

Description

CREATE TEXT SEARCH DICTIONARY creates a new text search dictionary. A text search dictionary specifies a way of recognizing interesting or uninteresting words for searching. A dictionary depends on a text search template, which specifies the functions that actually perform the work. Typically the dictionary provides some options that control the detailed behavior of the template's functions.

If a schema name is given then the text search dictionary is created in the specified schema. Otherwise it is created in the current schema.

The user who defines a text search dictionary becomes its owner.

Refer to Chapter 12 for further information.

Parameters

name

> The name of the text search dictionary to be created. The name can be schema-qualified.

template

> The name of the text search template that will define the basic behavior of this dictionary.

option

> The name of a template-specific option to be set for this dictionary.

value

> The value to use for a template-specific option. If the value is not a simple identifier or number, it must be quoted (but you can always quote it, if you wish).

The options can appear in any order.

Examples

The following example command creates a Snowball-based dictionary with a nonstandard list of stop words.

```
CREATE TEXT SEARCH DICTIONARY my_russian (
    template = snowball,
    language = russian,
    stopwords = myrussian
);
```

Compatibility

There is no `CREATE TEXT SEARCH DICTIONARY` statement in the SQL standard.

See Also

ALTER TEXT SEARCH DICTIONARY, DROP TEXT SEARCH DICTIONARY

CREATE TEXT SEARCH PARSER

CREATE TEXT SEARCH PARSER — define a new text search parser

Synopsis

```
CREATE TEXT SEARCH PARSER name (
    START = start_function ,
    GETTOKEN = gettoken_function ,
    END = end_function ,
    LEXTYPES = lextypes_function
    [, HEADLINE = headline_function ]
)
```

Description

CREATE TEXT SEARCH PARSER creates a new text search parser. A text search parser defines a method for splitting a text string into tokens and assigning types (categories) to the tokens. A parser is not particularly useful by itself, but must be bound into a text search configuration along with some text search dictionaries to be used for searching.

If a schema name is given then the text search parser is created in the specified schema. Otherwise it is created in the current schema.

You must be a superuser to use CREATE TEXT SEARCH PARSER. (This restriction is made because an erroneous text search parser definition could confuse or even crash the server.)

Refer to Chapter 12 for further information.

Parameters

name

> The name of the text search parser to be created. The name can be schema-qualified.

start_function

> The name of the start function for the parser.

gettoken_function

> The name of the get-next-token function for the parser.

end_function

> The name of the end function for the parser.

lextypes_function

> The name of the lextypes function for the parser (a function that returns information about the set of token types it produces).

headline_function

> The name of the headline function for the parser (a function that summarizes a set of tokens).

The function names can be schema-qualified if necessary. Argument types are not given, since the argument list for each type of function is predetermined. All except the headline function are required.

The arguments can appear in any order, not only the one shown above.

Compatibility

There is no **CREATE TEXT SEARCH PARSER** statement in the SQL standard.

See Also

ALTER TEXT SEARCH PARSER, DROP TEXT SEARCH PARSER

CREATE TEXT SEARCH TEMPLATE

CREATE TEXT SEARCH TEMPLATE — define a new text search template

Synopsis

```
CREATE TEXT SEARCH TEMPLATE name (
    [ INIT = init_function , ]
    LEXIZE = lexize_function
)
```

Description

CREATE TEXT SEARCH TEMPLATE creates a new text search template. Text search templates define the functions that implement text search dictionaries. A template is not useful by itself, but must be instantiated as a dictionary to be used. The dictionary typically specifies parameters to be given to the template functions.

If a schema name is given then the text search template is created in the specified schema. Otherwise it is created in the current schema.

You must be a superuser to use CREATE TEXT SEARCH TEMPLATE. This restriction is made because an erroneous text search template definition could confuse or even crash the server. The reason for separating templates from dictionaries is that a template encapsulates the "unsafe" aspects of defining a dictionary. The parameters that can be set when defining a dictionary are safe for unprivileged users to set, and so creating a dictionary need not be a privileged operation.

Refer to Chapter 12 for further information.

Parameters

name

>   The name of the text search template to be created. The name can be schema-qualified.

init_function

>   The name of the init function for the template.

lexize_function

>   The name of the lexize function for the template.

The function names can be schema-qualified if necessary. Argument types are not given, since the argument list for each type of function is predetermined. The lexize function is required, but the init function is optional.

The arguments can appear in any order, not only the one shown above.

Compatibility

There is no CREATE TEXT SEARCH TEMPLATE statement in the SQL standard.

See Also

ALTER TEXT SEARCH TEMPLATE, DROP TEXT SEARCH TEMPLATE

CREATE TRANSFORM

CREATE TRANSFORM — define a new transform

Synopsis

```
CREATE [ OR REPLACE ] TRANSFORM FOR type_name LANGUAGE lang_name (
    FROM SQL WITH FUNCTION from_sql_function_name [ (argument_type
[, ...]) ],
    TO SQL WITH FUNCTION to_sql_function_name [ (argument_type
[, ...]) ]
);
```

Description

CREATE TRANSFORM defines a new transform. CREATE OR REPLACE TRANSFORM will either create a new transform, or replace an existing definition.

A transform specifies how to adapt a data type to a procedural language. For example, when writing a function in PL/Python using the hstore type, PL/Python has no prior knowledge how to present hstore values in the Python environment. Language implementations usually default to using the text representation, but that is inconvenient when, for example, an associative array or a list would be more appropriate.

A transform specifies two functions:

- A "from SQL" function that converts the type from the SQL environment to the language. This function will be invoked on the arguments of a function written in the language.

- A "to SQL" function that converts the type from the language to the SQL environment. This function will be invoked on the return value of a function written in the language.

It is not necessary to provide both of these functions. If one is not specified, the language-specific default behavior will be used if necessary. (To prevent a transformation in a certain direction from happening at all, you could also write a transform function that always errors out.)

To be able to create a transform, you must own and have USAGE privilege on the type, have USAGE privilege on the language, and own and have EXECUTE privilege on the from-SQL and to-SQL functions, if specified.

Parameters

type_name

The name of the data type of the transform.

lang_name

The name of the language of the transform.

from_sql_function_name[(argument_type [, ...])]

The name of the function for converting the type from the SQL environment to the language. It must take one argument of type internal and return type internal. The actual argument will be of the type for the transform, and the function should be coded as if it were. (But it is not allowed to declare an SQL-level function returning internal without at least one argument of type internal.) The actual return value will be something specific to the language implementation. If no argument list is specified, the function name must be unique in its schema.

to_sql_function_name[(argument_type [, ...])]

The name of the function for converting the type from the language to the SQL environment. It must take one argument of type internal and return the type that is the type for the transform. The actual argument value will be something specific to the language implementation. If no argument list is specified, the function name must be unique in its schema.

Notes

Use DROP TRANSFORM to remove transforms.

Examples

To create a transform for type hstore and language plpythonu, first set up the type and the language:

```
CREATE TYPE hstore ...;

CREATE EXTENSION plpythonu;
```

Then create the necessary functions:

```
CREATE FUNCTION hstore_to_plpython(val internal) RETURNS internal
LANGUAGE C STRICT IMMUTABLE
AS ...;

CREATE FUNCTION plpython_to_hstore(val internal) RETURNS hstore
LANGUAGE C STRICT IMMUTABLE
AS ...;
```

And finally create the transform to connect them all together:

```
CREATE TRANSFORM FOR hstore LANGUAGE plpythonu (
    FROM SQL WITH FUNCTION hstore_to_plpython(internal),
    TO SQL WITH FUNCTION plpython_to_hstore(internal)
);
```

In practice, these commands would be wrapped up in an extension.

The contrib section contains a number of extensions that provide transforms, which can serve as real-world examples.

Compatibility

This form of CREATE TRANSFORM is a PostgreSQL extension. There is a CREATE TRANSFORM command in the SQL standard, but it is for adapting data types to client languages. That usage is not supported by PostgreSQL.

See Also

CREATE FUNCTION, CREATE LANGUAGE, CREATE TYPE, DROP TRANSFORM

CREATE TRIGGER

CREATE TRIGGER — define a new trigger

Synopsis

```
CREATE [ CONSTRAINT ] TRIGGER name { BEFORE | AFTER | INSTEAD OF }
{ event [ OR ... ] }
    ON table_name
    [ FROM referenced_table_name ]
    [ NOT DEFERRABLE | [ DEFERRABLE ] [ INITIALLY IMMEDIATE |
INITIALLY DEFERRED ] ]
    [ REFERENCING { { OLD | NEW } TABLE
[ AS ] transition_relation_name } [ ... ] ]
    [ FOR [ EACH ] { ROW | STATEMENT } ]
    [ WHEN ( condition ) ]
    EXECUTE { FUNCTION | PROCEDURE } function_name ( arguments )
```

where event can be one of:

```
INSERT
UPDATE [ OF column_name [, ... ] ]
DELETE
TRUNCATE
```

Description

CREATE TRIGGER creates a new trigger. The trigger will be associated with the specified table, view, or foreign table and will execute the specified function function_name when certain operations are performed on that table.

The trigger can be specified to fire before the operation is attempted on a row (before constraints are checked and the INSERT, UPDATE, or DELETE is attempted); or after the operation has completed (after constraints are checked and the INSERT, UPDATE, or DELETE has completed); or instead of the operation (in the case of inserts, updates or deletes on a view). If the trigger fires before or instead of the event, the trigger can skip the operation for the current row, or change the row being inserted (for INSERT and UPDATE operations only). If the trigger fires after the event, all changes, including the effects of other triggers, are "visible" to the trigger.

A trigger that is marked FOR EACH ROW is called once for every row that the operation modifies. For example, a DELETE that affects 10 rows will cause any ON DELETE triggers on the target relation to be called 10 separate times, once for each deleted row. In contrast, a trigger that is marked FOR EACH STATEMENT only executes once for any given operation, regardless of how many rows it modifies (in particular, an operation that modifies zero rows will still result in the execution of any applicable FOR EACH STATEMENT triggers).

Triggers that are specified to fire INSTEAD OF the trigger event must be marked FOR EACH ROW, and can only be defined on views. BEFORE and AFTER triggers on a view must be marked as FOR EACH STATEMENT.

In addition, triggers may be defined to fire for TRUNCATE, though only FOR EACH STATEMENT.

The following table summarizes which types of triggers may be used on tables, views, and foreign tables:

When	Event	Row-level	Statement-level
BEFORE	INSERT/UP-DATE/DELETE	Tables and foreign tables	Tables, views, and foreign tables
	TRUNCATE	—	Tables
AFTER	INSERT/UP-DATE/DELETE	Tables and foreign tables	Tables, views, and foreign tables
	TRUNCATE	—	Tables
INSTEAD OF	INSERT/UP-DATE/DELETE	Views	—
	TRUNCATE	—	—

Also, a trigger definition can specify a Boolean WHEN condition, which will be tested to see whether the trigger should be fired. In row-level triggers the WHEN condition can examine the old and/or new values of columns of the row. Statement-level triggers can also have WHEN conditions, although the feature is not so useful for them since the condition cannot refer to any values in the table.

If multiple triggers of the same kind are defined for the same event, they will be fired in alphabetical order by name.

When the CONSTRAINT option is specified, this command creates a *constraint trigger*. This is the same as a regular trigger except that the timing of the trigger firing can be adjusted using SET CONSTRAINTS. Constraint triggers must be AFTER ROW triggers on plain tables (not foreign tables). They can be fired either at the end of the statement causing the triggering event, or at the end of the containing transaction; in the latter case they are said to be *deferred*. A pending deferred-trigger firing can also be forced to happen immediately by using SET CONSTRAINTS. Constraint triggers are expected to raise an exception when the constraints they implement are violated.

The REFERENCING option enables collection of *transition relations*, which are row sets that include all of the rows inserted, deleted, or modified by the current SQL statement. This feature lets the trigger see a global view of what the statement did, not just one row at a time. This option is only allowed for an AFTER trigger that is not a constraint trigger; also, if the trigger is an UPDATE trigger, it must not specify a *column_name* list. OLD TABLE may only be specified once, and only for a trigger that can fire on UPDATE or DELETE; it creates a transition relation containing the *before-images* of all rows updated or deleted by the statement. Similarly, NEW TABLE may only be specified once, and only for a trigger that can fire on UPDATE or INSERT; it creates a transition relation containing the *after-images* of all rows updated or inserted by the statement.

SELECT does not modify any rows so you cannot create SELECT triggers. Rules and views may provide workable solutions to problems that seem to need SELECT triggers.

Refer to Chapter 39 for more information about triggers.

Parameters

name

> The name to give the new trigger. This must be distinct from the name of any other trigger for the same table. The name cannot be schema-qualified — the trigger inherits the schema of its table. For a constraint trigger, this is also the name to use when modifying the trigger's behavior using SET CONSTRAINTS.

BEFORE
AFTER
INSTEAD OF

Determines whether the function is called before, after, or instead of the event. A constraint trigger can only be specified as AFTER.

event

One of INSERT, UPDATE, DELETE, or TRUNCATE; this specifies the event that will fire the trigger. Multiple events can be specified using OR, except when transition relations are requested.

For UPDATE events, it is possible to specify a list of columns using this syntax:

UPDATE OF *column_name1* [, *column_name2* ...]

The trigger will only fire if at least one of the listed columns is mentioned as a target of the UPDATE command.

INSTEAD OF UPDATE events do not allow a list of columns. A column list cannot be specified when requesting transition relations, either.

table_name

The name (optionally schema-qualified) of the table, view, or foreign table the trigger is for.

referenced_table_name

The (possibly schema-qualified) name of another table referenced by the constraint. This option is used for foreign-key constraints and is not recommended for general use. This can only be specified for constraint triggers.

DEFERRABLE
NOT DEFERRABLE
INITIALLY IMMEDIATE
INITIALLY DEFERRED

The default timing of the trigger. See the CREATE TABLE documentation for details of these constraint options. This can only be specified for constraint triggers.

REFERENCING

This keyword immediately precedes the declaration of one or two relation names that provide access to the transition relations of the triggering statement.

OLD TABLE
NEW TABLE

This clause indicates whether the following relation name is for the before-image transition relation or the after-image transition relation.

transition_relation_name

The (unqualified) name to be used within the trigger for this transition relation.

```
FOR EACH ROW
FOR EACH STATEMENT
```

This specifies whether the trigger function should be fired once for every row affected by the trigger event, or just once per SQL statement. If neither is specified, FOR EACH STATEMENT is the default. Constraint triggers can only be specified FOR EACH ROW.

condition

A Boolean expression that determines whether the trigger function will actually be executed. If WHEN is specified, the function will only be called if the *condition* returns true. In FOR EACH ROW triggers, the WHEN condition can refer to columns of the old and/or new row values by writing OLD.*column_name* or NEW.*column_name* respectively. Of course, INSERT triggers cannot refer to OLD and DELETE triggers cannot refer to NEW.

INSTEAD OF triggers do not support WHEN conditions.

Currently, WHEN expressions cannot contain subqueries.

Note that for constraint triggers, evaluation of the WHEN condition is not deferred, but occurs immediately after the row update operation is performed. If the condition does not evaluate to true then the trigger is not queued for deferred execution.

function_name

A user-supplied function that is declared as taking no arguments and returning type trigger, which is executed when the trigger fires.

In the syntax of CREATE TRIGGER, the keywords FUNCTION and PROCEDURE are equivalent, but the referenced function must in any case be a function, not a procedure. The use of the keyword PROCEDURE here is historical and deprecated.

arguments

An optional comma-separated list of arguments to be provided to the function when the trigger is executed. The arguments are literal string constants. Simple names and numeric constants can be written here, too, but they will all be converted to strings. Please check the description of the implementation language of the trigger function to find out how these arguments can be accessed within the function; it might be different from normal function arguments.

Notes

To create a trigger on a table, the user must have the TRIGGER privilege on the table. The user must also have EXECUTE privilege on the trigger function.

Use DROP TRIGGER to remove a trigger.

A column-specific trigger (one defined using the UPDATE OF *column_name* syntax) will fire when any of its columns are listed as targets in the UPDATE command's SET list. It is possible for a column's value to change even when the trigger is not fired, because changes made to the row's contents by BEFORE UPDATE triggers are not considered. Conversely, a command such as UPDATE ... SET x = x ... will fire a trigger on column x, even though the column's value did not change.

In a BEFORE trigger, the WHEN condition is evaluated just before the function is or would be executed, so using WHEN is not materially different from testing the same condition at the beginning of the trigger function. Note in particular that the NEW row seen by the condition is the current value, as possibly modified by earlier triggers. Also, a BEFORE trigger's WHEN condition is not allowed to examine the system columns of the NEW row (such as oid), because those won't have been set yet.

In an AFTER trigger, the WHEN condition is evaluated just after the row update occurs, and it determines whether an event is queued to fire the trigger at the end of statement. So when an AFTER trigger's WHEN condition does not return true, it is not necessary to queue an event nor to re-fetch the row at end of statement. This can result in significant speedups in statements that modify many rows, if the trigger only needs to be fired for a few of the rows.

In some cases it is possible for a single SQL command to fire more than one kind of trigger. For instance an INSERT with an ON CONFLICT DO UPDATE clause may cause both insert and update operations, so it will fire both kinds of triggers as needed. The transition relations supplied to triggers are specific to their event type; thus an INSERT trigger will see only the inserted rows, while an UPDATE trigger will see only the updated rows.

Row updates or deletions caused by foreign-key enforcement actions, such as ON UPDATE CASCADE or ON DELETE SET NULL, are treated as part of the SQL command that caused them (note that such actions are never deferred). Relevant triggers on the affected table will be fired, so that this provides another way in which a SQL command might fire triggers not directly matching its type. In simple cases, triggers that request transition relations will see all changes caused in their table by a single original SQL command as a single transition relation. However, there are cases in which the presence of an AFTER ROW trigger that requests transition relations will cause the foreign-key enforcement actions triggered by a single SQL command to be split into multiple steps, each with its own transition relation(s). In such cases, any statement-level triggers that are present will be fired once per creation of a transition relation set, ensuring that the triggers see each affected row in a transition relation once and only once.

Statement-level triggers on a view are fired only if the action on the view is handled by a row-level INSTEAD OF trigger. If the action is handled by an INSTEAD rule, then whatever statements are emitted by the rule are executed in place of the original statement naming the view, so that the triggers that will be fired are those on tables named in the replacement statements. Similarly, if the view is automatically updatable, then the action is handled by automatically rewriting the statement into an action on the view's base table, so that the base table's statement-level triggers are the ones that are fired.

Creating a row-level trigger on a partitioned table will cause identical triggers to be created in all its existing partitions; and any partitions created or attached later will contain an identical trigger, too. Triggers on partitioned tables may only be AFTER.

Modifying a partitioned table or a table with inheritance children fires statement-level triggers attached to the explicitly named table, but not statement-level triggers for its partitions or child tables. In contrast, row-level triggers are fired on the rows in affected partitions or child tables, even if they are not explicitly named in the query. If a statement-level trigger has been defined with transition relations named by a REFERENCING clause, then before and after images of rows are visible from all affected partitions or child tables. In the case of inheritance children, the row images include only columns that are present in the table that the trigger is attached to. Currently, row-level triggers with transition relations cannot be defined on partitions or inheritance child tables.

In PostgreSQL versions before 7.3, it was necessary to declare trigger functions as returning the place-holder type opaque, rather than trigger. To support loading of old dump files, CREATE TRIGGER will accept a function declared as returning opaque, but it will issue a notice and change the function's declared return type to trigger.

Examples

Execute the function check_account_update whenever a row of the table accounts is about to be updated:

```
CREATE TRIGGER check_update
    BEFORE UPDATE ON accounts
    FOR EACH ROW
    EXECUTE FUNCTION check_account_update();
```

The same, but only execute the function if column `balance` is specified as a target in the `UPDATE` command:

```
CREATE TRIGGER check_update
    BEFORE UPDATE OF balance ON accounts
    FOR EACH ROW
    EXECUTE FUNCTION check_account_update();
```

This form only executes the function if column `balance` has in fact changed value:

```
CREATE TRIGGER check_update
    BEFORE UPDATE ON accounts
    FOR EACH ROW
    WHEN (OLD.balance IS DISTINCT FROM NEW.balance)
    EXECUTE FUNCTION check_account_update();
```

Call a function to log updates of `accounts`, but only if something changed:

```
CREATE TRIGGER log_update
    AFTER UPDATE ON accounts
    FOR EACH ROW
    WHEN (OLD.* IS DISTINCT FROM NEW.*)
    EXECUTE FUNCTION log_account_update();
```

Execute the function `view_insert_row` for each row to insert rows into the tables underlying a view:

```
CREATE TRIGGER view_insert
    INSTEAD OF INSERT ON my_view
    FOR EACH ROW
    EXECUTE FUNCTION view_insert_row();
```

Execute the function `check_transfer_balances_to_zero` for each statement to confirm that the `transfer` rows offset to a net of zero:

```
CREATE TRIGGER transfer_insert
    AFTER INSERT ON transfer
    REFERENCING NEW TABLE AS inserted
    FOR EACH STATEMENT
    EXECUTE FUNCTION check_transfer_balances_to_zero();
```

Execute the function `check_matching_pairs` for each row to confirm that changes are made to matching pairs at the same time (by the same statement):

```
CREATE TRIGGER paired_items_update
```

```
AFTER UPDATE ON paired_items
REFERENCING NEW TABLE AS newtab OLD TABLE AS oldtab
FOR EACH ROW
EXECUTE FUNCTION check_matching_pairs();
```

Section 39.4 contains a complete example of a trigger function written in C.

Compatibility

The `CREATE TRIGGER` statement in PostgreSQL implements a subset of the SQL standard. The following functionalities are currently missing:

- While transition table names for `AFTER` triggers are specified using the `REFERENCING` clause in the standard way, the row variables used in `FOR EACH ROW` triggers may not be specified in a `REFERENCING` clause. They are available in a manner that is dependent on the language in which the trigger function is written, but is fixed for any one language. Some languages effectively behave as though there is a `REFERENCING` clause containing `OLD ROW AS OLD NEW ROW AS NEW`.

- The standard allows transition tables to be used with column-specific `UPDATE` triggers, but then the set of rows that should be visible in the transition tables depends on the trigger's column list. This is not currently implemented by PostgreSQL.

- PostgreSQL only allows the execution of a user-defined function for the triggered action. The standard allows the execution of a number of other SQL commands, such as `CREATE TABLE`, as the triggered action. This limitation is not hard to work around by creating a user-defined function that executes the desired commands.

SQL specifies that multiple triggers should be fired in time-of-creation order. PostgreSQL uses name order, which was judged to be more convenient.

SQL specifies that `BEFORE DELETE` triggers on cascaded deletes fire *after* the cascaded `DELETE` completes. The PostgreSQL behavior is for `BEFORE DELETE` to always fire before the delete action, even a cascading one. This is considered more consistent. There is also nonstandard behavior if `BEFORE` triggers modify rows or prevent updates during an update that is caused by a referential action. This can lead to constraint violations or stored data that does not honor the referential constraint.

The ability to specify multiple actions for a single trigger using `OR` is a PostgreSQL extension of the SQL standard.

The ability to fire triggers for `TRUNCATE` is a PostgreSQL extension of the SQL standard, as is the ability to define statement-level triggers on views.

`CREATE CONSTRAINT TRIGGER` is a PostgreSQL extension of the SQL standard.

See Also

ALTER TRIGGER, DROP TRIGGER, CREATE FUNCTION, SET CONSTRAINTS

CREATE TYPE

CREATE TYPE — define a new data type

Synopsis

```
CREATE TYPE name AS
    ( [ attribute_name data_type [ COLLATE collation ] [, ... ] ] )

CREATE TYPE name AS ENUM
    ( [ 'label' [, ... ] ] )

CREATE TYPE name AS RANGE (
    SUBTYPE = subtype
    [ , SUBTYPE_OPCLASS = subtype_operator_class ]
    [ , COLLATION = collation ]
    [ , CANONICAL = canonical_function ]
    [ , SUBTYPE_DIFF = subtype_diff_function ]
)

CREATE TYPE name (
    INPUT = input_function,
    OUTPUT = output_function
    [ , RECEIVE = receive_function ]
    [ , SEND = send_function ]
    [ , TYPMOD_IN = type_modifier_input_function ]
    [ , TYPMOD_OUT = type_modifier_output_function ]
    [ , ANALYZE = analyze_function ]
    [ , INTERNALLENGTH = { internallength | VARIABLE } ]
    [ , PASSEDBYVALUE ]
    [ , ALIGNMENT = alignment ]
    [ , STORAGE = storage ]
    [ , LIKE = like_type ]
    [ , CATEGORY = category ]
    [ , PREFERRED = preferred ]
    [ , DEFAULT = default ]
    [ , ELEMENT = element ]
    [ , DELIMITER = delimiter ]
    [ , COLLATABLE = collatable ]
)

CREATE TYPE name
```

Description

CREATE TYPE registers a new data type for use in the current database. The user who defines a type becomes its owner.

If a schema name is given then the type is created in the specified schema. Otherwise it is created in the current schema. The type name must be distinct from the name of any existing type or domain in the same schema. (Because tables have associated data types, the type name must also be distinct from the name of any existing table in the same schema.)

There are five forms of CREATE TYPE, as shown in the syntax synopsis above. They respectively create a *composite type*, an *enum type*, a *range type*, a *base type*, or a *shell type*. The first four of these are discussed in turn below. A shell type is simply a placeholder for a type to be defined later; it is created by issuing CREATE TYPE with no parameters except for the type name. Shell types are needed as forward references when creating range types and base types, as discussed in those sections.

Composite Types

The first form of CREATE TYPE creates a composite type. The composite type is specified by a list of attribute names and data types. An attribute's collation can be specified too, if its data type is collatable. A composite type is essentially the same as the row type of a table, but using CREATE TYPE avoids the need to create an actual table when all that is wanted is to define a type. A stand-alone composite type is useful, for example, as the argument or return type of a function.

To be able to create a composite type, you must have USAGE privilege on all attribute types.

Enumerated Types

The second form of CREATE TYPE creates an enumerated (enum) type, as described in Section 8.7. Enum types take a list of quoted labels, each of which must be less than NAMEDATALEN bytes long (64 bytes in a standard PostgreSQL build). (It is possible to create an enumerated type with zero labels, but such a type cannot be used to hold values before at least one label is added using ALTER TYPE.)

Range Types

The third form of CREATE TYPE creates a new range type, as described in Section 8.17.

The range type's *subtype* can be any type with an associated b-tree operator class (to determine the ordering of values for the range type). Normally the subtype's default b-tree operator class is used to determine ordering; to use a non-default operator class, specify its name with *subtype_opclass*. If the subtype is collatable, and you want to use a non-default collation in the range's ordering, specify the desired collation with the *collation* option.

The optional *canonical* function must take one argument of the range type being defined, and return a value of the same type. This is used to convert range values to a canonical form, when applicable. See Section 8.17.8 for more information. Creating a *canonical* function is a bit tricky, since it must be defined before the range type can be declared. To do this, you must first create a shell type, which is a placeholder type that has no properties except a name and an owner. This is done by issuing the command CREATE TYPE *name*, with no additional parameters. Then the function can be declared using the shell type as argument and result, and finally the range type can be declared using the same name. This automatically replaces the shell type entry with a valid range type.

The optional *subtype_diff* function must take two values of the *subtype* type as argument, and return a double precision value representing the difference between the two given values. While this is optional, providing it allows much greater efficiency of GiST indexes on columns of the range type. See Section 8.17.8 for more information.

Base Types

The fourth form of CREATE TYPE creates a new base type (scalar type). To create a new base type, you must be a superuser. (This restriction is made because an erroneous type definition could confuse or even crash the server.)

The parameters can appear in any order, not only that illustrated above, and most are optional. You must register two or more functions (using CREATE FUNCTION) before defining the type. The support functions *input_function* and *output_function* are required, while the functions *receive_function*, *send_function*, *type_modifier_input_function*, *type_modifier_output_function* and *analyze_function* are optional. Generally these functions have to be coded in C or another low-level language.

The *input_function* converts the type's external textual representation to the internal representation used by the operators and functions defined for the type. *output_function* performs the reverse transformation. The input function can be declared as taking one argument of type cstring, or as taking three arguments of types cstring, oid, integer. The first argument is the input text as a C string, the second argument is the type's own OID (except for array types, which instead receive their element type's OID), and the third is the typmod of the destination column, if known (-1 will be passed if not). The input function must return a value of the data type itself. Usually, an input function should be declared STRICT; if it is not, it will be called with a NULL first parameter when reading a NULL input value. The function must still return NULL in this case, unless it raises an error. (This case is mainly meant to support domain input functions, which might need to reject NULL inputs.) The output function must be declared as taking one argument of the new data type. The output function must return type cstring. Output functions are not invoked for NULL values.

The optional *receive_function* converts the type's external binary representation to the internal representation. If this function is not supplied, the type cannot participate in binary input. The binary representation should be chosen to be cheap to convert to internal form, while being reasonably portable. (For example, the standard integer data types use network byte order as the external binary representation, while the internal representation is in the machine's native byte order.) The receive function should perform adequate checking to ensure that the value is valid. The receive function can be declared as taking one argument of type internal, or as taking three arguments of types internal, oid, integer. The first argument is a pointer to a StringInfo buffer holding the received byte string; the optional arguments are the same as for the text input function. The receive function must return a value of the data type itself. Usually, a receive function should be declared STRICT; if it is not, it will be called with a NULL first parameter when reading a NULL input value. The function must still return NULL in this case, unless it raises an error. (This case is mainly meant to support domain receive functions, which might need to reject NULL inputs.) Similarly, the optional *send_function* converts from the internal representation to the external binary representation. If this function is not supplied, the type cannot participate in binary output. The send function must be declared as taking one argument of the new data type. The send function must return type bytea. Send functions are not invoked for NULL values.

You should at this point be wondering how the input and output functions can be declared to have results or arguments of the new type, when they have to be created before the new type can be created. The answer is that the type should first be defined as a *shell type*, which is a placeholder type that has no properties except a name and an owner. This is done by issuing the command CREATE TYPE *name*, with no additional parameters. Then the C I/O functions can be defined referencing the shell type. Finally, CREATE TYPE with a full definition replaces the shell entry with a complete, valid type definition, after which the new type can be used normally.

The optional *type_modifier_input_function* and *type_modifier_output_function* are needed if the type supports modifiers, that is optional constraints attached to a type declaration, such as char(5) or numeric(30,2). PostgreSQL allows user-defined types to take one or more simple constants or identifiers as modifiers. However, this information must be capable of being packed into a single non-negative integer value for storage in the system catalogs. The *type_modifier_input_function* is passed the declared modifier(s) in the form of a cstring array. It must check the values for validity (throwing an error if they are wrong), and if they are correct, return a single non-negative integer value that will be stored as the column "typmod". Type modifiers will be rejected if the type does not have a *type_modifier_input_function*. The *type_modifier_output_function* converts the internal integer typmod value back to the correct form for user display. It must return a cstring value that is the exact string to append to the type name; for example numeric's function might return (30,2). It is allowed to omit the *type_modifier_output_function*, in which case the default display format is just the stored typmod integer value enclosed in parentheses.

The optional *analyze_function* performs type-specific statistics collection for columns of the data type. By default, ANALYZE will attempt to gather statistics using the type's "equals" and "less-than" operators, if there is a default b-tree operator class for the type. For non-scalar types this behavior is likely to be unsuitable, so it can be overridden by specifying a custom analysis function. The analysis function must be declared to take a single argument of type internal, and return a boolean result. The detailed API for analysis functions appears in src/include/commands/vacuum.h.

While the details of the new type's internal representation are only known to the I/O functions and other functions you create to work with the type, there are several properties of the internal representation that must be declared to PostgreSQL. Foremost of these is *internallength*. Base data types can be fixed-length, in which case *internallength* is a positive integer, or variable-length, indicated by setting *internallength* to VARIABLE. (Internally, this is represented by setting typlen to -1.) The internal representation of all variable-length types must start with a 4-byte integer giving the total length of this value of the type. (Note that the length field is often encoded, as described in Section 68.2; it's unwise to access it directly.)

The optional flag PASSEDBYVALUE indicates that values of this data type are passed by value, rather than by reference. Types passed by value must be fixed-length, and their internal representation cannot be larger than the size of the Datum type (4 bytes on some machines, 8 bytes on others).

The *alignment* parameter specifies the storage alignment required for the data type. The allowed values equate to alignment on 1, 2, 4, or 8 byte boundaries. Note that variable-length types must have an alignment of at least 4, since they necessarily contain an int4 as their first component.

The *storage* parameter allows selection of storage strategies for variable-length data types. (Only plain is allowed for fixed-length types.) plain specifies that data of the type will always be stored in-line and not compressed. extended specifies that the system will first try to compress a long data value, and will move the value out of the main table row if it's still too long. external allows the value to be moved out of the main table, but the system will not try to compress it. main allows compression, but discourages moving the value out of the main table. (Data items with this storage strategy might still be moved out of the main table if there is no other way to make a row fit, but they will be kept in the main table preferentially over extended and external items.)

All *storage* values other than plain imply that the functions of the data type can handle values that have been *toasted*, as described in Section 68.2 and Section 38.12.1. The specific other value given merely determines the default TOAST storage strategy for columns of a toastable data type; users can pick other strategies for individual columns using ALTER TABLE SET STORAGE.

The *like_type* parameter provides an alternative method for specifying the basic representation properties of a data type: copy them from some existing type. The values of *internallength*, *passedbyvalue*, *alignment*, and *storage* are copied from the named type. (It is possible, though usually undesirable, to override some of these values by specifying them along with the LIKE clause.) Specifying representation this way is especially useful when the low-level implementation of the new type "piggy-backs" on an existing type in some fashion.

The *category* and *preferred* parameters can be used to help control which implicit cast will be applied in ambiguous situations. Each data type belongs to a category named by a single ASCII character, and each type is either "preferred" or not within its category. The parser will prefer casting to preferred types (but only from other types within the same category) when this rule is helpful in resolving overloaded functions or operators. For more details see Chapter 10. For types that have no implicit casts to or from any other types, it is sufficient to leave these settings at the defaults. However, for a group of related types that have implicit casts, it is often helpful to mark them all as belonging to a category and select one or two of the "most general" types as being preferred within the category. The *category* parameter is especially useful when adding a user-defined type to an existing built-in category, such as the numeric or string types. However, it is also possible to create new entirely-user-defined type categories. Select any ASCII character other than an upper-case letter to name such a category.

A default value can be specified, in case a user wants columns of the data type to default to something other than the null value. Specify the default with the `DEFAULT` key word. (Such a default can be overridden by an explicit `DEFAULT` clause attached to a particular column.)

To indicate that a type is an array, specify the type of the array elements using the `ELEMENT` key word. For example, to define an array of 4-byte integers (`int4`), specify `ELEMENT = int4`. More details about array types appear below.

To indicate the delimiter to be used between values in the external representation of arrays of this type, *delimiter* can be set to a specific character. The default delimiter is the comma (`,`). Note that the delimiter is associated with the array element type, not the array type itself.

If the optional Boolean parameter *collatable* is true, column definitions and expressions of the type may carry collation information through use of the `COLLATE` clause. It is up to the implementations of the functions operating on the type to actually make use of the collation information; this does not happen automatically merely by marking the type collatable.

Array Types

Whenever a user-defined type is created, PostgreSQL automatically creates an associated array type, whose name consists of the element type's name prepended with an underscore, and truncated if necessary to keep it less than `NAMEDATALEN` bytes long. (If the name so generated collides with an existing type name, the process is repeated until a non-colliding name is found.) This implicitly-created array type is variable length and uses the built-in input and output functions `array_in` and `array_out`. The array type tracks any changes in its element type's owner or schema, and is dropped if the element type is.

You might reasonably ask why there is an `ELEMENT` option, if the system makes the correct array type automatically. The only case where it's useful to use `ELEMENT` is when you are making a fixed-length type that happens to be internally an array of a number of identical things, and you want to allow these things to be accessed directly by subscripting, in addition to whatever operations you plan to provide for the type as a whole. For example, type `point` is represented as just two floating-point numbers, which can be accessed using `point[0]` and `point[1]`. Note that this facility only works for fixed-length types whose internal form is exactly a sequence of identical fixed-length fields. A subscriptable variable-length type must have the generalized internal representation used by `array_in` and `array_out`. For historical reasons (i.e., this is clearly wrong but it's far too late to change it), subscripting of fixed-length array types starts from zero, rather than from one as for variable-length arrays.

Parameters

name

> The name (optionally schema-qualified) of a type to be created.

attribute_name

> The name of an attribute (column) for the composite type.

data_type

> The name of an existing data type to become a column of the composite type.

collation

> The name of an existing collation to be associated with a column of a composite type, or with a range type.

label

> A string literal representing the textual label associated with one value of an enum type.

subtype

> The name of the element type that the range type will represent ranges of.

subtype_operator_class

> The name of a b-tree operator class for the subtype.

canonical_function

> The name of the canonicalization function for the range type.

subtype_diff_function

> The name of a difference function for the subtype.

input_function

> The name of a function that converts data from the type's external textual form to its internal form.

output_function

> The name of a function that converts data from the type's internal form to its external textual form.

receive_function

> The name of a function that converts data from the type's external binary form to its internal form.

send_function

> The name of a function that converts data from the type's internal form to its external binary form.

type_modifier_input_function

> The name of a function that converts an array of modifier(s) for the type into internal form.

type_modifier_output_function

> The name of a function that converts the internal form of the type's modifier(s) to external textual form.

analyze_function

> The name of a function that performs statistical analysis for the data type.

internallength

> A numeric constant that specifies the length in bytes of the new type's internal representation. The default assumption is that it is variable-length.

alignment

> The storage alignment requirement of the data type. If specified, it must be char, int2, int4, or double; the default is int4.

storage

> The storage strategy for the data type. If specified, must be plain, external, extended, or main; the default is plain.

like_type

> The name of an existing data type that the new type will have the same representation as. The values of *internallength*, *passedbyvalue*, *alignment*, and *storage* are copied from that type, unless overridden by explicit specification elsewhere in this CREATE TYPE command.

category

> The category code (a single ASCII character) for this type. The default is 'U' for "user-defined type". Other standard category codes can be found in Table 52.63. You may also choose other ASCII characters in order to create custom categories.

preferred

> True if this type is a preferred type within its type category, else false. The default is false. Be very careful about creating a new preferred type within an existing type category, as this could cause surprising changes in behavior.

default

> The default value for the data type. If this is omitted, the default is null.

element

> The type being created is an array; this specifies the type of the array elements.

delimiter

> The delimiter character to be used between values in arrays made of this type.

collatable

> True if this type's operations can use collation information. The default is false.

Notes

Because there are no restrictions on use of a data type once it's been created, creating a base type or range type is tantamount to granting public execute permission on the functions mentioned in the type definition. This is usually not an issue for the sorts of functions that are useful in a type definition. But you might want to think twice before designing a type in a way that would require "secret" information to be used while converting it to or from external form.

Before PostgreSQL version 8.3, the name of a generated array type was always exactly the element type's name with one underscore character (_) prepended. (Type names were therefore restricted in length to one less character than other names.) While this is still usually the case, the array type name may vary from this in case of maximum-length names or collisions with user type names that begin with underscore.

Writing code that depends on this convention is therefore deprecated. Instead, use `pg_type.typarray` to locate the array type associated with a given type.

It may be advisable to avoid using type and table names that begin with underscore. While the server will change generated array type names to avoid collisions with user-given names, there is still risk of confusion, particularly with old client software that may assume that type names beginning with underscores always represent arrays.

Before PostgreSQL version 8.2, the shell-type creation syntax `CREATE TYPE` *name* did not exist. The way to create a new base type was to create its input function first. In this approach, PostgreSQL will first see the name of the new data type as the return type of the input function. The shell type is implicitly created in this situation, and then it can be referenced in the definitions of the remaining I/O functions. This approach still works, but is deprecated and might be disallowed in some future release. Also, to avoid accidentally cluttering the catalogs with shell types as a result of simple typos in function definitions, a shell type will only be made this way when the input function is written in C.

In PostgreSQL versions before 7.3, it was customary to avoid creating a shell type at all, by replacing the functions' forward references to the type name with the placeholder pseudo-type `opaque`. The `cstring` arguments and results also had to be declared as `opaque` before 7.3. To support loading of old dump files, `CREATE TYPE` will accept I/O functions declared using `opaque`, but it will issue a notice and change the function declarations to use the correct types.

Examples

This example creates a composite type and uses it in a function definition:

```
CREATE TYPE compfoo AS (f1 int, f2 text);

CREATE FUNCTION getfoo() RETURNS SETOF compfoo AS $$
    SELECT fooid, fooname FROM foo
$$ LANGUAGE SQL;
```

This example creates an enumerated type and uses it in a table definition:

```
CREATE TYPE bug_status AS ENUM ('new', 'open', 'closed');

CREATE TABLE bug (
    id serial,
    description text,
    status bug_status
);
```

This example creates a range type:

```
CREATE TYPE float8_range AS RANGE (subtype = float8, subtype_diff =
 float8mi);
```

This example creates the base data type **box** and then uses the type in a table definition:

```
CREATE TYPE box;
```

```
CREATE FUNCTION my_box_in_function(cstring) RETURNS box AS ... ;
CREATE FUNCTION my_box_out_function(box) RETURNS cstring AS ... ;

CREATE TYPE box (
    INTERNALLENGTH = 16,
    INPUT = my_box_in_function,
    OUTPUT = my_box_out_function
);

CREATE TABLE myboxes (
    id integer,
    description box
);
```

If the internal structure of box were an array of four float4 elements, we might instead use:

```
CREATE TYPE box (
    INTERNALLENGTH = 16,
    INPUT = my_box_in_function,
    OUTPUT = my_box_out_function,
    ELEMENT = float4
);
```

which would allow a box value's component numbers to be accessed by subscripting. Otherwise the type behaves the same as before.

This example creates a large object type and uses it in a table definition:

```
CREATE TYPE bigobj (
    INPUT = lo_filein, OUTPUT = lo_fileout,
    INTERNALLENGTH = VARIABLE
);
CREATE TABLE big_objs (
    id integer,
    obj bigobj
);
```

More examples, including suitable input and output functions, are in Section 38.12.

Compatibility

The first form of the CREATE TYPE command, which creates a composite type, conforms to the SQL standard. The other forms are PostgreSQL extensions. The CREATE TYPE statement in the SQL standard also defines other forms that are not implemented in PostgreSQL.

The ability to create a composite type with zero attributes is a PostgreSQL-specific deviation from the standard (analogous to the same case in CREATE TABLE).

See Also

ALTER TYPE, CREATE DOMAIN, CREATE FUNCTION, DROP TYPE

CREATE USER

CREATE USER — define a new database role

Synopsis

```
CREATE USER name [ [ WITH ] option [ ... ] ]

where option can be:

    SUPERUSER | NOSUPERUSER
  | CREATEDB | NOCREATEDB
  | CREATEROLE | NOCREATEROLE
  | INHERIT | NOINHERIT
  | LOGIN | NOLOGIN
  | REPLICATION | NOREPLICATION
  | BYPASSRLS | NOBYPASSRLS
  | CONNECTION LIMIT connlimit
  | [ ENCRYPTED ] PASSWORD 'password' | PASSWORD NULL
  | VALID UNTIL 'timestamp'
  | IN ROLE role_name [, ...]
  | IN GROUP role_name [, ...]
  | ROLE role_name [, ...]
  | ADMIN role_name [, ...]
  | USER role_name [, ...]
  | SYSID uid
```

Description

`CREATE USER` is now an alias for CREATE ROLE. The only difference is that when the command is spelled `CREATE USER`, `LOGIN` is assumed by default, whereas `NOLOGIN` is assumed when the command is spelled `CREATE ROLE`.

Compatibility

The `CREATE USER` statement is a PostgreSQL extension. The SQL standard leaves the definition of users to the implementation.

See Also

CREATE ROLE

CREATE USER MAPPING

CREATE USER MAPPING — define a new mapping of a user to a foreign server

Synopsis

```
CREATE USER MAPPING [ IF NOT EXISTS ] FOR { user_name | USER |
 CURRENT_USER | PUBLIC }
    SERVER server_name
    [ OPTIONS ( option 'value' [ , ... ] ) ]
```

Description

CREATE USER MAPPING defines a mapping of a user to a foreign server. A user mapping typically encapsulates connection information that a foreign-data wrapper uses together with the information encapsulated by a foreign server to access an external data resource.

The owner of a foreign server can create user mappings for that server for any user. Also, a user can create a user mapping for their own user name if USAGE privilege on the server has been granted to the user.

Parameters

IF NOT EXISTS

> Do not throw an error if a mapping of the given user to the given foreign server already exists. A notice is issued in this case. Note that there is no guarantee that the existing user mapping is anything like the one that would have been created.

user_name

> The name of an existing user that is mapped to foreign server. CURRENT_USER and USER match the name of the current user. When PUBLIC is specified, a so-called public mapping is created that is used when no user-specific mapping is applicable.

server_name

> The name of an existing server for which the user mapping is to be created.

OPTIONS (option 'value' [, ...])

> This clause specifies the options of the user mapping. The options typically define the actual user name and password of the mapping. Option names must be unique. The allowed option names and values are specific to the server's foreign-data wrapper.

Examples

Create a user mapping for user bob, server foo:

```
CREATE USER MAPPING FOR bob SERVER foo OPTIONS (user 'bob', password
 'secret');
```

Compatibility

`CREATE USER MAPPING` conforms to ISO/IEC 9075-9 (SQL/MED).

See Also

ALTER USER MAPPING, DROP USER MAPPING, CREATE FOREIGN DATA WRAPPER, CREATE SERVER

CREATE VIEW

CREATE VIEW — define a new view

Synopsis

```
CREATE [ OR REPLACE ] [ TEMP | TEMPORARY ] [ RECURSIVE ] VIEW name
  [ ( column_name [, ...] ) ]
    [ WITH ( view_option_name [= view_option_value] [, ... ] ) ]
    AS query
    [ WITH [ CASCADED | LOCAL ] CHECK OPTION ]
```

Description

CREATE VIEW defines a view of a query. The view is not physically materialized. Instead, the query is run every time the view is referenced in a query.

CREATE OR REPLACE VIEW is similar, but if a view of the same name already exists, it is replaced. The new query must generate the same columns that were generated by the existing view query (that is, the same column names in the same order and with the same data types), but it may add additional columns to the end of the list. The calculations giving rise to the output columns may be completely different.

If a schema name is given (for example, CREATE VIEW myschema.myview ...) then the view is created in the specified schema. Otherwise it is created in the current schema. Temporary views exist in a special schema, so a schema name cannot be given when creating a temporary view. The name of the view must be distinct from the name of any other view, table, sequence, index or foreign table in the same schema.

Parameters

TEMPORARY or TEMP

> If specified, the view is created as a temporary view. Temporary views are automatically dropped at the end of the current session. Existing permanent relations with the same name are not visible to the current session while the temporary view exists, unless they are referenced with schema-qualified names.

> If any of the tables referenced by the view are temporary, the view is created as a temporary view (whether TEMPORARY is specified or not).

RECURSIVE

> Creates a recursive view. The syntax

```
CREATE RECURSIVE VIEW [ schema . ] view_name (column_names) AS
  SELECT ...;
```

> is equivalent to

```
CREATE VIEW [ schema . ] view_name AS WITH RECURSIVE view_name
 (column_names) AS (SELECT ...) SELECT column_names FROM view_name;
```

A view column name list must be specified for a recursive view.

name

> The name (optionally schema-qualified) of a view to be created.

column_name

> An optional list of names to be used for columns of the view. If not given, the column names are deduced from the query.

WITH (*view_option_name* [= *view_option_value*] [, ...])

> This clause specifies optional parameters for a view; the following parameters are supported:

> check_option (string)

>> This parameter may be either local or cascaded, and is equivalent to specifying WITH [CASCADED | LOCAL] CHECK OPTION (see below). This option can be changed on existing views using ALTER VIEW.

> security_barrier (boolean)

>> This should be used if the view is intended to provide row-level security. See Section 41.5 for full details.

query

> A SELECT or VALUES command which will provide the columns and rows of the view.

WITH [CASCADED | LOCAL] CHECK OPTION

> This option controls the behavior of automatically updatable views. When this option is specified, INSERT and UPDATE commands on the view will be checked to ensure that new rows satisfy the view-defining condition (that is, the new rows are checked to ensure that they are visible through the view). If they are not, the update will be rejected. If the CHECK OPTION is not specified, INSERT and UPDATE commands on the view are allowed to create rows that are not visible through the view. The following check options are supported:

> LOCAL

>> New rows are only checked against the conditions defined directly in the view itself. Any conditions defined on underlying base views are not checked (unless they also specify the CHECK OPTION).

> CASCADED

>> New rows are checked against the conditions of the view and all underlying base views. If the CHECK OPTION is specified, and neither LOCAL nor CASCADED is specified, then CASCADED is assumed.

> The CHECK OPTION may not be used with RECURSIVE views.

> Note that the CHECK OPTION is only supported on views that are automatically updatable, and do not have INSTEAD OF triggers or INSTEAD rules. If an automatically updatable view is defined

on top of a base view that has INSTEAD OF triggers, then the LOCAL CHECK OPTION may be used to check the conditions on the automatically updatable view, but the conditions on the base view with INSTEAD OF triggers will not be checked (a cascaded check option will not cascade down to a trigger-updatable view, and any check options defined directly on a trigger-updatable view will be ignored). If the view or any of its base relations has an INSTEAD rule that causes the INSERT or UP-DATE command to be rewritten, then all check options will be ignored in the rewritten query, including any checks from automatically updatable views defined on top of the relation with the INSTEAD rule.

Notes

Use the DROP VIEW statement to drop views.

Be careful that the names and types of the view's columns will be assigned the way you want. For example:

```
CREATE VIEW vista AS SELECT 'Hello World';
```

is bad form because the column name defaults to ?column?; also, the column data type defaults to text, which might not be what you wanted. Better style for a string literal in a view's result is something like:

```
CREATE VIEW vista AS SELECT text 'Hello World' AS hello;
```

Access to tables referenced in the view is determined by permissions of the view owner. In some cases, this can be used to provide secure but restricted access to the underlying tables. However, not all views are secure against tampering; see Section 41.5 for details. Functions called in the view are treated the same as if they had been called directly from the query using the view. Therefore the user of a view must have permissions to call all functions used by the view.

When CREATE OR REPLACE VIEW is used on an existing view, only the view's defining SELECT rule is changed. Other view properties, including ownership, permissions, and non-SELECT rules, remain unchanged. You must own the view to replace it (this includes being a member of the owning role).

Updatable Views

Simple views are automatically updatable: the system will allow INSERT, UPDATE and DELETE statements to be used on the view in the same way as on a regular table. A view is automatically updatable if it satisfies all of the following conditions:

- The view must have exactly one entry in its FROM list, which must be a table or another updatable view.

- The view definition must not contain WITH, DISTINCT, GROUP BY, HAVING, LIMIT, or OFFSET clauses at the top level.

- The view definition must not contain set operations (UNION, INTERSECT or EXCEPT) at the top level.

- The view's select list must not contain any aggregates, window functions or set-returning functions.

An automatically updatable view may contain a mix of updatable and non-updatable columns. A column is updatable if it is a simple reference to an updatable column of the underlying base relation; otherwise the column is read-only, and an error will be raised if an INSERT or UPDATE statement attempts to assign a value to it.

If the view is automatically updatable the system will convert any INSERT, UPDATE or DELETE statement on the view into the corresponding statement on the underlying base relation. INSERT statements that have an ON CONFLICT UPDATE clause are fully supported.

If an automatically updatable view contains a WHERE condition, the condition restricts which rows of the base relation are available to be modified by UPDATE and DELETE statements on the view. However, an UPDATE is allowed to change a row so that it no longer satisfies the WHERE condition, and thus is no longer visible through the view. Similarly, an INSERT command can potentially insert base-relation rows that do not satisfy the WHERE condition and thus are not visible through the view (ON CONFLICT UPDATE may similarly affect an existing row not visible through the view). The CHECK OPTION may be used to prevent INSERT and UPDATE commands from creating such rows that are not visible through the view.

If an automatically updatable view is marked with the security_barrier property then all the view's WHERE conditions (and any conditions using operators which are marked as LEAKPROOF) will always be evaluated before any conditions that a user of the view has added. See Section 41.5 for full details. Note that, due to this, rows which are not ultimately returned (because they do not pass the user's WHERE conditions) may still end up being locked. EXPLAIN can be used to see which conditions are applied at the relation level (and therefore do not lock rows) and which are not.

A more complex view that does not satisfy all these conditions is read-only by default: the system will not allow an insert, update, or delete on the view. You can get the effect of an updatable view by creating INSTEAD OF triggers on the view, which must convert attempted inserts, etc. on the view into appropriate actions on other tables. For more information see CREATE TRIGGER. Another possibility is to create rules (see CREATE RULE), but in practice triggers are easier to understand and use correctly.

Note that the user performing the insert, update or delete on the view must have the corresponding insert, update or delete privilege on the view. In addition the view's owner must have the relevant privileges on the underlying base relations, but the user performing the update does not need any permissions on the underlying base relations (see Section 41.5).

Examples

Create a view consisting of all comedy films:

```
CREATE VIEW comedies AS
    SELECT *
    FROM films
    WHERE kind = 'Comedy';
```

This will create a view containing the columns that are in the film table at the time of view creation. Though * was used to create the view, columns added later to the table will not be part of the view.

Create a view with LOCAL CHECK OPTION:

```
CREATE VIEW universal_comedies AS
    SELECT *
    FROM comedies
    WHERE classification = 'U'
    WITH LOCAL CHECK OPTION;
```

This will create a view based on the comedies view, showing only films with kind = 'Comedy' and classification = 'U'. Any attempt to INSERT or UPDATE a row in the view will be rejected if the new row doesn't have classification = 'U', but the film kind will not be checked.

Create a view with CASCADED CHECK OPTION:

```
CREATE VIEW pg_comedies AS
    SELECT *
    FROM comedies
    WHERE classification = 'PG'
    WITH CASCADED CHECK OPTION;
```

This will create a view that checks both the kind and classification of new rows.

Create a view with a mix of updatable and non-updatable columns:

```
CREATE VIEW comedies AS
    SELECT f.*,
           country_code_to_name(f.country_code) AS country,
           (SELECT avg(r.rating)
            FROM user_ratings r
            WHERE r.film_id = f.id) AS avg_rating
    FROM films f
    WHERE f.kind = 'Comedy';
```

This view will support INSERT, UPDATE and DELETE. All the columns from the films table will be updatable, whereas the computed columns country and avg_rating will be read-only.

Create a recursive view consisting of the numbers from 1 to 100:

```
CREATE RECURSIVE VIEW public.nums_1_100 (n) AS
    VALUES (1)
UNION ALL
    SELECT n+1 FROM nums_1_100 WHERE n < 100;
```

Notice that although the recursive view's name is schema-qualified in this CREATE, its internal self-reference is not schema-qualified. This is because the implicitly-created CTE's name cannot be schema-qualified.

Compatibility

CREATE OR REPLACE VIEW is a PostgreSQL language extension. So is the concept of a temporary view. The WITH (...) clause is an extension as well.

See Also

ALTER VIEW, DROP VIEW, CREATE MATERIALIZED VIEW

DEALLOCATE

DEALLOCATE — deallocate a prepared statement

Synopsis

```
DEALLOCATE [ PREPARE ] { name | ALL }
```

Description

DEALLOCATE is used to deallocate a previously prepared SQL statement. If you do not explicitly deallocate a prepared statement, it is deallocated when the session ends.

For more information on prepared statements, see PREPARE.

Parameters

PREPARE

This key word is ignored.

name

The name of the prepared statement to deallocate.

ALL

Deallocate all prepared statements.

Compatibility

The SQL standard includes a DEALLOCATE statement, but it is only for use in embedded SQL.

See Also

EXECUTE, PREPARE

DECLARE

DECLARE — define a cursor

Synopsis

```
DECLARE name [ BINARY ] [ INSENSITIVE ] [ [ NO ] SCROLL ]
    CURSOR [ { WITH | WITHOUT } HOLD ] FOR query
```

Description

DECLARE allows a user to create cursors, which can be used to retrieve a small number of rows at a time out of a larger query. After the cursor is created, rows are fetched from it using FETCH.

Note

This page describes usage of cursors at the SQL command level. If you are trying to use cursors inside a PL/pgSQL function, the rules are different — see Section 43.7.

Parameters

name

The name of the cursor to be created.

BINARY

Causes the cursor to return data in binary rather than in text format.

INSENSITIVE

Indicates that data retrieved from the cursor should be unaffected by updates to the table(s) underlying the cursor that occur after the cursor is created. In PostgreSQL, this is the default behavior; so this key word has no effect and is only accepted for compatibility with the SQL standard.

SCROLL
NO SCROLL

SCROLL specifies that the cursor can be used to retrieve rows in a nonsequential fashion (e.g., backward). Depending upon the complexity of the query's execution plan, specifying SCROLL might impose a performance penalty on the query's execution time. NO SCROLL specifies that the cursor cannot be used to retrieve rows in a nonsequential fashion. The default is to allow scrolling in some cases; this is not the same as specifying SCROLL. See Notes for details.

WITH HOLD
WITHOUT HOLD

WITH HOLD specifies that the cursor can continue to be used after the transaction that created it successfully commits. WITHOUT HOLD specifies that the cursor cannot be used outside of the transaction that created it. If neither `WITHOUT HOLD` nor `WITH HOLD` is specified, `WITHOUT HOLD` is the default.

query

A SELECT or VALUES command which will provide the rows to be returned by the cursor.

The key words `BINARY`, `INSENSITIVE`, and `SCROLL` can appear in any order.

Notes

Normal cursors return data in text format, the same as a `SELECT` would produce. The `BINARY` option specifies that the cursor should return data in binary format. This reduces conversion effort for both the server and client, at the cost of more programmer effort to deal with platform-dependent binary data formats. As an example, if a query returns a value of one from an integer column, you would get a string of 1 with a default cursor, whereas with a binary cursor you would get a 4-byte field containing the internal representation of the value (in big-endian byte order).

Binary cursors should be used carefully. Many applications, including psql, are not prepared to handle binary cursors and expect data to come back in the text format.

Note

When the client application uses the "extended query" protocol to issue a `FETCH` command, the Bind protocol message specifies whether data is to be retrieved in text or binary format. This choice overrides the way that the cursor is defined. The concept of a binary cursor as such is thus obsolete when using extended query protocol — any cursor can be treated as either text or binary.

Unless `WITH HOLD` is specified, the cursor created by this command can only be used within the current transaction. Thus, `DECLARE` without `WITH HOLD` is useless outside a transaction block: the cursor would survive only to the completion of the statement. Therefore PostgreSQL reports an error if such a command is used outside a transaction block. Use BEGIN and COMMIT (or ROLLBACK) to define a transaction block.

If `WITH HOLD` is specified and the transaction that created the cursor successfully commits, the cursor can continue to be accessed by subsequent transactions in the same session. (But if the creating transaction is aborted, the cursor is removed.) A cursor created with `WITH HOLD` is closed when an explicit `CLOSE` command is issued on it, or the session ends. In the current implementation, the rows represented by a held cursor are copied into a temporary file or memory area so that they remain available for subsequent transactions.

`WITH HOLD` may not be specified when the query includes `FOR UPDATE` or `FOR SHARE`.

The `SCROLL` option should be specified when defining a cursor that will be used to fetch backwards. This is required by the SQL standard. However, for compatibility with earlier versions, PostgreSQL will allow backward fetches without `SCROLL`, if the cursor's query plan is simple enough that no extra overhead is needed to support it. However, application developers are advised not to rely on using backward fetches from a cursor that has not been created with `SCROLL`. If `NO SCROLL` is specified, then backward fetches are disallowed in any case.

Backward fetches are also disallowed when the query includes `FOR UPDATE` or `FOR SHARE`; therefore `SCROLL` may not be specified in this case.

> ### Caution
>
> Scrollable and WITH HOLD cursors may give unexpected results if they invoke any volatile functions (see Section 38.7). When a previously fetched row is re-fetched, the functions might be re-executed, perhaps leading to results different from the first time. One workaround for such cases is to declare the cursor WITH HOLD and commit the transaction before reading any rows from it. This will force the entire output of the cursor to be materialized in temporary storage, so that volatile functions are executed exactly once for each row.

If the cursor's query includes FOR UPDATE or FOR SHARE, then returned rows are locked at the time they are first fetched, in the same way as for a regular SELECT command with these options. In addition, the returned rows will be the most up-to-date versions; therefore these options provide the equivalent of what the SQL standard calls a "sensitive cursor". (Specifying INSENSITIVE together with FOR UPDATE or FOR SHARE is an error.)

> ### Caution
>
> It is generally recommended to use FOR UPDATE if the cursor is intended to be used with UPDATE ... WHERE CURRENT OF or DELETE ... WHERE CURRENT OF. Using FOR UPDATE prevents other sessions from changing the rows between the time they are fetched and the time they are updated. Without FOR UPDATE, a subsequent WHERE CURRENT OF command will have no effect if the row was changed since the cursor was created.
>
> Another reason to use FOR UPDATE is that without it, a subsequent WHERE CURRENT OF might fail if the cursor query does not meet the SQL standard's rules for being "simply updatable" (in particular, the cursor must reference just one table and not use grouping or ORDER BY). Cursors that are not simply updatable might work, or might not, depending on plan choice details; so in the worst case, an application might work in testing and then fail in production. If FOR UPDATE is specified, the cursor is guaranteed to be updatable.
>
> The main reason not to use FOR UPDATE with WHERE CURRENT OF is if you need the cursor to be scrollable, or to be insensitive to the subsequent updates (that is, continue to show the old data). If this is a requirement, pay close heed to the caveats shown above.

The SQL standard only makes provisions for cursors in embedded SQL. The PostgreSQL server does not implement an OPEN statement for cursors; a cursor is considered to be open when it is declared. However, ECPG, the embedded SQL preprocessor for PostgreSQL, supports the standard SQL cursor conventions, including those involving DECLARE and OPEN statements.

You can see all available cursors by querying the pg_cursors system view.

Examples

To declare a cursor:

```
DECLARE liahona CURSOR FOR SELECT * FROM films;
```

See FETCH for more examples of cursor usage.

Compatibility

The SQL standard says that it is implementation-dependent whether cursors are sensitive to concurrent updates of the underlying data by default. In PostgreSQL, cursors are insensitive by default, and can be made sensitive by specifying FOR UPDATE. Other products may work differently.

The SQL standard allows cursors only in embedded SQL and in modules. PostgreSQL permits cursors to be used interactively.

Binary cursors are a PostgreSQL extension.

See Also

CLOSE, FETCH, MOVE

DELETE

DELETE — delete rows of a table

Synopsis

```
[ WITH [ RECURSIVE ] with_query [, ...] ]
DELETE FROM [ ONLY ] table_name [ * ] [ [ AS ] alias ]
    [ USING using_list ]
    [ WHERE condition | WHERE CURRENT OF cursor_name ]
    [ RETURNING * | output_expression [ [ AS ] output_name ] [, ...] ]
```

Description

DELETE deletes rows that satisfy the WHERE clause from the specified table. If the WHERE clause is absent, the effect is to delete all rows in the table. The result is a valid, but empty table.

Tip

TRUNCATE provides a faster mechanism to remove all rows from a table.

There are two ways to delete rows in a table using information contained in other tables in the database: using sub-selects, or specifying additional tables in the USING clause. Which technique is more appropriate depends on the specific circumstances.

The optional RETURNING clause causes DELETE to compute and return value(s) based on each row actually deleted. Any expression using the table's columns, and/or columns of other tables mentioned in USING, can be computed. The syntax of the RETURNING list is identical to that of the output list of SELECT.

You must have the DELETE privilege on the table to delete from it, as well as the SELECT privilege for any table in the USING clause or whose values are read in the condition.

Parameters

with_query

> The WITH clause allows you to specify one or more subqueries that can be referenced by name in the DELETE query. See Section 7.8 and SELECT for details.

table_name

> The name (optionally schema-qualified) of the table to delete rows from. If ONLY is specified before the table name, matching rows are deleted from the named table only. If ONLY is not specified, matching rows are also deleted from any tables inheriting from the named table. Optionally, * can be specified after the table name to explicitly indicate that descendant tables are included.

alias

> A substitute name for the target table. When an alias is provided, it completely hides the actual name of the table. For example, given DELETE FROM foo AS f, the remainder of the DELETE statement must refer to this table as f not foo.

using_list

> A list of table expressions, allowing columns from other tables to appear in the WHERE condition. This is similar to the list of tables that can be specified in the FROM Clause of a SELECT statement; for example, an alias for the table name can be specified. Do not repeat the target table in the *using_list*, unless you wish to set up a self-join.

condition

> An expression that returns a value of type boolean. Only rows for which this expression returns true will be deleted.

cursor_name

> The name of the cursor to use in a WHERE CURRENT OF condition. The row to be deleted is the one most recently fetched from this cursor. The cursor must be a non-grouping query on the DELETE's target table. Note that WHERE CURRENT OF cannot be specified together with a Boolean condition. See DECLARE for more information about using cursors with WHERE CURRENT OF.

output_expression

> An expression to be computed and returned by the DELETE command after each row is deleted. The expression can use any column names of the table named by *table_name* or table(s) listed in USING. Write * to return all columns.

output_name

> A name to use for a returned column.

Outputs

On successful completion, a DELETE command returns a command tag of the form

DELETE *count*

The *count* is the number of rows deleted. Note that the number may be less than the number of rows that matched the *condition* when deletes were suppressed by a BEFORE DELETE trigger. If *count* is 0, no rows were deleted by the query (this is not considered an error).

If the DELETE command contains a RETURNING clause, the result will be similar to that of a SELECT statement containing the columns and values defined in the RETURNING list, computed over the row(s) deleted by the command.

Notes

PostgreSQL lets you reference columns of other tables in the WHERE condition by specifying the other tables in the USING clause. For example, to delete all films produced by a given producer, one can do:

```
DELETE FROM films USING producers
  WHERE producer_id = producers.id AND producers.name = 'foo';
```

What is essentially happening here is a join between `films` and `producers`, with all successfully joined `films` rows being marked for deletion. This syntax is not standard. A more standard way to do it is:

```
DELETE FROM films
  WHERE producer_id IN (SELECT id FROM producers WHERE name = 'foo');
```

In some cases the join style is easier to write or faster to execute than the sub-select style.

Examples

Delete all films but musicals:

```
DELETE FROM films WHERE kind <> 'Musical';
```

Clear the table `films`:

```
DELETE FROM films;
```

Delete completed tasks, returning full details of the deleted rows:

```
DELETE FROM tasks WHERE status = 'DONE' RETURNING *;
```

Delete the row of `tasks` on which the cursor `c_tasks` is currently positioned:

```
DELETE FROM tasks WHERE CURRENT OF c_tasks;
```

Compatibility

This command conforms to the SQL standard, except that the `USING` and `RETURNING` clauses are PostgreSQL extensions, as is the ability to use `WITH` with `DELETE`.

See Also
TRUNCATE

DISCARD

DISCARD — discard session state

Synopsis

```
DISCARD { ALL | PLANS | SEQUENCES | TEMPORARY | TEMP }
```

Description

DISCARD releases internal resources associated with a database session. This command is useful for partially or fully resetting the session's state. There are several subcommands to release different types of resources; the DISCARD ALL variant subsumes all the others, and also resets additional state.

Parameters

PLANS

> Releases all cached query plans, forcing re-planning to occur the next time the associated prepared statement is used.

SEQUENCES

> Discards all cached sequence-related state, including currval()/lastval() information and any preallocated sequence values that have not yet been returned by nextval(). (See CREATE SEQUENCE for a description of preallocated sequence values.)

TEMPORARY or TEMP

> Drops all temporary tables created in the current session.

ALL

> Releases all temporary resources associated with the current session and resets the session to its initial state. Currently, this has the same effect as executing the following sequence of statements:

```
SET SESSION AUTHORIZATION DEFAULT;
RESET ALL;
DEALLOCATE ALL;
CLOSE ALL;
UNLISTEN *;
SELECT pg_advisory_unlock_all();
DISCARD PLANS;
DISCARD SEQUENCES;
DISCARD TEMP;
```

Notes

DISCARD ALL cannot be executed inside a transaction block.

Compatibility

DISCARD is a PostgreSQL extension.

DO

DO — execute an anonymous code block

Synopsis

```
DO [ LANGUAGE lang_name ] code
```

Description

DO executes an anonymous code block, or in other words a transient anonymous function in a procedural language.

The code block is treated as though it were the body of a function with no parameters, returning void. It is parsed and executed a single time.

The optional LANGUAGE clause can be written either before or after the code block.

Parameters

code

> The procedural language code to be executed. This must be specified as a string literal, just as in CREATE FUNCTION. Use of a dollar-quoted literal is recommended.

lang_name

> The name of the procedural language the code is written in. If omitted, the default is plpgsql.

Notes

The procedural language to be used must already have been installed into the current database by means of CREATE EXTENSION. plpgsql is installed by default, but other languages are not.

The user must have USAGE privilege for the procedural language, or must be a superuser if the language is untrusted. This is the same privilege requirement as for creating a function in the language.

If DO is executed in a transaction block, then the procedure code cannot execute transaction control statements. Transaction control statements are only allowed if DO is executed in its own transaction.

Examples

Grant all privileges on all views in schema public to role webuser:

```
DO $$DECLARE r record;
BEGIN
    FOR r IN SELECT table_schema, table_name FROM
 information_schema.tables
             WHERE table_type = 'VIEW' AND table_schema = 'public'
```

```
    LOOP
        EXECUTE 'GRANT ALL ON ' || quote_ident(r.table_schema) || '.'
   || quote_ident(r.table_name) || ' TO webuser';
    END LOOP;
END$$;
```

Compatibility

There is no DO statement in the SQL standard.

See Also

CREATE LANGUAGE

DROP ACCESS METHOD

DROP ACCESS METHOD — remove an access method

Synopsis

```
DROP ACCESS METHOD [ IF EXISTS ] name [ CASCADE | RESTRICT ]
```

Description

DROP ACCESS METHOD removes an existing access method. Only superusers can drop access methods.

Parameters

IF EXISTS

Do not throw an error if the access method does not exist. A notice is issued in this case.

name

The name of an existing access method.

CASCADE

Automatically drop objects that depend on the access method (such as operator classes, operator families, and indexes), and in turn all objects that depend on those objects (see Section 5.13).

RESTRICT

Refuse to drop the access method if any objects depend on it. This is the default.

Examples

Drop the access method heptree:

```
DROP ACCESS METHOD heptree;
```

Compatibility

DROP ACCESS METHOD is a PostgreSQL extension.

See Also

CREATE ACCESS METHOD

DROP AGGREGATE

DROP AGGREGATE — remove an aggregate function

Synopsis

```
DROP AGGREGATE [ IF EXISTS ] name ( aggregate_signature ) [, ...]
 [ CASCADE | RESTRICT ]

where aggregate_signature is:

* |
[ argmode ] [ argname ] argtype [ , ... ] |
[ [ argmode ] [ argname ] argtype [ , ... ] ] ORDER BY [ argmode ]
 [ argname ] argtype [ , ... ]
```

Description

DROP AGGREGATE removes an existing aggregate function. To execute this command the current user must be the owner of the aggregate function.

Parameters

IF EXISTS

Do not throw an error if the aggregate does not exist. A notice is issued in this case.

name

The name (optionally schema-qualified) of an existing aggregate function.

argmode

The mode of an argument: IN or VARIADIC. If omitted, the default is IN.

argname

The name of an argument. Note that DROP AGGREGATE does not actually pay any attention to argument names, since only the argument data types are needed to determine the aggregate function's identity.

argtype

An input data type on which the aggregate function operates. To reference a zero-argument aggregate function, write * in place of the list of argument specifications. To reference an ordered-set aggregate function, write ORDER BY between the direct and aggregated argument specifications.

CASCADE

Automatically drop objects that depend on the aggregate function (such as views using it), and in turn all objects that depend on those objects (see Section 5.13).

`RESTRICT`

Refuse to drop the aggregate function if any objects depend on it. This is the default.

Notes

Alternative syntaxes for referencing ordered-set aggregates are described under ALTER AGGREGATE.

Examples

To remove the aggregate function `myavg` for type `integer`:

```
DROP AGGREGATE myavg(integer);
```

To remove the hypothetical-set aggregate function `myrank`, which takes an arbitrary list of ordering columns and a matching list of direct arguments:

```
DROP AGGREGATE myrank(VARIADIC "any" ORDER BY VARIADIC "any");
```

To remove multiple aggregate functions in one command:

```
DROP AGGREGATE myavg(integer), myavg(bigint);
```

Compatibility

There is no `DROP AGGREGATE` statement in the SQL standard.

See Also

ALTER AGGREGATE, CREATE AGGREGATE

DROP CAST

DROP CAST — remove a cast

Synopsis

```
DROP CAST [ IF EXISTS ] (source_type AS target_type) [ CASCADE |
 RESTRICT ]
```

Description

DROP CAST removes a previously defined cast.

To be able to drop a cast, you must own the source or the target data type. These are the same privileges that are required to create a cast.

Parameters

IF EXISTS

> Do not throw an error if the cast does not exist. A notice is issued in this case.

source_type

> The name of the source data type of the cast.

target_type

> The name of the target data type of the cast.

CASCADE
RESTRICT

> These key words do not have any effect, since there are no dependencies on casts.

Examples

To drop the cast from type text to type int:

```
DROP CAST (text AS int);
```

Compatibility

The DROP CAST command conforms to the SQL standard.

See Also
CREATE CAST

DROP COLLATION

DROP COLLATION — remove a collation

Synopsis

```
DROP COLLATION [ IF EXISTS ] name [ CASCADE | RESTRICT ]
```

Description

DROP COLLATION removes a previously defined collation. To be able to drop a collation, you must own the collation.

Parameters

IF EXISTS

Do not throw an error if the collation does not exist. A notice is issued in this case.

name

The name of the collation. The collation name can be schema-qualified.

CASCADE

Automatically drop objects that depend on the collation, and in turn all objects that depend on those objects (see Section 5.13).

RESTRICT

Refuse to drop the collation if any objects depend on it. This is the default.

Examples

To drop the collation named german:

```
DROP COLLATION german;
```

Compatibility

The DROP COLLATION command conforms to the SQL standard, apart from the IF EXISTS option, which is a PostgreSQL extension.

See Also

ALTER COLLATION, CREATE COLLATION

DROP CONVERSION

DROP CONVERSION — remove a conversion

Synopsis

```
DROP CONVERSION [ IF EXISTS ] name [ CASCADE | RESTRICT ]
```

Description

DROP CONVERSION removes a previously defined conversion. To be able to drop a conversion, you must own the conversion.

Parameters

IF EXISTS

Do not throw an error if the conversion does not exist. A notice is issued in this case.

name

The name of the conversion. The conversion name can be schema-qualified.

CASCADE
RESTRICT

These key words do not have any effect, since there are no dependencies on conversions.

Examples

To drop the conversion named myname:

```
DROP CONVERSION myname;
```

Compatibility

There is no DROP CONVERSION statement in the SQL standard, but a DROP TRANSLATION statement that goes along with the CREATE TRANSLATION statement that is similar to the CREATE CONVERSION statement in PostgreSQL.

See Also

ALTER CONVERSION, CREATE CONVERSION

DROP DATABASE

DROP DATABASE — remove a database

Synopsis

```
DROP DATABASE [ IF EXISTS ] name
```

Description

DROP DATABASE drops a database. It removes the catalog entries for the database and deletes the directory containing the data. It can only be executed by the database owner. Also, it cannot be executed while you or anyone else are connected to the target database. (Connect to postgres or any other database to issue this command.)

DROP DATABASE cannot be undone. Use it with care!

Parameters

IF EXISTS

Do not throw an error if the database does not exist. A notice is issued in this case.

name

The name of the database to remove.

Notes

DROP DATABASE cannot be executed inside a transaction block.

This command cannot be executed while connected to the target database. Thus, it might be more convenient to use the program dropdb instead, which is a wrapper around this command.

Compatibility

There is no DROP DATABASE statement in the SQL standard.

See Also
CREATE DATABASE

DROP DOMAIN

DROP DOMAIN — remove a domain

Synopsis

```
DROP DOMAIN [ IF EXISTS ] name [, ...] [ CASCADE | RESTRICT ]
```

Description

DROP DOMAIN removes a domain. Only the owner of a domain can remove it.

Parameters

IF EXISTS

Do not throw an error if the domain does not exist. A notice is issued in this case.

name

The name (optionally schema-qualified) of an existing domain.

CASCADE

Automatically drop objects that depend on the domain (such as table columns), and in turn all objects that depend on those objects (see Section 5.13).

RESTRICT

Refuse to drop the domain if any objects depend on it. This is the default.

Examples

To remove the domain box:

```
DROP DOMAIN box;
```

Compatibility

This command conforms to the SQL standard, except for the IF EXISTS option, which is a PostgreSQL extension.

See Also

CREATE DOMAIN, ALTER DOMAIN

DROP EVENT TRIGGER

DROP EVENT TRIGGER — remove an event trigger

Synopsis

```
DROP EVENT TRIGGER [ IF EXISTS ] name [ CASCADE | RESTRICT ]
```

Description

DROP EVENT TRIGGER removes an existing event trigger. To execute this command, the current user must be the owner of the event trigger.

Parameters

IF EXISTS

Do not throw an error if the event trigger does not exist. A notice is issued in this case.

name

The name of the event trigger to remove.

CASCADE

Automatically drop objects that depend on the trigger, and in turn all objects that depend on those objects (see Section 5.13).

RESTRICT

Refuse to drop the trigger if any objects depend on it. This is the default.

Examples

Destroy the trigger snitch:

```
DROP EVENT TRIGGER snitch;
```

Compatibility

There is no DROP EVENT TRIGGER statement in the SQL standard.

See Also

CREATE EVENT TRIGGER, ALTER EVENT TRIGGER

DROP EXTENSION

DROP EXTENSION — remove an extension

Synopsis

```
DROP EXTENSION [ IF EXISTS ] name [, ...] [ CASCADE | RESTRICT ]
```

Description

DROP EXTENSION removes extensions from the database. Dropping an extension causes its component objects to be dropped as well.

You must own the extension to use DROP EXTENSION.

Parameters

IF EXISTS

Do not throw an error if the extension does not exist. A notice is issued in this case.

name

The name of an installed extension.

CASCADE

Automatically drop objects that depend on the extension, and in turn all objects that depend on those objects (see Section 5.13).

RESTRICT

Refuse to drop the extension if any objects depend on it (other than its own member objects and other extensions listed in the same DROP command). This is the default.

Examples

To remove the extension hstore from the current database:

```
DROP EXTENSION hstore;
```

This command will fail if any of hstore's objects are in use in the database, for example if any tables have columns of the hstore type. Add the CASCADE option to forcibly remove those dependent objects as well.

Compatibility

DROP EXTENSION is a PostgreSQL extension.

See Also

CREATE EXTENSION, ALTER EXTENSION

DROP FOREIGN DATA WRAPPER

DROP FOREIGN DATA WRAPPER — remove a foreign-data wrapper

Synopsis

```
DROP FOREIGN DATA WRAPPER [ IF EXISTS ] name [, ...] [ CASCADE |
RESTRICT ]
```

Description

DROP FOREIGN DATA WRAPPER removes an existing foreign-data wrapper. To execute this command, the current user must be the owner of the foreign-data wrapper.

Parameters

IF EXISTS

Do not throw an error if the foreign-data wrapper does not exist. A notice is issued in this case.

name

The name of an existing foreign-data wrapper.

CASCADE

Automatically drop objects that depend on the foreign-data wrapper (such as foreign tables and servers), and in turn all objects that depend on those objects (see Section 5.13).

RESTRICT

Refuse to drop the foreign-data wrapper if any objects depend on it. This is the default.

Examples

Drop the foreign-data wrapper dbi:

```
DROP FOREIGN DATA WRAPPER dbi;
```

Compatibility

DROP FOREIGN DATA WRAPPER conforms to ISO/IEC 9075-9 (SQL/MED). The IF EXISTS clause is a PostgreSQL extension.

See Also

CREATE FOREIGN DATA WRAPPER, ALTER FOREIGN DATA WRAPPER

DROP FOREIGN TABLE

DROP FOREIGN TABLE — remove a foreign table

Synopsis

```
DROP FOREIGN TABLE [ IF EXISTS ] name [, ...] [ CASCADE | RESTRICT ]
```

Description

DROP FOREIGN TABLE removes a foreign table. Only the owner of a foreign table can remove it.

Parameters

IF EXISTS

> Do not throw an error if the foreign table does not exist. A notice is issued in this case.

name

> The name (optionally schema-qualified) of the foreign table to drop.

CASCADE

> Automatically drop objects that depend on the foreign table (such as views), and in turn all objects that depend on those objects (see Section 5.13).

RESTRICT

> Refuse to drop the foreign table if any objects depend on it. This is the default.

Examples

To destroy two foreign tables, films and distributors:

```
DROP FOREIGN TABLE films, distributors;
```

Compatibility

This command conforms to the ISO/IEC 9075-9 (SQL/MED), except that the standard only allows one foreign table to be dropped per command, and apart from the IF EXISTS option, which is a PostgreSQL extension.

See Also
ALTER FOREIGN TABLE, CREATE FOREIGN TABLE

DROP FUNCTION

DROP FUNCTION — remove a function

Synopsis

```
DROP FUNCTION [ IF EXISTS ] name [ ( [ [ argmode ] [ argname ] argtype
[, ...] ] ) ] [, ...]
    [ CASCADE | RESTRICT ]
```

Description

DROP FUNCTION removes the definition of an existing function. To execute this command the user must be the owner of the function. The argument types to the function must be specified, since several different functions can exist with the same name and different argument lists.

Parameters

IF EXISTS

Do not throw an error if the function does not exist. A notice is issued in this case.

name

The name (optionally schema-qualified) of an existing function. If no argument list is specified, the name must be unique in its schema.

argmode

The mode of an argument: IN, OUT, INOUT, or VARIADIC. If omitted, the default is IN. Note that DROP FUNCTION does not actually pay any attention to OUT arguments, since only the input arguments are needed to determine the function's identity. So it is sufficient to list the IN, INOUT, and VARIADIC arguments.

argname

The name of an argument. Note that DROP FUNCTION does not actually pay any attention to argument names, since only the argument data types are needed to determine the function's identity.

argtype

The data type(s) of the function's arguments (optionally schema-qualified), if any.

CASCADE

Automatically drop objects that depend on the function (such as operators or triggers), and in turn all objects that depend on those objects (see Section 5.13).

RESTRICT

Refuse to drop the function if any objects depend on it. This is the default.

Examples

This command removes the square root function:

```
DROP FUNCTION sqrt(integer);
```

Drop multiple functions in one command:

```
DROP FUNCTION sqrt(integer), sqrt(bigint);
```

If the function name is unique in its schema, it can be referred to without an argument list:

```
DROP FUNCTION update_employee_salaries;
```

Note that this is different from

```
DROP FUNCTION update_employee_salaries();
```

which refers to a function with zero arguments, whereas the first variant can refer to a function with any number of arguments, including zero, as long as the name is unique.

Compatibility

This command conforms to the SQL standard, with these PostgreSQL extensions:

* The standard only allows one function to be dropped per command.

* The IF EXISTS option

* The ability to specify argument modes and names

See Also

CREATE FUNCTION, ALTER FUNCTION, DROP PROCEDURE, DROP ROUTINE

DROP GROUP

DROP GROUP — remove a database role

Synopsis

```
DROP GROUP [ IF EXISTS ] name [, ...]
```

Description

DROP GROUP is now an alias for DROP ROLE.

Compatibility

There is no DROP GROUP statement in the SQL standard.

See Also

DROP ROLE

DROP INDEX

DROP INDEX — remove an index

Synopsis

```
DROP INDEX [ CONCURRENTLY ] [ IF EXISTS ] name [, ...] [ CASCADE |
    RESTRICT ]
```

Description

DROP INDEX drops an existing index from the database system. To execute this command you must be the owner of the index.

Parameters

CONCURRENTLY

Drop the index without locking out concurrent selects, inserts, updates, and deletes on the index's table. A normal DROP INDEX acquires exclusive lock on the table, blocking other accesses until the index drop can be completed. With this option, the command instead waits until conflicting transactions have completed.

There are several caveats to be aware of when using this option. Only one index name can be specified, and the CASCADE option is not supported. (Thus, an index that supports a UNIQUE or PRIMARY KEY constraint cannot be dropped this way.) Also, regular DROP INDEX commands can be performed within a transaction block, but DROP INDEX CONCURRENTLY cannot.

IF EXISTS

Do not throw an error if the index does not exist. A notice is issued in this case.

name

The name (optionally schema-qualified) of an index to remove.

CASCADE

Automatically drop objects that depend on the index, and in turn all objects that depend on those objects (see Section 5.13).

RESTRICT

Refuse to drop the index if any objects depend on it. This is the default.

Examples

This command will remove the index title_idx:

```
DROP INDEX title_idx;
```

Compatibility

DROP INDEX is a PostgreSQL language extension. There are no provisions for indexes in the SQL standard.

See Also

CREATE INDEX

DROP LANGUAGE

DROP LANGUAGE — remove a procedural language

Synopsis

```
DROP [ PROCEDURAL ] LANGUAGE [ IF EXISTS ] name [ CASCADE | RESTRICT ]
```

Description

DROP LANGUAGE removes the definition of a previously registered procedural language. You must be a superuser or the owner of the language to use DROP LANGUAGE.

Note

As of PostgreSQL 9.1, most procedural languages have been made into "extensions", and should therefore be removed with DROP EXTENSION not DROP LANGUAGE.

Parameters

IF EXISTS

Do not throw an error if the language does not exist. A notice is issued in this case.

name

The name of an existing procedural language. For backward compatibility, the name can be enclosed by single quotes.

CASCADE

Automatically drop objects that depend on the language (such as functions in the language), and in turn all objects that depend on those objects (see Section 5.13).

RESTRICT

Refuse to drop the language if any objects depend on it. This is the default.

Examples

This command removes the procedural language plsample:

```
DROP LANGUAGE plsample;
```

Compatibility

There is no DROP LANGUAGE statement in the SQL standard.

See Also

ALTER LANGUAGE, CREATE LANGUAGE

DROP MATERIALIZED VIEW

DROP MATERIALIZED VIEW — remove a materialized view

Synopsis

```
DROP MATERIALIZED VIEW [ IF EXISTS ] name [, ...] [ CASCADE |
 RESTRICT ]
```

Description

DROP MATERIALIZED VIEW drops an existing materialized view. To execute this command you must be the owner of the materialized view.

Parameters

IF EXISTS

Do not throw an error if the materialized view does not exist. A notice is issued in this case.

name

The name (optionally schema-qualified) of the materialized view to remove.

CASCADE

Automatically drop objects that depend on the materialized view (such as other materialized views, or regular views), and in turn all objects that depend on those objects (see Section 5.13).

RESTRICT

Refuse to drop the materialized view if any objects depend on it. This is the default.

Examples

This command will remove the materialized view called order_summary:

```
DROP MATERIALIZED VIEW order_summary;
```

Compatibility

DROP MATERIALIZED VIEW is a PostgreSQL extension.

See Also

CREATE MATERIALIZED VIEW, ALTER MATERIALIZED VIEW, REFRESH MATERIALIZED VIEW

DROP OPERATOR

DROP OPERATOR — remove an operator

Synopsis

```
DROP OPERATOR [ IF EXISTS ] name ( { left_type | NONE } , { right_type
 | NONE } ) [, ...] [ CASCADE | RESTRICT ]
```

Description

DROP OPERATOR drops an existing operator from the database system. To execute this command you must be the owner of the operator.

Parameters

IF EXISTS

   Do not throw an error if the operator does not exist. A notice is issued in this case.

name

   The name (optionally schema-qualified) of an existing operator.

left_type

   The data type of the operator's left operand; write NONE if the operator has no left operand.

right_type

   The data type of the operator's right operand; write NONE if the operator has no right operand.

CASCADE

   Automatically drop objects that depend on the operator (such as views using it), and in turn all objects that depend on those objects (see Section 5.13).

RESTRICT

   Refuse to drop the operator if any objects depend on it. This is the default.

Examples

Remove the power operator a^b for type integer:

```
DROP OPERATOR ^ (integer, integer);
```

Remove the left unary bitwise complement operator ~b for type bit:

```
DROP OPERATOR ~ (none, bit);
```

Remove the right unary factorial operator x! for type bigint:

```
DROP OPERATOR ! (bigint, none);
```

Remove multiple operators in one command:

```
DROP OPERATOR ~ (none, bit), ! (bigint, none);
```

Compatibility

There is no DROP OPERATOR statement in the SQL standard.

See Also

CREATE OPERATOR, ALTER OPERATOR

DROP OPERATOR CLASS

DROP OPERATOR CLASS — remove an operator class

Synopsis

```
DROP OPERATOR CLASS [ IF EXISTS ] name USING index_method [ CASCADE |
  RESTRICT ]
```

Description

DROP OPERATOR CLASS drops an existing operator class. To execute this command you must be the owner of the operator class.

DROP OPERATOR CLASS does not drop any of the operators or functions referenced by the class. If there are any indexes depending on the operator class, you will need to specify CASCADE for the drop to complete.

Parameters

IF EXISTS

> Do not throw an error if the operator class does not exist. A notice is issued in this case.

name

> The name (optionally schema-qualified) of an existing operator class.

index_method

> The name of the index access method the operator class is for.

CASCADE

> Automatically drop objects that depend on the operator class (such as indexes), and in turn all objects that depend on those objects (see Section 5.13).

RESTRICT

> Refuse to drop the operator class if any objects depend on it. This is the default.

Notes

DROP OPERATOR CLASS will not drop the operator family containing the class, even if there is nothing else left in the family (in particular, in the case where the family was implicitly created by CREATE OPERATOR CLASS). An empty operator family is harmless, but for the sake of tidiness you might wish to remove the family with DROP OPERATOR FAMILY; or perhaps better, use DROP OPERATOR FAMILY in the first place.

Examples

Remove the B-tree operator class widget_ops:

```
DROP OPERATOR CLASS widget_ops USING btree;
```

This command will not succeed if there are any existing indexes that use the operator class. Add CASCADE to drop such indexes along with the operator class.

Compatibility

There is no DROP OPERATOR CLASS statement in the SQL standard.

See Also

ALTER OPERATOR CLASS, CREATE OPERATOR CLASS, DROP OPERATOR FAMILY

DROP OPERATOR FAMILY

DROP OPERATOR FAMILY — remove an operator family

Synopsis

```
DROP OPERATOR FAMILY [ IF EXISTS ] name USING index_method [ CASCADE |
RESTRICT ]
```

Description

DROP OPERATOR FAMILY drops an existing operator family. To execute this command you must be the owner of the operator family.

DROP OPERATOR FAMILY includes dropping any operator classes contained in the family, but it does not drop any of the operators or functions referenced by the family. If there are any indexes depending on operator classes within the family, you will need to specify CASCADE for the drop to complete.

Parameters

IF EXISTS

> Do not throw an error if the operator family does not exist. A notice is issued in this case.

name

> The name (optionally schema-qualified) of an existing operator family.

index_method

> The name of the index access method the operator family is for.

CASCADE

> Automatically drop objects that depend on the operator family, and in turn all objects that depend on those objects (see Section 5.13).

RESTRICT

> Refuse to drop the operator family if any objects depend on it. This is the default.

Examples

Remove the B-tree operator family float_ops:

```
DROP OPERATOR FAMILY float_ops USING btree;
```

This command will not succeed if there are any existing indexes that use operator classes within the family. Add CASCADE to drop such indexes along with the operator family.

Compatibility

There is no `DROP OPERATOR FAMILY` statement in the SQL standard.

See Also

ALTER OPERATOR FAMILY, CREATE OPERATOR FAMILY, ALTER OPERATOR CLASS, CREATE OPERATOR CLASS, DROP OPERATOR CLASS

DROP OWNED

DROP OWNED — remove database objects owned by a database role

Synopsis

```
DROP OWNED BY { name | CURRENT_USER | SESSION_USER } [, ...] [ CASCADE
   | RESTRICT ]
```

Description

DROP OWNED drops all the objects within the current database that are owned by one of the specified roles. Any privileges granted to the given roles on objects in the current database and on shared objects (databases, tablespaces) will also be revoked.

Parameters

name

The name of a role whose objects will be dropped, and whose privileges will be revoked.

CASCADE

Automatically drop objects that depend on the affected objects, and in turn all objects that depend on those objects (see Section 5.13).

RESTRICT

Refuse to drop the objects owned by a role if any other database objects depend on one of the affected objects. This is the default.

Notes

DROP OWNED is often used to prepare for the removal of one or more roles. Because DROP OWNED only affects the objects in the current database, it is usually necessary to execute this command in each database that contains objects owned by a role that is to be removed.

Using the CASCADE option might make the command recurse to objects owned by other users.

The REASSIGN OWNED command is an alternative that reassigns the ownership of all the database objects owned by one or more roles. However, REASSIGN OWNED does not deal with privileges for other objects.

Databases and tablespaces owned by the role(s) will not be removed.

See Section 21.4 for more discussion.

Compatibility

The DROP OWNED command is a PostgreSQL extension.

See Also

REASSIGN OWNED, DROP ROLE

DROP POLICY

DROP POLICY — remove a row level security policy from a table

Synopsis

```
DROP POLICY [ IF EXISTS ] name ON table_name [ CASCADE | RESTRICT ]
```

Description

DROP POLICY removes the specified policy from the table. Note that if the last policy is removed for a table and the table still has row level security enabled via ALTER TABLE, then the default-deny policy will be used. ALTER TABLE ... DISABLE ROW LEVEL SECURITY can be used to disable row level security for a table, whether policies for the table exist or not.

Parameters

IF EXISTS

Do not throw an error if the policy does not exist. A notice is issued in this case.

name

The name of the policy to drop.

table_name

The name (optionally schema-qualified) of the table that the policy is on.

CASCADE
RESTRICT

These key words do not have any effect, since there are no dependencies on policies.

Examples

To drop the policy called p1 on the table named my_table:

```
DROP POLICY p1 ON my_table;
```

Compatibility

DROP POLICY is a PostgreSQL extension.

See Also

CREATE POLICY, ALTER POLICY

DROP PROCEDURE

DROP PROCEDURE — remove a procedure

Synopsis

```
DROP PROCEDURE [ IF EXISTS ] name [ ( [ [ argmode ] [ argname
] argtype [, ...] ] ) ] [, ...]
    [ CASCADE | RESTRICT ]
```

Description

DROP PROCEDURE removes the definition of an existing procedure. To execute this command the user must be the owner of the procedure. The argument types to the procedure must be specified, since several different procedures can exist with the same name and different argument lists.

Parameters

IF EXISTS

Do not throw an error if the procedure does not exist. A notice is issued in this case.

name

The name (optionally schema-qualified) of an existing procedure. If no argument list is specified, the name must be unique in its schema.

argmode

The mode of an argument: IN or VARIADIC. If omitted, the default is IN.

argname

The name of an argument. Note that DROP PROCEDURE does not actually pay any attention to argument names, since only the argument data types are needed to determine the procedure's identity.

argtype

The data type(s) of the procedure's arguments (optionally schema-qualified), if any.

CASCADE

Automatically drop objects that depend on the procedure, and in turn all objects that depend on those objects (see Section 5.13).

RESTRICT

Refuse to drop the procedure if any objects depend on it. This is the default.

Examples

```
DROP PROCEDURE do_db_maintenance();
```

Compatibility

This command conforms to the SQL standard, with these PostgreSQL extensions:

- The standard only allows one procedure to be dropped per command.

- The IF EXISTS option

- The ability to specify argument modes and names

See Also

CREATE PROCEDURE, ALTER PROCEDURE, DROP FUNCTION, DROP ROUTINE

DROP PUBLICATION

DROP PUBLICATION — remove a publication

Synopsis

```
DROP PUBLICATION [ IF EXISTS ] name [, ...] [ CASCADE | RESTRICT ]
```

Description

DROP PUBLICATION removes an existing publication from the database.

A publication can only be dropped by its owner or a superuser.

Parameters

IF EXISTS

> Do not throw an error if the publication does not exist. A notice is issued in this case.

name

> The name of an existing publication.

CASCADE
RESTRICT

> These key words do not have any effect, since there are no dependencies on publications.

Examples

Drop a publication:

```
DROP PUBLICATION mypublication;
```

Compatibility

DROP PUBLICATION is a PostgreSQL extension.

See Also

CREATE PUBLICATION, ALTER PUBLICATION

DROP ROLE

DROP ROLE — remove a database role

Synopsis

```
DROP ROLE [ IF EXISTS ] name [, ...]
```

Description

DROP ROLE removes the specified role(s). To drop a superuser role, you must be a superuser yourself; to drop non-superuser roles, you must have CREATEROLE privilege.

A role cannot be removed if it is still referenced in any database of the cluster; an error will be raised if so. Before dropping the role, you must drop all the objects it owns (or reassign their ownership) and revoke any privileges the role has been granted on other objects. The REASSIGN OWNED and DROP OWNED commands can be useful for this purpose; see Section 21.4 for more discussion.

However, it is not necessary to remove role memberships involving the role; DROP ROLE automatically revokes any memberships of the target role in other roles, and of other roles in the target role. The other roles are not dropped nor otherwise affected.

Parameters

IF EXISTS

> Do not throw an error if the role does not exist. A notice is issued in this case.

name

> The name of the role to remove.

Notes

PostgreSQL includes a program dropuser that has the same functionality as this command (in fact, it calls this command) but can be run from the command shell.

Examples

To drop a role:

```
DROP ROLE jonathan;
```

Compatibility

The SQL standard defines DROP ROLE, but it allows only one role to be dropped at a time, and it specifies different privilege requirements than PostgreSQL uses.

See Also

CREATE ROLE, ALTER ROLE, SET ROLE

DROP ROUTINE

DROP ROUTINE — remove a routine

Synopsis

```
DROP ROUTINE [ IF EXISTS ] name [ ( [ [ argmode ] [ argname ] argtype
[, ...] ] ) ] [, ...]
    [ CASCADE | RESTRICT ]
```

Description

DROP ROUTINE removes the definition of an existing routine, which can be an aggregate function, a normal function, or a procedure. See under DROP AGGREGATE, DROP FUNCTION, and DROP PROCEDURE for the description of the parameters, more examples, and further details.

Examples

To drop the routine foo for type integer:

```
DROP ROUTINE foo(integer);
```

This command will work independent of whether foo is an aggregate, function, or procedure.

Compatibility

This command conforms to the SQL standard, with these PostgreSQL extensions:

- The standard only allows one routine to be dropped per command.

- The IF EXISTS option

- The ability to specify argument modes and names

- Aggregate functions are an extension.

See Also

DROP AGGREGATE, DROP FUNCTION, DROP PROCEDURE, ALTER ROUTINE

Note that there is no CREATE ROUTINE command.

DROP RULE

DROP RULE — remove a rewrite rule

Synopsis

```
DROP RULE [ IF EXISTS ] name ON table_name [ CASCADE | RESTRICT ]
```

Description

DROP RULE drops a rewrite rule.

Parameters

IF EXISTS

Do not throw an error if the rule does not exist. A notice is issued in this case.

name

The name of the rule to drop.

table_name

The name (optionally schema-qualified) of the table or view that the rule applies to.

CASCADE

Automatically drop objects that depend on the rule, and in turn all objects that depend on those objects (see Section 5.13).

RESTRICT

Refuse to drop the rule if any objects depend on it. This is the default.

Examples

To drop the rewrite rule newrule:

```
DROP RULE newrule ON mytable;
```

Compatibility

DROP RULE is a PostgreSQL language extension, as is the entire query rewrite system.

See Also

CREATE RULE, ALTER RULE

DROP SCHEMA

DROP SCHEMA — remove a schema

Synopsis

```
DROP SCHEMA [ IF EXISTS ] name [, ...] [ CASCADE | RESTRICT ]
```

Description

DROP SCHEMA removes schemas from the database.

A schema can only be dropped by its owner or a superuser. Note that the owner can drop the schema (and thereby all contained objects) even if they do not own some of the objects within the schema.

Parameters

IF EXISTS

Do not throw an error if the schema does not exist. A notice is issued in this case.

name

The name of a schema.

CASCADE

Automatically drop objects (tables, functions, etc.) that are contained in the schema, and in turn all objects that depend on those objects (see Section 5.13).

RESTRICT

Refuse to drop the schema if it contains any objects. This is the default.

Notes

Using the CASCADE option might make the command remove objects in other schemas besides the one(s) named.

Examples

To remove schema mystuff from the database, along with everything it contains:

```
DROP SCHEMA mystuff CASCADE;
```

Compatibility

DROP SCHEMA is fully conforming with the SQL standard, except that the standard only allows one schema to be dropped per command, and apart from the IF EXISTS option, which is a PostgreSQL extension.

See Also

ALTER SCHEMA, CREATE SCHEMA

DROP SEQUENCE

DROP SEQUENCE — remove a sequence

Synopsis

```
DROP SEQUENCE [ IF EXISTS ] name [, ...] [ CASCADE | RESTRICT ]
```

Description

DROP SEQUENCE removes sequence number generators. A sequence can only be dropped by its owner or a superuser.

Parameters

IF EXISTS

> Do not throw an error if the sequence does not exist. A notice is issued in this case.

name

> The name (optionally schema-qualified) of a sequence.

CASCADE

> Automatically drop objects that depend on the sequence, and in turn all objects that depend on those objects (see Section 5.13).

RESTRICT

> Refuse to drop the sequence if any objects depend on it. This is the default.

Examples

To remove the sequence serial:

```
DROP SEQUENCE serial;
```

Compatibility

DROP SEQUENCE conforms to the SQL standard, except that the standard only allows one sequence to be dropped per command, and apart from the IF EXISTS option, which is a PostgreSQL extension.

See Also
CREATE SEQUENCE, ALTER SEQUENCE

DROP SERVER

DROP SERVER — remove a foreign server descriptor

Synopsis

```
DROP SERVER [ IF EXISTS ] name [, ...] [ CASCADE | RESTRICT ]
```

Description

`DROP SERVER` removes an existing foreign server descriptor. To execute this command, the current user must be the owner of the server.

Parameters

IF EXISTS

Do not throw an error if the server does not exist. A notice is issued in this case.

name

The name of an existing server.

CASCADE

Automatically drop objects that depend on the server (such as user mappings), and in turn all objects that depend on those objects (see Section 5.13).

RESTRICT

Refuse to drop the server if any objects depend on it. This is the default.

Examples

Drop a server `foo` if it exists:

```
DROP SERVER IF EXISTS foo;
```

Compatibility

`DROP SERVER` conforms to ISO/IEC 9075-9 (SQL/MED). The `IF EXISTS` clause is a PostgreSQL extension.

See Also
CREATE SERVER, ALTER SERVER

DROP STATISTICS

DROP STATISTICS — remove extended statistics

Synopsis

```
DROP STATISTICS [ IF EXISTS ] name [, ...]
```

Description

DROP STATISTICS removes statistics object(s) from the database. Only the statistics object's owner, the schema owner, or a superuser can drop a statistics object.

Parameters

IF EXISTS

Do not throw an error if the statistics object does not exist. A notice is issued in this case.

name

The name (optionally schema-qualified) of the statistics object to drop.

Examples

To destroy two statistics objects in different schemas, without failing if they don't exist:

```
DROP STATISTICS IF EXISTS
    accounting.users_uid_creation,
    public.grants_user_role;
```

Compatibility

There is no DROP STATISTICS command in the SQL standard.

See Also

ALTER STATISTICS, CREATE STATISTICS

DROP SUBSCRIPTION

DROP SUBSCRIPTION — remove a subscription

Synopsis

```
DROP SUBSCRIPTION [ IF EXISTS ] name [ CASCADE | RESTRICT ]
```

Description

DROP SUBSCRIPTION removes a subscription from the database cluster.

A subscription can only be dropped by a superuser.

DROP SUBSCRIPTION cannot be executed inside a transaction block if the subscription is associated with a replication slot. (You can use ALTER SUBSCRIPTION to unset the slot.)

Parameters

name

   The name of a subscription to be dropped.

CASCADE
RESTRICT

   These key words do not have any effect, since there are no dependencies on subscriptions.

Notes

When dropping a subscription that is associated with a replication slot on the remote host (the normal state), DROP SUBSCRIPTION will connect to the remote host and try to drop the replication slot as part of its operation. This is necessary so that the resources allocated for the subscription on the remote host are released. If this fails, either because the remote host is not reachable or because the remote replication slot cannot be dropped or does not exist or never existed, the DROP SUBSCRIPTION command will fail. To proceed in this situation, disassociate the subscription from the replication slot by executing ALTER SUBSCRIPTION ... SET (slot_name = NONE). After that, DROP SUBSCRIPTION will no longer attempt any actions on a remote host. Note that if the remote replication slot still exists, it should then be dropped manually; otherwise it will continue to reserve WAL and might eventually cause the disk to fill up. See also Section 31.2.1.

If a subscription is associated with a replication slot, then DROP SUBSCRIPTION cannot be executed inside a transaction block.

Examples

Drop a subscription:

```
DROP SUBSCRIPTION mysub;
```

Compatibility

DROP SUBSCRIPTION is a PostgreSQL extension.

See Also

CREATE SUBSCRIPTION, ALTER SUBSCRIPTION

DROP TABLE

DROP TABLE — remove a table

Synopsis

```
DROP TABLE [ IF EXISTS ] name [, ...] [ CASCADE | RESTRICT ]
```

Description

DROP TABLE removes tables from the database. Only the table owner, the schema owner, and superuser can drop a table. To empty a table of rows without destroying the table, use DELETE or TRUNCATE.

DROP TABLE always removes any indexes, rules, triggers, and constraints that exist for the target table. However, to drop a table that is referenced by a view or a foreign-key constraint of another table, CASCADE must be specified. (CASCADE will remove a dependent view entirely, but in the foreign-key case it will only remove the foreign-key constraint, not the other table entirely.)

Parameters

IF EXISTS

Do not throw an error if the table does not exist. A notice is issued in this case.

name

The name (optionally schema-qualified) of the table to drop.

CASCADE

Automatically drop objects that depend on the table (such as views), and in turn all objects that depend on those objects (see Section 5.13).

RESTRICT

Refuse to drop the table if any objects depend on it. This is the default.

Examples

To destroy two tables, films and distributors:

```
DROP TABLE films, distributors;
```

Compatibility

This command conforms to the SQL standard, except that the standard only allows one table to be dropped per command, and apart from the IF EXISTS option, which is a PostgreSQL extension.

See Also

ALTER TABLE, CREATE TABLE

DROP TABLESPACE

DROP TABLESPACE — remove a tablespace

Synopsis

```
DROP TABLESPACE [ IF EXISTS ] name
```

Description

DROP TABLESPACE removes a tablespace from the system.

A tablespace can only be dropped by its owner or a superuser. The tablespace must be empty of all database objects before it can be dropped. It is possible that objects in other databases might still reside in the tablespace even if no objects in the current database are using the tablespace. Also, if the tablespace is listed in the temp_tablespaces setting of any active session, the DROP might fail due to temporary files residing in the tablespace.

Parameters

IF EXISTS

Do not throw an error if the tablespace does not exist. A notice is issued in this case.

name

The name of a tablespace.

Notes

DROP TABLESPACE cannot be executed inside a transaction block.

Examples

To remove tablespace mystuff from the system:

```
DROP TABLESPACE mystuff;
```

Compatibility

DROP TABLESPACE is a PostgreSQL extension.

See Also

CREATE TABLESPACE, ALTER TABLESPACE

DROP TEXT SEARCH CONFIGURATION

DROP TEXT SEARCH CONFIGURATION — remove a text search configuration

Synopsis

```
DROP TEXT SEARCH CONFIGURATION [ IF EXISTS ] name [ CASCADE |
  RESTRICT ]
```

Description

DROP TEXT SEARCH CONFIGURATION drops an existing text search configuration. To execute this command you must be the owner of the configuration.

Parameters

IF EXISTS

> Do not throw an error if the text search configuration does not exist. A notice is issued in this case.

name

> The name (optionally schema-qualified) of an existing text search configuration.

CASCADE

> Automatically drop objects that depend on the text search configuration, and in turn all objects that depend on those objects (see Section 5.13).

RESTRICT

> Refuse to drop the text search configuration if any objects depend on it. This is the default.

Examples

Remove the text search configuration my_english:

```
DROP TEXT SEARCH CONFIGURATION my_english;
```

This command will not succeed if there are any existing indexes that reference the configuration in to_tsvector calls. Add CASCADE to drop such indexes along with the text search configuration.

Compatibility

There is no DROP TEXT SEARCH CONFIGURATION statement in the SQL standard.

See Also

ALTER TEXT SEARCH CONFIGURATION, CREATE TEXT SEARCH CONFIGURATION

DROP TEXT SEARCH DICTIONARY

DROP TEXT SEARCH DICTIONARY — remove a text search dictionary

Synopsis

```
DROP TEXT SEARCH DICTIONARY [ IF EXISTS ] name [ CASCADE | RESTRICT ]
```

Description

DROP TEXT SEARCH DICTIONARY drops an existing text search dictionary. To execute this command you must be the owner of the dictionary.

Parameters

IF EXISTS

Do not throw an error if the text search dictionary does not exist. A notice is issued in this case.

name

The name (optionally schema-qualified) of an existing text search dictionary.

CASCADE

Automatically drop objects that depend on the text search dictionary, and in turn all objects that depend on those objects (see Section 5.13).

RESTRICT

Refuse to drop the text search dictionary if any objects depend on it. This is the default.

Examples

Remove the text search dictionary english:

```
DROP TEXT SEARCH DICTIONARY english;
```

This command will not succeed if there are any existing text search configurations that use the dictionary. Add CASCADE to drop such configurations along with the dictionary.

Compatibility

There is no DROP TEXT SEARCH DICTIONARY statement in the SQL standard.

See Also

ALTER TEXT SEARCH DICTIONARY, CREATE TEXT SEARCH DICTIONARY

DROP TEXT SEARCH PARSER

DROP TEXT SEARCH PARSER — remove a text search parser

Synopsis

```
DROP TEXT SEARCH PARSER [ IF EXISTS ] name [ CASCADE | RESTRICT ]
```

Description

DROP TEXT SEARCH PARSER drops an existing text search parser. You must be a superuser to use this command.

Parameters

IF EXISTS

Do not throw an error if the text search parser does not exist. A notice is issued in this case.

name

The name (optionally schema-qualified) of an existing text search parser.

CASCADE

Automatically drop objects that depend on the text search parser, and in turn all objects that depend on those objects (see Section 5.13).

RESTRICT

Refuse to drop the text search parser if any objects depend on it. This is the default.

Examples

Remove the text search parser my_parser:

```
DROP TEXT SEARCH PARSER my_parser;
```

This command will not succeed if there are any existing text search configurations that use the parser. Add CASCADE to drop such configurations along with the parser.

Compatibility

There is no DROP TEXT SEARCH PARSER statement in the SQL standard.

See Also

ALTER TEXT SEARCH PARSER, CREATE TEXT SEARCH PARSER

DROP TEXT SEARCH TEMPLATE

DROP TEXT SEARCH TEMPLATE — remove a text search template

Synopsis

```
DROP TEXT SEARCH TEMPLATE [ IF EXISTS ] name [ CASCADE | RESTRICT ]
```

Description

DROP TEXT SEARCH TEMPLATE drops an existing text search template. You must be a superuser to use this command.

Parameters

IF EXISTS

> Do not throw an error if the text search template does not exist. A notice is issued in this case.

name

> The name (optionally schema-qualified) of an existing text search template.

CASCADE

> Automatically drop objects that depend on the text search template, and in turn all objects that depend on those objects (see Section 5.13).

RESTRICT

> Refuse to drop the text search template if any objects depend on it. This is the default.

Examples

Remove the text search template thesaurus:

```
DROP TEXT SEARCH TEMPLATE thesaurus;
```

This command will not succeed if there are any existing text search dictionaries that use the template. Add CASCADE to drop such dictionaries along with the template.

Compatibility

There is no DROP TEXT SEARCH TEMPLATE statement in the SQL standard.

See Also

ALTER TEXT SEARCH TEMPLATE, CREATE TEXT SEARCH TEMPLATE

DROP TRANSFORM

DROP TRANSFORM — remove a transform

Synopsis

```
DROP TRANSFORM [ IF EXISTS ] FOR type_name LANGUAGE lang_name
    [ CASCADE | RESTRICT ]
```

Description

DROP TRANSFORM removes a previously defined transform.

To be able to drop a transform, you must own the type and the language. These are the same privileges that are required to create a transform.

Parameters

IF EXISTS

Do not throw an error if the transform does not exist. A notice is issued in this case.

type_name

The name of the data type of the transform.

lang_name

The name of the language of the transform.

CASCADE

Automatically drop objects that depend on the transform, and in turn all objects that depend on those objects (see Section 5.13).

RESTRICT

Refuse to drop the transform if any objects depend on it. This is the default.

Examples

To drop the transform for type hstore and language plpythonu:

```
DROP TRANSFORM FOR hstore LANGUAGE plpythonu;
```

Compatibility

This form of DROP TRANSFORM is a PostgreSQL extension. See CREATE TRANSFORM for details.

See Also

CREATE TRANSFORM

DROP TRIGGER

DROP TRIGGER — remove a trigger

Synopsis

```
DROP TRIGGER [ IF EXISTS ] name ON table_name [ CASCADE | RESTRICT ]
```

Description

DROP TRIGGER removes an existing trigger definition. To execute this command, the current user must be the owner of the table for which the trigger is defined.

Parameters

IF EXISTS

> Do not throw an error if the trigger does not exist. A notice is issued in this case.

name

> The name of the trigger to remove.

table_name

> The name (optionally schema-qualified) of the table for which the trigger is defined.

CASCADE

> Automatically drop objects that depend on the trigger, and in turn all objects that depend on those objects (see Section 5.13).

RESTRICT

> Refuse to drop the trigger if any objects depend on it. This is the default.

Examples

Destroy the trigger if_dist_exists on the table films:

```
DROP TRIGGER if_dist_exists ON films;
```

Compatibility

The DROP TRIGGER statement in PostgreSQL is incompatible with the SQL standard. In the SQL standard, trigger names are not local to tables, so the command is simply DROP TRIGGER name.

See Also

CREATE TRIGGER

DROP TYPE

DROP TYPE — remove a data type

Synopsis

```
DROP TYPE [ IF EXISTS ] name [, ...] [ CASCADE | RESTRICT ]
```

Description

DROP TYPE removes a user-defined data type. Only the owner of a type can remove it.

Parameters

IF EXISTS

Do not throw an error if the type does not exist. A notice is issued in this case.

name

The name (optionally schema-qualified) of the data type to remove.

CASCADE

Automatically drop objects that depend on the type (such as table columns, functions, and operators), and in turn all objects that depend on those objects (see Section 5.13).

RESTRICT

Refuse to drop the type if any objects depend on it. This is the default.

Examples

To remove the data type box:

```
DROP TYPE box;
```

Compatibility

This command is similar to the corresponding command in the SQL standard, apart from the IF EXISTS option, which is a PostgreSQL extension. But note that much of the CREATE TYPE command and the data type extension mechanisms in PostgreSQL differ from the SQL standard.

See Also

ALTER TYPE, CREATE TYPE

DROP USER

DROP USER — remove a database role

Synopsis

```
DROP USER [ IF EXISTS ] name [, ...]
```

Description

DROP USER is simply an alternate spelling of DROP ROLE.

Compatibility

The DROP USER statement is a PostgreSQL extension. The SQL standard leaves the definition of users to the implementation.

See Also

DROP ROLE

DROP USER MAPPING

DROP USER MAPPING — remove a user mapping for a foreign server

Synopsis

```
DROP USER MAPPING [ IF EXISTS ] FOR { user_name | USER | CURRENT_USER
    | PUBLIC } SERVER server_name
```

Description

DROP USER MAPPING removes an existing user mapping from foreign server.

The owner of a foreign server can drop user mappings for that server for any user. Also, a user can drop a user mapping for their own user name if USAGE privilege on the server has been granted to the user.

Parameters

IF EXISTS

> Do not throw an error if the user mapping does not exist. A notice is issued in this case.

user_name

> User name of the mapping. CURRENT_USER and USER match the name of the current user. PUBLIC is used to match all present and future user names in the system.

server_name

> Server name of the user mapping.

Examples

Drop a user mapping bob, server foo if it exists:

```
DROP USER MAPPING IF EXISTS FOR bob SERVER foo;
```

Compatibility

DROP USER MAPPING conforms to ISO/IEC 9075-9 (SQL/MED). The IF EXISTS clause is a PostgreSQL extension.

See Also

CREATE USER MAPPING, ALTER USER MAPPING

DROP VIEW

DROP VIEW — remove a view

Synopsis

```
DROP VIEW [ IF EXISTS ] name [, ...] [ CASCADE | RESTRICT ]
```

Description

DROP VIEW drops an existing view. To execute this command you must be the owner of the view.

Parameters

IF EXISTS

> Do not throw an error if the view does not exist. A notice is issued in this case.

name

> The name (optionally schema-qualified) of the view to remove.

CASCADE

> Automatically drop objects that depend on the view (such as other views), and in turn all objects that depend on those objects (see Section 5.13).

RESTRICT

> Refuse to drop the view if any objects depend on it. This is the default.

Examples

This command will remove the view called kinds:

```
DROP VIEW kinds;
```

Compatibility

This command conforms to the SQL standard, except that the standard only allows one view to be dropped per command, and apart from the IF EXISTS option, which is a PostgreSQL extension.

See Also

ALTER VIEW, CREATE VIEW

END

END — commit the current transaction

Synopsis

```
END [ WORK | TRANSACTION ]
```

Description

END commits the current transaction. All changes made by the transaction become visible to others and are guaranteed to be durable if a crash occurs. This command is a PostgreSQL extension that is equivalent to COMMIT.

Parameters

WORK
TRANSACTION

> Optional key words. They have no effect.

Notes

Use ROLLBACK to abort a transaction.

Issuing END when not inside a transaction does no harm, but it will provoke a warning message.

Examples

To commit the current transaction and make all changes permanent:

```
END;
```

Compatibility

END is a PostgreSQL extension that provides functionality equivalent to COMMIT, which is specified in the SQL standard.

See Also
BEGIN, COMMIT, ROLLBACK

EXECUTE

EXECUTE — execute a prepared statement

Synopsis

```
EXECUTE name [ ( parameter [, ...] ) ]
```

Description

EXECUTE is used to execute a previously prepared statement. Since prepared statements only exist for the duration of a session, the prepared statement must have been created by a PREPARE statement executed earlier in the current session.

If the PREPARE statement that created the statement specified some parameters, a compatible set of parameters must be passed to the EXECUTE statement, or else an error is raised. Note that (unlike functions) prepared statements are not overloaded based on the type or number of their parameters; the name of a prepared statement must be unique within a database session.

For more information on the creation and usage of prepared statements, see PREPARE.

Parameters

name

The name of the prepared statement to execute.

parameter

The actual value of a parameter to the prepared statement. This must be an expression yielding a value that is compatible with the data type of this parameter, as was determined when the prepared statement was created.

Outputs

The command tag returned by EXECUTE is that of the prepared statement, and not EXECUTE.

Examples

Examples are given in the Examples section of the PREPARE documentation.

Compatibility

The SQL standard includes an EXECUTE statement, but it is only for use in embedded SQL. This version of the EXECUTE statement also uses a somewhat different syntax.

See Also

DEALLOCATE, PREPARE

EXPLAIN

EXPLAIN — show the execution plan of a statement

Synopsis

```
EXPLAIN [ ( option [, ...] ) ] statement
EXPLAIN [ ANALYZE ] [ VERBOSE ] statement

where option can be one of:

    ANALYZE [ boolean ]
    VERBOSE [ boolean ]
    COSTS [ boolean ]
    BUFFERS [ boolean ]
    TIMING [ boolean ]
    SUMMARY [ boolean ]
    FORMAT { TEXT | XML | JSON | YAML }
```

Description

This command displays the execution plan that the PostgreSQL planner generates for the supplied statement. The execution plan shows how the table(s) referenced by the statement will be scanned — by plain sequential scan, index scan, etc. — and if multiple tables are referenced, what join algorithms will be used to bring together the required rows from each input table.

The most critical part of the display is the estimated statement execution cost, which is the planner's guess at how long it will take to run the statement (measured in cost units that are arbitrary, but conventionally mean disk page fetches). Actually two numbers are shown: the start-up cost before the first row can be returned, and the total cost to return all the rows. For most queries the total cost is what matters, but in contexts such as a subquery in EXISTS, the planner will choose the smallest start-up cost instead of the smallest total cost (since the executor will stop after getting one row, anyway). Also, if you limit the number of rows to return with a LIMIT clause, the planner makes an appropriate interpolation between the endpoint costs to estimate which plan is really the cheapest.

The ANALYZE option causes the statement to be actually executed, not only planned. Then actual run time statistics are added to the display, including the total elapsed time expended within each plan node (in milliseconds) and the total number of rows it actually returned. This is useful for seeing whether the planner's estimates are close to reality.

Important

Keep in mind that the statement is actually executed when the ANALYZE option is used. Although EXPLAIN will discard any output that a SELECT would return, other side effects of the statement will happen as usual. If you wish to use EXPLAIN ANALYZE on an INSERT, UPDATE, DELETE, CREATE TABLE AS, or EXECUTE statement without letting the command affect your data, use this approach:

```
BEGIN;
```

```
EXPLAIN ANALYZE ...;
ROLLBACK;
```

Only the `ANALYZE` and `VERBOSE` options can be specified, and only in that order, without surrounding the option list in parentheses. Prior to PostgreSQL 9.0, the unparenthesized syntax was the only one supported. It is expected that all new options will be supported only in the parenthesized syntax.

Parameters

ANALYZE

Carry out the command and show actual run times and other statistics. This parameter defaults to `FALSE`.

VERBOSE

Display additional information regarding the plan. Specifically, include the output column list for each node in the plan tree, schema-qualify table and function names, always label variables in expressions with their range table alias, and always print the name of each trigger for which statistics are displayed. This parameter defaults to `FALSE`.

COSTS

Include information on the estimated startup and total cost of each plan node, as well as the estimated number of rows and the estimated width of each row. This parameter defaults to `TRUE`.

BUFFERS

Include information on buffer usage. Specifically, include the number of shared blocks hit, read, dirtied, and written, the number of local blocks hit, read, dirtied, and written, and the number of temp blocks read and written. A *hit* means that a read was avoided because the block was found already in cache when needed. Shared blocks contain data from regular tables and indexes; local blocks contain data from temporary tables and indexes; while temp blocks contain short-term working data used in sorts, hashes, Materialize plan nodes, and similar cases. The number of blocks *dirtied* indicates the number of previously unmodified blocks that were changed by this query; while the number of blocks *written* indicates the number of previously-dirtied blocks evicted from cache by this backend during query processing. The number of blocks shown for an upper-level node includes those used by all its child nodes. In text format, only non-zero values are printed. This parameter may only be used when `ANALYZE` is also enabled. It defaults to `FALSE`.

TIMING

Include actual startup time and time spent in each node in the output. The overhead of repeatedly reading the system clock can slow down the query significantly on some systems, so it may be useful to set this parameter to `FALSE` when only actual row counts, and not exact times, are needed. Run time of the entire statement is always measured, even when node-level timing is turned off with this option. This parameter may only be used when `ANALYZE` is also enabled. It defaults to `TRUE`.

SUMMARY

Include summary information (e.g., totaled timing information) after the query plan. Summary information is included by default when `ANALYZE` is used but otherwise is not included by default, but can be enabled using this option. Planning time in `EXPLAIN EXECUTE` includes the time required to fetch the plan from the cache and the time required for re-planning, if necessary.

FORMAT

Specify the output format, which can be TEXT, XML, JSON, or YAML. Non-text output contains the same information as the text output format, but is easier for programs to parse. This parameter defaults to TEXT.

boolean

Specifies whether the selected option should be turned on or off. You can write TRUE, ON, or 1 to enable the option, and FALSE, OFF, or 0 to disable it. The *boolean* value can also be omitted, in which case TRUE is assumed.

statement

Any SELECT, INSERT, UPDATE, DELETE, VALUES, EXECUTE, DECLARE, CREATE TABLE AS, or CREATE MATERIALIZED VIEW AS statement, whose execution plan you wish to see.

Outputs

The command's result is a textual description of the plan selected for the *statement*, optionally annotated with execution statistics. Section 14.1 describes the information provided.

Notes

In order to allow the PostgreSQL query planner to make reasonably informed decisions when optimizing queries, the pg_statistic data should be up-to-date for all tables used in the query. Normally the autovacuum daemon will take care of that automatically. But if a table has recently had substantial changes in its contents, you might need to do a manual ANALYZE rather than wait for autovacuum to catch up with the changes.

In order to measure the run-time cost of each node in the execution plan, the current implementation of EXPLAIN ANALYZE adds profiling overhead to query execution. As a result, running EXPLAIN ANALYZE on a query can sometimes take significantly longer than executing the query normally. The amount of overhead depends on the nature of the query, as well as the platform being used. The worst case occurs for plan nodes that in themselves require very little time per execution, and on machines that have relatively slow operating system calls for obtaining the time of day.

Examples

To show the plan for a simple query on a table with a single integer column and 10000 rows:

```
EXPLAIN SELECT * FROM foo;

                        QUERY PLAN
---------------------------------------------------------
 Seq Scan on foo  (cost=0.00..155.00 rows=10000 width=4)
(1 row)
```

Here is the same query, with JSON output formatting:

```
EXPLAIN (FORMAT JSON) SELECT * FROM foo;
          QUERY PLAN
```

```
------------------------------
 [                             +
   {                           +
     "Plan": {                 +
       "Node Type": "Seq Scan",+
       "Relation Name": "foo", +
       "Alias": "foo",         +
       "Startup Cost": 0.00,   +
       "Total Cost": 155.00,   +
       "Plan Rows": 10000,     +
       "Plan Width": 4         +
     }                         +
   }                           +
 ]
(1 row)
```

If there is an index and we use a query with an indexable WHERE condition, EXPLAIN might show a different plan:

```
EXPLAIN SELECT * FROM foo WHERE i = 4;

                      QUERY PLAN
--------------------------------------------------------------
 Index Scan using fi on foo  (cost=0.00..5.98 rows=1 width=4)
   Index Cond: (i = 4)
(2 rows)
```

Here is the same query, but in YAML format:

```
EXPLAIN (FORMAT YAML) SELECT * FROM foo WHERE i='4';
          QUERY PLAN
-------------------------------
 - Plan:                      +
     Node Type: "Index Scan"  +
     Scan Direction: "Forward"+
     Index Name: "fi"         +
     Relation Name: "foo"     +
     Alias: "foo"             +
     Startup Cost: 0.00       +
     Total Cost: 5.98         +
     Plan Rows: 1             +
     Plan Width: 4            +
     Index Cond: "(i = 4)"
(1 row)
```

XML format is left as an exercise for the reader.

Here is the same plan with cost estimates suppressed:

```
EXPLAIN (COSTS FALSE) SELECT * FROM foo WHERE i = 4;

          QUERY PLAN
```

```
----------------------------
 Index Scan using fi on foo
   Index Cond: (i = 4)
(2 rows)
```

Here is an example of a query plan for a query using an aggregate function:

```
EXPLAIN SELECT sum(i) FROM foo WHERE i < 10;

                             QUERY PLAN
---------------------------------------------------------------------
 Aggregate  (cost=23.93..23.93 rows=1 width=4)
   ->  Index Scan using fi on foo  (cost=0.00..23.92 rows=6 width=4)
         Index Cond: (i < 10)
(3 rows)
```

Here is an example of using EXPLAIN EXECUTE to display the execution plan for a prepared query:

```
PREPARE query(int, int) AS SELECT sum(bar) FROM test
    WHERE id > $1 AND id < $2
    GROUP BY foo;

EXPLAIN ANALYZE EXECUTE query(100, 200);

                                              QUERY PLAN
-----------------------------------------------------------------------------------
 HashAggregate  (cost=9.54..9.54 rows=1 width=8) (actual
time=0.156..0.161 rows=11 loops=1)
   Group Key: foo
   ->  Index Scan using test_pkey on test  (cost=0.29..9.29 rows=50
width=8) (actual time=0.039..0.091 rows=99 loops=1)
         Index Cond: ((id > $1) AND (id < $2))
 Planning time: 0.197 ms
 Execution time: 0.225 ms
(6 rows)
```

Of course, the specific numbers shown here depend on the actual contents of the tables involved. Also note that the numbers, and even the selected query strategy, might vary between PostgreSQL releases due to planner improvements. In addition, the ANALYZE command uses random sampling to estimate data statistics; therefore, it is possible for cost estimates to change after a fresh run of ANALYZE, even if the actual distribution of data in the table has not changed.

Compatibility

There is no EXPLAIN statement defined in the SQL standard.

See Also

ANALYZE

FETCH

FETCH — retrieve rows from a query using a cursor

Synopsis

```
FETCH [ direction [ FROM | IN ] ] cursor_name
```

where *direction* can be empty or one of:

```
NEXT
PRIOR
FIRST
LAST
ABSOLUTE count
RELATIVE count
count
ALL
FORWARD
FORWARD count
FORWARD ALL
BACKWARD
BACKWARD count
BACKWARD ALL
```

Description

FETCH retrieves rows using a previously-created cursor.

A cursor has an associated position, which is used by FETCH. The cursor position can be before the first row of the query result, on any particular row of the result, or after the last row of the result. When created, a cursor is positioned before the first row. After fetching some rows, the cursor is positioned on the row most recently retrieved. If FETCH runs off the end of the available rows then the cursor is left positioned after the last row, or before the first row if fetching backward. FETCH ALL or FETCH BACKWARD ALL will always leave the cursor positioned after the last row or before the first row.

The forms NEXT, PRIOR, FIRST, LAST, ABSOLUTE, RELATIVE fetch a single row after moving the cursor appropriately. If there is no such row, an empty result is returned, and the cursor is left positioned before the first row or after the last row as appropriate.

The forms using FORWARD and BACKWARD retrieve the indicated number of rows moving in the forward or backward direction, leaving the cursor positioned on the last-returned row (or after/before all rows, if the count exceeds the number of rows available).

RELATIVE 0, FORWARD 0, and BACKWARD 0 all request fetching the current row without moving the cursor, that is, re-fetching the most recently fetched row. This will succeed unless the cursor is positioned before the first row or after the last row; in which case, no row is returned.

Note

This page describes usage of cursors at the SQL command level. If you are trying to use cursors inside a PL/pgSQL function, the rules are different — see Section 43.7.3.

Parameters

direction

> *direction* defines the fetch direction and number of rows to fetch. It can be one of the following:

> NEXT

>> Fetch the next row. This is the default if *direction* is omitted.

> PRIOR

>> Fetch the prior row.

> FIRST

>> Fetch the first row of the query (same as ABSOLUTE 1).

> LAST

>> Fetch the last row of the query (same as ABSOLUTE -1).

> ABSOLUTE *count*

>> Fetch the *count*'th row of the query, or the abs(*count*)'th row from the end if *count* is negative. Position before first row or after last row if *count* is out of range; in particular, ABSOLUTE 0 positions before the first row.

> RELATIVE *count*

>> Fetch the *count*'th succeeding row, or the abs(*count*)'th prior row if *count* is negative. RELATIVE 0 re-fetches the current row, if any.

> *count*

>> Fetch the next *count* rows (same as FORWARD *count*).

> ALL

>> Fetch all remaining rows (same as FORWARD ALL).

> FORWARD

>> Fetch the next row (same as NEXT).

> FORWARD *count*

>> Fetch the next *count* rows. FORWARD 0 re-fetches the current row.

> FORWARD ALL

>> Fetch all remaining rows.

BACKWARD

Fetch the prior row (same as `PRIOR`).

BACKWARD *count*

Fetch the prior *count* rows (scanning backwards). `BACKWARD 0` re-fetches the current row.

BACKWARD ALL

Fetch all prior rows (scanning backwards).

count

count is a possibly-signed integer constant, determining the location or number of rows to fetch. For `FORWARD` and `BACKWARD` cases, specifying a negative *count* is equivalent to changing the sense of `FORWARD` and `BACKWARD`.

cursor_name

An open cursor's name.

Outputs

On successful completion, a `FETCH` command returns a command tag of the form

FETCH *count*

The *count* is the number of rows fetched (possibly zero). Note that in psql, the command tag will not actually be displayed, since psql displays the fetched rows instead.

Notes

The cursor should be declared with the `SCROLL` option if one intends to use any variants of `FETCH` other than `FETCH NEXT` or `FETCH FORWARD` with a positive count. For simple queries PostgreSQL will allow backwards fetch from cursors not declared with `SCROLL`, but this behavior is best not relied on. If the cursor is declared with `NO SCROLL`, no backward fetches are allowed.

`ABSOLUTE` fetches are not any faster than navigating to the desired row with a relative move: the underlying implementation must traverse all the intermediate rows anyway. Negative absolute fetches are even worse: the query must be read to the end to find the last row, and then traversed backward from there. However, rewinding to the start of the query (as with `FETCH ABSOLUTE 0`) is fast.

DECLARE is used to define a cursor. Use MOVE to change cursor position without retrieving data.

Examples

The following example traverses a table using a cursor:

```
BEGIN WORK;

-- Set up a cursor:
DECLARE liahona SCROLL CURSOR FOR SELECT * FROM films;
```

```
-- Fetch the first 5 rows in the cursor liahona:
FETCH FORWARD 5 FROM liahona;
```

```
 code  |          title          | did | date_prod  |   kind   |  len
-------+-------------------------+-----+------------+----------+-------
 BL101 | The Third Man           | 101 | 1949-12-23 | Drama    | 01:44
 BL102 | The African Queen       | 101 | 1951-08-11 | Romantic | 01:43
 JL201 | Une Femme est une Femme | 102 | 1961-03-12 | Romantic | 01:25
 P_301 | Vertigo                 | 103 | 1958-11-14 | Action   | 02:08
 P_302 | Becket                  | 103 | 1964-02-03 | Drama    | 02:28
```

```
-- Fetch the previous row:
FETCH PRIOR FROM liahona;
```

```
 code  | title   | did | date_prod  |  kind  |  len
-------+---------+-----+------------+--------+-------
 P_301 | Vertigo | 103 | 1958-11-14 | Action | 02:08
```

```
-- Close the cursor and end the transaction:
CLOSE liahona;
COMMIT WORK;
```

Compatibility

The SQL standard defines FETCH for use in embedded SQL only. The variant of FETCH described here returns the data as if it were a SELECT result rather than placing it in host variables. Other than this point, FETCH is fully upward-compatible with the SQL standard.

The FETCH forms involving FORWARD and BACKWARD, as well as the forms FETCH *count* and FETCH ALL, in which FORWARD is implicit, are PostgreSQL extensions.

The SQL standard allows only FROM preceding the cursor name; the option to use IN, or to leave them out altogether, is an extension.

See Also

CLOSE, DECLARE, MOVE

GRANT

GRANT — define access privileges

Synopsis

```
GRANT { { SELECT | INSERT | UPDATE | DELETE | TRUNCATE | REFERENCES |
 TRIGGER }
    [, ...] | ALL [ PRIVILEGES ] }
    ON { [ TABLE ] table_name [, ...]
          | ALL TABLES IN SCHEMA schema_name [, ...] }
    TO role_specification [, ...] [ WITH GRANT OPTION ]

GRANT { { SELECT | INSERT | UPDATE | REFERENCES } ( column_name
 [, ...] )
    [, ...] | ALL [ PRIVILEGES ] ( column_name [, ...] ) }
    ON [ TABLE ] table_name [, ...]
    TO role_specification [, ...] [ WITH GRANT OPTION ]

GRANT { { USAGE | SELECT | UPDATE }
    [, ...] | ALL [ PRIVILEGES ] }
    ON { SEQUENCE sequence_name [, ...]
          | ALL SEQUENCES IN SCHEMA schema_name [, ...] }
    TO role_specification [, ...] [ WITH GRANT OPTION ]

GRANT { { CREATE | CONNECT | TEMPORARY | TEMP } [, ...] | ALL
 [ PRIVILEGES ] }
    ON DATABASE database_name [, ...]
    TO role_specification [, ...] [ WITH GRANT OPTION ]

GRANT { USAGE | ALL [ PRIVILEGES ] }
    ON DOMAIN domain_name [, ...]
    TO role_specification [, ...] [ WITH GRANT OPTION ]

GRANT { USAGE | ALL [ PRIVILEGES ] }
    ON FOREIGN DATA WRAPPER fdw_name [, ...]
    TO role_specification [, ...] [ WITH GRANT OPTION ]

GRANT { USAGE | ALL [ PRIVILEGES ] }
    ON FOREIGN SERVER server_name [, ...]
    TO role_specification [, ...] [ WITH GRANT OPTION ]

GRANT { EXECUTE | ALL [ PRIVILEGES ] }
    ON { { FUNCTION | PROCEDURE | ROUTINE } routine_name
 [ ( [ [ argmode ] [ arg_name ] arg_type [, ...] ] ) ] [, ...]
          | ALL { FUNCTIONS | PROCEDURES | ROUTINES } IN
 SCHEMA schema_name [, ...] }
    TO role_specification [, ...] [ WITH GRANT OPTION ]

GRANT { USAGE | ALL [ PRIVILEGES ] }
```

```
        ON LANGUAGE lang_name [, ...]
        TO role_specification [, ...] [ WITH GRANT OPTION ]

GRANT { { SELECT | UPDATE } [, ...] | ALL [ PRIVILEGES ] }
        ON LARGE OBJECT loid [, ...]
        TO role_specification [, ...] [ WITH GRANT OPTION ]

GRANT { { CREATE | USAGE } [, ...] | ALL [ PRIVILEGES ] }
        ON SCHEMA schema_name [, ...]
        TO role_specification [, ...] [ WITH GRANT OPTION ]

GRANT { CREATE | ALL [ PRIVILEGES ] }
        ON TABLESPACE tablespace_name [, ...]
        TO role_specification [, ...] [ WITH GRANT OPTION ]

GRANT { USAGE | ALL [ PRIVILEGES ] }
        ON TYPE type_name [, ...]
        TO role_specification [, ...] [ WITH GRANT OPTION ]

where role_specification can be:

    [ GROUP ] role_name
  | PUBLIC
  | CURRENT_USER
  | SESSION_USER

GRANT role_name [, ...] TO role_name [, ...] [ WITH ADMIN OPTION ]
```

Description

The GRANT command has two basic variants: one that grants privileges on a database object (table, column, view, foreign table, sequence, database, foreign-data wrapper, foreign server, function, procedure, procedural language, schema, or tablespace), and one that grants membership in a role. These variants are similar in many ways, but they are different enough to be described separately.

GRANT on Database Objects

This variant of the GRANT command gives specific privileges on a database object to one or more roles. These privileges are added to those already granted, if any.

There is also an option to grant privileges on all objects of the same type within one or more schemas. This functionality is currently supported only for tables, sequences, functions, and procedures. ALL TABLES also affects views and foreign tables, just like the specific-object GRANT command. ALL FUNCTIONS also affects aggregate functions, but not procedures, again just like the specific-object GRANT command.

The key word PUBLIC indicates that the privileges are to be granted to all roles, including those that might be created later. PUBLIC can be thought of as an implicitly defined group that always includes all roles. Any particular role will have the sum of privileges granted directly to it, privileges granted to any role it is presently a member of, and privileges granted to PUBLIC.

If WITH GRANT OPTION is specified, the recipient of the privilege can in turn grant it to others. Without a grant option, the recipient cannot do that. Grant options cannot be granted to PUBLIC.

There is no need to grant privileges to the owner of an object (usually the user that created it), as the owner has all privileges by default. (The owner could, however, choose to revoke some of their own privileges for safety.)

The right to drop an object, or to alter its definition in any way, is not treated as a grantable privilege; it is inherent in the owner, and cannot be granted or revoked. (However, a similar effect can be obtained by granting or revoking membership in the role that owns the object; see below.) The owner implicitly has all grant options for the object, too.

PostgreSQL grants default privileges on some types of objects to PUBLIC. No privileges are granted to PUBLIC by default on tables, table columns, sequences, foreign data wrappers, foreign servers, large objects, schemas, or tablespaces. For other types of objects, the default privileges granted to PUBLIC are as follows: CONNECT and TEMPORARY (create temporary tables) privileges for databases; EXECUTE privilege for functions and procedures; and USAGE privilege for languages and data types (including domains). The object owner can, of course, REVOKE both default and expressly granted privileges. (For maximum security, issue the REVOKE in the same transaction that creates the object; then there is no window in which another user can use the object.) Also, these initial default privilege settings can be changed using the ALTER DEFAULT PRIVILEGES command.

The possible privileges are:

SELECT

> Allows SELECT from any column, or the specific columns listed, of the specified table, view, or sequence. Also allows the use of COPY TO. This privilege is also needed to reference existing column values in UPDATE or DELETE. For sequences, this privilege also allows the use of the currval function. For large objects, this privilege allows the object to be read.

INSERT

> Allows INSERT of a new row into the specified table. If specific columns are listed, only those columns may be assigned to in the INSERT command (other columns will therefore receive default values). Also allows COPY FROM.

UPDATE

> Allows UPDATE of any column, or the specific columns listed, of the specified table. (In practice, any nontrivial UPDATE command will require SELECT privilege as well, since it must reference table columns to determine which rows to update, and/or to compute new values for columns.) SELECT ... FOR UPDATE and SELECT ... FOR SHARE also require this privilege on at least one column, in addition to the SELECT privilege. For sequences, this privilege allows the use of the nextval and setval functions. For large objects, this privilege allows writing or truncating the object.

DELETE

> Allows DELETE of a row from the specified table. (In practice, any nontrivial DELETE command will require SELECT privilege as well, since it must reference table columns to determine which rows to delete.)

TRUNCATE

> Allows TRUNCATE on the specified table.

REFERENCES

> Allows creation of a foreign key constraint referencing the specified table, or specified column(s) of the table. (See the CREATE TABLE statement.)

TRIGGER

Allows the creation of a trigger on the specified table. (See the CREATE TRIGGER statement.)

CREATE

For databases, allows new schemas and publications to be created within the database.

For schemas, allows new objects to be created within the schema. To rename an existing object, you must own the object *and* have this privilege for the containing schema.

For tablespaces, allows tables, indexes, and temporary files to be created within the tablespace, and allows databases to be created that have the tablespace as their default tablespace. (Note that revoking this privilege will not alter the placement of existing objects.)

CONNECT

Allows the user to connect to the specified database. This privilege is checked at connection startup (in addition to checking any restrictions imposed by `pg_hba.conf`).

TEMPORARY
TEMP

Allows temporary tables to be created while using the specified database.

EXECUTE

Allows the use of the specified function or procedure and the use of any operators that are implemented on top of the function. This is the only type of privilege that is applicable to functions and procedures. The `FUNCTION` syntax also works for aggregate functions. Alternatively, use `ROUTINE` to refer to a function, aggregate function, or procedure regardless of what it is.

USAGE

For procedural languages, allows the use of the specified language for the creation of functions in that language. This is the only type of privilege that is applicable to procedural languages.

For schemas, allows access to objects contained in the specified schema (assuming that the objects' own privilege requirements are also met). Essentially this allows the grantee to "look up" objects within the schema. Without this permission, it is still possible to see the object names, e.g. by querying the system tables. Also, after revoking this permission, existing backends might have statements that have previously performed this lookup, so this is not a completely secure way to prevent object access.

For sequences, this privilege allows the use of the `currval` and `nextval` functions.

For types and domains, this privilege allows the use of the type or domain in the creation of tables, functions, and other schema objects. (Note that it does not control general "usage" of the type, such as values of the type appearing in queries. It only prevents objects from being created that depend on the type. The main purpose of the privilege is controlling which users create dependencies on a type, which could prevent the owner from changing the type later.)

For foreign-data wrappers, this privilege allows creation of new servers using the foreign-data wrapper.

For servers, this privilege allows creation of foreign tables using the server. Grantees may also create, alter, or drop their own user mappings associated with that server.

ALL PRIVILEGES

> Grant all of the available privileges at once. The PRIVILEGES key word is optional in PostgreSQL, though it is required by strict SQL.

The privileges required by other commands are listed on the reference page of the respective command.

GRANT on Roles

This variant of the GRANT command grants membership in a role to one or more other roles. Membership in a role is significant because it conveys the privileges granted to a role to each of its members.

If WITH ADMIN OPTION is specified, the member can in turn grant membership in the role to others, and revoke membership in the role as well. Without the admin option, ordinary users cannot do that. A role is not considered to hold WITH ADMIN OPTION on itself, but it may grant or revoke membership in itself from a database session where the session user matches the role. Database superusers can grant or revoke membership in any role to anyone. Roles having CREATEROLE privilege can grant or revoke membership in any role that is not a superuser.

Unlike the case with privileges, membership in a role cannot be granted to PUBLIC. Note also that this form of the command does not allow the noise word GROUP.

Notes

The REVOKE command is used to revoke access privileges.

Since PostgreSQL 8.1, the concepts of users and groups have been unified into a single kind of entity called a role. It is therefore no longer necessary to use the keyword GROUP to identify whether a grantee is a user or a group. GROUP is still allowed in the command, but it is a noise word.

A user may perform SELECT, INSERT, etc. on a column if they hold that privilege for either the specific column or its whole table. Granting the privilege at the table level and then revoking it for one column will not do what one might wish: the table-level grant is unaffected by a column-level operation.

When a non-owner of an object attempts to GRANT privileges on the object, the command will fail outright if the user has no privileges whatsoever on the object. As long as some privilege is available, the command will proceed, but it will grant only those privileges for which the user has grant options. The GRANT ALL PRIVILEGES forms will issue a warning message if no grant options are held, while the other forms will issue a warning if grant options for any of the privileges specifically named in the command are not held. (In principle these statements apply to the object owner as well, but since the owner is always treated as holding all grant options, the cases can never occur.)

It should be noted that database superusers can access all objects regardless of object privilege settings. This is comparable to the rights of root in a Unix system. As with root, it's unwise to operate as a superuser except when absolutely necessary.

If a superuser chooses to issue a GRANT or REVOKE command, the command is performed as though it were issued by the owner of the affected object. In particular, privileges granted via such a command will appear to have been granted by the object owner. (For role membership, the membership appears to have been granted by the containing role itself.)

GRANT and REVOKE can also be done by a role that is not the owner of the affected object, but is a member of the role that owns the object, or is a member of a role that holds privileges WITH GRANT OPTION on the object. In this case the privileges will be recorded as having been granted by the role that actually owns the object or holds the privileges WITH GRANT OPTION. For example, if table t1 is owned by role g1, of which role u1 is a member, then u1 can grant privileges on t1 to u2, but those privileges will appear to have been granted directly by g1. Any other member of role g1 could revoke them later.

If the role executing GRANT holds the required privileges indirectly via more than one role membership path, it is unspecified which containing role will be recorded as having done the grant. In such cases it is best practice to use SET ROLE to become the specific role you want to do the GRANT as.

Granting permission on a table does not automatically extend permissions to any sequences used by the table, including sequences tied to SERIAL columns. Permissions on sequences must be set separately.

Use psql's \dp command to obtain information about existing privileges for tables and columns. For example:

```
=> \dp mytable
                                Access privileges
 Schema |  Name   | Type  |   Access privileges   | Column access
 privileges
--------+---------+-------+-----------------------
+------------------------
 public | mytable | table | miriam=arwdDxt/miriam | col1:
                          : =r/miriam             :   miriam_rw=rw/
miriam
                          : admin=arw/miriam
(1 row)
```

The entries shown by \dp are interpreted thus:

```
rolename=xxxx -- privileges granted to a role
        =xxxx -- privileges granted to PUBLIC

            r -- SELECT ("read")
            w -- UPDATE ("write")
            a -- INSERT ("append")
            d -- DELETE
            D -- TRUNCATE
            x -- REFERENCES
            t -- TRIGGER
            X -- EXECUTE
            U -- USAGE
            C -- CREATE
            c -- CONNECT
            T -- TEMPORARY
       arwdDxt -- ALL PRIVILEGES (for tables, varies for other objects)
            * -- grant option for preceding privilege

        /yyyy -- role that granted this privilege
```

The above example display would be seen by user miriam after creating table mytable and doing:

```
GRANT SELECT ON mytable TO PUBLIC;
GRANT SELECT, UPDATE, INSERT ON mytable TO admin;
GRANT SELECT (col1), UPDATE (col1) ON mytable TO miriam_rw;
```

For non-table objects there are other \d commands that can display their privileges.

If the "Access privileges" column is empty for a given object, it means the object has default privileges (that is, its privileges column is null). Default privileges always include all privileges for the owner, and can include some privileges for PUBLIC depending on the object type, as explained above. The first GRANT or REVOKE on an object will instantiate the default privileges (producing, for example, {miriam=arwdDxt/miriam}) and then modify them per the specified request. Similarly, entries are shown in "Column access privileges" only for columns with nondefault privileges. (Note: for this purpose, "default privileges" always means the built-in default privileges for the object's type. An object whose privileges have been affected by an ALTER DEFAULT PRIVILEGES command will always be shown with an explicit privilege entry that includes the effects of the ALTER.)

Notice that the owner's implicit grant options are not marked in the access privileges display. A * will appear only when grant options have been explicitly granted to someone.

Examples

Grant insert privilege to all users on table films:

```
GRANT INSERT ON films TO PUBLIC;
```

Grant all available privileges to user manuel on view kinds:

```
GRANT ALL PRIVILEGES ON kinds TO manuel;
```

Note that while the above will indeed grant all privileges if executed by a superuser or the owner of kinds, when executed by someone else it will only grant those permissions for which the someone else has grant options.

Grant membership in role admins to user joe:

```
GRANT admins TO joe;
```

Compatibility

According to the SQL standard, the PRIVILEGES key word in ALL PRIVILEGES is required. The SQL standard does not support setting the privileges on more than one object per command.

PostgreSQL allows an object owner to revoke their own ordinary privileges: for example, a table owner can make the table read-only to themselves by revoking their own INSERT, UPDATE, DELETE, and TRUNCATE privileges. This is not possible according to the SQL standard. The reason is that PostgreSQL treats the owner's privileges as having been granted by the owner to themselves; therefore they can revoke them too. In the SQL standard, the owner's privileges are granted by an assumed entity "_SYSTEM". Not being "_SYSTEM", the owner cannot revoke these rights.

According to the SQL standard, grant options can be granted to PUBLIC; PostgreSQL only supports granting grant options to roles.

The SQL standard provides for a USAGE privilege on other kinds of objects: character sets, collations, translations.

In the SQL standard, sequences only have a USAGE privilege, which controls the use of the NEXT VALUE FOR expression, which is equivalent to the function nextval in PostgreSQL. The sequence privileges

SELECT and UPDATE are PostgreSQL extensions. The application of the sequence USAGE privilege to the currval function is also a PostgreSQL extension (as is the function itself).

Privileges on databases, tablespaces, schemas, and languages are PostgreSQL extensions.

See Also

REVOKE, ALTER DEFAULT PRIVILEGES

IMPORT FOREIGN SCHEMA

IMPORT FOREIGN SCHEMA — import table definitions from a foreign server

Synopsis

```
IMPORT FOREIGN SCHEMA remote_schema
    [ { LIMIT TO | EXCEPT } ( table_name [, ...] ) ]
    FROM SERVER server_name
    INTO local_schema
    [ OPTIONS ( option 'value' [, ... ] ) ]
```

Description

IMPORT FOREIGN SCHEMA creates foreign tables that represent tables existing on a foreign server. The new foreign tables will be owned by the user issuing the command and are created with the correct column definitions and options to match the remote tables.

By default, all tables and views existing in a particular schema on the foreign server are imported. Optionally, the list of tables can be limited to a specified subset, or specific tables can be excluded. The new foreign tables are all created in the target schema, which must already exist.

To use IMPORT FOREIGN SCHEMA, the user must have USAGE privilege on the foreign server, as well as CREATE privilege on the target schema.

Parameters

remote_schema

  The remote schema to import from. The specific meaning of a remote schema depends on the foreign data wrapper in use.

LIMIT TO (table_name [, ...])

  Import only foreign tables matching one of the given table names. Other tables existing in the foreign schema will be ignored.

EXCEPT (table_name [, ...])

  Exclude specified foreign tables from the import. All tables existing in the foreign schema will be imported except the ones listed here.

server_name

  The foreign server to import from.

local_schema

  The schema in which the imported foreign tables will be created.

OPTIONS (option 'value' [, ...])

  Options to be used during the import. The allowed option names and values are specific to each foreign data wrapper.

Examples

Import table definitions from a remote schema `foreign_films` on server `film_server`, creating the foreign tables in local schema `films`:

```
IMPORT FOREIGN SCHEMA foreign_films
    FROM SERVER film_server INTO films;
```

As above, but import only the two tables `actors` and `directors` (if they exist):

```
IMPORT FOREIGN SCHEMA foreign_films LIMIT TO (actors, directors)
    FROM SERVER film_server INTO films;
```

Compatibility

The `IMPORT FOREIGN SCHEMA` command conforms to the SQL standard, except that the `OPTIONS` clause is a PostgreSQL extension.

See Also

CREATE FOREIGN TABLE, CREATE SERVER

INSERT

INSERT — create new rows in a table

Synopsis

```
[ WITH [ RECURSIVE ] with_query [, ...] ]
INSERT INTO table_name [ AS alias ] [ ( column_name [, ...] ) ]
    [ OVERRIDING { SYSTEM | USER} VALUE ]
    { DEFAULT VALUES | VALUES ( { expression | DEFAULT } [, ...] )
[, ...] | query }
    [ ON CONFLICT [ conflict_target ] conflict_action ]
    [ RETURNING * | output_expression [ [ AS ] output_name ] [, ...] ]

where conflict_target can be one of:

    ( { index_column_name | ( index_expression ) } [ COLLATE collation
] [ opclass ] [, ...] ) [ WHERE index_predicate ]
    ON CONSTRAINT constraint_name

and conflict_action is one of:

    DO NOTHING
    DO UPDATE SET { column_name = { expression | DEFAULT } |
                    ( column_name [, ...] ) = [ ROW ] ( { expression |
DEFAULT } [, ...] ) |
                    ( column_name [, ...] ) = ( sub-SELECT )
                  } [, ...]
              [ WHERE condition ]
```

Description

INSERT inserts new rows into a table. One can insert one or more rows specified by value expressions, or zero or more rows resulting from a query.

The target column names can be listed in any order. If no list of column names is given at all, the default is all the columns of the table in their declared order; or the first N column names, if there are only N columns supplied by the VALUES clause or query. The values supplied by the VALUES clause or query are associated with the explicit or implicit column list left-to-right.

Each column not present in the explicit or implicit column list will be filled with a default value, either its declared default value or null if there is none.

If the expression for any column is not of the correct data type, automatic type conversion will be attempted.

ON CONFLICT can be used to specify an alternative action to raising a unique constraint or exclusion constraint violation error. (See ON CONFLICT Clause below.)

The optional RETURNING clause causes INSERT to compute and return value(s) based on each row actually inserted (or updated, if an ON CONFLICT DO UPDATE clause was used). This is primarily useful for obtaining values that were supplied by defaults, such as a serial sequence number. However, any expression using the table's columns is allowed. The syntax of the RETURNING list is identical to that of the output list of SELECT. Only rows that were successfully inserted or updated will be returned. For example, if a row was locked but not updated because an ON CONFLICT DO UPDATE ... WHERE clause *condition* was not satisfied, the row will not be returned.

You must have INSERT privilege on a table in order to insert into it. If ON CONFLICT DO UPDATE is present, UPDATE privilege on the table is also required.

If a column list is specified, you only need INSERT privilege on the listed columns. Similarly, when ON CONFLICT DO UPDATE is specified, you only need UPDATE privilege on the column(s) that are listed to be updated. However, ON CONFLICT DO UPDATE also requires SELECT privilege on any column whose values are read in the ON CONFLICT DO UPDATE expressions or *condition*.

Use of the RETURNING clause requires SELECT privilege on all columns mentioned in RETURNING. If you use the *query* clause to insert rows from a query, you of course need to have SELECT privilege on any table or column used in the query.

Parameters

Inserting

This section covers parameters that may be used when only inserting new rows. Parameters *exclusively* used with the ON CONFLICT clause are described separately.

with_query

> The WITH clause allows you to specify one or more subqueries that can be referenced by name in the INSERT query. See Section 7.8 and SELECT for details.
>
> It is possible for the *query* (SELECT statement) to also contain a WITH clause. In such a case both sets of *with_query* can be referenced within the *query*, but the second one takes precedence since it is more closely nested.

table_name

> The name (optionally schema-qualified) of an existing table.

alias

> A substitute name for *table_name*. When an alias is provided, it completely hides the actual name of the table. This is particularly useful when ON CONFLICT DO UPDATE targets a table named excluded, since that will otherwise be taken as the name of the special table representing rows proposed for insertion.

column_name

> The name of a column in the table named by *table_name*. The column name can be qualified with a subfield name or array subscript, if needed. (Inserting into only some fields of a composite column leaves the other fields null.) When referencing a column with ON CONFLICT DO UPDATE, do not include the table's name in the specification of a target column. For example, INSERT INTO table_name ... ON CONFLICT DO UPDATE SET table_name.col = 1 is invalid (this follows the general behavior for UPDATE).

OVERRIDING SYSTEM VALUE

> Without this clause, it is an error to specify an explicit value (other than DEFAULT) for an identity column defined as GENERATED ALWAYS. This clause overrides that restriction.

OVERRIDING USER VALUE

If this clause is specified, then any values supplied for identity columns defined as GENERATED BY DEFAULT are ignored and the default sequence-generated values are applied.

This clause is useful for example when copying values between tables. Writing INSERT INTO tbl2 OVERRIDING USER VALUE SELECT * FROM tbl1 will copy from tbl1 all columns that are not identity columns in tbl2 while values for the identity columns in tbl2 will be generated by the sequences associated with tbl2.

DEFAULT VALUES

All columns will be filled with their default values. (An OVERRIDING clause is not permitted in this form.)

expression

An expression or value to assign to the corresponding column.

DEFAULT

The corresponding column will be filled with its default value.

query

A query (SELECT statement) that supplies the rows to be inserted. Refer to the SELECT statement for a description of the syntax.

output_expression

An expression to be computed and returned by the INSERT command after each row is inserted or updated. The expression can use any column names of the table named by *table_name*. Write * to return all columns of the inserted or updated row(s).

output_name

A name to use for a returned column.

ON CONFLICT Clause

The optional ON CONFLICT clause specifies an alternative action to raising a unique violation or exclusion constraint violation error. For each individual row proposed for insertion, either the insertion proceeds, or, if an *arbiter* constraint or index specified by *conflict_target* is violated, the alternative *conflict_action* is taken. ON CONFLICT DO NOTHING simply avoids inserting a row as its alternative action. ON CONFLICT DO UPDATE updates the existing row that conflicts with the row proposed for insertion as its alternative action.

conflict_target can perform *unique index inference*. When performing inference, it consists of one or more *index_column_name* columns and/or *index_expression* expressions, and an optional *index_predicate*. All *table_name* unique indexes that, without regard to order, contain exactly the *conflict_target*-specified columns/expressions are inferred (chosen) as arbiter indexes. If an *index_predicate* is specified, it must, as a further requirement for inference, satisfy arbiter indexes. Note that this means a non-partial unique index (a unique index without a predicate) will be inferred (and thus used by ON CONFLICT) if such an index satisfying every other criteria is available. If an attempt at inference is unsuccessful, an error is raised.

ON CONFLICT DO UPDATE guarantees an atomic INSERT or UPDATE outcome; provided there is no independent error, one of those two outcomes is guaranteed, even under high concurrency. This is also known as *UPSERT* — "UPDATE or INSERT".

conflict_target

Specifies which conflicts ON CONFLICT takes the alternative action on by choosing *arbiter indexes*. Either performs *unique index inference*, or names a constraint explicitly. For ON CONFLICT DO NOTHING, it is optional to specify a *conflict_target*; when omitted, conflicts with all usable constraints (and unique indexes) are handled. For ON CONFLICT DO UPDATE, a *conflict_target must* be provided.

conflict_action

conflict_action specifies an alternative ON CONFLICT action. It can be either DO NOTHING, or a DO UPDATE clause specifying the exact details of the UPDATE action to be performed in case of a conflict. The SET and WHERE clauses in ON CONFLICT DO UPDATE have access to the existing row using the table's name (or an alias), and to rows proposed for insertion using the special excluded table. SELECT privilege is required on any column in the target table where corresponding excluded columns are read.

Note that the effects of all per-row BEFORE INSERT triggers are reflected in excluded values, since those effects may have contributed to the row being excluded from insertion.

index_column_name

The name of a *table_name* column. Used to infer arbiter indexes. Follows CREATE INDEX format. SELECT privilege on *index_column_name* is required.

index_expression

Similar to *index_column_name*, but used to infer expressions on *table_name* columns appearing within index definitions (not simple columns). Follows CREATE INDEX format. SELECT privilege on any column appearing within *index_expression* is required.

collation

When specified, mandates that corresponding *index_column_name* or *index_expression* use a particular collation in order to be matched during inference. Typically this is omitted, as collations usually do not affect whether or not a constraint violation occurs. Follows CREATE INDEX format.

opclass

When specified, mandates that corresponding *index_column_name* or *index_expression* use particular operator class in order to be matched during inference. Typically this is omitted, as the *equality* semantics are often equivalent across a type's operator classes anyway, or because it's sufficient to trust that the defined unique indexes have the pertinent definition of equality. Follows CREATE INDEX format.

index_predicate

Used to allow inference of partial unique indexes. Any indexes that satisfy the predicate (which need not actually be partial indexes) can be inferred. Follows CREATE INDEX format. SELECT privilege on any column appearing within *index_predicate* is required.

constraint_name

> Explicitly specifies an arbiter *constraint* by name, rather than inferring a constraint or index.

condition

> An expression that returns a value of type boolean. Only rows for which this expression returns true will be updated, although all rows will be locked when the ON CONFLICT DO UPDATE action is taken. Note that condition is evaluated last, after a conflict has been identified as a candidate to update.

Note that exclusion constraints are not supported as arbiters with ON CONFLICT DO UPDATE. In all cases, only NOT DEFERRABLE constraints and unique indexes are supported as arbiters.

INSERT with an ON CONFLICT DO UPDATE clause is a "deterministic" statement. This means that the command will not be allowed to affect any single existing row more than once; a cardinality violation error will be raised when this situation arises. Rows proposed for insertion should not duplicate each other in terms of attributes constrained by an arbiter index or constraint.

Note that it is currently not supported for the ON CONFLICT DO UPDATE clause of an INSERT applied to a partitioned table to update the partition key of a conflicting row such that it requires the row be moved to a new partition.

Tip

It is often preferable to use unique index inference rather than naming a constraint directly using ON CONFLICT ON CONSTRAINT constraint_name. Inference will continue to work correctly when the underlying index is replaced by another more or less equivalent index in an overlapping way, for example when using CREATE UNIQUE INDEX ... CONCURRENTLY before dropping the index being replaced.

Outputs

On successful completion, an INSERT command returns a command tag of the form

INSERT oid count

The count is the number of rows inserted or updated. If count is exactly one, and the target table has OIDs, then oid is the OID assigned to the inserted row. The single row must have been inserted rather than updated. Otherwise oid is zero.

If the INSERT command contains a RETURNING clause, the result will be similar to that of a SELECT statement containing the columns and values defined in the RETURNING list, computed over the row(s) inserted or updated by the command.

Notes

If the specified table is a partitioned table, each row is routed to the appropriate partition and inserted into it. If the specified table is a partition, an error will occur if one of the input rows violates the partition constraint.

Examples

Insert a single row into table films:

```
INSERT INTO films VALUES
    ('UA502', 'Bananas', 105, '1971-07-13', 'Comedy', '82 minutes');
```

In this example, the len column is omitted and therefore it will have the default value:

```
INSERT INTO films (code, title, did, date_prod, kind)
    VALUES ('T_601', 'Yojimbo', 106, '1961-06-16', 'Drama');
```

This example uses the DEFAULT clause for the date columns rather than specifying a value:

```
INSERT INTO films VALUES
    ('UA502', 'Bananas', 105, DEFAULT, 'Comedy', '82 minutes');
INSERT INTO films (code, title, did, date_prod, kind)
    VALUES ('T_601', 'Yojimbo', 106, DEFAULT, 'Drama');
```

To insert a row consisting entirely of default values:

```
INSERT INTO films DEFAULT VALUES;
```

To insert multiple rows using the multirow VALUES syntax:

```
INSERT INTO films (code, title, did, date_prod, kind) VALUES
    ('B6717', 'Tampopo', 110, '1985-02-10', 'Comedy'),
    ('HG120', 'The Dinner Game', 140, DEFAULT, 'Comedy');
```

This example inserts some rows into table films from a table tmp_films with the same column layout as films:

```
INSERT INTO films SELECT * FROM tmp_films WHERE date_prod <
'2004-05-07';
```

This example inserts into array columns:

```
-- Create an empty 3x3 gameboard for noughts-and-crosses
INSERT INTO tictactoe (game, board[1:3][1:3])
    VALUES (1, '{{" "," "," "},{" "," "," "},{" "," "," "}}');
-- The subscripts in the above example aren't really needed
INSERT INTO tictactoe (game, board)
    VALUES (2, '{{X," "," "},{" ",O," "},{" ",X," "}}');
```

Insert a single row into table distributors, returning the sequence number generated by the DEFAULT clause:

```
INSERT INTO distributors (did, dname) VALUES (DEFAULT, 'XYZ Widgets')
```

```
    RETURNING did;
```

Increment the sales count of the salesperson who manages the account for Acme Corporation, and record the whole updated row along with current time in a log table:

```
WITH upd AS (
  UPDATE employees SET sales_count = sales_count + 1 WHERE id =
    (SELECT sales_person FROM accounts WHERE name = 'Acme
 Corporation')
    RETURNING *
)
INSERT INTO employees_log SELECT *, current_timestamp FROM upd;
```

Insert or update new distributors as appropriate. Assumes a unique index has been defined that constrains values appearing in the did column. Note that the special excluded table is used to reference values originally proposed for insertion:

```
INSERT INTO distributors (did, dname)
    VALUES (5, 'Gizmo Transglobal'), (6, 'Associated Computing, Inc')
    ON CONFLICT (did) DO UPDATE SET dname = EXCLUDED.dname;
```

Insert a distributor, or do nothing for rows proposed for insertion when an existing, excluded row (a row with a matching constrained column or columns after before row insert triggers fire) exists. Example assumes a unique index has been defined that constrains values appearing in the did column:

```
INSERT INTO distributors (did, dname) VALUES (7, 'Redline GmbH')
    ON CONFLICT (did) DO NOTHING;
```

Insert or update new distributors as appropriate. Example assumes a unique index has been defined that constrains values appearing in the did column. WHERE clause is used to limit the rows actually updated (any existing row not updated will still be locked, though):

```
-- Don't update existing distributors based in a certain ZIP code
INSERT INTO distributors AS d (did, dname) VALUES (8, 'Anvil
 Distribution')
    ON CONFLICT (did) DO UPDATE
    SET dname = EXCLUDED.dname || ' (formerly ' || d.dname || ')'
    WHERE d.zipcode <> '21201';

-- Name a constraint directly in the statement (uses associated
-- index to arbitrate taking the DO NOTHING action)
INSERT INTO distributors (did, dname) VALUES (9, 'Antwerp Design')
    ON CONFLICT ON CONSTRAINT distributors_pkey DO NOTHING;
```

Insert new distributor if possible; otherwise DO NOTHING. Example assumes a unique index has been defined that constrains values appearing in the did column on a subset of rows where the is_active Boolean column evaluates to true:

```
-- This statement could infer a partial unique index on "did"
-- with a predicate of "WHERE is_active", but it could also
-- just use a regular unique constraint on "did"
```

```
INSERT INTO distributors (did, dname) VALUES (10, 'Conrad
 International')
     ON CONFLICT (did) WHERE is_active DO NOTHING;
```

Compatibility

INSERT conforms to the SQL standard, except that the RETURNING clause is a PostgreSQL extension, as is the ability to use WITH with INSERT, and the ability to specify an alternative action with ON CONFLICT. Also, the case in which a column name list is omitted, but not all the columns are filled from the VALUES clause or *query*, is disallowed by the standard.

The SQL standard specifies that OVERRIDING SYSTEM VALUE can only be specified if an identity column that is generated always exists. PostgreSQL allows the clause in any case and ignores it if it is not applicable.

Possible limitations of the *query* clause are documented under SELECT.

LISTEN

LISTEN — listen for a notification

Synopsis

```
LISTEN channel
```

Description

LISTEN registers the current session as a listener on the notification channel named *channel*. If the current session is already registered as a listener for this notification channel, nothing is done.

Whenever the command NOTIFY *channel* is invoked, either by this session or another one connected to the same database, all the sessions currently listening on that notification channel are notified, and each will in turn notify its connected client application.

A session can be unregistered for a given notification channel with the UNLISTEN command. A session's listen registrations are automatically cleared when the session ends.

The method a client application must use to detect notification events depends on which PostgreSQL application programming interface it uses. With the libpq library, the application issues LISTEN as an ordinary SQL command, and then must periodically call the function PQnotifies to find out whether any notification events have been received. Other interfaces such as libpgtcl provide higher-level methods for handling notify events; indeed, with libpgtcl the application programmer should not even issue LISTEN or UNLISTEN directly. See the documentation for the interface you are using for more details.

NOTIFY contains a more extensive discussion of the use of LISTEN and NOTIFY.

Parameters

channel

Name of a notification channel (any identifier).

Notes

LISTEN takes effect at transaction commit. If LISTEN or UNLISTEN is executed within a transaction that later rolls back, the set of notification channels being listened to is unchanged.

A transaction that has executed LISTEN cannot be prepared for two-phase commit.

Examples

Configure and execute a listen/notify sequence from psql:

```
LISTEN virtual;
NOTIFY virtual;
```

```
Asynchronous notification "virtual" received from server process with
    PID 8448.
```

Compatibility

There is no LISTEN statement in the SQL standard.

See Also

NOTIFY, UNLISTEN

LOAD

LOAD — load a shared library file

Synopsis

```
LOAD 'filename'
```

Description

This command loads a shared library file into the PostgreSQL server's address space. If the file has been loaded already, the command does nothing. Shared library files that contain C functions are automatically loaded whenever one of their functions is called. Therefore, an explicit LOAD is usually only needed to load a library that modifies the server's behavior through "hooks" rather than providing a set of functions.

The library file name is typically given as just a bare file name, which is sought in the server's library search path (set by dynamic_library_path). Alternatively it can be given as a full path name. In either case the platform's standard shared library file name extension may be omitted. See Section 38.10.1 for more information on this topic.

Non-superusers can only apply LOAD to library files located in `$libdir/plugins/` — the specified *filename* must begin with exactly that string. (It is the database administrator's responsibility to ensure that only "safe" libraries are installed there.)

Compatibility

LOAD is a PostgreSQL extension.

See Also

CREATE FUNCTION

LOCK

LOCK — lock a table

Synopsis

```
LOCK [ TABLE ] [ ONLY ] name [ * ] [, ...] [ IN lockmode MODE ]
[ NOWAIT ]
```

where `lockmode` is one of:

```
ACCESS SHARE | ROW SHARE | ROW EXCLUSIVE | SHARE UPDATE EXCLUSIVE
| SHARE | SHARE ROW EXCLUSIVE | EXCLUSIVE | ACCESS EXCLUSIVE
```

Description

LOCK TABLE obtains a table-level lock, waiting if necessary for any conflicting locks to be released. If NOWAIT is specified, LOCK TABLE does not wait to acquire the desired lock: if it cannot be acquired immediately, the command is aborted and an error is emitted. Once obtained, the lock is held for the remainder of the current transaction. (There is no UNLOCK TABLE command; locks are always released at transaction end.)

When a view is locked, all relations appearing in the view definition query are also locked recursively with the same lock mode.

When acquiring locks automatically for commands that reference tables, PostgreSQL always uses the least restrictive lock mode possible. LOCK TABLE provides for cases when you might need more restrictive locking. For example, suppose an application runs a transaction at the READ COMMITTED isolation level and needs to ensure that data in a table remains stable for the duration of the transaction. To achieve this you could obtain SHARE lock mode over the table before querying. This will prevent concurrent data changes and ensure subsequent reads of the table see a stable view of committed data, because SHARE lock mode conflicts with the ROW EXCLUSIVE lock acquired by writers, and your LOCK TABLE name IN SHARE MODE statement will wait until any concurrent holders of ROW EXCLUSIVE mode locks commit or roll back. Thus, once you obtain the lock, there are no uncommitted writes outstanding; furthermore none can begin until you release the lock.

To achieve a similar effect when running a transaction at the REPEATABLE READ or SERIALIZABLE isolation level, you have to execute the LOCK TABLE statement before executing any SELECT or data modification statement. A REPEATABLE READ or SERIALIZABLE transaction's view of data will be frozen when its first SELECT or data modification statement begins. A LOCK TABLE later in the transaction will still prevent concurrent writes — but it won't ensure that what the transaction reads corresponds to the latest committed values.

If a transaction of this sort is going to change the data in the table, then it should use SHARE ROW EXCLUSIVE lock mode instead of SHARE mode. This ensures that only one transaction of this type runs at a time. Without this, a deadlock is possible: two transactions might both acquire SHARE mode, and then be unable to also acquire ROW EXCLUSIVE mode to actually perform their updates. (Note that a transaction's own locks never conflict, so a transaction can acquire ROW EXCLUSIVE mode when it holds SHARE mode — but not if anyone else holds SHARE mode.) To avoid deadlocks, make sure all transactions acquire locks on the same objects in the same order, and if multiple lock modes are involved for a single object, then transactions should always acquire the most restrictive mode first.

More information about the lock modes and locking strategies can be found in Section 13.3.

Parameters

name

The name (optionally schema-qualified) of an existing table to lock. If ONLY is specified before the table name, only that table is locked. If ONLY is not specified, the table and all its descendant tables (if any) are locked. Optionally, * can be specified after the table name to explicitly indicate that descendant tables are included.

The command LOCK TABLE a, b; is equivalent to LOCK TABLE a; LOCK TABLE b;. The tables are locked one-by-one in the order specified in the LOCK TABLE command.

lockmode

The lock mode specifies which locks this lock conflicts with. Lock modes are described in Section 13.3.

If no lock mode is specified, then ACCESS EXCLUSIVE, the most restrictive mode, is used.

NOWAIT

Specifies that LOCK TABLE should not wait for any conflicting locks to be released: if the specified lock(s) cannot be acquired immediately without waiting, the transaction is aborted.

Notes

LOCK TABLE ... IN ACCESS SHARE MODE requires SELECT privileges on the target table. LOCK TABLE ... IN ROW EXCLUSIVE MODE requires INSERT, UPDATE, DELETE, or TRUNCATE privileges on the target table. All other forms of LOCK require table-level UPDATE, DELETE, or TRUNCATE privileges.

The user performing the lock on the view must have the corresponding privilege on the view. In addition the view's owner must have the relevant privileges on the underlying base relations, but the user performing the lock does not need any permissions on the underlying base relations.

LOCK TABLE is useless outside a transaction block: the lock would remain held only to the completion of the statement. Therefore PostgreSQL reports an error if LOCK is used outside a transaction block. Use BEGIN and COMMIT (or ROLLBACK) to define a transaction block.

LOCK TABLE only deals with table-level locks, and so the mode names involving ROW are all misnomers. These mode names should generally be read as indicating the intention of the user to acquire row-level locks within the locked table. Also, ROW EXCLUSIVE mode is a shareable table lock. Keep in mind that all the lock modes have identical semantics so far as LOCK TABLE is concerned, differing only in the rules about which modes conflict with which. For information on how to acquire an actual row-level lock, see Section 13.3.2 and the The Locking Clause in the SELECT reference documentation.

Examples

Obtain a SHARE lock on a primary key table when going to perform inserts into a foreign key table:

```
BEGIN WORK;
LOCK TABLE films IN SHARE MODE;
```

```
SELECT id FROM films
    WHERE name = 'Star Wars: Episode I - The Phantom Menace';
-- Do ROLLBACK if record was not returned
INSERT INTO films_user_comments VALUES
    (_id_, 'GREAT! I was waiting for it for so long!');
COMMIT WORK;
```

Take a SHARE ROW EXCLUSIVE lock on a primary key table when going to perform a delete operation:

```
BEGIN WORK;
LOCK TABLE films IN SHARE ROW EXCLUSIVE MODE;
DELETE FROM films_user_comments WHERE id IN
    (SELECT id FROM films WHERE rating < 5);
DELETE FROM films WHERE rating < 5;
COMMIT WORK;
```

Compatibility

There is no LOCK TABLE in the SQL standard, which instead uses SET TRANSACTION to specify concurrency levels on transactions. PostgreSQL supports that too; see SET TRANSACTION for details.

Except for ACCESS SHARE, ACCESS EXCLUSIVE, and SHARE UPDATE EXCLUSIVE lock modes, the PostgreSQL lock modes and the LOCK TABLE syntax are compatible with those present in Oracle.

MOVE

MOVE — position a cursor

Synopsis

```
MOVE [ direction [ FROM | IN ] ] cursor_name
```

where *direction* can be empty or one of:

```
NEXT
PRIOR
FIRST
LAST
ABSOLUTE count
RELATIVE count
count
ALL
FORWARD
FORWARD count
FORWARD ALL
BACKWARD
BACKWARD count
BACKWARD ALL
```

Description

MOVE repositions a cursor without retrieving any data. MOVE works exactly like the FETCH command, except it only positions the cursor and does not return rows.

The parameters for the MOVE command are identical to those of the FETCH command; refer to FETCH for details on syntax and usage.

Outputs

On successful completion, a MOVE command returns a command tag of the form

```
MOVE count
```

The *count* is the number of rows that a FETCH command with the same parameters would have returned (possibly zero).

Examples

```
BEGIN WORK;
DECLARE liahona CURSOR FOR SELECT * FROM films;

-- Skip the first 5 rows:
```

```
MOVE FORWARD 5 IN liahona;
MOVE 5

-- Fetch the 6th row from the cursor liahona:
FETCH 1 FROM liahona;
 code  | title  | did | date_prod  |  kind  |  len
-------+--------+-----+------------+--------+-------
 P_303 | 48 Hrs | 103 | 1982-10-22 | Action | 01:37
(1 row)

-- Close the cursor liahona and end the transaction:
CLOSE liahona;
COMMIT WORK;
```

Compatibility

There is no MOVE statement in the SQL standard.

See Also

CLOSE, DECLARE, FETCH

NOTIFY

NOTIFY — generate a notification

Synopsis

```
NOTIFY channel [ , payload ]
```

Description

The NOTIFY command sends a notification event together with an optional "payload" string to each client application that has previously executed LISTEN *channel* for the specified channel name in the current database. Notifications are visible to all users.

NOTIFY provides a simple interprocess communication mechanism for a collection of processes accessing the same PostgreSQL database. A payload string can be sent along with the notification, and higher-level mechanisms for passing structured data can be built by using tables in the database to pass additional data from notifier to listener(s).

The information passed to the client for a notification event includes the notification channel name, the notifying session's server process PID, and the payload string, which is an empty string if it has not been specified.

It is up to the database designer to define the channel names that will be used in a given database and what each one means. Commonly, the channel name is the same as the name of some table in the database, and the notify event essentially means, "I changed this table, take a look at it to see what's new". But no such association is enforced by the NOTIFY and LISTEN commands. For example, a database designer could use several different channel names to signal different sorts of changes to a single table. Alternatively, the payload string could be used to differentiate various cases.

When NOTIFY is used to signal the occurrence of changes to a particular table, a useful programming technique is to put the NOTIFY in a statement trigger that is triggered by table updates. In this way, notification happens automatically when the table is changed, and the application programmer cannot accidentally forget to do it.

NOTIFY interacts with SQL transactions in some important ways. Firstly, if a NOTIFY is executed inside a transaction, the notify events are not delivered until and unless the transaction is committed. This is appropriate, since if the transaction is aborted, all the commands within it have had no effect, including NOTIFY. But it can be disconcerting if one is expecting the notification events to be delivered immediately. Secondly, if a listening session receives a notification signal while it is within a transaction, the notification event will not be delivered to its connected client until just after the transaction is completed (either committed or aborted). Again, the reasoning is that if a notification were delivered within a transaction that was later aborted, one would want the notification to be undone somehow — but the server cannot "take back" a notification once it has sent it to the client. So notification events are only delivered between transactions. The upshot of this is that applications using NOTIFY for real-time signaling should try to keep their transactions short.

If the same channel name is signaled multiple times from the same transaction with identical payload strings, the database server can decide to deliver a single notification only. On the other hand, notifications with distinct payload strings will always be delivered as distinct notifications. Similarly, notifications from different transactions will never get folded into one notification. Except for dropping later instances of duplicate notifications, NOTIFY guarantees that notifications from the same transaction get delivered in the order they were sent. It is also guaranteed that messages from different transactions are delivered in the order in which the transactions committed.

It is common for a client that executes NOTIFY to be listening on the same notification channel itself. In that case it will get back a notification event, just like all the other listening sessions. Depending on the application logic, this could result in useless work, for example, reading a database table to find the same updates that that session just wrote out. It is possible to avoid such extra work by noticing whether the notifying session's server process PID (supplied in the notification event message) is the same as one's own session's PID (available from libpq). When they are the same, the notification event is one's own work bouncing back, and can be ignored.

Parameters

channel

Name of the notification channel to be signaled (any identifier).

payload

The "payload" string to be communicated along with the notification. This must be specified as a simple string literal. In the default configuration it must be shorter than 8000 bytes. (If binary data or large amounts of information need to be communicated, it's best to put it in a database table and send the key of the record.)

Notes

There is a queue that holds notifications that have been sent but not yet processed by all listening sessions. If this queue becomes full, transactions calling NOTIFY will fail at commit. The queue is quite large (8GB in a standard installation) and should be sufficiently sized for almost every use case. However, no cleanup can take place if a session executes LISTEN and then enters a transaction for a very long time. Once the queue is half full you will see warnings in the log file pointing you to the session that is preventing cleanup. In this case you should make sure that this session ends its current transaction so that cleanup can proceed.

The function pg_notification_queue_usage returns the fraction of the queue that is currently occupied by pending notifications. See Section 9.25 for more information.

A transaction that has executed NOTIFY cannot be prepared for two-phase commit.

pg_notify

To send a notification you can also use the function pg_notify(text, text). The function takes the channel name as the first argument and the payload as the second. The function is much easier to use than the NOTIFY command if you need to work with non-constant channel names and payloads.

Examples

Configure and execute a listen/notify sequence from psql:

```
LISTEN virtual;
NOTIFY virtual;
Asynchronous notification "virtual" received from server process with
 PID 8448.
```

```
NOTIFY virtual, 'This is the payload';
Asynchronous notification "virtual" with payload "This is the payload"
 received from server process with PID 8448.

LISTEN foo;
SELECT pg_notify('fo' || 'o', 'pay' || 'load');
Asynchronous notification "foo" with payload "payload" received from
 server process with PID 14728.
```

Compatibility

There is no NOTIFY statement in the SQL standard.

See Also

LISTEN, UNLISTEN

PREPARE

PREPARE — prepare a statement for execution

Synopsis

```
PREPARE name [ ( data_type [, ...] ) ] AS statement
```

Description

PREPARE creates a prepared statement. A prepared statement is a server-side object that can be used to optimize performance. When the PREPARE statement is executed, the specified statement is parsed, analyzed, and rewritten. When an EXECUTE command is subsequently issued, the prepared statement is planned and executed. This division of labor avoids repetitive parse analysis work, while allowing the execution plan to depend on the specific parameter values supplied.

Prepared statements can take parameters: values that are substituted into the statement when it is executed. When creating the prepared statement, refer to parameters by position, using $1, $2, etc. A corresponding list of parameter data types can optionally be specified. When a parameter's data type is not specified or is declared as unknown, the type is inferred from the context in which the parameter is first referenced (if possible). When executing the statement, specify the actual values for these parameters in the EXECUTE statement. Refer to EXECUTE for more information about that.

Prepared statements only last for the duration of the current database session. When the session ends, the prepared statement is forgotten, so it must be recreated before being used again. This also means that a single prepared statement cannot be used by multiple simultaneous database clients; however, each client can create their own prepared statement to use. Prepared statements can be manually cleaned up using the DEALLOCATE command.

Prepared statements potentially have the largest performance advantage when a single session is being used to execute a large number of similar statements. The performance difference will be particularly significant if the statements are complex to plan or rewrite, e.g. if the query involves a join of many tables or requires the application of several rules. If the statement is relatively simple to plan and rewrite but relatively expensive to execute, the performance advantage of prepared statements will be less noticeable.

Parameters

name

An arbitrary name given to this particular prepared statement. It must be unique within a single session and is subsequently used to execute or deallocate a previously prepared statement.

data_type

The data type of a parameter to the prepared statement. If the data type of a particular parameter is unspecified or is specified as unknown, it will be inferred from the context in which the parameter is first referenced. To refer to the parameters in the prepared statement itself, use $1, $2, etc.

statement

Any SELECT, INSERT, UPDATE, DELETE, or VALUES statement.

Notes

Prepared statements can use generic plans rather than re-planning with each set of supplied EXECUTE values. This occurs immediately for prepared statements with no parameters; otherwise it occurs only after five or more executions produce plans whose estimated cost average (including planning overhead) is more expensive than the generic plan cost estimate. Once a generic plan is chosen, it is used for the remaining lifetime of the prepared statement. Using EXECUTE values which are rare in columns with many duplicates can generate custom plans that are so much cheaper than the generic plan, even after adding planning overhead, that the generic plan might never be used.

A generic plan assumes that each value supplied to EXECUTE is one of the column's distinct values and that column values are uniformly distributed. For example, if statistics record three distinct column values, a generic plan assumes a column equality comparison will match 33% of processed rows. Column statistics also allow generic plans to accurately compute the selectivity of unique columns. Comparisons on non-uniformly-distributed columns and specification of non-existent values affects the average plan cost, and hence if and when a generic plan is chosen.

To examine the query plan PostgreSQL is using for a prepared statement, use EXPLAIN, e.g. EXPLAIN EXECUTE. If a generic plan is in use, it will contain parameter symbols n, while a custom plan will have the supplied parameter values substituted into it. The row estimates in the generic plan reflect the selectivity computed for the parameters.

For more information on query planning and the statistics collected by PostgreSQL for that purpose, see the ANALYZE documentation.

Although the main point of a prepared statement is to avoid repeated parse analysis and planning of the statement, PostgreSQL will force re-analysis and re-planning of the statement before using it whenever database objects used in the statement have undergone definitional (DDL) changes since the previous use of the prepared statement. Also, if the value of search_path changes from one use to the next, the statement will be re-parsed using the new `search_path`. (This latter behavior is new as of PostgreSQL 9.3.) These rules make use of a prepared statement semantically almost equivalent to re-submitting the same query text over and over, but with a performance benefit if no object definitions are changed, especially if the best plan remains the same across uses. An example of a case where the semantic equivalence is not perfect is that if the statement refers to a table by an unqualified name, and then a new table of the same name is created in a schema appearing earlier in the `search_path`, no automatic re-parse will occur since no object used in the statement changed. However, if some other change forces a re-parse, the new table will be referenced in subsequent uses.

You can see all prepared statements available in the session by querying the `pg_prepared_statements` system view.

Examples

Create a prepared statement for an INSERT statement, and then execute it:

```
PREPARE fooplan (int, text, bool, numeric) AS
    INSERT INTO foo VALUES($1, $2, $3, $4);
EXECUTE fooplan(1, 'Hunter Valley', 't', 200.00);
```

Create a prepared statement for a SELECT statement, and then execute it:

```
PREPARE usrrptplan (int) AS
```

```
      SELECT * FROM users u, logs l WHERE u.usrid=$1 AND u.usrid=l.usrid
      AND l.date = $2;
EXECUTE usrrptplan(1, current_date);
```

Note that the data type of the second parameter is not specified, so it is inferred from the context in which $2 is used.

Compatibility

The SQL standard includes a PREPARE statement, but it is only for use in embedded SQL. This version of the PREPARE statement also uses a somewhat different syntax.

See Also

DEALLOCATE, EXECUTE

PREPARE TRANSACTION

PREPARE TRANSACTION — prepare the current transaction for two-phase commit

Synopsis

```
PREPARE TRANSACTION transaction_id
```

Description

PREPARE TRANSACTION prepares the current transaction for two-phase commit. After this command, the transaction is no longer associated with the current session; instead, its state is fully stored on disk, and there is a very high probability that it can be committed successfully, even if a database crash occurs before the commit is requested.

Once prepared, a transaction can later be committed or rolled back with COMMIT PREPARED or ROLLBACK PREPARED, respectively. Those commands can be issued from any session, not only the one that executed the original transaction.

From the point of view of the issuing session, PREPARE TRANSACTION is not unlike a ROLLBACK command: after executing it, there is no active current transaction, and the effects of the prepared transaction are no longer visible. (The effects will become visible again if the transaction is committed.)

If the PREPARE TRANSACTION command fails for any reason, it becomes a ROLLBACK: the current transaction is canceled.

Parameters

transaction_id

> An arbitrary identifier that later identifies this transaction for COMMIT PREPARED or ROLLBACK PREPARED. The identifier must be written as a string literal, and must be less than 200 bytes long. It must not be the same as the identifier used for any currently prepared transaction.

Notes

PREPARE TRANSACTION is not intended for use in applications or interactive sessions. Its purpose is to allow an external transaction manager to perform atomic global transactions across multiple databases or other transactional resources. Unless you're writing a transaction manager, you probably shouldn't be using PREPARE TRANSACTION.

This command must be used inside a transaction block. Use BEGIN to start one.

It is not currently allowed to PREPARE a transaction that has executed any operations involving temporary tables or the session's temporary namespace, created any cursors WITH HOLD, or executed LISTEN, UNLISTEN, or NOTIFY. Those features are too tightly tied to the current session to be useful in a transaction to be prepared.

If the transaction modified any run-time parameters with SET (without the LOCAL option), those effects persist after PREPARE TRANSACTION, and will not be affected by any later COMMIT PREPARED or

ROLLBACK PREPARED. Thus, in this one respect PREPARE TRANSACTION acts more like COMMIT than ROLLBACK.

All currently available prepared transactions are listed in the pg_prepared_xacts system view.

Caution

It is unwise to leave transactions in the prepared state for a long time. This will interfere with the ability of VACUUM to reclaim storage, and in extreme cases could cause the database to shut down to prevent transaction ID wraparound (see Section 24.1.5). Keep in mind also that the transaction continues to hold whatever locks it held. The intended usage of the feature is that a prepared transaction will normally be committed or rolled back as soon as an external transaction manager has verified that other databases are also prepared to commit.

If you have not set up an external transaction manager to track prepared transactions and ensure they get closed out promptly, it is best to keep the prepared-transaction feature disabled by setting max_prepared_transactions to zero. This will prevent accidental creation of prepared transactions that might then be forgotten and eventually cause problems.

Examples

Prepare the current transaction for two-phase commit, using foobar as the transaction identifier:

```
PREPARE TRANSACTION 'foobar';
```

Compatibility

PREPARE TRANSACTION is a PostgreSQL extension. It is intended for use by external transaction management systems, some of which are covered by standards (such as X/Open XA), but the SQL side of those systems is not standardized.

See Also
COMMIT PREPARED, ROLLBACK PREPARED

REASSIGN OWNED

REASSIGN OWNED — change the ownership of database objects owned by a database role

Synopsis

```
REASSIGN OWNED BY { old_role | CURRENT_USER | SESSION_USER } [, ...]
                TO { new_role | CURRENT_USER | SESSION_USER }
```

Description

REASSIGN OWNED instructs the system to change the ownership of database objects owned by any of the *old_roles* to *new_role*.

Parameters

old_role

The name of a role. The ownership of all the objects within the current database, and of all shared objects (databases, tablespaces), owned by this role will be reassigned to *new_role*.

new_role

The name of the role that will be made the new owner of the affected objects.

Notes

REASSIGN OWNED is often used to prepare for the removal of one or more roles. Because REASSIGN OWNED does not affect objects within other databases, it is usually necessary to execute this command in each database that contains objects owned by a role that is to be removed.

REASSIGN OWNED requires membership on both the source role(s) and the target role.

The DROP OWNED command is an alternative that simply drops all the database objects owned by one or more roles.

The REASSIGN OWNED command does not affect any privileges granted to the *old_roles* for objects that are not owned by them. Use DROP OWNED to revoke such privileges.

See Section 21.4 for more discussion.

Compatibility

The REASSIGN OWNED command is a PostgreSQL extension.

See Also
DROP OWNED, DROP ROLE, ALTER DATABASE

REFRESH MATERIALIZED VIEW

REFRESH MATERIALIZED VIEW — replace the contents of a materialized view

Synopsis

```
REFRESH MATERIALIZED VIEW [ CONCURRENTLY ] name
    [ WITH [ NO ] DATA ]
```

Description

REFRESH MATERIALIZED VIEW completely replaces the contents of a materialized view. To execute this command you must be the owner of the materialized view. The old contents are discarded. If WITH DATA is specified (or defaults) the backing query is executed to provide the new data, and the materialized view is left in a scannable state. If WITH NO DATA is specified no new data is generated and the materialized view is left in an unscannable state.

CONCURRENTLY and WITH NO DATA may not be specified together.

Parameters

CONCURRENTLY

Refresh the materialized view without locking out concurrent selects on the materialized view. Without this option a refresh which affects a lot of rows will tend to use fewer resources and complete more quickly, but could block other connections which are trying to read from the materialized view. This option may be faster in cases where a small number of rows are affected.

This option is only allowed if there is at least one UNIQUE index on the materialized view which uses only column names and includes all rows; that is, it must not index on any expressions nor include a WHERE clause.

This option may not be used when the materialized view is not already populated.

Even with this option only one REFRESH at a time may run against any one materialized view.

name

The name (optionally schema-qualified) of the materialized view to refresh.

Notes

While the default index for future CLUSTER operations is retained, REFRESH MATERIALIZED VIEW does not order the generated rows based on this property. If you want the data to be ordered upon generation, you must use an ORDER BY clause in the backing query.

Examples

This command will replace the contents of the materialized view called order_summary using the query from the materialized view's definition, and leave it in a scannable state:

```
REFRESH MATERIALIZED VIEW order_summary;
```

This command will free storage associated with the materialized view `annual_statistics_basis` and leave it in an unscannable state:

```
REFRESH MATERIALIZED VIEW annual_statistics_basis WITH NO DATA;
```

Compatibility

`REFRESH MATERIALIZED VIEW` is a PostgreSQL extension.

See Also

CREATE MATERIALIZED VIEW, ALTER MATERIALIZED VIEW, DROP MATERIALIZED VIEW

REINDEX

REINDEX — rebuild indexes

Synopsis

```
REINDEX [ ( VERBOSE ) ] { INDEX | TABLE | SCHEMA | DATABASE |
   SYSTEM } name
```

Description

REINDEX rebuilds an index using the data stored in the index's table, replacing the old copy of the index. There are several scenarios in which to use REINDEX:

- An index has become corrupted, and no longer contains valid data. Although in theory this should never happen, in practice indexes can become corrupted due to software bugs or hardware failures. REINDEX provides a recovery method.

- An index has become "bloated", that is it contains many empty or nearly-empty pages. This can occur with B-tree indexes in PostgreSQL under certain uncommon access patterns. REINDEX provides a way to reduce the space consumption of the index by writing a new version of the index without the dead pages. See Section 24.2 for more information.

- You have altered a storage parameter (such as fillfactor) for an index, and wish to ensure that the change has taken full effect.

- An index build with the CONCURRENTLY option failed, leaving an "invalid" index. Such indexes are useless but it can be convenient to use REINDEX to rebuild them. Note that REINDEX will not perform a concurrent build. To build the index without interfering with production you should drop the index and reissue the CREATE INDEX CONCURRENTLY command.

Parameters

INDEX

Recreate the specified index.

TABLE

Recreate all indexes of the specified table. If the table has a secondary "TOAST" table, that is reindexed as well.

SCHEMA

Recreate all indexes of the specified schema. If a table of this schema has a secondary "TOAST" table, that is reindexed as well. Indexes on shared system catalogs are also processed. This form of REINDEX cannot be executed inside a transaction block.

DATABASE

Recreate all indexes within the current database. Indexes on shared system catalogs are also processed. This form of REINDEX cannot be executed inside a transaction block.

SYSTEM

> Recreate all indexes on system catalogs within the current database. Indexes on shared system catalogs are included. Indexes on user tables are not processed. This form of REINDEX cannot be executed inside a transaction block.

name

> The name of the specific index, table, or database to be reindexed. Index and table names can be schema-qualified. Presently, REINDEX DATABASE and REINDEX SYSTEM can only reindex the current database, so their parameter must match the current database's name.

VERBOSE

> Prints a progress report as each index is reindexed.

Notes

If you suspect corruption of an index on a user table, you can simply rebuild that index, or all indexes on the table, using REINDEX INDEX or REINDEX TABLE.

Things are more difficult if you need to recover from corruption of an index on a system table. In this case it's important for the system to not have used any of the suspect indexes itself. (Indeed, in this sort of scenario you might find that server processes are crashing immediately at start-up, due to reliance on the corrupted indexes.) To recover safely, the server must be started with the -P option, which prevents it from using indexes for system catalog lookups.

One way to do this is to shut down the server and start a single-user PostgreSQL server with the -P option included on its command line. Then, REINDEX DATABASE, REINDEX SYSTEM, REINDEX TABLE, or REINDEX INDEX can be issued, depending on how much you want to reconstruct. If in doubt, use REINDEX SYSTEM to select reconstruction of all system indexes in the database. Then quit the single-user server session and restart the regular server. See the postgres reference page for more information about how to interact with the single-user server interface.

Alternatively, a regular server session can be started with -P included in its command line options. The method for doing this varies across clients, but in all libpq-based clients, it is possible to set the PGOPTIONS environment variable to -P before starting the client. Note that while this method does not require locking out other clients, it might still be wise to prevent other users from connecting to the damaged database until repairs have been completed.

REINDEX is similar to a drop and recreate of the index in that the index contents are rebuilt from scratch. However, the locking considerations are rather different. REINDEX locks out writes but not reads of the index's parent table. It also takes an exclusive lock on the specific index being processed, which will block reads that attempt to use that index. In contrast, DROP INDEX momentarily takes an exclusive lock on the parent table, blocking both writes and reads. The subsequent CREATE INDEX locks out writes but not reads; since the index is not there, no read will attempt to use it, meaning that there will be no blocking but reads might be forced into expensive sequential scans.

Reindexing a single index or table requires being the owner of that index or table. Reindexing a schema or database requires being the owner of that schema or database. Note that is therefore sometimes possible for non-superusers to rebuild indexes of tables owned by other users. However, as a special exception, when REINDEX DATABASE, REINDEX SCHEMA or REINDEX SYSTEM is issued by a non-superuser, indexes on shared catalogs will be skipped unless the user owns the catalog (which typically won't be the case). Of course, superusers can always reindex anything.

Reindexing partitioned tables or partitioned indexes is not supported. Each individual partition can be reindexed separately instead.

Examples

Rebuild a single index:

```
REINDEX INDEX my_index;
```

Rebuild all the indexes on the table my_table:

```
REINDEX TABLE my_table;
```

Rebuild all indexes in a particular database, without trusting the system indexes to be valid already:

```
$ export PGOPTIONS="-P"
$ psql broken_db
...
broken_db=> REINDEX DATABASE broken_db;
broken_db=> \q
```

Compatibility

There is no REINDEX command in the SQL standard.

RELEASE SAVEPOINT

RELEASE SAVEPOINT — destroy a previously defined savepoint

Synopsis

```
RELEASE [ SAVEPOINT ] savepoint_name
```

Description

RELEASE SAVEPOINT destroys a savepoint previously defined in the current transaction.

Destroying a savepoint makes it unavailable as a rollback point, but it has no other user visible behavior. It does not undo the effects of commands executed after the savepoint was established. (To do that, see ROLLBACK TO SAVEPOINT.) Destroying a savepoint when it is no longer needed allows the system to reclaim some resources earlier than transaction end.

RELEASE SAVEPOINT also destroys all savepoints that were established after the named savepoint was established.

Parameters

savepoint_name

The name of the savepoint to destroy.

Notes

Specifying a savepoint name that was not previously defined is an error.

It is not possible to release a savepoint when the transaction is in an aborted state.

If multiple savepoints have the same name, only the one that was most recently defined is released.

Examples

To establish and later destroy a savepoint:

```
BEGIN;
    INSERT INTO table1 VALUES (3);
    SAVEPOINT my_savepoint;
    INSERT INTO table1 VALUES (4);
    RELEASE SAVEPOINT my_savepoint;
COMMIT;
```

The above transaction will insert both 3 and 4.

Compatibility

This command conforms to the SQL standard. The standard specifies that the key word SAVEPOINT is mandatory, but PostgreSQL allows it to be omitted.

See Also

BEGIN, COMMIT, ROLLBACK, ROLLBACK TO SAVEPOINT, SAVEPOINT

RESET

RESET — restore the value of a run-time parameter to the default value

Synopsis

```
RESET configuration_parameter
RESET ALL
```

Description

RESET restores run-time parameters to their default values. RESET is an alternative spelling for

```
SET configuration_parameter TO DEFAULT
```

Refer to SET for details.

The default value is defined as the value that the parameter would have had, if no SET had ever been issued for it in the current session. The actual source of this value might be a compiled-in default, the configuration file, command-line options, or per-database or per-user default settings. This is subtly different from defining it as "the value that the parameter had at session start", because if the value came from the configuration file, it will be reset to whatever is specified by the configuration file now. See Chapter 19 for details.

The transactional behavior of RESET is the same as SET: its effects will be undone by transaction rollback.

Parameters

configuration_parameter

Name of a settable run-time parameter. Available parameters are documented in Chapter 19 and on the SET reference page.

ALL

Resets all settable run-time parameters to default values.

Examples

Set the `timezone` configuration variable to its default value:

```
RESET timezone;
```

Compatibility

RESET is a PostgreSQL extension.

See Also

SET, SHOW

REVOKE

REVOKE — remove access privileges

Synopsis

```
REVOKE [ GRANT OPTION FOR ]
    { { SELECT | INSERT | UPDATE | DELETE | TRUNCATE | REFERENCES |
TRIGGER }
    [, ...] | ALL [ PRIVILEGES ] }
    ON { [ TABLE ] table_name [, ...]
         | ALL TABLES IN SCHEMA schema_name [, ...] }
    FROM { [ GROUP ] role_name | PUBLIC } [, ...]
    [ CASCADE | RESTRICT ]

REVOKE [ GRANT OPTION FOR ]
    { { SELECT | INSERT | UPDATE | REFERENCES } ( column_name
[, ...] )
    [, ...] | ALL [ PRIVILEGES ] ( column_name [, ...] ) }
    ON [ TABLE ] table_name [, ...]
    FROM { [ GROUP ] role_name | PUBLIC } [, ...]
    [ CASCADE | RESTRICT ]

REVOKE [ GRANT OPTION FOR ]
    { { USAGE | SELECT | UPDATE }
    [, ...] | ALL [ PRIVILEGES ] }
    ON { SEQUENCE sequence_name [, ...]
         | ALL SEQUENCES IN SCHEMA schema_name [, ...] }
    FROM { [ GROUP ] role_name | PUBLIC } [, ...]
    [ CASCADE | RESTRICT ]

REVOKE [ GRANT OPTION FOR ]
    { { CREATE | CONNECT | TEMPORARY | TEMP } [, ...] | ALL
[ PRIVILEGES ] }
    ON DATABASE database_name [, ...]
    FROM { [ GROUP ] role_name | PUBLIC } [, ...]
    [ CASCADE | RESTRICT ]

REVOKE [ GRANT OPTION FOR ]
    { USAGE | ALL [ PRIVILEGES ] }
    ON DOMAIN domain_name [, ...]
    FROM { [ GROUP ] role_name | PUBLIC } [, ...]
    [ CASCADE | RESTRICT ]

REVOKE [ GRANT OPTION FOR ]
    { USAGE | ALL [ PRIVILEGES ] }
    ON FOREIGN DATA WRAPPER fdw_name [, ...]
    FROM { [ GROUP ] role_name | PUBLIC } [, ...]
    [ CASCADE | RESTRICT ]
```

```
REVOKE [ GRANT OPTION FOR ]
    { USAGE | ALL [ PRIVILEGES ] }
    ON FOREIGN SERVER server_name [, ...]
    FROM { [ GROUP ] role_name | PUBLIC } [, ...]
    [ CASCADE | RESTRICT ]

REVOKE [ GRANT OPTION FOR ]
    { EXECUTE | ALL [ PRIVILEGES ] }
    ON { { FUNCTION | PROCEDURE | ROUTINE } function_name
 [ ( [ [ argmode ] [ arg_name ] arg_type [, ...] ] ) ] [, ...]
        | ALL { FUNCTIONS | PROCEDURES | ROUTINES } IN
  SCHEMA schema_name [, ...] }
    FROM { [ GROUP ] role_name | PUBLIC } [, ...]
    [ CASCADE | RESTRICT ]

REVOKE [ GRANT OPTION FOR ]
    { USAGE | ALL [ PRIVILEGES ] }
    ON LANGUAGE lang_name [, ...]
    FROM { [ GROUP ] role_name | PUBLIC } [, ...]
    [ CASCADE | RESTRICT ]

REVOKE [ GRANT OPTION FOR ]
    { { SELECT | UPDATE } [, ...] | ALL [ PRIVILEGES ] }
    ON LARGE OBJECT loid [, ...]
    FROM { [ GROUP ] role_name | PUBLIC } [, ...]
    [ CASCADE | RESTRICT ]

REVOKE [ GRANT OPTION FOR ]
    { { CREATE | USAGE } [, ...] | ALL [ PRIVILEGES ] }
    ON SCHEMA schema_name [, ...]
    FROM { [ GROUP ] role_name | PUBLIC } [, ...]
    [ CASCADE | RESTRICT ]

REVOKE [ GRANT OPTION FOR ]
    { CREATE | ALL [ PRIVILEGES ] }
    ON TABLESPACE tablespace_name [, ...]
    FROM { [ GROUP ] role_name | PUBLIC } [, ...]
    [ CASCADE | RESTRICT ]

REVOKE [ GRANT OPTION FOR ]
    { USAGE | ALL [ PRIVILEGES ] }
    ON TYPE type_name [, ...]
    FROM { [ GROUP ] role_name | PUBLIC } [, ...]
    [ CASCADE | RESTRICT ]

REVOKE [ ADMIN OPTION FOR ]
    role_name [, ...] FROM role_name [, ...]
    [ CASCADE | RESTRICT ]
```

Description

The REVOKE command revokes previously granted privileges from one or more roles. The key word PUBLIC refers to the implicitly defined group of all roles.

See the description of the GRANT command for the meaning of the privilege types.

Note that any particular role will have the sum of privileges granted directly to it, privileges granted to any role it is presently a member of, and privileges granted to PUBLIC. Thus, for example, revoking SELECT privilege from PUBLIC does not necessarily mean that all roles have lost SELECT privilege on the object: those who have it granted directly or via another role will still have it. Similarly, revoking SELECT from a user might not prevent that user from using SELECT if PUBLIC or another membership role still has SELECT rights.

If GRANT OPTION FOR is specified, only the grant option for the privilege is revoked, not the privilege itself. Otherwise, both the privilege and the grant option are revoked.

If a user holds a privilege with grant option and has granted it to other users then the privileges held by those other users are called dependent privileges. If the privilege or the grant option held by the first user is being revoked and dependent privileges exist, those dependent privileges are also revoked if CASCADE is specified; if it is not, the revoke action will fail. This recursive revocation only affects privileges that were granted through a chain of users that is traceable to the user that is the subject of this REVOKE command. Thus, the affected users might effectively keep the privilege if it was also granted through other users.

When revoking privileges on a table, the corresponding column privileges (if any) are automatically revoked on each column of the table, as well. On the other hand, if a role has been granted privileges on a table, then revoking the same privileges from individual columns will have no effect.

When revoking membership in a role, GRANT OPTION is instead called ADMIN OPTION, but the behavior is similar. Note also that this form of the command does not allow the noise word GROUP.

Notes

Use psql's \dp command to display the privileges granted on existing tables and columns. See GRANT for information about the format. For non-table objects there are other \d commands that can display their privileges.

A user can only revoke privileges that were granted directly by that user. If, for example, user A has granted a privilege with grant option to user B, and user B has in turn granted it to user C, then user A cannot revoke the privilege directly from C. Instead, user A could revoke the grant option from user B and use the CASCADE option so that the privilege is in turn revoked from user C. For another example, if both A and B have granted the same privilege to C, A can revoke their own grant but not B's grant, so C will still effectively have the privilege.

When a non-owner of an object attempts to REVOKE privileges on the object, the command will fail outright if the user has no privileges whatsoever on the object. As long as some privilege is available, the command will proceed, but it will revoke only those privileges for which the user has grant options. The REVOKE ALL PRIVILEGES forms will issue a warning message if no grant options are held, while the other forms will issue a warning if grant options for any of the privileges specifically named in the command are not held. (In principle these statements apply to the object owner as well, but since the owner is always treated as holding all grant options, the cases can never occur.)

If a superuser chooses to issue a GRANT or REVOKE command, the command is performed as though it were issued by the owner of the affected object. Since all privileges ultimately come from the object owner (possibly indirectly via chains of grant options), it is possible for a superuser to revoke all privileges, but this might require use of CASCADE as stated above.

REVOKE can also be done by a role that is not the owner of the affected object, but is a member of the role that owns the object, or is a member of a role that holds privileges WITH GRANT OPTION on the object. In this case the command is performed as though it were issued by the containing role that actually owns the object or holds the privileges WITH GRANT OPTION. For example, if table t1 is owned by role g1, of which role u1 is a member, then u1 can revoke privileges on t1 that are recorded as being granted by g1. This would include grants made by u1 as well as by other members of role g1.

If the role executing REVOKE holds privileges indirectly via more than one role membership path, it is unspecified which containing role will be used to perform the command. In such cases it is best practice to use SET ROLE to become the specific role you want to do the REVOKE as. Failure to do so might lead to revoking privileges other than the ones you intended, or not revoking anything at all.

Examples

Revoke insert privilege for the public on table films:

```
REVOKE INSERT ON films FROM PUBLIC;
```

Revoke all privileges from user manuel on view kinds:

```
REVOKE ALL PRIVILEGES ON kinds FROM manuel;
```

Note that this actually means "revoke all privileges that I granted".

Revoke membership in role admins from user joe:

```
REVOKE admins FROM joe;
```

Compatibility

The compatibility notes of the GRANT command apply analogously to REVOKE. The keyword RESTRICT or CASCADE is required according to the standard, but PostgreSQL assumes RESTRICT by default.

See Also

GRANT

ROLLBACK

ROLLBACK — abort the current transaction

Synopsis

```
ROLLBACK [ WORK | TRANSACTION ]
```

Description

ROLLBACK rolls back the current transaction and causes all the updates made by the transaction to be discarded.

Parameters

WORK
TRANSACTION

> Optional key words. They have no effect.

Notes

Use COMMIT to successfully terminate a transaction.

Issuing ROLLBACK outside of a transaction block emits a warning and otherwise has no effect.

Examples

To abort all changes:

```
ROLLBACK;
```

Compatibility

The SQL standard only specifies the two forms ROLLBACK and ROLLBACK WORK. Otherwise, this command is fully conforming.

See Also

BEGIN, COMMIT, ROLLBACK TO SAVEPOINT

ROLLBACK PREPARED

ROLLBACK PREPARED — cancel a transaction that was earlier prepared for two-phase commit

Synopsis

```
ROLLBACK PREPARED transaction_id
```

Description

ROLLBACK PREPARED rolls back a transaction that is in prepared state.

Parameters

transaction_id

    The transaction identifier of the transaction that is to be rolled back.

Notes

To roll back a prepared transaction, you must be either the same user that executed the transaction originally, or a superuser. But you do not have to be in the same session that executed the transaction.

This command cannot be executed inside a transaction block. The prepared transaction is rolled back immediately.

All currently available prepared transactions are listed in the `pg_prepared_xacts` system view.

Examples

Roll back the transaction identified by the transaction identifier `foobar`:

```
ROLLBACK PREPARED 'foobar';
```

Compatibility

ROLLBACK PREPARED is a PostgreSQL extension. It is intended for use by external transaction management systems, some of which are covered by standards (such as X/Open XA), but the SQL side of those systems is not standardized.

See Also

PREPARE TRANSACTION, COMMIT PREPARED

ROLLBACK TO SAVEPOINT

ROLLBACK TO SAVEPOINT — roll back to a savepoint

Synopsis

```
ROLLBACK [ WORK | TRANSACTION ] TO [ SAVEPOINT ] savepoint_name
```

Description

Roll back all commands that were executed after the savepoint was established. The savepoint remains valid and can be rolled back to again later, if needed.

ROLLBACK TO SAVEPOINT implicitly destroys all savepoints that were established after the named savepoint.

Parameters

savepoint_name

> The savepoint to roll back to.

Notes

Use RELEASE SAVEPOINT to destroy a savepoint without discarding the effects of commands executed after it was established.

Specifying a savepoint name that has not been established is an error.

Cursors have somewhat non-transactional behavior with respect to savepoints. Any cursor that is opened inside a savepoint will be closed when the savepoint is rolled back. If a previously opened cursor is affected by a FETCH or MOVE command inside a savepoint that is later rolled back, the cursor remains at the position that FETCH left it pointing to (that is, the cursor motion caused by FETCH is not rolled back). Closing a cursor is not undone by rolling back, either. However, other side-effects caused by the cursor's query (such as side-effects of volatile functions called by the query) *are* rolled back if they occur during a savepoint that is later rolled back. A cursor whose execution causes a transaction to abort is put in a cannot-execute state, so while the transaction can be restored using ROLLBACK TO SAVEPOINT, the cursor can no longer be used.

Examples

To undo the effects of the commands executed after my_savepoint was established:

```
ROLLBACK TO SAVEPOINT my_savepoint;
```

Cursor positions are not affected by savepoint rollback:

```
BEGIN;
```

```
DECLARE foo CURSOR FOR SELECT 1 UNION SELECT 2;

SAVEPOINT foo;

FETCH 1 FROM foo;
 ?column?
----------
        1

ROLLBACK TO SAVEPOINT foo;

FETCH 1 FROM foo;
 ?column?
----------
        2

COMMIT;
```

Compatibility

The SQL standard specifies that the key word SAVEPOINT is mandatory, but PostgreSQL and Oracle allow it to be omitted. SQL allows only WORK, not TRANSACTION, as a noise word after ROLLBACK. Also, SQL has an optional clause AND [NO] CHAIN which is not currently supported by PostgreSQL. Otherwise, this command conforms to the SQL standard.

See Also

BEGIN, COMMIT, RELEASE SAVEPOINT, ROLLBACK, SAVEPOINT

SAVEPOINT

SAVEPOINT — define a new savepoint within the current transaction

Synopsis

```
SAVEPOINT savepoint_name
```

Description

SAVEPOINT establishes a new savepoint within the current transaction.

A savepoint is a special mark inside a transaction that allows all commands that are executed after it was established to be rolled back, restoring the transaction state to what it was at the time of the savepoint.

Parameters

savepoint_name

   The name to give to the new savepoint.

Notes

Use ROLLBACK TO SAVEPOINT to rollback to a savepoint. Use RELEASE SAVEPOINT to destroy a savepoint, keeping the effects of commands executed after it was established.

Savepoints can only be established when inside a transaction block. There can be multiple savepoints defined within a transaction.

Examples

To establish a savepoint and later undo the effects of all commands executed after it was established:

```
BEGIN;
    INSERT INTO table1 VALUES (1);
    SAVEPOINT my_savepoint;
    INSERT INTO table1 VALUES (2);
    ROLLBACK TO SAVEPOINT my_savepoint;
    INSERT INTO table1 VALUES (3);
COMMIT;
```

The above transaction will insert the values 1 and 3, but not 2.

To establish and later destroy a savepoint:

```
BEGIN;
    INSERT INTO table1 VALUES (3);
    SAVEPOINT my_savepoint;
```

```
    INSERT INTO table1 VALUES (4);
    RELEASE SAVEPOINT my_savepoint;
COMMIT;
```

The above transaction will insert both 3 and 4.

Compatibility

SQL requires a savepoint to be destroyed automatically when another savepoint with the same name is established. In PostgreSQL, the old savepoint is kept, though only the more recent one will be used when rolling back or releasing. (Releasing the newer savepoint with `RELEASE SAVEPOINT` will cause the older one to again become accessible to `ROLLBACK TO SAVEPOINT` and `RELEASE SAVEPOINT`.) Otherwise, `SAVEPOINT` is fully SQL conforming.

See Also

BEGIN, COMMIT, RELEASE SAVEPOINT, ROLLBACK, ROLLBACK TO SAVEPOINT

SECURITY LABEL

SECURITY LABEL — define or change a security label applied to an object

Synopsis

```
SECURITY LABEL [ FOR provider ] ON
{
  TABLE object_name |
  COLUMN table_name.column_name |
  AGGREGATE aggregate_name ( aggregate_signature ) |
  DATABASE object_name |
  DOMAIN object_name |
  EVENT TRIGGER object_name |
  FOREIGN TABLE object_name
  FUNCTION function_name [ ( [ [ argmode ] [ argname ] argtype
[, ...] ] ) ] |
  LARGE OBJECT large_object_oid |
  MATERIALIZED VIEW object_name |
  [ PROCEDURAL ] LANGUAGE object_name |
  PROCEDURE procedure_name [ ( [ [ argmode ] [ argname ] argtype
[, ...] ] ) ] |
  PUBLICATION object_name |
  ROLE object_name |
  ROUTINE routine_name [ ( [ [ argmode ] [ argname ] argtype
[, ...] ] ) ] |
  SCHEMA object_name |
  SEQUENCE object_name |
  SUBSCRIPTION object_name |
  TABLESPACE object_name |
  TYPE object_name |
  VIEW object_name
} IS 'label'

where aggregate_signature is:

* |
[ argmode ] [ argname ] argtype [ , ... ] |
[ [ argmode ] [ argname ] argtype [ , ... ] ] ORDER BY [ argmode ]
  [ argname ] argtype [ , ... ]
```

Description

SECURITY LABEL applies a security label to a database object. An arbitrary number of security labels, one per label provider, can be associated with a given database object. Label providers are loadable modules which register themselves by using the function `register_label_provider`.

> ### Note
>
> `register_label_provider` is not an SQL function; it can only be called from C code loaded into the backend.

The label provider determines whether a given label is valid and whether it is permissible to assign that label to a given object. The meaning of a given label is likewise at the discretion of the label provider. PostgreSQL places no restrictions on whether or how a label provider must interpret security labels; it merely provides a mechanism for storing them. In practice, this facility is intended to allow integration with label-based mandatory access control (MAC) systems such as SE-Linux. Such systems make all access control decisions based on object labels, rather than traditional discretionary access control (DAC) concepts such as users and groups.

Parameters

object_name
table_name.column_name
aggregate_name
function_name
procedure_name
routine_name

The name of the object to be labeled. Names of tables, aggregates, domains, foreign tables, functions, procedures, routines, sequences, types, and views can be schema-qualified.

provider

The name of the provider with which this label is to be associated. The named provider must be loaded and must consent to the proposed labeling operation. If exactly one provider is loaded, the provider name may be omitted for brevity.

argmode

The mode of a function, procedure, or aggregate argument: `IN`, `OUT`, `INOUT`, or `VARIADIC`. If omitted, the default is `IN`. Note that `SECURITY LABEL` does not actually pay any attention to `OUT` arguments, since only the input arguments are needed to determine the function's identity. So it is sufficient to list the `IN`, `INOUT`, and `VARIADIC` arguments.

argname

The name of a function, procedure, or aggregate argument. Note that `SECURITY LABEL` does not actually pay any attention to argument names, since only the argument data types are needed to determine the function's identity.

argtype

The data type of a function, procedure, or aggregate argument.

large_object_oid

The OID of the large object.

`PROCEDURAL`

This is a noise word.

label

The new security label, written as a string literal; or NULL to drop the security label.

Examples

The following example shows how the security label of a table might be changed.

```
SECURITY LABEL FOR selinux ON TABLE mytable IS
  'system_u:object_r:sepgsql_table_t:s0';
```

Compatibility

There is no SECURITY LABEL command in the SQL standard.

See Also

sepgsql, src/test/modules/dummy_seclabel

SELECT

SELECT, TABLE, WITH — retrieve rows from a table or view

Synopsis

```
[ WITH [ RECURSIVE ] with_query [, ...] ]
SELECT [ ALL | DISTINCT [ ON ( expression [, ...] ) ] ]
    [ * | expression [ [ AS ] output_name ] [, ...] ]
    [ FROM from_item [, ...] ]
    [ WHERE condition ]
    [ GROUP BY grouping_element [, ...] ]
    [ HAVING condition [, ...] ]
    [ WINDOW window_name AS ( window_definition ) [, ...] ]
    [ { UNION | INTERSECT | EXCEPT } [ ALL | DISTINCT ] select ]
    [ ORDER BY expression [ ASC | DESC | USING operator ] [ NULLS
{ FIRST | LAST } ] [, ...] ]
    [ LIMIT { count | ALL } ]
    [ OFFSET start [ ROW | ROWS ] ]
    [ FETCH { FIRST | NEXT } [ count ] { ROW | ROWS } ONLY ]
    [ FOR { UPDATE | NO KEY UPDATE | SHARE | KEY SHARE }
[ OF table_name [, ...] ] [ NOWAIT | SKIP LOCKED ] [...] ]

where from_item can be one of:

    [ ONLY ] table_name [ * ] [ [ AS ] alias [ ( column_alias
[, ...] ) ] ]
                [ TABLESAMPLE sampling_method ( argument [, ...] )
[ REPEATABLE ( seed ) ] ]
    [ LATERAL ] ( select ) [ AS ] alias [ ( column_alias [, ...] ) ]
    with_query_name [ [ AS ] alias [ ( column_alias [, ...] ) ] ]
    [ LATERAL ] function_name ( [ argument [, ...] ] )
                [ WITH ORDINALITY ] [ [ AS ] alias [ ( column_alias
[, ...] ) ] ]
    [ LATERAL ] function_name ( [ argument [, ...] ] ) [ AS ] alias
( column_definition [, ...] )
    [ LATERAL ] function_name ( [ argument [, ...] ] ) AS
( column_definition [, ...] )
    [ LATERAL ] ROWS FROM( function_name ( [ argument [, ...] ] ) [ AS
( column_definition [, ...] ) ] [, ...] )
                [ WITH ORDINALITY ] [ [ AS ] alias [ ( column_alias
[, ...] ) ] ]
    from_item [ NATURAL ] join_type from_item [ ON join_condition |
USING ( join_column [, ...] ) ]

and grouping_element can be one of:

    ( )
    expression
    ( expression [, ...] )
```

```
ROLLUP ( { expression | ( expression [, ...] ) } [, ...] )
CUBE ( { expression | ( expression [, ...] ) } [, ...] )
GROUPING SETS ( grouping_element [, ...] )
```

and *with_query* is:

```
with_query_name [ ( column_name [, ...] ) ] AS ( select | values
| insert | update | delete )
```

```
TABLE [ ONLY ] table_name [ * ]
```

Description

SELECT retrieves rows from zero or more tables. The general processing of SELECT is as follows:

1. All queries in the WITH list are computed. These effectively serve as temporary tables that can be referenced in the FROM list. A WITH query that is referenced more than once in FROM is computed only once. (See WITH Clause below.)

2. All elements in the FROM list are computed. (Each element in the FROM list is a real or virtual table.) If more than one element is specified in the FROM list, they are cross-joined together. (See FROM Clause below.)

3. If the WHERE clause is specified, all rows that do not satisfy the condition are eliminated from the output. (See WHERE Clause below.)

4. If the GROUP BY clause is specified, or if there are aggregate function calls, the output is combined into groups of rows that match on one or more values, and the results of aggregate functions are computed. If the HAVING clause is present, it eliminates groups that do not satisfy the given condition. (See GROUP BY Clause and HAVING Clause below.)

5. The actual output rows are computed using the SELECT output expressions for each selected row or row group. (See SELECT List below.)

6. SELECT DISTINCT eliminates duplicate rows from the result. SELECT DISTINCT ON eliminates rows that match on all the specified expressions. SELECT ALL (the default) will return all candidate rows, including duplicates. (See DISTINCT Clause below.)

7. Using the operators UNION, INTERSECT, and EXCEPT, the output of more than one SELECT statement can be combined to form a single result set. The UNION operator returns all rows that are in one or both of the result sets. The INTERSECT operator returns all rows that are strictly in both result sets. The EXCEPT operator returns the rows that are in the first result set but not in the second. In all three cases, duplicate rows are eliminated unless ALL is specified. The noise word DISTINCT can be added to explicitly specify eliminating duplicate rows. Notice that DISTINCT is the default behavior here, even though ALL is the default for SELECT itself. (See UNION Clause, INTERSECT Clause, and EXCEPT Clause below.)

8. If the ORDER BY clause is specified, the returned rows are sorted in the specified order. If ORDER BY is not given, the rows are returned in whatever order the system finds fastest to produce. (See ORDER BY Clause below.)

9. If the LIMIT (or FETCH FIRST) or OFFSET clause is specified, the SELECT statement only returns a subset of the result rows. (See LIMIT Clause below.)

10.If FOR UPDATE, FOR NO KEY UPDATE, FOR SHARE or FOR KEY SHARE is specified, the SELECT statement locks the selected rows against concurrent updates. (See The Locking Clause below.)

You must have SELECT privilege on each column used in a SELECT command. The use of FOR NO KEY UPDATE, FOR UPDATE, FOR SHARE or FOR KEY SHARE requires UPDATE privilege as well (for at least one column of each table so selected).

Parameters

WITH Clause

The WITH clause allows you to specify one or more subqueries that can be referenced by name in the primary query. The subqueries effectively act as temporary tables or views for the duration of the primary query. Each subquery can be a SELECT, TABLE, VALUES, INSERT, UPDATE or DELETE statement. When writing a data-modifying statement (INSERT, UPDATE or DELETE) in WITH, it is usual to include a RETURNING clause. It is the output of RETURNING, *not* the underlying table that the statement modifies, that forms the temporary table that is read by the primary query. If RETURNING is omitted, the statement is still executed, but it produces no output so it cannot be referenced as a table by the primary query.

A name (without schema qualification) must be specified for each WITH query. Optionally, a list of column names can be specified; if this is omitted, the column names are inferred from the subquery.

If RECURSIVE is specified, it allows a SELECT subquery to reference itself by name. Such a subquery must have the form

```
non_recursive_term UNION [ ALL | DISTINCT ] recursive_term
```

where the recursive self-reference must appear on the right-hand side of the UNION. Only one recursive self-reference is permitted per query. Recursive data-modifying statements are not supported, but you can use the results of a recursive SELECT query in a data-modifying statement. See Section 7.8 for an example.

Another effect of RECURSIVE is that WITH queries need not be ordered: a query can reference another one that is later in the list. (However, circular references, or mutual recursion, are not implemented.) Without RECURSIVE, WITH queries can only reference sibling WITH queries that are earlier in the WITH list.

A key property of WITH queries is that they are evaluated only once per execution of the primary query, even if the primary query refers to them more than once. In particular, data-modifying statements are guaranteed to be executed once and only once, regardless of whether the primary query reads all or any of their output.

The primary query and the WITH queries are all (notionally) executed at the same time. This implies that the effects of a data-modifying statement in WITH cannot be seen from other parts of the query, other than by reading its RETURNING output. If two such data-modifying statements attempt to modify the same row, the results are unspecified.

See Section 7.8 for additional information.

FROM Clause

The FROM clause specifies one or more source tables for the SELECT. If multiple sources are specified, the result is the Cartesian product (cross join) of all the sources. But usually qualification conditions are added (via WHERE) to restrict the returned rows to a small subset of the Cartesian product.

The FROM clause can contain the following elements:

table_name

The name (optionally schema-qualified) of an existing table or view. If ONLY is specified before the table name, only that table is scanned. If ONLY is not specified, the table and all its descendant tables (if any) are scanned. Optionally, * can be specified after the table name to explicitly indicate that descendant tables are included.

alias

A substitute name for the FROM item containing the alias. An alias is used for brevity or to eliminate ambiguity for self-joins (where the same table is scanned multiple times). When an alias is provided, it completely hides the actual name of the table or function; for example given FROM foo AS f, the remainder of the SELECT must refer to this FROM item as f not foo. If an alias is written, a column alias list can also be written to provide substitute names for one or more columns of the table.

TABLESAMPLE *sampling_method* (*argument* [, ...]) [REPEATABLE (*seed*)]

A TABLESAMPLE clause after a *table_name* indicates that the specified *sampling_method* should be used to retrieve a subset of the rows in that table. This sampling precedes the application of any other filters such as WHERE clauses. The standard PostgreSQL distribution includes two sampling methods, BERNOULLI and SYSTEM, and other sampling methods can be installed in the database via extensions.

The BERNOULLI and SYSTEM sampling methods each accept a single *argument* which is the fraction of the table to sample, expressed as a percentage between 0 and 100. This argument can be any real-valued expression. (Other sampling methods might accept more or different arguments.) These two methods each return a randomly-chosen sample of the table that will contain approximately the specified percentage of the table's rows. The BERNOULLI method scans the whole table and selects or ignores individual rows independently with the specified probability. The SYSTEM method does block-level sampling with each block having the specified chance of being selected; all rows in each selected block are returned. The SYSTEM method is significantly faster than the BERNOULLI method when small sampling percentages are specified, but it may return a less-random sample of the table as a result of clustering effects.

The optional REPEATABLE clause specifies a *seed* number or expression to use for generating random numbers within the sampling method. The seed value can be any non-null floating-point value. Two queries that specify the same seed and *argument* values will select the same sample of the table, if the table has not been changed meanwhile. But different seed values will usually produce different samples. If REPEATABLE is not given then a new random sample is selected for each query, based upon a system-generated seed. Note that some add-on sampling methods do not accept REPEATABLE, and will always produce new samples on each use.

select

A sub-SELECT can appear in the FROM clause. This acts as though its output were created as a temporary table for the duration of this single SELECT command. Note that the sub-SELECT must be surrounded by parentheses, and an alias *must* be provided for it. A VALUES command can also be used here.

with_query_name

A WITH query is referenced by writing its name, just as though the query's name were a table name. (In fact, the WITH query hides any real table of the same name for the purposes of the primary query. If necessary, you can refer to a real table of the same name by schema-qualifying the table's name.) An alias can be provided in the same way as for a table.

function_name

Function calls can appear in the FROM clause. (This is especially useful for functions that return result sets, but any function can be used.) This acts as though the function's output were created as a temporary table for the duration of this single SELECT command. When the optional WITH

`ORDINALITY` clause is added to the function call, a new column is appended after all the function's output columns with numbering for each row.

An alias can be provided in the same way as for a table. If an alias is written, a column alias list can also be written to provide substitute names for one or more attributes of the function's composite return type, including the column added by `ORDINALITY` if present.

Multiple function calls can be combined into a single `FROM`-clause item by surrounding them with `ROWS FROM( ... )`. The output of such an item is the concatenation of the first row from each function, then the second row from each function, etc. If some of the functions produce fewer rows than others, null values are substituted for the missing data, so that the total number of rows returned is always the same as for the function that produced the most rows.

If the function has been defined as returning the `record` data type, then an alias or the key word `AS` must be present, followed by a column definition list in the form (*column_name data_type* [, ...]). The column definition list must match the actual number and types of columns returned by the function.

When using the `ROWS FROM( ... )` syntax, if one of the functions requires a column definition list, it's preferred to put the column definition list after the function call inside `ROWS FROM( ... )`. A column definition list can be placed after the `ROWS FROM( ... )` construct only if there's just a single function and no `WITH ORDINALITY` clause.

To use `ORDINALITY` together with a column definition list, you must use the `ROWS FROM( ... )` syntax and put the column definition list inside `ROWS FROM( ... )`.

join_type

One of

- `[ INNER ] JOIN`

- `LEFT [ OUTER ] JOIN`

- `RIGHT [ OUTER ] JOIN`

- `FULL [ OUTER ] JOIN`

- `CROSS JOIN`

For the `INNER` and `OUTER` join types, a join condition must be specified, namely exactly one of `NATURAL`, `ON` *join_condition*, or `USING` (*join_column* [, ...]). See below for the meaning. For `CROSS JOIN`, none of these clauses can appear.

A `JOIN` clause combines two `FROM` items, which for convenience we will refer to as "tables", though in reality they can be any type of `FROM` item. Use parentheses if necessary to determine the order of nesting. In the absence of parentheses, `JOIN`s nest left-to-right. In any case `JOIN` binds more tightly than the commas separating `FROM`-list items.

`CROSS JOIN` and `INNER JOIN` produce a simple Cartesian product, the same result as you get from listing the two tables at the top level of `FROM`, but restricted by the join condition (if any). `CROSS JOIN` is equivalent to `INNER JOIN ON (TRUE)`, that is, no rows are removed by qualification. These join types are just a notational convenience, since they do nothing you couldn't do with plain `FROM` and `WHERE`.

`LEFT OUTER JOIN` returns all rows in the qualified Cartesian product (i.e., all combined rows that pass its join condition), plus one copy of each row in the left-hand table for which there was no right-hand row that passed the join condition. This left-hand row is extended to the full width of the joined table by inserting null values for the right-hand columns. Note that only the JOIN clause's own condition is considered while deciding which rows have matches. Outer conditions are applied afterwards.

Conversely, RIGHT OUTER JOIN returns all the joined rows, plus one row for each unmatched right-hand row (extended with nulls on the left). This is just a notational convenience, since you could convert it to a LEFT OUTER JOIN by switching the left and right tables.

FULL OUTER JOIN returns all the joined rows, plus one row for each unmatched left-hand row (extended with nulls on the right), plus one row for each unmatched right-hand row (extended with nulls on the left).

ON *join_condition*

join_condition is an expression resulting in a value of type boolean (similar to a WHERE clause) that specifies which rows in a join are considered to match.

USING (*join_column* [, ...])

A clause of the form USING (a, b, ...) is shorthand for ON left_table.a = right_table.a AND left_table.b = right_table.b .... Also, USING implies that only one of each pair of equivalent columns will be included in the join output, not both.

NATURAL

NATURAL is shorthand for a USING list that mentions all columns in the two tables that have matching names. If there are no common column names, NATURAL is equivalent to ON TRUE.

LATERAL

The LATERAL key word can precede a sub-SELECT FROM item. This allows the sub-SELECT to refer to columns of FROM items that appear before it in the FROM list. (Without LATERAL, each sub-SELECT is evaluated independently and so cannot cross-reference any other FROM item.)

LATERAL can also precede a function-call FROM item, but in this case it is a noise word, because the function expression can refer to earlier FROM items in any case.

A LATERAL item can appear at top level in the FROM list, or within a JOIN tree. In the latter case it can also refer to any items that are on the left-hand side of a JOIN that it is on the right-hand side of.

When a FROM item contains LATERAL cross-references, evaluation proceeds as follows: for each row of the FROM item providing the cross-referenced column(s), or set of rows of multiple FROM items providing the columns, the LATERAL item is evaluated using that row or row set's values of the columns. The resulting row(s) are joined as usual with the rows they were computed from. This is repeated for each row or set of rows from the column source table(s).

The column source table(s) must be INNER or LEFT joined to the LATERAL item, else there would not be a well-defined set of rows from which to compute each set of rows for the LATERAL item. Thus, although a construct such as *X* RIGHT JOIN LATERAL *Y* is syntactically valid, it is not actually allowed for *Y* to reference *X*.

WHERE Clause

The optional WHERE clause has the general form

WHERE *condition*

where `condition` is any expression that evaluates to a result of type `boolean`. Any row that does not satisfy this condition will be eliminated from the output. A row satisfies the condition if it returns true when the actual row values are substituted for any variable references.

GROUP BY Clause

The optional `GROUP BY` clause has the general form

```
GROUP BY grouping_element [, ...]
```

`GROUP BY` will condense into a single row all selected rows that share the same values for the grouped expressions. An `expression` used inside a `grouping_element` can be an input column name, or the name or ordinal number of an output column (`SELECT` list item), or an arbitrary expression formed from input-column values. In case of ambiguity, a `GROUP BY` name will be interpreted as an input-column name rather than an output column name.

If any of `GROUPING SETS`, `ROLLUP` or `CUBE` are present as grouping elements, then the `GROUP BY` clause as a whole defines some number of independent `grouping sets`. The effect of this is equivalent to constructing a `UNION ALL` between subqueries with the individual grouping sets as their `GROUP BY` clauses. For further details on the handling of grouping sets see Section 7.2.4.

Aggregate functions, if any are used, are computed across all rows making up each group, producing a separate value for each group. (If there are aggregate functions but no `GROUP BY` clause, the query is treated as having a single group comprising all the selected rows.) The set of rows fed to each aggregate function can be further filtered by attaching a `FILTER` clause to the aggregate function call; see Section 4.2.7 for more information. When a `FILTER` clause is present, only those rows matching it are included in the input to that aggregate function.

When `GROUP BY` is present, or any aggregate functions are present, it is not valid for the `SELECT` list expressions to refer to ungrouped columns except within aggregate functions or when the ungrouped column is functionally dependent on the grouped columns, since there would otherwise be more than one possible value to return for an ungrouped column. A functional dependency exists if the grouped columns (or a subset thereof) are the primary key of the table containing the ungrouped column.

Keep in mind that all aggregate functions are evaluated before evaluating any "scalar" expressions in the `HAVING` clause or `SELECT` list. This means that, for example, a `CASE` expression cannot be used to skip evaluation of an aggregate function; see Section 4.2.14.

Currently, `FOR NO KEY UPDATE`, `FOR UPDATE`, `FOR SHARE` and `FOR KEY SHARE` cannot be specified with `GROUP BY`.

HAVING Clause

The optional `HAVING` clause has the general form

```
HAVING condition
```

where `condition` is the same as specified for the `WHERE` clause.

`HAVING` eliminates group rows that do not satisfy the condition. `HAVING` is different from `WHERE`: `WHERE` filters individual rows before the application of `GROUP BY`, while `HAVING` filters group rows created by `GROUP BY`. Each column referenced in `condition` must unambiguously reference a grouping column, unless the reference appears within an aggregate function or the ungrouped column is functionally dependent on the grouping columns.

The presence of HAVING turns a query into a grouped query even if there is no GROUP BY clause. This is the same as what happens when the query contains aggregate functions but no GROUP BY clause. All the selected rows are considered to form a single group, and the SELECT list and HAVING clause can only reference table columns from within aggregate functions. Such a query will emit a single row if the HAVING condition is true, zero rows if it is not true.

Currently, FOR NO KEY UPDATE, FOR UPDATE, FOR SHARE and FOR KEY SHARE cannot be specified with HAVING.

WINDOW Clause

The optional WINDOW clause has the general form

```
WINDOW window_name AS ( window_definition ) [, ...]
```

where *window_name* is a name that can be referenced from OVER clauses or subsequent window definitions, and *window_definition* is

```
[ existing_window_name ]
[ PARTITION BY expression [, ...] ]
[ ORDER BY expression [ ASC | DESC | USING operator ] [ NULLS { FIRST
  | LAST } ] [, ...] ]
[ frame_clause ]
```

If an *existing_window_name* is specified it must refer to an earlier entry in the WINDOW list; the new window copies its partitioning clause from that entry, as well as its ordering clause if any. In this case the new window cannot specify its own PARTITION BY clause, and it can specify ORDER BY only if the copied window does not have one. The new window always uses its own frame clause; the copied window must not specify a frame clause.

The elements of the PARTITION BY list are interpreted in much the same fashion as elements of a GROUP BY Clause, except that they are always simple expressions and never the name or number of an output column. Another difference is that these expressions can contain aggregate function calls, which are not allowed in a regular GROUP BY clause. They are allowed here because windowing occurs after grouping and aggregation.

Similarly, the elements of the ORDER BY list are interpreted in much the same fashion as elements of an ORDER BY Clause, except that the expressions are always taken as simple expressions and never the name or number of an output column.

The optional *frame_clause* defines the *window frame* for window functions that depend on the frame (not all do). The window frame is a set of related rows for each row of the query (called the *current row*). The *frame_clause* can be one of

```
{ RANGE | ROWS | GROUPS } frame_start [ frame_exclusion ]
{ RANGE | ROWS | GROUPS } BETWEEN frame_start AND frame_end
  [ frame_exclusion ]
```

where *frame_start* and *frame_end* can be one of

```
UNBOUNDED PRECEDING
```

```
offset PRECEDING
CURRENT ROW
offset FOLLOWING
UNBOUNDED FOLLOWING
```

and *frame_exclusion* can be one of

```
EXCLUDE CURRENT ROW
EXCLUDE GROUP
EXCLUDE TIES
EXCLUDE NO OTHERS
```

If *frame_end* is omitted it defaults to CURRENT ROW. Restrictions are that *frame_start* cannot be UNBOUNDED FOLLOWING, *frame_end* cannot be UNBOUNDED PRECEDING, and the *frame_end* choice cannot appear earlier in the above list of *frame_start* and *frame_end* options than the *frame_start* choice does — for example RANGE BETWEEN CURRENT ROW AND *offset* PRECEDING is not allowed.

The default framing option is RANGE UNBOUNDED PRECEDING, which is the same as RANGE BETWEEN UNBOUNDED PRECEDING AND CURRENT ROW; it sets the frame to be all rows from the partition start up through the current row's last *peer* (a row that the window's ORDER BY clause considers equivalent to the current row; all rows are peers if there is no ORDER BY). In general, UNBOUNDED PRECEDING means that the frame starts with the first row of the partition, and similarly UNBOUNDED FOLLOWING means that the frame ends with the last row of the partition, regardless of RANGE, ROWS or GROUPS mode. In ROWS mode, CURRENT ROW means that the frame starts or ends with the current row; but in RANGE or GROUPS mode it means that the frame starts or ends with the current row's first or last peer in the ORDER BY ordering. The *offset* PRECEDING and *offset* FOLLOWING options vary in meaning depending on the frame mode. In ROWS mode, the *offset* is an integer indicating that the frame starts or ends that many rows before or after the current row. In GROUPS mode, the *offset* is an integer indicating that the frame starts or ends that many peer groups before or after the current row's peer group, where a *peer group* is a group of rows that are equivalent according to the window's ORDER BY clause. In RANGE mode, use of an *offset* option requires that there be exactly one ORDER BY column in the window definition. Then the frame contains those rows whose ordering column value is no more than *offset* less than (for PRECEDING) or more than (for FOLLOWING) the current row's ordering column value. In these cases the data type of the *offset* expression depends on the data type of the ordering column. For numeric ordering columns it is typically of the same type as the ordering column, but for datetime ordering columns it is an interval. In all these cases, the value of the *offset* must be non-null and non-negative. Also, while the *offset* does not have to be a simple constant, it cannot contain variables, aggregate functions, or window functions.

The *frame_exclusion* option allows rows around the current row to be excluded from the frame, even if they would be included according to the frame start and frame end options. EXCLUDE CURRENT ROW excludes the current row from the frame. EXCLUDE GROUP excludes the current row and its ordering peers from the frame. EXCLUDE TIES excludes any peers of the current row from the frame, but not the current row itself. EXCLUDE NO OTHERS simply specifies explicitly the default behavior of not excluding the current row or its peers.

Beware that the ROWS mode can produce unpredictable results if the ORDER BY ordering does not order the rows uniquely. The RANGE and GROUPS modes are designed to ensure that rows that are peers in the ORDER BY ordering are treated alike: all rows of a given peer group will be in the frame or excluded from it.

The purpose of a WINDOW clause is to specify the behavior of *window functions* appearing in the query's SELECT List or ORDER BY Clause. These functions can reference the WINDOW clause entries by name in their OVER clauses. A WINDOW clause entry does not have to be referenced anywhere, however; if it is not used in the query it is simply ignored. It is possible to use window functions without any WINDOW clause at all, since a window function call can specify its window definition directly in its OVER clause. However, the WINDOW clause saves typing when the same window definition is needed for more than one window function.

Currently, FOR NO KEY UPDATE, FOR UPDATE, FOR SHARE and FOR KEY SHARE cannot be specified with WINDOW.

Window functions are described in detail in Section 3.5, Section 4.2.8, and Section 7.2.5.

SELECT List

The SELECT list (between the key words SELECT and FROM) specifies expressions that form the output rows of the SELECT statement. The expressions can (and usually do) refer to columns computed in the FROM clause.

Just as in a table, every output column of a SELECT has a name. In a simple SELECT this name is just used to label the column for display, but when the SELECT is a sub-query of a larger query, the name is seen by the larger query as the column name of the virtual table produced by the sub-query. To specify the name to use for an output column, write AS *output_name* after the column's expression. (You can omit AS, but only if the desired output name does not match any PostgreSQL keyword (see Appendix C). For protection against possible future keyword additions, it is recommended that you always either write AS or double-quote the output name.) If you do not specify a column name, a name is chosen automatically by PostgreSQL. If the column's expression is a simple column reference then the chosen name is the same as that column's name. In more complex cases a function or type name may be used, or the system may fall back on a generated name such as ?column?.

An output column's name can be used to refer to the column's value in ORDER BY and GROUP BY clauses, but not in the WHERE or HAVING clauses; there you must write out the expression instead.

Instead of an expression, * can be written in the output list as a shorthand for all the columns of the selected rows. Also, you can write *table_name.* as a shorthand for the columns coming from just that table. In these cases it is not possible to specify new names with AS; the output column names will be the same as the table columns' names.

According to the SQL standard, the expressions in the output list should be computed before applying DISTINCT, ORDER BY, or LIMIT. This is obviously necessary when using DISTINCT, since otherwise it's not clear what values are being made distinct. However, in many cases it is convenient if output expressions are computed after ORDER BY and LIMIT; particularly if the output list contains any volatile or expensive functions. With that behavior, the order of function evaluations is more intuitive and there will not be evaluations corresponding to rows that never appear in the output. PostgreSQL will effectively evaluate output expressions after sorting and limiting, so long as those expressions are not referenced in DISTINCT, ORDER BY or GROUP BY. (As a counterexample, SELECT f(x) FROM tab ORDER BY 1 clearly must evaluate f(x) before sorting.) Output expressions that contain set-returning functions are effectively evaluated after sorting and before limiting, so that LIMIT will act to cut off the output from a set-returning function.

> ## Note
>
> PostgreSQL versions before 9.6 did not provide any guarantees about the timing of evaluation of output expressions versus sorting and limiting; it depended on the form of the chosen query plan.

DISTINCT Clause

If SELECT DISTINCT is specified, all duplicate rows are removed from the result set (one row is kept from each group of duplicates). SELECT ALL specifies the opposite: all rows are kept; that is the default.

SELECT DISTINCT ON (expression [, ...]) keeps only the first row of each set of rows where the given expressions evaluate to equal. The DISTINCT ON expressions are interpreted using the same rules as for ORDER BY (see above). Note that the "first row" of each set is unpredictable unless ORDER BY is used to ensure that the desired row appears first. For example:

```
SELECT DISTINCT ON (location) location, time, report
    FROM weather_reports
    ORDER BY location, time DESC;
```

retrieves the most recent weather report for each location. But if we had not used ORDER BY to force descending order of time values for each location, we'd have gotten a report from an unpredictable time for each location.

The DISTINCT ON expression(s) must match the leftmost ORDER BY expression(s). The ORDER BY clause will normally contain additional expression(s) that determine the desired precedence of rows within each DISTINCT ON group.

Currently, FOR NO KEY UPDATE, FOR UPDATE, FOR SHARE and FOR KEY SHARE cannot be specified with DISTINCT.

UNION Clause

The UNION clause has this general form:

```
select_statement UNION [ ALL | DISTINCT ] select_statement
```

select_statement is any SELECT statement without an ORDER BY, LIMIT, FOR NO KEY UPDATE, FOR UPDATE, FOR SHARE, or FOR KEY SHARE clause. (ORDER BY and LIMIT can be attached to a subexpression if it is enclosed in parentheses. Without parentheses, these clauses will be taken to apply to the result of the UNION, not to its right-hand input expression.)

The UNION operator computes the set union of the rows returned by the involved SELECT statements. A row is in the set union of two result sets if it appears in at least one of the result sets. The two SELECT statements that represent the direct operands of the UNION must produce the same number of columns, and corresponding columns must be of compatible data types.

The result of UNION does not contain any duplicate rows unless the ALL option is specified. ALL prevents elimination of duplicates. (Therefore, UNION ALL is usually significantly quicker than UNION; use ALL when you can.) DISTINCT can be written to explicitly specify the default behavior of eliminating duplicate rows.

Multiple UNION operators in the same SELECT statement are evaluated left to right, unless otherwise indicated by parentheses.

Currently, FOR NO KEY UPDATE, FOR UPDATE, FOR SHARE and FOR KEY SHARE cannot be specified either for a UNION result or for any input of a UNION.

INTERSECT Clause

The INTERSECT clause has this general form:

select_statement INTERSECT [ALL | DISTINCT] *select_statement*

select_statement is any SELECT statement without an ORDER BY, LIMIT, FOR NO KEY UP-
DATE, FOR UPDATE, FOR SHARE, or FOR KEY SHARE clause.

The INTERSECT operator computes the set intersection of the rows returned by the involved SELECT
statements. A row is in the intersection of two result sets if it appears in both result sets.

The result of INTERSECT does not contain any duplicate rows unless the ALL option is specified. With
ALL, a row that has m duplicates in the left table and n duplicates in the right table will appear min(m,n)
times in the result set. DISTINCT can be written to explicitly specify the default behavior of eliminating
duplicate rows.

Multiple INTERSECT operators in the same SELECT statement are evaluated left to right, unless parentheses dictate otherwise. INTERSECT binds more tightly than UNION. That is, A UNION B INTERSECT
C will be read as A UNION (B INTERSECT C).

Currently, FOR NO KEY UPDATE, FOR UPDATE, FOR SHARE and FOR KEY SHARE cannot be
specified either for an INTERSECT result or for any input of an INTERSECT.

EXCEPT Clause

The EXCEPT clause has this general form:

select_statement EXCEPT [ALL | DISTINCT] *select_statement*

select_statement is any SELECT statement without an ORDER BY, LIMIT, FOR NO KEY UP-
DATE, FOR UPDATE, FOR SHARE, or FOR KEY SHARE clause.

The EXCEPT operator computes the set of rows that are in the result of the left SELECT statement but
not in the result of the right one.

The result of EXCEPT does not contain any duplicate rows unless the ALL option is specified. With ALL,
a row that has m duplicates in the left table and n duplicates in the right table will appear max(m-n,0)
times in the result set. DISTINCT can be written to explicitly specify the default behavior of eliminating
duplicate rows.

Multiple EXCEPT operators in the same SELECT statement are evaluated left to right, unless parentheses
dictate otherwise. EXCEPT binds at the same level as UNION.

Currently, FOR NO KEY UPDATE, FOR UPDATE, FOR SHARE and FOR KEY SHARE cannot be
specified either for an EXCEPT result or for any input of an EXCEPT.

ORDER BY Clause

The optional ORDER BY clause has this general form:

ORDER BY *expression* [ASC | DESC | USING *operator*] [NULLS { FIRST |
LAST }] [, ...]

The ORDER BY clause causes the result rows to be sorted according to the specified expression(s). If two
rows are equal according to the leftmost expression, they are compared according to the next expression

and so on. If they are equal according to all specified expressions, they are returned in an implementation-dependent order.

Each `expression` can be the name or ordinal number of an output column (SELECT list item), or it can be an arbitrary expression formed from input-column values.

The ordinal number refers to the ordinal (left-to-right) position of the output column. This feature makes it possible to define an ordering on the basis of a column that does not have a unique name. This is never absolutely necessary because it is always possible to assign a name to an output column using the AS clause.

It is also possible to use arbitrary expressions in the ORDER BY clause, including columns that do not appear in the SELECT output list. Thus the following statement is valid:

```
SELECT name FROM distributors ORDER BY code;
```

A limitation of this feature is that an ORDER BY clause applying to the result of a UNION, INTERSECT, or EXCEPT clause can only specify an output column name or number, not an expression.

If an ORDER BY expression is a simple name that matches both an output column name and an input column name, ORDER BY will interpret it as the output column name. This is the opposite of the choice that GROUP BY will make in the same situation. This inconsistency is made to be compatible with the SQL standard.

Optionally one can add the key word ASC (ascending) or DESC (descending) after any expression in the ORDER BY clause. If not specified, ASC is assumed by default. Alternatively, a specific ordering operator name can be specified in the USING clause. An ordering operator must be a less-than or greater-than member of some B-tree operator family. ASC is usually equivalent to USING < and DESC is usually equivalent to USING >. (But the creator of a user-defined data type can define exactly what the default sort ordering is, and it might correspond to operators with other names.)

If NULLS LAST is specified, null values sort after all non-null values; if NULLS FIRST is specified, null values sort before all non-null values. If neither is specified, the default behavior is NULLS LAST when ASC is specified or implied, and NULLS FIRST when DESC is specified (thus, the default is to act as though nulls are larger than non-nulls). When USING is specified, the default nulls ordering depends on whether the operator is a less-than or greater-than operator.

Note that ordering options apply only to the expression they follow; for example ORDER BY x, y DESC does not mean the same thing as ORDER BY x DESC, y DESC.

Character-string data is sorted according to the collation that applies to the column being sorted. That can be overridden at need by including a COLLATE clause in the `expression`, for example ORDER BY mycolumn COLLATE "en_US". For more information see Section 4.2.10 and Section 23.2.

LIMIT Clause

The LIMIT clause consists of two independent sub-clauses:

```
LIMIT { count | ALL }
OFFSET start
```

`count` specifies the maximum number of rows to return, while `start` specifies the number of rows to skip before starting to return rows. When both are specified, `start` rows are skipped before starting to count the `count` rows to be returned.

If the *count* expression evaluates to NULL, it is treated as `LIMIT ALL`, i.e., no limit. If *start* evaluates to NULL, it is treated the same as `OFFSET 0`.

SQL:2008 introduced a different syntax to achieve the same result, which PostgreSQL also supports. It is:

```
OFFSET start { ROW | ROWS }
FETCH { FIRST | NEXT } [ count ] { ROW | ROWS } ONLY
```

In this syntax, the *start* or *count* value is required by the standard to be a literal constant, a parameter, or a variable name; as a PostgreSQL extension, other expressions are allowed, but will generally need to be enclosed in parentheses to avoid ambiguity. If *count* is omitted in a `FETCH` clause, it defaults to 1. `ROW` and `ROWS` as well as `FIRST` and `NEXT` are noise words that don't influence the effects of these clauses. According to the standard, the `OFFSET` clause must come before the `FETCH` clause if both are present; but PostgreSQL is laxer and allows either order.

When using `LIMIT`, it is a good idea to use an `ORDER BY` clause that constrains the result rows into a unique order. Otherwise you will get an unpredictable subset of the query's rows — you might be asking for the tenth through twentieth rows, but tenth through twentieth in what ordering? You don't know what ordering unless you specify `ORDER BY`.

The query planner takes `LIMIT` into account when generating a query plan, so you are very likely to get different plans (yielding different row orders) depending on what you use for `LIMIT` and `OFFSET`. Thus, using different `LIMIT`/`OFFSET` values to select different subsets of a query result *will give inconsistent results* unless you enforce a predictable result ordering with `ORDER BY`. This is not a bug; it is an inherent consequence of the fact that SQL does not promise to deliver the results of a query in any particular order unless `ORDER BY` is used to constrain the order.

It is even possible for repeated executions of the same `LIMIT` query to return different subsets of the rows of a table, if there is not an `ORDER BY` to enforce selection of a deterministic subset. Again, this is not a bug; determinism of the results is simply not guaranteed in such a case.

The Locking Clause

`FOR UPDATE`, `FOR NO KEY UPDATE`, `FOR SHARE` and `FOR KEY SHARE` are *locking clauses*; they affect how `SELECT` locks rows as they are obtained from the table.

The locking clause has the general form

```
FOR lock_strength [ OF table_name [, ...] ] [ NOWAIT | SKIP LOCKED ]
```

where *lock_strength* can be one of

```
UPDATE
NO KEY UPDATE
SHARE
KEY SHARE
```

For more information on each row-level lock mode, refer to Section 13.3.2.

To prevent the operation from waiting for other transactions to commit, use either the `NOWAIT` or `SKIP LOCKED` option. With `NOWAIT`, the statement reports an error, rather than waiting, if a selected row cannot be locked immediately. With `SKIP LOCKED`, any selected rows that cannot be immediately locked are skipped. Skipping locked rows provides an inconsistent view of the data, so this is not suitable for general purpose work, but can be used to avoid lock contention with multiple consumers accessing a queue-like table. Note that NOWAIT and SKIP LOCKED apply only to the row-level lock(s) — the required ROW SHARE table-level lock is still taken in the ordinary way (see Chapter 13). You can use LOCK with the NOWAIT option first, if you need to acquire the table-level lock without waiting.

If specific tables are named in a locking clause, then only rows coming from those tables are locked; any other tables used in the SELECT are simply read as usual. A locking clause without a table list affects all tables used in the statement. If a locking clause is applied to a view or sub-query, it affects all tables used in the view or sub-query. However, these clauses do not apply to WITH queries referenced by the primary query. If you want row locking to occur within a WITH query, specify a locking clause within the WITH query.

Multiple locking clauses can be written if it is necessary to specify different locking behavior for different tables. If the same table is mentioned (or implicitly affected) by more than one locking clause, then it is processed as if it was only specified by the strongest one. Similarly, a table is processed as NOWAIT if that is specified in any of the clauses affecting it. Otherwise, it is processed as SKIP LOCKED if that is specified in any of the clauses affecting it.

The locking clauses cannot be used in contexts where returned rows cannot be clearly identified with individual table rows; for example they cannot be used with aggregation.

When a locking clause appears at the top level of a SELECT query, the rows that are locked are exactly those that are returned by the query; in the case of a join query, the rows locked are those that contribute to returned join rows. In addition, rows that satisfied the query conditions as of the query snapshot will be locked, although they will not be returned if they were updated after the snapshot and no longer satisfy the query conditions. If a LIMIT is used, locking stops once enough rows have been returned to satisfy the limit (but note that rows skipped over by OFFSET will get locked). Similarly, if a locking clause is used in a cursor's query, only rows actually fetched or stepped past by the cursor will be locked.

When a locking clause appears in a sub-SELECT, the rows locked are those returned to the outer query by the sub-query. This might involve fewer rows than inspection of the sub-query alone would suggest, since conditions from the outer query might be used to optimize execution of the sub-query. For example,

```
SELECT * FROM (SELECT * FROM mytable FOR UPDATE) ss WHERE col1 = 5;
```

will lock only rows having col1 = 5, even though that condition is not textually within the sub-query.

Previous releases failed to preserve a lock which is upgraded by a later savepoint. For example, this code:

```
BEGIN;
SELECT * FROM mytable WHERE key = 1 FOR UPDATE;
SAVEPOINT s;
UPDATE mytable SET ... WHERE key = 1;
ROLLBACK TO s;
```

would fail to preserve the FOR UPDATE lock after the ROLLBACK TO. This has been fixed in release 9.3.

Caution

It is possible for a SELECT command running at the READ COMMITTED transaction isolation level and using ORDER BY and a locking clause to return rows out of order. This is because ORDER BY is applied first. The command sorts the result, but might then block trying to obtain a lock on one or more of the rows. Once the SELECT unblocks, some of

---

the ordering column values might have been modified, leading to those rows appearing to be out of order (though they are in order in terms of the original column values). This can be worked around at need by placing the FOR UPDATE/SHARE clause in a sub-query, for example

```
SELECT * FROM (SELECT * FROM mytable FOR UPDATE) ss ORDER
 BY column1;
```

Note that this will result in locking all rows of mytable, whereas FOR UPDATE at the top level would lock only the actually returned rows. This can make for a significant performance difference, particularly if the ORDER BY is combined with LIMIT or other restrictions. So this technique is recommended only if concurrent updates of the ordering columns are expected and a strictly sorted result is required.

At the REPEATABLE READ or SERIALIZABLE transaction isolation level this would cause a serialization failure (with a SQLSTATE of '40001'), so there is no possibility of receiving rows out of order under these isolation levels.

TABLE Command

The command

```
TABLE name
```

is equivalent to

```
SELECT * FROM name
```

It can be used as a top-level command or as a space-saving syntax variant in parts of complex queries. Only the WITH, UNION, INTERSECT, EXCEPT, ORDER BY, LIMIT, OFFSET, FETCH and FOR locking clauses can be used with TABLE; the WHERE clause and any form of aggregation cannot be used.

Examples

To join the table films with the table distributors:

```
SELECT f.title, f.did, d.name, f.date_prod, f.kind
    FROM distributors d, films f
    WHERE f.did = d.did

        title       | did |    name      | date_prod  |  kind
--------------------+-----+--------------+------------+----------
 The Third Man      | 101 | British Lion | 1949-12-23 | Drama
 The African Queen  | 101 | British Lion | 1951-08-11 | Romantic
 ...
```

To sum the column len of all films and group the results by kind:

```
SELECT kind, sum(len) AS total FROM films GROUP BY kind;
```

```
  kind     | total
-----------+-------
 Action    | 07:34
 Comedy    | 02:58
 Drama     | 14:28
 Musical   | 06:42
 Romantic  | 04:38
```

To sum the column `len` of all films, group the results by `kind` and show those group totals that are less than 5 hours:

```
SELECT kind, sum(len) AS total
    FROM films
    GROUP BY kind
    HAVING sum(len) < interval '5 hours';

  kind     | total
-----------+-------
 Comedy    | 02:58
 Romantic  | 04:38
```

The following two examples are identical ways of sorting the individual results according to the contents of the second column (`name`):

```
SELECT * FROM distributors ORDER BY name;
SELECT * FROM distributors ORDER BY 2;

 did |       name
-----+------------------
 109 | 20th Century Fox
 110 | Bavaria Atelier
 101 | British Lion
 107 | Columbia
 102 | Jean Luc Godard
 113 | Luso films
 104 | Mosfilm
 103 | Paramount
 106 | Toho
 105 | United Artists
 111 | Walt Disney
 112 | Warner Bros.
 108 | Westward
```

The next example shows how to obtain the union of the tables `distributors` and `actors`, restricting the results to those that begin with the letter W in each table. Only distinct rows are wanted, so the key word `ALL` is omitted.

```
distributors:                 actors:
 did |     name                id |     name
-----+--------------          ----+----------------
 108 | Westward                 1 | Woody Allen
```

```
111 | Walt Disney          2 | Warren Beatty
112 | Warner Bros.         3 | Walter Matthau
...                        ...

SELECT distributors.name
    FROM distributors
    WHERE distributors.name LIKE 'W%'
UNION
SELECT actors.name
    FROM actors
    WHERE actors.name LIKE 'W%';

      name
----------------
 Walt Disney
 Walter Matthau
 Warner Bros.
 Warren Beatty
 Westward
 Woody Allen
```

This example shows how to use a function in the FROM clause, both with and without a column definition list:

```
CREATE FUNCTION distributors(int) RETURNS SETOF distributors AS $$
    SELECT * FROM distributors WHERE did = $1;
$$ LANGUAGE SQL;

SELECT * FROM distributors(111);
 did |     name
-----+-------------
 111 | Walt Disney

CREATE FUNCTION distributors_2(int) RETURNS SETOF record AS $$
    SELECT * FROM distributors WHERE did = $1;
$$ LANGUAGE SQL;

SELECT * FROM distributors_2(111) AS (f1 int, f2 text);
 f1  |     f2
-----+-------------
 111 | Walt Disney
```

Here is an example of a function with an ordinality column added:

```
SELECT * FROM unnest(ARRAY['a','b','c','d','e','f']) WITH ORDINALITY;
 unnest | ordinality
--------+----------
 a      |     1
 b      |     2
 c      |     3
 d      |     4
 e      |     5
 f      |     6
```

(6 rows)

This example shows how to use a simple `WITH` clause:

```
WITH t AS (
    SELECT random() as x FROM generate_series(1, 3)
  )
SELECT * FROM t
UNION ALL
SELECT * FROM t

        x
-------------------
  0.534150459803641
  0.520092216785997
 0.0735620250925422
  0.534150459803641
  0.520092216785997
 0.0735620250925422
```

Notice that the `WITH` query was evaluated only once, so that we got two sets of the same three random values.

This example uses `WITH RECURSIVE` to find all subordinates (direct or indirect) of the employee Mary, and their level of indirectness, from a table that shows only direct subordinates:

```
WITH RECURSIVE employee_recursive(distance, employee_name,
 manager_name) AS (
    SELECT 1, employee_name, manager_name
    FROM employee
    WHERE manager_name = 'Mary'
  UNION ALL
    SELECT er.distance + 1, e.employee_name, e.manager_name
    FROM employee_recursive er, employee e
    WHERE er.employee_name = e.manager_name
  )
SELECT distance, employee_name FROM employee_recursive;
```

Notice the typical form of recursive queries: an initial condition, followed by `UNION`, followed by the recursive part of the query. Be sure that the recursive part of the query will eventually return no tuples, or else the query will loop indefinitely. (See Section 7.8 for more examples.)

This example uses `LATERAL` to apply a set-returning function `get_product_names()` for each row of the `manufacturers` table:

```
SELECT m.name AS mname, pname
FROM manufacturers m, LATERAL get_product_names(m.id) pname;
```

Manufacturers not currently having any products would not appear in the result, since it is an inner join. If we wished to include the names of such manufacturers in the result, we could do:

```
SELECT m.name AS mname, pname
```

```
FROM manufacturers m LEFT JOIN LATERAL get_product_names(m.id) pname
 ON true;
```

Compatibility

Of course, the SELECT statement is compatible with the SQL standard. But there are some extensions and some missing features.

Omitted FROM Clauses

PostgreSQL allows one to omit the FROM clause. It has a straightforward use to compute the results of simple expressions:

```
SELECT 2+2;

 ?column?
----------
        4
```

Some other SQL databases cannot do this except by introducing a dummy one-row table from which to do the SELECT.

Note that if a FROM clause is not specified, the query cannot reference any database tables. For example, the following query is invalid:

```
SELECT distributors.* WHERE distributors.name = 'Westward';
```

PostgreSQL releases prior to 8.1 would accept queries of this form, and add an implicit entry to the query's FROM clause for each table referenced by the query. This is no longer allowed.

Empty SELECT Lists

The list of output expressions after SELECT can be empty, producing a zero-column result table. This is not valid syntax according to the SQL standard. PostgreSQL allows it to be consistent with allowing zero-column tables. However, an empty list is not allowed when DISTINCT is used.

Omitting the AS Key Word

In the SQL standard, the optional key word AS can be omitted before an output column name whenever the new column name is a valid column name (that is, not the same as any reserved keyword). PostgreSQL is slightly more restrictive: AS is required if the new column name matches any keyword at all, reserved or not. Recommended practice is to use AS or double-quote output column names, to prevent any possible conflict against future keyword additions.

In FROM items, both the standard and PostgreSQL allow AS to be omitted before an alias that is an unreserved keyword. But this is impractical for output column names, because of syntactic ambiguities.

ONLY and Inheritance

The SQL standard requires parentheses around the table name when writing ONLY, for example SELECT * FROM ONLY (tab1), ONLY (tab2) WHERE .... PostgreSQL considers these parentheses to be optional.

PostgreSQL allows a trailing * to be written to explicitly specify the non-ONLY behavior of including child tables. The standard does not allow this.

(These points apply equally to all SQL commands supporting the ONLY option.)

TABLESAMPLE Clause Restrictions

The TABLESAMPLE clause is currently accepted only on regular tables and materialized views. According to the SQL standard it should be possible to apply it to any FROM item.

Function Calls in FROM

PostgreSQL allows a function call to be written directly as a member of the FROM list. In the SQL standard it would be necessary to wrap such a function call in a sub-SELECT; that is, the syntax FROM *func(...) alias* is approximately equivalent to FROM LATERAL (SELECT *func(...)) alias*. Note that LATERAL is considered to be implicit; this is because the standard requires LATERAL semantics for an UNNEST() item in FROM. PostgreSQL treats UNNEST() the same as other set-returning functions.

Namespace Available to GROUP BY and ORDER BY

In the SQL-92 standard, an ORDER BY clause can only use output column names or numbers, while a GROUP BY clause can only use expressions based on input column names. PostgreSQL extends each of these clauses to allow the other choice as well (but it uses the standard's interpretation if there is ambiguity). PostgreSQL also allows both clauses to specify arbitrary expressions. Note that names appearing in an expression will always be taken as input-column names, not as output-column names.

SQL:1999 and later use a slightly different definition which is not entirely upward compatible with SQL-92. In most cases, however, PostgreSQL will interpret an ORDER BY or GROUP BY expression the same way SQL:1999 does.

Functional Dependencies

PostgreSQL recognizes functional dependency (allowing columns to be omitted from GROUP BY) only when a table's primary key is included in the GROUP BY list. The SQL standard specifies additional conditions that should be recognized.

LIMIT and OFFSET

The clauses LIMIT and OFFSET are PostgreSQL-specific syntax, also used by MySQL. The SQL:2008 standard has introduced the clauses OFFSET ... FETCH {FIRST | NEXT} ... for the same functionality, as shown above in LIMIT Clause. This syntax is also used by IBM DB2. (Applications written for Oracle frequently use a workaround involving the automatically generated rownum column, which is not available in PostgreSQL, to implement the effects of these clauses.)

FOR NO KEY UPDATE, FOR UPDATE, FOR SHARE, FOR KEY SHARE

Although FOR UPDATE appears in the SQL standard, the standard allows it only as an option of DECLARE CURSOR. PostgreSQL allows it in any SELECT query as well as in sub-SELECTs, but this is an extension. The FOR NO KEY UPDATE, FOR SHARE and FOR KEY SHARE variants, as well as the NOWAIT and SKIP LOCKED options, do not appear in the standard.

Data-Modifying Statements in WITH

PostgreSQL allows INSERT, UPDATE, and DELETE to be used as WITH queries. This is not found in the SQL standard.

Nonstandard Clauses

`DISTINCT ON ( ... )` is an extension of the SQL standard.

`ROWS FROM( ... )` is an extension of the SQL standard.

SELECT INTO

SELECT INTO — define a new table from the results of a query

Synopsis

```
[ WITH [ RECURSIVE ] with_query [, ...] ]
SELECT [ ALL | DISTINCT [ ON ( expression [, ...] ) ] ]
    * | expression [ [ AS ] output_name ] [, ...]
    INTO [ TEMPORARY | TEMP | UNLOGGED ] [ TABLE ] new_table
    [ FROM from_item [, ...] ]
    [ WHERE condition ]
    [ GROUP BY expression [, ...] ]
    [ HAVING condition [, ...] ]
    [ WINDOW window_name AS ( window_definition ) [, ...] ]
    [ { UNION | INTERSECT | EXCEPT } [ ALL | DISTINCT ] select ]
    [ ORDER BY expression [ ASC | DESC | USING operator ] [ NULLS
{ FIRST | LAST } ] [, ...] ]
    [ LIMIT { count | ALL } ]
    [ OFFSET start [ ROW | ROWS ] ]
    [ FETCH { FIRST | NEXT } [ count ] { ROW | ROWS } ONLY ]
    [ FOR { UPDATE | SHARE } [ OF table_name [, ...] ] [ NOWAIT ]
[...] ]
```

Description

SELECT INTO creates a new table and fills it with data computed by a query. The data is not returned to the client, as it is with a normal SELECT. The new table's columns have the names and data types associated with the output columns of the SELECT.

Parameters

TEMPORARY or TEMP

> If specified, the table is created as a temporary table. Refer to CREATE TABLE for details.

UNLOGGED

> If specified, the table is created as an unlogged table. Refer to CREATE TABLE for details.

new_table

> The name (optionally schema-qualified) of the table to be created.

All other parameters are described in detail under SELECT.

Notes

CREATE TABLE AS is functionally similar to SELECT INTO. CREATE TABLE AS is the recommended syntax, since this form of SELECT INTO is not available in ECPG or PL/pgSQL, because they interpret the INTO clause differently. Furthermore, CREATE TABLE AS offers a superset of the functionality provided by SELECT INTO.

To add OIDs to the table created by SELECT INTO, enable the default_with_oids configuration variable. Alternatively, CREATE TABLE AS can be used with the WITH OIDS clause.

Examples

Create a new table films_recent consisting of only recent entries from the table films:

```
SELECT * INTO films_recent FROM films WHERE date_prod >= '2002-01-01';
```

Compatibility

The SQL standard uses SELECT INTO to represent selecting values into scalar variables of a host program, rather than creating a new table. This indeed is the usage found in ECPG (see Chapter 36) and PL/pgSQL (see Chapter 43). The PostgreSQL usage of SELECT INTO to represent table creation is historical. It is best to use CREATE TABLE AS for this purpose in new code.

See Also

CREATE TABLE AS

SET

SET — change a run-time parameter

Synopsis

```
SET [ SESSION | LOCAL ] configuration_parameter { TO | = } { value |
'value' | DEFAULT }
SET [ SESSION | LOCAL ] TIME ZONE { timezone | LOCAL | DEFAULT }
```

Description

The SET command changes run-time configuration parameters. Many of the run-time parameters listed in Chapter 19 can be changed on-the-fly with SET. (But some require superuser privileges to change, and others cannot be changed after server or session start.) SET only affects the value used by the current session.

If SET (or equivalently SET SESSION) is issued within a transaction that is later aborted, the effects of the SET command disappear when the transaction is rolled back. Once the surrounding transaction is committed, the effects will persist until the end of the session, unless overridden by another SET.

The effects of SET LOCAL last only till the end of the current transaction, whether committed or not. A special case is SET followed by SET LOCAL within a single transaction: the SET LOCAL value will be seen until the end of the transaction, but afterwards (if the transaction is committed) the SET value will take effect.

The effects of SET or SET LOCAL are also canceled by rolling back to a savepoint that is earlier than the command.

If SET LOCAL is used within a function that has a SET option for the same variable (see CREATE FUNCTION), the effects of the SET LOCAL command disappear at function exit; that is, the value in effect when the function was called is restored anyway. This allows SET LOCAL to be used for dynamic or repeated changes of a parameter within a function, while still having the convenience of using the SET option to save and restore the caller's value. However, a regular SET command overrides any surrounding function's SET option; its effects will persist unless rolled back.

Note

In PostgreSQL versions 8.0 through 8.2, the effects of a SET LOCAL would be canceled by releasing an earlier savepoint, or by successful exit from a PL/pgSQL exception block. This behavior has been changed because it was deemed unintuitive.

Parameters

SESSION

Specifies that the command takes effect for the current session. (This is the default if neither SESSION nor LOCAL appears.)

LOCAL

> Specifies that the command takes effect for only the current transaction. After COMMIT or ROLL-BACK, the session-level setting takes effect again. Issuing this outside of a transaction block emits a warning and otherwise has no effect.

configuration_parameter

> Name of a settable run-time parameter. Available parameters are documented in Chapter 19 and below.

value

> New value of parameter. Values can be specified as string constants, identifiers, numbers, or comma-separated lists of these, as appropriate for the particular parameter. DEFAULT can be written to specify resetting the parameter to its default value (that is, whatever value it would have had if no SET had been executed in the current session).

Besides the configuration parameters documented in Chapter 19, there are a few that can only be adjusted using the SET command or that have a special syntax:

SCHEMA

> SET SCHEMA 'value' is an alias for SET search_path TO value. Only one schema can be specified using this syntax.

NAMES

> SET NAMES value is an alias for SET client_encoding TO value.

SEED

> Sets the internal seed for the random number generator (the function random). Allowed values are floating-point numbers between -1 and 1, which are then multiplied by 2^{31}-1.

> The seed can also be set by invoking the function setseed:

> SELECT setseed(value);

TIME ZONE

> SET TIME ZONE value is an alias for SET timezone TO value. The syntax SET TIME ZONE allows special syntax for the time zone specification. Here are examples of valid values:

'PST8PDT'

> The time zone for Berkeley, California.

'Europe/Rome'

> The time zone for Italy.

-7

> The time zone 7 hours west from UTC (equivalent to PDT). Positive values are east from UTC.

```
INTERVAL '-08:00' HOUR TO MINUTE
```

The time zone 8 hours west from UTC (equivalent to PST).

```
LOCAL
DEFAULT
```

Set the time zone to your local time zone (that is, the server's default value of `timezone`).

Timezone settings given as numbers or intervals are internally translated to POSIX timezone syntax. For example, after `SET TIME ZONE -7`, `SHOW TIME ZONE` would report `<-07>+07`.

See Section 8.5.3 for more information about time zones.

Notes

The function `set_config` provides equivalent functionality; see Section 9.26. Also, it is possible to UPDATE the `pg_settings` system view to perform the equivalent of `SET`.

Examples

Set the schema search path:

```
SET search_path TO my_schema, public;
```

Set the style of date to traditional POSTGRES with "day before month" input convention:

```
SET datestyle TO postgres, dmy;
```

Set the time zone for Berkeley, California:

```
SET TIME ZONE 'PST8PDT';
```

Set the time zone for Italy:

```
SET TIME ZONE 'Europe/Rome';
```

Compatibility

`SET TIME ZONE` extends syntax defined in the SQL standard. The standard allows only numeric time zone offsets while PostgreSQL allows more flexible time-zone specifications. All other `SET` features are PostgreSQL extensions.

See Also

RESET, SHOW

SET CONSTRAINTS

SET CONSTRAINTS — set constraint check timing for the current transaction

Synopsis

```
SET CONSTRAINTS { ALL | name [, ...] } { DEFERRED | IMMEDIATE }
```

Description

`SET CONSTRAINTS` sets the behavior of constraint checking within the current transaction. `IMMEDIATE` constraints are checked at the end of each statement. `DEFERRED` constraints are not checked until transaction commit. Each constraint has its own `IMMEDIATE` or `DEFERRED` mode.

Upon creation, a constraint is given one of three characteristics: `DEFERRABLE INITIALLY DEFERRED`, `DEFERRABLE INITIALLY IMMEDIATE`, or `NOT DEFERRABLE`. The third class is always `IMMEDIATE` and is not affected by the `SET CONSTRAINTS` command. The first two classes start every transaction in the indicated mode, but their behavior can be changed within a transaction by `SET CONSTRAINTS`.

`SET CONSTRAINTS` with a list of constraint names changes the mode of just those constraints (which must all be deferrable). Each constraint name can be schema-qualified. The current schema search path is used to find the first matching name if no schema name is specified. `SET CONSTRAINTS ALL` changes the mode of all deferrable constraints.

When `SET CONSTRAINTS` changes the mode of a constraint from `DEFERRED` to `IMMEDIATE`, the new mode takes effect retroactively: any outstanding data modifications that would have been checked at the end of the transaction are instead checked during the execution of the `SET CONSTRAINTS` command. If any such constraint is violated, the `SET CONSTRAINTS` fails (and does not change the constraint mode). Thus, `SET CONSTRAINTS` can be used to force checking of constraints to occur at a specific point in a transaction.

Currently, only `UNIQUE`, `PRIMARY KEY`, `REFERENCES` (foreign key), and `EXCLUDE` constraints are affected by this setting. `NOT NULL` and `CHECK` constraints are always checked immediately when a row is inserted or modified (*not* at the end of the statement). Uniqueness and exclusion constraints that have not been declared `DEFERRABLE` are also checked immediately.

The firing of triggers that are declared as "constraint triggers" is also controlled by this setting — they fire at the same time that the associated constraint should be checked.

Notes

Because PostgreSQL does not require constraint names to be unique within a schema (but only per-table), it is possible that there is more than one match for a specified constraint name. In this case `SET CONSTRAINTS` will act on all matches. For a non-schema-qualified name, once a match or matches have been found in some schema in the search path, schemas appearing later in the path are not searched.

This command only alters the behavior of constraints within the current transaction. Issuing this outside of a transaction block emits a warning and otherwise has no effect.

Compatibility

This command complies with the behavior defined in the SQL standard, except for the limitation that, in PostgreSQL, it does not apply to NOT NULL and CHECK constraints. Also, PostgreSQL checks non-deferrable uniqueness constraints immediately, not at end of statement as the standard would suggest.

SET ROLE

SET ROLE — set the current user identifier of the current session

Synopsis

```
SET [ SESSION | LOCAL ] ROLE role_name
SET [ SESSION | LOCAL ] ROLE NONE
RESET ROLE
```

Description

This command sets the current user identifier of the current SQL session to be `role_name`. The role name can be written as either an identifier or a string literal. After SET ROLE, permissions checking for SQL commands is carried out as though the named role were the one that had logged in originally.

The specified `role_name` must be a role that the current session user is a member of. (If the session user is a superuser, any role can be selected.)

The SESSION and LOCAL modifiers act the same as for the regular SET command.

The NONE and RESET forms reset the current user identifier to be the current session user identifier. These forms can be executed by any user.

Notes

Using this command, it is possible to either add privileges or restrict one's privileges. If the session user role has the INHERITS attribute, then it automatically has all the privileges of every role that it could SET ROLE to; in this case SET ROLE effectively drops all the privileges assigned directly to the session user and to the other roles it is a member of, leaving only the privileges available to the named role. On the other hand, if the session user role has the NOINHERITS attribute, SET ROLE drops the privileges assigned directly to the session user and instead acquires the privileges available to the named role.

In particular, when a superuser chooses to SET ROLE to a non-superuser role, they lose their superuser privileges.

SET ROLE has effects comparable to SET SESSION AUTHORIZATION, but the privilege checks involved are quite different. Also, SET SESSION AUTHORIZATION determines which roles are allowable for later SET ROLE commands, whereas changing roles with SET ROLE does not change the set of roles allowed to a later SET ROLE.

SET ROLE does not process session variables as specified by the role's ALTER ROLE settings; this only happens during login.

SET ROLE cannot be used within a SECURITY DEFINER function.

Examples

```
SELECT SESSION_USER, CURRENT_USER;
```

```
 session_user | current_user
--------------+--------------
 peter        | peter

SET ROLE 'paul';

SELECT SESSION_USER, CURRENT_USER;

 session_user | current_user
--------------+--------------
 peter        | paul
```

Compatibility

PostgreSQL allows identifier syntax ("*rolename*"), while the SQL standard requires the role name to be written as a string literal. SQL does not allow this command during a transaction; PostgreSQL does not make this restriction because there is no reason to. The SESSION and LOCAL modifiers are a PostgreSQL extension, as is the RESET syntax.

See Also

SET SESSION AUTHORIZATION

SET SESSION AUTHORIZATION

SET SESSION AUTHORIZATION — set the session user identifier and the current user identifier of the current session

Synopsis

```
SET [ SESSION | LOCAL ] SESSION AUTHORIZATION user_name
SET [ SESSION | LOCAL ] SESSION AUTHORIZATION DEFAULT
RESET SESSION AUTHORIZATION
```

Description

This command sets the session user identifier and the current user identifier of the current SQL session to be user_name. The user name can be written as either an identifier or a string literal. Using this command, it is possible, for example, to temporarily become an unprivileged user and later switch back to being a superuser.

The session user identifier is initially set to be the (possibly authenticated) user name provided by the client. The current user identifier is normally equal to the session user identifier, but might change temporarily in the context of SECURITY DEFINER functions and similar mechanisms; it can also be changed by SET ROLE. The current user identifier is relevant for permission checking.

The session user identifier can be changed only if the initial session user (the *authenticated user*) had the superuser privilege. Otherwise, the command is accepted only if it specifies the authenticated user name.

The SESSION and LOCAL modifiers act the same as for the regular SET command.

The DEFAULT and RESET forms reset the session and current user identifiers to be the originally authenticated user name. These forms can be executed by any user.

Notes

SET SESSION AUTHORIZATION cannot be used within a SECURITY DEFINER function.

Examples

```
SELECT SESSION_USER, CURRENT_USER;

 session_user | current_user
--------------+--------------
 peter        | peter

SET SESSION AUTHORIZATION 'paul';

SELECT SESSION_USER, CURRENT_USER;

 session_user | current_user
--------------+--------------
```

```
paul          | paul
```

Compatibility

The SQL standard allows some other expressions to appear in place of the literal *user_name*, but these options are not important in practice. PostgreSQL allows identifier syntax ("*username*"), which SQL does not. SQL does not allow this command during a transaction; PostgreSQL does not make this restriction because there is no reason to. The SESSION and LOCAL modifiers are a PostgreSQL extension, as is the RESET syntax.

The privileges necessary to execute this command are left implementation-defined by the standard.

See Also

SET ROLE

SET TRANSACTION

SET TRANSACTION — set the characteristics of the current transaction

Synopsis

```
SET TRANSACTION transaction_mode [, ...]
SET TRANSACTION SNAPSHOT snapshot_id
SET SESSION CHARACTERISTICS AS TRANSACTION transaction_mode [, ...]

where transaction_mode is one of:

    ISOLATION LEVEL { SERIALIZABLE | REPEATABLE READ | READ COMMITTED
  | READ UNCOMMITTED }
    READ WRITE | READ ONLY
    [ NOT ] DEFERRABLE
```

Description

The SET TRANSACTION command sets the characteristics of the current transaction. It has no effect on any subsequent transactions. SET SESSION CHARACTERISTICS sets the default transaction characteristics for subsequent transactions of a session. These defaults can be overridden by SET TRANSACTION for an individual transaction.

The available transaction characteristics are the transaction isolation level, the transaction access mode (read/write or read-only), and the deferrable mode. In addition, a snapshot can be selected, though only for the current transaction, not as a session default.

The isolation level of a transaction determines what data the transaction can see when other transactions are running concurrently:

READ COMMITTED

   A statement can only see rows committed before it began. This is the default.

REPEATABLE READ

   All statements of the current transaction can only see rows committed before the first query or data-modification statement was executed in this transaction.

SERIALIZABLE

   All statements of the current transaction can only see rows committed before the first query or data-modification statement was executed in this transaction. If a pattern of reads and writes among concurrent serializable transactions would create a situation which could not have occurred for any serial (one-at-a-time) execution of those transactions, one of them will be rolled back with a serialization_failure error.

The SQL standard defines one additional level, READ UNCOMMITTED. In PostgreSQL READ UNCOMMITTED is treated as READ COMMITTED.

The transaction isolation level cannot be changed after the first query or data-modification statement (SELECT, INSERT, DELETE, UPDATE, FETCH, or COPY) of a transaction has been executed. See Chapter 13 for more information about transaction isolation and concurrency control.

The transaction access mode determines whether the transaction is read/write or read-only. Read/write is the default. When a transaction is read-only, the following SQL commands are disallowed: INSERT, UPDATE, DELETE, and COPY FROM if the table they would write to is not a temporary table; all CREATE, ALTER, and DROP commands; COMMENT, GRANT, REVOKE, TRUNCATE; and EXPLAIN ANALYZE and EXECUTE if the command they would execute is among those listed. This is a high-level notion of read-only that does not prevent all writes to disk.

The DEFERRABLE transaction property has no effect unless the transaction is also SERIALIZABLE and READ ONLY. When all three of these properties are selected for a transaction, the transaction may block when first acquiring its snapshot, after which it is able to run without the normal overhead of a SERIALIZABLE transaction and without any risk of contributing to or being canceled by a serialization failure. This mode is well suited for long-running reports or backups.

The SET TRANSACTION SNAPSHOT command allows a new transaction to run with the same *snapshot* as an existing transaction. The pre-existing transaction must have exported its snapshot with the pg_export_snapshot function (see Section 9.26.5). That function returns a snapshot identifier, which must be given to SET TRANSACTION SNAPSHOT to specify which snapshot is to be imported. The identifier must be written as a string literal in this command, for example '000003A1-1'. SET TRANSACTION SNAPSHOT can only be executed at the start of a transaction, before the first query or data-modification statement (SELECT, INSERT, DELETE, UPDATE, FETCH, or COPY) of the transaction. Furthermore, the transaction must already be set to SERIALIZABLE or REPEATABLE READ isolation level (otherwise, the snapshot would be discarded immediately, since READ COMMITTED mode takes a new snapshot for each command). If the importing transaction uses SERIALIZABLE isolation level, then the transaction that exported the snapshot must also use that isolation level. Also, a non-read-only serializable transaction cannot import a snapshot from a read-only transaction.

Notes

If SET TRANSACTION is executed without a prior START TRANSACTION or BEGIN, it emits a warning and otherwise has no effect.

It is possible to dispense with SET TRANSACTION by instead specifying the desired *transaction_modes* in BEGIN or START TRANSACTION. But that option is not available for SET TRANSACTION SNAPSHOT.

The session default transaction modes can also be set by setting the configuration parameters default_transaction_isolation, default_transaction_read_only, and default_transaction_deferrable. (In fact SET SESSION CHARACTERISTICS is just a verbose equivalent for setting these variables with SET.) This means the defaults can be set in the configuration file, via ALTER DATABASE, etc. Consult Chapter 19 for more information.

Examples

To begin a new transaction with the same snapshot as an already existing transaction, first export the snapshot from the existing transaction. That will return the snapshot identifier, for example:

```
BEGIN TRANSACTION ISOLATION LEVEL REPEATABLE READ;
SELECT pg_export_snapshot();
 pg_export_snapshot
```

```
--------------------
 00000003-0000001B-1
(1 row)
```

Then give the snapshot identifier in a SET TRANSACTION SNAPSHOT command at the beginning of the newly opened transaction:

```
BEGIN TRANSACTION ISOLATION LEVEL REPEATABLE READ;
SET TRANSACTION SNAPSHOT '00000003-0000001B-1';
```

Compatibility

These commands are defined in the SQL standard, except for the DEFERRABLE transaction mode and the SET TRANSACTION SNAPSHOT form, which are PostgreSQL extensions.

SERIALIZABLE is the default transaction isolation level in the standard. In PostgreSQL the default is ordinarily READ COMMITTED, but you can change it as mentioned above.

In the SQL standard, there is one other transaction characteristic that can be set with these commands: the size of the diagnostics area. This concept is specific to embedded SQL, and therefore is not implemented in the PostgreSQL server.

The SQL standard requires commas between successive *transaction_modes*, but for historical reasons PostgreSQL allows the commas to be omitted.

SHOW

SHOW — show the value of a run-time parameter

Synopsis

```
SHOW name
SHOW ALL
```

Description

SHOW will display the current setting of run-time parameters. These variables can be set using the SET statement, by editing the postgresql.conf configuration file, through the PGOPTIONS environmental variable (when using libpq or a libpq-based application), or through command-line flags when starting the postgres server. See Chapter 19 for details.

Parameters

name

    The name of a run-time parameter. Available parameters are documented in Chapter 19 and on the SET reference page. In addition, there are a few parameters that can be shown but not set:

    SERVER_VERSION

        Shows the server's version number.

    SERVER_ENCODING

        Shows the server-side character set encoding. At present, this parameter can be shown but not set, because the encoding is determined at database creation time.

    LC_COLLATE

        Shows the database's locale setting for collation (text ordering). At present, this parameter can be shown but not set, because the setting is determined at database creation time.

    LC_CTYPE

        Shows the database's locale setting for character classification. At present, this parameter can be shown but not set, because the setting is determined at database creation time.

    IS_SUPERUSER

        True if the current role has superuser privileges.

ALL

    Show the values of all configuration parameters, with descriptions.

Notes

The function current_setting produces equivalent output; see Section 9.26. Also, the pg_settings system view produces the same information.

Examples

Show the current setting of the parameter DateStyle:

```
SHOW DateStyle;
 DateStyle
-----------
 ISO, MDY
(1 row)
```

Show the current setting of the parameter geqo:

```
SHOW geqo;
 geqo
------
 on
(1 row)
```

Show all settings:

```
SHOW ALL;
          name          | setting |                description

------------------------+---------
+-----------------------------------------------
 allow_system_table_mods | off     | Allows modifications of the
 structure of ...
    .
    .
    .
 xmloption              | content | Sets whether XML data in implicit
 parsing ...
 zero_damaged_pages      | off     | Continues processing past damaged
 page headers.
(196 rows)
```

Compatibility

The SHOW command is a PostgreSQL extension.

See Also

SET, RESET

START TRANSACTION

START TRANSACTION — start a transaction block

Synopsis

```
START TRANSACTION [ transaction_mode [, ...] ]

where transaction_mode is one of:

    ISOLATION LEVEL { SERIALIZABLE | REPEATABLE READ | READ COMMITTED
  | READ UNCOMMITTED }
    READ WRITE | READ ONLY
    [ NOT ] DEFERRABLE
```

Description

This command begins a new transaction block. If the isolation level, read/write mode, or deferrable mode is specified, the new transaction has those characteristics, as if SET TRANSACTION was executed. This is the same as the BEGIN command.

Parameters

Refer to SET TRANSACTION for information on the meaning of the parameters to this statement.

Compatibility

In the standard, it is not necessary to issue START TRANSACTION to start a transaction block: any SQL command implicitly begins a block. PostgreSQL's behavior can be seen as implicitly issuing a COMMIT after each command that does not follow START TRANSACTION (or BEGIN), and it is therefore often called "autocommit". Other relational database systems might offer an autocommit feature as a convenience.

The DEFERRABLE transaction_mode is a PostgreSQL language extension.

The SQL standard requires commas between successive transaction_modes, but for historical reasons PostgreSQL allows the commas to be omitted.

See also the compatibility section of SET TRANSACTION.

See Also

BEGIN, COMMIT, ROLLBACK, SAVEPOINT, SET TRANSACTION

TRUNCATE

TRUNCATE — empty a table or set of tables

Synopsis

```
TRUNCATE [ TABLE ] [ ONLY ] name [ * ] [, ... ]
    [ RESTART IDENTITY | CONTINUE IDENTITY ] [ CASCADE | RESTRICT ]
```

Description

TRUNCATE quickly removes all rows from a set of tables. It has the same effect as an unqualified DELETE on each table, but since it does not actually scan the tables it is faster. Furthermore, it reclaims disk space immediately, rather than requiring a subsequent VACUUM operation. This is most useful on large tables.

Parameters

name

> The name (optionally schema-qualified) of a table to truncate. If ONLY is specified before the table name, only that table is truncated. If ONLY is not specified, the table and all its descendant tables (if any) are truncated. Optionally, * can be specified after the table name to explicitly indicate that descendant tables are included.

RESTART IDENTITY

> Automatically restart sequences owned by columns of the truncated table(s).

CONTINUE IDENTITY

> Do not change the values of sequences. This is the default.

CASCADE

> Automatically truncate all tables that have foreign-key references to any of the named tables, or to any tables added to the group due to CASCADE.

RESTRICT

> Refuse to truncate if any of the tables have foreign-key references from tables that are not listed in the command. This is the default.

Notes

You must have the TRUNCATE privilege on a table to truncate it.

TRUNCATE acquires an ACCESS EXCLUSIVE lock on each table it operates on, which blocks all other concurrent operations on the table. When RESTART IDENTITY is specified, any sequences that are to be restarted are likewise locked exclusively. If concurrent access to a table is required, then the DELETE command should be used instead.

TRUNCATE cannot be used on a table that has foreign-key references from other tables, unless all such tables are also truncated in the same command. Checking validity in such cases would require table scans, and the whole point is not to do one. The CASCADE option can be used to automatically include all dependent tables — but be very careful when using this option, or else you might lose data you did not intend to!

TRUNCATE will not fire any ON DELETE triggers that might exist for the tables. But it will fire ON TRUNCATE triggers. If ON TRUNCATE triggers are defined for any of the tables, then all BEFORE TRUNCATE triggers are fired before any truncation happens, and all AFTER TRUNCATE triggers are fired after the last truncation is performed and any sequences are reset. The triggers will fire in the order that the tables are to be processed (first those listed in the command, and then any that were added due to cascading).

TRUNCATE is not MVCC-safe. After truncation, the table will appear empty to concurrent transactions, if they are using a snapshot taken before the truncation occurred. See Section 13.5 for more details.

TRUNCATE is transaction-safe with respect to the data in the tables: the truncation will be safely rolled back if the surrounding transaction does not commit.

When RESTART IDENTITY is specified, the implied ALTER SEQUENCE RESTART operations are also done transactionally; that is, they will be rolled back if the surrounding transaction does not commit. This is unlike the normal behavior of ALTER SEQUENCE RESTART. Be aware that if any additional sequence operations are done on the restarted sequences before the transaction rolls back, the effects of these operations on the sequences will be rolled back, but not their effects on currval(); that is, after the transaction currval() will continue to reflect the last sequence value obtained inside the failed transaction, even though the sequence itself may no longer be consistent with that. This is similar to the usual behavior of currval() after a failed transaction.

TRUNCATE is not currently supported for foreign tables. This implies that if a specified table has any descendant tables that are foreign, the command will fail.

Examples

Truncate the tables bigtable and fattable:

```
TRUNCATE bigtable, fattable;
```

The same, and also reset any associated sequence generators:

```
TRUNCATE bigtable, fattable RESTART IDENTITY;
```

Truncate the table othertable, and cascade to any tables that reference othertable via foreign-key constraints:

```
TRUNCATE othertable CASCADE;
```

Compatibility

The SQL:2008 standard includes a TRUNCATE command with the syntax TRUNCATE TABLE table-name. The clauses CONTINUE IDENTITY/RESTART IDENTITY also appear in that standard, but have slightly different though related meanings. Some of the concurrency behavior of this command is left implementation-defined by the standard, so the above notes should be considered and compared with other implementations if necessary.

See Also

DELETE

UNLISTEN

UNLISTEN — stop listening for a notification

Synopsis

```
UNLISTEN { channel | * }
```

Description

UNLISTEN is used to remove an existing registration for NOTIFY events. UNLISTEN cancels any existing registration of the current PostgreSQL session as a listener on the notification channel named *channel*. The special wildcard * cancels all listener registrations for the current session.

NOTIFY contains a more extensive discussion of the use of LISTEN and NOTIFY.

Parameters

channel

> Name of a notification channel (any identifier).

*

> All current listen registrations for this session are cleared.

Notes

You can unlisten something you were not listening for; no warning or error will appear.

At the end of each session, UNLISTEN * is automatically executed.

A transaction that has executed UNLISTEN cannot be prepared for two-phase commit.

Examples

To make a registration:

```
LISTEN virtual;
NOTIFY virtual;
Asynchronous notification "virtual" received from server process with
 PID 8448.
```

Once UNLISTEN has been executed, further NOTIFY messages will be ignored:

```
UNLISTEN virtual;
NOTIFY virtual;
-- no NOTIFY event is received
```

Compatibility

There is no UNLISTEN command in the SQL standard.

See Also

LISTEN, NOTIFY

UPDATE

UPDATE — update rows of a table

Synopsis

```
[ WITH [ RECURSIVE ] with_query [, ...] ]
UPDATE [ ONLY ] table_name [ * ] [ [ AS ] alias ]
    SET { column_name = { expression | DEFAULT } |
          ( column_name [, ...] ) = [ ROW ] ( { expression | DEFAULT }
 [, ...] ) |
          ( column_name [, ...] ) = ( sub-SELECT )
        } [, ...]
    [ FROM from_list ]
    [ WHERE condition | WHERE CURRENT OF cursor_name ]
    [ RETURNING * | output_expression [ [ AS ] output_name ] [, ...] ]
```

Description

UPDATE changes the values of the specified columns in all rows that satisfy the condition. Only the columns to be modified need be mentioned in the SET clause; columns not explicitly modified retain their previous values.

There are two ways to modify a table using information contained in other tables in the database: using sub-selects, or specifying additional tables in the FROM clause. Which technique is more appropriate depends on the specific circumstances.

The optional RETURNING clause causes UPDATE to compute and return value(s) based on each row actually updated. Any expression using the table's columns, and/or columns of other tables mentioned in FROM, can be computed. The new (post-update) values of the table's columns are used. The syntax of the RETURNING list is identical to that of the output list of SELECT.

You must have the UPDATE privilege on the table, or at least on the column(s) that are listed to be updated. You must also have the SELECT privilege on any column whose values are read in the *expressions* or *condition*.

Parameters

with_query

> The WITH clause allows you to specify one or more subqueries that can be referenced by name in the UPDATE query. See Section 7.8 and SELECT for details.

table_name

> The name (optionally schema-qualified) of the table to update. If ONLY is specified before the table name, matching rows are updated in the named table only. If ONLY is not specified, matching rows are also updated in any tables inheriting from the named table. Optionally, * can be specified after the table name to explicitly indicate that descendant tables are included.

alias

A substitute name for the target table. When an alias is provided, it completely hides the actual name of the table. For example, given UPDATE foo AS f, the remainder of the UPDATE statement must refer to this table as f not foo.

column_name

The name of a column in the table named by *table_name*. The column name can be qualified with a subfield name or array subscript, if needed. Do not include the table's name in the specification of a target column — for example, UPDATE table_name SET table_name.col = 1 is invalid.

expression

An expression to assign to the column. The expression can use the old values of this and other columns in the table.

DEFAULT

Set the column to its default value (which will be NULL if no specific default expression has been assigned to it).

sub-SELECT

A SELECT sub-query that produces as many output columns as are listed in the parenthesized column list preceding it. The sub-query must yield no more than one row when executed. If it yields one row, its column values are assigned to the target columns; if it yields no rows, NULL values are assigned to the target columns. The sub-query can refer to old values of the current row of the table being updated.

from_list

A list of table expressions, allowing columns from other tables to appear in the WHERE condition and the update expressions. This is similar to the list of tables that can be specified in the FROM Clause of a SELECT statement. Note that the target table must not appear in the *from_list*, unless you intend a self-join (in which case it must appear with an alias in the *from_list*).

condition

An expression that returns a value of type boolean. Only rows for which this expression returns true will be updated.

cursor_name

The name of the cursor to use in a WHERE CURRENT OF condition. The row to be updated is the one most recently fetched from this cursor. The cursor must be a non-grouping query on the UPDATE's target table. Note that WHERE CURRENT OF cannot be specified together with a Boolean condition. See DECLARE for more information about using cursors with WHERE CURRENT OF.

output_expression

An expression to be computed and returned by the UPDATE command after each row is updated. The expression can use any column names of the table named by *table_name* or table(s) listed in FROM. Write * to return all columns.

output_name

A name to use for a returned column.

Outputs

On successful completion, an UPDATE command returns a command tag of the form

```
UPDATE count
```

The count is the number of rows updated, including matched rows whose values did not change. Note that the number may be less than the number of rows that matched the condition when updates were suppressed by a BEFORE UPDATE trigger. If count is 0, no rows were updated by the query (this is not considered an error).

If the UPDATE command contains a RETURNING clause, the result will be similar to that of a SELECT statement containing the columns and values defined in the RETURNING list, computed over the row(s) updated by the command.

Notes

When a FROM clause is present, what essentially happens is that the target table is joined to the tables mentioned in the from_list, and each output row of the join represents an update operation for the target table. When using FROM you should ensure that the join produces at most one output row for each row to be modified. In other words, a target row shouldn't join to more than one row from the other table(s). If it does, then only one of the join rows will be used to update the target row, but which one will be used is not readily predictable.

Because of this indeterminacy, referencing other tables only within sub-selects is safer, though often harder to read and slower than using a join.

In the case of a partitioned table, updating a row might cause it to no longer satisfy the partition constraint of the containing partition. In that case, if there is some other partition in the partition tree for which this row satisfies its partition constraint, then the row is moved to that partition. If there is no such partition, an error will occur. Behind the scenes, the row movement is actually a DELETE and INSERT operation. However, there is a possibility that a concurrent UPDATE or DELETE on the same row may miss this row. For details see the section Section 5.10.2.3. Currently, rows cannot be moved from a partition that is a foreign table to some other partition, but they can be moved into a foreign table if the foreign data wrapper supports it.

Examples

Change the word Drama to Dramatic in the column kind of the table films:

```
UPDATE films SET kind = 'Dramatic' WHERE kind = 'Drama';
```

Adjust temperature entries and reset precipitation to its default value in one row of the table weather:

```
UPDATE weather SET temp_lo = temp_lo+1, temp_hi = temp_lo+15, prcp =
DEFAULT
  WHERE city = 'San Francisco' AND date = '2003-07-03';
```

Perform the same operation and return the updated entries:

```
UPDATE weather SET temp_lo = temp_lo+1, temp_hi = temp_lo+15, prcp =
 DEFAULT
   WHERE city = 'San Francisco' AND date = '2003-07-03'
   RETURNING temp_lo, temp_hi, prcp;
```

Use the alternative column-list syntax to do the same update:

```
UPDATE weather SET (temp_lo, temp_hi, prcp) = (temp_lo+1, temp_lo+15,
 DEFAULT)
   WHERE city = 'San Francisco' AND date = '2003-07-03';
```

Increment the sales count of the salesperson who manages the account for Acme Corporation, using the FROM clause syntax:

```
UPDATE employees SET sales_count = sales_count + 1 FROM accounts
   WHERE accounts.name = 'Acme Corporation'
   AND employees.id = accounts.sales_person;
```

Perform the same operation, using a sub-select in the WHERE clause:

```
UPDATE employees SET sales_count = sales_count + 1 WHERE id =
   (SELECT sales_person FROM accounts WHERE name = 'Acme Corporation');
```

Update contact names in an accounts table to match the currently assigned salesmen:

```
UPDATE accounts SET (contact_first_name, contact_last_name) =
    (SELECT first_name, last_name FROM salesmen
     WHERE salesmen.id = accounts.sales_id);
```

A similar result could be accomplished with a join:

```
UPDATE accounts SET contact_first_name = first_name,
                    contact_last_name = last_name
   FROM salesmen WHERE salesmen.id = accounts.sales_id;
```

However, the second query may give unexpected results if salesmen.id is not a unique key, whereas the first query is guaranteed to raise an error if there are multiple id matches. Also, if there is no match for a particular accounts.sales_id entry, the first query will set the corresponding name fields to NULL, whereas the second query will not update that row at all.

Update statistics in a summary table to match the current data:

```
UPDATE summary s SET (sum_x, sum_y, avg_x, avg_y) =
    (SELECT sum(x), sum(y), avg(x), avg(y) FROM data d
     WHERE d.group_id = s.group_id);
```

Attempt to insert a new stock item along with the quantity of stock. If the item already exists, instead update the stock count of the existing item. To do this without failing the entire transaction, use savepoints:

```
BEGIN;
-- other operations
SAVEPOINT sp1;
INSERT INTO wines VALUES('Chateau Lafite 2003', '24');
-- Assume the above fails because of a unique key violation,
-- so now we issue these commands:
ROLLBACK TO sp1;
UPDATE wines SET stock = stock + 24 WHERE winename = 'Chateau Lafite
  2003';
-- continue with other operations, and eventually
COMMIT;
```

Change the kind column of the table films in the row on which the cursor c_films is currently positioned:

```
UPDATE films SET kind = 'Dramatic' WHERE CURRENT OF c_films;
```

Compatibility

This command conforms to the SQL standard, except that the FROM and RETURNING clauses are PostgreSQL extensions, as is the ability to use WITH with UPDATE.

Some other database systems offer a FROM option in which the target table is supposed to be listed again within FROM. That is not how PostgreSQL interprets FROM. Be careful when porting applications that use this extension.

According to the standard, the source value for a parenthesized sub-list of target column names can be any row-valued expression yielding the correct number of columns. PostgreSQL only allows the source value to be a row constructor or a sub-SELECT. An individual column's updated value can be specified as DEFAULT in the row-constructor case, but not inside a sub-SELECT.

VACUUM

VACUUM — garbage-collect and optionally analyze a database

Synopsis

```
VACUUM [ ( option [, ...] ) ] [ table_and_columns [, ...] ]
VACUUM [ FULL ] [ FREEZE ] [ VERBOSE ] [ ANALYZE ] [ table_and_columns
[, ...] ]
```

where `option` can be one of:

```
FULL
FREEZE
VERBOSE
ANALYZE
DISABLE_PAGE_SKIPPING
```

and `table_and_columns` is:

```
table_name [ ( column_name [, ...] ) ]
```

Description

VACUUM reclaims storage occupied by dead tuples. In normal PostgreSQL operation, tuples that are deleted or obsoleted by an update are not physically removed from their table; they remain present until a VACUUM is done. Therefore it's necessary to do VACUUM periodically, especially on frequently-updated tables.

Without a `table_and_columns` list, VACUUM processes every table and materialized view in the current database that the current user has permission to vacuum. With a list, VACUUM processes only those table(s).

VACUUM ANALYZE performs a VACUUM and then an ANALYZE for each selected table. This is a handy combination form for routine maintenance scripts. See ANALYZE for more details about its processing.

Plain VACUUM (without FULL) simply reclaims space and makes it available for re-use. This form of the command can operate in parallel with normal reading and writing of the table, as an exclusive lock is not obtained. However, extra space is not returned to the operating system (in most cases); it's just kept available for re-use within the same table. VACUUM FULL rewrites the entire contents of the table into a new disk file with no extra space, allowing unused space to be returned to the operating system. This form is much slower and requires an exclusive lock on each table while it is being processed.

When the option list is surrounded by parentheses, the options can be written in any order. Without parentheses, options must be specified in exactly the order shown above. The parenthesized syntax was added in PostgreSQL 9.0; the unparenthesized syntax is deprecated.

Parameters

FULL

Selects "full" vacuum, which can reclaim more space, but takes much longer and exclusively locks the table. This method also requires extra disk space, since it writes a new copy of the table and doesn't release the old copy until the operation is complete. Usually this should only be used when a significant amount of space needs to be reclaimed from within the table.

FREEZE

Selects aggressive "freezing" of tuples. Specifying FREEZE is equivalent to performing VACUUM with the vacuum_freeze_min_age and vacuum_freeze_table_age parameters set to zero. Aggressive freezing is always performed when the table is rewritten, so this option is redundant when FULL is specified.

VERBOSE

Prints a detailed vacuum activity report for each table.

ANALYZE

Updates statistics used by the planner to determine the most efficient way to execute a query.

DISABLE_PAGE_SKIPPING

Normally, VACUUM will skip pages based on the visibility map. Pages where all tuples are known to be frozen can always be skipped, and those where all tuples are known to be visible to all transactions may be skipped except when performing an aggressive vacuum. Furthermore, except when performing an aggressive vacuum, some pages may be skipped in order to avoid waiting for other sessions to finish using them. This option disables all page-skipping behavior, and is intended to be used only when the contents of the visibility map are suspect, which should happen only if there is a hardware or software issue causing database corruption.

table_name

The name (optionally schema-qualified) of a specific table or materialized view to vacuum. If the specified table is a partitioned table, all of its leaf partitions are vacuumed.

column_name

The name of a specific column to analyze. Defaults to all columns. If a column list is specified, ANALYZE must also be specified.

Outputs

When VERBOSE is specified, VACUUM emits progress messages to indicate which table is currently being processed. Various statistics about the tables are printed as well.

Notes

To vacuum a table, one must ordinarily be the table's owner or a superuser. However, database owners are allowed to vacuum all tables in their databases, except shared catalogs. (The restriction for shared catalogs means that a true database-wide VACUUM can only be performed by a superuser.) VACUUM will skip over any tables that the calling user does not have permission to vacuum.

VACUUM cannot be executed inside a transaction block.

For tables with GIN indexes, VACUUM (in any form) also completes any pending index insertions, by moving pending index entries to the appropriate places in the main GIN index structure. See Section 66.4.1 for details.

We recommend that active production databases be vacuumed frequently (at least nightly), in order to remove dead rows. After adding or deleting a large number of rows, it might be a good idea to issue a VACUUM ANALYZE command for the affected table. This will update the system catalogs with the results of all recent changes, and allow the PostgreSQL query planner to make better choices in planning queries.

The FULL option is not recommended for routine use, but might be useful in special cases. An example is when you have deleted or updated most of the rows in a table and would like the table to physically shrink to occupy less disk space and allow faster table scans. VACUUM FULL will usually shrink the table more than a plain VACUUM would.

VACUUM causes a substantial increase in I/O traffic, which might cause poor performance for other active sessions. Therefore, it is sometimes advisable to use the cost-based vacuum delay feature. See Section 19.4.4 for details.

PostgreSQL includes an "autovacuum" facility which can automate routine vacuum maintenance. For more information about automatic and manual vacuuming, see Section 24.1.

Examples

To clean a single table onek, analyze it for the optimizer and print a detailed vacuum activity report:

```
VACUUM (VERBOSE, ANALYZE) onek;
```

Compatibility

There is no VACUUM statement in the SQL standard.

See Also

vacuumdb, Section 19.4.4, Section 24.1.6

VALUES

VALUES — compute a set of rows

Synopsis

```
VALUES ( expression [, ...] ) [, ...]
    [ ORDER BY sort_expression [ ASC | DESC | USING operator ]
[, ...] ]
    [ LIMIT { count | ALL } ]
    [ OFFSET start [ ROW | ROWS ] ]
    [ FETCH { FIRST | NEXT } [ count ] { ROW | ROWS } ONLY ]
```

Description

VALUES computes a row value or set of row values specified by value expressions. It is most commonly used to generate a "constant table" within a larger command, but it can be used on its own.

When more than one row is specified, all the rows must have the same number of elements. The data types of the resulting table's columns are determined by combining the explicit or inferred types of the expressions appearing in that column, using the same rules as for UNION (see Section 10.5).

Within larger commands, VALUES is syntactically allowed anywhere that SELECT is. Because it is treated like a SELECT by the grammar, it is possible to use the ORDER BY, LIMIT (or equivalently FETCH FIRST), and OFFSET clauses with a VALUES command.

Parameters

expression

A constant or expression to compute and insert at the indicated place in the resulting table (set of rows). In a VALUES list appearing at the top level of an INSERT, an expression can be replaced by DEFAULT to indicate that the destination column's default value should be inserted. DEFAULT cannot be used when VALUES appears in other contexts.

sort_expression

An expression or integer constant indicating how to sort the result rows. This expression can refer to the columns of the VALUES result as column1, column2, etc. For more details see ORDER BY Clause.

operator

A sorting operator. For details see ORDER BY Clause.

count

The maximum number of rows to return. For details see LIMIT Clause.

start

The number of rows to skip before starting to return rows. For details see LIMIT Clause.

Notes

VALUES lists with very large numbers of rows should be avoided, as you might encounter out-of-memory failures or poor performance. VALUES appearing within INSERT is a special case (because the desired column types are known from the INSERT's target table, and need not be inferred by scanning the VALUES list), so it can handle larger lists than are practical in other contexts.

Examples

A bare VALUES command:

```
VALUES (1, 'one'), (2, 'two'), (3, 'three');
```

This will return a table of two columns and three rows. It's effectively equivalent to:

```
SELECT 1 AS column1, 'one' AS column2
UNION ALL
SELECT 2, 'two'
UNION ALL
SELECT 3, 'three';
```

More usually, VALUES is used within a larger SQL command. The most common use is in INSERT:

```
INSERT INTO films (code, title, did, date_prod, kind)
    VALUES ('T_601', 'Yojimbo', 106, '1961-06-16', 'Drama');
```

In the context of INSERT, entries of a VALUES list can be DEFAULT to indicate that the column default should be used here instead of specifying a value:

```
INSERT INTO films VALUES
    ('UA502', 'Bananas', 105, DEFAULT, 'Comedy', '82 minutes'),
    ('T_601', 'Yojimbo', 106, DEFAULT, 'Drama', DEFAULT);
```

VALUES can also be used where a sub-SELECT might be written, for example in a FROM clause:

```
SELECT f.*
  FROM films f, (VALUES('MGM', 'Horror'), ('UA', 'Sci-Fi')) AS t
 (studio, kind)
  WHERE f.studio = t.studio AND f.kind = t.kind;

UPDATE employees SET salary = salary * v.increase
  FROM (VALUES(1, 200000, 1.2), (2, 400000, 1.4)) AS v (depno, target,
 increase)
  WHERE employees.depno = v.depno AND employees.sales >= v.target;
```

Note that an AS clause is required when VALUES is used in a FROM clause, just as is true for SELECT. It is not required that the AS clause specify names for all the columns, but it's good practice to do so. (The default column names for VALUES are column1, column2, etc in PostgreSQL, but these names might be different in other database systems.)

When VALUES is used in INSERT, the values are all automatically coerced to the data type of the corresponding destination column. When it's used in other contexts, it might be necessary to specify the correct data type. If the entries are all quoted literal constants, coercing the first is sufficient to determine the assumed type for all:

```
SELECT * FROM machines
WHERE ip_address IN (VALUES('192.168.0.1'::inet), ('192.168.0.10'),
  ('192.168.1.43'));
```

Tip

For simple IN tests, it's better to rely on the list-of-scalars form of IN than to write a VALUES query as shown above. The list of scalars method requires less writing and is often more efficient.

Compatibility

VALUES conforms to the SQL standard. LIMIT and OFFSET are PostgreSQL extensions; see also under SELECT.

See Also

INSERT, SELECT

PostgreSQL Client Applications

This part contains reference information for PostgreSQL client applications and utilities. Not all of these commands are of general utility; some might require special privileges. The common feature of these applications is that they can be run on any host, independent of where the database server resides.

When specified on the command line, user and database names have their case preserved — the presence of spaces or special characters might require quoting. Table names and other identifiers do not have their case preserved, except where documented, and might require quoting.

Table of Contents

clusterdb

clusterdb — cluster a PostgreSQL database

Synopsis

clusterdb [connection-option...] [--verbose | -v] [--table | -t table] ... [dbname]

clusterdb [connection-option...] [--verbose | -v] --all | -a

Description

clusterdb is a utility for reclustering tables in a PostgreSQL database. It finds tables that have previously been clustered, and clusters them again on the same index that was last used. Tables that have never been clustered are not affected.

clusterdb is a wrapper around the SQL command CLUSTER. There is no effective difference between clustering databases via this utility and via other methods for accessing the server.

Options

clusterdb accepts the following command-line arguments:

-a
--all

  Cluster all databases.

[-d] dbname
[--dbname=]dbname

  Specifies the name of the database to be clustered. If this is not specified and -a (or --all) is not used, the database name is read from the environment variable PGDATABASE. If that is not set, the user name specified for the connection is used.

-e
--echo

  Echo the commands that clusterdb generates and sends to the server.

-q
--quiet

  Do not display progress messages.

-t table
--table=table

  Cluster table only. Multiple tables can be clustered by writing multiple -t switches.

-v
--verbose

  Print detailed information during processing.

```
-V
--version
```

Print the clusterdb version and exit.

```
-?
--help
```

Show help about clusterdb command line arguments, and exit.

clusterdb also accepts the following command-line arguments for connection parameters:

```
-h host
--host=host
```

Specifies the host name of the machine on which the server is running. If the value begins with a slash, it is used as the directory for the Unix domain socket.

```
-p port
--port=port
```

Specifies the TCP port or local Unix domain socket file extension on which the server is listening for connections.

```
-U username
--username=username
```

User name to connect as.

```
-w
--no-password
```

Never issue a password prompt. If the server requires password authentication and a password is not available by other means such as a `.pgpass` file, the connection attempt will fail. This option can be useful in batch jobs and scripts where no user is present to enter a password.

```
-W
--password
```

Force clusterdb to prompt for a password before connecting to a database.

This option is never essential, since clusterdb will automatically prompt for a password if the server demands password authentication. However, clusterdb will waste a connection attempt finding out that the server wants a password. In some cases it is worth typing -W to avoid the extra connection attempt.

```
--maintenance-db=dbname
```

Specifies the name of the database to connect to discover what other databases should be clustered. If not specified, the `postgres` database will be used, and if that does not exist, `template1` will be used.

Environment

```
PGDATABASE
PGHOST
PGPORT
PGUSER
```

Default connection parameters

This utility, like most other PostgreSQL utilities, also uses the environment variables supported by libpq (see Section 34.14).

Diagnostics

In case of difficulty, see CLUSTER and psql for discussions of potential problems and error messages. The database server must be running at the targeted host. Also, any default connection settings and environment variables used by the libpq front-end library will apply.

Examples

To cluster the database `test`:

```
$ clusterdb test
```

To cluster a single table `foo` in a database named `xyzzy`:

```
$ clusterdb --table=foo xyzzy
```

See Also

CLUSTER

createdb

createdb — create a new PostgreSQL database

Synopsis

createdb [*connection-option*...] [*option*...] [*dbname* [*description*]]

Description

createdb creates a new PostgreSQL database.

Normally, the database user who executes this command becomes the owner of the new database. However, a different owner can be specified via the -O option, if the executing user has appropriate privileges.

createdb is a wrapper around the SQL command CREATE DATABASE. There is no effective difference between creating databases via this utility and via other methods for accessing the server.

Options

createdb accepts the following command-line arguments:

dbname

Specifies the name of the database to be created. The name must be unique among all PostgreSQL databases in this cluster. The default is to create a database with the same name as the current system user.

description

Specifies a comment to be associated with the newly created database.

-D *tablespace*
--tablespace=*tablespace*

Specifies the default tablespace for the database. (This name is processed as a double-quoted identifier.)

-e
--echo

Echo the commands that createdb generates and sends to the server.

-E *encoding*
--encoding=*encoding*

Specifies the character encoding scheme to be used in this database. The character sets supported by the PostgreSQL server are described in Section 23.3.1.

-l *locale*
--locale=*locale*

Specifies the locale to be used in this database. This is equivalent to specifying both --lc-collate and --lc-ctype.

`--lc-collate=`*`locale`*

Specifies the LC_COLLATE setting to be used in this database.

`--lc-ctype=`*`locale`*

Specifies the LC_CTYPE setting to be used in this database.

`-O` *`owner`*
`--owner=`*`owner`*

Specifies the database user who will own the new database. (This name is processed as a double-quoted identifier.)

`-T` *`template`*
`--template=`*`template`*

Specifies the template database from which to build this database. (This name is processed as a double-quoted identifier.)

`-V`
`--version`

Print the createdb version and exit.

`-?`
`--help`

Show help about createdb command line arguments, and exit.

The options `-D`, `-l`, `-E`, `-O`, and `-T` correspond to options of the underlying SQL command CREATE DATABASE; see there for more information about them.

createdb also accepts the following command-line arguments for connection parameters:

`-h` *`host`*
`--host=`*`host`*

Specifies the host name of the machine on which the server is running. If the value begins with a slash, it is used as the directory for the Unix domain socket.

`-p` *`port`*
`--port=`*`port`*

Specifies the TCP port or the local Unix domain socket file extension on which the server is listening for connections.

`-U` *`username`*
`--username=`*`username`*

User name to connect as.

`-w`
`--no-password`

Never issue a password prompt. If the server requires password authentication and a password is not available by other means such as a `.pgpass` file, the connection attempt will fail. This option can be useful in batch jobs and scripts where no user is present to enter a password.

```
-W
--password
```

Force createdb to prompt for a password before connecting to a database.

This option is never essential, since createdb will automatically prompt for a password if the server demands password authentication. However, createdb will waste a connection attempt finding out that the server wants a password. In some cases it is worth typing -W to avoid the extra connection attempt.

```
--maintenance-db=dbname
```

Specifies the name of the database to connect to when creating the new database. If not specified, the postgres database will be used; if that does not exist (or if it is the name of the new database being created), template1 will be used.

Environment

```
PGDATABASE
```

If set, the name of the database to create, unless overridden on the command line.

```
PGHOST
PGPORT
PGUSER
```

Default connection parameters. PGUSER also determines the name of the database to create, if it is not specified on the command line or by PGDATABASE.

This utility, like most other PostgreSQL utilities, also uses the environment variables supported by libpq (see Section 34.14).

Diagnostics

In case of difficulty, see CREATE DATABASE and psql for discussions of potential problems and error messages. The database server must be running at the targeted host. Also, any default connection settings and environment variables used by the libpq front-end library will apply.

Examples

To create the database demo using the default database server:

```
$ createdb demo
```

To create the database demo using the server on host eden, port 5000, using the template0 template database, here is the command-line command and the underlying SQL command:

```
$ createdb -p 5000 -h eden -T template0 -e demo
CREATE DATABASE demo TEMPLATE template0;
```

See Also

dropdb, CREATE DATABASE

createuser

createuser — define a new PostgreSQL user account

Synopsis

```
createuser [connection-option...] [option...] [username]
```

Description

createuser creates a new PostgreSQL user (or more precisely, a role). Only superusers and users with CREATEROLE privilege can create new users, so createuser must be invoked by someone who can connect as a superuser or a user with CREATEROLE privilege.

If you wish to create a new superuser, you must connect as a superuser, not merely with CREATEROLE privilege. Being a superuser implies the ability to bypass all access permission checks within the database, so superuserdom should not be granted lightly.

createuser is a wrapper around the SQL command CREATE ROLE. There is no effective difference between creating users via this utility and via other methods for accessing the server.

Options

createuser accepts the following command-line arguments:

username

> Specifies the name of the PostgreSQL user to be created. This name must be different from all existing roles in this PostgreSQL installation.

`-c` *number*
`--connection-limit=`*number*

> Set a maximum number of connections for the new user. The default is to set no limit.

`-d`
`--createdb`

> The new user will be allowed to create databases.

`-D`
`--no-createdb`

> The new user will not be allowed to create databases. This is the default.

`-e`
`--echo`

> Echo the commands that createuser generates and sends to the server.

`-E`
`--encrypted`

> This option is obsolete but still accepted for backward compatibility.

`-g role`
`--role=role`

Indicates role to which this role will be added immediately as a new member. Multiple roles to which this role will be added as a member can be specified by writing multiple `-g` switches.

`-i`
`--inherit`

The new role will automatically inherit privileges of roles it is a member of. This is the default.

`-I`
`--no-inherit`

The new role will not automatically inherit privileges of roles it is a member of.

`--interactive`

Prompt for the user name if none is specified on the command line, and also prompt for whichever of the options `-d/-D`, `-r/-R`, `-s/-S` is not specified on the command line. (This was the default behavior up to PostgreSQL 9.1.)

`-l`
`--login`

The new user will be allowed to log in (that is, the user name can be used as the initial session user identifier). This is the default.

`-L`
`--no-login`

The new user will not be allowed to log in. (A role without login privilege is still useful as a means of managing database permissions.)

`-P`
`--pwprompt`

If given, createuser will issue a prompt for the password of the new user. This is not necessary if you do not plan on using password authentication.

`-r`
`--createrole`

The new user will be allowed to create new roles (that is, this user will have CREATEROLE privilege).

`-R`
`--no-createrole`

The new user will not be allowed to create new roles. This is the default.

`-s`
`--superuser`

The new user will be a superuser.

`-S`
`--no-superuser`

The new user will not be a superuser. This is the default.

`-V`
`--version`

Print the createuser version and exit.

`--replication`

The new user will have the REPLICATION privilege, which is described more fully in the documentation for CREATE ROLE.

`--no-replication`

The new user will not have the REPLICATION privilege, which is described more fully in the documentation for CREATE ROLE.

`-?`
`--help`

Show help about createuser command line arguments, and exit.

createuser also accepts the following command-line arguments for connection parameters:

`-h host`
`--host=host`

Specifies the host name of the machine on which the server is running. If the value begins with a slash, it is used as the directory for the Unix domain socket.

`-p port`
`--port=port`

Specifies the TCP port or local Unix domain socket file extension on which the server is listening for connections.

`-U username`
`--username=username`

User name to connect as (not the user name to create).

`-w`
`--no-password`

Never issue a password prompt. If the server requires password authentication and a password is not available by other means such as a `.pgpass` file, the connection attempt will fail. This option can be useful in batch jobs and scripts where no user is present to enter a password.

`-W`
`--password`

Force createuser to prompt for a password (for connecting to the server, not for the password of the new user).

This option is never essential, since createuser will automatically prompt for a password if the server demands password authentication. However, createuser will waste a connection attempt finding out that the server wants a password. In some cases it is worth typing `-W` to avoid the extra connection attempt.

Environment

PGHOST
PGPORT
PGUSER

Default connection parameters

This utility, like most other PostgreSQL utilities, also uses the environment variables supported by libpq (see Section 34.14).

Diagnostics

In case of difficulty, see CREATE ROLE and psql for discussions of potential problems and error messages. The database server must be running at the targeted host. Also, any default connection settings and environment variables used by the libpq front-end library will apply.

Examples

To create a user `joe` on the default database server:

```
$ createuser joe
```

To create a user `joe` on the default database server with prompting for some additional attributes:

```
$ createuser --interactive joe
Shall the new role be a superuser? (y/n) n
Shall the new role be allowed to create databases? (y/n) n
Shall the new role be allowed to create more new roles? (y/n) n
```

To create the same user `joe` using the server on host `eden`, port 5000, with attributes explicitly specified, taking a look at the underlying command:

```
$ createuser -h eden -p 5000 -S -D -R -e joe
CREATE ROLE joe NOSUPERUSER NOCREATEDB NOCREATEROLE INHERIT LOGIN;
```

To create the user `joe` as a superuser, and assign a password immediately:

```
$ createuser -P -s -e joe
Enter password for new role: xyzzy
Enter it again: xyzzy
CREATE ROLE joe PASSWORD 'md5b5f5ba1a423792b526f799ae4eb3d59e'
 SUPERUSER CREATEDB CREATEROLE INHERIT LOGIN;
```

In the above example, the new password isn't actually echoed when typed, but we show what was typed for clarity. As you see, the password is encrypted before it is sent to the client.

See Also

dropuser, CREATE ROLE

dropdb

dropdb — remove a PostgreSQL database

Synopsis

```
dropdb [connection-option...] [option...] dbname
```

Description

dropdb destroys an existing PostgreSQL database. The user who executes this command must be a database superuser or the owner of the database.

dropdb is a wrapper around the SQL command DROP DATABASE. There is no effective difference between dropping databases via this utility and via other methods for accessing the server.

Options

dropdb accepts the following command-line arguments:

dbname

> Specifies the name of the database to be removed.

`-e`
`--echo`

> Echo the commands that dropdb generates and sends to the server.

`-i`
`--interactive`

> Issues a verification prompt before doing anything destructive.

`-V`
`--version`

> Print the dropdb version and exit.

`--if-exists`

> Do not throw an error if the database does not exist. A notice is issued in this case.

`-?`
`--help`

> Show help about dropdb command line arguments, and exit.

dropdb also accepts the following command-line arguments for connection parameters:

`-h host`
`--host=host`

> Specifies the host name of the machine on which the server is running. If the value begins with a slash, it is used as the directory for the Unix domain socket.

-p *port*
--port=*port*

> Specifies the TCP port or local Unix domain socket file extension on which the server is listening for connections.

-U *username*
--username=*username*

> User name to connect as.

-w
--no-password

> Never issue a password prompt. If the server requires password authentication and a password is not available by other means such as a `.pgpass` file, the connection attempt will fail. This option can be useful in batch jobs and scripts where no user is present to enter a password.

-W
--password

> Force dropdb to prompt for a password before connecting to a database.

> This option is never essential, since dropdb will automatically prompt for a password if the server demands password authentication. However, dropdb will waste a connection attempt finding out that the server wants a password. In some cases it is worth typing -W to avoid the extra connection attempt.

--maintenance-db=*dbname*

> Specifies the name of the database to connect to in order to drop the target database. If not specified, the `postgres` database will be used; if that does not exist (or is the database being dropped), `template1` will be used.

Environment

PGHOST
PGPORT
PGUSER

> Default connection parameters

This utility, like most other PostgreSQL utilities, also uses the environment variables supported by libpq (see Section 34.14).

Diagnostics

In case of difficulty, see DROP DATABASE and psql for discussions of potential problems and error messages. The database server must be running at the targeted host. Also, any default connection settings and environment variables used by the libpq front-end library will apply.

Examples

To destroy the database `demo` on the default database server:

```
$ dropdb demo
```

To destroy the database demo using the server on host eden, port 5000, with verification and a peek at the underlying command:

```
$ dropdb -p 5000 -h eden -i -e demo
Database "demo" will be permanently deleted.
Are you sure? (y/n) y
DROP DATABASE demo;
```

See Also

createdb, DROP DATABASE

dropuser

dropuser — remove a PostgreSQL user account

Synopsis

dropuser [*connection-option*...] [*option*...] [*username*]

Description

dropuser removes an existing PostgreSQL user. Only superusers and users with the CREATEROLE privilege can remove PostgreSQL users. (To remove a superuser, you must yourself be a superuser.)

dropuser is a wrapper around the SQL command DROP ROLE. There is no effective difference between dropping users via this utility and via other methods for accessing the server.

Options

dropuser accepts the following command-line arguments:

username

    Specifies the name of the PostgreSQL user to be removed. You will be prompted for a name if none is specified on the command line and the -i/--interactive option is used.

-e
--echo

    Echo the commands that dropuser generates and sends to the server.

-i
--interactive

    Prompt for confirmation before actually removing the user, and prompt for the user name if none is specified on the command line.

-V
--version

    Print the dropuser version and exit.

--if-exists

    Do not throw an error if the user does not exist. A notice is issued in this case.

-?
--help

    Show help about dropuser command line arguments, and exit.

dropuser also accepts the following command-line arguments for connection parameters:

-h *host*
--host=*host*

> Specifies the host name of the machine on which the server is running. If the value begins with a slash, it is used as the directory for the Unix domain socket.

-p *port*
--port=*port*

> Specifies the TCP port or local Unix domain socket file extension on which the server is listening for connections.

-U *username*
--username=*username*

> User name to connect as (not the user name to drop).

-w
--no-password

> Never issue a password prompt. If the server requires password authentication and a password is not available by other means such as a `.pgpass` file, the connection attempt will fail. This option can be useful in batch jobs and scripts where no user is present to enter a password.

-W
--password

> Force dropuser to prompt for a password before connecting to a database.

> This option is never essential, since dropuser will automatically prompt for a password if the server demands password authentication. However, dropuser will waste a connection attempt finding out that the server wants a password. In some cases it is worth typing **-W** to avoid the extra connection attempt.

Environment

PGHOST
PGPORT
PGUSER

> Default connection parameters

This utility, like most other PostgreSQL utilities, also uses the environment variables supported by libpq (see Section 34.14).

Diagnostics

In case of difficulty, see DROP ROLE and psql for discussions of potential problems and error messages. The database server must be running at the targeted host. Also, any default connection settings and environment variables used by the libpq front-end library will apply.

Examples

To remove user `joe` from the default database server:

```
$ dropuser joe
```

To remove user joe using the server on host eden, port 5000, with verification and a peek at the underlying command:

```
$ dropuser -p 5000 -h eden -i -e joe
Role "joe" will be permanently removed.
Are you sure? (y/n) y
DROP ROLE joe;
```

See Also

createuser, DROP ROLE

ecpg

ecpg — embedded SQL C preprocessor

Synopsis

```
ecpg [option...] file...
```

Description

ecpg is the embedded SQL preprocessor for C programs. It converts C programs with embedded SQL statements to normal C code by replacing the SQL invocations with special function calls. The output files can then be processed with any C compiler tool chain.

ecpg will convert each input file given on the command line to the corresponding C output file. Input files preferably have the extension .pgc. The extension will be replaced by .c to determine the output file name. The output file name can also be overridden using the -o option.

This reference page does not describe the embedded SQL language. See Chapter 36 for more information on that topic.

Options

ecpg accepts the following command-line arguments:

-c

Automatically generate certain C code from SQL code. Currently, this works for EXEC SQL TYPE.

-C mode

Set a compatibility mode. mode can be INFORMIX, INFORMIX_SE, or ORACLE.

-D symbol

Define a C preprocessor symbol.

-i

Parse system include files as well.

-I directory

Specify an additional include path, used to find files included via EXEC SQL INCLUDE. Defaults are . (current directory), /usr/local/include, the PostgreSQL include directory which is defined at compile time (default: /usr/local/pgsql/include), and /usr/include, in that order.

-o filename

Specifies that ecpg should write all its output to the given filename.

-r option

Selects run-time behavior. Option can be one of the following:

no_indicator

Do not use indicators but instead use special values to represent null values. Historically there have been databases using this approach.

prepare

Prepare all statements before using them. Libecpg will keep a cache of prepared statements and reuse a statement if it gets executed again. If the cache runs full, libecpg will free the least used statement.

questionmarks

Allow question mark as placeholder for compatibility reasons. This used to be the default long ago.

-t

Turn on autocommit of transactions. In this mode, each SQL command is automatically committed unless it is inside an explicit transaction block. In the default mode, commands are committed only when EXEC SQL COMMIT is issued.

-v

Print additional information including the version and the "include" path.

--version

Print the ecpg version and exit.

-?
--help

Show help about ecpg command line arguments, and exit.

Notes

When compiling the preprocessed C code files, the compiler needs to be able to find the ECPG header files in the PostgreSQL include directory. Therefore, you might have to use the -I option when invoking the compiler (e.g., -I/usr/local/pgsql/include).

Programs using C code with embedded SQL have to be linked against the libecpg library, for example using the linker options -L/usr/local/pgsql/lib -lecpg.

The value of either of these directories that is appropriate for the installation can be found out using pg_config.

Examples

If you have an embedded SQL C source file named prog1.pgc, you can create an executable program using the following sequence of commands:

```
ecpg prog1.pgc
cc -I/usr/local/pgsql/include -c prog1.c
cc -o prog1 prog1.o -L/usr/local/pgsql/lib -lecpg
```

pg_basebackup

pg_basebackup — take a base backup of a PostgreSQL cluster

Synopsis

pg_basebackup [*option*...]

Description

pg_basebackup is used to take base backups of a running PostgreSQL database cluster. These are taken without affecting other clients to the database, and can be used both for point-in-time recovery (see Section 25.3) and as the starting point for a log shipping or streaming replication standby servers (see Section 26.2).

pg_basebackup makes a binary copy of the database cluster files, while making sure the system is put in and out of backup mode automatically. Backups are always taken of the entire database cluster; it is not possible to back up individual databases or database objects. For individual database backups, a tool such as pg_dump must be used.

The backup is made over a regular PostgreSQL connection, and uses the replication protocol. The connection must be made with a superuser or a user having REPLICATION permissions (see Section 21.2), and pg_hba.conf must explicitly permit the replication connection. The server must also be configured with max_wal_senders set high enough to leave at least one session available for the backup and one for WAL streaming (if used).

There can be multiple pg_basebackups running at the same time, but it is better from a performance point of view to take only one backup, and copy the result.

pg_basebackup can make a base backup from not only the master but also the standby. To take a backup from the standby, set up the standby so that it can accept replication connections (that is, set max_wal_senders and hot_standby, and configure host-based authentication). You will also need to enable full_page_writes on the master.

Note that there are some limitations in an online backup from the standby:

- The backup history file is not created in the database cluster backed up.

- If you are using -X none, there is no guarantee that all WAL files required for the backup are archived at the end of backup.

- If the standby is promoted to the master during online backup, the backup fails.

- All WAL records required for the backup must contain sufficient full-page writes, which requires you to enable full_page_writes on the master and not to use a tool like pg_compresslog as archive_command to remove full-page writes from WAL files.

Options

The following command-line options control the location and format of the output.

`-D directory`
`--pgdata=directory`

> Directory to write the output to. pg_basebackup will create the directory and any parent directories if necessary. The directory may already exist, but it is an error if the directory already exists and is not empty.
>
> When the backup is in tar mode, and the directory is specified as – (dash), the tar file will be written to `stdout`.
>
> This option is required.

`-F format`
`--format=format`

> Selects the format for the output. `format` can be one of the following:
>
> `p`
> `plain`
>
> > Write the output as plain files, with the same layout as the current data directory and tablespaces. When the cluster has no additional tablespaces, the whole database will be placed in the target directory. If the cluster contains additional tablespaces, the main data directory will be placed in the target directory, but all other tablespaces will be placed in the same absolute path as they have on the server.
> >
> > This is the default format.
>
> `t`
> `tar`
>
> > Write the output as tar files in the target directory. The main data directory will be written to a file named `base.tar`, and all other tablespaces will be named after the tablespace OID.
> >
> > If the value – (dash) is specified as target directory, the tar contents will be written to standard output, suitable for piping to for example gzip. This is only possible if the cluster has no additional tablespaces and WAL streaming is not used.

`-r rate`
`--max-rate=rate`

> The maximum transfer rate of data transferred from the server. Values are in kilobytes per second. Use a suffix of `M` to indicate megabytes per second. A suffix of `k` is also accepted, and has no effect. Valid values are between 32 kilobytes per second and 1024 megabytes per second.
>
> The purpose is to limit the impact of pg_basebackup on the running server.
>
> This option always affects transfer of the data directory. Transfer of WAL files is only affected if the collection method is `fetch`.

`-R`
`--write-recovery-conf`

> Write a minimal `recovery.conf` in the output directory (or into the base archive file when using tar format) to ease setting up a standby server. The `recovery.conf` file will record the connection

settings and, if specified, the replication slot that pg_basebackup is using, so that the streaming replication will use the same settings later on.

-T *olddir=newdir*
--tablespace-mapping=*olddir=newdir*

> Relocate the tablespace in directory *olddir* to *newdir* during the backup. To be effective, *olddir* must exactly match the path specification of the tablespace as it is currently defined. (But it is not an error if there is no tablespace in *olddir* contained in the backup.) Both *olddir* and *newdir* must be absolute paths. If a path happens to contain a = sign, escape it with a backslash. This option can be specified multiple times for multiple tablespaces. See examples below.

> If a tablespace is relocated in this way, the symbolic links inside the main data directory are updated to point to the new location. So the new data directory is ready to be used for a new server instance with all tablespaces in the updated locations.

--waldir=*waldir*

> Specifies the location for the write-ahead log directory. *waldir* must be an absolute path. The write-ahead log directory can only be specified when the backup is in plain mode.

-X *method*
--wal-method=*method*

> Includes the required write-ahead log files (WAL files) in the backup. This will include all write-ahead logs generated during the backup. Unless the method `none` is specified, it is possible to start a postmaster directly in the extracted directory without the need to consult the log archive, thus making this a completely standalone backup.

> The following methods for collecting the write-ahead logs are supported:

n
none

> Don't include write-ahead log in the backup.

f
fetch

> The write-ahead log files are collected at the end of the backup. Therefore, it is necessary for the wal_keep_segments parameter to be set high enough that the log is not removed before the end of the backup. If the log has been rotated when it's time to transfer it, the backup will fail and be unusable.

> When tar format mode is used, the write-ahead log files will be written to the `base.tar` file.

s
stream

> Stream the write-ahead log while the backup is created. This will open a second connection to the server and start streaming the write-ahead log in parallel while running the backup. Therefore, it will use up two connections configured by the max_wal_senders parameter. As long as the client can keep up with write-ahead log received, using this mode requires no extra write-ahead logs to be saved on the master.

> When tar format mode is used, the write-ahead log files will be written to a separate file named `pg_wal.tar` (if the server is a version earlier than 10, the file will be named `pg_xlog.tar`).

This value is the default.

`-z`
`--gzip`

Enables gzip compression of tar file output, with the default compression level. Compression is only available when using the tar format, and the suffix `.gz` will automatically be added to all tar filenames.

`-Z level`
`--compress=level`

Enables gzip compression of tar file output, and specifies the compression level (0 through 9, 0 being no compression and 9 being best compression). Compression is only available when using the tar format, and the suffix `.gz` will automatically be added to all tar filenames.

The following command-line options control the generation of the backup and the running of the program.

`-c fast|spread`
`--checkpoint=fast|spread`

Sets checkpoint mode to fast (immediate) or spread (default) (see Section 25.3.3).

`-C`
`--create-slot`

This option causes creation of a replication slot named by the `--slot` option before starting the backup. An error is raised if the slot already exists.

`-l label`
`--label=label`

Sets the label for the backup. If none is specified, a default value of "`pg_basebackup base backup`" will be used.

`-n`
`--no-clean`

By default, when `pg_basebackup` aborts with an error, it removes any directories it might have created before discovering that it cannot finish the job (for example, data directory and write-ahead log directory). This option inhibits tidying-up and is thus useful for debugging.

Note that tablespace directories are not cleaned up either way.

`-N`
`--no-sync`

By default, `pg_basebackup` will wait for all files to be written safely to disk. This option causes `pg_basebackup` to return without waiting, which is faster, but means that a subsequent operating system crash can leave the base backup corrupt. Generally, this option is useful for testing but should not be used when creating a production installation.

`-P`
`--progress`

Enables progress reporting. Turning this on will deliver an approximate progress report during the backup. Since the database may change during the backup, this is only an approximation and may not end at exactly `100%`. In particular, when WAL log is included in the backup, the total amount of data cannot be estimated in advance, and in this case the estimated target size will increase once it passes the total estimate without WAL.

When this is enabled, the backup will start by enumerating the size of the entire database, and then go back and send the actual contents. This may make the backup take slightly longer, and in particular it will take longer before the first data is sent.

`-S` *slotname*
`--slot=`*slotname*

This option can only be used together with `-X stream`. It causes the WAL streaming to use the specified replication slot. If the base backup is intended to be used as a streaming replication standby using replication slots, it should then use the same replication slot name in `recovery.conf`. That way, it is ensured that the server does not remove any necessary WAL data in the time between the end of the base backup and the start of streaming replication.

The specified replication slot has to exist unless the option `-C` is also used.

If this option is not specified and the server supports temporary replication slots (version 10 and later), then a temporary replication slot is automatically used for WAL streaming.

`-v`
`--verbose`

Enables verbose mode. Will output some extra steps during startup and shutdown, as well as show the exact file name that is currently being processed if progress reporting is also enabled.

`--no-slot`

This option prevents the creation of a temporary replication slot during the backup even if it's supported by the server.

Temporary replication slots are created by default if no slot name is given with the option `-S` when using log streaming.

The main purpose of this option is to allow taking a base backup when the server is out of free replication slots. Using replication slots is almost always preferred, because it prevents needed WAL from being removed by the server during the backup.

`--no-verify-checksums`

Disables verification of checksums, if they are enabled on the server the base backup is taken from.

By default, checksums are verified and checksum failures will result in a non-zero exit status. However, the base backup will not be removed in such a case, as if the `--no-clean` option had been used.

The following command-line options control the database connection parameters.

`-d` *connstr*
`--dbname=`*connstr*

Specifies parameters used to connect to the server, as a connection string. See Section 34.1.1 for more information.

The option is called `--dbname` for consistency with other client applications, but because pg_basebackup doesn't connect to any particular database in the cluster, database name in the connection string will be ignored.

-h *host*
--host=*host*

> Specifies the host name of the machine on which the server is running. If the value begins with a slash, it is used as the directory for the Unix domain socket. The default is taken from the PGHOST environment variable, if set, else a Unix domain socket connection is attempted.

-p *port*
--port=*port*

> Specifies the TCP port or local Unix domain socket file extension on which the server is listening for connections. Defaults to the PGPORT environment variable, if set, or a compiled-in default.

-s *interval*
--status-interval=*interval*

> Specifies the number of seconds between status packets sent back to the server. This allows for easier monitoring of the progress from server. A value of zero disables the periodic status updates completely, although an update will still be sent when requested by the server, to avoid timeout disconnect. The default value is 10 seconds.

-U *username*
--username=*username*

> User name to connect as.

-w
--no-password

> Never issue a password prompt. If the server requires password authentication and a password is not available by other means such as a .pgpass file, the connection attempt will fail. This option can be useful in batch jobs and scripts where no user is present to enter a password.

-W
--password

> Force pg_basebackup to prompt for a password before connecting to a database.

> This option is never essential, since pg_basebackup will automatically prompt for a password if the server demands password authentication. However, pg_basebackup will waste a connection attempt finding out that the server wants a password. In some cases it is worth typing -W to avoid the extra connection attempt.

Other options are also available:

-V
--version

> Print the pg_basebackup version and exit.

-?
--help

> Show help about pg_basebackup command line arguments, and exit.

Environment

This utility, like most other PostgreSQL utilities, uses the environment variables supported by libpq (see Section 34.14).

Notes

At the beginning of the backup, a checkpoint needs to be written on the server the backup is taken from. Especially if the option `--checkpoint=fast` is not used, this can take some time during which pg_basebackup will be appear to be idle.

The backup will include all files in the data directory and tablespaces, including the configuration files and any additional files placed in the directory by third parties, except certain temporary files managed by PostgreSQL. But only regular files and directories are copied, except that symbolic links used for tablespaces are preserved. Symbolic links pointing to certain directories known to PostgreSQL are copied as empty directories. Other symbolic links and special device files are skipped. See Section 53.4 for the precise details.

Tablespaces will in plain format by default be backed up to the same path they have on the server, unless the option `--tablespace-mapping` is used. Without this option, running a plain format base backup on the same host as the server will not work if tablespaces are in use, because the backup would have to be written to the same directory locations as the original tablespaces.

When tar format mode is used, it is the user's responsibility to unpack each tar file before starting the PostgreSQL server. If there are additional tablespaces, the tar files for them need to be unpacked in the correct locations. In this case the symbolic links for those tablespaces will be created by the server according to the contents of the `tablespace_map` file that is included in the `base.tar` file.

pg_basebackup works with servers of the same or an older major version, down to 9.1. However, WAL streaming mode (`-X stream`) only works with server version 9.3 and later, and tar format mode (`--format=tar`) of the current version only works with server version 9.5 or later.

pg_basebackup will preserve group permissions in both the `plain` and `tar` formats if group permissions are enabled on the source cluster.

Examples

To create a base backup of the server at `mydbserver` and store it in the local directory `/usr/local/pgsql/data`:

```
$ pg_basebackup -h mydbserver -D /usr/local/pgsql/data
```

To create a backup of the local server with one compressed tar file for each tablespace, and store it in the directory `backup`, showing a progress report while running:

```
$ pg_basebackup -D backup -Ft -z -P
```

To create a backup of a single-tablespace local database and compress this with bzip2:

```
$ pg_basebackup -D - -Ft -X fetch | bzip2 > backup.tar.bz2
```

(This command will fail if there are multiple tablespaces in the database.)

To create a backup of a local database where the tablespace in `/opt/ts` is relocated to `./backup/ts`:

```
$ pg_basebackup -D backup/data -T /opt/ts=$(pwd)/backup/ts
```

See Also

pg_dump

pgbench

pgbench — run a benchmark test on PostgreSQL

Synopsis

pgbench -i [*option*...] [*dbname*]

pgbench [*option*...] [*dbname*]

Description

pgbench is a simple program for running benchmark tests on PostgreSQL. It runs the same sequence of SQL commands over and over, possibly in multiple concurrent database sessions, and then calculates the average transaction rate (transactions per second). By default, pgbench tests a scenario that is loosely based on TPC-B, involving five SELECT, UPDATE, and INSERT commands per transaction. However, it is easy to test other cases by writing your own transaction script files.

Typical output from pgbench looks like:

```
transaction type: <builtin: TPC-B (sort of)>
scaling factor: 10
query mode: simple
number of clients: 10
number of threads: 1
number of transactions per client: 1000
number of transactions actually processed: 10000/10000
tps = 85.184871 (including connections establishing)
tps = 85.296346 (excluding connections establishing)
```

The first six lines report some of the most important parameter settings. The next line reports the number of transactions completed and intended (the latter being just the product of number of clients and number of transactions per client); these will be equal unless the run failed before completion. (In -T mode, only the actual number of transactions is printed.) The last two lines report the number of transactions per second, figured with and without counting the time to start database sessions.

The default TPC-B-like transaction test requires specific tables to be set up beforehand. pgbench should be invoked with the -i (initialize) option to create and populate these tables. (When you are testing a custom script, you don't need this step, but will instead need to do whatever setup your test needs.) Initialization looks like:

```
pgbench -i [ other-options ] dbname
```

where *dbname* is the name of the already-created database to test in. (You may also need -h, -p, and/or -U options to specify how to connect to the database server.)

> ### Caution
>
> pgbench -i creates four tables pgbench_accounts, pgbench_branches, pg-bench_history, and pgbench_tellers, destroying any existing tables of these names. Be very careful to use another database if you have tables having these names!

At the default "scale factor" of 1, the tables initially contain this many rows:

```
table                    # of rows
-------------------------------
pgbench_branches         1
pgbench_tellers          10
pgbench_accounts         100000
pgbench_history          0
```

You can (and, for most purposes, probably should) increase the number of rows by using the -s (scale factor) option. The -F (fillfactor) option might also be used at this point.

Once you have done the necessary setup, you can run your benchmark with a command that doesn't include -i, that is

```
pgbench [ options ] dbname
```

In nearly all cases, you'll need some options to make a useful test. The most important options are -c (number of clients), -t (number of transactions), -T (time limit), and -f (specify a custom script file). See below for a full list.

Options

The following is divided into three subsections. Different options are used during database initialization and while running benchmarks, but some options are useful in both cases.

Initialization Options

pgbench accepts the following command-line initialization arguments:

-i
--initialize

Required to invoke initialization mode.

-I init_steps
--init-steps=init_steps

Perform just a selected set of the normal initialization steps. init_steps specifies the initialization steps to be performed, using one character per step. Each step is invoked in the specified order. The default is dtgvp. The available steps are:

d (Drop)

Drop any existing pgbench tables.

t (create Tables)

Create the tables used by the standard pgbench scenario, namely `pgbench_accounts`, `pgbench_branches`, `pgbench_history`, and `pgbench_tellers`.

g (Generate data)

Generate data and load it into the standard tables, replacing any data already present.

v (Vacuum)

Invoke `VACUUM` on the standard tables.

p (create Primary keys)

Create primary key indexes on the standard tables.

f (create Foreign keys)

Create foreign key constraints between the standard tables. (Note that this step is not performed by default.)

`-F fillfactor`
`--fillfactor=fillfactor`

Create the `pgbench_accounts`, `pgbench_tellers` and `pgbench_branches` tables with the given fillfactor. Default is 100.

`-n`
`--no-vacuum`

Perform no vacuuming during initialization. (This option suppresses the v initialization step, even if it was specified in `-I`.)

`-q`
`--quiet`

Switch logging to quiet mode, producing only one progress message per 5 seconds. The default logging prints one message each 100000 rows, which often outputs many lines per second (especially on good hardware).

`-s scale_factor`
`--scale=scale_factor`

Multiply the number of rows generated by the scale factor. For example, `-s 100` will create 10,000,000 rows in the `pgbench_accounts` table. Default is 1. When the scale is 20,000 or larger, the columns used to hold account identifiers (`aid` columns) will switch to using larger integers (`bigint`), in order to be big enough to hold the range of account identifiers.

`--foreign-keys`

Create foreign key constraints between the standard tables. (This option adds the f step to the initialization step sequence, if it is not already present.)

`--index-tablespace=index_tablespace`

Create indexes in the specified tablespace, rather than the default tablespace.

```
--tablespace=tablespace
```

Create tables in the specified tablespace, rather than the default tablespace.

```
--unlogged-tables
```

Create all tables as unlogged tables, rather than permanent tables.

Benchmarking Options

pgbench accepts the following command-line benchmarking arguments:

```
-b scriptname[@weight]
--builtin=scriptname[@weight]
```

Add the specified built-in script to the list of executed scripts. An optional integer weight after @ allows to adjust the probability of drawing the script. If not specified, it is set to 1. Available built-in scripts are: `tpcb-like`, `simple-update` and `select-only`. Unambiguous prefixes of built-in names are accepted. With special name `list`, show the list of built-in scripts and exit immediately.

```
-c clients
--client=clients
```

Number of clients simulated, that is, number of concurrent database sessions. Default is 1.

```
-C
--connect
```

Establish a new connection for each transaction, rather than doing it just once per client session. This is useful to measure the connection overhead.

```
-d
--debug
```

Print debugging output.

```
-D varname=value
--define=varname=value
```

Define a variable for use by a custom script (see below). Multiple -D options are allowed.

```
-f filename[@weight]
--file=filename[@weight]
```

Add a transaction script read from *filename* to the list of executed scripts. An optional integer weight after @ allows to adjust the probability of drawing the test. See below for details.

```
-j threads
--jobs=threads
```

Number of worker threads within pgbench. Using more than one thread can be helpful on multi-CPU machines. Clients are distributed as evenly as possible among available threads. Default is 1.

```
-l
--log
```

Write information about each transaction to a log file. See below for details.

-L *limit*
--latency-limit=*limit*

> Transaction which last more than *limit* milliseconds are counted and reported separately, as *late*.

> When throttling is used (**--rate=...**), transactions that lag behind schedule by more than *limit* ms, and thus have no hope of meeting the latency limit, are not sent to the server at all. They are counted and reported separately as *skipped*.

-M *querymode*
--protocol=*querymode*

> Protocol to use for submitting queries to the server:

> - **simple**: use simple query protocol.

> - **extended**: use extended query protocol.

> - **prepared**: use extended query protocol with prepared statements.
> The default is simple query protocol. (See Chapter 53 for more information.)

-n
--no-vacuum

> Perform no vacuuming before running the test. This option is *necessary* if you are running a custom test scenario that does not include the standard tables pgbench_accounts, pgbench_branches, pgbench_history, and pgbench_tellers.

-N
--skip-some-updates

> Run built-in simple-update script. Shorthand for **-b simple-update**.

-P *sec*
--progress=*sec*

> Show progress report every *sec* seconds. The report includes the time since the beginning of the run, the TPS since the last report, and the transaction latency average and standard deviation since the last report. Under throttling (**-R**), the latency is computed with respect to the transaction scheduled start time, not the actual transaction beginning time, thus it also includes the average schedule lag time.

-r
--report-latencies

> Report the average per-statement latency (execution time from the perspective of the client) of each command after the benchmark finishes. See below for details.

-R *rate*
--rate=*rate*

> Execute transactions targeting the specified rate instead of running as fast as possible (the default). The rate is given in transactions per second. If the targeted rate is above the maximum possible rate, the rate limit won't impact the results.

> The rate is targeted by starting transactions along a Poisson-distributed schedule time line. The expected start time schedule moves forward based on when the client first started, not when the previous transaction ended. That approach means that when transactions go past their original scheduled end time, it is possible for later ones to catch up again.

When throttling is active, the transaction latency reported at the end of the run is calculated from the scheduled start times, so it includes the time each transaction had to wait for the previous transaction to finish. The wait time is called the schedule lag time, and its average and maximum are also reported separately. The transaction latency with respect to the actual transaction start time, i.e. the time spent executing the transaction in the database, can be computed by subtracting the schedule lag time from the reported latency.

If `--latency-limit` is used together with `--rate`, a transaction can lag behind so much that it is already over the latency limit when the previous transaction ends, because the latency is calculated from the scheduled start time. Such transactions are not sent to the server, but are skipped altogether and counted separately.

A high schedule lag time is an indication that the system cannot process transactions at the specified rate, with the chosen number of clients and threads. When the average transaction execution time is longer than the scheduled interval between each transaction, each successive transaction will fall further behind, and the schedule lag time will keep increasing the longer the test run is. When that happens, you will have to reduce the specified transaction rate.

`-s` *scale_factor*
`--scale=`*scale_factor*

Report the specified scale factor in pgbench's output. With the built-in tests, this is not necessary; the correct scale factor will be detected by counting the number of rows in the `pgbench_branches` table. However, when testing only custom benchmarks (`-f` option), the scale factor will be reported as 1 unless this option is used.

`-S`
`--select-only`

Run built-in select-only script. Shorthand for `-b select-only`.

`-t` *transactions*
`--transactions=`*transactions*

Number of transactions each client runs. Default is 10.

`-T` *seconds*
`--time=`*seconds*

Run the test for this many seconds, rather than a fixed number of transactions per client. `-t` and `-T` are mutually exclusive.

`-v`
`--vacuum-all`

Vacuum all four standard tables before running the test. With neither `-n` nor `-v`, pgbench will vacuum the `pgbench_tellers` and `pgbench_branches` tables, and will truncate `pgbench_history`.

`--aggregate-interval=`*seconds*

Length of aggregation interval (in seconds). May be used only with `-l` option. With this option, the log contains per-interval summary data, as described below.

`--log-prefix=`*prefix*

Set the filename prefix for the log files created by `--log`. The default is `pgbench_log`.

--progress-timestamp

When showing progress (option **-P**), use a timestamp (Unix epoch) instead of the number of seconds since the beginning of the run. The unit is in seconds, with millisecond precision after the dot. This helps compare logs generated by various tools.

--random-seed=_SEED_

Set random generator seed. Seeds the system random number generator, which then produces a sequence of initial generator states, one for each thread. Values for _SEED_ may be: **time** (the default, the seed is based on the current time), **rand** (use a strong random source, failing if none is available), or an unsigned decimal integer value. The random generator is invoked explicitly from a pgbench script (**random...** functions) or implicitly (for instance option **--rate** uses it to schedule transactions). When explicitly set, the value used for seeding is shown on the terminal. Any value allowed for _SEED_ may also be provided through the environment variable **PGBENCH_RANDOM_SEED**. To ensure that the provided seed impacts all possible uses, put this option first or use the environment variable.

Setting the seed explicitly allows to reproduce a **pgbench** run exactly, as far as random numbers are concerned. As the random state is managed per thread, this means the exact same **pgbench** run for an identical invocation if there is one client per thread and there are no external or data dependencies. From a statistical viewpoint reproducing runs exactly is a bad idea because it can hide the performance variability or improve performance unduly, e.g. by hitting the same pages as a previous run. However, it may also be of great help for debugging, for instance re-running a tricky case which leads to an error. Use wisely.

--sampling-rate=_rate_

Sampling rate, used when writing data into the log, to reduce the amount of log generated. If this option is given, only the specified fraction of transactions are logged. 1.0 means all transactions will be logged, 0.05 means only 5% of the transactions will be logged.

Remember to take the sampling rate into account when processing the log file. For example, when computing TPS values, you need to multiply the numbers accordingly (e.g. with 0.01 sample rate, you'll only get 1/100 of the actual TPS).

Common Options

pgbench accepts the following command-line common arguments:

-h _hostname_
--host=_hostname_

The database server's host name

-p _port_
--port=_port_

The database server's port number

-U _login_
--username=_login_

The user name to connect as

-V
--version

Print the pgbench version and exit.

```
-?
--help
```

Show help about pgbench command line arguments, and exit.

Notes

What is the "Transaction" Actually Performed in pgbench?

pgbench executes test scripts chosen randomly from a specified list. They include built-in scripts with -b and user-provided custom scripts with -f. Each script may be given a relative weight specified after a @ so as to change its drawing probability. The default weight is 1. Scripts with a weight of 0 are ignored.

The default built-in transaction script (also invoked with -b tpcb-like) issues seven commands per transaction over randomly chosen aid, tid, bid and balance. The scenario is inspired by the TPC-B benchmark, but is not actually TPC-B, hence the name.

1. BEGIN;

2. UPDATE pgbench_accounts SET abalance = abalance + :delta WHERE aid = :aid;

3. SELECT abalance FROM pgbench_accounts WHERE aid = :aid;

4. UPDATE pgbench_tellers SET tbalance = tbalance + :delta WHERE tid = :tid;

5. UPDATE pgbench_branches SET bbalance = bbalance + :delta WHERE bid = :bid;

6. INSERT INTO pgbench_history (tid, bid, aid, delta, mtime) VALUES (:tid, :bid, :aid, :delta, CURRENT_TIMESTAMP);

7. END;

If you select the simple-update built-in (also -N), steps 4 and 5 aren't included in the transaction. This will avoid update contention on these tables, but it makes the test case even less like TPC-B.

If you select the select-only built-in (also -S), only the SELECT is issued.

Custom Scripts

pgbench has support for running custom benchmark scenarios by replacing the default transaction script (described above) with a transaction script read from a file (-f option). In this case a "transaction" counts as one execution of a script file.

A script file contains one or more SQL commands terminated by semicolons. Empty lines and lines beginning with -- are ignored. Script files can also contain "meta commands", which are interpreted by pgbench itself, as described below.

Note

Before PostgreSQL 9.6, SQL commands in script files were terminated by newlines, and so they could not be continued across lines. Now a semicolon is *required* to separate consecu-

---

tive SQL commands (though a SQL command does not need one if it is followed by a meta command). If you need to create a script file that works with both old and new versions of pgbench, be sure to write each SQL command on a single line ending with a semicolon.

There is a simple variable-substitution facility for script files. Variable names must consist of letters (including non-Latin letters), digits, and underscores. Variables can be set by the command-line -D option, explained above, or by the meta commands explained below. In addition to any variables preset by -D command-line options, there are a few variables that are preset automatically, listed in Table 241. A value specified for these variables using -D takes precedence over the automatic presets. Once set, a variable's value can be inserted into a SQL command by writing :*variablename*. When running more than one client session, each session has its own set of variables.

Table 241. Automatic Variables

Variable	Description
client_id	unique number identifying the client session (starts from zero)
default_seed	seed used in hash functions by default
random_seed	random generator seed (unless overwritten with -D)
scale	current scale factor

Script file meta commands begin with a backslash (\) and normally extend to the end of the line, although they can be continued to additional lines by writing backslash-return. Arguments to a meta command are separated by white space. These meta commands are supported:

\if *expression*
\elif *expression*
\else
\endif

> This group of commands implements nestable conditional blocks, similarly to psql's \if *expression*. Conditional expressions are identical to those with \set, with non-zero values interpreted as true.

\set *varname expression*

> Sets variable *varname* to a value calculated from *expression*. The expression may contain the NULL constant, Boolean constants TRUE and FALSE, integer constants such as 5432, double constants such as 3.14159, references to variables :*variablename*, operators with their usual SQL precedence and associativity, function calls, SQL CASE generic conditional expressions and parentheses.

> Functions and most operators return NULL on NULL input.

> For conditional purposes, non zero numerical values are TRUE, zero numerical values and NULL are FALSE.

> When no final ELSE clause is provided to a CASE, the default value is NULL.

> Examples:

```
\set ntellers 10 * :scale
\set aid (1021 * random(1, 100000 * :scale)) % \
          (100000 * :scale) + 1
\set divx CASE WHEN :x <> 0 THEN :y/:x ELSE NULL END
```

\sleep *number* [us | ms | s]

Causes script execution to sleep for the specified duration in microseconds (us), milliseconds (ms) or seconds (s). If the unit is omitted then seconds are the default. *number* can be either an integer constant or a :*variablename* reference to a variable having an integer value.

Example:

```
\sleep 10 ms
```

\setshell *varname command* [*argument* ...]

Sets variable *varname* to the result of the shell command *command* with the given *argument*(s). The command must return an integer value through its standard output.

command and each *argument* can be either a text constant or a :*variablename* reference to a variable. If you want to use an *argument* starting with a colon, write an additional colon at the beginning of *argument*.

Example:

```
\setshell variable_to_be_assigned command
 literal_argument :variable ::literal_starting_with_colon
```

\shell *command* [*argument* ...]

Same as \setshell, but the result of the command is discarded.

Example:

```
\shell command
 literal_argument :variable ::literal_starting_with_colon
```

Built-In Operators

The arithmetic, bitwise, comparison and logical operators listed in Table 242 are built into pgbench and may be used in expressions appearing in \set.

Table 242. pgbench Operators by increasing precedence

Operator	Description	Example	Result
OR	logical or	5 or 0	TRUE
AND	logical and	3 and 0	FALSE
NOT	logical not	not false	TRUE
IS [NOT] (NULL| TRUE|FALSE)	value tests	1 is null	FALSE

Operator	Description	Example	Result
ISNULL | NOTNULL	null tests	1 notnull	TRUE
=	is equal	5 = 4	FALSE
<>	is not equal	5 <> 4	TRUE
!=	is not equal	5 != 5	FALSE
<	lower than	5 < 4	FALSE
<=	lower or equal	5 <= 4	FALSE
>	greater than	5 > 4	TRUE
>=	greater or equal	5 >= 4	TRUE
|	integer bitwise OR	1 | 2	3
#	integer bitwise XOR	1 # 3	2
&	integer bitwise AND	1 & 3	1
~	integer bitwise NOT	~ 1	-2
<<	integer bitwise shift left	1 << 2	4
>>	integer bitwise shift right	8 >> 2	2
+	addition	5 + 4	9
-	subtraction	3 - 2.0	1.0
*	multiplication	5 * 4	20
/	division (integer truncates the results)	5 / 3	1
%	modulo	3 % 2	1
-	opposite	- 2.0	-2.0

Built-In Functions

The functions listed in Table 243 are built into pgbench and may be used in expressions appearing in \set.

Table 243. pgbench Functions

Function	Return Type	Description	Example	Result
abs(a)	same as a	absolute value	abs(-17)	17
debug(a)	same as a	print a to stderr, and return a	debug(5432.1)	5432.1
double(i)	double	cast to double	double(5432)	5432.0
exp(x)	double	exponential	exp(1.0)	2.718281828459045
greatest(a [, ...])	double if any a is double, else integer	largest value among arguments	greatest(5, 4, 3, 2)	5
hash(a [, seed])	integer	alias for hash_mur-mur2()	hash(10, 5432)	-5817877081768721 6
hash_fnv1a(a [, seed])	integer	FNV-1a hash[1]	hash_fn-v1a(10, 5432)	-7793829335365542 1

[1] https://en.wikipedia.org/wiki/Fowler%E2%80%93Noll%E2%80%93Vo_hash_function

Function	Return Type	Description	Example	Result
`hash_mur-mur2(a   [, seed ] )`	integer	MurmurHash2 hash[2]	`hash_mur-mur2(10, 5432)`	`-5817877081768721676`
`int(x)`	integer	cast to int	`int(5.4    + 3.8)`	`9`
`least(a    [, ... ] )`	double if any a is double, else integer	smallest value among arguments	`least(5,    4, 3, 2.1)`	`2.1`
`ln(x)`	double	natural logarithm	`ln(2.718281828459045)`	
`mod(i, j)`	integer	modulo	`mod(54, 32)`	`22`
`pi()`	double	value of the constant PI	`pi()`	`3.14159265358979323846`
`pow(x,    y), power(x, y)`	double	exponentiation	`pow(2.0,   10), power(2.0, 10)`	`1024.0`
`random(lb, ub)`	integer	uniformly-distributed random integer in `[lb, ub]`	`random(1, 10)`	an integer between 1 and 10
`random_expo-nential(lb, ub,    parame-ter)`	integer	exponentially-distributed random integer in `[lb, ub]`, see below	`random_expo-nential(1, 10, 3.0)`	an integer between 1 and 10
`random_gauss-ian(lb,    ub, parameter)`	integer	Gaussian-distributed random integer in `[lb,   ub]`, see below	`random_gauss-ian(1,    10, 2.5)`	an integer between 1 and 10
`random_zipfi-an(lb,    ub, parameter)`	integer	Zipfian-distributed random integer in `[lb, ub]`, see below	`random_zipfi-an(1,    10, 1.5)`	an integer between 1 and 10
`sqrt(x)`	double	square root	`sqrt(2.0)`	`1.414213562`

The `random` function generates values using a uniform distribution, that is all the values are drawn within the specified range with equal probability. The `random_exponential`, `random_gaussian` and `random_zipfian` functions require an additional double parameter which determines the precise shape of the distribution.

- For an exponential distribution, *parameter* controls the distribution by truncating a quickly-decreasing exponential distribution at *parameter*, and then projecting onto integers between the bounds. To be precise, with

  f(x) = exp(-parameter * (x - min) / (max - min + 1)) / (1 - exp(-parameter))

  Then value *i* between *min* and *max* inclusive is drawn with probability: `f(i) - f(i + 1)`.

  Intuitively, the larger the *parameter*, the more frequently values close to *min* are accessed, and the less frequently values close to *max* are accessed. The closer to 0 *parameter* is, the flatter (more

---

[2] https://en.wikipedia.org/wiki/MurmurHash

uniform) the access distribution. A crude approximation of the distribution is that the most frequent 1% values in the range, close to *min*, are drawn *parameter*% of the time. The *parameter* value must be strictly positive.

- For a Gaussian distribution, the interval is mapped onto a standard normal distribution (the classical bell-shaped Gaussian curve) truncated at `-parameter` on the left and `+parameter` on the right. Values in the middle of the interval are more likely to be drawn. To be precise, if `PHI(x)` is the cumulative distribution function of the standard normal distribution, with mean mu defined as `(max + min) / 2.0`, with

  f(x) = PHI(2.0 * parameter * (x - mu) / (max - min + 1)) /
     (2.0 * PHI(parameter) - 1)

  then value *i* between *min* and *max* inclusive is drawn with probability: `f(i + 0.5) - f(i - 0.5)`. Intuitively, the larger the *parameter*, the more frequently values close to the middle of the interval are drawn, and the less frequently values close to the *min* and *max* bounds. About 67% of values are drawn from the middle `1.0 / parameter`, that is a relative `0.5 / parameter` around the mean, and 95% in the middle `2.0 / parameter`, that is a relative `1.0 / parameter` around the mean; for instance, if *parameter* is 4.0, 67% of values are drawn from the middle quarter (1.0 / 4.0) of the interval (i.e. from `3.0 / 8.0` to `5.0 / 8.0`) and 95% from the middle half (`2.0 / 4.0`) of the interval (second and third quartiles). The minimum *parameter* is 2.0 for performance of the Box-Muller transform.

- `random_zipfian` generates an approximated bounded Zipfian distribution. For *parameter* in (0, 1), an approximated algorithm is taken from "Quickly Generating Billion-Record Synthetic Databases", Jim Gray et al, SIGMOD 1994. For *parameter* in (1, 1000), a rejection method is used, based on "Non-Uniform Random Variate Generation", Luc Devroye, p. 550-551, Springer 1986. The distribution is not defined when the parameter's value is 1.0. The function's performance is poor for parameter values close and above 1.0 and on a small range.

  parameter defines how skewed the distribution is. The larger the *parameter*, the more frequently values closer to the beginning of the interval are drawn. The closer to 0 *parameter* is, the flatter (more uniform) the output distribution. The distribution is such that, assuming the range starts from 1, the ratio of the probability of drawing *k* versus drawing *k+1* is `((k+1)/k)**parameter`. For example, `random_zipfian(1, ..., 2.5)` produces the value 1 about `(2/1)**2.5 = 5.66` times more frequently than 2, which itself is produced `(3/2)*2.5 = 2.76` times more frequently than 3, and so on.

Hash functions `hash`, `hash_murmur2` and `hash_fnv1a` accept an input value and an optional seed parameter. In case the seed isn't provided the value of `:default_seed` is used, which is initialized randomly unless set by the command-line `-D` option. Hash functions can be used to scatter the distribution of random functions such as `random_zipfian` or `random_exponential`. For instance, the following pgbench script simulates possible real world workload typical for social media and blogging platforms where few accounts generate excessive load:

```
\set r random_zipfian(0, 100000000, 1.07)
\set k abs(hash(:r)) % 1000000
```

In some cases several distinct distributions are needed which don't correlate with each other and this is when implicit seed parameter comes in handy:

```
\set k1 abs(hash(:r, :default_seed + 123)) % 1000000
\set k2 abs(hash(:r, :default_seed + 321)) % 1000000
```

As an example, the full definition of the built-in TPC-B-like transaction is:

```
\set aid random(1, 100000 * :scale)
\set bid random(1, 1 * :scale)
\set tid random(1, 10 * :scale)
\set delta random(-5000, 5000)
BEGIN;
UPDATE pgbench_accounts SET abalance = abalance + :delta WHERE aid
 = :aid;
SELECT abalance FROM pgbench_accounts WHERE aid = :aid;
UPDATE pgbench_tellers SET tbalance = tbalance + :delta WHERE tid
 = :tid;
UPDATE pgbench_branches SET bbalance = bbalance + :delta WHERE bid
 = :bid;
INSERT INTO pgbench_history (tid, bid, aid, delta, mtime) VALUES
 (:tid, :bid, :aid, :delta, CURRENT_TIMESTAMP);
END;
```

This script allows each iteration of the transaction to reference different, randomly-chosen rows. (This example also shows why it's important for each client session to have its own variables — otherwise they'd not be independently touching different rows.)

Per-Transaction Logging

With the -l option (but without the --aggregate-interval option), pgbench writes information about each transaction to a log file. The log file will be named *prefix.nnn*, where *prefix* defaults to pgbench_log, and *nnn* is the PID of the pgbench process. The prefix can be changed by using the --log-prefix option. If the -j option is 2 or higher, so that there are multiple worker threads, each will have its own log file. The first worker will use the same name for its log file as in the standard single worker case. The additional log files for the other workers will be named *prefix.nnn.mmm*, where *mmm* is a sequential number for each worker starting with 1.

The format of the log is:

```
client_id transaction_no time script_no time_epoch time_us
 [ schedule_lag ]
```

where *client_id* indicates which client session ran the transaction, *transaction_no* counts how many transactions have been run by that session, *time* is the total elapsed transaction time in microseconds, *script_no* identifies which script file was used (useful when multiple scripts were specified with -f or -b), and *time_epoch*/*time_us* are a Unix-epoch time stamp and an offset in microseconds (suitable for creating an ISO 8601 time stamp with fractional seconds) showing when the transaction completed. The *schedule_lag* field is the difference between the transaction's scheduled start time, and the time it actually started, in microseconds. It is only present when the --rate option is used. When both --rate and --latency-limit are used, the *time* for a skipped transaction will be reported as skipped.

Here is a snippet of a log file generated in a single-client run:

```
0 199 2241 0 1175850568 995598
0 200 2465 0 1175850568 998079
0 201 2513 0 1175850569 608
```

```
0 202 2038 0 1175850569 2663
```

Another example with --rate=100 and --latency-limit=5 (note the additional *schedule_lag* column):

```
0 81 4621 0 1412881037 912698 3005
0 82 6173 0 1412881037 914578 4304
0 83 skipped 0 1412881037 914578 5217
0 83 skipped 0 1412881037 914578 5099
0 83 4722 0 1412881037 916203 3108
0 84 4142 0 1412881037 918023 2333
0 85 2465 0 1412881037 919759 740
```

In this example, transaction 82 was late, because its latency (6.173 ms) was over the 5 ms limit. The next two transactions were skipped, because they were already late before they were even started.

When running a long test on hardware that can handle a lot of transactions, the log files can become very large. The --sampling-rate option can be used to log only a random sample of transactions.

Aggregated Logging

With the --aggregate-interval option, a different format is used for the log files:

```
interval_start num_transactions sum_latency sum_latency_2 min_latency max_l
 [ sum_lag sum_lag_2 min_lag max_lag [ skipped ] ]
```

where *interval_start* is the start of the interval (as a Unix epoch time stamp), *num_transactions* is the number of transactions within the interval, *sum_latency* is the sum of the transaction latencies within the interval, *sum_latency_2* is the sum of squares of the transaction latencies within the interval, *min_latency* is the minimum latency within the interval, and *max_latency* is the maximum latency within the interval. The next fields, *sum_lag*, *sum_lag_2*, *min_lag*, and *max_lag*, are only present if the --rate option is used. They provide statistics about the time each transaction had to wait for the previous one to finish, i.e. the difference between each transaction's scheduled start time and the time it actually started. The very last field, *skipped*, is only present if the --latency-limit option is used, too. It counts the number of transactions skipped because they would have started too late. Each transaction is counted in the interval when it was committed.

Here is some example output:

```
1345828501 5601 1542744 483552416 61 2573
1345828503 7884 1979812 565806736 60 1479
1345828505 7208 1979422 567277552 59 1391
1345828507 7685 1980268 569784714 60 1398
1345828509 7073 1979779 573489941 236 1411
```

Notice that while the plain (unaggregated) log file shows which script was used for each transaction, the aggregated log does not. Therefore if you need per-script data, you need to aggregate the data on your own.

Per-Statement Latencies

With the -r option, pgbench collects the elapsed transaction time of each statement executed by every client. It then reports an average of those values, referred to as the latency for each statement, after the benchmark has finished.

For the default script, the output will look similar to this:

```
starting vacuum...end.
transaction type: <builtin: TPC-B (sort of)>
scaling factor: 1
query mode: simple
number of clients: 10
number of threads: 1
number of transactions per client: 1000
number of transactions actually processed: 10000/10000
latency average = 15.844 ms
latency stddev = 2.715 ms
tps = 618.764555 (including connections establishing)
tps = 622.977698 (excluding connections establishing)
statement latencies in milliseconds:
        0.002   \set aid random(1, 100000 * :scale)
        0.005   \set bid random(1, 1 * :scale)
        0.002   \set tid random(1, 10 * :scale)
        0.001   \set delta random(-5000, 5000)
        0.326   BEGIN;
        0.603   UPDATE pgbench_accounts SET abalance = abalance
 + :delta WHERE aid = :aid;
        0.454   SELECT abalance FROM pgbench_accounts WHERE aid = :aid;
        5.528   UPDATE pgbench_tellers SET tbalance = tbalance + :delta
WHERE tid = :tid;
        7.335   UPDATE pgbench_branches SET bbalance = bbalance
 + :delta WHERE bid = :bid;
        0.371   INSERT INTO pgbench_history (tid, bid, aid, delta,
mtime) VALUES (:tid, :bid, :aid, :delta, CURRENT_TIMESTAMP);
        1.212   END;
```

If multiple script files are specified, the averages are reported separately for each script file.

Note that collecting the additional timing information needed for per-statement latency computation adds some overhead. This will slow average execution speed and lower the computed TPS. The amount of slowdown varies significantly depending on platform and hardware. Comparing average TPS values with and without latency reporting enabled is a good way to measure if the timing overhead is significant.

Good Practices

It is very easy to use pgbench to produce completely meaningless numbers. Here are some guidelines to help you get useful results.

In the first place, *never* believe any test that runs for only a few seconds. Use the -t or -T option to make the run last at least a few minutes, so as to average out noise. In some cases you could need hours to get numbers that are reproducible. It's a good idea to try the test run a few times, to find out if your numbers are reproducible or not.

For the default TPC-B-like test scenario, the initialization scale factor (-s) should be at least as large as the largest number of clients you intend to test (-c); else you'll mostly be measuring update contention. There are only -s rows in the pgbench_branches table, and every transaction wants to update one of them, so -c values in excess of -s will undoubtedly result in lots of transactions blocked waiting for other transactions.

The default test scenario is also quite sensitive to how long it's been since the tables were initialized: accumulation of dead rows and dead space in the tables changes the results. To understand the results you must keep track of the total number of updates and when vacuuming happens. If autovacuum is enabled it can result in unpredictable changes in measured performance.

A limitation of pgbench is that it can itself become the bottleneck when trying to test a large number of client sessions. This can be alleviated by running pgbench on a different machine from the database server, although low network latency will be essential. It might even be useful to run several pgbench instances concurrently, on several client machines, against the same database server.

Security

If untrusted users have access to a database that has not adopted a secure schema usage pattern, do not run pgbench in that database. pgbench uses unqualified names and does not manipulate the search path.

pg_config

pg_config — retrieve information about the installed version of PostgreSQL

Synopsis

pg_config [*option*...]

Description

The pg_config utility prints configuration parameters of the currently installed version of PostgreSQL. It is intended, for example, to be used by software packages that want to interface to PostgreSQL to facilitate finding the required header files and libraries.

Options

To use pg_config, supply one or more of the following options:

--bindir

    Print the location of user executables. Use this, for example, to find the `psql` program. This is normally also the location where the `pg_config` program resides.

--docdir

    Print the location of documentation files.

--htmldir

    Print the location of HTML documentation files.

--includedir

    Print the location of C header files of the client interfaces.

--pkgincludedir

    Print the location of other C header files.

--includedir-server

    Print the location of C header files for server programming.

--libdir

    Print the location of object code libraries.

--pkglibdir

    Print the location of dynamically loadable modules, or where the server would search for them. (Other architecture-dependent data files might also be installed in this directory.)

--localedir

Print the location of locale support files. (This will be an empty string if locale support was not configured when PostgreSQL was built.)

--mandir

Print the location of manual pages.

--sharedir

Print the location of architecture-independent support files.

--sysconfdir

Print the location of system-wide configuration files.

--pgxs

Print the location of extension makefiles.

--configure

Print the options that were given to the `configure` script when PostgreSQL was configured for building. This can be used to reproduce the identical configuration, or to find out with what options a binary package was built. (Note however that binary packages often contain vendor-specific custom patches.) See also the examples below.

--cc

Print the value of the `CC` variable that was used for building PostgreSQL. This shows the C compiler used.

--cppflags

Print the value of the `CPPFLAGS` variable that was used for building PostgreSQL. This shows C compiler switches needed at preprocessing time (typically, `-I` switches).

--cflags

Print the value of the `CFLAGS` variable that was used for building PostgreSQL. This shows C compiler switches.

--cflags_sl

Print the value of the `CFLAGS_SL` variable that was used for building PostgreSQL. This shows extra C compiler switches used for building shared libraries.

--ldflags

Print the value of the `LDFLAGS` variable that was used for building PostgreSQL. This shows linker switches.

--ldflags_ex

Print the value of the `LDFLAGS_EX` variable that was used for building PostgreSQL. This shows linker switches used for building executables only.

--ldflags_sl

> Print the value of the LDFLAGS_SL variable that was used for building PostgreSQL. This shows linker switches used for building shared libraries only.

--libs

> Print the value of the LIBS variable that was used for building PostgreSQL. This normally contains -l switches for external libraries linked into PostgreSQL.

--version

> Print the version of PostgreSQL.

-?
--help

> Show help about pg_config command line arguments, and exit.

If more than one option is given, the information is printed in that order, one item per line. If no options are given, all available information is printed, with labels.

Notes

The options --docdir, --pkgincludedir, --localedir, --mandir, --sharedir, --sysconfdir, --cc, --cppflags, --cflags, --cflags_sl, --ldflags, --ldflags_sl, and --libs were added in PostgreSQL 8.1. The option --htmldir was added in PostgreSQL 8.4. The option --ldflags_ex was added in PostgreSQL 9.0.

Example

To reproduce the build configuration of the current PostgreSQL installation, run the following command:

```
eval ./configure `pg_config --configure`
```

The output of pg_config --configure contains shell quotation marks so arguments with spaces are represented correctly. Therefore, using eval is required for proper results.

pg_dump

pg_dump — extract a PostgreSQL database into a script file or other archive file

Synopsis

pg_dump [*connection-option*...] [*option*...] [*dbname*]

Description

pg_dump is a utility for backing up a PostgreSQL database. It makes consistent backups even if the database is being used concurrently. pg_dump does not block other users accessing the database (readers or writers).

pg_dump only dumps a single database. To back up an entire cluster, or to back up global objects that are common to all databases in a cluster (such as roles and tablespaces), use pg_dumpall.

Dumps can be output in script or archive file formats. Script dumps are plain-text files containing the SQL commands required to reconstruct the database to the state it was in at the time it was saved. To restore from such a script, feed it to psql. Script files can be used to reconstruct the database even on other machines and other architectures; with some modifications, even on other SQL database products.

The alternative archive file formats must be used with pg_restore to rebuild the database. They allow pg_restore to be selective about what is restored, or even to reorder the items prior to being restored. The archive file formats are designed to be portable across architectures.

When used with one of the archive file formats and combined with pg_restore, pg_dump provides a flexible archival and transfer mechanism. pg_dump can be used to backup an entire database, then pg_restore can be used to examine the archive and/or select which parts of the database are to be restored. The most flexible output file formats are the "custom" format (-Fc) and the "directory" format (-Fd). They allow for selection and reordering of all archived items, support parallel restoration, and are compressed by default. The "directory" format is the only format that supports parallel dumps.

While running pg_dump, one should examine the output for any warnings (printed on standard error), especially in light of the limitations listed below.

Options

The following command-line options control the content and format of the output.

dbname

> Specifies the name of the database to be dumped. If this is not specified, the environment variable PGDATABASE is used. If that is not set, the user name specified for the connection is used.

-a
--data-only

> Dump only the data, not the schema (data definitions). Table data, large objects, and sequence values are dumped.

> This option is similar to, but for historical reasons not identical to, specifying --section=data.

-b
--blobs

Include large objects in the dump. This is the default behavior except when --schema, --table, or --schema-only is specified. The -b switch is therefore only useful to add large objects to dumps where a specific schema or table has been requested. Note that blobs are considered data and therefore will be included when --data-only is used, but not when --schema-only is.

-B
--no-blobs

Exclude large objects in the dump.

When both -b and -B are given, the behavior is to output large objects, when data is being dumped, see the -b documentation.

-c
--clean

Output commands to clean (drop) database objects prior to outputting the commands for creating them. (Unless --if-exists is also specified, restore might generate some harmless error messages, if any objects were not present in the destination database.)

This option is only meaningful for the plain-text format. For the archive formats, you can specify the option when you call pg_restore.

-C
--create

Begin the output with a command to create the database itself and reconnect to the created database. (With a script of this form, it doesn't matter which database in the destination installation you connect to before running the script.) If --clean is also specified, the script drops and recreates the target database before reconnecting to it.

With --create, the output also includes the database's comment if any, and any configuration variable settings that are specific to this database, that is, any ALTER DATABASE ... SET ... and ALTER ROLE ... IN DATABASE ... SET ... commands that mention this database. Access privileges for the database itself are also dumped, unless --no-acl is specified.

This option is only meaningful for the plain-text format. For the archive formats, you can specify the option when you call pg_restore.

-E *encoding*
--encoding=*encoding*

Create the dump in the specified character set encoding. By default, the dump is created in the database encoding. (Another way to get the same result is to set the PGCLIENTENCODING environment variable to the desired dump encoding.)

-f *file*
--file=*file*

Send output to the specified file. This parameter can be omitted for file based output formats, in which case the standard output is used. It must be given for the directory output format however, where it specifies the target directory instead of a file. In this case the directory is created by pg_dump and must not exist before.

-F `format`
--format=`format`

Selects the format of the output. `format` can be one of the following:

p
plain

Output a plain-text SQL script file (the default).

c
custom

Output a custom-format archive suitable for input into pg_restore. Together with the directory output format, this is the most flexible output format in that it allows manual selection and re-ordering of archived items during restore. This format is also compressed by default.

d
directory

Output a directory-format archive suitable for input into pg_restore. This will create a directory with one file for each table and blob being dumped, plus a so-called Table of Contents file describing the dumped objects in a machine-readable format that pg_restore can read. A directory format archive can be manipulated with standard Unix tools; for example, files in an uncompressed archive can be compressed with the gzip tool. This format is compressed by default and also supports parallel dumps.

t
tar

Output a `tar`-format archive suitable for input into pg_restore. The tar format is compatible with the directory format: extracting a tar-format archive produces a valid directory-format archive. However, the tar format does not support compression. Also, when using tar format the relative order of table data items cannot be changed during restore.

-j `njobs`
--jobs=`njobs`

Run the dump in parallel by dumping `njobs` tables simultaneously. This option reduces the time of the dump but it also increases the load on the database server. You can only use this option with the directory output format because this is the only output format where multiple processes can write their data at the same time.

pg_dump will open `njobs` + 1 connections to the database, so make sure your max_connections setting is high enough to accommodate all connections.

Requesting exclusive locks on database objects while running a parallel dump could cause the dump to fail. The reason is that the pg_dump master process requests shared locks on the objects that the worker processes are going to dump later in order to make sure that nobody deletes them and makes them go away while the dump is running. If another client then requests an exclusive lock on a table, that lock will not be granted but will be queued waiting for the shared lock of the master process to be released. Consequently any other access to the table will not be granted either and will queue after the exclusive lock request. This includes the worker process trying to dump the table. Without any precautions this would be a classic deadlock situation. To detect this conflict, the pg_dump worker process requests another shared lock using the NOWAIT option. If the worker process is not granted this shared lock, somebody else must have requested an exclusive lock in the meantime and there is no way to continue with the dump, so pg_dump has no choice but to abort the dump.

For a consistent backup, the database server needs to support synchronized snapshots, a feature that was introduced in PostgreSQL 9.2 for primary servers and 10 for standbys. With this feature, database clients can ensure they see the same data set even though they use different connections. `pg_dump -j` uses multiple database connections; it connects to the database once with the master process and once again for each worker job. Without the synchronized snapshot feature, the different worker jobs wouldn't be guaranteed to see the same data in each connection, which could lead to an inconsistent backup.

If you want to run a parallel dump of a pre-9.2 server, you need to make sure that the database content doesn't change from between the time the master connects to the database until the last worker job has connected to the database. The easiest way to do this is to halt any data modifying processes (DDL and DML) accessing the database before starting the backup. You also need to specify the `--no-synchronized-snapshots` parameter when running `pg_dump -j` against a pre-9.2 PostgreSQL server.

`-n` *schema*
`--schema=`*schema*

Dump only schemas matching *schema*; this selects both the schema itself, and all its contained objects. When this option is not specified, all non-system schemas in the target database will be dumped. Multiple schemas can be selected by writing multiple `-n` switches. Also, the *schema* parameter is interpreted as a pattern according to the same rules used by psql's `\d` commands (see Patterns), so multiple schemas can also be selected by writing wildcard characters in the pattern. When using wildcards, be careful to quote the pattern if needed to prevent the shell from expanding the wildcards; see Examples.

> ### Note
>
> When `-n` is specified, pg_dump makes no attempt to dump any other database objects that the selected schema(s) might depend upon. Therefore, there is no guarantee that the results of a specific-schema dump can be successfully restored by themselves into a clean database.

> ### Note
>
> Non-schema objects such as blobs are not dumped when `-n` is specified. You can add blobs back to the dump with the `--blobs` switch.

`-N` *schema*
`--exclude-schema=`*schema*

Do not dump any schemas matching the *schema* pattern. The pattern is interpreted according to the same rules as for `-n`. `-N` can be given more than once to exclude schemas matching any of several patterns.

When both `-n` and `-N` are given, the behavior is to dump just the schemas that match at least one `-n` switch but no `-N` switches. If `-N` appears without `-n`, then schemas matching `-N` are excluded from what is otherwise a normal dump.

`-o`
`--oids`

> Dump object identifiers (OIDs) as part of the data for every table. Use this option if your application references the OID columns in some way (e.g., in a foreign key constraint). Otherwise, this option should not be used.

`-O`
`--no-owner`

> Do not output commands to set ownership of objects to match the original database. By default, pg_dump issues ALTER OWNER or SET SESSION AUTHORIZATION statements to set ownership of created database objects. These statements will fail when the script is run unless it is started by a superuser (or the same user that owns all of the objects in the script). To make a script that can be restored by any user, but will give that user ownership of all the objects, specify `-O`.

> This option is only meaningful for the plain-text format. For the archive formats, you can specify the option when you call `pg_restore`.

`-R`
`--no-reconnect`

> This option is obsolete but still accepted for backwards compatibility.

`-s`
`--schema-only`

> Dump only the object definitions (schema), not data.

> This option is the inverse of `--data-only`. It is similar to, but for historical reasons not identical to, specifying `--section=pre-data --section=post-data`.

> (Do not confuse this with the `--schema` option, which uses the word "schema" in a different meaning.)

> To exclude table data for only a subset of tables in the database, see `--exclude-table-data`.

`-S username`
`--superuser=username`

> Specify the superuser user name to use when disabling triggers. This is relevant only if `--disable-triggers` is used. (Usually, it's better to leave this out, and instead start the resulting script as superuser.)

`-t table`
`--table=table`

> Dump only tables with names matching `table`. For this purpose, "table" includes views, materialized views, sequences, and foreign tables. Multiple tables can be selected by writing multiple `-t` switches. Also, the `table` parameter is interpreted as a pattern according to the same rules used by psql's \d commands (see Patterns), so multiple tables can also be selected by writing wildcard characters in the pattern. When using wildcards, be careful to quote the pattern if needed to prevent the shell from expanding the wildcards; see Examples.

> The `-n` and `-N` switches have no effect when `-t` is used, because tables selected by `-t` will be dumped regardless of those switches, and non-table objects will not be dumped.

Note

When −t is specified, pg_dump makes no attempt to dump any other database objects that the selected table(s) might depend upon. Therefore, there is no guarantee that the results of a specific-table dump can be successfully restored by themselves into a clean database.

Note

The behavior of the −t switch is not entirely upward compatible with pre-8.2 PostgreSQL versions. Formerly, writing −t tab would dump all tables named tab, but now it just dumps whichever one is visible in your default search path. To get the old behavior you can write −t '*.tab'. Also, you must write something like −t sch.tab to select a table in a particular schema, rather than the old locution of −n sch −t tab.

−T *table*
−−exclude-table=*table*

> Do not dump any tables matching the *table* pattern. The pattern is interpreted according to the same rules as for −t. −T can be given more than once to exclude tables matching any of several patterns.
>
> When both −t and −T are given, the behavior is to dump just the tables that match at least one −t switch but no −T switches. If −T appears without −t, then tables matching −T are excluded from what is otherwise a normal dump.

−v
−−verbose

> Specifies verbose mode. This will cause pg_dump to output detailed object comments and start/stop times to the dump file, and progress messages to standard error.

−V
−−version

> Print the pg_dump version and exit.

−x
−−no-privileges
−−no-acl

> Prevent dumping of access privileges (grant/revoke commands).

−Z *0..9*
−−compress=*0..9*

> Specify the compression level to use. Zero means no compression. For the custom archive format, this specifies compression of individual table-data segments, and the default is to compress at a moderate level. For plain text output, setting a nonzero compression level causes the entire output file to be compressed, as though it had been fed through gzip; but the default is not to compress. The tar archive format currently does not support compression at all.

--binary-upgrade

> This option is for use by in-place upgrade utilities. Its use for other purposes is not recommended or supported. The behavior of the option may change in future releases without notice.

--column-inserts
--attribute-inserts

> Dump data as `INSERT` commands with explicit column names (`INSERT INTO` *table* (*col-umn, ...*) `VALUES ...`). This will make restoration very slow; it is mainly useful for making dumps that can be loaded into non-PostgreSQL databases. However, since this option generates a separate command for each row, an error in reloading a row causes only that row to be lost rather than the entire table contents.

--disable-dollar-quoting

> This option disables the use of dollar quoting for function bodies, and forces them to be quoted using SQL standard string syntax.

--disable-triggers

> This option is relevant only when creating a data-only dump. It instructs pg_dump to include commands to temporarily disable triggers on the target tables while the data is reloaded. Use this if you have referential integrity checks or other triggers on the tables that you do not want to invoke during data reload.

> Presently, the commands emitted for **--disable-triggers** must be done as superuser. So, you should also specify a superuser name with **-S**, or preferably be careful to start the resulting script as a superuser.

> This option is only meaningful for the plain-text format. For the archive formats, you can specify the option when you call **pg_restore**.

--enable-row-security

> This option is relevant only when dumping the contents of a table which has row security. By default, pg_dump will set row_security to off, to ensure that all data is dumped from the table. If the user does not have sufficient privileges to bypass row security, then an error is thrown. This parameter instructs pg_dump to set row_security to on instead, allowing the user to dump the parts of the contents of the table that they have access to.

> Note that if you use this option currently, you probably also want the dump be in `INSERT` format, as the `COPY FROM` during restore does not support row security.

--exclude-table-data=*table*

> Do not dump data for any tables matching the *table* pattern. The pattern is interpreted according to the same rules as for **-t**. **--exclude-table-data** can be given more than once to exclude tables matching any of several patterns. This option is useful when you need the definition of a particular table even though you do not need the data in it.

> To exclude data for all tables in the database, see **--schema-only**.

--if-exists

> Use conditional commands (i.e. add an `IF EXISTS` clause) when cleaning database objects. This option is not valid unless **--clean** is also specified.

--inserts

Dump data as `INSERT` commands (rather than `COPY`). This will make restoration very slow; it is mainly useful for making dumps that can be loaded into non-PostgreSQL databases. However, since this option generates a separate command for each row, an error in reloading a row causes only that row to be lost rather than the entire table contents. Note that the restore might fail altogether if you have rearranged column order. The `--column-inserts` option is safe against column order changes, though even slower.

--load-via-partition-root

When dumping data for a table partition, make the `COPY` or `INSERT` statements target the root of the partitioning hierarchy that contains it, rather than the partition itself. This causes the appropriate partition to be re-determined for each row when the data is loaded. This may be useful when reloading data on a server where rows do not always fall into the same partitions as they did on the original server. That could happen, for example, if the partitioning column is of type text and the two systems have different definitions of the collation used to sort the partitioning column.

It is best not to use parallelism when restoring from an archive made with this option, because pg_restore will not know exactly which partition(s) a given archive data item will load data into. This could result in inefficiency due to lock conflicts between parallel jobs, or perhaps even reload failures due to foreign key constraints being set up before all the relevant data is loaded.

--lock-wait-timeout=*timeout*

Do not wait forever to acquire shared table locks at the beginning of the dump. Instead fail if unable to lock a table within the specified *timeout*. The timeout may be specified in any of the formats accepted by `SET statement_timeout`. (Allowed formats vary depending on the server version you are dumping from, but an integer number of milliseconds is accepted by all versions.)

--no-comments

Do not dump comments.

--no-publications

Do not dump publications.

--no-security-labels

Do not dump security labels.

--no-subscriptions

Do not dump subscriptions.

--no-sync

By default, `pg_dump` will wait for all files to be written safely to disk. This option causes `pg_dump` to return without waiting, which is faster, but means that a subsequent operating system crash can leave the dump corrupt. Generally, this option is useful for testing but should not be used when dumping data from production installation.

--no-synchronized-snapshots

This option allows running `pg_dump -j` against a pre-9.2 server, see the documentation of the -j parameter for more details.

`--no-tablespaces`

Do not output commands to select tablespaces. With this option, all objects will be created in whichever tablespace is the default during restore.

This option is only meaningful for the plain-text format. For the archive formats, you can specify the option when you call `pg_restore`.

`--no-unlogged-table-data`

Do not dump the contents of unlogged tables. This option has no effect on whether or not the table definitions (schema) are dumped; it only suppresses dumping the table data. Data in unlogged tables is always excluded when dumping from a standby server.

`--quote-all-identifiers`

Force quoting of all identifiers. This option is recommended when dumping a database from a server whose PostgreSQL major version is different from pg_dump's, or when the output is intended to be loaded into a server of a different major version. By default, pg_dump quotes only identifiers that are reserved words in its own major version. This sometimes results in compatibility issues when dealing with servers of other versions that may have slightly different sets of reserved words. Using `--quote-all-identifiers` prevents such issues, at the price of a harder-to-read dump script.

`--section=sectionname`

Only dump the named section. The section name can be `pre-data`, `data`, or `post-data`. This option can be specified more than once to select multiple sections. The default is to dump all sections.

The data section contains actual table data, large-object contents, and sequence values. Post-data items include definitions of indexes, triggers, rules, and constraints other than validated check constraints. Pre-data items include all other data definition items.

`--serializable-deferrable`

Use a `serializable` transaction for the dump, to ensure that the snapshot used is consistent with later database states; but do this by waiting for a point in the transaction stream at which no anomalies can be present, so that there isn't a risk of the dump failing or causing other transactions to roll back with a `serialization_failure`. See Chapter 13 for more information about transaction isolation and concurrency control.

This option is not beneficial for a dump which is intended only for disaster recovery. It could be useful for a dump used to load a copy of the database for reporting or other read-only load sharing while the original database continues to be updated. Without it the dump may reflect a state which is not consistent with any serial execution of the transactions eventually committed. For example, if batch processing techniques are used, a batch may show as closed in the dump without all of the items which are in the batch appearing.

This option will make no difference if there are no read-write transactions active when pg_dump is started. If read-write transactions are active, the start of the dump may be delayed for an indeterminate length of time. Once running, performance with or without the switch is the same.

`--snapshot=snapshotname`

Use the specified synchronized snapshot when making a dump of the database (see Table 9.82 for more details).

This option is useful when needing to synchronize the dump with a logical replication slot (see Chapter 49) or with a concurrent session.

In the case of a parallel dump, the snapshot name defined by this option is used rather than taking a new snapshot.

`--strict-names`

Require that each schema (`-n`/`--schema`) and table (`-t`/`--table`) qualifier match at least one schema/table in the database to be dumped. Note that if none of the schema/table qualifiers find matches, pg_dump will generate an error even without `--strict-names`.

This option has no effect on `-N`/`--exclude-schema`, `-T`/`--exclude-table`, or `--exclude-table-data`. An exclude pattern failing to match any objects is not considered an error.

`--use-set-session-authorization`

Output SQL-standard `SET SESSION AUTHORIZATION` commands instead of `ALTER OWNER` commands to determine object ownership. This makes the dump more standards-compatible, but depending on the history of the objects in the dump, might not restore properly. Also, a dump using `SET SESSION AUTHORIZATION` will certainly require superuser privileges to restore correctly, whereas `ALTER OWNER` requires lesser privileges.

`-?`
`--help`

Show help about pg_dump command line arguments, and exit.

The following command-line options control the database connection parameters.

`-d dbname`
`--dbname=dbname`

Specifies the name of the database to connect to. This is equivalent to specifying *dbname* as the first non-option argument on the command line.

If this parameter contains an = sign or starts with a valid URI prefix (`postgresql://` or `postgres://`), it is treated as a *conninfo* string. See Section 34.1 for more information.

`-h host`
`--host=host`

Specifies the host name of the machine on which the server is running. If the value begins with a slash, it is used as the directory for the Unix domain socket. The default is taken from the `PGHOST` environment variable, if set, else a Unix domain socket connection is attempted.

`-p port`
`--port=port`

Specifies the TCP port or local Unix domain socket file extension on which the server is listening for connections. Defaults to the `PGPORT` environment variable, if set, or a compiled-in default.

`-U username`
`--username=username`

User name to connect as.

-w
--no-password

>   Never issue a password prompt. If the server requires password authentication and a password is not available by other means such as a `.pgpass` file, the connection attempt will fail. This option can be useful in batch jobs and scripts where no user is present to enter a password.

-W
--password

>   Force pg_dump to prompt for a password before connecting to a database.

>   This option is never essential, since pg_dump will automatically prompt for a password if the server demands password authentication. However, pg_dump will waste a connection attempt finding out that the server wants a password. In some cases it is worth typing -W to avoid the extra connection attempt.

--role=rolename

>   Specifies a role name to be used to create the dump. This option causes pg_dump to issue a SET ROLE rolename command after connecting to the database. It is useful when the authenticated user (specified by -U) lacks privileges needed by pg_dump, but can switch to a role with the required rights. Some installations have a policy against logging in directly as a superuser, and use of this option allows dumps to be made without violating the policy.

Environment

    PGDATABASE
    PGHOST
    PGOPTIONS
    PGPORT
    PGUSER

>   Default connection parameters.

This utility, like most other PostgreSQL utilities, also uses the environment variables supported by libpq (see Section 34.14).

Diagnostics

pg_dump internally executes SELECT statements. If you have problems running pg_dump, make sure you are able to select information from the database using, for example, psql. Also, any default connection settings and environment variables used by the libpq front-end library will apply.

The database activity of pg_dump is normally collected by the statistics collector. If this is undesirable, you can set parameter track_counts to false via PGOPTIONS or the ALTER USER command.

Notes

If your database cluster has any local additions to the template1 database, be careful to restore the output of pg_dump into a truly empty database; otherwise you are likely to get errors due to duplicate definitions of the added objects. To make an empty database without any local additions, copy from template0 not template1, for example:

```
CREATE DATABASE foo WITH TEMPLATE template0;
```

When a data-only dump is chosen and the option --disable-triggers is used, pg_dump emits commands to disable triggers on user tables before inserting the data, and then commands to re-enable them after the data has been inserted. If the restore is stopped in the middle, the system catalogs might be left in the wrong state.

The dump file produced by pg_dump does not contain the statistics used by the optimizer to make query planning decisions. Therefore, it is wise to run ANALYZE after restoring from a dump file to ensure optimal performance; see Section 24.1.3 and Section 24.1.6 for more information.

Because pg_dump is used to transfer data to newer versions of PostgreSQL, the output of pg_dump can be expected to load into PostgreSQL server versions newer than pg_dump's version. pg_dump can also dump from PostgreSQL servers older than its own version. (Currently, servers back to version 8.0 are supported.) However, pg_dump cannot dump from PostgreSQL servers newer than its own major version; it will refuse to even try, rather than risk making an invalid dump. Also, it is not guaranteed that pg_dump's output can be loaded into a server of an older major version — not even if the dump was taken from a server of that version. Loading a dump file into an older server may require manual editing of the dump file to remove syntax not understood by the older server. Use of the --quote-all-identifiers option is recommended in cross-version cases, as it can prevent problems arising from varying reserved-word lists in different PostgreSQL versions.

When dumping logical replication subscriptions, pg_dump will generate CREATE SUBSCRIPTION commands that use the connect = false option, so that restoring the subscription does not make remote connections for creating a replication slot or for initial table copy. That way, the dump can be restored without requiring network access to the remote servers. It is then up to the user to reactivate the subscriptions in a suitable way. If the involved hosts have changed, the connection information might have to be changed. It might also be appropriate to truncate the target tables before initiating a new full table copy.

Examples

To dump a database called mydb into a SQL-script file:

```
$ pg_dump mydb > db.sql
```

To reload such a script into a (freshly created) database named newdb:

```
$ psql -d newdb -f db.sql
```

To dump a database into a custom-format archive file:

```
$ pg_dump -Fc mydb > db.dump
```

To dump a database into a directory-format archive:

```
$ pg_dump -Fd mydb -f dumpdir
```

To dump a database into a directory-format archive in parallel with 5 worker jobs:

```
$ pg_dump -Fd mydb -j 5 -f dumpdir
```

To reload an archive file into a (freshly created) database named `newdb`:

```
$ pg_restore -d newdb db.dump
```

To reload an archive file into the same database it was dumped from, discarding the current contents of that database:

```
$ pg_restore -d postgres --clean --create db.dump
```

To dump a single table named `mytab`:

```
$ pg_dump -t mytab mydb > db.sql
```

To dump all tables whose names start with `emp` in the `detroit` schema, except for the table named `employee_log`:

```
$ pg_dump -t 'detroit.emp*' -T detroit.employee_log mydb > db.sql
```

To dump all schemas whose names start with `east` or `west` and end in `gsm`, excluding any schemas whose names contain the word `test`:

```
$ pg_dump -n 'east*gsm' -n 'west*gsm' -N '*test*' mydb > db.sql
```

The same, using regular expression notation to consolidate the switches:

```
$ pg_dump -n '(east|west)*gsm' -N '*test*' mydb > db.sql
```

To dump all database objects except for tables whose names begin with `ts_`:

```
$ pg_dump -T 'ts_*' mydb > db.sql
```

To specify an upper-case or mixed-case name in `-t` and related switches, you need to double-quote the name; else it will be folded to lower case (see Patterns). But double quotes are special to the shell, so in turn they must be quoted. Thus, to dump a single table with a mixed-case name, you need something like

```
$ pg_dump -t "\"MixedCaseName\"" mydb > mytab.sql
```

See Also

pg_dumpall, pg_restore, psql

pg_dumpall

pg_dumpall — extract a PostgreSQL database cluster into a script file

Synopsis

pg_dumpall [*connection-option*...] [*option*...]

Description

pg_dumpall is a utility for writing out ("dumping") all PostgreSQL databases of a cluster into one script file. The script file contains SQL commands that can be used as input to psql to restore the databases. It does this by calling pg_dump for each database in the cluster. pg_dumpall also dumps global objects that are common to all databases, that is, database roles and tablespaces. (pg_dump does not save these objects.)

Since pg_dumpall reads tables from all databases you will most likely have to connect as a database superuser in order to produce a complete dump. Also you will need superuser privileges to execute the saved script in order to be allowed to add roles and create databases.

The SQL script will be written to the standard output. Use the [-f|file] option or shell operators to redirect it into a file.

pg_dumpall needs to connect several times to the PostgreSQL server (once per database). If you use password authentication it will ask for a password each time. It is convenient to have a `~/.pgpass` file in such cases. See Section 34.15 for more information.

Options

The following command-line options control the content and format of the output.

-a
--data-only

>   Dump only the data, not the schema (data definitions).

-c
--clean

>   Include SQL commands to clean (drop) databases before recreating them. DROP commands for roles and tablespaces are added as well.

-E *encoding*
--encoding=*encoding*

>   Create the dump in the specified character set encoding. By default, the dump is created in the database encoding. (Another way to get the same result is to set the PGCLIENTENCODING environment variable to the desired dump encoding.)

-f *filename*
--file=*filename*

>   Send output to the specified file. If this is omitted, the standard output is used.

`-g`
`--globals-only`

Dump only global objects (roles and tablespaces), no databases.

`-o`
`--oids`

Dump object identifiers (OIDs) as part of the data for every table. Use this option if your application references the OID columns in some way (e.g., in a foreign key constraint). Otherwise, this option should not be used.

`-O`
`--no-owner`

Do not output commands to set ownership of objects to match the original database. By default, pg_dumpall issues `ALTER OWNER` or `SET SESSION AUTHORIZATION` statements to set ownership of created schema elements. These statements will fail when the script is run unless it is started by a superuser (or the same user that owns all of the objects in the script). To make a script that can be restored by any user, but will give that user ownership of all the objects, specify `-O`.

`-r`
`--roles-only`

Dump only roles, no databases or tablespaces.

`-s`
`--schema-only`

Dump only the object definitions (schema), not data.

`-S username`
`--superuser=username`

Specify the superuser user name to use when disabling triggers. This is relevant only if `--disable-triggers` is used. (Usually, it's better to leave this out, and instead start the resulting script as superuser.)

`-t`
`--tablespaces-only`

Dump only tablespaces, no databases or roles.

`-v`
`--verbose`

Specifies verbose mode. This will cause pg_dumpall to output start/stop times to the dump file, and progress messages to standard error. It will also enable verbose output in pg_dump.

`-V`
`--version`

Print the pg_dumpall version and exit.

`-x`
`--no-privileges`
`--no-acl`

Prevent dumping of access privileges (grant/revoke commands).

--binary-upgrade

This option is for use by in-place upgrade utilities. Its use for other purposes is not recommended or supported. The behavior of the option may change in future releases without notice.

--column-inserts
--attribute-inserts

Dump data as `INSERT` commands with explicit column names (`INSERT INTO` *table* (*column,* ...) `VALUES` ...). This will make restoration very slow; it is mainly useful for making dumps that can be loaded into non-PostgreSQL databases.

--disable-dollar-quoting

This option disables the use of dollar quoting for function bodies, and forces them to be quoted using SQL standard string syntax.

--disable-triggers

This option is relevant only when creating a data-only dump. It instructs pg_dumpall to include commands to temporarily disable triggers on the target tables while the data is reloaded. Use this if you have referential integrity checks or other triggers on the tables that you do not want to invoke during data reload.

Presently, the commands emitted for **--disable-triggers** must be done as superuser. So, you should also specify a superuser name with **-S**, or preferably be careful to start the resulting script as a superuser.

--if-exists

Use conditional commands (i.e. add an `IF EXISTS` clause) to drop databases and other objects. This option is not valid unless **--clean** is also specified.

--inserts

Dump data as `INSERT` commands (rather than `COPY`). This will make restoration very slow; it is mainly useful for making dumps that can be loaded into non-PostgreSQL databases. Note that the restore might fail altogether if you have rearranged column order. The **--column-inserts** option is safer, though even slower.

--load-via-partition-root

When dumping data for a table partition, make the `COPY` or `INSERT` statements target the root of the partitioning hierarchy that contains it, rather than the partition itself. This causes the appropriate partition to be re-determined for each row when the data is loaded. This may be useful when reloading data on a server where rows do not always fall into the same partitions as they did on the original server. That could happen, for example, if the partitioning column is of type text and the two systems have different definitions of the collation used to sort the partitioning column.

--lock-wait-timeout=*timeout*

Do not wait forever to acquire shared table locks at the beginning of the dump. Instead, fail if unable to lock a table within the specified *timeout*. The timeout may be specified in any of the formats accepted by `SET statement_timeout`. Allowed values vary depending on the server version you are dumping from, but an integer number of milliseconds is accepted by all versions since 7.3. This option is ignored when dumping from a pre-7.3 server.

--no-comments

Do not dump comments.

--no-publications

Do not dump publications.

--no-role-passwords

Do not dump passwords for roles. When restored, roles will have a null password, and password authentication will always fail until the password is set. Since password values aren't needed when this option is specified, the role information is read from the catalog view `pg_roles` instead of `pg_authid`. Therefore, this option also helps if access to `pg_authid` is restricted by some security policy.

--no-security-labels

Do not dump security labels.

--no-subscriptions

Do not dump subscriptions.

--no-sync

By default, `pg_dumpall` will wait for all files to be written safely to disk. This option causes `pg_dumpall` to return without waiting, which is faster, but means that a subsequent operating system crash can leave the dump corrupt. Generally, this option is useful for testing but should not be used when dumping data from production installation.

--no-tablespaces

Do not output commands to create tablespaces nor select tablespaces for objects. With this option, all objects will be created in whichever tablespace is the default during restore.

--no-unlogged-table-data

Do not dump the contents of unlogged tables. This option has no effect on whether or not the table definitions (schema) are dumped; it only suppresses dumping the table data.

--quote-all-identifiers

Force quoting of all identifiers. This option is recommended when dumping a database from a server whose PostgreSQL major version is different from pg_dumpall's, or when the output is intended to be loaded into a server of a different major version. By default, pg_dumpall quotes only identifiers that are reserved words in its own major version. This sometimes results in compatibility issues when dealing with servers of other versions that may have slightly different sets of reserved words. Using `--quote-all-identifiers` prevents such issues, at the price of a harder-to-read dump script.

--use-set-session-authorization

Output SQL-standard SET SESSION AUTHORIZATION commands instead of ALTER OWNER commands to determine object ownership. This makes the dump more standards compatible, but depending on the history of the objects in the dump, might not restore properly.

-?
--help

    Show help about pg_dumpall command line arguments, and exit.

The following command-line options control the database connection parameters.

-d *connstr*
--dbname=*connstr*

    Specifies parameters used to connect to the server, as a connection string. See Section 34.1.1 for more information.

    The option is called --dbname for consistency with other client applications, but because pg_dumpall needs to connect to many databases, the database name in the connection string will be ignored. Use the -l option to specify the name of the database used for the initial connection, which will dump global objects and discover what other databases should be dumped.

-h *host*
--host=*host*

    Specifies the host name of the machine on which the database server is running. If the value begins with a slash, it is used as the directory for the Unix domain socket. The default is taken from the PGHOST environment variable, if set, else a Unix domain socket connection is attempted.

-l *dbname*
--database=*dbname*

    Specifies the name of the database to connect to for dumping global objects and discovering what other databases should be dumped. If not specified, the postgres database will be used, and if that does not exist, template1 will be used.

-p *port*
--port=*port*

    Specifies the TCP port or local Unix domain socket file extension on which the server is listening for connections. Defaults to the PGPORT environment variable, if set, or a compiled-in default.

-U *username*
--username=*username*

    User name to connect as.

-w
--no-password

    Never issue a password prompt. If the server requires password authentication and a password is not available by other means such as a .pgpass file, the connection attempt will fail. This option can be useful in batch jobs and scripts where no user is present to enter a password.

-W
--password

    Force pg_dumpall to prompt for a password before connecting to a database.

    This option is never essential, since pg_dumpall will automatically prompt for a password if the server demands password authentication. However, pg_dumpall will waste a connection attempt finding out that the server wants a password. In some cases it is worth typing -W to avoid the extra connection attempt.

Note that the password prompt will occur again for each database to be dumped. Usually, it's better to set up a ~/.pgpass file than to rely on manual password entry.

--role=*rolename*

Specifies a role name to be used to create the dump. This option causes pg_dumpall to issue a SET ROLE *rolename* command after connecting to the database. It is useful when the authenticated user (specified by -U) lacks privileges needed by pg_dumpall, but can switch to a role with the required rights. Some installations have a policy against logging in directly as a superuser, and use of this option allows dumps to be made without violating the policy.

Environment

PGHOST
PGOPTIONS
PGPORT
PGUSER

Default connection parameters

This utility, like most other PostgreSQL utilities, also uses the environment variables supported by libpq (see Section 34.14).

Notes

Since pg_dumpall calls pg_dump internally, some diagnostic messages will refer to pg_dump.

The --clean option can be useful even when your intention is to restore the dump script into a fresh cluster. Use of --clean authorizes the script to drop and re-create the built-in postgres and template1 databases, ensuring that those databases will retain the same properties (for instance, locale and encoding) that they had in the source cluster. Without the option, those databases will retain their existing database-level properties, as well as any pre-existing contents.

Once restored, it is wise to run ANALYZE on each database so the optimizer has useful statistics. You can also run vacuumdb -a -z to analyze all databases.

The dump script should not be expected to run completely without errors. In particular, because the script will issue CREATE ROLE for every role existing in the source cluster, it is certain to get a "role already exists" error for the bootstrap superuser, unless the destination cluster was initialized with a different boot-strap superuser name. This error is harmless and should be ignored. Use of the --clean option is likely to produce additional harmless error messages about non-existent objects, although you can minimize those by adding --if-exists.

pg_dumpall requires all needed tablespace directories to exist before the restore; otherwise, database creation will fail for databases in non-default locations.

Examples

To dump all databases:

```
$ pg_dumpall > db.out
```

To reload database(s) from this file, you can use:

```
$ psql -f db.out postgres
```

It is not important to which database you connect here since the script file created by pg_dumpall will contain the appropriate commands to create and connect to the saved databases. An exception is that if you specified `--clean`, you must connect to the `postgres` database initially; the script will attempt to drop other databases immediately, and that will fail for the database you are connected to.

See Also

Check pg_dump for details on possible error conditions.

pg_isready

pg_isready — check the connection status of a PostgreSQL server

Synopsis

pg_isready [*connection-option*...] [*option*...]

Description

pg_isready is a utility for checking the connection status of a PostgreSQL database server. The exit status specifies the result of the connection check.

Options

-d *dbname*
--dbname=*dbname*

  Specifies the name of the database to connect to.

  If this parameter contains an = sign or starts with a valid URI prefix (`postgresql://` or `post-gres://`), it is treated as a *conninfo* string. See Section 34.1.1 for more information.

-h *hostname*
--host=*hostname*

  Specifies the host name of the machine on which the server is running. If the value begins with a slash, it is used as the directory for the Unix-domain socket.

-p *port*
--port=*port*

  Specifies the TCP port or the local Unix-domain socket file extension on which the server is listening for connections. Defaults to the value of the `PGPORT` environment variable or, if not set, to the port specified at compile time, usually 5432.

-q
--quiet

  Do not display status message. This is useful when scripting.

-t *seconds*
--timeout=*seconds*

  The maximum number of seconds to wait when attempting connection before returning that the server is not responding. Setting to 0 disables. The default is 3 seconds.

-U *username*
--username=*username*

  Connect to the database as the user *username* instead of the default.

```
-V
--version
```

Print the pg_isready version and exit.

```
-?
--help
```

Show help about pg_isready command line arguments, and exit.

Exit Status

pg_isready returns 0 to the shell if the server is accepting connections normally, 1 if the server is rejecting connections (for example during startup), 2 if there was no response to the connection attempt, and 3 if no attempt was made (for example due to invalid parameters).

Environment

pg_isready, like most other PostgreSQL utilities, also uses the environment variables supported by libpq (see Section 34.14).

Notes

It is not necessary to supply correct user name, password, or database name values to obtain the server status; however, if incorrect values are provided, the server will log a failed connection attempt.

Examples

Standard Usage:

```
$ pg_isready
/tmp:5432 - accepting connections
$ echo $?
0
```

Running with connection parameters to a PostgreSQL cluster in startup:

```
$ pg_isready -h localhost -p 5433
localhost:5433 - rejecting connections
$ echo $?
1
```

Running with connection parameters to a non-responsive PostgreSQL cluster:

```
$ pg_isready -h someremotehost
someremotehost:5432 - no response
$ echo $?
2
```

pg_receivewal

pg_receivewal — stream write-ahead logs from a PostgreSQL server

Synopsis

pg_receivewal [*option*...]

Description

pg_receivewal is used to stream the write-ahead log from a running PostgreSQL cluster. The write-ahead log is streamed using the streaming replication protocol, and is written to a local directory of files. This directory can be used as the archive location for doing a restore using point-in-time recovery (see Section 25.3).

pg_receivewal streams the write-ahead log in real time as it's being generated on the server, and does not wait for segments to complete like archive_command does. For this reason, it is not necessary to set archive_timeout when using pg_receivewal.

Unlike the WAL receiver of a PostgreSQL standby server, pg_receivewal by default flushes WAL data only when a WAL file is closed. The option --synchronous must be specified to flush WAL data in real time.

The write-ahead log is streamed over a regular PostgreSQL connection and uses the replication protocol. The connection must be made with a superuser or a user having REPLICATION permissions (see Section 21.2), and pg_hba.conf must permit the replication connection. The server must also be configured with max_wal_senders set high enough to leave at least one session available for the stream.

If the connection is lost, or if it cannot be initially established, with a non-fatal error, pg_receivewal will retry the connection indefinitely, and reestablish streaming as soon as possible. To avoid this behavior, use the -n parameter.

In the absence of fatal errors, pg_receivewal will run until terminated by the SIGINT signal (**Control+C**).

Options

-D *directory*
--directory=*directory*

> Directory to write the output to.

> This parameter is required.

-E *lsn*
--endpos=*lsn*

> Automatically stop replication and exit with normal exit status 0 when receiving reaches the specified LSN.

> If there is a record with LSN exactly equal to *lsn*, the record will be processed.

--if-not-exists

> Do not error out when --create-slot is specified and a slot with the specified name already exists.

-n
--no-loop

> Don't loop on connection errors. Instead, exit right away with an error.

--no-sync

> This option causes `pg_receivewal` to not force WAL data to be flushed to disk. This is faster, but means that a subsequent operating system crash can leave the WAL segments corrupt. Generally, this option is useful for testing but should not be used when doing WAL archiving on a production deployment.

> This option is incompatible with `--synchronous`.

-s *interval*
--status-interval=*interval*

> Specifies the number of seconds between status packets sent back to the server. This allows for easier monitoring of the progress from server. A value of zero disables the periodic status updates completely, although an update will still be sent when requested by the server, to avoid timeout disconnect. The default value is 10 seconds.

-S *slotname*
--slot=*slotname*

> Require pg_receivewal to use an existing replication slot (see Section 26.2.6). When this option is used, pg_receivewal will report a flush position to the server, indicating when each segment has been synchronized to disk so that the server can remove that segment if it is not otherwise needed.

> When the replication client of pg_receivewal is configured on the server as a synchronous standby, then using a replication slot will report the flush position to the server, but only when a WAL file is closed. Therefore, that configuration will cause transactions on the primary to wait for a long time and effectively not work satisfactorily. The option `--synchronous` (see below) must be specified in addition to make this work correctly.

--synchronous

> Flush the WAL data to disk immediately after it has been received. Also send a status packet back to the server immediately after flushing, regardless of `--status-interval`.

> This option should be specified if the replication client of pg_receivewal is configured on the server as a synchronous standby, to ensure that timely feedback is sent to the server.

-v
--verbose

> Enables verbose mode.

-Z *level*
--compress=*level*

> Enables gzip compression of write-ahead logs, and specifies the compression level (0 through 9, 0 being no compression and 9 being best compression). The suffix `.gz` will automatically be added to all filenames.

The following command-line options control the database connection parameters.

-d *connstr*
--dbname=*connstr*

> Specifies parameters used to connect to the server, as a connection string. See Section 34.1.1 for more information.

> The option is called --dbname for consistency with other client applications, but because pg_receivewal doesn't connect to any particular database in the cluster, database name in the connection string will be ignored.

-h *host*
--host=*host*

> Specifies the host name of the machine on which the server is running. If the value begins with a slash, it is used as the directory for the Unix domain socket. The default is taken from the PGHOST environment variable, if set, else a Unix domain socket connection is attempted.

-p *port*
--port=*port*

> Specifies the TCP port or local Unix domain socket file extension on which the server is listening for connections. Defaults to the PGPORT environment variable, if set, or a compiled-in default.

-U *username*
--username=*username*

> User name to connect as.

-w
--no-password

> Never issue a password prompt. If the server requires password authentication and a password is not available by other means such as a .pgpass file, the connection attempt will fail. This option can be useful in batch jobs and scripts where no user is present to enter a password.

-W
--password

> Force pg_receivewal to prompt for a password before connecting to a database.

> This option is never essential, since pg_receivewal will automatically prompt for a password if the server demands password authentication. However, pg_receivewal will waste a connection attempt finding out that the server wants a password. In some cases it is worth typing -W to avoid the extra connection attempt.

pg_receivewal can perform one of the two following actions in order to control physical replication slots:

--create-slot

> Create a new physical replication slot with the name specified in --slot, then exit.

--drop-slot

> Drop the replication slot with the name specified in --slot, then exit.

Other options are also available:

```
-V
--version
```

Print the pg_receivewal version and exit.

```
-?
--help
```

Show help about pg_receivewal command line arguments, and exit.

Exit Status

pg_receivewal will exit with status 0 when terminated by the SIGINT signal. (That is the normal way to end it. Hence it is not an error.) For fatal errors or other signals, the exit status will be nonzero.

Environment

This utility, like most other PostgreSQL utilities, uses the environment variables supported by libpq (see Section 34.14).

Notes

When using pg_receivewal instead of archive_command as the main WAL backup method, it is strongly recommended to use replication slots. Otherwise, the server is free to recycle or remove write-ahead log files before they are backed up, because it does not have any information, either from archive_command or the replication slots, about how far the WAL stream has been archived. Note, however, that a replication slot will fill up the server's disk space if the receiver does not keep up with fetching the WAL data.

pg_receivewal will preserve group permissions on the received WAL files if group permissions are enabled on the source cluster.

Examples

To stream the write-ahead log from the server at **mydbserver** and store it in the local directory /usr/local/pgsql/archive:

```
$ pg_receivewal -h mydbserver -D /usr/local/pgsql/archive
```

See Also

pg_basebackup

pg_recvlogical

pg_recvlogical — control PostgreSQL logical decoding streams

Synopsis

`pg_recvlogical` [*option*...]

Description

`pg_recvlogical` controls logical decoding replication slots and streams data from such replication slots.

It creates a replication-mode connection, so it is subject to the same constraints as pg_receivewal, plus those for logical replication (see Chapter 49).

`pg_recvlogical` has no equivalent to the logical decoding SQL interface's peek and get modes. It sends replay confirmations for data lazily as it receives it and on clean exit. To examine pending data on a slot without consuming it, use `pg_logical_slot_peek_changes`.

Options

At least one of the following options must be specified to select an action:

`--create-slot`

Create a new logical replication slot with the name specified by `--slot`, using the output plugin specified by `--plugin`, for the database specified by `--dbname`.

`--drop-slot`

Drop the replication slot with the name specified by `--slot`, then exit.

`--start`

Begin streaming changes from the logical replication slot specified by `--slot`, continuing until terminated by a signal. If the server side change stream ends with a server shutdown or disconnect, retry in a loop unless `--no-loop` is specified.

The stream format is determined by the output plugin specified when the slot was created.

The connection must be to the same database used to create the slot.

`--create-slot` and `--start` can be specified together. `--drop-slot` cannot be combined with another action.

The following command-line options control the location and format of the output and other replication behavior:

`-E` *lsn*
`--endpos=`*lsn*

In `--start` mode, automatically stop replication and exit with normal exit status 0 when receiving reaches the specified LSN. If specified when not in `--start` mode, an error is raised.

If there's a record with LSN exactly equal to *lsn*, the record will be output.

The --endpos option is not aware of transaction boundaries and may truncate output partway through a transaction. Any partially output transaction will not be consumed and will be replayed again when the slot is next read from. Individual messages are never truncated.

-f *filename*
--file=*filename*

Write received and decoded transaction data into this file. Use – for stdout.

-F *interval_seconds*
--fsync-interval=*interval_seconds*

Specifies how often pg_recvlogical should issue fsync() calls to ensure the output file is safely flushed to disk.

The server will occasionally request the client to perform a flush and report the flush position to the server. This setting is in addition to that, to perform flushes more frequently.

Specifying an interval of 0 disables issuing fsync() calls altogether, while still reporting progress to the server. In this case, data could be lost in the event of a crash.

-I *lsn*
--startpos=*lsn*

In --start mode, start replication from the given LSN. For details on the effect of this, see the documentation in Chapter 49 and Section 53.4. Ignored in other modes.

--if-not-exists

Do not error out when --create-slot is specified and a slot with the specified name already exists.

-n
--no-loop

When the connection to the server is lost, do not retry in a loop, just exit.

-o *name*[=*value*]
--option=*name*[=*value*]

Pass the option *name* to the output plugin with, if specified, the option value *value*. Which options exist and their effects depends on the used output plugin.

-P *plugin*
--plugin=*plugin*

When creating a slot, use the specified logical decoding output plugin. See Chapter 49. This option has no effect if the slot already exists.

-s *interval_seconds*
--status-interval=*interval_seconds*

This option has the same effect as the option of the same name in pg_receivewal. See the description there.

-S *slot_name*
--slot=*slot_name*

> In --start mode, use the existing logical replication slot named *slot_name*. In --create-slot mode, create the slot with this name. In --drop-slot mode, delete the slot with this name.

-v
--verbose

> Enables verbose mode.

The following command-line options control the database connection parameters.

-d *database*
--dbname=*database*

> The database to connect to. See the description of the actions for what this means in detail. This can be a libpq connection string; see Section 34.1.1 for more information. Defaults to user name.

-h *hostname-or-ip*
--host=*hostname-or-ip*

> Specifies the host name of the machine on which the server is running. If the value begins with a slash, it is used as the directory for the Unix domain socket. The default is taken from the PGHOST environment variable, if set, else a Unix domain socket connection is attempted.

-p *port*
--port=*port*

> Specifies the TCP port or local Unix domain socket file extension on which the server is listening for connections. Defaults to the PGPORT environment variable, if set, or a compiled-in default.

-U *user*
--username=*user*

> User name to connect as. Defaults to current operating system user name.

-w
--no-password

> Never issue a password prompt. If the server requires password authentication and a password is not available by other means such as a .pgpass file, the connection attempt will fail. This option can be useful in batch jobs and scripts where no user is present to enter a password.

-W
--password

> Force pg_recvlogical to prompt for a password before connecting to a database.

> This option is never essential, since pg_recvlogical will automatically prompt for a password if the server demands password authentication. However, pg_recvlogical will waste a connection attempt finding out that the server wants a password. In some cases it is worth typing -W to avoid the extra connection attempt.

The following additional options are available:

```
-V
--version
```

Print the pg_recvlogical version and exit.

```
-?
--help
```

Show help about pg_recvlogical command line arguments, and exit.

Environment

This utility, like most other PostgreSQL utilities, uses the environment variables supported by libpq (see Section 34.14).

Notes

pg_recvlogical will preserve group permissions on the received WAL files if group permissions are enabled on the source cluster.

Examples

See Section 49.1 for an example.

See Also

pg_receivewal

pg_restore

pg_restore — restore a PostgreSQL database from an archive file created by pg_dump

Synopsis

pg_restore [*connection-option*...] [*option*...] [*filename*]

Description

pg_restore is a utility for restoring a PostgreSQL database from an archive created by pg_dump in one of the non-plain-text formats. It will issue the commands necessary to reconstruct the database to the state it was in at the time it was saved. The archive files also allow pg_restore to be selective about what is restored, or even to reorder the items prior to being restored. The archive files are designed to be portable across architectures.

pg_restore can operate in two modes. If a database name is specified, pg_restore connects to that database and restores archive contents directly into the database. Otherwise, a script containing the SQL commands necessary to rebuild the database is created and written to a file or standard output. This script output is equivalent to the plain text output format of pg_dump. Some of the options controlling the output are therefore analogous to pg_dump options.

Obviously, pg_restore cannot restore information that is not present in the archive file. For instance, if the archive was made using the "dump data as INSERT commands" option, pg_restore will not be able to load the data using COPY statements.

Options

pg_restore accepts the following command line arguments.

filename

> Specifies the location of the archive file (or directory, for a directory-format archive) to be restored. If not specified, the standard input is used.

-a
--data-only

> Restore only the data, not the schema (data definitions). Table data, large objects, and sequence values are restored, if present in the archive.
>
> This option is similar to, but for historical reasons not identical to, specifying --section=data.

-c
--clean

> Clean (drop) database objects before recreating them. (Unless --if-exists is used, this might generate some harmless error messages, if any objects were not present in the destination database.)

-C
--create

> Create the database before restoring into it. If --clean is also specified, drop and recreate the target database before connecting to it.

With --create, pg_restore also restores the database's comment if any, and any configuration variable settings that are specific to this database, that is, any ALTER DATABASE ... SET ... and ALTER ROLE ... IN DATABASE ... SET ... commands that mention this database. Access privileges for the database itself are also restored, unless --no-acl is specified.

When this option is used, the database named with -d is used only to issue the initial DROP DATABASE and CREATE DATABASE commands. All data is restored into the database name that appears in the archive.

-d dbname
--dbname=dbname

Connect to database dbname and restore directly into the database.

-e
--exit-on-error

Exit if an error is encountered while sending SQL commands to the database. The default is to continue and to display a count of errors at the end of the restoration.

-f filename
--file=filename

Specify output file for generated script, or for the listing when used with -l. Default is the standard output.

-F format
--format=format

Specify format of the archive. It is not necessary to specify the format, since pg_restore will determine the format automatically. If specified, it can be one of the following:

c
custom

The archive is in the custom format of pg_dump.

d
directory

The archive is a directory archive.

t
tar

The archive is a tar archive.

-I index
--index=index

Restore definition of named index only. Multiple indexes may be specified with multiple -I switches.

-j number-of-jobs
--jobs=number-of-jobs

Run the most time-consuming parts of pg_restore — those which load data, create indexes, or create constraints — using multiple concurrent jobs. This option can dramatically reduce the time to restore a large database to a server running on a multiprocessor machine.

Each job is one process or one thread, depending on the operating system, and uses a separate connection to the server.

The optimal value for this option depends on the hardware setup of the server, of the client, and of the network. Factors include the number of CPU cores and the disk setup. A good place to start is the number of CPU cores on the server, but values larger than that can also lead to faster restore times in many cases. Of course, values that are too high will lead to decreased performance because of thrashing.

Only the custom and directory archive formats are supported with this option. The input must be a regular file or directory (not, for example, a pipe). This option is ignored when emitting a script rather than connecting directly to a database server. Also, multiple jobs cannot be used together with the option `--single-transaction`.

`-l`
`--list`

> List the table of contents of the archive. The output of this operation can be used as input to the `-L` option. Note that if filtering switches such as `-n` or `-t` are used with `-l`, they will restrict the items listed.

`-L` *list-file*
`--use-list=`*list-file*

> Restore only those archive elements that are listed in *list-file*, and restore them in the order they appear in the file. Note that if filtering switches such as `-n` or `-t` are used with `-L`, they will further restrict the items restored.
>
> *list-file* is normally created by editing the output of a previous `-l` operation. Lines can be moved or removed, and can also be commented out by placing a semicolon (`;`) at the start of the line. See below for examples.

`-n` *schema*
`--schema=`*schema*

> Restore only objects that are in the named schema. Multiple schemas may be specified with multiple `-n` switches. This can be combined with the `-t` option to restore just a specific table.

`-N` *schema*
`--exclude-schema=`*schema*

> Do not restore objects that are in the named schema. Multiple schemas to be excluded may be specified with multiple `-N` switches.
>
> When both `-n` and `-N` are given for the same schema name, the `-N` switch wins and the schema is excluded.

`-O`
`--no-owner`

> Do not output commands to set ownership of objects to match the original database. By default, pg_restore issues `ALTER OWNER` or `SET SESSION AUTHORIZATION` statements to set ownership of created schema elements. These statements will fail unless the initial connection to the database is made by a superuser (or the same user that owns all of the objects in the script). With `-O`, any user name can be used for the initial connection, and this user will own all the created objects.

-P *function-name(argtype [, ...])*
--function=*function-name(argtype [, ...])*

> Restore the named function only. Be careful to spell the function name and arguments exactly as they appear in the dump file's table of contents. Multiple functions may be specified with multiple -P switches.

-R
--no-reconnect

> This option is obsolete but still accepted for backwards compatibility.

-s
--schema-only

> Restore only the schema (data definitions), not data, to the extent that schema entries are present in the archive.

> This option is the inverse of --data-only. It is similar to, but for historical reasons not identical to, specifying --section=pre-data --section=post-data.

> (Do not confuse this with the --schema option, which uses the word "schema" in a different meaning.)

-S *username*
--superuser=*username*

> Specify the superuser user name to use when disabling triggers. This is relevant only if --disable-triggers is used.

-t *table*
--table=*table*

> Restore definition and/or data of only the named table. For this purpose, "table" includes views, materialized views, sequences, and foreign tables. Multiple tables can be selected by writing multiple -t switches. This option can be combined with the -n option to specify table(s) in a particular schema.

Note

When -t is specified, pg_restore makes no attempt to restore any other database objects that the selected table(s) might depend upon. Therefore, there is no guarantee that a specific-table restore into a clean database will succeed.

Note

This flag does not behave identically to the -t flag of pg_dump. There is not currently any provision for wild-card matching in pg_restore, nor can you include a schema name within its -t. And, while pg_dump's -t flag will also dump subsidiary objects (such as indexes) of the selected table(s), pg_restore's -t flag does not include such subsidiary objects.

> **Note**
>
> In versions prior to PostgreSQL 9.6, this flag matched only tables, not any other type of relation.

`-T trigger`
`--trigger=trigger`

Restore named trigger only. Multiple triggers may be specified with multiple `-T` switches.

`-v`
`--verbose`

Specifies verbose mode.

`-V`
`--version`

Print the pg_restore version and exit.

`-x`
`--no-privileges`
`--no-acl`

Prevent restoration of access privileges (grant/revoke commands).

`-1`
`--single-transaction`

Execute the restore as a single transaction (that is, wrap the emitted commands in `BEGIN/COMMIT`). This ensures that either all the commands complete successfully, or no changes are applied. This option implies `--exit-on-error`.

`--disable-triggers`

This option is relevant only when performing a data-only restore. It instructs pg_restore to execute commands to temporarily disable triggers on the target tables while the data is reloaded. Use this if you have referential integrity checks or other triggers on the tables that you do not want to invoke during data reload.

Presently, the commands emitted for `--disable-triggers` must be done as superuser. So you should also specify a superuser name with `-S` or, preferably, run pg_restore as a PostgreSQL superuser.

`--enable-row-security`

This option is relevant only when restoring the contents of a table which has row security. By default, pg_restore will set row_security to off, to ensure that all data is restored in to the table. If the user does not have sufficient privileges to bypass row security, then an error is thrown. This parameter instructs pg_restore to set row_security to on instead, allowing the user to attempt to restore the contents of the table with row security enabled. This might still fail if the user does not have the right to insert the rows from the dump into the table.

Note that this option currently also requires the dump be in `INSERT` format, as `COPY FROM` does not support row security.

--if-exists

Use conditional commands (i.e. add an `IF EXISTS` clause) to drop database objects. This option is not valid unless `--clean` is also specified.

--no-comments

Do not output commands to restore comments, even if the archive contains them.

--no-data-for-failed-tables

By default, table data is restored even if the creation command for the table failed (e.g., because it already exists). With this option, data for such a table is skipped. This behavior is useful if the target database already contains the desired table contents. For example, auxiliary tables for PostgreSQL extensions such as PostGIS might already be loaded in the target database; specifying this option prevents duplicate or obsolete data from being loaded into them.

This option is effective only when restoring directly into a database, not when producing SQL script output.

--no-publications

Do not output commands to restore publications, even if the archive contains them.

--no-security-labels

Do not output commands to restore security labels, even if the archive contains them.

--no-subscriptions

Do not output commands to restore subscriptions, even if the archive contains them.

--no-tablespaces

Do not output commands to select tablespaces. With this option, all objects will be created in whichever tablespace is the default during restore.

--section=*sectionname*

Only restore the named section. The section name can be `pre-data`, `data`, or `post-data`. This option can be specified more than once to select multiple sections. The default is to restore all sections.

The data section contains actual table data as well as large-object definitions. Post-data items consist of definitions of indexes, triggers, rules and constraints other than validated check constraints. Pre-data items consist of all other data definition items.

--strict-names

Require that each schema (`-n`/`--schema`) and table (`-t`/`--table`) qualifier match at least one schema/table in the backup file.

--use-set-session-authorization

Output SQL-standard `SET SESSION AUTHORIZATION` commands instead of `ALTER OWNER` commands to determine object ownership. This makes the dump more standards-compatible, but depending on the history of the objects in the dump, might not restore properly.

-?
--help

    Show help about pg_restore command line arguments, and exit.

pg_restore also accepts the following command line arguments for connection parameters:

-h *host*
--host=*host*

    Specifies the host name of the machine on which the server is running. If the value begins with a slash, it is used as the directory for the Unix domain socket. The default is taken from the PGHOST environment variable, if set, else a Unix domain socket connection is attempted.

-p *port*
--port=*port*

    Specifies the TCP port or local Unix domain socket file extension on which the server is listening for connections. Defaults to the PGPORT environment variable, if set, or a compiled-in default.

-U *username*
--username=*username*

    User name to connect as.

-w
--no-password

    Never issue a password prompt. If the server requires password authentication and a password is not available by other means such as a .pgpass file, the connection attempt will fail. This option can be useful in batch jobs and scripts where no user is present to enter a password.

-W
--password

    Force pg_restore to prompt for a password before connecting to a database.

    This option is never essential, since pg_restore will automatically prompt for a password if the server demands password authentication. However, pg_restore will waste a connection attempt finding out that the server wants a password. In some cases it is worth typing -W to avoid the extra connection attempt.

--role=*rolename*

    Specifies a role name to be used to perform the restore. This option causes pg_restore to issue a SET ROLE *rolename* command after connecting to the database. It is useful when the authenticated user (specified by -U) lacks privileges needed by pg_restore, but can switch to a role with the required rights. Some installations have a policy against logging in directly as a superuser, and use of this option allows restores to be performed without violating the policy.

Environment

PGHOST
PGOPTIONS
PGPORT
PGUSER

    Default connection parameters

This utility, like most other PostgreSQL utilities, also uses the environment variables supported by libpq (see Section 34.14). However, it does not read `PGDATABASE` when a database name is not supplied.

Diagnostics

When a direct database connection is specified using the `-d` option, pg_restore internally executes SQL statements. If you have problems running pg_restore, make sure you are able to select information from the database using, for example, psql. Also, any default connection settings and environment variables used by the libpq front-end library will apply.

Notes

If your installation has any local additions to the `template1` database, be careful to load the output of pg_restore into a truly empty database; otherwise you are likely to get errors due to duplicate definitions of the added objects. To make an empty database without any local additions, copy from `template0` not `template1`, for example:

```
CREATE DATABASE foo WITH TEMPLATE template0;
```

The limitations of pg_restore are detailed below.

- When restoring data to a pre-existing table and the option `--disable-triggers` is used, pg_restore emits commands to disable triggers on user tables before inserting the data, then emits commands to re-enable them after the data has been inserted. If the restore is stopped in the middle, the system catalogs might be left in the wrong state.

- pg_restore cannot restore large objects selectively; for instance, only those for a specific table. If an archive contains large objects, then all large objects will be restored, or none of them if they are excluded via `-L`, `-t`, or other options.

See also the pg_dump documentation for details on limitations of pg_dump.

Once restored, it is wise to run `ANALYZE` on each restored table so the optimizer has useful statistics; see Section 24.1.3 and Section 24.1.6 for more information.

Examples

Assume we have dumped a database called `mydb` into a custom-format dump file:

```
$ pg_dump -Fc mydb > db.dump
```

To drop the database and recreate it from the dump:

```
$ dropdb mydb
$ pg_restore -C -d postgres db.dump
```

The database named in the `-d` switch can be any database existing in the cluster; pg_restore only uses it to issue the `CREATE DATABASE` command for `mydb`. With `-C`, data is always restored into the database name that appears in the dump file.

To reload the dump into a new database called `newdb`:

```
$ createdb -T template0 newdb
$ pg_restore -d newdb db.dump
```

Notice we don't use -C, and instead connect directly to the database to be restored into. Also note that we clone the new database from template0 not template1, to ensure it is initially empty.

To reorder database items, it is first necessary to dump the table of contents of the archive:

```
$ pg_restore -l db.dump > db.list
```

The listing file consists of a header and one line for each item, e.g.:

```
;
; Archive created at Mon Sep 14 13:55:39 2009
;     dbname: DBDEMOS
;     TOC Entries: 81
;     Compression: 9
;     Dump Version: 1.10-0
;     Format: CUSTOM
;     Integer: 4 bytes
;     Offset: 8 bytes
;     Dumped from database version: 8.3.5
;     Dumped by pg_dump version: 8.3.8
;
;
; Selected TOC Entries:
;
3; 2615 2200 SCHEMA - public pasha
1861; 0 0 COMMENT - SCHEMA public pasha
1862; 0 0 ACL - public pasha
317; 1247 17715 TYPE public composite pasha
319; 1247 25899 DOMAIN public domain0 pasha
```

Semicolons start a comment, and the numbers at the start of lines refer to the internal archive ID assigned to each item.

Lines in the file can be commented out, deleted, and reordered. For example:

```
10; 145433 TABLE map_resolutions postgres
;2; 145344 TABLE species postgres
;4; 145359 TABLE nt_header postgres
6; 145402 TABLE species_records postgres
;8; 145416 TABLE ss_old postgres
```

could be used as input to pg_restore and would only restore items 10 and 6, in that order:

```
$ pg_restore -L db.list db.dump
```

See Also

pg_dump, pg_dumpall, psql

psql

psql — PostgreSQL interactive terminal

Synopsis

psql [*option*...] [*dbname* [*username*]]

Description

psql is a terminal-based front-end to PostgreSQL. It enables you to type in queries interactively, issue them to PostgreSQL, and see the query results. Alternatively, input can be from a file or from command line arguments. In addition, psql provides a number of meta-commands and various shell-like features to facilitate writing scripts and automating a wide variety of tasks.

Options

-a
--echo-all

> Print all nonempty input lines to standard output as they are read. (This does not apply to lines read interactively.) This is equivalent to setting the variable ECHO to all.

-A
--no-align

> Switches to unaligned output mode. (The default output mode is otherwise aligned.) This is equivalent to \pset format unaligned.

-b
--echo-errors

> Print failed SQL commands to standard error output. This is equivalent to setting the variable ECHO to errors.

-c *command*
--command=*command*

> Specifies that psql is to execute the given command string, *command*. This option can be repeated and combined in any order with the -f option. When either -c or -f is specified, psql does not read commands from standard input; instead it terminates after processing all the -c and -f options in sequence.

> *command* must be either a command string that is completely parsable by the server (i.e., it contains no psql-specific features), or a single backslash command. Thus you cannot mix SQL and psql meta-commands within a -c option. To achieve that, you could use repeated -c options or pipe the string into psql, for example:

```
psql -c '\x' -c 'SELECT * FROM foo;'
```

> or

```
echo '\x \\ SELECT * FROM foo;' | psql
```

(\\ is the separator meta-command.)

Each SQL command string passed to -c is sent to the server as a single request. Because of this, the server executes it as a single transaction even if the string contains multiple SQL commands, unless there are explicit BEGIN/COMMIT commands included in the string to divide it into multiple transactions. (See Section 53.2.2.1 for more details about how the server handles multi-query strings.) Also, psql only prints the result of the last SQL command in the string. This is different from the behavior when the same string is read from a file or fed to psql's standard input, because then psql sends each SQL command separately.

Because of this behavior, putting more than one SQL command in a single -c string often has unexpected results. It's better to use repeated -c commands or feed multiple commands to psql's standard input, either using echo as illustrated above, or via a shell here-document, for example:

```
psql <<EOF
\x
SELECT * FROM foo;
EOF
```

-d *dbname*
--dbname=*dbname*

Specifies the name of the database to connect to. This is equivalent to specifying *dbname* as the first non-option argument on the command line.

If this parameter contains an = sign or starts with a valid URI prefix (postgresql:// or postgres://), it is treated as a *conninfo* string. See Section 34.1.1 for more information.

-e
--echo-queries

Copy all SQL commands sent to the server to standard output as well. This is equivalent to setting the variable ECHO to queries.

-E
--echo-hidden

Echo the actual queries generated by \d and other backslash commands. You can use this to study psql's internal operations. This is equivalent to setting the variable ECHO_HIDDEN to on.

-f *filename*
--file=*filename*

Read commands from the file *filename*, rather than standard input. This option can be repeated and combined in any order with the -c option. When either -c or -f is specified, psql does not read commands from standard input; instead it terminates after processing all the -c and -f options in sequence. Except for that, this option is largely equivalent to the meta-command \i.

If *filename* is - (hyphen), then standard input is read until an EOF indication or \q meta-command. This can be used to intersperse interactive input with input from files. Note however that Readline is not used in this case (much as if -n had been specified).

Using this option is subtly different from writing `psql < ` *`filename`*. In general, both will do what you expect, but using `-f` enables some nice features such as error messages with line numbers. There is also a slight chance that using this option will reduce the start-up overhead. On the other hand, the variant using the shell's input redirection is (in theory) guaranteed to yield exactly the same output you would have received had you entered everything by hand.

`-F` *`separator`*
`--field-separator=`*`separator`*

Use *`separator`* as the field separator for unaligned output. This is equivalent to `\pset fieldsep` or `\f`.

`-h` *`hostname`*
`--host=`*`hostname`*

Specifies the host name of the machine on which the server is running. If the value begins with a slash, it is used as the directory for the Unix-domain socket.

`-H`
`--html`

Turn on HTML tabular output. This is equivalent to `\pset format html` or the `\H` command.

`-l`
`--list`

List all available databases, then exit. Other non-connection options are ignored. This is similar to the meta-command `\list`.

When this option is used, psql will connect to the database `postgres`, unless a different database is named on the command line (option `-d` or non-option argument, possibly via a service entry, but not via an environment variable).

`-L` *`filename`*
`--log-file=`*`filename`*

Write all query output into file *`filename`*, in addition to the normal output destination.

`-n`
`--no-readline`

Do not use Readline for line editing and do not use the command history. This can be useful to turn off tab expansion when cutting and pasting.

`-o` *`filename`*
`--output=`*`filename`*

Put all query output into file *`filename`*. This is equivalent to the command `\o`.

`-p` *`port`*
`--port=`*`port`*

Specifies the TCP port or the local Unix-domain socket file extension on which the server is listening for connections. Defaults to the value of the `PGPORT` environment variable or, if not set, to the port specified at compile time, usually 5432.

-P *assignment*
--pset=*assignment*

> Specifies printing options, in the style of \pset. Note that here you have to separate name and value with an equal sign instead of a space. For example, to set the output format to LaTeX, you could write -P format=latex.

-q
--quiet

> Specifies that psql should do its work quietly. By default, it prints welcome messages and various informational output. If this option is used, none of this happens. This is useful with the **-c** option. This is equivalent to setting the variable QUIET to on.

-R *separator*
--record-separator=*separator*

> Use *separator* as the record separator for unaligned output. This is equivalent to \pset recordsep.

-s
--single-step

> Run in single-step mode. That means the user is prompted before each command is sent to the server, with the option to cancel execution as well. Use this to debug scripts.

-S
--single-line

> Runs in single-line mode where a newline terminates an SQL command, as a semicolon does.

Note

This mode is provided for those who insist on it, but you are not necessarily encouraged to use it. In particular, if you mix SQL and meta-commands on a line the order of execution might not always be clear to the inexperienced user.

-t
--tuples-only

> Turn off printing of column names and result row count footers, etc. This is equivalent to \t or \pset tuples_only.

-T *table_options*
--table-attr=*table_options*

> Specifies options to be placed within the HTML table tag. See \pset tableattr for details.

-U *username*
--username=*username*

> Connect to the database as the user *username* instead of the default. (You must have permission to do so, of course.)

```
-v assignment
--set=assignment
--variable=assignment
```

Perform a variable assignment, like the `\set` meta-command. Note that you must separate name and value, if any, by an equal sign on the command line. To unset a variable, leave off the equal sign. To set a variable with an empty value, use the equal sign but leave off the value. These assignments are done during command line processing, so variables that reflect connection state will get overwritten later.

```
-V
--version
```

Print the psql version and exit.

```
-w
--no-password
```

Never issue a password prompt. If the server requires password authentication and a password is not available by other means such as a `.pgpass` file, the connection attempt will fail. This option can be useful in batch jobs and scripts where no user is present to enter a password.

Note that this option will remain set for the entire session, and so it affects uses of the meta-command `\connect` as well as the initial connection attempt.

```
-W
--password
```

Force psql to prompt for a password before connecting to a database.

This option is never essential, since psql will automatically prompt for a password if the server demands password authentication. However, psql will waste a connection attempt finding out that the server wants a password. In some cases it is worth typing `-W` to avoid the extra connection attempt.

Note that this option will remain set for the entire session, and so it affects uses of the meta-command `\connect` as well as the initial connection attempt.

```
-x
--expanded
```

Turn on the expanded table formatting mode. This is equivalent to `\x` or `\pset expanded`.

```
-X,
--no-psqlrc
```

Do not read the start-up file (neither the system-wide `psqlrc` file nor the user's `~/.psqlrc` file).

```
-z
--field-separator-zero
```

Set the field separator for unaligned output to a zero byte. This is equivalent to `\pset field-sep_zero`.

```
-0
--record-separator-zero
```

Set the record separator for unaligned output to a zero byte. This is useful for interfacing, for example, with `xargs -0`. This is equivalent to `\pset recordsep_zero`.

```
-1
--single-transaction
```

> This option can only be used in combination with one or more -c and/or -f options. It causes psql to issue a BEGIN command before the first such option and a COMMIT command after the last one, thereby wrapping all the commands into a single transaction. This ensures that either all the commands complete successfully, or no changes are applied.
>
> If the commands themselves contain BEGIN, COMMIT, or ROLLBACK, this option will not have the desired effects. Also, if an individual command cannot be executed inside a transaction block, specifying this option will cause the whole transaction to fail.

```
-?
--help[=topic]
```

> Show help about psql and exit. The optional *topic* parameter (defaulting to options) selects which part of psql is explained: commands describes psql's backslash commands; options describes the command-line options that can be passed to psql; and variables shows help about psql configuration variables.

Exit Status

psql returns 0 to the shell if it finished normally, 1 if a fatal error of its own occurs (e.g. out of memory, file not found), 2 if the connection to the server went bad and the session was not interactive, and 3 if an error occurred in a script and the variable ON_ERROR_STOP was set.

Usage

Connecting to a Database

psql is a regular PostgreSQL client application. In order to connect to a database you need to know the name of your target database, the host name and port number of the server, and what user name you want to connect as. psql can be told about those parameters via command line options, namely -d, -h, -p, and -U respectively. If an argument is found that does not belong to any option it will be interpreted as the database name (or the user name, if the database name is already given). Not all of these options are required; there are useful defaults. If you omit the host name, psql will connect via a Unix-domain socket to a server on the local host, or via TCP/IP to localhost on machines that don't have Unix-domain sockets. The default port number is determined at compile time. Since the database server uses the same default, you will not have to specify the port in most cases. The default user name is your operating-system user name, as is the default database name. Note that you cannot just connect to any database under any user name. Your database administrator should have informed you about your access rights.

When the defaults aren't quite right, you can save yourself some typing by setting the environment variables PGDATABASE, PGHOST, PGPORT and/or PGUSER to appropriate values. (For additional environment variables, see Section 34.14.) It is also convenient to have a ~/.pgpass file to avoid regularly having to type in passwords. See Section 34.15 for more information.

An alternative way to specify connection parameters is in a *conninfo* string or a URI, which is used instead of a database name. This mechanism give you very wide control over the connection. For example:

```
$ psql "service=myservice sslmode=require"
$ psql postgresql://dbmaster:5433/mydb?sslmode=require
```

This way you can also use LDAP for connection parameter lookup as described in Section 34.17. See Section 34.1.2 for more information on all the available connection options.

If the connection could not be made for any reason (e.g., insufficient privileges, server is not running on the targeted host, etc.), psql will return an error and terminate.

If both standard input and standard output are a terminal, then psql sets the client encoding to "auto", which will detect the appropriate client encoding from the locale settings (`LC_CTYPE` environment variable on Unix systems). If this doesn't work out as expected, the client encoding can be overridden using the environment variable `PGCLIENTENCODING`.

Entering SQL Commands

In normal operation, psql provides a prompt with the name of the database to which psql is currently connected, followed by the string `=>`. For example:

```
$ psql testdb
psql (11.2)
Type "help" for help.

testdb=>
```

At the prompt, the user can type in SQL commands. Ordinarily, input lines are sent to the server when a command-terminating semicolon is reached. An end of line does not terminate a command. Thus commands can be spread over several lines for clarity. If the command was sent and executed without error, the results of the command are displayed on the screen.

If untrusted users have access to a database that has not adopted a secure schema usage pattern, begin your session by removing publicly-writable schemas from `search_path`. One can add `options=-csearch_path=` to the connection string or issue `SELECT pg_catalog.set_config('search_path', '', false)` before other SQL commands. This consideration is not specific to psql; it applies to every interface for executing arbitrary SQL commands.

Whenever a command is executed, psql also polls for asynchronous notification events generated by LISTEN and NOTIFY.

While C-style block comments are passed to the server for processing and removal, SQL-standard comments are removed by psql.

Meta-Commands

Anything you enter in psql that begins with an unquoted backslash is a psql meta-command that is processed by psql itself. These commands make psql more useful for administration or scripting. Meta-commands are often called slash or backslash commands.

The format of a psql command is the backslash, followed immediately by a command verb, then any arguments. The arguments are separated from the command verb and each other by any number of whitespace characters.

To include whitespace in an argument you can quote it with single quotes. To include a single quote in an argument, write two single quotes within single-quoted text. Anything contained in single quotes is furthermore subject to C-like substitutions for \n (new line), \t (tab), \b (backspace), \r (carriage return), \f (form feed), \\digits (octal), and \\xdigits (hexadecimal). A backslash preceding any other character within single-quoted text quotes that single character, whatever it is.

If an unquoted colon (:) followed by a psql variable name appears within an argument, it is replaced by the variable's value, as described in SQL Interpolation. The forms :'*variable_name*' and :"*variable_name*" described there work as well. The :{?*variable_name*} syntax allows testing whether a variable is defined. It is substituted by TRUE or FALSE. Escaping the colon with a backslash protects it from substitution.

Within an argument, text that is enclosed in backquotes (`) is taken as a command line that is passed to the shell. The output of the command (with any trailing newline removed) replaces the backquoted text. Within the text enclosed in backquotes, no special quoting or other processing occurs, except that appearances of :*variable_name* where *variable_name* is a psql variable name are replaced by the variable's value. Also, appearances of :'*variable_name*' are replaced by the variable's value suitably quoted to become a single shell command argument. (The latter form is almost always preferable, unless you are very sure of what is in the variable.) Because carriage return and line feed characters cannot be safely quoted on all platforms, the :'*variable_name*' form prints an error message and does not substitute the variable value when such characters appear in the value.

Some commands take an SQL identifier (such as a table name) as argument. These arguments follow the syntax rules of SQL: Unquoted letters are forced to lowercase, while double quotes (") protect letters from case conversion and allow incorporation of whitespace into the identifier. Within double quotes, paired double quotes reduce to a single double quote in the resulting name. For example, FOO"BAR"BAZ is interpreted as fooBARbaz, and "A weird"" name" becomes A weird" name.

Parsing for arguments stops at the end of the line, or when another unquoted backslash is found. An unquoted backslash is taken as the beginning of a new meta-command. The special sequence \\ (two backslashes) marks the end of arguments and continues parsing SQL commands, if any. That way SQL and psql commands can be freely mixed on a line. But in any case, the arguments of a meta-command cannot continue beyond the end of the line.

Many of the meta-commands act on the *current query buffer*. This is simply a buffer holding whatever SQL command text has been typed but not yet sent to the server for execution. This will include previous input lines as well as any text appearing before the meta-command on the same line.

The following meta-commands are defined:

\a

> If the current table output format is unaligned, it is switched to aligned. If it is not unaligned, it is set to unaligned. This command is kept for backwards compatibility. See \pset for a more general solution.

\c or \connect [-reuse-previous=*on*/*off*] [*dbname* [*username*] [*host*] [*port*] | *conninfo*]

> Establishes a new connection to a PostgreSQL server. The connection parameters to use can be specified either using a positional syntax, or using *conninfo* connection strings as detailed in Section 34.1.1.

> Where the command omits database name, user, host, or port, the new connection can reuse values from the previous connection. By default, values from the previous connection are reused except when processing a *conninfo* string. Passing a first argument of -reuse-previous=on or -reuse-previous=off overrides that default. When the command neither specifies nor reuses a particular parameter, the libpq default is used. Specifying any of *dbname*, *username*, *host* or *port* as - is equivalent to omitting that parameter.

> If the new connection is successfully made, the previous connection is closed. If the connection attempt failed (wrong user name, access denied, etc.), the previous connection will only be kept if psql

is in interactive mode. When executing a non-interactive script, processing will immediately stop with an error. This distinction was chosen as a user convenience against typos on the one hand, and a safety mechanism that scripts are not accidentally acting on the wrong database on the other hand.

Examples:

```
=> \c mydb myuser host.dom 6432
=> \c service=foo
=> \c "host=localhost port=5432 dbname=mydb connect_timeout=10
 sslmode=disable"
=> \c postgresql://tom@localhost/mydb?application_name=myapp
```

\C [*title*]

Sets the title of any tables being printed as the result of a query or unset any such title. This command is equivalent to `\pset title` *title*. (The name of this command derives from "caption", as it was previously only used to set the caption in an HTML table.)

\cd [*directory*]

Changes the current working directory to *directory*. Without argument, changes to the current user's home directory.

> # Tip
>
> To print your current working directory, use `\! pwd`.

\conninfo

Outputs information about the current database connection.

\copy { *table* [(*column_list*)] | (*query*) } { from | to } { *'filename'* | program *'command'* | stdin | stdout | pstdin | pstdout } [[with] (*option* [, ...])]

Performs a frontend (client) copy. This is an operation that runs an SQL COPY command, but instead of the server reading or writing the specified file, psql reads or writes the file and routes the data between the server and the local file system. This means that file accessibility and privileges are those of the local user, not the server, and no SQL superuser privileges are required.

When `program` is specified, *command* is executed by psql and the data passed from or to *command* is routed between the server and the client. Again, the execution privileges are those of the local user, not the server, and no SQL superuser privileges are required.

For `\copy ... from stdin`, data rows are read from the same source that issued the command, continuing until `\.` is read or the stream reaches EOF. This option is useful for populating tables in-line within a SQL script file. For `\copy ... to stdout`, output is sent to the same place as psql command output, and the `COPY count` command status is not printed (since it might be confused with a data row). To read/write psql's standard input or output regardless of the current command source or `\o` option, write `from pstdin` or `to pstdout`.

The syntax of this command is similar to that of the SQL COPY command. All options other than the data source/destination are as specified for COPY. Because of this, special parsing rules apply to the `\copy` meta-command. Unlike most other meta-commands, the entire remainder of the line is always taken to be the arguments of \copy, and neither variable interpolation nor backquote expansion are performed in the arguments.

Tip

Another way to obtain the same result as \copy ... to is to use the SQL COPY ... TO STDOUT command and terminate it with \g *filename* or \g |*program*. Unlike \copy, this method allows the command to span multiple lines; also, variable interpolation and backquote expansion can be used.

Tip

These operations are not as efficient as the SQL COPY command with a file or program data source or destination, because all data must pass through the client/server connection. For large amounts of data the SQL command might be preferable.

\copyright

Shows the copyright and distribution terms of PostgreSQL.

\crosstabview [*colV* [*colH* [*colD* [*sortcolH*]]]]

Executes the current query buffer (like \g) and shows the results in a crosstab grid. The query must return at least three columns. The output column identified by *colV* becomes a vertical header and the output column identified by *colH* becomes a horizontal header. *colD* identifies the output column to display within the grid. *sortcolH* identifies an optional sort column for the horizontal header.

Each column specification can be a column number (starting at 1) or a column name. The usual SQL case folding and quoting rules apply to column names. If omitted, *colV* is taken as column 1 and *colH* as column 2. *colH* must differ from *colV*. If *colD* is not specified, then there must be exactly three columns in the query result, and the column that is neither *colV* nor *colH* is taken to be *colD*.

The vertical header, displayed as the leftmost column, contains the values found in column *colV*, in the same order as in the query results, but with duplicates removed.

The horizontal header, displayed as the first row, contains the values found in column *colH*, with duplicates removed. By default, these appear in the same order as in the query results. But if the optional *sortcolH* argument is given, it identifies a column whose values must be integer numbers, and the values from *colH* will appear in the horizontal header sorted according to the corresponding *sortcolH* values.

Inside the crosstab grid, for each distinct value x of *colH* and each distinct value y of *colV*, the cell located at the intersection (x,y) contains the value of the colD column in the query result row for which the value of *colH* is x and the value of *colV* is y. If there is no such row, the cell is empty. If there are multiple such rows, an error is reported.

\d[S+] [*pattern*]

For each relation (table, view, materialized view, index, sequence, or foreign table) or composite type matching the *pattern*, show all columns, their types, the tablespace (if not the default) and any special attributes such as NOT NULL or defaults. Associated indexes, constraints, rules, and triggers are also shown. For foreign tables, the associated foreign server is shown as well. ("Matching the pattern" is defined in Patterns below.)

For some types of relation, \d shows additional information for each column: column values for sequences, indexed expressions for indexes, and foreign data wrapper options for foreign tables.

The command form \d+ is identical, except that more information is displayed: any comments associated with the columns of the table are shown, as is the presence of OIDs in the table, the view definition if the relation is a view, a non-default replica identity setting.

By default, only user-created objects are shown; supply a pattern or the S modifier to include system objects.

Note

If \d is used without a *pattern* argument, it is equivalent to \dtvmsE which will show a list of all visible tables, views, materialized views, sequences and foreign tables. This is purely a convenience measure.

\da[S] [*pattern*]

Lists aggregate functions, together with their return type and the data types they operate on. If *pattern* is specified, only aggregates whose names match the pattern are shown. By default, only user-created objects are shown; supply a pattern or the S modifier to include system objects.

\dA[+] [*pattern*]

Lists access methods. If *pattern* is specified, only access methods whose names match the pattern are shown. If + is appended to the command name, each access method is listed with its associated handler function and description.

\db[+] [*pattern*]

Lists tablespaces. If *pattern* is specified, only tablespaces whose names match the pattern are shown. If + is appended to the command name, each tablespace is listed with its associated options, on-disk size, permissions and description.

\dc[S+] [*pattern*]

Lists conversions between character-set encodings. If *pattern* is specified, only conversions whose names match the pattern are listed. By default, only user-created objects are shown; supply a pattern or the S modifier to include system objects. If + is appended to the command name, each object is listed with its associated description.

\dC[+] [*pattern*]

Lists type casts. If *pattern* is specified, only casts whose source or target types match the pattern are listed. If + is appended to the command name, each object is listed with its associated description.

\dd[S] [*pattern*]

Shows the descriptions of objects of type constraint, operator class, operator family, rule, and trigger. All other comments may be viewed by the respective backslash commands for those object types.

\dd displays descriptions for objects matching the *pattern*, or of visible objects of the appropriate type if no argument is given. But in either case, only objects that have a description are listed. By default, only user-created objects are shown; supply a pattern or the S modifier to include system objects.

Descriptions for objects can be created with the COMMENT SQL command.

`\dD[S+] [ pattern ]`

Lists domains. If *pattern* is specified, only domains whose names match the pattern are shown. By default, only user-created objects are shown; supply a pattern or the S modifier to include system objects. If + is appended to the command name, each object is listed with its associated permissions and description.

`\ddp [ pattern ]`

Lists default access privilege settings. An entry is shown for each role (and schema, if applicable) for which the default privilege settings have been changed from the built-in defaults. If *pattern* is specified, only entries whose role name or schema name matches the pattern are listed.

The ALTER DEFAULT PRIVILEGES command is used to set default access privileges. The meaning of the privilege display is explained under GRANT.

`\dE[S+] [ pattern ]`
`\di[S+] [ pattern ]`
`\dm[S+] [ pattern ]`
`\ds[S+] [ pattern ]`
`\dt[S+] [ pattern ]`
`\dv[S+] [ pattern ]`

In this group of commands, the letters E, i, m, s, t, and v stand for foreign table, index, materialized view, sequence, table, and view, respectively. You can specify any or all of these letters, in any order, to obtain a listing of objects of these types. For example, `\dit` lists indexes and tables. If + is appended to the command name, each object is listed with its physical size on disk and its associated description, if any. If *pattern* is specified, only objects whose names match the pattern are listed. By default, only user-created objects are shown; supply a pattern or the S modifier to include system objects.

`\des[+] [ pattern ]`

Lists foreign servers (mnemonic: "external servers"). If *pattern* is specified, only those servers whose name matches the pattern are listed. If the form `\des+` is used, a full description of each server is shown, including the server's ACL, type, version, options, and description.

`\det[+] [ pattern ]`

Lists foreign tables (mnemonic: "external tables"). If *pattern* is specified, only entries whose table name or schema name matches the pattern are listed. If the form `\det+` is used, generic options and the foreign table description are also displayed.

`\deu[+] [ pattern ]`

Lists user mappings (mnemonic: "external users"). If *pattern* is specified, only those mappings whose user names match the pattern are listed. If the form `\deu+` is used, additional information about each mapping is shown.

Caution

`\deu+` might also display the user name and password of the remote user, so care should be taken not to disclose them.

`\dew[+] [ `*`pattern`*` ]`

> Lists foreign-data wrappers (mnemonic: "external wrappers"). If *pattern* is specified, only those foreign-data wrappers whose name matches the pattern are listed. If the form `\dew+` is used, the ACL, options, and description of the foreign-data wrapper are also shown.

`\df[anptwS+] [ `*`pattern`*` ]`

> Lists functions, together with their result data types, argument data types, and function types, which are classified as "agg" (aggregate), "normal", "procedure", "trigger", or "window". To display only functions of specific type(s), add the corresponding letters `a`, `n`, `p`, `t`, or `w` to the command. If *pattern* is specified, only functions whose names match the pattern are shown. By default, only user-created objects are shown; supply a pattern or the `S` modifier to include system objects. If the form `\df+` is used, additional information about each function is shown, including volatility, parallel safety, owner, security classification, access privileges, language, source code and description.

> ---
> # Tip
>
> To look up functions taking arguments or returning values of a specific data type, use your pager's search capability to scroll through the `\df` output.
> ---

`\dF[+] [ `*`pattern`*` ]`

> Lists text search configurations. If *pattern* is specified, only configurations whose names match the pattern are shown. If the form `\dF+` is used, a full description of each configuration is shown, including the underlying text search parser and the dictionary list for each parser token type.

`\dFd[+] [ `*`pattern`*` ]`

> Lists text search dictionaries. If *pattern* is specified, only dictionaries whose names match the pattern are shown. If the form `\dFd+` is used, additional information is shown about each selected dictionary, including the underlying text search template and the option values.

`\dFp[+] [ `*`pattern`*` ]`

> Lists text search parsers. If *pattern* is specified, only parsers whose names match the pattern are shown. If the form `\dFp+` is used, a full description of each parser is shown, including the underlying functions and the list of recognized token types.

`\dFt[+] [ `*`pattern`*` ]`

> Lists text search templates. If *pattern* is specified, only templates whose names match the pattern are shown. If the form `\dFt+` is used, additional information is shown about each template, including the underlying function names.

`\dg[S+] [ `*`pattern`*` ]`

> Lists database roles. (Since the concepts of "users" and "groups" have been unified into "roles", this command is now equivalent to `\du`.) By default, only user-created roles are shown; supply the `S` modifier to include system roles. If *pattern* is specified, only those roles whose names match the pattern are listed. If the form `\dg+` is used, additional information is shown about each role; currently this adds the comment for each role.

`\dl`

> This is an alias for `\lo_list`, which shows a list of large objects.

`\dL[S+] [` *`pattern`* `]`

> Lists procedural languages. If *`pattern`* is specified, only languages whose names match the pattern are listed. By default, only user-created languages are shown; supply the `S` modifier to include system objects. If + is appended to the command name, each language is listed with its call handler, validator, access privileges, and whether it is a system object.

`\dn[S+] [` *`pattern`* `]`

> Lists schemas (namespaces). If *`pattern`* is specified, only schemas whose names match the pattern are listed. By default, only user-created objects are shown; supply a pattern or the `S` modifier to include system objects. If + is appended to the command name, each object is listed with its associated permissions and description, if any.

`\do[S+] [` *`pattern`* `]`

> Lists operators with their operand and result types. If *`pattern`* is specified, only operators whose names match the pattern are listed. By default, only user-created objects are shown; supply a pattern or the `S` modifier to include system objects. If + is appended to the command name, additional information about each operator is shown, currently just the name of the underlying function.

`\dO[S+] [` *`pattern`* `]`

> Lists collations. If *`pattern`* is specified, only collations whose names match the pattern are listed. By default, only user-created objects are shown; supply a pattern or the `S` modifier to include system objects. If + is appended to the command name, each collation is listed with its associated description, if any. Note that only collations usable with the current database's encoding are shown, so the results may vary in different databases of the same installation.

`\dp [` *`pattern`* `]`

> Lists tables, views and sequences with their associated access privileges. If *`pattern`* is specified, only tables, views and sequences whose names match the pattern are listed.
>
> The GRANT and REVOKE commands are used to set access privileges. The meaning of the privilege display is explained under GRANT.

`\drds [` *`role-pattern`* `[` *`database-pattern`* `] ]`

> Lists defined configuration settings. These settings can be role-specific, database-specific, or both. *`role-pattern`* and *`database-pattern`* are used to select specific roles and databases to list, respectively. If omitted, or if * is specified, all settings are listed, including those not role-specific or database-specific, respectively.
>
> The ALTER ROLE and ALTER DATABASE commands are used to define per-role and per-database configuration settings.

`\dRp[+] [` *`pattern`* `]`

> Lists replication publications. If *`pattern`* is specified, only those publications whose names match the pattern are listed. If + is appended to the command name, the tables associated with each publication are shown as well.

`\dRs[+] [` *`pattern`* `]`

> Lists replication subscriptions. If *`pattern`* is specified, only those subscriptions whose names match the pattern are listed. If + is appended to the command name, additional properties of the subscriptions are shown.

`\dT[S+] [ pattern ]`

> Lists data types. If `pattern` is specified, only types whose names match the pattern are listed. If + is appended to the command name, each type is listed with its internal name and size, its allowed values if it is an `enum` type, and its associated permissions. By default, only user-created objects are shown; supply a pattern or the S modifier to include system objects.

`\du[S+] [ pattern ]`

> Lists database roles. (Since the concepts of "users" and "groups" have been unified into "roles", this command is now equivalent to `\dg`.) By default, only user-created roles are shown; supply the S modifier to include system roles. If `pattern` is specified, only those roles whose names match the pattern are listed. If the form `\du+` is used, additional information is shown about each role; currently this adds the comment for each role.

`\dx[+] [ pattern ]`

> Lists installed extensions. If `pattern` is specified, only those extensions whose names match the pattern are listed. If the form `\dx+` is used, all the objects belonging to each matching extension are listed.

`\dy[+] [ pattern ]`

> Lists event triggers. If `pattern` is specified, only those event triggers whose names match the pattern are listed. If + is appended to the command name, each object is listed with its associated description.

`\e or \edit [ filename ] [ line_number ]`

> If `filename` is specified, the file is edited; after the editor exits, the file's content is copied into the current query buffer. If no `filename` is given, the current query buffer is copied to a temporary file which is then edited in the same fashion. Or, if the current query buffer is empty, the most recently executed query is copied to a temporary file and edited in the same fashion.

> The new contents of the query buffer are then re-parsed according to the normal rules of psql, treating the whole buffer as a single line. Any complete queries are immediately executed; that is, if the query buffer contains or ends with a semicolon, everything up to that point is executed. Whatever remains will wait in the query buffer; type semicolon or `\g` to send it, or `\r` to cancel it by clearing the query buffer. Treating the buffer as a single line primarily affects meta-commands: whatever is in the buffer after a meta-command will be taken as argument(s) to the meta-command, even if it spans multiple lines. (Thus you cannot make meta-command-using scripts this way. Use `\i` for that.)

> If a line number is specified, psql will position the cursor on the specified line of the file or query buffer. Note that if a single all-digits argument is given, psql assumes it is a line number, not a file name.

Tip

See under Environment for how to configure and customize your editor.

`\echo text [ ... ]`

> Prints the arguments to the standard output, separated by one space and followed by a newline. This can be useful to intersperse information in the output of scripts. For example:

```
=> \echo `date`
Tue Oct 26 21:40:57 CEST 1999
```

If the first argument is an unquoted −n the trailing newline is not written.

Tip

If you use the \o command to redirect your query output you might wish to use \qe-cho instead of this command.

\ef [*function_description* [*line_number*]]

This command fetches and edits the definition of the named function or procedure, in the form of a CREATE OR REPLACE FUNCTION or CREATE OR REPLACE PROCEDURE command. Editing is done in the same way as for \edit. After the editor exits, the updated command waits in the query buffer; type semicolon or \g to send it, or \r to cancel.

The target function can be specified by name alone, or by name and arguments, for example foo(integer, text). The argument types must be given if there is more than one function of the same name.

If no function is specified, a blank CREATE FUNCTION template is presented for editing.

If a line number is specified, psql will position the cursor on the specified line of the function body. (Note that the function body typically does not begin on the first line of the file.)

Unlike most other meta-commands, the entire remainder of the line is always taken to be the argument(s) of \ef, and neither variable interpolation nor backquote expansion are performed in the arguments.

Tip

See under Environment for how to configure and customize your editor.

\encoding [*encoding*]

Sets the client character set encoding. Without an argument, this command shows the current encoding.

\errverbose

Repeats the most recent server error message at maximum verbosity, as though VERBOSITY were set to verbose and SHOW_CONTEXT were set to always.

\ev [*view_name* [*line_number*]]

This command fetches and edits the definition of the named view, in the form of a CREATE OR REPLACE VIEW command. Editing is done in the same way as for \edit. After the editor exits, the updated command waits in the query buffer; type semicolon or \g to send it, or \r to cancel.

If no view is specified, a blank CREATE VIEW template is presented for editing.

If a line number is specified, psql will position the cursor on the specified line of the view definition.

Unlike most other meta-commands, the entire remainder of the line is always taken to be the argument(s) of \ev, and neither variable interpolation nor backquote expansion are performed in the arguments.

\f [*string*]

Sets the field separator for unaligned query output. The default is the vertical bar (|). It is equivalent to \pset fieldsep.

\g [*filename*]
\g [|*command*]

Sends the current query buffer to the server for execution. If an argument is given, the query's output is written to the named file or piped to the given shell command, instead of displaying it as usual. The file or command is written to only if the query successfully returns zero or more tuples, not if the query fails or is a non-data-returning SQL command.

If the current query buffer is empty, the most recently sent query is re-executed instead. Except for that behavior, \g without an argument is essentially equivalent to a semicolon. A \g with argument is a "one-shot" alternative to the \o command.

If the argument begins with | , then the entire remainder of the line is taken to be the *command* to execute, and neither variable interpolation nor backquote expansion are performed in it. The rest of the line is simply passed literally to the shell.

\gdesc

Shows the description (that is, the column names and data types) of the result of the current query buffer. The query is not actually executed; however, if it contains some type of syntax error, that error will be reported in the normal way.

If the current query buffer is empty, the most recently sent query is described instead.

\gexec

Sends the current query buffer to the server, then treats each column of each row of the query's output (if any) as a SQL statement to be executed. For example, to create an index on each column of my_table:

```
=> SELECT format('create index on my_table(%I)', attname)
-> FROM pg_attribute
-> WHERE attrelid = 'my_table'::regclass AND attnum > 0
-> ORDER BY attnum
-> \gexec
CREATE INDEX
CREATE INDEX
CREATE INDEX
CREATE INDEX
```

The generated queries are executed in the order in which the rows are returned, and left-to-right within each row if there is more than one column. NULL fields are ignored. The generated queries are sent literally to the server for processing, so they cannot be psql meta-commands nor contain psql variable references. If any individual query fails, execution of the remaining queries continues unless ON_ERROR_STOP is set. Execution of each query is subject to ECHO processing. (Setting ECHO to all or queries is often advisable when using \gexec.) Query logging, single-step mode, timing, and other query execution features apply to each generated query as well.

If the current query buffer is empty, the most recently sent query is re-executed instead.

\gset [*prefix*]

Sends the current query buffer to the server and stores the query's output into psql variables (see Variables). The query to be executed must return exactly one row. Each column of the row is stored into a separate variable, named the same as the column. For example:

```
=> SELECT 'hello' AS var1, 10 AS var2
-> \gset
=> \echo :var1 :var2
hello 10
```

If you specify a *prefix*, that string is prepended to the query's column names to create the variable names to use:

```
=> SELECT 'hello' AS var1, 10 AS var2
-> \gset result_
=> \echo :result_var1 :result_var2
hello 10
```

If a column result is NULL, the corresponding variable is unset rather than being set.

If the query fails or does not return one row, no variables are changed.

If the current query buffer is empty, the most recently sent query is re-executed instead.

\gx [*filename*]
\gx [|*command*]

\gx is equivalent to \g, but forces expanded output mode for this query. See \x.

\h or \help [*command*]

Gives syntax help on the specified SQL command. If *command* is not specified, then psql will list all the commands for which syntax help is available. If *command* is an asterisk (*), then syntax help on all SQL commands is shown.

Unlike most other meta-commands, the entire remainder of the line is always taken to be the argument(s) of \help, and neither variable interpolation nor backquote expansion are performed in the arguments.

> ### Note
>
> To simplify typing, commands that consists of several words do not have to be quoted. Thus it is fine to type **\help alter table**.

`\H` or `\html`

> Turns on HTML query output format. If the HTML format is already on, it is switched back to the default aligned text format. This command is for compatibility and convenience, but see `\pset` about setting other output options.

`\i` or `\include` *filename*

> Reads input from the file *filename* and executes it as though it had been typed on the keyboard.

> If *filename* is – (hyphen), then standard input is read until an EOF indication or `\q` meta-command. This can be used to intersperse interactive input with input from files. Note that Readline behavior will be used only if it is active at the outermost level.

> ## Note
>
> If you want to see the lines on the screen as they are read you must set the variable ECHO to `all`.

`\if` *expression*
`\elif` *expression*
`\else`
`\endif`

> This group of commands implements nestable conditional blocks. A conditional block must begin with an `\if` and end with an `\endif`. In between there may be any number of `\elif` clauses, which may optionally be followed by a single `\else` clause. Ordinary queries and other types of backslash commands may (and usually do) appear between the commands forming a conditional block.

> The `\if` and `\elif` commands read their argument(s) and evaluate them as a boolean expression. If the expression yields `true` then processing continues normally; otherwise, lines are skipped until a matching `\elif`, `\else`, or `\endif` is reached. Once an `\if` or `\elif` test has succeeded, the arguments of later `\elif` commands in the same block are not evaluated but are treated as false. Lines following an `\else` are processed only if no earlier matching `\if` or `\elif` succeeded.

> The *expression* argument of an `\if` or `\elif` command is subject to variable interpolation and backquote expansion, just like any other backslash command argument. After that it is evaluated like the value of an on/off option variable. So a valid value is any unambiguous case-insensitive match for one of: `true`, `false`, `1`, `0`, `on`, `off`, `yes`, `no`. For example, `t`, `T`, and `tR` will all be considered to be `true`.

> Expressions that do not properly evaluate to true or false will generate a warning and be treated as false.

> Lines being skipped are parsed normally to identify queries and backslash commands, but queries are not sent to the server, and backslash commands other than conditionals (`\if`, `\elif`, `\else`, `\endif`) are ignored. Conditional commands are checked only for valid nesting. Variable references in skipped lines are not expanded, and backquote expansion is not performed either.

> All the backslash commands of a given conditional block must appear in the same source file. If EOF is reached on the main input file or an `\include`-ed file before all local `\if`-blocks have been closed, then psql will raise an error.

> Here is an example:

```
-- check for the existence of two separate records in the database
 and store
-- the results in separate psql variables
SELECT
    EXISTS(SELECT 1 FROM customer WHERE customer_id = 123) as
 is_customer,
    EXISTS(SELECT 1 FROM employee WHERE employee_id = 456) as
 is_employee
\gset
\if :is_customer
    SELECT * FROM customer WHERE customer_id = 123;
\elif :is_employee
    \echo 'is not a customer but is an employee'
    SELECT * FROM employee WHERE employee_id = 456;
\else
    \if yes
        \echo 'not a customer or employee'
    \else
        \echo 'this will never print'
    \endif
\endif
```

\ir or **\include_relative** *filename*

The \ir command is similar to \i, but resolves relative file names differently. When executing in interactive mode, the two commands behave identically. However, when invoked from a script, \ir interprets file names relative to the directory in which the script is located, rather than the current working directory.

\l[+] or **\list[+]** [*pattern*]

List the databases in the server and show their names, owners, character set encodings, and access privileges. If *pattern* is specified, only databases whose names match the pattern are listed. If + is appended to the command name, database sizes, default tablespaces, and descriptions are also displayed. (Size information is only available for databases that the current user can connect to.)

\lo_export *loid filename*

Reads the large object with OID *loid* from the database and writes it to *filename*. Note that this is subtly different from the server function lo_export, which acts with the permissions of the user that the database server runs as and on the server's file system.

Tip

Use \lo_list to find out the large object's OID.

\lo_import *filename* [*comment*]

Stores the file into a PostgreSQL large object. Optionally, it associates the given comment with the object. Example:

```
foo=> \lo_import '/home/peter/pictures/photo.xcf' 'a picture of me'
lo_import 152801
```

The response indicates that the large object received object ID 152801, which can be used to access the newly-created large object in the future. For the sake of readability, it is recommended to always associate a human-readable comment with every object. Both OIDs and comments can be viewed with the `\lo_list` command.

Note that this command is subtly different from the server-side `lo_import` because it acts as the local user on the local file system, rather than the server's user and file system.

`\lo_list`

Shows a list of all PostgreSQL large objects currently stored in the database, along with any comments provided for them.

`\lo_unlink` *loid*

Deletes the large object with OID *loid* from the database.

+---+
| **Tip** |
| |
| Use `\lo_list` to find out the large object's OID. |
+---+

`\o` or `\out` [*filename*]
`\o` or `\out` [|*command*]

Arranges to save future query results to the file *filename* or pipe future results to the shell command *command*. If no argument is specified, the query output is reset to the standard output.

If the argument begins with |, then the entire remainder of the line is taken to be the *command* to execute, and neither variable interpolation nor backquote expansion are performed in it. The rest of the line is simply passed literally to the shell.

"Query results" includes all tables, command responses, and notices obtained from the database server, as well as output of various backslash commands that query the database (such as `\d`); but not error messages.

+---+
| **Tip** |
| |
| To intersperse text output in between query results, use `\qecho`. |
+---+

`\p` or `\print`

Print the current query buffer to the standard output. If the current query buffer is empty, the most recently executed query is printed instead.

`\password` [*username*]

Changes the password of the specified user (by default, the current user). This command prompts for the new password, encrypts it, and sends it to the server as an `ALTER ROLE` command. This makes sure that the new password does not appear in cleartext in the command history, the server log, or elsewhere.

`\prompt [ text ] name`

Prompts the user to supply text, which is assigned to the variable *name*. An optional prompt string, *text*, can be specified. (For multiword prompts, surround the text with single quotes.)

By default, `\prompt` uses the terminal for input and output. However, if the `-f` command line switch was used, `\prompt` uses standard input and standard output.

`\pset [ option [ value ] ]`

This command sets options affecting the output of query result tables. *option* indicates which option is to be set. The semantics of *value* vary depending on the selected option. For some options, omitting *value* causes the option to be toggled or unset, as described under the particular option. If no such behavior is mentioned, then omitting *value* just results in the current setting being displayed.

`\pset` without any arguments displays the current status of all printing options.

Adjustable printing options are:

border

The *value* must be a number. In general, the higher the number the more borders and lines the tables will have, but details depend on the particular format. In HTML format, this will translate directly into the `border=...` attribute. In most other formats only values 0 (no border), 1 (internal dividing lines), and 2 (table frame) make sense, and values above 2 will be treated the same as `border = 2`. The `latex` and `latex-longtable` formats additionally allow a value of 3 to add dividing lines between data rows.

columns

Sets the target width for the `wrapped` format, and also the width limit for determining whether output is wide enough to require the pager or switch to the vertical display in expanded auto mode. Zero (the default) causes the target width to be controlled by the environment variable `COLUMNS`, or the detected screen width if `COLUMNS` is not set. In addition, if `columns` is zero then the `wrapped` format only affects screen output. If `columns` is nonzero then file and pipe output is wrapped to that width as well.

expanded (or x)

If *value* is specified it must be either `on` or `off`, which will enable or disable expanded mode, or `auto`. If *value* is omitted the command toggles between the on and off settings. When expanded mode is enabled, query results are displayed in two columns, with the column name on the left and the data on the right. This mode is useful if the data wouldn't fit on the screen in the normal "horizontal" mode. In the auto setting, the expanded mode is used whenever the query output has more than one column and is wider than the screen; otherwise, the regular mode is used. The auto setting is only effective in the aligned and wrapped formats. In other formats, it always behaves as if the expanded mode is off.

fieldsep

Specifies the field separator to be used in unaligned output format. That way one can create, for example, tab- or comma-separated output, which other programs might prefer. To set a tab as field separator, type `\pset fieldsep '\t'`. The default field separator is `'|'` (a vertical bar).

`fieldsep_zero`

Sets the field separator to use in unaligned output format to a zero byte.

`footer`

If `value` is specified it must be either `on` or `off` which will enable or disable display of the table footer (the (`n rows`) count). If `value` is omitted the command toggles footer display on or off.

`format`

Sets the output format to one of `unaligned`, `aligned`, `wrapped`, `html`, `asciidoc`, `latex` (uses `tabular`), `latex-longtable`, or `troff-ms`. Unique abbreviations are allowed.

`unaligned` format writes all columns of a row on one line, separated by the currently active field separator. This is useful for creating output that might be intended to be read in by other programs (for example, tab-separated or comma-separated format).

`aligned` format is the standard, human-readable, nicely formatted text output; this is the default.

`wrapped` format is like `aligned` but wraps wide data values across lines to make the output fit in the target column width. The target width is determined as described under the `columns` option. Note that psql will not attempt to wrap column header titles; therefore, `wrapped` format behaves the same as `aligned` if the total width needed for column headers exceeds the target.

The `html`, `asciidoc`, `latex`, `latex-longtable`, and `troff-ms` formats put out tables that are intended to be included in documents using the respective mark-up language. They are not complete documents! This might not be necessary in HTML, but in LaTeX you must have a complete document wrapper. `latex-longtable` also requires the LaTeX `longtable` and `booktabs` packages.

`linestyle`

Sets the border line drawing style to one of `ascii`, `old-ascii`, or `unicode`. Unique abbreviations are allowed. (That would mean one letter is enough.) The default setting is `ascii`. This option only affects the `aligned` and `wrapped` output formats.

`ascii` style uses plain ASCII characters. Newlines in data are shown using a + symbol in the right-hand margin. When the `wrapped` format wraps data from one line to the next without a newline character, a dot (`.`) is shown in the right-hand margin of the first line, and again in the left-hand margin of the following line.

`old-ascii` style uses plain ASCII characters, using the formatting style used in PostgreSQL 8.4 and earlier. Newlines in data are shown using a `:` symbol in place of the left-hand column separator. When the data is wrapped from one line to the next without a newline character, a `;` symbol is used in place of the left-hand column separator.

`unicode` style uses Unicode box-drawing characters. Newlines in data are shown using a carriage return symbol in the right-hand margin. When the data is wrapped from one line to the next without a newline character, an ellipsis symbol is shown in the right-hand margin of the first line, and again in the left-hand margin of the following line.

When the `border` setting is greater than zero, the `linestyle` option also determines the characters with which the border lines are drawn. Plain ASCII characters work everywhere, but Unicode characters look nicer on displays that recognize them.

> Sets the string to be printed in place of a null value. The default is to print nothing, which can easily be mistaken for an empty string. For example, one might prefer `\pset null '(null)'`.

numericlocale

> If *value* is specified it must be either `on` or `off` which will enable or disable display of a locale-specific character to separate groups of digits to the left of the decimal marker. If *value* is omitted the command toggles between regular and locale-specific numeric output.

pager

> Controls use of a pager program for query and psql help output. If the environment variable `PSQL_PAGER` or `PAGER` is set, the output is piped to the specified program. Otherwise a platform-dependent default program (such as `more`) is used.

> When the `pager` option is `off`, the pager program is not used. When the `pager` option is `on`, the pager is used when appropriate, i.e., when the output is to a terminal and will not fit on the screen. The `pager` option can also be set to `always`, which causes the pager to be used for all terminal output regardless of whether it fits on the screen. `\pset pager` without a *value* toggles pager use on and off.

pager_min_lines

> If `pager_min_lines` is set to a number greater than the page height, the pager program will not be called unless there are at least this many lines of output to show. The default setting is 0.

recordsep

> Specifies the record (line) separator to use in unaligned output format. The default is a newline character.

recordsep_zero

> Sets the record separator to use in unaligned output format to a zero byte.

tableattr (or T)

> In HTML format, this specifies attributes to be placed inside the `table` tag. This could for example be `cellpadding` or `bgcolor`. Note that you probably don't want to specify `border` here, as that is already taken care of by `\pset border`. If no *value* is given, the table attributes are unset.

> In `latex-longtable` format, this controls the proportional width of each column containing a left-aligned data type. It is specified as a whitespace-separated list of values, e.g. `'0.2 0.2 0.6'`. Unspecified output columns use the last specified value.

title (or C)

> Sets the table title for any subsequently printed tables. This can be used to give your output descriptive tags. If no *value* is given, the title is unset.

tuples_only (or t)

> If *value* is specified it must be either `on` or `off` which will enable or disable tuples-only mode. If *value* is omitted the command toggles between regular and tuples-only output. Regular output

includes extra information such as column headers, titles, and various footers. In tuples-only mode, only actual table data is shown.

unicode_border_linestyle

Sets the border drawing style for the unicode line style to one of single or double.

unicode_column_linestyle

Sets the column drawing style for the unicode line style to one of single or double.

unicode_header_linestyle

Sets the header drawing style for the unicode line style to one of single or double.

Illustrations of how these different formats look can be seen in the Examples section.

Tip

There are various shortcut commands for \pset. See \a, \C, \f, \H, \t, \T, and \x.

\q or \quit

Quits the psql program. In a script file, only execution of that script is terminated.

\qecho *text* [...]

This command is identical to \echo except that the output will be written to the query output channel, as set by \o.

\r or \reset

Resets (clears) the query buffer.

\s [*filename*]

Print psql's command line history to *filename*. If *filename* is omitted, the history is written to the standard output (using the pager if appropriate). This command is not available if psql was built without Readline support.

\set [*name* [*value* [...]]]

Sets the psql variable *name* to *value*, or if more than one value is given, to the concatenation of all of them. If only one argument is given, the variable is set to an empty-string value. To unset a variable, use the \unset command.

\set without any arguments displays the names and values of all currently-set psql variables.

Valid variable names can contain letters, digits, and underscores. See the section Variables below for details. Variable names are case-sensitive.

Certain variables are special, in that they control psql's behavior or are automatically set to reflect connection state. These variables are documented in Variables, below.

> **Note**
>
> This command is unrelated to the SQL command SET.

`\setenv` *name* [*value*]

Sets the environment variable *name* to *value*, or if the *value* is not supplied, unsets the environment variable. Example:

```
testdb=> \setenv PAGER less
testdb=> \setenv LESS -imx4F
```

`\sf[+]` *function_description*

This command fetches and shows the definition of the named function or procedure, in the form of a CREATE OR REPLACE FUNCTION or CREATE OR REPLACE PROCEDURE command. The definition is printed to the current query output channel, as set by \o.

The target function can be specified by name alone, or by name and arguments, for example foo(integer, text). The argument types must be given if there is more than one function of the same name.

If + is appended to the command name, then the output lines are numbered, with the first line of the function body being line 1.

Unlike most other meta-commands, the entire remainder of the line is always taken to be the argument(s) of \sf, and neither variable interpolation nor backquote expansion are performed in the arguments.

`\sv[+]` *view_name*

This command fetches and shows the definition of the named view, in the form of a CREATE OR REPLACE VIEW command. The definition is printed to the current query output channel, as set by \o.

If + is appended to the command name, then the output lines are numbered from 1.

Unlike most other meta-commands, the entire remainder of the line is always taken to be the argument(s) of \sv, and neither variable interpolation nor backquote expansion are performed in the arguments.

`\t`

Toggles the display of output column name headings and row count footer. This command is equivalent to \pset tuples_only and is provided for convenience.

`\T` *table_options*

Specifies attributes to be placed within the table tag in HTML output format. This command is equivalent to \pset tableattr *table_options*.

`\timing` [*on* | *off*]

With a parameter, turns displaying of how long each SQL statement takes on or off. Without a parameter, toggles the display between on and off. The display is in milliseconds; intervals longer than 1 second are also shown in minutes:seconds format, with hours and days fields added if needed.

\unset *name*

> Unsets (deletes) the psql variable *name*.

> Most variables that control psql's behavior cannot be unset; instead, an \unset command is interpreted as setting them to their default values. See Variables, below.

\w or \write *filename*
\w or \write | *command*

> Writes the current query buffer to the file *filename* or pipes it to the shell command *command*. If the current query buffer is empty, the most recently executed query is written instead.

> If the argument begins with |, then the entire remainder of the line is taken to be the *command* to execute, and neither variable interpolation nor backquote expansion are performed in it. The rest of the line is simply passed literally to the shell.

\watch [*seconds*]

> Repeatedly execute the current query buffer (as \g does) until interrupted or the query fails. Wait the specified number of seconds (default 2) between executions. Each query result is displayed with a header that includes the \pset title string (if any), the time as of query start, and the delay interval.

> If the current query buffer is empty, the most recently sent query is re-executed instead.

\x [*on* | *off* | *auto*]

> Sets or toggles expanded table formatting mode. As such it is equivalent to \pset expanded.

\z [*pattern*]

> Lists tables, views and sequences with their associated access privileges. If a *pattern* is specified, only tables, views and sequences whose names match the pattern are listed.

> This is an alias for \dp ("display privileges").

\! [*command*]

> With no argument, escapes to a sub-shell; psql resumes when the sub-shell exits. With an argument, executes the shell command *command*.

> Unlike most other meta-commands, the entire remainder of the line is always taken to be the argument(s) of \!, and neither variable interpolation nor backquote expansion are performed in the arguments. The rest of the line is simply passed literally to the shell.

\? [*topic*]

> Shows help information. The optional *topic* parameter (defaulting to commands) selects which part of psql is explained: commands describes psql's backslash commands; options describes the command-line options that can be passed to psql; and variables shows help about psql configuration variables.

\;

> Backslash-semicolon is not a meta-command in the same way as the preceding commands; rather, it simply causes a semicolon to be added to the query buffer without any further processing.

Normally, psql will dispatch a SQL command to the server as soon as it reaches the command-ending semicolon, even if more input remains on the current line. Thus for example entering

```
select 1; select 2; select 3;
```

will result in the three SQL commands being individually sent to the server, with each one's results being displayed before continuing to the next command. However, a semicolon entered as `\;` will not trigger command processing, so that the command before it and the one after are effectively combined and sent to the server in one request. So for example

```
select 1\; select 2\; select 3;
```

results in sending the three SQL commands to the server in a single request, when the non-backslashed semicolon is reached. The server executes such a request as a single transaction, unless there are explicit `BEGIN`/`COMMIT` commands included in the string to divide it into multiple transactions. (See Section 53.2.2.1 for more details about how the server handles multi-query strings.) psql prints only the last query result it receives for each request; in this example, although all three SELECTs are indeed executed, psql only prints the 3.

Patterns

The various `\d` commands accept a *pattern* parameter to specify the object name(s) to be displayed. In the simplest case, a pattern is just the exact name of the object. The characters within a pattern are normally folded to lower case, just as in SQL names; for example, `\dt FOO` will display the table named `foo`. As in SQL names, placing double quotes around a pattern stops folding to lower case. Should you need to include an actual double quote character in a pattern, write it as a pair of double quotes within a double-quote sequence; again this is in accord with the rules for SQL quoted identifiers. For example, `\dt "FOO""BAR"` will display the table named FOO"BAR (not `foo"bar`). Unlike the normal rules for SQL names, you can put double quotes around just part of a pattern, for instance `\dt FOO"FOO"BAR` will display the table named `fooFOObar`.

Whenever the *pattern* parameter is omitted completely, the `\d` commands display all objects that are visible in the current schema search path — this is equivalent to using * as the pattern. (An object is said to be *visible* if its containing schema is in the search path and no object of the same kind and name appears earlier in the search path. This is equivalent to the statement that the object can be referenced by name without explicit schema qualification.) To see all objects in the database regardless of visibility, use `*.*` as the pattern.

Within a pattern, * matches any sequence of characters (including no characters) and ? matches any single character. (This notation is comparable to Unix shell file name patterns.) For example, `\dt int*` displays tables whose names begin with `int`. But within double quotes, * and ? lose these special meanings and are just matched literally.

A pattern that contains a dot (.) is interpreted as a schema name pattern followed by an object name pattern. For example, `\dt foo*.*bar*` displays all tables whose table name includes `bar` that are in schemas whose schema name starts with `foo`. When no dot appears, then the pattern matches only objects that are visible in the current schema search path. Again, a dot within double quotes loses its special meaning and is matched literally.

Advanced users can use regular-expression notations such as character classes, for example `[0-9]` to match any digit. All regular expression special characters work as specified in Section 9.7.3, except for `.` which is taken as a separator as mentioned above, * which is translated to the regular-expression notation `.*`, ? which is translated to `.`, and $ which is matched literally. You can emulate these pattern characters at need by writing ? for ., (R+|) for R*, or (R|) for R?. $ is not needed as a regular-expression character since the pattern must match the whole name, unlike the usual interpretation of regular expressions (in other words, $ is automatically appended to your pattern). Write * at the beginning and/or end if you don't wish the pattern to be anchored. Note that within double quotes, all regular expression special characters lose their special meanings and are matched literally. Also, the regular expression special characters are matched literally in operator name patterns (i.e., the argument of \do).

Advanced Features

Variables

psql provides variable substitution features similar to common Unix command shells. Variables are simply name/value pairs, where the value can be any string of any length. The name must consist of letters (including non-Latin letters), digits, and underscores.

To set a variable, use the psql meta-command \set. For example,

```
testdb=> \set foo bar
```

sets the variable foo to the value bar. To retrieve the content of the variable, precede the name with a colon, for example:

```
testdb=> \echo :foo
bar
```

This works in both regular SQL commands and meta-commands; there is more detail in SQL Interpolation, below.

If you call \set without a second argument, the variable is set to an empty-string value. To unset (i.e., delete) a variable, use the command \unset. To show the values of all variables, call \set without any argument.

Note

The arguments of \set are subject to the same substitution rules as with other commands. Thus you can construct interesting references such as \set :foo 'something' and get "soft links" or "variable variables" of Perl or PHP fame, respectively. Unfortunately (or fortunately?), there is no way to do anything useful with these constructs. On the other hand, \set bar :foo is a perfectly valid way to copy a variable.

A number of these variables are treated specially by psql. They represent certain option settings that can be changed at run time by altering the value of the variable, or in some cases represent changeable state of psql. By convention, all specially treated variables' names consist of all upper-case ASCII letters (and possibly digits and underscores). To ensure maximum compatibility in the future, avoid using such variable names for your own purposes.

Variables that control psql's behavior generally cannot be unset or set to invalid values. An \unset command is allowed but is interpreted as setting the variable to its default value. A \set command without a second argument is interpreted as setting the variable to on, for control variables that accept that value, and is rejected for others. Also, control variables that accept the values on and off will also accept other common spellings of Boolean values, such as true and false.

The specially treated variables are:

AUTOCOMMIT

When on (the default), each SQL command is automatically committed upon successful completion. To postpone commit in this mode, you must enter a BEGIN or START TRANSACTION SQL command. When off or unset, SQL commands are not committed until you explicitly issue COMMIT or END. The autocommit-off mode works by issuing an implicit BEGIN for you, just before any command that is not already in a transaction block and is not itself a BEGIN or other transaction-control command, nor a command that cannot be executed inside a transaction block (such as VACUUM).

Note

In autocommit-off mode, you must explicitly abandon any failed transaction by entering ABORT or ROLLBACK. Also keep in mind that if you exit the session without committing, your work will be lost.

Note

The autocommit-on mode is PostgreSQL's traditional behavior, but autocommit-off is closer to the SQL spec. If you prefer autocommit-off, you might wish to set it in the system-wide psqlrc file or your ~/.psqlrc file.

COMP_KEYWORD_CASE

Determines which letter case to use when completing an SQL key word. If set to lower or upper, the completed word will be in lower or upper case, respectively. If set to preserve-lower or preserve-upper (the default), the completed word will be in the case of the word already entered, but words being completed without anything entered will be in lower or upper case, respectively.

DBNAME

The name of the database you are currently connected to. This is set every time you connect to a database (including program start-up), but can be changed or unset.

ECHO

If set to all, all nonempty input lines are printed to standard output as they are read. (This does not apply to lines read interactively.) To select this behavior on program start-up, use the switch -a. If set to queries, psql prints each query to standard output as it is sent to the server. The switch to select this behavior is -e. If set to errors, then only failed queries are displayed on standard error output. The switch for this behavior is -b. If set to none (the default), then no queries are displayed.

ECHO_HIDDEN

When this variable is set to on and a backslash command queries the database, the query is first shown. This feature helps you to study PostgreSQL internals and provide similar functionality in your own programs. (To select this behavior on program start-up, use the switch -E.) If you set this variable to the value noexec, the queries are just shown but are not actually sent to the server and executed. The default value is off.

ENCODING

The current client character set encoding. This is set every time you connect to a database (including program start-up), and when you change the encoding with \encoding, but it can be changed or unset.

ERROR

`true` if the last SQL query failed, `false` if it succeeded. See also `SQLSTATE`.

FETCH_COUNT

If this variable is set to an integer value greater than zero, the results of `SELECT` queries are fetched and displayed in groups of that many rows, rather than the default behavior of collecting the entire result set before display. Therefore only a limited amount of memory is used, regardless of the size of the result set. Settings of 100 to 1000 are commonly used when enabling this feature. Keep in mind that when using this feature, a query might fail after having already displayed some rows.

Tip

Although you can use any output format with this feature, the default `aligned` format tends to look bad because each group of `FETCH_COUNT` rows will be formatted separately, leading to varying column widths across the row groups. The other output formats work better.

HISTCONTROL

If this variable is set to `ignorespace`, lines which begin with a space are not entered into the history list. If set to a value of `ignoredups`, lines matching the previous history line are not entered. A value of `ignoreboth` combines the two options. If set to `none` (the default), all lines read in interactive mode are saved on the history list.

Note

This feature was shamelessly plagiarized from Bash.

HISTFILE

The file name that will be used to store the history list. If unset, the file name is taken from the `PSQL_HISTORY` environment variable. If that is not set either, the default is `~/.psql_history`, or `%APPDATA%\postgresql\psql_history` on Windows. For example, putting:

```
\set HISTFILE ~/.psql_history- :DBNAME
```

in `~/.psqlrc` will cause psql to maintain a separate history for each database.

Note

This feature was shamelessly plagiarized from Bash.

HISTSIZE

> The maximum number of commands to store in the command history (default 500). If set to a negative value, no limit is applied.

> > # Note
> >
> > This feature was shamelessly plagiarized from Bash.

HOST

> The database server host you are currently connected to. This is set every time you connect to a database (including program start-up), but can be changed or unset.

IGNOREEOF

> If set to 1 or less, sending an EOF character (usually **Control+D**) to an interactive session of psql will terminate the application. If set to a larger numeric value, that many consecutive EOF characters must be typed to make an interactive session terminate. If the variable is set to a non-numeric value, it is interpreted as 10. The default is 0.

> > # Note
> >
> > This feature was shamelessly plagiarized from Bash.

LASTOID

> The value of the last affected OID, as returned from an INSERT or \lo_import command. This variable is only guaranteed to be valid until after the result of the next SQL command has been displayed.

LAST_ERROR_MESSAGE
LAST_ERROR_SQLSTATE

> The primary error message and associated SQLSTATE code for the most recent failed query in the current psql session, or an empty string and 00000 if no error has occurred in the current session.

ON_ERROR_ROLLBACK

> When set to on, if a statement in a transaction block generates an error, the error is ignored and the transaction continues. When set to interactive, such errors are only ignored in interactive sessions, and not when reading script files. When set to off (the default), a statement in a transaction block that generates an error aborts the entire transaction. The error rollback mode works by issuing an implicit SAVEPOINT for you, just before each command that is in a transaction block, and then rolling back to the savepoint if the command fails.

ON_ERROR_STOP

> By default, command processing continues after an error. When this variable is set to on, processing will instead stop immediately. In interactive mode, psql will return to the command prompt; otherwise, psql will exit, returning error code 3 to distinguish this case from fatal error conditions, which are

reported using error code 1. In either case, any currently running scripts (the top-level script, if any, and any other scripts which it may have in invoked) will be terminated immediately. If the top-level command string contained multiple SQL commands, processing will stop with the current command.

PORT

> The database server port to which you are currently connected. This is set every time you connect to a database (including program start-up), but can be changed or unset.

PROMPT1
PROMPT2
PROMPT3

> These specify what the prompts psql issues should look like. See Prompting below.

QUIET

> Setting this variable to on is equivalent to the command line option -q. It is probably not too useful in interactive mode.

ROW_COUNT

> The number of rows returned or affected by the last SQL query, or 0 if the query failed or did not report a row count.

SERVER_VERSION_NAME
SERVER_VERSION_NUM

> The server's version number as a string, for example 9.6.2, 10.1 or 11beta1, and in numeric form, for example 90602 or 100001. These are set every time you connect to a database (including program start-up), but can be changed or unset.

SHOW_CONTEXT

> This variable can be set to the values never, errors, or always to control whether CONTEXT fields are displayed in messages from the server. The default is errors (meaning that context will be shown in error messages, but not in notice or warning messages). This setting has no effect when VERBOSITY is set to terse. (See also \errverbose, for use when you want a verbose version of the error you just got.)

SINGLELINE

> Setting this variable to on is equivalent to the command line option -S.

SINGLESTEP

> Setting this variable to on is equivalent to the command line option -s.

SQLSTATE

> The error code (see Appendix A) associated with the last SQL query's failure, or 00000 if it succeeded.

USER

> The database user you are currently connected as. This is set every time you connect to a database (including program start-up), but can be changed or unset.

VERBOSITY

This variable can be set to the values `default`, `verbose`, or `terse` to control the verbosity of error reports. (See also `\errverbose`, for use when you want a verbose version of the error you just got.)

VERSION
VERSION_NAME
VERSION_NUM

These variables are set at program start-up to reflect psql's version, respectively as a verbose string, a short string (e.g., `9.6.2`, `10.1`, or `11beta1`), and a number (e.g., `90602` or `100001`). They can be changed or unset.

SQL Interpolation

A key feature of psql variables is that you can substitute ("interpolate") them into regular SQL statements, as well as the arguments of meta-commands. Furthermore, psql provides facilities for ensuring that variable values used as SQL literals and identifiers are properly quoted. The syntax for interpolating a value without any quoting is to prepend the variable name with a colon (`:`). For example,

```
testdb=> \set foo 'my_table'
testdb=> SELECT * FROM :foo;
```

would query the table `my_table`. Note that this may be unsafe: the value of the variable is copied literally, so it can contain unbalanced quotes, or even backslash commands. You must make sure that it makes sense where you put it.

When a value is to be used as an SQL literal or identifier, it is safest to arrange for it to be quoted. To quote the value of a variable as an SQL literal, write a colon followed by the variable name in single quotes. To quote the value as an SQL identifier, write a colon followed by the variable name in double quotes. These constructs deal correctly with quotes and other special characters embedded within the variable value. The previous example would be more safely written this way:

```
testdb=> \set foo 'my_table'
testdb=> SELECT * FROM :"foo";
```

Variable interpolation will not be performed within quoted SQL literals and identifiers. Therefore, a construction such as `':foo'` doesn't work to produce a quoted literal from a variable's value (and it would be unsafe if it did work, since it wouldn't correctly handle quotes embedded in the value).

One example use of this mechanism is to copy the contents of a file into a table column. First load the file into a variable and then interpolate the variable's value as a quoted string:

```
testdb=> \set content `cat my_file.txt`
testdb=> INSERT INTO my_table VALUES (:'content');
```

(Note that this still won't work if `my_file.txt` contains NUL bytes. psql does not support embedded NUL bytes in variable values.)

Since colons can legally appear in SQL commands, an apparent attempt at interpolation (that is, `:name`, `:'name'`, or `:"name"`) is not replaced unless the named variable is currently set. In any case, you can escape a colon with a backslash to protect it from substitution.

The :{?*name*} special syntax returns TRUE or FALSE depending on whether the variable exists or not, and is thus always substituted, unless the colon is backslash-escaped.

The colon syntax for variables is standard SQL for embedded query languages, such as ECPG. The colon syntaxes for array slices and type casts are PostgreSQL extensions, which can sometimes conflict with the standard usage. The colon-quote syntax for escaping a variable's value as an SQL literal or identifier is a psql extension.

Prompting

The prompts psql issues can be customized to your preference. The three variables PROMPT1, PROMPT2, and PROMPT3 contain strings and special escape sequences that describe the appearance of the prompt. Prompt 1 is the normal prompt that is issued when psql requests a new command. Prompt 2 is issued when more input is expected during command entry, for example because the command was not terminated with a semicolon or a quote was not closed. Prompt 3 is issued when you are running an SQL COPY FROM STDIN command and you need to type in a row value on the terminal.

The value of the selected prompt variable is printed literally, except where a percent sign (%) is encountered. Depending on the next character, certain other text is substituted instead. Defined substitutions are:

%M

> The full host name (with domain name) of the database server, or [local] if the connection is over a Unix domain socket, or [local:*/dir/name*], if the Unix domain socket is not at the compiled in default location.

%m

> The host name of the database server, truncated at the first dot, or [local] if the connection is over a Unix domain socket.

%>

> The port number at which the database server is listening.

%n

> The database session user name. (The expansion of this value might change during a database session as the result of the command SET SESSION AUTHORIZATION.)

%/

> The name of the current database.

%~

> Like %/, but the output is ~ (tilde) if the database is your default database.

%#

> If the session user is a database superuser, then a #, otherwise a >. (The expansion of this value might change during a database session as the result of the command SET SESSION AUTHORIZATION.)

%p

> The process ID of the backend currently connected to.

%R

In prompt 1 normally =, but @ if the session is in an inactive branch of a conditional block, or ^ if in single-line mode, or ! if the session is disconnected from the database (which can happen if \connect fails). In prompt 2 %R is replaced by a character that depends on why psql expects more input: – if the command simply wasn't terminated yet, but * if there is an unfinished /* ... */ comment, a single quote if there is an unfinished quoted string, a double quote if there is an unfinished quoted identifier, a dollar sign if there is an unfinished dollar-quoted string, or (if there is an unmatched left parenthesis. In prompt 3 %R doesn't produce anything.

%x

Transaction status: an empty string when not in a transaction block, or * when in a transaction block, or ! when in a failed transaction block, or ? when the transaction state is indeterminate (for example, because there is no connection).

%l

The line number inside the current statement, starting from 1.

%*digits*

The character with the indicated octal code is substituted.

%:*name*:

The value of the psql variable *name*. See the section Variables for details.

%`*command*`

The output of *command*, similar to ordinary "back-tick" substitution.

%[... %]

Prompts can contain terminal control characters which, for example, change the color, background, or style of the prompt text, or change the title of the terminal window. In order for the line editing features of Readline to work properly, these non-printing control characters must be designated as invisible by surrounding them with %[and %]. Multiple pairs of these can occur within the prompt. For example:

```
testdb=> \set PROMPT1 '%[%033[1;33;40m%]%n@%/%R%[%033[0m%]%# '
```

results in a boldfaced (1;) yellow-on-black (33;40) prompt on VT100-compatible, color-capable terminals.

To insert a percent sign into your prompt, write %%. The default prompts are '%/%R%# ' for prompts 1 and 2, and '>> ' for prompt 3.

> ## Note
>
> This feature was shamelessly plagiarized from tcsh.

Command-Line Editing

psql supports the Readline library for convenient line editing and retrieval. The command history is automatically saved when psql exits and is reloaded when psql starts up. Tab-completion is also supported, although the completion logic makes no claim to be an SQL parser. The queries generated by tab-completion can also interfere with other SQL commands, e.g. SET TRANSACTION ISOLATION LEVEL. If for some reason you do not like the tab completion, you can turn it off by putting this in a file named .inputrc in your home directory:

```
$if psql
set disable-completion on
$endif
```

(This is not a psql but a Readline feature. Read its documentation for further details.)

Environment

COLUMNS

If \pset columns is zero, controls the width for the wrapped format and width for determining if wide output requires the pager or should be switched to the vertical format in expanded auto mode.

PGDATABASE
PGHOST
PGPORT
PGUSER

Default connection parameters (see Section 34.14).

PSQL_EDITOR
EDITOR
VISUAL

Editor used by the \e, \ef, and \ev commands. These variables are examined in the order listed; the first that is set is used. If none of them is set, the default is to use vi on Unix systems or notepad.exe on Windows systems.

PSQL_EDITOR_LINENUMBER_ARG

When \e, \ef, or \ev is used with a line number argument, this variable specifies the command-line argument used to pass the starting line number to the user's editor. For editors such as Emacs or vi, this is a plus sign. Include a trailing space in the value of the variable if there needs to be space between the option name and the line number. Examples:

```
PSQL_EDITOR_LINENUMBER_ARG='+'
PSQL_EDITOR_LINENUMBER_ARG='--line '
```

The default is + on Unix systems (corresponding to the default editor vi, and useful for many other common editors); but there is no default on Windows systems.

PSQL_HISTORY

Alternative location for the command history file. Tilde (~) expansion is performed.

PSQL_PAGER
PAGER

If a query's results do not fit on the screen, they are piped through this command. Typical values are more or less. Use of the pager can be disabled by setting PSQL_PAGER or PAGER to an empty string, or by adjusting the pager-related options of the `\pset` command. These variables are examined in the order listed; the first that is set is used. If none of them is set, the default is to use `more` on most platforms, but `less` on Cygwin.

PSQLRC

Alternative location of the user's `.psqlrc` file. Tilde (~) expansion is performed.

SHELL

Command executed by the `\!` command.

TMPDIR

Directory for storing temporary files. The default is `/tmp`.

This utility, like most other PostgreSQL utilities, also uses the environment variables supported by libpq (see Section 34.14).

Files

psqlrc and ~/.psqlrc

Unless it is passed an `-X` option, psql attempts to read and execute commands from the system-wide startup file (`psqlrc`) and then the user's personal startup file (`~/.psqlrc`), after connecting to the database but before accepting normal commands. These files can be used to set up the client and/or the server to taste, typically with `\set` and `SET` commands.

The system-wide startup file is named `psqlrc` and is sought in the installation's "system configuration" directory, which is most reliably identified by running `pg_config --sysconfdir`. By default this directory will be `../etc/` relative to the directory containing the PostgreSQL executables. The name of this directory can be set explicitly via the `PGSYSCONFDIR` environment variable.

The user's personal startup file is named `.psqlrc` and is sought in the invoking user's home directory. On Windows, which lacks such a concept, the personal startup file is named `%APPDATA% \postgresql\psqlrc.conf`. The location of the user's startup file can be set explicitly via the `PSQLRC` environment variable.

Both the system-wide startup file and the user's personal startup file can be made psql-version-specific by appending a dash and the PostgreSQL major or minor release number to the file name, for example `~/.psqlrc-9.2` or `~/.psqlrc-9.2.5`. The most specific version-matching file will be read in preference to a non-version-specific file.

.psql_history

The command-line history is stored in the file `~/.psql_history`, or `%APPDATA%\postgresql\psql_history` on Windows.

The location of the history file can be set explicitly via the `HISTFILE` psql variable or the `PSQL_HISTORY` environment variable.

Notes

- psql works best with servers of the same or an older major version. Backslash commands are particularly likely to fail if the server is of a newer version than psql itself. However, backslash commands of the `\d` family should work with servers of versions back to 7.4, though not necessarily with servers newer than psql itself. The general functionality of running SQL commands and displaying query results should also work with servers of a newer major version, but this cannot be guaranteed in all cases.

If you want to use psql to connect to several servers of different major versions, it is recommended that you use the newest version of psql. Alternatively, you can keep around a copy of psql from each major version and be sure to use the version that matches the respective server. But in practice, this additional complication should not be necessary.

- Before PostgreSQL 9.6, the -c option implied -X (--no-psqlrc); this is no longer the case.

- Before PostgreSQL 8.4, psql allowed the first argument of a single-letter backslash command to start directly after the command, without intervening whitespace. Now, some whitespace is required.

Notes for Windows Users

psql is built as a "console application". Since the Windows console windows use a different encoding than the rest of the system, you must take special care when using 8-bit characters within psql. If psql detects a problematic console code page, it will warn you at startup. To change the console code page, two things are necessary:

- Set the code page by entering **cmd.exe /c chcp 1252**. (1252 is a code page that is appropriate for German; replace it with your value.) If you are using Cygwin, you can put this command in /etc/profile.

- Set the console font to Lucida Console, because the raster font does not work with the ANSI code page.

Examples

The first example shows how to spread a command over several lines of input. Notice the changing prompt:

```
testdb=> CREATE TABLE my_table (
testdb(>    first integer not null default 0,
testdb(>    second text)
testdb-> ;
CREATE TABLE
```

Now look at the table definition again:

```
testdb=> \d my_table
              Table "public.my_table"
 Column |  Type   | Collation | Nullable | Default
--------+---------+-----------+----------+---------
 first  | integer |           | not null | 0
 second | text    |           |          |
```

Now we change the prompt to something more interesting:

```
testdb=> \set PROMPT1 '%n@%m %~%R%# '
peter@localhost testdb=>
```

Let's assume you have filled the table with data and want to take a look at it:

```
peter@localhost testdb=> SELECT * FROM my_table;
 first | second
-------+--------
     1 | one
     2 | two
     3 | three
     4 | four
(4 rows)
```

You can display tables in different ways by using the \pset command:

```
peter@localhost testdb=> \pset border 2
Border style is 2.
peter@localhost testdb=> SELECT * FROM my_table;
+-------+--------+
| first | second |
+-------+--------+
|     1 | one    |
|     2 | two    |
|     3 | three  |
|     4 | four   |
+-------+--------+
(4 rows)

peter@localhost testdb=> \pset border 0
Border style is 0.
peter@localhost testdb=> SELECT * FROM my_table;
first second
----- ------
    1 one
    2 two
    3 three
    4 four
(4 rows)

peter@localhost testdb=> \pset border 1
Border style is 1.
peter@localhost testdb=> \pset format unaligned
Output format is unaligned.
peter@localhost testdb=> \pset fieldsep ","
Field separator is ",".
peter@localhost testdb=> \pset tuples_only
Showing only tuples.
peter@localhost testdb=> SELECT second, first FROM my_table;
one,1
two,2
three,3
four,4
```

Alternatively, use the short commands:

```
peter@localhost testdb=> \a \t \x
Output format is aligned.
Tuples only is off.
Expanded display is on.
peter@localhost testdb=> SELECT * FROM my_table;
-[ RECORD 1 ]-
first  | 1
second | one
-[ RECORD 2 ]-
first  | 2
second | two
-[ RECORD 3 ]-
first  | 3
second | three
-[ RECORD 4 ]-
first  | 4
second | four
```

When suitable, query results can be shown in a crosstab representation with the \crosstabview command:

```
testdb=> SELECT first, second, first > 2 AS gt2 FROM my_table;
 first | second | gt2
-------+--------+-----
     1 | one    | f
     2 | two    | f
     3 | three  | t
     4 | four   | t
(4 rows)

testdb=> \crosstabview first second
 first | one | two | three | four
-------+-----+-----+-------+------
     1 | f   |     |       |
     2 |     | f   |       |
     3 |     |     | t     |
     4 |     |     |       | t
(4 rows)
```

This second example shows a multiplication table with rows sorted in reverse numerical order and columns with an independent, ascending numerical order.

```
testdb=> SELECT t1.first as "A", t2.first+100 AS "B",
 t1.first*(t2.first+100) as "AxB",
testdb(> row_number() over(order by t2.first) AS ord
testdb(> FROM my_table t1 CROSS JOIN my_table t2 ORDER BY 1 DESC
testdb(> \crosstabview "A" "B" "AxB" ord
 A | 101 | 102 | 103 | 104
---+-----+-----+-----+-----
 4 | 404 | 408 | 412 | 416
 3 | 303 | 306 | 309 | 312
 2 | 202 | 204 | 206 | 208
 1 | 101 | 102 | 103 | 104
```

(4 rows)

reindexdb

reindexdb — reindex a PostgreSQL database

Synopsis

reindexdb [*connection-option*...] [*option*...] [--schema | -S *schema*] ... [--table | -t *table*] ... [--index | -i *index*] ... [*dbname*]

reindexdb [*connection-option*...] [*option*...] --all | -a

reindexdb [*connection-option*...] [*option*...] --system | -s [*dbname*]

Description

reindexdb is a utility for rebuilding indexes in a PostgreSQL database.

reindexdb is a wrapper around the SQL command REINDEX. There is no effective difference between reindexing databases via this utility and via other methods for accessing the server.

Options

reindexdb accepts the following command-line arguments:

-a
--all

   Reindex all databases.

[-d] *dbname*
[--dbname=]*dbname*

   Specifies the name of the database to be reindexed. If this is not specified and -a (or --all) is not used, the database name is read from the environment variable PGDATABASE. If that is not set, the user name specified for the connection is used.

-e
--echo

   Echo the commands that reindexdb generates and sends to the server.

-i *index*
--index=*index*

   Recreate *index* only. Multiple indexes can be recreated by writing multiple -i switches.

-q
--quiet

   Do not display progress messages.

-s
--system

   Reindex database's system catalogs.

`-S` *schema*
`--schema=`*schema*

> Reindex *schema* only. Multiple schemas can be reindexed by writing multiple `-S` switches.

`-t` *table*
`--table=`*table*

> Reindex *table* only. Multiple tables can be reindexed by writing multiple `-t` switches.

`-v`
`--verbose`

> Print detailed information during processing.

`-V`
`--version`

> Print the reindexdb version and exit.

`-?`
`--help`

> Show help about reindexdb command line arguments, and exit.

reindexdb also accepts the following command-line arguments for connection parameters:

`-h` *host*
`--host=`*host*

> Specifies the host name of the machine on which the server is running. If the value begins with a slash, it is used as the directory for the Unix domain socket.

`-p` *port*
`--port=`*port*

> Specifies the TCP port or local Unix domain socket file extension on which the server is listening for connections.

`-U` *username*
`--username=`*username*

> User name to connect as.

`-w`
`--no-password`

> Never issue a password prompt. If the server requires password authentication and a password is not available by other means such as a `.pgpass` file, the connection attempt will fail. This option can be useful in batch jobs and scripts where no user is present to enter a password.

`-W`
`--password`

> Force reindexdb to prompt for a password before connecting to a database.
>
> This option is never essential, since reindexdb will automatically prompt for a password if the server demands password authentication. However, reindexdb will waste a connection attempt finding out

that the server wants a password. In some cases it is worth typing -W to avoid the extra connection attempt.

--maintenance-db=*dbname*

Specifies the name of the database to connect to discover what other databases should be reindexed. If not specified, the `postgres` database will be used, and if that does not exist, `template1` will be used.

Environment

```
PGDATABASE
PGHOST
PGPORT
PGUSER
```

Default connection parameters

This utility, like most other PostgreSQL utilities, also uses the environment variables supported by libpq (see Section 34.14).

Diagnostics

In case of difficulty, see REINDEX and psql for discussions of potential problems and error messages. The database server must be running at the targeted host. Also, any default connection settings and environment variables used by the libpq front-end library will apply.

Notes

reindexdb might need to connect several times to the PostgreSQL server, asking for a password each time. It is convenient to have a ~/`.pgpass` file in such cases. See Section 34.15 for more information.

Examples

To reindex the database `test`:

```
$ reindexdb test
```

To reindex the table `foo` and the index `bar` in a database named `abcd`:

```
$ reindexdb --table=foo --index=bar abcd
```

See Also
REINDEX

vacuumdb

vacuumdb — garbage-collect and analyze a PostgreSQL database

Synopsis

vacuumdb [`connection-option`...] [`option`...] [--table | -t `table` [(`column` [,...])]] ...
[dbname]

vacuumdb [`connection-option`...] [`option`...] --all | -a

Description

vacuumdb is a utility for cleaning a PostgreSQL database. vacuumdb will also generate internal statistics used by the PostgreSQL query optimizer.

vacuumdb is a wrapper around the SQL command VACUUM. There is no effective difference between vacuuming and analyzing databases via this utility and via other methods for accessing the server.

Options

vacuumdb accepts the following command-line arguments:

-a
--all

> Vacuum all databases.

[-d] `dbname`
[--dbname=]`dbname`

> Specifies the name of the database to be cleaned or analyzed. If this is not specified and -a (or --all) is not used, the database name is read from the environment variable PGDATABASE. If that is not set, the user name specified for the connection is used.

-e
--echo

> Echo the commands that vacuumdb generates and sends to the server.

-f
--full

> Perform "full" vacuuming.

-F
--freeze

> Aggressively "freeze" tuples.

-j `njobs`
--jobs=`njobs`

> Execute the vacuum or analyze commands in parallel by running `njobs` commands simultaneously. This option reduces the time of the processing but it also increases the load on the database server.

vacuumdb will open *njobs* connections to the database, so make sure your max_connections setting is high enough to accommodate all connections.

Note that using this mode together with the -f (FULL) option might cause deadlock failures if certain system catalogs are processed in parallel.

```
-q
--quiet
```

Do not display progress messages.

```
-t table [ (column [,...]) ]
--table=table [ (column [,...]) ]
```

Clean or analyze *table* only. Column names can be specified only in conjunction with the --analyze or --analyze-only options. Multiple tables can be vacuumed by writing multiple -t switches.

Tip

If you specify columns, you probably have to escape the parentheses from the shell. (See examples below.)

```
-v
--verbose
```

Print detailed information during processing.

```
-V
--version
```

Print the vacuumdb version and exit.

```
-z
--analyze
```

Also calculate statistics for use by the optimizer.

```
-Z
--analyze-only
```

Only calculate statistics for use by the optimizer (no vacuum).

```
--analyze-in-stages
```

Only calculate statistics for use by the optimizer (no vacuum), like --analyze-only. Run several (currently three) stages of analyze with different configuration settings, to produce usable statistics faster.

This option is useful to analyze a database that was newly populated from a restored dump or by pg_upgrade. This option will try to create some statistics as fast as possible, to make the database usable, and then produce full statistics in the subsequent stages.

```
-?
--help
```

Show help about vacuumdb command line arguments, and exit.

vacuumdb also accepts the following command-line arguments for connection parameters:

```
-h host
--host=host
```

Specifies the host name of the machine on which the server is running. If the value begins with a slash, it is used as the directory for the Unix domain socket.

```
-p port
--port=port
```

Specifies the TCP port or local Unix domain socket file extension on which the server is listening for connections.

```
-U username
--username=username
```

User name to connect as.

```
-w
--no-password
```

Never issue a password prompt. If the server requires password authentication and a password is not available by other means such as a `.pgpass` file, the connection attempt will fail. This option can be useful in batch jobs and scripts where no user is present to enter a password.

```
-W
--password
```

Force vacuumdb to prompt for a password before connecting to a database.

This option is never essential, since vacuumdb will automatically prompt for a password if the server demands password authentication. However, vacuumdb will waste a connection attempt finding out that the server wants a password. In some cases it is worth typing `-W` to avoid the extra connection attempt.

```
--maintenance-db=dbname
```

Specifies the name of the database to connect to discover what other databases should be vacuumed. If not specified, the `postgres` database will be used, and if that does not exist, `template1` will be used.

Environment

```
PGDATABASE
PGHOST
PGPORT
PGUSER
```

Default connection parameters

This utility, like most other PostgreSQL utilities, also uses the environment variables supported by libpq (see Section 34.14).

Diagnostics

In case of difficulty, see VACUUM and psql for discussions of potential problems and error messages. The database server must be running at the targeted host. Also, any default connection settings and environment variables used by the libpq front-end library will apply.

Notes

vacuumdb might need to connect several times to the PostgreSQL server, asking for a password each time. It is convenient to have a ~/.pgpass file in such cases. See Section 34.15 for more information.

Examples

To clean the database test:

```
$ vacuumdb test
```

To clean and analyze for the optimizer a database named bigdb:

```
$ vacuumdb --analyze bigdb
```

To clean a single table foo in a database named xyzzy, and analyze a single column bar of the table for the optimizer:

```
$ vacuumdb --analyze --verbose --table='foo(bar)' xyzzy
```

See Also
VACUUM

PostgreSQL Server Applications

This part contains reference information for PostgreSQL server applications and support utilities. These commands can only be run usefully on the host where the database server resides. Other utility programs are listed in PostgreSQL Client Applications.

Table of Contents

initdb

initdb — create a new PostgreSQL database cluster

Synopsis

initdb [*option*...] [--pgdata | -D] *directory*

Description

initdb creates a new PostgreSQL database cluster. A database cluster is a collection of databases that are managed by a single server instance.

Creating a database cluster consists of creating the directories in which the database data will live, generating the shared catalog tables (tables that belong to the whole cluster rather than to any particular database), and creating the template1 and postgres databases. When you later create a new database, everything in the template1 database is copied. (Therefore, anything installed in template1 is automatically copied into each database created later.) The postgres database is a default database meant for use by users, utilities and third party applications.

Although initdb will attempt to create the specified data directory, it might not have permission if the parent directory of the desired data directory is root-owned. To initialize in such a setup, create an empty data directory as root, then use chown to assign ownership of that directory to the database user account, then su to become the database user to run initdb.

initdb must be run as the user that will own the server process, because the server needs to have access to the files and directories that initdb creates. Since the server cannot be run as root, you must not run initdb as root either. (It will in fact refuse to do so.)

For security reasons the new cluster created by initdb will only be accessible by the cluster owner by default. The --allow-group-access option allows any user in the same group as the cluster owner to read files in the cluster. This is useful for performing backups as a non-privileged user.

initdb initializes the database cluster's default locale and character set encoding. The character set encoding, collation order (LC_COLLATE) and character set classes (LC_CTYPE, e.g. upper, lower, digit) can be set separately for a database when it is created. initdb determines those settings for the template1 database, which will serve as the default for all other databases.

To alter the default collation order or character set classes, use the --lc-collate and --lc-ctype options. Collation orders other than C or POSIX also have a performance penalty. For these reasons it is important to choose the right locale when running initdb.

The remaining locale categories can be changed later when the server is started. You can also use --locale to set the default for all locale categories, including collation order and character set classes. All server locale values (lc_*) can be displayed via SHOW ALL. More details can be found in Section 23.1.

To alter the default encoding, use the --encoding. More details can be found in Section 23.3.

Options

-A *authmethod*
--auth=*authmethod*

> This option specifies the default authentication method for local users used in pg_hba.conf (host and local lines). initdb will prepopulate pg_hba.conf entries using the specified authentication method for non-replication as well as replication connections.
>
> Do not use trust unless you trust all local users on your system. trust is the default for ease of installation.

--auth-host=*authmethod*

> This option specifies the authentication method for local users via TCP/IP connections used in pg_hba.conf (host lines).

--auth-local=*authmethod*

> This option specifies the authentication method for local users via Unix-domain socket connections used in pg_hba.conf (local lines).

-D *directory*
--pgdata=*directory*

> This option specifies the directory where the database cluster should be stored. This is the only information required by initdb, but you can avoid writing it by setting the PGDATA environment variable, which can be convenient since the database server (postgres) can find the database directory later by the same variable.

-E *encoding*
--encoding=*encoding*

> Selects the encoding of the template database. This will also be the default encoding of any database you create later, unless you override it there. The default is derived from the locale, or SQL_ASCII if that does not work. The character sets supported by the PostgreSQL server are described in Section 23.3.1.

-g
--allow-group-access

> Allows users in the same group as the cluster owner to read all cluster files created by initdb. This option is ignored on Windows as it does not support POSIX-style group permissions.

-k
--data-checksums

> Use checksums on data pages to help detect corruption by the I/O system that would otherwise be silent. Enabling checksums may incur a noticeable performance penalty. This option can only be set during initialization, and cannot be changed later. If set, checksums are calculated for all objects, in all databases.

--locale=*locale*

> Sets the default locale for the database cluster. If this option is not specified, the locale is inherited from the environment that initdb runs in. Locale support is described in Section 23.1.

```
--lc-collate=locale
--lc-ctype=locale
--lc-messages=locale
--lc-monetary=locale
--lc-numeric=locale
--lc-time=locale
```

Like --locale, but only sets the locale in the specified category.

```
--no-locale
```

Equivalent to --locale=C.

```
-N
--no-sync
```

By default, initdb will wait for all files to be written safely to disk. This option causes initdb to return without waiting, which is faster, but means that a subsequent operating system crash can leave the data directory corrupt. Generally, this option is useful for testing, but should not be used when creating a production installation.

```
--pwfile=filename
```

Makes initdb read the database superuser's password from a file. The first line of the file is taken as the password.

```
-S
--sync-only
```

Safely write all database files to disk and exit. This does not perform any of the normal initdb operations.

```
-T config
--text-search-config=config
```

Sets the default text search configuration. See default_text_search_config for further information.

```
-U username
--username=username
```

Selects the user name of the database superuser. This defaults to the name of the effective user running initdb. It is really not important what the superuser's name is, but one might choose to keep the customary name postgres, even if the operating system user's name is different.

```
-W
--pwprompt
```

Makes initdb prompt for a password to give the database superuser. If you don't plan on using password authentication, this is not important. Otherwise you won't be able to use password authentication until you have a password set up.

```
-X directory
--waldir=directory
```

This option specifies the directory where the write-ahead log should be stored.

`--wal-segsize=size`

> Set the *WAL segment size*, in megabytes. This is the size of each individual file in the WAL log. The default size is 16 megabytes. The value must be a power of 2 between 1 and 1024 (megabytes). This option can only be set during initialization, and cannot be changed later.

> It may be useful to adjust this size to control the granularity of WAL log shipping or archiving. Also, in databases with a high volume of WAL, the sheer number of WAL files per directory can become a performance and management problem. Increasing the WAL file size will reduce the number of WAL files.

Other, less commonly used, options are also available:

`-d`
`--debug`

> Print debugging output from the bootstrap backend and a few other messages of lesser interest for the general public. The bootstrap backend is the program `initdb` uses to create the catalog tables. This option generates a tremendous amount of extremely boring output.

`-L directory`

> Specifies where `initdb` should find its input files to initialize the database cluster. This is normally not necessary. You will be told if you need to specify their location explicitly.

`-n`
`--no-clean`

> By default, when `initdb` determines that an error prevented it from completely creating the database cluster, it removes any files it might have created before discovering that it cannot finish the job. This option inhibits tidying-up and is thus useful for debugging.

Other options:

`-V`
`--version`

> Print the initdb version and exit.

`-?`
`--help`

> Show help about initdb command line arguments, and exit.

Environment

`PGDATA`

> Specifies the directory where the database cluster is to be stored; can be overridden using the `-D` option.

`TZ`

> Specifies the default time zone of the created database cluster. The value should be a full time zone name (see Section 8.5.3).

This utility, like most other PostgreSQL utilities, also uses the environment variables supported by libpq (see Section 34.14).

Notes

initdb can also be invoked via `pg_ctl initdb`.

See Also

pg_ctl, postgres

pg_archivecleanup

pg_archivecleanup — clean up PostgreSQL WAL archive files

Synopsis

pg_archivecleanup [*option*...] *archivelocation oldestkeptwalfile*

Description

pg_archivecleanup is designed to be used as an `archive_cleanup_command` to clean up WAL file archives when running as a standby server (see Section 26.2). pg_archivecleanup can also be used as a standalone program to clean WAL file archives.

To configure a standby server to use pg_archivecleanup, put this into its `recovery.conf` configuration file:

archive_cleanup_command = 'pg_archivecleanup *archivelocation* %r'

where *archivelocation* is the directory from which WAL segment files should be removed.

When used within archive_cleanup_command, all WAL files logically preceding the value of the %r argument will be removed from *archivelocation*. This minimizes the number of files that need to be retained, while preserving crash-restart capability. Use of this parameter is appropriate if the *archive-location* is a transient staging area for this particular standby server, but *not* when the *archivelocation* is intended as a long-term WAL archive area, or when multiple standby servers are recovering from the same archive location.

When used as a standalone program all WAL files logically preceding the *oldestkeptwalfile* will be removed from *archivelocation*. In this mode, if you specify a .partial or .backup file name, then only the file prefix will be used as the *oldestkeptwalfile*. This treatment of .backup file name allows you to remove all WAL files archived prior to a specific base backup without error. For example, the following example will remove all files older than WAL file name 000000010000003700000010:

pg_archivecleanup -d archive 000000010000003700000010.00000020.backup

pg_archivecleanup: keep WAL file "archive/000000010000003700000010"
  and later
pg_archivecleanup: removing file "archive/00000001000000370000000F"
pg_archivecleanup: removing file "archive/00000001000000370000000E"

pg_archivecleanup assumes that *archivelocation* is a directory readable and writable by the server-owning user.

Options

pg_archivecleanup accepts the following command-line arguments:

-d

    Print lots of debug logging output on `stderr`.

-n

    Print the names of the files that would have been removed on `stdout` (performs a dry run).

-V
--version

    Print the pg_archivecleanup version and exit.

-x *extension*

    Provide an extension that will be stripped from all file names before deciding if they should be deleted. This is typically useful for cleaning up archives that have been compressed during storage, and therefore have had an extension added by the compression program. For example: `-x .gz`.

-?
--help

    Show help about pg_archivecleanup command line arguments, and exit.

Notes

pg_archivecleanup is designed to work with PostgreSQL 8.0 and later when used as a standalone utility, or with PostgreSQL 9.0 and later when used as an archive cleanup command.

pg_archivecleanup is written in C and has an easy-to-modify source code, with specifically designated sections to modify for your own needs

Examples

On Linux or Unix systems, you might use:

```
archive_cleanup_command = 'pg_archivecleanup -d /mnt/standby/archive
%r 2>>cleanup.log'
```

where the archive directory is physically located on the standby server, so that the `archive_command` is accessing it across NFS, but the files are local to the standby. This will:

* produce debugging output in `cleanup.log`

* remove no-longer-needed files from the archive directory

See Also

pg_standby

pg_controldata

pg_controldata — display control information of a PostgreSQL database cluster

Synopsis

pg_controldata [*option*] [[--pgdata | -D] *datadir*]

Description

pg_controldata prints information initialized during initdb, such as the catalog version. It also shows information about write-ahead logging and checkpoint processing. This information is cluster-wide, and not specific to any one database.

This utility can only be run by the user who initialized the cluster because it requires read access to the data directory. You can specify the data directory on the command line, or use the environment variable PGDATA. This utility supports the options -V and --version, which print the pg_controldata version and exit. It also supports options -? and --help, which output the supported arguments.

Environment

PGDATA

  Default data directory location

pg_ctl

pg_ctl — initialize, start, stop, or control a PostgreSQL server

Synopsis

pg_ctl init[db] [-D *datadir*] [-s] [-o *initdb-options*]

pg_ctl start [-D *datadir*] [-l *filename*] [-W] [-t *seconds*] [-s] [-o *options*] [-p *path*] [-c]

pg_ctl stop [-D *datadir*] [-m s[mart] | f[ast] | i[mmediate]] [-W] [-t *seconds*] [-s]

pg_ctl restart [-D *datadir*] [-m s[mart] | f[ast] | i[mmediate]] [-W] [-t *seconds*] [-s] [-o *options*] [-c]

pg_ctl reload [-D *datadir*] [-s]

pg_ctl status [-D *datadir*]

pg_ctl promote [-D *datadir*] [-W] [-t *seconds*] [-s]

pg_ctl kill *signal_name process_id*

On Microsoft Windows, also:

pg_ctl register [-D *datadir*] [-N *servicename*] [-U *username*] [-P *password*] [-S a[uto] | d[emand]] [-e *source*] [-W] [-t *seconds*] [-s] [-o *options*]

pg_ctl unregister [-N *servicename*]

Description

pg_ctl is a utility for initializing a PostgreSQL database cluster, starting, stopping, or restarting the PostgreSQL database server (postgres), or displaying the status of a running server. Although the server can be started manually, pg_ctl encapsulates tasks such as redirecting log output and properly detaching from the terminal and process group. It also provides convenient options for controlled shutdown.

The init or initdb mode creates a new PostgreSQL database cluster, that is, a collection of databases that will be managed by a single server instance. This mode invokes the initdb command. See initdb for details.

start mode launches a new server. The server is started in the background, and its standard input is attached to /dev/null (or nul on Windows). On Unix-like systems, by default, the server's standard output and standard error are sent to pg_ctl's standard output (not standard error). The standard output of pg_ctl should then be redirected to a file or piped to another process such as a log rotating program like rotatelogs; otherwise postgres will write its output to the controlling terminal (from the background) and will not leave the shell's process group. On Windows, by default the server's standard output and standard error are sent to the terminal. These default behaviors can be changed by using -l to append the server's output to a log file. Use of either -l or output redirection is recommended.

stop mode shuts down the server that is running in the specified data directory. Three different shutdown methods can be selected with the -m option. "Smart" mode waits for all active clients to disconnect and any online backup to finish. If the server is in hot standby, recovery and streaming replication will be terminated once all clients have disconnected. "Fast" mode (the default) does not wait for clients to disconnect and will terminate an online backup in progress. All active transactions are rolled back and clients are forcibly disconnected, then the server is shut down. "Immediate" mode will abort all server processes immediately, without a clean shutdown. This choice will lead to a crash-recovery cycle during the next server start.

`restart` mode effectively executes a stop followed by a start. This allows changing the `postgres` command-line options, or changing configuration-file options that cannot be changed without restarting the server. If relative paths were used on the command line during server start, `restart` might fail unless pg_ctl is executed in the same current directory as it was during server start.

`reload` mode simply sends the `postgres` server process a SIGHUP signal, causing it to reread its configuration files (`postgresql.conf`, `pg_hba.conf`, etc.). This allows changing configuration-file options that do not require a full server restart to take effect.

`status` mode checks whether a server is running in the specified data directory. If it is, the server's PID and the command line options that were used to invoke it are displayed. If the server is not running, pg_ctl returns an exit status of 3. If an accessible data directory is not specified, pg_ctl returns an exit status of 4.

`promote` mode commands the standby server that is running in the specified data directory to end standby mode and begin read-write operations.

`kill` mode sends a signal to a specified process. This is primarily valuable on Microsoft Windows which does not have a built-in kill command. Use `--help` to see a list of supported signal names.

`register` mode registers the PostgreSQL server as a system service on Microsoft Windows. The `-S` option allows selection of service start type, either "auto" (start service automatically on system startup) or "demand" (start service on demand).

`unregister` mode unregisters a system service on Microsoft Windows. This undoes the effects of the `register` command.

Options

`-c`
`--core-files`

> Attempt to allow server crashes to produce core files, on platforms where this is possible, by lifting any soft resource limit placed on core files. This is useful in debugging or diagnosing problems by allowing a stack trace to be obtained from a failed server process.

`-D datadir`
`--pgdata=datadir`

> Specifies the file system location of the database configuration files. If this option is omitted, the environment variable `PGDATA` is used.

`-l filename`
`--log=filename`

> Append the server log output to `filename`. If the file does not exist, it is created. The umask is set to 077, so access to the log file is disallowed to other users by default.

`-m mode`
`--mode=mode`

> Specifies the shutdown mode. `mode` can be `smart`, `fast`, or `immediate`, or the first letter of one of these three. If this option is omitted, `fast` is the default.

-o *options*
--options=*options*

> Specifies options to be passed directly to the `postgres` command. `-o` can be specified multiple times, with all the given options being passed through.

> The *options* should usually be surrounded by single or double quotes to ensure that they are passed through as a group.

-o *initdb-options*
--options=*initdb-options*

> Specifies options to be passed directly to the `initdb` command. `-o` can be specified multiple times, with all the given options being passed through.

> The *initdb-options* should usually be surrounded by single or double quotes to ensure that they are passed through as a group.

-p *path*

> Specifies the location of the `postgres` executable. By default the `postgres` executable is taken from the same directory as `pg_ctl`, or failing that, the hard-wired installation directory. It is not necessary to use this option unless you are doing something unusual and get errors that the `postgres` executable was not found.

> In `init` mode, this option analogously specifies the location of the `initdb` executable.

-s
--silent

> Print only errors, no informational messages.

-t *seconds*
--timeout=*seconds*

> Specifies the maximum number of seconds to wait when waiting for an operation to complete (see option **-w**). Defaults to the value of the `PGCTLTIMEOUT` environment variable or, if not set, to 60 seconds.

-V
--version

> Print the pg_ctl version and exit.

-w
--wait

> Wait for the operation to complete. This is supported for the modes `start`, `stop`, `restart`, `promote`, and `register`, and is the default for those modes.

> When waiting, `pg_ctl` repeatedly checks the server's PID file, sleeping for a short amount of time between checks. Startup is considered complete when the PID file indicates that the server is ready to accept connections. Shutdown is considered complete when the server removes the PID file. `pg_ctl` returns an exit code based on the success of the startup or shutdown.

> If the operation does not complete within the timeout (see option **-t**), then `pg_ctl` exits with a nonzero exit status. But note that the operation might continue in the background and eventually succeed.

```
-W
--no-wait
```

Do not wait for the operation to complete. This is the opposite of the option -w.

If waiting is disabled, the requested action is triggered, but there is no feedback about its success. In that case, the server log file or an external monitoring system would have to be used to check the progress and success of the operation.

In prior releases of PostgreSQL, this was the default except for the stop mode.

```
-?
--help
```

Show help about pg_ctl command line arguments, and exit.

If an option is specified that is valid, but not relevant to the selected operating mode, pg_ctl ignores it.

Options for Windows

-e *source*

Name of the event source for pg_ctl to use for logging to the event log when running as a Windows service. The default is PostgreSQL. Note that this only controls messages sent from pg_ctl itself; once started, the server will use the event source specified by its event_source parameter. Should the server fail very early in startup, before that parameter has been set, it might also log using the default event source name PostgreSQL.

-N *servicename*

Name of the system service to register. This name will be used as both the service name and the display name. The default is PostgreSQL.

-P *password*

Password for the user to run the service as.

-S *start-type*

Start type of the system service. *start-type* can be auto, or demand, or the first letter of one of these two. If this option is omitted, auto is the default.

-U *username*

User name for the user to run the service as. For domain users, use the format DOMAIN\username.

Environment

PGCTLTIMEOUT

Default limit on the number of seconds to wait when waiting for startup or shutdown to complete. If not set, the default is 60 seconds.

PGDATA

Default data directory location.

Most `pg_ctl` modes require knowing the data directory location; therefore, the −D option is required unless `PGDATA` is set.

`pg_ctl`, like most other PostgreSQL utilities, also uses the environment variables supported by libpq (see Section 34.14).

For additional variables that affect the server, see postgres.

Files

`postmaster.pid`

> pg_ctl examines this file in the data directory to determine whether the server is currently running.

`postmaster.opts`

> If this file exists in the data directory, pg_ctl (in `restart` mode) will pass the contents of the file as options to postgres, unless overridden by the −o option. The contents of this file are also displayed in `status` mode.

Examples

Starting the Server

To start the server, waiting until the server is accepting connections:

```
$ pg_ctl start
```

To start the server using port 5433, and running without `fsync`, use:

```
$ pg_ctl -o "-F -p 5433" start
```

Stopping the Server

To stop the server, use:

```
$ pg_ctl stop
```

The −m option allows control over *how* the server shuts down:

```
$ pg_ctl stop -m smart
```

Restarting the Server

Restarting the server is almost equivalent to stopping the server and starting it again, except that by default, `pg_ctl` saves and reuses the command line options that were passed to the previously-running instance. To restart the server using the same options as before, use:

```
$ pg_ctl restart
```

But if **−o** is specified, that replaces any previous options. To restart using port 5433, disabling f sync upon restart:

```
$ pg_ctl -o "-F -p 5433" restart
```

Showing the Server Status

Here is sample status output from pg_ctl:

```
$ pg_ctl status
```

```
pg_ctl: server is running (PID: 13718)
/usr/local/pgsql/bin/postgres "-D" "/usr/local/pgsql/data" "-p" "5433"
 "-B" "128"
```

The second line is the command that would be invoked in restart mode.

See Also

initdb, postgres

pg_resetwal

pg_resetwal — reset the write-ahead log and other control information of a PostgreSQL database cluster

Synopsis

pg_resetwal [--force | -f] [--dry-run | -n] [option...] [--pgdata | -D] *datadir*

Description

pg_resetwal clears the write-ahead log (WAL) and optionally resets some other control information stored in the pg_control file. This function is sometimes needed if these files have become corrupted. It should be used only as a last resort, when the server will not start due to such corruption.

After running this command, it should be possible to start the server, but bear in mind that the database might contain inconsistent data due to partially-committed transactions. You should immediately dump your data, run initdb, and reload. After reload, check for inconsistencies and repair as needed.

This utility can only be run by the user who installed the server, because it requires read/write access to the data directory. For safety reasons, you must specify the data directory on the command line. pg_resetwal does not use the environment variable PGDATA.

If pg_resetwal complains that it cannot determine valid data for pg_control, you can force it to proceed anyway by specifying the -f (force) option. In this case plausible values will be substituted for the missing data. Most of the fields can be expected to match, but manual assistance might be needed for the next OID, next transaction ID and epoch, next multitransaction ID and offset, and WAL starting location fields. These fields can be set using the options discussed below. If you are not able to determine correct values for all these fields, -f can still be used, but the recovered database must be treated with even more suspicion than usual: an immediate dump and reload is imperative. *Do not* execute any data-modifying operations in the database before you dump, as any such action is likely to make the corruption worse.

Options

-f
--force

> Force pg_resetwal to proceed even if it cannot determine valid data for pg_control, as explained above.

-n
--dry-run

> The -n/--dry-run option instructs pg_resetwal to print the values reconstructed from pg_control and values about to be changed, and then exit without modifying anything. This is mainly a debugging tool, but can be useful as a sanity check before allowing pg_resetwal to proceed for real.

-V
--version

> Display version information, then exit.

```
-?
--help
```

Show help, then exit.

The following options are only needed when `pg_resetwal` is unable to determine appropriate values by reading `pg_control`. Safe values can be determined as described below. For values that take numeric arguments, hexadecimal values can be specified by using the prefix `0x`.

```
-c xid,xid
--commit-timestamp-ids=xid,xid
```

Manually set the oldest and newest transaction IDs for which the commit time can be retrieved.

A safe value for the oldest transaction ID for which the commit time can be retrieved (first part) can be determined by looking for the numerically smallest file name in the directory `pg_commit_ts` under the data directory. Conversely, a safe value for the newest transaction ID for which the commit time can be retrieved (second part) can be determined by looking for the numerically greatest file name in the same directory. The file names are in hexadecimal.

```
-e xid_epoch
--epoch=xid_epoch
```

Manually set the next transaction ID's epoch.

The transaction ID epoch is not actually stored anywhere in the database except in the field that is set by `pg_resetwal`, so any value will work so far as the database itself is concerned. You might need to adjust this value to ensure that replication systems such as Slony-I and Skytools work correctly — if so, an appropriate value should be obtainable from the state of the downstream replicated database.

```
-l walfile
--next-wal-file=walfile
```

Manually set the WAL starting location by specifying the name of the next WAL segment file.

The name of next WAL segment file should be larger than any WAL segment file name currently existing in the directory `pg_wal` under the data directory. These names are also in hexadecimal and have three parts. The first part is the "timeline ID" and should usually be kept the same. For example, if `00000001000000320000004A` is the largest entry in `pg_wal`, use `-l 00000001000000320000004B` or higher.

Note that when using nondefault WAL segment sizes, the numbers in the WAL file names are different from the LSNs that are reported by system functions and system views. This option takes a WAL file name, not an LSN.

Note

`pg_resetwal` itself looks at the files in `pg_wal` and chooses a default `-l` setting beyond the last existing file name. Therefore, manual adjustment of `-l` should only be needed if you are aware of WAL segment files that are not currently present in `pg_wal`, such as entries in an offline archive; or if the contents of `pg_wal` have been lost entirely.

-m *mxid,mxid*
--multixact-ids=*mxid,mxid*

Manually set the next and oldest multitransaction ID.

A safe value for the next multitransaction ID (first part) can be determined by looking for the numerically largest file name in the directory `pg_multixact/offsets` under the data directory, adding one, and then multiplying by 65536 (0x10000). Conversely, a safe value for the oldest multitransaction ID (second part of -m) can be determined by looking for the numerically smallest file name in the same directory and multiplying by 65536. The file names are in hexadecimal, so the easiest way to do this is to specify the option value in hexadecimal and append four zeroes.

-o *oid*
--next-oid=*oid*

Manually set the next OID.

There is no comparably easy way to determine a next OID that's beyond the largest one in the database, but fortunately it is not critical to get the next-OID setting right.

-O *mxoff*
--multixact-offset=*mxoff*

Manually set the next multitransaction offset.

A safe value can be determined by looking for the numerically largest file name in the directory `pg_multixact/members` under the data directory, adding one, and then multiplying by 52352 (0xCC80). The file names are in hexadecimal. There is no simple recipe such as the ones for other options of appending zeroes.

--wal-segsize=*wal_segment_size*

Set the new WAL segment size, in megabytes. The value must be set to a power of 2 between 1 and 1024 (megabytes). See the same option of initdb for more information.

> ## Note
>
> While `pg_resetwal` will set the WAL starting address beyond the latest existing WAL segment file, some segment size changes can cause previous WAL file names to be reused. It is recommended to use -l together with this option to manually set the WAL starting address if WAL file name overlap will cause problems with your archiving strategy.

-x *xid*
--next-transaction-id=*xid*

Manually set the next transaction ID.

A safe value can be determined by looking for the numerically largest file name in the directory `pg_xact` under the data directory, adding one, and then multiplying by 1048576 (0x100000). Note that the file names are in hexadecimal. It is usually easiest to specify the option value in hexadecimal too. For example, if 0011 is the largest entry in `pg_xact`, **-x 0x1200000** will work (five trailing zeroes provide the proper multiplier).

Notes

This command must not be used when the server is running. `pg_resetwal` will refuse to start up if it finds a server lock file in the data directory. If the server crashed then a lock file might have been left behind; in that case you can remove the lock file to allow `pg_resetwal` to run. But before you do so, make doubly certain that there is no server process still alive.

`pg_resetwal` works only with servers of the same major version.

See Also

pg_controldata

pg_rewind

pg_rewind — synchronize a PostgreSQL data directory with another data directory that was forked from it

Synopsis

pg_rewind [option...] { -D |--target-pgdata } directory { --source-pgdata=directory | --source-server=connstr }

Description

pg_rewind is a tool for synchronizing a PostgreSQL cluster with another copy of the same cluster, after the clusters' timelines have diverged. A typical scenario is to bring an old master server back online after failover as a standby that follows the new master.

The result is equivalent to replacing the target data directory with the source one. Only changed blocks from relation files are copied; all other files are copied in full, including configuration files. The advantage of pg_rewind over taking a new base backup, or tools like rsync, is that pg_rewind does not require reading through unchanged blocks in the cluster. This makes it a lot faster when the database is large and only a small fraction of blocks differ between the clusters.

pg_rewind examines the timeline histories of the source and target clusters to determine the point where they diverged, and expects to find WAL in the target cluster's `pg_wal` directory reaching all the way back to the point of divergence. The point of divergence can be found either on the target timeline, the source timeline, or their common ancestor. In the typical failover scenario where the target cluster was shut down soon after the divergence, this is not a problem, but if the target cluster ran for a long time after the divergence, the old WAL files might no longer be present. In that case, they can be manually copied from the WAL archive to the `pg_wal` directory, or fetched on startup by configuring `recovery.conf`. The use of pg_rewind is not limited to failover, e.g. a standby server can be promoted, run some write transactions, and then rewinded to become a standby again.

When the target server is started for the first time after running pg_rewind, it will go into recovery mode and replay all WAL generated in the source server after the point of divergence. If some of the WAL was no longer available in the source server when pg_rewind was run, and therefore could not be copied by the pg_rewind session, it must be made available when the target server is started. This can be done by creating a `recovery.conf` file in the target data directory with a suitable `restore_command`.

pg_rewind requires that the target server either has the wal_log_hints option enabled in `postgresql.conf` or data checksums enabled when the cluster was initialized with initdb. Neither of these are currently on by default. full_page_writes must also be set to `on`, but is enabled by default.

Warning

If pg_rewind fails while processing, then the data folder of the target is likely not in a state that can be recovered. In such a case, taking a new fresh backup is recommended.

pg_rewind will fail immediately if it finds files it cannot write directly to. This can happen for example when the source and the target server use the same file mapping for read-only SSL keys and certificates. If such files are present on the target server it is recommended to remove them before running pg_rewind. After doing the rewind, some of those files may

---

have been copied from the source, in which case it may be necessary to remove the data copied and restore back the set of links used before the rewind.

Options

pg_rewind accepts the following command-line arguments:

`-D directory`
`--target-pgdata=directory`

This option specifies the target data directory that is synchronized with the source. The target server must be shut down cleanly before running pg_rewind

`--source-pgdata=directory`

Specifies the file system path to the data directory of the source server to synchronize the target with. This option requires the source server to be cleanly shut down.

`--source-server=connstr`

Specifies a libpq connection string to connect to the source PostgreSQL server to synchronize the target with. The connection must be a normal (non-replication) connection with superuser access. This option requires the source server to be running and not in recovery mode.

`-n`
`--dry-run`

Do everything except actually modifying the target directory.

`-P`
`--progress`

Enables progress reporting. Turning this on will deliver an approximate progress report while copying data from the source cluster.

`--debug`

Print verbose debugging output that is mostly useful for developers debugging pg_rewind.

`-V`
`--version`

Display version information, then exit.

`-?`
`--help`

Show help, then exit.

Environment

When `--source-server` option is used, pg_rewind also uses the environment variables supported by libpq (see Section 34.14).

Notes

How it works

The basic idea is to copy all file system-level changes from the source cluster to the target cluster:

1. Scan the WAL log of the target cluster, starting from the last checkpoint before the point where the source cluster's timeline history forked off from the target cluster. For each WAL record, record each data block that was touched. This yields a list of all the data blocks that were changed in the target cluster, after the source cluster forked off.

2. Copy all those changed blocks from the source cluster to the target cluster, either using direct file system access (`--source-pgdata`) or SQL (`--source-server`).

3. Copy all other files such as `pg_xact` and configuration files from the source cluster to the target cluster (everything except the relation files). Similarly to base backups, the contents of the directories `pg_dynshmem/`, `pg_notify/`, `pg_replslot/`, `pg_serial/`, `pg_snapshots/`, `pg_stat_tmp/`, and `pg_subtrans/` are omitted from the data copied from the source cluster. Any file or directory beginning with `pgsql_tmp` is omitted, as well as are `backup_label`, `tablespace_map`, `pg_internal.init`, `postmaster.opts` and `postmaster.pid`.

4. Apply the WAL from the source cluster, starting from the checkpoint created at failover. (Strictly speaking, pg_rewind doesn't apply the WAL, it just creates a backup label file that makes PostgreSQL start by replaying all WAL from that checkpoint forward.)

pg_test_fsync

pg_test_fsync — determine fastest wal_sync_method for PostgreSQL

Synopsis

pg_test_fsync [option...]

Description

pg_test_fsync is intended to give you a reasonable idea of what the fastest wal_sync_method is on your specific system, as well as supplying diagnostic information in the event of an identified I/O problem. However, differences shown by pg_test_fsync might not make any significant difference in real database throughput, especially since many database servers are not speed-limited by their write-ahead logs. pg_test_fsync reports average file sync operation time in microseconds for each wal_sync_method, which can also be used to inform efforts to optimize the value of commit_delay.

Options

pg_test_fsync accepts the following command-line options:

-f
--filename

> Specifies the file name to write test data in. This file should be in the same file system that the pg_wal directory is or will be placed in. (pg_wal contains the WAL files.) The default is pg_test_fsync.out in the current directory.

-s
--secs-per-test

> Specifies the number of seconds for each test. The more time per test, the greater the test's accuracy, but the longer it takes to run. The default is 5 seconds, which allows the program to complete in under 2 minutes.

-V
--version

> Print the pg_test_fsync version and exit.

-?
--help

> Show help about pg_test_fsync command line arguments, and exit.

See Also

postgres

pg_test_timing

pg_test_timing — measure timing overhead

Synopsis

pg_test_timing [*option*...]

Description

pg_test_timing is a tool to measure the timing overhead on your system and confirm that the system time never moves backwards. Systems that are slow to collect timing data can give less accurate EXPLAIN ANALYZE results.

Options

pg_test_timing accepts the following command-line options:

-d *duration*
--duration=*duration*

> Specifies the test duration, in seconds. Longer durations give slightly better accuracy, and are more likely to discover problems with the system clock moving backwards. The default test duration is 3 seconds.

-V
--version

> Print the pg_test_timing version and exit.

-?
--help

> Show help about pg_test_timing command line arguments, and exit.

Usage

Interpreting results

Good results will show most (>90%) individual timing calls take less than one microsecond. Average per loop overhead will be even lower, below 100 nanoseconds. This example from an Intel i7-860 system using a TSC clock source shows excellent performance:

```
Testing timing overhead for 3 seconds.
Per loop time including overhead: 35.96 ns
Histogram of timing durations:
  < us   % of total      count
     1   96.40465     80435604
     2    3.59518      2999652
     4    0.00015          126
```

```
    8     0.00002        13
   16     0.00000         2
```

Note that different units are used for the per loop time than the histogram. The loop can have resolution within a few nanoseconds (ns), while the individual timing calls can only resolve down to one microsecond (us).

Measuring executor timing overhead

When the query executor is running a statement using EXPLAIN ANALYZE, individual operations are timed as well as showing a summary. The overhead of your system can be checked by counting rows with the psql program:

```
CREATE TABLE t AS SELECT * FROM generate_series(1,100000);
\timing
SELECT COUNT(*) FROM t;
EXPLAIN ANALYZE SELECT COUNT(*) FROM t;
```

The i7-860 system measured runs the count query in 9.8 ms while the EXPLAIN ANALYZE version takes 16.6 ms, each processing just over 100,000 rows. That 6.8 ms difference means the timing overhead per row is 68 ns, about twice what pg_test_timing estimated it would be. Even that relatively small amount of overhead is making the fully timed count statement take almost 70% longer. On more substantial queries, the timing overhead would be less problematic.

Changing time sources

On some newer Linux systems, it's possible to change the clock source used to collect timing data at any time. A second example shows the slowdown possible from switching to the slower acpi_pm time source, on the same system used for the fast results above:

```
# cat /sys/devices/system/clocksource/clocksource0/
available_clocksource
tsc hpet acpi_pm
# echo acpi_pm > /sys/devices/system/clocksource/clocksource0/
current_clocksource
# pg_test_timing
Per loop time including overhead: 722.92 ns
Histogram of timing durations:
  < us    % of total      count
     1     27.84870     1155682
     2     72.05956     2990371
     4      0.07810        3241
     8      0.01357         563
    16      0.00007           3
```

In this configuration, the sample EXPLAIN ANALYZE above takes 115.9 ms. That's 1061 ns of timing overhead, again a small multiple of what's measured directly by this utility. That much timing overhead means the actual query itself is only taking a tiny fraction of the accounted for time, most of it is being consumed in overhead instead. In this configuration, any EXPLAIN ANALYZE totals involving many timed operations would be inflated significantly by timing overhead.

FreeBSD also allows changing the time source on the fly, and it logs information about the timer selected during boot:

```
# dmesg | grep "Timecounter"
Timecounter "ACPI-fast" frequency 3579545 Hz quality 900
Timecounter "i8254" frequency 1193182 Hz quality 0
Timecounters tick every 10.000 msec
Timecounter "TSC" frequency 2531787134 Hz quality 800
# sysctl kern.timecounter.hardware=TSC
kern.timecounter.hardware: ACPI-fast -> TSC
```

Other systems may only allow setting the time source on boot. On older Linux systems the "clock" kernel setting is the only way to make this sort of change. And even on some more recent ones, the only option you'll see for a clock source is "jiffies". Jiffies are the older Linux software clock implementation, which can have good resolution when it's backed by fast enough timing hardware, as in this example:

```
$ cat /sys/devices/system/clocksource/clocksource0/
available_clocksource
jiffies
$ dmesg | grep time.c
time.c: Using 3.579545 MHz WALL PM GTOD PIT/TSC timer.
time.c: Detected 2400.153 MHz processor.
$ pg_test_timing
Testing timing overhead for 3 seconds.
Per timing duration including loop overhead: 97.75 ns
Histogram of timing durations:
   < us   % of total      count
      1     90.23734    27694571
      2      9.75277     2993204
      4      0.00981        3010
      8      0.00007          22
     16      0.00000           1
     32      0.00000           1
```

Clock hardware and timing accuracy

Collecting accurate timing information is normally done on computers using hardware clocks with various levels of accuracy. With some hardware the operating systems can pass the system clock time almost directly to programs. A system clock can also be derived from a chip that simply provides timing interrupts, periodic ticks at some known time interval. In either case, operating system kernels provide a clock source that hides these details. But the accuracy of that clock source and how quickly it can return results varies based on the underlying hardware.

Inaccurate time keeping can result in system instability. Test any change to the clock source very carefully. Operating system defaults are sometimes made to favor reliability over best accuracy. And if you are using a virtual machine, look into the recommended time sources compatible with it. Virtual hardware faces additional difficulties when emulating timers, and there are often per operating system settings suggested by vendors.

The Time Stamp Counter (TSC) clock source is the most accurate one available on current generation CPUs. It's the preferred way to track the system time when it's supported by the operating system and the TSC clock is reliable. There are several ways that TSC can fail to provide an accurate timing source, making it unreliable. Older systems can have a TSC clock that varies based on the CPU temperature, making it unusable for timing. Trying to use TSC on some older multicore CPUs can give a reported time that's inconsistent among multiple cores. This can result in the time going backwards, a problem this program checks for. And even the newest systems can fail to provide accurate TSC timing with very aggressive power saving configurations.

Newer operating systems may check for the known TSC problems and switch to a slower, more stable clock source when they are seen. If your system supports TSC time but doesn't default to that, it may be disabled for a good reason. And some operating systems may not detect all the possible problems correctly, or will allow using TSC even in situations where it's known to be inaccurate.

The High Precision Event Timer (HPET) is the preferred timer on systems where it's available and TSC is not accurate. The timer chip itself is programmable to allow up to 100 nanosecond resolution, but you may not see that much accuracy in your system clock.

Advanced Configuration and Power Interface (ACPI) provides a Power Management (PM) Timer, which Linux refers to as the acpi_pm. The clock derived from acpi_pm will at best provide 300 nanosecond resolution.

Timers used on older PC hardware include the 8254 Programmable Interval Timer (PIT), the real-time clock (RTC), the Advanced Programmable Interrupt Controller (APIC) timer, and the Cyclone timer. These timers aim for millisecond resolution.

See Also

EXPLAIN

pg_upgrade

pg_upgrade — upgrade a PostgreSQL server instance

Synopsis

pg_upgrade -b *oldbindir* -B *newbindir* -d *oldconfigdir* -D *newconfigdir* [*option*...]

Description

pg_upgrade (formerly called pg_migrator) allows data stored in PostgreSQL data files to be upgraded to a later PostgreSQL major version without the data dump/reload typically required for major version upgrades, e.g. from 9.5.8 to 9.6.4 or from 10.7 to 11.2. It is not required for minor version upgrades, e.g. from 9.6.2 to 9.6.3 or from 10.1 to 10.2.

Major PostgreSQL releases regularly add new features that often change the layout of the system tables, but the internal data storage format rarely changes. pg_upgrade uses this fact to perform rapid upgrades by creating new system tables and simply reusing the old user data files. If a future major release ever changes the data storage format in a way that makes the old data format unreadable, pg_upgrade will not be usable for such upgrades. (The community will attempt to avoid such situations.)

pg_upgrade does its best to make sure the old and new clusters are binary-compatible, e.g. by checking for compatible compile-time settings, including 32/64-bit binaries. It is important that any external modules are also binary compatible, though this cannot be checked by pg_upgrade.

pg_upgrade supports upgrades from 8.4.X and later to the current major release of PostgreSQL, including snapshot and beta releases.

Options

pg_upgrade accepts the following command-line arguments:

-b *bindir*
--old-bindir=*bindir*

    the old PostgreSQL executable directory; environment variable `PGBINOLD`

-B *bindir*
--new-bindir=*bindir*

    the new PostgreSQL executable directory; environment variable `PGBINNEW`

-c
--check

    check clusters only, don't change any data

-d *configdir*
--old-datadir=*configdir*

    the old database cluster configuration directory; environment variable `PGDATAOLD`

`-D` *configdir*
`--new-datadir=`*configdir*

the new database cluster configuration directory; environment variable `PGDATANEW`

`-j`
`--jobs`

number of simultaneous processes or threads to use

`-k`
`--link`

use hard links instead of copying files to the new cluster

`-o` *options*
`--old-options` *options*

options to be passed directly to the old `postgres` command; multiple option invocations are appended

`-O` *options*
`--new-options` *options*

options to be passed directly to the new `postgres` command; multiple option invocations are appended

`-p` *port*
`--old-port=`*port*

the old cluster port number; environment variable `PGPORTOLD`

`-P` *port*
`--new-port=`*port*

the new cluster port number; environment variable `PGPORTNEW`

`-r`
`--retain`

retain SQL and log files even after successful completion

`-U` *username*
`--username=`*username*

cluster's install user name; environment variable `PGUSER`

`-v`
`--verbose`

enable verbose internal logging

`-V`
`--version`

display version information, then exit

`-?`
`--help`

show help, then exit

Usage

These are the steps to perform an upgrade with pg_upgrade:

1. **Optionally move the old cluster**

    If you are using a version-specific installation directory, e.g. `/opt/PostgreSQL/11`, you do not need to move the old cluster. The graphical installers all use version-specific installation directories.

    If your installation directory is not version-specific, e.g. `/usr/local/pgsql`, it is necessary to move the current PostgreSQL install directory so it does not interfere with the new PostgreSQL installation. Once the current PostgreSQL server is shut down, it is safe to rename the PostgreSQL installation directory; assuming the old directory is `/usr/local/pgsql`, you can do:

    ```
    mv /usr/local/pgsql /usr/local/pgsql.old
    ```

    to rename the directory.

2. **For source installs, build the new version**

    Build the new PostgreSQL source with `configure` flags that are compatible with the old cluster. pg_upgrade will check `pg_controldata` to make sure all settings are compatible before starting the upgrade.

3. **Install the new PostgreSQL binaries**

    Install the new server's binaries and support files. pg_upgrade is included in a default installation.

    For source installs, if you wish to install the new server in a custom location, use the `prefix` variable:

    ```
    make prefix=/usr/local/pgsql.new install
    ```

4. **Initialize the new PostgreSQL cluster**

    Initialize the new cluster using `initdb`. Again, use compatible `initdb` flags that match the old cluster. Many prebuilt installers do this step automatically. There is no need to start the new cluster.

5. **Install custom shared object files**

    Install any custom shared object files (or DLLs) used by the old cluster into the new cluster, e.g. `pgcrypto.so`, whether they are from `contrib` or some other source. Do not install the schema definitions, e.g. `CREATE EXTENSION pgcrypto`, because these will be upgraded from the old cluster. Also, any custom full text search files (dictionary, synonym, thesaurus, stop words) must also be copied to the new cluster.

6. **Adjust authentication**

    `pg_upgrade` will connect to the old and new servers several times, so you might want to set authentication to `peer` in `pg_hba.conf` or use a `~/.pgpass` file (see Section 34.15).

7. **Stop both servers**

    Make sure both database servers are stopped using, on Unix, e.g.:

    ```
    pg_ctl -D /opt/PostgreSQL/9.6 stop
    ```

```
pg_ctl -D /opt/PostgreSQL/11 stop
```

or on Windows, using the proper service names:

```
NET STOP postgresql-9.6
NET STOP postgresql-11
```

Streaming replication and log-shipping standby servers can remain running until a later step.

8. **Prepare for standby server upgrades**

If you are upgrading standby servers using methods outlined in section Step 10, verify that the old standby servers are caught up by running pg_controldata against the old primary and standby clusters. Verify that the "Latest checkpoint location" values match in all clusters. (There will be a mismatch if old standby servers were shut down before the old primary or if the old standby servers are still running.) Also, change `wal_level` to `replica` in the `postgresql.conf` file on the new primary cluster.

9. **Run pg_upgrade**

Always run the pg_upgrade binary of the new server, not the old one. pg_upgrade requires the specification of the old and new cluster's data and executable (`bin`) directories. You can also specify user and port values, and whether you want the data files linked instead of the default copy behavior.

If you use link mode, the upgrade will be much faster (no file copying) and use less disk space, but you will not be able to access your old cluster once you start the new cluster after the upgrade. Link mode also requires that the old and new cluster data directories be in the same file system. (Tablespaces and `pg_wal` can be on different file systems.) See `pg_upgrade --help` for a full list of options.

The `--jobs` option allows multiple CPU cores to be used for copying/linking of files and to dump and reload database schemas in parallel; a good place to start is the maximum of the number of CPU cores and tablespaces. This option can dramatically reduce the time to upgrade a multi-database server running on a multiprocessor machine.

For Windows users, you must be logged into an administrative account, and then start a shell as the `postgres` user and set the proper path:

```
RUNAS /USER:postgres "CMD.EXE"
SET PATH=%PATH%;C:\Program Files\PostgreSQL\11\bin;
```

and then run pg_upgrade with quoted directories, e.g.:

```
pg_upgrade.exe
        --old-datadir "C:/Program Files/PostgreSQL/9.6/data"
        --new-datadir "C:/Program Files/PostgreSQL/11/data"
        --old-bindir "C:/Program Files/PostgreSQL/9.6/bin"
        --new-bindir "C:/Program Files/PostgreSQL/11/bin"
```

Once started, `pg_upgrade` will verify the two clusters are compatible and then do the upgrade. You can use `pg_upgrade --check` to perform only the checks, even if the old server is still running. `pg_upgrade --check` will also outline any manual adjustments you will need to make after the upgrade. If you are going to be using link mode, you should use the `--link` option with `--check` to enable link-mode-specific checks. `pg_upgrade` requires write permission in the current directory.

Obviously, no one should be accessing the clusters during the upgrade. pg_upgrade defaults to running servers on port 50432 to avoid unintended client connections. You can use the same port number for both clusters when doing an upgrade because the old and new clusters will not be running at the same time. However, when checking an old running server, the old and new port numbers must be different.

If an error occurs while restoring the database schema, `pg_upgrade` will exit and you will have to revert to the old cluster as outlined in Step 16 below. To try `pg_upgrade` again, you will need to modify the old cluster so the pg_upgrade schema restore succeeds. If the problem is a `contrib` module, you might need to uninstall the `contrib` module from the old cluster and install it in the new cluster after the upgrade, assuming the module is not being used to store user data.

10. **Upgrade Streaming Replication and Log-Shipping standby servers**

    If you used link mode and have Streaming Replication (see Section 26.2.5) or Log-Shipping (see Section 26.2) standby servers, you can follow these steps to quickly upgrade them. You will not be running pg_upgrade on the standby servers, but rather rsync on the primary. Do not start any servers yet.

    If you did *not* use link mode, do not have or do not want to use rsync, or want an easier solution, skip the instructions in this section and simply recreate the standby servers once pg_upgrade completes and the new primary is running.

    a. **Install the new PostgreSQL binaries on standby servers**

        Make sure the new binaries and support files are installed on all standby servers.

    b. **Make sure the new standby data directories do *not* exist**

        Make sure the new standby data directories do *not* exist or are empty. If initdb was run, delete the standby servers' new data directories.

    c. **Install custom shared object files**

        Install the same custom shared object files on the new standbys that you installed in the new primary cluster.

    d. **Stop standby servers**

        If the standby servers are still running, stop them now using the above instructions.

    e. **Save configuration files**

        Save any configuration files from the old standbys' configuration directories you need to keep, e.g. `postgresql.conf`, `recovery.conf`, because these will be overwritten or removed in the next step.

    f. **Run rsync**

        When using link mode, standby servers can be quickly upgraded using rsync. To accomplish this, from a directory on the primary server that is above the old and new database cluster directories, run this on the *primary* for each standby server:

        ```
        rsync --archive --delete --hard-links --size-only --no-inc-
        recursive old_cluster new_cluster remote_dir
        ```

where `old_cluster` and `new_cluster` are relative to the current directory on the primary, and `remote_dir` is *above* the old and new cluster directories on the standby. The directory structure under the specified directories on the primary and standbys must match. Consult the rsync manual page for details on specifying the remote directory, e.g.

```
rsync --archive --delete --hard-links --size-only --no-inc-
recursive /opt/PostgreSQL/9.5 \
      /opt/PostgreSQL/9.6 standby.example.com:/opt/PostgreSQL
```

You can verify what the command will do using rsync's `--dry-run` option. While rsync must be run on the primary for at least one standby, it is possible to run rsync on an upgraded standby to upgrade other standbys, as long as the upgraded standby has not been started.

What this does is to record the links created by pg_upgrade's link mode that connect files in the old and new clusters on the primary server. It then finds matching files in the standby's old cluster and creates links for them in the standby's new cluster. Files that were not linked on the primary are copied from the primary to the standby. (They are usually small.) This provides rapid standby upgrades. Unfortunately, rsync needlessly copies files associated with temporary and unlogged tables because these files don't normally exist on standby servers.

If you have tablespaces, you will need to run a similar rsync command for each tablespace directory, e.g.:

```
rsync --archive --delete --hard-links --size-only --no-inc-
recursive /vol1/pg_tblsp/PG_9.5_201510051 \
      /vol1/pg_tblsp/PG_9.6_201608131 standby.example.com:/
vol1/pg_tblsp
```

If you have relocated `pg_wal` outside the data directories, rsync must be run on those directories too.

g. **Configure streaming replication and log-shipping standby servers**

Configure the servers for log shipping. (You do not need to run `pg_start_backup()` and `pg_stop_backup()` or take a file system backup as the standbys are still synchronized with the primary.)

11. **Restore `pg_hba.conf`**

If you modified `pg_hba.conf`, restore its original settings. It might also be necessary to adjust other configuration files in the new cluster to match the old cluster, e.g. `postgresql.conf`.

12. **Start the new server**

The new server can now be safely started, and then any rsync'ed standby servers.

13. **Post-Upgrade processing**

If any post-upgrade processing is required, pg_upgrade will issue warnings as it completes. It will also generate script files that must be run by the administrator. The script files will connect to each database that needs post-upgrade processing. Each script should be run using:

```
psql --username=postgres --file=script.sql postgres
```

The scripts can be run in any order and can be deleted once they have been run.

> ## Caution
>
> In general it is unsafe to access tables referenced in rebuild scripts until the rebuild scripts have run to completion; doing so could yield incorrect results or poor performance. Tables not referenced in rebuild scripts can be accessed immediately.

14. **Statistics**

    Because optimizer statistics are not transferred by pg_upgrade, you will be instructed to run a command to regenerate that information at the end of the upgrade. You might need to set connection parameters to match your new cluster.

15. **Delete old cluster**

    Once you are satisfied with the upgrade, you can delete the old cluster's data directories by running the script mentioned when pg_upgrade completes. (Automatic deletion is not possible if you have user-defined tablespaces inside the old data directory.) You can also delete the old installation directories (e.g. bin, share).

16. **Reverting to old cluster**

    If, after running pg_upgrade, you wish to revert to the old cluster, there are several options:

    - If you ran pg_upgrade with --check, no modifications were made to the old cluster and you can re-use it anytime.

    - If you ran pg_upgrade with --link, the data files are shared between the old and new cluster. If you started the new cluster, the new server has written to those shared files and it is unsafe to use the old cluster.

    - If you ran pg_upgrade *without* --link or did not start the new server, the old cluster was not modified except that, if linking started, a .old suffix was appended to $PGDATA/global/pg_control. To reuse the old cluster, possibly remove the .old suffix from $PGDATA/global/pg_control; you can then restart the old cluster.

Notes

pg_upgrade does not support upgrading of databases containing table columns using these reg* OID-referencing system data types: regproc, regprocedure, regoper, regoperator, regconfig, and regdictionary. (regtype can be upgraded.)

All failure, rebuild, and reindex cases will be reported by pg_upgrade if they affect your installation; post-upgrade scripts to rebuild tables and indexes will be generated automatically. If you are trying to automate the upgrade of many clusters, you should find that clusters with identical database schemas require the same post-upgrade steps for all cluster upgrades; this is because the post-upgrade steps are based on the database schemas, and not user data.

For deployment testing, create a schema-only copy of the old cluster, insert dummy data, and upgrade that.

If you are upgrading a pre-PostgreSQL 9.2 cluster that uses a configuration-file-only directory, you must pass the real data directory location to pg_upgrade, and pass the configuration directory location to the server, e.g. -d /real-data-directory -o '-D /configuration-directory'.

If using a pre-9.1 old server that is using a non-default Unix-domain socket directory or a default that differs from the default of the new cluster, set PGHOST to point to the old server's socket location. (This is not relevant on Windows.)

If you want to use link mode and you do not want your old cluster to be modified when the new cluster is started, make a copy of the old cluster and upgrade that in link mode. To make a valid copy of the old cluster, use rsync to create a dirty copy of the old cluster while the server is running, then shut down the old server and run rsync --checksum again to update the copy with any changes to make it consistent. (--checksum is necessary because rsync only has file modification-time granularity of one second.) You might want to exclude some files, e.g. postmaster.pid, as documented in Section 25.3.3. If your file system supports file system snapshots or copy-on-write file copies, you can use that to make a backup of the old cluster and tablespaces, though the snapshot and copies must be created simultaneously or while the database server is down.

See Also

initdb, pg_ctl, pg_dump, postgres

pg_verify_checksums

pg_verify_checksums — verify data checksums in a PostgreSQL database cluster

Synopsis

pg_verify_checksums [*option*...] [[-D | --pgdata] *datadir*]

Description

pg_verify_checksums verifies data checksums in a PostgreSQL cluster. The server must be shut down cleanly before running pg_verify_checksums. The exit status is zero if there are no checksum errors, otherwise nonzero.

Options

The following command-line options are available:

-D *directory*
--pgdata=*directory*

> Specifies the directory where the database cluster is stored.

-v
--verbose

> Enable verbose output. Lists all checked files.

-r *relfilenode*

> Only validate checksums in the relation with specified relfilenode.

-V
--version

> Print the pg_verify_checksums version and exit.

-?
--help

> Show help about pg_verify_checksums command line arguments, and exit.

Environment

PGDATA

> Specifies the directory where the database cluster is stored; can be overridden using the -D option.

pg_waldump

pg_waldump — display a human-readable rendering of the write-ahead log of a PostgreSQL database cluster

Synopsis

pg_waldump [option...] [startseg [endseg]]

Description

pg_waldump displays the write-ahead log (WAL) and is mainly useful for debugging or educational purposes.

This utility can only be run by the user who installed the server, because it requires read-only access to the data directory.

Options

The following command-line options control the location and format of the output:

startseg

Start reading at the specified log segment file. This implicitly determines the path in which files will be searched for, and the timeline to use.

endseg

Stop after reading the specified log segment file.

-b
--bkp-details

Output detailed information about backup blocks.

-e end
--end=end

Stop reading at the specified WAL location, instead of reading to the end of the log stream.

-f
--follow

After reaching the end of valid WAL, keep polling once per second for new WAL to appear.

-n limit
--limit=limit

Display the specified number of records, then stop.

-p path
--path=path

Specifies a directory to search for log segment files or a directory with a pg_wal subdirectory that contains such files. The default is to search in the current directory, the pg_wal subdirectory of the current directory, and the pg_wal subdirectory of PGDATA.

`-r rmgr`
`--rmgr=rmgr`

> Only display records generated by the specified resource manager. If `list` is passed as name, print a list of valid resource manager names, and exit.

`-s start`
`--start=start`

> WAL location at which to start reading. The default is to start reading the first valid log record found in the earliest file found.

`-t timeline`
`--timeline=timeline`

> Timeline from which to read log records. The default is to use the value in *startseg*, if that is specified; otherwise, the default is 1.

`-V`
`--version`

> Print the pg_waldump version and exit.

`-x xid`
`--xid=xid`

> Only display records marked with the given transaction ID.

`-z`
`--stats[=record]`

> Display summary statistics (number and size of records and full-page images) instead of individual records. Optionally generate statistics per-record instead of per-rmgr.

`-?`
`--help`

> Show help about pg_waldump command line arguments, and exit.

Notes

Can give wrong results when the server is running.

Only the specified timeline is displayed (or the default, if none is specified). Records in other timelines are ignored.

pg_waldump cannot read WAL files with suffix `.partial`. If those files need to be read, `.partial` suffix needs to be removed from the file name.

See Also

Section 30.5

postgres

postgres — PostgreSQL database server

Synopsis

```
postgres [option...]
```

Description

postgres is the PostgreSQL database server. In order for a client application to access a database it connects (over a network or locally) to a running postgres instance. The postgres instance then starts a separate server process to handle the connection.

One postgres instance always manages the data of exactly one database cluster. A database cluster is a collection of databases that is stored at a common file system location (the "data area"). More than one postgres instance can run on a system at one time, so long as they use different data areas and different communication ports (see below). When postgres starts it needs to know the location of the data area. The location must be specified by the -D option or the PGDATA environment variable; there is no default. Typically, -D or PGDATA points directly to the data area directory created by initdb. Other possible file layouts are discussed in Section 19.2.

By default postgres starts in the foreground and prints log messages to the standard error stream. In practical applications postgres should be started as a background process, perhaps at boot time.

The postgres command can also be called in single-user mode. The primary use for this mode is during bootstrapping by initdb. Sometimes it is used for debugging or disaster recovery; note that running a single-user server is not truly suitable for debugging the server, since no realistic interprocess communication and locking will happen. When invoked in single-user mode from the shell, the user can enter queries and the results will be printed to the screen, but in a form that is more useful for developers than end users. In the single-user mode, the session user will be set to the user with ID 1, and implicit superuser powers are granted to this user. This user does not actually have to exist, so the single-user mode can be used to manually recover from certain kinds of accidental damage to the system catalogs.

Options

postgres accepts the following command-line arguments. For a detailed discussion of the options consult Chapter 19. You can save typing most of these options by setting up a configuration file. Some (safe) options can also be set from the connecting client in an application-dependent way to apply only for that session. For example, if the environment variable PGOPTIONS is set, then libpq-based clients will pass that string to the server, which will interpret it as postgres command-line options.

General Purpose

-B nbuffers

Sets the number of shared buffers for use by the server processes. The default value of this parameter is chosen automatically by initdb. Specifying this option is equivalent to setting the shared_buffers configuration parameter.

-c *name=value*

> Sets a named run-time parameter. The configuration parameters supported by PostgreSQL are described in Chapter 19. Most of the other command line options are in fact short forms of such a parameter assignment. **-c** can appear multiple times to set multiple parameters.

-C *name*

> Prints the value of the named run-time parameter, and exits. (See the **-c** option above for details.) This can be used on a running server, and returns values from `postgresql.conf`, modified by any parameters supplied in this invocation. It does not reflect parameters supplied when the cluster was started.

> This option is meant for other programs that interact with a server instance, such as pg_ctl, to query configuration parameter values. User-facing applications should instead use SHOW or the `pg_settings` view.

-d *debug-level*

> Sets the debug level. The higher this value is set, the more debugging output is written to the server log. Values are from 1 to 5. It is also possible to pass **-d 0** for a specific session, which will prevent the server log level of the parent `postgres` process from being propagated to this session.

-D *datadir*

> Specifies the file system location of the database configuration files. See Section 19.2 for details.

-e

> Sets the default date style to "European", that is DMY ordering of input date fields. This also causes the day to be printed before the month in certain date output formats. See Section 8.5 for more information.

-F

> Disables `fsync` calls for improved performance, at the risk of data corruption in the event of a system crash. Specifying this option is equivalent to disabling the fsync configuration parameter. Read the detailed documentation before using this!

-h *hostname*

> Specifies the IP host name or address on which `postgres` is to listen for TCP/IP connections from client applications. The value can also be a comma-separated list of addresses, or * to specify listening on all available interfaces. An empty value specifies not listening on any IP addresses, in which case only Unix-domain sockets can be used to connect to the server. Defaults to listening only on localhost. Specifying this option is equivalent to setting the listen_addresses configuration parameter.

-i

> Allows remote clients to connect via TCP/IP (Internet domain) connections. Without this option, only local connections are accepted. This option is equivalent to setting `listen_addresses` to * in `postgresql.conf` or via **-h**.

> This option is deprecated since it does not allow access to the full functionality of listen_addresses. It's usually better to set `listen_addresses` directly.

-k *directory*

> Specifies the directory of the Unix-domain socket on which `postgres` is to listen for connections from client applications. The value can also be a comma-separated list of directories. An empty value

specifies not listening on any Unix-domain sockets, in which case only TCP/IP sockets can be used to connect to the server. The default value is normally /tmp, but that can be changed at build time. Specifying this option is equivalent to setting the unix_socket_directories configuration parameter.

-l

Enables secure connections using SSL. PostgreSQL must have been compiled with support for SSL for this option to be available. For more information on using SSL, refer to Section 18.9.

-N *max-connections*

Sets the maximum number of client connections that this server will accept. The default value of this parameter is chosen automatically by initdb. Specifying this option is equivalent to setting the max_connections configuration parameter.

-o *extra-options*

The command-line-style arguments specified in *extra-options* are passed to all server processes started by this postgres process.

Spaces within *extra-options* are considered to separate arguments, unless escaped with a backslash (\); write \\ to represent a literal backslash. Multiple arguments can also be specified via multiple uses of -o.

The use of this option is obsolete; all command-line options for server processes can be specified directly on the postgres command line.

-p *port*

Specifies the TCP/IP port or local Unix domain socket file extension on which postgres is to listen for connections from client applications. Defaults to the value of the PGPORT environment variable, or if PGPORT is not set, then defaults to the value established during compilation (normally 5432). If you specify a port other than the default port, then all client applications must specify the same port using either command-line options or PGPORT.

-s

Print time information and other statistics at the end of each command. This is useful for benchmarking or for use in tuning the number of buffers.

-S *work-mem*

Specifies the amount of memory to be used by internal sorts and hashes before resorting to temporary disk files. See the description of the work_mem configuration parameter in Section 19.4.1.

-V
--version

Print the postgres version and exit.

--*name*=*value*

Sets a named run-time parameter; a shorter form of -c.

--describe-config

This option dumps out the server's internal configuration variables, descriptions, and defaults in tab-delimited COPY format. It is designed primarily for use by administration tools.

```
-?
--help
```

Show help about postgres command line arguments, and exit.

Semi-internal Options

The options described here are used mainly for debugging purposes, and in some cases to assist with recovery of severely damaged databases. There should be no reason to use them in a production database setup. They are listed here only for use by PostgreSQL system developers. Furthermore, these options might change or be removed in a future release without notice.

`-f { s | i | o | b | t | n | m | h }`

Forbids the use of particular scan and join methods: s and i disable sequential and index scans respectively, o, b and t disable index-only scans, bitmap index scans, and TID scans respectively, while n, m, and h disable nested-loop, merge and hash joins respectively.

Neither sequential scans nor nested-loop joins can be disabled completely; the -fs and -fn options simply discourage the optimizer from using those plan types if it has any other alternative.

`-n`

This option is for debugging problems that cause a server process to die abnormally. The ordinary strategy in this situation is to notify all other server processes that they must terminate and then reinitialize the shared memory and semaphores. This is because an errant server process could have corrupted some shared state before terminating. This option specifies that `postgres` will not reinitialize shared data structures. A knowledgeable system programmer can then use a debugger to examine shared memory and semaphore state.

`-O`

Allows the structure of system tables to be modified. This is used by `initdb`.

`-P`

Ignore system indexes when reading system tables, but still update the indexes when modifying the tables. This is useful when recovering from damaged system indexes.

`-t pa[rser] | pl[anner] | e[xecutor]`

Print timing statistics for each query relating to each of the major system modules. This option cannot be used together with the -s option.

`-T`

This option is for debugging problems that cause a server process to die abnormally. The ordinary strategy in this situation is to notify all other server processes that they must terminate and then reinitialize the shared memory and semaphores. This is because an errant server process could have corrupted some shared state before terminating. This option specifies that `postgres` will stop all other server processes by sending the signal `SIGSTOP`, but will not cause them to terminate. This permits system programmers to collect core dumps from all server processes by hand.

`-v protocol`

Specifies the version number of the frontend/backend protocol to be used for a particular session. This option is for internal use only.

-W *seconds*

A delay of this many seconds occurs when a new server process is started, after it conducts the authentication procedure. This is intended to give an opportunity to attach to the server process with a debugger.

Options for Single-User Mode

The following options only apply to the single-user mode (see Single-User Mode).

--single

Selects the single-user mode. This must be the first argument on the command line.

database

Specifies the name of the database to be accessed. This must be the last argument on the command line. If it is omitted it defaults to the user name.

-E

Echo all commands to standard output before executing them.

-j

Use semicolon followed by two newlines, rather than just newline, as the command entry terminator.

-r *filename*

Send all server log output to *filename*. This option is only honored when supplied as a command-line option.

Environment

PGCLIENTENCODING

Default character encoding used by clients. (The clients can override this individually.) This value can also be set in the configuration file.

PGDATA

Default data directory location

PGDATESTYLE

Default value of the DateStyle run-time parameter. (The use of this environment variable is deprecated.)

PGPORT

Default port number (preferably set in the configuration file)

Diagnostics

A failure message mentioning semget or shmget probably indicates you need to configure your kernel to provide adequate shared memory and semaphores. For more discussion see Section 18.4. You might be able to postpone reconfiguring your kernel by decreasing shared_buffers to reduce the shared memory consumption of PostgreSQL, and/or by reducing max_connections to reduce the semaphore consumption.

A failure message suggesting that another server is already running should be checked carefully, for example by using the command

```
$ ps ax | grep postgres
```

or

```
$ ps -ef | grep postgres
```

depending on your system. If you are certain that no conflicting server is running, you can remove the lock file mentioned in the message and try again.

A failure message indicating inability to bind to a port might indicate that that port is already in use by some non-PostgreSQL process. You might also get this error if you terminate postgres and immediately restart it using the same port; in this case, you must simply wait a few seconds until the operating system closes the port before trying again. Finally, you might get this error if you specify a port number that your operating system considers to be reserved. For example, many versions of Unix consider port numbers under 1024 to be "trusted" and only permit the Unix superuser to access them.

Notes

The utility command pg_ctl can be used to start and shut down the postgres server safely and comfortably.

If at all possible, *do not* use SIGKILL to kill the main postgres server. Doing so will prevent postgres from freeing the system resources (e.g., shared memory and semaphores) that it holds before terminating. This might cause problems for starting a fresh postgres run.

To terminate the postgres server normally, the signals SIGTERM, SIGINT, or SIGQUIT can be used. The first will wait for all clients to terminate before quitting, the second will forcefully disconnect all clients, and the third will quit immediately without proper shutdown, resulting in a recovery run during restart.

The SIGHUP signal will reload the server configuration files. It is also possible to send SIGHUP to an individual server process, but that is usually not sensible.

To cancel a running query, send the SIGINT signal to the process running that command. To terminate a backend process cleanly, send SIGTERM to that process. See also pg_cancel_backend and pg_terminate_backend in Section 9.26.2 for the SQL-callable equivalents of these two actions.

The postgres server uses SIGQUIT to tell subordinate server processes to terminate without normal cleanup. This signal *should not* be used by users. It is also unwise to send SIGKILL to a server process — the main postgres process will interpret this as a crash and will force all the sibling processes to quit as part of its standard crash-recovery procedure.

Bugs

The -- options will not work on FreeBSD or OpenBSD. Use -c instead. This is a bug in the affected operating systems; a future release of PostgreSQL will provide a workaround if this is not fixed.

Single-User Mode

To start a single-user mode server, use a command like

postgres --single -D /usr/local/pgsql/data *other-options* **my_database**

Provide the correct path to the database directory with **-D**, or make sure that the environment variable **PGDATA** is set. Also specify the name of the particular database you want to work in.

Normally, the single-user mode server treats newline as the command entry terminator; there is no intelligence about semicolons, as there is in psql. To continue a command across multiple lines, you must type backslash just before each newline except the last one. The backslash and adjacent newline are both dropped from the input command. Note that this will happen even when within a string literal or comment.

But if you use the **-j** command line switch, a single newline does not terminate command entry; instead, the sequence semicolon-newline-newline does. That is, type a semicolon immediately followed by a completely empty line. Backslash-newline is not treated specially in this mode. Again, there is no intelligence about such a sequence appearing within a string literal or comment.

In either input mode, if you type a semicolon that is not just before or part of a command entry terminator, it is considered a command separator. When you do type a command entry terminator, the multiple statements you've entered will be executed as a single transaction.

To quit the session, type EOF (**Control+D**, usually). If you've entered any text since the last command entry terminator, then EOF will be taken as a command entry terminator, and another EOF will be needed to exit.

Note that the single-user mode server does not provide sophisticated line-editing features (no command history, for example). Single-user mode also does not do any background processing, such as automatic checkpoints or replication.

Examples

To start postgres in the background using default values, type:

$ nohup postgres >logfile 2>&1 </dev/null &

To start postgres with a specific port, e.g. 1234:

$ postgres -p 1234

To connect to this server using psql, specify this port with the -p option:

$ psql -p 1234

or set the environment variable PGPORT:

$ export PGPORT=1234
$ psql

Named run-time parameters can be set in either of these styles:

```
$ postgres -c work_mem=1234
$ postgres --work-mem=1234
```

Either form overrides whatever setting might exist for work_mem in postgresql.conf. Notice that underscores in parameter names can be written as either underscore or dash on the command line. Except for short-term experiments, it's probably better practice to edit the setting in postgresql.conf than to rely on a command-line switch to set a parameter.

See Also

initdb, pg_ctl

postmaster

postmaster — PostgreSQL database server

Synopsis

`postmaster [option...]`

Description

`postmaster` is a deprecated alias of `postgres`.

See Also

postgres

Bibliography

Selected references and readings for SQL and PostgreSQL.

Some white papers and technical reports from the original POSTGRES development team are available at the University of California, Berkeley, Computer Science Department web site[1].

SQL Reference Books

[bowman01] *The Practical SQL Handbook*. Using SQL Variants. Fourth Edition. Judith Bowman, Sandra Emerson, and Marcy Darnovsky. ISBN 0-201-70309-2. Addison-Wesley Professional. 2001.

[date97] *A Guide to the SQL Standard*. A user's guide to the standard database language SQL. Fourth Edition. C. J. Date and Hugh Darwen. ISBN 0-201-96426-0. Addison-Wesley. 1997.

[date04] *An Introduction to Database Systems*. Eighth Edition. C. J. Date. ISBN 0-321-19784-4. Addison-Wesley. 2003.

[elma04] *Fundamentals of Database Systems*. Fourth Edition. Ramez Elmasri and Shamkant Navathe. ISBN 0-321-12226-7. Addison-Wesley. 2003.

[melt93] *Understanding the New SQL*. A complete guide. Jim Melton and Alan R. Simon. ISBN 1-55860-245-3. Morgan Kaufmann. 1993.

[ull88] *Principles of Database and Knowledge*. Base Systems. Jeffrey D. Ullman. Volume 1. Computer Science Press. 1988.

PostgreSQL-specific Documentation

[sim98] *Enhancement of the ANSI SQL Implementation of PostgreSQL*. Stefan Simkovics. Department of Information Systems, Vienna University of Technology. Vienna, Austria. November 29, 1998.

[yu95] *The Postgres95. User Manual*. A. Yu and J. Chen. University of California. Berkeley, California. Sept. 5, 1995.

[fong] *The design and implementation of the POSTGRES query optimizer*[2]. Zelaine Fong. University of California, Berkeley, Computer Science Department.

Proceedings and Articles

[olson93] *Partial indexing in POSTGRES: research project*. Nels Olson. UCB Engin T7.49.1993 O676. University of California. Berkeley, California. 1993.

[ong90] "A Unified Framework for Version Modeling Using Production Rules in a Database System". L. Ong and J. Goh. *ERL Technical Memorandum M90/33*. University of California. Berkeley, California. April, 1990.

[rowe87] "The POSTGRES data model[3]". L. Rowe and M. Stonebraker. VLDB Conference, Sept. 1987.

[seshadri95] "Generalized Partial Indexes[4]". P. Seshadri and A. Swami. Eleventh International Conference on Data Engineering, 6-10 March 1995. Cat. No.95CH35724. IEEE Computer Society Press. Los Alamitos, California. 1995. 420-7.

---

[1] http://db.cs.berkeley.edu/papers/
[2] http://db.cs.berkeley.edu/papers/UCB-MS-zfong.pdf
[3] http://db.cs.berkeley.edu/papers/ERL-M87-13.pdf
[4] http://citeseer.ist.psu.edu/seshadri95generalized.html

[ston86] "The design of POSTGRES[5]". M. Stonebraker and L. Rowe. ACM-SIGMOD Conference on Management of Data, May 1986.

[ston87a] "The design of the POSTGRES. rules system". M. Stonebraker, E. Hanson, and C. H. Hong. IEEE Conference on Data Engineering, Feb. 1987.

[ston87b] "The design of the POSTGRES storage system[6]". M. Stonebraker. VLDB Conference, Sept. 1987.

[ston89] "A commentary on the POSTGRES rules system[7]". M. Stonebraker, M. Hearst, and S. Potamianos. *SIGMOD Record 18(3)*. Sept. 1989.

[ston89b] "The case for partial indexes[8]". M. Stonebraker. *SIGMOD Record 18(4)*. Dec. 1989. 4-11.

[ston90a] "The implementation of POSTGRES[9]". M. Stonebraker, L. A. Rowe, and M. Hirohama. *Transactions on Knowledge and Data Engineering 2(1)*. IEEE. March 1990.

[ston90b] "On Rules, Procedures, Caching and Views in Database Systems[10]". M. Stonebraker, A. Jhingran, J. Goh, and S. Potamianos. ACM-SIGMOD Conference on Management of Data, June 1990.

---

[5] http://db.cs.berkeley.edu/papers/ERL-M85-95.pdf
[6] http://db.cs.berkeley.edu/papers/ERL-M87-06.pdf
[7] http://db.cs.berkeley.edu/papers/ERL-M89-82.pdf
[8] http://db.cs.berkeley.edu/papers/ERL-M89-17.pdf
[9] http://db.cs.berkeley.edu/papers/ERL-M90-34.pdf
[10] http://db.cs.berkeley.edu/papers/ERL-M90-36.pdf

Index

Symbols

A

Y

Z